# HANDBOOK
# OF
# MEDIA MANAGEMENT
# AND ECONOMICS

# HANDBOOK
# OF
# MEDIA MANAGEMENT
# AND ECONOMICS

Editor

## Alan B. Albarran
*University of North Texas*

Co-Editors

## Sylvia M. Chan-Olmsted
*University of Florida*

## Michael O. Wirth
*University of Denver*

**LEA** LAWRENCE ERLBAUM ASSOCIATES, PUBLISHERS
**2006** Mahwah, New Jersey                    London

Senior Acquisitions Editor:     Linda Bathgate
Assistant Editor:     Karin Wittig Bates
Cover Design:     Kathryn Houghtaling Lacey
Textbook Production Manager:     Paul Smolenski
Full-Service Compositor:     TechBooks
Text and Cover Printer:     Hamilton Printing Company

This book was typeset in 11/13 pt. Dante, Bold, Italic.
The heads were typeset in Franklin Gothic, Bold, and Bold Italic.

Lawrence Erlbaum Associates, Inc., Publishers
10 Industrial Avenue
Mahwah, New Jersey 07430
www.erlbaum.com

**Library of Congress Cataloging-in-Publication Data**

Handbook of media management and economics / editor Alan B. Albarran;
    co-editors Sylvia M. Chan-Olmsted, Michael O. Wirth.
      p.    cm.
    Includes bibliographical references and index.
    ISBN 0-8058-5003-1 (casebound)—ISBN 0-8058-5004-X (pbk.)
    1. Mass media—Management.    2. Mass media—Economic aspects.    I. Albarran,
Alan B.    II. Chan-Olmsted, Sylvia M.    III. Wirth, Michael O., 1951–

    P96.M34.H366    2006
    302.23′068—dc22

                                               2005011722

Printed in the United States of America
10   9   8   7   6   5   4   3   2   1

In memory of my uncle, William F. "Bill" McAlister, a member
of the greatest generation.

—*Alan B. Albarran*

To Lanya Toshiko Olmsted and Wesley Chan Olmsted.

—*Sylvia M. Chan-Olmsted*

To Alice, Michelle, Christina, and my parents.

—*Michael O. Wirth*

# MME Handbook Editorial Review Board

# Contents

## PART II.  ISSUES IN MEDIA MANAGEMENT AND ECONOMICS

# List of Contributors

**Alan B. Albarran** University of North Texas

**Kendra S. Albright** University of Tennessee

**Benjamin J. Bates** University of Tennessee

**Johannes M. Bauer** Michigan State University

**Randal A. Beam** Indiana University

**Todd Chambers** Texas Tech University

**Sylvia M. Chan-Olmsted** University of Florida

**Barbara A. Cherry** Federal Communications Commission

**Amy Jo Coffey** University of Georgia

**John Dimmick** Ohio State University

**Gillian Doyle** University of Stirling

**Douglas A. Ferguson** College of Charleston

**Simon Frith** University of Stirling

**Richard A. Gershon** Western Michigan University

**David H. Goff** University of West Georgia

**Phil Graham** University of Waterloo and University of Queensland

**Annelies Hogenbirk** Rabobank Nederland

**C. Ann Hollifield** University of Georgia

**Herbert H. Howard** University of Tennessee

**Hans van Kranenburg** University of Maastricht

**Stephen Lacy** Michigan State University

**Walter S. McDowell** University of Miami

**Bozena I. Mierzjewska** University of St. Gallen

**Philip M. Napoli** Fordham University

**Gary W. Ozanich** The Kelsey Group

**Patricia F. Phalen** George Washington University

**Robert G. Picard** Jönköping University

**Ángel Arrese Reca** University of Navarra

**James W. Redmond** The University of Memphis

**Ronald J. Rizzuto** University of Denver

**Alfonso Sánchez-Tabernero** University of Navarra

**Dan Shaver** The University of Central Florida

**Mary Alice Shaver** The University of Central Florida

**David Waterman** Indiana University

**Steven S. Wildman** Michigan State University

**Michael O. Wirth** University of Denver

# Preface

We are very pleased to have had the opportunity to oversee the first ever *Handbook of Media Management and Economics* published in the rapidly growing field of media management and economics research. This project was first discussed several years ago between Linda Bathgate, Communications Editor for Lawrence Erlbaum Associates, and Alan B. Albarran, at the time the editor of the *Journal of Media Economics* (JME).

Linda was the driving editorial force behind this work. Lawrence Erlbaum Associates has been committed to publishing a series of handbooks for different areas of the communications field, and media management and economics was a logical choice given Erlbaum's publishing of JME and a number of texts devoted to research topics in the field.

The challenge was getting this project going amid other research efforts and responsibilities. Finally, the project began to take shape in 2002 after a series of conversations and e-mails between Linda and Alan. It was determined that this needed to be as comprehensive a collection of research as possible that would accomplish two primary goals: assess the state of knowledge for the topics selected for inclusion in the Handbook, and set the research agenda needed for each topic and ultimately the field for the decade following publication.

Given this exciting opportunity, the next step was to identify at least two people who could assist as co-editors for the Handbook and help share the workload for this project. The good news is that there are a number of very capable and qualified scholars around the globe who are capable of handling this project. Although Linda was helpful in suggesting and discussing potential editorial collaborators, the decision on who to select was left up to Alan.

A short list of candidates was established, and the top two people on my list were Sylvia Chan-Olmsted of the University of Florida and Mike Wirth from the University of Denver. Both Sylvia and Mike are prolific and established scholars, with a good deal of editorial and publishing experience. Both graduated with their doctorates from Michigan State University, in my view the best graduate program related to media management and economics (MME) in the country.

Sylvia and I co-edited a book entitled *Global Media Economics* in 1998, and she served as Book Review Editor for the *Journal of Media Economics* for several years. Sylvia has great editorial skills, and I knew she would be a tremendous asset to this project—but knowing how busy she stays with her own research and strong commitment to her graduate students, I didn't know if she would be able to assist.

Mike Wirth has been publishing research in the area of MME since the 1970s. Mike also served as a guest editor for an issue of JME a few years ago, and he was, without doubt, the most organized guest editor I ever worked with during my tenure as JME Editor. Like Sylvia, Mike has his share of responsibilities as Director of the School of Communication and Chair of the Department of Mass Communications and Journalism Studies at the University of Denver, as well as being a Senior Fellow with The Cable Center, and his long-standing involvement with the academic seminar at the National Cable & Telecommunications Association (NCTA).

Luckily, Sylvia and Mike eagerly jumped on this project and were a tremendous help as we discussed and debated potential topics, potential authors for those topics, and other editorial issues. We worked for several weeks over e-mail and conference calls to get organized, divided up the work, and then began the task of putting this volume together. In addition to serving as editors, all of us contributed chapters as authors; Sylvia went the extra mile and contributed two chapters.

Just about everyone we asked to author a chapter was happy to learn of this project and eager to participate. Naturally, some scholars we sought were unable to participate because of other projects and responsibilities, but most of them volunteered to help out as part of our Handbook Editorial Board, and we thank them for their contribution to this work in that capacity. But to our individual contributors—established scholars from around the world—we thank you for the incredible work and care you provided in your individual contributions.

My hope is that this project will be appreciated and used by students, professors, and industry practitioners for years to come, and that the ideas presented in this initial Handbook will stimulate even greater research in the field of media management and economics research.

I thank Sylvia and Mike for their dedication to this project, their commitment to the field, their integrity, and their friendship. I thank Linda Bathgate for her passion for this project and giving us the time to pull this massive undertaking together. My research assistant, Jami Clayman, provided hours and hours of editorial assistance for which I am very appreciative. I am also grateful to my wife, Beverly, and my daughters, Beth and Mandy, who make my life so very fulfilling and special.

—ALAN B. ALBARRAN

In my years of working with graduate students who are interested in learning more about MME, I always had a difficult time coming up with an answer when they asked for a definitive source of readings that would introduce them to the discipline. I often found myself compiling lists of articles and books that tackle the fundamental theories, methodological issues, and empirical studies relating to MME from many different disciplines. However, the "borrowed" literatures from economics, management, sociology, marketing, and many other areas never approached an MME topic quite the way I thought was appropriate for media products or addressed the right issues in the context of media industries. I am delighted that the search for a basic literature source in MME is over. This Handbook is comprised of invaluable contributions from many established scholars in our field who are experts in the topics of the specific chapters over which they labored. It is significant in that the Handbook not only provides a comprehensive review of the literature and established theories relevant to our field, but also challenges readers to build on that knowledge. I am very grateful to have the opportunity to be part of the project.

I remember being at a conference that was geared toward traditional mass communication studies where one student was trying to articulate why she approached a certain mass communication topic from a business perspective (i.e., she used media management theories). One of the respondents to her paper blasted her study and insisted that she should stick to mass communication, which has established, "serious" literatures and leave the business stuff to the people from business schools. I hope this volume speaks of the substance and legitimacy of our field. I thank all of the contributors who have made this project possible. It is always hard to be the planters who work the field, linking disciplines and developing new knowledge. I applaud their contributions to the maturing of our discipline and invite you to join us in further enriching the field of MME.

—Sylvia Chan-Olmsted

I first became interested in MME when I was a graduate student at Michigan State University in the early 1970s. It's truly amazing to see how far the study of MME has advanced during the past 30 years and exciting to think about the future of this field going forward as it grows and matures.

Publication of the *Handbook of Media Management and Economics* represents a milestone for our field. I hope the careful work of so many outstanding scholars will prove useful to everyone who does research in this area. In particular, the Handbook should be of significant assistance to researchers as they place even greater emphasis on theoretically based and analytically focused MME scholarly inquiry going forward. The interdisciplinary nature of MME research is also underscored by the scholarly work contained herein. Specifically, the Handbook provides MME scholars with a useful tool for applying concepts and theories from other disciplines to the study of specific MME phenomenon. Related to this, I encourage MME researchers to seek out and work with colleagues from other disciplines.

I was honored by Alan Albarran's invitation to be part of this project, and I feel very privileged and thankful to have had the opportunity to work with so many dedicated MME scholars (including my fellow editors Alan and Sylvia, the authors of all the chapters, and the members of the Handbook Editorial Board) and with Linda Bathgate from Lawrence Erlbaum Associates. I also wish to thank my wife, Alice, and my daughters, Michelle and Christina, for their love and support over the years and especially during the completion of this project. Finally, I am thankful to my parents, Austin (who passed away during the middle of this project) and Kathleen, for their love, wisdom, and inspiration.

—Michael O. Wirth

# THEORETICAL DIMENSIONS IN MEDIA MANAGEMENT AND ECONOMICS

# 1

# Historical Trends and Patterns in Media Management Research

Alan B. Albarran
University of North Texas

Media management research became an area of interest and study during the 20th century as media conglomerates began to take shape, first in the newspaper industry, and later in the radio, motion picture, and television industry. The media industries are unique to society in many ways in that they are ubiquitous and pervasive in nature. The media is a primary source for information and entertainment and an important part of the function Laswell (1949) described as transmitting the culture of a society.

Lavine and Wackman (1988) identified five characteristics that differentiate media industries from other types of businesses. These include (a) the perishable commodity of the media product, (b) the highly creative employees, (c) the organizational structure, (d) the societal role of the media (e.g., awareness, influence) and (e) the blurring of lines separating traditional media. Ferguson (1997) also discussed these distinctions in a call for a domain of media management grounded in theoretical development. Caves (2000) offers a distinction between media firms and other businesses through the theory of contracts and the differences involved in dealing with creative individuals and demand uncertainty.

Given the unique nature of the media, the study of the management of media enterprises, institutions, and personnel evolved quite naturally over time. Today, media management is a global phenomenon, and research and inquiry in the field of media management crosses interdisciplinary lines, theoretical domains, and political systems.

To understand contemporary trends and patterns in media management research, it is first helpful to review the major historical contributions to general management theory. The study of management began near the start of the 20th century, in the United States and abroad. Among the first to be engaged in the study of what would someday be called *management* was the philosopher Mary Parker Follett (see Follett, Pauline, & Graham, 1995; Fox & Urwick, 1977; Tonn, 2003). Follett, labeled the "prophet of management" by Peter Drucker, produced a series of papers concerned with business conflict, authority, power, and the place of the individual in society and the group. Ironically, Follett's works were not appreciated until many years after her death, but her contributions to management thought and inquiry are now widely recognized as important foundation literature for the field of management.

Most management texts review the study of management by examining the major schools of thought that dominated early management science. These schools are reviewed in the following paragraphs, the earliest of which is referred to as the classical school of management.

## CLASSICAL SCHOOL OF MANAGEMENT

The classical school of management (the late 1800s–1920s) parallels the industrial revolution, which marked a major shift from agrarian-based to industrial-based societies. This philosophy of management centered primarily on improving the means of production and increasing productivity among workers. Three different approaches represent the classical school: scientific management, administrative management, and bureaucratic management.

### Scientific Management

Scientific management offered a systematic approach to the challenge of increasing production. This approach introduced several practices, including determination of the most effective way to coordinate tasks, careful selection of employees for different positions, proper training and development of the workforce, and introduction of economic incentives to motivate employees. Each part of the production process received careful scrutiny toward the goal of greater efficiency.

Frederick W. Taylor, by profession a mechanical engineer, is known as the father of scientific management. In the early 20th century, Taylor (1991) made a number of contributions to management theory, including the ideas of careful and systematic analysis of each job and task and identification of the best employee to fit each individual task.

Scientific management also proposed that workers would be more productive if they received high wages in return for their labor. This approach viewed the worker mechanistically, suggesting that management could guarantee more output if better wages were promised in return. Later approaches proposed that workers need more than just economic incentives to be productive. Nevertheless, many of Taylor's principles of scientific management are still found in modern organizations, such as detailed job descriptions and sophisticated methods of employee selection, training, and development.

### Administrative Management

Henri Fayol, a French mining executive, approached worker productivity differently from Taylor by studying the entire organization in hopes of increasing efficiency. Fayol (1949) introduced the POC[3] model, which detailed the functions of management the author identified as planning, organizing, commanding, coordinating, and control. In addition, the author established a list of 14 principles of management that must be flexible enough to accommodate changing circumstances. In that sense, Fayol was among the first theorists to recognize management as a continuing process. One can find Fayol's management functions and principles widely used in contemporary business organizations.

## Bureaucratic Management

German sociologist Max Weber focused on another aspect of worker productivity—organizational structure. Weber (1947) theorized that the use of a hierarchy or bureaucracy would enable the organization to produce at an optimal level. Weber called for a clear division of labor and management, strong central authority, a seniority system, strict discipline and control, clear policies and procedures, and careful selection of workers based primarily on technical qualifications. Weber's contributions to management are numerous, manifested in things like flow charts, job descriptions, and specific guidelines for promotion and advancement.

The classical school of management concentrated on how to make organizations more productive. Management was responsible for establishing clearly defined job responsibilities, maintaining close supervision, monitoring output, and making important decisions. Individual workers were thought to have little motivation to do their tasks beyond wages and economic incentives. These ideas would be challenged by the next major approach to management.

## HUMAN RELATIONS SCHOOL OF MANAGEMENT

The belief that workers were motivated only by wages and economic factors began to be challenged in the 1930s and 1940s, giving rise to the human relations school of management. The human relations school recognized that managers and employees were indeed members of the same organization and thus shared in the accomplishment of objectives. Further, employees had needs other than just wages and benefits; with these needs met, workers would be more effective and the organization would benefit.

Many theories relating to the behavioral aspects of management arose in this era from a micro perspective, centering on the individual rather than the organization. Key contributors include Elton Mayo, Abraham Maslow, Frederick Herzberg, Douglas McGregor, and William Ouchi. Their contributions to the human relations school are discussed in the following paragraphs.

## The Hawthorne Experiments

Perhaps the greatest influence on the development of the human relations approach to management involved this series of experiments conducted from 1924 to 1932 often identified with Harvard professor Elton Mayo. These experiments were actually commissioned by General Electric, with the goal of ultimately increasing the sale of light bulbs sold to business and industry.

In 1924, AT&T's Western Electric Hawthorne plant in Cicero, Illinois, was the location to investigate the impact of illumination (lighting) on worker productivity. Efficiency experts at the plant used two different groups of workers in the seminal experiment. A control group worked under normal lighting conditions while an experimental group worked under varying degrees of illumination. As lighting increased in the experimental group, productivity went up. However, productivity in the control group also increased, without any increase in light.

Mayo and other consultants were brought in to investigate and expand the study to other areas of the plant. Mayo concluded the human aspects of their work affected the productivity of the workers more than the physical conditions of the plant. In other words, worker behavior is not just physiological but psychological as well. The increased attention and interaction with supervisors led to greater productivity among employees. Workers felt a greater affinity to the company when management showed interest in the employees and their work.

The term *Hawthorne effect* has come to describe the impact of management attention on employee productivity. The Hawthorne experiments represent an important benchmark in management thought by recognizing that employees have social as well as physical and monetary needs. In this era, new insights were developed into ways that management could identify and meet employee needs as well as motivate workers, and the results of the experiments stimulated new ways of thinking about managing employees.

## The Hierarchy of Needs

Psychologist Abraham Maslow contributed to the human relations school through his efforts to understand employee motivation. Maslow (1954) theorized employees have many needs resembling a hierarchy. As basic needs are met, other levels of needs become increasingly important to the individual as the person progresses through the hierarchy.

Maslow identified five areas of need: physiological, safety, social, esteem, and self-actualization. Physiological needs are the essentials for survival: food, water, shelter, and clothing. Safety or security concerns the need to be free from physical danger and to live in a predictable environment. Social includes the need to belong and be accepted by others. Esteem is both self-esteem (feeling good about the self) and recognition from others. Self-actualization is the desire to become what one is capable of being—the idea of maximizing one's potential.

The utility of Maslow's hierarchy lies in its recognition that each individual is motivated by different needs, and individuals respond differently throughout the life cycle. Some people may have dominant needs at a particular level and not everyone moves through the entire hierarchy. Regardless, Maslow's hierarchy suggests managers may require different techniques to motivate people according to their needs.

## Hygiene and Motivator Factors

Psychologist Frederick Herzberg, studied employee attitudes through intensive interviews to determine which job variables determined worker satisfaction. Herzberg (1966) identified two sets of what the author called hygiene or maintenance factors, and motivators.

Hygiene factors were analogous with the work environment, including technical and physical conditions and factors such as company policies and procedures, supervision, the work itself, wages, and benefits. Motivators consisted of recognition, achievement, responsibility, and individual growth and development. Herzberg recognized that motivators positively influence employee satisfaction. Herzberg's work suggests managers must recognize a dual typology of employee needs—hygiene factors and the need for positive motivation—in order to maintain job satisfaction.

## Theory X and Theory Y

Whereas Maslow and Herzberg helped advance an understanding of motivation in management, industrial psychologist Douglas McGregor (1960) noted many managers still held traditional assumptions that workers held little interest in work and lacked ambition. McGregor labeled this style of management Theory X, which emphasized control, threat, and coercion to motivate employees.

McGregor offered a different approach to management called Theory Y. Managers did not rely on control or fear but instead integrated the needs of the workers with the organization. Employees could exercise self-control and self-direction and develop their own sense of responsibility. The manager's role in Theory Y centers on matching individual talents with the proper position in the organization and providing appropriate rewards.

## Theory Z

Ouchi (1981) used characteristics of both Theory X and Theory Y in contrasting management styles of American and Japanese organizations. Ouchi claimed U.S. organizations could learn much from a Japanese managerial model, which the author labeled as Theory Z.

Theory Z posits employee participation and individual development as key components of organizational growth. Interpersonal relations between workers and managers are stressed in Theory Z. Ouchi also drew from Theory X, in that management makes key decisions, and a strong sense of authority must be maintained.

The human relations school signified an important change in management thought as the focus moved to the role of employees in meeting organizational goals. In particular, the ideas of creating a positive working environment and attending to the needs of the employees represent important contributions of the human relations school to management science.

## CONTEMPORARY APPROACHES TO MANAGEMENT

By the 1960s, theorists began to integrate and expand concepts and elements of both the classical and human relations schools. This effort, which continues into the 21st century, has produced an enormous amount of literature on modern management thought in the areas of management effectiveness, leadership, systems theory, total quality management (TQM), and strategic management.

## Management Effectiveness

The classical and human relations schools share organizational productivity as a common goal, although they differ on the means. The former proposes efficiency and control, whereas the latter endorses employees and their needs and wants. Neither approach considers the importance of *effectiveness,* or the actual attainment of organizational goals. In both the classical and human relations schools, effectiveness is simply a natural and expected outcome.

Modern management theorists have questioned this assumption. Drucker (1973) claimed effectiveness is the very foundation of organizational success, more so than organizational efficiency. Drucker (1986) developed Management by Objectives (MBO), promoting exchange between managers and employees. In an MBO system, management identifies the goals for each individual and shares these goals and expectations with each unit and employee. The shared objectives are used to guide individual units or departments and serve as a way for management to monitor and evaluate progress.

An important aspect of the MBO approach is an agreement between employees and managers regarding performance over a set period of time (e.g., 90 days, 180 days, etc.). In this sense, management retains external control, whereas employees exhibit self-control over how to complete their objectives. The MBO approach has further utility in that one can apply it to any organization, regardless of size. Critics of MBO contend it is time-consuming to implement and difficult to maintain in organizations that deal with rapidly changing environments.

## Leadership

The interdependent relationship between management and leadership represents a second area of modern management thought. Considered a broader topic than management, *leadership* is commonly defined among management theorists as "the process of influencing the activities of an individual or a group in efforts toward goal achievement in a given situation" (Hersey & Blanchard, 1996, p. 94). Although leadership is not confined to management, there is wide agreement that the most successful organizations have strong, effective leaders. Most organizations contain both formal and informal leaders, some of which are in management positions, some are not.

Leadership can be studied from many different perspectives. Among the more significant scholars is Warren Bennis (1994) who claims leadership consists of three basic qualities: vision, passion, and integrity. Regarding vision, leaders have an understanding of where they want to go and will not let obstacles deter their progress. Passion is another trait of a good leader, whereas integrity is made up of self-knowledge, candor, and maturity.

Bennis makes several distinctions between someone who is a manager versus someone who is a leader. To Bennis, the leader innovates, whereas the manager administers. Leaders offer a long-range perspective, whereas managers exhibit a short-range view.

Leaders originate, managers imitate. The author argues that most business schools—and education in general—focus on narrow aspects of training rather than on development of leadership qualities in individuals. Only one study related to the media industries has dealt with leadership aspects; Perez-Latre and Sanchez-Tabernero (2003) conducted a qualitative study to assess how leadership affects change among Spanish media firms.

There is an emerging body of literature that deals with leadership that is more practical in nature and less theory-driven. Publications like *Strategy and Leadership*, *Fast Company*, and *Leadership Wired* (an online publication) provide articles related to leadership principles. *Strategy and Leadership* occasionally features specific articles that deal with the media industries (see Parker, 2004; Sterling, 2002).

## Systems Theory

Systems theory approaches management from a macro perspective, examining the entire organization and the environment in which the organization operates (Schoderbek, Schoderbek, & Kefalas, 1985). Organizations are engaged in similar activities involving inputs (e.g., labor, capital, and equipment), production processes (converting inputs into some type of product), and outputs (e.g., products, goods, and services). In a systems approach to management, organizations also study the external environment, evaluating feedback from the environment in order to recognize change and reassess goals.

Organizations are not isolated; they interact interdependently with other organizations in the environment. The systems approach recognizes the relationship between the organization and its external environment. Although managers cannot control this environment, they must be aware of environmental factors and the impact they may have on the organization. Covington (1997) illustrates the application of systems theory to television station management.

Another approach to systems theory is the resource dependence perspective developed by Pfeffer and Salancik (1978). An organization's survival is based on its utilization of resources, both internal and external. All organizations depend on the environment for resources, and media industries are no exception (Turow, 1992).

Much of the uncertainty organizations face is due to environmental factors. As Pfeffer and Salancik (1978) state, "Problems arise not merely because organizations are dependent on their environment, but because this environment is not dependable . . . [W]hen environments change, organizations face the prospect either of not surviving or of changing their activities in response to these environmental factors" (p. 3).

Organizations can alter their interdependence with other organizations by absorbing other entities or cooperating with other organizations to reach mutual interdependence (Pfeffer & Salancik, 1978). Mergers and acquisitions, vertical integration, and diversification are strategies organizations use to ease resource dependence.

## Total Quality Management

Another modern approach to management theory is total quality management (TQM). TQM is best described as a series of approaches to achieving quality in organizations, especially when producing products and serving customers (Weaver, 1991). Under TQM, managers combine strategic approaches to deliver the best products and services by continuously improving every part of an operation (Hand, 1992). Although management implements and leads TQM in an organization, every employee is responsible for quality.

A number of management scholars have contributed to an understanding of TQM, which is widely used. Considered the pioneer of modern quality control, Walter Shewart originally worked for Bell Labs, where early work focused on control charts built on statistical analyses. Juran (1988) and Deming (1982) contributed to Shewart's early work, primarily with Japanese industries. Deming linked the ideas of quality, productivity, market share, and jobs; Juran contributed a better understanding of planning, control, and improvement in the quality process. Other important contributors to the development of TQM include Philip Crosby, Armand Feigenbaum, and Karou Ishikawa (Kolarik, 1995).

The popularity of TQM in the United States increased during the late 1970s and early 1980s, when U.S. business and industry were suffering from what many industrial experts labeled declining quality. Organizations adopted quality control procedures and strategies to reverse the negative image associated with poor-quality products. TQM is still used as a way to encourage and demand high quality in the products and services produced by organizations.

## Strategic Management

The growth of companies and industries during the second half of the 20th century led to the importance of strategic management. Strategic management is concerned with developing the tools and techniques to analyze industries and competitors and developing strategies to gain competitive advantage. The most significant scholar in the area of strategic management is Harvard professor Michael Porter, whose seminal works *Competitive Strategy* (1980) and *Competitive Advantage* (1985) form the primary literature in studying strategy in business schools all over the world. There is an entire chapter in this Handbook devoted to the topic of strategic management and its application to media industries and organizations (see Chan-Olmsted, Chap. 8, this volume).

## Management in the 21st Century

How might management science evolve in the 21st century? Peter Drucker, one of the preeminent management scholars of the past century calls for a new management model, as well a new economic theory to guide business and industry (Drucker, 2000). The author claimed that schools have become antiquated, failing to prepare people for the new managerial environment.

In an earlier work, Drucker (1999) argued that, given the sweeping social, political, and economic changes affecting the world, there are few certainties in management and strategic thinking. Drucker states, "one cannot manage change . . . one can only be ahead of it" (1999, p. 73). Drucker claims managers must become change leaders, seizing opportunities and understanding how to effect change successfully in their organizations.

Clearly, media managers would agree with Drucker that in order to be successful, the ability to cope with change and use change to reach a competitive advantage is critical.

The challenge is how to embrace change successfully. A critical change issue for managers in the 21st century is determining when to focus on the external environment and when to focus on the internal environment.

At the end of the day, management is still concerned with working with and through other people to accomplish organizational objectives (Albarran, 2002). In a seminal study of over 400 companies and 80,000 individual managers across numerous industries, Buckingham and Coffman (1999) identified four key characteristics of great managers. Great managers were those who were particularly adept at selecting the right talent, defining clear expectations, focusing on each individual's strengths, and helping individuals find the right fit in the organization. The authors' findings have particular implications for media management, helping to focus attention on the importance of quality employees in meeting organizational objectives.

In summary, the different approaches to management reflected in the classical, behavioral, and modern schools all have limitations regarding their application to the media industries. Although the classical school emphasizes production, its understanding of management skills and functions are helpful. The human relations school makes an important contribution by emphasizing employee needs and proper motivation. Modern approaches clarify managerial effectiveness and leadership but also recognize the interdependency of media and other societal systems.

The evolving nature of the communication industries hinders the adoption of a universal theory of media management. The complex day-to-day challenges associated with managing a newspaper firm, radio or television station, a cable system, or a telecommunications facility makes identifying or suggesting a central theory challenging. Further, the variability of media firms in terms of the number of employees, market rankings, qualitative characteristics, globalization, and organizational culture requires individual analysis to discern what style of management will work best.

Having reviewed the key schools of thought in developing our knowledge of general management, our attention now shifts to examining how scholars have approached the study of media management and relevant findings. The focus will be on the following industries: newspapers, radio, television and cable, and converging media industries.

## NEWSPAPER MANAGEMENT

Newspapers are somewhat complex in their managerial structure in that management occurs throughout a newspaper firm at different levels. Typically at the top of the hierarchy is the publisher, who is accountable to the newspaper's ownership for the economic performance of the newspaper. The editor-in-chief, or managing editor, is responsible for the actual content of the newspaper. But throughout the organization there are editors for various sections (local/metropolitan, sports, business, etc.) that supervise reporters, writers, and other staff. There are also departments that have nothing to do with the content that provide support functions; among them are accounting and billing, retail and classified sales, personnel, and customer service. Hence, management can take place within and across numerous departments.

Books written in the mid-20th century were among the earliest efforts to study newspaper management. Wood (1952) focused exclusively on managing newspaper circulation, whereas Thayer (1954) provided a more comprehensive approach in explaining the business management of newspapers. Rucker and Williams (1955) considered the organizational structure of the newspaper industry and the impact it had on management; this work would be revised in four subsequent editions through 1978.

As newspaper chains and conglomerates began to rise in the 1950s and beyond, other works began to focus on publishing single-owned newspapers and community papers. Representative works include Wyckoff (1956), McKinney (1977) and Harvard Post (1978). Efforts to improve production aspects (Woods, 1963) and credit and collections (Institute of Newspaper Controllers, 1971) illustrate the importance of newspaper publishing as a business.

Books devoted to more analytical aspects of newspaper and newsroom management began to be published during the late 1970s, including Engwall's (1978) examination of newspapers as organizations, followed by works by Rankin (1986), Giles (1987), and Willis (1988). Fink (1988) authored the first book to look at newspapers and strategic management. A sociological examination of the newspaper work force and changes in the publishing area was conducted by Kalleberg, Wallace, Loscocco, Leicht, and Ehm (1987), following Kalleberg and Berg's analysis (1987) of work structures. Underwood's (1993) text illustrates how the newspaper industry had changed by the 1990s, with much more of an emphasis on business practices. Picard and Brody (1997) and Mogel (2000) offer more general overviews of newspaper publishing and less emphasis on newspaper management.

Scholars from other countries have addressed managerial aspects of newspaper publishing. Höyer, Hadednius and Weibull (1975) examined the development and economics of the press, whereas Hendricks (1999) compared strategic management of newspaper firms between the United States and the Netherlands. Dunnett (1988) probably offers one of the best overviews of global aspects of publishing.

In terms of articles in scholarly journals, only a few offer a specific look at management. Soloski (1979) and Litman and Bridges (1986) are each concerned with the economics of newspaper publishing, whereas Demers and Wackman (1988) discussed the impact of chain ownership on management practices. Olien, Tichenor and Donohue (1988) compared perceptions and attitudes between corporate owners and newspaper editors. Matthews (1997) offered the only-known study to examine how newspaper chains develop and promote publishers, the top managerial position in a newspaper. Several studies related to competition, chain ownership, organizational development, and diversity offer implications for newspaper management (see Adams, 1995; Akhavan-Majid & Boudreau, 1995; Gade, 2004; Gade & Perry, 2003; Lacy & Blanchard, 2003; Lacy, Shaver, & St. Cyr, 1996, Lacy & Simon, 1997).

An emerging area of newspaper studies involves Internet newspapers, especially online and offline relationships and their implications for management. Lichtenberg (1999) discussed the impact of online newspapers and the Internet on editors and publishers. Chyi and Lasorsa (1999, 2002) and Chyi and Sylvie (2001) provided the earliest empirical examinations of online newspaper usage, access, and comparisons to traditional papers. Wall, Schoenbach and Lauf (2004) surveyed 1,000 Dutch respondents to assess how newspapers are substitutes for traditional media, and Chyi (2004) surveyed Hong Kong residents to determine the viability of online subscription models.

The body of literature on newspaper management is varied and somewhat disjointed in that many topics are considered, but there is little depth of knowledge. The fact that management can occur at different levels within a newspaper certainly is responsible for part of the breadth, but there are few scholarly studies that focus on any particular area. Although newspaper scholars have been primarily interested in issues like advertising, circulation, competition, chain ownership, and actual editorial content, there is a great need for more contemporary studies on newspaper management, especially involving the continuing impact of chain ownership on management and examining how managers are affected in markets where media industries—and newsrooms—are converging. Likewise, additional research on the role of online newspapers and their impact on traditional papers deserve continuing scholarly attention as well.

## RADIO MANAGEMENT

Virtually all of our scholarly knowledge on radio management is drawn from the United States. This is due to a number of factors, among them the fact that America has the most radio stations of any nation on the globe and that the industry is commercially driven. Thus, this section centers on radio management from a U.S. perspective.

Radio management has undergone significant change since the 1980s primarily because of a series of regulatory changes that have steadily increased ownership limits to the point where there are no longer national limits, but limits at the local market level dependent on the number of station signals home to the market (see Albarran & Pitts, 2000). Over time, this has led to numerous changes in radio management, with the general manager—the top position in a radio station—being responsible for more than one station.

Historically, the earliest effort to detail specific aspects of radio station management is a book by broadcaster Leonard Reinsch (1948). Revised 12 years later (Reinsch & Ellis, 1960) the work nearly tripled in size but maintained a strong professional orientation. Reflecting the development of FM broadcasting in the 1960s, new works appeared, including Hoffer (1968) and Quall and Martin (1968), the latter also covering television broadcasting and revised three times in subsequent editions.

There are several texts designed for media management courses, most of which offer some discussion on radio management and other media. These include Albarran (2002), Albarran and Pitts (2000), Lavine and Wackman (1988), Marcus (1986), Pringle, Starr and McCavitt (1999), Sherman (1997), and Willis and Willis (1993).

Few scholarly articles exist that focus exclusively on radio station management. Hulbert (1962) looked at managerial employment in the broadcast industry, and Bohn and Clark (1972) profiled media managers in small markets. Abel and Jacobs (1975) collected data on radio station management's attitudes toward broadcasting. Hagin's dissertation (1994) provides the first study to examine management of radio duopolies. Chan-Olmsted (1995) looks at the economic implications of duopoly ownership, whereas Lacy and Riffe (1994) provide an analysis of the impact of competition and group ownership on radio news. Shane (1998) and Chambers (2001) analyze how regulatory changes are affecting radio, and Chambers (2003) examines the effects of consolidation on radio industry structure.

Efforts to understand the evolving role of market managers (individuals responsible for three or more stations) in the radio industry led to a survey of the top 25 radio groups conducted by Loomis and Albarran (2004). The authors found that managers responsible for a cluster of stations are working longer hours and focusing more on the financial aspects of management (e.g., sales and marketing). A key finding was that managers were delegating more tasks to mid-level managers (e.g., programming, sales, engineering) in order to handle increasing responsibilities. Given the influence of the U.S. media system on other countries, the authors in a separate study (Albarran & Loomis, 2004) illustrate how the regulatory experience in America may transfer to other developed nations.

Online radio and Internet radio business studies are emerging. Lind and Medoff (1999) authored the first examination of how radio stations were using the Internet. Evans and Smethers (2001) conducted a Delphi study of the impact of online radio on traditional radio. Ren and Chan-Olmsted (2004) analyze different business models for streaming terrestrial and Internet-based radio stations in the United States.

Our understanding of radio management is very limited, giving researchers plenty of opportunity to investigate many different avenues of inquiry. Clearly, additional work is needed not only to have a better understanding of the role of market and general managers, but also to learn more about the evolution of middle managers that are taking a much more prominent role in the day-to-day operations in the radio industry. Researchers will also need to examine managerial implications of Internet utilization and competition from Web-based radio services and subscription satellite radio services.

## TELEVISION AND CABLE MANAGEMENT

Although television came of age during the 1950s in most developed nations, the first books on television management would not appear until the 1960s. Roe (1964) authored the first book devoted to television management, followed by Quall and Martin (1968). These early works featured a predominant industry orientation with no theoretical foundation. Bunyan and Crimmins (1977), Dessart (1978), and Hillard (1989) also offered books of a descriptive nature detailing different aspects of television station management.

Cable television programming and production is the subject of a book by Schiller, Brock and Rigby (1979), whereas Oringel and Buske (1987) focused on managing a community access channel. Covington (1997) applied systems theory to television management and also addressed creativity in television and cable management and producing (Covington, 1999). Parsons and Frieden (1998) provided a comprehensive look at the cable and satellite industry, but the work is not specifically focused on management. As cited previously, textbooks for management courses also cover television and cable management, and most provide a basic theoretical orientation to the various schools of management (see Albarran, 2002; Lavine & Wackman, 1988; Marcus, 1986; Pringle et al., 1999; Sherman, 1997; Willis & Willis, 1993).

In terms of articles in scholarly journals, the literature devoted to television management is extremely limited, both from a domestic and a global perspective. Barber (1958) examined the decision-making process in covering news for television. Busby (1979) surveyed managers regarding changes in media regulatory policy. Geisler (2000) surveyed controllers in a census of German television stations and found they were instrumental in the planning and budgeting processes within the stations they serve. Tjernstrom (2002) argued for a theory of the media firm, especially for public service broadcasting. Schultz (2002) found differences among younger versus older religious broadcast managers in regards to background, attitude, management style, and digital implementation.

Changes in U.S. regulatory policy led to the creation of television duopolies beginning in 1999. Albarran and Loomis (2003) conducted a census of all known television duopoly managers at the time of the study and found that managing a duopoly led to a greater dependence on middle managers and more attention to sales and news performance. Managers also reported challenges in merging two stations and different cultures in establishing a duopoly. In a related article, the authors speculated on the implications of their findings for international television management (Albarran & Loomis, 2004).

Television station managers are also attempting to find innovative ways to utilize the Internet as part of their business operations. Chan-Olmsted and Ha (2003) offered an early analysis of Internet business models used by TV broadcasters, but much work and development on this topic remain to be done.

Although television has been the focus of thousands of studies, television management has been practically ignored by the scholarly community. Clearly, with the television industry experiencing rapid change as a result of regulatory and technological forces, academic researchers have an open door for future study. In regards to multichannel television (cable and satellite) even less is known about management practices and decision making. More research is needed to understand television managerial decision making in regards to economics and finance, programming and news, working with employees, and business uses of the Internet. These are just a few areas that are ripe for new research and study.

## CONVERGING MEDIA INDUSTRIES

The topic of convergence (the integration of data, media, and telecommunication systems) is often identified with the media industries, yet research on managing media convergence is in its infancy. Two studies provided the first glimpse at this subject.

Killebrew (2003) studied different aspects of convergence between newspaper and television station newsrooms and the challenges of integrating two distinct cultures (print versus broadcast). The author suggested that for convergence to be successful, efforts must follow a well-designed plan of action that addresses individual journalists rather than simply creating organizational efficiency. Lawson-Borders (2003) examined convergence activity among three media companies (Tribune, Belo, and Media General). The author presented seven observations of convergence identified as communication, commitment, cooperation, compensation, culture, competition, and customer as a result of the field research.

As more and more media organizations embrace convergence, opportunities abound for further study on managing media convergence. For example, studies could be conducted at various levels of analysis (local, national, global) using multiple methodological approaches.

## PROPOSITIONS REGARDING MEDIA MANAGEMENT RESEARCH

In reviewing the body of literature that forms our knowledge of trends and patterns in media management research, it is possible to offer the following propositions regarding our knowledge of the field. These propositions will be useful in establishing future directions for research in this area.

1. The literature on media management is limited in terms of both its practical and theoretical contributions to the field. Much of the early work (prior to the 1990s) is descriptive in nature, but helps provide a good orientation and foundation to the field.
2. There is no consensus among scholars on how to approach the study of management. Most media management is targeted toward the role of the editor/publisher in the newspaper industry or the general manager in the broadcast/cable industries. Consciously or not, researchers have ignored other levels of management (e.g., supervisory, middle management) in media operations.
3. Methodologies employed in studying media management rely almost exclusively on personal interviews, surveys, or secondary research sources. However, research conducted since the mid-1990s tends to be more sophisticated in that it is theoretically driven and analytically based.
4. The field is ripe for exploring new avenues of research, expanding the use of different methodologies, and developing new theoretical approaches.

## SETTING THE AGENDA FOR MEDIA MANAGEMENT RESEARCH

Given the existing state of the field of media management research, what are the next steps in further developing and refining the field? This section offers an agenda for scholars to consider regarding future research in media management for over the next decade and beyond.

1. The field needs management research conducted at multiple levels of analysis that also takes into consideration the macro and global (cross-cultural) implications. As the media industries continue to consolidate and expand their operations beyond domestic borders, media management research must follow this trend, and study management issues from the boardroom to the smallest unit in a media facility.
2. The field needs studies that are rigorous in the sense that they are theoretically grounded and methodologically sound and can further expand our knowledge of media management practices and decision making. Researchers need to take risks by testing new theoretical assumptions that challenge existing paradigms.

3. The field needs to be fully engaged in researching the challenges of managing media convergence, as the integration of various types of media forms represent a major shift in the application of media management.
4. The field needs studies to gain an understanding of the different strategies employed by media management to acquire market share, improve cash flow, develop new products, expand business models, implement new technologies, and respond to competition and external forces.
5. The field needs research that explicates our understanding of the interplay among management, economic, social, and regulatory forces.
6. The field needs research that expands beyond single-purpose studies to more longitudinal research that builds on existing knowledge and trends. There is little benchmarking data for researchers in the field to utilize.
7. The field needs greater interaction with other academic areas studying management, including business and the social and behavioral sciences. Likewise, the field would benefit greatly from collaborative research between media firms and academic scholars.
8. Researchers need to be more active in disseminating their work, not only through traditional conferences and scholarly publications, but also through working papers and research-in-progress made available to others via Web sites and discussion lists.

By following these suggestions, scholars will collectively move media management research into new and exciting directions through the next decade. Media management research stands at an important crossroads, building on a firm foundation through early research in the general area of management science and the growth of the media industries, to the multi-faceted, competitive global marketplace that media firms find themselves engaged in early in the 21st century.

## REFERENCES

Abel, J. D., & Jacobs, F. N. (1975). Radio station manager attitudes toward broadcasting. *Journal of Broadcasting, 14*(4), 411–421.

Adams, E. E. (1995). Chain growth and merger waves: A macroeconomic historical perspective on press consolidation. *Journalism and Mass Communication Quarterly, 72*(2), 376–389.

Akhavan-Majid, R., & Boudreau, T. (1995). Chain ownership, organizational size, and editorial role perceptions. *Journalism and Mass Communication Quarterly, 72*(4), 863–873.

Albarran, A. B. (2002). *Management of electronic media* (2nd ed.). Belmont, CA: Wadsworth.

Albarran, A. B., & Loomis, K. D. (2003). *Managing television duopolies: A first look*. Unpublished manuscript. The University of North Texas.

Albarran, A. B., & Loomis, K. D. (2004). Regulatory changes and impacts on media management in the United States: A look at early research. *The International Journal on Media Management, 6*(1–2), 131–138.

Albarran, A. B., & Pitts, G. G. (2000). *The radio broadcasting industry*. Needham Heights, MA: Allyn & Bacon.

Barber, R. B. (1958). Decisions behind the camera. *Journal of Broadcasting, 3*(4), 305–325.

Bennis, W. (1994). *On becoming a leader*. Reading, MA: Addison-Wesley.

Bohn, T. W., & Clark, R. K. (1972). Small market media managers: A profile. *Journal of Broadcasting, 16*(2), 205–215.

Buckingham, M., & Coffman, C. (1999). *First, break all the rules. What the world's greatest managers do differently*. New York: Simon & Schuster.

Bunyan, J. A., & Crimmins, J. C. (1977). *Television and management: The manager's guide to video.* White Plains, NY: Knowledge Industry.

Busby, L. J. (1979). Broadcast regulatory policy: The managerial view. *Journal of Broadcasting, 23*(3), 331–341.

Caves, R. E. (2000). *Creative industries. Contracts between art and commerce.* Cambridge, MA: Harvard University Press.

Chambers, T. (2001). Losing owners: Deregulation and small market radio. *The Journal of Radio Studies, 8*(2), 292–315.

Chambers, T. (2003). Structural changes in small media markets. *The Journal of Media Economics, 16*(1), 41–59.

Chan-Olmsted, S. M. (1995). A chance for survival or status quo? The economic implications of the radio duopoly ownership rules. *Journal of Radio Studies, 4,* 59–75.

Chan-Olmsted, S. M., & Ha, L. (2003). Internet business models for broadcasters: How television stations perceive and integrate the Internet. *Journal of Broadcasting & Electronic Media, 47*(4), 597–617.

Chyi, H. I. (2004, May). *Who would pay for online news? An empirical study on the viability of the subscription model.* Paper presented at the 6th World Media Economics Conference, Montreal, Canada.

Chyi, H. I., & Lasorsa, D. (1999). Access, use and preferences for online newspapers. *Newspaper Research Journal, 20*(4), 2–13.

Chyi, H. I., & Lasorsa, D. L. (2002). An explorative study on the market relation between online and print newspapers. *The Journal of Media Economics, 15*(2), 91–106.

Chyi, H. I., & Sylvie, G. (2001). The medium is global, the content is not: The role of geography in online newspaper markets. *The Journal of Media Economics, 14*(4), 231–248.

Covington, W. G. (1997). *Systems theory applied to television station management in the competitive marketplace.* Lanham, MD: University Press of America.

Covington, W. G. (1999). *Creativity in TV & cable managing and producing.* Lanham, MD: University Press of America.

Demers, D. P., & Wackman, D. B. (1988). Effect of chain ownership on newspaper management. *Newspaper Research Journal, 9,* 59–68.

Deming, W. E. (1982). *Out of crisis.* Cambridge, MA: Productivity Press.

Dessart, G. (1978). *Television in the real world: A case study course in broadcast management.* New York: Hastings House.

Drucker, P. F. (1974). *Management: Tasks, responsibilities, practices.* New York: Harper & Row.

Drucker, P. F. (1986). *Innovation and entrepreneurship: Practice and principles.* New York: Harper & Row.

Drucker, P. F. (1999). *Management challenges for the 21st century.* New York: HarperBusiness.

Drucker, P. (2000, January 1). Talking about tomorrow: Peter Drucker. Millennium Edition: Interactive Edition, *The Wall Street Journal.* Available online: http://interactive.wsj.com/archive/retrieve.cgi?id=SB944517413185622361.djm Accessed February 15, 2005.

Dunnett, P. J. S. (1988). *The world newspaper industry.* London: Croom Helm.

Engwall, L. (1978). *Newspapers as organizations.* Farnborough, UK: Saxon House.

Evans, C. L., & Smethers, S. (2001). Streaming into the future: A Delphi study of broadcasters' predictions about cyber radio's impact on traditional station operation procedures. *Journal of Radio Studies, 7*(1), 15–28.

Fayol, H. (1949). *General and industrial management* (C. Storrs, Trans.). London: Pittman.

Ferguson, D. A. (1997). The domain of inquiry for media management researchers. In C. Warner (Ed.), *Media management review* (pp. 177–184). Mahwah, NJ: Lawrence Erlbaum Associates.

Fink, C. C. (1988). *Strategic newspaper management.* New York: Random House.

Follett, M. P., Pauline, G., & Graham, P. (1995). *Mary Parker Follett, prophet of management.* Boston: Harvard Business School Press.

Fox, E. M., & Urwick, L. (1977). *Dynamic administration: The collected works of Mary Parker Follett* (2nd ed.). New York: Hippocrene Books.

Gade, P. J. (2004). Newspapers and organizational development: Management and journalist perceptions of newsroom cultural change. *Journalism and Mass Communication Monographs, 6*(1), 5–55.

Gade, P. J., & Perry, E. L. (2003). Changing the newsroom culture: A four-year case study of organizational development at the St. Louis Post-Dispatch. *Journalism and Mass Communication Quarterly, 80*(2), 327–347.

Giesler, R. (2000). Management control in German television: Delivering numbers for management decision. *The Journal of Media Economics, 13*(2), 123–143.

Giles, R. H. (1987). *Newsroom management: A guide to theory and practice.* Indianapolis, IN: R. J. Berg.

Hagin, L. A. (1994). *United States radio consolidation: An investigation of the structures and strategies of selected duopolies.* Unpublished doctoral dissertation, University of Tennessee, Knoxville.

Hand, M. (1992). Total quality management—One God but many prophets. In M. Hand and B. Plowman (Eds.), *Quality management handbook* (pp. 26–46). Oxford, UK: Butterworth-Heinemann.

Harvard Post. (1978). *How to produce a small newspaper.* Port Washington, NY: Harvard Common Press.

Hendricks, P. (1999). *Newspapers, a lost cause? Strategic management of newspaper firms in the United States and the Netherlands.* Boston: Kluwer Academic.

Hersey, P., & Blanchard, K. H. (1996). *Management of organizational behavior* (7th ed.). Englewood Cliffs, NJ: Prentice-Hall.

Herzberg, F. (1966). *Work and the nature of man.* New York: World Publishing.

Herzberg, F. (1987). One more time: How do you motivate employees? *Harvard Business Review, 67*(5), 109–117.

Hillard, R. L. (1989). *Television station operations and management.* Boston: Focal Press.

Hoffer, J. (1968). *Managing today's radio station.* Blue Ridge Summit, PA: Tab Books.

Höyer, S., Hadednius, S. & Weibull, L. (1975). *The practice and economics of the press: A developmental perspective.* London: Sage.

Hulbert, J. H. (1962). Broadcasting management: A report from the APBE-NAB employment study. *Journal of Broadcasting, 6*(3), 255–264.

Institute of Newspaper Controllers and Finance Officers. (1971). *Newspaper credit and collection management.* Fair Haven, NJ: Author.

Juran, J. M. (1988). *Juran on planning for quality.* Cambridge, MA: Productivity Press.

Kalleberg, A. L., & Berg, I. (1987). *Work and industry. Structures, markets and processes.* New York: Plenum.

Kalleberg, A. L., Wallace, M., Loscocco, K. A., Leicht, K., & Ehm, H. (1987). The eclipse of craft: The changing face of labor in the newspaper industry. In D. B. Cornfield (Ed.), *Workers, managers and technological change: Emerging patterns of labor relations* (pp. 47–71). New York: Plenum.

Killebrew, K. C. (2003). Culture, creativity and convergence: Managing journalists in a changing information workplace. *The International Journal on Media Management, 5*(1), 39–46.

Kolarik, W. J. (1995). *Creating quality.* New York: McGraw-Hill.

Lacy, S., & Blanchard, A. (2003). The impact of public ownership, profits, and competition on number of newsroom employees and starting salaries at mid-sized daily newspapers. *Journalism and Mass Communication Quarterly, 80*(4), 949–968.

Lacy, S., & Riffe, D. (1994). The impact of competition and group ownership on radio news. *Journalism Quarterly 71*, 583–593.

Lacy, S., Shaver, M. A., & St. Cyr, C. (1996). The effects of public ownership and newspaper competition on the financial performance of newspaper corporations: A replication and extension. *Journalism and Mass Communication Quarterly, 73*(2), 332–341.

Lacy, S., & Simon, T. F. (1997). Intercounty group ownership of daily newspapers and the decline of competition for readers. *Journalism and Mass Communication Quarterly, 74*(4), 814–825.

Laswell, H. D. (1949). The structure and function of communication in society. In W. Schramm (Ed.), *Mass communications* (pp. 102–115). Urbana: University of Illinois Press.

Lavine, J. M., & Wackman, D. B. (1988). *Managing media organizations.* New York: Longman.

Lawson-Borders, G. (2003). Integrating new media and old media: Seven observations of convergence as a strategy for best practices in media organizations. *The International Journal on Media Management, 5*(2), 91–99.

Lichtenberg, L. (1999). Influences of electronic developments on the role of editors and publishers—strategic issues. *The International Journal on Media Management, 1*(1), 23–34.

Lind, R. A., & Medoff, N. J. (1999). Radio stations and the World Wide Web. *Journal of Radio Studies, 6*(2), 203–221.

Litman, B. R., & Bridges, J. (1986). An economic analysis of daily newspaper performance. *Newspaper Research Journal, 7*, 9–26.

Loomis, K. D., & Albarran, A. B. (2004). Managing radio market clusters: Orientations of general managers. *The Journal of Media Economics, 17*(1), 51–69.

Marcus, N. (1986). *Broadcast and cable management.* Englewood Cliffs, NJ: Prentice-Hall.

Maslow, A. H. (1954). *Motivation and personality.* New York: Harper & Row.

Matthews, M. N. (1997). Pathway to the top: How the top newspaper chains train and promote publishers. In C. Warner (Ed.), *Media management review* (pp. 147–156). Mahwah, NJ: Lawrence Erlbaum Associates.

McGregor, D. (1960). *The human side of enterprise.* New York: McGraw-Hill.

McKinney, J. (1977). *How to start your own community newspaper.* Port Jefferson, NY: Meadow Press.

Mogel, L. (2000). *The newspaper: Everything you need to know to make it in the newspaper business.* Pittsburgh, PA: GATF Press.

Olien, C. N., Tichenor, P. J., & Donohue, G. A. (1988). Relation between corporate ownership and editor attitudes about business. *Journalism Quarterly, 65,* 259–266.

Oringel, R. S., & Buske, S. M. (1987). *The access manager's handbook: A guide for managing community television.* Boston: Focal Press.

Ouchi, W. G. (1981). *Theory Z: How American business can meet the Japanese challenge.* Reading, MA: Addison-Wesley.

Parker, N. (2004). The 30-hour day: The future for media and entertainment businesses. *Strategy and Leadership, 32*(2), 36–43.

Parsons, P. R., & Frieden, R. M. (1998). *The cable and satellite television industries.* Boston: Allyn & Bacon.

Perez-Latre, F. J., & Sanchez-Taberneo, A. (2003). Leadership, an essential requirement for effecting change in media companies: An analysis of the Spanish market. *The International Journal on Media Management, 5*(2), 199–208.

Pfeffer, G., & Salancik, G. (1978). *The external control of organizations: A resource dependence perspective.* New York: Harper & Row.

Picard, R. G., & Brody, J. H. (1997). *The newspaper publishing industry.* Boston: Allyn & Bacon.

Porter, M. E. (1980). *Competitive strategy.* New York: The Free Press.

Porter, M. E. (1985). *Competitive advantage.* New York: The Free Press.

Pringle, P., Starr, M., & McCavitt, W. (1999). *Electronic media management* (4th ed.). Boston: Focal Press.

Quall, W. L., & Martin, L. A. (1968). *Broadcast management: Radio, television.* New York: Hastings House.

Rankin, W. P. (1986). *The practice of newspaper management.* New York: Praeger.

Reinsch, J. L. (1948). *Radio station management.* New York: Harper.

Reinsch, J. L., & Ellis, E. I. (1960). *Radio station management* (2nd ed.). New York: Harper.

Ren, W., & Chan-Olmsted, S. M. (2004). Radio business on the World Wide Web: Comparing the online content of streaming terrestrial and Internet-based radio stations in the United States. *Journal of Radio Studies, 11*(1), 6–25.

Roe, Y. (1964). *Television station management: The business of broadcasting.* New York: Hastings House.

Rucker, F. W., & Williams, H. L. (1955). *Newspaper organization and management.* Ames: Iowa State College Press.

Schiller, D., Brock, B. E., & Rigby, F. (1979). *CATV program origination & production.* Blue Ridge Summit, PA: Tab Books.

Schoderbek, P. P., Schoderbek, C. D., & Kefalas, A. G. (1985). *Management systems: Conceptual considerations* (3rd ed.). Plano, TX: Business Publications.

Schultz, B. E. (2002). The effect of age and background of religious broadcasting executives on digital television implementation. *The Journal of Media & Religion, 1*(4), 217–230.

Shane, E. (1998). The state of the industry: Radio's shifting paradigm. *The Journal of Radio Studies, 5*(2), 1–7.

Sherman, B. (1997). *Telecommunications management* (3rd ed.). New York: McGraw-Hill.

Soloski, J. (1979). Economics and management: The real influence on newspaper groups. *Newspaper Research Journal, 1,* 19–27.

Sterling, J. (2002). Strategy development for the real world: A metro newspaper has nowhere to grow and lots of "new media" competition. *Strategy and Leadership, 30*(1), 10–17.

Taylor, F. W. (1991). *The principles of scientific management.* New York: Harper.

Thayer, F. (1954). *Newspaper business management.* New York: Prentice-Hall.

Tjernstrom, S. (2002). Theoretical approaches to the management of the public service media firm. *The Journal of Media Economics, 15*(4), 241–249.

Tonn, J. C. (2003). *Mary P. Follett: Changing democracy, transforming management.* New Haven, CT: Yale University Press.

Turow, J. (1992). *Media systems in society: Understanding industries, strategies, and power.* New York: Longman.

Underwood, D. (1993). *When MBAs rule the newsroom: How the marketers and managers are reshaping today's media.* New York: Columbia University Press.

Wall, E., Schoenbach, K., & Lauf, E. (2004, May). *Online newspapers: A substitute for print newspapers and other information channels?* Paper presented at the 6th World Media Economics Conference, Montreal, Canada.

Weaver, C. N. (1991). *TQM: A step-by-step guide to implementation.* Milwaukee, WI: Quality Press.

Weber, M. (1947). *The theory of social and economic organization* (A. M. Henderson and T. Parsons, Trans.). New York: Free Press.

Willis, J., & Willis, D. B. (1993). *New directions in media management.* Boston: Allyn & Bacon.

Willis, W. J. (1988). *Surviving in the newspaper business: Newspaper management in turbulent times.* New York: Praeger.

Woods, A. (1963). *Modern newspaper production.* New York: Harper & Row.

Wood, D. J. (1952). *Newspaper circulation management, a profession.* Oakland, CA: Newspaper Research Bureau.

Wyckoff, E. H. (1956). *Editing and producing the small publication.* Princeton, NJ: Van Nostrand.

# 2

# Historical Trends and Patterns in Media Economics

Robert G. Picard

Jönköping University

Media economics is the study of how economic and financial pressures affect a variety of communications activities, systems, organizations, and enterprises, including media and telecommunications. The area of inquiry has developed strongly since the 1970s, has more breadth and depth than many who are unfamiliar with its literature assume, and is based on a variety of economic theories and a wide range of analysis methods. This chapter reviews the development of the field of inquiry, its differing approaches, touchstones in its literature, and changing patterns in the focus of its research.

In a technical sense there is no such thing as media economics because it implies that the economic laws and theories for media are different than for other entities. Media economics is a specific application of economic laws and theories to media industries and firms, showing how economic, regulatory, and financial pressures direct and constrain activities and their influences on the dynamics of media markets.

Media economics is not only concerned with market-based activities because its base is the study of choices made in using resources at the individual, firm, industry, and society levels and how the benefits of those choices can be maximized. It provides means to examine the inner workings of media firms but goes on to provide methods for analyzing how choices and use of resources affect broader concepts such as consumer welfare and social welfare.

Media economics analyses are not only applicable for understanding free and open markets, but provide insight to media activities in a variety of market conditions including those operating in closed systems or with regulation and state support.

The field of inquiry is concerned with how these forces affect the kinds of media and communications available in society. It focuses on the way media behave and operate, explores the kinds of structures and content these forces create, and considers the implications of these factors on culture, politics, and society as a whole, and the role of media and communications in economic and social development.

Researchers in the field are guided by beliefs that financial and economic concerns are central to understanding communications systems and firms and to the formulation of public policies regarding communications.

## HISTORY OF MEDIA ECONOMICS INQUIRY

Since the beginning of the study of communications, attention has primarily focused on the roles, functions, and effects of communications. When media and other communications enterprises were studied, they were typically explored as social institutions, and much of the focus was on the social, political, legal, and technological influences on the enterprises and their operations.

Historically, media scholars ignored, or only lightly attended to, the effects of economic forces. This should not come as a surprise to anyone familiar with the history of communications inquiry, because communications scholars initially came from the disciplines of sociology, psychology, political science, history, and literary criticism. They passed on their approaches to studying media to new generations of communications scholars that were produced during the mid- and second half of the 20th century.

Media entities themselves permitted this lack of scholarly interest in economics and management because—for most of their history—large numbers of media executives had not considered media to be business enterprises. This is not to say that there were no commercial aspects. Many owners, however, operated publications and small commercial radio and television stations as a means of making modest livings, while enjoying a great deal of rewards from playing influential roles in the social, political, and cultural lives of the communities and nations in which they were published. Worldwide, public service and state-operated radio and television had operated outside the realm of the market economy, funded by government or legally required license fees and often protected by monopoly status.

In the second half of the 20th century, media of all kinds began taking on stronger commercial characteristics as their ability to produce large incomes increased with the explosion of advertising expenditures. Newspapers and magazines prospered, commercial radio and television became highly profitable, and even some public service broadcasters began accepting advertising as a means of increasing their revenues.

These changes and the increased competition with existing media created by additional competitors and newer media began creating new business and economic issues at the enterprise, industry, and social levels. Scholars, however, were slow to develop interest in these areas. Although a handful of economists began occasional inquiries, communication scholars generally ignored the phenomena.

Given the history of the discipline, communications departments and colleges in universities traditionally did not have courses in media economics. Only rare seminars on its concerns appeared, and these were typically in economics departments and business schools and colleges. Thus, little formal study of economic aspects has been offered to those who work in and operate media firms. This is not to say that economics and finance never caught the attention of communications educators, but that the topics were handled with brevity, in a disorganized fashion, and without significant depth and understanding. Only a few economics concerns would be haphazardly touched on in communications history courses, media and society courses, communications law courses, and the limited number of media management courses offered worldwide. For the most part, the approach to these topics in those courses was polemical rather than substantive, and it was often inappropriate for explaining modern communications developments. The result of this situation was that many communications scholars and—unfortunately—many of those who rose to positions in the management of communications enterprises or in government policymaking agencies had relatively little understanding of even basic economic forces affecting communications.

The earliest contributions to media economics literature were primarily from economists exploring newspaper competition and characteristics (Ray, 1951, 1952; Reddaway, 1963) and broadcasting structures and regulation (Coase, 1950, 1954, 1959, 1966; Levin, 1958; Steiner, 1952). Later communications scholars began exploring media economics using the political economy approach in the late 1960s and 1970s with a focus on the power structures affecting media. Notable contributions were made by Dallas Smythe (1969), Herbert Schiller (1969, 1976), and Armand Mattelart and Seth Seigelaub (1979).

In the 1970s an increasing number of economists and business scholars began exploring media, especially as the result of changes leading to the development of cable television and problematic trends appearing in the newspaper industry. Significant contributions about the economics and structure of television markets were made by Owen, Beebe, and Manning (1974) and Spence and Owen (1977). A few communications scholars with economic and business backgrounds began contributing their knowledge to understanding of media.

One of the earliest contributions in book form was made by Nadine Toussaint Desmoulins in France, who wrote the first known textbook to specifically analyze media industries from the economic viewpoint (Toussaint Desmoulins, 1978). Alfonso Nieto Tamargo produced early works on the magazine press in Spain (Nieto Tamargo, 1968, 1973) and a Spanish text on media economics was published in 1985 (López). In the United States, the work of Owen, Beebe, and Manning (1974) contributed an influential volume exploring economic issues in television and Owen (1975) explored the implications of economics on media and expression. Benjamin Compaine published a volume on the economics of book distribution (Compaine, 1978) and then edited a seminal volume on ownership of U.S. media and communication firms (Compaine, 1979).

It was not until the 1980s, however, that communications schools themselves began to give economic and financial forces and issues the significant attention that was due. Since that time, a coherent and growing body of knowledge about economic issues and problems and the financial strategies and behavior of communications enterprises has developed. That literature has begun to help explain how economic and financial forces and strategies affect media developments and operations.

This new avenue of inquiry has begun to significantly alter the imbalance that ignored the role of communications enterprises as business and financial institutions. In a relatively short period of time, a great deal of explanatory material and research provided the foundations for descriptions of communications business organizations and operations, methods of competition between media enterprises, choices of consumers and producers of communications products, and a broad range of economic and financial problems and performance issues, especially in the areas of concentration and monopoly.

Excellent analyses have considered the political economy of communications enterprises and its effects on society and vice versa (Dyson & Humphries, 1990; Garnham, 1990; & Mosco & Wasco, 1988). Several significant economic texts have emerged in the field, exploring the economic structure and organization of various communications industries (Albarran, 1996; Alexander, Owers, & Carveth, 1993 [3rd ed., 2003]; Picard, 1989; Toussaint Desmoulins, 1996), focusing on economic issues in media worldwide (Albarran & Chan-Olmsted, 1998) and in specific communications industries (Collins, Garnham, & Locksley, 1989; Dunnett, 1990; Lacy & Simon, 1993; McFadyen, Hoskins, & Gillen, 1980; Noam, 1985; Owen & Wildman, 1992; Picard, Winter, McCombs, & Lacy, 1988; Schmalensee, 1981; Vejanouski & Bishop, 1983; Webb, 1983), and revealing how basic economic laws and principles can be applied to the study and operation of media and media firms (Picard, 1989; 2002b).

Although interest in media economics was growing in the 1980s, the number of scholars active in the field was still limited and they were widely dispersed geographically and located in a range of academic programs including journalism, broadcasting, communications, economics, business, and political science faculties. It was rare for more than one person on a faculty to share the interest.

Scholarship was presented in general meetings of a variety of associations represented by the disciplines of those involved and published in a wide range of journals. The relative isolation of scholars was ultimately broken by the creation of an informal network of scholars that crossed disciplines. Meetings of members of the network were facilitated by gatherings of the Telecommunications Policy Research Conference (an annual U.S. forum for telecommunications and information policy issues), meetings of the Management and Sales Division of the Broadcast Education Association and, ultimately, the Media Management and Economics Division of the Association for Education in Journalism and Mass Communications.

In 1987 discussions among members of the network led to the establishment of *The Journal of Media Economics*, which published its first volume in the spring of 1988 and has since become the primary journal in the field of media economics.

In 1999 the position of media economics was clarified further when *the International Journal on Media Management* (JMM) appeared with a clearer focus on managerial rather than economic issues. Further segmentation in the field is evident with the establishment of *The Journal of Media Business Studies* in 2004, which focuses more closely on company issues.

The importance of journals in the fast-developing scholarship is seen in the fact that during the first decade of *The Journal of Media Economics*' existence, its articles were dominated by $2^1/_2$ as many citations for articles as for books (Chambers, 1998).

The trends in approaches and issues covered in the journals provide another indicator of the development of the field. Early literature was often oriented toward introducing basic concepts and approaches to analyzing media, exemplified by contributions that explored the spending on media (McCombs & Eyal, 1980; Wood, 1986), the financial performance of media (Litman & Bridges, 1986), revenue forecasting (Adams, 1987), welfare economics and media (Busterna, 1988), measurement of concentration (Picard 1988), measurement of quality through media firm expenditures (Lacy, 1992), consumer spending analysis (McCombs & Nolan, 1992), and the views from political economy (Gandy, 1992).

In the 1980s and early 1990s significant concern over structural changes in broadcast and cable media were explored using the industrial organization and competition approaches. Exemplary studies explored integration in the cable television industry (Chan-Olmsted & Litman, 1988), diversification (Albarran & Porco, 1990), television syndication markets (Chan-Olmsted, 1991), market effects of broadcasting entry barriers (Berry & Waldfogel, 1999; Fournier & Martin, 1983), telephone company entry into video distribution (Foley, 1992), vertical integration in information distribution (Waterman, 1993), and concentration (Albarran & Dimmick, 1996; Sparks, 1995; Neiva, 1996).

By the mid-1990s, scholarship was moving from basic market-oriented studies, and new concepts and methods were introduced to the field. These included more sophisticated analyses of strategies (Barrett, 1996; Blankenburg & Friend, 1994; Chan-Olmsted, 1997), explorations of the value of media firms (Bates, 1995; Miller, 1997); and pricing issues (Kalita & Ducoffe, 1995; Shaver, 1995).

In the 1990s internationalization of the field was represented by studies exploring international markets for U.S. media (Dupagne, 1992), the development of transnational firms (Gershon, 1993), and issues in entering specific markets (Holtz-Bacha, 1997). The introduction of economic analyses of media in other parts of the world included productivity in graphic arts industries (Paasio, Picard, & Toivonen, 1994), competition in changing European television markets (Powers, Kristjansdottir, & Sutton, 1995), magazine globalization methods (Hafstrand, 1995), and how public service broadcasting was being affected by policy and market changes (Boardman & Vining, 1996; Brown & Althaus, 1996; Cave, 1996). Macroeconomic issues such as the effects of recessions on media (Picard, 2001; Picard & Rimmer, 1999) and media constraints in the global economy (Sussman & Lent, 1999) also appeared.

An increasing emphasis on analyzing the economic context and behavior of media firms rather than markets alone emerged at the millennium through studies of media empires (Picard, 1996), company takeovers (Wolfe & Kapoor, 1998), mergers and acquisitions (Chan-Olmsted, 1998), comparative strategies of firms (Shrikhande, 2001), company choices (Picard, 2002b), and company economics and financing (Picard, 2002a). Exploration of revenue streams and business models for interactive television (Pagani, 2000), online content (Picard, 2000), and free newspapers (Bakker, 2002), appeared. These represented a stronger shift toward business economic approaches.

With the development of the body of knowledge, media economics and management education expanded beyond coursework to include full programs of study in the 1990s including the Executive MBA programs at Turku School of Economics and Business Administration in Finland, and MBA programs at the University of St. Gallen, Switzerland, and Fordham University and Northwestern University in the United States. Other master's degree specialty programs were established at the University of Navarra, Spain, University of Southern California, and University of Stirling, Scotland. Doctoral studies that permitted students to specialize in media economics and management emerged at Indiana University, Jönköping International Business School, Michigan State University, University of Cologne, University of Dortmund, University of Navarra, University of Florida, University of St. Gallen, University of Southern California, and other institutions.

Non-English textbooks on media economics expanded rapidly in the 1990s. Picard's 1989 text was translated into Chinese and Korean, and original textbooks were published in French (Le Floch & Sonnac, 2000; Paul, 1991; Toussant Desmoulins, 1996), German (Altmeppen, 1996; Bruck, 1993; Heinrich, 1994; Karmasin, 1998), Polish (Kowalski, 1998), Russian (Gurevich, 1999), and Hungarian (Gálik, 2001).

## TRADITIONS IN MEDIA ECONOMIC SCHOLARSHIP

Because the field of inquiry is maturing, it is useful to step back from the increases in knowledge and educational programs to gain broader understanding of its scope. Three traditions for the study of communications economics have emerged during the development of the discipline: a *theoretical tradition*, an *applied tradition*, and a *critical tradition* (see Table 2.1). The theoretical and applied traditions are often intertwined in the scholarship, but the critical tradition tends to stand aside from the others. The traditions developed from undertaking media economics research based on different academic foundations and from focusing on different subjects and issues.

### Theoretical Tradition

The theoretical tradition emerged from the work of economists who have tried to explain choices and decisions and other economic factors affecting producers and consumers of

**TABLE 2.1**
Fields of Inquiry in Communications Economics

| | Theoretical and Applied Traditions | | Critical Traditions |
|---|---|---|---|
| Level of Analysis | Microeconomics | Macroeconomics | Meta |
| Academic Foundations | Business economics and management | Economics and political economy | Communications, media studies and political economy |
| Foci of Analysis | Communication firms and consumers | Communication industries, government policies, general economy | Communications systems, culture, government policies |
| Issues Studied | Financial flow, cost structures, return issues, and decision making | Competition, consumption, efficiencies, and externalities | Social, political, and cultural effects of communications systems and policies |

communications goods and services. This approach is primarily based on neoclassical economics and uses that approach to explain the forces that constrain and compel actions involving communications systems and media. It very often emerges in studies designed to support forecasts of the prospects and effects of development of media, designed to theoretically identify optimal choices for media operators, or designed to explore optimal outcomes for policy choices. Important contributions in this tradition include Owen, Beebe and Manning (1974), Webb (1983), and Owen and Wildman (1992).

## Applied Tradition

The applied tradition emerged from business economics and management departments at universities and from researchers for communications industry associations. It is now the most common approach found when media economics study is located in university communications departments. This applied tradition has often explored the structure of communication industries and their markets, with an emphasis on understanding trends and changes. It has often had a response orientation, designed to help lead to the development of strategies or policies for firms or government to use in controlling or responding to the changes in the economy and consumer behavior. Studies using this tradition have explored consumer and advertising trends, specific firms, and sub-branches of the communications industries or the industries as a whole. Important contributions in this tradition include Compaine (1979), Picard (1989), Albarran (1996), Alexander, Owers, and Carveth (1998), and Picard (2002b).

## Critical Tradition

The critical tradition emerged from the work of political economists and social critics, primarily within communications studies, concerned about issues of welfare economics. These scholars have a strong cultural and social orientation that led to a focus on issues such as concentration and monopoly in communications, cultural effects issues, work and workers, and how society is being altered by shifts from the industrial to information economy. The approach is influenced by British cultural studies scholarship and neo-Marxist scholarship. Works by Mosco and Wasko (1988), Dyson and Humphreys (1990), and Garnham (1990) have been influential in developing this tradition.

The first two traditions have used both *microeconomic* and *macroeconomic* approaches to exploring communications institutions and interactions. The microeconomic approach tends to focus on market activities of producers and consumers in specific markets, both as individual and aggregate groups of producers and consumers. Macroeconomics approaches are used to explore the operations of economic systems, usually at the national level, but increasingly at regional and global levels as the nation-state becomes less the locus of economic activity. This latter approach is concerned with issues such as the production of goods and services, economic growth, employment, inflation, and public policies affecting markets.

Research using the microeconomic approach studies such issues as purchasing decisions, price behavior, financial flow, cost structures, and issues of financial returns. Central to the viewpoint is the idea that media are economic institutions that cannot be understood without recognizing that they operate in markets. They produce and market content to consumers and concurrently market opportunities for advertisers to reach those consumers. Macroeconomic-based studies of media often focus on broader industry concerns and market structures. They consider issues such as competition and monopoly, effects of changes in the economy on consumption of communications products and services, and the effects of government policies on communications industries.

Those who employ the critical approach to communications economics take a broader view that considers the overall effects of the economic, political, and social bases of the communications systems and the constraints that are placed on the systems. This approach explores the end results of those bases and constraints, identifies issues and problems arising from them, and seeks solutions—usually through public policies—to overcome deficiencies.

A tension between the proponents and practitioners of the three traditions is sometimes evident, but that conflict is unnecessary and counterproductive because each contributes important evidence and explanation that makes the others stronger and provides context on which each can build.

All three of these traditions provide means of analyzing and understanding communications and methods and approaches that are useful to the discipline. Although some distinctions among the traditions will remain constant, an overlap of methods and approaches is beginning to emerge as those who have been trained or began their studies in each tradition find value and explanation in some of the works of the others.

Despite differences in traditions, common approaches are evident in media economics scholarship, and they can be grouped together as industry and market studies, company studies, and effect studies (Table 2.2). These approaches provide the basic means of analyses and measurement of economic behavior in the industries, and most use theories and techniques common in economic and business inquiry. In recent years a large number of industrial organization studies have provided descriptive and explanatory information about media industries and firm behavior. Demand approaches have provided studies

TABLE 2.2
Common Approaches to Studying Media Economics

| Industry & Market Studies | Company Studies | Effects Studies |
|---|---|---|
| Industrial organization | Business strategy | Dependency |
| Demand | Company organization and culture | Financial commitment |
| Forecasting | Cost structures | Quality and diversity |
| Consumer spending | Financing and investment | Globalization and trade balances |
| Niche | Financial performance | Consumer and social welfare |
| Concentration | Productivity | |
| Relative constancy | Diversification | |
| Communications policy | | |

on consumer and advertiser behavior. Efficiency approaches have explored the internal operations of firms.

A few, such as the niche, dependency, and political economy approaches, have been adapted from other fields of inquiry, and the communications field itself has contributed the relative constancy and financial commitment approaches.

The list of approaches and methods of analysis are increasing as interest in media economics and the sophistication of the analysis increases. These approaches and others make it possible not only to gain an understanding of contemporary developments but also to make significant comparisons between specific communications industries and their problems and issues, and between strategies and performance of communications firms. They make it possible to compare companies by looking for factors, influences, and market mechanisms and processes that have created differences in success, by looking at differences in global and localized firms, or by comparing the behavior of conglomerates and specialized enterprises. Such studies and many different variations will help provide better understanding of the operation and effects of communications firms, industries, and systems.

## CONTEMPORARY AND FUTURE RESEARCH ISSUES

Issues gaining attention of scholars of media economics have tended to be contemporary to their times seeking to explore or answer questions raised by industry developments. Concerns in the early days of the field resulted from the appearance of cable and satellite services and their effects on broadcasting and on the decline of the newspaper industry. As time progressed, issues of deregulation, internationalization, and the appearance of new media became more significant.

Research in media economics today is being driven by massive changes in the nature of communications and the operations of communications systems and firms. Much of the research results from or focuses on changes in markets, changes in technology, changes in competition, increasing trade in communications products and services, capital flow into related industries, and changes in ownership.

The issues of changing markets result from alterations in the location and size of markets for communications products and services. Worldwide we are witnessing realignment and expansion of existing markets and the breakdown of traditional national markets. As a result, we are seeing the establishment of natural markets based on regional, continental, and global communications with less emphasis on the role of the nation-state in the markets. Two results of this change are that traditional public policy approaches to communications are becoming less effective and nationally based industrial organizational analyses are not as useful as when geographic market boundaries were clearer.

A great deal of change in communications is resulting from changing technologies and questions raised about those changes. The integration of telephone, computing, and broadcast technologies is changing the means of production and distribution of communications products and services by providing flexible, integrated, and multichannel capabilities. These changes raise significant questions about demand for technologies, distribution of and access to technologies, and the economic and social impact of these emerging and coordinated technologies. Difficulties of establishing workable markets and business models for mediated communications on the Internet, high definition and digital terrestrial television, and mobile content services all raise important avenues for inquiry.

Intensification of competition in communications is the inevitable result of changes in markets and new technologies. The changes have brought more media and communications systems that had been relatively protected from heavy competition into direct and, sometimes, fierce competition. These changes require companies and researchers to more clearly understand markets and competition and to find ways to create clear niches and specialized services because substitutability of communications products and services is rapidly growing. It is also forcing the adoption of internal cost management strategies and productivity planning in media companies so firms can survive and adapt.

Because markets have expanded beyond the artificial borders of nation-states, issues of trade in communications products and services are playing an increasingly important role in global politics. Concerns over trade barriers, protection of copyrights and trademarks, and whether communications should be considered as goods and services under bilateral and multilateral trade agreements are leading to significant international debate. Much of the debate is based on uncertainty and fear rather than knowledge, and further research about the bases and effects of changes can help establish the true nature of these developments, their effects, and appropriate policy responses.

The flow of capital into communications firms has increased as state entities have been privatized, and relatively small communications firms have grown large after seeking capital in stock markets. Questions over where and how capital is flowing globally, the roles of institutional investors, foreign ownership of communications, governance, and global concentration and monopoly are being increasingly raised. Additional research is needed to help explain such phenomena and to help companies and policymakers react to developments.

Significant changes are and will continue to occur as the distinctiveness of media industries and their markets continue breaking down because of the convergence of underlying production and distribution technologies. These changes are leading media firms to increasingly engaging in cross-media activities and to create conglomerate firms active in many media. The new environment is leading telephone, computer, and other firms to enter markets and engage in activities once carried out only by media firms. The economic and managerial implications of these developments are not yet clear, but it is obvious that the blurring of markets will affect companies and traditional markets, and create new types of markets and market structures that research can identify and explain. Further research on the effects of conglomerates and consolidation on markets and means for identifying and analyzing relevant markets will also be required.

Media economics is a fertile field of inquiry in which continually changing technologies, supply, consumption, and regulation alter markets and the operations and prospects for firms. It is a field that benefits from the breadth of approaches and questions being asked in a range of disciplines and with a wide variety of research methods. This interest will continue to widen the contributions and understanding of economic aspects of media in the years to come.

## SUMMARY

The need for media economics scholarship is growing concurrent with the growth and change in media and communications activities. In developed nations the rise of enormous commercial enterprises in communications, the rapid development of new electronic communication systems, and the commercialization of broadcasting are dramatically changing the communications landscape and the economic and financial pressures on media and communication systems. In Central and Eastern Europe changing market conditions caused by political changes in the late 1980s and early 1990s forced economic and financial concerns regarding media to the forefront. In Asia, heavy investment in communications systems and the manufacturing of media and communications equipment in countries such as Japan, South Korea, Singapore, China, and India, Malaysia, and Thailand are radically altering domestic communications. In many parts of the world media and communications systems still need a great deal of development, and there is a need to understand internal economic and financial forces but also how developed nations affect communications and media products and service availability worldwide.

These needs have led to increased emphasis on economics in journalism and communications education in Western nations. In many universities it has led to specific courses on media economics and the integration of economic and financial topics into existing media and society and media management courses. In economics and business schools, research groups and courses focusing on media communications are expanding and contributing to the growth of media economics education.

In the past 3 decades, the discipline has shown itself to be intellectually robust, durable, and central to the missions of a variety of types of educational institutions. Its ability to explain media and communication developments make it an essential discipline for analyzing activities in the field, for improving practices in media and communications firms, and for helping policymakers fashion effective means to achieve desirable outcomes.

Now well past its introduction and development stages, the media economics discipline is maturing and spreading worldwide. It is doing so because it provides profound insight that is built on solid theoretical bases and can be observed and tested in the media and communications environment.

## REFERENCES

Adams, P. D. (1987). A forecasting model for newspaper management. *Newspaper Research Journal, 8*(4), 43–50.

Albarran, A. B. (1996). *Media economics: Understanding markets, industries and concepts.* Ames: Iowa State University Press.

Albarran, A. B., & Chan-Olmsted, S. (1998). *Global media economics: Commercialization, concentration and integration of world media markets.* Ames: Iowa State University Press.

Albarran, A. B., & Dimmick, J. (1996). Concentration and the economics of multiformity in the communication industries. *Journal of Media Economics, 9*(4), 41–50.

Albarran, A. B., & Porco, J. F. (1990). Measuring and analyzing diversification of corporations involved in pay cable. *Journal of Media Economics, 3*(2), 3–14.

Alexander, A., Owers, J., & Carveth, R. (1998). *Media economics.* Hillsdale, NJ: Lawrence Erlbaum Associates.

Altmeppen, K.-D. (1996). *Ökonomie der medien und der mediensystems* [Economy of Media and Media Systems]. Wiesbaden, Germany: Gabler Verlag, Opladen.

Bakker, P. (2002). Free daily newspapers—Business models and strategies. *JMM—International Journal on Media Management, 4*(3), 180–187.

Barrett, M. (1996). Strategic behavior and competition in cable television: Evidence from two overbuilt markets. *Journal of Media Economics, 9*(2), 43–62.

Bates, B. J. (1995). What's a station worth? Models for determining radio station value. *Journal of Media Economics, 8*(1), 13–23.

Berry, S. T., & Waldfogel, J. (1999). Free entry and social inefficiency in radio broadcasting. *Rand Journal of Economics, 30*, 397–420.

Blankenburg, W. B., & Friend, R. L. (1994). Effects of cost and revenue strategies on newspaper circulation. *Journal of Media Economics, 7*(2), 1–13.

Boardman, A. E., & Vining, A. R. (1996). Public service broadcasting in Canada. *Journal of Media Economics, 9*(1), 49–63.

Brown, A., & Althaus, C. (1996) Public service broadcasting in Australia. *Journal of Media Economics, 9*(1), 31–47.

Bruck, P. (1993). *Okonomie und zukunft der printmedien* [Economy and Future of Print Media]. Munich, Germany: Fischer.

Busterna, J. C. (1988). Welfare economics and media performance. *Journal of Media Economics, 1*(1), 75–88.

Cave, M. (1996). Public service broadcasting in the United Kingdom. *Journal of Media Economics, 9*(1), 17–30.

Chambers, T. (1998). Who's on first? Studying the scholarly community of media economics. *The Journal of Media Economics, 11*(1), 1–12.

Chan-Olmsted, S. (1991). A structural analysis of market competition in the U.S. TV syndication industry, 1981–1990. *Journal of Media Economics, 4*(3), 9–28.

Chan-Olmsted, S. (1997).Theorizing multichannel media economics: An exploration of a group-industry strategic competition model. *Journal of Media Economics, 10*(1), 39–49.

Chan-Olmsted, S. (1998). Mergers, acquisitions, and convergence: The strategic alliances of broadcasting, cable television, and telephone services. *Journal of Media Economics, 11*(3), 33–46.

Chan-Olmsted, S., & Litman, B. R. (1988). Antitrust and horizontal mergers in the cable industry. *Journal of Media Economics, 1*(2), 3–28.

Coase, R. H. (1950). *British broadcasting. A study in monopoly.* London: Longman.

Coase, R. H. (1954). The development of the British television service. *Land Economics, 30*, 207–222.

Coase, R. H. (1959). The Federal Communications Commission. *Journal of Law and Economics, 2*, 1–40.

Coase, R. H. (1966). The economics of broadcasting and government policy. *American Economic Review, 56*, 440–447.

Collins, R., Garnham, N., & Locksley, G. (1989). *The economics of television: The UK case.* London: Sage.

Compaine, B. M. (1978). *The book industry in transition: An economic study of book distribution and marketing.* White Plains, NY: Knowledge Industry Publications.

Compaine, B. M. (1979). *Who owns the media?* White Plains, NY: Knowledge Industry Publications.

Dunnett, P. (1990). *The world television industry: An economic analysis.* New York: Routledge.

Dupagne, M. (1992) Factors influencing the international syndication marketplace in the 1990s. *Journal of Media Economics, 5*(3), 3–29.

Dyson, K., & Humphreys, P. (1990). *The political economy of information: International and European dimensions.* London: Routledge.

Foley, J. (1992). Economic factors underlying telephone companies' efforts to enter home video distribution. *Journal of Media Economics, 5*(3), 57–68.

Fournier, G., & Martin, D. (1983). Does government restricted entry produce market power: Evidence from the market for television advertising. *Bell Journal of Economics, 14*, 44–56.

Gálik, M. (2001). *Médiagazdaságtan* [Media Economics]. Budapest, Hungary: Aula Kiadó.

Gandy, O. H., Jr. (1992). The political economy approach: A critical challenge. *Journal of Media Economics, 5*(2), 23–42.

Garnham, N. (1990). *Capitalism and communication: Global culture and information economics.* London: Sage.

Gershon, R. A. (1993). International deregulation and the rise of transnational media corporations. *Journal of Media Economics, 6*(2), 3–22.

Gurevich, S. M. (1999). *Ekonomika i sredstv massovoi informatsii* [Economy and Mass Media]. Moscow: Izdatelstvo im. Sabashnikovykh.

Hafstrand, H. (1995). Consumer magazines in transition: A study of approaches to internationalization. *Journal of Media Economics, 8*(1), 1–12.

Heinrich, J. (1994). *Medienökonomie: Mediensystem, zeitung, zeitschrift, anzeignblatt* [Media Economics: Media System, Newspapers, Magazine, Free Sheets]. Westdeutscher Verlag, Opladen.

Holtz-Bacha, C. (1997). Development of the German media market: Opportunities and challenges for U.S. media firms. *Journal of Media Economics, 10*(4), 39–58.

Kalita, J. K., & Ducoffe, R. H. (1995). A simultaneous-equation analysis of pricing, circulation, and advertising revenue for leading consumer magazines. *Journal of Media Economics, 8*(4), 1–16.

Karmasin, M. (1998). *Mediaökonomie als theorie (massen-) medialer kommunikation: Kommunikationsökonomie und stakeholder theorie* [Media Economy as Mass Media Communication Theory: Communication Economics and Stakeholder Theory]. Nauser & Nauser.

Kowalski, T. (1998). Media i pieniądze: Ekonomiczne aspekty działalnołci środków komunikowania masowego [Media and Money: Economic aspects of Mass Communication]. Warsaw, Poland: Prezedsiebiorstwo Handlowe TEX.

Lacy, S. (1992). The financial commitment approach to news media competition. *Journal of Media Economics, 5*(2), 3–21.

Lacy, S., & Simon, T. F. (1993). *The economics and regulation of United States newspapers.* Norwood, NJ: Ablex.

Le Floch, P., & Sonnac, N. (2000). *Économie de la presse* [Economy of the Press]. Paris: Éditions La Découverte.

Levin, H. J. (1958). Economic structure and regulation of television. *Quarterly Journal of Economics, 72,* 445–456.

Litman, B., & Bridges, J. (1986). An economic analysis of daily newspaper performance. *Newspaper Research Journal, 7,* 9–26.

López, J. T. (1985). *Economia de la communicación de masas* [Economy of Mass Communication]. Madrid: Gruopo Zero.

Mattelart, A., & Siegelaub, S. (1979). *Communication and class struggle.* New York: International General.

McCombs, M. E., & Eyal, C. (1980). Spending on mass media. *Journal of Communication, 30*(1), 153–158.

McCombs, M., & Nolan, J. (1992). The relative constancy approach to consumer spending for media. *Journal of Media Economics, 5*(2), 43–52.

McFadyen, S., Hoskins, C., & Gillen, D. (1980). *Canadian broadcasting: Market structure and economic performance.* Montreal, Canada: Institute for Research on Public Policy.

Miller, I. R. (1997). Models for determining the economic value of cable television systems. *Journal of Media Economics, 10*(2), 21–33.

Mosco, V., & Wasko, J. (Eds.). (1988). *The political economy of information.* Madison: University of Wisconsin Press.

Neiva, E. M. (1996). Chain building: The consolidation of the American newspaper industry, 1953–1980. *Business History Review, 70,* 1–42.

Nieto Tamargo, A. (1968). *El concepto de empresa periodística* [The Concept of the Periodical Press]. Pamplona, Spain: Eunsa.

Nieto Tamargo, A. (1973). *La empressa periodística en España* [The Periodical Press in Spain]. Pamplona, Spain: Eunsa.

Noam, E. (1985). *Video media competition: Regulation, economics, and technology.* New York: Columbia University Press.

Owen, B. M. (1975). *Economics and freedom of expression: Media structure and the First Amendment.* Cambridge, MA: Ballinger.

Owen, B. M., Beebe, J. H., & Manning, W. G. (1974). *Television economics.* Lexington, MA: Heath.

Owen, B. M., & Wildman, S. S. (1992). *Video economics.* Cambridge, MA: Harvard University Press.

Paasio, A., Picard, R. G., & Toivonen, T. E. (1994). Measuring and engineering personnel productivity in the graphic arts industry. *Journal of Media Economics, 7*(2), 39–53.

Pagani, M. (2000). Interactive television: A model of business economic dynamics. *JMM—International Journal on Media Management, 2*(1), 25–37.

Paul, J.-P. (1991). *Économie de la communication TV-radio.* [The Economy of TV-Radio Communication] Paris: Presses Universitaires de France.

Picard, R. G. (1988). Measures of concentration in the daily newspaper industry. *Journal of Media Economics, 1*(1), 61–74.

Picard, R. G. (1989). *Media economics: Concepts and issues.* Newbury Park, CA: Sage.

Picard, R. G. (1996). The rise and fall of communication empires. *Journal of Media Economics, 9*(4), 23–40.

Picard, R. G. (2000). Changing business models of online content services: Their implications for multimedia and other content producers. *JMM—International Journal on Media Management, 2*(2), 60–68

Picard, R. G. (2001). Effects of recessions on advertising expenditures: An exploratory study of economic downturns in nine developed nations. *Journal of Media Economics, 14*(1), 1–14.

Picard, R. G. (2002a). *The economics and financing of media companies.* New York: Fordham University Press.

Picard, R. G. (Ed.). (2002b). *Media firms: Structures, operations, and performance.* Mahwah, NJ: Lawrence Erlbaum Associates.

Picard, R. G., & Rimmer, T. (1999). Weathering a recession: Effects of size and diversification on newspaper companies. *Journal of Media Economics, 12*(1), 1–18.

Picard, R. G., Winter, J. P., McCombs, M. E., & Lacy, S. (Eds.). (1988). *Press concentration and monopoly: New perspectives on newspaper ownership and operation.* Norwood, NJ: Ablex.

Powers, A., Kristjansdottir, H., & Sutton, H. (1995). Competition in Danish television news. *Journal of Media Economics, 7*(4), 21–30.

Ray, R. H. (1951). Competition in the newspaper industry. *Journal of Marketing, 43*, 444–456.

Ray, R. H. (1952). Economic forces as factors in daily newspaper competition. *Journalism Quarterly, 29*, 31–42.

Reddaway, W. B. (1963). The economics of newspapers. *Economic Journal, 73*, 201–218.

Schiller, H. I. (1969). *Mass communication and American empire.* New York: Augustus Kelly.

Schiller, H. I. (1976). *Communication and cultural domination.* White Plains, NY: M. E. Sharpe.

Schmalensee. R. (1981). *Economics of advertising.* Amsterdam, The Netherlands: North-Holland.

Shaver, M. A. (1995). Application of pricing theory in studies of pricing behavior and rate strategy in the newspaper industry. *Journal of Media Economics, 8*(2), 49–59.

Shrikhande, S. (2001). Competitive strategies in the internationalization of television: CNNI and BBC World in Asia. *Journal of Media Economics, 14*(3), 147–168.

Smythe, D. W. (1969). On the political economy of communications. *Journalism Quarterly, 69*(3), 563–572.

Sparks, C. (1995). Concentration and market entry in the UK national daily press. *European Journal of Communication, 10*(2), 179–206.

Spence, A. M., & Owen, B. M. (1977). Television programming, monopolistic competition and welfare. *Quarterly Journal of Economics, 91*, 103–126.

Steiner, P. O. (1952). Program patterns and preferences, and the workability of competition in radio broadcasting. *Quarterly Journal of Economics, 66*, 194–223.

Sussman, G., & Lent, J. A. (1999) Who speaks for Asia: Media and information control in the global economy. *Journal of Media Economics, 12*(2), 133–147.

Toussaint Desmoulins, N. (1978). *L'economie de medias* [The Economy of Media]. Paris: Press Universitaires de France

Toussaint Desmoulins, N. (1996). *L'economie de medias,* (4th ed.) [The Economy of Media]. Paris: Press Universitaires de France.

Vejanouski, C., & Bishop, W. D. (1983). *Choice by cable: The economics of a new area in television.* Lansing, UK: Institute of Economic Affairs.

Waterman, D. (1993). A model of vertical integration and economies of scale in information product distribution. *Journal of Media Economics, 6*(3), 23–35.

Webb, G. K. (1983). *The economics of cable television.* Lexington, MA: Lexington Books.

Wolfe, A. S., & Kapoor, S. (1998). The Matsushita takeover of MCA: A critical, materialist, historical, and First Amendment view. *Journal of Media Economics, 9*(4), 1–21.

Wood, W. C. (1986). Consumer spending on the mass media: The principle of relative constancy reconsidered. *Journal of Communication, 36*(2), 39–51.

# 3

# Theoretical Approaches in Media Management Research

Bozena I. Mierzjewska
University of St. Gallen

C. Ann Hollifield
University of Georgia

In the field of mass communication, the term *theory* is often loosely defined.[1] Paradigms,[2] conceptual frameworks, models, normative theories and, of course, actual theories are all frequently referred to as theory, although very different constructs are represented by those words. As traditionally defined in science, a theory is a systematically related set of statements about the causes or relationships underlying observable phenomena (Rudner, 1966). Theories are developed by abstracting from observation and are confirmed through repeated experiments designed to test hypotheses related to the theory. The result is often the development of law-like generalizations about underlying causes and relationships. The purpose of a theory is to increase scientific understanding through a systemized structure capable of both explaining and predicting phenomena (Christensen & Raynor, 2003; Hunt, 1991).

Accepted theories become a part of our understanding and are the basis for further explorations of less-understood areas. Even though not all phenomena can be replicated in experiments, quantified, and measured—a problem often faced in the social sciences—multiple observations and identified causal processes constitute the basis for theory. Good theories are valuable for making predictions. Being a statement of cause and effect, they help us predict with a certain degree of confidence future consequences of our current

---

[1] It has been observed by Jonathan Turner that there is an increasing tendency among social scientists to use the term theory in a "humpty-dumpty fashion." One of the often-cited examples is the mistaken notion that the theory "emerges" when sufficient number of facts are gathered about a subject (Turner, 1993).

[2] *Paradigms* are differences in the ontological and epistemological assumptions underlying scholarship. They are discussed in detail elsewhere in this volume.

actions. Sound theories also help to describe what is happening and why, hence, they are valuable tools for data interpretation.

In mass communication and social science research, theory is used in a broad sense and generally refers to conceptual explanation of phenomena. Among social scientists, a theory represents the way in which the observers see the environment and its forces rather than its specific causes, as is the case in the physical sciences. Few theories developed in the social sciences have met the physical sciences test of describing law-like causal forces, but social science theories do constitute a set of useful concepts and frameworks that contribute to general understanding.

For all of their usefulness, theories do have limitations:

- They are focused and very specific; therefore, they cannot give full explanations of all factors involved. This very characteristic usually results in deterministic explanations.
- They tend to be based on narrow, unrealistic assumptions. Theories aim to develop models used for predictions of future behaviour and consequences, but they need to deal with complications of the unpredictability of individual humans and social groups.

A theory represents a fairly advanced level of understanding in a particular area and emerges, if at all, only after considerable research on a specific topic. Consequently, much, if not most, social science and mass communication research is conducted without the benefit of fully developed theories. In the absence of a cohesive theory, the primary approach to abstracting relationships is to use conceptual frameworks. Conceptual frameworks draw on existing research that has revealed underlying relationships or variables relevant to the current research question and builds them into a new framework for understanding a specific situation. A conceptual framework may involve identifying and testing the interrelationship between variables that emerged in very diverse streams of research. It also may take the form of developing a systematic way of categorizing phenomena. As Ulrich (1984) points out, conceptual frameworks serve as a frame of reference where useful thoughts can be placed and organized systematically. Frameworks, in this understanding, identify the relevant variables and questions that an analyst should consider in order to develop conclusions tailored to a particular situation or company (Porter, 1991). The use of conceptual frameworks is often a step toward the development of a more fully tested theory.

A third approach to abstracting or understanding the variables related to a phenomenon is to develop and test models. Models are specific descriptive statements, often visually diagrammed, about the relationships among variables or the process through which something occurs. In communication sciences, models have been widely utilized and offer convenient ways to think about communication. As with theories, using models contains some risks. They tend to encourage scholars to harden their conceptions of how a process works, slowing further development and refinement, and they can be self-perpetuating, keeping alive questionable assumptions (McQuail & Windahl, 1993).

Finally, in addition to positive theories, that is, theories that describe real cause–effect relations, the social sciences also have developed *normative theories*. Normative theories are a subset of theories that describe norms and behaviours that *should* exist, rather than those that do exist. In essence, normative theories are prescriptive rather than predictive. Recommendations developed based on normative theories challenge existing systems and generate new points of view.

The common thread uniting research that utilizes theory, conceptual frameworks, models, or normative theories is the focus on abstracting underlying causal variables from observed phenomena. The results of such research can then be applied toward understanding events that involve similar variables but that may occur in entirely different contexts. In contrast to such a theoretically or conceptually based approach, atheoretical or descriptive research is research that describes phenomena or events without trying to identify anything more than direct, contextually specific factors. As a result, atheoretical research provides a detailed snapshot of the conditions at one particular place and time. However, because underlying forces are not abstracted, as soon as the conditions or context change, it can no longer be assumed that the findings are valid. Nor can it be assumed that the findings can be applied to other similar situations. Consequently, descriptive research has little long-term value to the scholarly community.

An example of atheoretical research would be a study that described the media mergers and acquisitions that occurred in a specific year. A conceptually based study of the same phenomenon might be one that applied strategic theory to understand the common market, competitive, or resource conditions among the companies that launched mergers and acquisitions in that year, rather than focusing on the details of the mergers themselves. Findings from the conceptually based study could be used to understand or predict future mergers and acquisitions in the industry, whereas the atheoretical study would be valuable primarily to business historians as documentation of the events in a particular year.

In summary then, in its abstraction from the specific to the general, theory allows us to recognize, understand, and solve problems that have similar underlying factors, even though on the surface the problems may seem dissimilar. Theory allows us to predict *probabilities,* but not certainties, in human behavior.

In media management research, most theory is drawn from the larger field of organizational studies and, in principle, is based on similar constructs. Management theory is considered distinct from economic theory, although both microeconomic and management theory focus on organizational-level phenomena. Also, management research often, although not always, includes economic performance among the dependent variables examined. Management science is seen as one of the applied sciences that would serve managers in a similar way as the physical sciences serve engineers. This particular positivist understanding of the practice of science is the main principle of research into management (Reed, 1996).

Management theory covers a spectrum of organizational topics that can be categorized along a structural-agency continuum. *Structural theories* focus on nonhuman organizational factors such as the organizational structure, market conditions, technologies of production, etc., whereas *agency theories* focus on the human influences in organizations: leadership, power, gender and racial diversity, decision making, culture, communication. The lines between this typology of management theories are, however, blurred because such areas as strategic management, although considered structural, clearly involve human elements as the very word strategy implies.

Although most of the theories and conceptual frameworks from which media management research draws are based in organizational studies, the field of media management is distinctive in a number of ways. First, media organizations produce information products rather than tangible products, and the underlying economic characteristics of information products differ from other types of goods in critical ways (Priest, 1994). These fundamental economic characteristics are related to crucial differences in demand, production, market, and distribution conditions, creating a very different management environment than is found in many industries.

Most important, media products have extremely high social externality value because of the central role information and media content plays in economic, political, and social processes. Because media are one of the critical infrastructure industries in society, media management practices have implications far beyond the purely economic concerns of corporate investors. Thus, although media management research shares with organizational studies a concern with financial outcomes, the field extends its focus to include the study of the effects of organizational management on media content and society. This very feature distinguishes the field of media management from the field of organizational studies. Indeed, Ferguson (1997) argued that until media management scholars develop distinctive theories that go beyond economics and applied management, it will be difficult to argue that media management is a domain of inquiry separate from either mass communication or organizational studies.

This extension of organizational theories to the study of content and social outcomes is not, however, without problems. Fu (2003) cautioned that when media management and economics researchers apply traditional organizational theories to research in which performance has been redefined as media content or social outcomes rather than financial performance, the theories may no longer be valid. Careful research is needed on this question. However, it is difficult to justify the need for specialized scholarly study of the media industry if the unique economic characteristics of media products and their larger role in society are not taken into account. Indeed, it could be argued that understanding the effects of management decisions on media content and, by extension, on society is explicitly or implicitly the raison d'etre of the field.

## THEORETICAL APPROACHES IN PUBLISHED MEDIA MANAGEMENT RESEARCH

An examination of 309 articles in the *Journal of Media Economics* (JME) and *The International Journal on Media Management* (JMM) was conducted to assess the last 15 years of research and the theoretical approaches used by media management scholars (Table 3.1). The time period was chosen because the *Journal of Media Economics*, the first refereed, academic journal focusing on issues relevant to media business, debuted in 1988. Studies relying on economic theory or management theory represented 77% of all the research published in those journals.

Among the articles based in management theories, strategic management was the conceptual approach most commonly used in both journals (Table 3.2). It must be noted, however, that the research analyzed here does not represent the full body of media

**TABLE 3.1**
Theoretical Approaches Used in Studies Published
in the *Journal of Media Economics* and *The
International Journal on Media Management*

| Theoretical Approaches | Percentage |
| --- | --- |
| Economic theories | 33 |
| Management theories | 44 |
| Communication theories | 5 |
| Atheoretical, applied or essay | 17 |

$n = 309$.

management research. A great deal of very influential research in media management has been published in other journals within the business, policy, journalism, and communication domains.

**TABLE 3.2**
Distribution of Media Management Theory Published in
the *Journal of Media Economics* and *The International
Journal on Media Management*

| Media Management Approach | Percentage |
| --- | --- |
| Strategic management theories | 54 |
| Technology, innovation, creativity theories | 21 |
| Contingency/efficiency theories | 9 |
| Audience/media consumer/behavior theories | 12 |
| Political economy/normative approaches | 5 |
| Organizational/professional culture theories | 3 |

$n = 137$.

## STRATEGIC MANAGEMENT THEORIES

Strategic management has been the most widely used theoretical or conceptual framework in media management studies to date. Numerous case studies and analyses have been conducted in an effort to understand why some media firms outperform others, which is the primary focus of strategic management research. Those studies have addressed such issues as explaining the strategy of media market concentration (Albarran, 2002; Compaine & Gomery, 2000), adapting to changing market conditions (Albarran & Gormly, 2004; Greco, 1999; Picard, 2004), and exploring strategic options for companies operating in various markets and regulatory settings (Gershon, 2000; Hoskins, Finn, & McFayden, 1994; Liu & Chan-Olmsted, 2003).

Two conceptual frameworks for studying strategic management are recognized as dominant (Chan-Olmsted, 2003). The first builds on industrial-organization concepts and what has come to be known as the structure-conduct-performance (SCP) framework. The SCP approach focuses on the structure of industries and the linkages among an industry's structure and organizational performance and conduct. Early work using the SCP approach was proposed by Bain (1968) and developed further by Porter (1991). According to the SCP framework, the *structure* of an industry (e.g., number, size, and location of firms) affects how firms behave (or their individual or collective "conduct"). In turn, the industry's *performance* is related to the conduct of firms.

For media management scholars, performance stands for both economic performance—the traditional measure in organizational studies—and social responsibilities that media need to fulfill for the betterment of society (Fu, 2003). Studies that have applied the SCP paradigm to the media industry are numerous (Busterna 1988; Gomery, 1989; Ramstad, 1997; Wirth & Bloch, 1995; Young, 2000).

The second strain of strategic management research, known as the resource-based-view (RBV), builds on the assumption that each firm is a collection of unique resources that enable it to conceive and implement strategies. RBV strategies suggest that firms should discover those assets and skills that are unique to their organizations and cannot be imitated, thus protecting the organization with knowledge barriers (Barney & Hesterly, 1996). This approach is especially important and meaningful in the media industry because of the unique economic characteristics of information products (Chan-Olmsted, & Kang, 2003; Priest, 1994). In a content analysis of media strategy research, Chan-Olmsted identified an even split between the SCP and RBV approaches in strategic management research on media companies (Chan-Olmsted, 2003).

A third important approach to studying strategic management that has emerged in the media management field is based on ecological niche theory from the biological sciences (Dimmick, 2003; Dimmick & Rothenbuhler, 1984). *Niche theory* posits that industries occupy market niches just as biological species occupy ecological niches. The theory has proved valuable in examining competition among media corporations for scarce resources such as advertisers and audiences. It also helps explain how sectors of the media industry adapt to new competition such as from the Internet or other new media and technologies.

Although the SCP and RBV approaches and niche theory represent the most frequently used theoretical approaches to studying strategic management, the study of strategy covers a wide range of other topics. Market-entry strategy, branding, joint venture management, and new-product development are only a few of the more specific topics that can be conceptualized and studied as elements of strategic management. As research on the strategic management of media companies continues, the field may succeed in developing strategic theories specific to the media industry that take into account the special economic, social, and regulatory environments in which media industries and organizations operate. Chan-Olmsted's (2003) proposed analytical framework for strategy formulation and implementation is one step in that direction, as is Dimmick's (2003) niche theory.

## STRUCTURAL THEORIES

The primary approach in organizational studies to the study of issues of organizational structure has been structural contingency theory. It describes the relationships between organizational structures and performance outcomes. Grounded in assumptions of economic rationality, structural contingency theory argues that organizations will adopt structures that maximize efficiency and optimize financial performance according to the specific contingencies that exist within the organization's market environment (Donaldson, 1996). Consequently, there is no single organizational structure that will be equally effective for all companies.

Structural contingency theory first emerged in organizational studies during the 1950s and subsequently generated a great deal of attention. Under the theory, organizational structures are deemed to include authority, reporting, decision and communication relationships, and organizational rules, among other elements. The primary contingency factors that influence organizational structures include organizational scale and task uncertainty. Small organizations and those facing low levels of uncertainty in their environments are theorized to operate most efficiently with simple, centralized structures, whereas larger organizations and those dependent on creativity and innovation are expected to perform better with more decentralized structures. The theory also predicts that if an organization adopts a structure that is not optimal given its specific contingencies, it will either evolve toward a more efficient structure or fail.

Structural contingency theory falls firmly on the structural end of the structural-agency continuum of organizational theory because it holds that, if human decisions lead to nonoptimal organizational structures, economic rationality eventually will reassert itself.

Within media management research, structural contingency theory in its classic form has been little used. This may change in the future as the structures of media organizations grow increasingly complex through media consolidation, and variances in performance across seemingly similar media corporations become more evident. But if media scholars have invested little effort in exploring the effects of organizational structures on economic performance, they have, instead, developed a related but unique stream of research. That research concerns the effects of media ownership structures on media content.

Research on the effects of media ownership structures on media content and organizational priorities first emerged in the 1970s in response to consolidation in the newspaper industry. By the 1980s the topic had become a major focus of research, and interest continued through the 1990s. Most research in the area has focused on the effects of newspaper chain ownership on media content as compared to independent ownership. The types of effects on content that have been studied have included endorsements of political candidates, editorial positions on current issues, hard news and feature news coverage, and coverage of conflict and controversy in the community (Akhavan-Majid,

Rife, & Gopinath, 1991; Busterna & Hansen, 1990; Donohue, Olien, & Tichenor, 1985; Gaziano, 1989; Glasser, Allen, & Blanks, 1989; Wackman, Gillmor, Gaziano, & Dennis, 1975). Although there have been some contradictory findings, most studies have concluded that ownership structures do affect content, although the mechanisms by which that influence occurs continues to be debated.

More recently, the focus of media management research on ownership structures has shifted from comparing the effects of chain and independent ownership to comparing the effects of public and private ownership (Blankenberg & Ozanich, 1993; Cranberg, Bezanson, & Soloski, 2001; Edge, 2003; Lacy & Blanchard, 2003; Lacy, Shaver, & St. Cyr, 1996). This research suggests that pressure from financial markets to maximize investor returns is reducing the resources publicly owned media corporations invest in newsrooms and content production. That, in turn, is presumed to reduce the quality of the news and entertainment products those companies produce, although the connection between reduced newsroom resources and reduced content quality has not yet been fully established.

Finally, another related area of research concerning the impact of media ownership structures focuses on the effects of such structures on news managers' professional values and priorities, which are assumed to shape news decisions and the organizational resources invested in news coverage (Demers, 1993, 1996).

Important to note is that the majority of research on the effects of ownership structures on media content has focused on newspaper content. Relatively few structural studies have examined broadcast content (Chambers, 2002). This, no doubt, has much to do with the affordability and accessibility of newspaper content as a subject of analysis compared to television and radio content. However, in the face of the rapid consolidation in the electronic sectors of the media industry since 1996, the increase in television and radio duopolies, and the development and diffusion of centralcasting models among broadcasters, there is a clear need to expand the samples used in media structure-content research to include broadcast organizations.

## TRANSNATIONAL MEDIA MANAGEMENT THEORIES

In the past 2 decades, the rapid movement of media companies into global markets has spurred a corresponding surge in research on transnational media management and economics. The topic has attracted interest for a number of reasons. There are many unanswered questions about how the kinds of consolidation and diversification involved in global expansion affect corporate financial returns; how globalization influences the content and quality of news, films, and other media products produced for a corporation's home market; how media management structures and practices shape the products and content produced for audiences in foreign markets and, subsequently, how that content then affects the politics, economics, cultures, and public interest in the countries that receive it.

The importance of research on transnational media management issues is unlikely to diminish as media corporations' global reach continues to expand. One of the challenges of transnational media management research is developing theoretical or conceptual frameworks through which the phenomenon can be studied. Because transnational management includes so many different management topics, there is no single theoretical base for approaching research. This problem is characteristic of international business research in general (Parker, 1996). Indeed, perhaps the only unifying conceptual element in transnational organizational research is the assumption that having operations in multiple national markets will affect organizations or organizational outcomes in some way.

From a conceptual standpoint, much of the early research on transnational media operations focused on international trade in media products or the industry-level structures and economics of overseas media markets (Donohue, 1987; Dupagne, 1992; Gershon, 1997; Hoskins & Mirus, 1988; Thompson, 1985). More recently, there has been increased interest in the effects of firm-level behaviors within and across international markets (Chan-Olmsted & Chang, 2003; Hollifield, 1999; Pathania-Jain, 2001; Shrikhande, 2001) and, to a lesser degree, in the effects of foreign market environments on transnational media organizational strategies and decisions (Chan-Olmsted & Chang, 2003; Gershon, 2000).

At best, transnational media management research can be considered to be in its infancy as an area of study. A meta-analysis of transnational media management research (Hollifield, 2001) found that organizational-economic perspectives and critical perspectives were the theoretical and conceptual frameworks most frequently used by scholars. The analysis also showed that a significant proportion of transnational media management research was atheoretical and descriptive, and only one study (Weinstein, 1977) formally tested a model for transnational media management.

Regardless of the specific theories used, the majority of the transnational media management studies examined in the meta-analysis were based in assumptions of economic rationality. Said another way, on the continuum between structure and agency theories in organizational studies, most transnational media management scholars have taken a structural approach. Research has tended to cluster around issues of organizational structure, strategy, and policy (Chan-Olmsted & Chang, 2003; Gershon, 1993, 2000; Shrikhande, 2001). Relatively few studies have addressed specific issues of functional management such as finance, cross-cultural personnel management, leadership, product development, and operational coordination (Hollifield, 1998; Hoskins & McFadyen, 1993; Lent, 1998; Pathania-Jain, 2001; Pendakur, 1998; Wasko, 1998; West, 1993). Few scholars have yet ventured into studies of human agency in transnational media management such as how leadership, social networks, and decisions influence global media expansion, product development, and outcomes.

The use of such a variety of conceptual and theoretical frameworks has created a rich and wide-ranging view of transnational media management issues. However, it also has created a smorgasbord of only marginally related findings that offer little in-depth understanding of any particular issue or phenomenon. Far more systematic, programmatic research in specific areas of organizational structure, strategy, function, and leadership will be necessary before the field can claim to have a true understanding of the management issues and challenges facing transnational media corporations and their host countries.

## ORGANIZATIONAL CULTURE THEORIES

Culture is a powerful force within organizations. Organizational culture shapes decisions, determines priorities, influences behaviors, and affects outcomes (Martin & Frost, 1996; Schein, 1992). It can be a source of organizational strength or a factor in organizational weakness. In media management, organizational culture became a topic of widespread research interest in the late 1990s and the early 21st century at least in part because journalists and financial analysts blamed organizational culture clashes for many of the problems that developed in major media corporations during that period (Ahrens, 2004; Klein, 2002; Landler & Kirkpatrick, 2002).

The concept of organizational culture has its roots in anthropology. Although the term *culture* has been defined many ways, most definitions recognize that culture is historically and socially constructed; includes shared practices, knowledge, and values that experienced members of a group transmit to newcomers through socialization; and is used to shape a group's processes, material output, and ability to survive (Bantz, McCorkle, & Baade, 1997; Bloor & Dawson, 1994; Linton, 1945; Ott, 1989; Schein, 1992).

Organizational cultures are the product of a number of influences including the national culture within which the organization operates, the long-term influence of the organization's founder or early dominant leaders as well as its current leadership, and the organization's operating environment. The company's primary line of business, the technologies of production it employs, and the market environment in which it competes are components of the operating environment. Thus, in the media industry, companies operating in the same industry sector, such as television stations, would be expected to share some characteristics of organizational culture because of the similarities in their products, markets, and technologies, whereas they would be expected to differ culturally from newspapers and radio stations for the same reasons.

Within most media organizations, there also exist multiple professional and occupational subcultures. Professional cultures unite individuals within the same occupation, even though they work for different organizations (Bloor & Dawson, 1994; Martin & Frost, 1996; Ott, 1989; Toren, 1969). The presence and mix of professional subcultures within an organization influences the culture of the overall organization, whereas the interaction between competing occupational subcultures within the company influences organizational behavior and climate. Research suggests that conflict between organizational and professional cultures is common (Bloor & Dawson, 1994; Ettema, Whitney, & Wackman, 1987). In general, organizational cultures are viewed by professionals as impinging on professional norms, freedom of action, and commitment to service of the public interest. Similar tensions occur between coexisting occupational subcultures within an organization.

National culture, the third element that shapes organizational culture, refers to the dominant cultural values and behaviors of the nation or region in which the organization is located. Also included under national culture are the individual national, religious, ethnic, and gender-based cultural differences that may exist among employees within the organization. Organizational culture theory can be used to address such questions as how the mix of multiple ethnic or regional cultures and their location within a dominant national or professional culture would shape organizational climate, behaviors, and outcomes.

In organizational studies, the surge in interest in studying culture dates back to the Japanese management revolution of the late 1970s (Martin & Frost, 1996). Initially, most organizational culture research focused on integrative strategies in organizations—also known as *values engineering*—but eventually research expanded to include the study of differences and conflicts between cultures. Cultural differences have been examined both in terms of actual occurrence and from a critical, normative perspective. The topic also has attracted scholars working from a postmodern perspective, who view organizational culture as a sea of endlessly changing, endlessly competing individual cultural narratives, rather than a single, unified organizational metanarrative (Martin & Frost, 1996).

As an approach to understanding organizations, organizational culture theory provides a bridge between the structural and agency camps of organizational studies. The definition of culture includes both structural influences such as the technologies of production, market conditions, and organizational and industry regulations, and human variables such as leadership style, socialization processes, communication norms, and the social construction of values.

Examination of media management research suggests that the application of organizational culture theory as a base for studying media organizations and management practices is relatively new, and the number of media management studies clearly grounded in culture theory remains small. Some examples of these studies include a comparative study of the roles that organizational and professional culture played in the hiring decisions of television news directors and newspaper editors (Hollifield, Kosicki, & Becker, 2001), an examination of the influence of corporate culture on the ability of news organizations to adapt to changing market conditions (Küng, 2000), and a study of the role that the *New York Times'* organizational culture played in the Jayson Blair plagiarism scandal of 2003 (Sylvie, 2003).

In fact, however, interest in the effects of organizational and professional culture on newsrooms and media content have been part of media research for decades, even if it has not always been explicitly defined as the study of organizational culture. Breed (1955) and Gieber (1964) wrote the seminal pieces on media organizational culture in studies of the processes by which news organizations maintain social control over semi-autonomous journalism professionals. Both projects reflect scholars' long-standing interest in the conflict—or cooperation—between the professional culture of journalists and the corporate cultures of the organizations that employ them.

In subsequent years, the underlying constructs of organizational and professional culture theory have infiltrated a wide range of media studies such as news construction, gatekeeping, ownership effects, and organizational innovation. News construction research is the study of how variables such as newsroom structures, news routines, the demographic profile of journalists, and journalists' relationships with sources affect the selection and framing of news stories. Within the news construction research tradition, research on news routines examines the processes journalists use in their work and the way those routines—or professional cultural norms—influence story and source selection (Ettema et al., 1987; Hirsch, 1977; Shoemaker & Reese, 1991; Tuchman, 1973). Another related area of study has been how the technologies of news production, a factor in organizational culture, influence the professional norms of news routines (Abbott & Brassfield, 1989; Atwater & Fico, 1986; Lasorsa & Reese, 1990; Peer & Chestnut, 1995).

In summary, the concept of organizational culture has been widely used in the popular press to explain media corporate behavior and performance, and the constructs underlying organizational culture theory have been applied in news construction research for decades. But organizational culture theory itself started being applied directly to media management research only in the late 1990s. However, in the future, organizational culture may well become a leading theoretical frame for understanding media performance and content because of its potential power to explain a wide variety of corporate problems and behaviors. Media merger outcomes, the effects of media ownership on media content, the values-based conflict between journalists and their employers, the ability to foster creativity and innovation in media organizations, and the effects of global media content on national and local cultures are just a few of the media management issues that might be usefully studied through the theoretical frame of culture.

## TECHNOLOGY, INNOVATION, AND CREATIVITY

The management of innovation has been identified as one of the most critical areas of research for the field of media management and economics (Picard, 2003). This assertion was supported by a surge in published research on the management of technology and innovation in media organizations, which began around 2000. Approximately 60% of the articles on media technology and innovation that were published by specialized media management and economics journals appeared after the turn of the century.

This research focus on technology and innovation reflects the fact that the media are one of a handful of industries facing the emergence of potentially "disruptive" technologies. Disruptive technologies are defined as "science-based innovations that have the potential to create a new industry or transform an existing one" (Day & Schoemaker, 2000, p. 2). The Internet, HDTV, and interactive television devices are examples of the types of communication technologies that, when they emerge, have the potential to significantly disrupt the underlying business models of existing sectors of the media industry.

Understanding the development, adoption, and economic and social impacts of new technologies on the media industry and its products is important to a wide range of stakeholders: media managers and professionals, economists, investors, policymakers, and consumers. Consequently, there is a need for programmatic research on technologies and innovations in media that will contribute to the development of innovation management theory.

The first step in developing systematic research that provides a foundation for theory development is to carefully define the nature of the phenomenon being studied. It is this step that may well be one of the most difficult obstacles in the study of technology and innovation in media. The process of building and testing theory requires that research be based around some consistent construct. If the phenomenon being examined is defined differently in different studies, then researchers are studying different things. This problem plagues organizational research on technology and innovation. In a 1996 study, Roberts and Grabowski identified seven different definitions of technology used by researchers up to that time. Those definitions ranged from purely material artifacts such as hardware and software to sweeping constructs that included all forms of invention, innovation, and human knowledge.

Even more complex is the notion of innovation. In some definitions, innovation was a subset of technology. In others, technology was a subset of the broader construct of innovation (Day & Schoemaker, 2000; Roberts & Grabowski, 1996). Finally, Day and Schoemaker further conceptualized technology as *disruptive* and *nondisruptive* and argued that organizations approached technology adoption and innovation management differently depending on the disruptive or nondisruptive potential of the technology or innovation in question.

Similar definitional problems have arisen during attempts to define the terms *emerging media* or *new media* in mass communication research (Dennis & Ash, 2001; Rawolle & Hess, 2000). Efforts to develop definitions for these terms have generated complex taxonomies ranging from such concepts as *interactivity*, *digitalization*, and *convergence*, to classification schemes based on usage such as *transport media* and *end devices* or *online/offline*, and even some approaches based on audience behavior while using the technology such as *user attention high/low*.

Such complex taxonomies can be important methodologically. It may be necessary to carefully define the nature of specific innovations before doing large-scale comparative studies of, for example, market structure-conduct-performance or market-entry strategies. However, as yet, no consensus has developed among scholars regarding how media technologies are to be defined or classified, and such consensus is likely to be difficult, if not impossible, to develop in the future. The absence of consistent classification schemes almost certainly will hinder the development of theory in the study of media technologies.

These definitional challenges notwithstanding, most research on technology and innovation in organizations is grounded in some underlying assumption about the nature of the technology and its role in the organization. Some of the more commonly used conceptual frameworks used to study technology and innovations in media organizations are discussed in the following sections.

## Economic Theory

New technologies present media organizations with a number of pressing economic questions. One is the issue of whether demand exists for a new product or service. Another is whether a feasible business model for producing the product can be found. Traditional economic theory provides a framework for studying such issues as demand, market competition, marginal costs, economies of scale and scope, the economic characteristics of information, marginal utilities, price discrimination, and so on. Economic theory has been widely used to study the market for emerging technologies and innovations (Chon, Choi, Barnett, Danowski, & Joo, 2003; Loebbecke & Falkenberg, 2002; Picard, 2000).

An equally critical question facing the media industry is how emerging technologies may disrupt existing media markets. Predicting with any accuracy the economic impact an emerging technology will have on existing media markets is extremely difficult. Nevertheless, some scholars have applied economic theory to the question (Rizzuto & Wirth, 2002; Shaver & Shaver, 2003).

## Strategic Management Theory

New products, technologies, and innovations are a primary strategic weapon, and strategic management theory has been a central framework through which innovation in the media industry has been examined by media management scholars.

Strategic management research is grounded in a fairly wide range of conceptual frameworks, as noted previously. Among the frameworks used to study the strategic management of innovation in media companies have been Porter's concept of the value-chain (Rolland, 2003), the industrial/organizational model (Chyi & Sylvie, 1998; Williams, 2002), marketing and branding theory (Ha & Chan-Olmsted, 2001; Johansson, 2002); market-entry strategies (Knyphausen-Aufsess, Krys, & Schweizer, 2002); strategic alliance and joint venture theory (Liu & Chan-Olmsted, 2003) and more mixed frameworks that incorporate several concepts.

## New Product Development Theory

Management research has long focused on the issues and processes of new product development, and a rich literature exists on the topic. The importance attached to new product development reflects the fact that an organization's ability to innovate successfully has been linked to financial performance. Among the issues of new product development that have been examined in the organizational literature have been product design processes (Bonner, 1999; Dougherty, 1996), technology and market forecasting, organizational commitment and goal-setting (Atuahene-Gima & Li, 2000), the effectiveness of the organizational structures and teams used in new product development (Day & Schoemaker, 2000; Wheelwright & Clark, 1992), leadership effects (Karlsson & Ahlstrom, 1997; Ruekert & Walker, 1995), and the effects of organizational, professional, and national cultures on innovation processes (Cheng, 1998).

Within the media management and mass communication literatures, there has been relatively little examination of new product development processes. Franke & Schreier (2002) studied how the Internet could be used as a new-product development tool for producers in all kinds of industries, and Saksena and Hollifield (2002) examined the internal organizational structures that U.S. newspapers had used to develop online editions as a new product. However, in general, organizational approaches to new product development in the media industry have been a neglected area of research.

## Diffusion Theory

Another conceptual approach to research on new media products is the use of diffusion theory, which is also known as adoption of innovations research. Diffusion theory is probably most frequently used to understand consumer behavior in response to new media technologies. The theory holds that the successful diffusion of innovations occurs according to a predictable pattern that moves from the *change agent*, who introduces the innovation, to the *laggards*, who refuse to accept it (Rogers, 1995). Demographic factors such as age, education, and income have been found to be at least somewhat related to consumers' willingness to adopt innovations. Diffusion theory helps explain a number of factors in new product development, including success, failure, and pricing.

Diffusion theory originated early in the 20th century with the study of farmers' adoption and nonadoption of new agricultural processes and technologies. Since then, the adoption of innovation framework has been widely applied across many fields as social scientists have sought to understand human responses to innovation and change. In media management and economics research, diffusion theory has been used to examine consumer behavior in relationship to a large number of new media products and technologies including broadband delivery of education (Savage, Madden, & Simpson, 1997), DVD technology (Sedman, 1998), digital cable (Kang, 2002), digital broadcast television (Atkin et al., 2003), high definition television (Dupagne, 1999), and the Internet (Hollifield & Donnermeyer, 2003; Kelly & Lewis, 2001), among others.

Diffusion theory also is a valuable theoretical framework for understanding organizations' decisions to adopt or not to adopt new technologies (Rogers, 1995). Research on organizational adoption of innovations has found that organizational adoption processes are more complex than individual adoption decisions. More people are involved, the decision is influenced by the organization's authority structure and existing rules and regulations, and decisions are contingent on previous decisions to adopt or to not adopt other innovations. However, relatively few media management scholars have used diffusion theory to look at organizational adoption issues within media companies (Lawson-Borders, 2003).

## Effects of Technology Adoption on Organizations and Employees

Although few media management scholars have examined the processes of organizational technology adoption, quite a few have studied the effects of organizational technology adoption on media work processes and media professionals (Daniels & Hollifield, 2002; Russial, 1994; Russial & Wanta, 1998; Stamm, Underwood, & Giffard, 1995). This research, although limited in scope, suggests that the introduction of new media production technologies decreases job satisfaction in the short-term, changes job roles, forces media professionals to learn new skills, increases production time, and decreases the time spent developing content. However, the studies also suggest that the negative effects of new technologies dissipate over time.

## Uses and Gratifications

Uses and gratifications is another framework through which consumer behavior in regards to new media products and services has been examined. The uses and gratifications approach looks at the ways consumers use media and the utilities they receive from that use. Uses and gratifications is a conceptual framework rather than a theory, and generally it is used to describe and classify audience behavior rather than to predict it.

Lacy and Simon (1993) identified five basic uses or gratifications that people receive from consuming media products: surveillance of the environment, decision making, entertainment and diversion, social cultural interaction, and self-understanding. Although uses and gratifications has been widely used to understand other aspects of media-use behavior, it has been less frequently applied as a framework for understanding consumers' use of new media technologies and products (Dans, 2000; Rao, 2001; Rose, Lees, & Meuter, 2001).

## Creativity

In the media management literature, creativity is a slightly different construct from innovation. Creativity is conceptualized as being the result of individual or small group effort, and generally is associated with content rather than products and services. Creativity is an issue of central concern to media companies, because the creation of content is the primary business of most media companies, and the development of content involves substantial financial investment and risk.

Even though creativity usually is conceptualized as an unpredictable outcome wholly dependent on human agency, most research on the management of creativity has focused on structural variables (Ettema, 1982; Küng, 2003; Newcomb & Alley, 1982; Turow, 1982). Far less research has been done in which individual or agency factors have been used as independent variables in studying creativity. However, the existing research supports the argument that leadership style affects the creative process (Hughes, Ginnett, & Curphy, 1999). Despite the importance of creativity to media corporate performance, few studies in the media management literature have examined the actual management of the creative process using the artist/producer as the unit of analysis (Newcomb & Alley, 1982).

## LEADERSHIP THEORIES

Arguably the single most neglected area of research and theory development in the field of media management is leadership. This is not to say that leadership is considered unimportant. Much of what is written by journalists, authors, investment analysts, and even scholars about the performance of media corporations contains assumptions—one might even say "underlying theories"—about the role that one or more media executives have played in events.

But despite assumptions about the relationship between leadership and media organizations' behavior and performance, there has been very little systematic research by media management scholars on leadership behavior and effects. Although the subject is generally well covered by media management textbooks (Albarran, 2002; Gershon, 2001; Redmond & Trager, 2004; Wicks et al., 2004), the number of scholarly studies of media leadership that have used primary data and have been published in media management journals has been surprisingly small.

Within organizational studies, leadership incorporates a fairly wide array of topics, all of which are focused on issues of human behavior. These issues include leadership traits and styles, follower traits and styles, leadership contingencies and situations, decision-making styles, communication styles, motivation and job satisfaction, the acquisition and use of power within organizations, and managing change, to name just a few. Most theories of leadership and associated subjects are based in psychological theory. On the continuum between structural theories and agency theories of organizational behavior, leadership and related topics fall firmly into the category of agency theory.

If leadership is a neglected subject among media management researchers, it is not so in the larger field of organizational studies. Leadership research originated among organizational scholars before World War I with the development of Taylor's principles of *scientific management*. The goal of scientific management was to maximize the efficiency of the work process through systematic management, but maximizing efficiency also included the need to motivate employees through both intrinsic and extrinsic rewards (Taylor, 1947). Consequently, embedded in the principles of scientific management were some fundamental approaches to leadership.

The study of leadership later evolved to focus on leaders themselves, rather than simply on the outcomes of leadership. In the 1940s, leadership research was dominated by the study of leadership traits, most of which were assumed to be inborn rather than learned (Bryman, 1996). The scholarly interest in leadership traits was followed in the 1960s by interest in leadership styles. In the late 1960s and early 1970s, the focus of leadership research changed again, moving to what is termed the *contingency approach*. The contingency approach recognized that successful leadership depends on more than just the leader alone. It is affected by the delicate interplay between an individual's personal leadership style, the style and traits of the individuals being led, and the variables of the situation that provide the context in which leadership is occurring (Hughes, Ginnett, & Curphy, 1999). For example, the contingency approach argues that an authoritarian, hierarchical approach to leadership probably is the most effective leadership style in situations where there are serious time pressures or where workers may face significant risks and dangers. Given these factors, broadcast newsrooms would be environments where authoritarian leadership might be more successful than consensus-based leadership.

In contrast, hierarchal, authoritarian approaches to leadership are thought to stifle creativity and innovation (Hughes, Ginnett, & Curphy, 1999). Consequently, it might be hypothesized that consensus-based leadership would be common to media companies that depend on innovation or creativity for success.

Another major stream of leadership research known as *new leadership* or *transformational leadership* emerged among organizational scholars in the 1980s. It focused on studying leaders who had proved transformational for their organizations. The primary variable of interest in the new leadership school is the *vision* of the transforming leader, which is posited as the defining leadership trait.

The new leadership approach achieved widespread support in the 1980s and 1990s, spawning many popular bestsellers. However, it has been criticized on grounds that it focuses exclusively on the top leader of an organization, ignoring other forms of leadership. It also ignores the context of the leadership situation, and it uses success as the criterion by which leadership is defined (Bryman, 1996). The leader who fails is, by definition, not a transformational leader and, therefore, is ignored as a subject of study.

In the media management literature, only a handful of studies have directly or indirectly examined leadership issues. These have looked at such topics as the relationship between leadership and change (Gade, 2004; Killebrew, 2003; Perez-Latre & Sanchez-Tabernero, 2003), organizational problems (Sylvie, 2003), and organizational values and priorities (Demers, 1993, 1994, 1996; Edge, 2003).

Related to leadership research is the study of human motivation. There are a number of theories commonly used to understand motivation in the workplace. All are based in psychological theory. The factors these theories predict are important to motivation and job satisfaction include (a) basic existence elements such as salary and safe working conditions; (b) social relationships in the office and a sense of belonging; and (c) opportunities for personal development and growth (Alderfer, 1972; Herzberg, Mausner, & Synderman, 1959; Maslow, 1954). Other theories of motivation describe the relationship between environmental conditions, the person's personal interpretation of those conditions, and the person's behavior (Bandura, 1986). Most motivation theory recognizes a difference between intrinsic motivations—the individual's drive to meet his or her own standards and goals for growth—and extrinsic motivations—direct rewards for behavior such as raises, bonuses, promotions, or other forms of recognition by others.

Motivation is another area of leadership research that has been largely ignored by media management scholars. The single area of motivation that has been seriously examined in the field is job satisfaction among journalists. The research shows that among journalists, the factors that contribute to job satisfaction vary by age and industry sector (Pollard, 1995). However, journalists are generally more satisfied when they believe they are producing a high-quality news product that keeps the public informed (Weaver & Wilhoit, 1991), they have good relationships with management, job autonomy (Bergen & Weaver, 1988), and higher social status (Demers, 1994). In other words, journalists tend to be intrinsically motivated and focus more on professional values than organizational values.

An area of leadership research that began attracting attention from media scholars early in the 21st century was change management. In a changing economic, regulatory, and technical environment, change has become almost the only constant in the organizational environment of media companies. Indeed, many economists and organizational scholars believe that only organizations that are able to constantly change and adapt will succeed in the 21st century.

Because high levels of uncertainty and instability are demotivating to employees and tend to lead to employee turnover, knowing how to effectively manage people during periods of change and uncertainty has become an essential skill for media managers, particularly because the quality of media products are largely dependent on the personal talents of the individuals who create them. A handful of scholars have studied change management in the media, usually focusing on the effects of change on newsrooms and journalists (Daniels & Hollifield, 2002; Gade, 2002, 2004; Gade & Perry 2003; Killebrew, 2003; Perez-Latre & Sanchez-Tabernero, 2003; Sylvie, 2003). Generally, these studies have found that change is disruptive. However, the research generally also indicates that leadership plays a central role in shaping change-management outcomes.

Given the prevalence of change in the media industry, there clearly is a need for more research on change management, job satisfaction, and motivation issues. Additionally, there is a need to expand these research streams beyond journalists and newsrooms to examine how change and motivation issues are affecting media professionals and media performance in other sectors of the media industry.

Other aspects of leadership such as power, decision making, and communication have, as yet, attracted little attention from media management researchers. Research on these topics would contribute immensely to understanding the factors of human agency that shape media content and organizational performance.

## MEDIA LABOR FORCE RESEARCH

The media labor force is a critical area of research in media management. Personnel is the largest single budget item for many, if not most, media corporations. For example, personnel compensation made up 42.4% of total company expenses in U.S. television stations on average in 2000—by far the biggest line item (National Association of Broadcasters, 2001). More important, because media products are information products, their quality and creativity is dependent on the knowledge, skills, and talents of the individuals who produce them. Consequently, knowledgeable, talented employees are the most valuable resource that media corporations control. A particularly talented employee is a resource that has the additional strategic advantage of being unique and hard to imitate.

The media labor force also is of interest from a public policy perspective. In the late 1960s, the Kerner Commission investigating the race riots that had occurred in U.S. cities during that decade argued that diversity in media personnel was important as a means of ensuring that minority populations and the issues important to them were accurately represented in the media. Since then, increasing ethnic diversity in the U.S. media work force has been both a public policy and industry priority, and some other countries with significant ethnic diversity also have adopted it as a priority.

Finally, labor issues are important to nations for economic reasons because the media industry is a growth industry worldwide. Consequently, the financial health of the industry and the size of its labor force are issues of concern to policymakers in nations around the world.

The U.S. media labor force has been the subject of intense study for a number of decades and similar research is beginning to appear on the media work force of other countries (Deuze, 2002). An assumption underlying virtually all media labor-market research is that there is a connection between the demographic and psychographic makeup of the media workforce and the content that reaches the public (Napoli, 1999; Shoemaker & Reese, 1991). Far rarer has been research that has examined the media labor force as a resource issue for media corporations.

In the United States, media labor force research has benefited from a number of well-funded, long-term research projects that have generated a wealth of valuable data. As a result, media labor force research is one of the few topics in the field of media management where significant theoretical development is beginning to emerge.

Since the early 1970s, mass communication scholars have been producing a decennial survey of U.S. media workers known as the "American Journalist Survey" (Johnstone, Slawski, & Bowman, 1976; Weaver, Beam, Brownlee, Voakes, & Wilhoit, 2003; Weaver & Wilhoit, 1991, 1996). The studies track the demographic and psychographic makeup of journalists in American newsrooms. Included are such variables as income, political affiliation, professional values, job satisfaction, and newsgathering techniques.

A second series of studies, known as the Annual Surveys of Journalism & Mass Communication Graduates, tracks trends in the labor pipeline going into journalism and other media professions. The studies, which have been conducted regularly since 1964, survey recent graduates of journalism and mass communication programs, reporting on their demographics, motivations for studying journalism, job seeking experiences, the nature of their entry-level positions in the industry, and their starting salaries and benefits (Becker, et al., 2004).

The existence of these rich longitudinal data sets contributes immensely to understanding the media labor force. The collaboration among scholars doing this research has contributed to some important conceptual breakthroughs. For example, the existence of longitudinal data on both graduates and employees makes it possible to examine the connection—or disconnection—between the profiles of students graduating from journalism programs and those who the industry hires and promotes. This has been particularly valuable in examining issues of diversity in newsrooms and media companies' ability to attract and retain personnel (Becker, Lauf, & Lowrey, 1999; Becker, Vlad, Huh, & Mace, 2003; Becker, Vlad, Daniels, & Martin, 2003).

In addition to these long-running surveys, other major studies of the labor market have examined such issues as media executives' hiring practices for entry-level personnel (Becker, Fruit, & Caudill, 1987; Hollifield, Kosicki, & Becker, 2001), the demographics of media personnel and their opportunities for advancement (Brooks, Daniels, & Hollifield, 2003; Papper & Gerhard, 1997, 1999, 2000, 2001; Stone, 1987, 1988, 1989; Warner & Spencer, 1990), and other labor and media personnel issues.

Beyond labor market research, there is an immense body of literature on other issues of diversity in media. These studies range from the experiences of women and minorities as employees of media companies to issues of representation of minorities and women in media content. Very little of this research has been framed in the context of media management and, in much of it, the assumption of the link between personnel characteristics and content diversity is explicit. However, such a link has yet to be conclusively demonstrated through research, at least in part because of the methodological problems involved in establishing causal links between journalists' individual demographic characteristics and the content they produce.

Far less well studied are the macroeconomic implications of media labor forces. In the 1990s, a few scholars examined the offshore outsourcing of jobs in the animation industry (Lent, 1998; Pendakur, 1998; Wasko, 1998). This phenomenon is likely to attract more attention from media management researchers in the future. Although the United States dominated the media industries in the 20th century and commanded the largest share of the media labor force, by the end of the century there were signs that dominance might change. If greater global parity in the production and trade of media products develops in the 21st century, the shift would have significant economic implications for the nations involved.

Although media labor force research is probably one of the most data-rich areas of the field, it still has a number of weaknesses. First, labor force research has focused disproportionately on journalists, leaving most other types of media employees unexamined. Second, much of the work rests on the assumption of a connection between the diversity of employment and diversity of content. A much greater effort needs to be made to test that hypothesis. Additionally, in contrast with much media management research, most media labor force research has been framed almost entirely in terms of its social implications. Research and theory development needs to expand to include the relationship between labor and the strategic management of the industry.

## SUMMARY AND CONCLUSIONS

If the emergence of media management and economics as a subfield of mass communication can be dated by the development of specialized journals and divisions within scholarly associations, then the field is, by any measure, young. Moreover, as a specialized area within a much larger discipline, media management is the focus of only a small group of scholars when compared to mass communication as a whole or to organizational studies. It is hardly surprising, then, that so little organizational theory has been fully applied in the study of media organizations and that some key areas of organizational research hardly have been examined at all.

Nevertheless, media management research has made remarkable progress in the development of theory in several areas. The strategic management of media companies has drawn the most consistent attention from scholars, resulting in the development of a strong body of research on the structures of media markets and the strategic management of the resources that media companies control. Although much of the research has been less systematic than is necessary for theory development, Dimmick's (2003) work on media market niches is just one example of theoretical development in the area of strategic management that has contributed significantly to understanding the behavior of media companies.

Another area in which media management scholars have made a unique contribution to theory development is on the implications and effects of organizational and corporate structures on media content. Finally, the rich, multifaceted longitudinal data gathered by scholars studying media labor force issues has labor-force research poised on the brink of important theoretical breakthroughs in terms of understanding such issues as the role of internal labor markets on industry's ability to recruit and retain workers and the effects of personnel diversity on media content and creativity.

These are the not the only areas, of course, in which media management research has contributed to theory development. However, analysis of media management literature shows that one of the weaknesses of the field is that research tends to be fragmented, unsystematic, and nonprogrammatic. Studies in the same general subject area often apply different conceptual frameworks, focus on different populations, or use different operational definitions. As a result, much of the research is of limited use in systematically developing and testing theory. In only a few areas of study are media management scholars developing programmatic research in which they carefully replicate and extend each other's or their own work. Theory development requires this type of methodical approach in which each study seeks to verify and refine the insights provided in the last and extends the research to answer new questions that might have been raised.

Another challenge in the development of media management theory is the need to carefully reevaluate the theoretical foundations on which most research in the field has been built. Although many of the management theories drawn from organizational science naturally have proven valuable in the study of media companies, the theories were developed primarily through the study of manufacturing and service industries—industries in which the fundamental economic characteristics and production processes differ from those of the media industry in crucial ways. As a result, many organizational theories—such as those in the areas of strategic management, structural contingency, and leadership—may not be completely transferable to media firms. Media management researchers should treat at least some organizational theories tentatively until they have been systematically re-examined in the media industry. More research that uses "normal" industries as a control group also might be valuable for purposes of theory development. Identifying differences between information-industries and consumer-product and service industries may help shed light on the management of media companies. This, in turn, should help strengthen both the predictive and prescriptive value of media management theory and research.

Media management almost certainly will continue to grow as a research specialty in coming decades. As media consolidation continues, there will be an increased demand for a better understanding of the relationships between media management, economics, content, and society. Additionally, as the competitive environment within the media industry changes in the face of new technologies, regulations, and market conditions, the industry itself will be seeking insights into effective management practices.

As a consequence, the strategic management of media companies is likely to continue to be a key area of study in the foreseeable future. Among the most pressing research questions facing those working in the area of strategic management will be the effectiveness of media consolidation and diversification as strategies and their effects on media content. Similarly, as scholars studying one of only a handful of industries that were impacted by truly disruptive technologies in the past decade, media management researchers are in a prime position to significantly advance the study of innovation management. The examination of technology from the standpoints of both new product development and organizational adoption almost certainly will be one of the central areas of research in media management and economics in the foreseeable future, as media managers struggle with the risks that emerging innovations pose to their markets and their corporate survival. For the industry, one of the critical needs will be to better understand effective organizational processes for evaluating, adopting, and innovating new technologies. Research suggests that managing innovation is a challenge for which relatively few media managers are adequately prepared.

Examination of the current state of media management shows that the most glaring omission in the field is in research on media organizational leadership and employee motivation. Clearly, this gap must be addressed. This area of study will be particularly important given the rapid changes overtaking the media industry and the industry's heavy reliance on human capital in the creative processes of production. Among the critical research questions about media leadership that need to be answered are the relationship between leadership and the ability of media companies to thrive in rapidly changing market environments, the effective management of change, creativity, innovation, and professional cultures, and the impact of media executives and their personal values on the content produced by their corporations.

Also in need of more systematic and theoretically grounded work is research on the management of transnational media corporations, including structural, functional, and performance issues. In an era of rapid media globalization, far too little is understood about the behavior of media corporations as they operate in different national markets. There is a need for much more empirical information about the relationship between corporate strategy and behavior and the impact that global media corporations may be having on the content, cultures, political systems, and economies of the nations in which they invest. The findings of such research have the potential not only to contribute to theory development but also to play a role in international policy processes.

Finally, media management scholars must continue to extend research on the outcomes of management decisions and behaviors beyond financial performance and organizational efficiency measures to include the quality of media content and social externalities. Given the media industry's role as a central infrastructure in global communication, political, and economic systems, it is simply inadequate for media management scholars to adopt the traditional approach in organizational studies of measuring company and industry performance primarily in terms of financial and competitive outcomes. To develop theory that effectively predicts and explains the likely effects of media management decisions and behaviors on media content and, by extension, society may well prove to be the central conceptual challenge facing the field. But if the decisions of media executives and the behavior of media organizations matter enough to generate specialized study, then certainly understanding the full impact of those decisions both within and beyond the industry must be a central focus of media management research.

## REFERENCES

Abbott, E. A., & Brassfield, L. T. (1989). Comparing decisions on releases by television and newspaper gatekeepers. *Journalism Quarterly, 66*, 853–856.

Ahrens, F. (2004, February 13). But would it work? Other media mergers provide lessons for Comcast-Disney. *The Washington Post*, p. E1.

Akhavan-Majid, R., Rife, A., & Gopinath, S. (1991). Chain ownership and editorial independence: A case study of Gannett Newspapers. *Journalism Quarterly, 68*(1/2) 59–66.

Albarran, A. B. (1998). Media economics: Research paradigms, issues, and contributions to mass communication theory. *Mass Communication and Society, 1*(3/4), 117–129.

Albarran, A. B. (2002). *Management of electronic media* (2nd ed.). Belmont, CA: Wadsworth.

Albarran, A. B., & Gormly, R. K. (2004). Strategic response or strategic blunder? An examination of AOL Time Warner and Vivendi Universal. In R. G. Picard, (Ed.), *Strategic responses to media market changes* (pp. 35–46). (JIBS Research Reports No. 2004-2). Jönköping International Business School, Sweden.

Alderfer, C. (1972). *Existence, relatedness, and growth: Human needs in organizational settings.* New York: Free Press.

Atkin, D. J., Neuendorf, K., & Jeffres, L. W. & Skalski, P. (2003). Predictors of audience interest in adopting digital television. *Journal of Media Economics, 16*(3), 159–173.

Atuahene-Gima, K., & Li , H. (2000). Marketing's influence tactics in new product development: A study of high technology firms in China. *Journal of Product Innovation Management, 17*(6), 451–470.

Atwater, T., & Fico, F. (1986). Source reliance and use in reporting state government: A study of print and broadcast practices. *Newspaper Research Journal, 8*(1), 53–61.

Bain, J. S. (1968). *Industrial Organization* (2nd ed.). New York: Wiley.

Bandura, A. (1986). *Social foundations of thought and action: A social cognitive theory.* Englewood Cliffs, NJ: Prentice-Hall.

Bantz, C. R., McCorkle, S., & Baade, R. C. (1997). The news factory. In D. Berkowitz (Ed.), *Social meaning of news: A text reader* (pp. 269–285). Thousand Oaks, CA: Sage.

Barney, J. B., & Hesterly, W. (1996). Organizational economics: Understanding the relationship between organizations and economic analysis. In S. R. Clegg, C. Hardy, & W. R. Nord (Eds.), *Handbook of organization studies* (pp. 115–147). London: Sage.

Becker, et al. (2004). *Annual surveys of journalism and mass communication graduates*. Retrieved March 15, 2004, from http://www.grady.uga.edu/annualsurveys

Becker, L. B., Fruit, J. W., & Caudill, S. L. (1987). *The training and hiring of journalists*. Norwood, NJ: Ablex.

Becker, L. B., Lauf, E., & Lowrey, W. (1999). Differential employment rates in the journalism and mass communication labor force based on gender, race and ethnicity: Exploring the impact of affirmative action. *Journalism & Mass Communication Quarterly, 76*, 631–645.

Becker, L. B., Vlad, T., Huh, J., & Mace, N. R., (2003). Gender equity elusive, surveys show. Retrieved December 15, 2003, from http://www.grady.uga.edu/centers/frame.CoxCenter.asp

Becker, L. B., Vlad, T., Daniels, G. L., & Martin, H. J. (2003, November.). *The impact of internal labor markets on newspaper industry diversification*. Paper presented at the annual meeting of the Midwest Association for Public Opinion Research, Chicago, IL. Retrieved Dec. 13, 2003, from http://www.grady.uga.edu/annualsurveys/Mapor%20Report%202003.pdf

Bergen, L. A., & Weaver, D. (1988). Job satisfaction of daily newspaper journalists and organization size. *Newspaper Research Journal, 9*(Winter), 1–13.

Blankenburg, W. B., & Ozanich, G. W. (1993). The effects of public ownership on the financial performance of newspaper corporations. *Journalism Quarterly, 70*(1), 68–75.

Bloor, G., & Dawson, P. (1994). Understanding professional culture in organizational context. *Organization Studies, 15*(2), 275–295.

Bonner, J. B. (1999). *Customer involvement in new product development: Customer interaction intensity and customer network issues*. Unpublished doctoral dissertation, University of Minnesota, Minneapolis.

Breed, W. (1955). Social control in the newsroom: A functional analysis. *Social Forces, 33*(4), 326–335.

Brooks, D. E., Daniels, G. L., & Hollifield, C. A. (2003). Television in living color: Racial diversity in the local commercial television industry. *Howard Journal of Communications, 14*(3), 123–146.

Bryman, A. (1996). Leadership in organizations. In S. R. Clegg, C. Hardy, & W. R. Nord (Eds.), *Handbook of organizational studies* (pp. 276–292). London: Sage.

Busterna, J. C. (1988). Welfare economics and media performance. *Journal of Media Economics, 1*(1), 75–88.

Busterna, J. C., & Hansen, K. A. (1990). Presidential endorsement patterns by chain-owned newspapers, 1976–84. *Journalism Quarterly, 67*(2), 286–294.

Chambers, T. (2002, August). *Measuring radio program diversity in the era of consolidation*. Paper presented to the annual meeting of the Association for Education in Journalism and Mass Communication, Miami, FL.

Chan-Olmsted, S. M. (2003). Fundamental issues and trends in media strategy research. *Journal of Media Economics & Culture, 1*(1), 9–35.

Chan-Olmsted, S. M., & Chang, B. H. (2003). Diversification strategy of global media conglomerates: Examining its patterns and determinants. *Journal of Media Economics, 16*(4), 213–233.

Chan-Olmsted, S. M., Kang, J. W. (2003). Theorizing the strategic architecture of a broadband television industry. *Journal of Media Economics, 16*(1), 3–21.

Cheng, J. L. C. (1998). Managing innovation in overseas labs: The effects of corporate, scientific, and local cultures on R&D performance. Retrieved March 10, 2004, from http://cims.nscu.edu/reports/Cheng-0598.pdf

Chon, B. S., Choi, J. H., Barnett, G. A., Danowski J. A., & Joo, S. H. (2003). A structural analysis of media convergence: Cross-industry mergers and acquisitions in the information industries. *Journal of Media Economics, 16*(3), 141–157.

Christensen, C. M., & Raynor M. E. (2003, September). Why hard-nosed executives should care about management theory. *Harvard Business Review,* 67–74.

Chyi, H. I., & Sylvie, G. (1998). Competing with whom? Where? And how? A structural analysis of the electronic newspaper market. *Journal of Media Economics, 11*(2), 1–18.

Compaine, B. M., & Gomery, D., (2000). *Who owns the media? Competition and concentration in the mass media industry*. Mahwah, NJ: Lawrence Erlbaum Associates.

Cranberg, G., Bezanson, R., & Soloski, J. (2001). *Taking stock: Journalism & the publicly traded newspaper company*. Ames: Iowa State University Press.

Daniels, G., & Hollifield, C. A. (2002). Times of turmoil: Short- and long-term effects of organizational change on newsroom employees. *Journalism and Mass Communication Quarterly, 79*(3), 661–680.

Dans, E. (2000). Internet newspapers: Are some more equal than others? *International Journal of Media Management, 2*(1), 4–13.

Day, G. S., & Schoemaker, P. J. H. (2000). *Wharton on managing emerging technologies.* New York: Wiley.

Demers, D. P. (1993). Effect of corporate structure on autonomy of top editors at U.S. dailies. *Journalism Quarterly, 70*(3), 499–508.

Demers, D. (1994). Effect of organizational size on job satisfaction of top editors at U.S. dailies. *Journalism Quarterly, 71*(4), 914–925.

Demers, D. P. (1996). Corporate newspaper structure, profits, and organizational goals. *Journal of Media Economics, 9*(2), 1–23.

Dennis, E. A., & Ash, J. (2001). Toward a taxonomy of new media: Management views of an evolving industry. *The International Journal on Media Management, 3*(1), 26–32.

Deuze, M. (2002). National news cultures: A comparison of Dutch, German, British, Australian, and U.S. journalists. *Journalism & Mass Communication Quarterly, 79*(1), 134–149.

Dimmick, J. W. (2003). *Media competition and coexistence: The theory of the niche.* Mahwah, NJ: Lawrence Erlbaum Associates.

Dimmick, J., & Rothenbuhler, E. (1984). The theory of the niche: Quantifying competition among media industries. *Journal of Communication, 34*(1), 103–119.

Donahue, G. A., Olien, C. N., & Tichenor, P. J. (1985). Reporting conflict by pluralism, newspaper type and ownership. *Journalism Quarterly, 62*(3), 489–499, 507.

Donahue, S. M. (1987). *American film distribution: The changing marketplace.* Ann Arbor, MI: UMI Research Press.

Donaldson, L. (1996). The normal science of structural contingency theory. In S. R. Clegg, C. Hardy, & W. R. Nord (Eds.), *Handbook of organizational studies* (pp. 57–76). London: Sage.

Dougherty, D. (1996). Organizing for innovation. In S. R. Clegg, C. Hardy, & W. R. Nord (Eds.), *Handbook of organizational studies* (pp. 424–439). London: Sage.

Dupagne, M. (1992). Factors influencing the international syndication marketplace in the 1990s. *Journal of Media Economics, 5*(3), 3–30.

Dupagne, M. (1999). Exploring the characteristics of potential high-definition television adopters. *Journal of Media Economics, 12*(1), 35–50.

Edge, M. (2003). The good, the bad and the ugly: Financial markets and the demise of Canada's Southam Newspapers. *The International Journal on Media Management, 5*(4), 227–236.

Ettema, J. S. (1982). The organizational context of creativity: A case study from Public Television. In J. S. Ettema & D. C. Whitney (Eds.), *Individuals in mass media organizations: Creativity and constraint* (pp. 91–106). Beverly Hills, CA: Sage.

Ettema, J. S., Whitney, D. C., & Wackman, D. B. (1987). Professional mass communicators. In C. R. Berger & S. H. Chaffee (Eds.), *Handbook of communication science* (pp. 747–780). Newbury Park, NJ: Sage.

Ferguson, D. A. (1997). The domain of inquiry for media management researchers. In C. Warner (Ed.), *Media management review* (pp. 177–184), Mahwah, NJ: Lawrence Erlbaum Associates.

Franke, N., & Schreier, M. (2002). Entrepreneurial opportunities with toolkits for user innovation and design. *The International Journal on Media Management, 4*(4), 225–234.

Fu, W. (2003). Applying the structure-conduct-performance framework in the Media Industry Analysis. *The International Journal on Media Management, 5*(4), 275–284.

Gade, P. J. (2002). Managing change: Editors' attitudes towards integrated marketing, journalism. *Newspaper Research Journal, 23*(2/3), 148–152.

Gade, P. J. (2004). Newspapers and organizational development: Management and journalist perceptions of newsroom cultural change. *Journalism & Communication Monographs, 6*(1).

Gade, P. J., & Perry, E. L. (2003). Changing the newsroom culture: A four-year case study of organizational development at the St. Louis Post-Dispatch. *Journalism & Mass Communication Quarterly, 80*, 327–347.

Gaziano, C. (1989). Chain newspaper homogeneity and presidential endorsements, 1972–1988. *Journalism Quarterly, 66*(4) 836–845.

Gershon, R. A. (1993). International deregulation and the rise of the transnational media corporation. *Journal of Media Economics, 6*(2), 3–21.

Gershon, R. A. (1997). *The transnational media corporation: Global messages and free market competition.* Mahwah, NJ: Lawrence Erlbaum Associates.

Gershon, R. A. (2000). The transnational media corporation: Environmental scanning and strategy formulation. *Journal of Media Economics, 13*(2), 81–101.

Gershon, R. A. (2001). *Telecommunications management: Industry structures and planning strategies.* Mahwah, NJ: Lawrence Erlbaum Associates.

Gieber, W. (1964). News is what newspapermen make it. In L. A. Dexter, & D. M. White (Eds.), *People, society and mass communication* (pp. 173–182). New York: Free Press.

Glasser, T. L., Allen, D. S., & Blanks, E. S. (1989). The influence of chain ownership on news play: A case study. *Journalism Quarterly, 66*(3), 607–614.

Gomery, D. (1989). Media economics: Terms of analysis. *Critical Studies in Mass Communication, 6*(1), 43–60.

Greco, A. (1999). The impact of horizontal mergers and acquisitions on corporate concentration in the U.S. book publishing industry, 1989–1994. *Journal of Media Economics, 12*(3), 165–180.

Ha, L., & Chan-Olmsted, S. M. (2001). Enhanced TV as brand extension: TV viewers' perception of enhanced TV features and TV commerce on broadcast networks' Web sites. *The International Journal on Media Management, 3*(4), 202–212.

Herzberg, F., Mausner, B., & Synderman, B. (1959). *The motivation to work.* New York: Wiley.

Hirsch, P. M. (1977). Occupational, organizational and institutional models in mass media research: Toward an integrated framework. In P. M. Hirsch, P. V. Miller, & F. G. Kline (Eds.), *Strategies for communication research* (pp. 13–42). Beverly Hills, CA: Sage.

Hollifield, C. A. (1998). The transnational tightrope: A case study in magazine management across borders. In A. B. Sohn, J. L. Wicks, & S. Lacy (Eds.), *Media management: A casebook approach* (2nd ed., pp. 211–229). Mahwah, NJ: Lawrence Erlbaum Associates.

Hollifield, C. A. (1999). Effects of foreign ownership on media content: Thomson's papers coverage of Quebec independence vote. *Newspaper Research Journal, 20*(1), 65–82.

Hollifield, C. A. (2001). Crossing borders: Media management in a transnational market environment. *Journal of Media Economics, 14*(3), 133–146.

Hollifield, C. A., & Donnermeyer, J. F. (2003). Creating demand: Influencing information technology diffusion in rural communities. *Government Information Quarterly, 20*(2), 135–150.

Hollifield, C. A., Kosicki, G. M., & Becker, L. B. (2001). Organizational vs. professional culture in the newsroom: Television news directors' and newspaper editors' hiring decisions. *Journal of Broadcasting and Electronic Media, 45*(1), 92–117.

Hoskins, C., & McFadyen, S. (1993). Canadian participation in international co-productions and co-ventures in television programming. *Canadian Journal of Communication, 18*, 219–236.

Hoskins, C., Finn, A., & McFayden, S. (1994). Marketing management and competitive strategy in the cultural industries. *Canadian Journal of Communication, 19*(3/4), 269–296.

Hoskins, C., & Mirus, R. (1988). Reasons for U.S. dominance of the international trade in television programmes. *Media, Culture, & Society, 10*, 499–515.

Hughes, R. L., Ginnett, R. C., & Curphy, G. J. (1999). *Leadership: Enhancing the lessons of experience.* Boston: Irwin/McGraw-Hill.

Hunt, S. D. (1991). *Modern marketing theory: Critical issues in the philosophy of marketing science.* Cincinnati, OH: South Western.

Johansson, T. (2002). Lighting the campfire: The creation of a community of interest around a media company. *The International Journal on Media Management, 4*(1), 4–12.

Johnstone, J. W. C., Slawski, E. J., & Bowman, W. W. (1976). *The news people: A sociological portrait of American journalists and their work.* Urbana: University of Illinois Press.

Kang, M. H. (2002). Digital cable: Exploring factors associated with early adoption. *Journal of Media Economics, 15*(3), 193–207.

Karlsson, C., & Ahlstrom, P. (1997). Perspective: Changing product development strategy—A managerial challenge. *Journal of Product Innovation Management, 14*(6), 473–484.

Kelly, R. E., & Lewis, P. E. T. (2001). Household demand for Internet connection. *Journal of Media Economics, 14*(4), 249–265.

Killebrew, K. C. (2003). Culture, creativity and convergence: Managing journalists in a changing information workplace. *The International Journal on Media Management, 5*(1), 39–46.

Klein, A. (2002, October 21). A merger taken AO-ill: Financials, culture, ideology divide Time Warner and its new media partner. *Washington Post*, p. E01.

Küng, L. (2000). Exploring the link between culture and strategy in media organisations: The cases of the BBC and CNN. *The International Journal on Media Management, 2*(2), 100–109.

Küng, L. (2004). *What makes media firms tick? Exploring the hidden drivers of firm performance.* In R. G. Picard (Ed.), *Strategic Responses to Media Market Changes* (pp. 65–82). (JIBS Research Reports No. 2004-2) Jönköping International Business School, Sweden.

Knyphausen-Aufsess, D., Krys, C., & Schweizer, L. (2002). Attacker's advantage in a homogenous market: The case of GSM. *The International Journal on Media Management, 4*(4), 212–224.

Lacy, S., & Blanchard, A. (2003). The impact of public ownership, profits, and competition on number of newsroom employees and starting salaries at mid-sized daily newspapers. *Journalism & Mass Communication Quarterly, 80*(4), 949–968.

Lacy, S., Shaver, M. A., & St. Cyr, C. (1996). The effects of public ownership and newspaper competition on the financial performance of newspaper corporations: A replication and extension. *Journalism & Mass Communication Quarterly, 73*(2), 332–341.

Lacy, S., & Simon, T. F. (1993). *The economics and regulation of United States newspapers.* Norwood, NJ: Ablex.

Landler, M., & Kirkpatrick, D. D. (2002, July 29). Bertelsmann's chief is fired after clash with ownership. *New York Times*, p. 1A.

Lasorsa, D. L., & Reese, S. D. (1990). News source use in the crash of 1987: A study of four national media. *Journalism Quarterly, 67*(1), 60–71.

Lawson-Borders, G. (2003). Integrating new media and old media: Seven observations of convergence as a strategy for best practices in media organizations. *The International Journal on Media Management, 5*(2), 91–99.

Lent, J. A. (1998). The animation industry and it offshore factories. In G. Sussman and J. A. Lent (Eds.), *Global productions: Labor in the making of the "information society"* (pp. 239–254). Cresskill, NJ: Hampton Press.

Linton, R. (1945). *The cultural background of personality.* New York: Appleton-Century-Crafts.

Liu, F., & Chan-Olmsted, S. M. (2003). Partnerships between the old and the new: Examining the strategic alliances between broadcast television networks and Internet firms in the context of convergence. *The International Journal on Media Management, 5*(1), 47–56.

Loebbecke, C., & Falkenberg, M. (2002). A framework for assessing market-entry opportunities for Internet-based TV. *The International Journal on Media Management, 4*(2), 95–104.

Martin, J., & Frost, P. (1996). The organizational culture war games: A struggle for intellectual dominance. In S. R. Clegg, C. Hardy, & W. R. Nord (Eds.), *Handbook of organization studies* (pp. 599–621). London: Sage.

Maslow, A. (1954). *Motivation and personality.* New York: Harper.

McQuail, D., & Windahl, S. (1993). *Communication models for the study of mass communication* (2nd ed.). London: Longman.

Napoli, P. M. (1999). Deconstructing the diversity principle. *Journal of Communication, 49*(4), 7–34.

National Association of Broadcasters. (2001). *Television financial report,* 2001. Washington, DC: Author.

Newcomb, H. M., & Alley, R. S. (1982). The producer as artist: Commercial television. In J. S. Ettema & D. C. Whitney (Eds.), *Individuals in mass media organizations: Creativity and constraint* (pp. 69–89). Beverly Hills, CA: Sage.

Ott, J. S. (1989). *The organizational culture perspective.* Chicago: Dorsey.

Papper, R., & Gerhard, M. (1997). Moving forward, falling back. Retrieved March 10, 2004, from http://www.rtndf.org/issues/articles/wmsurvey.htm

Papper, R., & Gerhard, M. (1999). Minority journalists: Making a difference. Retrieved March 10, 2004, from http://rtndf.org/issues/articles/wmsurvey99.htm#author

Papper, R., & Gerhard, M. (2000). Women & minorities: In radio and TV news. *Communicator, 54*(7), 36–38.

Papper, R., & Gerhard, M. (2001). Women & minorities: In radio and TV news. *Communicator, 55*(7), 37–41.

Parker, B. (1996). Evolution and revolution: From international business to globalization. In S. R. Clegg, C. Hardy, & W. R. Nord (Eds.), *Handbook of organization studies* (pp. 484–506). London: Sage.

Pathania-Jain, G. (2001). Global parents, local partners: A value-chain analysis of collaborative strategies of media firms in India. *Journal of Media Economics, 14*(3), 169–187.

Peer, L., & Chestnut, B. (1995). Deciphering media independence: The Gulf War debate in television and newspaper news. *Political Communication, 12*(1), 81–95.

Pendakur, M. (1998). Hollywood north: Film and tv production in Canada. In G. Sussman & J. A. Lent (Eds.), *Global productions: Labor in the making of the "information society"* (pp. 213–238). Cresskill, NJ: Hampton Press.

Perez-Latre, F. J., & Sanchez-Tabernero, A. (2003). Leadership, an essential requirement for effecting change in media companies: An analysis of the Spanish market. *The International Journal on Media Management, 5*(3), 199–208.

Picard, R. G. (2000). Changing business models of online content services: Their implications for multimedia and other content producers. *The International Journal on Media Management, 2*(2), 60–68.

Picard, R. G. (2003, July). *The transition of media economic studies: From industry to firm.* Presentation to the annual meeting of the Association for Education in Journalism & Mass Communication, Kansas City, MO.

Picard, R. (2004). Environmental and market changes driving strategic planning in media firms. In R. G. Picard (Ed.), *Strategic responses to media market changes* (pp. 65–82). (JIBS Research Reports No. 2004-2). Jönköping International Business School, Sweden.

Pollard, G. (1995). Job satisfaction among news workers: The influence of professionalism, perceptions of organizational structure, and social attributes. *Journalism and Mass Communication Quarterly, 72*(3), 682–697.

Porter, M. E. (1991). Towards a dynamic theory of strategy. *Strategic Management Journal, 12*(3), 95–117.

Priest, W. C. (1994). An information framework for the planning and design of "information highways." Retrieved November 2004, from http://www.eff.org/Groups/CITS/Reports/cits_nii_framework_ota.report

Ramstad, G. O. (1997). A model of structural analysis of the media market. *Journal of Media Economics, 10*(3), 45–50.

Rao, B. (2001). Broadband innovation and the customer experience imperative. *The International Journal on Media Management, 3*(2), 56–65.

Rawolle, J., & Hess, T. (2000). New digital media and devices: An analysis for the media industry. *The International Journal on Media Management, 2*(2), 89-99.

Redmond, J., & Trager, R. (2004). *Balancing on the wire: The art of managing media organizations* (2nd ed.). Cincinnati, OH: Atomic Dog.

Reed, M. (1996). Organizational theorizing: A historically contested terrain. In. S. R. Clegg, C. Hardy, & W. R. Nord (Eds.), *Handbook of organization studies* (pp. 31–56). London: Sage.

Rizzuto, R. J., & Wirth, M. O. (2002). Economics of video on demand: A simulation analysis. *Journal of Media Economics, 15*(3), 209–225.

Roberts, K. H., & Grabowski, M. (1996). Organizations, technology and structuring. In S. R. Clegg, C. Hardy, & W. R. Nord (Eds.), *Handbook of organization studies* (pp. 409–423). London: Sage.

Rogers, E. (1995). *Diffusion of innovations.* New York: Free Press.

Rolland, A. (2003). Convergence as strategy for value creation. *The International Journal on Media Management, 5*(1), 14–24.

Rose, G., Lees, J., & Meter, M. L. (2001). A refined view of download time impacts on E-consumer attitudes and patronage intentions towards E-retailers. *The International Journal on Media Management, 3*(2), 105–111.

Rudner, R. S. (1966). *Philosophy of social science.* Englewood Cliffs, NJ: Prentice-Hall.

Ruekert, R. W., & Walker, O. C. Jr. (1995). The effect of company policies and senior management intervention on product development, team behavior and performance. In R. Chandy & A. Stringfellow (Eds.), *Organizational innovation for effective new product development* (pp. 23–26). Cambridge, MA: Marketing Science Institute.

Russial, J. T. (1994). Pagination and newsroom: A question of time. *Newspaper Research Journal, 15*(1), 91–99.

Russial, J., & Wanta, W. (1998). Digital imaging skills and hiring and training of photojournalists. *Journalism and Mass Communication Quarterly, 75*(3), 593–605.

Saksena, S., & Hollifield, C. A. (2002). U.S. newspapers and the development of online editions. *The International Journal on Media Management, 4*(2), 75–84.

Savage, S., Madden, G., & Simpson, M. (1997). Broadband delivery of educational services: A study of subscription intentions in Australian provincial centres. *Journal of Media Economics, 10*(1), 3–15.

Schein, E. H. (1992). *Organizational culture and leadership* (2nd ed.). San Francisco: Jossey-Bass.

Sedman, D. (1998). Market parameters, marketing type, and technical standards: The introduction of the DVD. *Journal of Media Economics, 11*(1), 49–58.

Shaver, D., & Shaver, M. A. (2003). Books and digital technology: A new industry model. *Journal of Media Economics, 16*(2), 71–86.

Shoemaker, P. J., & Reese, S. D. (1991). *Mediating the message: Theories of influences on mass media content*. New York: Longman.

Shrikhande, S. (2001). Competitive strategies in the internationalization of television: CNNI and BBC World in Asia. *Journal of Media Economics, 14*(3), 147–168.

Stamm, K., Underwood, D., & Giffard, A. (1995). How pagination effects job satisfaction of editors. *Journalism and Mass Communication Quarterly, 72*(4), 851–862.

Stone, V. A. (1987). Changing profiles of news directors of radio and TV stations, 1972–1986. *Journalism Quarterly, 6*(4), 745–749.

Stone, V. A. (1988). Trends in the status of minorities and women in broadcast news. *Journalism Quarterly, 65*, 288–293.

Stone, V. A. (1989, September/October). Women gain as broadcast news directors in new RTNDA study. *Media Report to Women*, 6–7.

Sylvie, G. (2003). A lesson from the *New York Times*: Timing and the management of cultural change. *The International Journal on Media Management, 5*(4), 294–304.

Taylor, F. W. (1947). *Principles of scientific management*. New York: Harper & Row.

Thompson, K. (1985). *Exporting entertainment: America in the world film market, 1907–34*. London: BFI.

Toren, N. (1969). Semi-professionalism and social work: A theoretical perspective. In A. Etzioni (Ed.), *The semi-professions and their organization: teachers, nurses, social workers* (pp. 141–195). New York: The Free Press.

Tuchman, G. (1973). Making news by doing work: Routinizing the unexpected. *American Journal of Sociology, 79*(1), 110–131.

Turner, J. H. (1993). *Classical sociological theory: A positivist's perspective*. Chicago: Nelson Hall.

Turow, J. (1982). Unconventional programs on commercial television: An organizational perspective. In J. S. Ettema & D. C. Whitney (Eds.), *Individuals in mass media organizations: Creativity and constraint* (pp. 107–129). Beverly Hills, CA: Sage.

Turow, J. (1992). *Media systems in society: Understanding industries, strategies, and power*. New York: Longman.

Ulrich, H. (1984). *Management*. Bern, Switzerland/Stuttgart, Germany: Haupt.

Wackman, D. B., Gillmor, D. M., Gaziano, C., & Dennis, E. E. (1975). Chain newspaper autonomy as reflected in presidential campaign endorsements. *Journalism Quarterly, 52*(3), 411–420.

Warner, C., & Spencer, J. (1990). Radio and television sales staff profiles, compensation, and practices. Retrieved November 21, 1999, from http://www.missouri.edu/~jourcw/rtvsls.html

Wasko, J. (1998). Challenges to Hollywood's labor force in the 1990s. In G. Sussman & J. A. Lent (Eds.), *Global productions: Labor in the making of the "information society"* (pp. 173–190). Cresskill, NJ: Hampton Press.

Weaver, D., Beam, R., Brownlee, B., Voakes, P., & Wilhoit, G. C. (2003, August). *The American journalist in the 21st century: Key findings*. Paper presented to the Association for Education in Journalism & Mass Communication, Kansas City, MO.

Weaver, D. H., & Wilhoit, G. C. (1991). *The American journalist: A portrait of U.S. news people and their work* (2nd ed.). South Bend: Indiana University Press.

Weaver, D. H., & Wilhoit, G. C. (1996). *The American journalist in the 1990s: U.S. news people at the end of an era*. Mahwah, NJ: Lawrence Erlbaum Associates.

Weinstein, A. K. (1977). Foreign investments by service firms: The case of the multinational advertising agency. *Journal of International Business Studies, 8*(1), 83–91.

West, D. C. (1993). Cross-national creative personalities, processes and agency philosophies. *Journal of Advertising Research, 33*(5), 53–62.

West, D. C. (1996). The determinants and consequences of multinational advertising agencies. *International Journal of Advertising, 15*(2), 128–139.

Wheelwright, S. C., & Clark, K. B. (1992). *Revolutionizing product development.* New York: Free Press.

Wicks, J. L., Sylvie, G., Hollifield, C. A., Lacy, S., & Sohn, A. B. (2004). *Media management: A casebook approach* (3rd ed.). Mahwah, NJ: Lawrence Erlbaum Associates.

Williams, D. (2002). Structure and competition in the U.S. home video game industry. *The International Journal on Media Management, 4*(1), 41–54.

Wirth, M. O., & Bloch, H. (1995). Industrial organization theory and media industry analysis. *Journal of Media Economics, 8*(2), 15–26.

Young, D. P. T. (2000). Modeling media markets. How important is market structure. *Journal of Media Economics, 13*(1), 27–44.

# 4

# Paradigms and Analytical Frameworks in Modern Economics and Media Economics

Steven S. Wildman
Michigan State University

Theories are constructed to explain what we see or think we see. Since the publication of Kuhn's *Structure of Scientific Revolutions* in 1962, however, it has been generally appreciated that theories may also determine what we think we see because people interpret the world they observe in terms of the theories and models they carry in their heads. That is, observations are automatically classified according to the convenient categories provided by accepted theories. In the extreme, aspects of reality that do not neatly fit within the structures of existing theories may be overlooked entirely.

Economists are no different than practitioners of other scientific disciplines in their tendency to see the world in terms of the theories in which they were schooled, and the same must be said for those who study media economics as well. Kuhn (1996) referred to dominant analytical frameworks as paradigms and argued that scientific knowledge advanced in two ways: through incremental progress based on research inspired by a dominant paradigm and through the more radical advances that occur as one paradigm supplants another and opens new opportunities for further research. An example of such a paradigm shift was the replacement of Newtonian mechanics by Einstein's theory of relativity as the theoretical framework guiding advanced research in physics and astronomy after the publication of Einstein's theory of special relativity in 1906. Astronomers' use of classical methods to predict the periodicity of objects orbiting our sun is an example of work done within the Newtonian framework.

Up through the 1970s and somewhat beyond, it is fair to say that the overwhelming bulk of the research and writing in economics during the 20th century was inspired by an analytical framework commonly referred to as the neoclassical paradigm. Although the term neoclassical is still employed to describe portions of modern economics, it is increasingly rare to hear it referred to as a dominant paradigm in the Kuhnian sense. The primary reason is that the set of analytical tools and perspectives employed by economists has expanded enormously over the past 30 years, often in ways that are not obvious extensions of the framework established by the early neoclassical economists. The same economist may now employ the tools of several different analytical frameworks to address different economic questions.

Classified in terms of the economic methodologies employed, media economics is a subfield of industrial organization (IO), the branch of economics that applies microeconomic tools to study the functioning of markets (Tirole, 1988). By extension, this includes the behavior of market participants. This chapter provides an overview of the principle analytical frameworks employed by IO economists today and more briefly discusses their applications to the study of media firms and markets. The neoclassical approach, which is discussed in the next section, will receive the most attention. Although no longer the overwhelmingly dominant paradigm it once was, neoclassical economics is still the source of the intuition guiding much, if not most, of today's economic research, and the newer frameworks are still typically defined by how they differ from the neoclassical approach. Furthermore, the newer frameworks and tools often allow for actors that adhere to many or most of the neoclassical postulates about economic behavior. This section reviews the analytical foundations of the neoclassical paradigm and describes the principal models of market organization developed within the neoclassical tradition. The new analytical tools and frameworks that have achieved increasing prominence over the last 30 years are discussed in the next section. Applications of the various frameworks are considered in the final section.

## NEOCLASSICAL INDUSTRIAL ORGANIZATION

### Assumptions and Analytical Foundations of Neoclassical Economics

For an analytical framework that until recently was generally accorded dominant paradigm status, there is less agreement on the contours of neoclassical economics than might be expected. In a recent review of the origins of neoclassical economics, Ekelund and Hébert (2002) emphasized that the "essence of neoclassical economics is far from settled in the history of economic thought," (p. 198) and they listed reliance on mathematical methods, marginalism, subjective utility, and "the static analysis of efficient allocation" (p. 198) as four features of modern economic analysis that are often claimed to be defining attributes of neoclassical analysis. Common reliance on an analytical toolkit comprised of these elements is often dated to the publication of Alfred Marshall's *Principles of Economic Analysis* in 1890, although Ekelund and Hébert pointed out that all of the critical elements of the analytical framework codified by Marshall were developed by preceding generations of economists.

It would be hard to deny that marginalism, subjective utility, and static efficiency analysis are signature features of the body of literature identified with neoclassical economics.

Each is thus worth some attention in this discussion of neoclassical economics. Much of modern economic analysis, especially theory development, is also highly mathematical in character. However, I agree with Ekelund and Hébert's observation that, although prominently employed, use of mathematical methods is not a defining characteristic of neoclassical analysis because the fundamental assumptions and the defining analytical perspective are themselves not based in mathematics. Although the other attributes of the framework make the application of mathematical tools to economic problems a natural development, for many purposes, and perhaps most, mathematical formalism is not essential.

### Subjective Utility

In its simplest applications, utility refers to the pleasure or personal perception of benefit an individual consumer derives from consuming various products and services, which are commonly referred to as goods. Most common consumption items are goods. Economic bads are products and activities that reduce an individual's utility. Pollution, highway congestion, and other peoples' conversations during the feature film at the cinema are examples of bads. Modern economic analysis treats each individual's utility as personal and unique to that individual. Because utility is subjectively experienced, there is no common metric for comparing the utilities of different individuals. The relationship between the set of potential combinations of goods (and bads) consumed and an individual's utility is referred to as that individual's utility function, or, working in the opposite direction, the set of utility-based preferences among goods and combinations of goods determined by an individual's utility function is referred to as his or her preference function or preference ordering.

### Marginalism

Marginalism refers to a focus in analyses of both firms' and individual consumers' behavior on changes at the margin in variables economic agents control, such as output and consumption, and outcomes influenced by control variables, such as revenue, profits, and utility. Consumers are assumed to maximize utility and firms are assumed to maximize profis. Consumers maximize utility by adjusting their consumption of affordable goods and services in small (marginal) increments until a point is reached at which any further adjustments can only reduce their utility. Firms maximize profits through a similar process of incremental changes in outputs or prices until further change can only lower profits.

Utility theory is the foundation of the consumer side of demand theory. If, as is commonly assumed and generally believed, the utility derived from a unit consumed of a given good declines with the number of units already consumed (diminishing marginal utility), a seller will find it necessary to lower its price to get any individual consumer to purchase more of its product. Because economists typically place price on the vertical axis of diagrams of price–quantity relationships, a consequence of diminishing marginal utility is that demand curves slope downward from left to right so that sellers must lower their prices to get consumers to buy more of their products.[1] If individuals behave in

---

[1] I am ignoring here the possibility of a Giffen good, in which case a small region of its demand curve will slope upward. Giffen goods are theoretically possible because price changes, through their effects on buying power,

the aggregate as they do individually, the aggregate demand for a seller's good must also slope downward.

### Stable Preferences

Individual utility functions are typically taken as givens and stable in neoclassical analyses. Although this assumption simplifies demand analysis, it has also been criticized for ignoring evidence that individuals' preferences evolve over time and that individuals from different cultures may exhibit systematic differences in tastes. However, social system-level influences on demands for consumer goods do not preclude their being effectively stable from the perspective of sellers, and if preferences in any given culture evolve slowly over time, it may still be reasonable to assume that preferences are stable for models of market exchange. Furthermore, Stigler and Becker (1977) argue that with an appropriate reformulation of utility theory, what appear to be changes in preferences over time may, in fact, be consistent with a stable underlying function for transforming goods consumed into utility over time if consuming more of certain types of goods in the present increases the utility derived from their consumption in the future.

Demands for inputs and supplies by commercial buyers are also typically assumed to slope downward. Diminishing marginal productivity, which means that the marginal unit of an input contributes less to a firm's output the greater is the number of units of the input already employed, plays the role of diminishing marginal utility in consumer demand theory in making commercial buyers' demand curves slope downward.

### Static Optimization

The processes of utility maximization and profit maximization are commonly modeled as taking place in environments in which critical factors (e.g., incomes and prices of goods and services for consumers; prices of inputs, consumer demand, and competitors' prices or outputs for firms) are assumed constant. Analyses of consumer and firm behavior that employ these assumptions are thus exercises in static optimization, and comparisons of market outcomes when these and other factors taken as givens for an analysis are changed are referred to as comparative statics. Policy analysts are often concerned with the maximization of economic surplus, which is defined as the sum of consumer benefits (measured as aggregate willingness to pay for goods consumed minus payments to sellers) and firms' profits. A market's efficiency is assessed in terms of how close the market's participants come to collectively producing the theoretical maximum surplus attainable given consumers' demand functions and the costs of inputs to firms. Predictions of changes in a market's contribution to economic surplus because of changes in factors controlled by policymakers are also exercises in comparative statics within the neoclassical framework.

### Rational Actors

Economists describe agents who maximize their individual utilities or profits in the manner just described as rational, and the assumption of rational actors (sometimes

---

influence the effective incomes of individuals as well as the expense tradeoffs between different goods. For a fuller discussion of Giffen goods, see Varian (1984, pp. 119, 120).

referred to as the rationality postulate) may be the most singular defining characteristic of neoclassical economics. It is important to note, however, that the rational actor assumed in a typical neoclassical analysis is not simply rational in the sense of doing the best he or she can given the circumstances. An actor in a neoclassical model actually realizes the greatest utility (or highest profit) that is possible given the resources available to him or her by choosing the attainable combination of resources for which utility (or profit) is highest. This is why Williamson (2002) described neoclassical economics as the economics of choice. As Nobel laureate Herbert Simon (1987) put it, "[t]he rational person of neoclassical economics always reaches the decision that is objectively, or substantively, best in terms of the given utility function" (p. 27). The rational neoclassical actor reaches the objectively best decision because he or she knows with certainty the consequences of the various choices he or she might make. Simon contrasts the rational actor of economics with "the rational person of psychology [who] goes about making his or her decisions in a way that is procedurally reasonable in light of the available knowledge and means of computation" (p. 27).

The strong form of rationality employed in neoclassical analyses accounts for much of the mathematical precision of neoclassical economics and the power of its analytical tools, but it is also a source of persistent criticism of the neoclassical approach. Arrow (1987), like Simon, criticizes neoclassical economics for placing impossibly large informational demands on economic actors, and psychologists have identified general behavioral tendencies that result in choices that violate the rationality assumption. (Kahneman, 2003; Tversky & Kahneman, 1987). Defenders of the neoclassical approach typically acknowledge that there are circumstances for which the assumption of rational actors is not appropriate, but argue that the predictions of rational actor models are empirically supported in a remarkably wide range of settings and that experimental tests of rational actor models generally, although not always, produce results consistent with the models (Plott, 1986). Lucas (1987) suggested that in a wide range of situations economic actors may learn through experience what strategies produce the best (or at least acceptable) results and described his view of economics as the study of "decision rules that are steady states of some adaptive process, decisions rules that are found to work over a range of situations and hence are no longer revised appreciably as more experience accumulates" (p. 218). He, thus, sees economic models as predicting the outcomes of economic choices by assessing the consequences of alternatives, but not as descriptions of the processes by which choices are made.

Campbell (1987), echoing Alchian's (1950) defense of rational actor assumptions nearly 40 years earlier, also argued that it is inappropriate to interpret the decision rules ascribed to the rational actors of economic models as descriptions of the thought processes guiding real economic actors when they make choices. He pointed out that similar assumptions of rationality and intentionality are successfully employed in models of animal behavior, even though no one would argue that the animals described were consciously aware of the logic guiding their actions.[2] Rather, selection for fitness in nature and in markets produces agents with decision rules similar to those predicted by models employing neoclassical assumptions. Finally, defenders of the neoclassical approach claim that for

---

[2] Examples are models of foraging strategy and signaling models. Wildman (2004) provides a brief review of animal signaling models and parallel work on signaling theory in economics.

many applications there is no alternative theoretical framework that performs nearly so well in explaining economic behaviors and institutions. It is fair to say that few, if any, scholars working within the neoclassical tradition would defend the extreme rational actor assumptions often employed as wholly accurate depictions of economic agents. Instead they would argue that these assumptions produce more than adequate approximations to the behaviors of the real economic agents they study and that the gains in analytical tractability achieved more than compensate for whatever sacrifices are made in realism of description.

## Neoclassical Models of Market Organization

Most analyses of firms and markets within the neoclassical tradition build on one of several core models of markets organized in different ways. In describing them, it is convenient to begin with the model of perfect competition, as the other core neoclassical IO models can be described in terms of how they deviate from the model of a perfectly competitive market. The attractive efficiency properties of perfectly competitive markets have also been a major source of inspiration for policies promoting competition, even though no real world markets satisfy all the conditions assumed to hold in the model of a perfectly competitive market.

### Perfect Competition

Although different authors have combined them in different ways, the following seven assumptions are all essential to the model of perfect competition and are listed in one form or another in most textbook presentations of the model.[3]

1. Firms (sellers) seize every opportunity to maximize profits, and consumers, or more generally buyers, adjust their purchases of the market's product to maximize their individual utilities.
2. Firms produce a homogeneous product, which means consumers view each seller's product as a perfect substitute for any other firm's product.
3. Buyers appear identical to sellers in the sense that although the profits a firm realizes may be influenced by the number of customers it has, its profits are in no way affected by the identities of those customers.
4. There is a large number of firms, and each firm accounts for a small fraction of market output.
5. Consumers are also numerous, and each consumer accounts for only a small fraction of the market's sales.
6. All firms and all consumers are perfectly informed about the prices charged by every firm.
7. Entry into and exit from the market is costless for firms and for consumers.

The first three assumptions plus number six guarantee that all firms charge the same price, which of necessity is the market clearing price, as any firm charging more than any

---

[3] Compare with Henderson and Quandt (1971).

one of its competitors would have no customers. "Large numbers" and "numerous" in assumptions four and five refer to numbers of agents sufficiently large that coordinated behavior is infeasible. Together, assumptions four and seven guarantee that the market price will be the competitive zero profit price. The meaning of "small" in these two assumptions is that each player's contribution to demand or supply is so small that changes in that player's output or purchases will have a negligible effect on the market price.

Even in the absence of free entry, Stigler (1964) argued that with numerous buyers and sellers, communication costs will be high enough to render collusion ineffective, so the market price will be the outcome of uncoordinated actions by independent agents.[4] Thus, each player takes the market price as a given in maximizing its profits or utility. This guarantees that price will equal marginal cost, as firms can increase profits by increasing (decreasing) output if price exceeds (is less than) marginal cost. A consequence is that each firm contributes the maximum amount possible to the surplus created by the market. Assumption seven guarantees that industry output will be set at a level such that the total cost of expanding market output (including any fixed costs incurred by a firm entering the market) is just equal to the revenue generated. As each buyer is paying just what the product is worth to him or her at the margin, free entry (and exit) ensures that market output is also set at the level that maximizes the market's contribution to surplus.

Because all opportunities to increase surplus are exploited, a perfectly competitive market is also efficient. Much of the policy appeal of competition as a mechanism for governing markets reflects a belief that competition in real world markets can produce results that approximate the efficiency benefits of a perfectly competitive market.

### *Monopoly*

Other models developed within the neoclassical framework can be described as the modeling consequences of dropping one or more of the assumptions central to the model of perfect competition. Reducing the large number of firms in the perfectly competitive market to one produces the neoclassical monopolist.[5] For a monopolist, firm output is the same as market output. Because market price falls as market output increases, the monopolist sees price as a declining function of its own output. As price must be reduced to increase market sales, marginal revenue also declines with output and at a faster rate than price because the lower price applies to all units sold. Marginal revenue is thus less than price for a monopolist for all units sold except the first, and producing at the output for which marginal revenue equals marginal cost to maximize profits results in a price in excess of marginal cost. The fact that the monopolist's profit-maximizing price, which measures the value of the marginal unit of the monopolist's product to consumers, exceeds its marginal cost means that a monopolist sells less of its product than the amount required to maximize the total of consumer and producer surplus. This is the inefficiency of monopoly.

---

[4]Note, however, the tension between the assumption that large numbers make the communication required for coordination prohibitively costly and the assumption of perfectly informed agents. Baumol, Panzar and Willig (1982) demonstrated free entry alone may be sufficient to produce competitively efficient outcomes—even for a market served by a single active firm if an entrant can profit from a quick "hit and run" entry and exit strategy.

[5]The buyer-side analogue to monopoly is monopsony, which is a market with a single buyer. Although less frequently analyzed, monopsony may create inefficiencies analogous to those associated with monopoly.

### Monopolistic Competition

If we drop the assumption of a homogeneous product while keeping the numbers of firms and buyers large, the market described is monopolistically (or imperfectly) competitive. Chamberlin (1956) is credited with being the first to rigorously explore the properties of a market organized in this way. Firms in models of monopolistically competitive markets sell differentiated versions of a product that buyers view as close, but not perfect, substitutes for each other. Entry still drives profits to zero (at least for the marginal firm) as in the model of perfect competition, but because consumers do not view individual firms' products as perfect substitutes for each other, the demand for each firm's product is downward sloping. Revenue is equal to cost when profits are zero. Therefore, each firm's average revenue (which is equal to its price) is also equal to its average cost in a monopolistically competitive market when the marginal revenue equals marginal cost condition for profit maximization is satisfied, two conditions which also describe equilibrium in a perfectly competitive market. However, because each firm's demand curve is downward sloping with monopolistic competition, price exceeds marginal revenue and marginal cost just as it does for a monopolist. As monopolistically competitive firms earn zero profits, the excess of price over marginal cost is better viewed as an inevitable consequence of product differentiation than evidence of market power. Since Spence (1976) published his model of a monopolistically competitive market, the principal welfare question addressed in studies of monopolistic competition is whether competitive firms supply the optimal amount of product variety. Depending on demand and cost characteristics, monopolistically competitive markets may supply either too much or too little product variety.[6]

### Oligopoly

Between competition and monopoly when products are homogeneous and monopolistic competition and monopoly when products are differentiated is oligopoly. Oligopoly theory refers to a collection of models of strategic interaction that apply to markets served by a small number of firms, where small describes a number greater than one but not so large that firms pay no explicit attention to individual competitors in choosing their own courses of action. In contrast to a perfectly competitive market, in which each firm contributes such a small fraction of the market's supply that plausible changes in its output leave the market price and the profits of other firms effectively unchanged, each oligopolist is large enough relative to the market for its actions to have significant impact on the profits of the other firms in the market. Each firm is therefore compelled to design its strategy in anticipation of what it expects its competitors to do in the future. These strategic links are the key feature distinguishing oligopoly from the other forms of market structure discussed to this point[7] (Friedman, 1983) and make oligopoly

---

[6] Salop (1979) and Waterman (1990) presented models for which monopolistically competitive markets provide too much variety in equilibrium. Too little variety is a possibility in Spence's model.

[7] This may also be the case for some models of monopolistic competition where many firms offer differentiated products, but each firm has only a small number of competitors offering products that are close substitutes for its own. For example, spatial models of monopolistic competition have this property. In these models each firm is

theory a more complex undertaking than are theories of monopoly, competition, and monopolistic competition.

Oligopolists are always faced with the challenge of resolving the tension between their conflicting urges to compete and to collude. Joint profits are maximized when they collude, and if they collude perfectly they *may* be able to realize profits as large as would a monopolist serving the same market.[8] However, it is almost always the case that an individual firm can profit by deviating from a collusive arrangement, for example, by charging a price slightly below the agreed upon level to pick up a larger share of the market for itself. At one extreme, oligopolists may simply decide that coordination is too difficult to manage effectively, and each may try to maximize its own profits without regard for its competitors' profits. At the other extreme, oligopolists may able to work in complete harmony in devising a common course of action. In between are arrangements that are intermittently successful, with periods of cooperation broken by episodes of cartel cheating and intense competition, and arrangements that manage to sustain profits at above competitive levels on an ongoing basis, but still fall short of the level of profits that perfect coordination would produce.

### Applications to Competition Policy

Antitrust enforcement and competition policy more generally is primarily concerned with the effect of market structure—the number and relative sizes of competitors—on price, and oligopoly theory provides the foundation for investigations of this relationship for individual markets. It is generally believed that collusion is more likely to be effective in more concentrated markets,[9] but theory offers little, if any, guidance as to how concentrated a market must be for coordinated action to have an effect on price and the importance of factors other than market structure that also influence the likelihood of successful collusion. However, theory clearly demonstrates that an increase in concentration may lead to an increase in price even when competitors develop their strategies in a totally uncoordinated fashion, at least when competitors maintain Cournot-like beliefs about their rivals[10] (Farrell & Shapiro, 1990). Gurrea and Owen (in press) suggest that the relatively undeveloped state of economic theories of coordinated action may help explain a shift in emphasis in U.S. merger enforcement efforts from a focus on the effects of mergers on the likelihood of successful collusion to concern with the unilateral effects of merger on price beginning in the early 1990s.

The four sets of neoclassical theories just reviewed—monopoly, competition, monopolistic competition, and oligopoly—and empirical studies inspired by these models, constitute the primary foundation for the structure-conduct-performance (SCP) framework

---

strategically linked to those competitors providing the closest substitutes to its own products. See, for example, models of competition on a circle developed by Salop (1979) and Waterman (1990).

[8]I use *may* rather than *will* in this sentence because a monopolist serving the same market may not choose the same facilities employed by the oligopolists or it may choose a different selection of products if products are differentiated.

[9]See Stigler (1964) for an early, and still influential, discussion of the reasons why this should be so.

[10]Cournot competitors select their outputs on the assumption that their competitors will keep their outputs at their current levels.

that has guided industry analysis and competition policy in the United States and other economically advanced nations.[11] Although there is still considerable work being done to extend and refine these theories of industry structure, their basic outlines within the neoclassical tradition have been settled for some time. Starting in the 1970s, the analytical toolkit employed by IO economists began a period of rapid expansion fueled by new developments in economic theory and by a more widespread appreciation of the importance of earlier attempts to do work outside the analytical boundaries implicit in the constraints of the neoclassical paradigm. These new frameworks are briefly introduced and discussed in the next section. With the exception of the new work on network effects and networks industries, which might be viewed as a logical extension of neoclassical analysis, each can be interpreted as a methodological response to one or more of the criticisms of the neoclassical approach.

It would be incorrect to say that the new analytical frameworks have replaced neoclassical analysis. Rather, the neoclassical paradigm now occupies a highly visible spot in a growing smorgasbord of analytical approaches that economists employ to address different types of economic questions. However, as the new approaches have gained acceptance, economists have become more aware of the limitations imposed by the core assumptions of neoclassical economics. As a consequence, the range of topics to which it is applied has been somewhat curtailed while a host of new topics have been opened to analysis.

## POST-NEOCLASSICAL ADDITIONS TO THE IO TOOLKIT

### Mathematical Game Theory

Mathematical game theory is a collection of mathematical techniques employed to model strategies and the outcomes of strategic interactions. Although economists have contributed greatly to the development of game theory, game theory has many applications outside of economics, including politics and evolutionary biology. It has economic content only when applied to economic problems. As was mentioned earlier, oligopolists, by definition, recognize their interdependence, and theories of oligopoly must take this recognition of strategic interdependence into account. Nash (1950) supplied a critical conceptual breakthrough for modeling equilibria where firms base their strategies on their beliefs about other firms' strategies. Loosely speaking, in a Nash equilibrium the strategy predicted for a player by other players is that player's best response to its predictions of their strategies. A situation that satisfies this condition is an equilibrium because no player has an incentive to change his or her strategy. Nash's equilibrium concept is at the core of much of modern game theory.[12] With the obvious exception of monopoly,

---

[11] To keep this chapter to a manageable length, I have refrained from discussing the frequent use of these models to study vertical relationships such as the pricing strategy of a monopolist at one level of a value chain selling to competitive firms at the next lower level or the implications for the structure of a downstream market of the merger of one of several downstream firms with an upstream supplier of a critical input.

[12] Nash shared the 1994 Nobel Prize in Economics with another game theorist, Reinhard Selten, for this contribution to economic theory.

all of the standard neoclassical models of different types of markets can be described in terms of Nash equilibria of various types.[13]

A Nash equilibrium describes a market at a particular point in time. Because today's production typically depends on assets acquired and plans put in place in an earlier period, a description of an equilibrium as Nash tells us little by itself about the strategic choices and commitments market participants made in the past to bring the market to the observed equilibrium state. Much of the most important work in game theory following Nash involved the development of techniques for modeling the strategic choices made at the pre-equilibrium stages of a game. These choices are typically modeled through a process of backward induction, whereby market participants (or potential participants) project forward to the final (equilibrium) stage of the game to predict their opponents' responses to all strategies they might employ at that stage. If each strategy is contingent on a choice made at an earlier stage of the game, selecting the best final stage strategy determines the best strategy for the earlier stage as well. There is no limit to the number of stages to which this backward induction process might be applied. Because competitors also use backward induction to determine their strategies, the choices for all stages of the game (the entire set of strategic choices) are determined for all players in this manner. This process can be applied to games in which competitors are fully informed and games with less than complete information.

The methods of game theory permit a formal analysis of dynamic elements of competition that could not be examined with equivalent rigor with the tools of traditional neoclassical economics. Because they have such broad applicability, game theoretic techniques are also commonly employed by people working with some of the other post-neoclassical analytical frameworks. Chapter 11 of Tirole's (1988) text provides a concise introduction to the basic tools of game theory employed in the study of industrial organization. Gibbons' (1992) *Game Theory for Applied Economists* is a reader-friendly, graduate-level introduction to economic applications of game theory that starts at a fairly basic level.

## Network Industries and Two-Sided Markets

Two theoretical developments of particular interest for the study of media economics are the work on network effects and network industries that started in the 1970s (see, e.g., Rohlfs (1974)) and the related, but much more recent, work on models of two-sided markets. For certain types of products (and services), the value of the product to each individual user depends to some degree on the number of other individuals (or firms) using that product. Each user's decision to acquire the product thus affects the value of the product to other users, forming a *network* of individuals linked by this demand

---

[13] Nash equilibria are often described in terms of the strategic variable on which players focus their attention. For example, a market equilibrium may be described as Nash in price if firms select their strategies based on the prices they believe their competitors will charge. A Nash equilibrium may be defined for any strategic variable. Models that can be described as applications of the Nash equilibrium concept were developed long before Nash provided his generalized characterization of an equilibrium. For example, an equilibrium that is Nash in quantities (outputs) is often referred to as a Cournot equilibrium after the model of such an equilibrium first published by Augustin Cournot in 1838.

interdependency. The effect of one user on the consumption value realized by other users is referred to as a network effect, and industries for which network effects are important are called network industries. Telephony is a commonly used example of an industry for which network effects are important. The value of telephone service to any individual subscriber is a positive function of the number of other people who can be contacted by phone. The value of a phone system to individual subscribers thus increases with the size of the network as measured by the number of subscribers. In most situations analyzed, network effects are positive, although they may also be negative, as would be the case if network congestion increased with the number of subscribers.

The value of an additional telephone subscriber to other subscribers is a direct network effect as the subscriber itself is the source of added value. Subscribers may also benefit from a larger network if economies of scale lead to lower costs and prices or if third parties see the network's customers as an opportunity for creating new products or services that make the original service more valuable. Benefits associated with the provision of complementary products that increase as the number of users increases are referred to as indirect network effects. Answering machines are an example of positive indirect network effects for telephone service as they are supplied by third parties as an enhancement to basic telephone service. As with direct network effects, indirect network effects can also be negative. For most people, unsolicited calls from direct marketers are a negative indirect network effect. Indirect network effects, whether positive or negative, exist when two (or more) markets are linked because the demand for or supply of products in one market affects the demand for or supply of products in the other market(s).

Although game theory has played a major role in the development of this literature, many of the new models developed to analyze network industries can be seen as straight-forward extensions of the neoclassical framework to deal with the structural and strategic implications of network effects. Incorporation of network effects into analyses of market equilibria and competitive dynamics can be interpreted as a consequence of relaxing the unstated, but implicit, assumption of the earlier neoclassical models of market structure that the value of a product to a buyer is unaffected by other buyers' choices of which sellers to purchase from.

Most of the critical insights regarding the implications of network effects for market structure and strategy were established by the mid-1980s and are now well known. When competing products have their own distinct networks of users and there are positive network effects, the product with the largest user base has a competitive advantage over other products in the market independent of its relative technical merits. Given network effects, users may rationally choose a product with a large user base over a competing product with a smaller user base even when the technical specifications of the smaller base product are better suited to their needs because the network benefits outweigh the benefits of product superiority (Besen & Johnson, 1986). If users do not know other users' preferences, they may still make product choices based on beliefs about which product will have the larger user base in the long run. In such circumstances, *band wagons* may develop around products with an early lead in market share and such expectations can become self-fulfilling. There is no guarantee that markets will choose the best product in such circumstances (Besen & Johnson).

Network effects may also preserve the market positions of established firms with older products against entrants with superior new products if users are unable to engineer a coordinated switch (Farrel & Saloner, 1985). Firms competing for position in a market for a new type of product or service may choose to subsidize early adopters for the long-term competitive advantage of a larger group of users for their own version of the product (Katz & Shapiro, 1986). Dominant firms may try to protect their dominant positions by making their products incompatible with the products of smaller competitors, whereas firms with smaller networks may want to promote compatibility through shared networks to realize the benefits of increased network effects (Economides, 1991). As the technical standards supporting different products often determine the degree to which they are compatible, standard setting is an important topic addressed in this literature. Katz and Shapiro (1994) provide a very accessible review of the work on competitive dynamics in the presence of network effects. A small, but growing, empirical branch of this literature has verified the importance of network effects for several communication industries (see, e.g., Ohashi, 2003).

Indirect network effects are of particular relevance to the study of ad-supported media because the consumption value of a media product to its audience and the value of the audience to advertisers are linked if advertising provided with a media product affects consumer demand for it and the number of people consuming the product affects how much advertisers will pay to place advertising in it. Rosse's (1978) econometric study found positive feedback between consumers' demand for newspapers and advertisers' demands for newspaper ad space. This relationship was formally modeled by Blair and Romano (1993).

The existence of an agent, such as a newspaper firm, that creates a product or service, such as a newspaper, to exploit the connection between the two markets turns markets linked through indirect network externalities into a two-sided platform market. Two-sided platform markets exist for other products besides media and have recently become a subject of considerable interest from IO theorists. Wright (2004) reviewed the new research on this topic. Media economists may profit from following this literature as it develops.

## Information Economics

The perfectly informed actors of the neoclassical IO models are embodiments of the rationality assumption central to neoclassical economics. The assumption of rational actors in models of economic behavior itself rests on two supporting assumptions relating to the acquisition of information that are often left unstated. If we dispense with the notion that economic actors are innately endowed with the information they need to make optimal choices and assume instead that the information actors need to make rational choices is available somewhere in the environment, then satisfaction of the rational actor assumption requires that economic actors be able to acquire and process that information at zero cost. Furthermore, if the information relevant to a transaction is initially held by different individuals, then costless acquisition of information implies costless communication, as Hirschliefer (1980) noted in his popular text. The second information acquisition assumption is that individuals holding information are honest in disclosing it to other economic agents. The field of information economics reviewed in this subsection explores the implications of relaxing the two information acquisition assumptions implied by neoclassical rationality.

Information may be costly to acquire even though economic agents are honest, and a large literature on search explores the strategies for acquiring information when it is costly to do so. Closest to the neoclassical tradition are attempts to model information acquisition strategies as attempts to maximize the difference between the benefits of search (better products, lower prices) and the cost of repeated search. Although an early paper by Stigler (1961) is credited with inspiring work on this topic, Stigler's search model was quickly dropped in favor of sequential search models developed originally for applications in operations research. Search for lower prices is a simple illustration of the approach. In these models, economic agents search by sampling a known distribution of values for an economic good until the expected payoff from learning the value of one more item exceeds the search cost of doing so. Common applications are to searches over distributions of product prices or wages when the item sought is a job. McCall's (1965) description of this search strategy included an application to investment decisions, where the probability distribution of economic values was the set of prospective payoffs to investments in innovations. Weitzman (1979) generalized the approach to allow search among alternatives drawn from different distributions and Vishwanath (1988) examined strategies for conducting multiple simultaneous searches over different distributions.

The economic problems posed by incomplete information become much more complicated when critical information is held by agents with a personal stake in what is revealed. Analysis of these situations must account for the strategic interests involved. For example, a prospective buyer and a hopeful seller negotiating a price for the latter's used car may each try to mislead the other—the potential buyer by understating how much he or she wants the car and the owner by exaggerating its reliability. Each may also fully understand the other's incentive to mislead or withhold information and believe that its counterpart in the negotiation holds an equally sophisticated understanding of the situation (or not).

A large, and for the most part, mathematically challenging literature on the economics of asymmetric information has employed game theoretic techniques to analyze situations in which economic agents are differentially informed. The 2001 Nobel Prize in Economics shared by Michael Spence, George Akerlof, and Joseph Stiglitz recognized their pioneering contributions to this body of research beginning in the late 1960s and early 1970s. The versions of their Nobel lectures printed in the June 2002 issue of *The American Economic Review* provide excellent introductions to the origins of this literature and subsequent developments most directly related to their pioneering work (Akerlof, 2002; Spence, 2002, Stiglitz, 2002).

Akerlof's (1970) famous paper on the market for lemons (of the automotive type) illustrates the challenges asymmetric information poses for market organization and economic transactions more generally. He posited a hypothetical market for used cars in which sellers knew the true quality of the cars they wanted to sell, whereas buyers knew only the average quality for used cars. With no additional information, buyers would be willing to pay at most the value of an average quality used car. Akerlof pointed out that sellers of cars worth more than this amount would withdraw them from the market, leaving a smaller selection of cars with a lower average value. Cars worth more than the new average would then be withdrawn. In the end the market would collapse to the point where only the lowest quality cars were offered for sale. Of course, appropriate prices could be negotiated for all used cars if each owner honestly revealed the true quality of the car he or she was trying to sell. The problem is that owners of all but the highest quality cars have an incentive to represent their qualities as higher than they actually are. Furthermore, even a small fraction of dishonest sellers would lower the prices buyers were willing to pay for the cars of honest sellers, which could still threaten the viability of the market.

Some degree of informational asymmetry is present in virtually every transactional situation. Thus, it is not surprising that a large portion of the more theoretical work on industrial organization now deals with the strategic issues that arise from information asymmetries. Of particular interest are strategies honest agents might employ to credibly distinguish themselves from dishonest agents, mechanisms for inducing agents to reveal private information, and the design of incentives to motivate agents holding private information to perform optimally. Spence and Stiglitz were pioneers in the early work on mechanisms that might be employed to overcome the threat to commerce of self-interested, asymmetrically informed transactional partners. In his Nobel lecture, Stiglitz (2002) referred to information economics as a new paradigm. Although it may be too early to pass judgment on the paradigmatic status of this body of work, its techniques have certainly become part of the standard toolkit of the IO economist.

## Transaction Cost Economics and the New Institutional Economics

Asymmetric information and potentially dishonest agents also figure prominently in the field of economics known variously as transaction cost economics, the new institutionalism, and the economics of organization. However, although the optimizing agents described in the theories and models of the information economics literature can be seen as direct descendents of the rational optimizers of neoclassical economics, work in this field, although acknowledging roots in neoclassical economics, draws heavily on an intellectual lineage that focuses more on the institutions of governance broadly defined than on the choices made by individual actors.

Governance institutions fall into two broad categories. One is the set of coordination mechanisms that arise through the interaction of self-interested agents in an economic system based on private exchange. From this perspective, firms and markets are two among many types of governance institutions that might arise through private ordering. Other examples would include franchising and the multitude of relationships based on contracts. Each of these privately arranged mechanisms for governance are employed in an economic context defined by the laws and regulations of a nation-state (or a supranational governmental unit like the European Union) and the prevailing norms and traditions determining the application of state power to effect their enforcement. State-set rules and the norms governing their application are the second set of institutions studied as part of the new institutional economics. The terms *transaction cost economics* and the *economics of governance* are most closely associated with the study of institutions arranged through private ordering, whereas *new institutionalism* has been applied to both branches of this literature. For the branch of this literature most closely identified with transaction costs, the firms, markets, and other privately arranged governance institutions typically taken as givens in neoclassical analyses are themselves the subjects of investigation.

The existence of firms and other nonmarket forms of organization is an implicit challenge to completeness of the neoclassical framework. This challenge was first fully recognized by Coase (1937) in his pioneering paper on the nature of the firm. Coase's insight was that firms are comprised of individuals whose actions are coordinated by nonmarket mechanisms, yet, the neoclassical framework offers no explanation for why the work carried out within firms is not coordinated by markets as well. Coase argued that the coexistence of markets and hierarchical organizational forms like firms necessarily meant that each had a comparative advantage in coordinating different types of economic relationships. Coordination itself must be a costly activity, and different coordination mechanisms were "selected," though perhaps through a process of natural selection rather than deliberative choice, for their advantages in reducing coordination (or transaction) costs.

Although generally applauded, little was done to build on Coase's insight until Williamson started to develop a well-articulated framework for the comparative analysis of economic institutions approximately 30 years later. His 1975 book was the first comprehensive presentation of the emerging transaction cost framework. Williamson's framework posited that the coordination mechanisms that persist are the ones that best respond to the challenges posed to economic coordination by bounded rationality, opportunism, and the vulnerabilities that arise in exchange relationships.

Bounded rationality refers to inherent limitations in individuals' ability to acquire and process information relevant to making economic decisions. All economic actors are assumed to be boundedly rational because of a combination of cognitive limitations and the time and resource costs of acquiring information. As a consequence, economic choices are almost always less than fully informed. Opportunism refers to a tendency of some economic actors to take advantage of other actors when the opportunities to do so present themselves. Of course, such opportunities would not arise in the absence of bounded rationality. Opportunism may be a barrier to transactions when one or more of the transactional partners are vulnerable to exploitation by the other(s). Williamson's earlier work emphasized sunk costs (nonrecoverable costs incurred by one party as a necessary precondition for participating in an exchange) specific to a transactional relationship as an important source of vulnerability. However, vulnerability may arise in a number of ways. For example, the ability of one partner in an economic relationship to pursue her objectives may be contingent on the performance of one or more other partners.[14]

Because they are boundedly rational, economic agents are more vulnerable to opportunism when products are complex and technologies and/or market conditions are changing rapidly. Williamson predicts that markets will be employed to coordinate economic

---

[14]This situation characterizes the production of most media content. If this were not the case, talent could not withhold services to bargain for higher compensation.

activities when the informational demands on market participants are low and they have little to lose should other agents try to take advantage of them. More hierarchical forms will dominate in situations in which agents of necessity are less well-informed and have more at risk because protections can be built into hierarchical structures. Vertical integration, which replaces vertically linked markets with firms, creates the most hierarchical of forms. By enclosing the two sides of a potential market in a single organization, the opportunity for one party to take advantage of the other is eliminated, but lost in the process is the ability to take advantage of market incentives to perform efficiently. The organizational forms that survive in the long run do the best job of balancing these tradeoffs.

There is now a vast literature dealing with both the theory and empirical implications of transaction cost economics. Empirical findings have been generally supportive of the predictions. (See, e.g., Joskow, 1985, and Monteverde & Teece, 1982.) Williamson's 1985 book, *The Economic Institutions of Capitalism*, and any of his frequent articles surveying developments in the field (e.g., Williamson, 2002), are probably the best introductions to this literature.

Nobel laureate Douglas North is the scholar most prominently associated with the new institutional literature on the importance of the institutions of official governance and the unofficial norms governing their use for economic performance. His 1990 book, *Institutions, Institutional Change, and Economic Performance*, has become a touchstone for many working in this interdisciplinary field. Work by economists and political scientists has shown that the design of legislative, executive, and judicial institutions and their relative strengths in a political system can all influence the degree to which nations succeed in transforming their resources into wealth. The extent to which government institutions are corrupted and employed to further the interests of those in power and their supporters may have a dramatic effect on economic performance. Levy and Spiller's (1996) chapter in their edited volume on the comparative performance of the telecommunications industries of six nations provides an overview of the literature through the mid-1990s and shows how the framework can be applied to the study of the performance of specific industries as well as to national economies.

## Behavioral Economics

In addition to the information acquisition assumptions discussed earlier, the type of rationality assumed in neoclassical models rests on several assumptions regarding the psychological makeup of economic actors. Two critical psychological assumptions are that individual preference orderings are stable and transitive. Preference stability means that an economic actor expressing a preference for Good A over Good B one day will not choose Good B over Good A the next day if the circumstances in which the choice is made do not change. Transitivity requires that if A is preferred to B and B is preferred to C, then C will not be preferred to A. A third psychological assumption is that individuals possessing information relevant to their choices will use that information to make choices that further their long-term best interests. Behavioral economics explores the implications of relaxing these psychological assumptions.

Experimental work by psychologists has identified a number of behavioral regularities that seem inconsistent with the rational actor assumption (Kahneman, 2003). For example, experimental subjects have been consistently shown to value losses more than financially equivalent gains. There are also frequent violations of the transitivity requirement, preferences are revealed to be time inconsistent, and economic actors may systematically err in predicting the utility they will realize from substantial changes in their consumption, which raises questions about the rationality of long-term planning. Rabin (1998) provided a review of the psychological literature and assessed its implications for economic analysis. Tversky and Thaler (1990) provided a more tightly focused discussion of preference reversals and argued that the evidence is most compatible with a view of "preference as a constructive, context-dependent process" (p. 210). The testing and discovery of behavioral regularities involving economic choices is one facet of the behavioral economics research agenda. Another is the development of economic models that incorporate these regularities. Matthew Rabin has pioneered in developing these models. (See, e.g., Rabin, 1993.) Camerer and Thaler (2003) provided examples of ways economic models of preferences can be modified to incorporate the psychological findings in their review of Rabin's work. Most involved substantial modifications of traditional neoclassical modeling assumptions. For example, utility functions defined on wealth may have a kink at an individual's current endowment to reflect the higher value placed on wealth lost than wealth gained.

## Evolutionary Economics

Of the analytical frameworks reviewed in this chapter, evolutionary economics represents by far the biggest departure from the tenets of neoclassical economics. The fundamental tenet of evolutionary economics is that the survival of firms and the evolution of market structures can be studied as the outcomes of an evolutionary process in which "fitter" firms survive and weaker firms are eliminated either through financial failure or acquisition by competitors. The relative fitness of different firms is determined by the degree to which their business methods are appropriate to the conditions of the markets in which they compete. Just as once successful biological species may go extinct because traits that served them well in the climate and environmental conditions in which they evolved may leave them poorly adapted when climates or other features of their environments change, firms whose business methods once brought them success may also founder if market conditions change.

Sources of innovation, the nature of organizational problem solving, codification of knowledge, the nature of learning, and the importance of tacit knowledge are all studied in this literature as factors contributing to firm success. An important question is whether there are vehicles specific to firms that carry traits adaptive to markets at any given time into the future, similar to the role genes play in biological systems in preserving a species' traits from one generation to the next. In the seminal work that launched this field of inquiry, Nelson and Winter (1982) suggested that organizational routines might play this role. Nelson and Winter (2002) reviewed the work inspired by their pioneering effort. The August 2002 and April 2003 issues of the economics journal, *Industrial and Corporate*

**TABLE 4.1**

Major Analytical Frameworks Used by IO Economists

| Analytical Framework | Principle Assumptions and Guiding Perspectives |
|---|---|
| Traditional neoclassical economics | Rational actors who are typically fully informed, optimization at the margin, subjective utility, focus on static efficiency. |
| Network industries | The existence of network effects, which means that the value of a product or service to a user depends on the number of other users of the same product or service. |
| Two-sided markets | Demand and/or supply interdependencies create linkages between otherwise independent markets that make coordinated optimization desirable. |
| Information economics | Economic agents are imperfectly informed and sometimes asymmetrically informed. |
| Transaction cost economics and the new institutional economics | Economic actors are boundedly rational and at least some are opportunistic, which makes economic exchange risky. Governance institutions (both private and public) evolve to minimize the economic costs associated with these risks. |
| Behavioral economics | Explores the implications of observed violations of neoclassical assumptions of preference stability and rationality. |
| Evolutionary economics | The histories of firms and markets can be modeled as outcomes of an evolutionary process through which survivors are selected on the basis of fitness for their economic environments. |

*Change*, are special issues devoted to evolutionary economics and provide examples of the range of current work in this field.

## USE OF DIFFERENT ECONOMIC FRAMEWORKS IN THE STUDY OF MEDIA ECONOMICS: PAST PRACTICE AND NEW OPPORTUNITIES

Most of the work on the economics of media firms and markets to date has been inspired by the four major sets of neoclassical models of market structure, and much of this has been applications of the structure, conduct, performance (SCP) framework.[15] Picard's (1989) text provides excellent examples of the use of the SCP framework to analyze media industries. Game theory has been used rather sparingly, and most of this has been in single stage games exploring various Nash equilibria. Best known are studies of programming strategies by television networks, such as the models by Steiner (1952),

---

[15]I am excluding here work on managerial economics (which still relies heavily on models with rational actors) and strategy. Strategic analyses in particular draw on a more eclectic set of analytical traditions.

Beebe (1977), Spence and Owen (1977), and Waterman (1990). More recently this topic has been studied using models of multistage games (Doyle, 1998; Gal-Or & Dukes, 2003).

Modeling breakthroughs have been realized by relaxing some of the standard assumptions of neoclassical models of markets unrelated to the rational actor assumption that are at odds with critical features of media products and markets. In most neoclassical models, costs vary according to the incremental cost of serving additional customers with a prespecified product. Crandall (1974) and Park (1975) relaxed this assumption to consider the effects of the entry of a fourth broadcast network on the existing networks during the pre-Fox era in the United States when there were only three. They allowed a network's expenditures on programs (the products) to be a decision variable under the assumption that programs with larger production budgets attracted larger audiences. Later, Hoskins and Mirus (1988), Waterman (1988) and Wildman and Siwek (1987, 1988) developed models of trade in media products with variable content creation costs. Wildman (1995) argued that the theoretical perspective used to explain trade flows may also explain many other structural features of media markets.

As noted earlier, Rosse (1978) and Blair and Romano (1993) constructed models of monopoly newspaper firms with interdependent demands for newspapers and ad space. Although analogous demand interdependencies also exist for other media, there has been relatively little work exploring their implications. Wildman (1999) argued that demographic homogeneity for alternative media audiences does not force competitive sellers of ad space or time to all charge a common price as is the case in the model of perfect competition. The reason is that a second exposure to members of one firm's audience will not make the same contribution to an advertiser's sales as the first exposure to members of another firm's audience unless the members of the two audiences are exactly the same. The result is different competitive outcomes than in the standard neoclassical models that have guided research on advertising markets in the past. In general it would seem that the study of media economics would benefit from a systematic attempt to determine to what extent the assumptions, both explicit and implicit, underlying neoclassical models of markets apply to media products and industries (Wirth & Bloch, 1995).

Relatively little use has been made of the postneoclassical analytical frameworks reviewed earlier in research on media economics, but the opportunities are many and the payoff from doing so is likely to be as big for media studies as it has been for studies of other industries. I close this chapter by briefly discussing some of the more obvious opportunities.

Consumers make imperfectly informed choices among media products. The search models developed in the information economics literature might shed new light on the processes by which consumers select the television networks, periodicals, and Internet services they turn to on a regular basis and the strategies media services employ to influence the outcomes of consumer search. A more sophisticated understanding of how consumers select among media options could also lead to more realistic models of competition among content providers than those that have been employed in the program choice literature.

Studies of consumer choices among television programs might also benefit from the new thinking on behavioral economics. The findings on time inconsistency previously mentioned suggest that services such as video-on-demand that make it easier for viewers to find what they want when they want it and devices such as personal video recorders (PVRs) that make it easier for viewers to plan their viewing hours or days in advance may both significantly influence viewers' choices among programs, but perhaps in different ways. Video-on-demand makes the gratification of attractive programs more immediate. To the extent television is viewed as an enjoyable diversion from other more important activities, widespread availability of video-on-demand might lead to more regret among viewers over time spent watching TV. The instant availability of all sorts of diversions on the Internet might have a similar effect. On the other hand, the PVR enables viewing at a date or time after a program is first broadcast and might be viewed as a device that aids in impulse control.

The relationships between content producers and firms involved in distribution are fraught with informational asymmetries. Applications of the work on information economics should thus prove fruitful here as well. For example, networks can only imperfectly monitor producer efforts to uphold expected standards in quality of writing and acting, and producers have little control over the scheduling and promotion of their shows once the networks pick them up. To what extent can terms and clauses in network–producer contracts be explained as mechanisms for dealing with these sources of uncertainty and vulnerability?

There have been limited applications of transaction cost principles to media industries (Phalen, 1998; Williamson, 1976), but the prevalence of sunk costs in distribution infrastructure and content production for most media, not to mention vulnerabilities that are due to reliance on the performance of partners in the creation of content, suggest many more applications of this framework. Media firms' choices between producing content in-house or purchasing it from outside suppliers is perhaps the most obvious. Karamanis's (2003) study of the privatization of the Greek television industry makes very effective use of the political institutions branch of the new institutional economics to show how legal and regulatory infrastructure, along with the unwritten norms of governance, may have a dramatic impact on the development of a nation's media industries. Her findings suggest that there is much to be learned from applying this perspective to the study of media in other countries.

Finally, it would be interesting to see what insights might be produced by an evolutionary analysis of developments in media industries. New technologies and the new products and services that employ them are creating unprecedented opportunities to study new media industries as they evolve.

## REFERENCES

Alchian, A. (1950). Uncertainty, evolution and economic theory. *Journal of Political Economy, 58,* 211–221.

Akerlof, G. A. (1970). The market for "lemons": Quality uncertainty and the market mechanism. *Quarterly Journal of Economics, 84*(3), 488–500.

Akerlof, G. A. (2002). Behavioral macroeconomics and macroeconomic behavior. *American Economic Review, 92*(3), 411–433.

Arrow, K. J. (1987). Rationality of self and others in an economic system. In R. M. Hogarth & M. W. Reder (Eds.), *Rational choice: The contrast between economics and psychology* (pp. 201–216). Chicago: University of Chicago Press.

Baumol, W. J., Panzar, J. C., & Willig, R. D. (1982). *Contestible markets and the theory of industry structure*. New York: Harcourt Brace.

Beebe, J. H. (1977). Institutional structure and program choices in television markets. *Quarterly Journal of Economics, 91,* 15–37.

Besen, S. M., & Johnson, L. L. (1986). *Compatibility standards, competition, and innovation in the broadcasting industry*. R-3453-NSF. Santa Monica, CA: The RAND Corporation.

Blair, R., & Romano, R. (1993). Pricing decisions of a newspaper monopolist. *Southern Economics Journal, 59*(4), 721–732.

Camerer, C., & Thaler, R. H. (2003). In honor of Matthew Rabin: Winner of the John Bates Clark medal. *Journal of Economic Perspectives, 17*(3), 159–176.

Campbell, D. T. (1987). Rationality and utility from the standpoint of evolutionary biology. In R. M. Hogarth & M. W. Reder (Eds.), *Rational choice: The contrast between economics and psychology* (pp. 171–180). Chicago: University of Chicago Press.

Chamberlin, E. (1956). *The theory of monopolistic competition* (7th ed.). Cambridge, MA: Harvard University Press.

Coase, R. (1937). The nature of the firm. *Economica N.S., 4,* 386–405.

Cournot, A. (1938). Recherches sur les principes mathématiques de la théorie des richesses [Researches into the mathematical principles of the theory of wealth]. Paris: Hachette.

Crandall, R. W. (1974). The economic case for a fourth commercial network. *Public Policy, 12,* 513–536.

Doyle, C. (1998). Programming in a competitive broadcasting market: Entry, welfare and regulation. *Information Economics and Policy, 10*(1), 23–40.

Economides, N. (1991). Compatibility and the creation of shared networks. In M. E. Guerin-Calvert & S. S. Wildman (Eds.), *Electronic services networks: A business and public policy challenge* (pp. 39–55). New York: Praeger.

Ekelund, R. B., Jr. & Hébert, R. F. (2002). The origins of neoclassical microeconomics. *Journal of Economic Perspectives, 3,* 197–215.

Farrel, J., & Saloner, G. (1985). Standardization, compatibility, and innovation. *Rand Journal of Economics, 16,* 70–80.

Farrel, J., & Shapiro, C. (1990). Horizontal mergers: An equilibrium analysis. *American Economic Review, 80,* 107–126.

Friedman, J. (1983). *Oligopoly theory*. Cambridge, UK: Cambridge University Press.

Gal-Or, E., & Dukes, A. (2003). Minimum differentiation in commercial media markets. *Journal of Economics & Management Strategy, 12*(3), 291–325.

Gibbons, R. (1992). *Game theory for applied economists*. Princeton, NJ: Princeton University Press.

Gurrea, S. D., & Owen, B. M. (2003). Coordinated interaction and Clayton §7 enforcement. *George Mason Law Review, 12*(1), 89–118.

Henderson, J. M., & Quandt, R. E. (1971). *Microeconomic theory: A mathematical approach*. New York: McGraw-Hill.

Hirschliefer, J. (1980). *Price theory and applications* (2nd ed.). Englewood Cliffs, NJ: Prentice-Hall.

Hoskins, C., & Mirus, R. (1988). Reasons for the U.S. dominance of the international trade in television programmes. *Media, Culture, and Society, 10,* 499–515.

Joskow, P. L. (1985). Vertical integration and long-term contracts. *Journal of Law, Economics and Organization, 1,* 33–80.

Kahneman, D. (2003). Maps of bounded rationality: Psychology for behavioral economics. *American Economic Review, 93*(5), 1449–1475.

Karamanis, T. (2003). *The role of culture and political institutions in media policy: The case of tv privatization in Greece*. Cresskill, NJ: Hampton Press.

Katz, M. L., & Shapiro, C. (1986). Technology adoption in the presence of network externalities. *Journal of Political Economy, 94,* 822–841.

Katz, M. L., & Shapiro, C. (1994). Systems competition and network effects. *Journal of Economic Perspectives, 8*(2), 93–115.

Klein, B. (1980). Transaction cost determinants of "unfair" contractual arrangements. *American Economic Review, 70*(2), 356–362.

Kuhn, T. S. (1996), *The structure of scientific revolutions* (3rd ed.). Chicago: University of Chicago Press.

Levy, B., & Spiller, P. T. (1996). A framework for resolving the regulatory problem. In B. Levy & P. T. Spiller (Eds.), *Regulations, institutions, and commitments: Comparative studies of telecommunications* (pp. 1–35). Cambridge, UK: Cambridge University Press.

Lucas, R. E., Jr. (1987). Adaptive behavior and economic theory. In R. M. Hogarth & M. W. Reder (Eds.), *Rational choice: The contrast between economics and psychology* (pp. 217–242). Chicago: University of Chicago Press.

Marshall, A. (1961). *Principles of economics* (9th ed.). London: Macmillan.

McCall, J. J. (1965). The economics of information and optimal stopping rules. *Journal of Business, 38,* 300–317.

Monteverde, K., & Teece, D. (1982). Supplier switching costs and vertical integration in the automobile industry. *Bell Journal of Economics, 13,* 206–213.

Nash, J. F. (1950). Equilibrium points in n-person games. *Proceedings of the National Academy of Sciences, 36,* 48–49.

Nelson, R. R., & Winter, S. G. (1982). *An economic theory of economic change.* Cambridge, MA: Harvard University Press.

Nelson, S. G., & Winter, S. G. (2002). Evolutionary theorizing in economics. *Journal of Economic Literature, 16*(2), 23–46.

North, D. C. (1990). *Institutions, institutional change, and economic performance.* Cambridge, MA: Harvard University Press.

Ohashi, H. (2003). The role of network effects in the US VCR market, 1978–1986. *Journal of Economics & Management Strategy, 12*(2), 447–494.

Owen, B. M., & Wildman, S. S. (1992). *Video economics.* Cambridge, MA: Harvard University Press.

Park, R. E. (1975). New television networks. *Bell Journal of Economics, 6,* 607–620.

Phalen, P. F. (1998), The market information system and personalized exchange: Business practices in the market for television audiences. *Journal of Media Economics, 11*(4), 17–34.

Picard, R. G. (1989). *Media economics: Concepts and issues.* Newbury Park, CA: Sage.

Plott, C. R. (1986). Rational choice in experimental markets. *Journal of Business, 59*(4, pt. 2), 301–327.

Rabin, M. (1993). Incorporating fairness into game theory and economics. *American Economic Review, 83*(5), 1281–1302.

Rabin, M. (1998). Psychology and economics. *Journal of Economic Literature, 36,* 11–46.

Rohlfs, J. (1974). A theory of interdependent demand for a communication service. *Bell Journal of Economics, 5,* 16–37.

Rosse, J. N. (1978). The evolution of one-newspaper cities. In *Proceedings of the Symposium on Media Concentration,* Vol. 2 (pp. 429–471). Washington, DC: Federal Trade Commission.

Salop, S. (1979). Monopolistic competition with outside goods. *Bell Journal of Economics, 10* (Spring), 141–156.

Simon, H. A. (1987). Rationality in psychology and economics. In R. M. Hogarth & M. W. Reder (Eds.), *Rational choice: The contrast between economics and psychology* (pp. 25–40). Chicago: University of Chicago Press.

Spence, A. M. (1976). Product selection, fixed costs, and monopolistic competition. *Review of Economic Studies, 43,* 217–235.

Spence, A. M. (2002). Signaling in retrospect and the informational structure of markets. *American Economic Review, 92*(3), 434–459.

Spence, A. M., & Owen, B. M. (1977). Television programming, monopolistic competition, and welfare. *Quarterly Journal of Economics, 93,* 103–126.

Steiner, P. O. (1952). Program patterns and preferences, and the workability of competition in radio broadcasting. *Quarterly Journal of Economics, 66,* 194–223.

Stigler, G. J. (1961). The economics of information. *Journal of Political Economy, 69*(3), 213–225.

Stigler, G. J. (1964). A theory of oligopoly. *Journal of Political Economy, 72,* 44–61.

Stigler, G. J., & Becker, G. S. (1977). De gustibus non est disputatum. *American Economic Review, 67*(2), 76–90.

Stiglitz, J. E. (2002). Information and the change in the paradigm in economics. *American Economic Review, 92*(3), 460–501.

Tirole, J. (1988), *The theory of industrial organization.* Cambridge, MA: The MIT Press.

Tversky, A., & Kahneman, D. (1987). Rational choice and the framing of decisions. In R. M. Hogarth & M. W. Reder (Eds.), *Rational choice: The contrast between economics and psychology* (pp. 67–94). Chicago: University of Chicago Press.

Tversky, A., & Thaler, R. H. (1990). Anomalies: Preference reversals. *Journal of Economic Perspectives, 4*(2), 201–211.

Varian, H. R. (1984). *Microeconomic analysis* (2nd ed.). New York: Norton.

Vishwanath, T. (1988). Parallel search and information gathering. *American Economic Review, 78*(2), 110–116.

Waterman, D. (1988). World television trade: The economic effects of privatization and new technology. *Telecommunications Policy, 12*(2), 141–151.

Waterman, D. (1990). Diversity and quality of information products in a monopolistically competitive industry. *Information, Economics and Policy, 4,* 291–303.

Weitzman, M. (1979). Optimal search for the best alternative. *Econometrica, 47,* 637–654.

Wildman, S. S. (1995). Trade liberalization and policy for media industries: A theoretical examination of media flows. *Canadian Journal of Communication, 20,* 367–388.

Wildman, S. S. (1998). Toward a better integration of media economics and media competition policy. In R. G. Noll & M. E. Price (Eds.), *A communications cornucopia* (pp. 573–593). Washington, DC: Brookings Institution Press.

Wildman, S. S. (2004). Conditional expectations communication and the impact of biotechnology. In S. Braman (Ed.), *Biotechnology and communication: The meta-technologies of information* (pp. 63–95), Mahwah, NJ: Lawrence Erlbaum Associates.

Wildman, S. S., & Siwek, S. E. (1987). The privatization of European television: Effects on international markets for programs. *The Columbia Journal of World Business, 22*(3), 71–76.

Wildman, S. S., & Siwek, S. E. (1988). *International trade in films and television programs.* Cambridge, MA: Ballinger.

Williamson, O. E. (1975). *Markets and hierarchies: Analysis and antitrust implications.* New York: The Free Press.

Williamson, O. E. (1976). Franchise bidding for natural monopoly—In general and with respect to CATV. *Bell Journal of Economics, 7,* 73–104.

Williamson, O. E. (1985). *The economic institutions of capitalism.* New York: The Free Press.

Williamson, O. E. (2002). The theory of governance structure: From choice to contract. *Journal of Economic Perspectives, 16*(3), 171–195.

Wirth, M. O., & Bloch, H. (1995). Industrial organization theory and media industry analysis. *Journal of Media Economics, 8*(2), 15–26.

Wright, J. (2004). One-sided logic in two-sided markets. *Review of Network Economics*, March, 42–63. Retrieved March 7, 2005 from http://www.rnejournal.com/articles/wright_mar04.pdf

# 5

# Regulatory and Political Influences on Media Management and Economics

Barbara A. Cherry

Federal Communications Commission

Sustainable development of a nation's telecommunications infrastructure requires regulatory policies that satisfy *both* political feasibility and the economic conditions for maintaining a financially viable industry. Fulfilling the joint requirements of political feasibility and economic viability in the context of telecommunications deregulatory policies, in contrast to the traditional monopoly regimes, is becoming particularly difficult given the rapid rate of technological change, the growing complexities of communication technology, and the increasingly vital role of the information sector to global economies. In the United States, early warning signs of unsustainable deregulatory policies in the telecommunications industry include declining stock values and investments, bankruptcies, and growing customer service problems.

In addition, because of the development of digital technology, the telecommunications and mass media industries no longer serve fully separable economic markets. Rather, these industries now provide some substitutable services and uses. The economic interrelationships also create interdependencies among these industries' historically distinct regulatory regimes so that policy change within one regime may have spillover effects for the others.

Academic research purporting to offer policy recommendations must keep pace with the increasing difficulties of designing sustainable deregulatory policies in a world of digital convergence. To do so, analyses must become more interdisciplinary so as to simultaneously evaluate the interrelated economic and political constraints among the telecommunications and mass media industries.

This chapter seeks to contribute to the development of better interdisciplinary research by providing a framework for determining how economic viability and political feasibility problems jointly constrain the adoption and sustainability of reasonably achievable policy options for telecommunications regulation. Telecommunications scholars can use this framework to better identify attributes of policy options that facilitate or hinder sustainability, whether to develop new recommendations, critique others' recommendations, or evaluate the effectiveness of current policies. This chapter also seeks to improve scholars' understanding of the interrelationships of policy development among the telecommunications and mass media industries through illustrations of policy migration across regulatory regimes. For example, intermodal broadband competition introduces freedom of speech policy concerns to telecommunications and common carrier policy concerns to cable and the Internet.

This chapter is organized as follows. The next section reviews the necessity to address both economic and political constraints on policy choices. Based on prior research (Cherry & Wildman, 1999a, 2000), the third section reviews the economic viability constraints on policy choices that arise from the need to support private investment generally and to be compatible with the financial viability of specific firms or industries. The fourth section examines political feasibility constraints in three contexts: to support the legitimacy of government itself, to enable initial adoption of a policy, and to enable sustainability of a policy over time. This section also shows the interrelationship of political feasibility and economic viability constraints. In some cases, regulatory interventions may enhance governmental legitimacy as well as mitigate economic viability problems; in others, political feasibility constraints may require sacrifice of some economic efficiency objectives, or economic viability constraints may require modification or abandonment of some political objectives. The fifth section discusses some economic viability and political feasibility constraints on deregulatory telecommunication policies. The final section describes interrelated policy developments for telecommunications and mass media industries through examples of policy migration across regulatory regimes.

## ECONOMIC AND POLITICAL CONSTRAINTS ON POLICY CHOICES

To date much academic research evaluating deregulatory policies has focused on the need to properly design *regulatory incentives* affecting behavior of private parties to better achieve desired policy goals. More recently, research has also emphasized the need to focus on the attributes of *regulatory governance* restraining the behavior of regulators in order to create a suitable environment for infrastructure investment (Cherry & Wildman, 1999a; Levy & Spiller, 1996). Furthermore, Cherry and Wildman (1999a) showed that the need to properly design both regulatory incentives and regulatory governance may require the sacrifice of some economic efficiency goals.

Prior research has contributed to an improved understanding of how to design and enforce regulatory rules—both regulatory incentives and regulatory governance—that are compatible with achieving the desired economic behavior of private parties. Such research has encouraged government officials to better understand the constraints that the economic viability needs of firms and industries impose on public policy goals and associated regulatory designs. In so doing, many policy prescriptions have been made that appear, at least theoretically, to be quite straightforward.

Yet many such policy prescriptions—for example, rebalancing retail rates and funding universal service through explicit charges on consumers' bills—tend to pose politically infeasible solutions (Cherry, 2000; Cherry & Nystrom, 2000). *For this reason, it is important not only for policymakers to better understand the economic realities that limit achievability of policy goals, but also for all parties attempting to influence the policy process to be aware of the political constraints that limit policymakers' choices.* Likewise, academic research offering policy recommendations must integrate relevant economic and political constraints.

## ECONOMIC VIABILITY CONSTRAINTS ON POLICY CHOICES

The economic realities of providing goods and services through private entities place constraints on the design of regulatory rules, both regulatory incentives and regulatory governance, likely to achieve desirable social objectives. Cherry and Wildman (1999a, 2000) discussed the nature of the economic constraints that affect the design of regulatory rules to achieve policy objectives based on reliance on private investment to provide telecommunications infrastructure and services. Based on this prior research, this section provides an overview of the types of economic problems that must be satisfactorily addressed through appropriate regulatory design in order for public policy objectives to be economically sustainable over time. Although much of the prior work has been done through evaluation of economic problems in the context of governance under the U.S. Constitution, the fundamental types of economic problems remain the same across governance structures. This overview not only summarizes admonitions to policymakers of how to prevent economic problems through a better regulatory design, but it also lays a foundation for the discussion in the next section of how policy experts and stakeholders need to address mirror-image political sustainability problems that policymakers face.

### Supporting Private Investment Generally

This subsection reviews economic viability constraints on policy choices that arise from the need to support private investment generally. Cherry and Wildman (1999a, pp. 613–619; 2000, pp. 64–74, 81–85) provide a more in-depth discussion of the points covered in this subsection.

Government's own performance influences what can be achieved by private entities in a system of voluntary exchange. Through rules affecting transactions among parties, whether public or private, government affects the long-term certainty and risk that parties face. The levels of uncertainty and risk, in turn, affect the profitability of investment and commercial activities.

Government contributes to the viability of the market itself through definition and enforcement of private property rights and rules of contract. However, these rules must constrain government as well as private party behavior. For example, constraints on government's eminent domain power protect private party investment by reducing the risk of government confiscation of private property. Under the U.S. Constitution, both the federal and state governments are prohibited from taking private property for public use without providing just compensation.

Similarly, government must be held accountable for the breaches of contracts for which it is responsible. First, there need to be constraints on government action that impairs contracts between private parties. Second, government should be held liable for its breach of a contract to which it is a party. Such enforceability is necessary to ensure that government can, in fact, make credible commitments and thereby preserve its capacity to make contracts in the future. In the United States, state governments are constrained by the Contract Clause of the U.S. Constitution, with similar constraints imposed on the federal government by the U.S. Supreme Court in *United States v. Winstar Corporation* (1996).

Such constraints on government as well as private party behavior serve to generally support economic investments of individuals and firms relying on the underlying systems of property rights and contracts. These constraints are also critical for supporting private investment in utility infrastructures, such as telecommunications, that are characterized by high sunk costs. Differences in telecommunications sector performance among nations can be traced to problems in their respective regulatory governance structures (Levy & Spiller, 1996).

## Compatibility With Financial Viability of Firms or Industries

Even if a system of regulatory rules generally supports private investment in the market, rules applied to a specific sector or industry may not be compatible with the economic viability of the affected firms or industries. As a result, the desired economic performance and social consequences underlying policymakers' objectives may not be forthcoming. Cherry and Wildman first discussed these problems in the context of developing universal service policy for the telecommunications industry (1999b), and then expanded the analysis for public utilities and economic activities in general (2000). This subsection summarizes those attributes of regulatory design that create firm or industry viability problems that may undermine fulfillment of underlying or related policy objectives.

Regulatory rules may pose economic viability problems for a given firm or industry, among firms within a given industry, or among industries. For simplicity, the collective set of such economic viability problems will be referred to as interfirm or interindustry viability problems. These interfirm or interindustry viability problems may be either prospective or transition problems.

*Prospective problems* arise from the prospective effects of government rules that: (a) treat some firms or industries differently than others, whether on a per se or de facto basis; (b) impose unreasonable and fundamentally unremunerative financial obligations on firms or industries; or (c) require compliance with coexisting yet conflicting or incompatible rules. An example of the first type is the application of different tax laws to providers of competing services, such as facilities-based carriers and resellers. An example of the second type is a cross-subsidy requirement or price control that amounts to confiscation of property. The third type includes coexisting, conflicting federal and state requirements for which simultaneous compliance is impossible. Cherry and Wildman (2000) discussed how certain clauses of the U.S. Constitution provide protection and relief from some of these prospective problems.

*Transition problems* arise from changes in governmental rules that affect the earnings on preexisting investments, contracts, or conduct, and thereby the willingness of private actors to rely on government commitments in planning future economic endeavors. For example, elimination of an incumbent local exchange carrier's (ILEC's) monopoly rights and imposition of asymmetric requirements on an ILEC to provide access to its facilities to competitors will affect the ILEC's ability to recover preexisting investment made during the monopoly regime as well as its willingness to make future investments. Cherry and Wildman (2000) also discussed how certain clauses of the U.S. Constitution provide protection and relief from some transition problems.

To address these prospective and transition problems, specific remedies or adjustments to regulatory design are required. In some cases, monetary compensation may suffice to offset the nature of the financial inviability. In others, the offending rule(s) may need to be modified or even eliminated.

Analysis of regulatory rules for prospective and transition problems can be a useful tool to help government face the challenges of designing and enforcing regulatory rules in an increasingly technologically dynamic and unpredictable information economy. Such analysis illustrates how government's actions or inactions can create prospective and transition problems for particular firms or industries. It can also facilitate policymakers' ability to anticipate and prevent problems through more thoughtful, initial regulatory design.

## POLITICAL FEASIBILITY CONSTRAINTS ON POLICY CHOICES

Policy choices likely to fulfill underlying policy objectives are constrained by political feasibility problems. This section provides a framework to facilitate mutual understanding, among policymakers and those attempting to influence them (whether policy experts, industry members, or other stakeholders), of the political constraints inherent in the policymaking process.

In so doing, this section explains how certain political feasibility constraints arise from the need to support the legitimacy of the existing government itself, whereas others arise to enable a given policy to remain in force over time. These two types of situations can be thought of as mirror-images of the economic viability constraints arising from the needs to support private investment generally and to be compatible with the ongoing financial viability of the specific firms or industries. However, some political feasibility constraints are endemic to the initial adoption of any specific policy proposal that must be considered separately, and, in addition, to the sustainability of that policy over time. These constraints are discussed utilizing Kingdon's model (1995) of the policymaking process.

## Supporting the Legitimacy of Government Itself

Successful pursuit of policy objectives requires, perhaps most fundamentally, that regulatory intervention be constrained by those limitations on government action that support the legitimacy of the government itself. The legitimizing principle of political authority in the modern state is the principle of popular sovereignty, which contrasts with traditional bases of theocracy, divine right, noble birth, or caste (Finer, 1999, p. 1474). The principle of popular sovereignty

> affirms that no government is legitimate and hence obedience-worthy unless it can demonstrate to its subjects that its powers have been conferred by them. This dogma, it must be noted, is neutral—it does not predicate any particular form of regime; it will accommodate liberal-democracy, autocracy, oligarchy, even totalitarianism, providing only that the office-bearers are able to convince the public they have received office by popular mandate—whatever this is (and however contrived). (Finer, p. 1476)

Under a government based on popular sovereignty, the importance of a government's adherence to self-imposed limitations on its power to retain its legitimacy and stability has often been explained by social contract theory. Several philosophers—Hobbes, Locke, Rousseau, and Kant—are associated with the development of social contract theory. Interpretations of social contract theory differ, such as whether the social contract is merely a legal fiction for legitimizing a political community or represents historical fact (Allen, 1999; Kary, 1999; Priban, 2003; Rosenfeld, 1985). Nonetheless, the concept of social contract is a helpful analytical tool for understanding the development and maintenance of sovereign authority (Black, 1993; Hoepfl & Thompson, 1979).

Social contract theory can be defined as

> the view that human authorities are established by agreement with their subjects for specific tasks, that their legitimacy depends upon fulfillment of these tasks, and that such agreements may be enforced by clear, defined procedures, as one would enforce a contract in private law. (Black, 1993, p. 57)

The specific limitations to which a given nation's government has acceded will vary, of course, with the social contract and associated governance structure of that nation. Direct limitations consist of judicially enforceable guarantees that specifically deny government the right to engage in certain actions or to exercise certain types of authority. Indirect limitations consist of governance structures, such as separation of powers or a system of checks and balances among branches of government, that constrain use of government power (Strong, 1997, pp. 7–12). For a given nation, the core values expressed in direct or indirect limitations must be recognized as political (as well as legal) feasibility constraints on regulatory intervention.

In the United States, direct and indirect limitations of power are provided in the Federal Constitution. Some of the core values in the U.S. Constitution are found in the Bill of Rights, which directly limit any use of government power in order to protect specific individual rights and liberties. Other core values are reflected in U.S. constitutional principles designed to address specific problems of equity and fairness that correspond to the four sources of economic viability (prospective and transition) problems discussed in the previous section. More specifically, certain constitutional principles are based on values of equity and fairness that limit or prohibit:

1. Differential treatment of rules among persons, firms or industries.
2. Rules that impose unreasonable burdens.
3. Imposition of coexisting yet conflicting or incompatible rules.
4. Changes in rules affecting preexisting investment, contracts or conduct.

This interrelationship between economic viability and equity/fairness problems is depicted in Table 5.1, which is based on a rearrangement of the information in Tables 1 through 4 in Cherry and Wildman (2000, pp. 94–99).

*Thus, how government addresses problems of equity and fairness is directly related to potential sources of economic viability problems for specific firms or industries.* By recognizing this interrelationship, it may be possible—with appropriate judicial enforcement of constitutional principles—to design regulatory interventions that both enhance governmental legitimacy as well as mitigate economic viability problems faced by the regulated firms and industries. Conversely, some regulatory interventions may simultaneously undermine government legitimacy and policy objectives that depend on the economic viability of the regulated entities. In any event, the ability to design regulatory interventions with such dual properties is greatly enhanced not only if policymakers better understand the economic viability constraints on regulated firms and industries, but also if those attempting to influence policy choices, understand the equity and fairness constraints on policymakers (Cherry & Wildman, 2000, pp. 93–105).

Regulatory intervention in other nations requires a similar examination of the core values underlying the given nation's social contract. These values and their enforcement will necessarily create political constraints on the policy options that can be adopted and maintained over time. Examining the interrelationship among these political and associated economic viability constraints greatly enhances the opportunity to design policy options that satisfy all the constraints.

## Enabling Initial Adoption of a Policy

In addition to the political constraints arising from the need to support legitimacy of government itself, a policy choice is constrained by the circumstances prevailing at the time of its adoption. These constraints are endemic to the policy decision-making process itself. Kingdon (1995) has developed a model of this process. It has been applied to policy decision-making affecting the telecommunications industry. Zahariadis (1992, 1995) studied the political processes of privatization decisions in Britain and France. Cherry (2000) applied the model to explain the adoption of different rate rebalancing policies by the federal U.S. and European Union policymaking bodies.

Kingdon's model is utilized here to identify political constraints relevant to the initial adoption of a policy. Its components are briefly described here. The model is discussed more fully in Kingdon (1995) and Cherry (2000).

**TABLE 5.1**

Addressing Economic Viability and Political Feasibility Problems Through
Enforcement of Constitutional Principles

| Economic Viability and Equity/Fairness Problem | Enforcement Remedy Affecting Regulatory Design | Constitutional Direct Limitations on Power |
|---|---|---|
| Differential treatment of rules among persons, firms, or industries | Eliminate or reduce the asymmetry:<br>• Invalidate or repeal the rule<br>• Amend rule to restore symmetry<br>• Compensate, in whole or in part, those bearing burden of the asymmetry | • First Amendment<br>• Ex Post Facto/Bill of Attainder<br>• Equal Protection Clause<br>• Due Process Clause |
| Unreasonable burden of rule(s) | Eliminate or reduce the burden:<br>• Invalidate or repeal the rule<br>• Amend the rule to reduce the burden<br>• Compensate, in whole or in part, those bearing the burden | • First Amendment<br>• Equal Protection Clause<br>• Takings Clause |
| Impossibility of complying with coexisting, conflicting rules | Eliminate the conflict of rules:<br>• Invalidate or repeal one or more of the rules<br>• Amend one or more of the rules to remove conflict<br>• Compensate for losses incurred while bearing burden of conflicting rules | • Supremacy Clause<br>• Commerce Clause<br>• Takings Clause<br>• Tenth Amendment |
| Change in rules affecting preexisting investment, contracts, or conduct | Protect interest in preexisting investment:<br>• Invalidate or repeal the rule change<br>• Compensate for losses suffered because of the rule change | • Contract Clause, *U.S. v. Winstar* (1996)<br>• Ex Post Facto/Bill of Attainder<br>• Takings Clause |

Kingdon described policy decisions as the outcome of three processes—the problem, policy, and political streams—that are coupled during windows of opportunity. Each stream is affected by its own institutional structures, but they also interact. Windows of opportunity are created by changes in the problem or political streams, during which policy entrepreneurs attempt to couple the three streams to produce the policy outcomes they desire.

The *problem stream* is the process whereby policy problems are defined and rise to a sufficient level of urgency that they find a place on policymakers' agenda (Kingdon, 1995, pp. 113–114). The *policy stream* is the process of developing and selecting alternative policy solutions through consensus within the policy community. The criteria for acceptance of a policy solution are technical feasibility (economic and legal abilities to implement the solution), value acceptability (compatibility with values of members of the policy community) and anticipation of future constraints (anticipating acceptability of the solution in the political stream) (Kingdon, pp. 131–139). The *political stream* is the process of developing consensus on policy issues in the broader political environment through coalition building (Kingdon, pp. 144–149). *Windows of opportunity* are the opportunities for advocates of policy proposals to push their solutions or to draw attention to their special problems. A window of opportunity is created by a change in the problem or political stream, such as a crisis, a disaster, or a turnover in administrative or elected officials.

*Coupling* of the three streams by policy entrepreneurs during windows of opportunity is the critical step for producing policy outcomes. The coupling process is a challenging one: many windows of opportunity are unpredictable and open only for a limited time; policy entrepreneurs compete to exploit windows of opportunity for which outcomes are unpredictable; and the interdependence of the streams contributes to the complexity of their coupling (Kingdon, 1995, pp. 168–190).

The implications of understanding Kingdon's model are that *political considerations dominate the ability to develop and adopt policy outcomes.* For the problem stream, the policymakers' views of economic viability problems control the policy agenda. For the policy and political streams, the policymakers' views of political feasibility ultimately determine both the attributes of a proposed policy solution and the political strategy deemed necessary for its adoption.

### *Policymakers' Views of Economic Viability Problems*

Policymakers identify and define the policy problems of sufficient urgency to be placed on their agenda. For policy problems arising from economic viability problems of firms or industries, policymakers' views of economic viability problems are critical and affected by several factors. First, their views are influenced by their perceptions of prior policy choices and the impact on economic behavior of parties. Policymakers' reliance on prior experience contributes to path dependence, which explains why most policy change is incremental and major policy change requires the intervention of strong conjunctural forces (Hall, 1986; Wilsford, 1994).

Second, policymakers' perceptions of policy problems are influenced by various information sources, which are likely to provide a wide range of often conflicting perspectives. One source consists of the representatives of affected firms, industries, or other special interest stakeholders, who selectively produce and present information to reflect their respective strategies. Another source includes experts, who—whether on their own initiative or on behalf of affected parties—attempt to influence policymakers' perceptions through research and studies. Mass media may report relevant information or provide their own perspectives. Government entities may directly collect and evaluate relevant data.

Third, limited time and resources compel policymakers to compare and rank the importance of many, often unrelated, policy problems. This task is often further confused by actions of information sources on which policymakers rely.

### Policymakers' Views of Political Feasibility

Assuming that an economic viability problem ranks highly on the policy agenda, policymakers' views of political feasibility ultimately determine the attributes of the selected policy option and the political strategy deemed necessary for its adoption.

Policymakers select a political strategy based on their perceptions of what is politically possible under existing circumstances. In this regard, the process of coalition building in the *political stream* is essential. Kingdon's model identifies the critical components for developing consensus on policy issues in the broader political environment as: evaluation of the organization of political forces in support or opposition, perceived public opinion, and other politician approval.

Policymakers' assessment of these components is affected by prior experience with successful or failed policy initiatives and of constituent expectations of equity and fairness. Their assessment is also affected by their own political objectives, often posing principal–agent problems in which personal long-term political objectives may foreclose pursuit of more socially beneficial policy options. For example, policymakers favor *credit claiming strategies* when a policy option produces concentrated constituent benefits and diffuse losses and forces of political opposition. However, given the negativity bias of voters (i.e., constituents respond more to losses than to gains), policymakers favor *blame avoidance strategies* when a policy option requires retrenchment of substantial benefits from a concentrated group of constituents but confers relatively small benefits to a diffuse group of constituents, thereby imposing significantly lower transaction costs to organize political opponents rather than supporters (Pierson, 1994; Weaver, 1986). In contrast to credit claiming strategies, *blame avoidance strategies* consist of distinctive tactics to diffuse political opposition (Pierson, p. 8), such as obfuscatory tactics to decouple the relationship between the desired policy and its negative consequences; avoidance of deciding critical policy elements through delegation to other governmental entities; and compensation to victims of retrenchment (Pierson, pp. 19–26; Weaver, pp. 384–390). Blame avoidance strategies contribute to the path dependency of preexisting, even failing, policies (Weaver, pp. 393–395).

The selection of a political strategy is also interrelated with the attributes of the proposed policy solution selected from the *policy stream*. As previously mentioned, the criteria for acceptance of a policy solution in the policy stream are technical feasibility, value acceptability and anticipation of future constraints. To satisfy these criteria, members of the policy community need to incorporate the political problems of adopting a policy option (reflected in the perceived need to use credit claiming or blame avoidance strategies) into the substantive dimensions of proposed policy solutions. Failure to incorporate attributes of the political strategy into proposed policy options within the policy community may result in the lost opportunity to adopt beneficial policy options.

Of course, successful adoption of any policy option requires coupling of the problem stream, policy stream, and political stream during requisite windows of opportunity. Although some windows may open because of features of existing governance structure or policies, such as statutory sunset clauses, most are difficult to predict. However, sensitivity to conditions likely to open such windows, and "softening up" of policymakers to facilitate receptivity for desired action when a window opens, can enhance successful coupling (Kingdon, 1995, pp. 168–186).

## Enabling Sustainability of a Policy Over Time

Even if the problem stream, policy stream, and political stream are successfully coupled during a window of opportunity to enable initial adoption of a policy option, fulfillment of the underlying policy objectives requires sustainability of the policy over the relevant time frame. In this way, political feasibility constraints affecting effectiveness of policy choices over time is the mirror image of economic viability constraints. The ability to retain a policy over time requires analysis of the problems associated with subsequent efforts of retrenchment. This requires a dynamic, not static, assessment of the policy decision-making process over time.

Weaver (1986) and Pierson (1994) described the uniqueness and difficulties of retrenchment politics, some aspects of which have previously been discussed. Political scientists have also examined the characteristics of policies that tend to better withstand attacks of retrenchment. Perhaps most relevant to the consideration of adopting sustainable telecommunications deregulatory policies are the conclusions of research in the context of social welfare programs. Cherry (2003a) discussed how public utility regulation can be understood as an early form of welfare state regulation, bearing similar policy retrenchment problems.

In democracies, universalistic programs are more politically sustainable than targeted ones (Mishra, 1990; Skocpol, 1995; Wilson, 1987). The underlying reason is that the more broadly defined the group of beneficiaries, the broader will be the support from constituencies for maintaining the existing policy notwithstanding changes in circumstances affecting the problem stream, policy stream, or political stream. For this reason, universalistic programs are more politically sustainable even if they are more expensive than policies targeted solely on the poor or marginal groups (Skocpol, pp. 250–253). Consequently, some political scientists advocate "targeting within universalism," that is, addressing the needs of the less privileged through programs that include more advantaged groups (Skocpol, pp. 267–272; Wilson, pp. 118–124). This recommendation is in stark contrast to those of many economists who advocate, for example, narrowly targeted universal service programs as a component of telecommunications deregulatory policy in order to minimize the funding burden.

Skocpol (2000) also identified other characteristics associated with successful social policy programs in the United States. These are: (a) benefits provided in exchange for service rather than as entitlements; (b) policies nurtured by partnerships between government and popularly-rooted voluntary associations; and (c) programs backed by reliable public revenues. The validity of these characteristics may vary among nations, depending on differences among their institutional endowments (Levy & Spiller, 1996) and core values embedded in their social contracts as discussed earlier.

The importance of the discussion here is that factors affecting the political sustainability of a given policy option *over time* need to be contemplated when designing and selecting a policy option for adoption *at a given point in time*. Incorporation of the factors enabling sustainability of a policy over time into the analysis of the factors enabling initial adoption of a policy raises the likelihood of adopting a policy option that actually fulfills the desired policy objectives. Of course, the available options remain constrained by the overall set of options supportive of the legitimacy of government itself. In this way, compliance with all forms of political feasibility constraints described in this section must be achieved simultaneously.

## ECONOMIC VIABILITY AND POLITICAL FEASIBILITY CONSTRAINTS ON TELECOMMUNICATIONS POLICIES

Sustainable telecommunications policies require the simultaneous fulfillment of the various economic viability and political feasibility constraints described in the prior two sections. This section discusses some of the constraints on deregulatory telecommunications policies.

### Pre-Telecommunications Act of 1996—Historical Perspective

Given the dual jurisdictional nature of federal–state regulation of the U.S. telecommunications industry, pursuit of deregulatory policies requires coordination between the federal and state governments. Many policy changes to permit competition in telecommunications markets developed under the Communications Act of 1934 and federal antitrust law without the need for further federal legislation. FCC orders permitted entry into interstate long-distance telecommunications and customer premise equipment markets. The Modified Final Judgment (MFJ), settling the Department of Justice's antitrust case against AT&T, further changed market structure in the long distance, manufacturing, and information services markets. After the divestiture of AT&T, many states amended their laws to accommodate competition in intrastate long-distance telecommunications markets. However, removal of state legal barriers to competition in local exchange markets developed more slowly and unevenly among jurisdictions.

Yet, deregulatory approaches exposed some legal and economic problems that could not be adequately addressed without federal legislation. These problems include the following. First, legal barriers to entry in local exchange markets persisted in many states and could only be uniformly removed through federal preemption. Second, FCC efforts to detariff long-distance services had been held by the U.S. Supreme Court in *MCI v. AT&T* (1994) to be beyond the FCC's statutory authority under the 1934 Act. Third, competition was eroding the economic viability of artificially imposed implicit subsidies characteristic of traditional monopoly regulation, requiring a shift from primary reliance on implicit subsidies to explicit funding mechanisms and rate rebalancing (Cherry, 1998; Cherry & Wildman, 1999b). Fourth, the waiver process for seeking relief from conditions of the MFJ further fragmented decision-making processes affecting telecommunications regulation, and express coordination of MFJ-related issues, with or by the FCC, required Congressional action.

These problems, among others, induced intense Congressional activity that ultimately culminated in the passage of the Telecommunications Act of 1996 (TA96). As to the problems enumerated, TA96 preempted the states from maintaining or creating entry barriers (Section 253), provided the FCC with forbearance powers to address issues such as detariffing (Section 10), created a framework for universal service policy (Section 254), and codified conditions originating in the MFJ with oversight authority transferred to the

FCC (Sections 271–274). Among other things, it also provided a framework for addressing issues such as interconnection, unbundling, resale, and payphone competition.

## Post-Telecommunications Act of 1996

Federal and state government actions to implement the provisions of TA96, however, are creating new sustainability problems. Many difficulties are inherent in the statutory provisions of TA96. As stated by the U.S. Supreme Court in *AT&T v. Iowa Utilities Board* (1999): "It would be gross understatement to say that the 1996 Act is not a model of clarity. It is in many important respects a model of ambiguity or indeed even self-contradiction" (p. 738). Two examples are briefly discussed in the following.

### Sustainability of Universal Service Support

The first example concerns sustainability of the universal service framework established in Section 254 of TA96. Potential sustainability problems embedded in Section 254 and, particularly, in the rules promulgated by the FCC, were foreseen by Cherry (1998) and Cherry and Wildman (1999b). Cherry and Nystrom (2000) and Cherry (2001) also discussed why the universal service framework established in section 254 should be considered an unconstitutional delegation of legislative power by Congress to the FCC.

The long-term viability of the federal universal service support fund created under Section 254 is threatened by a combination of factors, as acknowledged by the FCC in its *Interim Contribution Methodology Order* (2002b). These factors include the overall size of the fund (approximately $5.9 billion in 2001), the statutory requirement that telecommunications providers' contributions to the fund be based on interstate revenues, and industry developments that are creating a declining assessable interstate revenue base. The long-term viability is also related to the difficulties of implementing rate rebalancing, which thus far has been a less politically feasible option in the United States than in the European Union (Cherry, 2000).

The *Interim Contribution Methodology Order* does provide interim measures in an attempt to maintain viability of universal service support in the near term while long-term reforms are considered. However, the components of a politically feasible policy that could provide long-term viable funding are unclear. Longstanding political resistance to rate rebalancing remains and, although reallocation of federal and state regulatory powers over telecommunications could better enable rate rebalancing options (Cherry, 2000), altering the federal–state balance of powers is fraught with political difficulties as described in the following subsection. Modifying the source of universal service support also faces political resistance. Federal government budget constraints have thus far blocked funding from general tax revenues, which is why sector-based funding was established in section 254 under TA96. However, there does appear to be increasing receptivity for expanding the assessable revenue base for existing sector-based funding to include intrastate revenues.

### Sustainability of Local Competition Through Unbundling

Another example concerns the sustainability of an unbundling regime as a means of encouraging viable local exchange competition. Several observations are highlighted here.

First, some difficulties arise from differing opinions as to how to design unbundling to better ensure economically viable local exchange competition. Put simply, ILEC's argue that their financial viability is threatened by policy options imposing greater unbundling obligations and lower prices for unbundled network elements; whereas competitive local exchange carriers (CLECs) argue that their financial viability is threatened by policy options favored by ILECs. Assessing the veracity of the respective assertions of ILECs and CLECs is a difficult task for the regulators.

Second, some difficulties arise from jurisdictional battles between the FCC and the states with regard to the FCC's attempts to establish unbundling rules under Section 251(c)(3). The first challenge, ultimately decided by the U.S. Supreme Court in *AT&T v. Iowa Utilities Board* (1999), was brought not only by industry members but by state commissions asserting that the FCC had unlawfully intruded on states' intrastate regulatory authority. Even though the U.S. Supreme Court upheld the FCC's jurisdictional authority in *AT&T v. Iowa Utilities Board*, the Court did invalidate as overbroad the FCC's application of the impairment standard in Section 251(d)(2) for determining what network elements needed to be unbundled. Upon remand, the FCC's revised rules were subsequently invalidated by the District Court of Columbia Circuit Court of Appeals in *United States Telecom Association v. FCC* (2002/2003) ("*USTA I*"). In relevant part, the D.C. Circuit invalidated the FCC's national uniform rule for finding impairment as an insufficiently nuanced approach and demanded that the FCC apply a more granular one. Disparate views of appropriate roles for the FCC and state commissions in implementing such a "granular" approach resulted in a contentiously debated and divided decision by the FCC in its *Triennial Review Order* (2003/2004) and in unprecedented delay in its issuance. Upon appeal, in *United States Telecom Association v. FCC* (2004) ("*USTA II*"), the D.C. Circuit yet again reversed and remanded that portion of the *Triennial Review Order* providing a revised approach for determining impairment. In this case, the D.C. Circuit found that the FCC's subdelegation of its decision-making authority—not merely a fact-finding function—of impairment determinations to state commissions was unlawful. In essence, the FCC insufficiently considered the states' perspectives in *USTA I*, but overdelegated consideration of the states' perspectives to state commissions in *USTA II*. Some parties have sought, but the FCC and the Solicitor General of the United States have declined to seek, an appeal of *USTA II* to the U.S. Supreme Court.

It is unclear whether local competition based on CLEC access to unbundled network elements is sustainable in such an environment. Particularly troublesome is the severity of the continuing delay and legal uncertainty created by federal–state jurisdictionally related battles, which are likely to be prolonged given the allocation of federal and state powers under the U.S. Constitution. Perhaps a more stable political and legal environment could be created through reassessment and realignment of federal and state regulatory powers over telecommunications. However, such realignment would require either Congress to more aggressively exercise its federal preemption powers or a constitutional amendment to override the presumption of powers reserved to the states under the Tenth Amendment. Either option poses daunting political obstacles. The former would invoke opposition based on states' rights and the latter would require no less than renegotiation of the social contract (U.S. Constitution).

## The Unique Legacy of Public Utility Regulation

The sustainability problems associated with universal service funding and unbundling are directly related to specific attributes and implementation of TA96. Yet, there are some political feasibility constraints impeding the adoption of sustainable deregulatory policy objectives that arise from prior policy choices embedded in traditional public utility regulation—the regime from which any deregulatory utility policy is attempting to transition—which long preceded and constrained the provisions deemed acceptable in TA96 itself.

More specifically, Cherry (2003a) discussed how the common law doctrines of *just price* and *businesses affected with a public interest* constrain the adoption of sustainable deregulatory models for public utility industries. These common law doctrines are derived from the medieval concepts of fairness in economic exchange and the sovereign's inherent power to regulate private party activity to protect the general welfare. These concepts form the basis for common carriage obligations—to charge reasonable prices, to serve without discrimination, and to provide service with adequate care—that originated under English common law during the Middle Ages and are a subset of the obligations borne by public utilities (Cherry, 2003a, 2003b). The associated obligations imposed on public utilities in the United States have also been long codified in federal and state statutes regulating the electricity and telecommunications industries.

Attempts to retrench from these common law doctrines to pursue deregulatory policies are politically hazardous. As Cherry (2003a) explains, this is because public utility regulation bears characteristics similar to other forms of welfare state regulation and faces similar political barriers associated with policy retrenchment that affect the sustainability of that policy over time. Furthermore, in attempting to transition from monopoly public utility regulation to a competitive regulatory regime, the conditions for political feasibility often conflict with those for economic viability—for example, political resistance to, but the economic necessity of, rate rebalancing. This conflict exacerbates the difficulty in adopting and maintaining sustainable—that is, reasonably achievable—deregulatory policy objectives. Examples include the electricity deregulatory efforts in California and implementation of section 254 of TA96 by the FCC (Cherry, 2003a). These retrenchment problems necessitate careful reevaluation of the design and efficacy of deregulatory policies.

## Possible New Windows of Opportunity for Policy Change

The sustainability problems arising under TA96, and further attempts to retrench from traditional public utility regulation previously discussed, illustrate the difficulties of simultaneously satisfying the political and economic conditions for a financially viable telecommunications industry under deregulatory policies. Under what circumstances can these difficulties be overcome? Kingdon's model provides some insights.

For adoption of a policy at a given point in time, a window of opportunity must open to enable coupling of the problem stream, policy stream, and political stream. Changes in the problem stream, such as crises or other major focusing events, can create such windows. There have been several recent events that have increased policymakers' perception of economic viability problems and may provide a window of opportunity for adoption of further regulatory reforms that to date have not been politically feasible.

For example, Cherry (2000) discussed changes in circumstances that could create windows of opportunity to better enable adoption in the United States of rate rebalancing policy more consistent with competitive markets. In addition, the terrorist attacks of September 11, 2001, exposed the vulnerability and importance of telecommunications infrastructure to the nation's economy and security. The economic vulnerability of the telecommunications industry has been further heightened by the dramatic downturn in the telecommunications sector, the rash of CLEC bankruptcies, and the questionable accounting practices and bankruptcy of WorldCom. Finally, recent events affecting other industries may also have spillover effects for the telecommunications industry (Kingdon, 1995, p. 190). These include the electricity crisis arising from deregulatory efforts on behalf of the electricity industry in California and the recent electricity blackout affecting more than 50 million people in the northeast part of the United States.

## INTERRELATIONSHIP OF TELECOMMUNICATIONS AND MASS MEDIA POLICY REGIMES

The previous section provided examples of the difficulties of simultaneously satisfying economic viability and political feasibility constraints in pursuit of deregulatory telecommunications policies based on problems evolving from within the traditional telecommunications sphere of activities. However, additional difficulties arise from the growing interrelationships between the telecommunications and mass media spheres of activity.

Most notably, with digital convergence, there is a growing tension among policy choices based on common carriage and free speech principles. Historically, telecommunications providers have been regulated as common carriers, and, as providers of transmission facilities only, they possess no First Amendment free speech rights. However, mass media have not been considered common carriers, and, as providers of information content, they do possess free speech rights. With the elimination of technological entry barriers between telecommunications and mass media, policymakers have faced free speech claims from telecommunications carriers and have thus far resisted extension of common carriage obligations to mass media competitors. What constitutes a *sustainable* balance of free speech rights and common carrier obligations for intermodal competitive providers, such as broadband access providers, has yet to be determined.

### Telecommunications Carriers' Free Speech Rights

In 1970, the FCC adopted a rule that prohibited any common carrier from providing video programming to subscribers in its telephone area because of concerns that telephone companies would monopolize video programming by favoring their affiliates in granting access to telephone poles and conduits. The telephone-cable cross-ownership ban was codified by Congress in Section 533(b) of the original Cable Communications Policy Act of 1984.

By the early 1990s, the nature of the cable television industry had changed enormously. In the Cable Television Consumer Protection and Competition Act of 1992, Congress found that the cable industry had become highly concentrated, resulting in undue market power that posed barriers to entry for new programmers. Furthermore, cable companies were permitted to provide telephony services over their cable facilities, for which their greater bandwidth provided a competitive advantage over telephone company facilities.

The telephone companies subsequently sought to eliminate the federal telephone-cable cross-ownership ban. They succeeded by seeking invalidation of the ban as an unconstitutional violation of their First Amendment free speech rights to provide video programming. Both the Fourth Circuit Court of Appeals in *Chesapeake & Potomac Tel. Co. v. United States* (1994 / 1996) and the Ninth Circuit Court of Appeals in *US West, Inc. v. United States* (1995 / 1996) found the cross-ownership ban to be insufficiently narrowly tailored under the intermediate scrutiny test of the First Amendment. While the Fourth Circuit case was on appeal to the U.S. Supreme Court, Congress repealed the cross-ownership ban in TA96.

Repeal of the federal telephone-cable cross-ownership ban eliminated a form of regulatory asymmetry among competing firms. In this respect, had the video programming ban not been found unconstitutional, the long-run economic viability of individual telephone companies in certain markets could have been seriously threatened (Cherry & Wildman, 2000). In this way, enforcement of telecommunications carriers' free speech rights has significantly impacted subsequent technological and market developments among the communications industries, as evidenced by substantial entry and merger / acquisition activities of telecommunications carriers into cable and Internet markets.

## Resistance to Extension of Common Carriage Obligations

New sustainability problems are also being created by the FCC's policy choices for regulation of broadband services under TA96. These problems are most apparent in recent service classification proceedings considered by the FCC, where the relevant regulatory treatment is driven by a service's classification as an information or telecommunications service.

First, in the *Cable Modem Access Order* (Federal Communications Commission, 2002a / 2003, par. 38), the FCC defined cable modem service to endusers as an information service with no separable telecommunications component under TA96. Thus, provision of cable modem service would not be subject to common carrier regulation. However, the FCC's ruling was recently reversed by the Ninth Circuit Court of Appeals in *Brand X Internet Services v. FCC* (2003), holding that it was bound by its earlier decision in *AT&T v. City of Portland* (2000) that the transmission element of cable broadband service constitutes telecommunications service under TA96.

Second, prior to the Ninth Circuit's decision in *Brand X Internet Services V. FCC*, the FCC issued a Notice of Proposed Rule Making (NPRM), *Wireline Broadband Internet Access NPRM* (FCC, 2002c). To avoid imposing asymmetric obligations between cable modem service providers and wireline broadband Internet access providers (i.e., DSL providers) in this NPRM, the FCC tentatively concluded that wireline broadband Internet access service to endusers is also an integrated information service with no separable telecommunications service (pars. 17–26). However, if the Ninth Circuit's opinion in *Brand X Internet Services v. FCC* stands, then the FCC will need to reverse its tentative conclusion—an option it has thus far declined to accept—in order to retain intermodal symmetry.

However, beyond the uncertainty created by the Ninth Circuit's reversal of the *Cable Modem Access Order*, examination of the cable modem access and wireline broadband access proceedings reveals a fundamental sustainability problem. By attempting to provide intermodal regulatory parity as non-common carriers between cable modem access and wireline broadband Internet access, the FCC would create *intramodal asymmetric regulation* between broadband (non-common carriage) and narrowband (common carriage) services over the networks of wireline carriers.

It is not clear whether such intramodal asymmetric regulation is sustainable (Cherry, 2003b). Wireline providers may not be able to provide both non-common carriage broadband and common carriage narrowband on an economically viable basis, at least for some customers, groups, or serving areas. To the extent such economic inviability exists, broadband and/or narrowband services will not be available for some customers, groups, or serving areas. Yet, such unavailability of service will pose political sustainability problems, particularly if the common carriage narrowband service is no longer available. The unavailability of *any* common carriage-provided service (whether broadband or narrowband) means that the customer is facing a service provider who may choose not to serve an area, refuse to serve a customer, discriminate among customers, or provide unaffordable service (relative to a customer's needs or means). The absence of any common carriage-provided communications service is likely to be a politically unsustainable scenario, given the unique political feasibility constraints on attempts to retrench from public utility regulation, as previously discussed. Thus, a politically sustainable policy may likely require the availability of *some* common carriage-provided service. However, joint satisfaction of economic viability and political feasibility may require the provision of *all* broadband and narrowband services on a common carriage basis in order to ensure that *some* common carriage-provided service is always ubiquitously available. In other words, the only sustainable policy may be one that simultaneously provides intermodal and intramodal regulatory symmetry.

## Sustainable Balance of Common Carriage Obligations and Free Speech Rights

Although non-exhaustive, the preceding examples illustrate policy migration across historically separate regulatory regimes. Intermodal competition implicates free speech rights for common carriers and consideration of common carriage obligations for combined facilities–content providers. The classification proceedings for cable modem access and wireline broadband Internet access services present early manifestations of frictions between free speech rights and common carrier obligations as applied to competing communication channel providers. Yet, posing problems of first impression, we understand little concerning the potentially conflicting effects among the legal mechanisms that developed to support free speech rights and common carriage objectives.

## FUTURE RESEARCH

At the very least, these issues raise questions as to what set of free speech rights and common carrier obligations for intermodal competitive providers are sustainable—both economically and politically. What are the potential tradeoffs among societal values underlying free speech and common carriage for sustainable provision of intermodal communications services? How might such tradeoffs change over time through technological innovation? Will free speech rights of communication channel providers have to yield to the needs, both economically and politically, of endusers? Or will the centuries-old legacy of common carriage obligations to protect customers have to yield to the free speech rights of communication channel providers? Will sustainable policy require both symmetric intermodal and intramodal service regulation? Does there exist a free speech/common carriage regime that can be stable over time, or will it need to be continually revisited as technological innovation proceeds? These are important, yet only beginning, research questions that telecommunications and mass media scholars need to explore in order to address the evolving interrelationships among the telecommunications and mass media spheres of activity. More broadly, research agendas must continually evolve to embrace new manifestations of policy migration among these historically separate regulatory regimes.

## REFERENCES

Allen, A. (1999). Social contract theory in American case law. *Florida Law Review, 51,* 1–40.

AT&T v. City of Portland, 216 F.3d 871 (9th Cir. 2000).

AT&T v. Iowa Utilities Board, 525 U.S. 366 (1999).

Black, A. (1993). The juristic origins of social contract theory. *History of Political Thought, 14,* 57–76.

Brand X Internet Services v. FCC, 345 F.3d 1120 (9th Cir. 2003).

Cable Communications Policy Act of 1984, Pub. L. No. 98–549, 98 Stat. 2779, amending Communications Act of 1934, 47 U.S.C.A. §151 *et seq.* (West 2001 & Supp. 2004).

Cable Television Consumer Protection and Competition Act of 1992, Pub. L. No. 102–385, 106 Stat. 1460, amending Communications Act of 1934, 47 U.S.C.A. §151 *et seq.* (West 2001 & Supp. 2004).

Cherry, B. (1998). Designing regulation to achieve universal service goals: Unilateral or bilateral rules. In. E. Bohlin & S. L. Levin (Eds.), *Telecommunications Transformation: Technology, strategy and policy* (pp. 343–359). Amsterdam: IOS Press.

Cherry, B. (2000). The irony of telecommunications deregulation: Assessing the role reversal in U.S. and EU Policy. In I. Vogelsang & B. Compaine (Eds.), *The Internet upheaval: Raising questions and seeking answers in communications policy* (pp. 355–385). Cambridge, MA: MIT Press.

Cherry, B. (2001). Challenging the constitutionality of universal service contributions: *Whitman v. American Trucking Associations, Inc. M.S.U.- D.C.L. L. Rev., 2001,* 423–426.

Cherry, B. (2003a). The political realities of telecommunications policies in the U.S.: How the legacy of public utilities regulation constrains adoption of new regulatory models. *M.S.U.-D.C.L. L. Rev., 2003,* 757–790.

Cherry, B. (2003b). Utilizing "essentiality of access" analyses to mitigate risky, costly and untimely government interventions in converging telecommunications technologies and markets. *CommLaw Conspectus, 11,* 251–275.

Cherry, B., & Nystrom, D. (2000). Universal service contributions: An unconstitutional delegation of taxing power. *M.S.U.-D.C.L. L. Rev., 2000,* 107–138.

Cherry, B., & Wildman, S. (1999a). Institutional endowment as foundation for regulatory performance and regime transitions: The role of the U.S. constitution in telecommunications regulation in the United States. *Telecommunications Policy, 23,* 607–623.

Cherry, B., & Wildman, S. (1999b). Unilateral and bilateral rules: A framework for increasing competition while meeting universal service goals in telecommunications. In B. Cherry, S. Wildman, & A. Hammond (Eds.), *Making universal service policy: Enhancing the process through multidisciplinary evaluation* (pp. 39–58). Mahwah, NJ: Lawrence Erlbaum Associates.

Cherry, B., & Wildman, S. (2000). Preventing flawed communication policies by addressing constitutional principles. *M.S.U.-D.C.L. L. Rev., 2000,* 55–105.

Chesapeake & Potomac Tel. Co. v. United States, 42 F.3d 181 (4th Cir. 1994), *cert granted sub nom,* United States v. Chesapeake & Potomac Tel. Co., 515 U.S. 1157 (1995), *judgment vacated,* 516 U.S. 415 (1996).

Federal Communications Commission. (2002a). Cable Modem Access Order, Declaratory Ruling and Notice of Proposed Rulemaking, In the Matter of Inquiry Concerning High-Speed Access to the Internet Over Cable and Other Facilities, 17 FCC Rcd 4798 (2002), *affirmed in part, vacated in part,* Brand X Internet Services v. FCC, 345 F.3d 1120 (9th Cir. 2003).

Federal Communications Commission. (2002b). Interim Contribution Methodology Order, Report and Order and Second Further Notice of Proposed Rulemaking, In the Matter of Federal-State Joint Board on Universal Service, 17 FCC Rcd 3752.

Federal Communications Commission. (2002c). Wireline Broadband Internet Access NPRM, Notice of Proposed Rulemaking, In the Matter of the Appropriate Framework for Broadband Access to the Internet Over Wireline Facilities, 17 FCC Rcd 3019.

Federal Communications Commission. (2003). Triennial Review Order, Report and Order and Order on Remand and Further Notice of Proposed Rulemaking, In the Matter of the Review of Section 251 Unbundling Obligations of Incumbent Local Exchange Carriers,18 FCC Rcd 16978, *judgment vacated in part, review dismissed in part,* United States Telecom Association v. FCC, 359 F.3d 554 (D.C. Cir. 2004).

Finer, S. E. (1999). *The history of government* (Vol. III). Oxford, UK: Oxford University Press.

Hall, P. (1986). *Governing the economy.* Oxford, UK: Oxford University Press.

Hoepfl, H., & Thompson, M. (1979). The history of contract as a motif in political thought. *The American Historical Review, 84,* 919–944.

Kary, J. (1999). Contract law and the social contract: What legal history can teach us about the political theory of Hobbes and Locke. *Ottawa Law Review, 31,* 73–91.

Kingdon, J. (1995). *Agendas, alternatives, and public policies* (2nd ed.). New York: HarperCollins.

Levy, B., & Spiller, P. (Eds.). (1996). *Regulations, institutions, and commitment: Comparative studies of telecommunications.* Cambridge, UK: Cambridge University Press.

MCI v. AT&T, 512 U.S. 218 (1994).

Mishra, R. (1990). *The welfare state in capitalist society: Policies of retrenchment and maintenance in Europe, North America and Australia.* Toronto, Ontario, Canada: University of Toronto Press.

Pierson, P. (1994). *Dismantling the welfare state: Reagan, Thatcher, and the politics of retrenchment.* Cambridge, UK: Cambridge University Press.

Priban, J. (2003). Stealing the natural language: The fiction of the social contract and legality in the light of Nietzsche's philosophy. *Cardozo L. Rev., 24,* 663–681.

Rosenfeld, M. (1985). Contract and justice: The relation between classical contract law and social contract theory. *Iowa Law Review, 70,* 769–899.

Skocpol, T. (1995). *Social policy in the United States.* Princeton, NJ: Princeton University Press.

Skocpol, T. (2000). *The missing middle.* New York: Norton.

Strong, F. (1997). *Judicial function in constitutional limitation of governmental power.* Durham, NC: Carolina Academic Press.

Telecommunications Act of 1996, Pub. L. No. 104–104, 110 Stat. 56, amending Communications Act of 1934, 47 U.S.C.A. §151 *et seq.* (West 2001 & Supp. 2004).

United States v. Winstar Corporation, 518 U.S. 839 (1996).

United States Telecom Association v. FCC, 290 F.3d 415 (D.C. Cir. 2002), *cert. denied sub nom,* WorldCom, Inc. v. United States Telecom Association, 538 U.S. 940 (2003).

United States Telecom Association v. FCC, 359 F.3d 554 (D.C. Cir. 2004).

US West, Inc. v. United States, 48 F.3d 1092 (9th Cir. 1995), *cert. granted, judgment vacated sub nom*, United States v. US West, Inc., 516 U.S. 1155 (1996).

Weaver, R. K. (1986). The politics of blame avoidance. *Journal of Public Policy 6*, 371–398.

Wilsford, D. (1994). Path dependency on why history makes it difficult but not impossible to reform health care systems in a big way. *Journal of Public Policy, 14*, 251–283.

Wilson, W. (1987). *The truly disadvantaged*. Chicago: University of Chicago Press.

Zahariadis, N. (1992). To sell or not to sell? Telecommunications policy in Britain and France. *Journal of Public Policy, 12*, 355–375.

Zahariadis, N. (1995). *Markets, states, and public policy: Privatization in Britain and France*. Ann Arbor, MI: The University of Michigan Press.

# ISSUES IN MEDIA MANAGEMENT AND ECONOMICS

# 6

# Issues in Human Relations Management

James W. Redmond

The University of Memphis

This chapter focuses on managing people in media organizations who work in an industry that has experienced radical operating environment changes. Since 1980, virtually every aspect of the media business has been altered by new technology and audience fragmentation. Other areas of this Handbook, notably those dealing with media market structure, competition, consolidation, and convergence, will bring perspective to the contemporary media challenge. To avoid duplication, this chapter will not discuss those areas in depth.

Despite increasing technological evolution, media organizations depend on human creativity more than ever. Machines are dumb things that can do only what the designer built into them. But human beings dream and create. They provide the critical element of innovation necessary to survive in the dynamic, contemporary operating environment (Dickson, 2003; Dobson, 2003; Garfield, 1992; Hellstrom & Hellstrom, 2002). A writer can create a grammatical sentence that is flat, boring, mundane, and a turnoff for the reader. Or that person can take us on a voyage to other places with images that drift within us like motion pictures of the mind. The complex bundles of hopes, fears, dreams, and frustrations known as human beings make up media organizations. Those human beings have most of the control over the *quality* of their work. Thus, the effective media manager must orchestrate traditional structural–functional aspects of the organization while dealing with the psychology of organizational members to help them be as creative and productive as possible. Shapiro (2002) likened this effort to that of creating excellent music. You need common knowledge and rules to keep everyone going in the same direction. But within those simple structures, artistry has a wide range in which to be expressed. "Like good jazz, businesses can operate within constraints that resemble sheet music, allowing for creativity within simple structures. This jazz metaphor seems particularly appropriate to the loose–tight combinations we should strive for in seeking innovative solutions" (p. 19).

## REVIEW OF HUMAN RELATIONS IN MEDIA ORGANIZATION LITERATURE

Human relations in media organizations encompasses a range of academic disciplines as well as the applied media arena. Although media organizations are in many ways similar to other kinds of human collectives, they have structural–functional and human dynamic differences that set them apart. For example, American journalistic media are a crucible within which the pragmatic business organization focused on capitalistic profit collides with the idealism of a free press specifically protected in the U.S. Constitution (Emery, Emery, & Roberts, 2000; Franklin & Franklin, 1990).

There is a wide range of media types, operational environments, audience trends, and innovations in technology. However, although the *context* of media production is varied and continually evolving, what is produced, the *content*, is generated by human constituencies. Thus, media organizations depend on the social capital of individual creativity. They are susceptible to the whims, emotions, hopes, fears, and idealism of the millions of people who labor within them. For example, a writer can turn out grammatically correct copy that cannot be faulted on its technical merits, but that has no "pop," no special twist of phrasing; the thing that sets apart Pulitzer prize-winning excellence from the merely mundane.

The discussion that follows is by no means an exhaustive review of the human relations' literature of interest to media management researchers. It is only intended to provide a sense of the breadth of available work that has been done on media organizations, or in other disciplines that can be of use to better understand the media organization context. This is a broad area of inquiry that must, by its very nature, synthesize knowledge from elsewhere. The literature of organizational behavior links to psychology, communication, mass communication, and journalism, with the latter focusing on the news and information sector. To consider human relations in media organizations is to consider a very large library with many rooms. Because human relations in media organizations is a relatively new field, there is a great deal to be learned giving the prospective researcher an open plain on which to wander.

Texts specific to the area of media management frequently contain chapters or cases about personnel management, human relations, and motivation (Lavine & Wackman, 1988; Redmond, 2004; Warner, 1994; Wicks, Sylvie, Hollifield, Lacy, & Sohn, 2004). The structural–functional approach to media typically analyzes the media systems, both technical and economic, within which media operate. This research provides understanding of the pragmatic world within which media-creative people engage in their profession along with the structural, functional, and economic parameters (Albarran & Chan-Olmsted, 1998; Albarran & Arrese, 2003; Sherman, 1995).

Any investigation of human relations in media management will uncover useful resources, continually evolving, on the Web sites of academic journals, trade associations, and nonprofit educational foundations. Universities are also developing research areas of focus in the media management field. It should be noted that much of research remains primarily structural–functional, and to date there is somewhat limited material concentrated on human relations in media management. This area of inquiry is ripe for further development, particularly in the area of qualitative studies. Two particularly useful university Web sites are the Grady College of Journalism and Mass Communication Broadcast Management Laboratory at the University of Georgia (http://www.grady.uga.edu/faherty/home.html) and Northwestern University's Media Management Center (http://www.mediamanagementcenter.org/center). Additionally, the nonprofit Poynter Institute attempts to span the boundary between applied journalism and the academic world. It maintains extensive bibliographies in a wide range of media studies (http://www.poynter.org/resource_center). Investigators into human relations in media management will find useful information and links regarding media ethics, media leadership, new media, and other topics including media professionals' perspectives on their careers and environments.

## Organizational Behavior

This research discipline rose out of classical management scholarship that initially attempted to understand the world from a structural–functional perspective (Fayol, 1949; Taylor, 1947/1967). Management style is a key factor in organizational performance, particularly whether that style fits the needs of those being managed. McGregor (1960) identified two opposing approaches to management, Theory X (authoritarian command and control) and Theory Y (employee-centered with minimal control). Participative management grew popular in the 1960s with the gradual shift from the early 20th century view of strict control to an understanding by mid-century that individuals who have a sense of power, responsibility, and expectancy about their work environment are often more productive (Likert, 1961; Mayo, 1960; Vroom, 1964).

With the rise of Japanese competitiveness, which became a serious threat to American business, considerable attention was paid to how Japanese culture fostered organizational citizenship, and how American companies could use the Japanese model to help workers feel more closely tied to an organization and its goals (Ouchi, 1981). Total Quality Management became fashionable with the idea that quality circle teams of employees, empowered to create and innovate, would mean organizational success (Marash, 1993). Building on this idea, substantial research has grown to foster the idea that it is positive to have personal and organizational goals and values in sync (Finegan, 2000), so the organization and individual reinforce each other in a holographic mirroring of one another (Mackenzie, 1991; Morgan, 1997).

Peters and Waterman (1982) argued that excellence should be the goal of an organization, which would result in greater productivity and competitiveness. Their work fed a trend of increased attention to social dynamics processes and of generating common themes and values within organizations and among organizational members. The human element is now considered to be among the most critical factors in organizational success with the organizational structure serving as a support mechanism (Garfield, 1992). Identification theory is a growing area investigating the way individuals derive meaning from organizational relationships and may thereby increase their contributions to the organization (Ravasi & Van Reckom, 2003; Whetten & Godfrey, 1998). In capitalist economies shareholders look for increasing stock value. Stock options are a popular way to compensate managers because they provide direct financial incentive to do whatever it takes to increase profits. Likewise, many organizations, including media organizations, use stock option plans, not only as a financial incentive, but to link shareholder values to individual employee behavior by helping employees identify their daily work as a way of increasing both their personal wealth and the company's stock performance (Greengard, 1999; Hannafey, 2003). In an environment geared toward steadily increasing stock value, maintaining high productivity while finding new ways to continually improve year after year is an omnipresent challenge (Drucker, 1988; Garmager & Shemmer, 1998; Greenberg, 1999; Hopkins-Doerr, 1989; Kanter, 1988; Schneider, 1983).

Recently organizational behaviorists have used the term *social capital* to refer to the human side of organizations (Clark, 2003; Oxman, 2002). The contemporary role of a leader or manager is to marshal that social capital in such a way that it carries the organization forward to accomplish management goals. Thus, in order to move the organization, a leader must find ways to inspire organizational members, who then actually move the organization (Fiorina et al., 2003). This is a very different perspective from early structural–functional, "classical" theorists who saw management as a driving force pushing benign workers who were paycheck-focused and perceived as willing to follow orders. Contemporary theorists see management's challenge as charting the course but empowering the organizational members to sail it as a highly motivated, innovative, and creative crew (Bolman & Deal, 1991; Fournies, 2000; Hellstrom & Hellstrom, 2002). Today, we better understand the critical nature of the nuances of human relations.

In strong organizational cultures, management may be more effective in a facilitating role rather than merely as a command and control function (Logan, Kiely, & Greer, 2003; Lucas, 1999; Way, 2000). An organization, in today's context, has great difficulty going anywhere the people within it do not want it to go. Long, standard organizational approaches such as goal setting are recognized as problematical, not always effective, and requiring considerable developmental care (Humphreys, 2003). Indeed, a fundamental question in the goal-setting equation is, as Levinson (2003) titled a recent article on this issue, "Management by Whose Objectives?" Thus, goal setting is a partnership activity. In a metaphorical sense, the organization is now viewed as a personality with human characteristics, including having a passion for the enterprise.

In the pursuit of organizational effectiveness, authors frequently provide checklists in an attempt to boil down the intricacies of organizational behavior to a list of manageable attributes (Juechter, Fischer, & Alford, 1998; Paulson, 2003). However, despite more concerted efforts toward consensus building, it has long been recognized that a degree of conflict can be healthy, even a positive impetus for innovation (Sutton, 2002). As we learn more about organizational behavior, we realize still more is left to be understood. The elusive human element is always challenging "Inside Our Strange World of Organizations" as Mintzberg (1989) subtitled one of his books on management.

## Psychology

Organizational member psychology is a daily factor in effectiveness that has been well established (Alderfer, 1972; Bandura, 1986; Herzberg, Mausner, & Snyderman, 1959; Vroom, 1964). Maslow (1954/1970) defined a hierarchy of human motivational needs in which a person moves up through levels from the bottom level of survival needs, to the top level of self-actualization—a sense of fulfillment, the deeper meaning of life. It is at the top of his hierarchy where individuals who feel safe will take risks, push innovative ideas, and feel free to create. Maslow perceived each level as resting on the former. Thus, if some unexpected event occurs, such as the firing of a favorite boss and replacement with someone feared, the self-actualizing employee may quickly drop back to the survival level. There, the tendency is to engage in a modern illusion of the survival-level employee telling the boss only what the employee thinks the boss wants to here; much like Hans Christian Anderson's fairy tale: sycophants telling the emperor how splendid he looks in his new clothes, while in reality he is naked and absurd before his subjects (Anderson, 1837/1949; Argyris, 1998).

Herzberg et al. (1959) argued that people react to two sets of forces in the workplace. One set comprises the extrinsic factors. These are external to the individual—the job context such as working conditions, salary, and company policy. The second set of motivators includes more abstract intrinsic factors. These satisfy the person from the inside—the job content including a sense of responsibility, recognition, achievement, meaningful work, and doing something for the greater good of society. People who consider their work a *calling*, such as members of the clergy, medical doctors, and many journalists (Auletta, 1991) have high intrinsic needs that may outweigh financial remuneration.

Alderfer (1972) used a three-part model to explain motivation. Things like food, water, working conditions, and monetary pay are the *existence needs*. Those things motivate human beings to work, but humans also have *growth needs*, the sense of being productive, creative, or doing something worthwhile. Humans also need personal and social relationships that are meaningful, called *relatedness needs*. The three needs groups—existence, growth, and relatedness—work together. The more perfect the balance among them, the higher the motivation.

Bandura's (1986) *social cognitive theory* posited that people are complex blends of their backgrounds, intelligence, social learning, and other factors. These cannot be separated into individual elements, but swirl together in a kind of soup of emotion, each ingredient flavoring the whole. Individuals engage in social learning in which "correlated experiences create expectations that regulate action" (p. 188), and these vary from one individual to another.

Human beings learn patterns of behavior from what succeeded in the past. Humans then do things to produce the results they expect, based on those past experiences. This *expectancy theory* was advanced by Victor Vroom (1964). Additionally, when organizational members feel there is unfairness in something, they may take steps to adjust the scales, to restore their sense of equity. That can mean slowing down, turning out adequate but not stunning work, or even actively working to make something fail by withholding service until the sense of fairness and balance is restored (Harder, 1991: Lamertz, 2002).

The psychology of the workplace, then, is inherently complicated. In group settings, people who are more prosocial, and not as self-absorbed, tend to be more interested in the larger context of organizational values (Nauta, de Dreu, & van der Vaart, 2002). Those who are positively motivated by a sense of ownership of the work, expanding themselves cognitively, and who are positively inclined to interrelating with others, are most effective in what are called self-managing work teams (Druskak & Pesconsolido, 2002). Recent work investigated psychological empowerment in the organizational context (Spreitzer, 1995), influencing behavior in the workplace (Brief & Weiss, 2002), the positive and negative effects of emotion in the organizational context (Kiefer & Briner, 2003), and how the rising number of so-called "knowledge workers" can be positively motivated by the work environment. These are the creative people who generate new things, ideas, or concepts. They have a great need to have the organization encourage them to accomplish their ideals and dreams, rather than to merely complete the required daily processes (Brenner, 1999). For many people the organization within which they work is a fundamental part of their very definition of self.

> To varying degrees, people derive part of the identity and sense of self from the organizations or workgroups to which they belong. Indeed, for many people their professional and/or organizational identity may be more pervasive and important than ascribed identities based on gender, age, ethnicity, race, or nationality. (Hogg & Terry, 2000, para. 2)

## Communication

Interpersonal and organizational communication provide a considerable body of research that is relevant to the study of human relations in managing media organizations. Jablin & Putnam (2000) and Jablin, Putnam, Roberts, & Porter (1987) provided extensive and particularly useful material in this area covering theoretical and methodological issues in organizational communication research, along with pertinent readings in organizational environments, structures, and communication flows. Clarity of messaging, lateral and vertical communication, and informal and formal communication channels all have an affect on people within the organizational envelope. The communication climate within an organization has a direct bearing on the conveyance of meaning among organizational members at all levels, including up and down the managerial hierarchy (Falcione, Sussman, & Herden, 1987; Poole, 1985; Trujillo, 1983). Analyzing the dominant communication paradigms in organizations is particularly useful in understanding the way leaders and subordinates negotiate meaning (Watson, 1982). Recent research with new entrants to the work force has underscored the critical role communication plays in maximizing employee and organizational effectiveness (Tulgan, 2000).

Morgan (1997) provided useful background in the history of management theory, the rise of machine organizations, and the concept of organizations as evolving organisms continually adapting to change. Particularly useful in Morgan's work are the following chapters: "Nature Intervenes: Organizations as Organisms," "Creating Social Reality: Organizations as Cultures," "Interests, Conflict, and Power: Organizations as Political Systems," and "Exploring Plato's Cave: Organizations as Psychic Prisons." A key element in Morgan's work, for the purposes of this discussion, is that "organizations and their members become trapped by constructions of reality that, at best, give an imperfect grasp of the world" creating "psychic prisons" that inhibit free thinking and creativity (p. 216). Morgan argued for more open, evolving organizational structures and used the metaphor of the brain as a growing, evolving, learning, adapting organization, contrary to the inherent rigidity of traditional corporate structures and cultures.

Because language is symbolic, it is inherently complicated (Burke, 1966). Organizations are challenging because the combination of climate, culture, communication patterns, management/leader and organizational member interface all combine to create an environment that can be conducive to excellent performance or contrary to achieving the desired goals (Akgun, Lynn, & Byrne, 2003; Balestracci, 2003; Falcione et al., 1987; Levy & Levy, 2000; Schein, 1985). The messages and the process through which they transfer intended meaning to others are critical factors in effectiveness (Stohl & Redding, 1987). Communication problems have been found to have a significant effect on organizations in trouble because information flow is necessary to respond and adapt to environmental changes, and because lack of information may feed the generation of misinformation and rumor accelerating organizational decline (Whetten, 1988). One of a manager's key functions is to communicate (Bennis & Nanus, 1985; Huczynski, 1992; Whetten & Cameron, 1995). Interpersonal communication helps build relationships, which is a fundamental principle of the long popular "management by walking around" (MBWA) strategy (Peters & Waterman, 1982; Taylor, 1994; Zahniser, 1994). It is essential to fostering climates of innovation, building the sense among employees that the manager is working for their best interests, and providing more individual contact with subordinates to both improve the quality of work and build a greater sense of mutual teaming to accomplish organizational objectives (Shapiro, 2002; Geisler, 1999, 2000).

## Mass Media

There is considerable literature regarding theories of mass media, beyond the scope of this discussion. Suffice it to say, it is particularly useful for the investigator in human relations in media organizations to be grounded in the underlying concepts of mass media communication, particularly the theories of audience engagement, mass media message filtering, agenda setting, and media influence. Mass media is such a fundamental part of the modern experience that debate about it continues in academic and public forums ranging from parental access controls, to media ownership, to content regulation. Academic areas of inquiry include the impact of mass media on society, powerful effects, limited effects, behavioral changes that may be attributed to mass media, mass-mediated realities that affect perception, and numerous other areas of interest (DeFleur & Ball-Rokeach, 1989; McQuail, 1994; Tan, 1985)

Mass media rose out of the dawn of the Industrial Revolution as part of the radical shift from agrarian-based to urban-centered society and the concurrent rise of literacy. Historical context is vital to understanding codes, rituals, and ethical systems within a culture. This is particularly true with the American media model, which is specifically protected in the U.S. Constitution and by more than 2 centuries of evolving case law. When The United States was created, the First Amendment was included in the Constitution to ensure a free press beyond control of the central government. The idea was based on the Miltonian concept of the press, as a kind of balance to the government, providing a marketplace of ideas for free discussion of issues important to the citizenry, regardless of the sentiment of those who held political power. In the Miltonian marketplace of ideas, it is presumed that if truth is in the marketplace, it will be in obvious contrast to falsity. By the mid-19th century new technology in the form of steam-driven presses enabled large circulation dailies to emerge. With the ability to quickly and easily reach tens of thousands of people to increase sales of virtually anything, advertising quickly became the economic engine driving mass distribution media, particularly those engaged in news and current events information (Emery, Emery, & Roberts, 2000; Fellow & Tebbel, 2004; Folkerts & Teeter, 2002; Franklin & Franklin, 1990).

The American model of journalism presumes objectivity of a free press not associated directly with political parties. Unlike the European model, where papers typically identify themselves as a social democratic paper or some other ideological alignment, the American model rose with an ideal of being a neutral critic to the political fray (Franklin & Franklin, 1990). The concept of *objectivity*, is a fundamental part of the professional journalist's ethic inside traditional newsrooms. The codes (formal and informal), rituals, and mythology of professional journalism are so entrenched that many news workers maintain a kind of illusion that they are separate from the money side of the enterprise. However, since the beginning of mass circulation newspapers nearly 2 centuries ago, the engine of mass media has been advertising.

## Journalism

Substantial research has been conducted regarding journalism processes, products, and effects. Academic publications provide extensive article collections with studies in virtually all aspects of media. For example, the 75-year-old *Journalism & Mass Communication Quarterly* lists 36 different content categories of publication. Among those are human relations-oriented articles on newsroom satisfaction (Stamm & Underwood, 1993), how working journalists respond to management styles (Gaziano & Coulson, 1988), and the clash of business and editorial interests when advertisers try to influence coverage (Hays & Reisner, 1991). Two publications, with great credibility in the field, are the *American Journalism Review*, based at the University of Maryland, and the *Columbia Journalism Review* produced by the Columbia University Graduate School of Journalism. Both publications offer a critical, applied journalism focus on the controversies, internal philosophical struggles, ethical challenges, and perspectives of working journalists' daily lives (e.g. Flournoy, 2004; Jenkins, 2003: Rosen, 2004; Smolkin, 2004). The Radio-TV News Directors Association (RTNDA) and the Associated Press Managing Editors Association (APME) also publish trade publications relevant to media management researchers. These include online access. Both the *RTNDA Communicator* and the *APME Update* frequently contain articles dealing with people management including techniques for improving creativity, productivity, and handling difficult employees and managerial situations. Some of the most useful research done on the environment of newsrooms has been initially reported in such trade publications.

Stone, a former RTNDA research director and Missouri professor emeritus, tracked television newsroom demographics during the 1970s and 1980s, including the frequency of news director turnover. News directors are the department heads of television station news operations. Stone found that news directors changed an average of every 2.5 years, with some slight annual fluctuations (RTNDA Survey, 2000; Stone, 1986, 1987, 1992). Papper, of Ball State University, has continued Stone's line of research by doing annual television newsroom surveys that provide insight into the way such environments function. In June 2004, he confirmed that the average life span of a news director at a station has moved up only slightly to 3 years (Papper, personal communication, June 20, 2004).

Typically, when a new manager is brought in, there are staff changes. As people decide to leave, new people are hired, and on-air personalities are adjusted. This contributes to an environment of continual uncertainty and change that can also be perceived as high risk. Stone's last survey, conducted in 1990–1991 found that a majority of local TV newsroom workers, 55%, had less than 3 years tenure at their current station (Stone, 1991). Undoubtedly, career development encourages some movement, but the data imply that when the boss changes, the people tend to change, creating an environment of uncertainty and risk.

By mid-20th century, there was growing interest in how news organizations determined what the public would read, hear, and see. White's (1950) classic study defined so-called gatekeeping or the decision-making process within a newsroom of what to publish. Breed (1955) provided insight into newsroom culture and the way new journalists are imbued with the rights, rituals, and mythology of their profession. For a thorough review of these two seminal works in the journalism field, see Reese and Ballinger (2001). After the Vietnam War ended, television news organizations scurried to find ways to retain audiences without the exciting battlefield footage. News consultants had already established themselves, and they grew to dominate the industry in the attempt to inflate ratings. Powers (1977) investigated the pervasive ways in which news consultants affect every aspect of news operations from the types of stories covered, to news sets, formats, series reports used to spike audiences during ratings periods, and the selection of anchor personnel based on their attractiveness; all of which remain relevant today. In this same period, Gans (1980) studied the three traditional broadcast network news operations, ABC, CBS, and NBC, along with news magazines *Newsweek* and *Time.* Gans articulated for the nonjournalist the normative behavior to which many journalists still idealistically ascribe including an excellent chapter titled "Objectivity, Values, and Ideology" (p. 182).

## News and Information as Business

Newspapers have historically been among the most successful businesses with profit margins typically exceeding 20% a year. Underwood (1995) argued that, despite their financial success, newspapers have increasingly emphasized profits, with an MBA mentality. Audience market research has increased in importance among all media to lure readers, listeners, viewers, and now Internet surfers. Thus, we are living in the age of what McManus (1994) dubbed market-driven journalism. His qualitative study of local television news provided great insight into the creation and packaging of current events information tailored to technical and marketing considerations. Technology dominates the way television stories are conceptualized and manufactured such as "live" introductions of stories actually covered much earlier. The live element is interjected to show off technology and to generate a greater sense of urgency, even though the actual event may have concluded hours before and is included as a prerecorded insert between a live open and close (p. 44).

Bagdikian (2004) documented the steady collapse of mass media ownership into the hands of five dominant conglomerates, Time Warner, Disney, Viacom, News Corporation, and Bertelsmann AG. The economic influences on mass media were his major focus. Bagdikian posed the obvious questions about whether limited ownership of all media with which we engage means limited "voices" in the "marketplace of ideas," and therefore is contrary to the intent of the framers in creating the "free" press clause of the U.S. Constitution. Is there less control of media if, instead of a king, all the power to control the flow of information and news is in the hands of a few corporations? The growth of conglomerate control of American media, combined with McManus' concept of market-driven journalism, against the historical context of the worst excesses in American journalism, causes one to ponder whether what has occurred recently is a new evolution in modern media, or a return to the past. As Emery & Emery (1996) described the 1890s:

> Yellow journalism, at its worst, was the new journalism without a soul. Trumpeting their concern for "the people," yellow journalists at the same time choked up the news channels on which the common people depended with a shrieking, gaudy, sensation-loving, devil-may-care kind of journalism. This turned the high drama of life into a cheap melodrama and led to stories being twisted into the form best suited for sales by the howling newsboy. Worst of all, instead of giving effective leadership, yellow journalism offered a palliative of sin, sex, and violence. (p. 194)

## Creative Media Workers

There is a continuing struggle between the idealism of practicing journalists and the for-profit organizations in which most of them work. Indeed, journalists receive positive benefits from those organizations (e.g., salaries and fringe benefits), and they are able to pursue their desired profession within fairly clear business-oriented parameters.

Media workers are often creative personalities who seek independence and a sense of ownership of their work. Efforts have been made to simplify the task of managing creative people (Loeb, 1995), generating more creativity by raising managerial expectations, thereby fueling the sense of creative employees that management cares about what they are doing (Tierney & Farmer, 2004), and understanding that a sense of empowerment can produce more positive behavior (Thomas & Velthouse, 1990). Research into the effect of both job-related and outside influences found creative performance is enhanced when the person has a sense of support in both sectors (Madjar, Oldham, & Pratt, 2002). Additionally, the environment of the organization needs to provide enough psychological space for creative people to come up with new ideas and to test them. When daily pressure to accomplish tasks is the focus, it can dampen creativity because the message is sent that thinking beyond the immediate task is not valued (Dickson, 2003). Ettema and Whitney (1982) brought together 13 perspectives on *Individuals in Mass Media*

*Organizations: Creativity and Constraint*, which address the inherent conflicts in mass media production within the context of a capitalist system. The conflicts they identified 2 decades ago appear to be increasing as media companies become more economically powerful (Bagdikian, 2004).

To many media workers, the organization is a kind of funding source, with a medical and benefits package, to pursue their creative interests. You can be paid to write, shoot still or video pictures, and/or perform in front of a camera. This sets up a not uncommon situation where a creative, idealistic journalist works for a pragmatic business concern focused on circulation (or ratings) and profit. The tension produced by such contrasting values appears inherent to the production of news and information, as Edward R. Murrow asserted a half century ago:

> One of the basic troubles with radio and television news is that both instruments have grown up as an incompatible combination of show business, advertising and news. Each of the three is a rather bizarre and demanding profession. And when you get all three under one roof, the dust never settles. (Sperber, 1986, p. xvi)

Numerous works have been published to cast light on the inside world of journalism. These are particularly useful for researchers in human relations in media organizations because they often focus on people within the context of the events they covered and include a subtext of perceptions of what journalism is, or in the authors' minds, should be. These range from critical works pointing out many of the problems in news and information work (e.g., Burns, 1993; Goldberg, 2002; Graham, 1990; Willis, 2003), to autobiographical efforts by celebrity journalists that often produce significant sales when released because of public curiosity about major news personalities (e.g., Brinkley, 1995; Brokaw, 2002; Kuralt, 1990; Rather, 1977). Other works range from journalistic narratives of the evolution of dominant networks (Slater, 1988), to well-researched biographies of significant figures in the history of mass media (e.g., Johnston, 2003; Sperber, 1986). Such works often provide a reporter's perspective of the sweep of historical events, how coverage was managed, and the philosophical struggles of the individuals involved.

Thus, the give and take that goes on in news operations—between journalistic principles and ethics, and monetary and technical considerations in determining coverage—is available to those who have never had the experience of working within such a context. As in anthropological research, it is one thing to use a survey instrument to gather qualitative data about a tribe, and quite another to live with a tribe for a period of time to learn the nuances of its rights, rituals, and context of meaning.

The context of media endeavor directly affects the human relations process. Differences occur in values and attitudes of media workers, depending on the industry sector being considered. A major issue in one media sector may not be important in another. In one area, the point may be to create illusion, fiction, and drama; in another type of media organization the goal may be to manage the image of something for a more favorable vantage point (i.e., spin); in still another type of media organization, such approaches would be major violations of ethics and considered abhorrent activities subjecting the person to firing or forced resignation in disgrace. For example, within traditional news organizations, at the newsroom level, there tends to be a working journalist perception of "a calling, not just a job" (Auletta, 1991, p. 559). However, at the organizational level, "the content of media outlets is developed to attract a specifically defined target audience, just as manufacturers create products designed to attract a target segment of consumers" (Wicks et al., 2004, p. 217). The ideal of informing the public, as part of the individual's calling may come into conflict with organizational goals to maximize ratings by pandering to marketing studies of what the audience *wants* while paying little attention to what the audience may *need*. This is a reaffirmation of the observation of Liebling (1961/1981) who observed that, "Freedom of the press is guaranteed only to those who own one" (p. 32).

Media are at once highly creative with increasing technology to manufacture images that appear real, while at the same time, confronted with a responsibility to be accurate, fair, and honest in serving the needs of society. Although flipping a photograph over to have the person in it look the other direction for layout considerations may be perfectly fine in advertising, in news that would be a firing offense because it would not be the same person, but an illusion. Indeed, in many aspects of media the specific individual is the critical element contributing to their success.

> A Sheryl Crow song covered by someone else isn't the same song, *Nightline* with Ted Koppel is recognizably different from other TV news and public affairs shows. What makes them different are individual differences among their creators—differences in talent, creativity, energy, and a host of other "individual difference" variables—the interests, values, gender and ethnicities of the individuals creating them. (Grossberg, Wartella & Whitney, 1998, p. 60)

## THE CONTEMPORARY MEDIA MANAGEMENT ENVIRONMENT

Understanding the operating context of contemporary media organizations is critical for researchers working in this area. Media organizations are sometimes thought of in the idealistic terms of the First Amendment with a view that the role of the press is to inform the public about important issues of the day. However, the reality of media organization endeavors is a clash between the aforementioned idealism and the reality of highly profitable businesses seeking to maximize return on investment in a conglomerate-dominated world. Much of what is covered by the media involves the attempt to maximize circulation or ratings. Failure to fully understand the economic engine of media organizations, which directly affects the behavior of media managers and employees, may produce incomplete or misinterpreted research.

As discussed elsewhere in this Handbook, the contemporary media context is radically different from what existed in the mid-20th century, and it continues to evolve worldwide with new technologies and audience fragmentation altering media economics and ownership (Albarran & Chan-Olmsted, 1998). Current media audience trends and analyses of issues of concern to the public and working journalists are available through The Project for Excellence in Journalism. It has launched what is planned to be an annual survey and analysis of contemporary American media trends. The inaugural report was published on the Internet in spring 2004 with free access to the public (State of the News Media, 2004). Economic and technology change pose enormous challenges for media funded primarily by mass advertising. To maintain profit margins, media businesses have coalesced into increasingly larger megacorporations that feature combined functions to take advantage of economies of scale. Thus, rather than a growing diversity of media forms fostering an increasingly diverse "marketplace of ideas" with highly varied programming, just the reverse has occurred. There is a kind of sameness of a handful of basic program offerings (former network reruns, movie services, sports, interview programs positioned as "news" product, music entertainment) with a striking similarity of content (Bagdikian, 2004).

To be a media manager at the beginning of the 21st century is to be a person caught in the middle: at the place where the pragmatic business focus on cost and profit collides with the idealism of creativity and working in an art form. For example, journalism, which is a significant part of media activity within a thriving democracy, rose to inform the public as a counter to governmental controls (Emery, Emery, & Roberts, 2000). However, even in the United States, where the concept of a free press was written into the Constitution, there has always been a strange relationship with the media ideal and the forces of the marketplace. When marketing studies designed to increase audience shares for advertisers drive the journalistic content, the free press vision of the framers of the Constitution is redefined, arguably, as just another form of commercial speech. In all Western model media embracing an "inform the public" ideal, there is tension between the business side and the creative side. Typically, the business side creates a set of walls of economic reality that do restrict the creative side to some degree, but within those walls media idealists are allowed considerable freedom. Each side tends to see the other as a necessary encumbrance. Advertising is the primary funding mechanism for the buildings, paper, ink, electricity, people, and other technology it takes to produce modern media in their many forms. This often means a preference for highly visual, fast-paced, simplistic, positive, and easy-to-comprehend content over the complex and seriously analytical. It is a marriage of information and entertainment into what is increasingly referred to as "infotainment" (Redmond, 2004). As mid-20th century newspaper columnist A. J. Liebling (1961/1981) so aptly put it, "The function of the press in society is to inform. But its role is to make money" (p. 6). The news or entertainment that makes it through the conduit of media in such a system is increasingly designed to deliver audience shares than to develop greater public understanding of complex issues.

## Media Managers Caught in the Middle

The media manager is a representative of the working journalist to the corporate world, and at the same time the representative of corporate back to the world of writers, photographers, and other creative professionals. All media managers operate under substantial stress in a highly competitive environment. The demands of the job, across media types, generally include implementing market research, selecting and motivating staffs, supervising media content, and managing budgetary issues with seemingly continuous pressure to trim budgets because of declining audience shares that focus owners and managers on the financial bottom line (Flander, 1986; Stone, 1992; Warner, 1998). Because of the nature of media work, and the clash of ideals and economic reality that frame it in the western model, those who manage these organizations

> must be extraordinarily strong in communicating a vision; they are, after all, speaking to employees who make their living by resisting spin and seeking truth. It takes a lot to inspire them. But even as they are trained to be skeptics, journalists, at their core, are idealists. They want leaders with visions. They follow those who creatively and honestly articulate it. (Geisler, 2000, p. 2)

## Media Organization Design Conflict

Media organizations are a combination of two organizational forms that are distinctly different. This squares the difficulty of managing them. Organizational structuralists have developed a characterization of these typologies as *machine* and *professional* organizations with specific attributes (Mintzberg, 1989; Walton, 1981).

On the one hand, media organizations are machine in that they have assembly lines with strict deadlines and involved processes that must be done in order, with speed, and with repetition. Everything is tightly controlled and meshed together like a set of gears, working according to Morgan's (1997, p. 13) machine organization metaphor: "They are designed like machines, and their employees are in essence expected to behave as if they were parts of the machine. . . . Organizations that are designed and operated as if they were machines are now usually called bureaucracies."

On the other hand, media organizations are also professional environments where employees have considerable creative control of their work. Media workers are typically more highly educated and do work that is full of judgment calls (Mintzberg, 1989). They tend to see their work in altruistic terms, as a higher calling, and to think of the product as their personal property even though the media organization owns the copyright. So you have factory workers—laboring under tight production line schedules—who are in many respects creative professionals with considerable individual control over their work, similar to doctors and lawyers. The *quality* of what is produced depends on *them* more than on the technology they use. The difference between merely doing *acceptable* work and striving for *exceptional* achievement is held closely within the hearts and minds of media workers, regardless of the machine context of the assembly line on which they work.

Among media workers, journalists, for example, have a kind of duality of expectancy in the workplace. On the one hand, they need freedom to develop ideas and make decisions, retaining a sense of personal achievement that is critical to their creative side. On the other hand, journalists typically have a strong need for feedback, including frequent personal communication with those who manage them directly. It is a kind of independence—dependence dichotomy where the loss of either side of the relationship can lead to discontent (Hansen, Neuzil, & Ward, 1997).

## MEDIA ORGANIZATIONS ARE HUMAN COLLECTIVES

It is important for researchers to consider the psychology of the media organization workplace. Media organizations are human collectives with considerable diversity in the way individuals frame their values and purpose in life. Unpacking those values, both organizationally and individually, is vital to more fully understanding the dynamics within those organizations and explaining both organizational and individual behavior.

The complexity of human interaction with the operating environment has been the focus of considerable research on motivation and organizational efficiency dependent on the individual members who make up the collective known as an organization. Various content theorists, such as Maslow (1954/1970), Herzberg, Mausner, and Synderman (1959), and Alderfer (1972), attempted to reconcile the external world to internal motivational considerations within the individual.

Bandura (1986) proposed a *social cognitive theory* in which the human being is seen as the junction of complex knowledge, perception, and desire strands, which are all affected by the particular environment at hand:

> In the social cognitive view people are neither driven by inner forces nor automatically shaped and controlled by external stimuli. Rather, human functioning is explained in terms of a model of triadic reciprocality in which behavior, cognitive and other personal factors, and environmental events all operate as interacting determinants of each other. (p. 18)

Bandura's *triadic reciprocality* is the view that the way we act (behavior), our knowledge acquisition (cognitive) processes and other personal factors, and the environment within which all of this occurs fold together interactively to create individualized meaning. Our personality and our way of engaging with the world around us cannot be separated into neat categories presumed to be mutually exclusive and unaffected by the others. All are contributors to, and products of, one another. This helps explain media industry workers who, while working within the context of a machine-like company, still retain a sense of professional independence and control over their work. Many media workers, particularly in creative areas, consider what they do as personalized (important and owned by them), not corporatized (merely something they do for the company to get money).

Several things come into play from Bandura's social cognitive theory. A *self-regulatory capability* allows individuals to govern much of their behavior by "internal standards and self-evaluative reactions to their own actions" (Bandura, 1986, p. 20). Additionally, there is a "capability for reflective self-consciousness," wherein people "think about their own thought processes" (p. 21). We are also "enactive learners" where our observations of what goes on, and the experiences we build up over time, exert strong influence on our decision making. When people have an outcome they particularly desire, they tend to use their organization or group experience to decide what action to take to attain it.

As the perceptions of threats, rewards, expected outcomes, and social learning come together in the human dynamic, we carefully watch for signals that predict the outcomes we desire. When we see those signals, we are positively reinforced that we're on track. But when we don't get those signals, or we get signals we don't expect, fear may escalate as we worry about how things will turn out (Bandura, 1986, p. 205).

## Media Culture and Climate Factors

Media organizations tend to be highly developed cultures with distinctive codes of behavior that, when violated, cause great turmoil (Jenkins, 2003). Thus, to understand a media organization you need to understand both its culture and climate.

Organizational culture is the framework of rituals, practices, and behavior patterns that set an organization apart. Schein (1985) defined it as the

> pattern of basic assumptions that a given group has invented, discovered, or developed in learning to cope with its problems of external adaptation and internal integration, which have worked well enough to be considered valid and, therefore, to be taught to new members as the correct way to perceive, think, and feel in relation to those problems. (p. 9)

As such, culture is an acquired knowledge base that evolves within the organization as it resolves problems and adapts to its environment. An organization's culture is wrapped up within its history, procedures, and people, and it is the fundamental definition of the organization and its purpose. At the same time, it is interconnected to its external environment as both continually evolve. (For a discussion of the concept of organizational culture see Eisenberg & Riley, 2000.)

Organizational climate is defined by Poole (1985) as, "collective beliefs, expectations, and values regarding communication, and is generated in interaction around organizational practices via a continuous process of structuration" (p. 107). For purposes of this discussion, think of organizational climate as the atmosphere of a company. This organizational weather system swirls through every corner of an organization, "continually interacting and evolving with organizational processes, structured around common organizational practices" (Falcione et al., 1987, p. 203). If organizational culture is thought of as the entity's personality, organizational climate is the current of emotional fluctuations that ebb and flow within it. The personality is more stable, defined, and therefore allows prediction. But the climate side is more variable and can be altered more quickly by sudden changes in the operating environment. It can have a profound effect on organizational performance because it "serves as a frame of reference for member activity and therefore shapes members' expectancies, attitudes, and behaviors; through these effects it influences organizational outcomes such as performance, satisfaction, and morale" (p. 96).

Research demonstrated that strong organizational cultures can have a positive impact on performance. Juechter et al. (1998) found clear relationships between the strength of an organizational culture and bottom line financial performance. Companies with a strong culture tend to have, among other things, wider involvement of organizational members in strategy development, lower than average turnover, significant investment in training and personnel development within the organization, and greater financial success (Garmager & Shemmer, 1998; Levy & Levy, 2000). However, when media organizations are combined strictly for initial financial benefit, the differences in the respective organizational structures, cultures, and climates may prove unwieldy causing substantial loss in overall effectiveness. Such a case was the much publicized AOL–Time Warner merger that quickly spun off billions in losses for investors as managers struggled to restructure the conglomerate (Rosenbloom, 2004).

Some organizations approach changes in the environment defensively, resisting making internal adjustments in the way they do things, whereas others seem to seek adaptive strategies readily. What makes the difference is the propensity of the particular corporate culture to depart from tradition in order "to replace existing methods with more productive ones" (Kanter, 1988, p. 406). However, this is often a very complex problem because of traditional ways of doing things, large and small. Grove (1988) termed *organizational inertia* that which is generated "when the day-to-day protocols and procedures of a company get in the way of employees trying to do their jobs (p. 418)." Grove asserts such inertia is more prevalent over time and that "the older and bigger an organization, the more inertia it will tend to have" (p. 418). When a new management approach is implemented that does not sync with what the organizational culture is prepared to embrace, serious dysfunction can result (Robertson, 2003). Indeed, when a change agent is brought in, the effort to rejuvenate an organization can backfire, unless existing organizational dynamics are considered (Paulson, 2003).

Mackenzie (1991) saw organizations as "complex living systems of interdependent processes, resources and people" that must work in concert to adapt to a constantly changing, dynamic environment (p. 51). Those organizations that can achieve a high level of internal compatibility have a competitive edge because they eliminate much of what stymies organizations with weaker cultures. When traditional bureaucratic layering of position and power permeate an organization, there is rigidity in adjustment to change and a kind of myopia of management based on past practices, which hinder adaptation. This results in managers relying on past experience to make future decisions. However, when the conditions of the marketplace have changed, the decisions will be flawed. Indeed, "organizations, like organisms, are 'open' to their environment and must achieve an appropriate relation with that environment if they are to survive" (Morgan, 1997, p. 39)

A media organization example of this occurred as Cap Cities was finalizing its takeover of the ABC network in late 1985. The top executives at Cap Cities grew impatient with then-ABC president Fred Pierce, a career employee of the network. At the time, audience fragmentation, which was due to cable and other television alternatives to the broadcast networks, was just beginning. However, while Cap Cities executives grew increasingly wary of the way ABC was spending money, the network president continued justifying his actions by concentrating on the bright spots in the network efforts and ignoring the accelerating overall financial erosion. Cap Cities chair Tom Murphy, and chief operating officer Dan Burke, finally decided to replace Pierce. The symptom was continuing financial erosion of the network, but the underlying cause of Pierce's increasing ineffectiveness was summed up by Burke, who said, "Fred was a hostage to his experience." It was discovered later that Pierce had even put a psychic on the ABC payroll to advise him on programming the network (Auletta, 1991, p. 114).

The case of the major television network reaction to new technology was an example of how organizations can become what Morgan (1997) termed *psychic prisons*. He defined these as a playing out of the classic Plato's Cave metaphor, wherein Socrates tells of inhabitants unable to cope with a different world outside the cave and thereby "tighten their grip on their familiar way of seeing." As Morgan points out, like the ancient cave dwellers from classic literature, "organizations and their members become trapped by constructions of reality that, at best, give an imperfect grasp on the world" (p. 216). Morgan also uses a brain metaphor, asserting that organizations, like human brains, are communication and information processing systems that develop personalities. They harbor a kind of corporate rationale and psyche that can drive them in positive or negative directions with a collective consciousness. Thus, organizations can learn and adapt. However, to do so, the "learning organization" cannot be trapped by mechanized bureaucracy but must "scan and anticipate change," while at the same time, it can "develop an ability to question, challenge and change operating norms and assumptions" (p. 90).

## Dealing With Perceptions

### Interpretation of Meaning

It is very important to understand that individual, "pre-formed frames of interpretation" decode message meaning based on personal experience (McQuail, 1987, p. 243). In other words, people interpret the messages they receive and evaluate what is *true* based on their belief system. Burke (1966) called these filters through which we interpret reality "terministic screens" that work similarly to photographic filters; they alter the color, contrast, and warmth of messages we receive, if not the basic facts of the message itself.

This means we are set up to believe something, based on past experience or trusted sources. Thus, rumors containing false information may quickly gain credibility as they are passed from one person to another. They take on a life of their own. Once widespread, they are very difficult to reverse because they become part of the *received truth*, acquired from others whom the person trusts. When information is restricted, the work culture creates its own information. Sometimes management has very good reasons for not disclosing things. However, unless information is kept confidential for competitive or legal reasons, all restricting information flow does is feed the rumor mill. When organizational members are concerned about something, the rumor mill starts up because, "in general, rumors are grounded in a combination of uncertainty and anxiety" (Stohl & Redding, 1987, p. 481). Employees worry and develop scenarios of what they think is probably happening. Then they pass those around, and, in the process, the illusions gain credibility. Thus, it is vital that managers have open lines of communication with organizational members to get continual feedback on their perceptions and to provide accurate information to diffuse the rumor mill (Rosnow, 1980; Watson, 1982).

Media managers serve a multiplicity of communicative roles. They monitor the various information channels available, disseminate the information to others, and serve as spokespersons for various factions within the organization, and often externally as organizational representatives to those outside (Trujillo, 1983). Whatever is communicated, or not communicated, by a media manager has an effect. "People want to know what the problem is, why they are being asked to do certain things, how they relate to the larger picture" (Gardner, 1988, p. 224).

Human beings tend to filter meaning relative to their basic beliefs. According to selective influence theory we sift out that with which we have less fundamental agreement. In other words, we pay more attention to that with which we agree, while discounting or ignoring that with which we disagree (DeFleur & Ball-Rokeach, 1989).

When something comes up, we naturally compare it, consciously or unconsciously, with what we have experienced before. This means we tend to look at new problems and new solutions within the context of old problems and old solutions. This happened in the American network television industry beginning in 1980. Where formerly there were tight controls by the government and very few networks, there quickly evolved a myriad of competitors at the national level with concurrent significant decline in governmental control. The result was what one critic termed, "an earthquake in slow motion" (Auletta, 1991, p. 4). As discussed earlier, because of the rise of new technology, and a radicalization of the operating environment, the old solutions simply failed. Media organizations continue to struggle with this. It is natural, in one sense, to do what worked in the past. However, with the environment undergoing rapid technological change, this is a trap that can lead to serious decline and, potentially, organizational death (Whetten, 1988).

### Equity, Expectancy and Malicious Compliance

How people perceive the fairness of their world, and what they expect it to provide, are major determinants of what they do and how they do it. We all make adjustments in our daily lives, our personal relationships, and our careers that depend on how we think things will turn out. We try to do what we hope will move matters toward a positive outcome and avoid what we fear will fail. We learn to anticipate various types of consequences from actions that are taken and the results they produce.

This area of organizational dynamics is important for those who want to be effective managers. By anticipating subordinates' sense of fairness and expectation, managers can set in motion opportunities for both personal and organizational growth. Ingersoll (1896/1980) once said, "In nature there are neither rewards nor punishments—there are consequences" (p. 615). Everything is a consequence of something else. As a result, it is clear that, to affect what consequences occur, we need to look for causes. Equity and expectancy are causal factors for many behavioral consequences in media organizations.

The basic assumption in equity theory (Adams, 1963) is that workers compare their tasks and rewards with the tasks and rewards of those around them. They then develop perceptions of whether they are fairly treated based on that comparison (Harder, 1991). Such perceptions may or may not be based on accurate information and analysis by the individual.

Tied into the issue of equity is expectancy theory, originally advanced by Vroom (1964). From our knowledge and experiences, we expect things to happen based on what we do. In other words, a certain type of behavior is expected to produce a predictable outcome. If you rob a bank and are caught, you can expect to go to prison. If you study hard, you expect to earn a good grade. Expectancy has a big effect on us when coupled with rewards we desire. People balance their personal values and anticipated rewards all the time, continually adjusting their performance to achieve the outcomes they desire. When people operate from an expectancy perspective, they have linear logic that says, "If I work harder, I will do a better job. If I do a better job, I will be rewarded."

An important aspect of maintaining equity and keeping expectancies realistic is using different rewards for different people. This is particularly important in media management because of the diverse nature of media employees and their tendency to feel personal ownership in their work (Geisler, 1999). Research demonstrated that recognition and a sense of accomplishment are preferred by many people to monetary rewards (Hellstrom & Hellstrom, 2002). Typically pay becomes a right, in a person's mind, within a relatively short time following a raise. Thus, pay is often merely the basic reason to show up for work rather than being perceived as a reward for doing that work well. So the reward effect of a raise is of limited duration and not automatically an incentive to work harder (Fournies, 2000). However, for a single mother with serious day care problems, flexibility in work hours can be a long-term motivator. One individual may seek overtime, but another person may prefer compensatory time off for extra hours he or she puts in. Media managers need to focus on the personalized environment within which people toil and the benefits they personally value. When a manager makes it apparent he or she cares about people and recognizes their needs, there is a positive effect throughout the work environment (Tulgan, 2000). Regardless of a person's position in the organizational hierarchy, there is a need to feel appreciated and have good work recognized. Such recognition can take many forms (Fournies).

When people do not believe things are equitable, or their expectancies are not realized, they move to restore the balance. They may slow down, reduce the quality of their work, or take other measures to get even for what they perceive is unfair (Harder, 1991). Taken to the extreme a syndrome called *malicious compliance* may result (Kennedy, 1992; Mariotti, 1996; Maurer, 1998). It is, in simple terms, doing the job well enough so it looks as if you are a *team member*, but in such a way you really are trying to harm the organization. Malicious compliance occurs when people do their job to the worst of their abilities, but only to the degree they won't get caught. Usually, it is a conscious effort, but sometimes it can be an unconscious reaction to negative feelings that build up toward management. It can be manifested in little things such as throwing away perfectly good pens to increase the cost of supplies or stopping work 30 minutes before your shift ends and just socializing while waiting to leave. It can grow into major attacks on the organization such as working to bring in a union, sending confidential information to competitors, or doing something to trigger investigations by the news media or regulatory authorities. In entrenched, large bureaucracies a typical technique is simply to do everything according to the bureaucratic rules that everyone has found ways to circumvent. The organization slows down very quickly. It can be caused by personal grudges, or, in the case of deeply committed media workers, by a sense the organization has "sold out" to generating a profit and is no longer committed to the ideals of journalism (Redmond, 2004). It is important to note that, "where an organization is going is not where someone says it is going but where its internal behavioral processes actually take it" (Schneider, 1983, p. 34).

## Effective Goal Setting as a Motivational Tool

Goal-based management has become endemic to American organizational culture. It is as if we don't know how to work without having goals set for us that we are then under significant pressure to attain (Gibson, Ivancevich, & Donnelly, 1997). Effective goal setting takes "hard thinking and hard work" (Fiorina et al., 2003, p. 41). When used correctly, goal setting builds motivation, provides direction, and blends communication flows from the bottom up, as well as the top down (Lucas, 1999; Nicholson, 2003).

Organizations use goal setting to maintain competitiveness and involve organizational members in continuous adaptation and improvement (Humphreys, 2003; Levinson, 2003). Goals must include the following to be effective: (a) relevance to the individual, (b) reliability as a measure over time, (c) discrimination between good and poor performers, and (d) practical application for the organization (Gibson et al., 1997).

Additionally, very specific, relatively short-term goals are more effective than broad, long-term ones. People respond positively to what's known as a *small-wins* strategy (Whetten & Cameron, 1995). Cutting large tasks into small, manageable pieces helps prevent frustration and gives people the sense things are moving along.

A major problem in goal setting is that both employer and employee have different ideas about appropriate goals, based on their individual motivations, values, and biases (Nicholson, 2003). To be maximally effective, goals must be set and accomplished in partnership with management and subordinates. Both sides have to buy-in to the goals, have a sense of ownership of them, have a clear idea of how the goal benefits them directly and/or personally, and have mutual responsibility for carrying them out (Denning, 1998; Humphreys, 2003; Lucas, 1999).

## Building "Stakeholder" Relationships

One of the most effective ways to increase media workers' dedication is to help them increase the perception of themselves as *stakeholders* in the success of the organization. Drucker (1988) coined the term to describe organizational members who are, in effect, psychological part owners. They see the success of the organization and their success tied together. When this occurs, a cause–effect relationship is developed that benefits both. However, a critical element in stakeholder development is building trust. In order for employees to buy into the organization as mutually beneficial partners, they have to have a sense of commitment from both management and their peers. However, this is particularly difficult when the operational environment is under stress.

Conflict is inherent in creative organizations, and people voicing different views and ideas contribute to innovation and adaptation (Sutton, 2002). Optimistic attitudes have been shown to foster greater creativity and innovation in the workplace, with a more relaxed environment bonding employees to one another and to the organization. In contrast, pessimistic attitudes tend to evolve in highly controlled, autocratic environments where the *bully syndrome* (also known as the *emperor's new clothes syndrome*) of management is common (Bolman & Deal, 1991; Logan et al., 2003). It is vital that managers encourage championing of new ideas and risk taking by subordinates to be effective in the contemporary media organization environment, which depends on innovation, creativity, and adaptability.

## Maintaining Managerial Presence While Encouraging Individual Creativity

### MBWA—Management by Walking Around

In media organizations creative people require trust relationships to be most effective. They are often wary of new managers, and it takes time to break down the natural defense mechanisms. The best way to do this is to understand the people in the organization fully and ensure they understand their managers. One of the most effective approaches is for managers to be highly visible and connect with the employees personally. The phrase that is used for that is *management by walking around*, or MBWA (Peters & Waterman,

1982). Some management consultants believe up to half a manager's time should be spent wandering around observing the work process. However, too many managers become prisoners of their offices dealing with bureaucratic and organizational clutter (Taylor, 1994).

As in all things involving management, there is a right way and a wrong way to practice MBWA. It cannot be done at the same time every day, or the manager will see the same few people and the same work processes at the same point. Managerial appearances have to be highly variable and unpredictable (Hopkins-Doerr, 1989).

This gets managers out among those working at frequent, unscheduled times (How to Successfully Practice MBWA, 1994). Too often when people become managers, they are given an office and are then trapped in it by the various organizational clutter that comes with being responsible for weekly reports to those higher up the management chain. Managers have to get out from behind their desks into the daily life of those they manage (Eckert, 2001). They need to be part of the ongoing atmosphere in order to design more effective ways of accomplishing the work (Zahniser, 1994).

It is imperative that, when managers move among subordinates, they know a little bit about them. For example, if you walk up to a person and ask, "How's the family?" to begin a little dialog, and that person is single, you may be perceived as a manipulator. It is vital the MBWA manager comes across as caring and involved with subordinates on their level including a personalized, friendly approach (Fournies, 2000). It does not mean a manager should be "your employee's best friend, or forgiving bad performance. . . . Friendliness means the little things you might think of as politeness and respect" (p. 94).

## Managing Yourself

One of the most difficult things for any leader or manager to achieve is life balance. Bennis and Nanus (1985) call this *deployment of self*. It is not uncommon for a person to be swept up by a career and see it as an end in itself. In contemporary American culture, a strong work ethic and dedication to the job are much admired attributes. However, our culture also has serious problems with divorce as well as alcoholism and other substance abuse. Personal lives are as challenging to manage as are our professional lives.

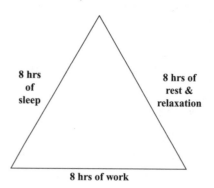

FIG. 6.1.   Triangle of a balanced life.
*Note.* From *Balancing on the wire: The Art of Managing Media Organizations* (p. 196), by J. Redmond, 2004, Cincinnati, OH: Atomic Dog. Copyright 2004 by Atomic Dog Publishing. Reprinted with permission.

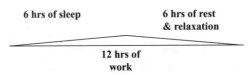

FIG. 6.2.   Twelve hour work day triangle.

*Note.* From *Balancing on the Wire: The Art of Managing Media Organizations* (p. 197), by J. Redmond, 2004, Cincinnati, OH: Atomic Dog. Copyright 2004 by Atomic Dog Publishing. Reprinted with permission.

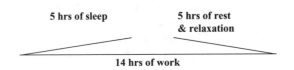

FIG. 6.3.   Fourteen hour work day triangle.

*Note.* From *Balancing on the Wire: The Art of Managing Media Organizations* (p. 198), by J. Redmond, 2004, Cincinnati, OH: Atomic Dog. Copyright 2004 by Atomic Dog Publishing. Reprinted with permission.

When people become obsessive about their work, they often fail to get enough sleep, or they don't sleep well. They tend to cut back on their extracurricular activities, becoming one-dimensional. Eventually their energy is eroded, their decisions become flawed (partly because of fatigue, both physical and mental), and failure becomes the ultimate price.

One of the best ways to keep life in balance is to understand it in the metaphor of the equilateral triangle. As is shown in Fig. 6.1, an equilateral triangle has equal length sides and equal angles. If each side has 8 units, you can see that they add up to 24, the hours in the day. Think of the baseline as 8 hours of work. You need a job to provide the support for everything else. The left side of the triangle is hours of sleep. The right side is the hours spent getting ready in the morning, commuting, relaxing with family, or pursuing outside interests and hobbies. So, along with 8 hours of work and 8 hours of sleep in a balanced life, you have 8 hours for rest, relaxation, and refreshing your perspective on what life, career, and those around you are all about (Redmond, 2004).

When you start working long hours, cutting back sleep, and not making time for yourself, life gets out of balance. Two other figures depict this scenario. Figure 6.2 shows a 12-hour work day. You can see that it squashes down, so there is little depth to the person's existence. In effect, this person works so much that trying to keep up is a constant struggle.

Figure 6.3 shows what happens when a person works more than 12 hours a day. There's not enough time left to get enough sleep, or have a life. So, there's a gap. This is where all the bad things happen: depression, alcoholism, drugs, divorce, etc. The feeling that comes over a person is like the title of an early 1980s movie, "I'm Dancing as Fast as I Can," and there's no keeping up. This is a person headed for a wreck in his career, personal life, or probably both.

It is possible, for relatively short durations, to be out of balance. Students get out of balance during finals week, professionals have those periods of brief crisis when they simply have to work long hours and there's no avoiding it. However, when it becomes *normal* and extends into years, managers can become burned out and lose effectiveness.

## SUMMARY

In sum, each of us has different experiences and knowledge that provide the foundation of our future development. The effective manager of media organizations understands that human relations is a key factor in effectiveness because of the reliance on creative people who tend to have a sense of ownership and pride in their work and see it as a reflection of themselves.

Media organizations are where the creative process collides with pragmatic business concerns. If not carefully managed, a media organization, depending on creative excellence, can quickly lose the competitive edge necessary to fend off competition in a highly volatile operating environment. That may occur when the overriding business concerns, or the focus on them, are allowed to dampen individual creativity on which the media organization depends.

Malicious compliance may be triggered by managerial lack of knowledge about, or sensitivity to, the ideals of creative workers. The wise manager understands the creative worker controls much of the quality of the thing being created, whether it is award winning or merely mundane. Being a manager in such an environment is a process of constant growth, learning, and maturing through experience and self-examination. In human relations in media organizations, the situation is always variable, the environment dynamic, and the creative individuals at work emotion laden and idealistic to one degree or another.

## SUGGESTIONS FOR FURTHER RESEARCH

In conclusion, most of the research into mass media, particularly mass media forms such as journalism, is quantitative. Although there is scholarship that is qualitative in nature, it is sparse compared to the quantitative research that has been published. This is a serious gap in our efforts to understand not just the structures and functions of media organizations but the human element within them—often driven by emotions that may not be reflected in numerical measures of circulation, actual content published or broadcast, or even analysis of how something like newsworthiness is defined. Analyzing newsworthiness on the basis of what is aired in television station newscasts does not tell us what kinds of arguments, employee resistance, and/or capitulation to autocratic consultants and managers may be at work, or not at work, within the newsroom.

We need to build a comprehensive body of research on the reality of the life of being a media worker and how that may warp perspectives. Media workers tend to be creative personalities often obsessed with their work as a calling. Most newspaper and television people, if they are successful, work afternoons and nights. They have great difficulty being "normal" people attending soccer games, parent–teacher conferences, and the like. We don't know enough about what media professionals' lives do to them. They may suffer higher incidents of personal problems—as other shift workers do. What are the long-term effects of the high stress, deadline-driven nature of their world? Are the media companies trading on dedicated employees and, in the process, contributing to problems both sociological and psychological in nature? Are those companies going to great lengths to help their employees with strong support and a nurturing environment? Do most newspaper and television people who begin their careers, change careers or stay to retirement?

We need more of an anthropological–sociological approach to understanding the culture of media workers. One problem is that this is very difficult. It is no simple task, for example, to gain access to do participant observation research in a television newsroom. Station managers and news directors are typically hesitant to provide open access without knowing, and trusting, the researcher. Is this because their high turnover rates keep them always feeling at risk, and they are thus wary of outsiders seeing what really goes on? Or is it because having a nontribal member asking questions about the dance will disturb the rhythm?

In one sense we may be trapped by our own predisposition in many journals for numbers. Statistics are always impressive. Another factor may be that qualitative research is often very time consuming, and, when an academic is trying to build a dossier toward tenure and/or promotion, numbers count. Yet, the reality is that we don't know enough about the *quality* of the career experience of media workers. The quality of the career experience may have significant bearing on how media workers perceive the world, cover it, reflect on it, and write about it.

## REFERENCES

Adams, J. S. (1963). Toward an understanding of equity. *Journal of Abnormal and Social Psychology, 67,* 422–436.

Akgun, A. E., Lynn, G. S., & Byrne, J. C. (2003). Organizational learning: A socio-cognitive framework. *Human Relations, 56,* 839–868. Retrieved June 28, 2004, from ABI/INFORM database: http://proquest.umi.com

Albarran, A., & Arrese, A. (2003). *Time and media markets.* Mahwah, NJ: Lawrence Erlbaum Associates.

Albarran, A., & Chan-Olmsted, S. (Eds.). (1998). *Global media economics: Commercialization, concentration, and integration of world media.* Ames: Iowa State University Press.

Alderfer, C. (1972). *Existence, relatedness, and growth: Human needs in organizational settings.* New York: Free Press.

Anderson, H. C. (1949). *The emperor's new clothes: Designed and illustrated by Virginia Lee Burton.* Boston: Houghton Mifflin. (Original fable published by Hans Christian Anderson 1837).

Argyris, C. (1998). Empowerment: The emperor's new clothes. *Harvard Business Review, 76*(3), 98–106.

Auletta, K. (1991). *Three blind mice: How the TV networks lost their way.* New York: Random House.

Bagdikian, B. (2004). *The new media monopoly.* Boston: Beacon Press.

Balestracci, D. (2003). Handling the human side of change. *Quality Progress, 36*(11), 38–45. Retrieved June 28, 2004, from ABI/INFORM database: http://proquest.umi.com

Bandura, A. (1986). *Social foundations of thought and action: A social cognitive theory.* Englewood Cliffs, NJ: Prentice-Hall.

Bennis, W., & Nanus, B. (1985). *Leaders: The strategies for taking charge.* New York: Harper & Row.

Bolman, L., & Deal, T. (1991). *Reframing organizations: Artistry, choice, and leadership.* San Francisco: Jossey-Bass.

Breed, W. (1955). Social control in the newsroom: A functional analysis. *Social Forces, 33,* 326–335.

Brenner, P. M. (1999). Motivating knowledge workers: The role of the workplace. *Quality Progress, 32*(1), 33–37.

Brief, A., & Weiss, H. (2002). Organizational behavior: Affect in the workplace. *Annual Review of Psychology, 53,* 279–307. Retrieved June 7, 2004, from InfoTrac OneFile database: http://infotrac.galegroup.com

Brinkley, D. (1995). *David Brinkley: 11 presidents, 4 wars, 22 political conventions, 1 moon landing, 3 assassinations, 2,000 weeks of news and other stuff on television and 18 years of growing up in North Carolina.* New York: Knopf.

Brokaw, T. (2002). *A long way from home: Growing up in the American heartland.* New York: Random House.

Burke, K. (1966). *Language as symbolic action: Essays on life, literature and method.* Berkeley, CA: University of California Press.

Burns, E. (1993). *Broadcast blues: Dispatches from the twenty-year war between a television reporter and his medium.* New York: HarperCollins.

Clark, J. M. (2003). Academics tout "social capital" as latest thing in strategic HR. *HR Magazine, 48*(2), 38.

DeFleur, M. L., & Ball-Rokeach, S. (1989). *Theories of mass communication* (5th ed.). New York: Longman.

Denning, S. L. (1998). *The practice of workplace participation: Management–employee relations at three participatory firms.* Westport, CT: Quorum Books.

Dickson, J. V. (2003). Killing creativity: How unspoken sentiments affect workplace creativity. *The Journal for Quality and Participation, 26*(2), 40.

Dobson, S. (2003). Executives decry lack of innovation. *Marketing Magazine, 108*(3), 2.

Drucker, P. (1988). Management: The problems of success. In J. Gibson, J. Ivancevich, & J. Donnelly, Jr. (Eds.), *Organizations close-up: A book of readings* (6th ed.; pp. 4–15). Plano, TX: Business Publications.

Druskak, V., & Pesconsolido, A. (2002). The content of effective teamwork mental models in self-managing teams: Ownership, learning and heedful interrelating. *Human Relations, 55,* 283–314. Retrieved June 7, 2004, from InfoTrac OneFile database: http://infotrac.galegroup.com

Eckert, R. A. (2001). Where leadership starts. *Harvard Business Review, 79*(10), 53–60.

Eisenberg, E. M., & Riley, P. (2000). Organizational culture. In F. M. Jablin & L. L. Putnam (Eds.), *The new handbook of organizational communication: Advances in theory, research, and methods* (pp. 291–322). Thousand Oaks, CA: Sage.

Emery, M., & Emery, E. (1996). *The press and America: An interpretive history of the mass media* (8th ed.). Boston: Allyn & Bacon.

Emery, M., Emery, E., & Roberts, N. (2000). *The press and America: An interpretive history of the mass media* (9th ed.). Boston: Allyn & Bacon.

Ettema, J., & Whitney, C. (1982). *Individuals in mass media organizations: Creativity and constraint.* Beverly Hills, CA: Sage.

Falcione, R. L., Sussman, L., & Herden, R. P. (1987). Communication climate in organizations. In F. Jablin, L. Putnam, K. Roberts, & L. Porter (Eds.), *Handbook of organizational communication: An interdisciplinary perspective* (pp. 195–227). Newbury Park, CA: Sage.

Fayol, H. (1949). *General and industrial management* (C. Storrs, Trans.). London: Pitman.

Fellow, A., & Tebbel, J. (2004). *American media history.* Belmont, CA: Wadsworth.

Finegan, J. (2000). The impact of person and organizational values on organizational commitment. *Journal of Occupational and Organizational Psychology, 73*(2), 149–170. Retrieved June 7, 2004, from InfoTrac OneFile database: http://infotrac.galegroup.com

Fiorina, C., Bangle, C., Veatch, C., Baker, L. M., Eckert, R. A., Butcher, S., Pillari, R. J., Baum, H., Mazzola, M., Ballard, R. D., Chuanzhi, L., & McKinnell, H. (2003). Moving mountains. *Harvard Business Review, 81*(1), 41–48.

Flander, J. (1986, May). Pressure and stress in the newsroom. *RTNDA Communicator,* 14.

Flournoy, C. (2004, May/June). Red dawn in Dallas. *Columbia Journalism Review.* Retrieved June 26, 2004, from www.cjr.org/issues/2004/3/fournoy-dallas.asp

Folkerts, J., & Teeter, D. (2002). *Voices of a nation: A history of mass media in the United States* (4th ed.). Boston: Allyn & Bacon.

Fournies, F. (2000). *Why employees don't do what they're supposed to do and what to do about it.* Blue Ridge Summit, PA: Liberty Hall Press.

Franklin, M. A., & Franklin, D. A. (1990). *Cases and materials on mass media law* (4th ed.). Westbury, NY: Foundation Press.

Gans, H. (1980). *Deciding what's news: A study of CBS Evening News, NBC Nightly News, Newsweek and Time.* New York: Vintage Books.

Gardner, J. (1988). The tasks of leadership. In J. Gibson, J. Ivancevich, & J. Donnelly, Jr. (Eds.), *Organizations close-up: A book of readings* (6th ed.; pp. 219–227). Plano, TX: Business Publications.

Garfield, C. (1992). *Second to none: How our smartest companies put people first*. Homewood, IL: Irwin.

Garmager, T., & Shemmer, L. (1998). Rich in culture, rich in profits. *HR Focus, 75*(10), 1–3.

Gaziano, C., & Coulson, D. (1988). Effect of newsroom management styles on journalists: A case study. *Journalism Quarterly, 65*, 869–880.

Geisler, J. (1999, March 15). The manager as coach: Tools for teaching. *Poynteronline*. Retrieved October 4, 2003, from http://poynter.org/content/content_view.asp?id=5498

Geisler, J. (2000, December 20). I'm your leader—What have I done for you lately? *Poynteronline*. Retrieved October 4, 2003, from http://poynter.org/content/content_print.asp?id=5792&custom=

Gibson, J., Ivancevich, J., & Donnelly, J., Jr. (1997). *Organizations: Behavior, structure, processes* (9th ed.). Homewood, IL: Irwin.

Goldberg, B. (2002). *Bias: A CBS insider exposes how the media distorts the news*. New York: Perennial.

Graham, F. (1990). *Happy talk: Confessions of a TV newsman*. New York: Norton.

Greenberg, J. (1999). *Managing behavior in organizations: Science in service to practice*. Upper Saddle River, NJ: Prentice-Hall.

Greengard, S. (1999). Stock options have their ups & downs. *Workforce, 78*(12), 44–47.

Grossberg, L., Wartella, E., & Whitney, C. (1998). *Mediamaking: Mass media in a popular culture*. Thousand Oaks, CA: Sage.

Grove, A. S. (1988). Elephants can so dance. In J. Gibson, J. Ivancevich, & J. Donnelly, Jr. (Eds.), *Organizations close-up* (pp. 418–424). Plano, TX: Business Publications.

Hannafey, F. T. (2003). Economic and moral criteria of executive compensation. *Business and Society Review, 108*, 405–415.

Hansen, K., Neuzil, M., & Ward, J. (1997, October). *Newsroom topic teams: Journalists' assessments of effects on news routines and newspaper quality*. Paper presented at AEJMC Mid-Year Conference, Central Michigan University, Mount Pleasant.

Harder, J. W. (1991). Equity theory versus expectancy theory: The case of major league baseball free agents. *Journal of Applied Psychology, 76*, 458–464.

Hays, R. G., & Reisner, A. E. (1991). Farm journalists and advertiser influence: Pressures on ethical standards. *Journalism Quarterly, 68*, 172–178.

Hellstrom, C., & Hellstrom, T. (2002). Highways, alleys, and by-lanes: Changing the pathways for ideas and innovation in organizations. *Creativity & Innovation Management, 11*(2), 1070–114.

Herzberg, F., Mausner, B., & Synderman, B. (1959). *The motivation to work*. New York: Wiley.

Hogg, M., & Terry, D. (2000). Social identity and self-categorization in organizational contexts. *Academy of Management Review, 25*(1), 121–141. Retrieved June 7, 2004, from InfoTrac OneFile database: http://infotrac.galegroup.com

Hopkins-Doerr, M. (1989). Getting more out of MBWA. *Supervisory Management, 34*(2), 17–19.

How to successfully practice MBWA. (1994). *Supervisory Management, 39*(1), 12. Retrieved September 12, 2004, from ABI/INFORM database: http://proquest.umi.com

Huczynski, A. (1992). Management guru ideas and the 12 secrets of their success. *Leadership & Organizational Development Journal, 13*(5), 15–21.

Humphreys, J. (2003). The dysfunctional evolution of goal setting. *MIT Sloan Management Review, 44*, 96–97. Retrieved October 18, 2003, from www.lexis-nexis.com

Ingersoll, R. (1980). Some reasons why. In E. Beck (Ed.), *Bartlett's Familiar Quotations: A collection of passages, phrases and proverbs traced to their sources in ancient and modern literature* (15th ed.; p. 615). Boston: Little, Brown. (Original published 1896)

Jablin, F. M., & Putnam, L. L. (Eds.). (2000). *The new handbook of organizational communication: Advances in theory, research, and methods*. Thousand Oaks, CA: Sage.

Jablin, F. M., Putnam, L. L., Roberts, K. H., & Porter, L. W. (Eds.). (1987). *Handbook of organizational communication: An interdisciplinary perspective*. Newbury Park, CA: Sage.

Jenkins, E. (2003, July/August). Perspectives on the Times: Fixing the system. *Columbia Journalism Review*. Retrieved December 29, 2003, from www.cjr.org/issues/2003/4/times-jenkins.asp

Johnston, L. (2003). *"Good night, Chet": A biography of Chet Huntley*. Jefferson, NC: McFarland.

Juechter, W. M., Fischer, C., & Alford, R. J. (1998). Five conditions for high performance cultures. *Training & Development, 52*, 63–65.

Kanter, R. (1988). Change masters and the intricate architecture of corporate culture change. In J. Gibson, J. Ivancevich, & J. Donnelly, Jr. (Eds.), *Organizations close-up: A book of readings* (6th ed.; pp. 400–417). Plano, TX: Business Publications.

Kennedy, M. (1992). The politics of mean. *Across the Board, 29*(9), 9–11.

Kiefer, T., & Briner, R. (2003). Handle with care: Emotion in the workplace can be a force for good, or it can be "toxic." That is why being able to understand feelings is vital for managers. *People Management, 9*(21), 48–50.

Kuralt, C. (1990). *A life on the road.* New York: G. P. Putnam's Sons.

Lamertz, K. (2002). The social construction of fairness: Social influence and sense making in organizations. *Journal of Organizational Behavior, 23*(1), 19–37.

Lavine, J., & Wackman, D. (1988). *Managing media organizations: Effective leadership of the media.* New York: Longman.

Levinson, H. (2003). Management by whose objectives? *Harvard Business Review, 81*(1), 107–117. Retrieved October 18, 2003, from http:// www.lexis-nexis.comwww.lexis-nexis.com

Levy, J., & Levy, M. (2000). Corporate culture, organizational health and human potential: Reflections for leaders. *Journal of Employee Assistance, 29*(1), 23. Exchange. Retrieved October 14, 2001, from www.lexis-nexis.com

Liebling, A. J. (1981). *The press.* New York: Pantheon. (Original work published 1961)

Likert, R. (1961). *New patterns of management.* New York: McGraw-Hill.

Loeb, M. (1995). Ten commandments for managing creative people. *Fortune, 131*(1), 135–136.

Logan, D., Kiely, L., & Greer, J. (2003). Getting your people to think. *Across the Board, 40*(1), 24–29.

Lucas, J. R. (1999). *The passionate organization: Igniting the fire of employee commitment.* New York: American Management Association.

Mackenzie, K. D. (1991). *The organizational hologram: The effective management of organizational change.* Norwell, MA: Kluwer.

Madjar, N., Oldham, G., & Pratt, M. (2002). There's no place like home? The contributions of work and non-work creativity support to employees' creative performance. *Academy of Management Journal, 45*, 757–767.

Marash, S. (1993). The key to TQM and world-class competitiveness—Part I. *Quality, 32*(9), 37–39.

Mariotti, J. (1996). Troubled by resistance to change? Don't fight it. First, try to understand it. *Industry Week, 245*(18), 30.

Maslow, A. (1970). *Motivation and personality.* New York: Harper & Row. (Original work published 1954)

Maurer, R. (1998). Is it resistance, or isn't it? *Manage, 50*(1) 28–29.

Mayo, E. (1960). *The human problems of an industrial civilization.* New York: Viking Press.

McGregor, D. (1960). *The human side of enterprise.* New York: McGraw-Hill.

McManus, J. (1994). *Market-driven journalism: Let the citizen beware?* Thousand Oaks, CA: Sage.

McQuail, D. (1987). *Mass communication theory: An introduction* (2nd ed.). London: Sage.

McQuail, D. (1994). *Mass communication theory: An introduction* (3rd ed.). Thousand Oaks, CA: Sage.

Mintzberg, H. (1989). *Mintzberg on management: Inside our strange world of organizations.* New York: The Free Press.

Morgan, G. (1997). *Images of organizations.* Thousand Oaks, CA: Sage.

Nauta, A., de Dreu, C. K. W., & van der Vaart, T. (2002). Social value orientation, organizational goal concerns and interdepartmental problem-solving behavior. *Journal of Organizational Behavior, 23*, 199–213.

Nicholson, N. (2003). How to motivate your problem people. *Harvard Business Review, 81*(1), 56–66. Retrieved October 18, 2003, from www.lexis-nexis.com

Ouchi, W. (1981). *Theory Z: How American business can meet the Japanese challenge.* New York: Avon.

Oxman, J. (2002). The hidden leverage of human capital. *MIT Sloan Management Review, 43*(4), 79–83.

Paulson, T. (2003). Change competencies: Ten sure-fire ways to fail as a change agent. Retrieved December 29, 2003, from www.changecentral.com / changeperspecten.html

Peters, T., & Waterman, R. (1982). *In search of excellence: Lessons from America's best-run companies.* New York: Warner.

Poole, M. S. (1985). Communication and organizational climates: Review, critique, and a new perspective. In R. D. McPhee & P. K. Tompkins (Eds.), *Organizational communication: Traditional themes and new dimensions* (pp. 79–108). Newbury Park, CA: Sage.

Powers, R. (1977). *The newscasters*. New York: St. Martin's Press.

Rather, D. (1977). *The camera never blinks: Adventures of a TV journalist*. New York: Morrow.

Ravasi, D., & Van Reckom, J. (2003). Key issues in organizational identity and identification theory. *Corporate Reputations Review, 6*(2), 118–132.

Redmond, J. (2004). *Balancing on the wire: The art of managing media organizations* (2nd ed.). Cincinnati, OH: Atomic Dog.

Reese, S. D., & Ballinger, J. (2001). The roots of a sociology of news: Remembering Mr. Gates and social control in the newsroom. *Journalism & Mass Communication Quarterly, 78*, 641–658.

Robertson, L. (2003, August/September). Down with top-down. *American Journalism Review*. Retrieved December 29, 2003, from www.ajr.org/archive.asp?Year=2003&Issue=61

Rosen, J. (2004, June/July). We mean business. *American Journalism Review*. Retrieved June 26, 2004, from www.ajr.org/Article.asp?id=3668

Rosenbloom, J. (2004, April 4). *A calamitous merger and the men who engineered it*. Boston Globe, p. C2.

Rosnow, R. (1980, May). Psychology in rumor reconsidered. *Psychological Bulletin, 89*, 578–591.

RTNDA Survey (2001). Retrieved October 22, 2001, from www.rtnda.org/research

Schein, E. (1985). *Organization culture and leadership*. San Francisco: Jossey-Bass.

Schneider, B. (1983). An interactionist perspective on organizational effectiveness. In K. Cameron & D. Whetten (Eds.), *Organizational effectiveness* (pp. 27–54). New York: Academic Press.

Shapiro, S. (2002). Innovate your organization. *Industrial Management, 44*(6), 18–22.

Sherman, B. (1995). *Telecommunications management: Broadcasting/cable and the new technologies* (2nd ed.). New York: McGraw-Hill.

Slater, R. (1988). This is CBS: A chronicle of sixty years. Englewood Cliffs, NJ: Prentice-Hall.

Smolkin, R. (2004, June/July). The expanding blogosphere. *American Journalism Review*. Retrieved June 26, 2004, from www.ajr.org/Article.asp?id=3682

Sperber, A. M. (1986). *Murrow, his life and times*. New York: Freundlich.

Spreitzer, G. (1995). Psychological empowerment in the workplace: Dimensions, measurement, and validation. *The Academy of Management Journal, 38*, 1442–1465.

Stamm, K., & Underwood, D. (1993). The relationship of job satisfaction to newsroom policy changes. *Journalism Quarterly, 70*, 528–541.

*State of the News Media 2004: An Annual Report on American Journalism*. (2004). Washington, DC: Project for Excellence in Journalism. Available from: www.stateofthenewsmedia.org/index.asp

Stohl, C., & Redding, W. (1987). Messages and message exchange processes. In F. Jablin, L. Putnam, K. Roberts, & L. Porter (Eds.), *Handbook of organizational communication: An interdisciplinary perspective* (pp. 451–502). Newbury Park, CA: Sage.

Stone, V. (1986, June). News directors profiled. *RTNDA Communicator*, 21–23.

Stone, V. (1987). Changing profiles of news directors of radio and TV stations, 1972–1986. *Journalism Quarterly, 64*, 745–749.

Stone, V. (1991). Age, experience and turnover in TV news: Years at present station. Retrieved June 24, 2004, from www.missouri.edu/~jourvs/tvyears.html#tenure

Stone, V. (1992). Women and men as news directors. *RTNDA Communicator, 54*(1), 143–144.

Sutton, R. I. (2002). Why innovation happens when happy people fight. *Ivey Business Journal, 67*(2), 1–6.

Tan, A. S. (1985). *Mass communication theories and research* (2nd ed.). New York: Wiley.

Taylor, C. (1994). OHBWA: Office hours by walking around. *Journal of Management Education, 18*, 270–272.

Taylor, F. (1967). *Scientific management*. New York: Norton. (Original work published 1947)

Thomas, K., & Velthouse, B. (1990). Cognitive elements of empowerment: An "interpretive" model of intrinsic task motivation. *Academy of Management Review, 15*, 666–681.

Tierney, P., & Farmer, S. (2004) The Pygmalion process and employee creativity. *Journal of Management, 30*, 413–432.

Trujillo, N. (1983). "Performing" Mintzberg's roles: The nature of managerial communication. In L. Putnam & M. Pacanowsky (Eds.), *Communication and organizations: An interpretative approach* (pp. 73–97). Newbury Park, CA: Sage.

Tulgan, B. (2000). *Managing generation X: How to bring out the best in young talent*. New York: Norton.

Underwood, D. (1995). *When MBAs rule the newsroom.* New York: Columbia University Press.

Vroom, V. (1964). *Work and motivation.* New York: Wiley.

Walton, E. (1981, January). The comparison of measures of organization structure. *Academy of Management Review, 6,* 155–160.

Warner, M. (1994). Organizational behavior revisited. *Human Relations, 47,* 1151–1167.

Warner, M. (Anchor/Moderator). (1998, July 1). *Unfit to print. The NewsHour with Jim Lehrer* [Television broadcast]. New York and Washington, DC: Public Broadcasting Service. Retrieved from www.pbs.org/newshour/bb/media/july-dec98/media_ethics_7-1.html

Watson, K. (1982, June). An analysis of communication patterns: A method for discriminating leader and subordinate roles. *Academy of Management Journal, 25*(1), 107–122.

Way, N. (2000). A new world of people power. *Business Review Weekly, 22*(23), 62–67.

Whetten, D. (1988). Sources, responses, and effects of organizational decline. In K. S. Cameron, R. I. Sutton, & D. A. Whetten (Eds.), *Readings in organizational decline: Frameworks, research, and prescriptions* (pp. 151–174). Boston: Ballinger.

Whetten, D., & Cameron, K. (1995). *Developing management skills* (3rd ed.). New York: HarperCollins.

Whetten, D. A., & Godfrey, P. (Eds). (1998). *Identity in organizations: Building theory through conversations.* Thousand Oaks, CA: Sage.

White, D. (1950). The gatekeeper: A case study in the selection of news. *Journalism Quarterly, 27,* 383–390.

Wicks, J., Sylvie, G., Hollifield, C. A., Lacy, S., & Sohn, A. (2004). *Media management: A casebook approach* (3rd ed.). Mahwah, NJ: Lawrence Erlbaum Associates.

Willis, J. (2003). *The human journalist: Reporters, perspectives, and emotions.* Westport, CT: Praeger.

Zahniser, R. (1994). Design by walking around. *Association for Computing Machinery: Communications of the ACM, 36*(10), 114–125. Retrieved June 21, 2004, from ABI/Inform database: http://proquest.umi.com

# 7

# Issues in Financial Management

Ronald J. Rizzuto
University of Denver

The media industry has a rich financial history. Virtually every form of financial engineering such as mergers, acquisitions, leveraged buy outs, equity carve outs, spin-offs, unfriendly takeovers, proxy fights, bankruptcies, and asset swaps have taken place somewhere in the media industry during the past 20 years. In addition, the industry has had a history of utilizing creative financing instruments and vehicles like limited partnerships, rights offerings, PIK (paid in kind) preferred stocks, and tracking stocks to name a few.

In addition to being the source of a great deal of innovative financial engineering and financing, the media industry provides an excellent research laboratory for the study of traditional finance issues such as: dividend policy, capital structure determination, and investment decision making. These financial topics represent fertile research areas for two reasons. First, the capital intensive nature of the media industry provides finance with a center role in all key decisions. Second, the reinvention that is taking place among media industry companies is necessitating a reevaluation of dividend and capital structure policies as well as decision-making methodologies. This reevaluation process provides researchers with a superb opportunity to compare theory to practice.

Historically, media researchers have neglected finance topics in their research. There are, of course, some notable exceptions including: Chan-Olmsted and Chang (2003); Dimpfel, Habann, and Algesheimer (2002); Gershon (2002); and Munk (2004). However, generally speaking, media researchers have not placed much focus on finance. Hence, a major purpose of this chapter is to review the relevant finance research literature and to identify possible finance research topics for media management and economics researchers.

The review of the current finance literature provided in the following focuses on topic areas that are particularly relevant to the media industry today. The literature review summarizes the current finance literature as well as any relevant research from media industry researchers. Suggestions for future media industry finance research are provided at the end of the chapter along with discussion and insights as to why this topic is particularly relevant for the media industry.

## LITERATURE REVIEW

Finance research includes several broad fields of inquiry including corporate finance, investments, financial institutions, and international finance. Like any discipline, each of these fields has multiple areas of research. The focus for this chapter is on research topics in the corporate finance field. The review provided focuses on the following topics within corporate finance research: dividend policy, capital structure theory, mergers and acquisitions, real options theory, and financial restructuring.

### Dividend Policy

There are two basic research questions with respect to dividend policy. The first question is—do dividends matter? In other words, can a company increase shareholder value by paying dividends to shareholders? The second question is—does it matter how the firm distributes cash to its shareholders? Also, do shareholders view the repurchase of stock from shareholders as a substitute for cash dividends?

#### Do Dividends Matter?

There are several ways to frame the question—do dividends matter?

1. Given a choice between dividends and future growth, do dividends matter?
2. Do dividends matter if a company has to borrow money in order to pay dividends so as not to sacrifice future growth opportunities?
3. Given no change in future growth and no change in financial leverage (debt), do dividends matter? In other words, do dividends matter if a company has to issue common stock in order to pay dividends?

Finance researchers have chosen this last alternative for framing the dividend relevance question. This alternative was selected because it neutralizes the impacts of the investment decision (i.e., growth) and financial leverage (i.e., debt vs. equity) on the dividend question.

Miller and Modigliani (1961) are credited with focusing finance researchers on framing the dividend question as a choice between financing with internal equity (i.e., retained earnings) or financing with external equity (i.e., new common stock issuance). Miller and Modigliani are also credited with the proof that in a world with perfect markets (i.e., no taxes, no transaction costs, no restrictions on the types of stocks investors could buy, and perfect information), dividends do not matter.

Miller and Modigliani's (1961) research focused finance researchers on the proposition that dividends per se did not matter, but that it was market imperfections that caused dividends to have value for shareholders. For example, in an imperfect world where shareholders are not privy to insider information, a dividend change by a board of directors represents a form of communication from insiders to shareholders. A dividend increase represents a favorable outlook, whereas a dividend decrease indicates a negative assessment of the future prospects of the company.

Dividend policy research, focused on market imperfections, has identified the following four imperfections and their impacts. First, taxes are imperfections, and, more important, the tax differential between dividends and capital gains argues for an inverse relationship between dividends and shareholder value or stock price. That is, historically, in the United States (i.e., prior to the 2003 tax law changes), dividends have been taxed as ordinary income, whereas capital appreciation gains from the sale of stock have been taxed at the capital gains rate. This tax differential imperfection argues for a company's retention of profits rather than the payment of dividends.

Second, transaction costs like the investment banking fees for issuing shares of common stock are market imperfections. If a company pays dividends, while maintaining its financial leverage and investment spending plans, then it will incur these investment underwriter's fees. The existence of these transaction costs argue for the retention of profits and the use of this internally generated equity rather than external equity for the company. Transaction costs like taxes suggest that there will be a negative relationship between dividends and stock price.

Third, in imperfect markets investors do not have access to all the information about a company. In particular, as noted, investors do not have access to insider information. Hence, a dividend increase is a way for insiders to signal their positive evaluation of the future prospects of the company, whereas a dividend decrease signals a negative outlook for the firm. This information imperfection argues for a positive relationship between dividends and stock price.

Fourth, in perfect markets there are no restrictions on investors with respect to buying and selling stocks. However, in an imperfect world there are restrictions. Many institutional investors cannot buy stocks unless they pay a dividend. Some individual investors who depend on their stock investments for income (e.g., widows and orphans) will not purchase a stock unless it pays dividends. Consequently, this *clientele effect* for dividend paying stocks broadens the market demand for dividend paying securities and creates a positive relationship between dividends and stock price.

The consequence of the differential impacts of these market imperfections is the dividend empirical controversy. Brealey and Myers (2003) summarized the three competing dividend theories as the *rightists*, the *leftists* and the *middle of the road*. The rightists argue that the information and buyer restriction imperfections outweigh the tax and transaction cost imperfections. The leftists believe the opposite is true, whereas the middle of the road think all the imperfections offset each other.

There has been much empirical work done testing these three theories. Miller (1986) as well as Kalay and Michaely (2000) did reviews of some of the empirical work in this area. In general, the empirical research has been inconclusive.

### Stock Repurchases as a Substitute for Cash Dividends

According to Grullon and Michaely (2002), there has been a large decrease in the number of firms paying dividends, although the number of firms buying back their shares has increased dramatically over the past 20 years. These trends raise the second dividend research question, previously noted, namely, are stock repurchases a substitute for cash dividends? Grullon and Michaely's research provided a comprehensive review of the literature regarding the substitution hypothesis as well as updated empirical research. They concluded that stock repurchases are substitutes for cash dividends and that share repurchase programs have become the preferred method of payout for firms.

One limitation of Grullon and Michaely's (2002) research was that their empirical analysis preceded the passage of the Jobs and Growth Tax Relief Reconciliation Act of 2003 in which most of the tax rate differential between dividends and capital gains was eliminated.

## Capital Structure–Financial Leverage

Capital structure research focuses on the question—is there an optimal capital structure for the firm, and, if so, how does a firm determine its optimal capital structure? In general, there is widespread agreement among finance researchers that: (a) leverage can enhance the value of the firm; (b) too much debt can destroy shareholder value; and (c) an optimal mix of debt and equity will maximize shareholder value.

### The Trade-Off Theory

The foundation of the theory that underpins these conclusions is the original work of Modigliani and Miller (1958, 1963). Modigliani and Miller's capital structure theory is frequently called the *trade-off theory*. In effect, these researchers theorized that debt per se has no value. Instead, they asserted that the imperfections in the market cause debt to have an impact on shareholder value. More specifically, Modigliani and Miller observed that debt enhances shareholder value because, in a world with corporate taxes as well as one in which corporations are allowed to deduct the interest expense on debt, interest expenses are subsidized by the government. Because this tax subsidy benefits the corporation, shareholder value is increased. Modigliani and Miller also observed that increased leverage has a negative impact because, in the real world there are costs associated with financial distress. Hence, the potential cost, as well as the probability of financial distress, increases with the amount of financial leverage.

Modigliani and Miller (1958, 1963) theorized that a firm optimizes firm and shareholder value when it strikes a balance between the competing impacts of leverage. That is, when the amount of leverage is low, the tax benefits are larger than the potential costs of distress. However, as leverage increases, the costs of distress increase and eventually become larger than the tax benefits. A firm's optimal capital structure is reached when these two impacts counterbalance one another.

Implicit in the *trade-off* theory is the implication that the optimal capital structure will vary by industry because the probability of financial distress will be different among industries. For example, in industries where there are few competitors, high barriers to entry, and inelastic demand for products and/or services, the optimal capital structure will include a high debt load. However, in industries with many competitors, few barriers to entry, and elastic demand for products and/or services, the leverage ratios should be low because of the greater probability of financial distress.

Some of the empirical research in this area (Barclay, Smith, & Watts, 1995; Myers, 2000), supported the trade-off theory of leverage. However, this research indicated that there were some companies for which the trade-off theory did not explain their behavior. This research showed that firms, like Microsoft, Pfizer and other highly profitable companies, tended to use little or no debt, when, in fact, the trade-off theory suggested that they should be using a significant amount of debt.

These anomalies inspired finance researchers such as Baskin (1989), Myers and Majluf (1984), and Shyam-Sunder and Myers (1999) to revisit capital structure theory. An additional theory called the *pecking order theory* emerged from this reinvestigation of companies' behavior in establishing their financing policies.

### The Pecking Order Theory

The pecking order theory starts with the observation that company managers have access to insider information. In effect, in a world in which there is asymmetric information between inside managers and outside investors, the financing decision becomes a form of communication from insiders. A decision to finance the growth of the business with internal sources, suggests that managers are optimistic about the future of the company's profitability, whereas a decision to finance with debt is an indication that the outlook for profitability is not as positive. These inferences with respect to financing decisions create a pecking order in the financing of corporations. In general, firms tend to finance in the following order:

1. Internal finance (i.e., reinvested profits).
2. Debt.
3. Hybrid securities like convertible bonds.
4. Issuance of common stock as a last resort.

Because firms tend to finance in this pecking order, a corporation's capital structure is a function of its profitability. In theory, highly profitable firms, like Microsoft and Pfizer, will use little or no debt, whereas less profitable firms will use more debt. Hence, the pecking order theory suggests an inverse relationship between leverage and shareholder value.

Currently, finance researchers recognize that neither the trade-off theory nor the pecking order theory completely explain the capital structure behavior of all corporations.

## Mergers and Acquisitions

Mergers and acquisitions constitute fundamental investment decisions for corporations. They are, however, much more complex than traditional capital investment decisions because they involve the integration of people, processes, products, shareholders and other stakeholders, and the financial policies of the two organizations. Finance research in the merger and acquisition area can take many forms: valuation methodologies, financing techniques, estimating and valuing synergies, accounting and tax structures utilized in the transaction, gains and losses for buyers and sellers, and success rates of mergers and acquisitions.

A key research question with special relevance for the media industry in this area is— do mergers succeed" (i.e., is the combined company more successful after the merger than before)?

Damodaran (2001) summarized several studies that considered this question for public companies that have merged. According to Damodaran, McKinsey and Company evaluated 58 acquisitions between 1972 and 1983 and concluded that 28 of these acquisitions did not generate a return in excess of the cost of capital, and they did not help the parent company outperform the competition. In a follow-up study, McKinsey and Company found that 60% of the 115 mergers in the United States and the United Kingdom during the 1990s earned a return that was less than the corporation's cost of capital, and, only 23% earned a return that was in excess of the cost of capital. KPMG (1999) examined 700 of the most expensive acquisitions between 1996 and 1998 and found that only 17% created value for the combined company, 30% were value neutral, and 53% destroyed value.

Other research approached the question of failure from the standpoint of whether the company acquired was divested sometime after the acquisition. Mitchell and Lehn (1990) found that 20.2% of the acquisitions between 1982 and 1986 were sold by 1988. Kaplan and Weisbach (1992) found that 44% of the mergers they studied were divested sometime after the merger.

Finance research regarding the success of mergers is quite sobering. The record of accomplishment for large public company mergers is mediocre, at best. However, these results are not an indictment of all mergers and acquisitions, just the larger ones. Many smaller, private companies boast that most of their acquisitions are successful. However, it is difficult to verify this conclusion because the required data are not readily available to researchers.

## Real Options Analysis

Discounted cash flow analysis, namely, net present value (NPV) and internal rate of return (IRR), are the primary capital investment techniques used by corporations around the world. These two techniques have been the analytical workhorses for business for more than 3 decades.

During the past 20 years, a new body of literature has developed that found some shortcomings in discounted cash flow analysis. This field of study is referred to as *real options analysis*. The primary shortcoming of discounted cash flow analysis is that it views investment decisions as passive. That is, it presumes the decision is to accept or reject the investment at a point in time. Traditional discounted cash flow techniques do not consider the value of active management or, in other words, the value of flexibility. Many investments provide management with the flexibility to change the investment decision when prices change or new information arrives.

To illustrate, an oil company is considering drilling an oil well assuming a price per barrel of oil of $30. On calculating the NPV, the company finds the project has a NPV of $10 million. Traditional discounted cash flow analysis would conclude that the company should drill the well now. However, if oil prices increase substantially in the future, the company could be better off deferring drilling the well. In effect, this investment has an option embedded in it. This investment provides the company with the option to wait. If there is a positive value for this option, then the company would be better off waiting to drill the well.

Discounted cash flow analysis techniques, given their predisposition to conclude yes or no, now or never, ignore the options embedded in an investment as well as fail to consider the value of these embedded options.

Real options theory is an adaptation of options valuation theory that was developed for the valuation of financial options to the valuation of real assets. Black and Scholes (1973) and Merton (1973) developed the options valuation model. The model helps in the pricing of call and put options. Call options are the right to purchase common stock at a specified price during a specified time period, whereas put options are the right to sell common stock at a specified price during a given time period. The option pricing model specifies that the option value is a function of five variables. These variables are:

1. The current price of the underlying stock.
2. The exercise price of the option.
3. The time to expiration of the option.
4. The risk-free interest rate.
5. The volatility of the stock.

Real options begin by viewing capital projects as analogous to options on financial assets. For example, one way to think about a capital project is to view it as a call option on an investment opportunity. The present value of the benefits of the project is the equivalent of the stock price, and the capital outlay for the project is the same thing as the exercise price. The variability of the project's present value of benefits is approximately equivalent to stock price volatility. Finally, the length of time the decision can be deferred is the same thing as the time to expiration, and the time value of money is equivalent to the risk-free rate in financial options.

Viewing capital budgeting projects as a call option is a simple real option analogy. Researchers in the real option area (Amran & Kulatilaka, 1999; Brennan & Schwartz, 1985; Copeland & Antikarov, 2001; Dixit & Pindyck, 1994, 1995; Kester, 1984; Kulatilaka, 1993; Luehrman, 1998; Mason & Merton, 1985; Mun, 2002; Triantis & Borison, 2001; and Trigeorgis, 1996) identified many types of options that are more complex than a call option. These include: option to wait, option to stage investments, option to contract, option to suspend and restart, option to abandon, option to switch input, option to expand, option to switch output, and option to grow.

The valuation of real options is one of the more complex aspects of applying options theory to real investments. The Black Scholes option valuation model is frequently used in valuing a simple call option. However, most of the options noted require more complex binominal models in valuing options. The basics of the binominal method for valuing real options can be found in standard corporate finance textbooks like Brealey and Myers (2003).

Finance researchers applied real options valuation in practical capital budgeting situations. Some of these efforts are summarized in the following: Brennan and Schwartz (1985), Kulatilaka (1993), Triantis and Borison (2001), McCormack, LeBlanc, and Heiser (2003), and Borison, Eapen, Mauboussin, and McCormack (2003).

This research underscores the progress made in the application of real options to capital budgeting as well as some of the problem areas. In general, the major difficulties in applying real options is in modeling complex options, estimating project volatility, and determining the time period for the option.

## Financial Restructuring

Another area of recent importance in financial research, particularly during the past decade, has been that of corporate restructurings. In this arena, often labeled *financial engineering*, public companies have undertaken the task of restructuring their assets and financial claims. This restructuring may include: equity carve outs, spin-offs, split-offs, asset sales or divestitures, leveraged buy outs, or tracking stocks.

An *equity carve out* is an initial public offering of a wholly owned subsidiary of the parent company. A *spin-off* involves the creation of a new independent company by detaching part of the parent company's assets and operations. In a spin-off the existing shareholders of the parent company receive shares in the new company based on their pro rata ownership of the parent.

A *split-off* is a transaction in which a company splits itself into two or more parts. In this transaction, some of the shareholders of the parent company receive shares in a subsidiary in return for relinquishing their shares in the parent company.

An *asset sale or divestiture* is simply a sale of a business unit or a group of assets. A *leveraged buy out* is frequently associated with taking a public company private. In this type of restructuring, some of the managers of the company borrow against the assets of the firm and buy out the equity of the remaining shareholders.

*Tracking stocks* are separate classes of the common stock of the parent corporation whose value is tied to a specific business unit or corporation. The creation of tracking stocks is a way for the company to remain intact while allowing the shareholders to have their investments track only a part, rather than all, of the company's performance. Typically, tracking stocks come into existence when the combined company has disparate businesses with differing financial characteristics.

The motivation behind use of all of these financial engineering techniques is that the parent company is not being fully valued by the public market. Specifically, in the case where a company is considering a tracking stock, the stock trades at a discount to the underlying fair market value of the assets because of a diversification discount, asymmetric information, and/or agency costs.

Berger and Ofek (1995) estimated that the stocks of conglomerate, diversified firms trade at a 13% to 15% discount to the fair market value of the assets of the business. This discount may be the result of market confusion regarding the economics of a company's businesses or the result of asymmetric information and agency costs.

A discount may result because managers of a business have more information about the individual businesses of the company than do the market and shareholders. Because this insider information cannot be shared directly with shareholders, there is a gap between the market's assessment of the value of the company and management's valuation of what the company is worth.

The management of a diversified corporation has to deal with business issues across a wide range of markets. Invariably, management may not have sufficient time or the expertise to deal with all the key issues. Consequently, the performance of some of the individual business units may suffer. This type of business neglect is an agency cost. This agency cost in turn translates into underperformance of the business and a lower valuation for the enterprise.

Much of the research on tracking stocks is empirical research focused on the question of whether the creation of a tracking stock unlocks shareholder value. If a tracking stock unlocks the trapped values of a company, the value of the company, after creation of the tracking stock, should be higher than before.

Empirical tracking studies (Billet & Mauer, 2000; Boone, Haushalter, & Mikkelson, 2003; D'Souza & Jacob, 2000; Elder & Westra, 2000; Harper & Madura, 2002) indicate that the combined value of the company and its tracking stock increase at the time of the announcement of the creation of the tracking stock. However, this research found that these positive impacts dissipate over time, indicating that tracking stocks do not have any long-term value in unlocking the hidden values of the company.

## SUGGESTIONS FOR FUTURE MEDIA FINANCE RESEARCH

This section provides a brief discussion of the current media industry situation with respect to each corporate finance research topic area included in the prior section. This discussion underscores the timeliness of each research topic from the perspective of the media industry. Suggestions for future academic research in the area of media finance are also provided.

### Dividend Policy Research

Historically, most of the firms in the media industry have paid no dividends or only nominal dividends (i.e., a small dividend relative to the stock price. For example, Disney currently pays a dividend of $.21 on a share price of $22.50). Charter Communications, Cox Communications, Comcast Corporation, Liberty Media, and Time Warner do not pay dividends. Other firms like Gannett, News Corporation, Tribune Company, The New York Times, Viacom, and Walt Disney only pay a nominal dividend.

One might look at the historic dividend behavior of media companies and conclude that they do not think dividends matter. In reality, most media companies have not paid dividends simply because they have needed the capital to fund growth. Because dividends for media companies have represented a trade-off between growth and dividends, researchers have not been able to isolate in on the question of whether media companies would issue common stock in order to pay dividends. Perhaps this phenomenon explains the lack of dividend policy research focused on the media industry.

The dividend situation for media companies will be different in the future. Shapiro (2004) argued that media companies will start to return significant amounts of capital because:

1. Paying down debt is not an option.
2. Reinvestment opportunities are limited.
3. Washington will not tolerate much more media consolidation.
4. Slowing secular growth is unlikely to reverse.
5. The market (i.e., investors) will no longer tolerate poor capital allocation decisions (i.e., big media mergers).

In view of these reasons, media researchers have the opportunity to consider the question—do dividends matter?—as media companies begin to address this question. In addition, academic researchers have the opportunity to focus on this question in an environment where the differential tax between dividends and capital gains market imperfection has been minimized as a result of the 2003 tax law changes.

Media researchers can also address the question of whether stock repurchases are a substitute for cash dividends. This could be a very interesting research area, particularly in view of the fact that some Wall Street analysts (e.g., Shapiro, 2004) are recommending that media companies opt for stock repurchases because they are accretive to free cash flow per share, and they give investors the option of participating.

## Capital Structure Research

The capital structure behavior of media companies can best be described by the trade-off theory of leverage. Traditionally, media companies have utilized leverage as a strategy for minimizing taxes as well as accelerating their rate of growth. Many media companies have opted for high degrees of financial leverage because of limited competition, high barriers to entry, and inelastic demand for their products. For example, the cable television industry has historically had leverage ratios, as measured by long-term debt/EBITDA (i.e., earnings before interest, taxes, depreciation, and amortization) of 6:1. In contrast, Regional Bell Operating Companies (RBOCs) have had long-term debt/EBITDA ratios of 2:1 or less.

Academic media researchers have several potential options for pursuing research in the capital structure area. First, researchers can test the validity of the trade-off theory vis-à-vis the pecking order theory for media companies. This research can be structured much like the research of Shyam-Sunder and Myers (1999). Second, researchers can document the change that is occurring in the optimal capital structure of various media companies. For example, cable television companies have been reducing their debt levels during the past few years because of increased competition. Media researchers can use this recalibration of leverage to shed light on the process and factors that contribute to a change in capital structure policy. Third, as media companies become free cash flow positive, as noted previously by Shapiro (2004), researchers may be interested in testing whether these firms change their capital structure philosophy from trade-off theory to pecking order theory. Alternatively, Hovakimian, Opler, and Titman's (2002) *dynamic trade-off theory* may come into play here. That is, companies may allow their leverage ratios to drift away from their targets for a time. However, when the distance between actual and targeted leverage ratios becomes large enough, managers will take steps to move back to the targets.

## Mergers and Acquisitions Research

There have been numerous mergers in the media industry (e.g., AOL and Time Warner, Comcast and AT&T Broadband, News Corporation and DirecTV, Viacom and Blockbuster, Disney and CapCities/ABC, NBC and Universal, etc). In fact, the media and communication industries account for 5 of the 10 largest transactions of all time: AOL/Time Warner—$165.9 billion, Vodafone/AirTouch—$62.8 billion, SBC Communications/Ameritech—$61.4 billion, AT&T/MediaOne—$55.8 billion, and Bell Atlantic/GTE—$52.8 billion.

The media industry, in particular, has been a hotbed of merger activity because of the search for scale, diversification of product lines, changing technology, and changing regulation. A number of media industry researchers have studied the area of media mergers and acquisitions (Chan-Olmsted & Chang, 2003; Compaine & Gomery, 2000; Gershon, 2002; Munk, 2004; Ozanich & Wirth, 2004). However, none of this research, except for Munk, has directly focused on the question addressed by finance researchers in this area, namely, is the combined company more successful after the merger than before?

Media research in the merger and acquisition arena might take the following approaches:

1. Compare the cost of capital of the acquirer at the time of the merger to the ex post rate of return of the combined company after the merger (i.e., a McKinsey [as discussed in Damodaran, 2001] or KPMG, 1999, type study).
2. Evaluate acquisitions from the perspective of which ones are reversed after the merger (i.e., a Mitchell & Lehn, 1990, or Kaplan & Weisbach, 1992, type study).
3. Conduct case studies focused on particular mergers and document the failures and successes of these mergers (a Munk, 2004, type study).

Research on the success or failure of media mergers will be useful in refuting or substantiating the claims of security analysts like Shapiro (2004) who concluded: "the market's perception is that big media mergers don't make sense (p. 2)." Shapiro noted that return on invested capital (ROIC) has trailed the weighted average cost of capital (WACC) for several of the large media companies for the past few years, driven largely by the poor returns of big media mergers. He thinks mergers, like AOL/Time Warner, Time Warner/Turner Broadcasting Systems, Comcast/AT&T Broadband and Viacom/Blockbuster/CBS/etc., have destroyed shareholder value. Shapiro calculated that Comcast would be trading at $35 per share without AT&T Broadband as compared to its October 2004 share price of $27, Time Warner without AOL and TBS would be trading at $43 as compared to $16, and Viacom without its string of acquisitions over the last decade would be close to $77 as compared to $35.

## Real Options Research

Some work in applying real options theory to media projects has been done by Mauboussin (1999), Shapiro (2001), and Dimpfel, Habann, and Algesheimer (2002).[1]

Mauboussin (1999) reported the application of real options to the valuation of cable television companies by Laura Martin, an analyst with Credit Suisse First Boston. Martin used real options to value the *stealth tier* (i.e., the available bandwidth above 648 megahertz) for a cable system. She reasoned that in 1999 cable systems only needed 648 megahertz of bandwidth for their operations, and, consequently, their decision to build 750 megahertz systems provided an embedded call option on future, undefined revenue opportunities. Martin used the Black Scholes option pricing model to value this call option.

Shapiro (2001) also applied real options theory to the cable television industry. Much like Martin, he was trying to value the bandwidth between 550 and 750 megahertz on a cable system. In Shapiro's case, he identified 10 call options for this bandwidth: digital classic, digital plus, video-on-demand, business communications, integrated digital video recorder, interactive, Internet protocol telephony, residential phone, t-commerce, and home networking. In valuing these options, however, Shapiro used a discounted present value approach instead of the option pricing model or a binominal model.

Dimpfel, Habann, and Algesheimer (2002) focused on the research opportunities in the media industry rather than on specific applications like Mauboussin and Shapiro. In their research, they discussed various types of options as well as which ones apply to various parts of the media industry. They argued that variable cost options (i.e., option to contract, option to suspend and restart, option to abandon, and option to switch input) are more applicable to the print industry. Whereas, fixed cost options (i.e., option to wait and option to stage investments) and sales options (i.e., option to expand, option to switch output, and option to grow) are more applicable to other sectors of the media industry.

A research agenda for academic media researchers with respect to real options might include: (a) empirical research focused on the extent to which media managers intuitively consider real options as well as the extent to which media companies include the valuation of real options in their capital budgeting process and (b) actual case studies, focused on individual media companies, illustrating the application of real options analysis.

## Financial Restructuring Research—Tracking Stocks

The media industry has done a great deal of financial engineering in the past. It is quite likely to do much more in the future given the current disparity between stock prices and the fair market value of the underlying assets. For example, in October 2004, Liberty Media was trading between $8 and $9 per share even though the fair market value of its assets was estimated to be 25% to 50% higher than this. All of the areas of financial restructuring identified should provide media researchers with ample research opportunities. However, the focus of this section is on tracking stock research.

---

[1]One other study of potential interest is Bughin (2001). This study focused on the management of real options in the broadcasting industry.

Historically, the media industry has been a frequent user of tracking stocks in restructuring companies. For example, General Motors issued its H stock to track the performance of Hughes after the acquisition of Hughes Electronics. Tele-Communications Inc. created a tracking stock for Liberty Media both when it was a stand-alone company and again as part of its merger with AT&T. US West issued its MediaOne tracking stock as part of its restructuring effort to separate the performance of the cable assets from its core telephone operations.

Several possible areas of academic inquiry are available to media researchers in the area of tracking stocks. First, researchers can replicate the research of Harper and Madura (2002) for media industry tracking stocks. This research could consider both the near-term and longer term benefits of tracking stocks in unlocking shareholder value. Likewise, such research will allow media researchers to compare the track record of tracking stocks in the media industry to that of other industries.

Second, media researchers have sufficient information on the utilization of tracking stocks by media companies to develop case studies that document the motivation, strategy, implementation, and success associated with the use of this restructuring technique. Besides contributing to scholarly knowledge in the area of financial restructuring, such case studies will be very helpful to those teaching media courses because financial engineering has played such a prominent role in the historical development of the media industry.

## CONCLUSION

This chapter provided a sampling of finance topics of possible interest to academic researchers interested in the media industry, but it did not provide an exhaustive inventory of possible finance research topics. The five topic areas discussed, however, (i.e., dividend policy, capital structure, mergers and acquisitions, real options, and financial restructuring) are considered to be the most important because they are key issues for any business and because so much has and is happening in the media industry with respect to these topics.

The media industry has a rich financial history and is an excellent laboratory for the study of finance. More important, financial strategy is central to the management of media enterprises. Going forward, media researchers should place greater focus on issues related to media finance so that this important area of academic inquiry can become a more significant part of the research literature related to the media industry.

## REFERENCES

Amran, M., & Kulatilaka, N. (1999). *Real options: Managing strategic investments in an uncertain world.* Boston: Harvard Business School Press.

Barclay, M. J., Smith, C. W., & Watts, R. L. (1995). The determinants of corporate leverage and dividend policies. *Journal of Applied Corporate Finance, 7*(4), 4–19.

Baskin, J. (1989). An empirical investigation of the pecking order hypothesis. *Financial Management, 18*(2), 26–35.

Berger, P., & Ofek, E. (1995). Diversification effect on firm value. *Journal of Financial Economics, 37*(1), 39–65.

Billett, M., & Mauer, D. (2000). Diversification and the value of internal capital markets: The case of tracking stocks. *Journal of Banking and Finance, 24,* 1457–1490.

Black, F., & Scholes, M. (1973). The pricing of options and corporate liabilities. *Journal of Political Economy, 81,* 637–654.

Boone, A., Haushalter, D., & Mikkelson, W. (2003). An investigation of the gains from specialized equity claims. *Financial Management, 32*(3), 67–83.

Borison, A., Eapen, G., Mauboussin, M., & McCormack, J. (2003). University of Maryland roundtable on real options and corporate practice. *Journal of Applied Corporate Finance, 15*(2), 8–23.

Brealey, R., & Myers, S. (2003). *Principles of corporate finance* (7th ed.). New York: McGraw-Hill/Irwin.

Brennan, M., & Schwartz, E. (1985). Evaluating natural resource investments. *Journal of Business, 58,* 135–157.

Bughin, J. (2001). Managing real options in broadcasting. *Communications and Strategies, 41,* 63–78.

Chan-Olmsted, S. M., & Chang, B. H. (2003). Diversification strategy of global media conglomerates: Examining its patterns and determinants. *Journal of Media Economics, 16,* 213–233.

Compaine, B., & Gomery, D. (2000). *Who owns the media? Competition and concentration in the mass media industry* ( 3rd ed.). Mahwah, NJ: Lawrence Erlbaum Associates.

Copeland, T., & Antikarov, V. (2001). *Real options: A practitioner's guide.* New York: Texere.

Damodaran, A. (2001). *Corporate finance: Theory and practice.* New York: Wiley.

Dimpfel, M., Habann, F., & Algesheimer, R. (2002). Real options theory, flexibility and the media industry. *The International Journal on Media Management, 4,* 261–272.

Dixit, A. K., & Pindyck, R. S. (1994). *Investment under uncertainty.* Princeton, NJ: Princeton University Press.

Dixit, A. K., & Pindyck, R. S. (1995). The options approach to capital investment. *Harvard Business Review, 72*(3), 105–115.

D'Souza, J., & Jacob, J. (2000). Why firms issue target stock. *Journal of Financial Economics, 56,* 459–483.

Elder, J., & Westra, P. (2000). The reaction of share prices to tracking stock announcements. *Journal of Economics and Finance, 24*(1), 36–55.

Gershon, R. A. (2002, September 29). *The deregulation paradox: The telecommunications industry in crisis.* Paper presented to the 30th Annual Telecommunications Policy Research Conference, Alexandria, VA.

Grullon, G., & Michaely, R. (2002). Dividends, share repurchases, and the substitution hypothesis. *Journal of Finance, 57,* 1649–1684.

Harper, J., & Madura, J. (2002). Sources of hidden value and risk within tracking stock. *Financial Management, 31*(3), 91–109.

Hovakimian, A., Opler, T., & Titman, S. (2002). The capital structure choice: New evidence for a dynamic tradeoff model. *Journal of Applied Corporate Finance, 15*(1), 24–30.

Kalay, A., & Michaely, R. (2000). Dividends and taxes: A re-examination. *Financial Management, 29*(2), 55–75.

Kaplan, S., & Weisbach, M. S. (1992). The success of acquisitions: The evidence from divestitures. *Journal of Finance, 47,* 107–138.

Kester, W. (1984). Today's options for tomorrow's growth. *Harvard Business Review, 62*(2), 153–160.

KPMG. (1999). *Unlocking shareholder value: The keys to success.* New York: Author.

Kulatilaka, N. (1993). The value of flexibility: The case of a dual-fuel industrial steam boiler. *Financial Management, 22*(3), 271–280.

Luehrman, T. (1998). Investment opportunities as real options: Getting started on the numbers. *Harvard Business Review, 76*(4), 51–67.

Mason, S., & Merton, R. (1985). The role of contingent claims analysis in corporate finance. In E. Altman, & M. Subrahmanyan (Eds.), *Recent advances in corporate finance* (pp. 175–193). Homewood, IL: Irwin.

Mauboussin, M. (1999, June 23). Get real. *Credit Suisse First Boston Equity Research.*

McCormack, J., LeBlanc, R., & Heiser, C. (2003). Turning risk into shareholder wealth in the petroleum industry. *Journal of Applied Corporate Finance, 15*(2), 67–72.

Merton, R. C. (1973). Theory of rational option pricing. *Bell Journal of Economics, 4,* 141–183.

Miller, M. H. (1986). Behavioral rationality in finance: The case of dividends. *Journal of Business, 59,* S451–S468.

Miller, M. H., & Modigliani, F. (1961). Dividend policy, growth, and the valuation of shares. *Journal of Business, 34,* 411–433.

Mitchell, M. L., & Lehn, K. (1990). Do bad bidders make good targets? *Journal of Applied Corporate Finance, 3*(2), 60–69.

Modigliani, F., & Miller, M. H. (1958). The cost of capital, corporation finance, and the theory of investment. *American Economic Review, 48*, 261–297.

Modigliani, F., & Miller, M. H. (1963). Corporate income taxes and the cost of capital: A correction. *American Economic Review, 53*, 433–443.

Mun, J. (2002). *Real options analysis.* Hoboken, NJ: Wiley.

Munk, N. (2004). *Fools rush in: Steve Case, Jerry Levin, and the unmaking of AOL Time Warner.* New York: Harper Business.

Myers, S. C. (1984). The capital structure puzzle. *Journal of Finance, 39*, 575–592.

Myers, S. C. (2000). The capital structure. *Journal of Economic Perspectives, 15*, 81–102.

Myers, S. C., & Majluf, N. S. (1984). Corporate financing and investment decisions when firms have information investors do not have. *Journal of Financial Economics, 13*, 187–222.

Ozanich, G., & Wirth, M. (2004). Structure and change: An industry overview. In A. Alexander, J. Owers, R. Carveth, A. Hollifield, & A. Greco (Eds.), *Media economics: Theory and practice* (3rd ed.; pp. 69–84). Mahwah, NJ: Lawrence Erlbaum Associates.

Real options and the new economy (2000). *Journal of Applied Corporate Finance, 13*(2), 1–128. (Entire publication)

Real options and the new economy. (2001). *Journal of applied Corporate Finance, 14*(2), 1–28.

Shapiro, D. S. (2001, June 21). The cable warrant. *Banc of America Securities Equity Research* (pp. 1–21).

Shapiro, D. S. (2004, July 7). Hey big media: The jig is up on big media mergers. *Banc of America Equity Research* (pp. 1–21).

Shyam-Sunder, L., & Myers, S. C. (1999). Testing static trade-off against pecking-order models of capital structure. *Journal of Financial Economics, 51*, 219–244.

Triantis, A., & Borison, A. (2001). Real options state of practice. *Journal of Applied Corporate Finance, 14*(2), 8–24.

Trigeorgis, L. (1996). *Real options.* Cambridge, MA: MIT Press.

# 8

# Issues in Strategic Management

Sylvia M. Chan-Olmsted
University of Florida

## FROM INDUSTRIAL MEDIA ECONOMICS TO STRATEGIC MEDIA MANAGEMENT

What makes a radio station initiate an aggressive Internet venture to deliver its programming product online? What makes an established cable television network develop multiple subniche networks to exploit the brand power of its existing network? What makes a broadcast television network merge with a movie studio? Many of these managerial decisions are a result of the dynamic relationship between a media organization, its environment, and its attempt to develop and implement activities that align its organizational resources with environmental changes. In a nutshell, the study of strategic management addresses the process and content of such alignment efforts.

When applied in a media industry setting, the emphasis in strategy, by nature, shifts the central question of how media firms, at the aggregated level, meet the needs of audiences, advertisers, and society and the factors that have an impact on the production and allocation of media goods / services to how individual media firms' various actions obtain competitive advantage and superior performance in the marketplace. In essence, strategic media management offers additional insights about the nature of mass media as business entities at the firm level, complementing existing media economics research that often provides the normative view of resource allocation of media goods. However, whereas media economics as a field of study has flourished in the last decade, a relatively limited amount of research has focused on the aspect of *media firms* (Picard, 2002a).

A media strategy study may be defined as the examination of one or more aspects of the financial, marketing, operations, and personnel functions that lead to the sustainable competitive advantage (SCA) of a firm or a group of firms in media industries. Scholarly investigation may focus on strategy formulation (content) or strategy implementation (process), conceptual or empirical, economic or noneconomic issues, or a combination of the aforementioned approaches. Various scholars have ventured into the study of media firms, discussing competition dynamics with the theory of the niche in explaining media competition and coexistence (Dimmick, 2003), introducing the essential aspects in evaluating media *firms* (Picard, 2002a; Picard 2002b), and applying strategic management concepts to assess media firm strategies (Chan-Olmsted & Jung, 2001; Chan-Olmsted & Li, 2002).

The first part of this chapter introduces the field of strategic management with discussions of its history, theoretical foundations, supporting analytical frameworks, and empirical investigation issues. The applicability of major strategic management paradigms in a media context are then examined. Next a media strategy analytical framework is integrated and proposed. Finally an array of future research directions are suggested. In this chapter, primary emphasis is placed on the resource-based view of strategic management rather than on other approaches to studying strategy, such as industrial economics, organizational management, culture, creativity, and leadership, which have been frequently investigated in the media economics and management literatures.

## HISTORY OF STRATEGY STUDIES

Strategy research or, more reflective of the academic discipline in higher education, strategic management is a relatively young field of study that surfaced in the late 1960s, often under the term *business policy*. Strategic management is primarily concerned with the integration of firm decisions with goals, products/services offered, competitive approaches in the market, business scopes and diversity, organization structure, etc. (Rumelt, Schendel, & Teece, 1996). The focus on the *strategy* component of a firm or a group of firms actually originated from the general capstone courses offered in many MBA programs in the United States. Such an origin has significant implications for the initial direction of strategic management as an academic field of inquiry. Unfortunately, the field's traditional emphasis on integrating disciplines and practical applications translated into limited theory construction during its early stage of development (Hoskisson, Hitt, Wan, & Yiu, 1999). The study of strategy went beyond the initial descriptive, prescriptive, and case study approach when a handful of scholars began researching the relationship between strategy and performance (Hatten & Schendel, 1977; Hatten, Schendel, & Cooper, 1978). The popularity of Porter's (1980) *five-forces framework* in offering a structured, analytical approach in integrating industrial economics and firm strategy established Industrial Organization (IO) as the first major paradigm for strategy research. As the field of strategic management matures, the theoretical frameworks constructed and examined have become more eclectic.

In fact, because of the complexity and breadth of this subject, many different theories on the studies and practice of strategic management have emerged. They may be summarized into two main approaches: the prescriptive and the evolutionary. Although the two basic approaches share some commonalities, the prescriptive approach stresses that the practice of strategic management is a rational and linear process with well-defined and developed elements before the strategy begins. By comparison, the evolutionary view does not present a clear, final objective for its strategy as it believes that strategy emerges, adapts, and evolves over time (Lynch, 1997). Chaffee (1985) further suggested that strategy can be studied from three distinct approaches: linear strategy, which focuses on planning and forecasting; adaptive strategy, which emphasizes the concept of *fit* and is most related to strategic management; and interpretive strategy, which sees strategy as a metaphor and thus views it in qualitative terms. After analyzing contemporary research and taking into consideration the historical perspectives in this area, Mintzberg, Ahlstrand and Lampel (1998) went on to identify 10 *schools* of strategy research that have developed since strategic management emerged as a field of study during the 1960s. These scholars proposed that the *design schools* see strategy as a process of conception; the *planning schools* treat strategy as a formal process; the *positioning schools* view strategy as an analytical process, the *entrepreneurial schools* regard strategy as a visionary process; the *cognitive schools* see strategy as a mental process; the *learning schools* treat strategy as an emergent process; the *power schools* view strategy as a process of negotiation; the *cultural schools* regard strategy as a collective process; the *environmental schools* see strategy as a reactive process; and the *configuration schools* treat strategy as a process of transformation. The contrasting definitions of the 10 emphases clearly show that the studies of strategy or strategic management have evolved tremendously over time.

## THEORETICAL FOUNDATIONS IN STRATEGIC MANAGEMENT

### From the Beginning: The Industrial Organization (IO) View of Strategy

As mentioned earlier, the study of strategic management has its roots in industrial economics. Based primarily on industrial organization concepts, the discipline has traditionally focused on the linkage between a firm's strategy and its external environment. Such a linkage is especially evident in the Structure-Conduct-Performance (SCP) paradigm proposed by Bain (1968) and popularized with a strategic flavor by Porter (1985). Specifically, the foundation of strategic management as a field may be traced to Chandler's definition of strategy as a set of managerial goals and choices, distinct from a structure, and the allocation of resources necessary for carrying out these goals (Chandler, 1962). In a sense, the industry structure in which a firm chooses to compete determines the state of competition, the context for strategies, and, thus, the resulting performance of the strategies (Collis & Montgomery, 1995; Grant, 1991). Process-wise, the IO approach of developing competitive advantage begins with examining the external environment, followed by locating an industry with high potential for above average returns. A strategy is then formulated to benefit from the exogenous factors, and assets and skills are developed to effectively implement the chosen strategy (Hitt, Ireland, & Hoskisson, 2001).

Some have argued that one of the most significant contributions to the development of strategic management came from industrial economics paradigms, especially the work of Michael Porter. His SCP model and the notion of strategic groups, where firms are clustered into groups of firms with strategic similarity within and differences across groups, have established a foundation for research on competitive dynamics (Hoskisson et al., 1999). As economics scholars gradually adopt other theories such as "game theory," "transaction costs economics," and "agency theory," strategic management research moves closer to firm level and competitive dynamics (Hoskisson et al.). Beginning in the late 1980s, business scholars, seeking to explain the impact of firm attributes/behavior, such as diversification, vertical integration, and technological experience, on performance (Lockett & Thompson, 2001), started investigating an inside–out, resource-based view of strategy.

## The Arrival of Internal Competency: The Resource-Based View (RBV) of Strategy

Emphasizing the critical value of the internal resources of a firm and the firm's capabilities to manage them, the resource-based view (RBV) assumes that each firm is a collection of unique resources that provide the foundation for its strategy and lead to the differences in each firm's performance (Hitt et al., 2001; Peteraf, 1993; Wernerfelt, 1984). The RBV of the firm grew out of a need to identify the sources of the differential performance of firms (Hoskisson et al., 1999). The RBV literature stresses that a firm's heterogeneous resources are the foremost factors influencing performance and sustainable competitive advantage.

According to the RBV, four specific attributes—value, rareness, nonsubstitutability, and inimitability—must work in tandem to increase performance. Valuable resources "exploit opportunities and/or neutralize threats in a firm's environment" (Barney, 1991, p. 105). A rare resource is one that is not easily located and implemented, moving firms beyond the *competitive parity* that is associated with common resources. Similarly, a nonsubstitutable resource has no strategic equivalents that perform the same function. The final factor—imperfect imitability—virtually guarantees a firm's sustainable competitive advantage, but it must work jointly with the aforementioned characteristics. That is, although a resource may be valuable, rare, and not easily substituted, it must be inimitable to bestow the firm with a sustained competitive advantage. Imperfect imitability may be the result of three factors: unique historical conditions, causal ambiguity, and/or social complexity (Barney, 1991).[1] The concurrent interactions, then, between these four resource attributes form the basis of a firm's superior performance.

Process-wise, an RBV approach begins with identifying and assessing a firm's resources and capabilities, locating an attractive industry in which the firm's resources and capabilities can be exploited, and finally selecting a strategy that best utilizes the firm's resources and capabilities relative to opportunities in that industry (Hitt et al., 2001). Scholars, such as McGahan and Porter (1997), examined the relationship between the comparative impact of firm (an RBV approach) and industry (an IO approach) attributes on firm performance and concluded that firm-related factors seem to carry more weight in influencing performance.

---

[1] That is, competitors may not be able to capture and recreate the historical conditions that have led the firm to experience success. They may not be able to understand the linkages between the firm's resources and its competitive advantage, or they may be unable to unravel the complex interactions among resources.

As a theoretical framework of investigation, the RBV approach has become more popular among strategic management scholars since the 1990s after the initial dominance of the IO approach. There seems to be an interesting parallel in such a progression between the general studies of strategic management and strategy studies in the context of media economics. As some media scholars pointed out, historically, there has been an overreliance on industrial organization studies in media economics (Picard, 2002a); examinations of the exogenous factors (i.e., the IO framework) that influence firm conduct have been the primary focus of many media industry studies. As we move toward the study of media firms, the RBV investigative approach might provide more insight into explaining the differential performance between individual media firms or various clusters of media firms.

## What Kind of Resources?

In examining a firm's strategy, the relationship between strategy and resources, and the linkage between strategy and performance, strategy scholars developed a number of resource categorization systems in an attempt to assess the differential contributions of various resources to performance in different market environments. Hofer and Schendel (1978) suggested that resources can be classified into six categories: financial resources, physical resources, human resources, technological resources, reputation, and organizational resources. Barney (1991) placed firm resources into three groups: physical capital resources, human capital resources, and organizational resources. Porter (1996) maintained resources are of three types: activities, skills/routines, and external assets, such as reputations and relationships. Black and Boal (1994) further argued that resources are best classified as operating in bundles—or network configurations—of two types: contained resources and system resources, based on the complexity of the network to which the resource belongs. Habann (2000), from a different perspective, divided firm resources into two sets according to their contents: competence, which refers to firm-specific capabilities, and strategic assets, which refer to tangible and intangible assets of strategic importance.

Nonetheless, Miller and Shamsie (1996) and Das and Teng (2000) maintained that the classification of resources is theoretically sound only when incorporated into the aforementioned four attributes. Specifically, because the basis of a sustainable competitive advantage lies mainly in the inimitability of a resource, categorization of resources therefore must incorporate this notion of imperfect imitability. Resources, thus, may be classified into two broad categories: property-based resources and knowledge-based resources, each based on the inimitability of property rights or knowledge barriers, respectively. Miller and Shamsie further incorporated Black and Boal's (1994) concept of resource configurations, thus subclassifying property-based and knowledge-based resources into discrete or systemic resources. That is, both property-based and knowledge-based resources may stand alone or compose part of a network of resources.

Specifically, property-based resources are inimitable because of the protection afforded by property rights. A firm may secure a competitive advantage based on the length of the protection, thus proscribing competitors from imitation and appropriation of the resource (Miller & Shamsie, 1996). Contractual agreements form the foundation of the two types of property-based resources. Discrete property-based resources, for example, "take the form of ownership rights or legal agreements that give an organization control over scarce and valuable inputs, facilities, locations, or patents" (Miller & Shamsie, p. 524). Disney, for example, has "international rights to about 853 feature films, 671 cartoon shorts and animated features, and tens of thousands of television productions" (Hollywood wired, 2001). Systemic property-based resources include configurations of physical facilities and equipment whose inimitability lies in the complexity of the network configurations. Viacom's television station group, which consists of 34 owned and operated (O&O) stations, is an example of systemic property-based resources (Viacom Television Stations Group, n.d.).

Knowledge-based resources refer to a firm's intangible know-how and skills, which cannot be imitated because they are protected by knowledge barriers. Competitors do not have the know-how to imitate a firm's processed resources, such as technical and managerial skill (Hall, 1992). McEvily and Chakravarthy (2002) attributed uncertain imitability to complexity, tacitness, and specificity of knowledge. Like property-based resources, knowledge-based resources are comprised of discrete and systemic resources. Discrete knowledge-based resources, such as technical, creative, and functional skills, stand alone. The management experience of specific media subsidiaries is an example of discrete knowledge-based resources. Systemic knowledge-based resources, on the other hand, "may take the form of integrative or coordinative skills required for multidisciplinary teamwork" (Miller & Shamsie, 1996, p. 527). Increasing attention in the strategy literature within the RBV framework has centered on the factor of *knowledge*. Many studies focused on how firms generate, leverage, transfer, integrate, and protect knowledge (Wright, Dunford, & Snell, 2001). Some went even further, arguing for a "knowledge-based" theory of the firm, under the notion that firms exist because they can better integrate, apply, and protect knowledge than can markets (Grant, 1991; Liebeskind, 1996). In recent years, knowledge-based competition has become a popular area of study among strategic management scholars and practitioners. Some researchers claim that knowledge is the most important source of sustainable competitive advantage and performance (McEvily & Chakravarthy, 2002).

## Resource Typology in Media Industries

The property–knowledge-based typology presents a meaningful system for classifying and analyzing media firms' resources because knowledge-related resources are particularly important in developing competitive advantages in a media industry: where the end product is mostly in the form of intangible content, where creativity and industry knowledge remain the essential elements in the production of the content product, and where content is often seen as the key to success in any media distribution system. Furthermore, because of the fact that today's media industries are entering a period of unprecedented changes brought about by emerging new technologies such as the Internet and digitization, examinations of knowledge-based resources for media firms are becoming more critical. For example, applying the property–knowledge resource typology, Landers and Chan-Olmsted (2002) studied the broadcast television networks' changing strategies longitudinally as the broadcast market becomes less stable because of many technological developments. The notion of market uncertainty might be another important factor to investigate. As Miller and Shamsie (1996) discovered in their study of

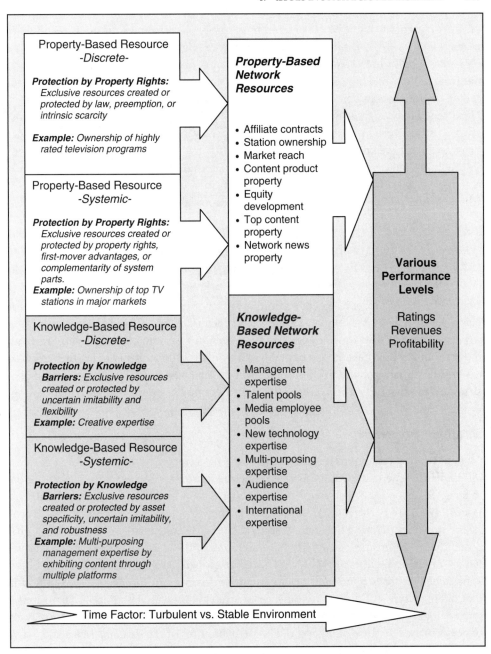

FIG. 8.1. A resource-based view framework for analyzing the network TV market.

the Hollywood film studios, property-based resources—both discrete and systemic—led to superior performance in the stable environment, whereas knowledge-based resources led to superior performance in the uncertain environment.

Figure 8.1 illustrates a possible resource typology as applied in the network television market (Landers & Chan-Olmsted, 2002). As depicted, resources such as affiliate contracts (or franchise agreements for cable television), station ownership, and content product copyright might be considered property-based resources, whereas technology management and content multipurposing expertise might be viewed as knowledge-based resources. Logically, the list of resources would be somewhat different depending on the nature and the value chain of the particular media market. For example, for the newspaper sector, distribution and printing properties represent essential property-based resources. Note that knowledge is a difficult resource to measure because of its fluidity. Most strategy studies used proxies for knowledge-related variables under the assumption that firms acquire more knowledge about activities they invest or engage in to a greater extent (McEvily & Chakravarthy, 2002). In the case of media industries, film / TV program awards and managers' average tenures were used as proxy measures for such a variable (Landers & Chan-olmsted, 2002). The drawback of such an empirical procedure will be discussed later.

## SUPPORTING ANALYTICAL FRAMEWORKS IN STRATEGIC MANAGEMENT

The IO and RBV perspectives for examining strategy establish the basic approaches for investigating a firm's functional, business, and corporate activities and their relationship to performance. Three more areas of study—strategic taxonomy, strategic network, and, more recently, strategic entrepreneurship—have also made a substantial contribution to the strategic management literature and will be reviewed next. These supporting constructs offer a rich theoretical base from which more media strategy studies might spring.

### Strategic Taxonomy

Classification of strategy types offers the utility of comparative analysis and systematic assessment of the relationship between different strategic postures and market performance. To this end, the strategy typologies proposed by Miles and Snow (1978) and Porter (1980) are perhaps the most popular frameworks used by strategic management researchers for analyzing business strategy (Slater & Olson, 2000). Whereas Porter proposed that most business strategies fall under one of the strategic types—*focus, differentiation,* or *low-cost leadership,* Miles and Snow developed a framework for defining firms' approaches in product market development, structures, and processes. The notion is that different types of firms have differential strategic preferences. Though firms in the same category might have a similar strategic tendency, they could achieve various levels of performance because of differential implementations of the strategy. Miles and Snow classified firms into four groups:

1. Prospectors, who continuously seek and exploit new products and market opportunities, often the first-to-market with a new product/service.
2. Defenders, who focus on occupying a market segment to develop a stable set of products and customers.
3. Analyzers, who have an intermediate position between prospectors and defenders by cautiously following the prospectors, while at the same time, monitoring and protecting a stable set of products and customers.

4. Reactors, who do not have a consistent product-market orientation but act or respond to competition with a more short-term focus. (Zahra & Pearce, 1990)

Despite the differences in strategic aggressiveness, empirical studies found that except for the reactors, the other three groups of firms achieve equal performance on average (Zahra & Pearce, 1990). The implication is that the implementation of the strategy is most critical to the performance variation within each strategy type. Strategic taxonomy might be applied in the media industries to empirically assess how organization factors/activities contribute to the effective implementation of different strategies. For example, how have different types of television stations, with their various organizational resources and capabilities, implemented their Internet-related strategies? The taxonomy approach also provides a useful framework for analyzing cross-media competition in an increasingly converged media world. For example, instead of investigating media corporations by sectors, which is becoming increasingly meaningless, one might use the Miles and Snow typology to examine these firms by analyzing their strategic preferences toward different media sectors.

## Strategic Networks

The media industries are among the top sectors for seeking out network relationships with other firms, both horizontally and vertically. This network orientation might be attributed to: media content's *public goods* nature; the media industries' need to be responsive to audience preferences and technological changes; and the symbiotic connection between media distribution and content.

Strategic networks may be defined as the "stable inter-organizational relationships that are strategically important to participating firms." These ties may take the form of joint ventures, alliances, and even long-term buyer-supplier partnerships (Amit & Zott, 2001, p. 498). In essence, firms might seek out such interorganizational partnerships to gain access to information, markets, and technologies, and to cultivate the potential to share risk, generate scale and scope economies, share knowledge, and facilitate learning (Gulati, Nohria, & Zaheer, 2000). Research in strategic networks often addresses questions that deal with such factors as the drivers and process of strategic network formation; the type of interfirm relationships that help participating firms compete; the sources of value creation in these networks; and the linkage between performance and participating firms' differential network positions and relationships (Amit & Zott, 2001).

Transaction cost economics provides the principal theoretical approach for explaining strategic network formation and development, particularly in the form of joint ventures (Ramanathan, Seth, & Thomas, 1997). Various theories (e.g., agency theory, resource-based view, organizational learning, and other strategic behavior perspectives) attempted to explain the factors influencing such networking strategies and their performance. Specifically, several drivers were proposed to influence a firm's adoption of a joint venture strategy. These include: competition reduction, access to resources or restricted markets, new business knowledge acquisition, market leadership maintenance, resource alliances for large projects, industry standards development, overcapacity reduction, and/or the increase of speed in product development or market entry (Hitt et al., 2001).

The most evident strategic network forms in the media industry are joint ventures and alliances. Many media firms have attractive core competencies such as the ownership of valuable content/talent and distribution outlets, but lack the size, access, or expertise to benefit from these unique resources and capabilities. Strategic networks not only offer an opportunity for access to a greater combination of competencies, but also reduce barriers to entry (e.g., scale economies and brand loyalty) in newer, technology-driven media markets such as the Internet and broadband sectors. Many recent studies in media industries found alliances to be a preferred method of entering the Internet, broadband, and wireless markets (Chan-Olmsted & Chang, 2003; Chan-Olmsted & Kang, 2003; Fang & Chan-Olmsted, 2003). The network strategy may also serve as a precurser for the essential merger and acquisition strategy. For example, Local Marketing Agreements (LMAs), which exist in many local television markets, offer participating stations access to expanded sales/marketing resources while, at the same time, reducing competition.

The notion of strategic networks also complements the strategic taxonomy research framework. Examination of firm resources and resource typology for media products are especially appropriate because of the tendency of media firms' to adopt alliance strategies that enhance the value of a content product through content repurposing, cross-promotion, and product windowing, and to pool resources together to compete in a fast changing information technology environment. In a sense, the RBV theory of strategic management provides the fundamental rationale for many alliance studies (Barney, 1986; Zahra, Ireland, Gutierrez, & Hitt, 2000). By the same token, RBV and the corresponding resource typology studies present an excellent opportunity for media scholars to examine alliances in the media industries with a more theory-driven framework. For example, Liu and Chan-Olmsted (2002) examined the strategic alliances between the U.S. broadcast television networks and Internet firms in the context of convergence using the aforementioned property–knowledge resource typology.

## Strategic Entrepreneurship

Media industries are fundamentally shaped by many entrepreneurs who took the risks required to introduce a media product in response to opportunities presented by environmental changes. From Disney to CNN to the DISH Network, media entrepreneurs such as Walt Disney, Ted Turner, Charlie Ergen, and many more have offered new products and/or developed new markets, and, in the process, become famous. In a sense, strategic entrepreneurship offers an excellent framework for investigating how media products evolve and develop over time.

Entrepreneurship is a well-established disciplinary area that is increasingly regarded as highly complementary to the study of strategic management. This is because both are primarily concerned with growth and wealth creation, albeit with slightly different emphases (Ireland, Hitt, & Sirmon, 2003). Whereas strategic management is based mostly on the theories of competitive advantage, entrepreneurship often concentrates on the theories of organizational creativity, innovation, and opportunity recognition/exploitation. Integrating entrepreneurial activities with strategic perspectives, strategic entrepreneurship may be defined as the strategic management and deployment of resources for identifying and exploiting opportunities to form competitive advantages and thus superior performance in established firms or new ventures.

Scholars suggested that strategic entrepreneurship manifests itself differently in established firms versus smaller firms or new ventures (Ireland et al., 2003). Although established firms are more skilled at developing sustainable competitive advantages, they are often less able to effectively identify new market opportunities. On the other hand, smaller firms or new ventures often excel at recognizing and exploiting new market opportunities, but they are often less capable of sustaining competitive advantages. Nevertheless, entrepreneurial attitudes and conduct are important for firms of all sizes to survive and prosper in competitive environments (Barringer & Bluedorn, 1999).

Ireland et al. (2003) suggested four dimensions of strategic entrepreneurship: entrepreneurial mindset, entrepreneurial culture and leadership, strategic management of resources, and development of creativity and innovation. Specifically, *entrepreneurial mindset* is defined as a way of approaching business with a focus on uncertainty in order to capture the benefits of uncertainty (McGrath & MacMillan, 2000). Such a mindset enables a firm to proactively and cognitively handle environmental risk and ambiguity because of its orientation toward growth opportunities and promotion of flexibility, creativity, innovation, and renewal. *Entrepreneurial culture* is defined as a set of shared entrepreneurial values that shape a firm's (and its members') behavioral norms and thus actions. The value system might include expectations of creativity, risk taking, occasional failure, learning and innovation, and continuous change. A related concept, *entrepreneurial leadership*, is the ability to influence others, nurture the aforementioned culture, and manage resources to both exploit opportunities and sustain competitive advantages. *Strategic management of resources* includes the functions of structuring, integrating, and leveraging of financial, human, and social capital to enhance entrepreneurial activities. Finally, the *development of creativity and innovation* involve the process of bisociation (i.e., the combining of previously unrelated information or skills; Koestler, 1964) that results in either disruptive (brand new) innovation or sustaining (improved) innovation (Ireland et al., 2003).

As discussed earlier, alliances and joint ventures have been a staple strategy in media industries. It would also be fruitful to investigate strategic entrepreneurship in the context of strategic network formation, especially the topic of alliance proactiveness, which might create access relationships to resources and capabilities that contribute to the exploitation of opportunities (Sarkar, Echambadi, & Harrison, 2001). Another concept that is especially suitable to incorporate in a media context is *entrepreneurial intensity*. Scholars found that firms in turbulent environments tend to be more innovative, risk taking, and proactive (Naman & Slevin, 1993). As the media environment continues to be infused with new technologies such as content digitization and the Internet, it would be interesting to examine how strategic entrepreneurship in the media sectors is influenced by external contexts, both in intensity and approaches (e.g., attitudes and activities).

## ISSUES IN STRATEGIC MANAGEMENT EMPIRICAL STUDIES

Strategic management researchers found it challenging to develop ways to empirically test the resource-based view of the firm because valuable resources, by nature, are less observable (Godfrey & Hill, 1995).[2] As previously stated, the resources and capabilities that create sustainable competitive advantages are valuable, rare, not substitutable, and imperfectly imitable. Such a definition seems to be fundamentally tautological and presents difficulties in strategy measurement and thus causality examination. It becomes even more challenging when intangible, knowledge-based assets are considered. Lockett and Thompson (2001) concluded that causal ambiguity and firm-specific opportunity sets have been the greatest challenges for empirical testing in such studies.

In response to such measurement challenges, early scholars focused on examining strategies using in-depth case studies, especially in instances in which less tangible resources are involved (Hoskisson et al., 1999). Although one might review a firm or a group of firms in their market context, by adopting detailed field-based case studies that incorporate both archival and interview data, the lack of large data sets to test theory and apply multivariate statistical tools creates significant challenges for strategic management researchers. It also makes it more difficult for media strategy studies to become a more mature, respected scholarly field of study. Finally, because it is difficult to measure many intangible resources, proxy variables such as awards (e.g., Emmys) and salaries (e.g., CEO's compensation) were used as measures of many intangible resources (Landers & Chan-Olmsted, 2002; Miller & Shamsie, 1996). Some strategic management researchers expressed reservations that proxies may not be valid measures for many underlying constructs (Godfrey & Hill, 1995).

In response to such empirical challenges, some strategy researchers tried combining quantitative questionnaires and qualitative interviews to increase the validity and reliability of their measures (Henderson & Cockburn, 1994). Some suggested a step-by-step approach—first, identify a potential resource; second, examine its properties theoretically based on previous research; then measure the effect of the resource on performance (Deephouse, 2000). Because of the multiplicity of methods needed to identify, measure, and understand firm characteristics, strategy might be best researched as a dynamic or evolutionary phenomenon and empirically approached with a combination of longitudinal, in-depth case studies and other quantitative measures.

In terms of the application of statistical techniques, cluster analysis, which groups observations into similar segments, has been used frequently in strategic management research since the 1970s. This multivariate technique is often used because the variables in strategy studies are complex and multidimensional. As a result, researchers need some way to identify sets of firms that share commonalities among a set of variables and to find configurations that capture the complexity of organizational reality (Ketchen & Shook, 1996). Nevertheless, cluster analysis has been heavily criticized by scholars in recent years because of its extensive reliance on researcher judgment and its lack of test statistics for hypothesis testing. In fact, many empirical studies in strategic management failed to find links between group membership and performance. As a result, strategic management scholars recommend limited use of this statistical technique and stress the importance of selecting variables inductively. When using this technique, researchers should also pay extra attention to determining and validating the number of clusters (Ketchen & Shook, 1996).

---

[2] A valuable resource would be easier to imitate and thus lose its value once it becomes observable.

## APPLICABILITY OF STRATEGIC MANAGEMENT IN MEDIA INDUSTRIES

This section will turn the focus from the more generic theoretical and empirical discussions in strategic management to the application of these same concepts and issues in media industries by introducing the unique characteristics of media products, certain media taxonomies, and an analytical framework for investigating strategic behavior of media firms.

### The Characteristics of Media Products

Strategic decisions are often resource dependent and rely on the specificity within a particular industry (Chatterjee & Wernerfelt, 1991). To this end, media products exhibit certain unique characteristics that shape the strategic directions of media firms. The major distinction between media and nonmedia products rests in the unique combination of a number of characteristics.

First, media firms offer dual, complementary products of *content* and *distribution*. The content component is intangible and inseparable from a tangible distribution medium. Second, most media content products are nonexcludable and nondepletable public goods whose consumption by one individual does not interfere with its availability to another but adds to the scale economies in production. Third, many media firms rely on dual revenue sources from consumers and advertisers. Fourth, many media content products use a windowing process to market content. For example, theatrical films are delivered to consumers via multiple outlets sequentially in different time periods (e.g., home video sales, home video rentals, cable and satellite television pay-per-view, pay cable networks, and broadcast networks). In a sense, the potential revenue for such a content product depends on the total number of distribution points and pricing at these points. Fifth, the market boundaries between various types of media products are becoming blurred (i.e., the degree of substitutability is increasing) because of technological advances. Sixth, each media content creation (not the distribution medium or a duplicated copy), by nature, is heterogeneous, nonstandardizable, and individually evaluated based on consumers' personal tastes. In other words, whereas Maytag may manufacture a new washing machine that contains certain standardized features, no movies can legally claim to contain identical content from the *Harry Potter and the Chamber of Secrets* movie. Even Ms. Rowland herself will not pen a standardized set of Harry Potter books. Finally, media products are subject to the cultural preferences and existing communication infrastructure of each geographic market/country and are often subject to more regulatory control from the host market because of how pervasive their impact is on individual societies.

The characteristics of media products listed earlier lead to a market environment in which certain strategies are often observed. For example, as intangibles, content-based media products may be stored and presented in various formats. A strategy of *related product diversification*, which extends a media firm's product lines into related content formats (e.g., print and online content), typically benefits firms by enabling content repurposing, marketing know-how, and sharing of production resources, and thus is likely to be preferred. It is also logical for media firms to seek out distribution products and content products that complement each other. The concept of resource alignment has been discussed extensively in the alliance literature. This concept emphasizes the importance of accessing resources that a firm does not already possess, but which are critical for improving its competitive position (Barney, 1991; Das & Teng, 2000). The symbiotic relationship between media content and distribution products provides a classic case of resource alignment. The fact that an existing product may be redistributed to and reused in different outlets, via a windowing process, reinforces the advantage of diversifying into multiple related distribution sectors in various geographical markets to increase the product's revenue potential. Furthermore, because of the importance of cultural sensitivity and understanding of the regulatory environment, media firms are more inclined to diversify into related product/geographic markets to take advantage of their acquired local knowledge and relationships.[3] The dependency on local communication/media infrastructure may also lead to a strategy that is geographically related (i.e., regionalized). This is because geographically clustered markets are often at similar stages of infrastructure development, and clusters of media distribution systems may lead to cost/resource-sharing benefits. For example, many U.S. cable systems and radio stations are geographically clustered.

The dual-revenue source mechanism and the public goods characteristic of media content products also create a driver for firms to offer media content that appeals to the largest possible group of marketable consumers. This is because the larger aggregated number of subscribers/audience adds to the value of advertising spots/space with minimal incremental costs for the firms. On the other hand, because of the heterogeneous, nonstandardizable, creative characteristic of media content products, intangible resources become especially essential in building competitive advantages. As a result, small firms that do not have access to a mass audience but which possess unique creative resources, still have the opportunity to achieve superior performance.

Media products are also especially sensitive to intangible resources by nature. Intangible resources, such as technology and brand loyalty, often lead to diversification so a media firm might exploit the *public goods* nature of these assets (Chatterjee & Wernerfelt, 1991).

## Media Product Taxonomy

As discussed earlier, technological development is constantly changing the degree of substitutability between different types of media products. For example, the increasing application of digitization is blurring radio product consumption patterns as more and more audiences begin listening to radio stations on the Internet. As a result, it might be fruitful to examine the audio product or the providers of the product from the perspective of the consumer rather than of the radio industry. In other words, as technology shifts more control and power to consumers, media strategies and competitive dynamics should be evaluated based on consumer, rather than industry, factors or definitions.

---

[3]Geographic market relatedness may also be examined in terms of language and cultural relatedness (e.g., Spanish language media content).

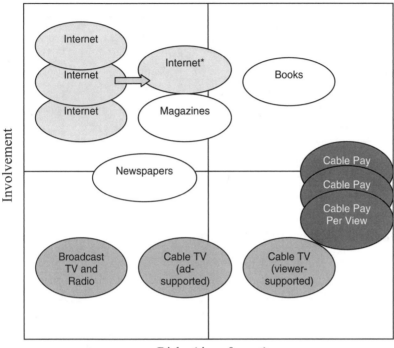

FIG. 8.2.   A proposed media product taxonomy.
  *This might be paid or personalized online content in which the audience has invested money and/or relatively more time.

One example would be to review the relative positions of different media firms using consumer-based concepts such as risk involved (i.e., time and cost invested) and degree of involvement. Figure 8.2 illustrates such a media product taxonomy. Media products—like the Internet, broadcast radio and television, cable television, books, and magazines—are classified based on how involved a typical consumer might be with the specific media product and how much time and cost are required to consume the product. These factors influence consumers' perceived risk and, thus, their assessment of the value of that product. For instance, although the Internet, by nature, is a relatively more involved product than broadcast television, pay cable is often perceived to involve more risks and is, therefore, subject to different value scales than the mostly free Internet content product. Alternatively, paid Internet content product is evaluated differently as it moves to the right on the risks scale. The taxonomy may be used to assess the competitive dynamics of various firms in a particular media market or a mixture of media markets. It may also be used as a tool for analyzing corporate strategy portfolios. The integrated factors of risks and involvement are only one example of a consumer-based framework for analyzing media products and firms. As technology continues to reshape the media landscape, strategy scholars need to construct more theoretically sound taxonomies to reflect the changing nature of media products and to take into consideration the factor of consumer choice and consumers' changing degree of control over the media products they consume.

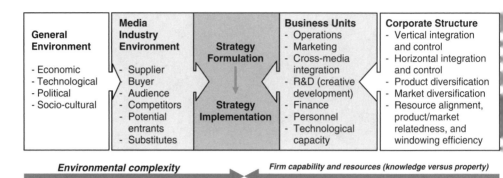

FIG. 8.3.   A proposed system of factors that affect strategy formulation and implementation.

## A Media Strategy Research Framework

Incorporating both the IO and RBV concepts, it is proposed that media strategy researchers utilize a system of factors that might affect the formulation and implementation of strategy in the media industries. This analytical framework integrates both exogenous and endogenous variables and serves as a beginning point to stimulate more media strategy inquiries (see Fig. 8.3). Theoretically, a media firm's strategy (formulation) and its ability to execute that strategy (implementation) are influenced by a combination of external factors relating to the general environment and a particular media market in which the media firm operates. General exogenous forces, such as the economy and technological advancement, affect the interplay of the six forces present in a specific media industry (e.g., changing audience preferences and the degree of substitution among different media products or altering the content-media outlet/supplier–buyer relationship), ultimately influencing the strategic behavior of a media firm. The environmental complexity is further complicated by a series of firm capabilities and resources at the business and corporate level, which shape the firm's strategy. Either property or knowledge-based, a media firm's corporate structure (e.g., its degree of vertical and horizontal integration with other media properties, its product and geographical diversification, and its windowing and resource alignment corporate capabilities) along with its specific business unit resources and capabilities (e.g., cross-media integration and marketing), directly determine the type of strategy formulated and implemented.

## FUTURE RESEARCH IN STRATEGIC MEDIA MANAGEMENT

To assess the development of media studies that address the issue of strategy at the firm level and to substantiate and integrate strategic management (a branch of management studies) into the field of media economics, this chapter elaborates on the general theories of strategy and discusses the application of these concepts to media products. As the field of media economics becomes a more mature area of study, it is essential for scholars to enhance the rigor of the discipline by developing theories that draw on new or modified paradigms from other established academic fields. To this end, the theoretical frameworks of IO and RBV provide a good starting point for communication scholars, who are interested in firm strategies, to empirically test the robustness of such concepts in unique media industries.

The field of media economics will benefit from more firm-based studies as it moves beyond inquiries focused on gaining a fundamental understanding of media industries and markets and their policy implications (Picard, 2002a). These firm-level investigations need to adopt an analytical framework that is more theory driven, such as paradigms from the field of strategic management.

This chapter suggested an array of strategic management theories for further applications in a media context. Media management and economics researchers should also survey the scholarly work published in the top strategy research academic journals: *Strategic Management Journal*, *Academy of Management Journal*, *Academy of Management Review*, the *Journal of Management*, and the *Journal of Management Studies* (Park & Gordon, 1996).

The fluidity of media industries, because of the continuous changes in communication technology, creative development, and audience preferences, requires media management and economics scholars to constantly introduce, incorporate, and test new paradigms. A multiplicity of theories is needed in this area of study because media management and economics, by nature, is a multidimensional discipline. In fact, some management scholars have begun to incorporate mass communication theoretical concepts into their application of resource-based theories. For example, Deephouse's (2000) *Journal of Management* article integrated mass communication and resource-based theories by viewing media reputation as a strategic resource.

## Future Research Directions

It is often useful to anticipate the course of an ongoing research agenda by first assessing the answers to the fundamental questions of—what highlights the presumptions and boundaries of the field? (Rumelt, Schendel, & Teece, 1996). A specific list of questions might be:

- How do a certain group of media firms behave?
- Why are these media firms different?
- What determines media firm success or failure?

Operationally, one might investigate the empirical patterns of media firms or propose theoretical assumptions to explain the observed behavioral patterns. The implications of these strategic patterns would then be empirically examined.

In the area of theory, it would be good to investigate the incorporation of *value chain* in the context of media industries. This would provide an excellent architecture for systematically understanding the sources of buyer value and thus approaches to differentiation. Researchers may also want to incorporate the aforementioned constructs of strategic networks, strategic entrepreneurship, and strategic taxonomy. These theories might help explain many firm behaviors such as mergers, acquisitions, and alliances, which occur frequently in media industries. Media taxonomy might be introduced to examine the relationship between specific business strategies (e.g., sales force management) and performance within each media firm type (e.g., prospectors versus defenders). Additionally, online or digital media ventures present an excellent avenue for the study of strategic entrepreneurship in a media setting because of the ventures' novelty and potential for generating new value through new product introduction and by changing the rules of competition.

Going back to the fundamental theories of strategic management, RBV theories present a fertile foundation through which to empirically investigate the behavior and performance of media firms. For example, one might adopt an RBV framework to understand the patterns of diversification and market entry in media industries both domestically and globally. One might also focus on human resource management (HRM) with an RBV approach, emphasizing people as strategically important to the success of a media firm. The RBV can also be used as a frame of reference for studying media marketing. Scholars might examine how changes in market-based assets and capabilities influence audience value creation. For example, the RBV can be used to assess inimitability through cross-selling and bundling.

In summary, the study of media strategy is a branch of media research that integrates the often industry-based, more macro issue-focused field of media economics with the traditional, personnel management/OB-oriented field (organizational behavior) of media management. It is an area of investigation that presents tremendous challenges and opportunities for the next phase of research in media economics.

# REFERENCES

Amit, R., & Zott, C. (2001). Value creation in e-business. *Strategic Management Journal, 22*, 493–520.

Bain, J. S. (1968). *Industrial organization* (2nd ed.). New York: Wiley.

Barney, J. (1986). Types of competition and the theory of strategy: Toward an integrative framework. *The Academy of Management Review, 11*, 791–800.

Barney, J. (1991). Firm resources and sustained competitive advantage. *Journal of Management, 17*, 99–120.

Barringer, B. R., & Bluedorn, A. C. (1999). The relationship between corporate entrepreneurship and strategic management. *Strategic Management Journal, 20*, 421–444.

Black, J. A., & Boal, K. B. (1994, Summer). Strategic resources: Traits, configurations and paths to sustainable competitive advantage [Special Issue—Strategy: Search for New Paradigms]. *Strategic Management Journal, 15*, 131–148.

Chaffee, E. (1985). Three models of strategy. *Academy of Management Review, 10*, 89–98.

Chandler, A. (1962). *Strategy and structure*. Cambridge, MA: MIT Press.

Chan-Olmsted, S. M., & Chang, B. (2003). Diversification strategy of global media conglomerates: Examining its patterns and drivers. *Journal of Media Economics, 16*, 213–233.

Chan-Olmsted, S. M., & Jung, J. (2001). Strategizing the net business: How television networks compete in the age of the Internet. *International Journal on Media Management, 3*. Retrieved August 3, 2002, from http://www.mediamanagement.org/modules/pub/view.php/mediajournal-57

Chan-Olmsted, S. M., & Kang, J. (2003). The emerging broadband television market in the United States: Assessing the strategic differences between cable television and telephone firms. *Journal of Interactive Advertising, 4*. Retrieved May 18, 2004, from http://jiad.org

Chan-Olmsted, S. M., & Li, C. C. (2002). Strategic competition in the multichannel video programming market: An intraindustry strategic group analysis . *Journal of Media Economics, 15*, 153–174.

Chatterjee, S., & Wernerfelt, B. (1991). The link between resources and type of diversification: Theory and evidence. *Strategic Management Journal, 12*, 33–48.

Collis, D. J., & Montgomery, C. A. (1995). Competing on resources: Strategy in the 1990s. *Harvard Business Review, 73,* 118–129.

Das, T. K., & Teng, B. (2000). A resource-based theory of strategic alliances. *Journal of Management, 26,* 31–61.

Deephouse, D. L. (2000). Media reputation as a strategic resource: An integration of mass communication and resource-based theories. *Journal of Management, 26,* 1091–1113.

Dimmick, J. W. (2003). *Media competition and coexistence.* Mahwah, NJ: Lawrence Erlbaum Associates.

Fang, L., & Chan-Olmsted, S. M. (2003). Partnerships between the old and the new: Examining the strategic alliances between broadcast television networks and Internet firms in the context of convergence. *International Journal on Media Management, 5,* 47–56.

Grant, R. M. (1991). The resource-based theory of competitive advantage: Implications for strategy formulation. *California Management Review, 33,* 114–135.

Godfrey, P. C., & Hill, C. W. (1995). The problem of unobservables in strategic management research. *Strategic Management Journal, 16,* 519–535.

Gulati, R., Nohria, N., & Zaheer, A. (2000). Strategic networks. [Special issue]. *Strategic Management Journal, 21,* 203–215.

Habann, F. (2000). Management of core resources: The case of media enterprises. *International Journal on Media Management, 2,* 14–24.

Hall, R. (1992). The strategic analysis of intangible resources. *Strategic Management Journal, 13,* 135–144.

Hatten, K. J., & Schendel, D. E. (1977, December). Heterogeneity within an industry. *Journal of Industrial Economics, 26,* 97–113.

Hatten, K. J., Schendel, D. E., & Cooper, A. C. (1978). A strategic model of the U.S. brewing industry: 1952–1971. *American Management Journal, 21,* 592–610.

Henderson, R., & Cockburn, I. (1994, Winter). Measuring competence? Exploring firm effects in pharmaceutical research. *Strategic Management Journal, 15,* 63–84.

Hitt, M. A., Ireland, R. D., & Hoskisson, R. E. (2001). *Strategic management: Competitiveness and globalization.* Cincinnati, OH: South-Western College Publishing/Thomson Learning.

Hofer, C. W., & Schendel, D. (1978). *Strategy formulation: Analytical concepts.* St. Paul, MN: West.

Hollywood wired. (2001, January). *Multichannel News International.* Retrieved June 21, 2002, from http://www.onesource.com

Hoskisson, R. E., Hitt, M. A., Wan, W. P., & Yiu, D. (1999). Theory and research in strategic management: Swings of a pendulum. *Journal of Management, 25,* 417–456.

Ireland, R. D., Hitt, M. A., & Sirmon, D. G. (2003). A model of strategic entrepreneurship: The construct and its dimensions. *Journal of Management, 29,* 962–989.

Ketchen, D. J., & Shook, C. L. (1996). The application of cluster analysis in strategic management research: An analysis and critique. *Strategic Management Journal, 17,* 441–458.

Koestler, A. (1964). The act of creation. New York: Dell.

Landers, D., & Chan-Olmsted, S. M. (2002, August). *Assessing the changing network television market: A resource-based analysis of broadcast television networks.* Paper submitted for presentation to the Media Management and Sales Division of the Broadcast Education Association, Miami, Florida.

Liebeskind, J. P. (1996). Knowledge, strategy, and the theory of the firm. *Strategic Management Journal, 17,* 93–109.

Liu, F., & Chan-Olmsted, S. M. (2002, April). *Partnerships between the old and the new: Examining the strategic alliances between broadcast television networks and Internet firms in the context of convergence.* Paper submitted for presentation to the Media Management and Sales Division of the Broadcast Education Association, Las Vegas, Nevada.

Lockett, A., & Thompson, S. (2001). The resource-based view and economics. *Journal of Management, 27,* 723–755.

Lynch, R. (1997). *Corporate strategy.* London England.

McEvily, S. K., & Chakravarthy, B. (2002). The persistence of knowledge-based advantage: An empirical test for product performance and technological knowledge. *Strategic Management Journal, 23,* 285–305.

McGahan, A. M., & Porter, M. E. (1997). How much does industry matter, really? *Strategic Management Journal 18,* 15–31.

McGrath, R., & MacMillan, I. C. (2000). *The entrepreneurial mindset.* Boston: Harvard Business School Press.

Miles, R. E., & Snow, C. C. (1978). *Organizational strategy, structure, and process*. New York: McGraw-Hill.

Miller, D., & Shamsie, J. (1996). The resource-based view of the firm in two environments: The Hollywood film studios from 1936 to 1965. *Academy of Management Journal, 39*, 519–543.

Mintzberg, H., Ahlstrand, B., & Lampel, J. (1998). *Strategy safari: A guided tour through the wilds of strategic management*. New York: The Free Press.

Naman, J., & Slevin, D. (1993). Entrepreneurship and the scope of fit: A model and empirical tests. *Strategic Management Journal, 14*, 137–153.

Park, S. H., & Gordon, M. E. (1996). Publication records and tenure decisions in the field of strategic management. *Strategic Management Journal, 17*, 109–128.

Peteraf, M. A. (1993). The cornerstones of competitive advantage: A resource-based view. *Strategic Management Journal, 14*, 179–190.

Picard, R. G. (2002a). *Media firms: Structure, operations, and performance*. Mahwah, NJ: Lawrence Erlbaum Associates.

Picard R. G. (2002b). *The economics and financing of media companies*. New York: Fordham University Press.

Porter, M. (1980). *Competitive strategy*. New York: The Free Press.

Porter, M. (1985). *Competitive advantage: Creating and sustaining superior performance*. New York: The Free Press.

Porter, M. (1996). Toward a dynamic theory of strategy. In R. P. Rumelt, D. E. Schendel, & D. J. Teece (Eds.), *Fundamental issues in strategy: A research agenda* (pp. 423–461). Cambridge, MA: Harvard Business School Press.

Ramanathan, K., Seth, A., & Thomas, H. (1997). Explaining joint ventures: Alternative theoretical perspectives. In P. W. Beamish & J. P. Killing (Eds.), *Cooperative strategies: North American perspectives* (pp. 51–85). San Francisco: New Lexington Press.

Rumelt, R. P., Schendel, D. E., & Teece, D. J. (1996). Fundamental issues in strategy. In R. P. Rumelt, D. E. Schendel, & D. J. Teece (Eds.), *Fundamental issues in strategy: A research agenda* (pp. 9–47). Cambridge, MA: Harvard Business School Press.

Sarkar, M., Echambadi, R., & Harrison, J. S. (2001). Alliance entrepreneurship and firm market performance. *Strategic Management Journal, 22*, 701–711.

Slater, S. F., & Olson, E. M. (2000). Strategy type and performance: The influence of sales force management. *Strategic Management Journal, 21*, 813–829.

Viacom Television Stations Group. Retrieved April 3, 2003, from http://www.viacom.com/prodbyunit1.tin?ixBusUnit=10000019

Wernerfelt, B. (1984). A resource-based view of the firm. *Strategic Management Journal, 52*, 171–180.

Wright, P. M., Dunford, B. B., & Snell, S. A. (2001). Human resources and the resource based view of the firm. *Journal of Management, 27*, 701–723.

Zahra, S. A., Ireland, R. D., Gutierrez, I., & Hitt, M. A. (2000). Privatization and entrepreneurial transformation: Emerging issues and a future research agenda. *The Academy of Management Review, 25*, 509–525.

Zahra, S. A., & Pearce, J. (1990). Research evidence on the Miles Snow typology. *Journal of Management, 16*, 751–768.

# 9

# Issues in Media Product Management

Ángel Arrese Reca
University of Navarra

The management of different media products constitutes a field of research and operational know-how posing numerous challenges, which, therefore, cannot be easily dealt with in a generic way. As in other areas of media management and economics, applying the general principles of management to the daily running of media companies has led to the discovery of a series of attributes characterizing the way that these products perform in the market. However, those features cannot be easily generalized for the whole media. The basic differences between products such as a free newspaper and a film, or between a musical performance and a television program, are so significant that any attempt to consider them as a whole would be very risky. Because of the varied nature of the media products themselves, it is wise to be cautious when putting forth ideas, theories, or universal principles. This becomes all the more evident as one examines the diverse literature and specific research on the subject. Concerning the management of newspapers, magazines, TV networks, programs, and films, there is a vast array of partial research that has already been carried out on specific aspects of that task, although very little thought and analysis have been bestowed on the handling of the media product itself.

This chapter, endeavors to widen our knowledge in this field of study, with due caution, by attempting to focus on a series of features borne in the management of any kind of media product. To achieve this, the chapter examines the special properties of media products, especially those found in varying degrees in all of them, which determine the fundamental decisions taken about them. Second, and as a result of the challenges posed by the media product, several essential operational issues regarding the product will be pinpointed—defining the formats, quality management, price schemes and content leverage. Finally, several areas of interest indicating how these products evolve in the markets and their effect on a number of organizational aspects will be highlighted.

## THE COMPLEX NATURE OF MEDIA PRODUCTS

Throughout economic and marketing literature, the product is generally defined by an arrangement of attributes or properties. Thus, product management plays a significant role in differentiating those attributes to meet the diverse needs and goals of target markets in a favorable, sustainable, and profitable way. Bearing this in mind, it stands to reason that any decision making affecting the product is intimately connected to its nature, which in the case of media products, is unique and complex.

On the whole, media products are comprised of two elements. On the one hand is the immaterial component (news, fiction, persuasive contents); on the other, the material component (the medium or means by which it reaches the consumer). Although both work jointly to meet the public's needs, the demand for media products depends primarily on its content elements and, to a smaller degree, on its transmission elements, despite the fact these are crucial when considering product accessibility. Therefore, the key feature of media products is their ability to satisfy their potential clients' needs and goals for contents of an informative, persuasive, or entertaining nature.

On this basis, the specificity of media products is defined by a set of basic components that distinguishes them from other products. Owing to their remarkable nature, some of these features are a result of the products as economic goods, whereas other characteristics stem from the particular social and cultural significance underlying the different types of content (Bates, 1988). Three basic aspects characterize media products from both perspectives: media products as information goods, media products as dual (multiple) goods, and media products as talent goods.

### Media Products as Information Goods

Varian (1999) defined information goods as "anything that can be digitized" (p. 3). From that point of view, Varian asserts that information goods carry three key properties: they are experience goods, they are subject to economies of scale, and they display features that resemble those of public goods.

To begin, media products are experience goods to a smaller or larger extent, which implies that they can only be valued once they have been consumed (Nelson, 1970). The uncertainty that arises from this standpoint can only be diminished by resorting to browsing, previewing, reviewing, as well as by building up a reputation through a strong brand. The fact that media products are experience goods very often means that product management must seek to win the customer's trust. This will be achieved by adequately exploring value perception (quality–price ratio), which will be boosted or altered over time with the aid of an ongoing learning process. Along these lines, many media products behave also as credence goods—consumers cannot judge the quality they receive compared to the quality they need (see Darby & Karni, 1973; Wolinsky, 1995).

The weight experience carries, along with the consumer's confidence in these products, play a vital role in their management.

Second, information goods are subject to *scale and scope economies*. Both phenomena are connected to the cost framework common to many of them: high fixed production costs for first copies and low variable costs, in some cases almost imperceptible, for reproduction. This structure enables marginal costs to be steadily reduced as the number of articles consumed grows (scale economies principle), besides securing substantial savings in both multiproduct commercialization strategies and in reselling ventures of a multiformated product (scope economies principle; Doyle, 2002, pp. 13–15). In addition, because of the unparalleled character of this economic structure, cross-financing is vital for a large number of media products (Ludwig, 2000), on the grounds that sales income is insufficient to finance their production.

Finally, information goods share, in varying degrees, qualities commonly found in public goods, those which depend on nonrival and nonexclusive consumption. As far as the media is concerned, there are a variety of ways to face rivalry and exclusiveness in consumption. Whereas free on-air television and radio have generally been regarded as public goods, newspapers, music, and cinema have more relation to private goods (i.e. their character bears a strong resemblance to that of private goods). The reason behind this is that although content consumption is nonrival in theory (nonrivalry means that if one individual consumes the good, this does not reduce the utility other individuals can derive from it), in reality rivalry appears through the use of a specific medium that is used for transmitting and receiving that content. Moreover, the different forms of payment have sparked the emergence of exclusion (in variable degrees). Taking these behavioral patterns into account, it is not surprising that over many years the debates that have flared over the efficiency of state or market provision of these goods as well as their economic impact have constituted a prime line of research (Anderson & Coate, 2000; Minasian, 1964; Samuelson, 1964).

However, when trying to determine whether media products are public or private, we must bear in mind that a large proportion of them are of a purely private nature, because they are contemplated as advertising media. According to Sjurts:

> In the advertising market, however, media content is a fully marketable private good. In this market there is rivalry between the advertisers for the advertising space, since the supply is limited for legal or cost reasons. The exclusion principle is practised in the advertising market through the price for printed and broadcast advertising space (Sjurts, 2002, p. 5).

On the basis of the circumstances mentioned, instead of referring to media products as public or private goods, we can refer to them as *shared goods* (Bakos, Brynjolfsson, & Lichtman, 1999; Goldfinger, 2000). They can be included in this category for several reasons: the coexistence of tangible and intangible elements in all of them; an ever-increasing capacity to reproduce content in numerous media outlets; and the possibility of consuming them sequentially or simultaneously, in diverse time or space frames.

Just as Goldfinger explains, "for tangible artefacts, purchase does not equal consumption (How many people read all the books they buy?) and consumption does not imply purchase: in newspapers or in broadcast television, the number of 'free riders' routinely exceeds that of paying consumers by a factor of three to four" (Goldfinger, 2000, p. 63). This hybrid or shared nature of media products is a source of specific problems in crucial areas such as handling content rights, not only with regard to those who own them, but also to those who receive the contents.

## Media Products as Dual (Multiple) Goods

Despite the fact that there is a vast range of media products, their multiple-purpose use is one of their basic common features. As a result, media products are usually called dual goods (Picard, 1989, pp. 17–19), because they are mainly made up of two supplementary products geared toward two very different markets: content for the audience and the time dedicated by the audience for the advertisers. This makes it easy to grasp the meaning of the metaphor that describes the media as "a bridge between advertisers and audiences" (Lavine & Wackman, 1988, p. 254).

Consequently, media product operations warrant, on the one hand, decision making that enables content products and audience products to blend together efficiently while, on the other hand, keeping in mind that each of them demands its own specific strategies encompassing design, product quality, price, distribution, and promotion. Research on media economics and management has traditionally sought to analyze the interrelations between these products by highlighting how management of one product is affected by the decision-making on the other. A few examples that illustrate this reality are the research on the degree of interdependence that news and ad content hold in the press (Gabszewicz, Laussel, & Sonnac, 2000), the analysis of the complexity of price decision making as a result of the interrelation between readers and advertisers' demands (Blair & Romano, 1993), and the notion that a media product is primarily an audience product, laying the groundwork to comprehend a product from a receptor's position (Napoli, 2001, 2003).

An integrating factor from both an advertising perspective and a reception viewpoint is to contemplate media products as attention goods. Simon synthesised this approach with his now famous words: "What information consumes is rather obvious: it consumes the attention of its recipients. Hence, a wealth of information creates a poverty of attention, and a need to allocate that attention efficiently among the overabundance of information sources that might consume it" (Simon, 1971, p. 40).

Media products compete in an economy of attention (Goldhaber, 1997), in which parameters such as time of consumption, repetition and frequency, compatibility or incompatibility with the consumption of other goods are of significant importance (Aigrain, 1997). Hence, media markets can be viewed as time markets (Albarran & Arrese, 2003; Vogel, 1998, pp. 3–8), where content and advertisements strive to draw that basic resource. That is the reason why both the manufacturing and commercialization stages of media products are greatly conditioned by time factors. Their differences lie not only in their time elasticity—which is more or less durable as far as consumption goes—but also in other time factors that have a bearing on their production and distribution. Picard and Grönlund (2003) state:

> Although a number of temporal issues affect the market structure and operations of media, the primary contributor is the time sensitivity of the medium or, more specifically, the

content that it conveys. Media industries vary greatly in terms of time sensitivity, reflecting the different roles they play for audiences. These differences in sensitivity affect the locations from which audiences can be served, the production and distribution operations of media, and the substitutability of media. (pp. 58–59)

Yet, in addition to these two basic dimensions that allows us to view them as dual goods found in most media products—content for audience and time attention for advertisers—there is a third dimension just as significant: one that justifies the public and political intervention in the sector. Apart from the specific content receptors and advertisers, media products have a third key client: society. Schultz commented, "a major difference between traditional consumer product and media products is the influence and impact of the community and the society in the entire system. The media must serve not only the media user and the advertiser but the community, too" (Schultz, 1993, p. 5). This idea is clearly reflected by the fact that the media are the only business specifically protected by Constitutional laws (First Amendment, free speech rights, etc.).

A cross-section of the media product content displays content of a cultural and symbolic nature, which is the fruit of human creativity, having come to be known as the cultural industries. Accordingly, along with their economic value, media products have socio-cultural value. Products such as films or music belong to the cultural heritage of society. As for the news media, several parameters such as the quantity, quality, and range of products may even alter the socio-political structure of our societies (Picard, 2000a, 2001).

On the whole, cultural industries are comprised of primarily symbolic goods, and as a consequence, their economic value can never be disassociated from their cultural value. In spite of numerous differences between media cultural products and other artistic cultural products (traditional art), it is becoming harder from an economic standpoint to keep the historic boundary separating art and commerce. As O'Connor (1999) stated, both deal in symbolic value whose ultimate test is within a circuit of cultural value that, whether meditated by market or bureaucracy, relies on a wider sense of it as meaningful or pleasurable. Towse (2002) expressed that one of the crucial elements that unifies all kinds of cultural industries is the fact that their creativity is protected by copyright.

To be able to even consider media products as cultural goods would require far more analysis; therefore, one way of overcoming the constant onslaught of an ideological debate is to view them as goods whose management can generate both positive and negative socio-cultural externalities. As McFadyen, Hoskins, and Finn (2000) explain:

> The tension between economic and cultural development approaches to examining cultural industries is in part due to misunderstandings; the external benefits concept can be used to reconcile many of the differences. The belief that indigenous programming and film processing desirable attributes can make viewers better citizens is at the heart of both the economic (external benefits) and "cultural" arguments. (p. 130)

This is precisely an example of the essential argument put forward in Europe to publicly "protect" the broadcast of certain events on free on-air television, such as soccer (Boardman & Heargreaves-Heap, 1999).

The cultural nature of media products, as well as their potential to be dealt with as public goods, have largely legitimated state intervention in the sector, either through ownership or concrete regulations that affect these markets. The provision of media products from either the market or the state obviously has a decisive bearing on how they are operated. Tjernström (2002) contends that traditional literature on media management, based on the audience–advertiser duality, has not earnestly taken into account the whole spectrum of features found in products supplied by state-controlled organizations. The duality of those organizations is mainly comprised of the consumers (TV viewers, radio listeners, etc.) and politicians (who set the rules).

In the light of these reflections, it stands to reason that most media products are endowed with a multiple nature, more than just a dual one, owing to the vast range of uses they are able to offer to different clients (or key stakeholders).

## Media Products as Talent Goods

On considering the features that media products embody, it is possible to draw a significant conclusion: Media products depend on people's talent to a large extent so it would be fair to consider media products as talent products. In fact, the media sector embodies the principle that states that the most important asset of a business is its people.

According to Wolf (1999), "the entertainment economy will place enormous demands on a finite humane resource: creativity. . . . In the high-tech entertainment economy, the old-fashioned, low-tech motivator of change and innovation still reigns supreme: The most valued commodity is the human imagination (pp. 293, 296)." Imagination, creativity and, talent are the ingredients that make content products so successful for several reasons—in some cases, the "stars" are capable of drawing massive attention, whereas in others a particular team of professionals has the drive to come up with genuinely valuable content at a given moment or on a continuous basis.

Those activities that constitute the creative industries sector depend heavily on talent. Activities that are specific to these industries have been defined by CITF Creative Industries Task Force (CITF) in the United Kingdom as "those (activities) which have their origin in individual creativity, skill and talent, and which have the potential for wealth and job creation through generation and exploitation of intellectual property" (CITF, 2001). In spite of the similarities between the concept of creative industry and that of cultural industry, the use of the former in this section denotes just how critical individual (or group) creativity is in media product management. Evidently, not all media products rely on an individual's talent to the same degree, but the way talent is used is at the root of their success or failure. According to this, all media products seem to fit Caves' definition of a creative product; "the product or service that contains a substantial element of artistic or creative endeavour" (Caves, 2000, p. vii).

In *Creative Industries*, Caves (2000) synthesized the major characteristics of a creative product, highlighting its erratic behavior in the market. The causes of this behavior are, on the one hand, the *demand* (uncertainty in the consumption itself of the experience goods) and, on the other hand, the *offer* (which has no previous or sometimes even posterior knowledge of the key to success or failure). This joint uncertainty or *symmetric ignorance,* besides having to accept high fixed costs and successive sunk costs, entails undertaking great economic risks to produce creative products. Unlike other sectors, another vital element of these type of products is that "creative workers care about their product" (Caves, 2000, p. 4). Journalists, singers, actors, scriptwriters, etc. strive to maintain their preferences, tastes, and professional views, which in turn have a direct impact on the number and quality of the features embodied in the creative product. The professionals' creative inputs, almost irreplaceable, must be coordinated and harmonized in high complex work groups. At the same time they must be integrated with what Caves (p. 4) defines as "humdrum (non-creative) inputs," for example those such as distribution. Last, creative products are gifted with the immense ability to differentiate themselves, which is conditioned in great measure by the number of distinct creative skills in the market.

In view of all this, it is no wonder that the economics of stars has the power to alter media product management (Adler, 1985; McDonald, 1988; Rosen, 1981). This phenomenon has been dealt with thoroughly in the film industry (Marvasti, 2000; Wallace, Seigerman, & Holbrook, 1993), yet its significance remains enormously visible in other markets, ranging from music to the news media. Cases such as the swelling of Martha Stewart's or Oprah Winfrey's creative businesses are but the tip of the iceberg of that phenomenon, and they are sufficient proof that stars and individual talent are bearing greater weight on this sector with the passage of time. There are other cases in which talented individuals constitute *ingredient brands* (Norris, 1992; Venkatesh & Mahajan, 1997); the success of some products depends primarily on these ingredient brands, a kind of "Intel Inside" with a range of content formats. This is also true of cases in which some of the talents associate themselves with specific media brands, thus setting up real brand partnerships (Rao & Ruekert, 1994).

Unfortunately, attempting to operate the dependency of media products on those essential talented individuals poses a tricky added risk. The fact that those individuals are gifted with the power to sway audiences from one media to another, from one firm to another, means they wield great bargaining power, which at times conditions the chances some companies have to compete and survive. Hence, all aspects of a contract pertaining to a professional's activities and work are of the utmost importance in this sector.

These features borne by the media products cause product operations to be of a more complex nature for a number of reasons, among them is the difficulty in determining the keys for assessing the quality and value of the products and selecting the basic resources (above all talent) because there are times when there is an oversupply of creative ambitions and proposals. Although operating a newspaper may seem, in principle, diametrically different to managing a movie project, the gap diminishes when we consider them both as information goods, with multiple purposes and being dependent on talent.

## KEYS TO MANAGING MEDIA PRODUCTS: FORMAT, QUALITY, PRICE, AND CONTENT LEVERAGE

If we consider that the media product attributes are capable of satisfying specific market needs, namely information and entertainment, then as keys to product management, media products are quite similar to other products. Consequently, product management is constituted by making decisions in several fundamental areas: (a) definiing an offer;

(b) setting and managing quality standards; (c) determining the product's interconnection with price; and (d) making the product available. In the realm of media products, focusing on these basic aspects gives rise to a number of operational challenges that should draw researcher's attention.

## Deciding Media Formats

Considering the numerous differences that exist among the vast array of media and content, and in an attempt to establish a common denominator for all of them, it could be asserted that contents compete in format markets. In order to be able to determine the position and perception of media products in the market, it is essential to carefully choose the format (type of newspaper or magazine, type of music or film, style of television programming, radio format, etc). We can resort to terms like formats, genres, or types of content in order to identify the differences among products within the same medium, or to establish the categories of content within conventional markets (see how the concept of format is applied in research on the variety of radio offerings, as explained by Berry & Waldfogel, 2001). The concept of format can also be used to analyze the competition of products by theme among various types of media, as in the case of specialized news in the press, radio, and television (Arrese & Medina, 2002).

This concept of format, employed to typify and categorize the range of content offers, could also be applied by analogy to other features of media product management, especially those related to the different business models and distribution technologies. However, we shall deal exclusively with the former, that of content formats.

Considering product operations from the standpoint of format requires a large degree of decision making on the building blocks of the offer. From a certain perspective, a media product is nearly always formed by a unique combination of ingredients. That is the reason why the menu analogy can be resorted to in this sector. Hence, in terms of economics, a large proportion of media products are a combination of products that could or do have value in themselves, whether they are newspaper articles, scripts, individual performances, music, programs, commercials, etc. As a result, because of the great potential new technologies wield, the chance to exploit subproducts of the media product is increasing day by day. At the other end of the spectrum, the multimedia firms are finding it easier and easier to aggregate formats in multiproduct offers.

Therefore, the economics of bundling and unbundling is the pivot of management in the case of a large number of media products, as it dictates the content formats that compete in the market. Bakos and Brynjolfsson (1999) explained the strategy of selling a bundling of many distinct information goods for a single price that often yields higher profits and greater efficiency than selling the same goods separately.

A successful television program format is the integration of talent capable of working harmoniously to come up with a captivating product for a particular audience. A TV channel product consists of orchestrating a vast array of different formats, which as a whole constitutes a specific television offering; similarly, the product of cable or satellite TV is a combination of channels that work together forming a menu from which the viewer selects programs. Herrero (2003), for example, carried out research on the implications of this approach for pay television.

The underlying logic for selecting and adding value, for working on a range of ways to present media products, is becoming more evident through multiple commercial transactions that span from the sale of film packs to exhibitors and broadcasters to the role of sales promotion contents as an essential element of newspapers and magazines (Argentesi, 2003).

Unbundling constitutes a reverse strategy. A product that has been traditionally commercialized as a unit is broken down into elements or subproducts capable of meeting an audience's urge for particular ingredients inherent to that product. This process of unbundling is the key to customizing many information goods, by decomposing them into services and personalized contents, as is the case affecting the customization of electronic information services of old and new media (Ritz, 2002).

To maximize the earnings of their content, most media management works simultaneously with bundling and unbundling strategies or mixed systems of format configuration. As with other aspects already examined, management of content rights (their quantity, quality, range, life span, etc.) is a central issue in developing these strategies because of its capability to set into motion bundling initiatives that are more or less complex and attractive.

## Managing Quality

Configuring media products in highly complex formats as already described, has a direct effect on setting the quality standards of the offer or offers that a company provides. The quality of a media product is often a sum of qualities, many of which are very difficult to assess. As mentioned before, the fact that media products are basically experience goods of an intangible nature and endowed with a strong creative component poses innumerable problems in this area.

When managing the quality of media products one must bring several elements to work in a harmonious way: (a) features of objective quality (defined, even if vaguely, by the professionals themselves); (b) features of subjective quality (based on how satisfactorily specific audience needs and expectations have been met); and (c) so-called social quality (the ability of media products to fulfil cultural, political, and social aims in democratic societies). Integrating these three views of quality in intangible experience or credence goods presents itself as a challenging task, therefore it is not surprising that people's opinions on quality range from "nobody knows" to "I know it when I see it." The difficulty of integrating professional quality with financial feasibility and social gain is also at the root of much jostling among designers, managers, and social representatives over these products.

In the light of all these difficulties, much of the research conducted on media product quality is mainly from an industrial organization perspective rather than from a management perspective. Some of the outcomes of this perspective are the analysis of how several factors have a bearing on the quality offers, factors such as competitive structure (Waterman, 1989; Zaller, 1999), interrelation within demand because of its dual nature (Dewenter, 2003), market size (Berry & Waldfogel, 2003), degree of resource investment (Lacy, 1992), media ownership models (Coulson, 1994), and even audience diversity in the news media market (Mullainathan & Shleifer, 2003). Simultaneously, and owing to the importance of the social role the media plays, the concept of quality has been coupled with that of pluralism and diversity of offers in the market.

Yet though all these issues are undoubtedly of interest, what we are concerned about from a media product management angle is determining quality measures or parameters that can be reasonably used to improve quality. A research effort must guarantee that each one of the media products is dealt with individually as these products are to be considered on a format basis. In the case of newspapers, this line of research has produced interesting results. To name just two examples, Meyer and Kim (2003) shed light on the ties between journalism quality and business success, and Schoenbach (2000) dealt with the key to success for local newspapers in Germany. In the case of TV programming, pioneering work was carried out by Hoggart (1989) and Medina (1999) who tried to put forward quality criteria for TV programming. One further example, significant research in movies by Litman (1983), Thorsby (1990) and Ginsburgh and Weyers (1999) examined factors that predict success and quality of a film.

Most initiatives that are aimed at analyzing and managing the quality of media product somehow take the three dimensions just mentioned into account—quality defined by experts, quality based on audience satisfaction, and quality as social value.

An interesting approach to determine how those different views on the quality of a media product are related, and considered jointly, is taking into account how important the experts' role is with regard to their assessment, prescription, or reinforcement. Another approach is by resorting to other procedures that assess the offers before and after their consumption, thus influencing the audience's expectations or experience (Eliashberg & Shugan, 1997; Faber & O'Guinn, 1984).

Those views on quality are fundamental as media management work toward establishing a brand and building up the reputation of the product and its basic ingredients (programs, actors, anchors, journalists, etc.). There are a number of vital mechanisms for managing both the quality and the degree of importance in the success of the product, such as the role played by film critics (Reinstein & Snyder, 2000; Wyatt & Badger, 1984), the function of the director or actors or actresses starring in a movie as a mark of quality (Albert, 1998; Ravid, 1999), the winning of specific awards, for example, an Oscar, a Pulitzer, etc. (Nelson, Donihue, Waldman, & Wheaton, 2001), or a host of other ways to mark the so-called "chart business" (Jeffcutt & Pratt, 2002, p. 228).

Only by means of these marking devices, which are part of an ever-increasing marketing effort, will a media product be capable of reaching a critical mass, which in turn will trigger a number of network effects (changes in the benefit, or surplus, that an agent derives from a good when the number of other agents consuming the same kind of good changes). These effects, which are of an economic-technological and psycho-social nature, make that saying, "success breeds success," a process that is characteristic of specific fashion dynamics in some product categories or formats (Kretschmer, Klimis, & Choi, 1999). The significant role played by size—linked to success—and therefore to one aspect of quality, has undergone analysis in other markets, as in the case of some newspaper markets, in which network effects may partly be responsible for a tendency of media concentration, as a consequence of a circulation spiral (Gabszewicz, Laussel & Sonnac, 2002; Gustafsson, 1978).

On the basis of what has been pointed out with regard to marking and highlighting the significant role of size in quality management, it becomes evident that a score of multimedia strategies launched by the big multimedia groups have been aimed at aiding efforts to achieve synergies by means of diversification, cross-promotion activities, and by setting up complex gatekeeping systems in various market areas that reinforce each other. However, the success or failure of those strategies, and the specific outcomes of multimedia synergies, should be analyzed carefully. They usually depend more on right or wrong management decisions than on the benefits of theoretical mantras. As Jung (2003) explains, "more diversification does not always seem to be better. Hence, rather than pursuing diversification for its own sake, the management of a firm needs to choose businesses that lead to real economic gains" (p. 247).

At the same time a system geared toward marking quality and taking advantage of network effects may also have its drawbacks because of the difficulty in assessing quality objectively. To sustain a certain degree of quality over a length of time, above all in media products that depend on repetitive purchasing or loyalty (printed or audiovisual media), involves establishing a highly leveraged cost framework—one in which the profit margin can soar high above the break-even point. However, when that mark is not reached, then great losses can emerge. The temptation to strike out against basic resources affecting product quality is high throughout either advertising crisis spells or the need to improve results, especially when the audience's capability to assess quality is uncertain. In reference to the press market, Meyer commented, "the bottom-line benefits of reducing newspaper quality are immediate and visible. The long-term costs in reduced reader loyalty are slower to materialize" (Meyer & Kim, 2003, p. 9). This problem deserves special attention in the case of big media conglomerates. Jung (2003) states:

> From the perspective of the public, whether the fat media conglomerates would invest money to provide quality information and entertainment product is questionable. Even worse, if these same conglomerates are struggling financially due to their rampant diversification through mergers and acquisitions, which might lead to excessive debt levels, ultimately it is the public who will suffer. Big is not necessarily bad, but uncontrolled ambitious big, which may cause financial difficulty, might well conceive the seeds of disaster that can hurt the public, who need fair and high-quality media products and services. (p. 247)

Apart from product quality, another vital parameter that can assess the market behavioral patterns of firms and consumers is price. As far as the media products are concerned, the quality–price relation presents a range of peculiar features worth looking into as they affect price strategies for products.

## Pricing Policies

In reference to the nature of media products, as previously mentioned, there are several coexisting demands and price managers must strive to optimize several prices simultaneously to sell the product at a profit and meet the clients' value expectations. This can easily be detected in the newspaper, magazine, or pay television market, in which the price of the product has to be optimized with respect to advertising rates. In some cases, (e.g. several European public TV networks), this price structure must also bear in mind that some competitors receive government funding to produce their goods, thus making the traditional market price fixing framework more complex. Last, devising the range of pricing policies for the media and consequently the range of income systems is based on various schemes of free-use or payment by the end consumers, all of which are subject to third-party financing (mainly advertisers and public funding).

Pricing policies in this sector are challenged seriously not only by the financial properties of the media products (above all their cost framework and intangibility), but also because the media product competes in an attention-drawing economy. We must take into consideration that, in the media world, what interests the audience greatly today may be worthless tomorrow (as is the case of most current news) and vice-versa, something that drew no attention yesterday may end up in the spotlight today thanks to the revival of a trend, a remake of a film or song, etc. Yet the very same product may have the potential to be commercialized in various markets within a wide price range according to its life span. Therefore, the pricing of media products constitutes a managing tool that is highly dynamic, volatile, subject to a myriad of market or other kinds of forces, and unrelated to product cost. Furthermore, pricing policies become tremendously flexible once the initial investment on the first copy of the product is recovered and the lowest possible cost scheme for reproduction and distribution is established. So much so, that only very effective means to safeguard copyright can stop pirate sales markets that offer huge discounts or free consumption from emerging.

Based on these findings, the peculiarities that intangible goods embody render scores of traditional assessment mechanisms for transactions and pricing inadequate. Goldfinger (2000) claimed that applying the two traditional methods for pricing simply on the basis of production costs and on clients' value perception was quite difficult in the case of intangible goods.

On the one hand, a production cost scheme is useless in order to set up a pricing policy because inputs and outputs hold no proportionality. Samples of this phenomenon are content goods such as a book, song, or even a film, many of which are produced by means of very small creative teams but whose earnings may hold no relation to what we could call their standard cost. Scale economies in media products are determined by massive consumption, not by massive production.

On the other hand, the technique consisting in establishing consumers' willingness to pay is also limited when we consider how easy it is to reproduce and transmit content (consider the vast amount of musical piracy or the appropriation of news content from Internet Web sites) and how hard it is to evaluate that content before being consumed.

Considering these ideas, three main avenues about price decisions can be explored, which hold special interest for media markets: (a) adoption of pricing or free-use schemes; (b) pricing per unit or pricing per use; (c) resorting to price discrimination.

Throughout the commercialization and distribution phases, almost any media content is susceptible to a combination of these three schemes. Whether we choose a specific one or a combination of the three will determine the business framework because of the fact that its repercussions bear weight on the income system that is attempting to achieve the highest possible profit. Consequently, that may be the reason why, over the last few years, the releasing of content goods through the Internet has drawn great interest on the performance of different business models, based on varied price schemes (free-use, direct payment, or combinations of them; Picard, 2000b; Waterman, 2001).

The duality between products that are essentially financed by advertising as opposed to those financed mainly by the audience, with a great range of mixed financing systems, is beginning to sprout far more easily in scores of other markets, ranging from television to printed media. In terms of direct payment, all markets are endeavoring to create circumstances that will enable them to resort to mixed payment schemes consisting of charging for content use and content units, thus maximizing earnings (Fishburn, Odlyzko, & Siders, 1997). At the same time, the potential to work with a variety of price discrimination options (setting a range of prices for a product in the case of unjustified cost differences) is growing rapidly, as it could be expected with information goods (Varian, 1999). As a matter of fact, the content held by a large extent of media can be priced by drawing on the heterogeneous market assessment of their value. Discrimination based on consumption volume, various bundles of products, moment of consumption, client traits, or location are all becoming more widespread chiefly in the multimedia firm sphere thanks to not only their potential to develop intensive cross-selling activities, but also to their growing understanding of purchase preferences and clients' willingness to pay.

Serious setbacks affecting market perception, besides the fact that clients have always found it difficult to evaluate the range of offers, can be brought about by introducing price discrimination strategies, mixed schemes of payment based on use and units, and different offers of pay and free contents. The disorientation consumers suffer when the products undergo price alterations can lead to price wars, and, as a result diminish, the profit margins in that sector. That is probably the reason why price discrimination has always been the best option whenever there is a monopoly or clear-cut differentiation among products, because the producer can exploit different willingness to pay in the market. This is the logic underlying the creation of giant multimedia groups that aim to hold sufficient market power and grasp the largest possible portion of the audience, enabling them to have the widest price policies to maximize their earnings and profitability.

The spawning of this volume business (Vizjak & Ringlstetter, 2001, pp. 8–11) has meant the use of open distribution strategies, giving rise to *channel agnosticism*, whose main aim is to make content available to clients under whatever conditions they wish.

## Managing Content Leverage

As Hirsch (2000) explained "as the cost of technologies for making a record, printing a book, or filming a movie continues to decrease, control over their distribution becomes more critical for organizations seeking to reduce uncertainty over the outcome of their investments" (p. 356). Although this is not the place to discuss the essential role that distribution plays in the commercialization of media products, it is important to search to display content by means of all existing channels with the range of leverage strategies seeking to tap the potential of each media format as well as its elements or ingredients.

Accepting the idea of format as the crucial element in media content management, and taking the most basic format "the idea, the creative element of copyright works" (p. 5) as the starting point, Vizjak and Ringlstetter (2001) highlighted three content syndication levels. In the first level, additional usage applications are added to the existing content. The content format remains unchanged, however, the reception format undergoes alterations just like in the process of windowing movies. In the second level, product differentiation for market segments is achieved through versioning. Content digitization enables the design and commercialization of different versions from a basic content, in order to satisfy specific needs of different consumer segments. Finally, in the third level, "additional marketing potential is unlocked. A highly differentiated product portfolio can be marketed and used across and beyond media segments by means of cross-promotion and cross-selling" (p. 7). Perhaps the most visible proof of the expansion potential held by format or the original idea is that it has the power to go beyond the media sphere and help other products become worthwhile (by means of merchandising) in diverse economy sectors.

One of the prime features characterizing product managing in multimedia firms is the ability to exploit formats and ideas in such a manner that they are able to travel across media and technological boundary lines. The range of opportunities granted by content leverage almost equals the challenges posed by the quest to manage, in an efficient way, content capable of satisfying a host of formal and technological demands. Just to mention one example, the emergence of new hybrid devices, such as interactive set top boxes and personal digital video recorders, like TiVo, requires a range of new media formats that combine a variety of static and interactive multimedia content into a single media stream that can be differentiated for each market segment or individual. To reach that goal, work processes, existing technological systems, the organizational arrangement of the creative, marketing, and distribution areas, apart from the web of product and service suppliers, will need to be transformed in many cases.

In a world of multiformat offers, content leverage becomes brand leverage. It is becoming increasingly imperative to build strong brands with the potential to deal with a range of content offers but at the same time hold a consistent identity, especially in markets riddled with an overabundance of offers, low entrance barriers (regarding above all content production), and a highly volatile demand. These brands need to be characterized by a number of features: (a) the potential to deal with a range of content offers but, at the same time, hold a consistent identity; (b) the ability to undergo constant renewal yet hold on to relevant values and ties within the market; (c) the ability to set fine professional and creative standards, achieve public status, and aid consumers in the ever-increasing number of choices.

Hence, the striking thing, as already pointed out by Chan-Olmsted and Kim (2001), is the limited research and comprehension that exists on how media product brands, or at least those in subsectors such as news media, are managed or work. This is all the more surprising if we consider that the importance of the brands can only grow in the future. Likewise, there is little known about how to assess what type of brand will be the most appropriate in certain content spheres, and what kind of promotional campaigns will be needed in each case. Incomprehensibly, none of these aspects have been dealt with in depth by researchers.

This apparent paradox looming over brand managing—on the one hand, its importance yet, on the other hand, its falling into oblivion—is very likely to be caused by the behavioral patterns of the media products in the market. Although brands require stability, coherence, and consistency over a period of time, the truth of the matter is that most media products are subject to the laws of novelty, change, ongoing innovation, and perishability. Only when decisions are made regarding the evolution of media products in the market can we readily observe the consequences of that paradox.

## MANAGING THE LIFE OF MEDIA PRODUCTS AND PROJECTS

Academic literature on media economics and management conducted, from different angles, research on several issues concerning the introduction and development of a new media in the market, the substitution and complementarity between new media and old media, the diffusion of distribution technologies, and other factors that have an impact on market evolution. The majority of these analyses apply diffusion of innovation theories and marketing theories on product and life cycles to a range of media (press, radio, TV, Internet, etc.), but not to content types or formats (see Cohen-Avigdor & Lehman-Wilzig, 2002). Moreover, the life cycles of specific products, such as movies, has undergone in-depth study, from the degree of market seasonality in the sector (Radas & Shugan, 1998), to the timing for launching a new film (Krider & Weinberg, 1998).

From a more generic standpoint, which is underlying this chapter, the most stunning feature about the life of a media product is the need to make novelty and the relatively short life of each copy compatible with the consistency and durability of the brand format. There are newspapers over 100 years old but whose existence—owing to the nature of the medium—consists in updating an editorial project comprised of content that is born and dies practically on the same day. Because of the creative nature of media products, managing them becomes a nonstop innovation task whose time framework fluctuates from the real time in some online information contents to several years in film projects. Evidently each product has it own particular degree of creative intensity and complexity, though these tend to be overwhelmingly higher in both fiction and entertainment content compared to those of news content. In fact, each product is necessarily a new creation in the world of both audiovisual and cinema fiction, whereas in the sphere of news products, the format remains unaltered in spite of the winds of change brought about by daily events.

On these grounds, the concept of format innovation acquires special significance for media products. This innovation finds itself halfway between the longer cycles of the technological innovation and renovation of the medium and the shorter cycles belonging to the life span of each copy (whether it is a newspaper, a news broadcast, a CD, or a film). In view of this distinction, a series of relevant concepts in the world of contents acquire special meaning, as it happens with the concept of *stylistic innovation* (Schweizer, 2002, p. 18). According to Schweizer, a media product can be broken down into three elements: core product (issues, messages, etc.), inner form (which would be equivalent to the concept of format used in this chapter), and outer form (the technologically specific tangible form that helps content reach the consumers). Stylistic innovation could affect all three elements but seems to be best suited for inner form innovations. This idea of style applied to the media products does not differ much from the one used in other consumption areas, which are also creative ones, characterized by being highly dependent on the design and whose products have a life span mainly determined by fashion cycles, network effects, and information cascades (Bikchandani, Hirschleifer, & Welch, 1992, 1993).

Furthermore, the almost confusing intimate relationship between innovation and creativity processes in media products hinders this sector from acquiring innovation processes and systems found in other markets. Actually, in most cases, standardized prototypes that have been successfully tested cannot be resorted to in these markets. The prototype issue of a new magazine or the pilot program for a new TV series can be tested, but their results can only vaguely forecast the outcome of the launching of the new product. Once in the market, each new magazine issue and each new episode of a series is subject to creativity and innovation; each one is a new project.

Based on these findings, perhaps it can be asserted that managing products as projects is quite logical in the media world. This view becomes clearly visible in subsectors such as films (DeFillippi & Arthur, 1998), although it can be applied easily to other audiovisual media, even to print. Ekinsmyth (2002) conducted research on the editing techniques employed in various British magazine firms, concluding that in most cases the organizational and work framework—of their daily activity as well as the launching of new products—seemed to correspond to those used in project management. An example of this type of organization is the hiring of freelance labor on a cyclic and creative basis, an approach that is quite important to many other media products.

Besides requiring a project management approach, media product managing and its relentless urge for change demand flexible organizational approaches capable of being used in complex relationships networks. Starkey, Barnatt, and Tempest (2000), analyzing the case of British television firms, referred to the peculiar "latent organizations" that go into action as soon as a key project needs to be launched:

> In industries where transactions focus upon intermittent projects, networks can best sustain their effectiveness if they are sustained between projects by what we call *latent organizations*. Latent organizations are forms of organization that bind together configurations of key actors in ongoing relationships that become active/manifest as and when new projects demand. Because latent organizations offer the means of reuniting key actors for specific projects, they constitute an important source of continuity and of guaranteed quality of output in industries ostensibly characterized by impermanence and change. (p. 299)

That organizational flexibility and the emergence of key actor configurations to trigger new projects are essential in areas such as the media product field for a number of reasons: (a) the media product is subject to novelty; (b) the substitution of products has taken an increasing pace; and (c) there is a need to work with a range of different and varied projects, knowing full well that only a fraction of them will eventually succeed in the market. Only flexible organizations or those with unconventional work structures and frameworks have the chance to survive in an environment with a high degree of uncertainty, risk, and ubiquity of failure, all of which are characteristic drawbacks in the world of content.

The attributes of the media product life cycles and their management as collective works, in flexible organizations, are an example of the consequences derived from the special features of the media products. As an area of research, the organizational factors of the management of these products is one of a wide range of areas to study in media management.

## A RESEARCH CHALLENGE IN MEDIA PRODUCT MANAGEMENT

In this chapter we did not try to deal with all key issues pertaining to media product management. On the contrary, we attempted to cast light on crucial issues that reflect that media product management is, on the one hand, different from management of other types of products, but is also similar to management of products that contrast sharply to those produced by content firms. On the basis of this idea, we looked into aspects of media products regarded as information and cultural goods. It is important to note that the contrast between news and entertainment business, printed and electronic outlets, or film-making and music recording activities, deserves more individualized and comprehensive research.

The somewhat risky generic approach to media management is increasingly being called for because of the expansion of the multimedia industry, characterized by the facts that technology and formats converge, business diversification is taking gigantic leaps, and any offer can become a multiproduct, multiformat, and multimedia offering. This is an industry where a product becomes a joint multicompany project, in which diverse corporate and professional cultures, along with brands and talent endowed with a strong personality, blend together and work hand in hand today, and tomorrow they may be competing against each other. In the light of these facts, there must be ongoing research into the common managing principles of products that to some extent seek to integrate professional value, economic and commercial value, as well as societal value (political, social, and cultural) in a well-balanced way.

Earlier in this chapter, when discussing the range of possible sources and research paths, we highlighted that this generic kind of approach to media product managing emphasized the need for interdisciplinary work, taking into account the role played by a variety of disciplines in the creation and commercialization of cultural or creative goods. The media represent an economic and business subsector within an extensive realm that could be defined as the *symbolic economy* or, as Nieto (2001) calls it, the "appearance economy" (p. 120). Yet this subsector is growing in importance day by day and shares with ones that have traditionally been considered to belong to high culture far more special properties than we can imagine.

Where does the key decision making on media management lie? It basically lies at the crossroads of a series of elements, the spot where the paths of both elements meet—between ideas and commerce, between individuals' intelligence and creativity and financial resources invested by the firms and organizations, between meeting specific individuals or audiences' wishes and dealing with citizens' needs. Media economics research has dealt with that confluence of interests, on the grounds that it constitutes the specificity focus of the sector. In view of this fact, there has been serious concern for a number of aspects, among others, the impact that market structures have on the variety of offers, the effects of regulation and state intervention, and the analysis of different ownership structures. Perhaps, it's time for media management research, and more specifically content management, to take its peculiar nature more seriously and consider it essential.

Even though a media product is far more than an intangible content, in reality that is what it is. Neither must we overlook the fact that the emergence of that content is thanks to individuals or teams who struggled to come up with the idea and then gave it a specific format. Likewise, an audience is much more than concrete individuals, although deep down it is a collection of individuals. It is on this basis, that we have attempted to look into media product management of those original aspects, the ones in which people and ideas generate all other processes. Ongoing serious thought and work needs to be carried out on media product management in a bid to comprehend these aspects even further from multidisciplinary angles. In the last decade, that is precisely what some of the most productive research approaches on media management (managing copyright issues, creative contracts, content and brand leverage, personalizing media and products, etc.) has accomplished.

## REFERENCES

Adler, M. (1985). Stardom and talent. *American Economic Review, 75*(1), 208–212.

Aigrain, P. (1997). Attention, media, value and economics. *First Monday, 2*(9). Retrieved February 10, 2004 from http://www.firstmonday.dk/issues/issue2_9/index.html

Albarran, A. B., & Arrese, A. (2003). *Time and media markets.* Mahwah, NJ: Lawrence Erlbaum Associates.

Albert, S. (1998). Movie stars and the distribution of financially successful films in the motion picture industry. *Journal of Cultural Economics, 22,* 249–270.

Anderson, S., & Coate, S. (2000). Market provision of public goods: The case of broadcasting. (NBER Working Paper No. 7513). Cambridge, MA: National Bureau of Economic Research.

Argentesi, E. (2003, October). *Non-price competition in the Italian newspaper market. Bundling as a promotional device.* Paper presented at the 2nd Workshop on Media Economics. How do media markets work?, Norwegian School of Economics and Business Administration (NHH)/Institute for Research in Economics and Business Administration (SNF), Bergen, Norway. Retrieved January 20, 2004 from http://www.snf.no/MediaEcon/pdf/Argentesi.pdf

Arrese, A., & Medina, M. (2002). Competition between new and old media in economic and financial news markets. In R. G. Picard (Ed.), *Media firms: Structures, operations and performance* (pp. 59–75). Mahwah, NJ: Lawrence Erlbaum Associates.

Bakos, J., Brynjolfsson, E., & Lichtman, D. (1999). Shared information goods. *Journal of Law & Economics, 42*(1), 117–155.

Bakos, Y., & Brynjolfsson, E. (1999). Bundling information goods: Pricing, profits and efficiency. *Management Science, 45*(12), 1.613–1.630.

Bates, B. J. (1988). Information as an economic good: Sources of individual and social value. In V. Mosco & J. Wasko (Eds.), *The political economy of information* (pp. 76–94). Madison: University of Wisconsin Press.

Berry, S., & Waldfogel, J. (2001). Do mergers increase product variety? Evidence from radio broadcasting. *Quarterly Journal of Economics, 116*(3), 1009–1025.

Berry, S., & Waldfogel, J. (2003). Product quality and market size. (NBER Working Paper No. 9675). Cambridge, MA: National Bureau of Economic Research.

Bikchandani, S., Hirschleifer, D., & Welch, I. (1992). A theory of fads, fashion, custom, and cultural change in informational cascades. *Journal of Political Economy, 100*(5), 992–1026.

Bikchandani, S., Hirschleifer, D., & Welch, I. (1993). The blind leading the blind: Social influence, fads and information cascades. (UCLA Working Paper No. 24–93). Los Angeles, CA: Anderson School of Management.

Blair, R. D., & Romano, R. E. (1993). Pricing decisions of the newspaper monopolist. *Southern Economic Journal, 59*(4), 723–732.

Boardman, A. E., & Heargreaves-Heap, D. P. (1999). Network externalities and government restrictions on satellite broadcasting of key sporting events. *Journal of Cultural Economics, 23,* 167–181.

Caves, R. E. (2000). *Creative industries. Contracts between art and commerce.* Cambridge, MA: Harvard University Press.

Chan-Olmsted, S. M., & Kim, Y. (2001). Perceptions of branding among television station managers: An exploratory analysis. *Journal of Broadcasting & Electronic Media, 45*(1), 75–91.

CITF (2001). *Creative industry task force mapping document.* Retrieved February 10, 2004 from http://www.culture.gov.uk/creative/mapping.html

Cohen-Avigdor, N., & Lehman-Wilzig, S. (2002). *A life cycle model of media development: The Internet as case study.* Paper presented at the annual conference of the Association for Education in Journalism and Mass Communications (AEJMC). Miami Beach, FL.

Coulson, D. C. (1994). Impact of ownership on newspaper quality. *Journalism Quarterly, 71*(2), 403–410.

Darby, M., & Karni, E. (1973). Free competition and the optimal amount of fraud. *Journal of Law and Economics, 16*, 67–88.

DeFillipi, R. J., & Arthur, M. B. (1998). Paradox in project-based enterprise: The case of film making. *California Management Review, 40*(2), 125–139.

Dewenter, R. (2003). Quality provision in interrelated markets. (Discussion paper No. 7). Hamburg, Germany: University of the Federal Armed Forces.

Doyle, G. (2002). *Understanding media economics.* London: Sage.

Ekinsmyth, C. (2002). Project organization, embeddedness and risk in magazine publishing. *Regional Studies, 36*(3), 229–243.

Eliashberg, J., & Shugan, S. M. (1997). Film critics: Influencers or predictors? *Journal of Marketing, 61*, 68–78.

Faber, R., & O'Guinn, T. (1984). Effect of media advertising and other sources on movie selection. *Journalism Quarterly, 61*, 371–377.

Fishburn, P., Odlyzko, A. M., & Siders, R. C. (1997). Fixed fee versus unit pricing for information goods: Competition, equilibria and price wars. *First Monday, 2*(7). Retrieved January 8, 2004 from http://www.firstmonday.dk/issues/issue2_7/odlyzko/index.html

Gabszewicz, J. J., Laussel, D., & Sonnac, N. (2000). Press advertising and the ascent of the "Pensée Unique"? *European Economic Review, 45*, 641–651.

Gabszewicz, J. J., Laussel, D., & Sonnac, N. (2002). Concentration in the press industry and the theory of the "circulation spiral." (CORE Discussion Paper, No. 64). Louvain, Belgium: Center for Operations Research and Econometrics.

Ginsburgh, V., & Weyers, S. (1999). On the perceived quality of movies. *Journal of Cultural Economics, 23*, 269–283.

Goldfinger, C. (2000). Intangible economy and financial markets. *Communications & Strategies, 40*(4), 59–89.

Goldhaber, M. H. (1997). The attention economy and the net. *First Monday, 2*(4). Retrieved January 8, 2004 from http://www.firstmonday.dk/issues/issue2_4/goldhaber/

Gustafsson, K. E. (1978). The circulation spiral and the principle of household coverage. *The Scandinavian Economic History Review, 26*(1), 1–14.

Herrero, M. (2003). *Programming and direct viewer payment for television. The case of Canal plus Spain.* Pamplona, Spain: Eunsa.

Hirsch, P. A. (2000). Culture industries revisited. *Organizational Science, 11*(3), 356–361.

Hoggart, R. (Ed.) (1989). *Quality in television. Programmes, programme-makers, systems,* London: Libbey.

Jeffcutt, P., & Pratt, A. C. (2002). Managing creativity in the cultural industries. *Creativity and Innovation Management, 11*(4), 225–233.

Jung, J. (2003). The bigger, the better? Measuring the financial health of media firms. *The International Journal on Media Management, 5*(4), 237–250.

Kretschmer, M., Klimis, G. M., & Choi, C. (1999). Increasing returns and social contagion in cultural industries. *British Journal of Management, 10*, S61–S72.

Krider, R. E., & Weinberg, C. B. (1998). Competitive dynamics and the introduction of new products: The motion picture timing game. *Journal of Marketing Research, 35*, 1–15.

Lacy, S. (1992). The financial commitment approach to news media competition. *Journal of Media Economics, 5*(2), 5–21.

Lavine, J. M., & Wackman, D. B. (1988). *Managing media organizations. Effective leadership of the media.* New York: Longman.

Litman, B. R. (1983). Predicting success of theatrical movies: An empirical study. *Journal of Popular Culture, 16*, 159–175.

Ludwig, J. (2000). The essential economic problem of the media: Working between market failure and cross-financing, *Journal of Media Economics, 13*(3), 187–200.

Marvasti, A. (2000). Motion pictures industry: Economics of scale and trade. *International Journal of the Economics of Business, 7*(1), 99–114.

McDonald, G. M. (1988). The economics of rising stars. *American Economic Review, 78*, 155–166.

McFadyen, S., Hoskins, C., & Finn, A. (2000). Cultural industries from an economic/business research perspective. *Canadian Journal of Communication, 25*, 127–144.

Medina, M. (1999). *Valoración publicitaria de los programas de televisión* [Advertising value of television programs]. Pamplona, Spain: Eunsa.

Meyer, P., & Kim, K-H. (2003). Quantifying newspaper quality: "I know it when I see it." Retrieved January 15, 2004 from http://www.unc.edu/~pmeyer/Quality_Project/quantifying_newspaper_quality.pdf

Minasian, J. (1964). Television pricing and the theory of public goods. *Journal of Law and Economics, 7*, 71–80.

Mullainathan, S., & Shleifer, A. (2003). *The market for news.* Retrieved February 15, 2004 from http://post.economics.harvard.edu/faculty/shleifer/papers/marketnews.pdf

Napoli, P. M. (2001). The audience product and the new media environment. *International Journal of Media Management, 3*(2), 66–73.

Napoli, P. M. (2003). *Audience economics.* New York: Columbia University Press.

Nelson, P. (1970). Information and consumer behavior. *Journal of Political Economy, 78*, 311–329.

Nelson, R. A., Donihue, M. R., Waldman, D. M., & Wheaton, C. (2001). What's an Oscar worth? *Economic Inquiry, 39*, 1–16.

Nieto, A. (2001). Economía de la apariencia y mercado de la información [Appearance economics and information markets]. *Comunicación y Sociedad, 14*(2), 117–142.

Norris, D. G. (1992). Ingredient branding: A strategy option with multiple beneficiaries. *Journal of Consumer Research, 9*, 19–31.

O'Connor, J. (1999). The definition of cultural industries. Manchester, UK: Manchester Insitute for Popular Culture. Retrieved December 10, 2003 from http://www.mipc.mmu.ac.uk/iciss/reports/defin.pdf

Picard, R. G. (1989). *Media economics. Concepts and issues.* Newbury Park, CA: Sage.

Picard, R. G. (2000a). *Measuring media content, quality, and diversity: Approaches and issues in content research.* Turku, Finland: Turku School of Economics and Finance.

Picard, R. G. (2000b). Changing business models of online content providers. *International Journal on Media Management, 2*(2), 60–68.

Picard, R. G. (2001). Relations among media economics, content, and diversity. *Nordicom Review, 22*(1), 65–69.

Picard, R. G., & Grönlund, M. (2003). Temporal aspects of media distribution. In A. B. Albarran & A. Arrese (Eds.), *Time and media markets* (pp. 49–60). Mahwah, NJ: Lawrence Erlbaum Associates.

Radas, S., & Shugan, S. M. (1998). Seasonal marketing and timing new product introductions. *Journal of Marketing Research, 35*, 296–315.

Rao, A. R., & Ruekert, R. W. (1994). Brand alliances as signals of product quality. *Sloan Management Review, 36*, 87–97.

Ravid, S. A. (1999). Information, blockbusters, and stars: A study of the film industry. *The Journal of Business, 72*(4), 463–492.

Reinstein, D. A., & Snyder, C. M. (2000). The influence of expert reviews on consumer demand for experience goods: A case study of movie critics. (Working paper). Washington, DC: George Washington University. Retrieved February 8, 2004 from http://home.gwu.edu/~csnyder/movies3.pdf

Ritz, T. (2002). Modeling production of personalized information services and their delivery on multiple distribution channels. Retrieved February 15, 2004 from http://www.dimi.uniud.it/~mizzaro/AH2002/proceedings/pdfs/2ritz.pdf

Rosen, S. (1981). The economics of superstars. *American Economic Review, 73*, 757–775.

Samuelson, P. (1964). Public goods and subscription TV: Correction of the record. *Journal of Law and Economics, 7*, 81–83.

Schoenbach, K. (2000). Factors of newspaper success: Does quality count? A study of German newspapers. In R. G. Picard (Ed.), *Measuring media content, quality, and diversity: Approaches and issues in content research* (pp. 85–96). Turku, Finland: Turku School of Economics and Business Administration.

Schultz, D. E. (1993). *Strategic newspaper marketing* (2nd ed.). Reston, VA: International Newspaper Marketing Association.

Schweizer, T. S. (2002). Managing interactions between technological and stylistic innovation in the media industries. (ERIM Report Series Research in Management, ERS-2002-16-ORG). Rotterdam, The Netherlands: Erasmus Research Institute of Management.

Simon, H. (1971). Designing organizations for an information-rich world. In M. Greenberged (Ed.), *Computers, communications and the public interest* (pp. 37–72). Baltimore: The Johns Hopkins Press.

Sjurts, I. (2002, May 9–11). *Similarity despite variety. An economic explanation of the tendency towards standarisation in the media markets*. Paper presented at the 5th World Media Economics Conference, Turku, Finland.

Starkey, K., Barnatt, C., & Tempest, S. (2000). Beyond networks and hierarchies: Latent organizations in the UK television industry. *Organization Science, 11*(3), 299–305.

Thorsby, D. (1990). Perception of quality in the demand for theatre. *Journal of Cultural Economics, 14,* 65–82.

Tjernström, S. (2002). Theoretical approaches to the management of the public service media firm. *Journal of Media Economics, 15*(4), 241–258.

Towse, R. (2002, May 9–11). *Copyright and creativity in cultural industries*. Paper presented at the 5th World Media Economics Conference, Turku, Finland.

Varian, H. (1999). *Markets for information goods*. Retrieved December 10, 2003, from http://www.sims.berkeley.edu/~hal/Papers/japan/japan.pdf

Venkatesh, R., & Mahajan, V. (1997). Products with branded components: An approach for premium and partner selection. *Marketing Science, 16*(2), 146–165.

Vizjak, A., & Ringlstetter, M. (Eds.). (2001). *Media management. Leveraging content for profitable growth*. Berlin: Springer.

Vogel, H. L. (1998). *Entertainment industry economics. A guide for financial analysis* (4th ed.). Cambridge, UK: Cambridge University Press.

Wallace, W. T., Seigerman, A., & Holbrook, M. B. (1993). The role of actors and actresses in the success of films: How much is a star worth? *Journal of Cultural Economics, 17,* 1–27.

Waterman, D. (1989). Diversity and quality of information products in a monopolistically competitive industry. *Information Economics and Policy, 4,* 291–301.

Waterman, D. (2001, October 27–29). Internet TV: Business models and programme content. Paper presented at the 29th Annual TPRC Research Conference on Information, Communication, and Internet Policy, Washington, DC.

Wolf, M. J. (1999). *The entertainment economy. How mega-media forces are transforming our lives*. New York: Time Books.

Wolinsky, A. (1995). Competition in markets for credence goods. *Journal of Institutional and Theoretical Economics, 151,* 117–131.

Wyatt, R. O., & Badger, D. P. (1984). How reviews affect interest in and evaluation of films. *Journalism Quarterly, 61,* 874–878.

Zaller, J. (1999, September). *Market competition and news quality*. Paper presented at the annual meeting of the American Political Science Association, Atlanta, GA.

# 10

# Issues in Transnational Media Management

Richard A. Gershon
Western Michigan University

The transnational corporation is a nationally based company with overseas operations in two or more countries. One distinctive feature of the transnational corporation (TNC) is that strategic decision making and the allocation of resources are predicated on economic goals and efficiencies with little regard to national boundaries. What distinguishes the transnational media corporation (TNMC) from other types of TNCs is that the principal commodity being sold is information and entertainment. It has become a salient feature of today's global economic landscape (Albarran & Chan-Olmsted, 1998; Demers, 1999; Gershon, 1997, 2000; Herman & McChesney, 1997).

The TNMC is the most powerful economic force for global media activity in the world today. As Herman and McChesney (1997) point out, transnational media are a necessary component of global capitalism. Through a process of foreign direct investment, the TNMC actively promotes the use of advanced media and information technology on a worldwide basis. This chapter will consider some of the critical issues facing today's TNMC. Table 10.1 identifies the seven leading TNMCs, including information pertaining to their country of origin and principal business operations.

## THE TNMC: ASSUMPTIONS AND MISCONCEPTIONS

During the past two decades, scholars and media critics alike have become increasingly suspicious of the better known, high-profile media mergers. Such suspicions have given way to a number of misconceptions concerning the intentions of TNMCs and the people

**TABLE 10.1**
The Transnational Media Corporation

| Companies | World Hdq. | Principal Business Operations |
| --- | --- | --- |
| Bertelsmann AG | Germany | Book & Record Clubs, Book Publishing, Magazines, Music and Film Entertainment |
| NBC Universal | USA | Television and Film Entertainment, Cable Programming, Theme Parks |
| News Corp. Ltd. | Australia/USA | Newspapers, Magazines, Television and Film Entertainment, Direct Broadcast Satellite |
| Sony | Japan | Consumer Electronics, Videogame Consoles, and Software, Music and Film Entertainment |
| Time-Warner | USA | Cable, Magazines, Publishing, Music and Film Entertainment, Internet Service Provision |
| Viacom | USA | Television and Film Entertainment, Cable Programming, Broadcast Television, Publishing, Videocassette and DVD Rental & Sale |
| Walt Disney | USA | Theme Parks, Film Entertainment, Broadcasting, Cable Programming, Consumer Merchandise |

who run them. The first misconception is that such companies are monolithic in their approach to business. In fact, just the opposite is true. Researchers like Gershon & Suri, (2004), Gershon, (1997, 2000), Morley & Shockley-Zalabak (1991) and Bennis (1986) argue that the business strategies and corporate culture of a company are often a direct reflection of the person (or persons) who were responsible for developing the organization and its business mission.

The Sony Corporation, for example, is a company that was largely shaped and developed by its founders Masaru Ibuka and Akio Morita. Together, they formed a unique partnership that has left an indelible imprint on Sony's worldwide business operations. As a company, Sony is decidedly Japanese in its business values. Senior managers operating in the company's Tokyo headquarters identify themselves as Japanese first and entrepreneurs second (Sony, 1996). By contrast, Bertelsmann A.G. is a TNMC that reflects the business philosophy of its founder, Reinhard Mohn, who believed in the importance of decentralization. Bertelsmann's success can be attributed to long-range strategic planning and decentralization, a legacy that Mohn instilled in the company before his retirement in 1981.

A second misconception is that the TNMC operates in most or all markets of the world. While today's TNMCs are indeed highly global in their approach to business, few companies operate in all markets of the world. Instead, the TNMC tends to operate in preferred markets with an obvious preference (and familiarity) toward one's home market (Gershon, 1997, 2000). News Corporation Ltd, for example, generates 76% of its total revenues inside the United States and Canada followed by Europe 16% and Australasia

8% respectively (News Corporation, 2003, p. 6). Similarly, Viacom generates an estimated 84% of its revenues inside the United States and Canada (Viacom International, 2002, p. 2).

## THE GLOBALIZATION OF MARKETS

The world has become a series of economic centers consisting of both nation states and transnational corporations. The globalization of markets involves the full integration of transnational business, nation-states and technologies operating at high speed. Globalization is being driven by a broad and powerful set of forces including: worldwide deregulation and privatization trends, advancements in new technology, market integration (such as the European Community, NAFTA, Mercosur, etc.) and the fall of communism. It is admittedly a fast-paced and uncertain world. The basic requirements for all would-be players are free trade and a willingness to compete on an international basis. According to German political theorist Carl Schmitt, "The Cold War was a world of friends and enemies. The globalization world, by contrast, tends to turn all friends and enemies into competitors" (Friedman, 1999, p. 11).

### Foreign Direct Investment

Foreign direct investment (FDI) refers to the ownership of a company in a foreign country. This includes the control of assets. As part of its commitment, the investing company will transfer some of its managerial, financial, and technical expertise to the foreign-owned company (Grosse & Kujawa, 1988). The decision to engage in FDI is based on the profitability of the market, growth potential, regulatory climate and existing competitive situation (Behrman & Grosse, 1990; Grosse & Kujawa, 1988). The TNMC is arguably better able to invest in the development of new media products and services than are smaller, nationally based companies or government supported industries. There are five reasons that help to explain why a company engages in FDI. They include:

#### Proprietary Assets and Natural Resources

Some TNCs invest abroad for the purpose of obtaining specific proprietary assets and natural resources. The ownership of talent or specialized expertise can be considered a type of proprietary asset. Sony Corporation's purchase of CBS Records in 1988 and Columbia Pictures in 1989 enabled the company to become a formidable player in the field of music and entertainment. Rather than trying to create an altogether new company, Sony purchased proprietary assets in the form of exclusive contracts with some of the world's leading musicians and entertainers. The company also holds the copyright to various music recordings and films (Gershon, 2000).

#### Foreign Market Penetration

A second consideration is the obvious need to expand into new markets. Some TNMCs invest abroad for the purpose of entering a foreign market and serving it from that location. The market may exist or may have to be developed. The ability to buy an existing media property is the easiest and most direct method for market entry. This was the strategy employed by Bertelsmann A.G. when it entered the United States in 1986 and purchased Doubleday Publishing ($475 million) and RCA Records ($330 million). One year later, Bertelsmann consolidated its U.S. recording labels by forming the Bertelsmann Music Group which is headquartered in New York City. Today, the United States is responsible for 24.4% of the company's revenues worldwide.

### Research, Production and Distribution Efficiencies

The cost of research, production, and labor are important factors in the selection of foreign locations. Some countries offer significant advantages such as a well-trained work-force, lower labor costs, tax relief, and technology infrastructure. India, for example, is fast becoming an important engineering and manufacturing facility for many computer and telecommunications companies located in the United States. Companies like Texas Instruments and Intel use India as a research and development hub for microprocessors and multimedia chips. Similarly, companies like IBM and Oracle use Indian IT engineers to develop new kinds of software applications. By some estimates, there are more information technology engineers in Bangalore, India (150,000) than in Silcon Valley (120,000). Research studies performed by Deloitte Research and the Gartner Group report that outsourcing and work performed in India have reduced costs to U.S. companies by an estimated 40% to 60% ("The Rise of India," 2003, p. 69).

### Overcoming Regulatory Barriers to Entry

Some TNCs invest abroad for the purpose of entering into a market that is heavily tar-iffed. It is not uncommon for nations to engage in various protectionist policies designed to protect local industry. Such protectionist policies usually take the form of tariffs or import quotas. On October 3, 1989, the European Community (EC), in a meeting of the 12 nations' foreign ministers, adopted by a 10 to 2 vote the *Television Without Frontiers* directive. Specifically, EC Directive 89/552 was intended to promote European television and film production. The plan called for an open market for television broadcasting by reducing barriers and restrictions placed on cross-border transmissions. The EC was concerned that the majority of broadcast airtime be filled with European programming. The *Television Without Frontiers* directive required member states to insure, where practical and by appropriate means that broadcasters reserve for European works a majority of their transmission time excluding the time allocated for news, sports and games (Cate, 1990; Kevin, 2003).

For TNMCs (and other television and film distributors), the EC Directive was initially viewed as a form of trade protectionism. In order to offset the potential effects of program quotas, TNMCs and second tier television and film distributors adjusted to the EC Directive by forming international partnerships and/or engaging in coproduction ventures. By becoming a European company (or having a European affiliate), a TNMC is able to circumvent perceived regulatory barriers and is able to exercise greater control over international television/film trade matters (Litman, 1998).

### *Empire Building*

Writers like Bennis (1986) contend that the CEO is the person most responsible for shaping the beliefs, motivations, and expectations for the organization as a whole. The importance of the CEO is particularly evident when it comes to the formation of business strategy. For CEOs like Rupert Murdoch (News Corp.), Sumner Redstone (Viacom), and John Malone (Liberty Media), there is a certain amount of personal competitiveness and business gamesmanship that goes along with managing a major company. Success is measured in ways that go beyond straight profitability. A high premium is placed on successful deal making and new project ventures. Today's generation of transnational media owners and CEOs are risk takers at the highest level, willing and able to spend billions of dollars in order to advance the cause of a new project venture. Viacom's Sumner Redstone, for example, is known for his aggressive leadership style and his tenacity as a negotiator. He is a fierce competitor. Redstone's competitive style can be seen in a comment he made in *Fortune* magazine.

> There are two or three of us who started with nothing. Ted Turner started with a half-bankrupt billboard company. Rupert Murdoch started with a little newspaper someplace in Australia. I was born in a tenement, my father became reasonably successful, and I started with two drive-in theaters before people knew what a drive-in theater was . . . So I do share that sort of background with Rupert. People say I want to emulate him [Murdoch]. I don't want to emulate him. I'd like to beat him . . . ("There's No Business," 1998, p. 104)

## The Risks Associated with FDI

The decision to invest in a foreign country can pose serious risks to the company operating abroad. The TNC is subject to the laws and regulations of the host country. It is also vulnerable to the host country's politics and business policies. What are the kinds of risks associated with FDI? There are the problems associated with political instability including wars, revolutions, and coups. Less dramatic, but equally important, are changes stemming from the election of socialist or nationalist governments that may prove hostile to private business and particularly to foreign-owned business (Ball & McCulloch, 1996). Changes in labor conditions and wage requirements are also relevant factors in terms of a company's ability to do business abroad. Foreign governments may impose laws concerning taxes, currency convertibility, and/or impose requirements involving technology transfer. FDI can only occur if the host country is perceived to be politically stable, provides sufficient economic investment opportunities, and if its business regulations are considered reasonable. In light of such issues, the TNC will carefully consider the potential risks by doing what is called a country risk assessment before committing capital and resources.

## TRANSNATIONAL MEDIA AND BUSINESS STRATEGY

The main role of strategy is to plan for the future as well as to react to changes in the marketplace. Strategic planning is the set of managerial decisions and actions that determine the long-term performance of a company or organization. A competitive business strategy is the master plan, including specific product lines and approaches to be used by the organization in order to reach a stated set of goals and objectives. Porter (1985) argues that a firm's competitive business strategy needs to be understood in terms of scope, that is, the breadth of the company's product line as well as the markets it is prepared to serve. Strategy formulation presupposes an ongoing willingness to enlarge and improve the flow of a company's products and services.

Strategic planning presupposes the use of environmental scanning to monitor, evaluate, and disseminate information from both the internal and external business environments for the key decision makers within the organization. Researchers like Wheelen and Hunger (1998), suggest that the need for strategic planning is sometimes caused by triggering events. A triggering can be caused by changes in the competitive marketplace, changes in the management structure of an organization, or changes associated with internal performance and operations.

## The Purpose of a Global Business Strategy

Most companies do not set out with an established plan for becoming a major international company. Rather, as a company's exports steadily increase, it establishes a foreign office to handle the sales and services of its products. In the beginning stages, the foreign office tends to be flexible and highly independent. As the firm gains experience, it may get involved in other facets of international business such as licensing and manufacturing abroad. Later, as pressures arise from various international operations, the company begins to recognize the need for a more comprehensive global strategy (Gershon, 1997; Robock & Simmonds, 1989). In sum, most companies develop a global business strategy through a process of gradual evolution rather than by deliberate choice.

## Understanding Core Competency

The term *core competency* describes something that an organization does well (Hitt, Ireland, & Hoskisson 1999). The principle of core competency suggests that a highly successful company is one that possesses a specialized production process, brand recognition, or ownership of talent that enables it to achieve higher revenues and market dominance when compared to its competitors (Daft, 1997). Core competency can be measured in many ways, including: brand identity (Disney, ESPN, CNN), technological leadership (Cisco, Intel, Microsoft), superior research and development (Sony, Philips), and customer service (Dell, Amazon.com). Sony Corporation, which specializes in consumer electronics, is a good example of core competency. Consumer electronics represent 60% of Sony's worldwide business operations.

Historically, the TNMC begins as a company that is especially strong in one or two areas. At the start of the 1980s, for example, Time Inc. (prior to its merger with Warner Communication) was principally in the business of magazine publishing and pay cable television, whereas News Corporation Ltd. (News Corp.), parent company to Fox Television, was primarily a newspaper publisher. Today, both companies are transnational in scope with a highly diverse set of media products and services. Over time, the

TNMC develops additional sets of core competencies. News Corp., for example, has become the world's preeminent company in the business of direct broadcast satellite communication. News Corp. either fully owns or is a partial investor in five DBS services worldwide.

## Global Media Brands

Branding has emerged as a specialized field of marketing and advertising, and the burgeoning field of business literature reflects this pattern. Aaker's seminal work, *Managing Brand Equity* (1991), suggests that a highly successful brand is one that creates a strong resonance connection in the consumer's mind and leaves a lasting impression. According to Aaker, brands can be divided into five key elements: brand loyalty, brand awareness, perceived quality, brand associations, and proprietary brand assets. Global media brands, like Sony, Disney, HBO, Microsoft, and MTV, represent hardware and software products used by consumers worldwide. Such products are localized to the extent that they are made to fit into the local requirements (i.e., language, manufacturing, marketing style) of the host nation and culture. To that end, a successful brand name creates a resonance or connection in the consumer's mind toward a company's product or service.

### Profiling the Sony Walkman

Through the years, Sony has introduced a number of firsts in the development of new communication products. In some cases, the products were truly revolutionary in terms of a planning and design concept (Beamish 1999). Words like *Trinitron*, *Walkman*, and *Playstation* have become part of the public lexicon of terms to describe consumer electronics. Yet several of these products are more than just products. They have contributed to a profound change in consumer lifestyle. This, more than anything else, has contributed to Sony's brand identity.

The creation of Sony's highly popular Walkman portable music player was highly serendipitous in its origins. From 1966 onward, Sony and other Japanese manufacturers began the mass production of cassette tapes and recorders in response to growing demand. At first, cassette tape recorders could not match the sound quality of reel-to-reel recorders and were mainly used as study aids and for general purpose recording. By the late 1970s, audio quality had steadily improved and the stereo tape cassette machine had become a standard fixture in many homes and automobiles (Nathan, 1999).

It so happened that Masaru Ibuka (who was then honorary Chairman of Sony) was planning a trip to the United States. Despite its heaviness as a machine, Ibuka would often take a TC-D5 reel-to-reel tape machine when he traveled. This time, however, he asked Sony President, Norio Ohga for a simple, stereo playback version. Ohga contacted Kozo Ohsone, general manager of the tape recorder business division. Ohsone had his staff alter a Pressman stereo cassette by removing the recording function and had them convert it into a portable stereo playback device. The problem at that point was to find a set of headphones to go with it. Most headphones at the time were quite large. When Ibuka returned from his U.S. trip he was quite pleased with the unit, even if it had no recording capability (Gershon & Kanayama, 2002).

Ibuka soon went to Morita (then Chairman) and said, "Try this. Don't you think a stereo cassette player that you can listen to while walking around is a good idea?" (Sony, 1996, p. 207). Morita took it home and tried it out over the weekend. He immediately saw the possibilities. In February 1979, Morita called a meeting that included a number of the company's electrical and mechanical design engineers. He instructed the group that this product would enable someone to listen to music anytime, anywhere.

Akio Morita was the quintessential marketer. He understood how to translate new and interesting technologies into usable products (Gershon & Kanayama, 2002; Nathan, 1999). After rejecting several names, the publicity department came up with the name "Walkman." The product name was partially inspired by the movie *Superman* and Sony's existing *Pressman* portable tape cassette machine (Sony, 1996). The Walkman created a totally new market for portable music systems. By combining the features of mobility and privacy, the Walkman has contributed to an important change in consumer lifestyle. Today, portable music systems have become commonplace ranging from major urban subways to health and recreation facilities to city parks worldwide.

### Profiling MTV

Music Television channel (MTV) is an advertiser supported music entertainment cable channel that began as a joint venture between American Express and Warner Amex Communications; then a subsidiary of Warner Communications. It was conceived by John A. Lack in 1980 who was then vice president of Warner Amex. Lack recruited Robert Pittman (who would later oversee the AOL/Time Warner merger) to assemble a team responsible for developing the MTV concept. MTV was launched on August 1, 1981. By 1983, MTV had become successful and achieved profitability a year later. MTV's originator, John Lack, left the network in 1984. Robert Pittman rose to the position of president and CEO of MTV before leaving in 1986. In March 1986, MTV, Nickelodeon, and VH1 were sold to Viacom for $513 million. Shortly thereafter, Viacom CEO Sumner Redstone appointed Tom Freston as CEO. Freston was the last remaining member of Pittman's original development team. MTV's global success is in part due to the innovative management and programming strategies that Freston implemented early on in his tenure (Ogles, 1993).

In 1987, MTV launched its first overseas channel in Europe, which was a single feed consisting of American music programming hosted by English-speaking artists. MTV soon discovered that although American music was popular in Europe, it could not offset differences in language and culture and an obvious preference for local artists. European broadcasters, however, quickly understood the importance of MTV as a new programming concept. They soon adapted the MTV format and began broadcasting music videos in various languages throughout the whole of Europe. This, in turn, negatively affected MTV's financial performance in Europe.

In 1995, MTV was able to harness the power of digital satellite communications in order to create regional and localized programming. MTV's international programming draws on the talent, language, and cultural themes from localized regions which are then satellite fed to that same geographic area. Approximately 70% of MTV's content is generated locally. MTV airs more than 22 different feeds around the world, all tailored to their respective markets. They comprise a mixture of licensing agreements, joint ventures, and wholly owned operations, with MTV International still holding the creative control of these programs ("Sumner's Gemstone," 2000).

Today, the music video has become a staple of modern broadcast and cable television. Presently MTV has a huge market share in Asia, Europe, China, Japan, and Russia. MTV International is organized into 6 major divisions, including MTV Asia (Hindi, Mandarin), MTV Australia, MTV Brazil (Portuguese), MTV Europe, MTV Latin America (Spanish), and MTV Russia ("Sumner's Gemstone," 2000). The management of MTV's international operations is highly decentralized, which allows local managers the ability to develop programming and marketing strategies to fit the needs of each individual market.

## Vertical Integration and Complementary Assets

There are several ways that a major corporation can strategically plan for its future. One common growth strategy is vertical integration, whereby a company will control most or all of its operational phases. In principle, the TNMC can control an idea from its appearance in a book or magazine, to its debut in domestic and foreign movie theaters, as well as later distribution via cable, satellite, or DVD (Albarran, 2002). The rationale is that vertical integration will allow a large-size company to be more efficient and creative by promoting combined synergies between (and among) its various operating divisions. To that end, many of today's TNMCs engage in cross-media ownership, that is, owning a combination of news, entertainment and enhanced information services. Cross-media ownership allows for a variety of efficiencies, such as news gathering as well as cross licensing and marketing opportunities between company-owned properties.

### Profiling News Corporation Ltd

The desire to control most or all of a company's operational phases and thereby create internal synergies is a primary goal for any company or organization. Rupert Murdoch is a master of the vertical integration game. In April 1987, Murdoch's Australian based News Corporation Ltd. launched the Fox Television Network with 108 affiliates. In the process, Murdoch became a U.S. citizen. In the years that followed, Murdoch steadily improved the position of Fox television by combining a steady source of programming with greatly improved distribution outlets (Lee & Litman, 1991). In 1993, for example, News Corp. acquired the rights to televise the National Football League (NFL). The NFL established Fox as a highly credible player in the field of television entertainment. Shortly thereafter, News Corp. negotiated with New World Communications for partial ownership of 12 VHF stations in key markets throughout the United States, thus improving Fox Network's affiliation and direct viewer access. News Corp. has taken the philosophy of vertical integration (and complementary assets) to a whole new level by producing films and television programs that can be seen worldwide, including the Fox Television Network (USA); British Sky Broadcasting (U.K & Ireland); Star Television (including 40 program services in 7 languages in 53 countries—Asia); and DirecTV (USA). According to Peter Chernin (2003), News Corp's COO:

> About 75% of the world's population is covered by satellite and television platforms we control . . . mostly in Asia . . . We believe that in this period of global expansion, there are some important strategic bets to make. And we've been making them. (p. 92)

## The Strategic Necessity of Owning Both Software and Distribution Links

The once clear lines and historic boundaries that separated media and telecommunications are becoming less distinct. The result is a convergence of modes, whereby technologies and services are becoming more fully integrated. The main driving force behind convergence is the digitalization of media and information technology. Digital technology improves the quality and efficiency of switching, routing, and storing of information. It increases the potential for manipulation and transformation of data. As researcher Ithiel de Sola Poole (1990) writes, the organization that owns both software content as well as the means of distribution to the home represents a formidable player in the new world of telecommunications and residential services. Today's TNMC wants to own both software and the means of distribution into people's homes. A clear example of this was Viacom's 1999 decision to purchase CBS for $37 billion. For Viacom, the purchase of CBS represented an opportunity to obtain a well-established television network as well as a company that owned more than 160 U.S. radio stations (i.e., Infinity Broadcasting). For its part, Viacom already owned several well-established cable network services, including MTV, Nickelodeon, and Showtime. So, the purchase of CBS provided it with a steady distribution outlet for Viacom programs and offered it numerous cross licensing and marketing opportunities (Gershon & Suri, 2004).

### Broadband Communication

The term *broadband* communication is used to describe the ability to distribute multichannel information and entertainment services to the home. The goal for both cable operators and local exchange carriers is to offer consumers a whole host of software products via an electronic supermarket (i.e., broadband cable) to the home. Broadband is also a term used to describe the delivery of high speed Internet access via a cable modem or digital subscriber line (DSL). The issue of convergence becomes an important consideration in describing the ability to deliver information and entertainment services to the home using a variety of information delivery platforms, including cable television, telephony, and direct broadcast satellite as well as combined multimedia formats, the Internet, Web TV, online videogames, etc. (Chan-Olmsted & Kang, 2003). The future of tomorrow's so-called "smart home" will allow for the full integration of voice, data and video services and give new meaning to the term *programming*.

## Diversification

Diversification is a growth strategy that recognizes the value of owning a wide variety of related and unrelated businesses. In principle, a company that owns a diverse portfolio of businesses is spreading the risk of its investment. Thus, a downturn in any one business during a fiscal year is more than offset by the company's successful performance in other areas. The disadvantage, however, is that some companies can become too large and unwieldy in order to be properly managed. The General Electric Corporation, for example, is consistently ranked as one of the world's leading TNCs. The company is comprised of 11 major divisions including GE Consumer Industrial (appliances, home electronics),

GE Healthcare (medical imaging and diagnostics equipment), GE Commercial Finance and NBC Universal (television and media entertainment) to name only a few.

As a business strategy, diversification can also occur within the parameters of a general product line (Albarran & Dimmick, 1996). Accordingly, some TNMCs are more diverse than others; the differences being a matter of product relatedness and geographical location. In one study performed by Chan-Olmsted & Chang (2003), the authors examined the diversity of product line and geographical operations among seven leading TNMCs. Companies like Vivendi Universal and Bertelsmann were found to be more diverse in terms of product line than companies like Disney and Viacom, which were considered less diverse. Non-U.S.-based companies like Bertelsmann, Sony, and News Corp. were found to be the most geographically diverse. The same study points to the fact that the North American market is especially important from the standpoint of FDI and creating strategic alliances.

News Corp. is an example of a highly diverse TNC, but whose product line falls within the general scope of media news and entertainment. It is also a company whose FDI strategies reflect an abiding philosophy of preferred markets (see Table 10.2).

## TRANSNATIONAL MEDIA AND GLOBAL COMPETITION

The decades of the 1990s and the early 21st century have witnessed a new round of international mergers and acquisitions that have brought about a major realignment of business players. Concerns for antitrust violations seem to be overshadowed by a general acceptance that such changes are inevitable in a global economy. The result has been a consolidation of players in all aspects of business, including banking, aviation, pharmaceuticals, media and telecommunications (Albarran & Chan-Olmsted, 1998; Compaine & Gomery, 2000; Gershon, 1997, 2000). The communication industries, in particular, have taken full advantage of deregulatory trends to make ever-larger combinations. Some of the more high-profile mergers and acquisitions include: Viacom's purchase of CBS for $37 billion (in 1999), America Online's (AOL) purchase of Time Warner for $162 billion (in 2001) and Comcast's $54 billion purchase of AT&T Broadband in 2002 (Compaine & Gomery, 2000). The goal, simply put, is to possess the size and resources necessary in order to compete on a global playing field. Table 10.3 identifies the major mergers and acquisitions of media and telecommunications companies for the years 1999 to 2005.

### When Mergers and Acquisitions Fail

Not all mergers and acquisitions are successful. As companies feel the pressures of increased competition, they embrace a somewhat faulty assumption that increased size makes for a better company. Yet on closer examination, it becomes clear that this is not always the case. Often, the combining of two major firms creates problems that no one could foresee. A failed merger or acquisition can be highly disruptive to both organizations in terms of lost revenue, capital debt, and decreased job performance. The inevitable result is the elimination of staff and operations as well as the potential for bankruptcy. In addition, the effects on the support (or host) communities can be quite

**TABLE 10.2**
News Corporation Ltd.
Primary Media News and Entertainment Divisions (2004)
(Select Examples)

| | |
|---|---|
| **Filmed Entertainment** | 20th Century Fox |
| | 20th Century Fox International |
| | Fox Television Studios |
| **Television** | Fox Broadcasting Company |
| | Fox Sports Australia |
| | Fox Television Stations |
| | Foxtel |
| **Cable Television** | Fox Movie Channel |
| | Fox News Channel |
| | Fox Sports Digital |
| | Fox Sports en Espanol |
| **Direct Broadcast Satellite** | BSkyB |
| | DirecTV |
| | FoxTel |
| | Sky Italia |
| | Star TV |
| **Magazines and Inserts** | Gemstar TV-Guide International |
| | The Weekly Standard |
| | Smart Source |
| | News America Marketing |
| **Newspapers** | **AUSTRALASIA** |
| | Daily Telegraph |
| | Sunday Herald Sun |
| | Post Courier |
| | The Australian |
| | **UNITED KINGDOM** |
| | News International |
| | News of the World |
| | The Sun |
| | The Sunday Times |
| | The Times |
| **Books** | HarperCollins Publishers |
| **Other Assets** | National Rugby League |

*Source:* News Corporation Ltd.

destructive (Wasserstein, 1998). There are four reasons that help to explain why mergers and acquisitions can sometimes fail. They include: the lack of a compelling strategic rationale, failure to perform due diligence, post-merger planning and integration failures, and financing and the problems of excessive debt ("The Case Against Mergers," 1995).

### The Lack of a Compelling Strategic Rationale

In the desire to be globally competitive, both companies go into the proposed merger (or acquisition) with unrealistic expectations of complementary strengths and presumed

**TABLE 10.3**
Mergers and Acquisitions: Media and Telecommunication Companies
(1999–2005)

| Company Name | Description | Price | Date |
|---|---|---|---|
| Verizon and MCI | Verizon will purchase long distance carrier MCI and expand both its local and long distance telephone service. | $6.7 Bil. | 2005 pending |
| SBC and AT&T | SBC will purchase long distance carrier AT&T and expand both its local and long distance telephone service. | $16.7 Bil. | 2005 pending |
| NewsCorp and DirecTV | News Corp. paid Hughes Communication $6.1 billion in order to obtain the DirecTV satellite network. | $6.1 Bil. | 2004 |
| NBC and Universal | NBC acquired Universal Studios from Vivendi Inc. for $3.8 billion. | $3.8 Bil. | 2004 |
| Comcast and AT&T | Comcast acquired AT&T Broadband (cable) for $54 billion. The combinded company is now the largest cable television operator in the U.S. | $54.0 Bil. | 2002 |
| Vivendi S. A. and Seagrams (Universal and Polygram) | French media group Vivendi S. A. purchased Seagrams which owns Universal Studios and Polygram Records for $43.3 billion. | $43.3 Bil. | 2001 |
| America Online and Time Warner | AOL acquired Time Warner Inc for $162 billion. This was the first combination of a major ISP with a traditional media company. | $162.0 Bil. | 2001 |
| Verizon Bell Atlantic and GTE | Bell Atlantic purchased independent telephone Company GTE for $52.8 billion. The combined company was later renamed Verizon. | $52.8 Bil. | 2000 |
| Viacom and CBS | Viacom purchased CBS Inc. for $37 billion. Viacom has major investments in cable programming and film production. | $37.0 Bil. | 2000 |
| AT&T & TeleCommunications Inc. (TCI) | AT&T purchased TCI Inc. for $48 billion thus enabling AT&T to offer cable television, local and long distance telephone service. | $48.0 Bil. | 1999 |
| SBC Communications & Ameritech | SBC purchased RBOC Ameritech for $62 billion which allowed SBC to increase its telephone network in the midwest and eastern US. | $62.0 Bil. | 1999 |

*Sources:* R. Gershon and Company Reports

synergies. As Ozanich & Wirth (1998) point out, once a target company has been identified, a price level must be established. The challenging aspect to this is the valuation to be placed on the target company. Once negotiations are underway, there is sometimes undue pressure brought to bear to complete the deal. Unwarranted optimism regarding future performance can sometimes cloud critical judgment. The negotiation process suffers from what some observers call *winners curse*. The acquiring company often winds up paying too much for the acquisition. In the worst case scenario, the very issues and problems that prompted consideration of a merger in the first place become further exacerbated once the merger is complete.

### Failure to Perform Due Diligence

In the highly charged atmosphere of intense negotiations, the merging parties will sometimes fail to perform due diligence prior to the merger agreement. Both companies only later discover that the intended merger or acquisition may not accomplish the desired objectives ("The Case Against Mergers," 1995). The lack of due diligence can result in the acquiring company paying too much for the acquisition and/or later discovering hidden problems and costs. An example of this problem can be seen in AT&T's 1998 acquisition of TCI Cable for $48 billion. The stock and debt transaction gave AT&T direct connections into 33 million U.S. homes through TCI-owned and affiliated cable systems. For AT&T, the merger agreement represented an opportunity to enter the unregulated business of cable television. It was an intriguing strategy that earned CEO Michael Armstrong respect from all quarters of the telecommunications field for its sheer breadth of vision. The plan, however, did not work out as originally conceived. In October 2000, Armstrong, in a stunning reversal of strategy, announced plans to discontinue AT&T's original broadband strategy by dividing the company into four separate companies ("Armstrong's Vision," 2000). In the final analysis, AT&T was unable to surmount the continuing decline in long distance revenues coupled with the enormous costs of transforming TCI's cable operation into a state-of-the-art broadband network. In 2001, AT&T agreed to sell its broadband division to Comcast Corporation for $54 billion.

### Postmerger Planning and Integration Failures

One of the most important reasons that mergers fail is due to bad postmerger planning and integration. If the proposed merger does not include an effective plan for combining divisions with similar products, the duplication can be a source of friction rather than synergy. Turf wars erupt and reporting functions among managers become divisive. The problem becomes further complicated when there are significant differences in corporate culture.

The postmerger difficulties surrounding AOL and Time Warner, for example, demonstrate the difficulty of joining two very different kinds of organizational culture. AOL typified the fast and loose dot-com culture of the 1990s, whereas Time Warner demonstrated a staid, more button down approach to media management. The AOL–Time Warner merger was promoted as the marriage of old media and new media. In the end, the once hoped for synergies did not materialize, leaving the company with an unwieldy structure and bitter corporate infighting. Once the value of AOL stock began to plummet, Time Warner soon took control of the company, and those people associated with AOL were quickly overlooked when it came to strategic decision making. Adding to the tension were new questions about AOL's accounting practices and the way ad revenues were recorded ("You've Got New Management," 2002).

### Financing and the Problem of Excessive Debt

In order to finance the merger or acquisition, some companies will assume major amounts of debt through short-term loans. If or when performance does not meet expectations, such companies may be unable to meet their loan obligations. The company may then be forced to sell off entire divisions in order to raise capital or, worse still, default on its payment altogether.

Rupert Murdoch, president and CEO of News Corp. Ltd., is unique in his ability to structure debt and to obtain global financing. The Murdoch formula was to carefully build cash flow while borrowing aggressively. Throughout the early 1980s, Murdoch's excellent credit rating proved to be the essential ingredient to this formula. Each major purchase was expected to generate positive cash flow and thereby pay off what had been borrowed. Each successive purchase was expected to be bigger than the one before, thereby, ensuring greater cash flow. In his desire to maintain control over his operations, Murdoch developed a special ability to manage debt at a higher level than most companies (Gershon, 1997).

The problem with News Corp's debt financing, however, reached crisis proportions in 1991 when the company was carrying an estimated debt of $8.3 billion. The problem was compounded by the significant cash drains from Fox Television and the BSkyB DBS service. All this came at a time when the media industries (in general) were experiencing a worldwide economic recession. Murdoch was finally able to restructure the company's debt after several long and difficult meetings with some 146 investors. He nearly lost the company. Murdoch was able to obtain the necessary financing but not before the divestment of some important assets and an agreement to significantly pare down the company's debt load. In summarizing Murdoch's business activities and propensity for debt, the *Economist* magazine wrote, "Nobody exploited the booming media industry in the late 1980's better than Mr. Rupert Murdoch's News Corporation—and few borrowed more money to do it" ("Murdoch's Kingdom," 1990, p. 62).

### Profiling the AOL Time Warner Merger

On January 10, 2000, AOL, the largest Internet service provider in the United States, announced that it would purchase Time Warner Inc. for $162 billion. What was particularly unique about the deal was that AOL, with one fifth of the revenue and 15% of the workforce of Time Warner, was planning to purchase the largest TNMC in the world. Such was the nature of Internet economics that allowed Wall Street to assign a monetary value to AOL well in excess of its actual value. What is clear, however, is that AOL president Steve Case recognized that his company was ultimately in a vulnerable position. Sooner or later, Wall Street would come to realize that AOL was an overvalued company with little in the way of substantive assets.

At the time, AOL had no major deals with cable companies for delivery. Cable modems were just beginning to emerge as the technology of choice for residential users wanting high speed Internet access. AOL was completely dependent on local telephone lines and satellite delivery of its service; nor did AOL have any real content. As a company, AOL pursued what Aufderheide (2002) describes as a "walled gardens" strategy, whereby, the company attempted to turn users of the public Internet into customers of a proprietary environment. In looking to the future, AOL needed something more than a well-constructed first screen experience. Time Warner was well positioned in both media content as well as high speed cable delivery. In principle, an AOL–Time Warner combination would provide AOL with broadband distribution capability to Time Warner's 13 million cable households. AOL Time Warner cable subscribers would have faster Internet service as well as access to a wide variety of interactive and Internet software products (Faulhaber, 2002).

The AOL Time Warner merger may well be remembered as one of the worst mergers in U.S. corporate history. The first signs of trouble occurred in the aftermath of the dot-com crash beginning in March 2000. AOL, like most other Internet stocks, took an immediate hit. AOL's ad sales experienced a free fall and subscriber rates flattened out. By 2001, AOL Time Warner stock was down 70% ("AOL, You've Got Misery," 2002). AOL's Robert Pittman was assigned the task of overseeing the postmerger integration.

In the weeks and months that followed, the economic downturn and subsequent loss of advertising had a strong, negative impact on AOL's core business. AOL found itself financially weaker than it was a year earlier because of rising debt and a falling share price that left it without the financial means to pursue future deals. In the end, Time Warner CEO Gerald Levin bet the future of the company on the so-called marriage of old media and new media, leaving employees, investors, and consumers questioning his judgment as well as having to sort through the unintended consequences of that action. Why didn't the board of directors at Time Warner Inc. question (or challenge) the strategy in the first place? According to one senior AOL Time Warner official, "Gerry had a firm grip on the board" ("AOL's Board Digging In," 2002).

> This deal was a big leap of faith, says a person who was at the meeting. Yet the board jumped, assured by Time Warner CEO Gerry Levin that convergence of new and old media and the growth it would produce were real. (p. 46)

In the aftermath of the AOL Time Warner merger, the company's new board of directors has overseen a dramatic shake-up at the senior executive level, including Levin's retirement from the company and Pittman's forced resignation in July 2002 ("Failed Effort," 2002). In January 2003, Steve Case stepped down as Co-CEO claiming that he did not want to be a further distraction to the company. In their place, company directors installed Richard Parsons as Chairman and CEO and two longtime Time Warner executives as his co-chief operating officers. In January 2003, AOL Time Warner reported a $99 billion loss from the previous year making it the highest recorded loss in U.S. corporate history. Perhaps the most symbolic aspect of AOL Time Warner as a failed business strategy was the decision in September 2003 by the company's board to change the name AOL Time Warner back to its original form, Time Warner Inc.

# TRANSNATIONAL MEDIA AND GLOBAL COMPETITION

Global competition has engendered a new competitive spirit that cuts across nationalities and borders. A new form of economic Darwinism abounds, characterized by a belief that size and complementary strengths are crucial to business survival. As today's media and telecommunication companies continue to grow and expand, the challenges of staying globally competitive become increasingly difficult (Dimmick, 2003). The relentless pursuit of profits (and the fear of failure) have made companies around the world vigilant in their attempts to right-size, reorganize, and reengineer their business operations. Thus, no company, large or small, remains unaffected by the intense drive to increase profits and decrease costs.

## The Deregulation Paradox

In principle, deregulation is supposed to foster competition and thereby open markets to new service providers. The problem, however, is that complete and unfettered deregulation can sometimes create the very problem it was meant to solve; namely, a lack of competition. Researchers like Mosco (1990) call it the "mythology of telecommunications deregulation." Other writers such as Demers (1999) refer to it as the "great paradox of capitalism." This author simply calls it the deregulation paradox. Instead of fostering an open marketplace of new players and competitors, too much consolidation can lead to fewer players and, hence, less competition (Demers, 1999; Gershon, 2000; Mosco, 1990). As Demers points out:

> The history of most industries in so-called free market economies is the history of the growth of oligopolies, where a few large companies eventually come to dominate. The first examples occurred during the late 1800s in the oil, steel and railroad industries . . . Antitrust laws eventually were used to break up many of these companies but oligopolistic tendencies continue in these and most other industries. (p. 1)

In all areas of media and telecommunications, there has been a steady movement toward economic consolidation. The exponential increase in group and cross-media ownership is the direct result of media companies looking for ways to increase profits and achieve greater internal efficiencies. The TNMC of the 21st century is looking to position itself as a full service provider of media and telecommunication products and services (see Table 10.4). The same set of transnational media companies are prominent in each of the six categories listed.

# CORPORATE AND ORGANIZATIONAL CONDUCT

The challenges and difficulties faced by today's media and telecommunications companies call into question some basic assumptions regarding deregulation and the principle of self-regulation. This reality challenges several decades of conventional wisdom about the efficiency of free markets (Kuttner, 2002). The primary difficulty is that market discipline

**TABLE 10.4**

Transnational and Second Tier Media Companies Cross-Media Ownership
in the U.S. by Area

**Top 10 Television Broadcast Groups**
**(by market reach)**
- **Viacom Inc.** (CBS Television Network)
- **News Corp. Ltd.** (Fox Television Network)
- Paxson Communications Corp.
- **General Electric Co.** (NBC Tel. Network)
- Tribune Co.
- **Walt Disney Co.** (ABC Television Network)
- Univision Communications Inc.
- Gannett Company
- Hearst Corp. (Hearst-Argyle Television, Inc.)
- Trinity Broadcasting Network

**Top 10 Radio Broadcast Groups**
**(by revenue)**
- Clear Channel Communications, Inc.
- **Viacom Inc.** (Infinity)
- Cox Enterprises, Inc. (Cox Communications)
- Entercom Communications Corp.
- **Walt Disney Co.** (ABC Radio)
- Citadel Communications Corp.
- Radio One, Inc.
- Cumulus Media Inc.
- Univision Communications Inc.
- Emmis Communications Corp.

**Top 7 Film Production Companies**
**(by revenue)**
- **News Corp. Ltd.** (20th Century Fox)
- **Viacom Inc.** (Paramount Pictures)
- **Sony Corporation** (Columbia TriStar)
- **Walt Disney Co.** (Walt Disney Pictures)
- **Sony Corporation** (Metro-Goldwyn-Mayer)
- **NBC Universal** (Universal Studios)
- **Time Warner, Inc.** (Warner Bros.)

**Top 15 Cable Network Services**
**(by subscribers)**
- **Time Warner, Inc.** (TBS)
- **Walt Disney Co.** (ESPN)
- (C-SPAN)
- (Discovery Channel)
- (USA Network)
- **Time Warner, Inc.** (CNN)
- **Time Warner, Inc.** (TNT)
- **Disney** (Lifetime Television)
- **Viacom Inc.** (Nickelodeon)
- **Disney** (A&E Network)
- **Time Warner, Inc.** (Spike TV)
- (The Weather Channel)
- **Viacom Inc.** (MTV)
- (QVC)
- **Walt Disney Co.** (ABC Family Channel)

**Top 10 Cable Operating Systems**
**(by subscribers)**
- Comcast Corporation
- **Time Warner, Inc.** (Time Warner Cable)
- Charter Communications, Inc.
- Cox Enterprises, Inc. (Cox Communica...
- Adelphia Communications
- Cablevision Systems Corp.
- Bright House Networks
- Mediacom Communications Corp.
- Insight Communications Company, Inc
- Washington Post Co. (Cable One, Inc.)

**Satellite (by subscribers)**
- **News Corp. Ltd.** (DIRECTV)
- EchoStar Communications (Dish Netw...

*Sources:* NCTA, NAB, MPAA

and self-regulation noticeably failed in several instances when it came to unscrup
deal making, failed business strategy and deceptive accounting practices. Durir
high-water mark years of the 1990s, investors went along for the ride, delighted a
as stock performance kept rising. U.S. regulators and corporate boards were unv
(or unable) to spot and regulate fraud when it occurred. And given the respect acc

deregulation and the low esteem placed on government regulation, the U.S. Congress would not permit regulatory agencies (i.e., the FCC, SEC, and FTC) to challenge the activities of corporate America (Crew & Kleindorfer, 2002).

Today, falling markets and accounting scandals have tarnished the once iconic image of the chief executive officer. The self-dealing that characterized a handful of CEOs has fostered public resentment and called into question a system that would allow senior level executives to pursue high-risk strategies and personal enrichment schemes at the public's expense. As Charran & Useem (2002) point out, management decision-making, under such circumstances, becomes an incremental descent into poor judgment.

## Corporate Governance

The role of a corporate board of directors is to provide independent oversight and guidance to a CEO and his or her staff of senior executives. This can involve everything from approving new strategic initiatives to reviewing CEO performance. Corporate boards provide a level of professional oversight that embodies the principles of *self regulation*. One of the important goals, of corporate governance should be to prevent significant mistakes in corporate strategy and to ensure that when mistakes happen, they can be corrected quickly (Pound, 2002). The problem occurs when a corporate board of directors ignores its fiduciary responsibility to company stockholders and employees by failing to challenge questionable corporate strategy and/or by permitting unethical business practices to occur. More problematic, is when a corporate board loses its sense of independence. In recent years, many CEOs have tended to operate with corporate boards that have proven highly compliant rather than objective. This was the case with the Walt Disney Company where major investment groups criticized the company's board for failing to challenge (or hold accountable) the financial performance of the company and its CEO, Michael Eisner. There are several contributing reasons that help to explain why corporate governance systems sometime fail. They include: (a) senior management providing corporate boards with limited information; (b) the pursuit of sub-goals by senior managers that are contrary to the best interests of the company or organization; (c) corporate cultures of intimidation where questioning senior management is met with unremitting resistance and the possibility of job loss; and (d) corporate board members who provide consulting services and are, thereby, beholden to senior management (Monks & Minow, 1996; Siebens, 2002). In the worst case scenario, failures in corporate governance can lead to what Cohan (2002) describes as a diffusion of authority, where neither company nor person is fully aware of or takes responsibility for the actions of senior management.

## The Walt Disney Company and Corporate Governance

Events surrounding Walt Disney Corporation call into question the rights of investors and the obligations of a corporate board of directors to provide responsible corporate oversight. Throughout the decade of the 1980s and well into the 1990s, Disney's Michael Eisner was a highly respected CEO. Starting in 1984, he had managed to take an otherwise under-managed company and transform it into one the most highly successful media companies in the world. For the first 8 years, Michael Eisner and President Frank Wells were praised for their executive leadership and marketing savvy. In April 1994, Wells was killed in a helicopter skiing accident in Nevada. His death left Eisner with a personal loss and a difficult void to fill.

One possible choice to fill that vacancy was Jeffrey Katzenberg, then head of Disney Studios. In September 1994, after a long and difficult power struggle, Katzenberg re-signed his position and left the company in a highly visible and emotionally charged departure. He later sued Disney for moneys owed him, and eventually reached an out-of-court settlement of $250 million. Over the next few years, things would go from bad to worse as the company's financial performance did not improve. In 1992, the Walt Disney Company unveiled its Euro Disneyland theme park (later re-named Disneyland Paris). The park was beautifully designed but proved to be a huge financial drain on the company. In 1995, the Walt Disney Company acquired Cap/Cities ABC for $19 billion. Shortly thereafter, ratings at the newly acquired ABC television network plummeted. Gate admissions at the company theme parks were falling, and the company's overall financial performance lagged behind several of its peer TNMCs. The one bright spot was the financial performance of its cable sports subsidiary, ESPN.

That same year, Eisner hired his long-time friend, Michael S. Ovitz, as president, and agreed to pay him a $140 million severance package 14 months later when things didn't work out. The Walt Disney Company was later sued in 2004 and 2005 by a group of investors who felt that the company had been derelict in its financial handling of assets. Testimony during the trial has included a number of depositions revealing several embarrassing facts, including $2 million given to Mr. Ovitz for office renovation; $76,413 for limousines and rental cars; and $6,100 for a home X-ray machine. According to an internal financial audit, Mr. Ovitz spent $48,305 of the company's money for a home screening room and $6,500 for Christmas tips.

Throughout Eisner's tenure at Walt Disney, the company's board of directors has been routinely criticized for its lack of independence. In both 1999 and 2000, *Business Week* named the Disney board of directors the worst board in America ("The Best and Worst Corporate Boards," 2000). In May 2003, while deciding whether a shareholder lawsuit challenging the $140 million payout to Michael Ovitz should go forward, Delaware Chancellor William Chandler noted several governance failures by the Disney board, including:

1. Allowing CEO Michael Eisner to unilaterally make the decision to hire Ovitz, who was a close personal friend of Eisner. They did not get involved in the details or consider Mr. Ovitz's fitness for the position.
2. Failing to exercise proper oversight of the process by which Ovitz was both hired and later terminated, including the $140 million severance package (In The Walt Disney Company Derivative Litigation, 825 A.2d 275, 289 (Del. Ch. 2003)

According to UCLA Law Professor Stephen Bainbridge:

The facts suggest that Eisner hired his buddy Ovitz, fell out with Ovitz and wanted him gone, cut very lucrative deals for his friend Ovitz both on the way in and on the way out, all the while railroading the deals past a complacent and compliant board. The story that emerges is one of cronyism and backroom deals in which preservation of face was put ahead of the corporation's best interests ("Disney, Ovitz's Compensation," 2004).

The aforementioned problems were further exacerbated in 2004 when Eisner unilaterally turned down a $54 billion offer to acquire Disney by Comcast, Inc. Finally, under Eisner's leadership, the Disney company has also estranged its relationship with Steven Jobs's Pixar Animation Studio officials; producers of *Toy Story, Finding Nemo Monsters, Inc.* and *The Incredibles.* In 2004, the computer-animation giant elected not to renew its contact with Disney when its distribution deal expires in 2005.

The question should therefore be asked: Why was Disney's corporate board of directors so negligent in performing its duties? The answer, in part, has to do with what Collins (2001) describes as the problem of charismatic leadership and strong personalities. As Collins points out, highly successful CEOs are sometimes used to getting their way. To that end, Eisner was very adept at selecting board members who would prove compliant, including various friends and acquaintances. According to Business Week:

> Disney's sagging fortunes have turned up the pressure on CEO Eisner, who has tried to soothe critics by making several governance changes ... Eisner has steadfastly refused to rid Disney's board of his many friends and acquaintances. The board still includes Eisner's attorney, his architect, the principal of an elementary school once attended by his children, and the president of a university that received a $1 million Eisner donation. That's why many view the changes as token gestures, rather than real reform ("The Best and Worst Corporate Boards," 2000).

Most of Disney' outside directors board did not have direct access or get involved with the company's day-to-day business operations. They had little or no contact with company employees other than during presentations at board meetings. When problems did occur, most of the board members felt powerless or were so beholden to CEO Eisner, that no one felt confident to come forward and raise the kinds of questions that needed asking concerning the company's business practices and finances. In response to the *Business Week* article and outside investor lawsuit, the company did undergo some reforms of its corporate governance structure. Yet, it becomes clear that Eisner managed to turn those reforms to his own advantage. Roy Disney was forced out by a mandatory retirement provision and the only other persistent critic, Stanley Gold, was kept off key committee assignments because of his business dealings with the firm. Both men subsequently resigned from the Disney board and in a sign of protest created a Web site called SaveDisney.com. In the final analysis, shareholder activism failed because it never made a serious dent in the board's complacency. Eisner was good at boardroom politics and was able to use such reforms to further secure his own position.

The problems associated with Eisner's leadership reached its culmination point in May 2004 at the company's annual stockholders meeting in Philadelphia. Never before in corporate America have shareholders expressed such an enormous loss of confidence in a CEO. Before a highly vocal crowd of more than 3000 investors—some wearing Disney costumes and handing out anti Eisner pamphlets—the company announced that

43% of the nearly two billion votes cast by investors withheld support for Eisner in his post as Disney chairman ("Disney Strips Chairmanship," 2004). According to Christiana Wood, chief investment officer for the California Public Employees Retirement System, "The fact is, we have just lost confidence in Michael Eisner." ("Now its Time to Say Goodbye," 2004, pp. 31–32). In an effort to placate angry shareholders, the board voted to keep Eisner in place as CEO while taking away his title as chairman of the board. Former Maine Senator (and Disney board member) George Mitchell was appointed to the position of chairman. The board was correct in recognizing the need to separate the two top positions, including the decision to appoint a new chairman. That said, 24% the company's investors also withheld their support for Mitchell: a clear indication that many don't think he's the man for the job either. In 2004, Eisner agreed to relinquish his position as CEO in 2006, at the board's urging.

## SUGGESTIONS FOR FUTURE RESEARCH

Research in the field of transnational media management has increased markedly during the past decade. Such studies have tended to focus on strategic planning questions as well as market entry strategies (Hollifield, 2001). Until recently, there were only a select number of studies that looked at the TNMC in terms of cross-cultural personnel management, supply chain management, leadership, corporate conduct and governance issues, etc. This is beginning to change. As Hollifield (2001) points out:

> [It is necessary] to begin moving away from simply describing and discussing the global expansion of media enterprises and toward an increased focus on developing models of organizational and managerial behavior that are grounded in theory and can be used to explain and predict the behavior of media enterprises in transnational markets. (p. 142)

As we look to the future, the study of transnational media management and strategic decision making will change in light of two emerging trends. The first trend is the growing importance of the second tier TNMC that now provides an abundance of the world's media information and entertainment product. In Europe, Asia, and Latin America, the demand for new sources of programming has increased dramatically given worldwide privatization trends and new media technologies. In the past, the purchase of U.S. and TNMC made television and film products represented a less costly approach than producing one's own programs. Today, this is no longer the case.

In Europe alone, U.S.-made television programs account for less than 3% of primetime programming and less than 1% worldwide (Chernin, 2003). Although the TNMC is still a major player in the export of television and film products, several research studies have noted the continued increase in regional production capability in both Latin America (Anatola & Rogers, 1984) and Asia (Waterman & Rogers, 1994). If given the choice, most television consumers prefer programs that are nationally and/or locally produced. Straubhaar (1991, 2003) refers to this as the principle of cultural proximity; that is, a desire for cultural products that reflect a person's own language, culture, history, and values. Language is often the most important criteria in a host nation's decision to import foreign television programming (Wildman & Siwek, 1988). In Austria, for example, almost 12% of the country's television imports come from neighboring Germany. Similarly, Belgium and Switzerland are both major importers of French programming (Kevin, 2003). The principle of cultural proximity holds equally true in Latin America. The Dominican Republic imports a large percentage of its television programs from Mexico-based Televisa, a major producer for the Latin American market.

The second important trend is the demassification of media and entertainment product made possible by the Internet and advanced recording and storage technologies. For marketers, the steady shift from mass to micromarketing is being driven by a combination of technological change as well as strategic opportunity. Increasingly, consumers now have the ability to compile, edit, and customize the media they use. This does not bode well for traditional mass media and the companies who own them (Napoli, 2001). From a marketing standpoint, the value of broadcasting (and large circulation newspapers) are no longer seen as the primary or best means of advertising to smaller niche audiences.

Instead, more and more companies are using the Internet to create Web experiences for a younger generation of users. As Chan-Olmsted (2000) points out, the Internet's interactive capability changes the basic relationship between the individual and media, challenging marketers to shift their emphasis from persuasion to relationship building. "As communication channels continue to proliferate and fragment, successful media firms will have to focus on consumers, rather than on systems of distribution or types of media content" (p. 112). One indication of this trend was a comment made by Coca Cola President, Steven J. Heyer, when he declared that Coke was moving away from broadcast television as "the anchor medium" toward more direct experience-driven marketing (Heyer, 2003). At the same time, the Internet offers complementary opportunities for business organizations to extend their brand as is the case with personalized marketing and online shopping. Perhaps most important, the Internet dramatically changes the traditional business supply chain by allowing information to flow in all directions, thereby enabling faster communication and improved exchange efficiency (Porter, 2001). For researchers, understanding the underlying strategy and full impact of the Internet and micromarketing is still very much in the beginning stages.

Finally, a few research questions researchers should consider in conducting future studies focused on this area of inquiry include:

• To what extent do geographical location and cultural differences affect the ability of TNMCs to implement strategy on a local level?

• To what extent does intelligent networking affect supply chain management in the production and distribution of media products and services by TNMCs?

• During the past decade, researchers like Straubhaar have shown that audiences prefer locally produced television and film products. How do we gauge the growing importance of the second-tier media companies in satisfying the wants and needs of local audiences? To what extent can we expect increased partnership agreements between TNMCs and such second-tier media companies?

• The demassification of media and entertainment products, made possible by the Internet and advanced recording and storage technologies, will likely change the business of TNMC marketing and production. What are some of the likely new marketing and production strategies TNMCs can be expected to employ in the years ahead? How will these new business strategies affect the profitability and operational efficiency of TNMCs?

• As mentioned earlier, TNMCs are not as global as they would seemingly appear. For companies like Viacom and Time Warner who do a disproportionate share of their business in North America, there will be increased pressure to become more global in scope. Researchers may want to consider some of the important emerging markets for the future and what it means from a strategy standpoint. Researchers should also evaluate the impact of increased globalization of this type on the overall business strategy of TNMCs.

## REFERENCES

Aaker, D. (1991). *Managing brand equity: Capitalizing on the value of a brand name.* New York: The Free Press.

Albarran, A. B. (2002). *Media economics* (2nd ed.). Ames: Iowa State Press.

Albarran, A. B, & Chan-Olmsted, S. (Eds.). (1998). *Global media economics.* Ames: Iowa State Press.

Albarran, A. B., & Dimmick, J. (1996). Economics of multiformity and concentration in the communications industries. *Journal of Media Economics, 9*, 41–49.

Anatola, L., & Rogers, E. (1984). Television flows in Latin America. *Communication Research, 11*, 183–202.

AOL's board is digging in. (2002, August 19). *Newsweek*, pp. 46–47.

AOL, you've got misery. (2002, April 8). *Business Week*, pp. 58–59.

Armstrong's vision of AT&T cable empire unravels on the ground. (2000, October 8). *Wall Street Journal*, pp. 1., A-11.

Aufderheide, P. (2002). Competition and commons: The public interest in and after the AOL–Time Warner merger. *Journal of Broadcasting & Electronic Media, 46*, 515–531.

Ball, D., & McCulloch, W. H. (1996). *International business: The challenge of global competition* (6th ed.). Chicago: Irwin.

Beamish, P. (1999). Yoshide Nakamura on structure and decision-making. *Academy of Management Executive, 13*, 12–16.

Behrman, J., & Grosse, R. E. (1990). *International business and governments: Issues and institutions.* Columbia: University of South Carolina Press.

Bennis, W. (1986). *Leaders and visions: Orchestrating the corporate culture.* New York: Conference Board.

Cate, F. (1990). The European broadcasting directive. *Communications Committee Monograph Series.* Washington, DC: American Bar Association.

Chan-Olmsted, S. (2000). Marketing mass media on the world wide web. In Alan Albarran & David Goff (Eds.), *Understanding the Web: Social political and economic dimensions of the Internet* (pp. 95–116). Ames: Iowa University Press.

Chan-Olmsted, S., & Chang, B. H. (2003). Diversification strategy of global media conglomerates: Examining its patterns and determinants. *Journal of Media Economics, 16*, 213–233.

Chan-Olmsted, S., & Kang, J. W. (2003). Theorizing the strategic architecture of a broadband television industry. *Journal of Media Economics, 16*, 3–21.

Charran, R., & Useem, J. (2002, May 27). Why companies fail. *Fortune*, 50–62.

Chernin, P. (2003, October 11). *MIPCOM award acceptance speech.* Presentation given at the 2003 MIPCOM conference. Cannes, France.

Cohan, J. (2002). I didn't know and I was only doing my job: Has corporate ethics governance careened out of control? A case study of Enron's information myopia. *Journal of Business Ethics, 40*, 275–299.

Collins, J. (2001). *Good to great.* New York: HarperCollins.

Compaine, B., & Gomery, D. (2000). *Who owns the media?* (3rd ed.). Mahwah, NJ: Lawrence Erlbaum Associates.

Crew, M., & Kleindorfer, P. (2002). Regulatory economics: Twenty years of progress? *Journal of Regulatory Economics, 21*, 5–22.

Daft, R. (1997). *Management* (4th ed.). New York: Harcourt Brace.

Demers, D. (1999). *Global media: Menace or messiah.* Cresskill, NJ: Hampton Press.

Dimmick, J. W. (2003). Media competition and coexistence. The theory of niche. Mahwah, NJ: Lawrence Erlbaum Associates.

Disney, Ovitz's compensation, and the business judgment rule. (2004, September 28). Available at: http://www.professorbainbridge.com/2004/09/disney_ovitzs_c.html Retrieved February 15, 2005.

Disney strips chairmanship from Eisner. (2004, March 4). *USA Today*, 1B.

Failed effort to coordinate ads signals deeper woes at AOL. (2002, July 18). *The Wall Street Journal*, 1, A6.

Faulhaber, G. (2002). Network effects and merger analysis: Instant messaging and the AOL Time Warner case. *Telecommunications Policy, 26*, 311–333.

Friedman, T. (1999). *The Lexus and the olive tree.* New York: Farrar, Straus & Giroux.

Gershon, R. A. (1997). *The transnational media corporation: Global messages and free market competition.* Mahwah, NJ: Lawrence Erlbaum Associates.

Gershon, R. A. (2000). The transnational media corporation: Environmental scanning and strategy formulation. *Journal of Media Economics, 13*, 81–101.

Gershon, R. A., & Kanayama, T. (2002). The SONY corporation: A case study in transnational media management. *The International Journal on Media Management, 4*, 44–56.

Gershon, R. A., & Suri, V. R. (2004). Viacom Inc.: A case study in transnational media management. *Journal of Media Business Studies, 1*, 47–70.

Grosse, R., & Kujawa, D. (1988). *International business: Theory and application.* Homewood, IL: Irwin.

Heyer, S. (2003). *Keynote remarks.* Presentation given at the Advertising Age Madison + Vine Conference, Beverly Hills, CA. Available at: http://www2.coca-cola.com/presscenter/viewpointsvine conference.html

Hitt, M., Ireland, R., & Hoskisson, R. (1999). *Strategic management.* Cincinnati, OH: South-Western College Publishing.

Hollifield, C. A. (2001). Crossing borders: Media management research in a transnational market environment. *Journal of Media Economics, 14*, 133–146.

Kevin, D. (2003). *Europe in the media.* Mahwah, NJ: Lawrence Erlbaum Associates.

Kuttner, R. (2002, July 29). Today's markets need new rules. *Business Week*, p. 26.

Lee, L. T., & Litman, B. (1991). Fox Broadcasting company, why now? An economic study of the rise of the fourth network. *Journal of Broadcasting and Electronic Media, 35*, 139–157.

Litman, B. (1998). *The motion picture industry.* Boston: Allyn & Bacon.

Monks, R., & Minow, N. (1996). *Watching the watchers: Corporate governance for the 21st century.* Cambridge, MA: Blackwell.

Morley, D., & Shockley-Zalabak, P. (1991). Setting the rules: An examination of the influence of organizational founder values. *Management Communication Quarterly, 4*, 422–449.

Mosco, V. (1990, Winter). The mythology of telecommunications deregulation. *Journal of Communication, 40*, 36–49.

Murdoch's kingdom. (1990, August 7). *The Economist*, 62.

Napoli, P. (2001). The audience product and the new media environment: Implications for the economics of media industries. *The International Journal on Media Management, 3*, 66–73.

Nathan, J. (1999). *Sony: The private life.* Boston: Houghton Mifflin.

News Corporation, Inc. (2003). *Annual report.* New York: News Corporation.

Now it's time to say goodbye. (2004, March 15). *Business Week*, 31–32.

Ogles, R. (1993). Music television (MTV). In R. Picard (Ed.), *The cable networks handbook* (pp. 137–142). Riverside, CA: Carpelan Press.

Ozanich, G. W., & Wirth, M. O. (1998). Media mergers and acquisitions: A communications industry overview. In A. Alexander, J. Owers, & R. Carveth (Eds.), *Media economics: Theory and practice* (2nd ed., pp. 95–107). Mahwah, NJ: Lawrence Erlbaum Associates.

Poole, I. (1990). *Technologies without boundaries.* Cambridge, MA: Harvard University Press.

Porter, M. E. (1985). *Competitive advantage: Creating and sustaining superior performance.* New York: Free Press.

Porter, M. E. (2001, March). Strategy and the Internet. *Harvard Business Review*, 3–18.

Pound, J. (2002). The promise of the governed corporation. In *Harvard business review on corporate governance*. Cambridge, MA: Harvard Business School Press.

Robock, S., & Simmonds, K. (1989). *International business and multinational enterprises* (4th ed.). Homewood, IL: Irwin.

Siebens, H. (2002). Concepts and working instruments for corporate governance. *Journal of Business Ethics, 39*, 109–116.

Sony Corporation, Inc. (1996). *Genryu* (2nd ed.). Tokyo: Sony Corporation.

Straubhaar, J. (1991). Beyond media imperialism: Asymmetrical interdependence and cultural proximity. *Critical Studies in Mass Communication, 8*, 39–59.

Straubhaar, J. (2003). Choosing national TV: Cultural capital, language and cultural proximity. In M. Elasmar (Ed.), *The impact of international television: A paradigm shift* (pp. 77–110). Mahwah, NJ: Lawrence Erlbaum Associates.

Sumner's gemstone. (2000, February 21). *Forbes*, 105–111.

The best and worst corporate boards. (2000, January 24). Available at: http://www.businessweek.com/2000/00_04/b3665022.htm Retrieved December 10, 2004.

The case against mergers. (1995, October 30). *Business Week*, 122–126.

The Walt Disney Company derivative litigation, 825 A.2d 275, 289 (Del. Ch. 2003).

There's no business like show business. (1998, June 22). *Fortune*, 92–104.

The rise of India. (2003, December 8). *Business Week*, 66–76.

Viacom International Inc. (2002). *10-K report*. New York: Viacom Inc.

Wasserstein, B. (1998). *Big deal: The battle for control of America's leading corporations*. New York: Warner Books.

Waterman, D., & Rogers, E. (1994). The economics of television program production and trade in Far East Asia. *Journal of Communication, 44*(3), 89–111.

Wheelen T., & Hunger, D. (1998). *Strategic management and business policy*, Reading, MA: Addison-Wesley/Longman.

Wildman, S., & Siwek, S. (1988). *International trade in films and television programs*. Cambridge, MA: Ballinger.

You've got new management. (2002, July 29). *Newsweek*, 34–35.

# 11

# Issues in Marketing and Branding

Walter S. McDowell
University of Miami

## COMPETITION CHANGES EVERYTHING

The primary motivation for a business to embrace the principles of brand management is *competition*, and although the notion of branding is not new to most American consumer goods, it is relatively new to media brands. One of the first occasions where the concept of *media as brands* was presented in a public forum was within a speech made in 1993 by David Bender, president and CEO of Mediamark Research. He asserted that "media vehicles are one of the few examples of brands which don't, for the most part, conceive of themselves as brands; as a result, they often are not able to take advantage of the insight that accrues to those aware of the thinking and research on brands" (Bender, 1993, p. 2). A mere 2 years later, as network prime time ratings began to lose ground to cable, the notion of media as brands began to take form. An editorial in *Broadcasting and Cable* trumpeted that "Branding has become the buzzword of the day ... more is riding on the success or failure of broadcast branding than at any time in the medium's history" (Editorial, 1995). Practical branding guides for broadcast professionals began to emerge, such as Dickey (1994) and McDowell and Batten (1999). A decade later, the lexicon of media brand management is pervasive among media executives, such as Cecile Frot-Coutaz, producer of the wildly popular "American Idol," who insists that "we don't look at shows purely as television programs. We look at the shows as brands (Albiniak, 2004, p. 1)."

In recent decades, academic research covered a number of different issues that collectively advanced our understanding of brands. In the simplest of terms, brand research addresses the effects of a brand name on the thoughts and behavior of consumers. However, branding authority Kevin Keller (2001) warns:

> There is an inherent complexity with brands themselves as brand names, logos, symbols, slogans, etc. all have multiple dimensions which each can produce differential effects on consumer behavior. As a result, brand management challenges can be especially thorny. (p. 4)

Regardless of how thorny the research challenges might be, brands are important to people because they help simply life.

## Why Consumers Like Brands

Because consumers often lack the motivation, capacity, or opportunity to process all product information to which they are exposed in a thoughtful or deliberative manner, they opt for quick resolution techniques stored in memory. Strong brands assist in this heuristic process. Biel (1991) offers the following insight:

> On a very practical level consumers like brands because they package meaning. They form a kind of shorthand that makes choice easier. They let one escape from a feature-by-feature analysis of category alternatives, and so, in a world where time is an ever-diminishing commodity, brands make it easier to store evaluations. (p. 6)

Typically, consumers arrive at a small grouping of brands that are acceptable for purchase called a consideration set. How consideration sets are formed and maintained is a research area unto itself (Laroche, Kim, & Matsui, 2003).

Aside from easing the cognitive workload, strong brands also reduce risk and uncertainty for consumers. Hoeffler and Keller (2003) asserted that when consumers have limited prior experience with a product category and the consequences of making a poor decision are significant, brand familiarity can reduce unwanted purchase anxiety. Many companies leverage the familiarity and comfort level of an established brand name to a new product line. This brand *extension* is intended to reduce the consumer's perception of risk (Gronhaug, Hem, & Lines, 2002).

A behavioral outcome of relying on brands is the cultivation of habits. In repetitive decision-making situations, habits save time and reduce the mental effort and apprehension of decision making. For marketing researchers, habitual purchase behavior is synonymous with the concept of brand loyalty.

## Media Embrace Brand Management

Researchers stated repeatedly that in a competitive marketplace, brand equity enhances the effectiveness and efficiency of marketing activities and, therefore, increases profit margins (Hoeffler & Keller, 2003). It was not until the early 1990s that electronic media, in the form of radio, television, cable, satellite, telephony, and Internet delivery systems, began to experience massive competition for the attention of scarce audiences. Therefore, the specific study of media brands is relatively new and fertile ground for research.

Dramatic changes in media technology are revolutionizing the way media content is created, distributed, and consumed. For example, the following is an excerpt from a CNN sales presentation.

CNN touches more people in more places through more distribution platforms than any other news organization. CNN branded news and information content, distributed in and out-of-home, on broadcast unwired networks, radio, websites and wireless distribution platforms, has the potential to deliver 1.5 billion people daily around the world (CNN Advertising, 2003, p. C24).

For decades, conventional media, such as newspapers, magazines, books, radio programs, television programs, movies, and sound recordings were distinct technologies that fostered equally distinct consumer behaviors and brand marketing strategies. However, with expanding digital technology, the partitions separating one medium from another are disappearing (i.e., CNN can no longer be branded simply as a cable network). This blurring of media boundaries has fostered the concept of *media convergence* (Grant & Meadows, 2002).

The ramifications of competition and convergence are directed not only at the creators and distributors of media content, but also at the end users. For audiences, the ultimate consequence of these actions is abundant choice. *Multitasking* has become part of the new lexicon of modern media. Simultaneous activities, such as instant messaging, playing video games, downloading music files, and watching television have become second nature to young people (Elkin, 2003). Furthermore, these simultaneous media experiences are enhanced by the development of media-on-demand technology. Emerging video delivery technology, such as cable and satellite video-on-demand (VOD) channels and personal video recorders (PVRs) are cultivating a new media marketplace where audiences can select program content at will, without the shackles of program scheduling or having to drive to a rental store or movie theater. Of course the interaction with media is no longer relegated to the homestead. Wireless access to the Internet and other branded multichannel services enable people to remain electronically connected regardless of their physical location. Also, new media have been adopted eagerly by business (it is not surprising that more people watch CNBC at work than at home). More than ever, the criteria for audiences choosing media content are based on the perceived knowledge of a media brand, rather than on availability and convenience.

The decades-old assumptions surrounding mass communication have fragmented into the far more complex world of satisfying the esoteric needs of audiences. The old homogenous mass audience is becoming divided and subdivided into an ever-changing array of new demographic and psychographic *niche* categories (Bianco, 2004; Zyman, 1999). Coinciding with the increased empowerment for audiences is a growing concern that abundant choice has become overwhelming choice. Marketing experts, such as Henry (2001), talked about the hard-wired "certainties of human nature" that may be impossible to alter, implying that limitless options can reach a point of diminishing returns, where the mind seeks out heuristics to simplify decision making. One common heuristic is to depend on brand names to uncomplicate and accelerate consumer decision making.

Adding fuel to the fire of this exploding competitive media marketplace has been the unsettling fact that, although the number of available options has increased enormously in recent years, the number of such options actually used has not kept pace. Cable television offers the most poignant example. Ten years ago, when most cable operators offered between 30 and 53 analog channels, the typical household watched an average of 10 channels. Today with over 100-channel capacity, that same household watches a mere 14.8. channels. Furthermore, in homes capable of receiving 200 or more channels, actual viewership struggles to only 18.9. (FCC, 2004). This is a classic example of the law of diminishing returns, where more choice has not translated directly into more usage. Borrowing a term from retail marketing, one can surmise that audience viewing in the United States has evolved into a *zero sum market*, where the number of available customers for a product category does not expand in proportion to the number of brands entering the market.

Competing in a zero sum market demands that a business take customers away from competing brands. Consequently, the name of the game for most contemporary media businesses is *share of market* (Aaker, 1991).

## GETTING STARTED

A meaningful body of knowledge on media branding is beginning to take shape, but this relatively newfound research domain is still experiencing growing pains. Before embarking on a major research project in this field, a researcher needs to understand how the game is played within the halls of academia.

### Issues of Academic Parochialism and Jargon

In recent years, the study of mass communication, and particularly media management, encompassed several academic disciplines, each of which covets its own intellectual territory and esoteric language. Departments of psychology, sociology, economics, marketing, advertising, history, political science, and law all feel sufficiently competent to study the actions and impact of mass media. According to Grubb and McDowell (2003), even among communication schools that offer majors or concentrations in media management, there is little consensus as to departmental objectives and course content. Furthermore, there has been a decades-old tension between communication schools and business schools as to the proper place to study media management. For example, Northwestern University supports an independent School of Communication, offering a variety of majors, but a degree in media management must be obtained from the university's prestigious Kellogg School of Business. Furthermore, this business school emphasis appears more pronounced outside the United States. For instance, the Institute for Media and Communications Management at University of St. Gallen, Switzerland, is an extension of the university's business school. Similarly, the Media Management and Transformation Centre at the Jönköping International Business School, Sweden, is integrated into the departments of Economics, Business Administration, and Law.

To the new media researcher, the jargon of marketing can be confusing because conceptual and operational definitions of common terms often are not consistent across disciplines or professions. One of the most disconcerting examples is the semantic battle between the terms *marketing* and *promotion*. Business schools tend to envision promotion as a subcategory of marketing. Additionally, advertising and public relations are seen as subservient divisions of promotion. On the other hand, communications schools tend to see promotion and marketing as having the same function. That is, both are intended to provide ways to attract audiences and advertisers. From a teaching perspective, this is underscored by an introductory statement found in the popular textbook on media promotion written by Eastman, Ferguson, and Klein (2002).

> Promotion generally is considered a "smaller" term than marketing, but the broadcast industry continues to use *promotion* while the cable industry uses the term *marketing*. This book generally combines the terms and uses them interchangeably. (p. 1)

Most media trade organizations, such as PROMAX (2004) envision promotion and marketing as essentially identical professions. For instance, the PROMAX annual Brand Builder Awards competition "recognizes marketing and promotion executives responsible for building today's leading broadcast and cable companies." Additionally, the term branding is not used consistently across all academic disciplines. Although some authors address it as a singular topic, others place it within a wider context. For example, Bellamy and Traudt (2000) used the phrase "branding as promotion" (p. 127). Because the study of brand management has its theoretical and applied roots in retail package goods, the study of media brands requires an ecumenical, cross-disciplinary approach that seeks common ground between communication and business paradigms.

## Branding and the Marketing Mix

For the purposes of this chapter branding falls under the rubric of marketing, which, in simple terms, is the art and science of recognizing and satisfying consumer needs. Key marketing activities traditionally have been categorized into the Four Ps of *product, price, place,* and *promotion*. Product denotes product development. Price deals with product pricing strategies. Place is synonymous with distribution channels, and promotion addresses communication tools, such as advertising and public relations (Burnett & Moriarty, 1998). As will be elaborated later, brand equity is the capacity of a brand name to cause consumers to respond differently to marketing activities.

## Brand Management Concepts

The terminology and jargon of branding is often more perplexing than enlightening, but year by year there seems to be a growing consensus among researchers. The following is a brief clarification of some common brand management concepts. Acknowledging that no two researchers would agree on the definitions of all of these items, this is a synthesis of conceptualizations derived from many sources, including Aaker (1991), Keller (1993), de Chernatony and McDonald (1998). The intent was to create a list or topology that would be appropriate for the unique study of media brands. A certain amount of conceptual overlap was inevitable, but hopefully, this effort will disentangle most of the confusion surrounding these commonly used terms.

- *A brand* is a name, term, sign, design, or a unifying combination of them intended to identify and distinguish a product or service from its competitors. Brand names communicate thoughts and feelings that are designed to enhance the value of a product beyond its product category and functional value.
- *Brand Awareness* (also commonly referred to as brand identity) refers to the simple familiarity (recall or recognition) of a brand name relative to its product category.
- *Brand Image* goes beyond mere awareness and deals with the thoughts and feelings (meaning) of the brand to a consumer. It can be conceived as a cluster of attributes and associations.
- *Brand Knowledge* is characterized by many researchers, most notably Kevin Keller (1993), as a combination of the previously mentioned brand awareness and brand image. In tandem, these two dimensions become the essential infrastructure of brand equity. For some brand researchers, brand knowledge consists only of factual information with no evaluations.
- *Brand Attitude* refers to not only known facts about the brand but *evaluations*. A positive or negative attitude about a brand can be nurtured either directly through personal experience or indirectly through marketing communications such as advertising and public relations.
- *Brand Preference* is often seen as a derivation of brand attitude in that the consumer is asked to disclose not only evaluations about a brand but, also, the position of that brand relative to its competition. A caution; preference does not always translate into predictable brand purchase behavior.
- *Brand Consideration Set* recognizes the common fact that a consumer might not have a single brand preference but, rather, an array of brands that are equally acceptable for purchase. For media, this consideration set sometimes has been referred to as a *channel repertoire* (see Ferguson & Perse, 1993). The criteria for becoming eligible for a person's consideration set can vary, depending on many factors, including perceived quality and pricing.
- *Brand Loyalty*, although sometimes conceptualized as an attitudinal measure, is more often utilized by researchers as a *behavioral* metric with no entangling psychological components. That is, loyalty is the degree to which a consumer purchases repeatedly a single brand. Using this definition, loyalty (habitual repeat purchasing) may not reveal a vulnerability to switch brands in that it is not a true measure of brand commitment.
- *Brand Commitment*, although similar to brand loyalty in terms of observable outcomes, takes in more of the psychology of branding in that it is the expressed degree of fidelity to a brand. Strong commitment implies the consumer holds such strong, positive, and unique brand associations that the temptations of discounts, coupons, promotions, and other competitive marketing activities cannot seduce a loyal customer.

- *Brand Trial (or brand sampling)* is the initial consumer purchase or experience with a brand. Unlike brand awareness, where a consumer may be familiar with a brand because of advertising or word of mouth, a trial means direct personal usage.
- *Brand Satisfaction (Dissatisfaction)* is associated directly with trial and usage in that it is the evaluative result of experiencing a brand. In this respect, the term resembles aspects of brand attitude, but satisfaction is grounded in the idea of consumer *expectations*, which lies at the heart of brand management. Brand satisfaction asks the question, does this brand live up to its promises? Logically, satisfaction drives commitment, which in turn, drives loyalty.
- *Brand Equity* is the holy grail of brand management and therefore deserving of more elaboration. It is difficult to find agreement among scholars or professionals on its proper conceptualization.

The conceptual definition chosen to be the theoretical underpinning for this chapter comes from Hoeffler and Keller (2003) and Keller (1993), who see brand equity as the response of consumers to marketing activities that are uniquely attributable to the brand. Accordingly, there are two kinds of memory associations, brand *awareness and* brand *image*. As presented earlier, awareness is the first step in the equity building process, where measures of familiarity (such as recall and recognition) are introduced. Image is more complex and deals with the meaning of a brand to a consumer. The two dimensions in combination are called *brand knowledge*. All things being equal in terms of marketing mix activities (namely, product, price, place, and promotion), a product exhibiting strong brand equity will foster different consumer responses than those fostered by a weak or anonymous brand. The specific responses can be derived from a range of attitudinal and behavior measures, such as perceptions of quality and repeat purchasing. Again, what sets apart brand equity from other marketing concepts is that knowledge of the *brand name alone* is identified as the causal factor in altering consumer responses to marketing activities. In this respect, strong brands become shortcut devices for simplifying decision making. Brand-conscious consumers do not burden themselves with extensive cognitive effort. Instead, they rely on brand knowledge stored in memory to make quick, stress-free purchase decisions.

The enemy of brand equity is the notion of *equivalent substitutes*, wherein several competing brands are perceived by the consumer as equally satisfying. Under these conditions of no genuine brand differentiation, businesses often succumb to mutually destructive marketing battles, such as pricing wars, and extravagant, but ineffectual, advertising campaigns.

- *Brand Extension* is an attempt to leverage the equity of an established brand by *extending* the brand name to a new product. If executed properly, capitalizing on the familiarity and reputation of a known brand can be a huge competitive asset. A more in-depth discussion of media brand extensions will be presented in an upcoming section.

All of the previously mentioned brand management concepts can be applied readily to media brands. Throughout much marketing literature, by changing the word *consumer* to *audience* and recognizing that *purchase behavior* can be synonymous with *watching*, *listening*, or *reading*, many conventional marketing concepts can serve as useful research tools for the study of media brands.

## Methodology Considerations

Methodological approaches to brand research vary depending on the type of information desired. The following is a brief overview of typical approaches coupled with relevant reference examples. Because research directed specifically at media brands is so rare, some examples were taken from conventional brand studies.

### Surveys

Surveys or questionnaire studies, the most common brand research approach, provide knowledge about the frequency of occurrence of specified variables and the degree of association among these variables. For instance, from a managerial perspective, Chan-Olmstead and Kim (2001) conducted a mail survey of several hundred television station general managers, asking how they perceived the notion of branding within the context of their station operations. From an audience point of view, Bellamy and Traudt (2000) assessed the recall and recognition power of an array of broadcast and cable network brand names. Surveys can also be conducted using secondary data. For instance, Chambers (2003) used FCC data on radio station program formats and ownership to evaluate the status of program diversity in an era of massive consolidation.

### Experiments

Although experiments typically lack the external validity of large surveys, they do provide the advantage of testing causal theory. An example of such a design can be found in a study by Kim (2003) that evaluated the effect of different communication message strategies on consumer perceptions of brand extensions. Similarly, a news branding study conducted by McDowell and Dick (2002), manipulated the supposed market rankings ("We're number #1" etc.) of an unfamiliar local newscast to induce changes in news credibility evaluations. As will be discussed later, an experimental approach is the preferred way to measure properly the presence and magnitude of brand equity. One such venture was a quasi-experimental study conducted by McDowell and Sutherland (2000) that analyzed daily lead-in news audience behavior of three competing stations for an entire year in an effort to validate a new diagnostic tool for assessing program brand equity.

### Content Analysis

For decades, content analysis has been used as a methodological tool for understanding all types of mass media. Most such analyses are quantitative in nature, involving the counting of instances of certain types of content or techniques used to convey messages about a brand. An example would be an analysis of broadcast station Web sites conducted by Chan-Olmsted and Park (2000) or a comparison of advertising presence and practice between national TV network Web Sites and stand-alone dot-com portals conducted by

Ha (2003). There is also justification for qualitative analysis, emphasizing the meanings associated with the messages as exemplified by McDowell (2004b), who performed a qualitative content analysis of brand differentiation strategies used by cable networks in their business-to-business trade advertising. Recognizing that advertising, consumer brands, and culture are intertwined, Mastro and Stern (2003) conducted a content analysis of racial and ethnic minority representations found in over 2,000 prime-time commercials.

### Case Studies

Case studies encompass a wide range of techniques. In their most common form, cases have been used as a time-honored teaching tool in business schools, whereby a real world business situation is analyzed to stimulate discussion of specific principles. One example is an examination of how, several years ago, Fox outbid CBS for the network broadcast rights to NFL games (Anand & Conneely, 2003). In addition to a classroom function, case studies are also conducted as primary research, intended to reveal new knowledge and foster theory development. For instance, Dong and Helms (2001) suggested a brand name translation model derived from a case analysis of U.S. brands in China. Finally, a case approach can be used to examine policy issues affecting media, such as the gradual privatization and commercialization of the PBS brand observed by Hoynes (2003).

Today, many media studies take a hybrid approach of capitalizing on the advantages of both quantitative and qualitative paradigms. Gunter (2000) stated that increasingly, researchers are attempting to develop a complex thematic analysis of transcripts that combines interpretive sensitivity of qualitative work with systematic coding that leans more toward quantitative analysis. Some studies take a two-step approach, beginning with a qualitative exercise and then using this knowledge to create a quantitative survey instrument. Hausman (2000) offered a prime example of what the author calls a "multi-method investigation" of consumer impulse buying that could be transposed readily to a media decision-making environment.

## Measuring Brand Equity

First, it should be understood that not all brand marketing research attempts to measure the overarching construct of brand equity. Instead, there are dozens of other brand concepts (see prior list of brand management concepts) worthy of study without necessarily becoming part of a brand equity inquiry.

Recall that brand equity looks at *differential responses* by consumers that are uniquely attributable to a brand name. Based on this conceptual underpinning, the most crucial component for any equity measurement procedure, regardless of the variables chosen to be studied, is *control*. That is, the researcher must create a level playing field whereby brand strength is revealed cleanly, with no confounding marketing mix variables distorting the results. For example, an equity brand study of two competing brands of soup must be equivalent in terms of flavor category, price, size/quantity, availability, and testing situation. The only independent variable manipulated by the researcher should the brand names. A typical blind experiment might have respondents evaluate the taste of various soups, while the researcher surreptitiously switches brand labels. If taste evaluations vary by label, with all other reasonable factors held constant, the researcher has found evidence of brand equity. Media brands need to be explicated in a similar manner, so that measured differences in audience responses are the sole result of altering the name of the program, station, network, Web site, etc. In this respect, true brand equity studies must be experimental or quasi-experimental in designs. Other methodologies, such as straight surveys, content analysis, and case studies can all enhance the body of knowledge about branding but an experimental configuration, where brand names can be manipulated, provides the most persuasive evidence of differential response.

Audiences seek all kinds of gratifications from media, including companionship, escape, arousal, information, and relaxation (Rubin, 1994). Therefore, the measurement of audience-based media brand equity must respond accordingly. For example, is it appropriate to apply the same satisfaction measure to both a television newscast and a sitcom? Similarly, when audiences surf the Internet, are they seeking the same gratifications from all Web sites or, more plausibly, do audience expectations change, depending on the Web site found.

Along this same line of thought, media brand equity must include *appropriate brand competitors*. Proper identification can be complicated, particularly when brand benefits are more abstract than utilitarian. For instance, does a brand researcher for CNN look at only other cable news channels as direct competitors or should he or she include news sources found among broadcast networks, newspapers, and the Internet? Bergan and Peteraf (2002) offered valuable insights into creating brand competitor identification schemes.

Typically, brand equity studies take one of two approaches:

- *Indirect*—Measures of attitudinal or perceptual measures of brand knowledge.
- *Direct*—Measures of the impact of brand knowledge on market behavior.

Beyond these broadly defined approaches, the specific variables included can vary greatly. Hoeffler and Keller (2003) provided an excellent overview of available studies that demonstrate the ways different types of brand associations can affect consumer responses. These include product evaluations, perceptions of quality, product preference, consumer confidence, purchase intention, purchase rates, and overall market share. From a media standpoint, many of these measures could be worthwhile tools, depending on the nature of the content and audience expectations (e.g., measures of consumer confidence and perceptions of quality may not be applicable for a TV sitcom, but perfect for a TV newscast).

A quasi-experiment conducted by McDowell and Sutherland (2000) provided one of only a few attempts at measuring media brand equity using a new diagnostic tool that is unique to media; lead-in programming effects. There remains much more work to be done. Keller (2001) asserted that despite the progress that has been made in the field, "There remains a need to develop more insightful, diagnostic measures of branding phenomena.... it is especially important to develop highly reliable valuation techniques and means of assessing returns on brand investments (p. 4)." The study of media brand equity is no exception. Only the first steps have been taken to establish it as a worthwhile research domain.

## Media Brand Extensions

In recent years, rather than support an array of individual brands, many companies, including media conglomerates, are shifting toward greater use of corporate branding, attempting to bring all products and services under a unifying parent brand (Aaker & Keller, 1990). Looking at a channel line-up for a typical cable system, one could testify that a good third of the content options are derivations or extensions of a parent brand. At the forefront of this trend are companies, such as Discovery and ESPN, that seem to find endless ways to clone their brands, from magazines to restaurants. Because extensions have become so common and so important, a separate section of this chapter has been set aside for this singular topic.

As presented in an abbreviated form earlier, a brand extension is an application of an established brand name beyond its original designated product or service. It is an attempt to leverage a brand's equity to other products bearing the same brand name. Positive, strong and unique associations of a strong brand can be extended to a new product or service (Keller, 1993). For instance, ESPN has extended itself into ESPN magazine, ESPN Sports Zone Web site, ESPN merchandise, and ESPN restaurant franchises (Media Groups, 2003).

A special case of brand extension is *co-branding* in which two established brands are extended to a new product (Leuthesser, Kohli, & Suri, 2003). A media example would be the creation of cable channel MSNBC from a partnership extension between Microsoft and NBC. Both pure brand extension and cobranding raise the same basic issues, namely how to capitalize on the extension without harming the integrity of the originating brands.

The academic study of media extensions is scant but growing. For example, Ha and Chan-Olmsted (2001) examined TV viewers' perceptions of enhanced TV offerings on broadcast network Web sites. For the most part, knowledge of brand extensions still must be acquired from studies of conventional consumer goods. A pervasive message emanating from almost all such research is that extending a brand can have serious risks as well as rewards. On the positive side, studies and overviews, such as Aaker & Keller (1990) and Hoeffler & Keller (2003) showed how well-known and reputable brands can extend their equity into new products. However, on the negative side, several published studies, including John, Loken, & Joiner (1998) and Martinez, & Pina (2003), attested to the potential hazards of implementing a poorly executed brand extension. Even the simple public announcement of a planned corporate brand extension can influence stock market performance as found by Lane and Jacobson (1995).

In succinct terms, most brand extension studies concentrate on the notion, if not the exact terminology of *fit*. Studies may use terms, such as similarity, consistency, or congruency, but the common theoretical thread running throughout these studies is that in order for a new product to take full advantage of an extension, it must fit properly within the brand equity of the parent or master brand. Otherwise, the newly extended brand will not inherit sufficient equity to propel the new product through the rigors of a competitive marketplace. Furthermore, a worst case scenario, the originating brand becomes contaminated from the failed endeavor. Perhaps, the best conceptualization of this quandary is expressed by Zimmer and Bhat (2004), when they maintained that brand extensions involve *reciprocal effects*.

Carrying this idea a step further, Kim (2003) and McEnally and de Chernatony (1999) pointed out that a brand can change its meaning in consumers' minds as the company matures and develops more diverse product lines. As a result, companies often cultivate brand communication strategies that dwell more on abstract and intangible associations, enabling the brand to be extended across somewhat dissimilar products. A media example would be CNN's expansion into multiple distribution platforms, but still promoting itself as "The Most Trusted Source for News."

## Brands as Niches

The notions of segmentation go hand in hand with those of niche marketing. McEnally and de Chernatony (1999) maintained that consumer markets in general will become ever more splintered as needs-based segmentation becomes more common. The consequence is a greater number of brands designed to meet the needs of smaller customer segments or niches. James Stengel, global marketing officer for consumer brand giant Proctor and Gamble, maintains that its bulging portfolio of big brands contains "not one mass market brand . . . every one of our brands is targeted." (Bianco, 2004, p. 61). Media brands are evolving into a similar configuration where the goal is to attract highly defined niche audiences and advertisers. Dimmick (2003) looked at media competition and co-existence from the perspective of niche theory, asserting that niche differentiation leads to coexistence and survival in highly competitive media markets. Rather than competing head to head with all brands within a product category, niches are created that allow the brand to sidestep direct confrontation. Communicating the niche attributes and benefits to audiences and advertisers is the goal of brand management.

## The Psychology Versus Behavior Dilemma in Brand Research

Now that we have established some basic brand management concepts and examples of the methodological approaches, it is worthwhile to acknowledge a long-standing dilemma that permeates all brand research—the disparities between consumer psychology (what people say) and consumer behavior (what people actually do). Callingham and Baker (2002) posed the core question in the title of their work "We Know What They Think, but Do We Know What They Do?" Although most research in consumer-based brand equity assumes that attitudes beget behavior, many psychological components of branding, such as awareness, knowledge, and preference, are not necessarily good predictors of observable purchase behavior. For any number of reasons, a person may prefer a Lincoln but drive a Ford. Similarly, opinion surveys may rank the PBS brand a media treasure, but in terms of popularity, Nielsen audience behavior ratings indicate a far different story.

Along these same lines, there has been a long-standing discussion and debate over the ways marketing researchers classify people into meaningful consumer *segments* for analysis. A market segment is a group within a market that is clearly identifiable based on certain measurable criteria, which range from tangible or overt behavior characteristics, such as demographic grouping to more intangible or abstract psychographic characteristics, such as values and lifestyles (Callingham & Baker, 2002; Lin, 2002). Consumer segments are assumed to have many similar needs and desires that permit brand marketers to create highly targeted selling strategies. Media brands are just beginning to segment audiences beyond the conventional age/sex demographics provided by audience measurement companies such as Nielsen and Arbitron.

In addition to classifying the consumers of brands according to tangible and intangible criteria, the perceived characteristics of the brand itself can be analyzed in a similar fashion. That is, consumers can develop brand associations that can range from physical product attributes to more abstract and symbolic characteristics. One of the most renowned examples of a rather mundane consumer product being elevated into a cultural icon has been Nike. The brand's "Just do it" marketing strategies say far more about the character of the person who wears the footwear than the functionality of the shoe itself. The head of a major national advertising agency described the essential difference between Nike and Reebok, its nearest competitor, as "Reebok is about selling shoes, and Nike is about the soul of the athlete" (Buss, 2000, p. 45).

In an effort to differentiate one brand from another, many branding experts assert that symbolic values and meaning are often the only means by which brands are perceived as truly unique from their category competitors (Tan Tsu Wee & Chua Han Ming, 2003). Similarly, decades of media uses and gratifications research substantiates the premise that audiences seek certain media to gratify needs that, in many cases, are entirely psychological (Rubin, 1994). In this vein, McDowell (2004a) explored the feasibility of using a free association methodology to capture and differentiate abstract media brand associations for three cable news networks.

## Recognizing Differences Between Conventional Consumer Brands and Media Brands

Although much knowledge of brand management can be transposed readily to media brands, there are several areas where, from an audience perspective, the correspondence between branded conventional consumer goods and branded media products is not perfect. The following is an itemization of some significant differences.

First, whereas much of the literature available about typical consumer brands dwells on the dynamics of *pricing*, most media brands are not particularly price sensitive. The reason is that they are distributed typically via an advertising-based business model, wherein the only real cost for the audience is its time and attention. Of course, cash subscription models do exist for cable and satellite services offering a la carte or pay-per-play offerings, but so far, most channels remain bundled with many other brands that share little in common.

Coinciding with this lack of emphasis on unit pricing is a similar lack of focus on *risk reduction*. Indeed, consumers depend on familiar brands to reduce the risk of bad purchases, but the problem with applying this to media brands is that consequences of a bad purchase are seldom important (e.g., the consequences of watching a disappointing television program are tiny compared to those of buying a defective automobile or even spoiled groceries). Therefore, this low-risk media consumption has been considered by researchers, such as de Chernatony and McDonald (1998) and Keller (2003) as a *low-involvement* experience, similar to buying chewing gum, in that audiences are not motivated to invest substantial cognitive effort in brand decision making.

Another difference is the accessibility of competing brands. For most consumer goods, brand trials require repeated trips to a retail purchase location in order to sample multiple competitors. Furthermore, the time interval between trials might be weeks or months (e.g., how often to people purchase detergent?). Conversely, the physical act of sampling dozens of competitive media brands is remarkably easy, typically requiring a mere click of a remote control device or computer mouse. The combination of low risk and easy access forces media brand managers to cope with the esoteric problems of commercial zapping and channel grazing.

Although brand experts emphasize often the tangible versus intangible benefits of a brand (such as the Nike example presented earlier), one could argue that essentially all benefits from media brands are intangible, at least in terms of being able to experience physically the branded product or service. As McDowell (2004a) suggested, media brands associations can still be categorized according to a rough continuum ranging from associations addressing factual attributes (e.g., CNN provides news around the clock) to more attitudinal evaluations (e.g., CNN does the best job).

Perhaps the most significant aspect that makes media brands special is that they are *media* and, therefore, can be utilized as communication tools for self-branding. For instance, as Eastman, Ferguson, and Klein (2002) and other experts attested, the greatest brand marketing asset possessed by a major broadcast network or station is its own air time. Frozen peas do not have such an advantage. An important element of media brand management is developing strategies concerning what the brand communicates about itself.

## Seeking Worthwhile Topics for Academic Research

Given the above caveat that some aspects of conventional brand research may not be as appropriate for media brands, the best sources for research topics remain within the conventional brand research circles. The key is to have the skills to translate the theory, methodologies, and findings of these business studies into meaningful jumping off points for media management study. Reputable journals and conference papers are excellent sources for research topics. Scanning literature reviews and references of published or presented work often can stimulate ideas. Additionally, most discussion sections of academic work recommend specific futures studies.

*Replication* of a conventional brand business study is a good starting point, where known branding constructs and theoretical frameworks can be tested using media products. In some cases the focus might be more on methodology than theory, wherein the research challenge is how to come up with media-based operational definitions that replicate in spirit those found in a conventional brand study. Another reason for replication is that most published marketing studies typically concentrate on only one product category (e.g., soap, automobiles, liquor, etc.), and, therefore, the findings lack external validity. Until the body of knowledge encompassing media brand management becomes more substantial, researchers will continue to borrow from their branding "cousins" working in more traditional business areas.

In addition to the communications journals, such as the *Journal of Broadcasting and Electronic Media, Journal of Media Economics, The Journal of Radio Studies, The International Journal of Media Management,* and the newly formed *Journal of Media Business Studies,* there are many business-oriented academic journals that can provide valuable insight into marketing and branding. These include the *Journal of Brand Management, Journal of Product and Brand Management, Journal of Consumer Research, Journal of Consumer Marketing, Journal of Market Research, Journal of Marketing,* and the *Journal of Business Research.* Also, the Harvard Business School offers academics a wealth of teaching and research items, including its renowned case study archives.

Criticism of academic research in this field stems usually from two contradictory mindsets. The first accuses academic studies of being overly theoretical and abstract and, therefore, of little value to the real world of commerce. In this case, the demand is for more applied research. The opposing school of thought accuses academic studies of being overly concerned with mundane industry issues and not addressing loftier intellectual goals. In this case, the demand is for more basic or theoretical research. Scholarly work in marketing and branding is especially perplexing because the research in this social science domain would not exist if it were not for the everyday happenings in private business. Media trade publications, such as *Broadcasting and Cable, Advertising Age,* and *Mediaweek* can also stimulate ideas for scholarly research.

## LOOKING BACK BEFORE LOOKING FORWARD

As the adage goes, what is past is prelude and so, before looking to the future, it is appropriate to examine the scholarly work that already exist on media branding. There has been considerable work done about media promotion in general (Eastman, 2000) but only a small handful of studies have used media brand management as the centerpiece of the inquiry. For example, in broadcasting studies, Bellamy and Traudt (2000) explored the notion of television networks as brands; Chan-Olmsted and Kim (2001) investigated the perceptions of branding among television station managers; Hoynes (2003) looked at branding public service through the privatization of public television; McDowell and Dick (2002) studied perceived market rankings in inducing a brand placebo effect in news credibility evaluations; and McDowell and Sutherland (2000) examined the use of brand equity theory in explaining TV audience lead-in effects. In the cable area, Chan-Olmsted and Kim (2002) compared the PBS brand with cable brands; McDowell (in press) conducted a qualitative content analysis of cable network business-to-business advertising; and McDowell (2004) also explored a free association methodology to capture and differentiate abstract media brand associations in a study of three cable news networks. Looking at the role of branding in a new media environment, Chan-Olmsted and Ha (2003) investigated the Internet business models for broadcasters with a branding flavor. Chan-Olmsted and Jung (2001) examined how the U.S television networks diversify, brand, and compete in the age of the Internet. Finally, Ha and Chan-Olmsted (2001) looked at how enhanced TV might be used as brand extension by assessing TV viewers' perceptions of enhanced TV features and TV commerce on broadcast networks' Web sites. These studies, particularly their literature reviews, can serve as intellectual launching pads for choosing new topics.

## NECESSITY AND ESSENCE OF MEDIA BRAND STUDIES

### The Need for Strategy

At the very beginning of this chapter, it was posited that brand management is the inevitable result of fierce competition in a zero sum market. Rather than merely guessing what the best management decisions should be, well-designed and well-executed media brand studies provide managers with necessary empirical knowledge that can increase the odds of making the right decision. In other words, knowledge enables strategy and strategy is the essence of brand management in that it *points the way*. In this respect, strategy fosters discipline. Serio Zyman, former chief marketing officer for Coca-Cola, maintained that "Strategies provide the gravitational pull that keeps you from popping off in a million directions" (Zyman, 1999, p. 32). This is no truer than for media companies coping with multiple content and distribution components.

### Strategy Is About Being Different

The ultimate purpose of brand strategy is to nurture a powerful and sustainable competitive advantage, or as Kapferer (1992) asserted "There is only one strategic purpose: creating a difference ... brands are built up by persistent differences over the long run" (p. 11). Whereas these assertions may seem self-evident on paper, many businesses, including media businesses, often concentrate too much of their strategic thinking on the product and not enough on the brand. The result can be the squandering of time, talent, and money on a variety of inappropriate marketing efforts that yield consumers' confusion or, the worst of all branding sins, indifference.

Strategy guru Michael Porter of the Harvard Business School echoes the same thought, when he asserted that "Competitive strategy is about being different. It means deliberately choosing a different set of activities to deliver a unique mix of value" (Porter, 1996, p. 64). Along this same line, researchers in marketing have long been aware of the inherent problems of measuring simple consumer satisfaction in that consumers often are satisfied with the performance of most brands and, therefore, in terms of simple functionality, one brand becomes an equivalent substitute for several others (i.e., a huge consideration set).

Porter (1996) maintained that the challenge is to reconcile the differences between *operational effectiveness* with real strategy. Without actually using the exact terminology of branding, the author warns that:

> Few companies have competed successfully on the basis of operational effectiveness over extended periods ... the most obvious reason for that is the rapid diffusion of best practices. Competitors can quickly imitate management techniques, new technologies, input improvements and superior ways of meeting customers. (p. 63)

When all competitors become preoccupied with operational effectiveness at the expense of genuine strategic planning, the results are "mutually destructive battles wherein the competitors loose their distinctiveness in an effort to be all things to all customers" (Porter, 1996, p. 63).

Returning to niche theory terminology coined by Dimmick (2003), one can say that this brand substitution phenomenon can be defined as the *niche-breadth* of one brand overlapping too much with that of one or more category competitors. This notion can be integrated readily with the concept of brand differentiation. Keller (2003) recommended that strategy formulation begin with an analysis of what he called *points of parity* versus *points of difference*. As the names imply, points of parity consist of a list of derived associations that are common to several competing brands, while points of difference include a list of associations that are unique to a particular brand. As emphasized earlier, these unique brand associations can range from utilitarian attributes to symbolic imagery.

Porter (1996) maintained that competitive advantages come from the way a company's activities fit and reinforce one another and that just as a four-legged stool is sturdier than a three-legged stool, a company can achieve more stability in a competitive marketplace when it has multiple parts all working in harmony. In an era of unforgiving media competition, well-conceived brand-driven marketing strategies are essential for survival.

## Audience Strategy Versus Business-to-Business Strategy

Adams (2002) reminded media observers and researchers that although the most visible forms of marketing and promotion are aimed at the general public to attract audiences, there is a second target group that is equally important to most media businesses and that is the business community. Using the term *business-to-business* branding, De Chernatony and McDonald (1998) maintained that the notions of brand equity can be cultivated among this elite group of customers. For radio and television broadcasters, this means capturing primarily the attention of advertisers. For cable, satellite, and many online businesses, the goal is obtaining channel or Web site distribution (Warner & Buchman, 2004). Consequently, media brands must generate two sets of brand strategies. For example, unlike prior discussions concerning audience response to pricing, within a business-to-business context, pricing can be a pivotal variable for managing brand equity. That is, the more added values a brand name evokes to a media buyer, the more likely he or she will pay a premium price for a commercial or advertisement. To date, academic research in this area of business-to-business media brand marketing has been sparse. One recent contribution is McDowell (2004) who analyzed cable network business-to-business selling strategies from a niche brand differentiation viewpoint.

## Brand Strategy and Corporate Culture

The preceding discussion in this chapter so far has dealt with branding primarily in terms of external communications aimed at audiences and business people, but there is an additional internal dimension to branding that deals with managing the human resources involved with marketing a brand. According to Powers (2004), determining how the parts of an organization fit one another in terms of unity of command, span of control, division of labor, and departmentalization has become a daunting challenge, especially for media conglomerates attempting to manage several diverse media brands. For example, the recent merger of Vivendi Universal Entertainment with NBC (General

Electric) will create a giant synergistic multimedia conglomerate that, according to NBC sources, will require a unique "brand management structure" (Higgins, 2003, p. 44). However, business success means more than organizing properly the more tangible media assets of a diversified company. It also means dealing with human assets. Ind (2003) maintained that employees must buy into the brand ideology of their employer. This ideology often has been referred to as a *corporate culture*. Schein (1992) contended that at the heart of every organization there is a paradigm of interrelated and unconscious shared assumptions, which directs how members think, feel, and act. According to McEnally and de Chernatony (1999), brand management requires a corporate culture where:

> Employees must understand the brand's vision, its core values . . . and perform in a manner consistent with the brand's identity and be empowered to take actions that enhance it . . . this requires extensive training and a comprehensive explanation of the brand's meaning and strategy. (p. 29)

Kung (2000) conducted one of the few corporate culture studies addressing specifically media companies and found that at both the BBC and CNN, this internal culture can be a valuable strategic marketing asset. Today, marketing professionals must acquire new management strategies that can nurture brand-conscious corporate cultures. In many cases these skill sets will come initially from academic research.

## THE FUTURE OF MEDIA BRAND STUDY

The opening paragraphs of this chapter set the stage for discussing the challenges for the first decade of 21st century media brand management. The intermingled factors of technology, economics, and regulation are about to usher in another tumultuous era of media evolution and revolution. More than ever, the art and science of marketing and, in particular, branding will be crucial for companies to survive and prosper.

In addition to a dramatic increase in the number of competitors entering the media marketplace each year, the two interrelated factors of technological convergence and ownership consolidation are challenging many of the long-held principles and practices of media marketing. The unprecedented increase in media channels often has been referred to as an *explosion*, but on reflection, one could argue that that media are also experiencing an *implosion*. That is, media experiences for content creators, distributors, and audiences are coming together not pulling away.

As discussed earlier, technological convergence, fostered by the transition from analog to digital communication, has blurred the once familiar distinctions among all types of communication platforms. Traditional print and electronic media can now be digitized and offered to consumers through a variety of conduits, including over-the-air broadcast, satellite Direct to Home (DTH), microwave, cable, DSL telephone, fiber optics, and the Internet. Essentially, content is no longer inexorably attached to any particular delivery system. Furthermore, buzzwords such as time-shifting, multitasking, zapping, and wireless access are indicative of a world only a few visionaries saw coming.

More than 40 years ago, media philosopher Marshall McLuhan predicted what we are beginning to experience today:

> Information pours upon us, instantaneously and continuously. As soon as information is acquired, it is rapidly replaced by still newer information. Our electronically configured world has forced us to move from the habit of data classification to the mode of pattern recognition. We can no longer build serially, block by block, step by step, because instant communication insures that all factors of the environment and of experience coexist in a state of active interplay. (McLuhan and Fiori, 1967, p. 27)

Coinciding with the convergence of media technologies has been the convergence of media businesses, commonly referred to as *consolidation*. In fact, one could argue that the remarkable flexibility of cross-platform digital communication has been a catalyst for sharing facilities and personnel among mass media. For example, this new parsimony is attractive particularly for news operations, where in a matter of seconds, one reporter can send a digitized image and text of a news report to any number of media platforms. These types of functional interactions have spawned a new industry term "digital-asset management" (Kerschbaumer, 2002, p. 35).

Ozanich and Wirth (1998) maintained that merger and acquisition activity is driven by a combination of technological change, available capital, and a liberalization of ownership restrictions. In recent years, all three of these factors have materialized in the United States. Of special importance have been recent policy initiatives designed to relax decades-old media ownership barriers. Beginning with the groundbreaking 1996 Telecommunications Act and continuing into 2003 with FCC proposals to dismantle cross-ownership restrictions among TV stations, radio stations, and newspapers, there has been an unprecedented incentive to invest in cross-media properties (Federal Communications Commission, 2003). As with technological convergence, these shared business endeavors provide synergies whereby content is no longer relegated to a single isolated company. Instead, the content is reconfigured or "repurposed" to another branded platform (Vizjak & Ringlstetter, 2003). This leveraging of content is not always a function of outright ownership of diverse media. For example, Liu and Chan-Olmsted (2002) examined how broadcast networks create strategic alliances with independent Internet firms.

Technological convergence and business consolidation in tandem have provided media companies with operational advantages and cost efficiencies, but these cross-media amalgamations require brand researchers and professionals to be alert to the new complexities of today's media environment.

Against this dynamic background, researchers will continue to grapple with conceptualizing and measuring brand equity. After a particularly disappointing car-selling season for General Motors, a frustrated GM market analyst admitted that "even though brand equity may sometimes be hard to define, it's pretty clear when you've lost it" (Wilkie, 1996, p. 267). The fact that there are so many definitions and operationalizations of brand equity (and other related concepts) is not necessarily a bad circumstance. After all, every theory is partial, always leaving something out in favor of bringing something else in. As a result, one should not expect the creation of some unified theory of media brand equity. Instead, we should expect the ongoing development of many approaches, each offering special insight.

This chapter provided an overview of the current status of media brand research and alerted scholars and students to promising areas for future work in this burgeoning field. Although recognizing the unrivaled complexities of this brave new media world, the primary goal for researchers should be to *uncomplicate things*, to seek simplicity and elegance in our new theories and methodologies. Ironically, these are the same goals of a brand.

## REFERENCES

Aaker, D. A. (1991). *Managing brand equity. Capitalizing on the value of a brand name*. New York: Free Press.

Aaker. D. A., & Keller, K. L. (1990). Consumer evaluations of brand extensions. *Journal of Marketing, 54*, 27–41.

Adams, W. J. (2002). Marketing to affiliates, buyers, and advertisers. In S. T. Eastman, D. A. Ferguson, & R. Klein (Eds.), *Promotion and marketing for broadcasting, cable and the Web* (pp. 195–210). Boston: Focal Press.

Albiniak, P. (2004, April 19). New ways to get rich. *Broadcasting and Cable,* 1.

Anand, B., & Conneely, C. (2003). Fox and the NFL—1998 (Case Study No. 9-707-44). Cambridge, MA: Harvard Business School.

Burnett, J., & Moriarty, S. (1998). *Marketing communications. An integrated approach*. Upper Saddle River, NJ: Prentice-Hall.

Bellamy, R. V., & Traudt, P. J. (2000). Television branding as promotion. In S. T. Eastman (Ed.), *Research in media promotion* (pp. 265–296). Mahwah, NJ: Lawrence Erlbaum Associates.

Bender, D. C. (1993, March 24). *Media as brands.* Paper presented at Advertising Research Foundation 39th Annual Conference, New York.

Bergan, M., & Peteraf, M. (2002). Competitor identification and competitor analysis: A broad-based managerial approach. *Managerial and Decision Economics, 23*, 157–169.

Bianco, A. (2004, July 12). The vanishing mass market. *BusinessWeek,* p. 60.

Biel, A. L. (1991). How brand image drives brand equity. *Journal of Advertising Research, 6,* RC6–RC12.

Buss, D. (2000, December). Nike: Biography of a brand. *Brand Marketing, 2,* 45.

Callingham, M., & Baker, T. (2002). We know what they think, but do we know what they do? *International Journal of Market Research, 44,* 299–337.

Chambers, T. (2003). Radio programming diversity in the era of consolidation. *Journal of Radio Studies, 10,* 33–45.

Chan-Olmsted, S., & Ha, L. (2003). Internet business models for broadcasting: How television stations perceive and integrate the Internet. *Journal of Broadcasting and Electronic Media, 47,* 597–617.

Chan-Olmsted, S., & Kim, Y. (2002). The PBS brand versus cable brands: Assessing the brand image of public television in a multi-channel environment. *Journal of Broadcasting and Electronic Media, 46,* 300–321.

Chan-Olmsted, S., & Jung, J. (2001). Strategizing the net business: How the U.S. television networks diversify, brand, and compete in the age of the Internet. *International Journal of Media Management, 3,* 213–223.

Chan-Olmsted, S., & Kim, Y. (2001). Perceptions of branding among television station managers: An exploratory analysis. *Journal of Broadcasting and Electronic Media, 45,* 75–91.

Chan-Olmsted, S., & Park, J. (2000). From on-air to on-line world: Examining the content and structures of broadcast TV stations' Websites. *Journalism and Mass Communication, 77,* 321–340.

CNN Advertising (2003, May 19). Cable 2003 (Special advertising section). *Advertising Age, 74,* C24.

De Chernatony, L., & McDonald, M. (1998). *Creating strong brands in consumer service and industrial markets*. Oxford, UK: Butterworth/Heinemann.

Dickey, L. (1994). *The franchise. Building radio brands*. Washington, DC: National Association of Broadcasters.

Dimmick, J. W. (2003). *Media competition and coexistence. The theory of the niche*. Mahwah, NJ: Lawrence Erlbaum Associates.

Dong, L. C., & Helms, M. M. (2001). Brand name translation model: A case analysis of U.S. brands in China. *Journal of Brand Management, 9,* 99–115.

Eastman, S. T. (2000). *Research in media promotion.* Mahwah, NJ: Lawrence Erlbaum Associates.

Eastman, S. T., Ferguson, D. A., & Klein, R. A (2002). *Promotion and marketing for broadcasting, cable and the Web* (3rd ed.). Boston: Focal Press.

Editorial. (1995, June 12). Editorial. Stay Tuned. *Broadcasting and Cable,* 58.

Elkin, T. (2003, April 28). Study: Gen Y is key to convergence. *Advertising Age,* 61.

Federal Communications Commission (FCC). (2003, June 9). Out with the old. How the FCC modified its media-ownership rules. *Broadcasting and Cable,* 20.

Federal Communications Commission (FCC). (2004). *Annual assessment of the status of competition in the market for the delivery of video programming* (MB Docket No. 03-172). Washington, DC: Author.

Ferguson, D. A., & Perse, E. M. (1993). Media and audience influences on channel repertoire. *Journal of Broadcasting and Electronic Media, 37,* 31–48.

Grant, A. E., & Meadows, J. H. (2002). *Communication technology update.* Boston: Focal Press.

Gronhaug, K., Hem, L., & Lines, R. (2002). Exploring the impact of product category risk and consumer knowledge in brand extensions. *Journal of Brand Management, 9,* 463–476.

Grubb, M. V., & McDowell, W. S. (2003). Media management. In M. D. Murray, & R. L. Moore (Eds.), *Mass communication education* (pp. 413–423). Ames, Iowa State Press.

Gunter, B. (2000). *Media research methods.* London: Sage.

Ha, L. (2003). Crossing offline and online media: A comparison of online advertising on TV Websites and online portals. *Journal of Interactive Advertising, 3,* 1–18.

Ha, L., & Chan-Olmsted, S. (2001). Enhanced TV as brand extension: TV viewers' perceptions of enhanced TV features and TV commerce on broadcast networks' Websites. *International Journal of Media Management, 4,* 202–212.

Hausman, A. (2000). A multi-method investigation of consumer motivations in impulse buying. *Journal of Consumer Marketing, 17,* 403–417.

Henry, P. (2001). Evaluating implications for new media and information technologies. *The Journal of Consumer Marketing, 18,* 121–131.

Higgins, J. M. (2003, September 8). Who says synergy is a bad word? *Broadcasting and Cable,* 44.

Hoeffler, S., & Keller, K. L. (2003). The marketing advantages of strong brands. *Journal of Brand Management, 10,* 421–445.

Hoynes, W. (2003). Branding pubic service. The "new PBS" and the privatization of public television. *Television and New Media, 4,* 117–130.

Ind, N. (2003). Inside out: How employees build value. *Journal of Brand Management, 10,* 393–401.

John, D. R., Loken, B., & Joiner, C. (1998). The negative impact of extensions: Can flagship products be diluted? *Journal of Marketing, 62,* 19–33.

Kapferer, J. N. (1992). *Strategic brand management. New approaches to creating and evaluating brand equity.* New York: The Free Press.

Keller, K. L. (1993). Conceptualizing, measuring and managing brand equity. *Journal of Marketing, 57,* 1–22.

Keller, K. L. (2001). Editorial: Brand research imperatives. *Journal of Brand Management, 9,* 4–6.

Keller, K. L. (2003). *Strategic brand management: Building, measuring and managing brand equity.* Upper Saddle River, NJ: Prentice-Hall.

Kerschbaumer, K. (2002, November 25). Where tech meets workflow. Controlling content requires a new way of thinking about process. *Broadcasting and Cable,* 35.

Kim, J. Y. (2003). Communication message strategies for brand extensions. *Journal of Product and Brand Management, 12,* 462–476.

Kung, L. (2000). Exploring the link between culture and strategy in media organizations: The cases of BBC and CNN. *International Journal of Media Management, 2,* 100–109.

Lane, V., & Jacobson, R. (1995). Stock market reactions to brand extension announcements: The effects of brand attitude and familiarity. *Journal of Marketing, 59,* 63–77.

Laroche, M., Kim, C., & Matsui, T. (2003). Which decision heuristics are used in consideration set formation? *Journal of Consumer Marketing, 20,* 192–209.

Leuthesser, L., Kohli, C., & Suri, R. (2003). 2 + 2 = 5? A framework for using co-branding to leverage a brand. *Journal of Brand Management, 11,* 35–47.

Liu, F., & Chan-Olmsted, S. (2002). Partnerships between the old and the new: Examining the strategic alliances between broadcast television networks and Internet firms in the context of convergence. *International Journal on Media Management, 5*, 47–56.

Lin, C. F. (2002). Segmenting customer brand preference: Demographics or psychographic. *Journal of Product and Brand Management, 11*, 249–268.

Martinez, E., & Pina, J. M. (2003). The negative impact of brand extensions on parent brand image. *Journal of Product and Brand Management, 12*, 432–448.

Mastro, D. E., & Stern, S. R. (2003). Representations of race in television commercials: A content analysis of prime time advertising. *Journal of Broadcasting and Electronic Media, 47*, 638–647.

McLuhan, M., & Fiori, Q. (1967). *The medium is the message.* New York: Bantam Books.

McDowell, W. S. (2004a). Exploring a free association methodology to capture and differentiate abstract media brand associations: A study of three cable news networks. *Journal of Media Economics, 17*, 304–320.

McDowell, W. S. (2004b). Selling the niche: A qualitative content analysis of cable network business-to-business advertising. *International Journal on Media Management, 6*, 217–225.

McDowell, W. S, & Batten, A. (1999). *Branding TV: Principles and practices.* Washington, DC: National Association of Broadcasters.

McDowell, W. S., & Dick, S. J. (2002). We're number one: Manipulating perceived market rankings to induce a placebo effect in news credibility evaluations. *Atlantic Journal of Communication, 10*, 228–241.

McDowell, W. S., & Sutherland, J. (2000). Choice vs. chance: Using brand equity theory to explain TV audience lead-in effects. *Journal of Media Economics, 13*, 233–247.

McEnally, M. R., & de Chernatony, L. (1999). The evolving nature of branding: Consumer and managerial considerations. *Journal of Consumer and Marketing Research, 99*, 1–30.

Media Groups. (2003). Special report: Top 25 media groups. *Broadcasting and Cable*, 12.

Orezanich, G. W., & Wirth, M. O. (1998). Mergers and acquisitions: A communications industry overview. In A. Alexander, J. Owens, & R. Carveth (Eds.), *Media economics. Theory and practice* (pp. 95–107). Mahwah, NJ: Lawrence Erlbaum Associates.

Porter, M. E. (1996, November–December). What is strategy? *Harvard Business Review*, 61–78.

Powers, A. (2004). The global structure of media organizations. In J. L. Wicks, G. Sylvie, C. A. Hollifield, S. Lacey, & A. B. Sohn (Eds.), *Media management. A casebook approach* (3rd ed., pp. 74–98). Mahwah, NJ: Lawrence Erlbaum Associates.

PROMAX (2004). Promotion and marketing executives Web Site at www.promax.org.

Rubin, A. M. (1994). Media uses and effects: A uses and gratifications perspective. In J. Bryant, & D. Zillmann (Eds.), *Media Effects. Advances in theory and research* (pp. 417–436). Hillsdale, NJ: Lawrence Erlbaum Associates.

Schein, E. H. (1992). *Organizational culture and leadership.* San Francisco, CA: Jossey-Bass.

Tan Tsu Wee, T., & Chua Han Ming, M. (2003). Leveraging on symbolic values and meanings in branding. *Journal of Brand Management, 10*, 208–218.

Vizjak, A., & Ringlstetter, M. (2003). *Media management: Leveraging content for profitable growth.* New York: Springer.

Warner, C., & Buchman, J. (2004). *Media selling. Broadcast, cable, print and interactive.* Ames: Iowa State Press.

Wilkie, W. L. (1996). *Consumer behavior.* New York: Wiley.

Zimmer, M. R., & Bhat, S. (2004). The reciprocal effects of extension quality and fit on parent brand attitude. *Journal of Product and Brand Management, 13*, 37–46.

Zyman, S. (1999). *The end of marketing as we know it.* New York. Harper Business.

# 12

# Issues in Media Management and Technology

Sylvia M. Chan-Olmsted
University of Florida

The 20th century was marked by the incredible impact of mass media on the lives of the American people and its powerful role in the U.S. society and economy. At the beginning of the 21st century, new media technologies like the Internet are becoming mainstream media. Likewise, a growing number of media firms are extending their global reach as well as contemplating how to best realize the potential of a new digital media environment (Doyle, 2002; Herman & McChesney, 1997). It is evident that the diffusion of communication technologies has become a critical force in shaping not only American society but also the future of its media industries.

The literature in the adoption of innovation popularized by Rogers (1995) played an important role in explaining the process and determinants of consumer adoption of new communication technologies. Whereas the bulk of the innovation adoption research concerning new media has emphasized adoptions at the individual level, Lin (2003), in her proposed interactive communication technology adoption model, suggested that *system factors*, such as market competition, influence the development of market infrastructure for technology diffusion, mold the types of technology products available in an environment, and establish social and market trends influencing technology adoption. It is a fair assessment that the adoption of a communication technology by media firms, or more specifically, the commercialization of a new media product/service, plays not only a complementary but also an antecedent role to the adoption and diffusion of that technology in a society.

There have been numerous studies examining the introduction and impact of new communication technologies on media markets. From the arrival of the printing press to radio, broadcast television, multichannel television, the Internet, and now interactive, broadband television, new media technologies have always been developed, received, and commercialized with various degrees of enthusiasm, resource commitment, and success by media firms. For example, whereas CBS, ABC, and NBC decided to utilize the high definition television (HDTV) format to broadcast most of their primetime programs, Fox chose to limit its investment and deliver its programming at a resolution level below the high definition mode (Snider, 2003). Although all media firms are well aware of the potential advantage of being the first company to introduce a new product to a market (i.e., the so-called first mover advantage), many media firms are risk averse and avoid early entry into new product markets or the early incorporation of a new communication technology into their existing systems. Those companies that do attempt to develop or adopt the new technology are not all successful in reaping benefits from their adoption. For example, NBC's failed attempt to establish an online gateway to multimedia content through the acquisition of a once-popular search engine, SNAP.com, is illustrative of the performance variability associated with such investments. The factors influencing the decisions, rates, processes, and eventual success of such adoptions by media firms are of major interest going forward.

New media technologies often have the potential to generate additional revenues or to reduce costs; they might also transform the rules of competition in existing media markets. The arrival of the Internet and digitization clearly illustrate the diversity of strategies exhibited by different media firms and the magnitude of change brought about by communication technologies. Nevertheless, the media management and economics literature has not adequately explored the subject of innovation or technology adoption in the context of firm behavior and the drivers of that behavior. This chapter articulates the issues that play a role in this process, and develops a theoretical framework of inno-vation/technology adoption that captures the unique characteristics of media products and firms. The proposed framework addresses the adoption of new media technologies through the integration of various theoretical perspectives including entrepreneurship, strategic management, and innovation adoption. *New media technologies*, in the context of this chapter, refer to a product, service, system, or process that might be used to change or enhance the consumption of a mass media product and is perceived as new by the adopting firm. Examples include videotex, Internet radio, digital television (DTV), high definition television (HDTV), interactive television (ITV), satellite radio, and digital video recorders (DVR) such as TiVo. New media technologies here exclude internal ideas or processes (e.g., technologies that merely enhance internal production efficiency) that do not impact the final output or consumption of a media service or product.

## THEORETICAL PERSPECTIVES OF THE PROPOSED ADOPTION FRAMEWORK

The decision and process of innovation adoption logically differ between a consumer and a firm. Although noneconomic factors (e.g., personality, perceptions, and attitudes) and adoption stages (e.g., persuasion and self-confirmation) play an important role in the consumer adoption process (Rogers, 1995), they are less likely to influence the adoption decision of a firm. Rather, environmental forces (e.g., regulation) that shape the range of strategic behavior a firm might adopt, and internal characteristics (e.g., resources) that determine the type and amount of utilities that a firm's strategy might derive, play a more significant role in the firm's adoption process. Thus, to investigate the drivers of new media adoption at the firm level or, specifically, the business decision to commercialize a new media product/service, this chapter begins with a review of some theoretical perspectives in entrepreneurship, innovation adoption, and strategic management that ground the development of the proposed theoretical framework.

## Schumpeterism, Innovation, and Firms

The relationship between innovation and firms is well elucidated by the notion of *creative destruction* advocated by Schumpeter almost 70 years ago. As he argued, the primary driver of growth in an economy is the process of creative destruction brought about by entrepreneurs who continuously introduce new products, new ways of production, and other innovations, which create greater buyer utility and stimulate economic activity (Schumpeter, 1936, 1950). From this perspective, the entrepreneurial behavior of a firm in commercializing innovations is crucial not only to the success of the firm but also to the economic progress in a society.

The significant role of innovation can also be illustrated by its impact on the basic structure of an industry. For example, the arrival of new technology often changes an industry's existing value chain, forcing firms to attempt to create more value using the traditional system or to learn how to create value by incorporating the new technology into the existing system (Hitt, Ireland, Camp, & Sexton, 2001). Hamel (2000) argued that innovation is the most critical component of a company's strategy. The importance of innovation is stressed by many researchers. Whereas some found that early and fast movers (i.e., firms that are first to introduce new goods or services) often obtain higher returns, others discovered a positive relationship between the ability to develop and commercialize a new product and global strategic success (Lee, Smith, Grimm, & Schomburg, 2000; Subramaniam & Venkatraman, 1999). The economic value and extent of change, brought about by the introduction of new media, are evident as can be seen from how cable television transformed the format and content of television programming and how the Internet is revolutionizing the distribution of music products.

## Strategic Entrepreneurship

As discussed earlier, the entrepreneurial behavior of a firm is an essential component of the creative destruction process. Lumpkin and Dess (1996) argued that the key dimension of entrepreneurship is a focus on innovation. In fact, because entrepreneurial behavior entails the creation of new resources or the combination of existing resources in news ways to develop and commercialize new products, move into new markets, and/or service new customers (Hitt et al., 2001), it is at the heart of new technology adoption by media firms.

It is important to note that entrepreneurship is more than the phenomenon of startups. Some have suggested that the essence of entrepreneurship is opportunity recognition and exploitation (Brown, Davidsson, & Wiklund, 2001). Thus, entrepreneurial values, attitudes, and behaviors are necessary in organizations of any size (Zahra, 1993). Researchers asserted that a company's degree of entrepreneurship is determined by the degree of compatibility between its strategic management practices and its entrepreneurial ambitions and the extent to which it innovates, takes risks, and acts proactively (Miller, 1983; Murray, 1984). Barringer and Bluedorn (1999) proposed three specific enablers of firm-level entrepreneurial behavior: opportunity recognition, organizational flexibility, and the ability to measure, encourage, and reward innovative and risk-taking behavior.

### Assessment of Entrepreneurship

Fundamentally, entrepreneurship can be examined as a firm-level behavioral phenomenon. Thus, a firm's intensity of entrepreneurship falls along a conceptual continuum ranging from highly entrepreneurial to highly conservative (Barringer & Bluedorn, 1999). Brown et al. (2001) summarized a series of conceptual dimensions that might be used to assess the different approaches associated with management of entrepreneurial conduct. The first dimension is *strategic orientation*. On the one hand, a more entrepreneurial firm bases its behavior on the perceived opportunities that exist in a market not on the resources that might be required to exploit them. On the other hand, a less entrepreneurial firm focuses on available resources and opportunities that allow it to utilize its resources efficiently. The second dimension is *commitment to opportunity*. Here, a more entrepreneurial firm is action-oriented and pursues opportunities quickly to examine their value, whereas a less entrepreneurial firm is analysis-oriented taking a more risk-averse approach that requires slower, multiple levels of long-term commitments.

The third and fourth conceptual dimensions are the *commitment and control of resources*. In this case, a more entrepreneurial firm prefers incremental, minimal commitment of resources, to allow for flexibility in changing directions, and it is more interested in using and exploiting resources than in owning them. Conversely, a less entrepreneurial firm favors a thorough advance analysis with a complete commitment of less reversible investments and ownership control of resources. The fifth and six dimensions are about *management structure and reward philosophy*. A more entrepreneurial firm has a flatter organizational structure and is made up of multiple informal networks to encourage flexibility and opportunity exploitation. As a result, an entrepreneurial firm develops a reward system based on value creation in the form of ideas, experimentation, and creativity. A less entrepreneurial firm is likely to have a more hierarchical management structure with clearly defined lines of authority and with compensation related to seniority and the level of resources under an employee's control. The seventh dimension is *growth orientation*. A more entrepreneurial firm aims for rapid growth and accepts the risks associated with the growth opportunity, whereas a less entrepreneurial firm opts for a slow, safe, and steady growth. The last dimension is *entrepreneurial culture*. A more entrepreneurial firm promotes ideas, experimentation, and creativity to identify a broad range of opportunities, whereas a less entrepreneurial firm confines its flow of ideas to the resources it controls, and it penalizes failure more substantially than does its entrepreneurial counterpart.

### *Entrepreneurship, Firm Sizes, and Uncertain Environment*

Entrepreneurial attitudes and conduct are important for firms of all sizes to survive and prosper in competitive environments (Barringer & Bluedorn, 1999). A historical examination of some major media corporations reveals that media industries are often shaped by entrepreneurs who took the risks required to introduce a media product in response to opportunities introduced by environmental changes.

Scholars also suggested that strategic entrepreneurship materializes differently in established firms versus smaller firms or new ventures (Ireland, Hitt, & Sirmon, 2003). Whereas the former are more skilled in developing sustainable competitive advantages, they are often less effective in identifying new market opportunities. On the other hand, smaller firms or new ventures might excel in recognizing and exploiting new opportunities, but they are often less capable of sustaining competitive advantages.

In addition to the size factor, researchers found that firms in turbulent, uncertain environments tend to be more innovative, risk taking, and proactive (Naman & Slevin, 1993). Increasing intensity of competition, as measured by the general progression of time, also has a positive effect on the level of firm innovativeness (Kotabe & Swan, 1995). It seems that the external context plays an important role in affecting approaches to and intensity of entrepreneurial activities. The notion of uncertainty and its impacts on innovation adoption at the firm level, are especially relevant in today's media environment, which continues to be infused by the growth of digital communication technologies and a revolutionary new medium, the Internet. In fact, new digital and online technologies have altered the way many media firms conduct business, extended the range of opportunities available, and raised the complexity of commercializing new media products. Overall, this has added to the degree of uncertainly in media markets. The notion of uncertainty (and its accompanying risk factor) is an especially important consideration for certain types of media firms that offer less stable content product based on their reliance on varying audience tastes and expectations. For example, book publishers, recording firms, and motion picture producers offer individual content products that carry greater risks than newspapers or broadcasters, which typically have more stable consumer consumption patterns and revenue sources (Picard, 2002).

## Strategic Networks

Strategic networks may be defined as the "stable inter-organizational relationships that are strategically important to participating firms." These ties may take the form of joint ventures, alliances, and even long-term buyer–supplier partnerships (Amit & Zott, 2001, p. 498). In essence, firms might seek out such interorganizational partnerships to gain access to information, markets, and technologies, and to cultivate the potential to share risk, generate scale and scope economies, share knowledge, and facilitate learning (Gulati, Nohria, & Zaheer, 2000). Strategic networks' research often addresses questions related to such issues as the drivers and process of strategic network formation, the type of interfirm relationships that help participating firms compete, the sources of value creation in these networks, and the linkage between performance and participating firms' differential network positions and relationships (Amit & Zott, 2001); all are important variables that might affect a firm's entrepreneurial behavior, including its process of innovation adoption.

Media industries are one of the leading sectors for seeking out network relationships with other firms, both horizontally and vertically. This network orientation might be attributed to: media content's *public goods* characteristic, the need to be responsive to an audience's preferences and technological changes, the desire to spread risk among different holdings (Picard, 2002), and the symbiotic connection between media distribution and content. Strategic networks' theory plays an important supporting role to the success of entrepreneurial behavior because alliances and joint ventures, two major strategic network forms, have been a staple strategy in the media sector (Compaine & Gomery, 2000; Woodhull & Snyder, 1997). Additionally, proactiveness toward partnership formation often results in access relationships to resources and capabilities that contribute to the exploitation of opportunities (Sarkar, Echambadi, & Harrison, 2001). For example, studies found that broadcasting firms often prefer forming strategic partnerships with Internet firms to explore online opportunities rather than initiating a Greenfield-style investment (i.e., wholly owned new ventures; Chan-Olmsted & Jung, 2001; Liu & Chan-Olmsted, 2003). In essence, newer, smaller media firms might have attractive core competencies such as the ownership of valuable content/talents or innovative services, but they lack the size, access, distribution, or expertise to benefit from these unique resources and capabilities. Strategic networks not only offer an opportunity for access to a greater combination of competencies, but also reduce barriers to entry (e.g., scale economies and brand loyalty) in newer, technology-driven media markets such as the Internet and broadband sectors.

Finally, a focus on complementarities and cross-industry product development seem to be positively related to innovativeness in the context of strategic networks. For example, in forming strategic partnerships, firms that emphasized exploiting complementary assets outperformed those that concentrated on exploring the new technology. Scholars also concluded that cross-industry product offerings and cross-industry cooperation are good indicators of higher product innovativeness (Kotabe & Swan, 1995).

## Adoption of Innovation/Technology

Most research on the adoption or diffusion of communication technologies examined individual-level determinants, especially consumers' personality traits and perceptions of new media (Eastlick, 1993; Jeffres & Atkin, 1996; Lin, 1998, 2001). A meta-analysis of 42 studies concerning the adoption of communication technologies found that consumer perceptions about the relative advantages, motivations, and expectations about a new communication technology often affect the adoption of that innovation. Additionally, media usage, media repertoires, and demographics such as income, education, family size, and age were related to the adoption decisions of many new media technologies (Kang, 2003). More systematically, Lin proposed that antecedent technology factors such as innovation attributes, audience factors such as innovativeness, social factors such as opinion leadership, and system factors such as market competition are all part of a theoretical framework that explains a consumer's adoption decision, with outcomes ranging from adoption, likely adoption, nonadoption, discontinuance, to reinvention (Lin, 2003). Some of these determinants, in a modified form that reflects an institutional decision-making process, might play a role in the adoption of innovation at the firm level.

Some studies have empirically investigated the predictors of firm-level adoption of technological advances (Dong & Saha, 1998; Goel & Rich, 1997; Hannan & McDowell, 1984; Levin, Levin, & Meisel, 1987; Romeo, 1975). Goel and Rich found that degree of market competition, complementarities with current product characteristics, magnitude of expected substitution gains relative to existing technology, and prior adoptions are important determinants of technology adoption. Amit and Zott (2001), in their study about the sources of value in an e-business environment, suggested that the adoption of an online venture might create value through four interrelated factors: novelty, lock-in, complementarities, and efficiency. In a sense, these four elements might also serve as the drivers of different adoption strategies, at least in the case of Internet-related technologies.

## The Uniqueness of Media Products

Research in strategic management has concluded that strategic decisions are often re-source dependent and rely on the specificity within a particular industry (Chatterjee & Wernerfelt, 1991). To this end, media products exhibit certain unique characteristics that shape the approaches and intensity of innovation adoption by media firms. The major distinction between media and nonmedia products rests in the unique combination of seven characteristics.

First, media firms offer dual, complementary media products of *content* and *distribution*. The content component is intangible and inseparable from a tangible distribution medium. Such a symbiotic relationship increases the complexity and risks of an adoption decision. For example, the value of terrestrial television stations converting to DTV is largely determined by their local cable system's DTV capacity and strategy. In addition, the benefit associated with the allocation of DTV spectrum capable of delivering HDTV signals cannot be realized without the availability of HDTV programming. The software–hardware dependency present here also tends to lead to adoption via strategic networks.

In an analysis of innovation adoption by media firms, it is essential to examine the two types of products separately because a new media technology is likely to have an impact on a content producer differently from a distribution system. To this end, one might utilize the concept of value chains to assess the role of an innovation for media firms. For example, a media producer's value chain includes acquiring and creating content; selecting, organizing, packaging, and processing content; and producing, manufacturing, and transforming content into distributable form. A distribution value chain also includes marketing, advertising, promoting, and distributing the media service (Picard, 2002). One way to evaluate the potential of an adoption by a media firm is to examine the core value the firm brings to its value chain and the role of a new technology in that process.

Second, most media content products are nonexcludable and nondepletable public goods whose consumption by one individual does not interfere with its availability to another but adds to the scale economies in production (Albarran, 2002; Picard, 1989).

This characteristic might present a problem for smaller firms that lack the infrastructure to take advantage of such a cost benefit. In a sense, these firms are more likely to adopt or commercialize a product/service that requires fewer resources and appeals to more defined consumer segments. As a result, strategic partnerships might represent a viable option in a firm's adoption process.

Third, many media firms rely on dual revenue sources from consumers and advertisers (Picard, 1989). The need to identify a hybrid business model that generates sufficient revenues from both sources and capitalizes on the unique characteristics of a new media technology presents a tremendous challenge. This is because the lack of initial profitability might lead to expenditure reduction in improving the product, which is likely to lead to less desirable audiences and eventually lower revenue/profits (Picard, 2002). For example, most broadcast television stations have yet to profit from the integration of their online and on-air products, and many television networks have scaled back their online ventures.

Fourth, many media content products are marketed through a windowing process in which content, such as a theatrical film, is delivered to consumers via multiple outlets sequentially in different time periods (e.g., theatrical release, home video, DBS, pay-per-view, premium pay cable networks, and broadcast television networks) (Owen & Wildman, 1992). In a sense, the total potential revenue for such a content product depends on the total number of windows and pricing at these distribution points. This adds to the strategic complexity of commercializing a new media product. In this context, the adoption of a new media technology often has a significant impact on the value chain of an existing windowing system.

Fifth, media products are subject to changing audience and cultural preferences and the existing communication infrastructure of each geographic market. They are also often subject to more regulatory control because of the media's pervasive impact on society. The volatility of these environmental factors raises the risks associated with innovation adoption by media firms. The variability of audience tastes and preferences creates even more uncertainty for firms offering high price elasticity products that are not subscription-based.

Sixth, unlike many consumer goods that have a clear product category (making it easier to identify market and competitive concerns), media products are consumed in a repertoire fashion. In other words, media consumers rarely use only one medium or one media outlet. Instead, they are likely to develop a repertoire of media and media outlets that they regularly consume. As a result, media firms often provide products that complement as well as compete with their competitors' offerings. This makes the assessment of the potential utility of a new media technology more difficult.

Finally, the type of media industries in which a firm operates is likely to have an impact on the adoption of new media technology. Picard (2002) noted that a variety of characteristics influence the business models, operations, and environments in which media industries function. These characteristics compel and constrain firm actions and affect market opportunities as well as further development (e.g., new media technology adoption). Accordingly, different media industries' tendencies toward innovation adoption can be evaluated relatively based on these characteristics. Specifically, an individual media sector's propensity to innovate can be assessed through examination of its external, that

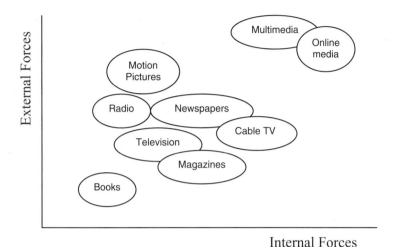

FIG. 12.1. The impact of external and internal forces on the adoption tendency of different media sectors.

is, market-based characteristics and its internal, that is, financial, cost, and operational attributes (see Fig. 12.1) (Picard, 2002).

To this end, online media and multimedia firms are likely to be more proactive when it comes to innovation adoption because their markets (i.e., external factors) are younger, have lower entry barriers, have high levels of direct competition and elasticity of demand, and have less stable/proven audience preferences. In addition, these firms might be more aggressive in innovation adoption because their businesses (i.e., internal forces) need to exploit new products to add value to existing offerings and to increase marketing appeals. By comparison, motion picture firms are under less internal pressure to be innovative. However, faced with a global market and growing secondary markets such as video-on-demand (i.e., external forces), these firms may need to focus on the adoption of distribution-related innovations. Radio firms, similar to their film counterparts, encounter strong, external market pressure (e.g., high levels of competition and elasticity of advertising demand) but less financial or operational (internal) reasons to innovate. Broadcast television firms have slightly lower innovation needs (as compared with motion picture and radio firms) from market drivers because their entry barriers are relatively high and competition is moderate. However, the moderate-to-high cost of operation (internal) might compel television firms to adopt new technologies to increase their audience base and/or to lower their per unit content costs. Internal factors are even more critical innovation drivers for cable television systems because they typically have very high capital requirements. Newspaper firms are motivated to innovate because they are faced with immediate threats from new technologies, a mature market with limited growth potential, and high capital requirements on all fronts. Book publishing firms are generally less inclined to adopt new innovations because they encounter lower threats from new technologies than do newspapers and magazines. Finally, because of their high distribution cost structures, it is likely that all print media firms will seek new technologies capable of reducing distribution costs.

# A PROPOSED FRAMEWORK OF NEW MEDIA ADOPTION
# BY MEDIA FIRMS

The constructs and theories reviewed thus far point to a number of antecedent variables that, individually and collectively, shape the outcome of a media firm's adoption decision. Specifically, it is proposed that eight sets of factors affect the adoption of new media technology by a media firm. They include: firm and media technology characteristics, strategic networks, perceived strategic value, available alternatives, market conditions, competition, and regulation/policy (see Fig. 12.2). Each of these factors is discussed in the following.

## Firm Characteristics

Just like many audience personality traits that play a role in consumers' adoption of new communication technologies (Lin, 2003), the collective qualities of an organization might also affect its new media technology adoption strategies.

Similar to personality trait factors that influence individual predispositions toward innovativeness, novelty, venturesomeness, and risk, it is proposed that two sets of media firm characteristics—organizational strategic traits (which describe a firm's strategic tendency toward a new media product/market), and degree of entrepreneurship (which depicts a firm's attitude toward opportunities and risks)—play a role in the adoption process.

### Organizational Strategic Traits

Classification of firms based on their strategic predisposition offers a useful conceptual framework to assess a firm's organizational traits in a strategic context. To this end, the strategy typologies proposed by Miles and Snow (1978) and Porter (1980) are the frameworks most often used by strategic management researchers to analyze a firm's organizational traits (Slater & Olson, 2000). Whereas Porter proposed that most business strategies fall under one of three strategic types—*focus, differentiation*, and *low cost leadership*, Miles and Snow developed a framework for defining firms' approaches to product market development, structures, and processes by theorizing that firms with different organizational traits have differential strategic preferences.

Specifically, the Miles and Snow taxonomy classifies firms into four groups:

1. Prospectors that continuously seek and exploit new products and market opportunities and are often the first-to-market with a new product/service.

2. Defenders that focus on occupying a market segment to develop a stable set of products and customers.

3. Analyzers that have an intermediate position between prospectors and defenders by cautiously observing and following the prospectors, while at the same time, monitoring and protecting a stable set of products and customers.

4. Reactors that do not have a consistent product-market orientation but act or respond to competition with a more short-term focus. (Zahra & Pearce, 1990)

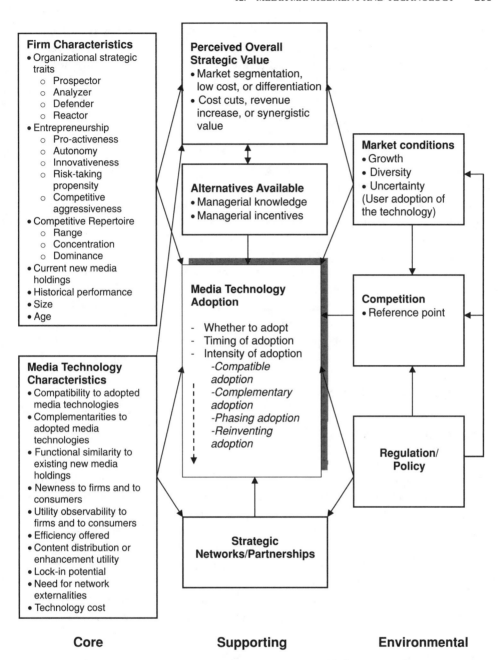

**Firm Characteristics**
- Organizational strategic traits
  - Prospector
  - Analyzer
  - Defender
  - Reactor
- Entrepreneurship
  - Pro-activeness
  - Autonomy
  - Innovativeness
  - Risk-taking propensity
  - Competitive aggressiveness
- Competitive Repertoire
  - Range
  - Concentration
  - Dominance
- Current new media holdings
- Historical performance
- Size
- Age

**Media Technology Characteristics**
- Compatibility to adopted media technologies
- Complementarities to adopted media technologies
- Functional similarity to existing new media holdings
- Newness to firms and to consumers
- Utility observability to firms and to consumers
- Efficiency offered
- Content distribution or enhancement utility
- Lock-in potential
- Need for network externalities
- Technology cost

**Perceived Overall Strategic Value**
- Market segmentation, low cost, or differentiation
- Cost cuts, revenue increase, or synergistic value

**Alternatives Available**
- Managerial knowledge
- Managerial incentives

**Media Technology Adoption**
- Whether to adopt
- Timing of adoption
- Intensity of adoption
  - *Compatible adoption*
  - *Complementary adoption*
  - *Phasing adoption*
  - *Reinventing adoption*

**Strategic Networks/Partnerships**

**Market conditions**
- Growth
- Diversity
- Uncertainty (User adoption of the technology)

**Competition**
- Reference point

**Regulation/ Policy**

**Core**           **Supporting**           **Environmental**

FIG. 12.2.   Toward a theory of media firm innovation development and adoption.

Despite differences in strategic aggressiveness, empirical studies have concluded that, except for the reactors, the other three groups of firms achieve equal performance on average (Zahra & Pearce, 1990). The implication is that the implementation of the strategy is most critical to the performance variation within each strategy type.

Such an organizational strategic taxonomy can be applied effectively to the media industries to assess how firms with different strategic predispositions approach new media technologies. The taxonomy approach also provides a useful framework for analyzing the adoption of new media technologies that affect multiple traditional media sectors in an increasingly converging media world or media conglomerates that have holdings in multiple media markets.

### Degree of Entrepreneurship

Another firm predisposition, degree of entrepreneurship, is likely to affect how a media firm approaches a new technology. Entrepreneurial characteristics, according to previous literature about this subject, might include a firm's proactiveness, autonomy, innovativeness, risk-taking propensity, and competitive aggressiveness. When considering these qualities in the context of media products / services, it is also important to determine whether adopting media firms have a core content or distribution product. On the one hand, entrepreneurship, from the perspective of a content firm, is largely defined by the quality of innovativeness or creativity. On the other hand, risk-taking propensity might be a better measurement of the entrepreneurial spirit of a distribution firm because new media technology adoption often takes the form of investments that require larger scale and scope and greater coordination.

A media firm's past competitive and new media technology behavior, as well as its resulting performance, logically influences its future decisions regarding new media technology adoption. Accordingly, the next set of firm characteristics focus on a media firm's current new media and competitive profiles.

### Competitive Repertoires

Competitive repertoires are a set of concrete market decisions adopted by a firm to attract, serve, and maintain customers in a given year (Miller & Chen, 1996). Competitive repertoires can be assessed across three dimensions: range, which refers to the number of types of market actions taken by a firm; concentration, which indicates the degree to which repertoires tend to be focused on a few main types of actions; and dominance, which is the extent to which a firm depends on its single most common type of market action (Miller & Chen, 1996). In the context of media products, the repertoires are greatly influenced by the type of media markets in which a firm operates. Many media firms operate in an oligopolistic market. This limits the range of their competitive repertoire. Media repertoires of the audience also affect the competitive repertoires of media firms.

### Current New Media Holdings and Historical Performance

Similar to the concept of new media ownership as a predictor of a consumer's adoption of new communication technologies, a firm's current new media holdings might also serve as an indicator of its predisposition to adopt additional new media technology because the firm might acquire experience that helps its future adoption decision-making process. As for the factor of historical performance, past output records are indicative of the resources a firm has available for commercializing a new media technology. They also point to possible directions or areas that a firm needs to enhance.

The last two firm characteristics, size and age, present the fundamental attributes of a firm in terms of its available resources and experience.

### Firm Size

In the world of innovation adoption, *size* is sometimes a liability. Christensen and Bower (1996) suggested that some firms are too successful to allocate resources to new technologies that initially cannot find application in mainstream markets. These types of firms are more likely to focus on providing products or services demanded by current customers in existing markets. In other words, when an innovation addresses the needs of only a small group of customers, it rarely warrants the appropriation of resources because it lacks the requisite impetus for resource allocation. The newer the product, the more likely the innovation will be brought to market by new entrants with an *attacker's advantage* over incumbent firms (Christensen & Bower, 1996). For example, Internet dial-up service was popularized by what was then a new firm, America Online, rather than by established computing or media incumbents.

Christensen and Bower (1996) further suggested that disruptive technologies tend to be initially saleable in markets with distinct economic and financial characteristics. This may be unattractive to certain established firms because adopting the technology would require a change in strategy to enter a very different market. For example, even though a top multiple system operator (MSO) such as Time Warner Cable might have the technological competency needed to commercialize interactive television services, it may be unable to do so because of the lack of impetus from customers in some of its systems. The essence here is a firm's inability to change strategy, not to adopt technology. Nevertheless, size does have its advantages as larger firms have a line of products that they can extend through continuous improvement. They also have more resources, marketing channels, and scale economies to commercialize new technologies.

### Firm Age

Just like size, the length of a firm's existence in a market can be both positive and negative. Although age is often positively related to acquired experience and resources, it might also spell inflexibility in opportunity identification and strategic adjustment, as well as a tendency toward risk aversion. In the context of media products, more experienced firms, especially those with branded content and established customer relationship and loyalty (e.g., Time Warner and its brands of CNN and *Time* magazine), might be in a better position to assess the needs of their customers and to exploit the market potential of a new media technology, either alone or via a strategic network.

## Media Technology Characteristics

Besides firm characteristics, the nature of a new media technology is likely to play an instrumental role in determining a media firm's adoption choice. Similar to the technology factors in the case of audience adoption, which basically indicate an adopter's perceptions and expectations about a new technology such as its relative advantage, complexity, and compatibility (Lin, 2003), the author proposes that the following characteristics influence the technology adoption decision of a media firm: the technology's compatibility, complementarities, and functional similarity to current media products that the firm offers; newness; utility observability; efficiency; content distribution or enhancement utility; lock-in potential; the need for network externalities; and technology cost.

### Compatibility, Complementarities, and Functional Similarity

The value of a new media technology can be first assessed by the degree of disruptiveness of its integration into the existing organization. A good gauge here would be the degree of its compatibility to currently adopted media technologies. Taking a step further, complementarities refer to situations where a bundle of goods together provides more value than consuming the goods separately (Brandenburger & Nalebuff, 1996). In other words, the degree of complementarity provides insight into how a new technology might add value to an organization. For example, a new media technology might be horizontally complementary by adding more media content choices or vertically complementary by improving content and distribution seamlessness. The last concept, functional similarity (i.e., how a new technology is perceived by consumers as being able to satisfy needs similar to those currently being fulfilled by an existing technology), indicates the new product's degree of substitutability as perceived by consumers. Logically, a media firm's assessment of this substitutability will affect its adoption decision. It is essential for media firms to consider these three factors because of the aforementioned concept of media repertoire, which complicates the boundaries between substitution, supplement, and complement.

### Newness

An innovation can also be examined by analyzing its degree of newness to the firm, newness to the market, or a combination thereof (Kotabe & Swan, 1995). Logically, the newer the technology, the greater the uncertainty and the more hesitant a firm will be to invest in the technology. Booz, Allen, & Hamilton (1982) suggested six levels of product innovativeness:

1. Cost reduction—new products that offer similar performance at lower cost (which is not applicable in the context of this study).
2. Repositionings—new products targeted at new markets or new market segments (which are not considered true innovations in the context of this study).
3. Improvements in existing products—new products that provide improved performance or greater perceived value such as digital cable.
4. Additions to existing product lines—new products that supplement a firm's established product lines such as a broadcaster's streaming news online.
5. New product lines—new products that allow a firm to enter an established market for the first time such as the adoption of satellite radio by Sirius.
6. New-to-the-world products—new products that create an entirely new market such as the introduction of dial-up Internet services.

An innovation can also be classified by its impact on established consumer consumption patterns (Robertson, 1967). In this case, a *continuous innovation* is one with characteristics that create little disruption in consumers' consumption patterns. A *dynamically continuous innovation* does not change the consumption pattern but creates some disruption. A *discontinuous innovation* is a new product that requires a consumer to establish new consumption patterns (Robertson, 1967). In the context of media products, Krugman (1985) suggested that, using over-the-air television as a technology base, basic cable might be regarded as a continuous innovation, pay cable as a dynamically continuous innovation, and interactive services, such as online shopping and video-on-demand, as discontinuous innovations.

### Utility Observability and Efficiency

Similar to the concept of *observability* proposed by Rogers (1995), a media firm's adoption decision is likely to be affected by the apparent utility displayed by the technology. For example, the utility of migrating to digital television might not be as observable or concrete to a broadcaster as compared to the utility of adopting a new technology that leads to new sales revenues. The efficiency offered by a new media technology might also drive an adoption decision. In the context of media products, increased economic efficiency might be attained through better content delivery systems (e.g., broadband distribution) or through scale economies achieved from demand aggregation or packaging (e.g., digital cable tiers).

### Content Distribution or Enhancement Utility

Many have claimed that *content* plays a significant role in a media market (Owen & Wildman, 1992). It is likely that a new media technology, which in some way improves the delivery of a content product (e.g., broadband distribution) or enhances the appeal of a content product (e.g., high definition TV), will increase its adoption probability. As discussed previously, the desire to distribute a content product more efficiently is a major driver for many media firms to consider the adoption of new media technologies.

### Lock-in and Need for Network Externalities

Lock-in refers to the ability of a service to create strong incentives for repeat transactions, thus preventing the migration of customers to competitors (Amit & Zott, 2001). For example, a new media technology that requires more upfront equipment investment by a consumer is likely to achieve a higher probability of lock-in (e.g., satellite TV as opposed to cable TV subscription when Direct Broadcast Satellite (DBS) subscribers were required to purchase all of their reception equipment). A technology that increases the lock-in potential of a media service is typically regarded as more valuable. Network externalities are defined as a change in the benefit or consumer surplus that consumers derive from a product when more consumers purchase the product (e.g., fax machines). Though network externalities tend to be more important for telephony services, they are becoming a more significant factor for cable entrepreneurs as more interactive media services are being introduced and as cable firms venture into the telecommunications sector.

### Technology Cost

Adopting a new media technology might bring in new revenues by attracting a new audience segment or improving the loyalty of existing media consumers; however, it is not costless. The technology cost factor certainly affects a media firm's desire to adopt a new technology. In fact, because of the uncertainty of returns for a new technology, even firms with sufficient resources might choose not to adopt a particular innovation if it is too costly.

## Strategic Networks

Strategic networks are important because they can provide a firm with access to information, resources, markets, technologies, credibility, and legitimacy (Cooper, 2001; Gulati, et al., 2000). This is especially important for new media firms that possess new technologies and seek to commercialize them. For established media corporations, the benefit might be access to technologies and learning/sharing of information. Alliances or strategic networks are especially important for smaller innovative firms because such partnerships offer access to financial/marketing resources and scale/scope economies. Because technical resources are often less available than financial and marketing resources, alliances may give innovative, small firms bargaining power (Sarkar et al., 2001). This might explain the frequent formations of strategic alliances between established media firms such as NBC, CNN, and Disney with small Internet-based start-ups (Chan-Olmsted & Jung, 2001; Liu & Chan-Olmsted, 2003).

## Perceived Strategic Value

The value of a new media technology can be assessed by examining its perceived contribution to a firm's overall strategic posture. Porter (1980) suggested that there are three major strategic approaches: market segmentation, low cost, and differentiation. Depending on a media firm's strategic goal at the time of adoption, certain technologies might provide more utility in accomplishing that objective than others. For instance, the value of a new media technology might be evaluated by analyzing how it helps a media firm reduce costs, increase revenue, and/or create synergistic advantage.

## Managerial Knowledge of and Incentives to Seek Alternatives

Though we typically assume a rational managerial decision-making process, the agency theory clearly points to the important role a manager plays in determining a firm's strategic directions (Frankforter, Berman, & Jones, 2000). In essence, innovation adoption might be influenced by a manager's knowledge of alternatives from his or her previous experience or through observation of his or her competitors. It could also be influenced by the incentives a manager has to search for and try out new alternatives because of poor performance or other threats and uncertainties. Internally, past performance, breadth of managerial experience, and firm age / size are expected to influence managerial incentives and knowledge. Externally, market diversity, growth, and uncertainty are likely to influence the incentives and knowledge associated with various innovation alternatives (Miller & Chen, 1996). This factor might be an even more critical driver for innovation adoption, in the context of media industries, because many media practitioners are people with diverse backgrounds and creative, strong personalities (Redmond & Trager, 1998).

## Market Conditions, Competition, and Regulation/Policy

Besides the core firm and product factors and supporting strategic drivers, environmental variables such as market growth, diversity, and uncertainty make up the condition of the market and affect a firm's needs to adopt a new media technology. The degree of user adoption critically shapes the overall condition of that market. In the case of competition, Goel and Rich (1997) investigated the incentives for private firms to adopt new technologies. They found that companies facing increased product market competition have a higher propensity to adopt technological innovations. In general, the research literature suggests that a positive relationship exists between innovativeness and both market turbulence/uncertainty and competition.

### Competition Reference Point

Borrowing from the prospect theory in which individuals use reference points in evaluating options, Fiegenbaum and Thomas (1988) proposed a reference point theory to explain firm behavior. They noted that a firm behaves as a risk taker when it perceives itself to be below its selected reference point and vice versa. Thus, a firm's performance will be influenced by management's choice of reference points (Fiegenbaum, Hart, & Schendel, 1996). The reference point concept can be expected to play a significant role in a firm's decision regarding how to approach a new media technology. For example, many local television stations decided to jump on the Internet bandwagon before formulating an online strategy simply because their competitors had established a presence online (Chan-Olmsted & Ha, 2003).

## New Media Technology Adoption

The first level of an adoption decision is whether to adopt a new media technology. Nevertheless, researchers argued that the innovation adoption rate cannot be fully explained by examining the relationship between the decision to adopt and a series of internal factors. Additional factors that must be analyzed include the timing and intensity of adoption. Thus, innovation adoption should not be analyzed simply as a dichotomous decision (Dong & Saha, 1998).

### Timing of Adoption

Timing of an adoption is often a strategic game of waiting for more information. In fact, the value of the wait might be proportional to the fixed adoption costs, potential reversal expenses, and the likelihood that the new technology will be unprofitable (Dong

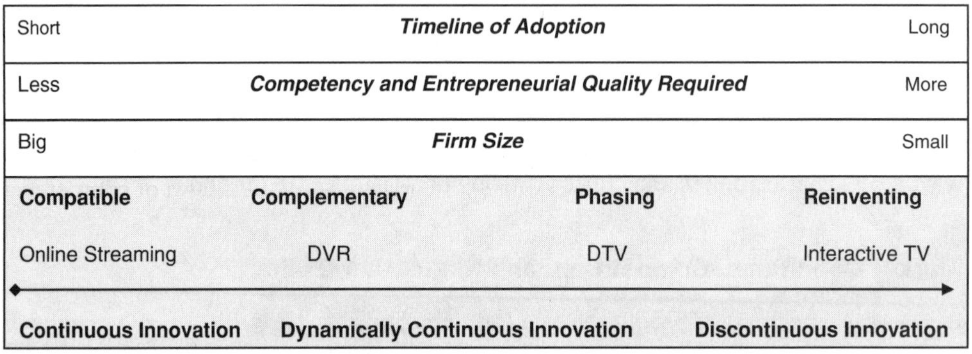

| Short | Timeline of Adoption | | | Long |
|---|---|---|---|---|
| Less | Competency and Entrepreneurial Quality Required | | | More |
| Big | Firm Size | | | Small |
| **Compatible** | **Complementary** | **Phasing** | | **Reinventing** |
| Online Streaming | DVR | DTV | | Interactive TV |
| **Continuous Innovation** | **Dynamically Continuous Innovation** | | **Discontinuous Innovation** | |

FIG. 12.3.   Spectrum of new media innovation adoption.

& Saha, 1998). For example, not all broadcasters embraced high definition television programming and not all cable systems invested the capital required to offer interactive television (ITV) functions via their broadband services. Of course, this does not mean these broadcasters and cablecasters will never offer HDTV and ITV services.

### Intensity of Adoption

The choice of timing is further complicated by the choice of adoption intensity. Lin (2003) suggested the outcome of technology adoption at the audience level could entail a decision of nonadoption, discontinuance, likely adoption, adoption, and reinvention. Whereas discontinuance refers to the phasing out of an adoption and consideration of a replacement, reinvention is defined as new uses of a technology made available through some form of purposeful modification. In the context of this chapter, subscribing to a similar spectrum of adoption intensity, it is proposed that the adoption of new media technology at the firm level ranges from compatible, complementary, phasing, and finally reinventing adoption. A firm might go through all four of these phases progressively in its adoption of a new media technology or it might decide to adopt the technology using one or more of these approaches.

Incorporating the factors of adoption timeline, types of innovation, competency, and entrepreneurial quality required, Fig. 12.3 illustrates a proposed spectrum of new media innovation adoption. As depicted, a compatible adoption would likely require the least amount of firm competency (i.e., resources and capability) and entrepreneurial quality, and take less time to adopt because the focus would be on making the new media technology fit into the existing product and operating systems. An example of a compatible adoption would be when a radio station simply streams its local content online. A complementary adoption, although still emphasizing the existing product, moves a step forward in attempting to capture the new technology's benefits in the context of the existing product and audience base. Comparatively, this adoption decision requires more competency, entrepreneurial quality, and time than a compatible adoption. For example, a cable system's incorporation of DVR technology, as a means of enhancing its cable service, would be an example of a complementary adoption. A phasing adoption occurs when a firm decides to invest and commercialize a new media technology over time, but cautiously phases out an existing platform. An example of this type of adoption is the gradual introduction of DVDs to replace VHS tapes for home video distribution by movie studios. Such an adoption decision takes even more competency, entrepreneurial quality, and time. Finally, reinvention adoption refers to modifying and/or using a technology for new purposes for which it was not originally designed. An example of reinvention adoption would be the many interactive television functions that might be introduced via broadband systems. This type of adoption requires the greatest level of competency, entrepreneurial quality, and time.

On the one hand, it is more likely for a firm to approach a continuous innovation with a compatible or complementary adoption strategy such as the carriage of over-the-air broadcast signals in the early days of basic cable adoption. On the other hand, discontinuous innovations are more likely to be adopted with a phasing or reinventing approach. Dynamically continuous innovations might move between complementary and phasing adoption depending on a firm's competency, entrepreneurial quality, and market conditions. Finally, because they serve a large existing customer base and because they are less able to make quick strategic changes, bigger firms are more likely to choose compatible or complementary adoptions over the other more drastic adoption approaches.

## Taxonomic and Relational Propositions

Now that the components of the proposed model have been introduced, this section elaborates on some taxonomical and relational propositions based on these components. Similar to Rogers' proposed diffusion of innovations curve that classifies adopters of innovations into the categories of innovators, early adopters, early majority, late majority, and laggards (Rogers, 1995), this chapter incorporates the concept of entrepreneurship, organizational strategic traits, and innovation adoption to suggest a taxonomy of new media adopters along an adoption timeline (see Fig. 12.4). Specifically, new media firm adopters may be categorized as follows. *Innovative prospectors* are innovative, proactive, smaller firms that continuously experiment with new products and market

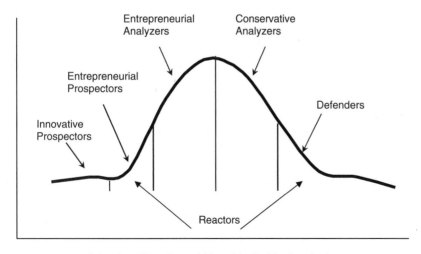

Adoption Timeline of New Media Technologies

FIG. 12.4.   Time of adoption and types of adopters.

opportunities, regardless of currently available resources. *Entrepreneurial prospectors* are aggressive, growth-seeking, risk takers that attempt to exploit new products, perhaps incrementally with a goal to be one of the early firms in successfully commercializing a new product. *Entrepreneurial analyzers* cautiously match the new technology with their available resources but are eager to pursue new business opportunities. *Conservative analyzers* often opt for a wait-and-see approach and prefer a slower, more complete adoption. *Defenders* prefer to adopt the technology when it has become a proven, stable product. *Reactors* focus on short-term outcomes and might opt to take advantage of the early commercialization opportunities with the entrepreneurial prospectors or wait and join the defenders when the dust settles.

The type of adopter a media firm might be and the kind of adoption timing and intensity a media firm might choose are influenced by a collection of factors. As proposed earlier, firm and media technology characteristics are essential, core antecedents to the adoption decision, whereas market conditions, competition, and regulatory issues are external forces that also shape a media firm's adoption options. The ability to form alliances and partnerships, the managerial incentives and knowledge of alternatives, and the perceived strategic value of the technology to a firm's overall strategic posture are all supporting factors that might enhance or diminish the value of an adoption (see Fig. 12.2). With this background, some propositions regarding the adoption decision and many internal factors that firms can control are now discussed.

First, media firms that are more entrepreneurial (e.g., the prospectors) are more likely to adopt earlier and more intensely. Considering the factor of competitive repertoire, media firms that rely on dual revenues from both the audience and advertisers (e.g., basic cable as opposed to pay cable services) might be more cautious in adopting new technologies because of the complexity associated with appealing to both audiences and advertisers. It is expected that current media holdings will play a significant role in a media firm's adoption decision, especially in the case of a new distribution technology, considering the importance of access to multiple distribution technologies according to the windowing principle. Although smaller and younger media firms are more likely to be more aggressive in adopting new media technologies, the author believes that the advantage of size and age might materialize more for firms in media-related sectors. This is because distribution firms need the size for resources to implement new technologies and a more experienced content firm might be able to exploit new media technology in a fashion more responsive to audiences. It is also proposed that a more entrepreneurial media firm will prefer a complementary and later a phasing adoption because of the media repertoire concept, which stresses the importance of competing while complementing. In general, smaller media firms are expected to be more likely to use phasing and reinventing adoption, whereas bigger firms are expected to be more likely to opt for compatible and complementary adoptions because of the importance of serving their current, established constituents.

As for media technology characteristics, consistent with the literature reviewed, it is expected that compatibility, complementarities, functional similarity, utility observability, efficiency, content distribution or enhancement utility, and lock-in potential will be positively related to the adoption decision. Conversely, the factors of newness, need for network externalities, and technology cost are expected to negatively impact adoption timing and intensity. Media firm managers who are more knowledgeable and motivated increase the likelihood that media firm's will adopt early and intensely.

Finally, a media firm that prefers a strategic posture of market segmentation or differentiation and / or that has a goal to generate additional revenues or create synergistic benefits is more likely to place greater value on a new media technology. The perceived overall strategic value of a new technology is also influenced by the perceptions of alternatives and by firm/media technology characteristics. The factor of strategic networks is expected to be positively related to a media firm's new technology adoption decision. As indicated earlier, the public goods and content-distribution connection often compel a media firm to seek partnerships as part of the adoption process.

## FUTURE RESEARCH IN MEDIA MANAGEMENT AND TECHNOLOGY

The proposed framework for analyzing the adoption of new media technology at the firm level incorporates various theoretical constructs in innovation adoption, strategic management, and entrepreneurship. The factors proposed as the antecedents to the adoption decisions can be tested empirically based on the propositions suggested. The roles of different firm and media characteristics can also be assessed empirically against an established technology to estimate the relative weight of each determinant in influencing the adoption decisions of different media firms. The relationship between adoption intensity and the formation of strategic networks should also be investigated because this supporting factor seems to be an especially critical antecedent for media industries. Finally, the connection between audience adoption of a communication technology and the adoption of that technology by media firms should also be examined.

This chapter also suggests a spectrum of new media innovation adoption and taxonomy of firm adopters. Careful case studies, which compare the development of various new media technologies and the firms that have adopted these technologies at different points in time and with different intensities, might provide useful insights regarding the validity of the proposed spectrum. As for the categorization of adopters, cluster analyses of media firms based on a number of core communication technologies over the last couple of decades might offer corroboration or possible refinements of the suggested adopter type profiles.

Communication technologies have become the driving force behind many media industry changes. This chapter proposes a theoretical framework for conducting technology adoption research at the firm level. It is hoped that the framework presented will provide a foundation for more empirical endeavors, eventually contributing to an increased understanding of a critical driver that propels the economic growth of society.

## REFERENCES

Albarran, A. B. (2002). *Media economics: Understanding markets, industries and concepts* (2nd ed.). Ames: Iowa State Press.

Amit, R., & Zott, C. (2001). Value creation in e-business. *Strategic Management Journal, 22*, 493–520.

Barringer, B. R., & Bluedorn, A. C. (1999). The relationship between corporate entrepreneurship and strategic management. *Strategic Management Journal, 20*, 421–444.

Brandenburger, A. M., & Nalebuff, B. J. (1996). *Co-opetition.* New York: Doubleday.

Brown, T. E., Davidsson, P., & Wiklund, J. (2001). An operationalization of Stevenson's conceptualization of entrepreneurship as opportunity-based firm behavior. *Strategic Management Journal, 22,* 953–968.

Booz, Allen, & Hamilton. (1982). *New product management for the 1980s.* New York: Author.

Chan-Olmsted, S. M., & Ha, L. (2003). Internet business models for broadcasters: How television stations perceive and integrate the Internet. *Journal of Broadcasting & Electronic Media.*

Chan-Olmsted, S. M., & Jung, J. (2001). Strategizing the net business: How television networks compete in the age of the Internet. *International Journal on Media Management, 3,* 213–225.

Chatterjee, S., & Wernerfelt, B. (1991). The link between resources and type of diversification: Theory and evidence. *Strategic Management Journal, 12,* 33–48.

Christensen, C. M., & Bower, J. L. (1996). Customer power, strategic investment and the failure of leading firms. *Strategic Management Journal, 17,* 197–219.

Compaine, B. M., & Gomery, D. (2000). *Who owns the media? Competition and concentration in the mass media industry* (3rd ed.). Mahwah, NJ: Lawrence Erlbaum Associates.

Cooper, A. C. (2001). Networks, alliances, and entrepreneurship. In M. A. Hitt, R. D. Ireland, S. M. Camp, & D. L. Sexton (Eds.), *Strategic entrepreneurship: Creating a new integrated mindset* (pp. 203–217). Oxford, UK: Blackwell.

Dong, D., & Saha, A. (1998). He came, he saw, and he waited: An empirical analysis of inertia in technology adoption. *Applied Economics, 30,* 893–905.

Doyle, G. (2002). *Understanding media economics.* London: Sage.

Eastlick, M. A. (1993). Predictors of videotex adoption. *Journal of Direct Marketing, 7,* 66–74.

Fiegenbaum, A., Hart, S., & Schendel, D. (1996). Strategic reference point theory. *Strategic Management Journal, 17,* 216–236.

Fiegenbaum, A., & Thomas, H. (1988). Attitudes toward risk and the risk–return paradox: Prospect theory explanations. *Academy of Management Journal, 31,* 85–106.

Frankforter, S. A., Berman, S. L., & Jones, T. M. (2000). Boards of directors and shark repellents: Assessing the value of an agency theory perspective. *Journal of Management Studies, 37,* 321–348.

Goel, R. K., & Rich, D. P. (1997). On the adoption of new technologies. *Applied Economics, 29,* 513–518.

Gulati, R., Nohria, N., & Zaheer, A. (2000). Strategic networks. *Strategic Management Journal Special Issue, 21,* 203–215.

Hamel, G. (2000). *Leading the revolution.* Boston: Harvard Business School Press.

Hannan, T. H., & McDowell, J. M. (1984). The determinants of technology adoption: The case of the banking firm. *Rand Journal of Economics, 15,* 328–335.

Herman, E. S., & McChesney, R. W. (1997). *Global media: The new missionaries of corporate capitalism.* London: Cassell.

Hitt, M. A., Ireland, R. D., Camp, S. M., & Sexton, D. L. (2001). Strategic entrepreneurship: Entrepreneurial strategies for wealth creation. *Strategic Management Journal, 22,* 479–491.

Ireland, R. D., Hitt, M. A., & Sirmon, D. G. (2003). A model of strategic entrepreneurship: The construct and its dimensions. *Journal of Management, 29,* 963–989.

Jeffres, L. W., & Atkin, D. J. (1996). Predicting use of technologies for communication and consumer needs. *Journal of Broadcasting & Electronic Media, 40,* 318–330.

Kang, J. (2003). *Predicting "prototype" interactive television use in a contemporary media environment: An innovation-adoption model.* Unpublished doctoral dissertation, University of Florida, Gainesville.

Kotabe, M., & Swan, K. S. (1995). The role of strategic alliances in high-technology new product development. *Strategic Management Journal, 16,* 621–636.

Krugman, D. (1985). Evaluating the audiences of the new media. *Journal of Advertising, 14,* 21–27.

Lee, H., Smith, K. G., Grimm, C. M., & Schomburg, A. (2000). Timing, order and durability of new product advantages with imitation. *Strategic Management Journal, 21,* 23–30.

Levin, S. G., Levin, S. L., & Meisel, J. B. (1987). A dynamic analysis of the adoption of new technology: The case of optical scanners. *Review of Economics and Statistics, 69,* 12–17.

Lin, A. L. (1998). Exploring personal computer adoption dynamics. *Journal of Broadcasting and Electronic Media, 42,* 95–112.

Lin, A. L. (2001). Audience attributes, media supplementation, and likely online service adoption. *Mass Communication and Society, 4,* 19–38.

Lin, A. L. (2003). An interactive communication technology adoption model. *Communication Theory, 13*, 345–365.

Liu, F., & Chan-Olmsted, S. M. (2003). Partnerships between the old and the new: Examining the strategic alliances between broadcast television networks and Internet firms in the context of convergence. *International Journal on Media Management, 5*, 47–56.

Lumpkin, G. T., & Dess, G. G. (1996). Clarifying the entrepreneurial orientation construct and linking it to performance. *Academy of Management Review, 21*, 135–172.

Miles, R. E., & Snow, C. C. (1978). *Organizational strategy, structure, and process.* New York: McGraw-Hill.

Miller, D. (1983). The correlates of entrepreneurship in three types of firms. *Management Science, 29*, 770–791.

Miller, D., & Chen, M. (1996). The simplicity of competitive repertoires: An empirical analysis. *Strategic Management Journal, 17*, 419–439.

Murray, J. A. (1984). A concept of entrepreneurial strategy. *Strategic Management Journal, 5*, 1–13.

Naman, J., & Slevin, D. (1993). Entrepreneurship and the scope of fit: A model and empirical tests. *Strategic Management Journal, 14*, 137–153.

Owen, B. M., & Wildman, S. S. (1992). *Video economics.* Cambridge, MA: Harvard University Press.

Picard, R. G. (1989). *Media economics.* Newbury Park, CA: Sage.

Picard, R. G. (2002). *The economics and financing of media companies.* New York: Fordham University Press.

Porter, M. (1980). *Competitive strategy.* New York: The Free Press.

Redmond, J., & Trager, R. (1998). *Balancing on the wire: The art of managing media organizations.* Boulder, CO: Coursewise.

Robertson, T. S. (1967). The process of innovation and the diffusion of innovation. *Journal of Marketing, 31*, 14–19.

Rogers, E. M. (1995). *Diffusion of innovations* (4th ed.). New York: The Free Press.

Romeo, A. A. (1975). Interindustry and interfirm differences in the rate of diffusion of an innovation. *Review of Economics and Statistics, 57*, 311–319.

Sarkar, M. B., Echambadi, R., & Harrison, J. S. (2001). Alliance entrepreneurship and firm market performance. *Strategic Management Journal, 22*, 701–711.

Schumpeter, J. A. (1936). *The theory of economic development.* Cambridge, UK: Cambridge University Press.

Schumpeter, J. A. (1950). *Capitalism, socialism, and democracy* (3rd ed.). New York: Harper & Row.

Slater, S. F., & Olson, E. M. (2000). Strategy type and performance: The influence of sales force management. *Strategic Management Journal, 21*, 813–829.

Snider, M. (2003, January 16). A defining moment for TV. *USA Today.* Retrieved January 15, 2004, from www.usatoday.com

Subramaniam, M., & Venkatraman, N. (1999). The influence of leveraging tacit overseas knowledge for global new product development capability: An empirical examination. In M. A. Hitt, P. G. Clifford, R. D. Nixon, & K. P. Coyne (Eds.), *Dynamic strategic resources* (pp. 373–401). New York: Wiley/Chichester.

Woodhull, N. J., & Snyder, R. W. (1997). *Media mergers.* New Brunswick, NJ: Transaction Books.

Zahra, S. A. (1993). Environment, corporate entrepreneurship, and financial performance: A taxonomic approach. *Journal of Business Venturing, 8*, 319–340.

Zahra, S. A., & Pearce, S. (1990). Research evidence on the Miles Snow typology. *Journal of Management, 16*, 751–768.

# 13

# Issues in Media Management and the Public Interest

Philip M. Napoli

Fordham University

Media management stands apart as a distinct subfield of management for two primary reasons. The first is that, from an economic standpoint, the products produced by media firms are quite distinct from the products produced by firms in other industries. Media firms produce content for distribution to audiences and audiences for distribution to advertisers (Napoli, 2003a). Both of these products—content and audiences—have a number of distinctive economic characteristics that effectively differentiate the media industries from other industries in the United States and global economies (see Hamilton, 2004; Owen & Wildman, 1992). Consequently, managers operating in the content and audience markets require specialized training and a specialized understanding of the unique dynamics of the marketplaces in which they are operating in order to make effective strategic and managerial decisions (Herrick, 2004; Napoli, 2003b).

The second reason that media management stands apart as a distinct subfield of management has to do with the unique position that media firms—and their output—occupy in the political and cultural life of the nations in which they operate. Media firms are, of course, more than economic entities (Cook, 1998; Napoli, 1997; Sparrow, 1999). Media firms also have the ability—and, in some contexts, the obligation—to have a profound impact on the political and cultural attitudes, opinions, and behaviors of the audiences who consume their products (Croteau & Hoynes, 2001).

It is because of this unique potential for cultural and political influence, and the enormous responsibility that accompanies it, that the concept of the *public interest* long has been central to the operation of media organizations and to the decision making of media managers (Barkin, 2002; Croteau & Hoynes, 2001; McCauley, Peterson, Artz,

Halleck, & Schiller, 2003; McQuail, 1992). The public interest concept encompasses those concerns beyond audience or profit maximization that are at the core of what media managers must consider in their day-to-day decision making. More so than in most other industries, managers in media firms must think about the impact of their decisions on the political and cultural welfare of their consumers. The nature of these concerns can be far reaching, involving issues such as the possible effects of violent television programming on children (Hamilton, 1998), the effects of news coverage (or lack thereof) of political campaigns on political knowledge and political participation (Entman, 1989; Gans, 2003; Patterson, 1994), or whether programming is effectively serving the needs and interests of all segments of the community, including minority segments (Einstein, 2004; Napoli, 2002).

Given the broader political and cultural significance of just these few representative areas of concern, it is perhaps not surprising that the public interest long has been the central guiding principle in the regulation of electronic media in the United States. Since the advent of broadcasting, policymakers have been aware of the unique potential for political and cultural influence that resides within the electronic media and have felt compelled to impose a variety of behavioral and structural regulations in an effort to increase the likelihood that media firms serve the public interest (Napoli, 1999). As previous research has noted, the term public interest appears 11 times in the Communications Act of 1934, and 40 times in the Telecommunications Act of 1996, indicating that the public interest remains central to the regulation of the U.S. media system (Napoli, 2001a, p. 66).

Thus, for media managers, the concept of the public interest exists both as an ethical imperative (borne of the social responsibility dimension of media management) and a regulatory mandate that they must follow. To a certain degree, these two manifestations of the public interest can overlap, as regulatory mandates may take the form of behavioral obligations that media managers must follow; or media managers' own ethical imperatives in the conduct of their work may correspond with the conceptualization of the public interest articulated by regulators.

Despite this potential for overlap in the ethical and regulatory aspects of the public interest, there remains an inherent tension between these two dimensions of the concept. Specifically, the public interest as regulatory mandate arises from the presumption that media managers are not effectively fulfilling the public interest as ethical imperative in their day-to-day decision making. Indeed, many debates in the media regulation and policy realm have revolved around the extent to which government-imposed public interest obligations are necessary to supplement existing industry practices (Advisory Committee, 1998; McQuail, 1992). It is this tension between the public interest as ethical imperative and the public interest as regulatory mandate that will serve as the focal point of this chapter, as this tension is implicit in almost any research addressing the subject area of media management and the public interest.

This chapter will explore the public interest concept from the standpoint of both an ethical imperative for media managers and a regulatory mandate imposed on them by government via an examination of the meaning of the term and an overview of the key issue areas (and their associated research) where the tensions surrounding the appropriate meaning and application of the public interest principle are most intense. Underlying the entirety of this review will be the additional tension that exists between media firms' identities as economic actors (where the primary managerial concerns are revenues and profits) and their identities as political and cultural actors (where the primary managerial concerns are the political and cultural welfare of the audience; see Croteau & Hoynes, 2001; Hamilton, 2004). Finally, this chapter will conclude with an assessment of how research can inform debates and discussions of the appropriate meaning and application of the public interest as both ethical imperative and regulatory mandate and will suggest specific avenues of research that can help better inform both a scholarly and an applied understanding of the public interest dimensions of media management.

## THE PUBLIC INTEREST AS ETHICAL IMPERATIVE AND REGULATORY MANDATE

Whether the concept of the public interest is approached as an ethical imperative or as a regulatory mandate, the first key issue that needs to be addressed is what the term actually means. In addressing this complex (and long-debated) issue, Napoli (2001a) broke the public interest principle down into three definitional levels: conceptual, operational, and applicational. At the conceptual level (the broadest of the three), the debate revolves around the general meaning behind public interest in terms of how public interest determinations are made. The fundamental question at this level of analysis is: How should an institution charged with serving the public interest make its public interest determinations? As Napoli illustrated, within the context of the behavior (and regulation) of media industries, the public interest typically has been conceptualized as a unitary, coherent scheme of values or principles (Held, 1970).

This conceptualization naturally leads to the operational level, which is the level at which specific values or principles associated with serving the public interest are identified. That is, this is the level at which the specific objectives to be pursued are defined. This level has been associated with identifying "indicators that we may use to determine empirically whether something is in the public interest" (Mitnick, 1976, p. 5). Finally, there is the applicational level, which is the level at which the particular values and principles delineated at the operational level are translated into specific behavioral objectives or regulatory standards. These different levels (particularly the latter two) provide a useful framework for exploring the meaning of the public interest concept both as ethical imperative and regulatory mandate.

### Public Interest as Ethical Imperative

When we turn to the meaning of the public interest principle as an ethical imperative for media managers, we must look to media industry ethical and behavioral guidelines. First, however, it is important to note that the public interest as an ethical imperative for media managers extends beyond its fairly narrow confines as a regulatory mandate (where it is limited to the electronic media—primarily radio and television broadcasting). The entire field of journalism (regardless of the technology via which news is disseminated) is infused with an ethical obligation to serve the public interest (Allen, 1995; Barkin, 2002; Iggers, 1999). This ethical imperative is well-illustrated in Siebert, Peterson, and Schramm's (1963) landmark study of the role of journalism in society, in which the authors outlined two theories of the press that are directly relevant to the behavior of media firms (and media managers) in a democracy.[1] The first (and most relevant to the current discussion) is the *libertarian* theory of the press. Under this theory, the underlying purpose of the mass media is to "help discover truth, to assist in the process of solving political and social problems by presenting all manner of evidence and opinion as the basis for decisions" (Siebert, 1963, p. 51). In addition, "The characteristic of the libertarian concept of the function of the press which distinguishes it from the other theories . . . is the right and duty of the press to serve as an extralegal check on government" (p. 56). Ultimately, under the libertarian approach, the public can "be trusted to digest the whole, to discard that not in the public interest and to accept that which served the needs of the individual and of the society of which he is a part" (p. 51).

In these statements, we begin to see an articulation of the key components of an operationalization of the public interest as an ethical imperative for media organizations (and media managers), with the press having obligations to contribute to the solving of political and social problems and to protect citizens from governmental abuses. Consequently, the various sectors of the media industry have, traditionally, maintained self-designed and self-imposed behavioral codes that typically embody the public interest concept to varying degrees.[2] For instance, many of the components of the press' public interest obligations previously described are clearly reflected in Article I (titled "Responsibility") of the Statement of Principles of the American Society of Newspaper Editors (2004):

> The primary purpose of gathering and distributing news and opinion is to serve the general welfare by informing the people and enabling them to make judgments on the issues of the time. . . . The American press was made free not just to inform or just to serve as a forum for debate but also to bring an independent scrutiny to bear on the forces of power in society, including the conduct of official power at all levels of government. (p. 1)

Here, we see the public service objectives of aiding citizens in their decision making and protecting them against governmental abuses of power again clearly articulated. We find

---

[1] The other two theories of the press discussed in the book—the *authoritarian* theory and the *soviet communist* theory are generally not applicable to the structure and behavior of the news media in a democracy such as the United States.

[2] See Campbell (1999), MacCarthy (1995), and Linton (1987) for detailed discussions of media industry self-regulatory codes. These authors devote particular attention to the rather unusual history of the National Association of Broadcasters' Radio and Television Codes, which were in place for roughly 50 and 30 years, respectively, before being eliminated in the early 1980s. Their elimination came about as a result of a Department of Justice (DOJ) suit that charged that the advertising provisions in the Television Code that limited commercial minutes and the total number of commercials per broadcast hour manipulated the supply of commercial time and, thus, violated the Sherman Antitrust Act. It is interesting to note that although the DOJ suit addressed only the advertising guidelines contained in the Code—and not the programming guidelines—the National Association of Broadcasters abandoned the entirety of the Code in the wake of the DOJ action (see Campbell, 1999).

similar values reflected in the Preamble of the Code of Ethics of the Society of Professional Journalists (2004), which states: "Members of the Society of Professional Journalists believe that public enlightenment is the forerunner of justice and the foundation of democracy" (p. 1). Here, the tie between the activities of the press and the effective functioning of the democratic process is made most explicit.

The public interest as ethical imperative is perhaps most clearly articulated in the Code of Ethics of the Radio and Television News Directors Association (2004), whose Preamble states: "Professional electronic journalists should operate as trustees of the public" (p. 1). The Code of Ethics goes on to state that "any commitment other than service to the public undermines trust and credibility," and that professional electronic journalists should "Provide a full range of information to enable the public to make enlightened decisions" (p. 1).

The public interest as ethical imperative, of course, extends beyond the realm of news and into entertainment programming as well, where the key concerns facing media managers do not typically involve serving the informational needs of the audience, but rather effectively and responsibly serving their cultural tastes and preferences. This fact is well-reflected in the Statement of Principles of Radio and Television Broadcasters, issued by the Board of Directors of the National Association of Broadcasters (2004a). This document reflects somewhat different values than the journalistic statements of principles previously described, given the very different functions of news and entertainment content, and focuses instead on the exercise of responsibility, sensitivity to community needs, and concern for the welfare of children—particularly in terms of the depiction of violence, sexuality, and drug abuse.

These statements help to identify the broad set of values associated with the public interest as an ethical imperative for media managers (i.e., the operational level). The next question that needs to be addressed is how are the values expressed in these behavioral codes translated into specific behavioral obligations or guidelines (i.e., the applicational level)?

If we look, for instance, at the following excerpt from the Statement of Principles for the American Society of Newspaper Editors (2004), we find a number of specific behavioral guidelines outlined, including:

*Independence.* Journalists must avoid impropriety and the appearance of impropriety as well as any conflict of interest or the appearance of conflict. They should neither accept anything nor pursue any activity that might compromise or seem to compromise their integrity. *Truth and Accuracy.* Good faith with the reader is the foundation of good journalism. Every effort must be made to assure that the news content is accurate, free from bias and in context, and that all sides are presented fairly. Editorials, analytical articles and commentary should be held to the same standards of accuracy with respect to facts as news reports. Significant errors of fact, as well as errors of omission, should be corrected promptly and prominently.
*Impartiality.* To be impartial does not require the press to be unquestioning or to refrain from editorial expression. Sound practice, however, demands a clear distinction for the reader between news reports and opinion. Articles that contain opinion or personal interpretation should be clearly identified.

*Fair Play.* Journalists should respect the rights of people involved in the news, observe the common standards of decency and stand accountable to the public for the fairness and accuracy of their news reports. Persons publicly accused should be given the earliest opportunity to respond. Pledges of confidentiality to news sources must be honored at all costs, and therefore should not be given lightly. Unless there is clear and pressing need to maintain confidences, sources of information should be identified. (pp. 2–3)

We see comparable behavioral obligations outlined in the codes of ethics of the Society of Professional Journalists (2004) and the Radio and Television News Directors Association (2004). In the Statement of Principles of Radio and Television Broadcasters (National Association of Broadcasters, 2004a), the emphasis is placed on "specific program principles," such as being aware of the composition and preferences of particular communities and audiences; portraying violence responsibly; avoiding glamorizing or encouraging drug use, and avoiding broadcasting programming with sexual themes during hours when significant numbers of children are likely to be in the audience. Explicit in all of these codes are not only sets of values but also the appropriate behaviors for maximizing the extent to which the mass media serve the political and cultural needs of media consumers.

Despite the emphasis on social responsibility reflected in both the values and the behavioral guidelines expressed in these codes, there is a fairly long history of research and criticism that raises questions regarding the extent to which media firms uphold their own ethical imperatives (Commission on Freedom of the Press, 1947; Fuller, 1997; Iggers, 1999; Napoli, 2001b; Patterson, 1994; Rosenstiel & Kovach, 2001). Much of this criticism and analysis hinges on the increasing difficulty that journalists and media managers seem to have in effectively negotiating media organizations' bifurcated nature as both economic and political-cultural institutions (Gans, 2003; Kaiser & Downie, 2003; McManus, 1992). Hamilton (2004) provided one of the most thorough analyses of the interaction between a media organization's economic and public service imperatives, showing how economic forces have historically affected the news product—often in directions that run counter to traditional public interest values. This situation has led to an intense reexamination within the journalistic community of what the notion of public service—and journalism's status as a public trust—actually means (Rosenstiel & Kovach, 2001).

## Public Interest as Regulatory Mandate

Just as the public interest as ethical imperative seems to be in a period of reexamination, so too does the public interest as regulatory mandate. As was mentioned earlier, the public interest as regulatory mandate has more limited applicability—as it is directed only at those sectors of the electronic media (primarily radio and television broadcasting, and, to a lesser degree, cable and satellite) that fall within the regulatory authority of the Federal Communications Commission (FCC). The relationship between the FCC, media organizations, and the public interest principle is well-expressed in the *social responsibility* theory of the press (see Peterson, 1963). Under the social responsibility theory, "the general normative principles and social responsibilities of the libertarian theory are even more prominent, representing the core of the press' function" (Peterson, 1963, p. 74).[3] In addition, unlike under the libertarian approach, "To the extent that the press does not assume its responsibilities, some other agency must see that the essential functions of mass communication are carried out" (p. 74).

This, obviously, is where the public interest as regulatory mandate acts as a supplement to the public interest as ethical imperative, and where the principles of public service and commitment to the democratic process have been translated into specific government-imposed requirements to serve the "public interest, convenience, or necessity" (see Communications Act of 1934). These obligations reflect the FCC's long-standing philosophy that "It is axiomatic that one of the most vital questions of mass communication in a democracy is the development of an informed public opinion through the public dissemination of news and ideas" (Federal Communications Commission, 1949, p. 1249).

When we look at the public interest principle as regulatory mandate at the operational level, there is the key question of identifying and prioritizing which principles best exemplify service in the public interest. During the 70-plus-year history of the FCC and its predecessor, the Federal Radio Commission, different sets of guiding principles have been articulated. The specific values associated with the public interest principle began to take shape as early as 1928, in a statement by the Federal Radio Commission (FRC). In this statement, the FRC identified "key principles which have demonstrated themselves in the course of the experience of the commission and which are applicable to the broadcasting band" (Federal Radio Commission, 1928, p. 59). These key principles included: (a) freedom of signal interference; (b) a fair distribution of different types of service; (c) localism; (d) diversity of program type; and (e) high levels of character and integrity on the part of broadcast licensees (Federal Radio Commission).

We see some of these values recur over time, indicating their relative stability as key elements of the public interest. For instance, through interviews with FCC commissioners and staff, Krugman and Reid (1980) identified five key components of the public interest. These included: (a) balance of opposing viewpoints; (b) heterogeneity of interests; (c) dynamism, in terms of technology, the economy, and the interests of stakeholders; (d) localism; and (e) diversity, in terms of programming, services, and ownership. In recent years, the diversity and localism values, in particular, have crystallized as key components of regulators' operationalization of the electronic media's public interest obligations (see Napoli, 2001a).

This is not to say that, historically, there has been strong and stable consensus in the regulatory realm as to how to operationalize or apply the public interest principle. Rather, the meaning of the public interest standard has been one of the defining controversies in media regulation and policy (Hundt, 1996; Krasnow & Goodman, 1998; Mayton, 1989; Sophos, 1990). Consider, for instance, the well-known *marketplace* approach to the public

---

[3]Peterson (1963) associates six obligations with the social responsibility theory of the press: (a) servicing the political system; (b) enlightening the public in order to facilitate self-government; (c) safeguarding the rights of the individual by serving as a watchdog against government; (d) servicing the economic system via advertising; (e) providing entertainment; (f) maintaining financial self-sufficiency in order to remain free from special interest pressures (p. 74).

interest typically associated with Reagan-era FCC Chairman Mark Fowler and echoed in statements by recently-departed FCC Chairman Michael Powell (2001). According to the marketplace approach:

> Communications policy should be directed toward maximizing the services the public desires. Instead of defining public demand and specifying categories of programming to serve this demand, the Commission should rely on the broadcasters' ability to determine the wants of their audiences through the normal mechanisms of the marketplace. The public's interest, then, defines the public interest. (Fowler & Brenner, 1982, pp. 3–4)

Clearly, the guiding principles underlying this operationalization of the public interest are market forces and consumer sovereignty. Although it may be the case that regulators' reliance on market forces and consumer sovereignty will effectively preserve and promote other traditional public interest values such as diversity and localism, strict adherents to the marketplace approach to the public interest typically will not prioritize such values to such an extent as to impose regulations or policies designed specifically to preserve or promote them.

In contrast, adherents of the *trustee* approach to the public interest (e.g., Hundt, 1996; Minow, 1978; Sunstein, 2000) advocate placing the FCC in the position of identifying and defining specific values (such as diversity and localism) that typically extend into the role and function of media organizations as contributors to the political and cultural well-being of the citizenry; and then, of course, having the Commission establish specific criteria for media firms to meet on behalf of these values.

As might be expected, differences between the marketplace and trustee approach can become particularly pronounced at the applicational level, where the key question involves what specific regulatory requirements to impose in the name of the values associated with the public interest. The applicational component of the public interest as a regulatory mandate is in a near-constant state of flux (see Federal Communications Commission, 1946, 1960, 1999a, 1999b; National Telecommunications and Information Administration, 1997), both because of changes in the hierarchy of values held by different administrations, as well as changes in the media environment and regulators' perceptions of how best to pursue these values (Napoli, 2001a).

One of the earliest efforts by the FCC to establish specific public interest performance criteria for broadcast licensees was the 1946 statement on the *Public Service Responsibilities of Broadcast Licensees* (commonly referred to as the *Blue Book*; see Federal Communications Commission, 1946). The *Blue Book* emphasized four basic components of public interest service: live local programs, public affairs programs, limits on advertising, and "sustaining" programs (defined as unsponsored network programs with experimental formats or appealing to niche audiences; see Federal Communications Commission, 1946). These requirements evolved dramatically in the Commission's much more extensive *Programming Policy Statement*, released in 1960, which outlined 14 "major elements usually necessary to the public interest" (Federal Communications Commission, 1960, p. 274). These included: the development and use of local talent; religious, children's educational, agricultural, news, and public affairs programming; editorializing by licensees;

political broadcasts; weather and market services; and service to minority groups (Federal Communications Commission, 1960).

Such an explicit listing of public interest obligations would seem to provide a reasonably clear set of guidelines to broadcast managers in terms of how to serve the public interest in ways that will satisfy regulators. However, it is important to note that these obligations typically have not taken the form of explicit quantitative requirements (particularly in recent years), though there have been some exceptions. For instance, in the wake of Congress' passage of the Children's Television Act of 1990, the FCC adopted specific programming requirements (3 hours of educational children's programming per week) after acknowledging its "imprecision in defining the scope of a broadcaster's obligation under the Children's Television Act" in its initial efforts to implement the Act (Federal Communications Commission, 1996, p. 10661). This imprecision led the Commission to conclude that the existing regulations did not effectively contribute to broadcasters' fulfillment of their public interest obligations (see Kunkel, 1998).

Napoli (2001a) outlined the current state of broadcasters' public interest obligations. It should be emphasized that the current state of broadcasters' public interest obligations represents a dramatic reduction in the scope of these obligations over the past 2 decades. Today, broadcasters' public interest obligations are limited primarily to the educational children's television requirement just mentioned, indecency and obscenity restrictions, and providing access to broadcast facilities and audiences to political candidates. Explicit requirements for locally produced programming, as well as news and public affairs programming have been eliminated, as have requirements to ascertain the needs and interests of local communities, to provide balanced coverage of controversial issues of public importance (the well-known Fairness Doctrine; see Donahue, 1989), and to allow political candidates the opportunity to respond on-air to "personal attacks" (Napoli, 2001a).

These public interest obligations have been eliminated or reduced for a variety of reasons. In some instances, the regulations were seen as counterproductive. For instance, in the case of the Fairness Doctrine, the FCC believed that requiring broadcasters to devote time to alternative perspectives on controversial issues of public importance actually discouraged broadcasters from covering such issues at all (Aufderheide, 1990; Hazlett & Sosa, 1997; Jung, 1996). That is, broadcast managers felt overly burdened by the Fairness Doctrine requirements (i.e., providing equal opportunity for opposing views) to such an extent that they would avoid covering controversial issues of public importance. In other cases, however, public interest obligations were eliminated by the Commission because of the belief that the regulations were not necessary to ensure that broadcasters would effectively serve the public interest, and that market forces and internal ethical imperatives would provide the necessary incentives for broadcasters to do so (Horwitz, 1989). In other cases, the courts have stepped in, declaring certain public interest obligations overly burdensome from a First Amendment standpoint, or arbitrary and capricious (Napoli, 1999; Trauth & Huffman, 1989).

Broadcasters frequently have argued that they are sufficiently attentive to public service and that government mandates are not necessary (e.g., National Association of Broadcasters, 2000, 2002). Some government and public interest representatives, as well as many scholars, have argued that broadcasters neglect their public service obligations.

Dating back to then-Federal Communications Commission Chairman Newton Minow's (1978) 1961 critique of television as a "vast wasteland," regulators, citizens, and public interest groups frequently have been critical of broadcasters' commitment to public service, to enhancing the democratic process, and to serving the cultural needs of the audience (e.g., Aufderheide, 1992; Benton Foundation 1998; Minow & LaMay 1995; Rainey 1993; Washburn, 1995). Some analyses suggested that as the burden of government-imposed public interest obligations has been reduced, broadcaster performance has deteriorated further (Bishop & Hakanen, 2002).

## CURRENT ISSUES IN MEDIA MANAGEMENT AND THE PUBLIC INTEREST

The previous section explored the meaning of the public interest principle as both an ethical imperative for media managers and as a regulatory mandate that they must follow, and indicated that both aspects of the principle are undergoing periods of change and reexamination. This section reviews a number of current issues that serve as focal points of concern for the future of the public interest principle. Not surprisingly, these issue areas represent points where the tension between the economic imperatives of media firms and their public interest imperatives is particularly intense.

### Market Conditions, Media Management, and the Public Interest

As was emphasized earlier, media organizations are both economic and political-cultural institutions. In a privatized, commercial media system, it is therefore incumbent on media organizations to simultaneously serve the financial needs of media owners and stockholders as well as the informational needs of the citizenry (Barkin, 2002). These distinct institutional objectives can frequently come into conflict—and whereas this has always been the case, a growing body of research suggests that this conflict has grown more intense in recent years as the media marketplace has undergone dramatic changes.

The increased competition for audience attention that has resulted from the increased channel capacity of cable television and the arrival of new content delivery technologies such as Direct Broadcast Satellite and the Internet, has fragmented the media audience, making it more difficult for individual media outlets to attract large audiences (Napoli, 2003a). Where there was once one 24-hour national cable news network (CNN) there are now four (CNN, FOX News, MSNBC, CNBC), as well as a host of regional cable news networks (Lieberman, 1998). Today, the average home receives over 100 television channels, in addition to the content abundance of the Internet. These massive increases in the content options available to media consumers have not been accompanied by proportional increases in the amount of time or money that consumers spend on media (Veronis Suhler Stevenson, 2003). Such an environment places greater pressures on media managers in their efforts to attract audience attention and maintain profitability, and many criticisms and analyses suggest that these pressures have compelled media managers to increasingly neglect public service in favor of content that is cheaper, less sophisticated, less informative, or more sensationalistic (Ehrlich, 1995; Lacy, Coulson, & St. Cyr, 1999; Tjernstrom, 2000).

Journalism frequently has been the target of such critiques (e.g., Gans, 2003; Kovach & Rosenstiel, 1999). McManus' (1994) well-known study of the newspaper industry illustrated how, in an era of declining newspaper readership (because of audience erosion to alternative news sources), newspaper managers increasingly are relying on market research and focus groups to determine the content of their newspapers; and as a result hard news coverage (i.e., coverage of current events, politics, and public affairs) is diminishing relative to soft news topics such as entertainment, lifestyles, and travel. This, and related work (see Patterson, 1994; Rosenstiel & Kovach, 2001; Sabato, 1994; Underwood, 1993), raises questions about whether the market pressures of the contemporary media environment can sustain a media system in which the news values that are central to serving the political and informational needs of the citizenry are given adequate priority (Fuller, 1997; Patterson, 1994). However, some research has suggested that increased competition can increase media outlets' output of public service-oriented content such as news and public affairs (Lacy & Riffe, 1994; Napoli, 2001c). Generally, these inconsistencies in the literature can be attributed to the differentiation between studies that examined output quantity as opposed to output quality; the latter, of course, being the more subjective component to measure.

Marketplace pressures also may compel media managers to neglect certain segments of the media audience—particularly those segments that advertisers consider less valuable (Napoli, 2002). For instance, research has suggested that advertisers' higher valuations of wealthier readers led newspapers to skew editorial content in ways that attract high-income readers and intentionally repel lower-income readers (Baker, 1994). Some newspapers have abandoned certain news categories, such as urban news, and expanded attention to other news categories, such as business news. These moves often led to declines in circulation in addition to an overall demographic composition that is more appealing to advertisers (Baker). The disturbing irony of this situation is that one of the audience segments most in need of the informational and educational benefits of newspaper readership (i.e., lower income citizens) is the one newspapers are least interested in serving.

A growing body of analysis of managerial decision making suggests that the pressure to satisfy advertiser demand for particular audience segments compels media firms to neglect the needs and interests of minority audience segments (Gandy, 2000; Rodriguez, 2001; Wildman & Karamanis, 1998). As one recent analysis concluded, the emphasis on attracting valuable audience segments that has become increasingly prominent in the television news industry has meant that, "Every week—every day—stories about African-Americans, Hispanics, and Asians are kept off the air" (Westin, 2001, p. 83). Obviously, such contentions raise questions concerning the extent to which media firms are serving any sort of inclusive notion of the public interest in the contemporary media marketplace.

Comparable concerns regarding the relationship between market conditions and the public interest extend into the realm of entertainment content as well. One key aspect of the public interest in entertainment media traditionally has been a concern for children—specifically, protecting children from exposure to adult-oriented content such as violent or sexually explicit programming (see National Association of Broadcasters,

2004a). However, the economic incentives for providing such content can overwhelm such concerns. Hamilton (2000), for instance, demonstrated how television programmers faced particularly powerful economic incentives to air violent programming, given that those demographic groups most highly valued by advertisers (men and women, ages 18–34) demonstrated the strongest affinity for violent programming. Consequently, a byproduct of programmers' pursuit of these valuable demographic groups is an abundance of violent programming, much of which is consumed by demographic groups outside of the target market (i.e., children).

The high-profile scandal (and subsequent flurry of activity within the FCC and Congress) surrounding the Janet Jackson breast-bearing incident during the 2004 Super Bowl halftime show can similarly be seen as an unintended consequence of programmers' efforts to attract a greater proportion of the most desirable audience segments. As Super Bowl ratings have declined amidst an increasingly fragmented television environment, programmers have worked at expanding the appeal of the event beyond its traditional audience base by incorporating high-profile musical performers across many different genres both before the game as well as at halftime.

The key point here is that as the media marketplace becomes increasingly fragmented, media managers must become increasingly aggressive in their efforts to attract a sufficient audience to remain economically viable, and these efforts may not conform with articulations of the public interest principle as either ethical imperative or regulatory mandate. As of this writing, both Congress and the FCC are considering increasing the sanctions imposed on broadcasters that violate indecency standards, and also considering whether to extend indecency regulations to cable television (which traditionally has been immune from such regulations). At the same time, the National Association of Broadcasters has formed a Task Force on Responsible Programming to assess industry rights and responsibilities from a programming standpoint (National Association of Broadcasters, 2004b). A similar reassessment of industry efforts to protect children from exposure to adult content was undertaken by the National Cable and Telecommunications Association (2004). This reexamination of current regulatory and ethical standards was prompted in large part by the Janet Jackson Super Bowl incident, as well as by growing concerns about indecency in talk radio (the Howard Stern Show being the focal point of such concerns).

## Ownership Concentration, Media Management, and the Public Interest

Research frequently has addressed the relationship between the ownership of media outlets and the content that media outlets provide (see Compaine, 1995; Shoemaker & Reese, 1996). From a management perspective, the key questions have involved if, or to what extent, owners are able to exert control over those directly involved in content production (Shoemaker & Reese), and what are the mechanisms by which such control is exerted (Epstein, 1974; Fishman, 1980; Gans, 1979; Shoemaker & Reese)?

Questions such as these have grown more important as concentration of ownership in certain sectors of the media industry has increased (see Compaine & Gomery, 2000; Gershon, 1997). Such increased concentration also has given rise to the question of the possible relationship between concentration of ownership in the media industries and the ability of media outlets to effectively serve the public interest (Davis & Craft, 2000; Lacy, 1991; Lacy & Riffe, 1994; Litman, 1978; Napoli, 2001d). This issue has risen to prominence in recent years, in large part because of the FCC's biennial media ownership review (the most recent review was completed in June 2003; see Federal Communications Commission, 2003). In the Telecommunications Act of 1996, Congress required the FCC to reassess all of its media ownership regulations every 2 years (recently changed to every 4 years) and to eliminate those "no longer necessary in the public interest as a result of competition" (Telecommunications Act of 1996). Under then FCC Chairman Michael Powell, in 2001 the Commission initiated its most thorough review of its ownership regulations to date, consolidating a review of six different media ownership rules into a single proceeding (Federal Communications Commission, 2003) and touching off an unusually high profile political battle over the ownership rules (a battle that, as of this writing, remains unresolved).

From a media management standpoint, the key question is whether different ownership structures bear any relationship to media mangers' incentives or abilities to provide public service-oriented content or services (Compaine, 1995). On one side of the debate, there is the argument that the greater economic efficiencies associated with more concentrated ownership provide media managers with greater resources to devote to public service (Demers, 2001). Support for this line of reasoning could be found in the FCC's analysis of the relationship between ownership and the provision of local news and public affairs programming (the two program types that regulators traditionally have tied most directly to the idea of serving the public interest). This study (conducted in conjunction with the FCC's biennial ownership review) found that television stations with newspaper holdings generally provided more local news and public affairs programming than stations without newspaper holdings (Spavins, Denison, Roberts, & Frenette, 2002).[4] These results contrast with those of earlier research, which found no significant relationship between news and public affairs programming provision and ownership variables such as group ownership and newspaper–TV cross-ownership (Wirth & Wollert, 1978), suggesting that the economics of the media marketplace have changed dramatically over the past 25 years. The more recent results suggest that the economies of scope associated with gathering and disseminating news and public affairs content across multiple distribution technologies may, in fact, encourage the production of such "public interest" programming (Spavins et al., 2002; see also Napoli, 2004).

On the other side of this debate is the argument that media outlets that become part of large national, or multinational, media conglomerates lose much of their ability and/or incentive to effectively serve the public interest (Gans, 2003). One of the most commonly articulated concerns is the possibility that media outlets owned by large media conglomerates will not have the same knowledge of—and commitment to—the needs and interests of the communities they serve as will media outlets operated by locally based owners (Napoli, 2000, 2001d). Another common concern is that media outlets

---

[4]Subsequent reanalysis of the FCC's data found that, when news and public affairs programming were analyzed separately, the relationship between newspaper–television station cross-ownership and news and public affairs programming held only for news, but not for public affairs programming. This distinction is likely attributable to the fundamentally different economic characteristics of news and public affairs programming (Napoli, 2004).

that are part of large, publicly held corporations will place a greater emphasis on profits than independent media outlets, to the neglect of public interest content such as hard news and public affairs (Beam, 2002; Cranberg, Bezanson, & Soloski, 2001; Gans, 2003; Underwood, 1993). FCC Commissioner Michael Copps (2003) even suggested that the increasing amount of violence and indecency presented on television may be a function of the increasing concentration of ownership in the media industries, though no research has yet been conducted to support this contention.

## New Technologies, Media Management, and the Public Interest

The new media environment raises a number of vital questions about the future of our media system. Perhaps among the most important of these is the question of how the public interest should be defined and applied in the new media environment (Bollier, 2002; Breen, 1998). This is a question being asked by both media managers and regulators, as it is central to both the ethical and regulatory dimensions of the public interest principle.

Should, for example, the same norms of social responsibility and ethical principles that characterize print and television journalism apply in the online realm, or should they be revised in some way to reflect the unique characteristics of the medium (Deuze, 2003)? Does the Internet offer the opportunity for journalism to better serve the public interest (Pavlik & Topping, 2001)? Questions such as these take time to resolve, as it often takes time for new media technologies to gain acceptance as legitimate sources of journalistic information. Just as it took time for television and radio to be considered a component of "the press" on par with newspapers (Baughman, 1997), so too it is taking time for the Internet to become established as a legitimate and reliable component of the press (Martin & Hansen, 1996; Tumber, 2001).

Similar questions can arise as existing technologies evolve and become more advanced. For instance, in the late 1990s, a fair amount of attention was devoted to the question of what, if any, public interest obligations should be imposed on broadcasters once they have made the transition from the analog to the digital broadcasting platform (Napoli, 2003c). In some quarters, the feeling was that the transition to digital broadcasting would provide the opportunity to correct for the regulatory mistakes made in the analog realm, where many felt the concept of the public interest had been drained of most of its meaning (Benton Foundation, 1998; Sunstein, 2000). The industry perspective was that the transition to digital broadcasting was too early in its progress to warrant the immediate imposition of public interest obligations, particularly in light of the uncertain financial prospects facing digital broadcasting (Decherd, 1998).

In March 1997, the Clinton administration established the Advisory Committee on the Public Interest Obligations of Digital Television Broadcasters. The Committee, a mix of industry executives, academics, and public interest advocates, was charged with the task of "determining how the principles of public trusteeship that have governed broadcast television for more than 70 years should be applied in the new television environment" (Advisory Committee, 1998, p. 136). The Committee met eight times over the next 15 months in different venues around the country to solicit input from the general public and from outside experts, and ultimately produced a set of recommendations that was submitted to the White House (Advisory Committee).

These recommendations addressed a variety of issues, such as disability access, the promotion of diversity, disaster warnings, funding for public broadcasting, and the establishment of a voluntary code of conduct for broadcasters. The Committee's report did not, for the most part, move very far beyond the regulatory framework and requirements that have been in place for analog broadcasters, and generally avoided providing specific details in regard to its recommendations. Many of these recommendations became part of then-FCC Chairman William Kennard's (2001) *Report to Congress on the Public Interest Obligations of Television Broadcasters as They Transition to Digital Television.* Since then, however, very little progress has been made on this issue (Napoli, 2003c), though effectively resolving this issue requires a careful balancing of the cultural and informational needs of the citizenry with the economic realities (and burdens) associated with a government-imposed, industrywide migration to a new broadcast system.

## SUGGESTIONS FOR FUTURE RESEARCH

As this review has suggested, the concept of the public interest may be losing ground both as an ethical imperative and a regulatory mandate. Regulators have been reducing the range and rigor of public interest obligations placed on the electronic media, while media firms face increasingly intense market pressures to prioritize audience maximization and cost savings over public service. In such an environment, the need for research addressing the relationship between media management and the public interest becomes more pronounced, as such research could potentially help in preserving—and possibly rehabilitating—the role of the public interest as both ethical imperative and regulatory mandate. It is particularly important that debates and discussions about the relationship between media management and the public interest be informed less by anecdotal examples of the poor—or exemplary—performance of media outlets, and more by rigorous assessments of media organization performance and analyses of the market and structural factors that may affect such performance. Toward this end, the development of more thorough and robust *metrics* of media performance is particularly desirable.

Regulators, in particular, are in need of a stronger empirical record demonstrating the relationship between market and structural conditions and the extent to which media firms serve the public interest. It is not only behavioral (or conduct) regulations that are often promulgated with the objective of improving the extent to which individual media outlets serve the public interest. Structural regulations (such as ownership regulations) often are adopted for the same reasons. Thus, regulators not only need research examining the extent to which media firms adhere to specific behavioral guidelines (e.g., to what extent are broadcast stations adhering to the requirement that they air 3 hours of educational children's programming per week), but also research illuminating whether the extent to which individual media outlets fulfill public interest principles is a function of factors such as ownership type, market conditions, or other potentially relevant characteristics of the organizations being studied or the markets in which the organizations operate.

The research needs of regulators explain why most research that examines media organization or industry performance in relation to public interest values typically assesses such performance (and its determinants) within the context of the public interest as regulatory imperative—that is, are media organizations meeting the behavioral standards established by regulators, and if not, why not? In contrast, surprisingly little research examines media performance in relation to the performance guidelines established by the media organizations themselves. That is, do media firms act in accordance with their own behavioral guidelines? As this chapter has illustrated, the various sectors of the media industry have developed quite explicit behavioral codes and guidelines, which can form the foundation for robust behavioral assessments as effectively as (if not better than) the typically vague behavioral requirements outlined by regulators. This emphasis on examining media performance within the context of internally generated behavioral guidelines and statements of principles (e.g., Napoli, 2001b) is particularly vital today, given the extent to which (as this chapter has illustrated) the public interest as regulatory mandate is receding in terms of its scope and intensity.

Ultimately, when we consider the notion of the public interest from the perspective of media management research, we are talking about a line of inquiry that addresses the following questions:

1. To what extent are media managers engaging in practices that serve the public interest?
2. What factors affect media managers' ability or willingness to engage in practices that serve the public interest?
3. How does public interest service affect media firms' profitability?
4. How should media managers define and apply the public interest principle in their daily activities?
5. How should policymakers define and measure the public interest performance of media firms?
6. How can media managers better serve the public interest?

As is suggested by this list of questions, research addressing the relationship between media management and the public interest can serve a variety of functions. It can be descriptive in nature, documenting if or how media firms are adhering to particular public interest principles. Or, it can be explanatory, examining whether particular market or structural conditions bear any relationship to media firms' public interest performance. Or, it can be normative, addressing how regulators or media managers should define and apply the public interest principle.

In the end, just as the unique capacity for political and cultural influence is what distinguishes the management of media firms from the management of other types of commercial organizations, research that addresses media organizations' management and performance in terms of their service to the political and cultural needs of the citizenry is ultimately what distinguishes media management research from other areas of management research. Continued attention to this core element of media management research can contribute to maintaining and strengthening those attributes that fundamentally—and necessarily—distinguish media organizations from other organizations in the American and global economies and can maintain the vital focus on improving our understanding of the relationship between media management and the public interest.

# REFERENCES

Advisory Committee on the Public Interest Obligations of Digital Broadcasters. (1998). *Charting the digital broadcasting future.* Washington, DC: U.S. Government Printing Office.

Allen, D. S. (1995). Separating the press and the public. *Journal of Mass Media Ethics, 10,* 197–209.

American Society of Newspaper Editors. (2004). *Statement of principles.* Retrieved January 10, 2004, from http://www.asne.org/index.cfm?ID=888

Aufderheide, P. (1990). After the fairness doctrine: Controversial broadcast programming and the public interest. *Journal of Communication, 40*(3), 47–72.

Aufderheide, P. (1992). Cable television and the public interest. *Journal of Communication, 42,* 52-65.

Baker, C. E. (1994). *Advertising and a democratic press.* Princeton, NJ: Princeton University Press.

Barkin, S. M. (2002). *American television news: The media marketplace and the public interest.* Armonk, NY: Sharpe.

Baughman, J. L. (1997). *The republic of mass culture: Journalism, filmmaking, and broadcasting in America since 1941.* Baltimore: Johns Hopkins University Press.

Beam, R. A. (2002). Size of corporate parent drives market orientation. *Newspaper Research Journal, 23,* 46–63.

Benton Foundation. (1998). *What's local about local broadcasting.* Retrieved January 14, 2004, from http://www.benton.org/publibrary/television/whatslocal.html

Bishop, R., & Hakanen, E. A. (2002). In the public interest? The state of local television programming fifteen years after deregulation. *Journal of Communication Inquiry, 26,* 261–276.

Bollier, D. (2002). *In search of the public interest in the new media environment.* Washington, DC: Aspen Institute.

Breen, M. (1998). Moving to jelly beans: Public interest theory for the Internet. *Electronic Journal of Communication, 8.* Retrieved February 25, 2005 from http://www.cios.org/getfile/Breen_u8n298.

Campbell, A. J. (1999). Self-regulation and the media. *Federal Communications Law Journal, 51,* 711–771.

Commission on Freedom of the Press. (1947). *A free and responsible press.* Chicago: University of Chicago Press.

Communications Act of 1934, Pub. L. No. 416, 48 Stat. 1064 (1934).

Compaine, B. M. (1995). The impact of ownership on content: Does it matter? *Cardozo Arts & Entertainment Law Journal, 13,* 755–780.

Compaine, B. M., & Gomery, D. (2000). *Who owns the media? Competition and concentration in the mass media industry* (3rd ed.). Mahwah, NJ: Lawrence Erlbaum Associates.

Cook, T. (1998). *Governing with the news: The news media as a political institution.* Chicago: University of Chicago Press.

Copps, M. J. (2003, January 22). Remarks before the NATPE 2003 family programming forum, New Orleans, LA. Retrieved January 10, 2004, from http://www.fcc.gov/Speeches/Copps/2003/spmjc301.pdf

Cranberg, G., Bezanson, R., & Soloski, J. (2001). *Taking stock: Journalism and the publicly traded newspaper company.* Ames, IA: Blackwell.

Croteau. D., & Hoynes, W. (2001). *The business of media: Corporate media and the public interest.* Thousand Oaks, CA: Pine Forge Press.

Davis, C., & Craft, S. (2000). New media synergy: Emergence of institutional conflicts of interest. *Journal of Mass Media Ethics, 15,* 219–231.

Decherd, R. (1998). Public interest obligations of digital television broadcasters: An examination of possible regulatory models. Retrieved January 14, 2004, from http://www.ntia.doc.gov/pubintadvcom/aprmtg/Belo-Regulatory.htm

Demers, D. (2001). *Global media: Menace or messiah?* (2nd ed.). Cresskill, NJ: Hampton Press.

Deuze, M. (2003). The Web and its journalisms: Considering the consequences of different types of news media online. *New Media and Society, 5,* 203–230.

Donahue, H. C. (1989). *The battle to control broadcast news: Who owns the First Amendment.* Cambridge, MA: MIT Press.

Ehrlich, M. C. (1995). The ethical dilemma of television news sweeps. *Journal of Mass Media Ethics, 10,* 37–48.

Einstein, M. (2004). *Media diversity: Economics, ownership, and the FCC.* Mahwah, NJ: Lawrence Erlbaum Associates.

Entman, R. M. (1989). *Democracy without citizens: Media and the decay of American politics*. New York: Oxford University Press.

Epstein, E. J. (1974). *News from nowhere*. New York: Vintage Books.

Federal Communications Commission. (1946). Public service responsibilities of broadcast licensees, 11 FCC 1458.

Federal Communications Commission. (1949). Editorializing by broadcast licensees. 13 FCC 1246.

Federal Communications Commission. (1960). Network programming inquiry, report and statement of policy, 25 Fed. Reg. 7291. (Reprinted from *Documents of American Broadcasting*, pp. 262–278, by F. J. Kahn, Ed., 1978, Englewood Cliffs, NJ: Prentice-Hall).

Federal Communications Commission. (1996). Policies and rules concerning children's television programming: Revision of programming policies for television broadcast stations, 11 FCC Rcd. 10660.

Federal Communications Commission. (1999a). *Public interest obligations of TV broadcast licensees*. 1999 FCC LEXIS 6487.

Federal Communications Commission. (1999b). *The public and broadcasting*. Washington, DC: Author.

Federal Communications Commission. (2003). In the Matter of 2002 Biennial Regulatory Review—Review of the Commission's Broadcast Ownership Rules and Other Rules Adopted Pursuant to Section 202 of the Telecommunications Act of 1996; Cross-Ownership of Broadcast Stations and Newspapers; Rules and Policies Concerning Multiple Ownership of Radio Broadcast Stations in Local Markets; Definition of Radio Markets; Definition of Radio Markets for Areas Not Located in an Arbitron Survey Area, 18 FCC Rcd. 13620.

Federal Radio Commission. (1928). Statement made by the Commission on August 23, 1928, relative to the public interest, convenience, or necessity. (Reprinted from) *Documents of American broadcasting*, 4th ed., pp. 57–62, by F. J. Kahn, Ed., 1978, Englewood Cliffs, NJ: Prentice-Hall).

Fishman, M. (1980). *Manufacturing the news*. Austin, TX: University of Texas Press.

Fowler, M. S., & Brenner, D. L. (1982). A marketplace approach to broadcast regulation. *Texas Law Review, 60*, 1–51.

Fuller, J. (1997). *News values: Ideas for an information age*. Chicago: University of Chicago Press.

Gandy, O. H. (2000, May). *Audience construction: Race, ethnicity and segmentation in popular media*. Paper presented at the annual meeting of the International Communication Association, Acapulco, Mexico.

Gans, H. J. (1979). *Deciding what's news*. New York: Vintage Books.

Gans, H. J. (2003). *Democracy and the news*. New York: Oxford University Press.

Gershon, R. A. (1997). *The transnational media corporation: Global messages and free market competition*. Mahwah, NJ: Lawrence Erlbaum Associates.

Hamilton, J. T. (Ed.). (1998). *Television violence and public policy*. Ann Arbor: University of Michigan Press.

Hamilton, J. T. (2000). *Channeling violence*. Princeton, NJ: Princeton University Press.

Hamilton, J. T. (2004). *All the news that's fit to sell: How the market transforms information into news*. Princeton, NJ: Princeton University Press.

Hazlett, T. A., & Sosa, D. W. (1997). Was the fairness doctrine a "chilling effect?" Evidence from the post-deregulation radio market. *Journal of Legal Studies, 26*, 279–301.

Held, V. (1970). *The public interest and individual interests*. New York: Basic Books.

Herrick, D. (2004). *Media management in the age of giants: The business dynamics of journalism*. Ames, IA: Blackwell.

Horwitz, R. B. (1989). *The irony of regulatory reform: The deregulation of American telecommunications*. New York: Oxford University Press.

Hundt, R. E. (1996). The public's airwaves: What does the public interest require of television broadcasters. *Duke Law Journal, 45*, 1089–1129.

Iggers, J. (1999). *Good news, bad news: Journalism ethics and the public interest*. Boulder, CO: Westview Press.

Jung, D. J. (1996). *The Federal Communications Commission, the broadcast industry, and the Fairness Doctrine, 1981–1987*. Lanham, MD: University Press of America.

Kaiser, R., & Downie, L. (2003). *News about the news: American journalism in peril*. New York: Vintage Books.

Kennard, W. E. (2001). *Report to Congress on the public interest obligations of television broadcasters as they transition to digital television*. Washington, DC: Federal Communications Commission.

Kovach, B., & Rosenstiel, T. (1999). *Warp speed: America in the age of mixed media.* New York: The Century Foundation.

Krasnow, E. G., & Goodman, J. N. (1998). The "public interest" standard: The search for the holy grail. *Federal Communications Law Journal, 50,* 605–636.

Krugman, D. M., & Reid, L. R. (1980). The "public interest" as defined by FCC policy makers. *Journal of Broadcasting, 24,* 311–325.

Kunkel, D. (1998). Policy battles over defining children's educational television. *Annals of the American Academy of Political and Social Sciences, 557,* 39–53.

Lacy, S. (1991). Effects of group ownership on daily newspaper content. *Journal of Media Economics, 4,* 35–47.

Lacy, S., Coulson, D., & St. Cyr, C. (1999). The impact of beat competition on city hall coverage. *Journalism & Mass Communication Quarterly, 76,* 325–340.

Lacy, S., & Riffe, D. (1994). The impact of competition and group ownership on radio news. *Journalism Quarterly, 71,* 583–593.

Lieberman, D. (1998, November/December). The rise and rise of 24-hour local cable news. *Columbia Journalism Review.* Retrieved November 14, 2002, from http://www.crj.org/year/98/tvnews.asp

Linton, B. A. (1987). Self-regulation in broadcasting revisited. *Journalism Quarterly, 64,* 483–490.

Litman, B. M. (1978). Is network ownership in the public interest? *Journal of Communication, 28,* 51–59.

MacCarthy, M. M. (1995). Broadcast self-regulation: The NAB codes, family viewing hour, and television violence. *Cardozo Arts & Entertainment Law Journal, 13,* 667–696.

Martin, S., & Hansen, K. A. (1996). Examining the "virtual" publication as a "newspaper of record." *Communication Law & Policy, 1,* 579–594.

Mayton, W. T. (1989). The illegitimacy of the public interest standard at the FCC. *Emory Law Journal, 38,* 715–769.

McCauley, M. P., Peterson, E. E., Artz, B. L., Halleck, D., & Schiller, D. (Eds.). (2003). *Public broadcasting and the public interest.* Armonk, NY: Sharpe.

McManus, J. (1992). Serving the public and serving the market: A conflict of interest? *Journal of Mass Media Ethics, 7,* 196–208.

McManus, J. (1994). *Market-driven journalism: Let the citizen beware?* Thousand Oaks, CA: Sage.

McQuail, D. (1992). *Media performance: Mass communication and the public interest.* London: Sage.

Minow, N. N. (1978). Address by Newton N. Minow to the National Association of Broadcasters. In F. Kahn (Ed.), *Documents of American broadcasting,* (4th ed., pp. 207–217). Englewood Cliffs, NJ: Prentice-Hall.

Minow, N. N., & LaMay, C. L. (1995). *Abandoned in the wasteland: Children, television and the First Amendment.* New York: Hill and Wang.

Mitnick B. M. (1976). A typology of conceptions of the public interest. *Administration & Society, 8,* 5–28.

Napoli, P. M. (1997). A principal–agent approach to the study of media organizations: Toward a theory of the media firm. *Political Communication, 14,* 207–219.

Napoli, P. M. (1999). The unique nature of communications regulation: Evidence and implications for communications policy analysis. *Journal of Broadcasting & Electronic Media, 43,* 565–581.

Napoli, P. M. (2000). The localism principle under stress. *Info: The Journal of Policy, Regulation, and Strategy for Telecommunications, Information and Media, 2,* 573–582.

Napoli, P. M. (2001a). *Foundations of communications policy: Principles and process in the regulation of electronic media.* Cresskill, NJ: Hampton Press.

Napoli, P. M. (2001b). Social responsibility and commercial broadcast television: An assessment of public affairs programming. *International Journal on Media Management, 3,* 226–233.

Napoli, P. M. (2001c). Market conditions and public affairs programming: Implications for digital television policy. *Harvard International Journal of Press/Politics, 6,* 15–29.

Napoli, P. M. (2001d, October 29). Diversity and localism: A policy analysis perspective. Presented before the Federal Communications Commission's Media Ownership Roundtable, Washington, DC.

Napoli, P. M. (2002). Audience valuation and minority media: An analysis of the determinants of the value of radio audiences. *Journal of Broadcasting & Electronic Media, 46,* 169–184.

Napoli, P. M. (2003a). *Audience economics: Media institutions and the audience marketplace.* New York: Columbia University Press.

Napoli, P. M. (2003b). Environmental assessment in a dual-product marketplace: A participant–observation perspective on the broadcast television industry. *International Journal on Media Management, 5*, 100–108.

Napoli, P. M. (2003c). The public interest obligations initiative: Lost in the digital television shuffle. *Journal of Broadcasting & Electronic Media, 47*, 153–156.

Napoli, P. M. (2004). Television station ownership characteristics and news and public affairs programming: An expanded analysis of FCC data. *Info: The Journal of Policy, Regulation, and Strategy for Telecommunications, Information, and Media. 6*(2), 112–121.

National Association of Broadcasters. (2000). *Bringing community service home.* Washington, DC: Author.

National Association of Broadcasters. (2002). *A national report on local broadcasters' community service.* Washington, DC: Author.

National Association of Broadcasters. (2004a). Statement of principles of radio and television broadcasters. Retrieved January 10, 2004, from http://www.nab.org/newsroom/Issues/NAB%20Statement%20of%20Principles.html

National Association of Broadcasters. (2004b). NAB to form task force on responsible programming. Retrieved June 10, 2004, from http://www.nab.org/Newsroom/PressRel/Releases/RP_Task_Force040104.htm

National Cable and Telecommunications Association. (2004). Cable industry efforts to empower television viewers: Choice, control, and education. Retrieved June 10, 2004, from http://www.ncta.com/pdf_files/whitepapers/TVControl.pdf

National Telecommunications and Information Administration. (1997). A primer on the public interest obligations of television broadcasters. Washington, DC: U.S. Government Printing Office.

Owen, B. M., & Wildman, S. S. (1992). *Video economics.* Cambridge, MA: Harvard University Press.

Patterson, T. E. (1994). *Out of order.* New York: Vintage Books.

Pavlik, J. V., & Topping, S. (2001). *Journalism and new media.* New York: Columbia University Press.

Peterson, T. (1963). The social responsibility theory. In F. Siebert, T. Peterson, & W. Schramm, *Four theories of the press* (pp. 73–105). Chicago: University of Illinois Press.

Powell, M. (2001, February 6). Press conference. Available: from FCC Web site, www.fcc.gov/realaudio/pc020601/ram

Radio and Television News Directors Association. (2004). *Code of ethics.* Retrieved January 10, 2004, from http://www.rtnda.org/ethics/coe.shtml

Rainey, R. R. (1993). The public's interest in public affairs discourse, democratic governance, and fairness in broadcasting: A critical review of the public interest duties of the electronic media. *Georgetown Law Journal, 82*, 269–372.

Rodriguez, A. (2001). *Reinventing minority media for the 21st century.* Washington, DC: Aspen Institute.

Rosenstiel, T., & Kovach, B. (2001). *The elements of journalism: What newspeople should know and what the public should expect.* New York: Three Rivers Press.

Sabato, L. J. (1994). *Feeding frenzy: How attack journalism has transformed American politics.* New York: Free Press.

Shoemaker, P. J., & Reese, S. D. (1996). *Mediating the message: Theories of influences on mass media content* (2nd ed.). White Plains, NY: Longman.

Siebert, F. S. (1963). The libertarian theory. In F. Siebert, T. Peterson, & W. Schramm (Eds.), *Four theories of the press* (pp. 39–72). Chicago: University of Illinois Press.

Siebert, F., Peterson, T., & Schramm, W. (Eds.). (1963). *Four theories of the press.* Chicago: University of Illinois Press.

Society of Professional Journalists. (2004). *Code of ethics.* Retrieved January 10, 2004, from http://www.spj.org/ethics_code.asp

Sophos, M. (1990). The public interest, convenience, or necessity: A dead standard in an era of broadcast deregulation? *Pace Law Review, 10*, 661–705.

Sparrow, B. H. (1999). *Uncertain guardians: The news media as a political institution.* Baltimore: Johns Hopkins University Press.

Spavins, T. C., Denison, L., Roberts, S., & Frenette, J. (2002). The measurement of local television news and public affairs programs. Washington, DC: Federal Communications Commission.

Sunstein, C. R. (2000). Television and the public interest. *University of California Law Review, 88*, 499–564.

Telecommunications Act of 1996, Pub. L. No. 104-104, 110 Stat. 56 (1996), (codified in scattered sections of 47 U.S.C.).

Tjernstrom, D. (2000). Public service management: Toward a theory of the media firm. *International Journal on Media Management, 2*, 153–164.

Trauth, D. M., & Huffman, J. L. (1989). A case study of a difference in perspectives: The DC Circuit Court of Appeals and the FCC. *Journal of Broadcasting and Electronic Media, 33*, 247–272.

Tumber, H. (2001). Democracy in the information age: The role of the fourth estate in cyberspace. *Information, Communication & Society, 4*, 95–112.

Underwood, D. (1993). *When MBAs rule the newsroom.* New York: Columbia University Press.

Veronis Suhler Stevenson (2003). *Communications industry report.* New York: Author.

Washburn, P. C. (1995). Top of the hour radio newscasts and the public interest. *Journal of Broadcasting & Electronic Media, 39*, 73–91.

Westin, A. (2001, April). The color of ratings. *Brill's Content,* 82–85, 129–131.

Wildman, S. S., & Karamanis, T. (1998). The economics of minority programming. In A. Garmer (Ed.), *Investing in diversity: Advancing opportunities for minorities in media* (pp. 47–65). Washington, DC: Aspen Institute.

Wirth, M. O., & Wollert, J. A. (1978). Public interest programming: FCC standards and station performance. *Journalism Quarterly, 55*, 554–561.

# 14

# Industry-Specific Management Issues

Douglas A. Ferguson

College of Charleston

This chapter analyzes the most significant management issues facing various segments of the media industry (i.e., broadcast television, radio, multichannel television, newspapers, magazines, books, film, and recording). Some issues are universal and warrant close attention by all media managers. Many more issues are particular to a specific medium.

The SWOT (strengths, weaknesses, opportunities, threats) analysis considers present-day strengths and weaknesses to construct present and future issues (opportunities and threats). The following analysis presumes the reader understands the relative advantages of one medium over another. On the one hand, broadcast and multichannel television dominates the advertiser-supported media because it combines sight, sound, and motion (Lafayette, 2004). On the other hand, radio is inexpensive and therefore does a better job with products or services that need repetition to reach the customer in ways that advertiser-supported television cannot. The other media also have unique advantages that determine many of their strengths (and weaknesses for others) within the SWOT analysis. Because internal strengths and weaknesses of each medium are more readily apparent, they are omitted in this discussion.

The utility of studying threats and opportunities is in identifying the key issues, rather than an exhaustive list of problems and benefits. Media managers need to stay focused on the most important considerations at any given time, because there is not time to pay attention to every detail in every situation. Opportunities and threats are future-oriented and focused on external forces, which are features closely associated with the planning function of management.

| Specific Medium | Threats | Opportunities |
|---|---|---|
| Broadcast Television | Cost of conversion to HDTV<br>Loss of revenue streams<br>Direct delivery of video content<br>Demise of traditional TV news<br>Audience fragmentation | Multicasting<br>Interactivity |
| Radio | Alternative forms of distribution<br>Loss of local identity | Talk formats<br>Companionship |
| Multichannel Television | Alternative forms of distribution<br>Government reregulation<br>Cost of technology<br>Programming expense | New revenue streams<br>Changes in the advertising<br>    process/model |
| Newspapers | Production costs<br>Competition from the Internet<br>Declining readership | Local dominance |
| Magazines | Competition from within<br>Competition from niche media<br>Postal rates | Fresh approaches<br>Cross-promotion |
| Books | Competition from cheap printers<br>Media consolidation<br>Declining reading skills<br>Advent of personal printing (C2C) | Electronic publishing<br>Online printing<br>Printing on demand |
| Film | Copyright protection<br>VOD<br>Home theater systems | Control of production<br>Strategic alliances & mergers |
| Recordings | Peer-to-peer file sharing | Internet-based delivery<br>Cross-promotion of products |

FIG. 14.1.   Summary of media threats and opportunities.

The first section of this chapter examines each medium according to its opportunities and threats—the last half of the traditional SWOT analysis. For example, studies of TiVo users confirm that asynchronous television viewing defeats much of the advertising revenue stream, which for the dominant television industry is the only real source of profit. This looming threat creates a real management issue for television stations and networks alike. Figures 14.1 and 14.2 provide a summary of these challenges and opportunities.

The second section of this chapter briefly summarizes the major challenges as they relate to many segments of the media industry. For example, direct digital delivery of content threatens all established media. The removal of the middleman function, a trend sometimes called disintermediation, is a recurring theme in the discussion.

## BROADCAST TV: THREATS

The five main threats to the broadcast television industry encompass the following: cost of conversion to HDTV, loss of revenue streams, direct delivery of video content, competition from digitally enabled print, and audience fragmentation at the hands of cable and satellite video. The implicit threats stand in stark contrast to the rich opportunities available to a medium whose ubiquitous audience is accustomed to vivid video messages.

| | Broadcast Television | Radio | Multichannel Television | Newspapers | Magazines | Books | Film | Recordings |
|---|---|---|---|---|---|---|---|---|
| Competition from alternative forms of distribution | X | X | X | X | X | X | X | X |
| Loss of key advantage | X | X | | | | | X | |
| Cost of technology | X | | X | | | | | |
| Cost of programming | | | X | | | | | |
| Cost of production | X | | | | X | | X | |
| Declining reading | | | | | X | X | | |
| Copyright and piracy | | | | | | X | X | X |
| Audience fragmentation | X | | | | X | | | |
| New ideas | X | | | | X | | | |
| New technology | X | | | | | | | |
| New revenue streams | | | | X | | X | | |
| Cross-promotion | | | | | X | | | X |
| Localism | X | | | X | | | | |
| Alliances | | | | X | | | X | |
| Continued strengths | | X | | X | | | | |

FIG. 14.2.   Matrix of media threats and opportunities.

## Cost of Conversion

The cost of moving from the old standard-definition system to high-definition continues to drain the resources of broadcast television stations, many of whom see no short-term benefit to digital-quality conversion, other than satisfying a Federal mandate to accomplish the switchover by 2007, a deadline that likely will be extended. Managers are stuck with a service for which there is low demand and sparse content. Eventually, however, the transition will be complete and the medium will be even more vivid in terms of video resolution and audio.

## Loss of Revenue Streams

A simple Google search of the threats to conventional broadcast television points primarily to new viewing technologies that facilitate the skipping of commercials. If the 30-second spot has been the linchpin of the broadcast television business, then the prospect of asynchronous viewing by means of a TiVo-like device is the hurricane wind. Sometimes called a PVR (personal video recorder), sometimes a DVR (digital video recorder), it promises to change the way people watch broadcast television.

Much has been written about the future of broadcast network television in a world where viewers set their own viewing schedules. A hard-drive storage device, whether it is built into the receiver, bundled with set-top boxes, or a stand-alone TiVo device, empowers the viewer to get a season pass to programs regardless of their competition within a set schedule and allows the same viewer to jump over, not merely fast-forward past, entire pods of commercials. It's what you want to watch, when you want to watch it, most likely without commercial interruption.

Network executives (e.g., Jamie Kellner, chairman of The WB) have railed against the DVR (McClellan, 2003a), industry analyst Tom Wolzien has recommended regulatory action to protect advertiser-supported television (Higgins, 2004b), and programmers have studied ways to defeat the DVR. For example, NBC has experimented with starting top-rated shows a few minutes earlier than the break point at the top of the hour, to interfere with the recording of the end of programs that lead up to the break point. Other networks have encouraged long-form or embedded messages (McCarthy, 2003). Still others propose serial mini-movies interspersed in primetime to discourage ad-skipping.

The strong reaction against DVRs is the best evidence of the threat they pose. However, the eventual demise of the conventional primetime schedule creates an opportunity for networks that own vast libraries of drama and comedy series. NBC proposes to use materials from its Vivendi-Universal vaults to supply on-demand shows to viewers with a few hundred megabytes of storage space to spare.

The economics of broadcast television have changed little over the years (Ferguson, 1998, 2003), but competition and technology are forcing a shift in the way managers can produce enough revenue to show a profit. How will the economic model change? Some point to pay-per-view schemes and others propose subscribing to NBC or CBS in the same way that cable subscribers presently subscribe to HBO or another premium service. Program sponsorship will remain to defray the cost of production, similar to the mix of advertising and subscription cost for cable television and most print media.

## Direct Content Delivery

Another example of discontinuous change for complacent broadcast television broadcasters involves the near completion of the evolution of wireless broadcast television to *direct delivery* of video, via satellite, Internet, wired cable, or even DVD. In his book *Being Digital*, Nicholas Negroponte predicted that telephones and television would "switch" delivery systems. Tom Hazlett (2001) wrote an analysis that proposes the final switch by subsidizing the handful of homes that do not receive direct connections. Even Reed Hundt, former FCC chairman, proposed that HDTV be accomplished via broadband rather than broadcast (McConnell, 2003). Colossal shifts of business models could result from the migration of homes to wired or direct-to-home (DTH) delivery. Moreover, DVD versions of serialized TV shows (e.g., *The Sopranos*) threaten schedulers by giving the viewers more control, but also offer opportunities to make money off unsuccessful series that garnered critical acclaim but low viewing (Higgins, 2003c).

## Demise of the Traditional Television News

Another threat to broadcast television involves the demise of localism as a unique selling proposition for broadcasters (Friedman, 2003). If viewers want local TV news, the local broadcast stations have always had an oligopoly; no other medium could cover local news with video with sufficient resources. The Associated Press announced plans in 2003, however, to help its member newspapers provide video stories on their Web sites (McClellan, 2003b). As broadband (high-speed) Internet connections reach a plurality of homes, the potential for newspapers to spread their excess capacity into video is substantial. Already, schools of journalism are preparing students for a convergence of media. Few have doubted the superiority of local newsgathering by print journalists, but only the availability of video distribution kept the reports from reaching broadcast television sets. Streaming video and overnight delivery of asynchronous video to DVR set-top boxes could create real competition for audiences that warm to the idea of on-demand video news.

Another viewpoint is that the dominant television news station in each market is doing so well that competition is actually limited, and that managers would be well-advised to expand their number of newscasts. Powers (2001) argued that there has been a movement from oligopolistic to monopolistic competition, at least in the top 10 markets. If this is true, broadcast television news may be more entrenched than has been previously thought.

## Loss of Viewing Primacy and Audience Fragmentation

In November 2003, for the first time, the advertiser-supported cable networks drew larger audiences than the broadcast networks (Dempsey, 2003). After years of paying more for smaller audiences, the advertising agencies began to question seriously the future of upfront buying from four networks that could no longer account for at least half the viewing (i.e., a 50 share).

Previously, the major networks were able to charge increasing amounts for smaller slivers of the audiences. Advertising agencies played along because they needed the huge audiences that networks could deliver. What has changed is that broadcast television networks no longer provide the dominant video vehicle. Advertisers still need broadcast, but they now wonder why the cost should continue to rise.

A case in point is the "disappearance" of the 18 to 34-year-old demographic, particularly the males. In September 2003, the networks noticed that Nielsen was underreporting the viewing of young males. Although the explanation is still being debated at this writing, a compelling case has been made that two systemic shifts have taken place. First, fewer males are entering the primetime viewing patterns, opting instead for cable channels that cater to their demographic and choosing to begin their viewing at 10 p.m. or 11 p.m. as they did when they were teenagers. Second, a growing number of young males are returning to their parents' homes and spending less time with traditional media, in effect continuing their adolescence well into their 20s and early 30s.

The most serious cable-related threat is the use of interconnects (i.e., geographically linking cable operators and their programs) to beat broadcasters at their own game (Mermigas, 2003a). Forecasts estimate that cable could double its $4 billion spot revenue, causing a sizable shift in the share of local advertising. Broadcast television at the local level is seeing its profit potential slide away, especially at a time when the share of viewing has shifted toward cable channels. Broadcast sales managers will have to finally compete head-on with the growing cable threat.

One predicted threat, the Internet, may or may not be affecting broadcast television much, either helping create more discretionary time for television viewing according to one source (Downey, 2001), or diverting time away from TV according to another source (Chmielewski, 2003). Broadcasters are treating the Web as a threat, by adding news content to their own Web sites to leverage their excess capacity and repurpose their newscasts. Chan-Olmstead and Ha (2003) offered research on how television broadcasters perceive the Internet. Most television stations have used the Internet to build audience relationships, rather than selling advertising online. This research suggested that broadcast television managers are missing an opportunity to generate revenue.

A looming threat for broadcast television is the growth of local people meters, which tend to decrease estimates of viewing to broadcast channels and increase the same for cable channels. Regardless of whether the new measurements are underestimates or improved estimates, the net effect is lower viewing to network affiliated stations (Karrfalt, 2003).

Another threat to broadcast television is digital television in the form of video-on-demand (VOD). Some fear that viewing will become channel-less and content will find its way to the screen in unscheduled formats (Mandese, 2004). The impetus is technology: By spring 2004, DVRs, digital satellite, digital cable, digital TV, and DVD saw their respective penetration figures reach 3.6%, 21.0%, 18.0%, 5.9%, and 56.0% (Knowledge Networks, 2004).

## BROADCAST TV: OPPORTUNITIES

The main opportunities for broadcast TV require that stations make the most of their bandwidth and that program producers (often the networks themselves) find enhanced ways to deliver their content. Enhanced content options further require that managers develop ways for the audience to become more actively involved in the programming, rather than being passive viewers (Ferguson, 2003). The key strength for stations (and therefore the biggest potential opportunity) is the ability to provide local attention in a way that national media cannot (Heaton, 2003).

### Multicasting

If fragmentation of the audience is inevitable, then broadcasters need to provide specialized programming that emphasizes localism (Slattery, Hakanen, and Doremus, 1996). Even when broadcasting high-definition content (roughly 14 Mbps [megabits per second] of the available 19.4 Mbps bandwidth), stations can split their programming effort to create at least one additional single-definition channel that targets well-defined viewing interests related to several dominant themes: news, weather, entertainment, personality-driven talk, and sports (Eggerton & Kerschbaumer, 2003). A good example of multicasting would be a sporting event where a station could choose to telecast the important game in high-definition and another lesser interest game in single-definition. In those day parts when they are not broadcasting in high-definition, stations can divide the digital spectrum even further, especially for such limited-motion programming as weather (2 Mbps). (Eggerton & Kerschbaumer, 2003).

That niche channels like The Weather Channel can draw a cumulative audience is a clue that a local weather channel can succeed with local talent and local advertiser sponsorship. Local news is another opportunity for a full-time niche channel that is fed by the excess capacity of expensive newsroom operations. Again, local sponsorships are the key to spreading revenue across day parts rather than concentrated in a single newscast or two (Eggerton & Kerschbaumer, 2003). The issue for broadcast television managers is how to choose, create, market, and cross-promote the extra content.

## Interactivity

An enduring view of television is that the audience and the viewing experience is passive (Jankowski & Fuchs, 1995). A whole generation of cell-phone users, instant-messaging addicts, and video-game players is finally chipping away at this commonly held view that the typical viewer prefers to be passive. Broadcast (and multichannel) television can bring home the full range of experiences found by young people in recent decades at the mall: the socializing, the gaming, the shopping, the widescreen theater experience, and the pursuit of entertainment.

## RADIO: THREATS

The main threats to music radio are competition from alternate forms of distribution and loss of local identity. Competition comes in the form of satellite radio providers, the Internet, independent retailers, and new personal technology options. Paul Kagan (2003) forecasted a host of competitive threats to radio, such as subscription-based Internet radio, customized CDs, and satellite radio. Automobile manufacturers have already begun to integrate personal music devices (e.g., the iPod) into their newer models.

## Alternative Forms of Distribution

It took TiVo at least 4 years to reach 1 million subscribers, but it only took XM radio half that long to achieve the same audience penetration (Gough, 2003b). Such is the allure of satellite radio, which has proven that people are willing to pay for radio, even when some of the 100 or so music formats being offered contain commercials (Claybaugh, 2002). Paying for radio must seem as strange to radio managers as paying for television did to broadcast television managers 20 years ago, but the trend is real. Radio managers should plan accordingly and treat satellite radio as a genuine competitor. They must look for ways to differentiate their programming, such as localized content, although XM satellite radio began offering local weather and traffic reports in 2004.

## Internet Competition

Again, direct delivery of content removes the need for a content provider. Radio is threatened by the Internet is three ways, according to the editors of *G2 News* (2003). First, the ability of radio to make money promoting music is threatened more and more by peer-to-peer (P2P) networks. Small, independent record labels pay P2P networks like Altnet to promote artists. Altnet uses Microsoft's digital rights management (DRM) to guard against unauthorized duplication.

Second, free and low-cost streaming music on the Internet threatens conventional radio. Arbitron and Nielsen rating services both measure such streaming media services as MusicMatch, listen.com, Microsoft's Windows Media Player's Radio Tuner, AOL's spinner.com, and RealNetworks' Jukebox, which is testimony to their popularity.

Third, portable radios are threatened by comparably sized portable MP3 players like the Sonicblue Rio S35S and the Apple iPod that hold hours and hours of music inexpensively. Time spent listening to radio will decline once listeners figure out they can choose their own songs and play them they way they want (*G2 Computer Intelligence*, 2003). B. Eric Rhoads, *Radio Ink* Magazine publisher, states:

> What will happen four years from now [2007 based on 2003], when every cell phone, Palm Pilot and car radio receives 20,000 online stations? Will you be prepared when agencies demand that you provide interactivity, which is physically impossible with radio? Will you be ready for the day when FM listeners move to Internet, as AM migrated to FM? (Rhoads, 2003).

### Fewer Independent Retailers

Local radio stations depend heavily on local advertisers, but chain-owned retailers are growing faster than locally owned independents (Radio Advertising Bureau, 2003a). The problem is compounded by the growing influence of Internet shopping. For example, 20% of credit card purchases for the 2003 end-of-year holiday buying season were done online, a nearly 30% increase over the previous year (Jessell, 2004). November online sales alone grew 55% from 2002 to 2003, at $8.5 billion. As local retailers lose business to chains and online sellers that use national advertising media, local media like radio and newspapers will lose revenue (Albarran, 2004).

### Personal Music Technologies

Many observers worry that MP3 and customized CDs will supplant music formats, but some see an opportunity for radio stations that tout www.mp3.com to cross-promote local music groups (Fybush, 2003). Even so, if syndicators can readily package their music wares directly to consumers, where is the need for live radio in the long term? If local radio moves farther toward voice-tracked content that sounds live and local, but is not, where is the desire for live radio?

Even for those managers who embrace the digital streaming world, there are still pitfalls. For example, the cost of copyright for online streaming is an ongoing issue (National Association of Broadcasters, 2003). Many of the problems center on the inconsistent operations of the Copyright Arbitration Royalty Panel (CARP) system. Until the controversy is resolved, most radio stations have discontinued streaming their content.

## RADIO: OPPORTUNITIES

Still, radio has a bright future as it moves to its own digital standard—in-band on-channel (IBOC) that allows analog and digital listeners to receive terrestrial broadcasts.

As long as listeners desire a specific sound, regardless of the music format, radio provides a convenient, ubiquitous source of programming that requires no effort on the part of its audience.

Talk radio continues to provide a unique source of political discussion that broadcast television and the Internet have not matched. Again, the content is created for the listener, requiring no effort on the part of the audience. Broadcast television political discussion adds little by showing the talking heads. Radio discussion is much more personal.

It is a small wonder that radio makes the perfect companion. Radio goes anywhere and everywhere. Radio is inexpensive and flexible. Revenues continue to be relatively healthy. Most of all, it is the most personal of local media, provided that programmers provide useful local information. Radio managers need to focus on the strengths and opportunities of their medium.

## MULTICHANNEL VIDEO: THREATS

The main threats to multichannel video are competition from alternative forms of delivery, government reregulation, cost of technology, and programming expense. Because multichannel video is primarily delivered via coaxial cable, most of the relevant literature is cable-centric (thus, the focus of this section). According to Mermigas (2003c), for example, other threats include the following: financial consequences of the industry converting to a largely pay-for-play model (e.g., tiered sports channels) and interference with the advertiser-support model from such interactive devices as the DVR (but also including set-top boxes, wireless 3G video phones, and server-based streaming media on the Internet).

### Satellite Competition

The successful merger in 2004 of DirecTV with Rupert Murdoch's Fox empire has completely awakened a sleeping giant in the form of DTH delivery of channels usually sent over coaxial or fiber cables (Shields, 2004).

At this writing, only 20% of homes get their multichannel content from a small dish antenna, compared to the 70% of homes that are wired. Yet, it is possible that cable and satellite penetration stands at the same division that AM and FM radio saw in the early 1970s, when only 20% of the listening was to a superior signal delivered by FM. If this analogy holds, it is conceivable that 20 years from now, expensive old technology will be substantially supplanted by DTH delivery.

It is more likely that cable will survive with a large share of homes, but with more fierce competition from DTH. The economics of cable is rooted in monopoly market structure. The adjustment to a shared customer base will create competition issues for cable managers.

Cable is often more expensive than satellite although it typically provides a lower quality analog signal. In 2003 the typical cable subscriber paid $40 per month, but DISH offered 50 channels for $25 per month. As local channels are added to most satellite channel lineups, the competitive advantage for cable will dim. In 2003, J. D. Power and Associates reported that satellite customers were far more satisfied than cable subscribers, but reported a different average monthly cost for satellite and cable, $48.93 and $49.62, respectively, when other services beyond basic service were included (Higgins, 2003a).

Two kinds of telephone competition exist: point-to-point (broadband Internet and telephone service) and multipoint (video). These pose a threat to cable companies in the broadband arena, especially with regard to digital subscriber line (DSL) competition. Also, telcos (telephone companies) being entrenched as telephone service providers makes it difficult for Voice over Internet Protocol (VoIP) to penetrate many homes. The telephone companies loom large as competitors to cable and other multichannel providers who wish to take over information services.

Video competition from the telephone companies, however, has failed to materialize as a present threat, even after the many years following the Telecommunications Act of 1996 that gave telcos the right to compete with cable. One can wonder if there is much of a future threat, given the lackluster inroads made by any form of telco-sponsored program distribution. It would seem that the telcos have figured out that the "one wire" home is likely to be the wire that can carry the most bandwidth. Given their sheer size, however, the telcos may simply buy their way into multichannel video by acquiring major cable providers, especially if wireless phones and VoIP can possibly whittle away their share. Telcos may also find relief in the reregulation of cable.

## Regulation

Cable has been deregulated and reregulated more than once in the past 20 years. The monthly cost to the average cable subscriber has grown from under $20 before deregulation in 1984 to well over $40 in 2004. Rates have risen 40% from 1998 to 2003 (Radio Advertising Bureau, 2003b).

Local regulation is another management issue. Before satellite competitors appeared, cable was king and local communities often profited from exclusive franchises. The growing penetration of satellite homes, especially with further consolidation and the provision of local channels, may cause friction between municipalities and cable providers.

## Rising Costs

Like all media, the cost of programming cuts into profit. The threat is less for multichannel video because recycled materials are more accepted and quality expectations are lower (Carter, 2004). This claim is unsupported by research but reasonable nevertheless, especially given the relative newcomer status of cable and satellite channels. Audiences seem to appreciate the additional choice, even if it is poker and celebrities (or both).

The cost of technology, however, is a real concern. An immense amount of capital is required to support cable and satellite distribution systems. As expensive as it is to launch and maintain geostationary satellites, it is more expensive to replace miles of fiber cable.

The expense of technology is less a threat now because the multiple system operator (MSO) companies have finished paying for major upgrades throughout the United States.

## Other Threats

Multichannel video is not particularly threatened by audience fragmentation because it sells advertising across channels rather than within a particular channel. Where broadcasters have seen their value to advertisers shrink as audiences get smaller, multichannel video providers can more easily reach all their subscribers, particularly with roadblocking techniques that position a commercial on all advertiser-supported channels at the same time, something broadcasters have not yet figured out.

## MULTICHANNEL VIDEO: OPPORTUNITIES

The main opportunities for conventional cable operators are broadband connections, VoIP phone service (in addition to circuit-switched telephony), VOD (video-on-demand), set-top DVR rentals, and changes in the advertising process/model via interconnect (especially in conjunction with Ad Tag/Ad Copy, which permits individual household targeting). The main opportunities for satellite television are achieving greater parity with cable through the addition of local channels and the program leverage that comes from Fox ownership (now that nearly all satellite service is controlled by Fox, which also owns a production studio).

## Broadband Connections

According to www.websiteoptimization.com, U.S. household broadband (i.e., high-speed Internet) penetration has reached 41.5%, compared to 74.2% penetration in the workplace. For people whose household income is greater than $75,000, the penetration figure is 46% at the end of 2003 (Fadner, 2004). Technological breakthroughs are often based on 35 to 40% saturation levels, so it appears that broadband has fully arrived, but the pace of growth had begun to slow somewhat in December 2003. Nevertheless, an extrapolation of the adoption curve shows that broadband share in the United States should exceed 50% by June 2004 (Web Site Optimization, 2003).

Cable is a major player, competing with DSL, and had 15 million subscribers at the end of 2003 (National Cable Television Association, 2003) based on 80% of homes passed. At the same time, this base compares to a little over 7 million DSL subscribers and about 9 million for DTH satellite providers (whose service is high-speed download and low-speed upload) for the same time period. Clearly, cable has an advantage to further exploit.

Another viewpoint on the convergence of cable television and broadband is that the two platforms will remain distinct from one another (Chan-Olmstead & Kang, 2003). The argument is that the unique features of each medium work against the merger of services. If this is true, it would go a long way to explaining why most attempts to bring interactivity into the multichannel television marketplace have failed.

## VoIP

Cable providers have begun to offer inexpensive Internet-based phone systems to businesses, a service that competes with expensive circuit-switched telephony. The Telecommunications Act of 1996 opened the door for cable to compete with telephone companies (and vice versa), but it was cable's very gradual deployment of fiber cables that finally offered a significant new revenue stream. Given the massive resources of telephone companies, it is a little surprising that the competition has been so one-sided, even considering the percentage of DSL high-speed Internet subscribers that compete with cable modems. Cable's advantage is that it can cherry-pick customers much more easily than the phone companies can, because cable's new service is merely point-to-point communication. Offering video entertainment and information that can compete with cable networks is a much taller order for the telcos.

The major implication of VoIP is that another revenue stream is created for cable. A decade ago, broadcasters complained when cable had a dual revenue stream (advertising and subscriptions), when they had just advertising revenue. Today one could argue that multichannel has doubled its revenue streams, to include telephone service and broadband Internet. If a medium can add newer services as older offerings mature, the growth potential is greater.

## Video-on-Demand

Subscription video-on-demand (SVOD) is discussed more fully later in this chapter in its role as a threat to the motion picture industry, but it certainly portends to be an opportunity for cable. Cable subscribers are more accustomed to tiers of services than pay-per-view, and SVOD successfully bridges the two models. Anyone who has had the option of a single price for all amusement rides at a county fair, versus a per ride cost, understands the appeal of SVOD over VOD. According to Jupiter Research's latest report, the VOD market will grow from $293 million in 2003 to $1.4 billion in 2007; SVOD revenues will top $800 million, up from $56 million in 2003. Collectively, this market will grow 58% annually, from $349 million in 2003 to $2.2 billion in 2007 (Radio Advertising Bureau, 2003b). Even if these figures are optimistic, multichannel video has clear potential to expand its subscription revenue stream via VOD (Rizzuto & Wirth, 2002).

## Set-Top DVRs

As discussed earlier, the TiVo stand-alone DVR threatened advertiser-supported broadcast television stations and networks. Although stand-alone DVRs were initially slow to diffuse, reaching only 2 to 3 million homes in their first 4 years, the bundling (for a fee) of optional DVRs (either built into set-top boxes or attached as "sidecars") offers additional revenues for cable operators. Many expect that the DVR will only become commonplace in homes when cable operators (and manufacturers of higher-price television sets) quickly roll them out. If operators can charge extra for the devices, cable can create another source of revenue (perhaps even a stream if the subscriber views the additional function as desirable). The telephone companies play a similar game with add-on features like call waiting and caller-ID.

## Changes in Advertising Process/Model Via Interconnect

Cable advertising has always promised to be a substantial second revenue stream for the MSO, but the use of sophisticated insertion equipment and interconnected cable systems puts the whole idea on steroids. Since the beginning, broadcast advertising has been based on broadcast markets guaranteed by grade-B signal contours. Cable interconnects, however, allow cable systems to gerrymander their own ad-hoc markets. Whereas broadcast television stations must rotate advertising taglines for co-op advertising, cable interconnects can insert taglines by neighborhood (similar to, but better than, zoned editions for print). One advertising executive for WPP Group media-buying service Mindshare says, "Most people don't know how to use it yet, but it will become more prolific. When it does, it begs the question: When is broadcast going to be able to do this? They'll have to have a relationship with cable in order to do it" (Haley, 2003).

With system upgrades in place by 2004, cable operators have the digital fiber technology to be competitive. More important, the capital spending is in the past and the cash flow has begun. Cable operators are free to reduce debt somewhat and look for acquisitions (Higgins, 2004b).

According to Mermigas (2003c), cable is no longer a single-product, basic subscriber-based industry, but a bundled service, tiered user-based industry. She writes, "Despite the broad loss of basic subscribers, cable operators actually are growing their significantly more valuable nonvideo subscribers—which are typically high-speed data-only customers—faster than they are losing video subscribers. So, counting all of its varied services, cable's overall basic subscriber rolls are actually rising" (¶11).

## NEWSPAPERS: THREATS

The main threats to newspapers are production costs, competition from the Internet, and declining readership. According to the industry's economic data from the Newspaper Association of America, national and retail advertising has recovered after the post-9/11 slump to the levels in 2000, however, classified advertising is down 20% from 2000 to 2003, or about $1 billion. Classified advertising was always a huge source of revenue for newspapers, but the advent of person-to-person contact via Ebay.com or Monster.com has shrunk the demand for print ads helping people sell their unwanted items or locate a job. The main implication of this unprecedented advertising competition is that newspapers can no longer count on a near-monopoly for employment and sale advertising.

### Production Costs

Newsprint costs are a major threat to newspaper profit, considering that they account for about 20% of cash operating expenses. Picard (2004) identified these costs as a major issue for newspapers. For example, the *New York Times* saw costs rise 13.1% in a single year (Graybow, 2003). In recent years, most newspapers have gone to narrower page widths to cut losses.

## Internet Competition

Christie, Di Senso, Gold, and Rader (2000) explained that the Internet threat to newspapers in the United States is two-fold. First, domestic newspapers rely more on advertising for revenue than do foreign newspapers, especially with regard to classified ads that are threatened by Internet competition. Second, the consumer is also lured away by the Internet, in terms of discretionary time and competition for viewpoints. They concluded that displacement is a major threat because readership is already down because of both declining literacy and increasing media choice.

Online classifieds, particularly in the form of help-wanted and auction Web sites, continues to threaten an important source of revenue for newspapers. Most newspapers have been improving their own Web sites to improve revenue. For example, New York Times Digital showed substantial growth in 2003 in employment and automotive classified, thanks in part to deals with AOL and General Motors (Gough, 2003a).

The issue, of course, is whether or not the competition for classified advertising serves as a significant threat to the viability of daily and weekly newspapers. Some observers noted the resilience of the newspaper industry to change (Picard, 2004) and others were less sanguine (Albarran, 2002). Chyi and Lasorsa (2002) examined reader attitudes toward online editions and found that most preferred the print editions, suggesting that the newspaper medium is not likely to change in the near future.

## Declining Readership

According to Scarborough data from the Newspaper Association of America (2003), daily adult readership declined from 55.8% in 1998 to 52.8% in 2002. Sunday readership also declined, from 68.1% to 64.5%. The clear challenge for management is to stem the losses, while competing media see gains in consumption.

Functional illiteracy is a growing threat (Picard & Brody, 1997). People can read, but some so poorly that they cannot enjoy a newspaper. Ninety million American have low-level reading skills (Terry, 1996). Over time, the No Child Left Behind Act will improve basic skills, but functional illiteracy is a current threat to newspaper circulation.

## NEWSPAPERS: OPPORTUNITIES

The greatest opportunity for newspapers lies in leveraging their dominant position in local communities. Newspapers, regardless of declining readership and circulation, are central to the culture and zeitgeist of their metropolitan areas. Radio talk shows feed off of newspaper content, and broadcast television news producers get their agenda delivered daily to their front porch. Despite the old technology, newspapers function as the official journal of events for a community, and no one should underestimate the importance of what gets printed in the paper each day (Picard, 2004).

As a result, newspaper editorial operations have tremendous capacity to inform and persuade, but typically only once per day in traditional format. As previously mentioned, as a threat to broadcast television, newspapers in a video streaming era have the unique opportunity to provide visual stories that individual TV stations only wish they could or pretend they can. For decades local broadcast television news had a monopoly on vivid and visceral impact. With a few notable exceptions, broadcast television news is superficial and sensationalistic. Soon it will have a formidable competitor as journalism schools are already training a generation of news practitioners who can write clearly as well as construct compelling images.

Newspapers have numerous opportunities to use the Internet. In many cities, the local Internet portal with the most information belongs to the local newspaper. The "journal" function of daily newspapers lends itself to online chronicling of news, events, and directories. Studies on Internet opportunities portray a bright future for newspapers, despite competition from other media (Lacy, Coulson, & Cho, 2002).

"Watching" a daily newspaper will be different from just reading it. The form and content will offer not just new business opportunities for managers and owners, but also change the way reality is socially constructed. And if IBM ever perfects an inexpensive, portable display technology based on flexible transistors, the newspaper may become the dominant electronic medium in the future.

## MAGAZINES: THREATS

The main threats to magazines are competition for talented writers and editors from within the magazine industry and competition from Internet and traditional media, especially niche cable. Rising postal rates are a continuing threat because preferential second-class handling had long made subscriptions affordable (Daly, Henry, & Ryder, 1997). Greco (2004) noted that declining circulation issues make it difficult for magazine publishers to make money.

### Internal Competition

Top editors, publishers, circulation directors, and other executives move among periodicals so that the industry feeds on itself. It is a corollary of product diversity that industries will find a shortage of talented employees. Turnover is an ongoing problem in magazines because of internecine competition.

### External Competition

The Internet itself is like a giant newsstand, with many more dedicated topical Web sites than the number of available magazine titles. Many sites are tied to fledgling print content providers who hope to make it onto the mainstream newsstands. For established print magazines, however, competition from a free Web source providing a near substitute can lure away paying subscribers. In the case of such men's magazines as *Playboy* and *Penthouse*, adult content on the Internet has killed an entire category of magazine content.

### Circulation Issues

Greco (2004) reported that proliferation of magazine titles threatens the profits per title. Readership per title declined 10% between 1996 and 2002, whereas the cost per single copy at the newsstand rose 35%. The implication is that advertisers are not willing to pay more for fewer readers.

## MAGAZINES: OPPORTUNITIES

The major opportunities for magazines lie in renewing long-standing target audiences with fresh approaches and in cross-promotion among competing media. First, a mature medium like magazines requires renewal (e.g., reinventing *Redbook* as *Rosie*). Second, despite how competition from other media is a threat under normal circumstances, magazines find a giant opportunity in cooperating with those same media to launch new titles (Lagorce, 2003). Thus, cross-promotion has become a key vehicle for magazines to cut through the clutter of offerings.

For example, *O*, the Oprah Winfrey magazine, and *Martha Stewart Living* are both successful because the audience is tied to the broadcast or multichannel television product. Cross-promotion is a way to overcome the odds against a new title floundering before its third birthday, which is the usual insurmountable hurdle (Greco, 2004). Another "safe" opportunity in new magazine titles is the use of brand extensions. For example, *Teen Vogue* capitalizes on the main brand but focuses on a younger readership. Another spinoff title is *Sports Illustrated on Campus*.

## BOOKS: THREATS

Rawlins (1998) identified several threats to (and opportunities for) the book publishing industry. For example, cheap, fast, high-quality paper copying threatens copyrighted books, especially those with expensive per-copy prices. He writes:

> Imagine a world of small cheap personal copiers, where you can rent, then copy, expensive paper books just as you can rent music, software, or movies today. Imagine a world where one student in a class buys a copy of a textbook, then copies it for all the others. Imagine a world where publishers in Pacific Rim and Middle Eastern countries buy one copy of a book then sell duplicates just above the duplicating cost (¶ 23).

Other threats to the book publishing industry are media consolidation, declining reading skills, and the advent of Creator to Consumer (C2C) printing.

### Media Consolidation

Although the sheer number of book publishers has mushroomed to 73,000 (many of whom only publish one title), the number of major book publishers continues to decline as larger companies acquire smaller publishers. Desktop publishing may have decreased the cost of press runs, but the cost of being large has fueled mergers.

### Declining Readership Skills

Functional illiteracy probably threatens book reading to a greater degree than newspaper reading. Print journalism has headlines and photographs, sentences are shorter, and the required attention span to complete a newspaper is far less than the average bestselling book. As a result, book retailing has changed over the years. A customer is just as likely to purchase a magazine, a video, or a music CD as they are to purchase a book.

### Creator to Consumer

C2C is an issue for book publishers because it limits the amount of control publishers have over what gets printed and what does not: Readers simply bypass the publishers. Disintermediation, a new concept abetted by new digital technologies, removes the middleman when the Internet becomes the distribution channel. In the book industry, fledgling authors find few barriers to entry on the Web. Vanity press opportunities still abound for those who want to hold the book in their hands, but there is a growing market for book titles with very light demand.

Traditional publishers have responded by printing books on demand, using the same digital efficiencies that spawned the Web. Such micropublishing, as well as experiments with e-books, may turn the threat of C2C into an opportunity. Even so, the digitization of books makes piracy an even greater threat than in the past (Greco, 2004).

## BOOKS: OPPORTUNITIES

The main opportunities for the book publishing industry are electronic publishing, online printing, and printing on demand.

### Electronic Publishing

Rawlins (1998) wrote:

> The problems facing the publishing industry seem insurmountable, if publishing proceeds as it does today except that books are electronic instead of on paper. But with a new view of publishing the apparently severe problems become opportunities. The only viable long-term solution is for publishers to make book buying cheaper or more convenient than book copying, as it used to be 5 years ago. Publishers can do so if they keep a stable number of captive readers and amortize costs over their entire list. (¶ 29)

Rawlins further explained that the same 500-page textbook that costs 10 cents a page (or 5 cents second-hand) only costs 3 cents a page on a large copier or 1 cent a page on a large printer. Electronic distribution brings the cost down to 1/5 cent per page. The electronic text content can be augmented with video/sound or automatically cross-referenced: "Electronic books can be easier to distribute, less expensive, less risky, more powerful, more flexible, more immediate, and easier to search and collate. They can also be interactive, changeable, and adaptive" (Rawlins, 1998, ¶ 6). Small wonder that electronic books have become more popular. But as easy as is to distribute books electronically, it is harder for publishers to guard against piracy. Greco (2004) noted that the success of e-books is at least a decade away and that technology has its limits.

### Online Printing

Rather than try to keep a wide selection of books in stock, retailers could provide electronic copies to customers. Assuming a reliable encryption scheme, books could be read on electronic devices, even cell phones or laptop computers. Bookstores could cut their inventory to just one hardcopy of every available title.

### Printing on Demand

Another option is to print books in the store on demand. For $200,000 a high-speed, high-quality printer could produce an attractive bound book in under an hour, similar to 1-hour photo labs. The high cost of the printers would be offset by the reduced costs in inventory and shipping.

### Online Book Sales

Once books are in print, the retailing function is influenced by e-commerce sites (e.g., Amazon.com). Booksellers like Barnes & Noble or Waldenbooks see competition from online book sales. Greco (2004) described the competition as intense, not just for distributors and retailers, but for the publishers themselves.

## FILM: THREATS

The main threats to the film industry are copyright protection, VOD, and the rise of home theater systems. The first threat is real and also applies to other video industries. The second threat is more subtle because the movie industry will still produce content that is feature-length and high-cost, what most people conceive as a movie or film. But as movies become less of an out-of-home phenomenon, the identity of the film industry will suffer. People will still look on movie attendance as a social outing, but the number of theatrical releases may decline. The trend according to the Motion Picture Association of America (2003) shows an 8.3% decline in the number of films released each year in the United States, from 509 in 1998 to 467 in 2002.

### Copyright Issues

Once a film becomes a stream of digital bits, it can be copied from DVDs (with the help of readily available decryption keys posted on the Internet) or digitized from stolen prints.

Once a movie becomes a computer file, pirates can share the content with anyone in the world, much like MP3 music files but with an immensely greater file size and download time. The Motion Picture Association of America (MPAA) estimates that piracy costs the film industry $3.5 billion a year, with 350 thousand to 400 thousand films illegally swapped on the Internet each day (Graser, 2003).

Fortunately for Hollywood, downloaded files are most frequently those media that enjoy repeated play, such as video games and songs ripped from CDs, rather than movies. Films are less likely to be played again and again, and therfore, obtaining a free copy is less attractive to the consumer. The cost in time and effort to steal an entire feature film is greater than buying a legal copy, in the event that someone wants an archival file to enjoy multiple times. Still, the cost of DVD burners is under $200, compared with $3,000 in 2001 and will likely become standard equipment on many desktop computers (Graser, 2003).

## Video-on-Demand

VOD is an exhibition window for theatrical films that comes long after the Cineplex and the video rental store. Yet, the marketing of subscription video-on-demand (SVOD) overcomes some consumer resistance by bridging the pay-per-view concept and the premium channel (pay-per-month) concept. According to one industry enthusiast, "By reinforcing the benefits of the subscription business model and emphasizing that there is no payment for each use and no separate purchase decision by the consumer, psychological hurdles are removed" (Starz Encore Group, 2003).

The film industry has yet to discover if more profits can be achieved by releasing VOD movies earlier, immediately following (or instead of) theatrical release. As discussed earlier, the diffusion of in-home theater projection systems may eventually prove a threat. One wonders if someone with a video system with surround sound and a 50-inch high-definition picture will still be willing to pay box office prices to see new releases. Perhaps movie studios will alter the release window schedule to benefit the high-tech user.

No one is predicting the demise of big screen theaters. The social opportunity for young people is not easily substituted by other media distribution. However, the future of video rental stores is far less certain. To the extent that the film industry competes with video rentals, alternative distribution is a threat. But it can also be a huge opportunity.

## FILM: OPPORTUNITIES

If content is king, then the relationship between co-owned studios and networks should eventually favor the producers. With new technologies, the old triumvirate of production, distribution, and exhibition is being broken down. The exhibition function is becoming less meaningful, especially in filmed entertainment, as consolidation and technology tighten their grip. Hollywood unions like the Writers Guild of America (WGA) foresee the demise of the license-based residual system, if content is simply placed on a giant video server for audiences to retrieve using broadband or fiber delivery, according to WGA East President, Mona Mangan (personal communication, January 7, 2004).

Whatever labor sees as a threat, management may see as an opportunity. Strategic alliances and mergers have always been a huge opportunity for the film industry. The sale of Vivendi-Universal to General Electric (GE) subsidiary NBC is hailed as a way to repurpose thousands of hours of filmed entertainment. The film libraries of major studios have always had high value, but extracting the value was a problem because of the shelf space of channels and the ability of content packagers to schedule the material. When the audience can pay a single subscription fee, a kind of library card, the value is easier to realize.

Even if the SVOD model fails to capture the fancy of viewers everywhere, the incredible success of sell-through DVDs in 2002 and 2003 is making the video rental industry nervous. According to Amdur (2004), "services such as Netflix, as well as deep sell-through discounting at Wal-Mart and other mass-market retailers, may be stealing some of the traffic [from video rental stores]" (¶ 4). Blockbuster insists that the movie industry is beholden to the video window opening before the VOD window, owing to $12 billion in gross profits from home video and DVD, far greater than the $500 million generated by pay-per-view and VOD.

## RECORDING INDUSTRY: THREATS

The main threat to the recording industry is not some wolf at the door, but one already roaming the hallways: peer-to-peer file sharing. Although Napster has been neutered, off-shore services like Kazaa still provide the means for music lovers to download copyrighted materials without paying anyone. As a result, recording studios and retailers alike are reeling from the losses.

This threat is not without its critics, because it is not reasonable to assume that everyone is a thief. Indeed, economist Stan Leibowitz argued that the recording industry is not suffering as much as the RIAA would have the public believe. The losses, he claimed, are substantially less than what one should expect. Leibowitz attributed the stability of sales to basic honesty among CD buyers, "It's not that say, 10 percent of record sales is a trivial amount of money, but it's not going to be the death of the record industry" (Cave, 2002, ¶ 13).

## RECORDING INDUSTRY: OPPORTUNITIES

The main opportunity for the recording industry lies in Internet-based digital music delivery systems. For example, record companies can join forces with the digital music services that are selling songs for 88 cents (Wal-mart) to 99 cents (Apple's iTunes). Another opportunity may be the continued cross-promotion of music-related media products.

The recording industry is beginning to recognize that its original retail chain is not the only way to make money. Rack jobbers (who supply CDs to mass retailers) will still provide a convenient outlet for the casual buyer of music, but legal music downloads and digital rights management (DRM) are becoming the means to keep the industry healthy. Leibowitz argues that the consumer is willing to pay for the convenience, "It may be the cost of putting these collections of songs together. Even though it seems low, it's more effort than the typical person is willing to go through. That may be what the salvation of the record industry is—that it's simply too hard to do on your own what they do for you" (Cave, 2002, ¶ 18).

## SYNTHESIS

Media managers have a lot more in common than what the foregoing discussion implies. As media converge and ownership consolidates, the issues look the same except from the functional level. Ferguson (1997) identified some unique concerns facing media managers in a global sense (e.g., operating in a fishbowl of public attention).

Lavine and Wackman (1988) foresaw five primary management issues of the 1990s and the new millennium: increasing competition, rising fragmentation, human productivity, technology as a change agent, and increasing ownership concentration. The foregoing discussion of industry-specific issues includes three of the five; productivity and concentration are concerns common to all. Competition is felt the most by media industries that were functionally unique (broadcast television, multichannel television, and newspapers), but shared by the rest to varying degrees. Fragmentation is a common problem for today's media, largely owing to the tremendous change brought about by new media (e.g., the Internet) and by new technologies (e.g., compressed digital media).

Turow (2003) identified six trends for the new millennium: media fragmentation, audience segmentation, distribution of products across media boundaries, globalization, conglomeration, and digital convergence. Audience segmentation, or targeting, is more important for radio and magazines than broadcast television and newspapers, but some degree of segmentation is important to all media. Media managers will need to treat segmentation as a separate issue. Globalization of media is increasingly important to all as a means of finding new markets for media products whose value is diminished by fragmentation and segmentation.

From the preceding industry-specific analysis, I can posit 10 enduring themes that emerge within and across the various media. These management issues can be clustered in at least ten areas that fall into four broad categories of issues, related to the resources of the sender, the technology, the demands of the receiver, and regulation. All of the clusters are discussed in the following with regard to what we already know and what managers need to understand and learn about the possible scenarios.

### Consolidation

With the exception of cable (Higgins, 2003b), all media continue to move to a smaller number of dominant corporations. The number of individual radio station owners is the most dramatic example, falling 24% from 5,222 in 1995 (before the Telecommunications Act of 1996) to 3,829 by the end of 1999 (Corporation for Public Broadcasting, 2001).

Clustered media ownership is becoming prevalent in the newspaper industry. According to Martin (2003), one third of all United States dailies are part of a cluster. Clustered newspapers tend to compete less aggressively, and they have higher advertising and subscription prices than nonclustered papers. Radio also does clusters and cable interconnects are based on clusters.

### Competition

Competition is a key macro-level variable for all media industries (Albarran, 2002). The four types are monopoly, oligopoly, monopolistic competition, and perfect competition.

These categories fit the media in clear patterns: cable and most local newspapers have monopoly structure; broadcast networks and stations operate as an oligopoly; radio and magazines exist in monopolistic competition; and the Internet approximates perfect competition because it has few, if any, barriers to entry. The greater opportunities depend on whether the media product comes from an established company or a newcomer. Perfect competition favors the latter and monopoly favors the former. Although a barrier to entry is an important element of market structure, economies of scale and scope protect the largest and most vertically integrated firms. Nevertheless, all media managers must differentiate their products to survive.

## Convergence

Mermigas (2003b) wrote that there is a lot of fear among the mature media industries, and for good reason. A key management issue will be how to combat slow (or no) growth. Being big enough to compete with the other giant corporations is crucial, but not becoming the next AOL Time Warner is equally important.

## Digital Conversion

Managers in all the media industries must contend with offering their content online. For some, it is a matter of keeping up with the competition and trying to grow new revenue streams. For others, the goal is to build a new business model that takes advantage of the 24/7 nature of information in the digital age. Deadline pressures, for example, are entirely different for media that offer information continuously. Interactive advertising opportunities are redefining the nature of the media. Managers must focus on the basic function of their particular medium rather than the discrete product it was before the digital age. Change is coming fast, and no one really knows what the media landscape will look like in 10 years, or even 5. Apparently, media use in the home will be very different as broadband connections become ubiquitous and high-tech devices become cheaper. Microsoft and others are shifting their focus away from the home office and into the living room, a trend that promises more change in the immediate future.

Digital rights management (DRM) portends to be a sea change for media audiences and media managers alike. DRM models allow content to be sold for a specific period of time, like a subscription. In the music industry, a lifetime license to a particular song can now be bought for under a dollar, but the term could just as easily be 3 months. The listener would receive a digital key that would unlock an encrypted file, but the key could be made to expire after awhile (offering an opportunity for renewal or conversion to lifetime access). Some unusual promotion opportunities also exist. For example, licensed users could be permitted to share brief, unencrypted portions of the content with their friends and be paid a bounty if the friend purchases a license.

Digital conversion is especially an issue for managers whose digital media content is provided free to the audience in anticipation that advertisers will pay the freight. Pop-up ad blockers and DVRs are effective ways for the audience to skip commercial messages.

The implication for managers is how to carefully gauge the demand for products. In the case of music, consumers will want the flexibility to listen again and again. Conversely, in the case of movies, the demand for repeat showings is less important.

## Piracy

Although piracy is primarily an issue to media that get repeated play (e.g., music), theft has always been an issue to media managers. Digitization has exacerbated the problem and further expanded the definition of intellectual property. Encryption schemes are frequently thwarted by hackers, who believe that all data (copyrighted or not) should be free. Once the decryption codes are posted on the World Wide Web, the battle is lost (Kerschbaumer, 2001). Piracy is particularly dangerous for media that are easily rendered (e.g., books) versus those with greater complexity (e.g., video).

## Asynchronous Viewing

Per-use pricing causes managers who have been focused on advertising support, even among subscription-supported media, to think differently about the audience. Indeed, the broadcast and multichannel television scheduling function is subverted when viewers empowered by DVRs or SVOD eventually choose their content from a menu, or choose their channels a la carte (Eastman & Ferguson, 2002). Books and music have always been an asynchronous experience, but radio and video can expect more discontinuous change, especially when the product relies on an advertising revenue stream.

## Automation

Technology-driven tactics like radio voice tracking and broadcast television centralcasting will continue to be important opportunities for media managers. As in most businesses, personnel costs are substantial for all media. Labor-saving methods help cut these expenses. Menu-driven, server-based distribution of video content may take the food analogy (Eastman & Ferguson, 2002) a step further: Like fast-food restaurants that moved the soft-drink dispenser from behind the counter out into dining areas where customers pour their own, video channels can move their schedule-based content from behind the network curtain of program scheduling out into the living room, where viewers can choose their own shows from a menu. In choosing their channels or restaurants, consumers can opt for self-service or full-service, depending on the situation.

## Demassification

One measure of advertiser-supported media is how efficiently it reaches a mass (albeit targeted) audience. As audiences become demassified, media managers must contend with increasingly fragmented audiences. To make matters worse, some functions within the media become less crucial (e.g., the program scheduling function), requiring different strategies and a realignment of talent. Ultimately, the media become more product driven than service driven in the age of disintermediation (where middlemen are less necessary).

## Audience Measurement

Another consequence of audience fragmentation is the increased cost and complexity of audience measurement. The portable people meter is a necessary solution, but an expensive one. If Nielsen Media Research, for example, moves from a national people meter sample of 5,000 homes to 10,000 homes (as it did in 2003) to keep up with smaller and smaller audiences, broadcast television managers must find a way to pay more for essentially the same service and make the declining ratings sufficiently attractive to advertisers. Perhaps measuring audiences for advertisers will be less important in media that are forced by technology (and new opportunities) to rely less on advertising.

## Regulation

Regardless of the medium, managers need to be wary of legal and regulatory problems. Less a problem for the entertainment media, the information media continue to guard against liabilities brought on by libel and newsroom diversity. All media managers must be wary of litigation (e.g., harassment) in some form. The complexity of contracts and union negotiations challenges all media managers in a world with more interlocking alliances among content owners and producers.

Finally, all the technology in the world is powerless against the will (and whim) of government regulators. A case in point is the opportunity of VoIP. The promise of yet another revenue stream for cable can be quickly undone if the government decides the threats to tax revenue or subsidized 911 service are reasons to restrict VoIP, or remove its competitive advantage. Anyone wistful for advertising-supported media might welcome government protection for disadvantaged audiences that may rely on free over-the-air channels, by requiring DVRs to limit or prevent ad skipping. A different FCC could decide that pay-per-view or viewing empowerment must not threaten the status quo. A different Justice Department or Supreme Court could break up the media conglomerates as easily as with the 1948 Paramount case or the 1984 AT&T divestiture.

Any one of these 10 issues is cause for concern among media managers, but they must contend with all of them to varying degrees. The challenges get greater with each new innovation and with every ownership consolidation. However, as Mermigas (2004) wrote: "Too many media companies and executives are content with simply acknowledging or dismissing the threat and challenge of VOD, PVR, intellectual property piracy, commercial ad skipping and anything else that smacks of a new competitive landscape that further fragments and even alienates viewers and advertisers" (¶ 23).

## REFERENCES

Albarran, A. B. (2002). *Media economics: Understanding markets, industries and concepts* (2nd ed.). Ames: Iowa State Press.
Albarran, A. B. (2004). The economics of the contemporary radio industry. In A. Alexander, J. Owers, R. Carveth, A. Hollifield, & A. Greco (Eds.), *Media economics: Theory and practice* (3rd ed., pp. 207–220). Mahwah, NJ: Lawrence Erlbaum Associates.

Amdur, M. (2004, January 6). Vidstore shares fall as DVD sales bite biz. *Variety.* Retrieved February 21, 2005, from http://www.variety.com/article/VR1117897892

Carter, B. (2004, June 29). At Fox, reality robbery mastermind or just playing the game? *New York Times.* Retrieved February 21, 2005, http://www.nytimes.com/2004/06/29/arts/television/29FOX.html

Cave, D. (2002, June 13). *File sharing: Innocent until proven guilty.* Retrieved February 21, 2005, from http://www.salon.com/tech/feature/2002/06/13/liebowitz/index.html.

Chan-Olmsted, S. M., & Ha, L. (2003). Internet business models for broadcasters: How television stations perceive and integrate the Internet. *Journal of Broadcasting & Electronic Media, 47*(4), 597–617.

Chan-Olmstead, S., & Kang, J-W. (2003). Theorizing the strategic architecture of a broadband television industry. *Journal of Media Economics, 16*(1), 3–21.

Chmielewski, D. C. (2003, January 30). The Net is cutting into TV time, study finds. *Mercury News.* Retrieved February 21, 2005, from http://www.siliconvalley.com/mld/siliconvalley/5071191.htm

Christie, E., Di Senso, P., Gold, M., & Rader, D. (2000, March). Print versus electronic media: The threat to newspapers and newsprint. *Digital Futures.* Retrieved February 21, 2005, from http://www.sric-bi.com/DF/oldMFsummaries/PrintToC.shtml

Chyi, H. I., & Lasorsa, D. L. (2002). An explorative study on the market relation between online and print newspapers. *Journal of Media Economics, 15*(2), 91–107.

Claybaugh, J. (2002, July 1). XM satellite radio "on track." *Washington Business Journal.* Retrieved February 21, 2005, from http://www.bizjournals.com/washington/stories/2002/07/01/daily1.html

Corporation for Public Broadcasting. (2001). CPB scan. Retrieved February 21, 2005, from http://stations.cpb.org/pdfs/radio/2001/aimhigher/cpb-scan.pdf

Daly, C. P., Henry, P., & Ryder, E. (1997). *The magazine publishing industry.* Boston: Allyn & Bacon.

Dempsey, J. (2003, December 5). Cable overtakes b'cast nets. *Variety.* Retrieved February 21, 2005, from http://www.variety.com/article/VR1117896663

Downey, K. (2001, June 21). Cable fast overtaking broadcast networks. *Media Life.* Retrieved February 21, 2005, from http://www.medialifemagazine.com/news2001/june01/june18/4_thurs/news1thursday.html

Eastman, S. T., & Ferguson, D. A. (2002). *Broadcast/cable/web programming: Strategies and practices* (6th ed.). Belmont, CA: Wadsworth.

Eggerton, J., & Kerschbaumer, K. (2003, December 8). *Broadcasting & Cable.* Retrieved February 21, 2005, from http://www.broadcastingcable.com/article/CA340330

Fadner, R. (2004, January 9). Giving new meaning to "rich" media, broadband achieves critical mass among affluent users. *Media Daily News..* Retrieved February 21, 2005, from http://publications.com/index.cfm?fuseaction=articles.showarticle&art_aid=6501

Ferguson, D. A. (1997). The domain of inquiry for media management researchers. *Media Management Review, 1,* 177–184.

Ferguson, D. A. (1998). The economics of broadcast television. In J. R. Walker & D. A. Ferguson (Eds.), *The broadcast television industry* (pp. 42–63). Boston: Allyn & Bacon.

Ferguson, D. A. (2003). The broadcast television networks. In A. Alexander, J. Owers, R. Carveth, A. Hollifield, & A. Greco (Eds.), *Media economics: Theory and practice* (3rd ed., pp. 149–171). Mahwah, NJ: Lawrence Erlbaum Associates.

Friedman, R. (2003). *The hidden and dangerous new threat to television news.* Retrieved February 21, 2005, from http://www.haleisner.com/from_field/ftfrickfriedman.htm

Fybush, S. (2003). MP3: Why radio should care. Retrieved April 15, 2004, from http://www.rwonline.com/reference-room/special-report/rwx-mp3.shtml

G2 News. (2003, January 4). Clear Channel radio network fighting pirates too. *The OnlineReporter.* Retrieved February 21, 2005, from http://www.onlinereporter.com/torbackissues/TOR329.htm#13

Gough, P. (2003a, October 17). The nation's top-ranked online newspaper site continued to fly high in the third quarter. *Media Daily News.* Retrieved February 21, 2005, from http://www.mediapost.com/dtls_dsp_onlineminute.cfm?fnl=031017

Gough, P. (2003b, November 7). XM: Satellite radio pace accelerates, surpasses PVRs. *Media Daily News.* Retrieved February 21, 2005, from http://publications.mediapost.com/index.cfm?fuseaction=articles.showarticle&art_aid=17761

Graser, M. (2003, December 7). Coming DVD recorders will speed copying. *Variety*. Retrieved April 15, 2004, from http://www.variety.com/ev_article/VR1117896688

Graybow, M. (2003, October 16). Tribune, NY Times earns slip as newsprint costs rise. *Forbes*. Retrieved February 21, 2005, from http://www.forbes.com/business/newswire/2003/10/16/rtr1111934.html

Greco, A. N. (2004). The economics of books and magazines. In A. Alexander, J. Owers, R. Carveth, A. Hollifield, & A. Greco (Eds.), *Media economics: Theory and practice* (3rd ed., pp. 127–147). Mahwah, NJ: Lawrence Erlbaum Associates.

Haley, K. (2003, November 24). New strategies target faster growth for '04. *Broadcasting & Cable*. Retrieved February 21, 2005, from http://www.broadcastingcable.com/article/CA337601

Hazlett, T. (2001, November). *The U.S. digital TV transition: Time to toss the Negroponte switch.* (Working Paper 01-15). Washington, DC: AEI-Brookings Joint Center for Regulatory Studies. Retrieved February 21, 2005, from http://www.aei.brookings.org/publications/working/working_01_15.pdf

Heaton, T. (2003, September 29). Technology is not the enemy. *TV News in a Postmodern World*. Retrieved February 21, 2005, from http://donatacom.com/papers/pomo5.htm

Higgins, J. M. (2003a, August 25). DBS customers happier than cable users. *Broadcasting & Cable*. Retrieved February 21, 2005, from http://www.broadcastingcable.com/article/CA318497

Higgins, J. M. (2003b, November 10). A pause in consolidation. *Broadcasting & Cable*. Retrieved February 21, 2005, from http://www.broadcastingcable.com/article/CA334596

Higgins, J, M, (2003c, December 22). Fast forward. *Broadcasting & Cable, 133*(51), 1, 22.

Higgins, J. M. (2004a, January 5). Cable cash flow flows. *Broadcasting & Cable, 134*(1), 33.

Higgins, J. M. (2004b, January 5). TiVo's got a gun. *Broadcasting & Cable, 134*(1), 32.

Jankowski, G. F., & Fuchs, D. C. (1995). *Television today and tomorrow.* New York: Oxford University Press.

Jessell, H. A. (2004, January 5). Dotcom redux. *Broadcasting & Cable, 134*(1), 32.

Kagan, P. (2003). *Radio financial databook 2003.* Retrieved February 21, 2005, from http://www.kagan.com/cgi-bin/pkcat/rfd03_toc.html

Karrfalt, W. (2003, November 24). Local people meters, headed for more cities, have changed the game in Boston. *Broadcasting & Cable*. Retrieved February 21, 2005, from http://www.broadcastingcable.com/article/CA337604

Kerschbaumer, K. (2001, January 29). Get serious about piracy. *Broadcasting & Cable*. Retrieved February 21, 2005, from http://www.broadcastingcable.com/article/CA61197

Knowledge Networks, Inc. (2004, June 30). 2004 ownership and trend report. In *The Home Technology Monitor* (pp. 1–20). Cranford, NJ: Author.

Lacy, S., Coulson, D. C., & Cho, H. (2002). Competition for readers among U.S. metropolitan, nonmetropolitan, daily, and weekly newspapers. *Journal of Media Economics, 15*(1), 21–40.

Lafayette, J. (2004). ABC makes the case for broadcast. *TV Week*. Retrieved April 15, 2004, from http://www.tvweek.com/topstorys/011204abc.html

Lavine, J. M., & Wackman, D. B. (1988). *Managing media organizations: Effective leadership of the media.* New York: Longman.

Lagorce, A. (2003, October 15). Magazines turn to TV for inspiration. *Forbes*. Retrieved February 21, 2005, from http://www.forbes.com/home_europe/2003/10/15/cx_al_1015magazines.html

Martin, H. J. (2003, August). *Some effects from horizontal integration of daily newspapers on markets, prices, and competition.* Paper presented at the annual meeting of the Association for Education in Journalism and Mass Communication, Kansas City.

Mandese, J. (2004, July 1). Universe collapses: Well, TV's, anyway. *MediaDailyNews*. Retrieved April 15, 2004, from http://www.mediapost.com/dtls_dsp_news.cfm?newsID=257842

McCarthy, M. (2003, October 26). "24" includes 6-minute film-ercial. *USA Today*. Retrieved February 21, 2005, from http://www.usatoday.com/money/advertising/2003-10-26-ford_x.htm

McClellan, S. (2003a, September 29). Will TiVo kill television, or are viewers too lazy to zap? *Broadcasting & Cable*. Retrieved February 21, 2005, from http://www.broadcastingcable.com/article/CA325815

McClellan, S. (2003b, October 27). The venerable AP is mulling new Curley cues. *Broadcasting & Cable*. Retrieved February 21, 2005, from http://www.broadcastingcable.com/article/CA331482

McConnell, B. (2003, December 31). Former FCC chief touts "big broadband." *Broadcasting & Cable*. Retrieved February 21, 2005, from http://www.broadcastingcable.com/article/CA372489

Mermigas, D. (2003a, September 22). Television ad model under pressure on two fronts. *TV Week*. Retrieved April 15, 2004, from http://www.tvweek.com/deals/092203dicolumn.html

Mermigas, D. (2003b, October 20). A flurry of media deals ahead. *TV Week*. Retrieved April 5, 2004, from http://www.tvweek.com/deals/102003dicolumn.html

Mermigas, D. (2003c, December 1). Cable faces multiple challenges. *TV Week*. Retrieved February 21, 2005, from http://www.tvweek.com/article.cms?articleid=21034

Mermigas, D. (2004, January 12). A wake-up call for old-line media. *TV Week*. Retrieved February 21, 2005, from http://www.tvweek.com/article.cms?articleid=18023

Motion Picture Association of America (2003). *U.S. entertainment industry: 2002 MPA market statistics*. Retrieved April 15, 2004, from http://www.mpaa.org/useconomicreview/2002/2002_Economic_Review.pdf

National Association of Broadcasters. (2003). Internet streaming issues. Retrieved April 15, 2004, from http://www.nab.org/Newsroom/Issues/issuepapers/streamingissues.pdf

National Cable Television Association. (2003). *2003 year-end industry overview*. Retrieved April 15, 2004, from http://www.ncta.com/pdf_files/Overview.pdf

Newspaper Association of America. (2003). Scarborough circulation data. Retrieved April 15, 2004, from http://www.naa.org/artpage.cfm?AID=1614&SID=1022

Picard, R. G. (2004). The economics of the daily newspaper industry. In A. Alexander, J. Owers, R. Carveth, A. Hollifield, & A. Greco (Eds.), *Media economics: Theory and practice* (3rd ed., pp. 109–125). Mahwah, NJ: Lawrence Erlbaum Associates.

Picard, R. G., & Brody, J. H. (1997). *The newspaper publishing industry*. Boston: Allyn & Bacon.

Powers, A. (2001). Toward monopolistic competition in U.S. local television news. *Journal of Media Economics, 14*(2), 77–87.

Radio Advertising Bureau. (2003a). Report reveals shift in retail environment—Independent merchants give way to national chains. Retrieved February 21, 2005, from http://www.rab.com/newrst/article_view.cfm?id=348&type=article3

Radio Advertising Bureau (2003b, March 14). RAB archives. Retrieved April 15, 2004, from http://www.rab.com

Rawlins, G. J. E. (1998, July 25). The new publishing: Technology's impact on the publishing industry over the next decade. Retrieved February 15, 2005, from http://www.roxie.org/papers/publishing/pub.ascii

Rhodes, B. E. (2003). [untitled]. Retrieved November 2, 2004, from http://digitaldeliverance.8k.com

Rizzuto, R. J., & Wirth, M. O. (2002). The economics of video on demand: A simulation analysis. *Journal of Media Economics, 15*(3), 209–226.

Shields, T. (2004, January 15). FCC: Satellite gaining on cable. *Mediaweek*. Retrieved April 15, 2004, from http://www.mediaweek.com/mediaweek/headlines/article_display.jsp?vnu_content_id=2071038

Slattery, K. L., Hakanen, E. A., & Doremus, M. E. (1996). The expression of localism: Local TV news coverage in the new video marketplace. *Journal of Broadcasting & Electronic Media, 40*(3), 403–413.

Starz Encore Group's Clasen calls 'brand transformation' of linear pay television and subscription VOD key to unlocking economic potential of on-demand platform (2003, October 1). *PR Newswire*. Retrieved April 15, 2004, from http://www.prnewswire.com

Terry, C. (1996). Reading the signs. Retrieved February 21, 2005, from http://www.naa.org/presstime/96/PTIME/p996lit.html

Turow, J. (2003). *Media today: An introduction to mass communication* (2nd ed.). Boston: Houghton Mifflin.

Web Site Optimization. (2003). *Home connectivity in the U.S.* Retrieved February 21, 2005, from www.websiteoptimization.com/bw/0312/

# 15

# Issues in Market Structure

**Hans van Kranenburg**
University of Maastricht

**Annelies Hogenbirk**
Rabobank Nederland

How do media firms and the market structure of media industries change over time? This is the central question in this chapter. When media industries are new, in the introduction stage of their life cycle, a lot of entry takes place, firms offer many different versions of the industry's product, the rate of product innovation is high, and market shares change rapidly. Over time, competition increases because of the large possible profits in the industry. The industry's output expands and the price decreases. When a dominant product design is accepted and production becomes standardized, the industry's firms generally have to become more price and cost conscious. As a consequence, the innovative activities of many firms gradually shift from product to process innovations. The emergence of economies of scale in production, sales, and R&D result in a sharp increase in market concentration. Firms that cannot keep up with the changes go bankrupt. Over their evolution many media industries may, therefore, experience a shake-out period during which the number of firms declines strongly. The industry then reaches maturity, a stage where new entry is difficult resulting in a relatively stable competitive environment. The remaining firms make high profits and reach most interested customers. Hence, the character of industries evolves over time, hand-in-hand with the changes in market structure. The process by which this co-evolution occurs involves a selection between different firms, which have different ideas, that are embodied in the different products and services that they offer (see Geroski, 1991, p. 264).

This chapter presents a number of theories that explain the evolution of media industries. We discuss the generic factors that help explain the entry, exit, and survival chances of firms in media industries. We consider both new entrants and incumbent firms and the effect of their behavior on the existing market structure. We illustrate the theoretical viewpoints with many examples from media industries. We start off with a brief explanation of the industry life cycle and some overall characteristics of the media industries. After that, we present the ideas of two groups of economic theories of organizational behavior that focus on understanding the dynamics of industrial evolution: organizational ecology (OE) and industrial organization (IO). Broadly speaking, organizational ecologists look for universal similarities, whereas IO scholars focus on the differences between and within industries. Both perspectives are, therefore, useful when trying to understand the dynamics in media industries. Based on the developed understanding, we discuss the implications of the developments and features on the media industries, and we also provide directions for further research.

## INDUSTRY LIFE CYCLE OF MEDIA INDUSTRIES

Media industries, like most industries, usually evolve along a general path from birth/introduction, growth, and shake-out to maturity and eventually to decline. As an industry experiences these successive stages, changes in sales, costs, consumers, profits, and competition occur. These changes are common to all industries. Knowing the position of an industry in the industry life cycle helps to understand the dynamics of market structure and the entry, exit, and survival patterns of firms. Table 15.1 presents some major developments in different stages of media industry life cycles.

The initial phase is characterized by a low output volume at high costs. Profits are negative because of low sales to customers that are characterized as innovators. Furthermore, a high degree of uncertainty exists, because the potential market is not clear and predictions on the potential success vary widely. An important example is the online video business.

The succeeding stage shows a swift entry of new firms that are attracted by the rapidly expanding sales and rising profits in the industry. The relevant market becomes clear, uncertainty gradually declines, and product designs proliferate and become standardized. Output grows rapidly in response to newly recognized product designs and unsatisfied market demands from early adopters. In this stage, the industry's firms generally have to become more price and cost conscious, resulting in a shift from product to process innovations. Media industries in this growth stage are satellite television, online media, and multimedia.

Firms that cannot keep up with the changes go bankrupt, resulting in a shake-out period where the number of firms active in the industry decreases substantially. Then a peak is reached in the sales volume, when the industry reaches maturity. Profits are still high because the mature media market continues to grow, but does so at a more regular and predictable rate. The media products or services are well known to both customers and suppliers. Market shares are changing slowly and entry and exit barriers are relatively high. Most print media (books and magazines) are in this mature stage. Their industry life cycle is one of the longest known cycles of any manufacturing industry (Picard, 2002).

The next phase of the life cycle is inconclusive. The number of firms may decrease further with declining demand. This development would imply the end of the industry.

**TABLE 15.1**

Location and Characteristics in Different Phases of Media Industry Life Cycles

| Phase of Life Cycle | Characteristics of Markets | | | | | | |
| | Sales | Profits | Customers | Barriers | | Competitors | Media Industries |
| | | | | Entry | Exit | | |
| Introduction | Low | Negative | Innovators | Low | Low | Few | "Streaming" or online video |
| Growth | Rapidly rising | Rising | Early adopters | Moderate | Moderate | Growing rapidly | Satellite Television; Online Media; Multimedia |
| Maturation | Peak | High | Majority | High | High | Relatively Stable and at Late Stage Declining | Audio Recordings; Books; Magazines; Motion Pictures; Radio; Television; Cable Television; Recorded Video |
| Decline | Declining | Declining | Laggards | High | High | Declining | Newspapers |

*Note:* From *The Economics and Financing of Media Companies* (pp. 24–25), by R. G. Picard, 2002, New York: Fordham University Press. Copyright 2002 by R. G. Picard. Adapted with permission.

Among all media industries, the newspaper industry is nearing decline because audiences and advertisers are becoming familiar and comfortable with newer information and communications technology. Because the history of newspapers is very well documented and long, newspapers have been part of our lives for more than 300 years, its history contributed significantly to the development of the media life cycle theory. Therefore, this industry is frequently cited as exemplifying the media life cycle.

The evolution of the daily newspaper industry in The Netherlands shows the existence of the industry life cycle. The initial phase begins with the introduction of the first daily newspaper in 1618 and ends in 1848, when 30 newspapers are printed. In 1848, freedom of the press was incorporated into the new Constitution of the Netherlands, marking the beginning of the growth period. The second phase is characterized by a period of sharp increase with an exceptional expansion in the number of newspapers in the period after 1869. In 1869 the Dutch government repealed the special tax system for newspapers, known as *Dagbladzegel*. The abolition of this tax system stimulated economic activity for the newspaper publishing companies. The costs for a publishing company to produce a newspaper decreased enormously with the abolition decision of the government. This abolition not only provided an economic incentive to increase the circulation of the incumbent newspapers, it also boosted the potential profits and consequently survival probabilities for the incumbents as well as for potential entrants (Pfann & Kranenburg, 2003). This is illustrated in Fig. 15.1.

The mature phase can be split into two subphases. The first is characterized by a net entry of approximately zero, and corresponds to the period 1900 to 1939. In the post-World War II period, the number of daily newspapers in The Netherlands experienced a continuous decline that coincided with an increase in total circulation (see Fig. 15.1). After World War II, the scale of production enlarged significantly, possibly because of technological innovations. Evidence of increasing scale economies is also found in other country's newspaper industries such as in Argentina, Denmark, Ireland, and the United

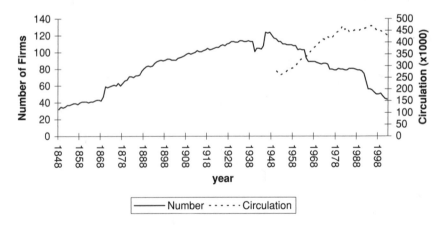

FIG. 15.1.   Life cycle of the daily newspaper industry in The Netherlands. From "The Life Cycle of Daily Newspapers in The Netherlands: 1848–1997," by H. L. van Kranenburg, F. C. Palm, and G. A. Pfann, 1998, *De Economist, 146*, p. 483. Copyright 1998 by Kluwer Academic Publishers. Reprinted with permision.

States (see Carroll, 1987; Gustafsson, 1993; Rosse, 1967; Sollinge, 1999). The declining stage for the newspaper industry in The Netherlands starts with the decrease in aggregated circulation in 1999 and continues to the present.

However, unlike perhaps in the case of the newspaper industry, maturity does not have to end in decline. Entry may also cease and the number of firms may stabilize until new developments significantly alter the evolution of the industry. An industry may even demonstrate a revival. A revival can occur when the established incumbents are successfully challenged by other firms, in particular the later entrants. These challenges are generally based on product and process innovations. An example of an industry that showed such a revival was the U.S. television manufacturing industry (Klepper & Simons, 2000). The demand for black and white televisions was declining for a few years in the 1970s as the market became saturated. The industry revived with the introduction of color television. New competition came mainly from Asian firms. The U.K. television industry also showed a revival in the last 2 decades. Twenty years ago, integration of a wide range of staff and production facilities under a single monolithic firm umbrella was the norm. Because of global forces and government interventions, the incumbents, among them British Broadcasting Corporation (BBC) and Independent TV (ITV), have to source at least 25% of their programming from independent producers. As a result, the number of listed independent producers in the United Kingdom has increased from a handful of firms in the late 1970s to around, 1,000 firms commercially active in the production of all genres of first-run television programming (Starkey, Barnatt, & Tempest, 2000).

The first stages of the media industry life cycle concept are closely related to the product life cycle. The four stages of the two cycles are introduction, growth, maturity, and decline (Gort & Klepper, 1982; Kuznets, 1930; Vernon, 1966). These concepts develop simultaneously. However, a media product or product group may have its own life cycle within a broadly defined market, as the example of televisions programs. The evolution of mature media industries may, therefore, significantly depart from the product life cycle.

Scholars in different disciplines have studied firm behavior and developments in markets over the industry life cycle. The most relevant research fields are organizational ecology (OE) and industrial organization (IO). OE is a relatively new strand of organization studies that over the last 30 years focused on the development of populations of organizational forms over time. Contrary to the IO scholars, OE focuses on the interaction among groups, and not so much on the behavior of an individual organization. IO has studied the development of market structures in specific industries for more than a century, emphasizing the particular conduct and performance of individual firms. These complementary theories are discussed in the remainder of this chapter.

## ORGANIZATIONAL ECOLOGY

Organizational ecology is a sociology-based approach that studies the evolution of industries (see e.g., Carroll, 1987, 1997; Hannan & Freeman, 1989). OE attempts to explain why so many different kinds of organizations exist. OE, therefore, offers an interesting perspective to analyze the dynamics of specific organizations that are tied to their membership in a particular industry (organizational populations). Two perspectives of the organizational ecology literature are relevant to media industries: density dependence and resource partitioning.

## Density Dependence Model

One of the important research areas in organizational ecology concerns the study of vital rates such as the entry and exit rates of organizations in a particular industry. These rates are strongly influenced by environmental forces, embodied in the number of firms (density) operating in any industry. This relationship is formulated in the density dependence model of competition and legitimation that refers to the status of an organizational form as a taken-for-granted feature of the society (Hannan & Carroll, 1992). Density dependence is defined as the effect of the number of organizations (density) on entry, exit, or survival processes of firms in industries. The effect of the number of firms on legitimation, competition, and entry and exit rates changes systematically as the industry ages (see Carroll, 1997; Hannan, 1997; Hannan & Freeman, 1977). According to the density dependence model, entry of media firms is an inversed U-shaped function of the number of incumbent media firms. For instance, Kranenburg, Palm, and Pfann (1998) showed that the annual entry rate of daily newspaper firms followed an inversed U-shaped pattern. The aggregate annual number of entrants increased from the establishment of the newspaper industry in The Netherlands until the end of the 20th century. After the year 1900, the annual number of newspaper births gradually decreased.

The rate of entry is proportional to the degree to which an organizational form is legitimate and inversely proportional to the level of competition. During the introduction of a new media industry, when the number of firms is low, the entry rate is low because the organizational form is not fully legitimate. The increase in the number of firms accelerates the entry rate by increasing the form's legitimacy. When the number of incumbent firms is high, the inhibiting effects of competition prevail and the entry rate slows down. An entry into the industry is based on the scarcity of material resources for which media firms compete.

The availability of particular environmental resources influences both the expansion of the number of firms and the level of competition between firms (Hannan & Freeman, 1989). Changes in competition and environmental resources determine a ceiling on the expansion of the number of firms. This ceiling is defined as the carrying capacity of the industry (Hannan & Freeman, 1977). When the number of media firms nears the carrying capacity, the entry of a new firm greatly intensifies competition. Moreover, the number of incumbent firms and the carrying capacity of the media industry influence the entry of firms in a media market.

Organizational ecologists strongly emphasize the existence of inertia in markets. Firms are assumed to be relatively inert and unable to undertake quick reorganizations of goals, authority, technology, and market segments. This inertia is assumed to be caused by past performance and market growth, by competitive experience and the diversity of the media market environment, and by the firm's age and size (Miller & Chen, 1994). This assumption of inertia sets OE theories aside from most organizational theories that tend to assume adaptability of firms.

## Resource Partitioning Model

Resource partitioning is the strand of organizational ecology that deals with the explanations for the observed declines and renewals of organizational populations in an industry. These observations have to do with the specific resources used by the organizations, including technology and consumer base (Carroll, 1997). Resource partitioning is originally developed in the context of newspapers and publishers (Carroll, 1985). It is also used to interpret the developments in other media industries such as the book publishing and music recording industries.

The resource partitioning model investigates the competition among large generalist media firms. Competition is strongly determined by economies of scale. Scale economies operate primarily for the generalist firms. However, when markets are highly concentrated and dominated by a few generalist firms, opportunities for specialist media firms arise. Because of the development of economies of scale, more resource space is left for niche players. These specialized firms may generate enough profits to survive, although they will usually stay relatively small in size. The more resource space is available, the higher the entry and exit rates will be in a particular media industry. This process of resource partitioning generates a dual market structure. In an ongoing tendency of firms to grow in size, the intensive competition occurs in the most abundant media market segments. The surviving media firms become larger and less specialized. Firms that are established in a specialist's niche can shelter against this heavy competition, increasing their survival opportunities. Empirical studies for the newspaper industries have supported this theory (Carroll, 1985; Kranenburg, Palm, & Pfann, 2002).

These dual media market structures refer to highly concentrated media industries with, on the one hand, a group of sizeable, center media firms and, on the other hand, a group of small, periphery media firms holding only a very small market share. This dual market is illustrated for the publishing industry in The Netherlands. Table 15.2 presents an overview of the number of firms in the book and maps, papers and magazines publishing industries in The Netherlands for the period 1996 and 2002. It indicates clearly

**TABLE 15.2**
Number of Firms According to Their Size and Forms in the Dutch
Publishing Industries

| | Number of Employees in 1996 | | | | Number of Employees in 2002 | | | |
|---|---|---|---|---|---|---|---|---|
| Publishing Industry | 0–10 | 11–50 | 51–100 | Larger than 100 | 0–10 | 11–50 | 50–100 | Larger than 100 |
| Books & Maps | 960 | 75 | 10 | 10 | 1030 | 90 | 10 | 10 |
| Papers | 185 | 25 | 10 | 30 | 220 | 40 | 5 | 35 |
| Magazines | 635 | 80 | 5 | 10 | 720 | 85 | 10 | 15 |

Note:  All information retrieved from Dutch Central Bureau of Statistics (CBS): StatLine databank, January 30, 2004.

the highly disproportion number of small, in general, specialist publishing firms. What is also intriguing about these industries is that at the same time the aggregated number of firms increased in this period. In general the majority of these, in particular small, publishing firms follow a focused strategy.

Most media industries are dominated by a relatively small group of generalist firms that are very large in terms of their economic size as measured, for instance, by number of employees, total assets, and yearly sales or circulations (Averitt, 1968; Carroll, 1994; Sutton, 1992). In general, the superior financial position and their strong capabilities in production, marketing, and distribution enable large generalist media firms to quickly transform new discoveries into well-established, profitable product and to enter new related and unrelated media markets and businesses. The history of the United Kingdom's music industry provides interesting evidence of how large incumbents overcame the challenges of entrants and invested in new activities and businesses (Huygens, Baden-Fuller, van den Bosch, & Volberda, 2001). In many cases, major music companies could overcome these challenges by purchasing the small, entrepreneurial and local publishing houses. In fact, in general, mature media industries are dominated by a small group of large companies. But they contain a preponderance of small and mid-size firms whose numbers may have increased over the last few decades.

The Dutch radio and television markets illustrate resource partitioning in the media landscape. Table 15.3 shows the distribution of generalist and specialist radio stations in The Netherlands. Next to the national offer of public and commercial stations aimed at The Netherlands, the television market includes a large number of stations operating in niche market segments. Furthermore, each province has a regional public broadcasting organization with Zuid-Holland an exception with two regional stations. The dual market structure is even more visible in the radio industry. A total of 21 large national radio stations operates in the market, whereas the smaller specialist stations provide 347 programs in The Netherlands.

**TABLE 15.3**
Number of Television and Radio Stations in
The Netherlands in 2002

| Media Type | Radio Stations | Television Stations |
|---|---|---|
| National public | 6 | 3 |
| National commercial | 15 | 17 |
| Regional public | 13 | 13 |
| Non-national commercial | 47 | 18 |
| Local public | 287 | 102 |

Note: All information was taken from Dutch Media Authority: Concentration and Diversity of the Dutch Media 2002.

## INDUSTRIAL ORGANIZATION

The Industrial Organization literature has developed over more than a century. IO studies contribute significantly to the understanding of how a market works from birth to maturity, focusing on individual firm behavior and success.

## Structure-Conduct-Performance Framework

Until the 1980s, the central framework of IO studies was Structure-Conduct-Performance, introduced by Bain in 1956. The SCP framework explains the relationship between alternate forms of market structure, firms' conduct, and firms' performance. Within Bain's pioneering SCP approach, it was theorized that a one-way causation runs from structure to conduct to performance, but it turns out to overlap or to be interdependent. Many studies link structure of a market to the conduct and performance of its firms. They show that the impact of the behavior of firms depends on the market structure, referring to the number and distribution of firms in a market. The majority of these studies investigate the impact of strategic behavior of firms in the four basic forms of market structure used for decades by economists: perfect competition, monopoly, monopolistic competition, and oligopoly (see Tirole, 1990).

In the theory of perfect competition, there are many firms, each of which is small relative to the entire market. The firms have access to the same technologies and produce identical products or services. Because there is perfect information, consumers know the quality and price of each firm's product or service. Hence, in a perfectly competitive market no individual firm or customer has a perceptible impact on the market price, quantity, or quality of the product produced or service in the market. When there is only a single provider of a product or service in a relevant market, then the firm is known as a monopolist. For example, some towns have a single movie theater that serves the entire local market. In the monopolistic markets, there is a tendency for the firm to capitalize on the monopoly position by restricting output and charging a price above marginal cost. However, in a monopolistically competitive market, there are many firms and consumers, and each firm sells a product that is slightly different from the services or products produced by other firms. As a result, a firm has some control over the price charged for the product or service. By raising the price, some customers remain loyal to the firm because of preference for the particular characteristics of its product or service. For instance, the independent producers in the U.K. television industry are operating in a monopolistically competitive market. Around 1,000 firms are commercially active in the production of all genres of first-run television programming (Starkey, Barnatt, & Tempest, 2000). Each individual producer tries to produce a product that is slightly different from its competitors.

Finally, in an oligopoly market, a few large firms tend to dominate. The distinguishing feature of this market structure is mutual interdependence among firms. Firms must consider the likely impact of their decisions on the decisions of other firms in the industry. When one firm changes its conduct, other firms in the market have an incentive to react to the change by altering their own conduct. The mutual interdependence in an oligopoly gives rise to strategic interaction among firms. For instance, for many years two Australian newspapers (the *Sun* and *Daily Mirror*) dominated the newspaper market in Sydney. The newspapers competed for the same readers and were close substitutes for one another. When the price leader *Sun* announced a price change, it was matched within days by the *Daily Mirror*. Suddenly, the *Daily Mirror* decided not to follow a price increase. As a consequence, the *Daily Mirror* stole market share from *Sun* and became the price leader in Sydney's afternoon newspaper market (Merrilees, 1983).

During the last 25 years, however, the focus in IO studies has shifted away from the SCP approach to new, more theoretical approaches. New perspectives emphasize that there is considerable short-run entry and exit turnover in most industry markets, even though the long-run market structure is relatively stable (see e.g., Bresnahan & Reiss, 1987, 1990, 1993; Dunne, Roberts, & Samuelson, 1988). The entry and exit rates of firms are positively correlated, but comparisons in both expanding and declining industries reveal that they may differ substantially (e.g., Baldwin, 1995; Geroski, 1991). This can be illustrated with the data from the Dutch daily newspaper industry. The aggregate correlation between entry and exit rates over time is 0.388, whereas the correlations between entry and exit for the subperiods 1848 to 1900, 1901 to 1939, 1940 to 1945, 1946 to 1997 are 0.146, 0.164, 0.595, and 0.292 respectively. With respect to the effects of these correlations, they are positive and significant for all periods (Kranenburg, Palm, & Pfann, 1998).

## Sunk Costs and Contestability Theory

The entry and exit rates in an industry are highly affected by the existence of entry and exit barriers. The higher the entry and exit thresholds, the lower the entry or exit rates respectively. The positive correlation between entry and exit rates can be explained by the fact that exit barriers can be viewed as entry barriers. This argument is based on the observation that if a potential entrant knows that the fraction of malleability and mobility of initial capital is low, the firm would be less inclined to enter the market than if the investments are less sunk. Sunk costs, therefore, influence a firm's decision to enter or exit the market. Sunk costs are firm- or industry-specific expenditures that cannot be (fully) recovered when the activity is ended (Dixit & Pindyck, 1994; Eaton & Lipsey, 1980, 1981; Sutton, 1992).[1]

Book publishers, audio recording firms, multimedia producers, and motion picture producers face high risks each time they introduce a new book, recording, production, or film. The investments in R&D, marketing, and advertising are mainly sunk costs that have to be made, whether the book, recording, or film turns out to be successful or not. However, with media products, the content is not stable from product to product, consumer consumption patterns vary, and it is difficult to determine how audiences will receive the combination of elements in each product (Picard, 2002). Therefore, the costs occur before the success is determined and may deter new entrants from the industry. Another example is investments in cable systems. It requires large capital to develop and implement a cable system. If the industry is reasonable competitive, the value of a cable system will be about the same for all firms in the industry, so there would be little to gain

---

[1]The distinction between fixed costs and sunk costs is one of degree, not one of nature, because fixed costs are also sunk in the short run (Tirole, 1990).

from selling it (Dixit & Pindyck, 1994), and, therefore, not many new firms are interested in entering the market. If the industry is in a recession and the developed system has become a bad investment for the firm, it will also be viewed as a bad investment by the other firms, and the ability to sell the system will not be compromised. No new firms will invest in the industry.

Irreversibility of an investment can also arise because of government regulations or institutional arrangements. Regulatory forces involve approval for media operations or requirements placed on media to avoid or to behave in certain ways. Government may politically and legally intervene in creating the framework within which media firms must operate by creating and enforcing property, contracts, corporate, and other rights necessary for media markets to function. This is illustrated by radio frequency license systems. Governments provide licenses to radio stations to use radio frequencies. In general, the acquisition of a radio license is quite expensive and, therefore, deters new entrants to the industry. The system may make it impossible for a radio station to sell its license to another firm. Hence, major investments are in large part irreversible.

Under the contestability doctrine the market structure, conduct, and performance of firms have been associated with the existence of sunk costs (see Baumol & Willig, 1981; Stiglitz, 1987; Tirole, 1990). This doctrine implies that media firms may behave competitively because of the threat provided by potential entrants even when the market is characterized by a limited number of incumbents. In other words, both the number of existing firms and the potential entrants determine the force of competition. The existence of sunk costs determines the entry and exit thresholds of a market, and competitive interaction arises when sunk costs exist, particularly when sunk costs are relatively small. According to the contestability doctrine four regularities emerge from the presence of sunk costs (Stiglitz, 1987):

1. Concerning the existence of profits—entrants are not inclined to enter the market, although the incumbents show positive profits.
2. Concerning competition—entry may lead to exit of one or more firms from the market, or the entrant(s) and incumbents will collude, but entry may not entail competition.
3. Concerning interaction between market participants—incumbents will take strategic and tactical actions to deter entry, and entrants will take actions to ease collusions.
4. Concerning misallocation and efficiency—even when markets are competitive and firms may entail zero-profits, these markets are characterized by misallocation and inefficiencies.

## Evolution of Industries

IO theories contributed many explanations for the development of industries. Gort and Klepper (1982) emphasized the diffusion of innovations over the industry life cycle. The authors showed that the time path of the diffusion of product innovations determines not only the pattern of entry and exit, but also the ultimate market structure. The number of firms is connected to the age of the product or industry and to the evolution of the structure of the market. The number of firms in a market changes over time. The industries considered by Gort and Klepper (1982), Klepper and Graddy (1990), and Jovanovic and MacDonald (1994b) demonstrated that output rises and prices fall with the age of the industry. These empirical findings stimulated the development of theoretic models of industry evolution.

The selection and learning model of Jovanovic (1982) was influential in shaping literature. In the Jovanovic model, a sequence of firms enters the market. Each firm has a level of efficiency that is characterized by its unit cost of production. Firms learn about their efficiency as they operate in the industry. Over time, the efficient firms grow and survive, whereas the inefficient ones decline and exit. Hence, the longer firms remain in the industry, the more they learn about their true costs and their relative efficiency, and the less likely they are to exit. Other models of innovation and capability adoption or entry decisions also derive an S-shaped diffusion path as the outcome of an assumed heterogeneity across firms (Jovanovic & Lach, 1989; Jovanovic & MacDonald, 1994a). Because of learning by doing, firms reduce their costs. If the learning effect cannot be fully appropriated by the incumbent firms, then unit production costs decrease further as the number of firms grows. As a result of the new lower industry costs, less efficient firms decline and exit the industry.

The empirical and theoretical evidence of life cycles indicates that shake-outs are a common phenomenon in the evolution of many industries. New theories have been proposed to explain the extent and timing of shake-outs across industries. One approach emphasized the role of precipitating events, such as major exogenous technological changes (e.g., Jovanovic & MacDonald, 1994b). The new technology offers low unit costs, but at a higher level of output per firm. Firms that are able to implement the new large-scale technology early increase their output and thus are able to produce efficiently. Consequently, the exit rate rises sharply until the less efficient firms are forced out of the market.

Another group interprets shake-outs as part of a gradual evolutionary process (Klepper, 1996; Klepper & Graddy, 1990; Nelson & Winter, 1982; Winter, 1984). These evolutionary theorists emphasized the differences in firms' innovative capabilities and the importance of firm size in appropriating the return from innovation to explain how entry, exit, growth, and market structure evolve over the life cycle of an industry. Innovations can be related to products or processes (Utterback & Abernathy, 1975). The majority of product innovations are introduced in the expanding phase of the industry life cycle by all firms, whereas process innovations, occurring in latter phases, are more likely to originate from large size firms. Over the industry life cycle, the increase in competition forces firms to become more price and cost conscious, and as a consequence, the innovative activities of firms gradually shift from product to process innovations. Process innovations increase the firm's optimal scale and reduce production costs. The technological improvement compresses the profit of the less efficient firms. In general, the smaller firms, who are not able to imitate the new innovation, exit, generating the shake-out (Cohen & Klepper, 1996).

Evolutionary economics studies also emphasized routines and capabilities (Winter, 1984). The incumbent firms have relative innovative advantages over entrants. Successful routines are replicated, leading to growth, while unsuccessful routines disappear.

However, successful incumbent firms can fall into so-called *competence traps*. Capabilities are refined at the firm level once firms have managed to adapt to major changes in their competitive environment. When the need to adapt to major changes in the competitive environment arises again, inertia and lack of absorptive capacity can preclude the firm's effective adaptation to the new developments. Finally, these firms will exit the industry. The history of the music industry shows many examples of how incumbent firms could overcome inertia and adapt. Huygens, Baden-Fuller, van den Bosch, & Volberda (2001) conducted a longitudinal study of the music industry with a time span of more than 100 years. The authors found, in particular, small and entrepreneurial record firms launched new capabilities and innovations that replaced the existing business models, products, and competition in the history of the music industry.

These developments induced incumbent firms to react to new technologies, business models, and entrants, but also took the industry to the next round of competitive dynamics. As the major record firms recognized the significance of the developments, they turned their attention to the small and entrepreneurial firms, and they purchased these firms. The major firms also created new capabilities and dissociated themselves from established practice. Hence, they were able to regain strength after they had undertaken a sequence of activities. Firms that were not able to manage to adapt to the new competitive environment were taken over or ceased production.

As an industry or market evolves from birth to maturity, the rate of demand growth and the minimum efficient size of firms are both likely to change. These structural changes influence the entry, exit, and survival rates of firms. It has been shown that both entry and exit rates depend systematically on the phase of the industry's life cycle (see Carroll, 1997; Gort & Klepper, 1982; Hannan & Carroll, 1992; Klepper, 1997; Klepper & Miller, 1995). Closely related to the relationship between entry and exit and the evolution of the industry is that between evolution of firms and survival. For the entering, surviving, and exiting firms in the 25 product markets Agarwal and Gort (1996) studied, firms' survival rates increased with the age of the firm but fell with the age of the industry. This result is in line with the findings by Carroll (1987) and Kranenburg and Pfann (2002), who also found a positive relation between newspaper and publisher firm age and survival throughout the observed age range for U.S. and Dutch data. According to Jovanovic (1998), these empirical stylized facts about survival rates suggest that older incumbent firms are more efficient and that the threshold of efficiency for viable operations in the industry rises as the industry matures.

The empirical literature also shows that entry in most industries is easy, but survival is difficult (Baldwin, 1995; Caves, 1998; Geroski, 1991, 1995). Recent empirical studies investigating the survival rates of entrants found a negative relation between starting size of firms and the probability of exit. Mata (1994), for instance, showed that the survival rates of incumbents and entrants are considerably lower for smaller than for larger firms. Furthermore, the results showed that 4 years after entry, 47% of the entrants had failed, whereas only 27% of incumbents exited in the same period. Audretsch and Mahmood (1995) also found that the survival rates of firms were positively related to size. A comparison between survival rates of entrants into a product or a process innovative industry by Audretsch (1991) revealed that the survival rates were determined by the conditions of technology, scale economies, and demand underlying the industry.

TABLE 15.4

Entry and Exit of Newspaper Firms and Survival Rates of New Newspaper
Firms Over the Daily Newspaper Life Cycle in The Netherlands: 1848–1994

| | | | Survival Rates | | |
|---|---|---|---|---|---|
| Period | Number of Entrants | Number of Exiting Firms | ≤5 years | ≤10 years | ≤15 years |
| 1848–1857 | 14 | 6 | 0.79 | 0.71 | 0.64 |
| 1858–1867 | 11 | 7 | 0.64 | 0.64 | 0.55 |
| 1868–1877 | 41 | 20 | 0.59 | 0.51 | 0.46 |
| 1878–1887 | 32 | 14 | 0.77 | 0.77 | 0.71 |
| 1888–1897 | 18 | 8 | 0.77 | 0.73 | 0.59 |
| 1898–1907 | 13 | 6 | 1.00 | 0.82 | 0.73 |
| 1908–1917 | 12 | 5 | 1.00 | 0.92 | 0.92 |
| 1918–1927 | 13 | 7 | 0.86 | 0.86 | 0.79 |
| 1928–1937 | 6 | 4 | 0.86 | 0.57 | 0.29 |
| 1938–1947 | 49 | 42 | 0.74 | 0.64 | 0.57 |
| 1948–1957 | 5 | 17 | 0.80 | 0.80 | 0.60 |
| 1958–1967 | 6 | 25 | 0.71 | 0.57 | 0.57 |
| 1968–1977 | 3 | 13 | 1.00 | 1.00 | 1.00 |
| 1978–1987 | 6 | 6 | 0.50 | 0.50 | 0.33 |
| 1988–1994 | 3 | 27 | 0.67 | — | — |

Note:  The survival rate is defined as the number of firms surviving in a given year, as a percentage of the total number of new newspapers established in the defined period. From "The Life Cycle of Daily Newspapers in The Netherlands: 1848–1997," by H. L. van Kranenburg, F. C. Palm, and G. A. Pfann, 1998, De Economist, 146, p. 485 and "Government Policy and the Evolution of the Market for Dutch Daily Newspapers," by H. L. van Kranenburg and G. A. Pfann, 2002, De Economist, 150, p. 237. Copyright 2002 by Kluwer Academic Publishers. Reprinted with permission.

In process innovative industries the survival opportunities for potential entrants are generally lower than for the entrants into product innovative industries. Agarwal and Gort (1996) showed that the survival opportunities for potential entrants decreased as the industry matured. Only the strongest newcomers enter the market as the industry matures or when it had already reached maturity. Newcomers in industries have more difficulty surviving when the industry matures, even though at later stages of the industry life cycle only the strongest firms actually do enter the market. This fact is illustrated by a longitudinal study of the daily newspaper industry in The Netherlands.

Table 15.4 presents the number of new newspapers and the number of exiting newspapers in the defined subperiods over the industry life cycle. It also contains the survival rates of the newly established newspapers over 5, 10, and 15 years. Table 15.4 confirms the low entry rates and high survival rates for entrants in the periods between 1900 and 1938, and from 1950 to 1994. This indicates that only the strongest newspaper firms entered the market in The Netherlands.

Overall, the survival rates for entrants are low (Geroski, 1995). This is consistent with the view of learning by doing and the size of firms. Entrants accumulate knowledge through learning by doing. The larger this base of knowledge, the larger the minimum efficient size of firms. Geroski recognized that even for successful entrants, it takes more than a decade to achieve a size comparable to the average incumbent. Hence, both firm size and age are correlated with the survival and growth of entrants.

Sutton (1997) and Caves (1998) summarized the empirical facts about entry, exit, and survival of entrants and incumbent firms. Their studies mentioned the following main findings:

- The probability of survival increases with firm size, and the rate of growth of a firm, given that it survives, is decreasing in size.
- The growth rate of a firm is smaller as the firm becomes older, but the probability of survival is greater.
- The number of firms in an industry tends to rise to a peak and later fall to some lower level (according to Jovanovic, 1998, the number of firms stabilizes at a level of about 40% below the peak).
- Across industries there is a positive correlation between gross entry rates and gross exit rates.
- Entry is more likely to occur into smaller size classes, and the initially smaller entrants generally have a lower survival rate.
- A firm's survival rate increases with the age of the firm but falls with the age of the industry.
- During the growth phase, the most recent entrants account for a disproportionate share of product innovations, and the number of major product innovations reaches a peak in this phase.

In general, the main findings indicated that the age and stage of the industry life cycle can explain a significant part of the firms' entry and survival rate differences over time. Because entry seems to have an important influence on the evolution of industry structure, many studies investigated which factors influence the number of entrants. These factors include the preentry profit rate of incumbents, the minimum efficient scale of entry, the rate of demand growth, the elasticity of demand, and the magnitude of sunk costs (Caves, 1998; Geroski, 1995; Kessides, 1990; Sutton, 1997).

According to Mata (1991), the expected lifetime of firms in a market, if entry fails, is probably influenced by two main factors: the active rivalry by the incumbent firms, and the entrant's ability to fight and to take action to ease collusions after entry has taken place. Tirole (1990) provided an impressive survey of the literature on entry and strategic and tactical actions of incumbent firms. Firms may utilize a variety of business strategies, depending on whether they want to deter entry, induce exit of immediate rivals, battle for market shares, or increase sunk costs. In general, the larger the scale at which entry must be attempted, the smaller the number of firms in the market and the higher the reduction in incumbents' output as a result of successful entry of new firms. The behavior of incumbents is, therefore, determined by the incentives they face and the market form of the industry. In a not concentrated or expanding market with a large number of firms, the initiation of retaliatory measures against an entrant is low. However, in a concentrated market, like an oligopoly, the incumbents have an incentive to engage in collusive punitive actions against new firms (Baldwin, 1995; Geroski, 1991; Sutton, 1992).

The empirical analyses provide a better understanding of the dynamic processes of the entry and the exit of firms, the growth and the decline of incumbent firms, and merger and acquisition processes over time. These studies showed that decreases in concentration are associated with higher entry and exit rates and that increases in concentration are not so much associated with lower rates of entry but with shake-outs of incumbent firms. The shake-out theory presumes that economies of scale increase the survival opportunities of the more efficient large-scale plants and firms (Jovanovic & MacDonald, 1994b). However, the shake-out theory in the previous evolutionary industry models assumes that aggregate output increases, while an industry's demand may decline and eventually become extinct.

## Declining Industries

A small number of theoretical studies has recently been conducted to investigate the competitive process in industries that are characterized by declining demand. In this stage, most firms' competitive actions pertain to divestment rather than investment. An industry experiencing a decline in market demand must reduce its capacity in order to remain profitable for its firms. Firms can divest by cutting capacity incrementally or by exiting. Incremental reductions can be carried out by closing part of an ongoing firm. The pattern of capacity reduction and exit of firms depends on the industry structure and the market's decline (Whinston, 1988).

Some studies emphasized that large firms are more efficient (Jovanovic & MacDonald, 1994b; Klepper, 1996). The differences in efficiency would cause smaller firms to be shaken out relatively early if prices fall during the declining phase. However, in declining industries the competitive process can also generate another effect. In the absence of cost differences in efficiency between firms, smaller firms can remain profitable over a longer period as market demand is declining. Controlling for plant size as the industry devolves, larger firms would rationally choose to exit early or reduce capacity by a greater percentage than smaller firms. This process is known as *stake-out*.

Ghemawat and Nalebuff (1985) theoretically showed that shrinking demand creates pressure for capacity to be reduced or eliminated to maintain profitability. If firms have different market shares and firms are perfectly informed about their competitors' costs, then the survival chances of firms depend on the size ordering of the incumbent firms; the largest firm is the first to exit the industry. Londregan (1990) generalized the Ghemawat and Nalebuff result for exit from a declining industry to cases in which reentry is a costly but feasible option. The outcome was in line with Ghemawat and Nalebuff's findings. Other extensions of the Ghemawat and Nalebuff model show that large (multiplant) firms that anticipate an eventual decline in demand of a specific product begin to close plants or merge with their rivals to provide a revenue increase of the remaining plants (Baden-Fuller, 1989; Reynolds, 1988; Whinston, 1988). In a subsequent article, Ghemawat and Nalebuff (1990) postulated a model in which firms divest continuously as demand declines. Large firms experience a greater pressure to reduce their capacity incrementally to the size of the smaller firms. Largest firms will reduce capacity first because they have lower marginal revenue and, hence, greater incentives to reduce capacity. The larger firms can increase their survival chances by closing plants. If this happens, the concentration in the declining industry diminishes over time, as firms' sizes become more equal. The convergence in size of firms occurs under both the shakeout and stakeout processes (Lieberman, 1990). Whinston (1988) showed that it is difficult to reach any general conclusions about the pattern of firms' capacity reduction and exit. The results strongly indicated that knowledge of the industry and pattern of shrinking demand over time are necessary to predict which firms reduce their capacity or exit.

Empirical evidence on the pattern of media firms exit and capacity reductions in declining industries has primarily been obtained from case studies. The majority of studies found higher rates of exit for small firms and plants, but only limited evidence was found to support stakeouts. For example, the evidence of the newspaper industry in The Netherlands showed that, in general, small-size firms exited the market disproportionately, whereas the large-share firms made more frequent incremental reductions of number of newspapers. Only two large publishing companies, Reed Elsevier and VNU, sold their newspaper business during the early years of decline (Kranenburg, Palm, & Pfann, 2002).

## CONCLUSION

This chapter reviewed the most important theories that may contribute to a deeper understanding of the evolution of media industries. They explain why entry, exit, and survival rates of media firms are what they are, why they change, when they do, and how innovations and interventions influence the market structures. Both organizational ecology and industrial organization theories of industry evolution contribute to this overall understanding. It appears that a combination of the various concepts would enrich the insights in entry, exit, and survival processes of firms and the market structure over media industry life cycles. Although the organizational ecology research and industrial organization research dealing with the evolution of industries differ significantly in approach, they confirm the importance of the industry life cycle on the entry, exit, and survival rates of firms.

The evidence in this chapter shows that entry, exit, and survival rates of media firms depend systematically on the stage of development of the industry in the life cycle. Moreover, the effects of macroeconomic, industry-specific and firm-specific developments on the selection of media firms and industry dynamics are time dependent. Hence, managers, policymakers, scholars, and other professionals should acknowledge the cyclical characteristics of industries.

Although research on the selection of firms and the evolution of media market structures and industries has a long tradition, primary data on industries over a long time period are scarce. To date, most studies have adopted a static approach of entry, exit, and survival analysis across industries. More detailed historical research of industries and case studies are needed to provide a better understanding of why and how media industries evolve, and perhaps even more important, explain their present market structure. By building up a detailed historical profile of the industry, a better explanation and understanding of the evolution of media industries can be given than would be possible solely on the basis of static analyses.

Another important issue for further research is to investigate what determines entry and exit within market niches and how media firm specialization evolves. A more extensive analysis in tracing the evolution of firm specialization and the entry and exit decisions of specialized firms in niche markets, taking into account the underlying circumstances, the range of media-related products or services, and technological change, seems a fruitful approach to explore this issue further. Because of liberalization, privatization, and globalization, media firms start to reconfigure their value chain to survive in the dynamic media landscape. The increasing integration of value-chain activities may cause specialized media firms focusing on one or just a few activities in the value chain to find it increasingly difficult to survive, and entry of new media firms will become limited or cease. To make inferences about successful strategies of media firms and evolution of media markets, further understanding of the connection between market niches, specialization, generalization, and entry and survival of media firms is likely to be quite valuable.

Related to the need of specialization or generalization and similar developments in other industries, such as the telecommunications and consumer electronics markets, a final issue for further research is undoubtedly the convergence of media and communications markets. The convergence fundamentally changes both market and competition conditions as well as consumer preferences. This leads to higher intensity of competition, entry of new competitors from outside the industry, and the need for different strategic behavior of incumbents. More detailed theoretical and empirical research needs to be made into the consequences of integration of various media and communications markets.

## REFERENCES

Agarwal, R., & Gort, M. (1996). The evolution of markets and entry, exit and survival of firms. *Review of Economics and Statistics, 78*, 489–497.

Audretsch, D. B. (1991). New-firm survival and the technological regime. *Review of Economics and Statistics, 73*, 441–450.

Audretsch, D. B., & Mahmood, T. (1995). New firm survival: New results using a hazard function. *Review of Economics and Statistics, 76*, 97–103.

Averitt, R. (1968). *The dual economy: The dynamics of American industry structure.* New York: Norton.

Baden-Fuller, C. W. F. (1989). Exit from declining industries and the case of steel casting. *Economic Journal, 99*, 949–961.

Bain, J. S. (1956). *Barriers to new competition.* Cambridge, MA: Harvard University Press.

Baldwin, J. R. (1995). *The dynamics of industrial competition.* Cambridge, UK: Cambridge University Press.

Baumol, W. J., & Willig, R. D. (1981). Fixed costs, sunk costs, entry barriers, and sustainability of monopoly. *Quarterly Journal of Economics, 96*, 405–431.

Bresnahan, T. F., & Reiss, P. C. (1987). Do entry conditions vary across markets? *Brookings Papers on Economic Activity, 3*, 833–881.

Bresnahan, T. F., & Reiss, P. C. (1990). Entry in monopoly markets. *Review of Economic Studies, 57*, 531–553.

Bresnahan, T. F., & Reiss, P. C. (1993). Measuring the importance of sunk costs. *Annales d'Economie et de Statistique, 31*, 181–217.

Carroll, G. R. (1985). Concentration and specialization: Dynamics of niche width in populations of organizations. *American Journal of Sociology, 90*, 1262–1283.

Carroll, G. R. (1987). *Publish and perish: The organizational ecology of newspaper industries.* Greenwich, CT: JAI Press.

Carroll, G. R. (1994). Organizations . . . the smaller they get. *California Management Review, 37*, 28–41.

Carroll, G. R. (1997). Long-term evolutionary change in organizational populations: Theory, models and empirical findings in industrial demography. *Industrial and Corporate Change, 6*, 119–143.

Caves, R. E. (1998). Industrial organization and new findings on the turnover and mobility of firms. *Journal of Economic Literature, 36*, 1947–1982.

Cohen, W. M., & Klepper, S. (1996). Firm size and the nature of innovation within industries: The case of process and product R&D. *Review of Economics and Statistics, 78*, 232–243.

Dixit, A. K., & Pindyck, R. S. (1994). *Investment under uncertainty.* Princeton, NJ: Princeton University Press.

Dunne, T., Roberts, M. J., & Samuelson, L. (1988). Patterns of firm entry and exit in U.S. manufacturing industries. *Rand Journal of Economics, 19*, 495–515.

Dutch Central Bureau of Statistics: Statline databank (2004). Retrieved from the World Wide Web, January 30, 2004: www.cbs.nl/nl/cybers/statline/index.htm

Dutch Media Authority: Concentration and Diversity of the Dutch Media 2002 (2003). Retrieved from the World Wide Web, February 18, 2004: www.cvdm.nl/pages/mediaconc.asp

Eaton, B. C., & Lipsey, R. G. (1980). Exit barriers are entry barriers: The durability of capital as a barrier to entry. *Bell Journal of Economics, 11*, 721–729.

Eaton, B. C., & Lipsey, R. G. (1981). Capital, commitment, and entry equilibrium. *Bell Journal of Economics, 12*, 593–604.

Geroski, P. A. (1991). *Market dynamics and entry.* Oxford, UK: Basil Blackwell.

Geroski, P. A. (1995). What do we know about entry. *International Journal of Industrial Organization, 13*, 421–440.

Ghemawat, P., & Nalebuff, B. (1985). Exit. *Rand Journal of Economics, 16*, 184–194.

Ghemawat, P., & Nalebuff, B. (1990). The devolution of declining industries. *Quarterly Journal of Economics, 105*, 167–186.

Gort, M., & Klepper, S. (1982). Time paths in the diffusion of product innovations. *Economic Journal, 92*, 630–653.

Gustafsson, K. E. (1993). Government policies to reduce newspaper entry barriers. *Journal of Media Economics, 6*, 37–43.

Hannan, M. T. (1997). Inertia, density and the structure of organizational populations: Entries in European automobile industries, 1886–1981. *Organization Studies, 18*, 193–228.

Hannan, M. T., & Carroll, G. R. (1992). *Dynamics of organizational populations: Density, legitimation, and competition.* New York: Oxford University Press.

Hannan, M. T., & Freeman, J. (1977). The population of ecology of organizations. *American Journal of Sociology, 82*, 929–964.

Hannan, M. T., & Freeman, J. (1989). *Organizational ecology.* Cambridge, MA: Harvard University Press.

Huygens, M., Baden-Fuller, C., van den Bosch, F. A. J., & Volberda, H. W. (2001). Co-evolution of firm capabilities and industry competition: Investigating the music industry, 1877–1997. *Organization Studies, 22*, 971–1011.

Jovanovic, B. (1982). Selection and the evolution of industry. *Econometrica, 50*, 649–670.

Jovanovic, B. (1998). Michael Gort's contribution to economics. *Review of Economic Dynamics, 1*, 327–337.

Jovanovic, B., & Lach, S. (1989). Entry, exit, and diffusion with learning by doing. *American Economic Review, 79*, 690–699.

Jovanovic, B., & MacDonald, G. M. (1994a). Competitive diffusion. *Journal of Political Economy, 102*, 24–52.

Jovanovic, B., & MacDonald, G. M. (1994b). The life cycle of a competitive industry. *Journal of Political Economy, 102*, 323–347.

Kessides, I. N. (1990). Towards a testable model of entry: A study of the U.S. manufacturing industries. *Economica, 57*, 219–238.

Klepper, S. (1996). Entry, exit, growth, and innovation over the product life cycle. *American Economic Review, 86*, 562–583.

Klepper S. (1997). Industry life cycles. *Industrial and Corporate Change, 6*, 145–181.

Klepper, S., & Graddy, E. (1990). The evolution of new industries and the determinants of market structure. *Rand Journal of Economics, 21*, 27–44.

Klepper, S., & Miller, J. H. (1995). Entry, exit, and shakeout in the United States in new manufactured products. *International Journal of Industrial Organization, 13*, 567–591.

Klepper, S., & Simons, K. L. (2000). Dominance by birthright: Entry of prior radio producers and competitive ramifications in the U.S. television receiver industry. *Strategic Management Journal, 21*, 997–1016.

Kranenburg, H. L. van, Palm, F. C., & Pfann, G. A. (1998). The life cycle of daily newspapers in the Netherlands: 1848–1997. *De Economist, 146*, 475–494.

Kranenburg, H. L. van, Palm, F. C., & Pfann, G. A. (2002). Exit and survival in a concentrating industry: The case of daily newspapers in the Netherlands. *Review of Industrial Organization, 21*, 283–303.

Kranenburg, H. L. van, & Pfann, G. A. (2002). Government policy and the evolution of the market for Dutch daily newspapers. *De Economist, 150*, 233–250.

Kuznets, S. (1930). *Secular movements in production and prices*. Boston: Houghton Mifflin, Riverside Press. (Reprinted 1967, New York: Augustus M. Kelly).

Lieberman, M. B. (1990). Exit from declining industries: "Shakeout" or "stakeout"? *Rand Journal of Economics, 21*, 538–554.

Londregan, J. (1990). Entry and exit over the industry life cycle. *Rand Journal of Economics, 21*, 446–458.

Mata, J. (1991). Sunk costs and entry by small and large plants. In P. A. Geroski & J. Schwalbach (Eds.), *Entry and market contestability: An international comparison* (pp. 49–62). Oxford, UK: Blackwell.

Mata, J. (1994). Firm growth during infancy. *Small Business Economics, 6*, 27–39.

Miller, D., & Chen, M. J. (1994). Sources and consequences of competitive inertia: A study of the U.S. airline industry. *Administrative Science Quarterly, 39*, 1–39.

Merrilees, W. (1983). Anatomy of a price leadership challenge: An evaluation of pricing strategies in the Australian newspaper industry. *Journal of Industrial Economics, 31*, 291–311.

Nelson, R. R., & Winter, S. G. (1982). *An evolutionary theory of economic change*. Cambridge, MA: Harvard University Press.

Pfann, G. A., & Kranenburg, H. L. van (2003). Tax policy, location choices, and market structure. *Journal of Law and Economics, 46*, 61–83.

Picard, R. G. (2002). *The economics and financing of media companies*. New York: Fordham University Press.

Reynolds, S. S. (1988). Plant closing and exit behaviour in declining industries. *Economica, 55*, 493–503.

Rosse, J. N. (1967). Daily newspapers, monopolistic competition, and economies of scale. *American Economic Review, 57*, 522–533.

Sollinge, J. D. (1999). Danish newspapers: Structure and developments. *Nodicom Review, 1999*(1), 31–76.

Starkey, K., Barnatt, C., & Tempest, S. (2000). Beyond network and hierarchies: Latent organizations in the U.K. television industry. *Organization Science, 11*, 299–305.

Stiglitz, J. E. (1987). Technological change, sunk costs, and competition. *Brookings Papers on Economic Activity, 3*, 883–947.

Sutton, J. (1992). *Sunk cost and market structure: Price competition, advertising, and the evolution of concentration*. Cambridge, MA: MIT Press.

Sutton, J. (1997). Gibrat's legacy. *Journal of Economic Literature, 35*, 40–59.

Tirole, J. (1990). *The theory of industrial organization*. Cambridge, MA: MIT Press.

Utterback, J. M., & Abernathy, W. J. (1975). A dynamic model of process and product innovation. *Omega, 3*, 639–656.

Vernon, R. (1966). International investment and international trade in the product life cycle. *Quarterly Journal of Economics, 80*, 190–207.

Whinston, M. D. (1988). Exit with multiplant firms. *Rand Journal of Economics, 19*, 568–588.

Winter, S. G. (1984). Schumpeterian competition in alternative technological regimes. *Journal of Economic Behavior and Organization, 5*, 287–320.

# 16

# Media Competition and Levels of Analysis

John Dimmick
Ohio State University

## INTRODUCTION

In the industrial organization (IO) model familiar to students of media economics and management (Albarran, 2002; Picard, 1989), competition is conceptualized as emanating from the number of firms in an industry and the type of products produced by the firms within the industry. In the IO model, competition is at its strongest in the market structure called pure or perfect competition, which exhibits a large number of firms producing homogeneous products. By contrast, competition is weakest in such market structures as differentiated oligopolies, which are characterized by a small number of firms producing differentiated products.

The IO concept of competition is a very restrictive definition. Albarran (2002) points out there are no examples of pure or perfect competition among media industries. Does this mean there is little competition among media firms and industries? Probably not. Even the most superficial conversations with media executives reveal that they believe they live in a highly competitive environment. Further, the IO model conceptualizes competition as occurring only *within* industries, ignoring the many other contexts in which competition occurs. Two decades ago, Dimmick and Rothenbuhler (1984) demonstrated that competition also occurs between media industries. Nor is between-industry competition limited to media industries. For example, it is apparent to even the most casual student of U.S. history that the transportation industries changed from waterborne travel and commercial shipping by river and canal when such travel and shipping were displaced by landborne transport via the railroad and the internal combustion engine.

In turn, these modes of transport were displaced by airborne transport. Displacement, of course, implies that at some points in their history the transportation industries were in competition.

Thus, the IO definition of competition focuses only on a special case, pure or perfect competition, and this restriction excludes many behaviors of firms and industries that are competitive in nature. This chapter uses a definition of competition drawn from ecology, which views the phenomenon as the striving among economic units such as firms or industries for scarce resources such as consumer time and money as well as advertising dollars. The author of one influential industrial organization economics text (Scherer, 1980) would view this striving as "rivalry" rather than competition. However, the ecological definition is closer to dictionary definitions and commonsense meanings of the word competition.

The ecological definition is an inclusive one and therefore risks defining competition too broadly: In doing so; it may conflate trivial with important competitive phenomena. This risk is ameliorated by the ability to measure the degree of competition among economic units. The concept of niche overlap, defined later in this chapter, provides the conceptual basis for distinguishing between weak and strong competition by emphasizing the necessity for actual measures of the strength of competition. These measures are more precise than simply classifying industries into one of several market structures.

Competition is therefore ubiquitous: It occurs between multinational companies and indigenous media organizations as the multinationals enter former socialist countries or regions such as China or Eastern Europe, marketing entertainment products that compete for consumer time and money within each country. Within countries it occurs between industries such as broadcast television and cable television. It occurs between multidivisional firms who operate in several industries such as music, publishing, or movies, for example, Time Warner, News Corporation, or Bertelsmann. It occurs between firms within industries such as network television, and it occurs between firms in the same or different industries in local markets. Even this brief sketch of the contexts in which competition takes place suggests the complexity of the topic. The question, then, is how to portray a complex and multifaceted topic such as competition within the confines of a handbook chapter?

The solution chosen by the author is to organize the chapter around levels of analysis based loosely on Dimmick and Coit (1982). The problem is how to make complex phenomena such as media competition analytically tractable. As McPhee (1963, p. 8) observed, the key question is "how to have our complexity and analyze it too." Herbert Simon's (1969) solution to the problem was to propose that complexity is often manifested in the form of hierarchy such as levels of analysis. Simon's work shows that hierarchies or hierarchic systems occur in such disparate fields of inquiry as biology, chemistry, and history. As defined by Simon, hierarchic systems are composed of subsystems arrayed in a hierarchical manner. The taxonomy presented in this chapter utilizes the concept of hierarchy by ordering the levels (subsystems) from the most molar or supranational level to the most molecular, the level of the individual firm or organization. One way of visualizing the multileveled hierarchy is as a set of Chinese boxes or Russian dolls with the smaller units nested within the larger. This nested hierarchy consists of five levels, and at each level I attempt to specify some of the influences operating to influence competition or the competitive situation of firms and industries.

The taxonomic system of levels of competition is hierarchical in two senses of the word. First, as noted previously, it is hierarchic in the sense that the unit of analysis increases in size as one ascends the hierarchy. It is also hierarchic in the sense that the levels higher in the hierarchy constitute the environment, or rather, set of environments, within which units at the lower levels operate. Firms, for example, operate within the environment formed by the ownership or supraorganization as well as the environment constituted by industry to which they belong. Although rivalry between individual firms may be the most familiar form of competition, the parameters of competition are often formed at higher levels in the hierarchy. For example, competition within a country between firms and industries occurs within the context of that country's media policies, which both provide opportunities and impose constraints on firm behavior.

Within the hierarchy, influence flows in two directions. It may ascend or descend in the hierarchy. Descendant influence is exemplified by the media policies, laws, and regulations formulated by bodies at the nation-state level to rule or guide the behavior of media firms and industries, within their borders. Ascendant influence, on the other hand, is exemplified by the fact that firms and industries, through trade associations, may attempt to influence legislation or rulemaking by regulatory bodies at the societal level on issues affecting their interests.

The taxonomy aims at completeness in specifying the levels of analysis but is necessarily incomplete in specifying all the variables operating at the various levels. Limitations of space preclude reviewing all the literature that could be relevant at the five levels of analysis. The literature reviewed at each level is that which I believe is most germane. Researchers who wish to use the taxonomy in their own work can readily classify the variables they are utilizing into the levels of analysis provided in this chapter. The purpose of the chapter is not to offer a complete theory, but rather to outline a systematic approach to conceptualizing and researching competition.

## LEVEL 1: SUPRANATIONAL

At this level of analysis there originate policies that set the parameters or limits as the ground rules of competition for media firms worldwide or within certain geographic regions such as Europe, Asia, or North America. Several decades ago the major supra-national influence on international media competition was a unit of the United Nations, UNESCO, which stimulated research in communication policy and planning as an initial phase in the formulation of national-level policies that affected media competition at the level within national borders (see Beltran, 1977; Rahim, 1977). In the contemporary world this nation-by-nation approach to formulation of media competitive policy has been replaced by broader policy bodies and policymaking at the world or regional level. For example, the World Trade Organization requires an open market in telecommunications, and this act has resulted in the opening of the huge Chinese market to competition from non-Chinese-media firms (Li & Dimmick, 2004). In addition to such global bodies as the WTO there are regional trade zones such as North America under the aegis of the North American Free Trade Agreement, the European Union, or Asian countries allied in the Southeast Asian Free Trade Area that set policies affecting competition by outside media firms (Chan-Olmstead & Albarran, 1998).

## LEVEL 2: NATIONAL

At this level of analysis two broad influences operate to influence competition. The first of these is national media policies; the second is the economy of the country in question.

### The Role of Policy

Like the supranational level, the national level is an environment within which media policies of nation-states set the parameters of competition for firms and industries and whose economies influence the availability of resources such as advertising and the intensity of competition for those resources.

Nations vary substantially in their media policies, ranging from countries such as Nigeria, which has no telecommunications policy at all (Amienyi, 1998), to countries such as the Netherlands (Hendriks, 1998), which has a strong and highly developed policy. Obviously, the degree of public versus private ownership also strongly affects the intensity of media competition within a country.

Contemporary media policy in the United States seems to operate somewhere between these extremes (Corn-Rovere & Carveth, 1998). One major feature of the regulatory environment in the United States that has affected competition is the 1996 Telecommunication Act, which eliminated many of former limits on media ownership and, in addition, eliminated a number of restrictions on cross-industry ownership in the electronic media industries. As a result of the 1996 Act firms have exploited the opportunity through merger and acquisition (Chon, Choi, Barnett, Danowski, & Joo, 2003). However, a thorough empirical assessment of the competitive effect of this M & A activity has yet to be conducted. The literature on competition and the field of media economics would greatly benefit from such an analysis. Detractors claim that the result has been to lessen competition, whereas proponents point to the improved competitive abilities of the formerly independent firms as well as their greater economic efficiency.

In addition to media policies of nation-states, national economies are another aspect of the environment inhabited by media firms and industries, and this economic environment provides the macroeconomic context within which competition for advertisers and consumer expenditures takes place. Obviously, if macroeconomic variables affect the monetary resources such as advertising available to the media, then the intensity of competition among the media will also be affected. McCombs (1972) was the first to suggest that the US economy influences spending on the media. McCombs' results have been thrown into question by later research (Demers, 1994; Wood, 1986; Wood & O'Hare, 1991). However, it is common knowledge in the U.S. media industries that firms tend to reduce advertising budgets during economic downturns.

Evidence of the relationship between a nation's economy and media spending is sparse. Apparently, Picard (2001) is the only researcher to attempt to document this relationship outside the United States. Picard found a relationship between recessions and advertising spending in developed countries, which included several European nations as well as Japan, the United Kingdom, and the United States. Picard concluded that a number of variables such as type of economies, national economic policies, and the severity of the recession, as well as other factors, probably play a role in advertising expenditures. Further research aimed at clarifying the role of national economies on the monetary resources available to media firms and industries would add significantly to our knowledge of media competition.

## LEVEL 3: THE GUILD, THE DOMAIN, AND THE NICHE: COMPETITION BETWEEN INDUSTRIES

This level is about comparisons between industries. Although significant competition occurs within industries, competition also occurs between industries, especially when a new industry emerges. At this level the theory of the niche (Dimmick, 2003) provides conceptual and measurement tools to map competition within guilds and domains.

### The Guild and the Domain

Competition occurs among industries or populations of organizations within communities composed of members of many industries. Communities may be defined at many levels or geographic areas, which might be a country, a region of a country such as a state, or a market or metropolitan area. An *industry* is a population or group of organizations that shares many attributes in common, and the firms within the industry are more like each other than they are like firms in other industries. For example, a newspaper resembles other newspapers more than it resembles cable systems. Media industries can be defined by their technologies (Dimmick, 2003), specifically their production technologies. Although all the media in the future may be digitally distributed, their production technologies will continue to make each industry distinct and recognizable.

Within the industries that constitute communities, some sets of firms or organizations constitute guilds or domains, and it is within the guild or domain that competition may be most intense. A *guild* is a group of industries that use a common resource such as advertising. Recall that competition is defined as taking place among firms or industries that use the same or similar resources. Dimmick and Rothenbuhler (1984) used the term *guild* to characterize the set of media industries that depend on advertising, in whole or in part, for their survival. Dimmick (2003) used the term *domain* to describe a set of media industries that serve the same or similar gratification utilities or that satisfy roughly the same consumer needs. The domains identified by Dimmick (2003) include the video entertainment media; the daily news media; business and economic news; and an interactive domain consisting of telephone, e-mail, and instant messaging. The gratification-utility domains are, not coincidentally, correspondent to content domains.

It is within the guild or the domain that competition may be at its most intense. The reason is fairly obvious. For the advertisers, the media firms that are members of the guild that depend on advertising constitute alternatives or potential substitutes for placement of messages (Dimmick, 2003). Similarly, to the consumer the content of the media that make up a domain are potential, if partial, substitutes. Similarly, within a domain the media are alternative means of spending time in pursuit of utility or gratification. Because the media within a guild or domain are at least partial substitutes, they are competitors.

## Competition, Guilds, and Domains

Within domains one can speak of three ways in which competition is manifested: diffuse competition, serial competition, and dominance. Later in this chapter the reader will see that competition is usually measured between each pair of industries within a guild or domain. However, it is also possible to conceptualize competition as the combined effect of the other members of a guild or domain on a focal industry. Ecologists such as Pianka (1983) have found that the combined but weaker competitive effect of a number of populations on a focal population can be equivalent to strong pairwise competition. This is called *diffuse competition*. If this is the case, one observable consequence might be a reduction in niche breadth (defined later in the chapter) in the focal population overtime. This reduction in niche breadth could occur without the invasion of the guild by new industries. The reduction in niche breadth is an outcome of competition.

A construct closely related to diffuse competition is the concept of serial competition. *Serial competition* occurs when a guild or domain is successively invaded by new industries over a long period of time. Dimmick (2003, p. 115) defined serial competitions as "the combined or cumulative effects of successive invasions on an older local population or populations." As an example of serial competition, Dimmick (2003) found that the share of all U.S. advertising garnered by newspapers dropped steadily from 1935 through 2000, while the combined advertising share of industries that had invaded the guild during this time period (radio, TV, and cable) rose concomitantly. The reduction in newspapers' share of advertising is a clear outcome of competition.

*Dominance* is the degree to which one industry in a guild is able to attain a commanding position in garnering a particular resource or resources. For example, on the time-spent-by-consumers dimension, television commands more of U.S. consumers' leisure time than any other medium and is therefore dominant on this dimension. Dominant industries occupy their status as a result of superior competitive ability.

Dimmick (2003) used a version of the Simpson index as a measure of dominance in the advertising guild in the period 1935–2000 and found that whereas the newspaper was the dominant industry at the beginning of the period, the medium's commanding position on the advertising dimension declined precipitously over the time period because of competition from newer media.

One unanswered question concerning dominance is an explanation of why it occurs. For example, if television were found to be dominant on the advertising dimension in the contemporary United States, is this because of a corresponding dominance on the consumer-time-spent dimension? If this question can be answered in the affirmative, is the dominance in consumer time spent with television related to the diversity of content available on the broadcast and cable channels as well as VCR and DVD?

## THE THEORY OF THE NICHE

Dictionaries usually define a niche as an opening or recess in a wall designed to hold a statue, an urn, or some other object. Although this architectural definition conveys the conventional meaning of the term, the theory of the niche is a body of constructs and research that originated in the field of bioecology. The word *niche* may have been first applied to natural phenomena by the American naturalist George Bird Grinnell in the 19th century but was also used by social scientists such as Robert Park in the early 20th century. The niche concept was first incorporated into a systematic theory, however, by the bioecologist G. Evelyn Hutchinson (1958).

The theory of the niche was first applied to problems of competition among media firms and industries by Dimmick and Rothenbuhler (1984) and has since been elaborated by Dimmick (2003).

## Competition and Resources

The theory of the niche takes as its province competition and coexistence among ecological units contending for the same or similar resources. As noted at the beginning of this chapter, *competition* is defined as rivalry between firms or industries in the pursuit of scarce resources such as advertising expenditures or consumer time.

The resources that are the object of rivalry are the following:

Gratification utilities and gratification opportunities.
Media content.
Consumer spending.
Time spent by consumers on the media.
Advertising expenditures.

*Gratification utilities* are the satisfactions expected and/or derived by consumers from their use of media content. *Gratification opportunities*, on the other hand, bear on the probability that a consumer can satisfy media-related needs in a particular time and place such as the household at 8:00 on a Tuesday evening or on the freeway or subway during the morning or evening commute to work, or while working at the computer in the office. To date, studies have assessed gratification utilities and gratification opportunities in several domains including video entertainment (Dimmick, 2003), the daily news media (Dimmick, Chen, & Li, 2004), and the interactive media such as telephone, e-mail and instant messaging (Dimmick, Kline, & Stafford, 2000; Ramirez, Lin, & Dimmick, 2004). The resource dimensions of media content and consumer spending, on the other hand, have been little studied. Similarly, time spent on the media by consumers is a resource dimension that has received little attention. Advertising expenditures have received a good deal of attention, but the studies have been mostly focused on the principle of relative constancy. These studies were briefly reviewed earlier in this chapter. Dimmick (2003) attempted to systematically formulate the relationships among all the niche dimensions, but a recapitulation of this synthesis is beyond the scope of this chapter.

The resource dimensions such as media content or advertising expenditures are termed *macrodimensions*. Some of the resource or niche dimensions may be subdivided further into microdimensions. The gratification utilities and gratification opportunities, for example, are defined by factor analysis, and each factor is a macrodimension while the items or questions scaling on a factor are the microdimensions. Similarly, media content within a domain can be subdivided into various content categories. For example, news content as a macrodimension can be subdivided into microdimensions such as national, international, and local news. Likewise, the advertising macrodimension is composed of microdimensions such as national advertising, classified advertising, and local retail advertising. Time spent by consumers with the media, on the other hand, cannot be subdivided into microdimensions.

## Niche Concepts: Breadth, Overlap, and Superiority

There are three central concepts in niche theory: niche breadth, niche overlap, and competitive superiority. In empirical studies, each of these concepts is measured along one or more of the resource dimensions.

*Niche breadth* refers to the position occupied by an industry on a particular resource dimension. Measures drawn from ecology were used by Dimmick and Rothenbuhler (1984) to measure the breadth of various media on the advertising dimension, because the microdimensions are at the nominal level of measurement. On the content dimension these same formulas appropriate for nominal measurement could be used to compute breadth. Dimmick (2003) formulated breadth measures appropriate for the ordinal/interval scales used for gratification utilities and gratification opportunities. Breadth measures are interpreted in terms of the degree of generalism/specialism that they denote. For example, on the advertising dimensions TV is a relative generalist. TV utilizes four microdimensions— network or national, local, spot, and syndication—and the proportion of its revenues is spread across these categories. Radio, by way of contrast, is clearly a specialist. Although the medium draws revenues from three categories or microdimensions—national, local, and spot—most of its revenues are drawn from the local category.

In ecological thought, niche breadth bears on the efficiency and survivability of competitors. It is believed that specialists are more efficient at exploiting resources because their energy and expertise are concentrated within a narrow range of endeavor. For example, the energies and knowledge of management in a specialist firm can be focused on a narrower range of activities, whereas a generalist firm's management is required to focus on a broader range of activities and a broader knowledge is necessary. Although the specialist may be more efficient, the generalist may be better equipped to survive an environmental change that alters resource availability. For example, before to the advent of TV, radio was a generalist with a broad niche using several categories of advertising. Radio's generalism was a key factor in its survival of competition from television. When outdone for national advertising by TV, radio used another microdimension (local advertising) more intensively. Within a decade after TV's impact, radio revenues had rebounded to their former levels. In contrast, the U.S. movie industry, which was solely dependent on consumer spending, was devastated by the impact of television in the 1950s.

Recall from the earlier exposition that the definition of competition is the use of the same or similar resources by firms or industries. This pattern of similar resource use is termed *ecological similarity*. The more firms and industries make their living in the same way, the more strongly they compete. It follows, therefore, that just as ecological similarity leads to strong competition, differences in resource use lead to reduced competition and, as a result, to what might be termed "peaceful coexistence" between firms and industries. *Niche overlap* is a measure of the ecological similarity or competition between firms or industries provided that resources are limited or scarce. Obviously if resources are abundant firms or industries may overlap strongly and yet the high overlap will not be indicative of strong competition. However, Dimmick (2003) shows that resources on which media organizations survive are generally limited.

Measures of niche overlap are available for nominal scales such as categories of advertising or media content (Dimmick & Rothenbuhler, 1984) and for gratification utilities and gratification opportunities (Dimmick, 2003) that require interval-level measures. Overlap measures are computed for each pair of industries within a guild or domain or for each pair of firms in the set under analysis.

## Competitive Superiority

Overlap measures yield information concerning whether firms or industries are in close competition but they cannot, by themselves, indicate which of each pair of competitors is the superior. It is extremely useful to be able to compute the relative superiority of each pair of competitors, because this will bear on the consequences of competition that are outlined in the next section of the chapter. Measures of competitive superiority are available for use with advertising data and in addition are available for gratification utilities and gratification opportunities. (See Dimmick, 2003.)

## CONSEQUENCES OF COMPETITION

There are three possibilities or outcomes if media firms or industries are competitors. First, if competition is not terribly strong, then firms and industries coexist without severe economic harm. If, on the other hand, competition is relatively strong, then competitive displacement or competitive exclusion may occur.

Displacement occurs when the superior competitor of a pair appropriates resources formerly allocated by, for example, consumers or advertisers to the other member of a competitive pair. Displacement is manifested in a narrowing of the niche of the outdone member of the pair. Dimmick (2003) documents a number of examples of displacement. It should be noted that displacement is direct evidence of the existence of limited resources. The appropriation by the television medium of national or network advertising dollars formerly spent on radio is one example of displacement. Another example of displacement was recorded by Dimmick, Kline, and Stafford (2000), who found that e-mail had displaced some usage of the long-distance telephone. It should be noted that the process of displacement results in differentiation of competitors, which, in turn, usually results in coexistence of formerly strong competitors.

The third consequence of competition—competitive exclusion—seems to have occurred only rarely in the realm of media firms and industries. The sole example of exclusion seems to be the case of vaudeville, a species of live variety entertainment, which was apparently excluded or driven entirely out of business by the newer entertainment media of movies and radio.

The conditions for competitive displacement or exclusion are, first, there must be high overlap or ecological similarity and, second, one competitor of the pair must be clearly superior to the other. With current theory and measures it is not possible to predict, in advance, whether displacement or exclusion will occur. Present knowledge allows the analyst to measure niche breadth, overlap, and superiority and to document displacement contemporaneously or ex post facto.

## INDUSTRY LEVEL

At the level of the industry there are two topics that are important to understanding competitive processes among media firms and industries. The first topic is market structure, the traditional way of conceptualizing competition within industries. The second is the concept of strategic groups, a newer approach to the topic of competition within an industry.

In traditional economics, the theory of the firm puts forward four types of market structure, which are the result of a two-dimensional classification, the number of firms in the industry and the relative differentiation of the products produced by the firms (Albarran, 2002). Pure or perfect competition is characterized by many firms producing homogeneous products. Oligopolies are composed of a few firms that may produce differentiated or undifferentiated products. Monopolistic industries are composed of many firms producing differentiated products, whereas monopolies consist of a single firm producing either a homogeneous or a differentiated product.

In applying the concept of market structure to competition within media industries it is immediately apparent that the four market structures are reduced to two, oligopoly and monopolistic market structures. There are no examples of media industries that can be classified as pure competition (Albarran, 2002) and, of course, a monopoly, such as most daily newspapers, is not a market structure characterized by competition. In the case of monopolistic industries such as magazines, radio, or cable (see Albarran, 2002), the differentiated nature of these firms preserves them from strong competition. Aside from a generalized competition for consumer time, magazines such as *Sports Illustrated* or *The English Home* do not strongly compete for the same readers or advertisers.

Oligopolies, on the other hand, may produce either differentiated or homogeneous products. Whereas differentiated firms do not strongly compete, the media firms in homogeneous oligopolies are in strong competition.

The case of competition in oligopolies in the realm of media industries may be explained using the examples of the broadcast industries, radio and television. The question one first encounters is how to quantify homogeneity/differentiation? In the broadcast industries this has been accomplished using the concept of diversity (Litman, 1992; Napoli, 1999). The encouragement of program diversity in broadcasting has been a hallmark of policies fomented by the U.S. Federal Communications Commission. It is possible to measure diversity in a number of different ways, and most of the measures such as the Simpson index or the information theory measure yield similar results (Dimmick & McDonald, 2002).

The medium of network TV as the dominant entertainment medium in the United States succeeded the formerly dominant network radio medium in the 1950s. Both media, on the basis of the number of firms, qualify as oligopolies. In radio there were four networks, and in the television industry there were only three networks until the emergence of Fox in the 1980s. The two industries differed, however, in the homogeneity of their product and, hence, in the intensity of competition.

In an unpublished study, Dimmick and McDonald used the Simpson index to calculate program diversity across the history of both the broadcast oligopolies from 1926 through 1995. When these data are graphed the result is a curve shaped like an inverted U. Diversity rose steadily over the history of network radio to a plateau corresponding to the heyday of the medium. High diversity also marked the beginning of the history of the TV network in the 1950s as radio programs were transferred to TV and the new medium experimented in creating new programs. Diversity then began a long and steady decline across the history of TV. Clearly, network radio was a differentiated industry, whereas network TV quickly became characterized by an increasingly homogeneous product. The key question, of course, is why the two oligopolies produced products differing in their homogeneity.

The answer to this question lies in the differences in economic goals, firm interdependence, and the breadth of the talent pool utilized by the two oligopolies. First, in network radio the economic goal was to maximize the size of the target audience for individual programs, whereas for most of the history of network television the goal of each network has been to maximize its ratings across the entire network schedule. Second, this difference in economic goals resulted in a difference in firm interdependence in program decision-making. Although network radio exhibited some interdependence in pricing and corporate structure, Dimmick and McDonald (2001) found little evidence of rivalrous imitation in programming, the network's product. The stars and advertising agencies who controlled programming seem to have acted relatively independently; the network role was that of a time broker who provided program slots. In television, however, control of programming passed from the advertising agencies and stars to the networks themselves. It is well known that rivalrous imitation is the hallmark of decision-making in network television. This rivalrous imitation includes imitation of programs or genres that are currently successful and using producers and writers with a track record of success in the medium. Whereas the relative independence of program decisionmaking in network radio resulted in the utilization of a relatively broad range of production talent, the interdependence in network TV has mandated reliance on a relatively small group of producers. The result was that network radio produced a differentiated product, whereas network television has become characterized by a relatively homogeneous product. In short, network radio was characterized by relatively weaker competition among the networks while network TV is marked by relatively stronger competition.

Hence, a set of related variables such as economic goals, decisionmaking patterns and the number of content providers has resulted in different patterns of diversity in the radio and television oligopolies. Strong competition for audiences across a TV network's schedule has resulted in rivalrous imitation, which, in turn, has led to homogeneous content.

The prevalence of oligopolistic market structures in media industries raises the possibility of anticompetitive practices such as collusion among firms within an industry on such matters as pricing. In the U.S. broadcast network TV industry, for example, the prices of commercial availabilities on the networks (their cost-per-thousand) are quite similar. Scholar van Kranenburg (personal communication, July 2004) has suggested the use of the Cournot and Stackelberg (see Carlton & Perloff, 1994) models to illuminate the problem of collusion in media oligopolies.

Corporations that form an industry are more similar to each other than they are to firms in other industries, as noted earlier in this chapter. But there may still be significant variation from firm to firm in an industry on many attributes. One of the ways in which firms within an industry are likely to differ is in their competitive strategy. An industry may be composed of strategic groups which vary in their strategy. According to Porter (1980) competitive strategy consists of a firm's goals and its chosen means for realizing those goals. The notion of a strategic group grew out of the fields of industrial organization economics and strategic management beginning in the 1970s. The origin of the concept is attributed to the work of Hunt (1972) and its elaboration by Porter (1980). A strategic group is a set of firms within an industry pursuing the same or similar strategies. For example, daily newspapers in the United States are generalists purveying local, regional, and international news as well as sports and entertainment, whereas weekly papers are specialists focusing on local events. There have been two approaches to isolating strategic groups. The oldest approach uses cluster analysis of firms' financial data to identify groups within an industry (see Barney & Hoskesson, 1990; Reger & Huff, 1993). A newer method called the cognitive approach uses the verbal reports of informants such as executives within an industry. As Peteraf and Shanley (1997, p. 166) wrote, "Studies of managerial cognition show that executives tend to view their industries in terms of groups of firms." Within the media management and economics literature the strategic group concept has been employed by Chan-Olmstead and Li (2002) and by Dimmick (2003).

Chan-Olmstead and Li (2002) studied the multichannel video programming market. These researchers used variables such as pricing, operating efficiency, differentiation, size, and vertical integration to identify seven strategic groups that ranged from commercial-free movie programmers such as AMC and established programmers such as CNN and USA cable networks to a group of "integrated programmers" such as MTV and ESPN. Chan-Olmstead and Li found a relationship between group membership and financial performance, but found that size and vertical integration were unrelated to financial performance.

Dimmick (2003) proposed that the largest communication firms such as News Corp and Disney constitute a strategic group defined by their pursuit of the niche breadth strategy. The firms pursuing the niche breadth strategy are characterized by large scale, diversification, their exploitation of economies of scope, and international operation. In addition, some of these firms consciously employ management tactics such as fostering interdivisional cooperation, which helps ensure exploitation of diversification and the resulting economies of scope. Dimmick (2003) also proposed research to investigate the hypothesis that the various umbrella layers in the newspaper industry such as national dailies, metro dailies, satellite city dailies, and weeklies (see Picard, 1989) are actually strategic groups.

The importance of strategic groups for competition in media industries lies in their ability to explain how firms within an industry may compete and yet coexist. In an industry characterized by pure competition, the existence of firms is precarious at best. Given the large number of firms and the lack of strong entry barriers, the competitive situation is aptly described in the Hobbesian phrase as a "war of all against all." Differentiation of firms in an industry into strategic groups, on the other hand, reduces the number of a firm's effective competitors to those within its group or niche and, ceteris paribus, is likely to enhance the financial performance and likelihood of survival of all firms in the industry.

Of the two theoretical frameworks reviewed at the industry level of analysis market structure and strategic groups, the latter is the most likely to yield productive research in the future. As media markets grow more concentrated in the United States and throughout the world, this trend is likely in the long term to reduce the efficacy of market structure in explaining patterns of competition because of the reduction in variation. The most common market structure that has emerged in the United States, for example, seems to be the oligopoly. The strategic group concept, on the other hand, seems to have great potential for the understanding of competitive relations among media firms. Although relatively few studies have utilized the strategic group construct, the approach appears to hold promise for explaining competitive patterns of behavior within industries.

## SUPRAORGANIZATIONAL LEVEL

The media firm that produces a single product in a single market is largely a relic of the 19th century. Although such firms may still exist as small start-up enterprises in newer media markets such as the Internet, the contemporary media landscape in the United States and much of the rest of the world is dominated by firms that operate in multiple markets, selling multiple products on an international scale. Firms such as Vivendi, Bertelsmann, AOL-Time Warner, and News Corporation operate in many media industries on the global scene. Aside from these global giants there are large firms that operate on a national level within a single industry such as Clear Channel in the United States. The individual business units such as cable channels or magazine firms do not operate in a totally autonomous fashion with respect to their competitors. The business units within these firms are likely to receive a greater or lesser degree of direction from their parent firm or supraorganization. Unfortunately, there is a dearth of research on this aspect of management of media firms. Fruitful research could be conducted on the relationship between parent firms and their business units.

According to Williamson (1975), the emergence of the multidivisional form of corporate organizational is characterized by two forms of control over its constituent business units. First, financial control is exercised through the budgetary process, and operating units may be given specific financial goals in terms of profits or revenues. The existence of financial controls, however, is not sufficient to define a firm as a modern multidivisional corporation. A firm whose operating units are in unrelated businesses subject to only financial control by the parent firm is called a *holding company* by Williamson (1975). The second form of control that a truly multidivisional firm utilizes is in the form of strategy or strategic planning formulated by a planning staff at corporate headquarters, which reports to the CEO and the Board of Directors. It is clear that both the financial controls and strategic plans form the context within which the corporation's business units compete. If the parent company is a true multidivisional corporation with both financial controls and strategic plans, its operating units will have a greater or lesser zone of autonomy within which it may formulate its own strategy vis-à-vis its external competitors.

As noted previously, academic research on this aspect of media corporations is lacking. In the absence of such research examples of firm strategy may be drawn from the writings of corporate executives and business journalists. Specifically, it will be useful to contrast the corporate control strategies of Disney and Time Warner before its merger with America Online.

Both Disney and Time Warner are multidivisional firms that produce media content in several industries. Hence, both firms are capable of realizing economies of scope from their operations. However, the approaches to these possibilities of scope by firm management to have been at opposite ends of the spectrum.

On the one hand, Disney has sought explicitly to encourage the interdivisional cooperation necessary to realize scope economies by employing four tactics (Eisner, 1999). First, executives are compensated not on the basis of how their business unit performs but on the basis of overall corporate performance. Second, communication between divisions is encouraged through regular meetings between division executives and corporate-level executives. Third, there are programs to inform all executives, and indeed all employees, on the activities of each division of the firm. Third, there is a "synergy czar" who tries to ensure that ideas created in one division can be utilized by other divisions.

The approach at Time Warner before the merger, on the other hand, could be described as one of laissez-faire: Time Warner divisions had almost complete autonomy as long as they met financial goals. In fact, competition between divisions was an accepted part of the climate (Klein, 2003). Rather than cooperate in ways that would realize scope economies, executives in different divisions fought over such issues as the price HBO would pay for Time Warner movies. According to Klein (2003) it once took a year for two Time Warner divisions to negotiate an internal contract. After the merger with AOL there were attempts to institute an executive compensation similar to Disney's for the new company as well as an attempt to foster interdivisional communication through regular meetings of executives, but these efforts apparently have failed to accomplish the goal of interdivisional cooperation in pursuit of economies of scope.

The implications of supraorganization or parent company strategy for competition are fairly obvious. The firm that can realize efficiencies such as economies of scope and scale will be more efficient than its competitors and, hence, more likely to survive and prosper.

## RESEARCH ON LEVELS OF COMPETITION

Whereas the five levels of analysis identified in the previous sections of the chapter are an attempt to catalog all of the system levels that influence competitive relations among media firms and industries, no such claim is made concerning the variables that influence competition at each level. The variables that influence competition at each level were drawn from previous research or suggested by my own analysis, and no claim is made concerning their completeness. Future research will no doubt unearth new variables influencing competition at the various levels.

One import of this chapter is that researchers in media economics and management should give greater attention to the influence of levels of analysis and competitive relationships. Whereas researchers have been quite cognizant of some levels (as measured by the amount of research), other levels have not been the object of research. For example, the effects of policy at the national level or the effects of industry structure routinely inform published research, yet the effects of supraorganization or firm strategy have been less intensively researched. However, beyond the necessity of explicitly recognizing the need for multilevel research, there is the question of how to engage in research utilizing multiple levels of analysis.

This chapter closes by attempting to sketch an outline for the conduct of research which incorporates, in the same research design, multiple levels of analysis. Since influences on competition may operate at several levels of analysis, it is important to be able to incorporate different levels into a research design. What is required is a research strategy that enables one to engage in an active search for level variables that influence competition. The social science literature, however, provides only a sparse treatment of this problem. However, researchers in comparative politics (Przeworksi & Teune, 1970) have offered one solution to the problem of multileveled research, and their work provides a basis for suggesting another.

The design logic that seems most appropriate to the problem is what these authors call the "most different systems," design which is defined in opposition to the "most similar systems" design. The latter analytic paradigm is based on the belief that the best samples are composed of systems that are similar in as many attributes as possible. The design logic of the "most similar systems" paradigm is that elements or attributes that systems such as firms have in common are conceived as being controlled, whereas differences between systems are seen as possible explanations. Differences that emerge from research on similar systems will be small and, hence, qualify as explanations. Both designs can operate with variables from different levels, but the important difference is that the "most similar systems" design requires an assumption before the research is conducted, concerning the level at which the important influences are operating. Once the data have been collected, other levels cannot be considered.

The "most different systems" design, on the other hand, does not require such an assumption as to which level is most important. Rather, this design seeks an empirical answer to the question. The design begins by measuring behavior at the most molecular level possible. Generally, this would be the firm level, but, depending on the research question, variables could be measured at the subunit or even the individual level. Rather than assuming that influence on competition emanates from particular levels of analysis, the researcher conducts an intensive search for the levels at which influence takes place. If a relationship is found at the most molecular level, the next question is whether the relationship is the same across all levels of analysis. As Przeworksi and Teune state (1970; material in brackets added by me):

> To the extent that identifying the social system [level of analysis] does not help predict individual characteristics, systemic factors [levels] are not important. The total population is homogeneous, and further research is not distinct from investigations conducted primarily within a single social system [level of analysis]. The analysis can proceed without resorting to any system-level [levels of analysis] variables. (p. 40)

On the other hand, if the assumption that the relationship in question does not vary across levels of analysis can be rejected, then levels of analysis are relevant to the explanation of the differences. A simple, brief example illustrates the "most different systems" design as it might be used in a study of competition.

The hypothetical study would begin by measuring the relationship between audience size and share of local advertising for each newspaper, TV or radio station, and cable system in a sample of Consolidated Metropolitan Statistical Areas in the United States. The levels of analysis used in the study would include the market (indexed by size and geographic location), the supraorganizational or ownership level (indexed by whether the media organization is owned locally or by a regional or national group, chain, or MSO and by size or the revenues of the parent firm), and the industry level. If a relationship between audience size and share of local advertising is found, the next question is whether it varies by level of analysis. Statistical techniques such as hierarchical regression could be used to assess whether any of the level variables make a contribution to the advertising shares. It is likely that one or more of the level variables would make such a contribution. If they do not, however, then it is the characteristics of the individual firms themselves that account for the relationship and levels of analysis and irrelevant to the explanation.

Designs like the one in the foregoing brief example would be costly and time-consuming if the researcher were required to actually gather all the information required as primary data. However, the large databases compiled by industries and trade groups and other organizations are a rich source for data that could be used to conduct studies incorporating multiple levels of analysis.

## ACKNOWLEDGMENT

The author is grateful to Hans van Kranenburg for his comments on an earlier draft of the chapter.

## REFERENCES

Albarran, A. (2002). *Media economics*. Ames: Iowa State University Press.

Amieny, O. (1998). Nigeria. In A. Albarran & S. Chan-Olmsted (Eds.), *Global media economics* (pp. 197–216). Ames: Iowa State University Press.

Barney, J., & Hoskisson, R. (1990). Strategic groups: Untested assertions and research proposals. *Managerial and decision economics, 11*, 187–198.

Beltran, S. (1977). National communication policy in Latin America: A glance at the first steps. In S. Rahim & J. Middleton (Eds.), *Perspectives in communication policy and planning* (pp. 185–234). Honolulu, HI: East-West Center.

Carlton, D., & Perloff, J. (1994). *Modern industrial organization*. New York: Harper Collins.

Chan-Olmsted, S., & Albarran, A. (1998). A framework for the study of global media economics. In A. Albarran & S. Chan-Olmsted (Eds.), *Global media economics* (pp. 3–16). Ames: Iowa State University Press.

Chan-Olmsted, S., & Li, J. (2002). Strategic competition in the multichannel video programming market: An intraindustry strategic group study of cable programming networks. *Journal of Media Economics, 15*, 153–174.

Chon, B., Choi, J., Barnett, G., Danowski, J., & Joo, S. (2003). A structural analysis of media convergence: Cross-industry mergers and acquisitions in the information industries. *Journal of Media Economics, 16*, 141–158.

Corn-Rovere, R., & Carveth, R. (1998). Economics and media regulation. In A. Alexander, J. Owens, & R. Carveth (Eds.), *Media economics*. Mahwah, NJ: Laurence Erlbaum Associates.

Demers, D. (1994). Relative constancy hypothesis, structural pluralism, and national advertising expenditures. *Journal of Media Economics, 7*, 31–48.

Dimmick, J. (2003). *Media competition and coexistence: The theory of the niche*. Mahwah, NJ: Lawrence Erlbaum Associates.

Dimmick, J., Chen, Y., & Li, Z. (2004). Competition between the internet and traditional news media: The gratification opportunities niche dimension. *Journal of Media Economics, 17*, 19–33.

Dimmick, J., & Coit, P. (1982). Levels of analyses in mass media decision-making: A taxonomy, research strategy and illustrative data analysis. *Communication Research, 9*, 3–32.

Dimmick, J., Kline, S., & Stafford, L. (2000). The gratification niches of personal e-mail and telephone: Competition, displacement and complementarity. *Communication Research, 27*(2), 227–248.

Dimmick, J., & MacDonald, D. (2001). Network radio as oligopoly, 1926–1956: Rivalrous imitation and program diversity. *Journal of Media Economics, 14*, 197–212.

Dimmick, J., & McDonald, D. (2003). "Diversification as an element of Corporate Structure." Paper presented at 5th World Media Economics Conference, Turku, Finland.

Dimmick, J., & Rothenbuhler, E. (1984). The theory of the niche: Quantifying competition among media industries. *Journal of Communications, 34*, 103–119.

Eisner, M. (1999). *Work in progress*. New York: Random House.

Hendriks, P. (1998). The Netherlands. In Albarran & S. Chan-Olmsted (Eds.), *Global media economics* (pp. 164–179). Ames: Iowa State University Press.

Hunt, M. (1972). *Competition in the major home appliance industry*. Unpublished doctoral dissertation, Harvard University.

Hutchinson, G. (1958). Concluding remarks. *Cold Spring Harbor Symposium on Quantitative Biology, 22*, 415–427.

Klein, A. (2003). *Stealing time*. New York: Simon and Schuster.

Li, A., & Dimmick, J. (2004, May) *Western media corporations strategic behavior in transitional and emerging markets*. Paper presented at the 6th World Media Economics Conference, Montreal.

Litman, B. (1992). Economic aspects of program quality: The case for diversity. *Studies of Broadcasting, 24*, 393–409.

McCombs, M. (1972). *Mass media in the market place* (*Journalism monographs* No. 24).

McDonald, D., & Dimmick, J. (2003). The conceptualization and measurement of diversity. *Communication Research, 30*, 60–79.

McPhee, W. (1963). *Formal theories of mass behavior*. New York: Free Press.

Napoli, P. (1999). Reconstructing the diversity principle. *Journal of Communication, 49*, 7–34.

Owens, J., Carveth, R., & Alexander, A. (1998). An introduction to media economics theory and practice. In A. Alexander, J. Owens, & R. Carveth (Eds.), *Media economics*. Mahwah, NJ: Lawrence Erlbaum Associates.

Peteraf, M., & Shanley, M. (1997). Getting to know you: A theory of strategic group identity. *Strategic Management Journal, 18*, 165–186.

Pianka, E. (1983). *Evolutionary ecology* (3rd ed.). New York: Harper and Row.

Picard, R. (1989). *Media economics*. Newbury Park, CA: Sage.

Picard, R. (2001). Effects of recessions on advertising expenditures: An exploratory study of economic downturns in nine developed nations. *Journal of Media Economics, 14*, 1–14.

Porter, M. (1980). *Competitive strategy*. New York: Free Press.

Przeworksi, A., & Teune, H. (1970). *The logic of comparative social inquiry*. New York: Wiley Interscience.

Rahim, S. (1977). The scope of communication policy and planning research. In S. Rahim and J. Middleton (Eds.), *Perspectives in communication policy and planning*. Honolulu, HI: East-West Center.

Ramirez, A., Lin, S., & Dimmick, J. (2004, May). *Revisiting interactive media competition: The gratification niches of instant messaging, e-mail and the telephone*. Paper presented at the International communication association conference, New Orleans, LA.

Reger, R., & Huff, A. (1993). Strategic groups: A cognitive perspective. *Strategic Management Journal, 14,* 103–123.

Scherer, F. M. (1980). *Industrial market structure and economic performance.* Chicago: Rand McNally.

Simon, H. (1969). *The sciences of the artificial.* Cambridge, MA: MIT Press.

Williamson, O. (1975). *Markets and hierarchies.* New York: Free Press.

Wood, W. (1986). Consumer spending on the mass media: The principle of relative constancy reconsidered. *Journal of Communication, 36,* 39–51.

Wood, W., & O'Hare, S. (1991). Paying for the video revolution: Consumer spending on the mass media. *Journal of Communication 41,* 24–30.

# 17

# The Economics of Media Consolidation

### Todd Chambers
Texas Tech University

### Herbert H. Howard
University of Tennessee

A hallmark of the American political system is the promise of the First Amendment that the government shall not abridge the freedom of the press. The free press has evolved from printed news pamphlets and the penny press to the wired and wireless forms of electronic mass media. In general, the modern media have been recognized as participants in a theoretical marketplace of ideas where information commodities are offered for public consumption and debate. Democracy demands a free and wide exchange of information from a diverse and antagonistic pool of information sources (*Associated Press v. United States*, 1945). When there is a threat to the number of diverse and antagonistic information sources, such as in the case of consolidation, some policymakers, scholars, and others call for government regulation or deregulation to satisfy the public interest in the marketplace of ideas. There is no doubt that the information in the marketplace of ideas has social, political, and economic value. It is in the economic framework that this chapter seeks to answer questions related to the economics of media consolidation. This chapter seeks to provide an examination of the economics of media consolidation by exploring some of the key issues related to changes in media market structures. Specifically, we define media consolidation, highlight historical trends in the regulation of media ownership, analyze past research dealing with media ownership and the effects of structural changes in media markets, and make recommendations regarding the future of research in the economics of media consolidation.

## DEFINING MEDIA CONSOLIDATION

The merger between America Online (AOL) and Time Warner in 2000 represented the new age of synergy consolidation in the media world. One of new media's largest companies in the Internet world merged with one of old media's largest companies in the movie, cable, magazine, and television world to realize all of the efficiencies that the merger promised to offer—for the business and for the consumers. The Federal Communications Commission (FCC) approved the merger and argued that consumers would receive better service and technology in terms of broadband content and distribution (Federal Communications Commission [FCC], 2001a). After the announcement of the merger in 2000, the new company realized some notable setbacks including billions of dollars in revenue losses. By 2003, the company had decided to drop "AOL" from its company name (Creamer, 2003). This merger as well as dozens of others by companies such as News Corp., Clear Channel Communications, and Viacom has fueled debate and criticism about mergers at the local, regional, national and global level.

The debate about media consolidation has spilled over from the traditional communities of academics and policymakers into the neighborhoods of average citizens. During the 20-month period (Oct. 2001 to May 2003) that the FCC reviewed the broadcast ownership rules, the Commission sifted through more than 520,000 public comments about the issue (FCC, 2003). A Pew Research Center poll found that 48% of respondents to a telephone survey in July 2003 knew about the decision by the FCC to relax the cross-media ownership rule—up from only 26% in February 2003 (Johnson, 2003). In addition, the same poll found that half of the respondents felt that the decision to relax the cross-media ownership rules would be bad for America (Johnson, 2003). The changes in the broadcast rules combined with the growing public interest in the issues of media ownership have highlighted the need to review the specifics of media consolidation and its perceived and actual effects on the welfare of the public.

Overall, media consolidation is a difficult concept to define, much less study. In economic terms, consolidation is a form of merger activity used by firms to combine properties in "a type of merger in which both companies cease to exist after the transaction and an entirely new corporation is formed which retains the assets and liabilities of both companies" (Ozanich & Wirth, 1993, p. 117). From a media perspective, Compaine (1982) concluded there are three general types of mergers in the media industry: horizontal, vertical, and conglomerate. The type of merger is determined by the product markets of the companies involved. If a company merges with another company with similar products in the same market, then the merger is typically characterized as a horizontal merger. A vertical merger can best be described as a company that produces a product buying another company that distributes the product. Finally, a conglomerate merger involves companies with multiple products in different product markets. Since the mid-1990s, there has been a spotlight on media merger activity with companies such as AT&T, TCI, AOL, Time Warner, News Corp., and DirecTV. Overall, these merger activities have created a new media environment with new questions about the consequences of consolidation.

## CURRENT TRENDS IN MEDIA CONSOLIDATION

Advances in new technologies such as the Internet, digital broadcast and cable television, and other communication technologies have created new outlets for information. According to the National Cable Television Association, there were 255 national cable television networks in January 2004 (National Cable Television Association, 2004). The FCC reported that there has been a 5% increase in the number of commercial radio stations since the passage of the 1996 Telecommunications Act ("FCC's Adelstein Urges Caution," 2003). Between 1990 and 2000, the number of broadcast television stations experienced a double-digit increase of 12.3% (Levy, Ford-Livene, & Levine, 2002). At the same time, the number of owners for media outlets has decreased in the radio (Williams & Roberts, 2002), television (Howard, 2003) and cable industries (FCC, 2002). According to Howard (2003), almost 86% of all television stations in the United States are owned by multiple-station or group ownership. Likewise, 87% of all cable systems are controlled by the top 10 multiple system operators (MSOs) (FCC, 2002). For radio, one company, Clear Channel Communications, controls more than 1,200 radio stations. Table 17.1 describe the number and value of radio and television transactions since 1994. Based on the transaction information, the spike for radio occurred in 2000 and 2001, whereas there was a jump for television between 2001 and 2002. Since mergers decrease the number of companies in a particular market and may have negative effects on the degree of competition in a market, policymakers evaluate and administer policies related to consolidation activity.

**TABLE 17.1**
Radio and Television Station Transactions, 1994–2002

| Year | Radio | Radio Value | TV | TV Value |
| --- | --- | --- | --- | --- |
| 1994 | 494 | 970,400,000 | 89 | 2,200,000 |
| 1995 | 524 | 792,440,000 | 112 | 4,740,000 |
| 1996 | 671 | 2,840,820,000 | 99 | 10,488,000,000 |
| 1997 | 630 | 2,461,570,000 | 108 | 6,400,000,000 |
| 1998 | 589 | 1,596,210,000 | 90 | 7,120,000,000 |
| 1999 | 382 | 1,718,000,000 | 86 | 4.720,000,000 |
| 2000 | 1,794 | 24,900,000,000 | 154 | 8,800,000,000 |
| 2001 | 1,000 | 3,800,000,000 | 108 | 4,900,000,000 |
| 2002 | 836 | 5,594,141,000 | 249 | 2,529,039,000 |

*Note:* Adapted from *Broadcasting & Cable Yearbook* (2003). Newton, MA: Reed Publishing.

## MEDIA CONSOLIDATION FROM A REGULATION PERSPECTIVE

The ideals of the Sherman Antitrust Act of 1890 embody the core concepts when dealing with merger activity in the media industry. Section 2 of the Sherman Act prohibits the monopolization of free trade in the United States. Historically, government agencies devoted to regulating the broadcasting industry have used the same ideals to prevent one company from monopolizing the content within the marketplace of ideas.

The U.S. Department of Justice and other agencies such as the U.S. Federal Trade Commission administer the policies of the Sherman Act and attempt to preserve competition within industries. The agency bases its regulatory decisions about mergers using a set of evaluative criteria known as the *Horizontal Merger Guidelines* (Federal Trade Commission [FTC], 1997). These guidelines help regulators evaluate the potential harm to competition and negative consequences on the consumer welfare from the merger of two companies. Specifically, the guidelines outline issues of market concentration, entry barriers, efficiency gains, and economic failure (FTC, 1997). These measures have been used to help shape and formulate policy related to the industries of mass media.

To help prevent the monopolization of ideas, various agencies and branches of the government have used laws and regulations to sustain a diverse marketplace of ideas. The First Amendment guarantees a "freedom of the press" that has been used by all types of organizations claiming "press" status. The general theme behind policies related to ownership is that the more independent owners there are, the better it is for society.

### Newspapers

Outside of economic factors, the freedom of the press clause guarantees that anyone can become a newspaper publisher. Unlike the broadcasting industry where a station owner must obtain a license to broadcast and even the cable industry where an individual or company must apply for a local franchise to operate a system, individuals wanting to publish a newspaper do not go through any type of application process. Despite this freedom, the government has argued that it has an interest in protecting the public interest when newspapers attempt to use anticompetitive practices to prevent other papers from operating. In one of the most widely discussed and cited cases, the U.S. Supreme Court upheld the right of competitive newspapers in its *Associated Press v. United States* (1945). According to the Court, the First Amendment "rests on the assumption that the widest dissemination of information from diverse and antagonistic sources is essential to the welfare of the public" (*Associated Press v. United States*, 326 U.S. 1, 1945). Part of the reasoning was to prevent the Associated Press from keeping its services from members' competitors. Although the Court wanted to maintain competition in the daily newspaper industry, it could not account for the economic conditions throughout the 20th century that decimated the number of markets with competitive newspapers.

As a result, Congress passed the *Newspaper Preservation Act* of 1970 that allowed newspaper competitors to form joint operating agreements (JOAs). A JOA permitted a newspaper in a market to take over the business operations of a failing newspaper in order to preserve the publication of both newspapers. According to Lacy (1988), Albuquerque's

*Journal* and *Tribune* formed the first JOA in 1933. Throughout the Act's history, there were joint operating agreements in 25 different cities; in 2003, there were 12 JOAs operating in markets such as Cincinnati, Ohio, and Las Vegas, Nevada (Newspaper Association of America, 2003).

## Broadcasting

Regulation of broadcasting in the United States was based on several principles including a limited broadcast spectrum that belongs to the public and is legally available through licensing by the government. Consequently, the Federal Radio Commission (FRC) (later the FCC) was granted the power to develop criteria for awarding licenses to applicants for broadcast stations. Under powers granted by the Radio Act of 1927, the FRC determined that broadcast licenses could be issued to business enterprises for commercial purposes, as well as to noncommercial organizations. Both types of licensees are expected to operate stations entrusted to them in the public interest, convenience, and necessity. No policy making action was taken regarding the multiple ownership of stations until much later.

Multiple station ownership has a long history, extending back to the licensee (Westinghouse Electric) of the first commercial radio station, KDKA, Pittsburgh, Pennsylvania. From 1920 to 1940, the regulatory commissions granted numerous licenses for group-owned radio stations. Ownership of radio stations and radio networks became a heated political issue in the late 1930s when the Mutual Broadcasting System sought governmental intervention to reduce the control that NBC and CBS had over numerous stations they operated for other owners. It was Mutual's contention that it was at an unfair advantage in gaining affiliate stations as outlets for its programming. Mutual also asked the government to break up the dual network operation of the National Broadcasting Company.

With the release of the FCC's ownership study, the *Report on Chain Broadcasting* (1941), the Commission expanded its powers to regulate the broadcast industry by exercising a rule that a company should not operate more than one national radio network. Although the FCC had no direct control over the "networks," the Commission used network affiliation to justify regulations in the public interest. Subsequently, after the U.S. Supreme Court upheld the Commission's new network broadcasting rules in *NBC v. United States* (1943), the FCC forced NBC to break up its dual Red and Blue networks. In complying with the Commission's order, NBC sold its Blue Network in 1943 and retained its more popular NBC Red network. In addition, the FCC forced NBC and CBS to stop operating stations licensed to other entities. Further, in 1943, the Commission adopted an antiduopoly rule, which required that no licensee own two stations of the same broadcast service in the same market area. This rule solidified the FCC's doctrine of localism, which had been developing since the 1920s.

With the network case prominent in its activity, in 1940 the FCC adopted rules to limit multiple station ownership in the two new broadcast services, FM radio and television. In this action, owners were limited to six FM stations and three TV stations per licensee. Although no limits were imposed on AM radio stations at that time, the Commission applied the duopoly principle to the new FM and television services. In 1944, the FCC, responding to a filing by NBC, increased the maximum to five TV stations per licensee.

Critics of multiple station ownership argued that unrestrained group ownership of stations could result in undue control of the communications media that could result in monopoly control of the flow of information received by the public, as well as undue economic control of the media by a few owners. For example, it was said that the latter could result in artificially high advertising rates and other types of trade restraint activity within the radio industry.

The debate concerning multiple station ownership resumed during the post–World War II years and, in 1952–53, the Commission adopted comprehensive rules that limited each owner to seven AM, seven FM, and seven television stations. The arbitrary number of seven stations thus became the FCC's operational limit for acceptable concentration of control of the broadcast media. Unfortunately, the 1952–53 rules did not take into account such relevant matters as station power or the size of markets served by stations. As a result, owners frequently sold stations in order to buy other stations in larger and more economically promising markets while staying within the limit of seven stations. These rules remained in effect until 1986, when the Commission relaxed the ownership limits to 12 stations of each type (AM, FM, and TV). This action also restricted television group owners to coverage of a maximum of 25% of the households in the United States. The relaxation of limits was justified by the fact that the number of stations in each broadcast service had increased by manifold numbers. Group ownership of both radio and television stations expanded greatly following the rules change of 1986.

Whenever more than one applicant sought a broadcast channel, the FCC customarily held comparative hearings to determine which applicant should be awarded the facility. Prominent among the Commission's criteria was its preference for local ownership of stations, which the agency favored as a means of promoting a more diverse body of station owners. As a result, the Commission usually favored local owners over owners of groups of stations. A second preference of the Commission in its comparative hearings was its desire to promote ownership diversity within a market. This preference became manifest in two ways in the agency's comparative hearings, particularly those for new television stations during the 1950s. First, the FCC usually preferred applicants who were not connected with dominant media outlets in a market. The agency, therefore, looked closely at each applicant's other broadcast holdings in a market when granting a new facility. Thus, a TV applicant who had a dominant radio station in the market was less likely to be favored than the owner of a smaller radio station, provided both had a good record of public service. Second, the FCC usually favored applicants who did not have an ownership interest in a local daily newspaper over those who were involved in local publishing.

Concerns were expressed quite strongly about cross-media ownership of newspapers and broadcast stations during the 1930s. The critics believed that a combination of a local broadcast station and a local newspaper could powerfully influence the public on matters of civic importance. No restrictions on local cross-media ownership of a broadcast station and a newspaper were adopted during the 1930s. However, after television became an established medium, controversy arose again concerning local newspaper–broadcast cross-media ownership in the 1960s. The debate climaxed in 1974 when the FCC issued cross-media ownership rules that forbade the formation of new combinations of local broadcast stations and daily newspapers. Established combinations, with a few exceptions, were allowed to remain unaffected by the rule. However, from 1974 forward, the number of newspaper–broadcast combinations declined sharply as many owners decided to sell off one of their properties, usually the broadcasting stations. Most owners who sold either a newspaper or a broadcasting station in the same community received favorable tax inducements to bring about compliance with the Commission's 1974 ruling.

## Cable

Prior to 1992, cable system operators had no upper cap on the number or percentage of subscribers they could serve. However, the 1992 Cable Act directed the FCC to establish limits on the number of subscribers a multiple system cable operator (MSO) may serve. The FCC implemented such rules in 1993, allowing operators to serve up to a 30% share of nationwide cable and direct broadcast satellite (DBS) subscribers. Although the U.S. Supreme Court upheld the constitutionality of the Cable Act, the U.S. Court of Appeals for the District of Columbia in 2001 remanded the FCC's limits for cable ownership the following year for further review. The lower court said the Commission "failed to explain why the specific restrictions were justified given the infringement on cable companies' free speech rights" (McConnell, 2001, p. 8). After the court's remanding order, the FCC, in September 2001, launched a proceeding to review its horizontal and vertical limits for cable companies ("FCC Begins Reviewing Cable Ownership Limits," 2001). Early in 2003, FCC Chairman Michael Powell told reporters that the agency would soon review recommendations from the Mass Media Bureau on revising cable-ownership limits. As of August 2004, no further Commission action had occurred on cable ownership limits. In effect, the District Court's order in 2001 abolished the 30% cap on the number of households a cable company could reach.

## Deregulation

Since the 1970s, Congress and the FCC have been deregulating the rules and regulations related to the broadcasting and cable industries. The FCC began to allow time brokerage agreements for radio broadcasters in 1971 (Hagin, 1994). A time brokerage or local marketing agreement (LMA) "allows the licensee of another broadcast facility to operate a station in return for a share of the profits" (Creech, 1993, p. 84). Another area of deregulation slowly relaxed restrictions on duopoly arrangements for radio and television. The duopoly rules for radio stations existed until 1992, when the Commission allowed radio duopolies in all markets. According to the duopoly rules, in markets with more than 14 stations an operator could control two AM and two FM stations (FCC, 1992). In smaller markets, the duopoly rules allowed an owner to operate three stations—two of the same service—as long as the duopoly does not attract more than 50% of the audience share of the market (Hagin, 1994). The Commission first relaxed the television duopoly rules for large markets in the fall of 1999 and expanded into other types of markets in June 2003.

In the *Telecommunications Act of 1996*, Congress changed the national market structure for both television and radio by lifting the limit on the number of properties one company can own on a national basis. For radio, this allowed the development of major radio groups such as Clear Channel Communications and Cumulus Broadcasting. For television, however, the rules retained a national audience reach cap. Under the former rules, a single television group owner could not reach more than 35% of the total potential national audience with no limit on the number of stations. By law, the FCC is required to review ownership rules every 2 years with the provision that any unnecessary rules should be eliminated. In 2003, the Commission voted to raise the cap to 45%. However, Congress and the Bush Administration revised the percentage to 39% in early 2004. In addition, the Act allowed cross-ownership between the cable and telephone industries.

Other decisions by the FCC have stirred public debate among industry, political, and academic communities about the effects of deregulation on media consolidation. After 20 months of review, the FCC adopted broadcast ownership rules in June 2003 that replaced the *Cross Media Ownership Rules* of 1975. In markets with at least nine television stations, the cross-ownership ban between the local newspaper and a local radio and/or a local television station was eliminated, and the local television duopoly rules were further relaxed. At the time of writing, a U.S. Appeals court was scheduled to review the cross-media and duopoly provisions of the FCC's rules changes of 2003.

## MEDIA CONSOLIDATION FROM AN ECONOMIC PERSPECTIVE

Media economists applied industrial organization theory as an acceptable framework to analyze media markets (Busterna, 1988a; Wirth & Bloch, 1995). According to the theory, the structure of a market determines the conduct of firms and subsequent performance of a particular market (Scherer, 1980; Sheperd, 1985; Stern & Grabner, 1970). In practical terms, this theory explains that the number and characteristics of organizations will determine the competitive behavior of these firms in the marketplace.

### The Market

One of the most important applications of the industrial organization model of economics is the ability to link market structure with market power. If a market contains a firm with market power, then the market might experience certain types of conduct from the dominant firm, resulting in an overall decrease in the market's performance (Ferguson & Ferguson, 1988). In particular, the dominant firm may use various pricing strategies to exclude current or potential competitors; or, a firm may use its power to differentiate its products or services to prevent other firms from entering the market. Through horizontal mergers and/or vertical integration, media companies can benefit from economic efficiencies and leverage market power in either or both of the market for audiences and the market for advertisers.

Economists classify a market as a group of buyers and sellers exchanging substitutable goods and services (Picard, 1989; Sheperd, 1985). Unlike other industries, local media not only exist in geographic markets, but also operate in a product market that is commonly referred to as the dual product market—the market for audience and the market for advertisers (Picard, 1989). Daily newspapers, local television stations and local radio stations compete for audience time at both the intraindustry and an intermedium level. Within a media industry, each medium competes with similar medium types for audience and advertising revenue. For example, a radio station will produce a differentiated product, or format, to attract a listener. Each station will compete against other radio stations for listeners and advertisers. At the intermedium level, each medium type will compete with different medium types for audiences and advertisers. At this level, a radio station might compete with a newspaper in terms of time spent listening rather than time spent reading the newspaper. Likewise, the radio station will compete with a daily newspaper for a share of the local advertising revenue.

## Ownership in the Market

Consolidation manifests itself in several different forms within the mass media. In the global or national marketplace, media companies typically combine for mergers, acquisitions, and joint ventures. For local markets, consolidation occurs when companies form joint operating agreements, local marketing agreements, shared service agreements, and duopoly. Although the media may operate like other types of industries in terms of geographic markets, the dual product nature of the media creates unique economic consequences for market conduct and performance.

Studies of media consolidation have typically explored the nature of ownership in descriptive studies or analyzed specific economic effects of ownership in analytical studies. In general, the descriptive studies have focused on identifying the national or local market structure from an intra- or intermedium industry perspective (Compaine, 1982; Compaine & Gomery, 2000; Nixon & Ward, 1961; Sterling, 1975; Waterman, 1991). These studies have used both simple and sophisticated tools to identify market structure. From counts of the number and types of owner in a market to calculations of the Hirschman–Herfindahl index (HHI) or the four- or eight-firm concentration ratios (CR4, CR8), there are a variety of methods available to analyze market structure in media markets (Albarran, 2003). These measures allow analysts to identify the concentration of ownership and evaluate the degree of competition in a market. Market concentration "shows the extent to which production of a particular good or service is confined to a few large firms" (Ferguson & Ferguson, 1988, p. 39). If a market has a dominant firm, that firm will lead to entry barriers and prevent competitors from offering consumers an alternative product or service.

The analytical tools for measuring market structure require clear and precise definitions of the geographic and product markets that will be studied. While all media companies exist in some type of geographic market, not all media companies will compete in the same product market(s). Bates (1993b) emphasized the importance of precision in defining geographic markets and measuring the product market for audiences separately from the product market for advertisers. For example, newspapers such as *The New York Times*, *The Wall Street Journal*, *USA Today*, and *The Los Angeles Times* are typically considered as newspapers with a nationwide market. These papers have a nationwide distribution where they are read and compete for reading time among subscribers in hundreds of other daily newspapers existing in local markets. Table 17.2 provides information about selected studies and how the authors measured market structure.

In addition, a key to exploring the issues of market structure, conduct, and performance is defining the nature of the media firm. In the dual product market, there is a distinction between the market for audiences and the market for advertisers at the firm level. Specifically, all media firms technically act as outlets for information in the audience and advertiser product markets. From this perspective, research in the area of source

**TABLE 17.2**
Selected Geographic and Product Market Definitions

| Author | Topic | Geographic Market(s) | Product Market(s) | Market Structure |
|---|---|---|---|---|
| Bates (1993b) | Television | Local TV markets | Viewers and advertisers | HHI |
| Larson (1980) | Television | National TV market | Viewers and advertisers | CR4, CR8, CR20 |
| Lacy & Davenport (1994) | Newspaper | Local daily newspaper markets | Subscribers | HHI, CR1, CR2, CR3 |
| Drushel (1998) | Radio | Top 50 local radio markets | Listeners | HHI |
| Berry & Waldfogel (2001) | Radio | Local radio markets | Listeners | HHI |

diversity has considered daily newspapers, local television stations, and local radio stations as participants in a marketplace of ideas (Lacy & Riffe, 1994; Levin, 1954). Whereas all media firms in a market technically act as outlets of information, not all firms exist as independent voices. Economists highlight the need to identify the source of programming or control of access to information (Owen, 1978). Sterling (1975) and Nixon and Ward (1961) defined a media voice as a separate, antagonistic owner of a media property within a local market. It is in this distinction between voices and outlets that the classic debate concerning media consolidation generates the most discussion.

Some scholars have attempted to link diversity of opinion with the number of different media outlets within a local market (Loevinger, 1979). A media outlet differs from a media voice because an owner controls the value of the license through management decisions. Former FCC Commissioner Loevinger (1979) argued that the increasing number of different media outlets ensures diversity within the marketplace of ideas. From this perspective, it would appear that the more outlets available to a market, the greater the diversity of information choices in the market. Another perspective spotlights the need to consider the ownership of these outlets to determine true diversity within the marketplace of ideas.

The primary issue in research related to media ownership is the effect of ownership on the performance of a media market. If a company controls the majority of the media outlets, then that company can monopolize the dual product of media—the audience and the advertiser. Scholars such as Bagdikian (1997) warned of the consolidation and conglomeration of the mass media. Beginning in 1983, Bagdikian (1983, 1990, 1997) argued that there have been a decreasing number of large conglomerates controlling the media content available to consumers. In most of Bagdikian's work, the findings are based on trend data from several different types of media industries to argue the majority of information and entertainment media are controlled by a handful of companies.

Bagdikian (1997) feared that monopoly control of information outlets would prevent the free expression of ideas in the American democracy. For critics of media concentration, the public interest is not served by monopoly control of local information outlets in all types of media industries. Essentially, this debate focuses on the development of ownership patterns in media markets.

When considering the mass media from an interindustry context, several scholars have addressed the general development and ownership of mass media industries (Compaine, 1982; Compaine & Gomery, 2000; Nixon & Ward, 1961; Sterling, 1975; Waterman, 1991). Most of these studies have focused on general information related to the number of outlets and owners as well as attempting to differentiate as many technical and organizational differences. In general, these studies focused on a national geographic market and included daily newspapers, broadcast television, radio, cable television multiple system operators and cable television networks, motion pictures, magazines and more recently, the top Internet companies. Other studies such as Albarran and Dimmick (1996) and Waterman (1991) added comparative analyses of the degree of ownership concentration across multiple media industries by using HHI and CR4 and CR8 ratios to compare the media industries. Overall, these studies cataloged valuable information related to the type of media owner and level of competition within the industries.

From an intraindustry perspective, studies have dealt with the issues of ownership in the newspaper (Lacy & Davenport, 1994), broadcast television (Howard, 2003; Larson, 1980), radio (Drushel, 1998; Riffe & Shaw, 1990; Rogers & Woodbury, 1996) and cable television industries (Chan-Olmsted & Litman, 1988; Waterman & Weiss, 1997). These studies addressed issues ranging from the concentration of ownership to the effects of market structure on a variety of dependent measures related to consumer welfare. Other researchers addressed the issues of media ownership by exploring mergers and acquisitions (Ozanich & Wirth, 1993). In most cases, the studies focused on the link between the type of media ownership structure and its effect on the diversity of information provided from the outlets controlled by those organizations.

## Market Structure

The structure of a market can be defined in terms of the size and distribution of owners, the amount of product differentiation, and the number of entry barriers within a market (Albarran, 2003; Picard, 1989). According to theory, the greater number of similar firms leads to a more competitive market (Picard, 1989). Markets are described using the theoretical framework known as the *theory of the firm*. This framework explains that markets operate in perfect competition, monopolistic competition, oligopoly, or monopoly.

In general, media economists have used the theory of the firm to classify the daily newspaper industry as monopoly (Albarran, 2003; Picard, 1989), the broadcast television industry as an oligopoly (Larson, 1980), and radio as moving from monopolistic competition to oligopoly (Drushel, 1998). In most markets, the newspaper industry has developed into a natural monopoly where one firm becomes so efficient in producing and delivering its product that it becomes difficult for a competitor to exist in the same market. Researchers have examined the status of newspaper market structure (Busterna, 1988a; Lacy & Davenport, 1994; Picard, 1994; Udell, 1990). Overall, the general trend within the newspaper industry indicated that the number of chain newspapers has doubled since 1960 (Busterna, 1988a). In addition, Lacy and Davenport (1994) concluded that the daily newspaper market was highly concentrated. Litman (1988) attributed the monopolization of the daily newspaper market to economies of scale and joint operating agreements. These results support the notion that the newspaper industry exists within a monopoly market.

The broadcast industries have wavered between oligopoly and monopolistic competition. The majority of research describing the structure of the broadcast industry focused on television (Bates, 1993b; Howard, 2003, 1998; Larson, 1980; Powers, 2001). On a national level, Howard (2003) found that more than 80% of all commercial television stations are under group ownership. At the local level, Bates (1993b) analyzed local television market structure in terms of the audience and advertiser markets, concluding that concentration levels were lower in the audience market than in the advertising market. For cable television, research indicated increases in ownership concentration for the overall industry (Chan-Olmsted, 1996).

Because of the changes in radio ownership rules, there has been a renewed interest in the structure of the radio industry (Berry & Waldfogel, 2001; Chan-Olmsted, 1995; Drushel, 1998; Rogers & Woodbury, 1996; Williams, 1998). Drushel (1998) reported movement toward oligopoly in the Top 50 radio markets. Chan-Olmsted (1995) found support for the notion that the relaxation of duopoly rules was leading to an expansion of ownership within local markets. Overall, the results of broadcast ownership studies suggested higher levels of consolidation at the national and local level. Overall, it appears that each of the traditional, local media industries—daily newspapers, local radio, local television stations, and cable systems—have maintained or moved toward moderate or high levels of ownership concentration. In other words, fewer owners of local media are controlling larger numbers of local media outlets. In addition, it seems the research indicates that the type of media owner is changing as well. Past research indicated that local markets were dominated by chain ownership of newspapers (Lacy & Davenport, 1994), group ownership of television stations (Howard, 2003), and absentee ownership in radio (Chambers, 2003). These policy changes related to television ownership and cross-media ownership will create more opportunities for research into the effects of market structure on the conduct of individual firms in an industry.

## Market Conduct

According to the theory of the firm, market structure is characterized by the activities, or conduct, of both the sellers and buyers in the market. In general, market structure predicts specific types of firm conduct such as pricing, product strategy and advertising, research and innovation, plant investment, and legal tactics (Albarran, 2003). From a monopoly market where a single product seller dominates the market and is able to set the price to maximize profits, to a perfect competition market where several sellers of similar products react as price takers in the competitive environment (Albarran, 2003), media exist in various market structures. Monopolistic competition shares some similarities with oligopoly. Under monopolistic competition, a market must have a large number of producers, a degree of product differentiation, no entry barriers, no firm interdependence, and no market share above 10% (Sheperd, 1985). In addition, firms in this environment will have control over the pricing of its products and services; however, these prices will be related to competitors' prices (Organisation for Economic Co-operation and Development, 1993a). Under an oligopoly market structure, the market will have small number of leading firms, some fringe competitors, and a degree of interdependence among firms (Picard, 1989; Sheperd, 1985). Since participants in an oligopoly have control over price, cooperative behavior can lead to joint maximization of prices (Organisation for Economic Co-operation and Development, 1993b). Although all elements are important elements when evaluating media markets, the majority of studies have focused on the pricing and price strategies of firms.

After the passage of the Telecommunications Act of 1996, one of the first responses from the U.S. Department of Justice was to investigate radio mergers in Boston, Philadelphia, Rochester, and Cincinnati to evaluate how radio consolidation affected the market for advertising (Department of Justice, 1996a, 1996b, 1996c). In particular, the Department of Justice wanted to prevent anticompetitive behavior in the pricing of advertising that may or may not have resulted from the radio mergers. Initial industry evidence suggested that consolidation defined as radio duopolies had not raised the price of radio advertising (Price, 1997). Examinations of advertising pricing in media markets have been a popular method of research in media economics.

Scholarly research in the area of advertising pricing and market structures has been mixed. Masson, Mudambi, and Reynolds (1990) studied radio and television advertising prices in terms of viewers and listeners. Overall, the results indicated that prices rise with increased competition. In a study about the Canadian radio industry, McFadyen, Hoskins, and Gillen (1980) found a strong positive relationship between market concentration and the cost of radio pricing. As the number of owners declines in a market, there is an increase in the cost for the price of a commercial. In other words, the dominant firms develop market power and increase the price of advertising.

There have been a variety of approaches to exploring pricing issues in the newspaper industry. Shaver (1995) examined theoretical perspectives of pricing theory by considering the rapidly changing competitive environment for newspapers. Empirical studies of the industry have found mixed results related to market structure and pricing differences between different types of newspaper structures. Picard (1988) reviewed research related to the pricing behavior of newspapers and reported that newspaper monopolies and newspapers in common ownership arrangements such as a joint operating agreement or part of a chain charge higher prices for advertising. A recent study about the economic effects of newspaper joint operating agreements found that newspapers in joint operating agreements actually have advertising rates that are similar to those of newspapers in competitive markets (Romeo, Pittman, & Familant, 2003). These findings highlight the difficulty in measuring issues of conduct related to an evolving media marketplace.

Although advertising pricing is an important component of market conduct, the audience can also enjoy or suffer consequences from changes in pricing behavior. After Congress initially deregulated cable television rates in 1984, consumers called on Congress to reregulate the industry as a result of increasing subscription rates. Jaffe and Kanter (1990) found that after deregulation in the 1980s there was a relationship between markets with more and less competition; in particular, it appeared that in smaller markets the price for cable was higher during deregulation than during regulation. Furthermore, Yan (2002) reported that firm size in the cable industry had negative consequences for consumers in terms of must-carry rules. Specifically, the author found "larger MSOs dropped a larger number of over-the-air television stations to add more cable networks to their lineups" (p. 188). As a natural monopoly, these types of results seem to confirm the exercise of market power by firms in this type of market structure.

Another popular area for research related to market conduct has been in the area of product strategy decisions in terms of newspapers, television, and radio. Several scholars have investigated issues of newspaper product strategy in terms of editorial aspects (Hale, 1988), wire services (Lacy, 1990, 1989), reporting aspects (Picard, 1989), and news content (Wanta & Johnson, 1994). For broadcast television, the research focused on content of television news (Besen & Johnson, 1985) and public interest programming (Busterna, 1988b; Prisuta, 1977; Wirth & Wollert, 1979). For radio, research topics in product strategy have focused on the effect of group ownership on news programming (Lacy & Riffe, 1994; McKean & Stone, 1992; Riffe & Shaw, 1990) and radio formats (Berry & Waldfogel, 2001; Greve, 1996; Rogers & Woodbury, 1996; Romeo & Dick, 2003). A U.S. Department of Justice study about the effect of market structure on radio programming found that major format changes occurred more frequently among radio stations with below-average market shares (Romeo & Dick, 2003). One reason for this trend is that the majority of the stations are large, group-owned radio stations. These studies provided mixed results related to the effect of ownership structure on variables related to market conduct.

## Market Performance

Market performance revolves around the concept of efficiency for the firm and for the public. Albarran (2003) outlines the components of market performance as technical and allocative efficiency, equity, and progress. In general, studies in this area have used a variety of measures for performance from both the firm and the market perspective. From a newspaper framework, studies of have measured performance at the firm level by looking at profits (Blankenburg & Ozanich, 1993; Demers, 1998, 1996, 1991) and the market level by examining the effects of a recession on the newspaper economy (Picard & Rimmer, 1998) and the long-term effects of consolidations in The Netherlands newspaper market (van Kraneburg, 2001). Many of these studies focused on public versus private companies and the differences each organizational type has on the various measures of performance. Demers (1998) found that although corporate newspapers are more profitable, they actually place *less* emphasis on profits than do independent newspapers.

At the firm and market levels for the broadcasting and cable industries, the studies focused on the rate of return for Canadian radio (McFadyen, Hoskins, & Gillen, 1980), station trafficking in television and radio (Bates, 1993a, 1993b), and consumer welfare in cable television (Crawford, 2000). McFadyen et al. (1980) found the overall rate of return for Canadian radio companies in 1975 was 18%. Bates (1993a) valued the use of multiples as an indicator of station financial performance. For radio, Bates (1993a) reported multiples averaged about 6–8 for AM, 8.5–10 for FM, and 7–10 for AM/FM combinations (p. 108). In related research about radio station trafficking, Bates (1993a) suggested that the FM radio industry was providing higher than average prices.

Throughout most of the research dealing with market performance issues has been the question: Is monopoly or competition better for consumer choice?

## THE STEINER MODEL

The seminal study concerning the effect of monopoly control of a media outlet and its effect on the performance of the market for media content was Steiner's (1952) work in the area of radio program choice. Based on Steiner's 1949 dissertation, the study focused on the degree of competition in the radio industry. Steiner hypothesized that a market operating with a discriminating monopolist would provide a better service to the public than a market operating with a set of competitors. According to the hypothesis, a discriminating monopolist, working with the assumption of audience maximization, has more incentive than participants in a competitive market to provide differentiated products to the entire market. The competitors, working with the assumption of audience maximization, will duplicate their programming according to the most popular program choice available; in other words, in a competitive market, economic theory suggests that competitors will duplicate the most popular program choice because the incentive lies in dividing the audience of the most popular station. Steiner argued that the public welfare was better served under the monopoly model for program choice.

Since Steiner, there have been several attempts to study the effects of broadcast competition and radio program choice (Berry & Waldfogel, 2001; Glasser, 1984; Greve, 1996; Haring, 1975; Owen, 1977; Rogers & Woodbury, 1996). The majority of research in the area of broadcast competition and program choice has focused primarily on television with specific analyses in the structural aspects of advertiser-supported and pay television (Noll, 1978; Noll, Peck, & McGowan, 1973; Owen, 1975; Owen, Beebe, & Manning, 1974; Owen & Wildman, 1992; Spence, 1976; Spence & Owen, 1975, 1977), the number of channels available on cable television (De Jong & Bates, 1991), content aspects related to the conduct of various media such as television and cable television (Grant, 1994), and the home video and theatrical marketplace (Hellman & Soramaki, 1994). Overall, explicit tests of the Steiner model have provided mixed results in studies dealing with program choices.

For the most part, studies dealing with television have rejected the Steiner theory on the basis of audience preferences and the mechanics of the television broadcast industry. Economists such as Noll (1978), Spence and Owen (1975), and Owen and Wildman (1992) have refuted the Steiner examples by analyzing the advertiser-based and pay television-based systems of delivery in terms of audience preferences. Recent studies in radio have suggested confirmation of the initial Steiner hypothesis. Berry and Waldfogel (2001) reported results that showed consolidation increasing the number of radio format choices in local radio markets. Likewise, Rogers and Woodbury (1996) demonstrated that it would take an unrealistic number of new competitors in a radio market to retrieve more diversity in the number of radio program choices. From a theoretical perspective, Gal-Or and Dukes (2003) explored the relationships between product differentiation and the level of advertising in commercial media markets. Because of the nature of an industry that competes for both advertising and audiences, the authors concluded that commercial media outlets involved in a competitive market situation have an interest in a minimum level of product differentiation because it allows stations to sell advertising at a higher rate. Gal-Or and Dukes argued the media have incentives to minimize product differentiation to allow producers to choose a lower level of advertising, consequently paying a higher price for the advertising space.

Overall, the program choice literature indicates the importance of the dual product nature of broadcast programming. Audiences and more important, advertisers, play an integral part in the media diversity equation. In addition, initial tests of the Steiner theory suggested that a monopolist would provide more diversity than a competitor because of the nature of program duplication. Finally, the results showed that although an increase to the number of stations in a market provides some increase in the level of program diversity, it requires a large number of stations in the market. The program choice literature expanded the theoretical basis for analyzing media consolidation.

## THE SCP PARADIGM

Overall, the structure-conduct-performance paradigm provides a useful framework for analyzing economic markets. Despite the successful application of industrial organization theory to studies of the media industry, contemporary research suggests the need to reexamine the basic premise of the paradigm because of rapid changes in media market structures (Young, 2000). In particular, convergence and concentration have created new types of multichannel media markets (Chan-Olmsted, 1997). In the cable industry, companies such as Cox Communications represent this type of converged media environment with a portfolio that includes newspapers, radio, television, cable systems, cable networks, Internet network distribution, and production capabilities. The mixed findings related to the consequences of ownership on conduct and performance variables make it difficult to anchor arguments solidly against or in favor of consolidation. In fact, recent studies in radio programming suggest that, contrary to the popular belief that consolidation would be bad for diversity of program choice, there have been increases in overall choice for radio formats. But, as others have pointed out, consolidation does seem to increase the cost of advertising and subscription prices to consumers.

Future studies should consider advancing the theoretical relationships between structure, conduct and performance. After finding that traditional models related to efficiency and market power did not fit data related to vertical integration in the cable industry, Ahn and Litman (1997) argued that consumer welfare was an important consideration when considering cable rate regulation. Few studies have attempted to examine the interplay between market structure, price competition, and the effect of advertising on media consumers within a media market. Häckner and Nyberg (2000) developed a model for analyzing price competition in different market structures while accounting for the nature of the product, advertising externalities, and product differentiation. In theory, the model suggested that exploring the link between the demands of media's dual audiences, the advertiser and the consumer, may reveal policy concerns about excessive media concentration in the public good media marketplace.

Based on a strict interpretation of the industrial organization theory, there are no mechanisms to deal with the product markets of multiple media industries. Outside of HHI and CR calculations using market share, very little research has focused on the effects of the audience on market structure. When the FCC released its Diversity Index with the new ownership rules in 2003, it hoped the index could be used to evaluate the amount of viewpoint diversity in local markets. The index included all of the major variables needed when considering the effects of consolidation—type of media, number of owners, and market share of medium. Despite the fact that it acknowledged the Internet, the Diversity Index assigned weights to media types that may be based on dated information about media use.

## A RESEARCH AGENDA

Convergence and policy changes are creating new types of media organizations that, by definition, will behave differently than the media organizations of old. The relaxation of broadcast ownership rules changed the structure of the local media market. Television duopolies, cross-media ownership, radio market clusters, and other new ownership types have restructured the media marketplace. These new ownership structures blur the lines between product markets for media and will require new methods for defining and analyzing market structure, conduct, and performance. Conceptually, these new structures require theoretical development at the firm level.

New technologies such as the Internet are changing the nature of traditional media. There is no doubt that the individual industries of radio, television, newspaper, and cable are becoming more concentrated—but how do you measure the degree of competition among all of these industries in a single market? Part of the problem might be solved by new methods of examining competition, such as the amount of time spent with various media types. Studies by McDonald and Dimmick (2003) and Shaver and Shaver (2003) have considered time as a crucial variable when thinking of issues of competition among the new media and the consequences of market concentration. By examining a variable such as time, researchers might be able to address issues related to global media concentration and intercultural communication patterns as well. These types of studies, combined with works by Napoli dealing with the role of the audience in economics (Napoli, 2001, 2002), could provide new frameworks for exploring market structures with new types of consequences on both industries and audiences.

The research agenda in the area of media ownership and consolidation must move past cataloguing trends and patterns of ownership and address issues related not only to shifts in the structures of media and media industries but also to the fundamental changes in the nature of media consumers in global, national, regional, and local media markets. In general, media economists might deal with these transitions from a variety of disciplines and contexts including strategic and organizational management, audience measurement, and policy assessment.

Future research in the area of media consolidation will continue expanding into the areas of organizational behavior and strategic management to deal with the new combinations of media organizations. In terms of organizational behavior and competitive strategy, researchers can address localism in a variety of contexts ranging from firm strategy to market performance. Young (2000) concluded that future research in industrial organization must get past the interpretation of the relationship between market structure and performance and observe the strategic interactions between competitive firms. Wirth and Bloch (1995) argued: "Strategic behavior undermines the direct links between market structure and conduct, such as those associated with static equilibrium models of perfect competition, monopoly and oligopoly" (p. 24). During the 1970s, research in cross-media ownership (Wirth & Allen, 1979) sought to understand the market structure of organizations with multiple-media platforms. As more markets experience new types of cross-media ownership, future research will apply new understanding about strategic behavior to these models of media organizations.

Already, studies attempting to move in this direction have explored strategic management theory about strategic group interaction between different organizational types of media types (Chan-Olmsted, 1998) as well as cable television (Chan-Olmsted & Li, 2002; Barrett, 1996). Napoli (1997) applied agency theory in an effort to explain the reasons media firms behave the way they do. These types of studies are necessary to deal with the new management models in the media industries.

Although the literature provided some general themes about the effects of consolidation on the conduct and performance of media markets, emerging media technologies raise new questions about an important issue—measurement. From simple geographical definitions of a market to complex definitions of the product market, researchers in the area of media consolidation will need to address new methods for measuring the effects of concentration. At the global level, more research is needed to identify ownership patterns of global media organizations. At the same time, technologies such as the Internet continue to blur the lines of clear product market distinctions and raise issues of being able to clearly identify the audience. Therefore, refinements in the area of audience measurement will need to account for audience mobility and time spent with media, as well as basic reliability and validity concerns.

Finally, the future of media consolidation research will include new methods for assessing the impact of communication policies. International concerns about intellectual property, cross-border information flows, and cultural imperialism will drive more research into the area of media ownership concentration. At the domestic level, policy organizations such as the FCC will continue to ask for assessments to gauge the success or failure related to changes in broadcasting, cable, and other telecommunications. There are numerous opportunities for longitudinal studies using various time series analysis techniques of single or multiple media industries.

In conclusion, the forecasts continue to show increases in the amount of time spent with media. As governments change policies related to market structure and as media industries adapt to technological developments, audiences will both enjoy and suffer from the mechanics of the economic markets. More important, however, is that the same market mechanics that determine the price of the monthly cable bill also determine the number of voices found within the market for ideas. Therefore, it is important for media economists and others to continue asking the questions related to different ownership structures brought about by consolidation and examine the consequences for the audience.

# REFERENCES

Ahn, H., & Litman, B. (1997). Vertical integration and consumer welfare in the cable industry. *Journal of Broadcasting & Electronic Media, 41*(4), 453–477.

Albarran, A. (2003). *Media economics: Understanding markets, industries and concepts* (2 ed.). Ames: Iowa State University Press.

Albarran, A., & Dimmick, J. (1996). Concentration and economies of multiformity in the communication industries. *Journal of Media Economics, 9*(4), 41–50.

*Associated Press v. United States*, 326 U.S. 1 (1945).

Bagdikian, B. (1983). *The media monopoly* (1st ed.). Boston: Beacon Press.

Bagdikian, B. (1990). *The media monopoly* (3rd ed.). Boston: Beacon Press.

Bagdikian, B. (1997). *The media monopoly* (5th ed.). Boston: Beacon Press.

Barrett, M. (1996). Strategic behavior and competition in cable television: Evidence from two overbuilt markets. *Journal of Media Economics, 9*(2), 43–62.

Bates, B. (1993a). Station trafficking in radio: The impact of deregulation. *Journal of Broadcasting & Electronic Media, 37*(1), 21–30.

Bates, B. (1993b). Concentration in local television markets. *Journal of Media Economics, 6*(3), 3–21.

Berry, S., & Waldfogel, J. (2001). Do mergers increase product variety? Evidence from radio broadcasting. *The Quarterly Journal of Economics*, 1009–1024.

Besen, S., & Johnson, L. (1985). Regulation of broadcast station ownership: Evidence and theory. In E. M. Noam (Ed.), *Video media competition* (pp. 364–389). New York: Columbia University Press.

Blankenburg, W., & Ozanich, G. (1993). The effects of public ownership on the financial performance of newspaper corporations. *Journalism Quarterly, 70*(1), 68–75.

*Broadcasting & cable yearbook* (2003). Newton, MA: Reed Publishing.

Busterna, J. C. (1988a). Concentration and the industrial organization model. In R. G. Picard, J. P. Winter, M. E. McCombs, & S. Lacy (Eds.), *Press concentration and monopoly: new perspectives on newspaper ownership and operation* (pp. 35–53). Norwood, NJ: Ablex.

Busterna, J. (1988b). Television station ownership effects on programming and idea diversity: Baseline data. *Journal of Media Economics, 1*(2), 63–74.

Chambers, T. (2001). Losing owners: Deregulation and small radio markets. *Journal of Radio Studies, 8*(2), 292–315.

Chambers, T. (2003). Structural changes in small media markets. *Journal of Media Economics, 16*(1), 41–59.

Chan-Olmsted, S. (1995). A chance for survival or status quo? The economic implications of the radio duopoly ownership rules. *Journal of Radio Studies, 3*, 59–75.

Chan-Olmsted, S. (1996). Market competition for cable television: Re-examining its horizontal mergers and industry concentration. *Journal of Media Economics, 9*(2), 25–41.

Chan-Olmsted, S. M. (1997). Theorizing multichannel media economics: An exploration of a group-industry strategic competition model. *Journal of Media Economics, 10*(1), 39–49.

Chan-Olmsted, S. (1998). Mergers, acquisitions, and convergence: The strategic alliances of broadcasting, cable television and telephone services. *Journal of Media Economics, 11*(3), 33–46.

Chan-Olmsted, S., & Li, J. (2002). Strategic competition in the multi-channel video programming market: an intra-industry strategic group analysis. *Journal of Media Economics, 15*(3), 153–174.

Chan-Olmsted, S., & Litman, B. (1988). Antitrust and horizontal mergers in the cable industry. *Journal of Media Economics, 1*(1), 63–74.

Compaine, B. (1982). *Who owns the media?* (2nd ed.). New York: Harmony Press.

Compaine, B., & Gomery, D. (2000). *Who owns the media? Competition and concentration in the mass media industry.* Mahwah, NJ: Lawrence Erlbaum Associates.

Crawford, G. (2000). The impact of the 1992 Cable Act on consumer demand and welfare: a discrete-choice, differentiated products approach. *RAND Journal of Economics, 31*(3), 422–449.

Creamer, M. (2003, October 6). AOL Time Warner stresses name change practicality. *PR Week*, Online Edition. Retrieved January 4, 2004, from Lexis-Nexis Academic Universe.

Creech, K. (1993). *Electronic media law and regulation.* Boston: Focal Press.

De Jong, A., & Bates, B. (1991). Channel diversity in cable television. *Journal of Broadcasting & Electronic Media, 35,* 159–166.

Demers, D. (1991). Corporate structures and emphasis on profits and product quality at U.S. daily newspapers. *Journalism Quarterly, 68,* 15–26.

Demers, D. (1996). Corporate newspaper structure, profits, and organizational goals. *Journal of Media Economics, 9*(2), 1–23.

Demers, D. (1998). Revisiting corporate newspaper structure and profit making. *Journal of Media Economics, 11*(2), 19–45.

Department of Justice. (1996a, August 5). *Justice Department requires Jacor to sell Cincinnati radio station* [News release]. Washington, DC: U.S. Department of Justice.

Department of Justice. (1996b, October 24). *Justice Department requires Boston-based American Radio Systems Corp. to divest three Rochester, New York radio stations* [News release]. Washington, DC: U.S. Department of Justice.

Department of Justice. (1996c, November 12). *Justice Department requires Westinghouse and Infinity to divest radio stations in Boston and Philadelphia in order to go ahead with largest radio industry merger in history* [News release]. Washington, DC: U.S. Department of Justice.

Drushel, B. (1998). The *Telecommunications Act of 1996* and radio market structure. *Journal of Media Economics, 11*(3), 3–20.

FCC's Adelstein urges caution on media ownership rules. (2003, January 13). *Television Digest.* Retrieved November 24, 2003, from Lexis-Nexis Academic Universe.

Federal Communications Commission. (1992). *Radio multiple ownership rule reconsidered.* 7 F.C.C. Rcd. 6387 (1992).

Federal Communications Commission. (1997). Report on chain broadcasting. FCC Pocket No. 5060. Washington, DC.: FCC.

Federal Communications Commission. (2001a). *Fact sheet: FCC's conditioned approval of AOL Time Warner merger.* Retrieved June 24, 2002, from http://www.fcc.gov/Bureaus/Cable/Public_Notices/2001/fcc01011_fact.doc

Federal Communications Commission (2001b, September 13). *FCC begins reviewing cable ownership limits* [News release]. Retrieved June 24, 2002, from www.fcc.gov/Bureaus/Cable/News_Releases/2001

Federal Communications Commission. (2002, January 14). *8th annual video competition report.* Retrieved June 24, 2002, from http://hraunfoss.fcc.gov/edocs_public/attachmatch/FCC-01-389A1.pdf

Federal Communications Commission. (2003, June 2). *FCC sets limits on media concentration* [News release]. Retrieved January 7, 2004, from http://hraunfoss.fcc.gov/edocs_public/attachmatch/DOC-235047A1.pdf

Federal Trade Commission. (1997). *1992 horizontal merger guidelines.* Retrieved December 15, 2003, from http://www.ftc.gov/bc/docs/horizmer.htm

Ferguson, P., & Ferguson, G. (1988). *Industrial economics. Issues and perspectives.* (2nd ed.). London: Macmillan.

Gal-Or, E., & Dukes, A. (2003). Minimum differentiation in commercial media markets. *Journal of Economics & Management Strategy, 12*(3), 291–325.

Glasser, T. (1984). Competition and diversity among radio formats: Legal and structural issues. *Journal of Broadcasting, 28*(2), 127–145.

Grant, A. (1994). The promise fulfilled? An empirical analysis of program diversity on television. *Journal of Media Economics, 7*(1), 51–64.

Greve, H. (1996). Patterns of competition: The diffusion of a market position in radio Broadcasting. *Administrative Science Quarterly, 41,* 29–60.

Häckner, J., & Nyberg, S. (2000). *Price competition, advertising and media market concentration.* Stockholm, Sweden: Stockholm University, Department of Economics.

Hagin, L. (1994). *U.S. radio consolidation: An investigation of the structures and strategies of selected radio duopolies.* Unpublished doctoral dissertation, University of Tennessee, Knoxville.

Hale, F. D. (1988). Editorial diversity and concentration. In R. Picard, J. Winter, M. E. McCombs, & S. Lacy (Eds.), *Press concentration and monopoly: New perspectives on newspaper ownership and operation* (pp. 161–176). Norwood, NJ: Ablex.

Haring, J. (1975). *Competition, regulation and performance in the commercial radio broadcasting industry.* Unpublished doctoral dissertation. New Haven, CT: Yale University.

Hellman, H., & Soramaki, M. (1994). Competition and content in the U.S. video market. *Journal of Media Economics, 7*(1), 29–49.

Hickey, N. (2002, May–June). Behind the mergers. *Columbia Journalism Review*. Retrieved December 5, 2003, from www.archives.cjr.org/year/02/3/hickey.asp

Howard, H. (1998). The Telecommunications Act and TV station ownership: One year later. *Journal of Media Economics, 11*(3), 21–32.

Howard, H. (2003). *Television station ownership in the U.S.: A comprehensive study (1950–2002)* (Final Report). National Association of Broadcasters.

Jaffe, A., & Kanter, D. (1990). Market power of local cable television franchises: Evidence from the effects of deregulation. *RAND Journal of Economics, 21*(2), 226–234.

Johnson, P. (2003, July 16). Public unsettled by media consolidation, poll shows. *USA Today*, p. 3D. Retrieved January 7, 2004, from Lexis-Nexis Academic Database.

Lacy, S. (1988). Content of joint operation newspapers. In R. G. Picard, J. P. Winter, M. E. McCombs, & S. Lacy (Eds.), *Press concentration and monopoly: New perspectives on newspaper ownership and operation* (pp. 147–160). Norwood, NJ: Ablex.

Lacy, S. (1989). A model demand for news: impact of competition on newspaper competition. *Journalism Quarterly, 68*(1), 40–48, 128.

Lacy, S. (1990). Newspaper competition and number of news services carried: A replication. *Journalism Quarterly, 69*(1), 79–82.

Lacy, S., & Davenport, L. (1994). Daily newspaper market structure, concentration, and competition. *Journal of Media Economics, 7*(3), 33–46.

Lacy, S., & Riffe, D. (1994). The impact of competition and group ownership on radio news. *Journalism Quarterly, 71*(3), 583–593.

Larson, T. (1980). The U.S. television industry: Concentration and the question of network divestiture of owned and operated television stations. *Communication Research, 7*(1), 23–44.

Levin, H. (1954). Competition among the mass media and the public interest. *Public Opinion Quarterly, 18*(1), 62–79.

Levy, J., Ford-Livene, M., & Levine, A. (2002). *Broadcast television: A survivor in a sea of competition* (Working Paper Series 37, Office of Plans and Policy). Washington, DC: Federal Communications Commission.

Litman, B. R. (1988). Microeconomic foundations. In R. G. Picard, J. P. Winter, M. E. McCombs, & S. Lacy (eds.), *Press concentration and monopoly: New perspectives on newspaper ownership and operation* (pp. 3–34). Norwood, NJ: Ablex.

Loevinger, L. (1979). Media concentration: Myth and reality. *The Antitrust Bulletin, 24*(3), 479–498.

Masson, R., Mudambi, R., & Reynolds, R. (1990). Oligopoly in advertiser-supported media. *Quarterly Review of Economics and Business, 30*(2), 3–16.

McConnell, B. (2001, March 5). Court scraps cap. *Broadcasting & Cable*. Retrieved January 7, 2004, from Lexis-Nexis Academic Database.

McDonald, D., & Dimmick, J. (2003). Time as a niche dimension: Competition between the Internet and television. In A. Albarran & A. Arrese (Eds.), *Time and media markets* (pp. 29–47). Mahwah, NJ: Lawrence Erlbaum Associates.

McFadyen, S., Hoskins, C., & Gillen, D. (1980). *Canadian broadcasting: Market structure and economic performance*. Montreal: The Institute for Research on Public Policy.

McKean, M. L. & Stone, V. A. (1992). Deregulation and competition: Explaining the absence of local broadcast news operations. *Journalism Quarterly, 69*(3), 713–723.

Napoli, P. (1997). Rethinking program diversity assessment: An audience-centered Approach. *Journal of Media Economics, 10*(4), 59–74.

Napoli, P. (2001). The audience product and the new media environment: Implications for the economics of media industries. *International Journal on Media Management, 3*(2), 66–73.

Napoli, P. (2002). Audience valuation and minority media: An analysis of the determinants of the value of radio audiences. *Journal of Broadcasting & Electronic Media, 46*(2), 169–184.

National Broadcasting Company v. United States 319 U.S. 190 (1943).

National Cable Television Association (2004). Industry overview, cable program networks. Retrieved January 9, 2004, from http://www.ncta.com/industry_overview/programList.cfm

Newspaper Association of America. (2003). Facts about newspapers. Retrieved December 19, 2003, from http://www.naa.org/info/facts03/17_facts2003.html

Nixon, R., & Ward, J. (1961). Trends in newspaper ownership and inter-media competition. *Journalism Quarterly, 38,* 3–14.

Noll, R. (1978). Television and competition. In Federal Trade Commission (Ed.), *Proceedings of the Symposium on Media Concentration* (pp. 243–259). Washington, DC: Federal Trade Commission.

Noll, R., Peck, M., & McGowan, J. (1973). *Economic aspects of television regulation.* (Brookings Institution). Washington, DC: U.S. Government Printing Office.

Organisation for Economic Co-operation and Development. (1993a). *Glossary of industrial organisation economics and competition law.* Paris: Author.

Organisation for Economic Co-operation and Development. (1993b). *Competition policy and a changing broadcast industry.* Paris: Author.

Owen, B. (1975). *Economics and freedom of expression: Media structure and the First Amendment.* Cambridge, MA: Ballinger.

Owen, B. (1977). Regulating diversity: The case of radio formats. *Journal of Broadcasting, 21*(3), 305–319.

Owen, B. (1978). The economic view of programming. *Journal of Communication, 28*(2), 43–47.

Owen, B., Beebe, J., & Manning, W. (1974). *Television economics.* Lexington, MA: Lexington Books.

Owen, B., & Wildman, S. (1992). *Video economics.* Cambridge, MA: Harvard University Press.

Ozanich, G., & Wirth, M. (1993). Media mergers and acquisitions: an overview. In A. Alexander, J. Owers, and R. Carveth (Eds.), *Media economics: Theory and Practice* (1st ed., pp. 116–133). Hillsdale, NJ: Lawrence Erlbaum Associates.

Picard, R. (1988). Pricing behavior of newspapers. In R. G. Picard, J. P. Winter, M. E. McCombs, & S. Lacy (Eds.), *Press concentration and monopoly: New perspectives on newspaper ownership and operation* (pp. 147–160). Norwood, NJ: Ablex.

Picard, R. (1989). *Media economics.* Newbury Park, CA: Sage.

Picard, R. (1994). Institutional ownership of publicly traded U.S. newspaper companies. *Journal of Media Economics, 7*(4), 49–64.

Picard, R., & Rimmer, T. (1998). Weathering a recession: Effects of size and diversification on newspaper companies. *Journal of Media Economics, 12*(1), 1–18.

Powers, A. (2001). Toward monopolistic competition in U.S. local television news. *Journal of Media Economics, 14*(2), 77–86.

Price, C. (1997, March). Status quo. Consolidation has little effect on cost per point. *Gavin GM. Radio's Business Edge, 2*(3), 23–24.

Prisuta, R. (1977). The impact of media concentration and economic factors on broadcast public interest programming. *Journal of Broadcasting, 21*(3), 321–337.

Riffe, D., & Shaw, E. (1990). Ownership, operating, staffing and content characteristics of 'news radio' stations. *Journalism Quarterly, 67*(4), 684–691.

Rogers, R. P., & Woodbury, J. R. (1996). Market structure, program diversity and radio audience size. *Contemporary Economic Policy, 14,* 81–91.

Romeo, C., & Dick, A. (2003). The effect of format changes and ownership consolidation on radio station outcomes. Unpublished manuscript.

Romeo, C., Pittman, R., & Familant, N. (2003). Do newspaper JOAs charge monopoly advertising rates? *Review of Industrial Organization, 22*(2), 121–138.

Scherer, F. (1980). *Industrial market structure and economic performance* (2nd ed.). Chicago: Rand McNally.

Shaver, M. (1995). Application of pricing theory in studies of pricing behavior and rate strategy in the newspaper industry. *Journal of Media Economics, 8*(2), 49–59.

Shaver, D., & Shaver, M. (2003). The impact of concentration and convergence on managerial efficiencies of time and cost. In A. Albarran & A. Arrese (eds.), *Time and media markets,* (pp. 29–47). Mawah, NJ: Lawrence Erlbaum Associates.

Sheperd, W. (1985). *The economics of industrial organization.* Englewood Cliffs, NJ: Prentice-Hall.

Spence, M. (1976). Product selection, fixed costs and monopolistic competition. *Review of Economic Studies, 43*(2), 217–235.

Spence, M., & Owen, B. (1975). Television programming, monopolistic competition and welfare. In B. Owen (Ed.), *Economics and freedom of expression: Media structure and the First Amendment* (pp. 143–165). Cambridge, MA: Ballinger.

Spence, M., & Owen, B. (1977). Television programming, monopolistic competition, and welfare. *Quarterly Journal of Economics, 51*(1), 103–125.

Steiner, P. (1952). Program patterns and preferences, and the workability of competition in radio broadcasting. *Quarterly Journal of Economics, 66*(2), 194–223.

Sterling, C. (1975). Trends in daily newspaper and broadcast ownership, 1922–1970. *Journalism Quarterly, 52*(2), 247–256, 320.

Stern, L., & Grabner, J. (1970). *Competition in the marketplace.* Glenview, IL: Scott Foresman.

Udell, J. G. (1990). Recent and future economic status of U.S. newspapers. *Journalism Quarterly, 67*(2), 331–339.

van Kraneburg, H. (2001). Economic effects of consolidations of publishers and newspapers in The Netherlands. *Journal of Media Economics, 14*(2), 61–76.

Wanta, W., & Johnson, T. (1994). Content changes in the St. Louis *Post-Dispatch* during different market situations. *Journal of Media Economics, 7*(1), 13–28.

Waterman, D. (1991). A new look at media chains and groups: 1977–1989. *Journal of Broadcasting & Electronic Media, 35*(2), 167–178.

Waterman, D., & Weiss, A. (1997). *Vertical integration in cable television.* Cambridge, MA: MIT Press.

Williams, W. (1998). The impact of ownership rules and the Telecommunications Act of 1996 on a small radio market. *Journal of Radio Studies, 5*(2), 8–18.

Williams, G., & Roberts, S. (2002). *Radio industry review 2002: trends in ownership format and finance* (Media Bureau Staff Working Paper, Federal Communications Commission). Retrieved November 15, 2002, from http://www.fcc.gov/ownership/studies.html.

Wirth, M., & Allen, B. (1979). Another look at cross-media ownership. *The Antitrust Bulletin, 24*(1), 87–103.

Wirth, M., & Bloch, H. (1995). Industrial organization theory and media industry analysis. *Journal of Media Economics, 8*(2), 15–26.

Wirth, M., & Wollert, J. (1979). Public interest programming: taxation by regulation. *Journal of Broadcasting, 23*(3), 319–330.

Yan, M. (2002). Market structure and local signal carriage decisions in the cable television industry: Results from count analysis. *Journal of Media Economics, 15*(3), 175–191.

Young, D. (2000). Modeling media markets: How important is market structure? *Journal of Media Economics, 13*(1), 27–44.

# 18

# The Economics of Media Programming

David Waterman
Indiana University

This chapter is generally about how economic forces determine market outcomes in media industries, especially the electronic media. Of course, that is a very broad subject, and our focus is on certain aspects of it. Among the main questions we ask: How do market structure (e.g., competition versus monopoly) and the economic system of support (e.g., advertising versus direct payment) affect the prices, audience sizes, and especially the diversity, quality, and certain other content characteristics of media products? How do the costs and technologies of media production and distribution affect these outcomes?

Underlying these questions are important issues of social welfare and government policy. Government determines the type of market system we employ to produce and distribute media products. Throughout the world, a variety of government regulations or other policies have attempted to control or modify outcomes of the market, such as by promoting greater program diversity, or by ensuring the availability of certain types of programs. Publicly funded radio and television systems have had similar objectives. Thus, a policy focus is inherent in our analysis.

This chapter is both a theoretical and an empirical investigation. We begin in the first section by establishing some criteria for evaluation, in terms of measurable market outcomes and social welfare, followed by discussion of fundamental economic trade-offs in the program production and distribution process. In the second section, we proceed to review and evaluate the theoretical literature in media program/product economics as it has evolved both in the economics and communications literatures. In the third section, we review and evaluate the related empirical research. Discussion of social welfare and public policy issues is interwoven throughout. Finally, in the fourth section, we set out some ideas about future research needs.

At the outset, some limitations exist. We primarily focus on electronic media, along with some consideration of motion pictures. We do not attempt to cover a large literature on the economics of newspaper and other print media content. Also outside the scope is a substantial literature on the economics of international trade in media products that involves issues of product quality, diversity, and content.[1] The review of theoretical and empirical literature in this chapter is also inherently incomplete, even within its electronic media focus. Only English language works are within this author's reach, and even inside that range, there is an unquestionable bias toward articles and books that are most readily available in the United States or that involve U.S. media.

## ECONOMIC AND POLICY FUNDAMENTALS

### Evaluation Criteria and Public Policy Concerns

Media program economics is fundamentally about outcomes of the market process. Those outcomes can be defined in terms of four basic variables: price, quantity, quality, and diversity. All of these variables are related to social welfare, which is most often defined by media economists in terms of economic satisfaction.

Concerns about the prices and quantities of media products parallel those that economics has in the case of nonmedia products more generally. Just as we want to know how many bicycles are produced and sold at what prices, we are interested in how DVDs, pay TV subscriptions, etc., are priced and how many sold, and how many people watch or listen to various programs. Thus, quantities are usually defined in media economics in terms of the number of buyers, viewers, listeners, or readers who consume a particular product or class of products. A complicating aspect of pricing and consumption in most media is the involvement of advertisers. In general, advertisers' willingness to pay for audience exposure encourages low or even zero prices of media products. For this reason, they tend to have very large audiences. From an economic welfare perspective, low prices and high levels of consumption are generally desirable, although as we discuss further, advertising has other effects that may be socially detrimental.

Product quality is of fundamental, general interest in economics. Other things equal, we want bicycles, cars, and cell phones to be reliable and last a long time. Product quality has a different, somewhat touchier meaning in media economics. Of course, media quality has aesthetic or other subjective dimensions about which economics has, so far at least, little to say. Along at least one dimension, though, media product quality can be explicitly and usefully defined—in terms of "first copy" investments, or product creation costs. In general, the more resources that are invested in a movie, a TV program, etc., the more attractive it becomes to audiences or consumers. Media quality can also be defined in terms of the physical product in which the information itself is embodied, such as the

---

[1] Economic studies of international trade in media products are surveyed in Waterman (2003).

exhibition quality of DVD versus a VHS tape. In most cases, though, the most important dimension of media quality for purposes of this chapter is first copy investment.

Turning to diversity (or product variety), questions about how many different auto models, types of restaurants, etc., appear in the market are a significant subject of general economic research. Market outcomes in terms of product variety or diversity, however, are a central focus of media economics. The diversity of media products affects the satisfaction of viewers because they desire variety, as opposed to "sameness." Diversity also has rather sensitive First Amendment and other political overtones. Does the spectrum of available news and opinion programs, for example, appropriately reflect the diversity of viewpoints in our society?

Media product diversity can be defined along three dimensions.[2] One easily measured dimension is simply a *count* of the number of different products available at some point in time, or over a period of time. The second, and by far the most heavily researched dimension of media diversity is often labeled as "type" diversity and measures *how different* the available media products are from each other, or whether they appeal to different groups. As we will see, such differences are inherently subjective and difficult to define. This dimension of diversity is intrinsically tied, though, to questions of whether consumers with minority tastes, including ethnic and racial minorities, are adequately served. A distinct third dimension of diversity is the number of different *owners* of the available products. If, for example, four news programs are available, but three are offered by outlets under the common ownership of one corporation, then "ownership" diversity would number two. Ownership diversity parallels industry concentration and, from that perspective, has important effects on market outcomes, including count and type diversity. As an outcome in itself, however, ownership diversity primarily involves matters of social and political equity and is mainly outside the scope of this analysis. Our focus in this chapter on diversity as an outcome is thus primarily in terms of count and type diversity measures.

All four of the variables describing media market outcomes—prices, quantity, quality, and diversity—are related to our ultimate interest, social welfare. How well off are viewers or listeners as a result of the market outcomes? For many purposes, economic welfare can be defined theoretically in fairly simple terms: the sum of the prices that viewers or users would be willing to pay (for a TV program, let us say), less the opportunity cost of the economic resources that go into the program's production and distribution. If a consumer (here for illustration the only consumer) would be willing to pay $8 to watch a pay TV program, but actually pays $6, and the program costs only $5 to produce and distribute, then the total "surplus" of $3 ($2 consumer surplus + $1 producer surplus) serves as a measure of economic welfare.

Although such simple measures will sometimes be used in this chapter, there are great practical limitations to the economic welfare concept. The real world is complicated, notably involving benefits and costs of advertising, and market imperfections that result

---

[2]These three dimensions generally correspond to those set out in Chapter 3 of Levin (1980) and are commonly distinguished in more recent literature. See Napoli (1999) for a recent survey and analysis of an extensive literature on the diversity concept.

in actual costs that do not reflect true opportunity costs. In any case, we usually have little way of knowing whether someone would have been willing to pay a higher price for something than he or she actually did. Welfare measures are especially difficult to make in differentiated product markets. Also, of course, most of us believe that media have important social, political, or cultural effects on their users as well as on society as a whole. All of these broader effects can be put under the rubric of economic "externalities." Still, that label doesn't contribute much. Often in this chapter, we just stick with the outcomes in terms of the objective measures we can make, and let readers arrive at their own judgments about the social welfare.

## Economic Fundamentals and Trade-offs

Media products have fundamental economic characteristics that limit the ability of free markets to achieve socially optimal outcomes in terms of the foregoing variables, or that require trade-offs among them.

The most important of these characteristics is familiar: relatively high first copy costs of production, combined with relatively low, or even zero, marginal costs of distribution. As a result, average costs per viewer or listener tend to decline indefinitely as more and more users of the same product are served.

One implication of this "public good" characteristic of media products, as it is often labeled, is a tradeoff between price and diversity. The larger the number of different products offered, the smaller the audiences of each, and thus the higher the price of each (to consumers and/or to advertisers) has to be in order to support production costs. Diversity is thus expensive to achieve. A second implied tradeoff is between diversity and first copy costs. The higher are first copy production investments, the more expensive it is to achieve diversity.

The economic tradeoffs involving first copy production costs, prices, and product variety also have important implications for market structure in media markets. Declining average costs per user imply a force toward monopoly. Counteracting that tendency is the demand for diversity. If consumers have strong preferences and are willing to pay enough to satisfy them, competition among providers offering differentiated products can prevail in spite of economies of scale.

Whether provided by a single firm or several firms, however, there are especially strong economic pressures in media industries toward "one-size-fits-all" products. It can be prohibitively expensive to design media products that perfectly suit individual or very small group tastes. The widespread dissatisfactions with media products that media critics, academics and others have expressed—and that are in fact a motivating theme of many of the economic models of the media reviewed below—can probably be traced to the one-size-fits-all tendency that results from extreme economies of scale.

The trade-offs among production investments, prices, and diversity also create basic social welfare trade-offs that are very difficult to resolve. Are we better off, for example, with two news programs at a $10 price per subscriber for each one, or with a single, "homogenized" news program at a price of $7.50 per subscriber? Usually, we have no way of usefully answering this question beyond just observing what the market produces and applying our judgment to that.

## ECONOMIC THEORIES OF PROGRAM CHOICE

The primary line of research into how demand conditions and market structure determine final outcomes of media markets in terms of prices, quantities, quality, and diversity is called the *theory of program choice*. Under what conditions does the marketplace offer few programs instead of many programs, very similar versus very different programs, cheaply produced versus expensive programs, etc.? What types of programs tend to be offered by alternative regimes of monopoly versus competition, advertiser versus pay support, etc.? And of central significance, how does, or how can, government policy affect those outcomes?

Owen and Wildman (1992) offer an extensive and rigorous review of program choice models up to about 1990, with detailed numerical examples. Although the perspective of our presentation differs, we focus on summarizing key results of the models up to that time, reserving more emphasis for later contributions.

## Alternative Regimes of Support and Market Structures

Beginning in the 1950s, a series of program choice models have compared market outcomes and consumer welfare under the alternative regimes of advertiser support versus direct consumer payment, and under alternative market structures of competition versus monopoly. Many of these studies were advanced in the context of political debates inspired by dissatisfaction with the system of limited-channel, advertiser support that initially governed the television industry, at least in the United States. Although there have been important technological constraints throughout, government spectrum allocation and other policies have fundamentally influenced what means of economic support, as well as what degree of competition, prevails in these industries.

From an early date, academics and others advocated replacing or supplementing the advertiser-supported broadcasting system in the United States with pay television. In practice, that meant multichannel cable television, which has always had a natural tendency toward geographically based monopoly because of the high fixed costs of building cable systems at the local level. Publicly supported television was also a hotly debated alternative. In Europe, Asia, and elsewhere, mostly very different political choices for the market structure and means of support for television were made, at least initially. The same political debates are relevant, though, because the introduction of advertising, pay television systems, privatization of public channels, and expansion of channel capacity in those countries during the past half century has also involved fundamental government decisions.

### Discrete Demand Models

Early program choice models were discrete in form, by which we mean that consumers are assumed to fit into a finite number of groups, within which all individuals have identical tastes. Most of these models specify distinct program "types" (perhaps labeled by their genre) that cost certain amounts to produce and are offered at particular prices, etc. Discrete demand models are limited in the robustness and refinement of their results,

**TABLE 18.1**
Program Choice Model 1: Basic Steiner Version

|  | Viewer Group I (600) | Viewer Group II (160) |
| --- | --- | --- |
| Program Type A | 1st choice | — |
| Program Type B | — | 1st choice |

especially with respect to economic welfare. Still, most of the basic theoretical results and insights into the economics of programming can be demonstrated using them.

The first study to systematically deal with issues of means of support and media market structure was Steiner's (1952) seminal demonstration that competition in advertiser-supported broadcasting tends to result in program type duplication. Contrary to all expectations suggested by general economic theory, a media monopoly might actually serve consumers better than does competition. Ironically, Steiner's model was inspired by radio programming, which at the time was dominated by four national networks and was similar in format to the series TV programming of today.

Steiner's basic insight can be represented by a very simple example in which there exist two homogeneous viewer groups, whose sizes are indicated in Table 18.1. Group I prefers a "majority" type program, A, whereas a smaller group, II, is identified by its members' preference for a "minority" type of programming, B. The dashed lines indicate that neither Group I nor Group II is willing to watch any but their first choice program. Advertiser support is assumed to prevail, with a set advertising rate per viewer. Program costs are fixed and are assumed not to be a constraint.

If only one channel is permitted to operate, the majority program, Type A, will be offered. If a second, competing channel enters the market, however, and it is assumed that two stations offering the same program type will split the audience, then two versions of Type A will be offered at 300 viewers each. In fact, there would have to be four channels for the minority type program, B, to be offered at all (three channels of type A at 200 viewers each, and one channel of type B at 160 viewers).

If there were as many as two channels, however, a monopolist could better serve consumers. In the two-channel case, for example, both A and B would be offered, serving 760 viewers in total, compared with 600 in the competitive case.

Later contributions by Wiles (1963), Rothenberg (1962), and Noll, Peck, and McGowan (1973) examined outcomes of monopoly versus competition, and of advertiser versus pay support, under a variety of alternative demand and cost assumptions. Beebe's (1977) contribution, first reported with extensions in Owen, Beebe, and Manning (1974), generalized discrete program choice models with computer simulations showing how different assumptions about market structure, means of support, viewer preferences, program costs, and channel capacity affect diversity and consumer welfare.

Beebe's study and those preceding it demonstrated a variety of economic trade-offs, such as between production costs and diversity, and between the skew of viewer

**TABLE 18.2**
Program Choice Model 2: Lowest Common Denominator
Program Choice Version

|  | Viewer Group I (300) | Viewer Group II (200) |
| --- | --- | --- |
| Program Type A | 1st choice | — |
| Program Type B | — | 1st choice |
| Program Type C | 2nd choice | 2nd choice |

preferences and the achievement of service to viewer minorities. Especially notable was the introduction into models of less preferred, "lowest common denominator" programs that certain consumers do not prefer, but are willing to watch before walking away from their sets. Consider, for example, a simple modification of Model 1 (Table 18.2).

In Model 2, a third program type, C, is introduced as a common alternative that all viewers are willing to watch before turning off their sets. The group sizes are also changed from Model 1 as shown. In this case, a single channel would produce the common denominator, Type C, satisfying no one but still serving all viewers. If a competing second channel entered, though, types A and B would both be produced, serving both groups with their first choices.[3] With more channels, that is, Type C disappears from the market.

It is easy to see as well how a pay TV system could better respond to viewer preferences than advertiser support in either of these models. If members of the 160-person minority group in Model 1, for example, were willing to pay three times as much to watch their preferred program as those in the 600-person majority group, then a first channel would still offer A, but a second channel B, thus resulting in diversity rather than duplication of A.

The political backdrop of these academic contributions was the famous speech of FCC chairman Newton Minow (1961) describing program output of the three main U.S. broadcast television networks as a "vast wasteland," tending to offer duplicative, monotonous mass-appeal entertainment programs, with little public-affairs or other socially beneficial fare. Also at this time, there was budding support in the United States for the introduction of pay TV systems and the deregulation of multichannel cable television. In 1967, a national public television system was formally introduced in the United States to supplement fare of the three commercial networks, following a long period of public debate.[4]

---

[3]If a second channel attempted to split the audience for C at 250 viewers each, it would be optimal for one of those channels to instead offer A, attracting 300 viewers, leaving 200 for B or C. A channel offering B, however, could attract all of the latter viewers away from C. The competitive equilibrium result with two channels is thus A and B.

[4]See Noll, Peck, and McGowan (1973) for citations and discussions of the public debates on pay television and public TV in the United States. Wiles (1963) was a British author writing in the context of a limited channel system partially supported by advertising.

Results of these models thus suggested justification for political initiatives to convert the vast wasteland of television into a cornucopia of channels satisfying diverse tastes and social needs of viewers. From an academic perspective, though, the studies also showed that results are sensitive to basically arbitrary assumptions about the structure of preferences and program costs. As our own examples have suggested, program choice models can be contrived to produce practically any outcome.

Nevertheless, two reasonably broad generalizations appearing to emerge from these models are:

1. A transition from competitive advertiser to competitive pay support favors "preferred" programs and tends to reduce lowest-common-denominator types.

As consumers become able to express the intensity of their demands in the market, that is, producer incentives to homogenize or produce "least objectionable" programs in order to maximize audience size are diminished.

2. Other things equal, higher channel capacity increases diversity and the prevalence of minority taste programs, and also tends to eliminate lowest common denominators.

As long as program cost constraints are not encountered, opportunities to segment television audiences more finely will obviously result in greater selection for consumers. More channels also provide incentives for producers to refine content to the tastes of smaller groups, thus drawing their demand away from lowest-common-denominator program content. At least in a competitive market, this mechanism works for advertiser- as well as pay-supported systems because consumers are always attracted to more appealing programs.

Steiner's basic insight that competing channels tend to offer similar or duplicative programming compared with monopoly was generally confirmed by Beebe's and other studies as well. But although a monopoly supplier never has an incentive to repeat program types, the option of common-denominator program types will also induce the profit-maximizing monopolist to reduce count diversity in order to save on production costs. The benefits of multichannel, direct payment TV systems therefore remain ambiguous when a tendency toward local market monopoly in cable is considered.

Given the limited-channel, advertiser-supported system that dominated television into the 1970s in the United States, tax-based funding for public television seemed justified by program choice models for three basic reasons. One was the tendency toward program duplication in advertiser-supported systems, and their particular failure to offer minority appeal programs such as Type B in the model examples given earlier. Second, there was an underlying presumption that viewers necessarily had more intense demands for minority-appeal programs such as B. In the absence of a viable pay TV system, however, they could not express those demands in the market. Third, there was a presumption that some small-audience programs, such as public affairs, had socially beneficial effects, so that even if price demands for them were low, their presentation on public media was justified.

### Continuous Demand Models

Models that assume arbitrarily fine gradations in consumer willingness to pay for programs, or fine gradations in viewer preferences for certain elements of program content, generally permit more refined or robust conclusions. Most such works have been published after the discrete models. Like discrete models, the continuous demand models have centered on characterizing the types of programs that are chosen by profit-making firms under alternative means of support or alternative market structures. The continuous demand models, however, are better equipped to demonstrate welfare implications of those choices.

Before proceeding to discuss individual contributions, a basic framework in Fig. 18.1 illustrates some of the conclusions that can be demonstrated with continuous demand models. Program X has a relatively steep demand curve, or in the terminology of Chae and Flores (1998), "intensive" demand. Program Y has "extensive" demand; it has a potentially larger total audience, but its viewers generally have more lukewarm demand for it. For purposes of this example, say that the program cost is zero, which is just a simplifying convenience to ensure there is no cost constraint. We also assume that the advertising rate is $0.50 per viewer.

How does the means of support determine program choice? Under advertiser support, the broader appeal Program Y will be offered, yielding total revenue of $30 (60 viewers at $0.50) versus income of $20 for X. Under pay support, however, the intensive-demand Program X will be selected since that choice yields revenue of $80 (20 sales at $4), versus $60 for Y. As the example illustrates, the choice dichotomy results because advertisers are just in the business of counting eyeballs, whereas pay TV responds directly to viewer demands.

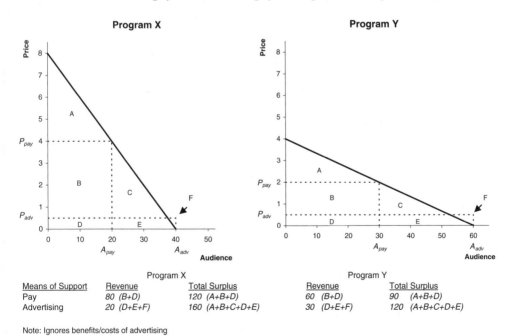

| Program X | | | | Program Y | | | |
|---|---|---|---|---|---|---|---|
| Means of Support | Revenue | | Total Surplus | | Revenue | | Total Surplus |
| Pay | 80 (B+D) | | 120 (A+B+D) | | 60 (B+D) | | 90 (A+B+D) |
| Advertising | 20 (D+E+F) | | 160 (A+B+C+D+E) | | 30 (D+E+F) | | 120 (A+B+C+D+E) |

Note: Ignores benefits/costs of advertising

FIG. 18.1. Advertiser versus pay support: continuous demand model.

Which of these systems is better for society? The debate on this subject dates to an exchange of articles published by Samuelson (1964) and Minasian (1964). Samuelson portrayed advertiser support for TV as fortuitous because the zero marginal cost of distributing a TV program called for a socially optimal price to consumers of zero. Minasian argued that subscription TV offered a superior mechanism for response by producers to the intensity of viewer preferences. As Samuelson recognized in this final reply, though, the debate cannot be settled by abstract reasoning: "Imperfections of one arrangement must be weighted against the imperfections of another" (1964, p. 83).

This basic welfare trade-off is illustrated by the Fig. 18.1 example. The direct pricing of Program X at $4 limits size of the audience, resulting in a "deadweight" loss of C + E, since the 20 excluded consumers would have been willing to pay more than the true zero marginal cost of distributing the program to them. Total surplus of A + B + D = $120 is still realized. Selection of Program X under pay support, however, reflects a better response to the intensity of viewer demands. As the examples are constructed, total viewer welfare turns out the same under pay or advertiser support, given the programs selected, at $120 (for Program Y, A + B + C + D + E = $120, the total area under the curve). The essential welfare shortcoming of both systems, however, is illustrated by the fact that the highest potential benefit to consumers would result from offering Program X under advertiser support, yielding a total surplus of $160 (the total area under the Program X demand curve). That choice cannot be realized, however, by the private market.

One other assumption widely held by pay TV's advocates at the time is illustrated by this model, namely that viewers were generally willing to pay more to watch TV programs than advertisers will pay to reach them.[5] For both Programs X and Y, pay support results in a higher flow of economic resources into television production. Although not shown by the model directly, that flow would presumably result in production of a larger variety of television programs that are better tailored to viewer demands.

In an elegant comparative statics model, Spence and Owen (1977) compared welfare results of alternative regimes of advertising versus pay support and alternative market structures in a world of differentiated television products. Spence and Owen demonstrated that from a social welfare perspective, both pay and ad-supported TV are "biased" against programs having certain demand and cost characteristics, but they were able to reach few general conclusions. A basic reason for the ambiguity of their economic welfare results is the irresolvable trade-off between the benefits of achieving maximum distribution and those of responding to the intensity of preferences. Of course, the magnitude of that trade-off can potentially be measured and weighed, as we have done for Fig. 18.1. The fundamental problem, however, is that we generally have no way of knowing the actual shapes of these demand curves.

To illustrate the basic welfare ambiguity problem in the Spence and Owen model, imagine that demand for Program X were $4 for all 20 of the highest value consumers, making the demand function flat between 0 and 20 consumers, instead of having the upward-sloping shape that creates the Fig. 18.1 region labeled A. Optimal price for the

---

[5] Noll, Peck, and McGowan (1973) present often-quoted evidence from early pay TV experiments in the United States that this was the case for certain program types.

program is still $4, generating 20 sales, but total surplus under pay support for program X would fall from $120 to $80, now resulting in less rather than more social benefit in comparison to advertiser support of Program Y. By having to offer a single price to all consumers, even pay TV suppliers take no account of the intensity of demand above that price and thus may select the "wrong" program from a welfare perspective.[6]

Wildman and Owen (1985) supplemented the Spence and Owen model by considering the possibility of pay and advertiser support at the same time, also including a variable for viewer aversion to commercials. Their welfare results are also ambiguous, but suggest that viewers would be better off if we had a combination of advertiser- and pay-supported systems. A combination would allow consumers to self-select according to their willingness to pay and their aversion to advertising.

A key element of such a combined system is price discrimination. That is, high-value viewers are induced to pay a high price for A and remaining viewers a low (here zero) price for B. It can be easily seen, in fact, that if a seller could perfectly price discriminate in selling a program, there would be no bias in program selection and viewer welfare would be optimized. Considering Program A in Fig. 18.1, for example, perfect price discrimination would imply that the entire area under the demand curve ($120) would be collected, an amount necessarily equal to the aggregate audience satisfaction from watching the program. Although no author has to our knowledge formally demonstrated its welfare benefits, the system by which movies and some other programs are released over time to a variety of different media at progressively lower prices would appear to be the closest approach to perfect price discrimination—and thus perfect program choice and maximum social welfare—that can be achieved by media program suppliers.[7]

Using a framework similar to that illustrated by Fig. 18.1, Chae and Flores (1998) investigate characteristics of programs selected under pay versus advertiser support. Consistent with earlier models, they find that more "extensive" demand programs (i.e., wide but shallow demand) are favored by advertiser support, and that a given program is more likely to be selected by advertiser-supported broadcasting as advertising rates rise, as advertising nuisance parameters fall, and as costs of pay revenue collection rise. Measures of welfare are ambiguous for reasons similar to those discussed earlier. Notably in Chae and Flores' analysis, though, welfare also depends on whether advertising is informative (having a positive effect) or merely persuasive (having a negative effect).

Papandrea (1997) investigates program choice and welfare trade-offs for extensive- versus intensive-demand programs in a circular demand model, as originally developed by Salop (1979). As illustrated in Fig. 18.2, consumers are positioned along a circle according to the intensity of their tastes for (unspecified) elements of program content. Distance above the circle measures each consumer's demand for the program nearest to his or her particular tastes. A consumer at Point C, for example, has the maximum possible willingness to pay for Program Z. Demand intensity of adjacent consumers falls off to zero according to the slope of intensity function, alternatively shown as $\beta$ or $\gamma$ in Fig. 18.2.

---

[6] See Owen and Wildman (1992) and Lence (1978) for more detailed discussion and examples.
[7] For related discussion of this issues, see Waterman (1992) and Owen and Wildman (1992).

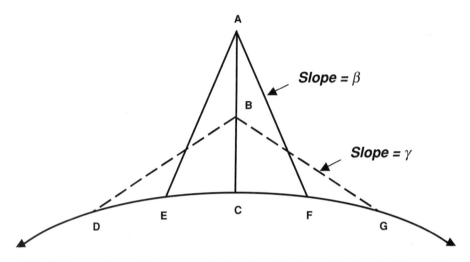

FIG. 18.2.   Circular model of program choice: alternative demand functions for Program Z.

Using this framework, Papandrea compares price and nonprice (i.e., advertiser support) systems under alternative market structures. He confirms results of previous models that since advertiser-supported channels ignore the intensity of demand, they are biased toward "broad appeal" types of programs. He also finds that competition has a greater tendency to duplicate programming than does monopoly if the number of channels is restricted. Welfare results are ambiguous, although Papandrea notes that if it is assumed that programs with relatively intense demand generate greater external benefits to the society as a whole, then advertiser support is to that extent an inferior system.

Doyle (1998) addresses similar questions with a framework in which program distributors can use advertiser support, pay support, or both. Advertiser-supported systems tend to offer large-audience programs, whereas diversity is more likely to occur with pay support. With a combination of advertising and pay support, program diversity is even more likely. Doyle explicitly considers policy issues from a British perspective. She points out the advantages of using profit taxes conditional on the types of programs produced as a means to enhance diversity in ad-supported systems. She also discusses the possible benefits of controlling subscription fees of pay TV systems as a means to minimize the welfare-reducing effects of viewer exclusion.

In an article inspired by high-priced boxing matches on PPV TV such as Tyson versus Ruddock in 1991, Holden (1993) shows straightforwardly that presenting such an event on pay-per-view television instead of free broadcasting reduces consumer surplus. With PPV, that is, consumers have to pay the supplier, whereas if the event were on broadcast TV they do not. Hansen and Kyhl (2001) address this issue from a European perspective, inspired by recent European Union bans on PPV exhibition of certain sports events. They show a similar result—that the ban increases consumer surplus, but they also find that it reduces copyright holder income. Both of these models appear to support government restrictions on PPV-exhibited sports events, although as Hansen and Kyhl note, that holds true only if the lower income to copyright holders would not have prevented the event from being staged in the first place.

A further line of theoretical research in this category involves public television. Using a model in which viewer preferences are distributed along a line, Noam (1987) shows that the presence of public TV might have the ironic effect of discouraging or driving out the future provision of similar programming by commercial stations. If public TV offers programs that appeal to relatively small minorities, for example, profit-making market entrants might choose to offer broader appeal programs than they otherwise would have.[8] Noam's analysis leads into empirical studies of this question that we consider later.

## Endogenous Product Quality Models

Although some of the models just reviewed permit first copy costs to vary, those variations serve only as simplistic constraints on variety. That is, for example, an assumption of higher television program production costs implies that less variety can be achieved because the higher costs eliminate profits for marginal programs. Another group of program choice models, however, explicitly recognizes that media product quality is embodied in first copy costs. First copy investments are thus a decision variable that program producers can use to raise or lower demand by increasing attractiveness of their products. In reality, variations in the first copy quality of media products are in fact so extreme that simply counting them up often has little meaning as a measure of product variety or industry output.

Endogenous product quality models have a general theoretical origin in the work of Shaked and Sutton (1983). For industries in which product quality is embodied in setup costs rather than marginal costs, these authors show that if marginal costs are low enough, industry concentration does not necessarily diminish as size of the market (i.e., the volume of demand) increases. The intuition of this result follows from economies of scale. As demand grows, a single producer may be able to continuously undercut would-be entrants by increasing product quality, thereby offering a wide range of consumers better value for their money than could an entrant with a differentiated product.[9]

Wildman and Lee (1989) recognize the media quality–variety trade-off in a model of television network programming strategy that predicts cheaper programming, or more program repetition, as channel capacity expands.

Understanding the basic effects of channel proliferation on program quality is useful for interpreting recent trends toward cheaper television genres, such as reality TV. Imagine, for example, an initial situation in which there are three advertiser support channels and a total audience of 30 million viewers that is fixed in size. Let the advertising rate be 10 cents per viewer. If these channels equally split the audience three ways, each can earn $1 million. Competition to attract viewers will induce each of them to invest in a program costing $1 million, which might, say, result in three reasonably high-quality dramas. Now say that technology or regulatory change permits six television channels

---

[8]See Owen and Wildman (1992) for a more detailed discussion of Noam's model.

[9]Berry and Waldfogel (2003) provide a clear exposition of Shaked and Sutton's (1987) model to empirically demonstrate that the average quality of daily newspapers increases with local market size, but that market fragmentation does not occur. That result contrasts with the increasing fragmentation as market size grows that they find in the case of restaurants, a product in which quality primarily depends upon variable costs.

to compete. Since advertising rates and total audience size are fixed, each station can now earn only $500,000, inducing them to switch to cheaper program forms, such as game shows, variety, or reality programs. The option of pay support may mitigate the quality-reducing effects of channel proliferation, but not by much unless viewer demands for differentiated programs are very intense. The key feature of the model is the evidently plausible assumption that in the initial situation, government or technology artificially restricts the supply of channel capacity. When that restriction is relaxed, entry moves the market outcome toward a new equilibrium of reduced program quality.

Using a model in which consumer tastes are distributed along a circle and program production costs are endogenous, Waterman (1990) shows that a shift from advertiser to pay television support in a competitive market does not necessarily lead to greater product variety, as earlier models with exogenous production costs suggested would happen. Rather, the result may only be higher cost programs, with no increase in product variety. In effect, the quality–variety trade-off in this model depends on the elasticity of consumer demand with respect to product quality versus the elasticity of demand with respect to product variety. If the former is stronger, then higher costs rather than greater variety tend to result when demand rises.

In a related paper, Waterman (1992) attempts to explain why technologies such as multichannel cable have not only appeared to segment audiences more finely with narrow-appeal programs, but have also offered relatively expensive broad-appeal programs, such as some major Hollywood movies, that are typically repeated on different media over time. This program choice model shows that a conversion to pay support, or the addition of greater channel capacity, may not only induce a producer with monopoly power to offer more expensive programs rather than greater product variety, but contrary to results of previous models, those programs may have increasingly lowest-common-denominator content. Owen and Wildman (1992) also construct a model to show how multimedia distribution opportunities may induce producers to increase their production budgets, but they do not address the product variety issue in that context.

Although the example in Table 18.3 abstracts from the product quality–variety trade-off by assuming that no entry is possible, it illustrates an essential idea of endogenous product quality models: why an expansion in potential market size—whether that occurs through population growth, rising income levels, or the accessibility of larger audiences

**TABLE 18.3**
Model 3: Product Quality and Market Size

| (a) *Program Cost Options* | (b) *Initial Market Demand* | (c) *Initial Demand* × 2 |
|---|---|---|
| Low (5) | 6 | 12 |
| High (10) | 9 | 18 |

due to new media outlets—tends to induce media producers to offer more expensively produced, higher quality media products.

We assume that there are two program cost options, low $= 5$ and high $= 10$, which can respectively generate initial market demand of 6 and 9, respectively (Column b). Notice that the doubling of production investment from 5 to 10 results in less that a doubling of demand—an assumption that, reasonably, reflects diminishing marginal returns to those investments. Under these conditions, a monopoly producer offering the high-cost program will lose money (at a profit of $9 - 10 = -1$), and will thus offer the low-cost program (at a profit of $6 - 5 = 1$).

Now say that market size doubles, as indicated by column (c). The producer will now make higher profits with the high-cost program (profit $= 18 - 10 = 8$ versus $12 - 5 = 7$ for the low-cost program). The basic reason for the producer's incentive to increase production costs can be traced to the extreme economies of scale in media product distribution. When market size doubles, the marginal productivity of investing another dollar in the production automatically doubles, inducing the producer to expand investment until the marginal return of that spending again falls to $1. Or in other words, the lump sum cost of moving from one quality level to a higher one becomes cheaper on a per-viewer basis as the potential audience increases.

Endogenous cost models based on Shaked and Sutton (1983) have been applied in several papers by Waldfogel and colleagues to issues of radio and television content. These are basically empirical papers, however, and we consider them in the following section.

Among other authors working with endogenous media quality models, Wright's (1994) research is presented in the context of regulations in Australia and the UK that limit the number of minutes per hour that television advertisements can be shown. He shows that such regulations will cause program quality to fall in a competitive market because higher investment levels can no longer be sustained. Such regulation benefits consumers to the extent that they may be averse to watching TV ads, but that must be weighed against the detrimental effects on consumers due to the lower program quality.

A classic result in the general economic literature on product differentiation is that firms have an incentive to differentiate their products in order to soften price competition. Two recent program choice modeling papers highlight the influence of this result on the advertiser versus pay TV support trade-off when program quality is endogenous.

Using a straight line-type duopoly model, Bourreau (2003) shows that pay support generally leads to greater program differentiation than does ad support because of the price softening motive. Under advertiser support (assuming that ad rates are exogenous), the two stations tend to mimic each other's content because they cannot use price as a competition softening device. To compensate for this inflexibility, the stations engage in relatively intense program quality competition. Program quality and differentiation outcomes under ad support vary with advertising rates. If ad prices are relatively low, lower quality and less differentiation results compared to pay support, whereas sufficiently high ad prices can result in program quality greater than that under pay support. The notable feature of this model is that although results are similar to the Steiner-type models, a different, more complex economic mechanism is at work.

The second article, Mangáni (2003), also investigates the effects of advertising in a duopoly broadcasting model with endogenous program production costs, but comes to a different conclusion. With the added assumption that viewers dislike advertising, he shows theoretically that an audience size maximization strategy pursued as a consequence of advertiser support can actually promote diversity. The mechanism at work in the Mangáni model is that the amount of advertising works something like a price. The farther the programs are from each other in product space, the more likely it is that a given viewer has satisfactory content, and thus the more minutes of advertising that the average viewer is willing to endure. The higher ad revenues in turn permit higher quality programs to be produced, which further attract viewers, etc. Contrary to earlier papers, Mangáni thus identifies a mechanism by which advertising can encourage rather than discourage program diversity.

Economic welfare results of endogenous media program quality models are mostly ambiguous, depending on parameter values. Bourreau (2003) and Waterman (1990) both find that program variety (or the degree of differentiation) is overproduced relative to the social optimum—a finding common to differentiated product models in the general economic literature—while quality is underproduced. These results, however, are not necessarily robust to alternative demand assumptions. As in the case of program choice models with fixed first copy costs, perfect price discrimination is generally impossible, and we do not know shapes of the demand curves that incorporate consumer valuations.

## Summary

Theoretical program choice models have offered relatively few unambiguous predictions about market outcomes or consumer welfare, mostly because the models are dependent on largely unverifiable assumptions about audience preferences. The models have, however, provided useful devices for describing economic trade-offs involving prices, audience sizes, diversity, quality, the quantity of advertising, and other aspects of program content, and how those trade-offs differ under alternative assumptions about channel capacity, means of support, and market structure. In that context, the models have suggested a variety of generally beneficial outcomes that would be likely to result from public policies encouraging higher channel capacities, availability of direct pricing mechanisms, and, with qualifications, from more centralized control of program menu decisions. Also with qualification due to potential crowding-out effects, program choice models have theoretically justified publicly funded media as well.

## EMPIRICAL STUDIES

We first consider broadly focused empirical studies that relate changes in channel capacity, market structure, or the means of support, to market outcomes, especially program diversity. We then turn in a second section to research that has been targeted toward individual types of programs, namely ethnic/racial minority–oriented programming, news and information, culture, and children's programming. In a third section, we consider empirical evidence of economic constraints on the narrowcasting model of television. Finally, we discuss evidence relevant to the appropriate role of publicly funded media.

Although containing less detail about individual studies in most cases, a recent book by Napoli (2003) usefully reviews or references a broader range of empirical studies involving the economics of the media and media audiences.

## Market Structure, Means of Support, and Diversity

Beginning in the 1960s, scholars have sought to measure the effects of higher channel capacity, or alternative means of support, on diversity and other aspects of program content.

Litman (1992) surveys empirical studies of TV program diversity. Our focus is on the extent to which these studies may confirm, refute, or otherwise inform the results of theoretical program choice models surveyed earlier. Of particular interest: What insights do empirical studies offer into how successful higher channel capacity and alternative means of payment have been in generating diverse, minority-appeal programming? Some studies addressing these questions have evaluated programming across local markets or across countries, whereas others have measured changes over time within the same markets.

Cross-sectional studies of diversity in local U.S. broadcast markets provide a natural laboratory to measure the effects of channel capacity expansion because larger markets have more channels than smaller markets. In an early academic study, Levin (1971) used 20 standard program "types" ("feature film," "cartoon," "situation comedy," "sports event," "religious," etc.) and showed that the number of different TV program types available over a 1-week period increased, though at a decreasing rate, as the number of commercial stations in the market rose. He also showed that public TV stations (then called Educational Television, or ETV) had a decisively higher positive impact on diversity than did commercial stations—one suggestion, at least, that public TV is socially beneficial. Levin's results generally confirmed the findings of a National Association of Broadcasters study by Herman W. Land Associates (1968), using a similar coding scheme and a more complex diversity measure. In a later and more elaborate diversity study, Levin (1980) also reports an increase in the amount of aggregate television viewing both as the number of stations rises, and as the number of program types rises—indications that viewers value and benefit from diversity.

A study by Grant (1994) evaluates the performance of multichannel television media using 1986 data. He defines 25 different program type categories and uses a measure of diversity that varies inversely with the concentration of individual program types in the sample.[10] Grant finds that basic cable networks have greater "horizontal" diversity (measured at a given point in time) than three other separate categories of channels: superstations, pay cable networks, and broadcast networks. As Grant acknowledges, his results are clouded by a possible bias in the diversity index with respect to the number of channels measured within each channel group. Also, choice of program categories may bias the results if certain categories tend to be more prevalent on basic or pay cable, for example, than on broadcast networks.

---

[10]Grant uses the following formula $Div = 1 - \sum_{i=1}^{n} S_i^2$, in which $S_i$ is the proportion of all the program types offered for the $i$th program type. The index decreases as the number of program types offered decreases or if one program type is offered for a disproportionately large number of times.

Grant's study nevertheless offers a degree of confirmation that multichannel cable does fragment audiences and that cable menus are more diverse than broadcast menus. The exact relationship between cable's performance and the predictions of theoretical models remains murky, however. On the one hand, cable operators tend to be local monopolists, which, as we discussed earlier, theory predicts will have less incentive to offer similar programs than will competitive suppliers. Theory also predicts, though, that a monopolist will tend to restrict the amount of programming offered and may tend to offer lowest common denominator types. In reality, of course, cable operators are not true monopolists because they compete with broadcast and other media, now including DBS. It seems evident that cable's competitive environment has been sufficient to prevent any major reduction in channel capacity or reversion to LCD programming.

Ishikawa et al. (1996) reports results of a large scale international study of programming diversity covering the 1990–1993 period, conducted under auspices of the NHK Broadcasting Culture Research Institute. Litman and Hasegawa (1996) measured diversity of programming on 22 U.S. broadcast and cable networks, based on 15 program type categories. They primarily used a "relative entropy"[11] measure of diversity, which, like Grant's measure, rises with lower concentrations of the same program types. Litman and Hasegawa found that overall diversity (measured over a full week of time) tended to be highest among a group of "narrowly targeted" basic cable networks, although results were somewhat different using a differently defined diversity index.

Ishikawa et al. (1996) also compared TV programming diversity in five major countries for the year 1992, considering only a more limited group of 26 public service and commercial channels in total, including the four commercial broadcast networks and PBS in the United States. Using the relative entropy measure, they found the UK system to have the highest overall diversity, followed respectively by Sweden, Japan, and Canada, with the U.S. networks bringing up the rear. The Ishikawa et al. study showed that public television networks contributed positively to diversity in all five countries, but especially so in the United States. As the authors acknowledge, however, their results remain tentative because the relative entropy index is sensitive to the number of channels covered within each country.

A series of other studies have measured trends in program diversity over time. In a well-known paper, Dominick and Pearce (1976) showed that the diversity of prime-time major broadcast network programming in the United States, as measured by 14 programming categories, steadily fell from 1953 to 1974. During this time, networks also turned away from news, public affairs, and interview/talk formats toward "entertainment" formats. Litman (1979) then showed a slight increase in major broadcast network diversity from 1973 to 1978. That paper was followed by Lin (1995), who found no overall trend in prime-time diversity among the major networks from 1980 to 1989.

The use of different program type classifications and diversity measures makes it difficult to interpret results of these studies as a continuous period of time. Also, although

---

[11] The Relative Entropy Index is defined as $H = \sum -p_i \log_2 p$, where $P_i$ indicates the probability of each category being selected. Relative entropy reaches its minimum value (0) when the probability of selection concentrates on a single category (minimum diversity) and it rises with the variance of probability of each category being selected. The maximum value (1) is obtained when the probability of selection is equal in all categories (maximum diversity).

oligopolistic interaction, competition from other media, and other external pressures are mentioned, these studies seem to lack compelling explanations for the trends. Especially after 1980, there was also significant entry of local stations and new networks not covered by the studies. To that extent, trends over time measured only for a subset of available channels become less meaningful.

Wakshlag and Adams (1985) studied prime-time broadcast network programming variety over a longer interval, 1950–1982. Using an entropy-based measure and 37 programming categories, they found no overall trend in diversity over the 33-year period, but noted a sharp and sustained decline coinciding with promulgation of the 1971 Prime Time Access Rule (PTAR). Essentially, the PTAR prohibited network-affiliated TV stations in the top 50 TV markets from showing more than 3 hours of network or "off-network" programs between 7 and 11 p.m., thus reducing the number of daily network-delivered prime-time programs after 1970. An ostensible purpose of the PTAR was to promote program diversity. Wakshlag and Adams found, however, a substantial decline in type diversity following the rule's introduction. Although they did not report evidence of a direct or straightforward effect that the rule had on diversity, Wakslag and Adams concluded that the PTAR (eventually repealed by the FCC in 1995) had apparently not served the public well with respect to the diversity of prime-time network programming that remained.

A recent study focusing on effects of the PTAR is Einstein's (2002) FCC-sponsored study of prime-time network program diversity. Einstein used 22 program categories to measure "before and after" diversity trends within two defined historical intervals: 1966 to 1974—during which the PTAR came into effect—and 1989 to 2002—during which the rule ended. Diversity was calculated in various ways, and for the latter period, the six most significant broadcast networks were included for some measures and only CBS, NBC, and ABC for others. Like Wakslag and Adams (1985), Einstein found a substantial decline in diversity right after the PTAR's 1971 debut. She also found a substantial rise in diversity after its 1995 repeal. While acknowledging that a number of economic factors had intervened, Einstein concluded that the PTAR appeared not to have achieved, or that it had been counterproductive to, its diversity objectives.

Einstein also reported that in spite of the strong trends within the separate time periods studied, there were no evident long-term trends in average diversity between the 1966–74 and the 1989–2002 periods. Both the Wachslag and Adams and the Einstein studies thus partly addressed shortcomings of other historical trend studies of diversity by using consistent measures over longer time intervals. They also, however, left unmeasured the trends in overall diversity due to the entry of cable and other programming that occurred over their study periods.

A study by De Jong and Bates (1991) compared programming diversity for a more complete, expanding menu of U.S. broadcast and cable networks for the years 1976, 1981, and 1986. They sampled the menus of 413 cable systems, which offered average capacities of approximately 14, 16, and 27 channels at the three respective points in time. Using 32 program type categories, their study showed an increase not only in absolute diversity, but in relative diversity, where the latter is defined as absolute diversity divided by the number of available channels. The rise in relative diversity is a more interesting result than the rise in absolute diversity since the former implies a more segmented array of programming options. Comparable to the earlier Levin and Herman Land & Associates studies, however, relative diversity did not increase as fast as the number of available channels. That is, absolute diversity tends to increase, but at a decreasing rate, as channel capacity expands.

Some more recent studies measure time trends in TV program diversity within other countries. Li and Chiang (2001) find that the three main networks in Taiwan responded to market entry and greater competition from cable and satellite channels over the 1986 to 1996 period by reducing the diversity of their programming menus. Wurff and Cuilenburg (2001) conducted a similar study of nine public and general-interest commercial channels supported primarily by advertising in the Netherlands, covering the period from 1988 to 1999. Using alternative measures, the authors generally find that up to about 1995, type diversity of programming on the subject networks increased. As competition intensified after this date, diversity declined. As explained by the authors, established networks appeared to respond to competition from "special interest" channels by reverting to menus of more "popular" program types.[12] These studies may suggest that competition among advertiser-supported networks promotes "sameness," as some program choice models implied. In both of these studies, though, the programming of only a limited number of channels was analyzed in the midst of substantial market entry by cable or satellite networks. Thus, although the strategic response of established networks may be to offer less diverse programming when confronted with competition, the impact of entry on the overall menu of programming available to consumers may be quite different.

The large number of localized radio markets in the United States, along with the dominant tendency of radio stations to segment audiences by selecting distinct programming formats, offer a convenient means to investigate how population size and other market characteristics affect media diversity and use. Such studies have intrinsic policy interest because the FCC has pursued a controversial practice of attempting to influence diversity by favoring license applications of radio stations that promise to offer certain differentiated formats. The FCC's station ownership rules may also affect diversity for reasons that we detail further hereafter.

Rogers and Woodbury (1996) use 1987–88 cross-sectional data for 115 local radio markets to investigate the relationship between the number of stations, format availability, and listening. They report that a 10% increase in the number of stations increases format availability by about 2%, but increases aggregate listening by only about 0.5%. Other things equal, a 10% rise in format availability lead to a 2% rise in listening, but more stations within a given format had no effect on listening. Rogers and Woodbury's results involving radio formats are limited by their use of only 11 format categories—fewer than the radio industry defines. As the authors observe, their results are generally consistent with predictions of program choice models that higher channel capacity under advertiser support leads to greater diversity. Their results confirm that at least to some extent, listeners value diversity.

A more recent empirical study by Berry and Waldfogel (2001) assesses effects of relaxing the radio ownership rules, as mandated by the 1996 Telecommunications Act, on entry in radio station markets, and on the mix of radio formats. Berry and Waldfogel first

---

[12]Note that some of the channels covered in this study entered during the period, so their programming was covered for only part of the 1988–99 interval.

present theoretical examples using a traditional line segment model to show how the effects of horizontal media mergers on product variety can differ depending on consumer preferences and the size of fixed costs. Based on these models, the authors conduct a "before and after" comparative study of 243 radio markets in 1993 and 1997, during which time substantial increases in local and national radio station ownership concentration took place. Forty-six different formats are considered.

Berry and Waldfogel's principal finding is that although greater ownership concentration within local markets tended to reduce the number of stations in operation, the ratio of formats to diversity (i.e., formats per station) rose over the period. They also found a weak tendency for absolute format diversity—that is, the total number of different formats offered—to rise. Berry and Waldfogel's interpretation of the apparent paradox that diversity rises while the number of stations falls is that locally co-owned stations tend to choose different, but still "nearby" formats as a strategy to crowd out entry of competing stations. Their results are also generally consistent with the predictions of classic program choice models that under advertiser support, co-owned stations have a greater tendency to differentiate their programming than do competing stations.

Three other studies have considered the effects of market concentration on radio programming diversity using more recent data. An FCC Staff Research Paper by Williams and Roberts (2002) reported that the variety of radio formats available to consumers had held steady since the 1996 Act. In another FCC study, Williams, Brown, and Alexander (2002) investigated the effects of substantially increasing station ownership concentration over the 1996–2001 period on the diversity of rock and roll station play lists. Although these authors stop short of a definitive conclusion about whether concentration affects radio program diversity, they report that play-list diversity generally remained stable over the 5-year time period, suggesting that rising concentration has had little effect by that measure. Chambers (2003) studies the relationship between radio program diversity and market structure in the top 50 radio markets, using a cross-section of 2001–2002 data. He found positive relationships between the degree of competition in local markets (as measured by the HHI) and both the variety of different available formats and the diversity of song titles.

The different results reported by both the FCC and Chambers studies in comparison to Berry and Waldfogel's paper may reflect more recent changes in radio markets. Both of the more recent studies, however, were based only on descriptive data and/or simple correlations, so it is difficult to be certain of the complete picture.

## Specialized Diversity Studies

Other academic works have been concerned with how economic factors affect the availability and consumption of particular program types. Although some of these studies also deal with general program diversity issues, they are included here if they substantially focus on specialized programming.

### Ethnic/Racial Minority Programming

Among economic studies of specialized programming types, a disproportionate number have involved racial/ethnic programming. As Wildman and Karamanis (1996) observe, there has been a general presumption in the United States that minorities are "underserved" by radio or television programming that is directly oriented toward their preferences. At least in part, that perception in the United States has apparently motivated a history of taxation and FCC licensing provisions that give preference to minority station owners (Mason, Bachen, & Craft, 2001).

Using data from 246 radio markets, Waldfogel (2003) investigates the effects of White, Black, and Hispanic population sizes on the availability of programming oriented toward these racial/ethnic groups, and also on their listening rates. He presents a simple discrete program choice model involving the concept of "preference externalities." Since there are fixed costs, the number of Black-oriented stations, for example, is expected to increase with an increase in the Black population, as should the aggregate level of Black listening. Additional Blacks in the population, that is, have a positive externality effect on other Blacks by increasing the incentives for commercial firms to supply Black-oriented programs. For a Black population of a given size, however, a growth in the number of Whites may reduce the availability of Black-oriented programming to the extent that more ambivalent Black listeners are siphoned off by the wider availability of White-oriented programming. In his empirical analysis, Waldfogel confirmed that Black-, Hispanic-, and White-oriented program availability and listening rise significantly with the size of those racial/ethnic populations, respectively; he showed weak evidence of negative externalities in the case of White population size on the Black listening share. More generally, Waldfogel reported that Blacks and Hispanics have sharply distinct radio listening preferences, a finding that was also suggested by a result from Rogers and Woodbury's (1996) study that both Black and Hispanic population sizes significantly encourage radio format diversity.

Other authors have focused more specifically on the "undersupply" issue by studying how audiences having different racial/ethnic compositions are valued by advertisers. Webster and Phalen (1997) found a significant negative relationship between the proportion of non-Whites in a market and advertising rates, and an FCC-sponsored study by Ofori (1999) reported lower CPMs for radio stations targeting minority audiences. In an individual radio station–level study, Napoli (2002) reported significantly lower advertiser valuations for Black and Hispanic audiences. In explaining these differences, Napoli cites lower average income levels of both Blacks and Hispanics in the United States, but he had insufficient data to statistically isolate the effects of income.

In a related paper, Brown and Cavazos (2002) studied advertising rates and their relationship to African-American representation in prime-time broadcast television program casts. They find strong preferences by Black audiences for programs with African-American casts, and also that such programs statistically underrepresent the proportion of Blacks in the general U.S. population. Having corrected for audience purchasing power, however, Brown and Cavazos find that this bias disappears. They nevertheless make a case that advertiser-supported broadcasting would result in an undersupply of Black-oriented programs even in the absence of these income differences. Their logic is that Black audiences' interests in Black-oriented programs are relatively intense, but advertiser-supported broadcast television does not offer them the means to express those intensities of interest. A higher intensity of interest in television programming among Blacks is also suggested by survey data reported in Albarran and Humphrey (1993).

Several authors have also directly studied the relationship between minority station ownership and programming content, but results have varied widely. In an early article, Schement and Singleton (1981) reported that ownership made no significant differences in the amount of news, public affairs, or other nonentertainment programming offered by Spanish-language radio stations. Similarly, Singleton (1981) found no significant differences in amounts of public service programming offered by Black-owned versus non-Black-owned radio stations. A later study of the effects of minority ownership on television programming content by Spitzer (1991) suggested positive relationships between minority ownership and the amount of minority program content, but did not report definitive results. A paper by Mason, Bachen, and Craft (2001) reported on a nationwide telephone survey of news directors at radio and television stations. They found that at least minority-owned radio stations put greater emphasis on issues of presumed interest to minorities than did other stations. Overall, the body of these studies appear to offer little policy guidance as to the desirability of minority radio and TV station ownership.

### News, Culture, and Children's Programming

An eclectic group of economic studies has focused on the availability and viewership of these distinct types of programming.

An extensive analysis of television news programming by Hamilton (2004) is loosely based on a program choice model involving numbers of channels, costs per program, audience demand prices, and audience sizes. Among other points, Hamilton argues that television news has become softer and more personality-driven over time because of the proliferation of channels and the relatively high production cost of hard news. Although channel proliferation does favor politically differentiated channels such as Fox News, he argues that the predominant effect is fragmentation of audiences and thus budgets, favoring softer news because it is cheaper. Hamilton also cites the pressures of more competition on the need to "brand" news programs, a strategy that tends to favor personality- and entertainment-driven forms.

One other recent study by Bae (1999) considered how the cable news networks, CNN, Fox, and MSNBC, differentiated their programming as of 1997. He found substantial differences among these channels in terms of programming style or format, but did not report significant political differentiation at that time.

A type of programming often cited in the 1970s and even before as holding out the highest hopes of commercial viability on multichannel, pay-supported television systems was "high culture." In an attempt to explain why cable TV networks fell short of these expectations in the early 1980s, Waterman (1986) cited high costs of production, very small audiences, and a lack of interest by advertisers. His findings contrasted with a popular assumption that cultural program viewers were a distinct group of intense, high-willingness-to-pay viewers with demand for large quantities of televised performing arts.

Children's programs are a category of television fare that has attracted a great deal of policy interest in the United States. FCC regulations have been based on requirements by the Children's Television Act of 1990 that television stations affiliated with any of the three main broadcast networks offer certain minimum quantities of "educational" programming for children. Although numerous authors have studied children's programming, few of those research efforts are from an economic perspective. In an extensive early study, Melody (1973) argued that the commercial television networks were biased against offering socially beneficial children's television programming, largely because of the advertisers' incentives. Chan-Olmsted (1996) documents the proliferation of children's programming on cable television and measures the extent of market concentration among its broadcast and cable providers. She did not, however, study diversity issues directly.

## Narrowcasting Constraints: Audience Composition and Advertiser Incentives

A series of studies by Goodhardt and Ehrenberg (1969) and Barwise and Ehrenberg (1982, 1987, 1988) have provided valuable insights into the potential for narrowcast types of programming by revealing the intensity of interest that various television audiences have in the programs that they watch. These studies, which the authors describe to be about the "liking and viewing" of television programs, were based on surveys conducted in Britain and the United States. In general, they interpret their findings to suggest that audience involvement in television programs is relatively low. Only a minority of series program viewers (about 40%) reported watching the previous episode, suggesting relatively casual interest. A 1982 Markle Foundation study by Barwise and Ehrenberg found that only about half of the typical program audience reported that they enjoyed the program they had just watched at the "extremely" or "very much" level.

Of most interest, Barwise and Ehrenberg report a significant positive correlation between the size of a program's audience and the average viewers' enjoyment of the program. That is, smaller audiences generally appear to have *less* intense demand for the programs they watch. That finding seems to challenge a fundamental assumption of some program choice models: namely, that more sharply focused program content can necessarily be more successfully tailored to the tastes of smaller groups because those tastes are more homogeneous. An alternative explanation for the positive correlation between audience size and average enjoyment, however, is that television audiences enjoy smaller audience programs less because those programs tend to be more cheaply produced than are large-audience programs. Nevertheless, the findings of Ehrenberg and colleagues are not encouraging to the narrowcasting model.

A study by Waterman and Yan (1999) is also somewhat discouraging to the narrowcasting model of cable television from an advertiser's perspective. Contrary to expectations generated by the pattern of higher cost per thousand advertising rates for more specialized, smaller circulation magazines, basic cable networks have historically tended to have lower CPM rates than their larger "mass audience" broadcast network counterparts. Waterman and Yan attribute that discrepancy to a disadvantage that cable networks have had in the advertising market because they have lower national audience reach than free broadcasting. Elasticity estimates suggest, however, that this disadvantage will continue to diminish as direct broadcast satellite and other technologies expand the reach of advertiser-supported cable networks.

## The Role of Public Media

How well have publicly supported radio and television systems served to enhance diversity or otherwise supply programs not offered by the private market? As discussed in the second section of this chapter, early program choice models suggested public media to be an ideal supplement to correct the bias of limited-channel, advertiser-supported commercial television systems in the United States against high-demand, minority-appeal programs, including those that might have wider social benefits. As we also noted earlier, the Levin (1971, 1980) and Ishikawa et al. (1996) studies showed that public television stations have tended to add more to diversity, especially in the United States, than have commercial stations. As Grant (1994) observed in his content analysis, though, cable networks have come to provide substantial quantities of much of the same program fare, including culture, public affairs, and racial/ethnically oriented programs, that PBS distributes. Noam's (1987) model also offered a formal theoretical argument to suggest that public TV might crowd out commercial TV, presumably a socially undesirable outcome.

Systematic empirical studies addressing these issues are sparse. Berry and Waldfogel (1999) concentrate on the potential commercial program displacement effect of publicly funded radio stations. They examine formats, play-list overlaps, and audience listening for jazz, classical music and news/talk stations in 165 U.S. local markets. By comparing commercial format availability and listening behavior in markets with and without public television stations that provide similar types of programming, Berry and Waldfogel find evidence of significant displacement of commercial media effects in classical music and to a lesser extent, the jazz format, in larger markets. They do not conclude that public expenditure on radio programming is necessarily undesirable, however, because they do not have direct evidence on the degree of actual similarity between public and commercial programming.

An examination of TV ratings data shows that PBS programs consistently outdraw, often by large margins, similar program types offered on basic cable networks, although these gaps have generally narrowed over the past decade.[13] Of course, such ratings differences could also reflect a crowding-out effect. Taken at face value, however, these ratings contrasts might demonstrate an inability of commercial cable networks to provide programs that are truly comparable to those of public television. Observations that cable networks provide similar programming to public TV stations may also do more to highlight the shortcomings of program format definitions than to demonstrate crowding-out effects. Public TV stations may provide higher benefits than private stations because of the absence of commercials, and these stations may have positive social externalities as well.

Another more pragmatic element of the policy debate in public broadcasting has been brought to the fore by the spread of cable: public TV program duplication. At the same time that cable has offered competitive program choices, it has dramatically enhanced the range and quality of public station signals, many of which have been handicapped by assignment to the UHF spectrum. Partly due to the FCC's "must-carry" rules, several

---

[13] See, for example, cable network ratings reports in *Cable Programming Investor* (Kagan World Media) and PBS ratings in *PBS Audience, Corporate Facts* (www.pbs.org).

different public television stations originally licensed to different communities within large television markets have often become available to individual cable households. One study by Phillips, Griffiths, and Tarbox (1991) found that 15% of public television program hours were duplicated within the same television market during a given week, although only 2% were actually shown simultaneously on the same day and time.

## Summary

Insights from empirical studies into how variations in channel capacity, different regimes of support, and different market structures actually affect market outcomes, especially in terms of program diversity, have been substantial. Most of the diversity or other program content studies, however, have at best been loosely based on the predictions of theoretical program choice models. They have also been hindered by the notorious difficulty of measuring program diversity, as illustrated by the use of nearly as many program content coding schemes as there have been program content studies. Both of these shortcomings present challenges for future empirical studies to meet.

## RESEARCH NEEDS

By their nature, the need for theoretical advances in program economics cannot be easily identified. The most evident promise for expanding our knowledge about the economics of programming is empirical, theory-based research. We suggest several areas of empirical study in which potential rewards seem in our judgment to be high.

One prediction of program choice models that appears to hold under a range of assumptions is that pay mechanisms and higher channel capacity should tend to reduce or eliminate lowest-common-denominator, or "least-objectionable," program types. The weight of empirical evidence is that greater channel capacity and/or direct payment mechanisms increase program diversity, and in some studies, diversity per channel. Although these results are suggestive, they do not directly address the "LCD" question. More direct evidence might be, for example, that certain radio formats or types of television programs tend to disappear from the market when capacity rises or when pay mechanisms are introduced. Although the arbitrariness of program type or format definitions are limiting to such an investigation, an alternative methodology may be to define programming focus in terms of the sharpness of their demographic appeal. As cable, DBS, and other multichannel media have proliferated, for example, has programming on the three major U.S. broadcast networks become more finely segmented toward certain demographic categories? Or, have the networks responded with even more broadly focused content, as Wurff and Cuilenburg's (2001) study suggests in the Dutch case?

There is also a need for empirical economic studies of specialized programming, especially of types that involve policy interest. The several studies of how market size and other economic factors determine the supply and usage of Black- and Hispanic-oriented radio and television programming provide a useful model for studies about programming directed to other minorities, such as foreign-language-speaking groups. How has the supply of foreign-language or other racial/ethnic programming changed with the advent of satellites, and other more efficient distribution technologies including the Internet? How do audience characteristics, advertising markets, channel capacity, and other factors affect the supply and usage of children's or other types of programming that have arguable social benefits as well as policy interest?

A third important subject is the role of publicly funded media. Studies of crowding-out effects, such as Berry and Waldfogel's analysis (1999) of public radio, might be applied, for example, to public television by making use of local variations in program availability. Of most significance, empirical research on public broadcasting must recognize that these organizations are not merely dependent on federal and other government funds. Rather, public TV and radio stations have complex objective functions that follow from dependence on corporate, individual, and other contributors, the pursuit of which has undoubted effects on their program choices.

Finally, we note an unresolved empirical issue of fundamental importance: that is, the relationship between the intensity of audience demand and breadth of appeal. Other things equal, what is the elasticity of demand with respect to the sharpness of content focus? Can audiences really be better satisfied by sharper focus toward fewer individuals, or are "mass appeal" programs more satisfying for some reason? Although the "liking and viewing" studies by Ehrenberg and colleagues have made important strides in this respect, further research is needed to distinguish the effects of content appeal from the effects of programming budget levels. In order to conduct studies in these and other areas, perhaps the thorniest difficulty is useful definition of program types, and of diversity more generally. In addition to using demographic characteristics of audiences as a proxy, diversity can also be defined in terms of actual perceptions by audiences of how different programs are from each other. Nearly a half century ago, Lang (1957) used surveys in which respondents were asked to rank order radio program preferences as a method to infer the perceived degree of similarly between programs. Perhaps that or another methodology could be used to overcome the most formidable obstacle to empirical studies of media program diversity.

## ACKNOWLEDGMENTS

I am grateful to Xiaofei Wang for exceptionally capable research assistance and to the editors for comments.

## REFERENCES

Albarran, A. B., & Humphrey, D. (1993). An examination of television motivation and program preferences by Hispanics, Blacks, and Whites. *Journal of Broadcasting & Electronic Media*, 95–103.

Bae, H.-S. (1999). Product differentiation in cable programming: The case of the cable national all-news networks. *Journal of Media Economics, 12*(4), 265–277.

Barwise, P., & Ehrenberg, A. (1988). *Television and its audience*. London: Sage.

Barwise, T. P., & Ehrenberg, A. S. C. (1982). *The liking and viewing of regular TV programs* (Study supported by the John & Mary R. Markle Foundation). London: London Business School.

Barwise, T. P., & Ehrenberg, A. S. C. (1987). The liking and viewing of regular TV series. *The Journal of Consumer Research, 14*(1), 63–70.

Beebe, J. H. (1977). Industrial structure and program choices in television markets. *Quarterly Journal of Economics, XCI*(1), 15–37.

Berry, S. T., & Waldfogel, J. (1999). Public radio in the United States: Does it correct market failure or cannibalize commercial stations? *Journal of Public Economics, 71*, 189–211.

Berry, S. T., & Waldfogel, J. (2001). Do mergers increase product variety? Evidence from radio broadcasting. *The Quarterly Journal of Economics, 116*(3), 1009–1025.

Berry, S. T., & Waldfogel, J. (2003, May). *Product Quality and Market Size*, Working paper 9675, NBER.

Bourreau, M. (2003). Mimicking vs. counter-programming strategies for television programs. *Information Economics & Policy, 15*(1), 35–54.

Brown, K. S., & Cavazos, R. J. (2002). Network revenues and African American broadcast television programs. *Journal of Media Economics, 15*(4), 227–239.

Chae, S., & Flores, D. (1998). Broadcasting versus narrowcasting. *Information Economics and Policy, 10*, 41–57.

Chambers, T. (2003). Radio programming diversity in the era of consolidation. *Journal of Radio Studies, 10*(1), 33–45.

Chan-Olmsted, S. (1996). From Sesame Street to Wall Street: An analysis of market competition in commercial children's television. *Journal of Broadcasting & Electronic Media, 40*(1), 30–45.

De Jong, A. S., & Bates, B. J. (1991). Channel diversity in cable television. *Journal of Broadcasting & Electronic Media, 35*(2), 159–167.

Dominick, J. R., & Pearce, M. C. (1976). Trends in network prime-time programming, 1953–74. *Journal of Communication, 26*(1), 70–80.

Doyle, C. (1998). Programming in a competitive broadcasting market: Entry, welfare and regulation. *Information Economics and Policy, 10*, 23–39.

Einstein, M. (2002). *Program diversity and the program selection process on broadcast network television* (FCC Media Ownership Working Group Studies). Retrieved November 10, 2003, from http://www.fcc.gov/ownership/studies.html

Goodhardt, G. J., & Ehrenberg, A. S. C. (1969). Duplication of television viewing between and within channels. *Journal of Marketing Research, VI*, 169–178.

Grant, A. E. (1994). The promise fulfilled? An empirical analysis of program diversity on television. *Journal of Media Economics, 7*(1), 51–64.

Hamilton, J. T. (2004). *All the news that's fit to sell: How the market transforms information into news*. Princeton, NJ: Princeton University Press.

Hansen, C. T., & Kyhl, S. (2001). Pay-per-view broadcasting of outstanding events: Consequences of a ban. *International Journal of Industrial Organization, 19*, 589–609.

Herman W. L., and Associates, I. (1968). *Television and the wired city*. Washington, DC: National Association of Braodcasters.

Holden, S. (1993). Network or pay-per-view? A welfare analysis. *Economics Letters, 43*, 59–64.

Ishikawa, S., Leggatt, T., Litman, B., Raboy, M., Rosengren, K. E., & Kambara, N. (1996). Diversity in television programming: Comparative analysis of five countries. In S. Ishikawa (Ed.), *Quality assessment of television* (pp. 253–263). Luton, UK: John Libbey Media.

Lang, K. (1957). Areas of radio preferences: A preliminary inquiry. *Journal of Applied Psychology, 41*(1), 7–14.

Lence, R. (1978). Theories of television program selection: A discussion of the Spence–Owen model. *Studies in Industry Economics #94*; Stanford University Dept. of Economics.

Levin, H. J. (1971). Program duplication, diversity, and effective viewer choices: Some empirical findings. *American Economic Review*, 81–88.

Levin, H. J. (1980). *Fact and fancy in television regulation: An economic study of policy alternatives*. New York: Russell Sage Foundations.

Li, S.-C. S., & Chiang, C.-C. (2001). Market competition and programming diversity: A study of the TV market in Taiwan. *Journal of Media Economics, 14*(2), 105–119.

Lin, C. A. (1995). Diversity of network prime-time program formats during the 1980s. *Journal of Media Economics, 8*(4), 17–28.

Litman, B., & Hasegawa, K. (1996). Measuring diversity in U.S. television programming: New evidence. In S. Ishikawa (Ed.), *Quality assessment of television* (pp. 203–230). Luton, UK: John Libbey Media.

Litman, B. R. (1979). The television networks, competition and program diversity. *Journal of Broadcasting, 23*(4), 393–409.

Litman, B. R. (1992). Economic aspects of program quality: The case for diversity. *Studies of Broadcasting, 28*, 121–156.

Mangáni, A. (2003). Profit and audience maximization in broadcasting markets. *Information Economics and Policy, 15*(3), 305–315.

Mason, L., Bachen, C. M., & Craft, S. (2001). Support for FCC minority ownership policy: How broadcast station owner race or ethnicity affects news and public affairs programming diversity. *Communication Law & Policy, 6*(1), 37–73.

Melody, W. (1973). *Children's television: The economics of exploitation.* New Haven, CT: Yale University Press.

Minasian, J. R. (1964). Television pricing and the theory of public goods. *Journal of Law and Economics, 7*, 71–80.

Minow, N. N. (1961). "The Vast Wasteland," address by Newton N. Minow to the National Association of Broadcasters, Washington, D.C., May 9, 1961, in F. Kahn (Ed.), 1978, Documents of American Broadcasting (4th ed., pp. 207–217). Englewood Cliffs, NJ: Prentice Hall.

Napoli, P. M. (1999). Deconstructing the diversity principle. *Journal of Communication*, 7–34.

Napoli, P. M. (2002). Audience valuation and minority media: An analysis of the determinants of the value of radio audiences. *Journal of Broadcasting & Electronic Media*, 169–183.

Napoli, P. M. (2003). Audience economics: Media institutions and the audience marketplace. New York: Columbia University Press.

Noam, E. M. (1987). A public and private-choice model of broadcasting. *Public Choice, 55*, 163–187.

Noll, R. G., Peck, M. J., & McGowan, J. J. (1973). *Economic aspects of television regulation.* Washington, DC: The Brookings Institution.

Ofori, K. A. (1999). *When being no. 1 isn't enough: The impact of advertising practices on minority-formatted and minority-owned broadcasters.* Federal Communication Commission, Released January 13, 1999. Washington, DC.

Owen, B. M., Beebe, J., & W. G. Manning, J. (1974). *Television economics.* Washington, DC: Health.

Owen, B. M., & Wildman, S. S. (1992). *Video economics.* Cambridge, MA: Harvard University Press.

Papandrea, F. (1997). Modelling television programming choices. *Information Economics and Policy, 9*, 203–218.

Phillips, T. M., Griffiths, T. A., & Tarbox, N. C. (1991). Public television efficiency versus diversity. *Journal of Media Economics, 4*(1), 19–33.

Rogers, R. P., & Woodbury, J. R. (1996). Market structure, program diversity, and radio audience size. *Contemporary Economic Policy, 14*(1), 81–91.

Rothenberg, J. (1962). Consumer sovereignty and the economics of TV programming. *Studies in Public Communication, 4*, 45–54.

Salop, S. (1979). Monopolistic competition with outside goods. *Bell Journal of Economics, 10*, 141–156.

Samuelson, P. A. (1964). Public goods and subscription TV: Correction of the record. *Journal of Law and Economics, VII*, 81–83.

Schement, J. R., & Singleton, L. A. (1981). The onus of minority ownership: FCC policy and Spanish-language radio. *Journal of Communication, 31*(2), 78–83.

Shaked, A., & Sutton, J. (1983). Natural oligopolies. *Econometrica, 51*, 1469–1484.

Singleton, L. A. (1981). FCC minority ownership policy and non-entertainment programming in Black-oriented radio stations. *Journal of Broadcasting, 25*, 195–201.

Spence, M., & Owen, B. M. (1977). Television programming, monopolistic competition and welfare. *Quarterly Journal of Economics, 91*(1), 103–126.

Spitzer, M. L. (1991). Justifying minority preferences in broadcasting. *Southern California Law Review, 64*, 293–361.

Steiner, P. O. (1952). Program patterns and preferences and the workability of competition in radio broadcasting. *Quarterly Journal of Economics, 66*(2), 194–223.

Wakshlag, J., & Adams, W. J. (1985). Trends in program variety and the prime time access rule. *Journal of Broadcastig and Electronic Media, 29*(1), 23–34.

Waldfogel, J. (2003). Preference externalities: An empirical study of who benefits whom in differentiated-product markets. *The Rand Journal of Economics, 34*(3), 557–568.

Waterman, D. (1986). The failure of cultural programming on cable TV: An economic interpretation. *Journal of Communication, 36*(3), 92–107.

Waterman, D. (1990). Diversity and quality of information products in a monopolistically competitive industry. *Information Economics and Policy, 4*(4), 291–303.

Waterman, D. (1992). "Narrowcasting" and "broadcasting" on nonbroadcast media: A program choice model. *Communication Research, 19*(1), 3–28.

Waterman, D. (2003). Economic explanations of American media trade dominance: Contest or contribution? *Journal of Media Economics & Culture, 1*(1), 38–63.

Waterman, D., & Yan, M. Z. (1999). Cable advertising and the future of basic cable networking. *Journal of Broadcasting & Electronic Media,* 645–658.

Webster, J. G., & Phalen, P. F. (1997). *The mass audience: Rediscovering the dominant model.* Mahwah, NJ: Lawrence Erlbaum Associates.

Wildman, S. S., & Karamanis, T. (1996). The economics of minority programming. In *Investing in Diversity.* Washington, DC: The Aspen Institute.

Wildman, S. S., & Lee, N. Y. (1989). *Program choice in a broadband environment.* Paper presented at the Integrated Broadband Networks Conference, Columbia University.

Wildman, S. S., & Owen, B. M. (1985). Program competition in the new video industry. In E. Noam (Ed.), Video Media Competition: *Rivalry among the video transmission media.* New York: Columbia University Press.

Wiles, P. (1963). Pilkington and the theory of value. *The Economic Journal, 73,* 183–200.

Williams, G., Brown, K., & Alexander, P. (2002). Radio market structure and music diversity (FCC Media Bureau Staff Research Paper, Media Ownership Working Group Studies) Retrieved November 10, 2003 from http://www.fcc.gov/ownership/studies.html

Williams, G., & Roberts, S. (2002). Radio industry review 2002: Trends in ownership, format, and finance (FCC Media Bureau Staff Research Paper, Media Ownership Working Group Studies). Retrieved November 10, 2003 from http://www.fcc.gov/ownership/studies.html

Wright, D. J. (1994). Television advertising regulation and program quality. *The Economic Record, 70*(211), 361–367.

Wurff, R. v. d., & Cuilenburg, J. v. (2001). Impact of moderate and ruinous competition on diversity: The Dutch television market. *Journal of Media Economics, 14*(4), 213–229.

# 19

# Issues in Network/Distribution Economics

Benjamin J. Bates and Kendra S. Albright
University of Tennessee

This chapter begins with a review of the basic economics of information networks and other distribution systems used for media products. Networks can be physical or nonphysical, permanent or temporary, ranging from the global telecommunications net to a group of friends chatting over drinks after work. They can incorporate one-way distribution of information goods, enable interactions, or permit a wide range of communication types (as evidenced by the Internet). The products distributed may be physical or not, and the information at its heart can often be embodied and distributed in a variety of forms. Although a wide range of distribution and transportation systems can be seen as networks, for our purposes we focus on information networks, systems that allow the sharing or distribution of information goods and services. We could also use the generic term "media," although this more commonly refers to a set of mass communication systems.

This chapter introduces the reader to several general concepts and economic features of such systems. One feature is the wide range of information products that are distributed by a number of networks and media, many with distinctive economic features and attributes. Thus, we also examine the more specific economics of different types of networks and distribution systems, focusing on those related to media and information goods and services. We then examine a number of issues facing media, and media managers, with regard to networks and distribution systems.

## ECONOMIC IMPLICATIONS OF INFORMATION PROPERTIES

Information is a fairly distinctive economic good, one that differs from typical physical products in a number of important ways (Bates, 1990; DeLong & Froomkin, 2000; Kingma, 2001). Several of these distinctions have an impact on the economics of networks, and therefore are important from the perspective of this chapter. Perhaps most important is that most of what we tend to think of as information goods and services are actually joint products: the combination of the information itself (which is nonphysical), and the distribution medium for that information (which uses a physical form and/or network to distribute the information content). Each component has its own distinctive economic nature and can display certain attributes typically associated with public goods. The information itself clearly shows properties of nonrivalrous consumption; that is, that consumption by one does not prohibit consumption by others. One way of looking at it is that while information is used, it is not consumed (used up) per se; the core information remains. Thus, the information may be shared across many users without diminishing the availability of the information to others. Some information networks and distribution systems also exhibit the other main property of public goods, nonexcludability, in that it is difficult to prevent consumption by nonpayers (think radio and TV). Although these properties pose certain difficulties on their own, they also contribute to externalities in the form of used markets, piracy, and the sharing of information products. In addition, information production exhibits considerable economies of scale; although it is costly to produce the initial information, there is little or no direct cost associated with replicating the information itself. Thus, most information goods and services evince continually declining average costs.

Markets for information goods and services are also distinctive from those of more typical economic goods. Shy (2001) notes several distinguishing characteristics: complementarity of goods and services and the impact of compatibility and standards; the presence of consumption externalities; the presence of switching costs and the related consequence of lock-in; and the prevalence of significant economies of scale in production and distribution. Information goods and services not only tend to have substitutes (alternative ways of obtaining the information), but in many cases also exhibit degrees of complementarity (links with other goods and services). Some of these involve the use of standards (for recording and playback, for example), or compatibility among components in the consumption process. There are also significant consumption externalities at work—at the very least, consuming information goods and services takes time and attention. Consumption may also require access to costly equipment or networks, and acquisition of relevant literacy skills. Some of these factors lead to the presence of switching costs (the need to acquire new skills and or equipment), with the resulting tendency to lock in to certain standards.

A second important distinction is that not only does the value of information goods and services arise from their use, but the value is shaped by the conditions and attributes of the particular use. Some of these reflect the market externalities mentioned by Shy (2001), such as the fact that the value of a network tends to grow as the number of connections increases (a phenomenon termed *network* or *adoption externalities*). In addition, in many cases there are what can be called ancillary values beyond the straight exchange value of the good or service (Bates, 1988; Kingma, 2001; Shapiro & Varian, 1998). Often, the value of information is related to noneconomic impacts, such as enjoyment of a recording, book, or a good conversation with an old friend. Advertising, for example, has value by seeking to influence future perceptions and behaviors, which, it is hoped, will create future value for advertisers. In the world of art, literature, and music, existing work affects the perceived value of future efforts. An informed population helps markets function more smoothly and allows for effective democratic governance, reflecting the creation of what could be called social value from information creation and use. These values, however, are difficult to measure precisely, contributing to another major market externality—uncertainty—the fact that the value of the information is not certain until after it is consumed.

These attributes of information goods and services, and their markets, make it difficult to achieve what economists tend to view as optimal competitive equilibria. Thus, they tend to suggest that such markets evidence *market failure* (not that they fail per se, but that they do not necessarily achieve socially or economically optimal results). DeLong and Froomkin (2000) suggest that this failure is systematic and derived from the particular nature of information goods and services. This is the primary rationale used to call for government intervention and regulation of information networks and markets.

## BASIC ECONOMICS OF NETWORKS

Networks are basically distribution systems. They can be defined broadly as any mechanism or system that connects people or things, but the goal and value of the connection is its potential for exchange. It is the combination of product (information good or service) and its distribution, and both the products and the networks can incorporate and accommodate a broad range of forms, markets, cost structures, and demand characteristics. Thus, it will be difficult to talk about network and distribution economics in the abstract.

### General Attributes

For networks to be viable, they generally must have some form of infrastructure that permits connection/distribution, and an operations component that does the actual distribution of information goods and services (that is, the use of the network). The network, though, is there to distribute a product or service, and the design and cost structures of the network are based on the nature and attributes of that product, as are the operating costs. These three components need to be considered separately, although they are interlinked.

In general, the infrastructure must be in place before the networks can be used, and the cost of operations is related to the actual amount of use. These two components generally correspond with what economists call fixed costs (infrastructure) and variable costs (operations). Infrastructure costs depend on the scope of the network and the form of distribution/connection, and networks are generally designed to facilitate the distribution of a particular product, although they may be adapted for other forms and formats. Infrastructure can further be broken into two components: the system of links, and the mechanisms necessary to distribute goods and services along the links. To use the phone system as an example, you have the wires connecting everyone, and then you have the switching system, amplifiers, phones, and related electronics needed to move calls from one user to another. The specific costs of these components tend to vary widely, depending on the type of network and information goods and services being distributed. They are also tied to the capacity of the system, setting an upper limit on the ability to use the network.

Once the network is established, it can be used. The use of the network entails a range of variable costs, tied to the amount of use, and the particular distribution paths utilized on the network. That is, the operations costs depend on the actual number and type of goods and services being distributed, as well as the nature and scope of the distribution paths along the network infrastructure. Although fixed and variable costs are often treated separately, with networks and distribution systems there is a trade-off between fixed and variable costs involved in the design of network infrastructure (that is, higher expenditures in infrastructure can reduce operating costs, and vice versa). Further, there can be additional trade-offs between what components of the system the consumer provides to the network (for instance, owning a television receiver or cellphone handset), which can affect cost and demand structures.

In general, there are two distinctive economic consequences that emerge from the growth of networks. The first of these are what are termed *network* or *adoption economies*: the fact that as networks embrace larger and larger markets, the network tends to increase in value to users. Part of this is related to the general growth of the market for those information goods and services being distributed. Another part is related more to access—the larger the network, the greater the opportunities for use (the more people to talk with, or the greater choice in information goods and services). This value can be further increased by the adoption of standards that facilitate compatibility and interconnection between systems.[1]

People tend to see this value as increasing ad infinitum, but some argue that there is a point where diseconomies kick in. Although in general the value of access increases with network size, not all additions to the network are equally valuable (and some may have no additional value at all), and the cost of finding the person/good you're looking for increases as the network grows. At some point, it is argued, the added search costs outweigh the added value of the network expansion, creating a network diseconomy.

Another factor contributing to network diseconomies is a result of the fact that networks and their use may not grow consistently. In particular, if the use of the network outstrips its capacity, users may experience *network congestion*. Congestion disrupts network operations, reducing the usability, and thus value, of the network to at least some users. Congestion can occur at any scale, if the amount of use approaches or surpasses the capacity of the existing network.

There are also a variety of what are known as *scale* and *scope economies* evidenced in networks and media. For any good, the particular mix of fixed and variable costs combine to produce a situation in which there are increases and/or decreases in the

---

[1] The adoption of standards can have additional economic impacts in terms of reducing risk and uncertainty, and aggregating demand, in equipment markets.

average cost of the good as the amount of goods produced increase. For goods with high fixed costs and relatively low variable costs, as is often the case with information goods and services, networks, and media, there tends to be a long period of declining average costs as production increases, producing what are generally known as *economies of scale*. The efficiencies associated with expanding networks, particularly in terms of the numbers of connections, can also contribute to scale economies. However, there also tends to be a point of diminishing returns, where the costs involved in reaching the next user, or in creating the next node, outweigh its added value. If networks or producers saturate the market before they reach that point, they create a situation where it is cheaper and more efficient to have only one producer of the good or service, creating what is called a *natural monopoly*. Fixed networks such as telephone and cable systems have, in the past, been considered local natural monopolies, in large part because the fixed costs of the network infrastructure were significantly higher than the operational costs, raising doubts about the efficiency of building multiple infrastructures, if one system could adequately service the market.

If the good or service has complements, or may be involved in multiple markets, there may also be what are known as *scope economies*. These may be related to larger firms' greater ability to average risk, obtain capital, and operate in multiple markets for goods and services. Vertically integrated firms can reduce risks involved in producing intermediate products and services considerably. Horizontally integrated firms can share products across markets, can engage in cross-promotion, and in some cases can centralize some organizational functions. In both cases, conglomerates can be in a position to reduce risks and spread costs over a larger group of markets, reducing costs and enhancing markets.

These economies of scale and scope and the generally limited geographic size of network markets have tended to limit the ability of these markets to satisfy Wheatley's (1999) four conditions for perfect markets. In addition, in many cases governments have imposed market entry limits. Thus, many network market structures lean toward local monopolies, whereas in those cases where some market entry is permitted and market demand is sufficient, oligopoly or monopolistic competition structures emerge.

## Basic Economics of Media Distribution Networks

As noted in the introduction, the range and variation in information products, networks, and other distribution systems preclude the presentation of a generic economic network/distribution market model, even though there are some general attributes that can be identified. In this section, we will first discuss the basics of distribution networks, and then consider the specific economic aspects of several broad categories of networks. Specifically, we will discuss the economics of distributing physical information goods, then the economics of a range of networks developed for transmitting information products in electronic forms (including wired and wireless networks, and the employment of dedicated, broadcast, and packet-switched technologies). Each of these has some distinctive economic attributes and consequences. We will also address the consequences of the digital/fiber technological revolution for cost and market structures in networks.

What we normally identify as media can also be described as networks that distribute media (information) products to a general audience. Within a particular medium, product forms tend to be standardized, and often the networks and distribution systems are designed specifically for those standards and specific products. Although there are a few generalizations that can be made about the economics of media distribution, the wide variety of information products (newspapers, books, CDs, movies, television programs, Internet sites) and distribution systems (home delivery, retail stores, theaters, broadcast networks) also suggest that there is significant variability within these general structures.

One of the generalizations that can be made has to do with the essence of the information product, the information content itself. The content is the primary source of value, and the various distribution systems are intermediaries. The physical forms and networks used to distribute the information tend to contribute very little inherent value, from a consumer perspective.[2] All information is inherently costly to produce, although those costs can vary significantly. The information content is also fairly inexpensive to reproduce, although costly to produce in physical formats and to distribute. As discussed earlier, the information content tends to be characterized by a constantly declining average cost curve. On the other hand, distribution systems, while also having fixed costs that tend to generate declining average costs initially, all tend to reach a point where marginal costs once again begin to rise. In the following sections, we will describe a range of general distribution networks, and their cost structures.

First, we can distinguish between systems that need to distribute physical copies of the information goods and services, and those that use nonphysical media. Dealing with physical goods imposes certain structural requirements, and costs, upon the production and distribution system. We will focus our consideration of nonphysical media forms on electronic networks, and further differentiate them between wired and wireless networks. The development of digital media and networks is also having a transforming effect, as the cost structures for digital are significantly different from analog and physical systems, and further benefits from a continuing decline in costs. The impact of the diffusion of digital technologies and systems throughout networks and media is addressed within each section.

## Physical Goods (Printed/Prerecorded Materials)

When the information is distributed in a distinctive physical format, such as a book or CD, there is a clear separation between the production of the good (itself a joint product), and the distribution system.[3] The supply chain can also be broken down into components: the production of the physical good, and the distribution system utilized to distribute goods to consumers. To produce multiple copies of information goods, it is typically necessary to invest in duplication equipment, contributing to fixed costs. There are also significant variable costs in terms of the materials required to reproduce each

---

[2]The one aspect of a network that might affect value is the usability of the form. Convenience, permanence, and the ability to format-shift can all add marginal value to information products.

[3]There is, on the other hand, also a relationship between the two, in that the production stage can be decentralized, in effect moving the production down the distribution chain.

unit. In general, there are economies of scale at work in terms of both equipment and materials, suggesting once again a declining average cost curve—at least until that point where the duplication equipment exceeds optimum efficiency, where it meets capacity (at which point additional capital costs are incurred), or where the use of materials is sufficient to deplete supplies and raise costs. There are similar general implications for the distribution of physical media. The distribution of physical products is inherently distance and size dependent; that is, the greater the distance involved, and the greater the size of the product, the higher the distribution cost and the longer the time involved. Another general rule for physical distribution is the faster the transportation, the higher the transport cost. In addition, there are often several different systems available for the transportation of goods (for example, rail, truck, and air), with different costs and levels of scale economies, and a distribution network may rely on one or a combination of specific distribution mechanisms, systems, and firms in the supply chain.

## TRADITIONAL MASS PRODUCTION/DISTRIBUTION

The joint product nature of information goods and services requires that we distinguish between the information content and its physical manifestation. As discussed earlier, the nature of information is that there is a high fixed cost in terms of the initial production, and a low to zero variable cost for replication of the information itself. On the other hand, the physical manifestation of the good as required for its distribution evidences the more traditional properties of physical goods. In addition, there are often a variety of ways in which the information content can be replicated in physical form. For example, music can be manifested in a variety of physical formats—records, tapes, CDs, live performances, radio broadcasts, etc. Similarly, the production can be in a limited run or mass produced, and produced in a central location or at multiple locations distributed throughout the network. There are, however, some general aspects that can be described.

The economic advantage of mass production has been for goods that evidence both a high ratio of fixed to variable costs of production and sizable demand. When production is relatively capital intensive, and the variable (marginal) costs tend to decline over a fairly large production run, there are significant economies of scale. If anticipated demand falls in the range of scale economies, a single centralized production house tended to be most cost efficient for most cases. Historically, centralization was useful for another reason as well. If the information was timely, such as a newspaper, there were certain efficiencies involved in locating the production facilities physically near where the information content was produced, to avoid delays caused by the transportation of the information goods to the duplication facility. On the other hand, one drawback of traditional centralized production models for physical goods is that physical copies are physical—they have bulk and weight and must be carried from the producer to the consumer, and both costs and the time necessary to transport the copies increased with distance.

Thus, there are two limits to the efficiencies of a centralized production and distribution system. First, if the product is timely, there is a limit to effective distribution: a point at which the production and distribution delays in getting the product to the consumer so reduce its value that it is no longer economically viable to try to reach that market (think daily newspapers, and their value if it takes 2 days to reach the consumer). Second, there is a trade-off point where the added costs of distribution of the basic information good or service from production sites outweigh the scale efficiencies of centralized production. These factors tend to limit the range of centralized markets. The range of the viable market is determined not only by the level of anticipated demand, but by the mix of production and distribution costs (which may include time).

## DISTRIBUTED PRODUCTION

As noted earlier, if there are economically viable means of transporting the information content to multiple production sites, this can be used not only to take advantage of scale economies, it can make it possible to extend the natural markets for products by having multiple production sites and distribution hubs, each serving a geographic market.

Three factors have promoted the rise of distributed production in recent years. The development of digital information processing and electronic transmission systems has made it possible to distribute the information content quickly, reliably, and cheaply to multiple sites. Second, developments in the production sector, fed by the same shift to digital information processing, have led to the situation where the optimal scale for production runs has tended to decline. That is, production efficiencies tend to peak at a smaller scale, making smaller production runs cheaper and more efficient and con-tributing to the efficiencies of distributed production. Third, while production costs are tending to decline and favor smaller production runs, transportation costs are generally increasing. The impact of these three shifts is to move the trade-off point for central-ized distribution to smaller production runs and distribution over smaller areas. This has favored the transition in many networks to a distributed production and distribution sys-tem, particularly for those media where the shift in costs is greatest, and where timeliness is a key component of value.

Of course, this distributed model is favored only for those goods where the size of the market is significantly greater than the point of scale efficiency for the product. On the other hand, the ability to distribute content economically to distributed production centers has also allowed for markets to expand. Although this suggests that distributed production will continue to spread for some goods, centralized production may still make sense where the production shifts have been minimal, where transportation costs are subsidized, or where the demand for the product is low.

## ON-DEMAND DISTRIBUTION

As the costs of digital distribution and production continue to decline, some products are getting to the point where it is economically viable to engage in what is called *on-demand distribution*. The ultimate in distributed production, this is where the physical copy is individually made to order, usually at the point of sale. Think of a kiosk in a record store that will burn a CD and print a cover to order. Although efficiencies of scale are not at the point where these are the cheapest production points for any physical product, there are other cost savings that can offset the added production cost.

On-demand production eliminates transportation costs, as well as inventory costs for the distribution point, particularly if the site can be linked to a network with access to inventories of product. It eliminates the costs and risks associated with trying to estimate production runs for products, with the concomitant likelihood of having surplus inventory to dispose of, or of losing sales because of lack of sufficient immediate supply. For the consumer, on-demand distribution can reduce the delays in getting materials that may need to be specially ordered, and can also offer the flexibility to customize the product. As single-unit production costs continue to decline, expect more on-demand distribution to fill certain niche products and markets.

Several economic factors are likely to slow the growth of on-demand production, however. First, there are concerns that such systems reduce the producers' control over content and contribute to fears of hacking and piracy. Transaction and marketing costs may also be higher and more complex; one advantage of distributing through middlemen is that these concerns and costs are shifted to them, rather than the content producer (and middlemen can also end up with lower costs through scale efficiencies and the aggregation of risk). Finally, the flexibility of such systems challenges traditional business norms and threatens traditional competitive and monopoly advantages for firms in the distribution chain.[4] Thus, there is likely to be some resistance to on-demand distribution networks in the near term.

## Electronic Networks

Electronic networks differ primarily in that they distribute information goods and services in an electronic, non-physical, form. Such forms tend to exhibit traditional public good attributes of nonrivalry and nonexclusivity, as well as marginal costs near zero for the electronic form. Between these features and the problem of uncertainty over the value of messages, it becomes difficult to efficiently charge for individual items and goods. Thus, pricing in electronic networks tends to be based not as much on the specific value of the information, but in terms of access to a set of generally valued goods or network services. In addition, electronic-based network distribution systems must be designed to accommodate specific signal forms and features. Network features can enhance or counteract certain of these attributes and can have differing cost structures, making market economics different for different types of network/signals mixes.

There are three distinctive forms that describe most electronic network distribution systems. First, there are dedicated transmission path networks, such as the basic telephone network. A second basic structure is the broadcast structure (such as radio and television), where the information goods and services are meant to be available to large numbers of users simultaneously. A third basic structure emerged with the development of digital packet-switching technology and the interconnected systems structure of the Internet. In this structure (commonly referred to as IP [Internet Protocol] systems), content is

---

[4]For example, on-demand CD production could remove the need for music companies, distributors, and music stores, allowing artists to sell directly to consumers.

distributed openly and widely, although it can also be directed and targeted to individual consumers by the use of addresses embedded in the packets. Electronic networks can also deploy a range of wired and wireless structures to distribute systems.[5]

## Wired Networks

Wired networks exhibit several general attributes, linked to their fixed physical nature. The first of these is that the physical structure of the network delimits the market, both geographically and in terms of capacity.[6] Users must be individually connected to the physical network. Wired networks tend to be designed to provide a cost-efficient system to meet specific signal and service requirements for a certain area; to expand either, one must in essence reconstruct the network.

Second, a wired network infrastructure is fairly expensive, with the cost determined by market size, geography, signal and distribution type, and system capacity. There are two main infrastructure components: the equipment needed to obtain and distribute the information networks, and the physical (wired) network itself. Construction costs for the physical network tend to be based on the amount (distance) of wire laid, but also depend on the physical characteristics of the wire and the geography of the area and can be fairly expensive. However, infrastructure consists of both the wire carrying the electronic content and the equipment needed to distribute the content. Depending on the design needs of a particular system, these equipment costs can be sizable as well. Thus, there tends to be a fairly high fixed cost to wired networks.

Furthermore, operational costs of wired network systems tend to be fairly minimal, so that marginal costs tend to be very low, at least until that point where system capacity is reached. At that point, additional investments in infrastructure must be made before additional users or services can be accommodated; thus, at the congestion point, there is a large jump in marginal costs equal to the additional infrastructure investment.

These attributes have led wired networks to generally be considered as local monopolies. To the extent that one infrastructure can meet market capacity, there is no inherent reason to build another, particularly if the monopoly is price-regulated in an efficient manner or if there are sufficient substitutes to minimize monopoly power. On the other hand, the low variable (marginal) costs suggest that once there is a second network, the firms will tend to engage in price competition, thereby reducing costs to consumers. Although this can be a short-term benefit to consumers, it also will likely limit additional infrastructure investment and expansion, if not eventually drive one or more firms out of the market.

This leads us to a consideration of two other common aspects to wired systems. With the high fixed costs of wired infrastructure, the economic incentives are to attempt to

---

[5]Although we use the terms *wired* and *wireless*, each actually embodies a wide range of technologies. We use *wired* to refer to any network where the signal is conducted through a physical medium, whether wire, fiber optic cable, or piece of string. *Wireless* is used to refer to technologies where signals are radiated without the need for a physical connection (radio spectrum, lasers, voice).

[6]Every transmission medium exhibits a natural bandwidth limit, as well as a level of resistance that causes electronic signals to degrade over distance. Electronic distribution systems are generally designed to enable reliable transmissions up to a certain bandwidth over a certain distance. Exceeding that limit can make the signal unusable.

maximize use of the system, at least to the point where it nears capacity. As it nears capacity, however, short-term strategy shifts to limiting growth, or shifting usage patterns to low-demand periods. In addition, these wired systems all use electronic signals to distribute content. With the continued development and diffusion of digital systems, a wide range of information goods and services (content) can be transmitted in electronic format, creating a situation where traditionally separate services can be offered along the same network, thus substantially heightening demand. Although increasing demand might pose problems with systems with limited capacity, technology is also transforming that aspect of electronic networks. Digital technology offers the ability to compress signals, thereby increasing the capacity of existing systems, and the shift to fiber optics as the distribution medium provides a network with significantly increased, and more readily scalable, system capacity.

Thus, shifting infrastructure to digital and fiber-optic technologies (at least in certain aspects of the network) offer not only lower costs, but also significant increases in capacity and network flexibility. If a network has excess capacity, one growth strategy is to offer additional information services. This can offer a back door to competing in those markets, as the firm can enter the market with an infrastructure already in place. In other words, although individual network systems might traditionally be considered natural monopolies because of the high cost of market entry through overbuilds, those old networks are increasingly capable of entering each other's markets. Thus, the market for a particular service or product might turn competitive with the available of multiple infrastructures capable of offering that service. For example, both cable and telephone industries compete in the broadband Internet access market, and increasingly, cable systems have the capability to offer telephone services, and telephone companies have the ability to offer multichannel video (cable) products. In contrast to the overbuild example, in this case, with the infrastructure already in place for their primary product, there is strong incentive to enter new markets in order to distribute those infrastructure costs over a wide range of markets and products.

As noted previously, there are significant differences among dedicated, broadcast, and IP distribution structures. We now discuss those in terms of what are perhaps their most familiar forms: telephony, cable, and the Internet.

## Telephone (POTS)

The traditional telephone system began as a fully wired network, one that differentiated itself from the telegraph not only by the form of the information carried, but by its use of a switched distribution system. With its emphasis on synchronous bi-directional transmission (i.e., people talking to one another), the telephone network worked by constructing a physical link between users, at least temporarily. The system also evolved into a hierarchical structure to take advantage of scale economies. On one hand, switch complexity and cost increase substantially with the number of lines, making it more cost efficient to connect a series of smaller switches rather than to centralize switching. Further, as most connections are temporary, aggregating calls locally could allow the system to use fewer lines between local switches. Similar efficiencies work at regional, national, and international levels, continuing the trend towards hierarchical systems.

On the operating side, we can note that operating costs are relatively small, and since the basic product of the phone is to communicate with others, that there will be significant network economies at work. The service aspect of telephony also means that the network does not have to acquire content for distribution, as that content is supplied by the users. This avoids one significant cost component of information media and networks.

This structure has several economic implications. On the cost side, the most obvious is the fact that fixed costs are quite high, with the greater part in the wires, and the lesser in the switching system. Actual use-based costs are marginal, in essence amounting to just the cost of operating the system (i.e., the electricity used in automated systems). This leads to the situation where marginal costs are negligible and average costs are constantly declining, at least to the point where the system nears capacity. Thus, it is reasonable to treat switched telephony as a natural monopoly. In most countries, the state started treating telephony as a regulated monopoly, both to encourage its development and spread to high-cost areas, and in order to have control over prices. Prices were often set to meet social goals rather than in response to specific cost factors, although there was generally consideration given to recouping actual costs.

On the demand side, the presence of network economies suggested that the value of the network was based on the size of the market. The value will also vary significantly among users, making price discrimination possible. On the other hand, when the market nears the point of congestion, where it is more difficult to obtain the connection, the value to the consumer drops. This initially led to the situation where price discrimination was used to maximize return, and, where needed, to keep use below system capacity, at least to the point where infrastructure investment increased capacity. Under regulation (or state ownership), the monopoly profits that this generated allowed a degree of cross-subsidy for lower-demand users, helping to maximize the network economies.

## Traditional Cable

Traditional cable resembles, in some basic ways, the traditional telephone system. Both require an extensive wired network connecting users to the system. Both also tend to have relatively low operational costs, other than maintenance and repair. On the other hand, there are several distinct differences at play. First, cable is a broadcast distributor of content. Therefore, cable must acquire that content, adding a cost that tends to be based on the number of consumers, and thus is treated as a variable cost. The broadcast aspect means that switches are not necessary, avoiding one large set of fixed costs, although there are additional fixed costs involved with the development of the headend (reception and retransmission equipment). Another factor is that the value of cable to the consumer is based, not on the number of users, but on the value of the offered programming. Thus, there are no network economies at work on the consumer side.

On the other hand, like broadcast stations, cable can operate in multiple markets, offering access to its subscribers to advertisers as well as programming to subscribers. For this aspect of the network operations, the value of the service (advertising) is based on the size of the audience, providing some network economies. The growing size of the advertising market (Bates & Chambers, 2004) and the broadcast focus also push cable network structure away from the hierarchical structure of telephony.

Whereas advertising demand may be based on audience size and makeup, subscriber demand is related to the amount, variety, and quality of content offered. As the number of cable programming sources increase, this puts pressure on the cable system to continue to upgrade its network and expand its capacity. Thus, the capacity (bandwidth) of cable systems is significantly larger than that of telephone networks and has tended to require significant, and regular, upgrading over time, with the result that the wired infrastructure costs are likely to be considerably higher. A single television channel uses the same bandwidth as about 6,000 telephone lines.

The pressure to accommodate the growing number of cable programming channels pushed cable systems through several levels of infrastructure upgrades. Taking advantage of the high bandwidth and declining costs of fiber-optic networks, cable systems in the United States, at any rate, tend to have a significantly higher capacity than other wired networks, and many incorporate bi-directional information flows, facilitated by the fact that it is more economical to install fiber in bundles, rather than individually. This has enabled cable firms to offer a range of additional services, including pay-per-view, broadband Internet connectivity, and even telephone services.

## Internet

The Internet as a network has several distinctive components that create a distinctive set of economic attributes (Egan, 1991; McKnight & Bailey, 1997). Its primary distinction is that the Internet is a network of networks. It was built as a conglomeration of information systems and telecommunications networks able to accommodate a specific communication protocol (TCP/IP). Systems utilized a range of distinctive networks, including telephone, cable, and computer/information networks to distribute signals. The Internet is also distinctive in that it is designed to handle virtually any type of information good or service that can be digitized. The Internet was designed to distribute information goods and services over an open distributed architecture using addressable packet-switching.[7] This gives the Internet a great deal of flexibility, limited in essence only by bandwidth.[8] It can be seen as a hybrid of the telephone and cable systems, using both as components, and offering the potential to also compete with their services. It is also a system where network economies are readily evident, both in terms of connectivity and in terms of the provision of content and services.

The history of the Internet as a network of networks and its flexibility also has some implications for its cost structure. Early expansion was able to take advantage of existing networks and infrastructure, and thus the cost of expansion was minimal, essentially simply the added cost of connecting to the existing networks. This reduction in apparent fixed costs was enhanced by the fact that many of the early, and central, networks

---

[7]Packet-switching involves breaking down a digital file into a number of smaller packets, each containing a portion of the larger file as well as control information on how to reassemble the file and addresses. With packet-switching, files of any size can be distributed over any bandwidth channel (larger files simply take more time). Packet-switching bypasses traditional bandwidth and format limitations, providing a more flexible and scalable transmission protocol.

[8]Specifically, the practical bandwidth available is limited to the most restricted bandwidth among the networks used.

forming the backbone of the Internet were subsidized. In addition, the system's use of packet addressing allowed the use of computers as routers, providing a substantial cost savings over switches. Thus, the fixed costs of the Internet were significantly lower that those of its competitors. The system also tends to be much more easily scalable, meaning that upgrading capacity is less expensive. Variable costs also tended to be low, because of the ever-reducing costs of digital computers and equipment. The privatization of the Internet backbone in 1994, however, introduced a new higher level of connectivity costs. The rapid development of the Internet requires that network components must continually upgrade the system to accommodate rapidly expanding demand. Information flow over the Internet is doubling every year or so, and the Internet's scope and reach continue to expand. This has mandated near-continual investment in upgrading the Internet backbone, and in expanding broadband connectivity to individual users. Further, while per-unit operations costs have tended to decline over time, both individual and aggregate demand has increased at a faster pace (that is, we're using the Internet more, and to access bigger files), leading to increased aggregate operating costs.

The historical development of the Internet also has implications on the demand and pricing side of the market. Early Internet use was centered in academia and in the business world, where individual use was subsidized by the larger entity. Private access to the old BBS (computer bulletin board systems) and private networks was often free, or handled on a subscription basis. In either case, the apparent cost of using the Internet was based on access or connection charges, rather than tied directly to the value of the information good or service, establishing consumer expectations for that pricing mechanism.

### Emerging Broadband "Intelligent Network" (Multiple Services)

As discussed previously, the advent of digital systems and high-capacity fiber-optic cable has also provided a quantum leap in terms of the capabilities and capacity of wired networks. The cost differentials are considerable and growing, threatening to disrupt traditional telecommunications and network cost structures (Crandall & Alleman, 2002; DeLong & Froomkin, 2000). Most of the wired networks discussed earlier are increasingly employing fiber in their infrastructure and shifting to an IP network architecture, suggesting that, over time, the networks will become increasingly similar in their capacity, and in the range of information goods and services that they can offer to consumers. As telephony, cable, and the Internet all transition toward what has been called the "Advanced Intelligent Network," it is likely that, despite the tendency of wired networks toward natural monopoly, there will likely be greater competition and substitution in coming years as each system develops independent capacity.

### Wired Structures as Media

As mentioned earlier, wired networks were designed to meet different service needs, and thus evolved distinctive structures. The telephone network developed a hierarchical switched structure to accommodate narrow-bandwidth interpersonal conversation.

Cable developed a broadcast (unswitched, undifferentiated, and unidirectional) distribution system for high-bandwith television signals. The Internet developed to accommodate addressable, largely asynchronous computer communications. Each design was very efficient for that form of communications, and would have been very inefficient in serving other functions even if it was technologically possible. Cable had the bandwidth to handle video signals that telephony and the early Internet didn't, but didn't have an ability to target signals to specific users or accommodate return signals. Telephony didn't have the bandwidth in its switched system to handle even moderate bandwidth signals, much less multiple channels of video. The Internet largely connected systems, and it did not have the last leg of the distribution chain, to the individual users. The Internet was also hampered by bandwidth limitations and the asynchronous nature of packet-switching.

Over time, however, technological improvements in digital computing and telecommunications not only have created new communication products and services, but have fostered a convergence of structural design. For example, technology has permitted the Internet to utilize first the local phone system, and then cable systems, to serve as the last leg of the Internet distribution system. Thus, what used to be very separate and distinct media structures are converging, as wired networks switch from copper to fiber, and from analog to digital.

During this transition period, however, certain networks still retain certain structural advantages. Cable, while offering a degree of interactivity, still is the most efficient local distributor of very high bandwidth content. On the other hand, it remains a largely local network, with significantly more bandwidth going downstream than upstream. The telephone system remains the network that can offer dedicated transmission paths for synchronous bi-directional communication, and its hierarchical nature efficiently links local markets offering an expanded global access. Those dedicated paths require the use of switches, which are considerably more expensive than the use of addressable routers.[9] The Internet offers the greater flexibility and cost efficiencies of a digital network, but at the moment is constrained by bandwidth and a focus on asynchronous system structure that limits its ability to offer differentiated services. For example, the Internet does not allow for "prioritized" or guaranteed communications.

In the short term, this suggests that the various networks will continue to have competitive advantages in their traditional markets, and in those new services that are seen as emerging from those traditional services. For example, in the short term, cable will have an advantage in offering video on demand, from both a structural efficiency perspective and a marketing perspective. On the other hand, it should be more difficult to enter and compete against traditional networks in their traditional markets, unless price differentials grow too large. The shifting costs of digital and fiber, however, suggest that as networks expand or are rebuilt, the structural distinctions will tend to diminish over time, suggesting that the structural competitive advantages of the various wired networks will also tend to disappear in the long run, as networks and structures converge.

---

[9] In particular, even modestly "broadband" switches have proven to be extremely expensive, while the ability of routers to process more information quickly and cheaply has increased. Thus, the cost discrepancy between switches and routers continues to grow.

## Wireless Networks

Wireless networks primarily employ the radio spectrum to distribute signals containing information goods and services over a wide area.[10] Like wired networks, they exhibit the need for establishing the network before goods and services can be offered, with concomitant high fixed costs (for construction of the transmission system). Wireless networks, however, have one significant temporary advantage over wired networks: The wireless infrastructure can be installed more rapidly, and once installed, the services it offers are available immediately to everyone within signal range, whereas a wired network takes time to be built out and may evidence differential costs to reach all areas.[11] There are also similarities in the trade-offs involved between transmitter and receiver costs. They differ from wired networks, however, in aspects of operating costs. To some degree, operating costs are related to distance, as power needs increase with distance. Also, as wireless generally requires line-of-sight, and the curvature of the earth mandates that the greater the range, the higher above ground the transmitting antenna needs to be. On the other hand, operating costs are generally not linked to the number of users within the signal range, at least for broadcast-based systems. Wireless reception and use are nonrivalrous, and congestion is not a problem (at least within signal range). Wireless systems are also somewhat more limited in terms of bandwidth and scalability. To maintain compatability between transmitters and receivers, wireless systems tend to require fixed standards and bandwidth, reducing flexibility. The most flexible aspect is the range of the transmitted signal, although that is also limited by physical constraints.

What this implies is that, for a given wireless transmission system, both fixed and variable costs are tied to signal strength, range, and bandwidth, and not necessarily the number of users. In other words, costs of adding new customers at the margin are zero, until the limits of signal and range are reached. At that point, the marginal cost is the cost of upgrading the system to that next level. Thus, wireless networks have an incentive to try to maximize reach and use, up to the design limits of the infrastructure base. As demand nears that level, however, the incentives shift to limiting growth in order to avoid the need upgrade the system.

The scale and scope of the market (i.e., number of potential users) does come into play with the relative efficiencies of different wireless network structures. As a result of the nature of electromagnetic waves, any set of spectra can be used only once in a transmitter's range. Most terrestrial wireless systems are constrained in terms of the distance that their signals can reach, and are thus best suited for local markets. Although local markets can be networked to create larger markets, the problems created by interference make for relatively inefficient use of spectrum, and in general, the larger the range of the broadcast signal, the greater the relative inefficiencies. Thus, when the market is fairly large (geographically), it generally becomes much more efficient to move to a satellite-based wireless system. At the other end, unless the signal needs to reach numerous users

---

[10]Technically, one can employ radio spectrum (also light from lasers) in a narrow focused beam between two points. However, in terms of economic structures, these tend to mimic wired networks more than broadcast wireless networks. Thus, we will focus on broadcast-based networks in this section.

[11]In fact, costs may be so high that some users will not be linked to the network.

over a large geographic area, a network of small signal areas (i.e., a cellular system) tends to be more efficient.

## Wireless Broadcast Networks

The emphasis on broadcasting is on distributing a common set of information goods and services, from which users can select which they want to acquire and use. As it distributes a common set of goods to all consumers, broadcasting takes advantage of the nonrivalrous nature of electronic information goods and services, suggesting, as noted earlier, that marginal costs within a given market approach zero. In addition, although it is possible to exclude users (through encryption, technology, or legal constraints), it is generally expensive and difficult to do so. Thus, traditional broadcast networks exhibit public good attributes and are generally treated as such. One result is the problematic nature of pricing and revenues.

From a social efficiency perspective (i.e., marginal costs = marginal revenue), optimal pricing for broadcast goods is zero. However, there are positive network distribution costs, as well as the first unit costs for producing the goods themselves. Thus, broadcast networks must come up with alternative revenue sources. One common public good solution is for government to use its power to collect, in the form of taxes or fees, sufficient revenues to ensure production of the public good. This was adopted in many countries through the imposition of a license fee for receivers. Another solution is to identify joint markets or products that can subsidize costs. Initially, such subsidies were granted by receiver manufacturers, who realized that set sales required the presence of something valuable to receive, to justify the cost of receiver purchases. Advertising increasingly serves such a function for radio and television networks around the world. Advertisers seek the audiences who give their time and attention in the consumption of broadcast programming. The audience is willing to put up with advertising to obtain "free" programming, and advertisers are willing to pay for access to that audience. One consequence of relying on such subsidies is that the programming will be driven by the needs of the joint product, rather than directly by consumer interest and demand.

With the transition to digital, it becomes easier, and somewhat less expensive, to develop technical means to exclude nonpayers from use of the broadcast content. Both the exclusion systems and the legal enforcement of it do bear costs, however, which must be added on top of the existing content and distribution costs. The use of such systems, therefore, will reduce effective demand (by raising costs), and will likely be viable only for high-value content, and only to the extent that consumers are willing to tolerate it.

## Wireless (Interactive) Networks

Wireless systems can also be used for individual or targeted transmissions, although the basic nature of the transmissions remain nonrivalrous and nonexclusive. Wireless networks are also relatively inefficient systems for the distribution of such forms of content, leading to generally higher costs. Thus they have been tended to be restricted to those information goods and services where the value of reaching mobile or other unwired users outweighed greater operational costs, and the costs of lack of privacy or the use of encryption systems.

The advent of digital packet-switching has reduced the inefficiencies through the development of cellular systems, which use the addressability feature and distributed processing to permit smaller transmission areas (i.e., cellular) and minimize inefficiencies. Digital computing and the use of packet-switching also makes encryption cheaper and more secure. In addition, IP-based networks tend to have significantly lower operating costs than traditional switched networks. Thus, the advent of digital systems has, once again, transformed the relative cost structures of a network, bringing cellular telephony within range of the cost structure of wired systems.

A summary of the main characteristics of each type of network is outlined in Table 19.1.

**TABLE 19.1**
A Typology of Network Characteristics

| Network Type | Main Characteristics |
|---|---|
| Telephone (POTS) | Switched distribution |
| | Bidirectional transmission |
| | Economies of scale |
| | High fixed costs |
| | Low operating costs |
| | Value rises with the number of users |
| Traditional cable | Content distribution |
| | High variable costs |
| | High fixed costs |
| | Low operational costs |
| | Value based on the programming offered |
| | Value to advertisers |
| Internet | Network of networks |
| | Signal distribution (telephone, cable, computer networks) |
| | Packet-switching of digital goods |
| | Bandwidth limitations |
| | Low fixed costs |
| | Scalable |
| | Low variable costs |
| | Increasing operating costs |
| Wireless broadcast | Nonrivalrous |
| | Low marginal costs |
| | Public good attributes |
| | Positive network distribution costs |
| | Inexpensive exclusionary mechanisms |
| Wireless interactive | Individual or targeted transmission |
| | Nonrivalrous |
| | Cellular transmission |
| | Lack of privacy may require encryption |
| | Low operating costs |

## IMPINGING ISSUES AND POLICY

There are a number of major issues confronting networks today, some lingering, some brought about by the continuing development of technology, markets, and cost and demand structures. Primary among them are questions about (socially) optimal market structure (regulated monopoly or limited competition, private or government ownership), appropriate pricing mechanisms, how to incorporate intellectual property rights protections in digital networks, and Universal Service issues. Another important trend is the continuing convergence to IP network structures, and the implications of a dominant, digital Internet. In this section we will address the economic aspects related to several of those issues.

### Market Structures

For most of the last century, the tendency to focus on limited sets of network products and services in relatively small geographic (i.e., local) markets kept market scopes small enough that scale economies pushed network markets into monopoly market structures. In fact, most of these markets could qualify as natural monopolies. Network markets thus tended to evidence monopoly power, allowing some control by firms over prices. By definition, this is likely to lead to nonoptimal prices and levels of consumption. On the other hand, the very low marginal costs for most network products and services suggest that socially optimal pricing is unlikely to generate sufficient revenues to cover production and distribution costs. Thus, it would seem that that network markets are doomed to market failure, thus requiring some degree of intervention in order to operate.

The initial response to this was for the government to intervene in the market, either by ownership of the monopoly, or through intervening in market operations. Market intervention could take place through price regulation, through the creation of alternative revenue sources or other subsidies, or by permitting the "failed" market to link (via joint products) with another, less problematic, market. Each strategy had its own economic implications.

Government monopolies could afford to price optimally (at marginal cost) and arrange to finance operations through other revenue sources. Although economically efficient, this is politically problematic, as the large fixed costs must be born by alternative revenue sources, which tends to limit infrastructure investment. Thus, historically, government ownership has acted as a disincentive to regular investment and innovation (Bates, 1997). On the other hand, government can use pricing to advance related policy goals (preserving certain services, limiting access, etc.), or as a source of general revenues. Government operations also tend to not be very efficient or responsive to consumer preferences. Thus, government ownership, per se, is not a guarantee of economic optimality or efficiency.

Government price regulation of a private monopoly can satisfy some of the same economic and policy concerns as government ownership. Further, the private firm has greater incentive toward efficiency and responding to consumer preferences. The pricing, though, has to be able to cover both operating costs and continuing investment needs, so prices are likely to be somewhat higher than might be possible under government ownership. Governments can still use prices to foster policy goals, through cross-subsidies and the determination of appropriate costs. Government intervention, by the setting of standards and other direct subsidies, can facilitate market growth and expansion for network products.

The natural monopoly status of network markets is disappearing, however. The rise of digital technology is altering cost structures and tending to lower the levels at which scale economies are found. Similarly, the distinctiveness of network product forms is disappearing as all become convertible to digital forms. There is little question that the continuing development of digital and telecommunications technologies and systems is changing market structures and operations. Economides (1996) notes that technological advances are increasing the complementarity of network components, leading to an increase in their substitutability, which, combined with decreasing production costs and a shift in scale efficiencies to lower production levels, is leading the market away from monopoly structures. With the implementation of IP network structures by multiple existing networks (telephone, cable, etc.), the time is coming when there will be multiple networks in place for most services, making local monopoly structures problematic.

The extensive presence of complements, substitutes, and multiple distribution networks for information goods and services suggests that attempts to maintain monopoly structures will become increasingly unviable. The "optimality" question then becomes one of whether the degree of competition in the new network markets will be sufficient to make market pricing more effective than price regulation in terms of promoting social welfare. As noted earlier, regulation can be used to minimize monopoly profit-taking in monopoly structures, although with a key social cost: Price setting tends to lag costs. In other words, regulated prices tend to be set according to recent or current costs and demand estimates. In markets where costs tend to decline rapidly, and demand is extremely volatile, this means that prices are often set by obsolete criteria. On the other hand, price regulation (again as noted earlier) can also be used to achieve a variety of policy goals.

Thus, we know that there are costs associated with price regulation, and that there are benefits associated with competitive markets. Competitive pressures are likely to decrease prices and hasten innovation and reactions to market changes. However, such pressures are also likely to lead to higher costs due to duplications in infrastructure and the push to innovate. We also know that there are social costs associated with the presence of monopoly pricing power, when competitive markets are not perfect.[12] The key issue is whether the network market will be sufficiently competitive to limit monopoly pricing power. The 1996 Telecommunications Act in the United States assumed that they would, although the evidence to date for most markets suggests that that goal has not yet been reached.

Government policy on network market structure intervention thus rests on two primary considerations: first, whether the markets in question are natural monopolies or are more or less competitive; and second, whether the government argues that price

---

[12]Although market power gives the ability to earn monopoly profits, it does not preclude firms from pursuing non-profit-maximizing strategies. For instance, a firm may keep prices and profits low to discourage other firms from entering the market.

regulation is an effective means to promote related social policies. In the case of a natural monopoly, the key issue is one of investment. The greater the need for investment in either infrastructure or content development, the less appropriate is government ownership as an intervention strategy. Some government oversight of pricing is vital under monopoly structures, but becomes more problematic the more competitive the market. There is no easy cutoff point for determining when a market is "sufficiently" competitive, although the more volatile the market, the more flexible the pricing mechanisms should be.

On the other hand, pricing regulations can also be used to promote other social policy goals. Take, for example, the issue of Universal Service. Universal Service refers to a policy decision that it is important to provide a certain level of some network product or service to everyone. In the United States, that has meant promoting the idea that every individual should have access to affordable basic telephone service (Mueller, 1997). From the perspective of networking economies, and the wide range of economic benefits that can be attributed to better communications, a fairly clear case could be made that Universal Service contributed to social welfare and the economy. Under the old regulated monopoly structure, the government could require that service be made available to everyone as a condition of the franchise, and used cross-subsidies from low-cost areas to subsidize high-cost areas, and high-value services to cross-subsidize basic service prices. It was argued, and fairly effectively, that any loss in social welfare due to these price distortions was outweighed by the benefits. However, it is difficult to maintain such subsidies in a competitive market, as new entrants can price at cost and consumers will shift to the lower cost network. Thus, there are now several serious Universal Service issues under debate.

Of course, using prices to promote alternative social policy goals (a positive social good, one hopes) simultaneously distorts the network market (a negative social good). In other words, there are costs as well as possible benefits to using prices as a policy device. From an economic perspective, though, price manipulations should only be used when the policy benefits clearly outweigh the likely costs of market distortions.

## Pricing Strategies

Whether or not pricing strategies are an issue depends, in part, on market structure. Under perfect competition, price is determined by the interaction of buyers and sellers in the marketplace. There is, thus, no real opportunity for strategy. With the presence of monopoly power, however, comes the ability to influence prices, and thus engage in pricing strategies. With information goods and services, including network products, the presence of multiple formats, multiple distribution systems, complements, substitutes, and joint products opens the potential for a wide range of pricing and marketing strategies. We will discuss a few that relate directly to network products.

In addition to the issue of whether or not the government should engage in price regulation of some form or another (discussed previously), there is the question of how network products should be priced. This breaks down into two key issues: first, whether prices can (or should) be tied to consumption; and second, the strategies that can be pursued in the setting of prices. The issue of whether prices should be usage-based depends primarily on whether the seller can enforce exclusivity: that is, whether the seller can prevent those who do not pay for the product directly from using it.

There are two common pricing practices used in electronic networks: flat-rate (access-based) and usage-based. Flat-rate pricing refers to the user paying a single fee for access to the network infrastructure and/or to the operational content that is accessed. Usage-based pricing refers to the user paying only for what is consumed either based on the time spent on the network infrastructure or on the volume of content that is accessed or some combination of the two.

### Usage-Based Pricing

Usage-based pricing tends to more directly link price to the specific individual value of the product. Thus, it has two economic implications: first, that production and allocation of the goods and services will be more efficient; and second, that usage pricing permits a generally higher degree of price discrimination, thereby allowing sellers to extract more of surplus value. Although arguably more efficient, usage-based pricing also imposes a generally higher level of transaction costs, particularly for electronic goods. Transaction costs for physical goods are incorporated with the physical transfer of the product. However, for electronic goods, the individual uses must be tracked and billed, imposing some additional costs.

Usage-based pricing is most useful when products exhibit exclusivity, when transaction costs are fairly low, and when there is evidence of value differentials that can be exploited by price discrimination. Usage-based pricing can also be used from a policy or demand-management perspective as a way to shift usage patterns.[13] This can be an effective strategy in highly congested markets such as the Internet, allowing firms to make more efficient use of infrastructure. It allows users who desire access the most to pay a higher price in order to obtain that access. Pricing differentials are based on priority of access by allocating different service classes to different users. The result is a more efficient network in both congestion and price where the value to the user is exchanged for the higher price of prioritized access. There is a drawback to usage-based pricing, however. Although it accounts for the actual costs incurred by a user based on how much he or she uses the network, it does not account for the value that is associated with the externalities that come from an increased subscriber base.

### Access-Based Pricing

Access-based pricing abandons the goal of linking price to individual item consumption, in favor of a fee that is tied to the ability to use a network and its products. Access-based pricing encompasses a range of specific strategies, including what is commonly referred to as flat-rate pricing, subscriptions, licensing, and even the licensing and taxation strategies associated with public goods. This strategy tends to be most effective when exclusivity is hard to enforce, when transaction costs are high, and when there is uncertainty about the value of specific network products. Often, it is easier to restrict

---

[13] For example, making long-distance rates cheaper in nonbusiness hours helps to shift traffic from peak periods.

access to a network than it is to control or even track consumption of individual products, making access the point at which exclusivity can be enforced. Using access-based pricing thus allows for a more efficient capture of value. Further, access-based pricing simplifies transactions, reducing transaction costs. Finally, the use of access-based pricing allows individual use values to be aggregated or averaged when individual values are uncertain. Such aggregation tends to reduce the perceived risk of purchasing and increasing perceived value.

Access-based pricing has several more negative implications. First, by removing the direct link between product use and costs, it encourages overconsumption of those goods.[14] Aggregation also makes it more difficult to maximize allocative efficiency. It is also somewhat more difficult to engage in efficient price discrimination under access-based pricing, requiring the ability to differentiate levels of access or differentiate user groups.

Access-based pricing is most appropriate when there is uncertainty over value and when one wants to maximize adoption and use, such as in the early stages of new network and product development. In such cases, the small loss in allocative efficiency is likely to be offset by network efficiencies and the general social benefits of increased production and use of network products. It is also a viable alternative when transaction and exclusion enforcement costs are high, when the allocative efficiency loss can be offset by the increases in demand (and/or profits) resulting from the lower transaction costs.

## Price Discrimination

Price discrimination refers to the strategy of differential pricing. The ability to engage in this strategy depends on the ability to differentiate either products or groups of consumers, and to enforce price discrimination. The effectiveness of this strategy also depends on there being sufficiently different levels of perceived value to justify differential pricing. Price discrimination allows firms to capture more of the social surplus in the market, although with added enforcement costs.

Price discrimination among buyers is a fairly common phenomenon and tends to be effective when one group has a relatively inelastic demand curve. There are several product differentiation strategies that are more specific to network products, including bundling and versioning. Suppliers can market different bundles of access, goods, or services as different sets of products. If the bundles are perceived to have different values, then price discrimination is possible. Versioning refers to the ability to market different versions of a network product or service, with different perceived value. Versioning can be a particularly effective strategy for network products, as the initial production costs of the good have already been undertaken, and it is usually relatively cheap to remove or disable certain aspects, making the production of alternative versions relatively inexpensive. Having an inexpensive version, or sample, of a product can also help to overcome uncertainty about the value of the full version, increasing its perceived value.

---

[14]This may actually be a benefit, if the information goods and services being consumed are socially valuable.

## Price Regulation Strategies

When states regulate prices in private markets, there are usually several goals to be met. First, they need to ensure that costs are sufficiently covered, including a basic level of profit, and continuing infrastructure investment. Second, they can use prices as a means of fostering policy goals. When the markets are monopolies, it is relatively easy to measure costs as they all occur within a single firm, although there are often debates over what costs and investment needs are appropriate. Even in this simple example, though, there are a large number of strategies that can be used for determining prices (and a large literature examining those strategies). Considering specific strategies would fill several chapters, and so we will raise only general concerns here.

Any specific criterion or strategy will have an impact on producer behaviors, especially in terms of investment, and so it is important to consider not only covering costs, but what the implications are for the determination of those costs and returns. Basing prices in terms of returns on investment, for example, will encourage investment, whereas basing it on operating costs will discourage investment. Usage-based pricing may be more directly linked to actual costs of services, but may discourage use, particularly compared to access-based pricing.

When networks become interconnected, and when markets become competitive, however, pricing becomes much more complex, for now costs have to be broken down among the various component parts of the network, prices assigned, and mechanisms developed for compensating the various component parts of the network for their contribution to the transmission / distribution of products. Falling prices, increased interconnection, and packet-switching all add additional complexity to the system. Trying to deal with such complexity (and the ensuing potential for litigation) raises the cost of the pricing mechanism, contributing to even more market distortions.

Simple pricing strategies may not allow for the full capture of value, or the most efficient allocation of resources, but the cost of developing pricing mechanisms (particularly in the public sector) may result in even greater market distortions, particularly in complex and integrated networks.

## Intellectual Property Rights in Digital Networks

Information goods and services are protected by intellectual property rights, principally copyright. The essence of copyright is the granting of a legal monopoly right to make copies of information products, providing a mechanism for securing returns to creators of covered works.[15] This system worked reasonably well when such goods and services were distributed in physical form, and copies were fixed, costly, and traceable. However, with the development of digital technology, copying is simple, inexpensive, and difficult to prevent or trace without costly copy protection technologies. Combine this with an expanding interconnected global telecommunications network, and making and distributing unauthorized copies, that is, engaging in content piracy, becomes cheap and easy.

---

[15] In other words, intellectual property rights provide a legal mechanism for enforcing excludability and controlling consumption of information goods and services. It grants monopoly power to owners, allowing them to extract consumer surplus from markets for their work.

Piracy makes economic sense when the costs of unauthorized duplication are significantly less than the monopoly pricing for those goods. As improvements in digital technology and telecommunications lower copying costs, and monopolists resist concomitant price reductions in their products (their reproduction and distribution costs are also declining), copyright violations are likely to increase. One way of attempting to control piracy is to make it more costly, by utilizing legal enforcement and penalties or through the use of copy protection schemes that make duplication more expensive. The problem with that is that it makes the primary good more expensive as well. In addition, these costs are a dead-weight loss to network product markets.

Strong, or excessive, intellectual property rights enforcement can also have serious economic implications for networks, as there is the question of liability for content distributed over networks. If networks are involved with enforcement, either as being held liable for distribution of allegedly illegal copies, or in terms of having to monitor or provide information on suspected violators, this not only will impose added costs, but adds considerable risk that can threaten the viability of networks. Thus, copyright enforcement can severely disrupt the efficient functioning of network markets, with little concomitant creation of social benefits.

It is important, however, to maintain some degree of enforceable intellectual property rights, to ensure that creators have the ability to benefit commercially from their work. The issue facing governments and the industry, however, is not how to enhance legal enforcement of copyright limits (which only distorts and damages markets), but how to promote a balance among creators, distributors, and users of intellectual property in a digital world. One possible approach is Digital Rights Management (DRM), a scheme that uses technology to identify conditions of use for intellectual property. DRM systems can mimic traditional copyright, but also permit alternative approaches that may be more flexible and supportive of digital networks. As a technological fix, though, it still imposes additional costs on products and networks and will lead to some market distortions. The nature and degree of the distortions will depend on the actual manifestation of Digital Rights Management.

## Universal Service

As discussed earlier, the idea of Universal Service is that a certain level of network products and services should be made generally available at an affordable price. With the presence of network economies and the general social benefits of information diffusion, there has been relatively little debate over the value of Universal Service as a policy goal. What has become an issue in recent years is the particular set of products and services that should be included, and how to ensure widespread availability in nonmonopoly markets. Until recently, Universal Service considerations focused on basic telephony. With the advent of cable, the Internet, and broadband digital networks, some have argued that the minimum set of services under the Universal Service umbrella needs to be expanded. This is not the place to discuss all the various options; we note, however, that any expansion of definitions is likely to involve a more costly set of services. In addition, any Universal Service formulation is likely to involve some form of subsidies, and thus will require some mechanism for creating those subsidies, and some market distortion.

## IMPLICATIONS FOR MEDIA MANAGERS

When it comes to electronic networks, the digital and fiber optic revolutions have given considerable economic advantages to broadband packet-switched (IP) networks. Digital media forms offer a degree of flexibility and processing potential unmatched by analog forms, and use creation, transmission, and storage technologies that continue to advance in speed, capabilities, and capacity, while costs continue to decline. Fiber systems also continue to evidence declining costs while capacity expands, and are also scalable (to a degree unmatched by "copper" systems). IP system designs offer unmatched flexibility and scalability, and the ability to use routers rather than switches offers significant cost savings. These networks are likely to continue to develop and converge as their cost advantages increase, replacing other telecommunication network structures, and interconnecting in the formation of what's been dubbed the Global Information Infrastructure.

Therefore, managers should not expect to continue to do business as usual in single network product markets over the long run. Digital telecommunications is removing market barriers and radically transforming cost structures. Consumer expectations are also changing, as they come to value flexibility and the ability to exert greater control over their consumption of information goods and services. The mechanics of distribution are increasingly transparent to consumers, whose value is increasingly associated with content rather than format.

Network markets are evolving, and the pace of change is likely to only get faster, and the changes more significant. Absent major governmental intervention, the new market and cost structures will force convergence and competition among a range of network products, complements, and substitutes. Managers need to recognize that they are increasingly in a competitive, multiproduct market, and try to take advantage of the opportunities that presents. The increased competition will also tend to reduce firms' ability to engage in monopoly pricing and price discrimination. As marginal costs decline in a digital work, maximizing revenues (and profits) is likely to result more from maximizing the number of customers rather than extracting the maximum value from a smaller number of consumers. When considering the increasing costs of enforcing exclusivity and transaction costs, this suggests the value of shifting from usage-based pricing to access-based pricing for many goods and services. The major challenges for media managers can be summarized as follows:

- Increasing pace of change in network markets
- Increasing convergence and competition across network products, complements, and substitutes
- Increasing competition that will reduce the ability to engage in monopoly pricing and price discrimination
- Shift toward access-based pricing rather than usage-based pricing
- Profits likely to result from maximizing the number of consumers (due to declining marginal costs)

In sum, network markets are in a period of radical transformation, with a "new economics" emerging—new, that is, in the sense that traditional market and cost structures are being radically transformed, resulting in the development of new economic relationships and implications. Managers need to be able to be able to recognize and take advantage of these new economic relationships, by being flexible in terms of their operations and strategies.

# REFERENCES

Bates, B. J. (1988). Information as an economic good: Sources of individual and social value. In V. Mosco & J. Wasko (Eds.), *The political economy of information* (pp. 76–94). Madison: University of Wisconsin Press.

Bates, B. J. (1990). Information as an economic good: A re-evaluation of theoretical approaches. In B. D. Ruben & L. A. Lievrouw (Eds.), *Mediation, information, and communication. Information and behavior.* (Vol. 3, pp. 379–394). New Brunswick, NJ: Transaction.

Bates, B. J. (1997). Learning from the evolution of telecommunications in the developed world. In P. S.-N. Lee (Ed.), *Telecommunications and development in China* (pp. 21–54). Creskill, NJ: Hampton Press.

Bates, B. J., & Chambers, L. T. (2004). The economics of the cable industry. In A. Alexander, J. Owers, R. Carveth, C. A. Hollifield, & A. N. Greco (Eds.), *Media economics: Theory and practice* (3rd ed., pp. 173–192). Mahwah, NJ: Lawrence Erlbaum Associates.

Crandall, R. W., & Alleman, J. H. (2002). *Broadband: Should we regulate high-speed Internet access?* Washington, DC: Brookings Institution Press.

DeLong, J. B., & Froomkin, A. M. (2000). Speculative microeconomics for tomorrow's economy." In B. Kahin and H. R. Varian (Eds.), *Internet publishing and beyond: The economics of digital information and intellectual property* (pp. 6–44). Cambridge, MA: The MIT Press.

Economides, N. (1996). The economics of networks. *International Journal of Industrial Organization, 14*(6), 673–699.

Egan, B. I. (1991). *Information superhighways: The economics of advanced public communication networks.* Norwood, MA: Artech House.

Kingma, B. R. (2001). *The economics of information: A guide to economic and cost-benefit analysis for information professionals* (2nd ed.). Englewood, CO: Libraries Unlimited.

McKnight, L. W., & Bailey, J. P. (1997). *Internet economics.* Cambridge, MA: MIT Press.

Mueller, M. M. (1997). *Universal service: Competition, interconnection, and monopoly in the making of the American telephone system.* Cambridge, MA: MIT Press.

Shapiro, C., & Varian, H. (1998). *Information rules: A strategic guide to the network economy.* Cambridge, MA: Harvard University Press.

Shy, Oz. (2001). *Economics of network industries.* Cambridge, UK: Cambridge University Press.

Wheatley, J. J. (1999). *World telecommunications economics.* London: The Institution of Electrical Engineers.

# Issues in Media Convergence

Michael O. Wirth
University of Denver

This chapter is devoted to a discussion of the multifaceted concept of media convergence. Media economics and management scholars and communication professionals have become increasingly interested in convergence over the past 15 years. There are many driving forces behind convergence and the increased interest in the concept. Driving forces include (a) technological innovation, including the rise of the Internet and the digital revolution; (b) deregulation / liberalization and globalization, including passage of the Telecommunications Act of 1996, formation of the European Union and the privatization of telecommunications and media around the world; (c) changing consumer tastes and increased consumer affluence; (d) technological standardization; (e) the search for synergy (i.e., $1 + 1 = 3$); (f) the fear of being left behind and big egos (which have resulted in high levels of merger and acquisition activity among media and telecommunication companies around the world); and (g) repurposing of old media content for distribution via various forms of new media (Wirth, 2003b).

One of the challenges of studying media convergence is that the concept is so broad that it has multiple meanings. As a result, the academic literature in this area is diverse and underdeveloped from both a theoretic and an empirical perspective. The chapter begins with a brief history of convergence including a review of various alternative definitions of the concept. The media management and economics literature in this area is then reviewed. Finally, questions/ideas/issues related to future research focused on media convergence are provided at the end of the chapter.

## BRIEF HISTORY OF CONVERGENCE

Sometime in the 1920s, Father Pierre Teilhard de Chardin, a Jesuit priest, came up with the concept of convergence.

> "With the evolution of man . . . a new law of Nature has come into force—that of convergence." Biological evolution had created step one, "expansive convergence." Now, in the 20th century, by means of technology, God was creating "compressive convergence." Thanks to technology . . . *Homo sapiens* [are] being united . . . by a single "stupendous thinking machine" . . . that would cover the earth like "a thinking skin," a "noo-sphere." (Wolfe, 2001, pp. 206–207, quoting Father Pierre Teilhard de Chardin)

In 1964, McLuhan (1964) renamed Teilhard's "noo-sphere" the "global village," which has become a foundation for discussions and inquiries focused on global connectivity via various media and telecommunication distribution systems. Rosenberg (1963) introduced the concept of technological convergence in his study of the machine tool industry from 1840 to 1910. Winseck (1999) concluded that the development of the telegraph as a news and information service, also from 1840 to 1910, provides an early example of media convergence with useful parallels to what's going on today. Kyrish (2001) points to videotex as a failed attempt to achieve convergence in the early 1980s. Yoffie's (1997a) edited volume on digital convergence provides a valuable theoretic underpinning for media and telecommunication scholarly inquiry focused on economic and managerial aspects of convergence. Jenkins (2001) identified five different media convergence processes.

> *Technological Convergence*: . . . the digitization of all media content; . . . *Economic Convergence*: the horizontal integration of the entertainment industry; . . . *Social or Organic Convergence*: consumers' multitasking strategies for navigating the new information environment; . . . *Cultural Convergence*: . . . encourages transmedia storytelling, the development of content across multiple channels; . . . *Global Convergence*: . . . the cultural hybridity that results from the international circulation of media content . . . reflect[ing] the experience of being a citizen of the "global village." (p. 93)

Dennis (2003, p. 7) identified four stages of communication industry convergence: "incremental awakening"—the 1980s, "early adoption"—early to mid-1990s, "uncritical acceptance"—late 1990s, and "presumptions of failure"—early 2000s. Frieden (2003, p. 25) indicates, "Between 1996 and 2001 over $1.3 trillion dollars was invested in information and telecommunications industries. . . . Since 2001 investment has substantially shrunk along with expectations about growth and new opportunities in converging information, communications and entertainment industries."

### Defining Convergence

As suggested by Jenkins' (2001), scholars wishing to study some aspect of media convergence must begin by defining the meaning of the concept. *Merriam-Webster's Dictionary* defines the general concept of convergence as "the act of converging and esp[ecially] moving toward union or uniformity" (Mish, 1993, p. 253). Definitions of media convergence focus on technological convergence, functional convergence, competitive/complementary convergence, and strategic/industry structure convergence.

For example, Yoffie (1997b, p. 2) views convergence as "the unification of functions—the coming together of previously distinct products that employ digital technologies." Collis, Bane, and Bradley (1997, p. 161) indicate that "convergence implies the creation of a common distribution network that will replace previously discrete telephone, television, and personal computing networks, and will transform the distribution of many other products and services." Greenstein and Khanna (1997, pp. 203–204) define convergence in terms of substitutes and complements: "Two products converge in substitutes when users consider either product interchangeable with the other. . . . Two products converge in complements when the products work better together than separately or when they work better together now than they worked together formerly." Fidler (1997, p. 278) describes convergence as the "Crossing of paths or combination that results in the transformation of each converging technology or entity as well as the creation of new technologies or entities." Allison, DeSonne, Rutenbeck, and Yadon (2002, p. 61) say that convergence is a "business trend where previously separate industries . . . are converging through mega-mergers, buyouts, partnerships and strategic alliances." Conversely, Noll (2003, pp. 12–13) contends that the "term "convergence" is so all encompassing [that] . . . convergence is nothing more than an over hyped illusion . . . a myth and not a mantra to be followed."

In spite of the bad decisions and hype that have been a major part of the history of convergence, Dennis (2003, p. 10) believes that the mistakes of the past have laid the groundwork for a converged future within the media industries.

## REVIEW OF LITERATURE

The digitization of media and telecommunication systems and content is principally responsible for technological media convergence (Abe, 2000; Baldwin, McVoy, & Steinfield, 1996; National Research Council, 2002; Sacconaghi et al., 2004). Without technological convergence, most types of media management and economic convergence would not be possible. However, because the area of media convergence is so diverse and divergent, the literature review provided below focuses exclusively on convergence-related scholarly studies in the areas of media economics and management. Table 20.1 provides a summary classification of the media convergence scholarly studies reviewed next. (Note: Studies that deal with multiple aspects of convergence are listed more than once.)

### Convergence in Substitutes/Complements

A good place to begin the study of media convergence from an economic and managerial perspective is to develop an understanding of the extent to which industries either are or are not coming together. The economic concepts of complements (i.e., the extent to which two goods are used together, such as coffee and sugar) and substitutes (i.e., the extent to which two goods compete with each other, such as coffee and tea) provide a useful starting place to begin to define the extent to which the boundaries between

**TABLE 20.1**
Summary Classification of Media Convergence Scholarly Studies

*Convergence in Substitutes/Complements*
- Weedon (1996)—*The Book Trade and Internet Publishing: A British Perspective*
- Greenstein & Khanna (1997)—What does industry convergence mean?
- Steemers (1997)—Broadcasting is dead. Long live digital choice: Perspectives from the United Kingdom and Germany
- Yoffie (1997b)—Introduction: Chess and competing in the age of digital convergence
- Dowling, Lechner, & Thielmann (1998)—Convergence—Innovation and change of market structures between television and online services
- Thielmann & Dowling (1999)—Convergence and innovation strategy for service provision in emerging web-TV markets
- Garrison (2000)—Diffusion of a new technology: On-line research in newspaper newsrooms
- Chan-Olmsted & Kang (2003)—Theorizing the strategic architecture of a broadband television industry

*Media Industry Structure and Convergence*
*Vertical/Horizontal Business Structure/Transformation*
- Collis, Bane, & Bradley (1997)—Winners and losers: Industry structure in the converging world of telecommunications, computing and entertainment
- Thielmann & Dowling (1999)—Convergence and innovation strategy for service provision in emerging web-TV markets
- Wirtz (1999)—Convergence processes, value constellations and integration strategies in the multimedia business
- Chan-Olmsted & Kang (2003)—Theorizing the strategic architecture of a broadband television industry

*Media and Telecommunication Mergers and Acquisitions*
- Chan-Olmsted (1998)—Mergers, acquisitions, and convergence: The strategic alliances of broadcasting, cable television, and telephone services
- Tseng & Litman (1998)—The impact of the Telecommunications Act of 1996 on the merger of RBOCs and MSOs: Case study: The merger of U.S. West and Continental Cablevision
- Wheeler (2002)—Tuning into the new economy: The European Union's competition policy in a converging communications environment
- Chon, Choi, Barnett, Danowski, & Joo (2003)—A structural analysis of media convergence: Cross-industry mergers and acquisitions in the information industries

*Convergence and Strategic Management*
*Convergence and the Industrial Organization (IO) View*
- Chan-Olmsted (1998)—Mergers, acquisitions, and convergence: The strategic alliances of broadcasting, cable television, and telephone services
- Dowling, Lechner, & Thielmann (1998)—Convergence—Innovation and change of market structures between television and online services
- Thielmann & Dowling (1999)—Convergence and innovation strategy for service provision in emerging web-TV markets
- Wirtz (1999)—Convergence processes, value constellations and integration strategies in the multimedia business
- Chan-Olmsted & Jung (2001)—Strategizing the Net business: How the U.S. television networks diversify, brand, and compete in the age of the Internet
- Chan-Olmsted & Kang (2003)—Theorizing the strategic architecture of a broadband television industry

*(continued)*

**TABLE 20.1**
*(continued)*

---

- Chon, Choi, Barnett, Danowski, & Joo (2003)—A structural analysis of media convergence: Cross-industry mergers and acquisitions in the information industries
- Rolland (2003)—Convergence as strategy for value creation

*Convergence and the Resource-Based View (RBV)*
- Liu & Chan-Olmsted (2003)—Partnerships between the old and the new: Examining the strategic alliances between broadcast television networks and Internet firms in the context of convergence

**Convergence and Consumer Demand**
- Yoffie (1997b)—Introduction: Chess and competing in the age of digital convergence
- Dowling, Lechner, & Thielmann (1998)—Convergence—Innovation and change of market structures between television and online services
- Lin & Jeffres (1998)—Factors influencing the adoption of multimedia cable technology
- Stipp (1999)—Convergence now?
- Picard (2000)—Changing business models of online content services: Their implications for multimedia and other content producers
- Carroll (2002)—Newspaper readership v. news emails: Testing the principle of relative constancy

**Convergence and Culture**
- Singer (1997)—Still guarding the gate?: The newspaper journalist's role in an online world
- Cottle (1999)—From BBC newsroom to BBC newscentre: On changing technology and journalist practices
- Palmer & Eriksen (1999)—Digital news—Paper, broadcast and more converge on the Internet
- Chyi & Sylvie (2000)—Online newspapers in the U.S.: Perceptions of markets, products, revenue, and competition
- Killebrew (2003)—Culture, creativity and convergence: Managing journalists in a changing information workplace
- Lawson-Borders (2003)—Integrating new media and old media: Seven observations of convergence as a strategy for best practices in media organizations
- MacGregor (2003)—Mind the gap: Problems of multimedia journalism

---

industries are beginning to converge or dissolve (Chan-Olmsted & Kang, 2003; Dowling, Lechner, & Thielmann, 1998; Greenstein & Khanna, 1997).

Greenstein and Khanna (1997, p. 203) indicate that two products converge in substitutes when a given number of consumers view the, often formerly unrelated, products as competitors for an increasing number of tasks and/or when an increasing number of consumers view the products as competitors for a given set of tasks. Dowling et al. (1998, p. 34) refer to this market situation as "competitive convergence" and suggest that, over time, "a new single industry" will emerge from this type of convergence (i.e., $1 + 1 = 1$). The increasing substitutability between the video services provided by direct broadcast satellite entrepreneurs and cable television entrepreneurs has led to the formation of the multichannel video market (Wirth, 2002). This is an example of convergence in substitutes.

Two goods converge in complements when "different firms develop products within a standard bundle that can increasingly work together to form a larger system" (Greenstein & Khanna, 1997, p. 204). In such a cooperative paradigm, new "synergistic" products and/or markets emerge in which the amount produced exceeds the "sum of the parts" (i.e., $1 + 1 = 3$) (Greenstein & Khanna, 1997, p. 204; Dowling et al., 1998, p. 34). The emergence of the broadband industry, in which voice, video, and data services are bundled together and marketed to consumers via a common distribution platform, is an example of convergence in complements.

Yoffie (1997b, p. 2) contends that, based on his research in the computer industry, "success is more likely to emerge from *creative combinations* that build on complementary technologies." This suggests that market entry is initially easier as a complement than as a substitute. New products that are complementary in one part of the value chain, but substitutes in another part, also have an easier time with respect to market entry. An examination of the history of video distribution via satellites provides a good example of this. Shortly after Time Inc. began to distribute HBO to U.S. cable systems via satellite on September 30, 1975, satellite distribution became the norm for cable programmers (Gershon & Wirth, 1993). Video satellite distribution at this point served a complementary role with respect to cable's distribution of video product into homes. So, video satellite distribution developed quickly as a complement. It took almost 20 years for a successful direct broadcast satellite service to be launched by DirecTV in 1994 (Southwick, 1998), which has now developed into a successful video distribution substitute for cable.

Chan-Olmsted and Kang (2003, p. 18) apply the concept of convergence in complements to develop a strategic architecture for the broadcast television market. They conclude that, at least in the foreseeable future, the broadband market will not become a "truly converged system" and that broadband entrepreneurs (i.e., multichannel television and telephone companies) will continue "to offer telecommunications and video programming products under two separate interfacing devices and different distribution infrastructures." Dowling et al. (1998, pp. 34–35) utilize convergence in substitutes and complements along with Porter's (1980) five competitive forces (with the focal point on customer needs) to examine convergence between the television industry and online services. They assert that, at least initially, complementary convergence will exist between television and online services. However, over time, as consumer needs change, competitive convergence may begin to emerge (Thielmann & Dowling, 1999, p. 8). Rapid improvements in digital signal compression via MPEG-4 (Wirth, 2003b), combined with increased penetration of high-speed Internet service ("Is Price All That Matters," 2004) and expansion of home digital networks (Sacconaghi et al., 2004), suggest that online video services will one day converge in substitutes with multichannel video distribution.

A number of additional academic studies focus on the competitive/complementary relationship between new media/new media forms and traditional media without using Greenstein and Khanna's (1997) paradigm. For example, Steemers (1997) conducted a qualitative analysis of the impact of digital television on public service broadcasting in the U.K. and Germany. She concludes that public service broadcasters and policy makers were ill prepared strategically for the potential impact of the convergence of broadcasting and telecommunications on the public interest in diversity and plurality (competitive convergence) (p. 67). Weedon (1996) compared the evolution of the format and distribution mechanisms utilized by Great Britain's book trade in the early part of the 20th century to the impact of the Internet on traditional book production, distribution, and marketing in the U.K. He concludes that the market structure of the U.K.'s book industry will likely be affected by the fact that "Competition and convergence . . . [are creating] new synergies . . . between publishers, software houses and on-line bookstores to develop and market electronic formats" (complementary convergence for book publishers initially/competitive convergence for traditional bookstores) (p. 98). Garrison (2000) conducted a longitudinal mail survey of U.S. newspapers (1994–1998) and used diffusion of innovation theory (Rogers, 1995) to assess journalists' adoption of the Internet as an online research tool (complementary convergence). The study's results confirm his expectations based on diffusion theory, and that the Internet has "become the dominant on-line research tool for journalists" (p. 84).

In sum, utilization of Greenstein and Khanna's (1997) convergence in complements and substitutes paradigm provides a useful way to determine if the boundaries between industries are coming closer together (i.e., converging) and, if they are, whether this can be expected to lead to increased market competitiveness (convergence in substitutes) or in new products and/or markets (convergence in complements).

## Media Industry Structure and Convergence

The impact of convergence on media industry structure represents a second area of interest among media economics and management scholars. Utilizing a functional rather than a technological framework to examine the impact of convergence on multimedia business structures allows researchers to more precisely dissect, analyze, and understand multimedia business strategies. It also provides researchers with insights into business models, which might prove to be more/less effective in this area.

Studies here have focused on two primary areas: the notion that convergence is transforming the media and telecommunication industries from vertical businesses into horizontal segments (including the strategic implications of this transformation) and the impact of convergence on media and telecommunication merger and acquisition strategies.

### *Vertical/Horizontal Business Structure Transformation*

Collis et al. (1997, pp. 160, 166–167) theorize that convergence is transforming the multimedia industry from "three vertical businesses (telephone, television, and computer) to five horizontal segments"—content, packaging, transmission network, manipulation infrastructure, and terminals. Similarly, Wirtz (1999) divides the multimedia value chain into five stages: "Content and Services Creators . . . , Content/Services Aggregators . . . , value added service providers . . . , access/connecting stage [transmission] . . . , [and the] Navigation/Interfacing stage" (p. 17).

Thielmann and Dowling (1999, p. 5) utilize the approach of Collis et al. (1997) to analyze "vertical convergence between content and service provision" in the multimedia value chain through a case study analysis of Web-TV Networks. They conclude that, to successfully innovate toward convergence as a service provider (part of Collis et al.'s packaging segment), Web-TV Networks must forge vertical strategic alliances with key multimedia value chain partners (e.g., content, packaging, processing, transmission, and devices) to develop distinctive competencies. They also recommend that Web-TV expand horizontally to get more involved in packaging (pp. 6–7).

Wirtz's (1999) qualitative examination of the impact of convergence on media migration and integration strategies comes to the conclusion that vertical and horizontal "strategic alliances in the form of capital integrations, joint ventures, and long-term contracts and agreements are being closed in order to secure know-how" up and down the multimedia value chain (p. 20). These alliances are due, at least in part, to the significant financial risks associated with "independent technological leadership."

Chan-Olmsted and Kang (2003) assert that broadband television value chain participants "have strong incentives to form partnerships with" access service providers to obtain "access to customer information and relationships" (p. 19). They also believe that, over time, packagers will gain market power relative to distributors (because of the complex nature of broadband service packages), and that the broadband industry will continue to trend toward total vertical integration up and down the value chain (among content creators, packagers, access service providers, distributors, and facilitators) (p. 19).

### Media and Telecommunication Mergers and Acquisitions

Placing the focus on various aspects of mergers and acquisitions provides researchers with a useful focal point for analyzing the impact of media convergence on M&A activity. Traditional industrial organization economics concepts related to market structure and concentration are particularly important in this area of inquiry.

Convergence-based mergers and acquisitions reached their zenith with the merger of AOL and Time Warner. As Huber (2000, p. A26) wrote, the AOL–Time Warner merger "is the beginning of the end of the old mass media and the end of all serious debate about the new." Many of the mergers that occurred during what Dennis (2003) calls the uncritical acceptance or "marriages of convergence" stage of convergence (i.e., the latter part of the 1990s) were justified and/or driven by "old media's" need to develop a "new media" strategy." When coupled with deregulation, very high telecommunication and media company valuations, globalization, and the desire to vertically integrate to leverage content and create barriers to new competition, all of the merger and acquisition activity that took place during this time period is not surprising (Ozanich & Wirth, 2004, pp. 76–77). However, for the most part, the promise of convergence has yet to be obtained (Wirth, 2003a). As Owen (1999) indicates:

> Convergence is a possibility not a reality, because it is much too expensive. One way to think about the future is to ask which technology is most likely, at scale, to reduce the costs of these services to levels consumers will find attractive. . . . Is such a system possible? Technically, yes. It is already being done. . . . But how about costs? And consumer demand? (pp. 192, 313)

In spite of the challenges associated with many convergence-based mergers/acquisitions (see for example, "AOL Disaster," 2003; Fransman, 2002; Lewis, 2003), "the allure of convergence remains very powerful for entrepreneurs, policy makers, and technologists" (Wirth, 2003a, p. 5).

To study the impact of convergence and industry deregulation on mergers and acquisitions in the information industries, Chon, Choi, Barnett, Danowski, and Joo (2003) utilize centrality analysis, cluster analysis, and Galileo analysis to conduct a network analysis of the information industry ownership transactions that took place before and after 1996. Their findings indicate that information industry consolidation has been facilitated "by deregulation and digitization . . . [and that] digital technologies including the Internet appear to have led to digital convergence among cable, telephony, and computer related industries" (p. 154). They also find that "delivery-based" companies drove post-1996 consolidation, whereas "content-based" companies were important M&A players prior to (but not after) 1996 (p. 155). In order to gain insights into industry convergence trends, Chan-Olmsted (1998) examines M&A strategies for broadcast, cable, and telephone entrepreneurs from 1991 to 1996 by classifying the M&A transactions of all communication industries (SIC code 48) during this time period as "horizontal, vertical, concentric, or conglomerate" (pp. 37–38). She concludes that M&A activity among radio, TV, cable TV, and telephone entrepreneurs was primarily internal (i.e., within each industry segment) from 1991 to 1996, and that cross-segment strategic alliances (i.e., attempts to truly converge) were limited to "nonpermanent, trial-format alliances such as partnerships in joint ventures . . . [at least partially due to] great differences in corporate cultures between cable TV and telephone companies" (pp. 44–45).

Tseng and Litman's (1998) case study analysis of the U.S. West/Continental Cablevision merger uses the industrial organization paradigm to discuss the economics and strategy behind the merger. In particular, Tseng and Litman conclude that "vertical integration for market power of programming, and . . . synergies" from converging "video, voice and data" were major factors behind the merger, and RBOCs could be expected to pursue multimedia services-based mergers to offset increased competition from new entrants (p. 63).

Wheeler (2002) examines three attempts by media and telecommunication companies to achieve convergence through mergers/acquisitions, by assessing the ability of the European Commission (EC) to appropriately regulate concentration in the European Union (EU). Based on his examination of these three cases, he concludes that the effectiveness of the EC's competition policy, with respect to the converging information industries, is limited, and that the EU should expand its evaluation of proposed mergers and acquisitions to "ensure the enhancement and diversity of . . . information services, as well as market openness and competitive fairness" (p. 115).

## Convergence and Strategic Management

Theories emanating from the field of strategic management represent a third area which has been applied to convergence-based research. Liu and Chan-Olmsted (2003) identify two major types of strategic management research studies: those that focus "on the linkage between strategy and the external environment" and those that use a resource-based approach to analyze firm strategy and performance resulting from the unique resources possessed by the firm (p. 48). The former strategic approach is labeled the *industrial organization* (IO) view and the latter strategic approach is labeled the *resource-based view* (RBV). There are many examples of strategic management studies that utilize an IO view and which provide some focus on convergence. They include Rolland (2003), Chan-Olmsted and Jung (2001), Chan-Olmsted (1998), Wirtz (1999), Chan-Olmsted and Kang (2003), Chon et al. (2003), Thielmann and Dowling (1999), and Dowling et al. (1998). However, Liu and Chan-Olmsted (2003) provide the only example of a convergence-based article with an RBV focus.

### Convergence and the Industrial Organization (IO) View

Through use of the IO view, strategic management researchers are able to classify and analyze the impact of various industry structure variables on media firm convergence-based strategies. Porter's (1980, 1985) work lays the foundation for much of the research that has gone on in this area of inquiry.

Because six of the eight IO view strategic management articles have already been reviewed in specific subareas related to the IO view (i.e., convergence in substitutes/complements and media industry structure and convergence, including vertical/horizontal business structure transformation and media and telecommunication mergers and acquisitions), only Rolland (2003) and Chan-Olmsted and Jung (2001) are reviewed here.

Rolland (2003, p. 14) contends that convergence is in a "pre-paradigmatic stage of development" and that convergence is ultimately a media firm "strategy for value creation." To increase our understanding of value configurations among mass media, in the converged information, communication and technology (ICT) environment, Rolland uses Stabell and Fjeldstad's (1998) value configuration analysis to classify media from a value creation perspective (i.e., how media create value via the value chain, value shop and value network). His analysis suggests that "digitalisation implies that [media] products become more similar and interchangeable. This calls for convergence of their organizational form" (i.e., industrial convergence) and of "the economic challenges they are facing" (i.e., value creation convergence) (p. 23). Rolland believes that when the media industries "digitize, merge, and become available as interchangeable commodities in the same transmission network," content creation will be the media's only value creation driver (p. 23).

Chan-Olmsted and Jung (2001) utilize the ICDT (information, community, distribution, transaction) model to conduct a case study analysis of convergence-based Internet strategies of U.S. broadcast and cable television networks. The ICDT model divides the Internet business virtual space into four segments—"a virtual information space (VIS), a virtual communication space (VCS), a virtual distribution space (VDS), and a virtual transaction space (VTS) (Angehrn, 1997)" (Chan-Olmsted & Jung, 2001, p. 215). Chan-Olmsted and Jung conclude that:

> U.S. television networks are in an initial strategic stage that focuses on ventures in the "marketing space" (VIS and VCS) of the Internet. . . . Their goal is to penetrate (i.e., market penetration strategy) the existing market with better customer service via the Internet and more online features that would enhance the networks' off-line products. . . . To be successful at this stage, it is essential for the networks to build upon their current core business strengths. . . . As the networks solidify their Internet presence . . . , they are likely to enter a second phase of Internet ventures with more investments in the commerce space (VDS and VTS), working toward a market/product development strategy. (pp. 222–223)

### Convergence and the Resource-Based View (RBV)

It is only recently that strategic management researchers began to apply the resource-based view (RBV) approach to analyze convergence-based media firm strategies. Application of this theoretical approach, which emphasizes the value of firms' internal resources and their ability to manage them, holds great promise for providing researchers with a different, and potentially very rich, analytical frame for examining such strategies.

Liu and Chan-Olmsted (2003) study convergence-based alliance formation between U.S. broadcast television networks and Internet companies through utilization of an RBV strategy framework. They find that "television networks primarily contribute property-based resources, while the Internet firms primarily offered knowledge-based resources" to these alliances (p. 54). The majority of network alliances were minority equity alliances with content-based niche Web sites. This was at least partially due to the fact that broadcast networks and Internet companies "still exhibit very different core competencies and business models" (Liu & Chan-Olmsted, 2003, p. 55). Liu and Chan-Olmsted conclude that broadcast networks with a larger number of alliances, both quantitatively and magnitudinally, also have a greater Internet presence.

## Convergence and Consumer Demand

A fourth area of focus with respect to convergence-based media management and economics academic inquiry is consumer demand. Dowling et al. (1998) indicate that convergence-based consumer need/demand issues will be even more important in the future as television moves "away from mass communication to more user specific communication" (p. 35). As a result, convergence-based research, which focuses on various aspects of consumer demand, should become an increasingly important area of inquiry for media economics and management scholars.

Dowling et al. (1998, p. 33) identify three dimensions of convergence: technology, needs (consumer demand), and industries/firms (supply). The development of convergence-based products, capable of fulfilling new and/or existing consumer needs in novel and/or less expensive ways (than such needs are currently being fulfilled), is key to the development of viable business models in this area (Dowling et al., 1998; Picard, 2000; Yoffie, 1997b). Understanding Porter's (1985) concept of the value chain is critical here. As Picard (2000) indicates:

> A business model . . . embraces the concept of the value chain . . . the value that is added to a product or service in each step of its acquisition, transformation, management, marketing and sales, and distribution. . . . This value chain concept is particularly important in understanding market behaviour because it places the emphasis on the value created for the customer who ultimately makes consumption decisions.[1] (p. 62)

In this regard, it is critical to develop consumer-driven, as opposed to technology-driven, convergence-related products (Picard, 2000, p. 61).

Picard (2000) explores the evolution and future prospects of ICT industry convergence-based business models for online content service providers. As part of his analysis, he argues that "convergence . . . is not producing any revolutionary change in communication. Rather, its primary effect is increasing the speed and flexibility of

---

[1] Consumer demand is also a major element of Porter's (1980) Five Forces Model through both the "threat of new entrants" (which includes consumer loyalty to existing brands as a major element) and the "threat of substitutes" (which is viewed in a similar fashion to a new entrant as products become increasingly substitutable).

communication ... creat[ing] new economies of scope and integration that change the economics of content distribution" (p. 60). Convergence has resulted in increased "choice and control" for consumers by "creating faster, easier, and more flexible means for consumers to do what they are already doing" (Picard, 2000, pp. 60–61). To be successful, new products, made possible through convergence, must create value for consumers and businesses by fulfilling existing needs at a lower cost or in a more convenient manner (than they are currently being met) and/or by fulfilling unmet consumer and/or business needs (p. 61).

Stipp's (1999) analysis of the convergence taking place between computers and television, places primary focus on consumer behavior convergence (p. 11). Through an examination of viewership data generated by various audience ratings organizations, Stipp concludes that the PC and TV serve different functions for consumers, that Internet usage is not reducing the amount of time spent watching TV, and that changes in consumer behavior as a result of convergence will be evolutionary rather than revolutionary (pp. 11–12).

Carroll (2002) empirically tests McCombs and Eyal's (1980) theory of relative constancy (i.e., consumers spend a fixed amount of time and money on media) by conducting a survey of users of both the weekly print edition and daily e-mail news updates of a furniture industry trade publication. In the short run, because the "eDaily" and the print edition of the trade publication serve different consumer needs, Carroll concludes that the "eDaily" was not cannibalizing the print edition's readership to any great extent (i.e., most consumers viewed the "eDaily" and the print version as complementary) (pp. 88–89). However, as the "eDaily" evolves and consumer tastes change, an increasing number of consumers could begin to view the "eDaily" as a substitute for the print version of the publication, which would lead to confirmation of the theory of relative constancy (p. 89).

Lin and Jeffres (1998) utilize diffusion theory and functional substitution theory to analyze survey data collected to explore audience intentions to adopt "multimedia" cable service (i.e., voice, data, and video). Their canonical correlation results suggest that consumers were more likely to indicate interest in experimenting/adopting "multimedia" cable service, made possible by convergence, if they were less satisfied with their present cable and television services (i.e., functional substitution), cable nonsubscribers, "more satisfied and heavier radio listeners, ... better able to keep up with new technology, ... married, better educated, wealthier, heavier newspaper readers and ... lighter television viewers" (pp. 347–348).

## Convergence and Culture

Media economics and management scholars are also interested in the impact of convergence on media culture (i.e., the development of content for distribution across different media channel forms and/or the repurposing of existing media content) (Jenkins, 2001). Media corporations are expected to continue to expand convergence-based strategies focused on the delivery of news content along with many other types of content. As a result, studies focused on media convergence and various aspects of media culture represent an increasingly fertile area for future research.

Most research in this area has focused on examining the managerial challenges and strategies related to moving toward multimedia convergence in the newsroom (i.e., attempting to achieve convergence with respect to print, broadcast, and online news operations and personnel). Studies in this area include Singer (1997), Cottle (1999), Palmer and Eriksen (1999), Chyi and Sylvie (2000), Killebrew (2003), and Lawson-Borders (2003).

Singer (1997) utilizes a case study approach along with Q methodology to examine the impact of beginning to deliver newspaper stories electronically via the Internet on how reporters and editors at three metropolitan U.S. newspapers view their role as gatekeepers. Singer concludes that journalists see a modified future role in which their "function changes from someone who chooses what information to make available to someone who . . . seeks to provide information whose quality distinguishes it from the rest and . . . makes sense of the information that *is* out there" (p. 86). Cottle's (1999) case study of a multimedia BBC newscenter assesses the degree to which multimedia convergence in the newsroom has been successfully implemented by the BBC. His findings suggest that, from the journalists' perspective, the primary impact of multimedia convergence in the newsroom has been to create increased pressure on and work expectations for journalists in "an impinging context of cost reduction and management's sought [after] efficiency gains through multi-skilled, multimedia work practices" (pp. 38–39).

Palmer and Eriksen (1999) examine the redesign of radio, TV and newspaper news content for redistribution on the Internet. They believe that news distribution via the Web "can take much of the best of the [old] media," but that it will be challenging to find a profitable business model for convergence-based distribution (p. 33). Specialized content (including historical content) coupled with the ability to offer consumers "goal-driven" multimedia integration appear to be promising avenues for developing a workable business model here (pp. 33–34). Chyi and Sylvie (2000) conducted qualitative interviews with managers from 14 U.S. online newspapers. Those interviewed believe that specialization is a key success factor for online newspapers, that no cannibalization exists between traditional and online newspapers (as of 1998–99), and that shovelware (i.e., the redistribution of newspaper stories online with minimal or no changes) will be a major component of online newspaper content for the foreseeable future (Chyi & Sylvie, 2000, p. 75; see also, MacGregor, 2003, for a recent examination of why PC-based news delivery has yet to realize its potential with respect to multimedia storytelling).

Killebrew (2003) draws on theories from organizational psychology, organizational communication, and traditional management to examine the major management challenges presented by convergence with respect to "culture, climate, and creativity" in the changing information workplace (p. 39). Based on his analysis, Killebrew recommends that if media firms attempting to implement convergence-based activities want to "create an organizational value shift among the participants [in] the upcoming enterprise," they should identify organizational risk takers, provide proper training for those who will be working on the converged activities (prior to launch), and, where possible, "beta" test the convergence activities in small markets (p. 45). Lawson-Borders (2003) uses the theory of diffusion of innovations (Rogers, 1995) and innovation management theory (Frambach, 1993) along with case-study results from three pioneering media groups to identify the best management practices for integrating old and new media. For convergence to succeed, Lawson-Borders (2003) believes that media firms must (a) engage in high-quality communication about what the organization is trying to accomplish (see also Killebrew, 2003); (b) be committed to incorporating convergence into their organizational mission and philosophy; (c) promote cooperation among everyone involved in the journalistic process "to share stories and ideas;" (d) revise compensation plans to fairly compensate multimedia journalists for taking on the new roles and responsibilities required by convergence; (e) facilitate the blending of different cultures in the newsroom (i.e., print, radio, television, and online) (see also Killebrew, 2003); (f) develop strategies and alliances capable of allowing media firms to successfully compete in local markets and globally; and (g) develop convergence strategies capable of serving evolving consumer needs in a dynamic and increasingly competitive/challenging marketplace (pp. 94–96).

## SUGGESTIONS FOR FUTURE RESEARCH

Technological advances affecting the economic viability of convergence continue apace. Likewise, there has been a dramatic increase in high speed data service subscribership (nearly tripling from 9.6 million HSD subscribers in June 2001 to 28.2 million in December 2003 in the U.S. according to the FCC; Hearn, 2004), and in the marketing of bundled services (i.e., voice, data, and video) to cable and telecommunication consumers. "Convergence involving the distribution of the same content across different channels . . . has [also] proven its worth" (Dennis, 2003, p. 9). So, it seems clear that media entrepreneurs will continue to pursue various types of convergence-based business strategies.

Thus, as a result of significant shifts in marketplace realities, convergence-based impacts and strategies are likely to become increasingly important elements of the studies conducted by media economics and management scholars. This means that media researchers need to continue to expand and improve their work in this area. Specific suggestions for improvement include the following.

- Those doing research in this area need to provide a stronger theoretic base for convergence-based studies. Research in this area should be shaped and driven by theory. Although interesting, additional ad hoc analyses will be of limited value in advancing knowledge and the quality of inquiry in this area.
- Although providing a theoretical base for convergence-related analyses is critical, it is equally critical that the theoretical base provided be utilized by scholars to inform and interpret their analyses.
- Researchers need to do more in the way of empirical research in this area. Surprisingly, only one of the convergence-based studies reviewed in this chapter provided hypotheses (Collis et al., 1997), and none of the studies tested hypotheses. Going forward, scholars need to design sophisticated empirical studies capable of quantitatively measuring and testing convergence-based theories and impacts.
- As scholars plan future work focused on identifying the impact of media convergence, they need to pose and attempt to answer analytical, as opposed to descriptive, research questions.

Some possible research questions scholars might utilize as a basis for future empirical research in this area include:

- How have old media/new media/telecommunication companies affected convergence-based strategic alliances?
- How have various types of convergence affected old media/new media/telecommunication company performance (e.g., profitability, customer satisfaction, customer retention, consumer demand, market concentration)?
- How have the value chains of old media/new media/telecommunication companies been affected by media convergence?
- How has the value creation process of old media/new media/telecommunication companies been affected by media convergence?
- How have the business models of old media/new media/telecommunication companies been affected by convergence?
- How has media/telecommunication market competition been affected by convergence?
- How has convergence affected the availability of substitutes within the media/telecommunication marketplace?
- How has convergence affected the availability of complements within the media/telecommunication marketplace?
- How have the globalization strategies pursued by media/telecommunication firms been affected by convergence?
- How have the corporate financial strategies pursued by media/telecommunication firms been affected by convergence?
- How have the merger and acquisition strategies pursued by media/telecommunication firms been affected by convergence?
- How have the media's information repurposing strategies been affected by convergence?
- How have the organizational management strategies of media/telecommunication firms been affected by convergence?
- How have the marketing strategies of media/telecommunication firms been affected by convergence?

In sum, convergence-based studies of media and telecommunications are still in an early stage of development. As a result, there are a wide array of possible studies and research directions available for scholars to pursue. One of the major challenges faced by researchers as they conduct research in this area is to clearly define what they mean by *convergence*, and to then operationalize and measure convergence so that they can assess its impact on the phenomenon under study.

## REFERENCES

Abe, G. (2000). *Residential broadband* (2nd ed.). Indianapolis, IN: Cisco Press.

Allison, A. W. III, DeSonne, M. L., Rutenbeck, J., & Yadon, R. E. (2002). *Tech terms* (2nd ed.). Washington, DC: National Association of Broadcasters.

Angehrn, A. A. (1997). Designing mature Internet business strategies: The ICDT model. *European Management Journal, 15*, 361–369.

AOL disaster a timely reminder. (2003, January 31). *Australian Financial Review*, p. 82. Retrieved March 21, 2003, from www.lexis-nexis.com/universe

Baldwin, T. F., McVoy, D. S., & Steinfield, C. (1996). *Convergence: Integrating media, information & communication.* Thousand Oaks, CA: Sage.

Carroll, B. (2002). Newspaper readership v. news emails: Testing the principle of relative constancy. *Convergence, 8*, 78–96.

Chan-Olmsted, S. M. (1998). Mergers, acquisitions, and convergence: The strategic alliances of broadcasting, cable television, and telephone services. *Journal of Media Economics, 11*, 33–46.

Chan-Olmsted, S. M., & Jung, J. (2001). Strategizing the Net business: How the U.S. television networks diversify, brand, and compete in the age of the Internet. *International Journal on Media Management, 3*, 213–225.

Chan-Olmsted, S. M., & Kang, J. W. (2003). Theorizing the strategic architecture of a broadband television industry. *Journal of Media Economics, 16*, 3–21.

Chon, B. S., Choi, J. H., Barnett, G. A., Danowski, J. A., & Joo, S. H. (2003). A structural analysis of media convergence: Cross-industry mergers and acquisitions in the information industries. *Journal of Media Economics, 16*, 141–57.

Chyi, H. I., & Sylvie, G. (2000). Online newspapers in the U.S.: Perceptions of markets, products, revenue, and competition. *International Journal on Media Management, 2*, 69–77.

Collis, D. J., Bane, P. W., & Bradley, S. P. (1997). Winners and losers: Industry structure in the converging world of telecommunications, computing and entertainment. In D. B. Yoffie (Ed.), *Competing in the age of digital convergence* (pp. 159–200). Boston: Harvard Business School Press.

Cottle, S. (1999). From BBC newsroom to BBC newscentre: On changing technology and journalist practices. *Convergence, 5*, 22–43.

Dennis, E. E. (2003). Prospects for a big idea—Is there a future for convergence? *International Journal on Media Management, 5*, 7–11.

Dowling, M., Lechner, C., & Thielmann, B. (1998). Convergence—Innovation and change of market structures between television and online services. *Electronic Markets, 8*(4), 31–35.

Fidler, R. (1997). *Mediamorphosis: Understanding new media.* Thousand Oaks, CA: Pine Forge Press.

Frambach, R. T. (1993). An integrated model of organizational adoption and diffusion of innovations. *European Journal of Marketing, 27*(5), 22–41.

Fransman, M. (2002). *Telecoms in the Internet age: From boom to bust to . . . ?* Oxford, UK: Oxford University Press.

Frieden, R. M. (2003). Fear and loathing in information and telecommunications industries: Reasons for and solutions to the current financial meltdown and regulatory quagmire. *International Journal on Media Management, 5*, 25–38.

Garrison, B. (2000). Diffusion of a new technology: On-line research in newspaper newsrooms. *Convergence, 6*, 84–105.

Gershon, R. A., & Wirth, M. O. (1993). Home Box Office. In R. G. Picard (Ed.), *The cable networks handbook* (pp. 114–122). Riverside, CA: Carpelan.

Greenstein, S., & Khanna, T. (1997). What does industry convergence mean? In D. B. Yoffie (Ed.), *Competing in the age of digital convergence* (pp. 201–226). Boston: Harvard Business School Press.

Hearn, T. (2004, September 13). Broadband surges: FCC: High-speed subs tripled since '01. *Multichannel News*, p. 40.

Huber, P. (2000, January 11). The death of old media. *The Wall Street Journal*, p. A26.

Is price all that matters in high-speed? (2004, June 21). *CableFax databriefs.*

Jenkins, H. (2001, June). Convergence? I diverge. *Technology Review*, p. 93.

Killebrew, K. C. (2003). Culture, creativity and convergence: Managing journalists in a changing information workplace. *International Journal on Media Management, 5*, 39–46.

Kyrish, S. (2001). Lessons from a "predictive history": What videotext told us about the World Wide Web. *Convergence, 7*, 10–29.

Lawson-Borders, G. (2003). Integrating new media and old media: Seven observations of convergence as a strategy for best practices in media organizations. *International Journal on Media Management, 5,* 91–99.

Lewis, P. (2003, March 10). The problem with convergence. *Fortune.* Retrieved March 23, 2003, from www.lexis-nexis.com/universe

Lin, C. A., & Jeffres, L. W. (1998). Factors influencing the adoption of multimedia cable technology. *Journalism & Mass Communication Quarterly, 75,* 341–352.

Liu, F., & Chan-Olmsted, S. (2003). Partnerships between the old and the new: Examining the strategic alliances between broadcast television networks and Internet firms in the context of convergence. *International Journal on Media Management, 5,* 47–56.

MacGregor, P. (2003). Mind the gap: Problems of multimedia journalism. *Convergence, 9,* 8–17.

McCombs, M. E., & Eyal, C. H. (1980). Spending on mass media. *Journal of Communication, 30*(1), 153–158.

McLuhan, M. (1964). *Understanding media: The extensions of man.* New York: McGraw-Hill.

Mish, F. C. (Ed.). (1993). *Merriam-Webster's Collegiate Dictionary* (10th ed.). Springfield, MA: Merriam-Webster.

*National Research Council. (2002). Broadband: Bringing home the bits.* Washington, DC: National Academy Press.

Noll, A. M. (2003). The myth of convergence. *International Journal on Media Management, 5,* 12–13.

Owen, B. M. (1999). *The Internet challenge to television.* Cambridge, MA: Harvard University Press.

Ozanich, G., & Wirth, M. O. (2004). Structure and change: A communications industry overview. In A. Alexander, J. Owers, R. Carveth, C. A. Hollifield, & A. N. Greco (Eds.), *Media economics: Theory and practice* (3rd ed., pp. 69–84). Mahwah, NJ: Lawrence Erlbaum Associates.

Palmer, J. W., & Eriksen, L. (1999). Digital news—Paper, broadcast and more converge on the Internet. *International Journal on Media Management, 1,* 31–34.

Picard, R. G. (2000). Changing business models of online content services: Their implications for multimedia and other content producers. *International Journal on Media Management, 2,* 60–68.

Porter, M. E. (1980). *Competitive strategy: Techniques for analyzing industries and competitors.* New York: Free Press.

Porter, M. E. (1985). *Competitive advantage: Creating and sustaining superior performance.* New York: Free Press.

Rogers, E. M. (1995). *Diffusion of innovations* (4th ed.). New York: Free Press.

Rolland, A. (2003). Convergence as strategy for value creation. *International Journal on Media Management, 5,* 14–24.

Rosenberg, N. (1963). Technological change in the machine tool industry, 1840–1910. *Journal of Economic History, 23,* 414–443.

Sacconaghi, A. M., Jr., Colledge, J. A., Wolzien, T., Mackenzie, M., Feldman, J. H., Parker, A. A., Dupree, N., Di Bona, C. J., II, & McGranahan, C. (2004, May). *The digital home.* New York: Bernstein Research.

Singer, J. B. (1997). Still guarding the gate?: The newspaper journalist's role in an on-line world. *Convergence, 3,* 72–89.

Southwick, T. (1998). *Distant signals.* Overland Park, KS: Primedia Intertec.

Stabell, C. B., & Fjeldstad, Ø. D. (1998). Configuring value for competitive advantage: On chains, shops, and networks. *Strategic Management, 19,* 413–437.

Steemers, J. (1997). Broadcasting is dead. Long live digital choice: Perspectives from the United Kingdom and Germany. *Convergence, 3,* 51–70.

Stipp, H. (1999). Convergence now? *International Journal on Media Management, 1,* 10–13.

Telecommunications Act of 1996, Pub. L. 104-104, 110 Stat.56, amending Communications Act of 1934, 47 U.S.C.A. §151 *et seq.* (West 2001 & Supp. 2004).

Thielmann, B., & Dowling, M. (1999). Convergence and innovation strategy for service provision in emerging web-TV markets. *International Journal on Media Management, 1,* 4–9.

Tseng, K. F., & Litman, B. (1998). The impact of the Telecommunications Act of 1996 on the merger of RBOCs and MSOs: Case study: The merger of U.S. West and Continental Cablevision. *Journal of Media Economics, 11,* 47–64.

Weedon, A. (1996). The book trade and Internet publishing: A British perspective. *Convergence, 2,* 76–102.

Wheeler, M. (2002). Tuning into the new economy: The European Union's competition policy in a converging communications environment. *Convergence, 8,* 98–116.

Winseck, D. (1999). Back to the future: Telecommunications, online information services and convergence from 1840-1910. *Media History, 5*, 137–157.

Wirth, M. O. (2002). Introduction: Economics of the multichannel video program distribution industry. *Journal of Media Economics, 15*, 151–152.

Wirth, M. O. (2003a). Editorial—The future of convergence. *International Journal on Media Management, 5*, 4–6.

Wirth, M. O. (2003b, July 31). *New media strategy: Convergence-based driving forces & challenges*. Paper presented at the annual convention of the Association for Education in Journalism and Mass Communication, Kansas City, KS.

Wirtz, B. W. (1999). Convergence processes, value constellations and integration strategies in the multimedia business. *International Journal on Media Management, 1*, 14–22.

Wolfe, T. (2001). Digibabble, fairy dust, and the human anthill. In *Forbes ASAP* (Eds.), *Big issues: The examined life in the digital age* (pp. 204–224). New York: Wiley.

Yoffie, D. B. (Ed.). (1997a). *Competing in the age of digital convergence*. Boston: Harvard Business School Press.

Yoffie, D. B. (1997b). Introduction: Chess and competing in the age of digital convergence. In D. B. Yoffie (Ed.), *Competing in the age of digital convergence* (pp. 1–35). Boston: Harvard Business School Press.

# Issues in Media Globalization

Alfonso Sánchez-Tabernero
University of Navarra

## THE GLOBAL SOCIETY: ECONOMICS, POLITICS, CULTURE, AND THE MEDIA

How the ordinary person in the street views globalization is an enigma still to be unraveled. Opinion leaders and organized movements have not been slow to express their opinions either for or against and to call for policies to safeguard rights they feel are under threat. But it is harder to know how ordinary men and women regard this phenomenon, whether it is with hope, fear, or indifference.

Undoubtedly, one of the most significant developments this turn of the century has witnessed has been "the shortening of distances," the fact that now the public have other people, events, products, and cultural icons located or originating far away from them right on their doorstep. This process, in which the media play a crucial role, has had a major effect on how media firms are run.

### The Old System

Traditionally, the same media companies competed in the same marketplace over a long period of time; the "rules of play" were clear and did not undergo abrupt changes; senior management knew their rivals; they knew what resources they could count on, what the editorial project was; and they knew their staff. In short, they were confident about how to compete.

In these markets, family-owned companies had a leading role: newspaper and magazine companies were passed on from one generation to the next, and if the heirs possessed the same talent and determination as the founders, then media groups were formed. These would gradually grow and expand, venturing into the radio and television sector.

In this competitive paradigm it was rare for new blood to make an uninvited appearance because there were different types of barriers that prevented these sudden incursions. First, legislation prevented or, at least, seriously hindered the presence of foreign capital in the mass media. Second, the pace of technological change was slow so that the chance of new businesses suddenly appearing overnight was slight; also, the transport system, for people and products, was antiquated, so few advantages could be derived from a scale economy and the costs of coordinating activities spread out over a wide geographical area were excessive. Moreover, consumer behavior in markets widely different from other countries and regions was not easy to ascertain. Finally, the most prestigious companies had good commercial relationships with suppliers and distributors, making it difficult for other companies to attempt to compete with them.

Traditional media companies operated in markets with some sort of stability, controlled risk, and shared loyalty among the media, intermediaries, and the public. In this context, the absence of innovation, strategic errors, and the lack of professionalism were not always excessively penalized by citizens: frequently, there were some opportunities to rectify, because competitors were thin on the ground and they often committed the same mistakes and shared similar flaws.

However, in the closing decades of the 20th century the media landscape began to change. The barriers that held back competition weakened; the media started to find it increasingly difficult to hold on to leadership positions. Media markets became more versatile, and many news and entertainment media brands gained an international presence.

This change in the paradigm is defined as globalization. Space is no longer the determining factor for social, information, and commercial relationships and distance becomes relative. In marketing, the concept of globalization was introduced by Levitt (1983), who, in a controversial study, stated that companies should operate as if the world were a huge market without great regional and national differences. And, years earlier, McLuhan (1960, p. 20) had formulated his celebrated proposal of the "global village": "The electronic media of post-literate man have shrunk the world to a village or tribe where everything happens to everyone at the same time."

In the field of sociology, the term globalization was coined in the mid-1980s by Robertson to refer to "both the understanding of the world and the intensification of the awareness of the world as a whole" (1992, p. 8). Giddens (1994, p. 67-68) defined globalization along similar lines: "an intensification of social relationships, in the whole world, by which far-off places are linked together so that local events are shaped by something that has taken place at many kilometers away or viceversa."

## Three Key Facts

Globalization, then, has been the subject of theoretical analyses for a number of decades. Even in its infant stage, the causes and effects of globalization were analyzed from different academic perspectives. But the beginning of a new era of globalization was marked by three events that occurred at the end of the 1990s: in the political field, the fall of the Berlin Wall; in the economic one, the establishment of the World Trade Organization (WTO); and in the technological area, the development of the Internet.

From the political perspective, the fall of the communist regimes meant that the international community was no longer at dialectical loggerheads. With the breaking down of the antagonistic blocs there was a greater chance for cooperation. There is no doubt that the tragic events of September 11, 2001, and the subsequent wars in Afghanistan and Iraq introduced new elements of uncertainty and division. The confrontation between capitalist and communist countries seems to have been replaced by conflict between the Christian West and extremist Muslim groups; but this new threat to peace has features quite different from those of the so-called "cold war." It is a struggle between ideological blocs made up, not of states, but of groups, organized to a greater or lesser extent— in some cases with the explicit or implicit backing of some governments—seeking to destroy the economic and military hegemony of the United States and its allies.

However, and without wishing to downplay the seriousness of terrorist threats, more and more countries are regulated by free economy markets because "option B" has largely ceased to be an option: namely, the chance to choose the model based on state planning and control of the production and distribution of goods and services.

In the economic arena, the most significant boost for globalization was the General Agreement on Tariffs and Trade (GATT), originating in the WTO, signed in 1947. The fundamental principle of GATT was that there should be no discriminatory tariffs between countries. In contrast to GATT, which is regulated by rules and multilateral agreements, in the WTO, created in 1995, decisions are adopted by consensus.

Globalization has provoked criticism and popular movements opposed to what they see as the danger of the strong dominating the weak. However, in the WTO, which at the close of 2003 had a membership of 148 countries, each state, regardless of size or its level of wealth, has the right of veto.

Alongside the development of international trade, which has a common basis, the past few years have seen the emergence of certain "clubs of countries" that seek greater economic union and, in some cases, political union as well. These include NAFTA, MERCOSUR, ASEAN, and the European Union, now made up of 25 member states and with a population of 450 million.

From the technological point of view, the Internet, more than any other advance in industry, science, or communication, is the most potent symbol of globalization. The fact that any number of citizens from around the globe can have access to up-to-the-minute information simultaneously, regardless of whether they are far from or near to events, had never been possible until now.

It is true that the Internet's penetration in the poorest countries is less than 20%; but its ease of use, ubiquity, and low price mean that numbers will grow quickly, especially in urban areas. The Internet has become the world's shop window, where all the ideas, products, and commercial offers are analyzed, compared, measured, and judged by people from a wide range of countries and cultures.

Greater globalization in the political, economic, and technological fields has led to a new media map and a new way of competing in media markets. The most controversial issue has been the possible uniformity of content and the hegemony of North-American culture: Minc (1994, p. 55), for instance, states that "The United States will not own the world but will be of its copy."

The hypothesis stating that supply has become less and less diversified is now a well-rehearsed metaphor: the McDonaldization of culture and the media. Ritzer (1996) uses this expression to define the process whereby "the ruling principles of fast-food restaurants have come to dominate an ever greater number of aspects of American society, as in the rest of the world" (p. 15).

Standardized processes obviously have great economic advantages: You don't need to know how to cook to work at McDonald's; all that is required is to follow the established procedures. The French fries do not depend on the worker's subjective opinion; when they are ready a buzzer sounds and they are automatically taken out of the fryer (Orihuela, 1997).

Among other reasons for success, companies with highly standardized manufacturing and sales processes, such as McDonald's, can beat their rivals in areas such as scale economy, process control, elimination of the unexpected, and predictability of supply. The key issue, then, lies in determining to what extent and in which cases this competitive strategy is becoming a common trend in the media; or rather, which type of company is more likely to be successful: media companies that are run along the lines of the fast-food chains or those that resemble restaurants where you can eat à la carte.

## FACTORS OF MEDIA GLOBALIZATION

This section analyzes the main external elements that have contributed to the globalization of media companies: legislation reform, which weakens the strength of national boundaries to keep markets apart; market globalization, with technological innovations creating new products that are consumed around the world; and the development of giant advertising agencies and intermediaries.

### The Legal Framework

As previously mentioned, in the media industry the erosion of national boundaries has been a contributory factor to globalization. The opening up of markets is good for everyone—companies and citizens—as long as the principles of plurality and reciprocity are respected and the rights of the weakest and minorities are safeguarded. Plurality implies that nobody can abuse a position of dominance in the market. Reciprocity means that if a state opens its doors to investors from other countries, then these countries, in their turn, must also allow the entry of foreign companies. The protection of the rights of the weakest and minorities includes a wide range of duties such as making sure that less wealthy or smaller countries are not dominated by wealthier or larger ones or safeguarding the rights of ethnic minorities and children.

In practice, the globalization of the legal framework is at once the cause and consequence of market globalization. For instance, in the area of the concentration of media companies, there is a growing interdependence between countries. Indeed, how

European legislation has evolved can only be explained by the modifications made to the legal framework of the media in the United States.

In 1996 the Telecommunications Act was passed, the most thorough-going reform of American audiovisual policy since 1934. This law, along with other liberalizing measures, eliminated certain restrictions on the maximum number of radio stations that one company could own. Until then, the limit had once been fixed at seven radio stations on FM and seven on AM for the whole country. Under the new law there was only one restriction: A certain number of radio stations could be owned in the same market, between two and eight, depending on the size of the market. According to Veronis, Suhler, and Associates (1999), the seven largest radio companies in the United States, which earned 17% of total revenues in 1995, went on to obtain 40% in 1998.

In 1999, the Federal Communications Commission reduced the restrictions on the ownership of television stations that had been in force with very few modifications since the 1940s. The new regulations established that a company, under certain conditions, could own two television stations in the same metropolitan area; the limitations on the control of cable systems and vertical integration between the production and broadcasting of audiovisual programs were also relaxed.

The new legal framework for the media in the United States has permitted the growth of the giant American groups that, with a strong position in the most prosperous market in the world, have reinforced their international development strategies (Sánchez-Tabernero & Carvajal, 2002). The necessary response from the other side of the Atlantic has been to promote a similar relaxing of the rules and procedures regulating the concentration of media companies.

The priority of those who have taken part in the modification of the rules of play in the Old Continent has been to promote the growth of large European companies, able to stand up to the giant American corporations, while seeking situations of a dominant position in Europe. At the same time, the European Union's Competition Directorate is working jointly with the Department of Justice of the United States to analyze concentration operations that affect both sides of the Atlantic.

From the early years of the 21st century the regulations barring the entry of foreign capital into media companies in Latin America and many Asian countries have also been relaxed. This trend is the result of several factors: the need to attract capital for the development of industries with high costs in fixed assets, such as cable and satellite television; the internationalization of capital and companies, especially those quoted on the stock market; and the abandonment of self-sufficiency policies or state control of the economy.

With regard to the new legal framework, it can be seen there are certain common trends and points of consensus. However, there are also areas of disagreement on how to approach the internationalization and concentration of media companies, and each country has different ways of addressing them (Croteau & Hoynes, 2001):

1. Is it more effective to establish highly detailed rules or legislate only on general aspects and allow the commissions charged with watching over the proper functioning of the free market enough room for maneuver? Legal texts may not be flexible enough, but commissions pose other risks such as lack of independence.

2. What is the ideal number of competitors in a market? It might seem that pluralism is directly proportional to the number of existing media companies; but if there were thousands of automakers in the world, very few people would be car owners: if scale economies disappeared, the rise in prices would be exorbitant.

3. Should the authorities act when there is a risk of a position of dominance or when that risk is confirmed and continues over a period of time?

4. How can we determine who has effective control over a media company, especially when the capital is highly diversified and, for example, no one owns more than 5% of the shares?

5. How should we deal with concentration operations of the new media whose business model is still unfamiliar, such as the Internet?

6. What are the real bottlenecks in each media sector? Which bodies should be in charge of watching out for the possible distortion of competition exerted by the gatekeepers, especially in the audiovisual sector?

The range of responses to these questions mark the differences between the legal frameworks for media in each country. It is important for companies competing on a global stage to be aware of and take on board these different approaches.

## Competing in a Global Marketplace

Media companies aim to produce or transmit news and entertainment messages. They can carry out both tasks at the same time: construct the product or service and place it in the hands of the public. Depending on their place in the value chain, some are intermediary companies such as production companies and news agencies, whose clients are other media companies; still others have a direct relationship with the public, the owners of end-user media.

Both the intermediaries and the end-user products manage to survive in the market if they gain a sustained competitive advantage (Porter, 1985): They have to be able to offer something that has value for the public and which is not easily copied by their real or potential rivals. One type of competitive advantage stems from a team's know-how or skills: experience in producing content, proximity to the market, technological prowess, an innovative spirit, or the ability to be quick off the mark in spotting what their competitors are doing.

Another form of differentiation lies in collecting high-profile brands, associated with ideas or values that are attractive to a certain public: when there is a surfeit of choice consumers become confused and disconcerted, as can be seen in the frenetic use of the remote control in multichannel households. In a context of unlimited choice, the high-value brands stand out above their mass of rivals.

However, the competitive advantages based on either know-how or prestigious brand names have shown themselves to have become more vulnerable; companies and media that, until a few years ago, seemed unbeatable on an international scale—such as CNN, National Geographic, Disney, or MTV—have seen their positions threatened by similar offers that add new advantages. They are cheaper, closer to the public, take different editorial lines, or are more imaginative.

Media companies are increasingly aware of the weakness of any position of hegemony. They compete with many other rivals who are constantly thinking up new ways of getting news and entertainment to the public; this means that lack of initiative and dynamism can very quickly lead to stagnation and decline.

Small organizations with a low international profile are unable to compete in certain areas—the music sector, the film industry, or cable and satellite television—with the giant media groups. This is why growth strategies are the route they choose in their endeavor to avoid being pushed out by larger competitors.

There is no ideal strategy that can be made to fit any company. The priorities and growth model can only be decided on after an internal and external analysis has been conducted, and no one company finds itself in an identical position to another. This means that simply trying to imitate a competitor—apart from demonstrating that ideas are in short supply—does not usually bring lasting success.

Growth often leads to new markets. Companies tend to open up new territories for the distribution of their messages. Some technological innovations favor this trend, such as the Internet, the use of satellites for transmitting radio and television signals, and sending newspaper pages to print works located far from where the newspaper is edited. With the weakening of protectionist systems, cultural differences have become the main barrier to the internationalization of products (Martín Barbero, 2002). As will be seen, this has greater implications for news media than for the entertainment media.

## Global Brands and Global Advertising

The structure of the advertising market is another factor which has helped to stimulate the international growth of media companies. In this sector, some aspects have hardly been modified at all (De Mooij, 2002). The United States, Europe, and Japan still attract more than 80% of world advertising investment. If we look at how investment is distributed in the different sectors, a certain balance has been maintained between print media and audiovisual media notwithstanding a rise in the percentage of investment in television as opposed to a slow decline in daily press. Up to now, the new media have managed to attract a marginal part of investments; and periods of advertising growth—such as most of the 1990s—have been followed by fairly brief episodes of deep recession, such as the one caused by the financial bubble in 2000.

But an analysis of how advertising investment has evolved on a global scale also shows it has undergone a major change in the past few years: There is a greater concentration of the sector (McChesney, 1999). On the one hand, the media-buying companies have accumulated more purchasing power in each country; and, on the other hand, many national advertising companies have been bought up by giant multinational companies, with headquarters in New York, Chicago, London, Paris, and Tokyo.

This is the result of the growing internationalization of the advertisers. In numerous cases, they will only negotiate with those advertising groups that can purchase advertising space and time in the media of a varied range of countries. This has given rise to group networks made up of national agencies that have been partially or totally absorbed but still retain a certain amount of independence. Often, after the concentration operation has

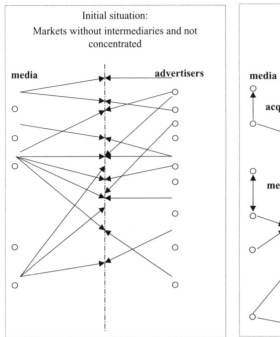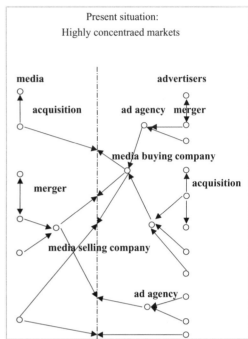

FIG. 21.1. Evolution of bargaining power of media and advertisers.

been completed, local managers continue to head the agency because of their knowledge of the market and their good commercial relations with the media and advertisers.

The rise in the number of intermediaries in the process of buying and selling advertising is related to the growing complexity of the media industry and the resulting audience fragmentation. The media buying companies have a good knowledge of the market and possess analytical tools that enable them to pinpoint the most profitable advertising investment decisions for advertisers.

An added advantage for the media buying companies is the huge discounts they can obtain from the media by negotiating large investment volumes. Media companies whose size has been an obstacle to obtaining favorable deals have followed similar concentration processes or have linked up with other companies to use joint advertising sales teams.

Hence, the old relationship between the local advertiser and local medium has given way to a much more complicated arrangement that not only involves advertisers and media but also includes advertising agencies, media buying companies, and media selling networks (Fig. 21.1).

Thus, the media and media companies with a more global reach can offer better solutions to advertisers and media buying companies seeking to launch their commercial messages over a wide range of countries. Although Nike, Coca-Cola, Benetton, Gillette, or Nokia can use smaller media for local or national advertising campaigns, they can only reach really lasting and wide-ranging agreements with media such as CNN, *The Economist, Elle,* or *The International Herald Tribune* because they are all global brand names.

## BARRIERS TO GLOBALIZATION

As will be seen, there are three factors that slow down or limit the scope of globalization processes: the pressure of organized groups, which influences the political action a country may take; citizens' interest in local issues; and the difficulty involved in running large multinational corporations.

### Ideology: Defending Cultural Identities

The globalization of the media and media companies can come up against obstacles of an ideological nature—these can take the form of political action, which may lead to legislation, and also practical difficulties, such as the peculiarities of each market.

The first problem has been typified in the thesis of "cultural imperialism," which also allows for different doctrinal variations. Schiller (1976) was one of the first to denounce the cultural domination of the United States, and in subsequent years insisted that "we are still not in the post-imperialist era" (1991, p. 13). Other authors, such as Mattelart (1994) or Boyd-Barret (1998), have used quantitative analyses to show that the strong dominate and endanger the cultural diversity of the weak.

In the media, analyses on globalization have often been linked to another similar phenomenon: concentration, which can pose a threat to news pluralism. Along these lines, Bagdikian's classic study (1990) has been followed by a number of monographs, with important contributions from Alger (1998) and McChesney (1999), who argue that there are fewer independent voices in the market.

As well as these critical approaches, other scholars have taken a more balanced and less dramatic viewpoint on the risk of cultural uniformity and have pointed out some of the advantages of globalization. It gives greater access to new content and more developed technologies, and it can contribute to greater professionalism and competence in markets (La Porte & Sádaba, 2002).

Paradoxically, the most global of all the media, the Internet, is also the most accessible and is better placed to promote diversity in viewpoints, ideas, and cultural contexts. Any citizen can be a content producer and send messages anywhere in the world at a low cost with access to a network.

On the other hand, globalization affects the traditional power struggle between the center and the perimeters that can arise in states and organizations. Hence, when a national government declares that its cultural identity is threatened by giant multinationals, regions and communities in the same country may also believe their own respective identities to be undermined by media companies whose headquarters are based in the capital city and whose news and entertainment products have a national slant.

These theoretical perspectives can influence government policies and are thus important for the repercussions they may have for companies. Globalization, then, rather than being perceived as a threat or a blessing, should be considered as a challenge that calls for ways of dealing with the problems and making the most of the opportunities it has to offer.

Most countries take a balanced approach with regard to the effects of globalization. The main risk identified in many cases is the United States' hegemony in the production of audiovisual content and the problems faced by small markets when exporting these products to other countries.

The revenue generated by North American companies in film distribution, video, and TV program sales and rentals in Europe is 10 times greater than its imports from Europe. The film industry throws up another interesting figure: In all the countries in Europe, the screen share of North American films is between 60% and 90% of all box-office takings.

Since 1989, the European Union has drawn up several plans designed to correct this commercial imbalance between Europe and the United States: the MEDIA program, to promote the production and distribution of European programs; the creation of a European television channel, an idea that led to the launching of the Euronews channel in 1993; the quota system, which stipulates that a minimum number of European-produced programs be broadcast on television channels; and a similar quota system for cinemas.

These policies have not been free from criticism. They have had little effect on the trade imbalance mentioned previously. There is no consensus on whether the content of European television channels and films shown in cinemas are what the public actually prefers or whether their preference is mediated by the defense policies of the European audiovisual industry.

However, there are other situations that also affect cultural identities in Europe. For instance, Ireland, Belgium, and Austria all have more powerful neighbors who share the same language: Great Britain, France, and Germany. The Irish, Belgian and Austrian governments, then, have encouraged the development of their own domestic companies so they can gain a dominant position in their respective local markets and the media companies from the neighboring countries do not get too big a slice of the market. Policymakers regard a high level of market concentration as preferable to foreign companies gaining too great an influence.

In contrast, in other countries that share the same language—such as Latin America—there are no strong trade imbalances. The greater capacity to produce and export telenovelas in Brazil, Mexico, and Venezuela is not perceived as a threat by their neighbors; thus there is no protectionist policy in this field.

In Asia, linguistic diversity means that governments do not need to take action to control media content. At the end of the 20th century, two problems have emerged: the dissemination of print and audiovisual content in English, aimed at the cultural and economic élites; and the launching of media broadcast in the local language such as Rupert Murdoch's Star TV. Until now, the possible discrepancies or differences in criteria between foreign companies and local governments have been solved by the use of pressure, threats, dialogue, and lobbying.

## The Market: Interest in Local Issues

The second great check on media globalization stems from the public's tastes and interests. As a rule, citizens prefer "the near" to "the far." They are more interested in local news than in what is happening in far-flung corners of the world; they prefer the viewpoint of somebody who shares their cultural register to a more distant outlook divorced from the reality of their community; and they place more value on fiction stories that unfold in easily recognizable scenarios, rather than in unfamiliar settings.

All these elements should constitute barriers to globalization. However, in many cases, European or Asian citizens will be more familiar with the streets of New York, Chicago, or Los Angeles—because they have watched so many films where the action takes place in these cities—than a city from their own country different from where they live. The songs of Elton John, Eminem, Madonna, or Gloria Estefan may be more familiar than those of singers native to their own country. And searching for information on the Internet, perhaps they will use Google and not a national search engine whose existence they are not even aware of.

In this regard, the media industry is very similar to other sectors. Coca-Cola is the most well-known cola drink in many countries in the world. The same occurs in the PC market with Microsoft, in the tobacco industry with Marlboro, and among fast-food chains with McDonald's.

These two phenomena appear to be contradictory. In many cases, citizens show a clear preference for what is closest; but, on other occasions, they are more familiar with and more likely to consume with greater alacrity the far as opposed to the near.

In truth, this ambivalence has always existed and is fundamentally based on two facts. First, in some sectors huge scale economies emerge, meaning that mass production brings with it advantages in quality and price. Second, in some areas the local perspective is more vital than in others. The daily newspaper must reflect the life of the community, told by someone with a good knowledge of the circumstances, history, and cultural environment. In contrast, what does it matter if a doll or a packet of sugar is made in Costa Rica or Taiwan, as long as the quality is good?

In this context, the key issue is to ascertain whether globalization and the subsequent convergence of income, available technology, and ways of life generates a more homogeneous behavior in consumers. In other words, is there a trend for consumers to be less interested in local issues or not?

Most international marketing courses take for granted the concept of the growing homogenization of consumer habits. Greater opportunities for interpersonal communication and the development of the media, brand names, and advertising campaigns on a global scale seem to support this thesis.

Levitt (1983) had already predicted that consumers would prefer standard products of high quality at low prices instead of more personalized and expensive products. The arguments were based on the premise that consumer behavior is rational in that consumers are logical in the way they look for what will give them the biggest advantage. But the rationalist conception of consumption does not consider other highly significant variables, such as cultural context or emotional impulses.

In fact, there is very little scientific evidence to support the thesis of the growing convergence in consumer behavior. As Inkeles (1998) suggests, convergence on a macro level—for example, rent per capita or the penetration of the Internet and the mobile phone—does not necessarily reflect convergence in consumer choice.

The problem in finding correlations between globalization and the convergence of consumer habits arises from the fact that in the choices citizens make there are factors that work in the other direction. On the one hand, we share a common cultural landscape, we buy certain universal brands, we choose certain media of a global scope, and we listen to commercial messages that reach us from a wide range of countries. But despite this, higher living standards and better education and the realization that the world has become more globalized mean that we tend to give greater importance to the local, to what differentiates us from a distant and unfamiliar group and to what binds us to our community.

Some empirical analyses confirm this. For example, De Mooij (2002), following Hofstede (2000), has shown that rent per capita is a good predictor for the purchase of computers and mobile phones; however, the consumption of print media and the use of the Internet are more mediated by the cultural variants of each country than by the purchasing power of their citizens.

The main application of these findings for media companies is that they can avoid making wrong assumptions based on macroeconomic analyses. There are already enough examples of advertising campaigns, fiction series, program planning, news products, marketing strategies, production processes, and personnel policies that have been successful in some countries and failures in others.

Management's task is to determine when rent per capita is a predictor for consumption and when cultural differences are decisive for the success of products in one market and their failure in another with supposedly—at least in the macroeconomic aspect—highly similar characteristics.

One of the most effective ways of avoiding falling into errors of perception when entering new markets is to develop joint venture policies. An international company's co-operation—bringing with it its scale economies, its knowledge of the business, and its scope—with a local partner—with its knowledge of the market and good trade relations with suppliers and distributors—combines the advantages of size with the benefits of proximity. Or, to put it another way, it is a good way to follow Levitt's old aphorism: to think global, act local.

## Size and Growth as Problems

If there are no internal problems—such as outdated products, debt burdens, uncommitted staff, or prestige loss—media companies decide on growth as a way of cashing in on opportunities and increasing their value in the market. However, growth strategies can also pose certain problems.

In the first place, growth may affect the company's level of specialization, which, in turn, can have an adverse impact on efficiency. Moreover, corporate culture may be undermined as result of internal communication difficulties, which can have negative repercussions for staff motivation. Bigger size can bring in its wake complacency, less experimentation, and less innovative zeal.

It is also true that some managers are capable of managing small or medium-sized companies, but are not so good at running large, highly diversified corporations: Different skills are needed for motivating a small editing team working in a local radio station than for mobilizing tens of thousands of employees of Time Warner, Disney, Bertelsmann, or News Corp.

Large companies usually turn into bureaucratic organizations generating high costs in co-ordination between departments and becoming slower to respond to changes around them. Some authors (Christensen, 1997) argue that big companies are expert in serving their clients, but this in itself then limits their ability to make the most of the potential offered by the new technologies.

Most concentration operations pose financial problems. Takeovers usually mean taking on more debt, either because they are funded by bank loans or because the acquired company already has large debt commitments.

Many multimedia groups have not achieved significant synergies. On paper—that is, during the decision process prior to a takeover or the launching of a new medium on the market—the integration of several media from different countries in one group seems to offer numerous advantages: advertising exchanges, joint use of production assets and news sources, block selling and purchasing, etc. However, these results are not always obtained, among other reasons, because any kind of coordination calls for managers from each country and business unit to be prepared to accept points of view different from their own and to surrender a certain amount of authority to their colleagues.

The fact of extending the geographical boundaries can be a problem in itself: Often, one of a media group's most valuable assets is its thorough knowledge of its own market, so when media groups venture into new countries they discover—with greater or lesser cost to their spreadsheets—the negative effects of being unfamiliar with the "rules of play."

A similar phenomenon occurs when companies specialized in one type of media acquire a different set of products. For example, the initial incursions into the Internet by traditional media groups have thrown up more failures than success stories.

The 21st century has seen most media groups in the world—of a size that gives them a strong competitive advantage—in crisis owing to one or other of the causes already mentioned: Time Warner (unrealistic expectations for the future of the Internet in general and AOL in particular), Disney (internal disputes, fall in efficiency and creativity), Vivendi (financial problems, overdiversification, takeovers at exorbitant prices), Bertelsmann (internal disputes, profitability losses in the music sector and the Internet), Kirch's Beta-Taurus (overoptimism regarding the development of pay television in Germany and high debts), and Telefónica Media (lack of leadership and managerial capacity, and takeovers at unjustifiable prices).

The route companies with successful growth strategies usually take is the following. At the initial stage, the promoters' drive gains them market entry and allows them to put up a challenge to larger rivals; the company then goes about obtaining competitive production tools and distribution systems that help to reinforce their position and raise profits. This is followed by a period of expansion into new markets or by a greater range of products offered in their own market. This is when the characteristic problems already mentioned can arise: growth crises. For some companies (such as Kirch's Beta-Taurus) this can spell their end; others, in contrast, manage to adapt and continue to progress until a new crisis occurs.

When media groups enter new markets they assume risks and take on new tasks for which the ability to adapt and learn are vital. In an increasingly globalized landscape, these qualities have acquired an essential value.

## GLOBAL STRATEGIES

Companies commit themselves to growth because they are sure they can overcome any disadvantage caused by an increase in size. Stagnation is regarded as the worse option because it dissatisfies both investors and employees, the former because no growth will mean a fall in the value of their shares, and the latter because their hopes of progress and professional development within the company will be limited.

In some media businesses, creativity and proximity to the public are more important creative advantages than size (Albarran & Dimmick, 1996). In contrast, others such as the publishing, audiovisual, and music industries require scale economies and international distribution networks.

## National and International Media Products

It is important for media companies to assess whether, depending on the nature of their activities, they should be close to the reader, listener, and viewer or whether, in contrast, standardized products will be well received in geographically dispersed markets. To gain a clearer picture, a first distinction can be made between news media and entertainment media.

Although fringe zones and hybrid products (such as television "infotainment") exist, when citizens consume media their basic aim is to find out what is happening in the world and to be entertained. From the product point of view, day-to-day news needs to be more personalized than entertainment: Even events of world interest, such as the war in Iraq and the fall of Saddam Hussein's regime, call for different analytical perspectives for an American, French, Russian, or Iraqi citizen; and within these countries, the ethnical, regional, or ideological differences mean there should be even more differentiated news coverage. In contrast, these citizens, when they watch an episode of *The Simpsons* or of *Friends*, or see a Disney film, or read a copy of *The Economist*, all share a similar interest.

From the beginnings of modern democracy, information on public issues has been perceived as a basic right of citizens. In 1787, Jefferson, in a letter, wrote one of the world's most quoted texts on the function of the press: "Seeing that the basis of our government is the opinion of the people, the primordial goal should be to uphold this right; and if I had to decide between a government without newspapers or newspapers without a government, I would not hesitate for a moment in preferring the latter" (School of Cooperative Individualism, 2004).

The interrelation between the daily press and its community makes it is one of the most indigenous of all media sectors. In many countries, such as the United States, local dailies predominate, although they are often owned by national chains. In Europe, the classic model consists of regional daily newspapers with differentiated local editions. In other countries, most daily newspapers are edited in the capital city; this fact is due to a variety of reasons: sometimes, because most of the population—and especially, the educated and ruling class—is concentrated in the capital, such as in most of Latin America; in other cases, such as Great Britain and Japan, because of their high density of population companies, located in the capital, can ensure delivery to subsidiary distribution points around the country.

As Picard and Brody (1997) have explained, whereas the generalist news press has hardly any foreign capital, the economic–financial newspapers are much more globalized. In this sector scale economies can be found in the area of newsgathering; moreover, the value of the most prestigious international brand names instills trust in their readers, who frequently use their financial newspaper to make decisions on spending and investments. Thus, Dow Jones is present in Europe and Asia with its respective editions of *The Wall Street Journal*, and the British group Pearson is leader of the economic press in Great Britain (*Financial Times*), France (*Les Echos*), Spain (*Expansión*), Portugal (*Diário Economico*), Argentina (*El Cronista*), and Chile (*Diario Financiero*).

The 24-hour news channels are on the way to becoming more local. This sector was dominated by CNN in the last two decades of the 20th century. The high cost of news production and distribution generated a quasi-natural worldwide monopoly. However, new technology has introduced greater efficiency quotas, which explains why competition in the American market and in the more developed countries with their own news channels has become greater. In this area, alliances and joint ventures are increasingly commonplace between giant multinational companies and local companies, dovetailing the advantages of proximity to viewers with the benefits of scale economies.

In the radio sector it is important to distinguish between predominately news-based radio stations and music stations. Radio news is basically local, with connections to the national network as needed. In contrast, the music radio station, more and more commonplace because of low production costs, usually offers the same type of content for the whole country. Regardless of what radio stations have to offer, most of their capital is not international because companies gain few advantages from amassing stations in different countries.

In contrast, the music industry is one of the sectors with the highest concentration and internationalization of capital. The giant companies in this sector are extraordinary marketing and distribution machines of their products. Major stars will only sign contracts with the biggest corporations, able to stage huge promotional campaigns and ensure their songs will be distributed around the world. This explains why, in the past few decades, five companies—Universal, Sony Music, BMG, Warner Music, and EMI (the latter two in the process of merging)—have been responsible for 80% of all world sales. The development of the Internet has given independent companies more opportunities because it brings down the value of physical distribution and permits a more personalized type of marketing (Hughes & Lang, 2003).

Like the rest of the entertainment sector, the publishing industry and the magazine sector are also prone to the internationalization of their capital because scale economies are highly important and some brands are exportable to other countries. It is significant that a German company, Bertelsmann, is the biggest publisher of books in English in the world. And certain magazines on women's issues, IT, science and nature, cars, and other thematic contents are distributed in dozens of countries.

Finally, the audiovisual sector offers many possibilities for internationalization. Film and television production companies, especially in the United States, broadcast their products on screens and channels across the world or launch themed channels in other countries; media companies acquire cable systems and satellite channels with international coverage (in this case the most outstanding example is the News Corp. Company); television channels buy up production companies from other countries, as has been the case in most European countries; and giant television companies—such as Mediaset or CLT-Ufa—have gained control of generalist channels in other markets.

## Scale Economies and Diversification of Risk

The pursuit of scale economies—which, as we have seen, is more important in some sectors than in others—is a determining factor for the growth strategies of media companies (Picard, 2002). As more units are sold the unitary cost of products is less because fixed costs are distributed among a higher volume of units. Thus, in businesses with very high running costs—such as the daily press, cable and satellite television systems management, and the music and publishing industries—the giants tend to control a large slice of the market.

Company growth encourages the generation of synergies; these are obtained when a corporation's structure acts as a multiplying factor for the effectiveness of its assets. In several departments—for example, content production, distribution, technology, or marketing—different media that belong to the same company join forces to get the most from their resources (Sánchez-Tabernero & Carvajal, 2002).

Newspapers save on costs by producing sections in centralized editorial units; they can also syndicate column writers and share foreign correspondents and services from news agencies. This is similar to what occurs in the radio and television industries. Radio stations and television companies join together to share production costs of news and programming.

Another advantage to size is the opportunity it gives for forging alliances and joint ventures with partners. Many cooperation agreements between companies of one or more countries follow this pattern. One company supplies its knowledge of the business (content, marketing plan, type of relations established between suppliers and distributors, etc.); the other company contributes with its knowledge of the market and its power to influence the government of the country, in cases where the prospective commercial activity requires previous authorization or administrative concessions.

This model has been followed, for instance, by the growth strategies of HBO and Canal + in pay television; Pearson and Dow Jones in economic news; the giant majors of Hollywood in film production and distribution; Bertelsmann and Hachette in book and magazine publishing; RTL in the radio industry; and America Online as a content supplier through the Internet. All of these companies, before undertaking international development, had reached a strong position in their respective domestic markets.

Large companies are better placed to have an influence on the political system. They can, for example, condition decisions referring to the labor framework, to taxes or legislation on free competition. But, above all, they have a lobbying function on all aspects directly related to the media industry and to their own corporate interests: the adjudication of radio and television channels, aid concessions, decisions taken by the antimonopoly commissions, measures regulating media content, and advertising guidelines.

Company growth is also a result of an attempt to diversify risk. Corporations that own media of a similar kind (for example, television channels, production companies, or magazines) located in the same geographical area accumulate enormous business risks. At the other extreme, as far as assumed risk is concerned, are the companies present in a wide range of markets, grouping together print, audiovisual, and interactive media, and whose business units are not in all cases heavily dependent on advertising.

Sony belongs to this latter growth model. Toward the end of the 1990s, with the economic crisis in Asia jeopardizing the future of many companies in the region, this

Japanese corporation balanced its falling sales in its domestic market by a strong presence in the film industry in the United States, which happened to be in a period of expansion.

Up to the end of the 20th century, the shockwaves caused by a regional economic crisis, an increase in the price of newsprint on the international markets, alterations to the legal framework of the audiovisual sector, or the inflation of the price of television programs could be felt even by the world's largest companies. However, today, the leading global media companies obtain an ever-smaller percentage of their revenue from their domestic markets because of their strategies of international expansion.

This means that the giant corporations have erected strong protection barriers against possible crises brought on by external factors: only a worldwide recession or a fall in the demand for news and entertainment could threaten the survival of well-run large media companies that are highly diversified in countries and in media.

## Seeking Out Opportunities and Attractive Markets

New markets offering investment opportunities are yet another stimulus for growth strategies. When a company finds that its own country no longer offers clear opportunities for higher earnings or profits—either because of intense competition or because legislation hampers growth—then it begins to look further afield.

A media group is ideally placed to introduce itself into another country under these circumstances: (a) the company has know-how that is not easily copied by the competition; (b) its unfamiliarity with the new market is not an obstacle if it forms alliances with local partners; (c) the target country is politically and socially stable and maintains high consumption levels; and (d) the entry barriers are weak, because the main operators either are uninnovative or show deficiencies in their management of products and services.

This set of circumstances is not a frequent occurrence because in the most attractive markets for investors—developed economies with legal frameworks that protect freedom of enterprise—competition is fierce. There are many companies seeking to innovate and incorporate technology, content, and production and distribution systems and marketing plans that have been successful in other countries.

Therefore, most markets are still at an early stage in their development or have high entry barriers. However, maturing markets represent an exception to this general rule. These are countries that do not offer as many incentives because of either economic underdevelopment or lack of political stability, but that can overcome this situation in a short time. Here, two crucial elements are present for foreign investors: vulnerable local companies and high profitability outlook.

Such was the case of the Spanish media firms when they invested heavily in Latin America at the end of the 1990s (Medina, 2001). The fall of the communist regimes in Central and Eastern Europe in the early 1990s also saw the entry of British, French, and German companies into these new markets.

Growth strategies are also useful for weakening the strength of rival companies. When companies stand still they run the risk of losing ground to those companies that have improved on sales and accumulated assets. There are many valuable competitive advantages to being a market leader. Companies and their commercial brands are more widely known; privileged trade relations can be maintained—for example, contracts of exclusivity—with suppliers and distributors; their role is fundamental for setting prices;

and, as mentioned previously, alliances can be forged with corporations from other countries.

In the media industry, newspaper companies were the first to use these defensive strategies: to maintain their leadership as the main suppliers of daily news, they began publishing free newspapers. They also acquired shares in the capital of other news suppliers: radio stations, television channels, and on-line services.

Television channels, too, seeking to retain their position as the leading entertainment supplier, have invested in the interactive content industry. In most industrialized countries, the average daily television consumption per person is between 3 and 4 hours, but the arrival of the Internet in the late 1990s has meant that television channels have found themselves having to compete for audience time, particularly among young audiences (Thompson, 1999). The major television companies, seeking to stay ahead as the leading entertainment content suppliers to households, have signed agreements with on-line content producers and software companies.

With the aim of maintaining their position as suppliers of basic services to households in different countries, a number of telephone companies and, to a lesser extent, water, gas, and electricity companies have diversified into the content industry, becoming cable television operators. These multinational corporations have access to huge economic resources, which enables them to make a swift entry into sectors requiring extremely costly fixed assets.

Media companies can grow by means of mergers, takeovers, and the launching of new media. They can also strengthen their position in the market by following a policy of joint ventures. Table 21.1 shows these growth processes. It also shows under what conditions they occur and what are their effects.

In practice, media companies grow and become more international because their senior executives seek to gain several advantages at the same time. For this reason, mergers, takeovers, and the launching of new media are usually based on both offensive and defensive reasons; they seek to maintain their market quotas while benefiting from investment opportunities; and they also stem from the wish to grow in size and the need to diversify business risk.

## Internationalization in Stages

Most media companies do not question whether they should widen their field of action or not. It is rather a question of when and how they should undertake expansion plans. In some circumstances it may be preferable to gain more presence in the same market and reinforce multimedia diversification; in other cases, international development may precede diversification. Either route leads to a global strategy: multimedia and international (Le Champion, 1991).

Several stages can be identified in the internationalization of media companies: strengthening of their competitive position in their own domestic market; their first venture abroad; consolidation of their international presence; and the configuration of transnational groups.

1. Initially, companies seek to start off from a strong position before venturing abroad. At this stage there are at least three different starting points: national multimedia

**TABLE 21.1**
Internal and External Processes of Growth

| System of Media Concentration and Diversification | General Conditions Required | Effects (Companies and Market) |
|---|---|---|
| Mergers | Crisis in the industry | Decrease in level of competition in the market |
| | | More favorable conditions for the companies |
| Acquisitions | Financial, industrial and commercial superiority (buyer) | Quick growth of the companies that invest large sums of money |
| | Need to improve competitive ability (seller) | Less "voices" in the market |
| Media expansion (new outlets) | Market changing, growing or with new possibilities (i.e., new media) | Slow growth of the company |
| | | More diversity in the market |
| Deals between companies | Maturity of the industry and considerable entry barriers | Dangerous competition in the market avoided |
| | | Power sharing |

companies; highly specialized companies, leaders in their sector; and hegemonic regional groups that launch or acquire media in the capital city and in other cities.

In any of the three cases, companies consolidate their position in their domestic market. Thus, they improve their efficiency, accumulate economic resources, increase their prestige, and begin to generate scale economies. All of this will contribute to their subsequent entry into foreign markets.

2.   The second stage sees the first international presence of companies. There is always some trigger that sparks off the idea of going farther afield when a company is doing well in the domestic market. The first steps are usually tentative and cautious, because owners and management feel uncertain about investing in a largely unfamiliar market.

When a company decides on international expansion, its first step must be the choice of country—normally one with greater geographical or cultural ties or where profit outlooks are favorable—and then the entry strategy must be designed. The product may be exported unmodified (*The Economist*); new content may be added (*The Wall Street Journal*) or a part of the programs may be changed (CNN or MTV); the brand name may be kept but the product may have to be adapted for the new market (such as women's magazines); or a new commercial name may be adopted (the financial newspapers of the Pearson group).

When a company embarks on a process of internationalization, the kind of relationship it has established with its foreign partners is another key element. Foreign partners may take on the role as the main operator, adopting the commercial name and receiving some help from the exporting company; they can agree to share management; or the foreign partner's role may simply be one of opening doors: facilitating contacts with economic agents and the most relevant politicians. It is normal at this phase for the local partners to take on more of the responsibilities.

3. A company's international presence is consolidated when the volume of its exports makes up at least 25% of its business. Management no longer regards incursion into foreign soil as a gamble for the future. The company begins to turn profits and finds itself in a position to initiate its own growth strategies. It now extends itself into other countries, normally no fewer than 10; retreat is no longer considered an option.

This process leads to a change in the organizational structure. Some activities are centralized, such as research and development, and perhaps part of production and marketing activities, whereas business units are given more independence. However, companies still retain their national aspect because their planning, financial, design, production, and sales centers remain in the home country.

4. In contrast, when transnational groups are formed, the domestic market becomes "just one more." The organizational structure undergoes further changes. The business units become totally independent and tend to depend on the national corporations that form part of the transnational company.

The subsidiary companies in each country are transformed into strategic partners whose skills and know-how help to give organizations worldwide competitive advantages. Companies act in the same way as flexible, coordinated integrated networks and seek to facilitate the exchange of expertise.

## THE INTEGRATION OF MEDIA GROUPS

Media groups can put their growth and internationalization strategies into practice through processes of horizontal and vertical integration. They can also develop other forms of integration at the same time. The following section attempts to describe and point out the advantages of each option.

### Vertical Integration

Vertical integration occurs when a corporation has control over the production and commercialization phases of a business, either because it does not wish to have to depend on suppliers and distributors or because it seeks to raise profits. The first of these aims is automatically achieved; if a company cultivates or makes the raw materials and then processes, packages, commercializes, and distributes them, the likelihood that an intermediary may have any detrimental effect on the products and services offered to the public is nonexistent (Markides & Williamson, 1994).

But, in practice, companies find it hard to achieve full vertical integration, because they do not have the experience, know-how, and financial capacity to control all the manufacturing and commercialization stages of their business. In some way or other they always depend on outside companies.

The second priority aim of vertical integration—to increase profits—is based on a logical approach. The total sum of the profit margins earned by all the middlemen present at the different phases of the process of production and commercialization could be obtained by just one company.

However, this argument does not take into account a key problem. Vertical integration implies a loss in specialization, it means a rise in fixed costs, and the way the company is organized becomes more complex. In the 1990s the importance of these negative factors was used as an argument by the most well-known of those who argued in favor of reengineering processes, such as Hammer (1996), to promote the farming out of functions and jobs.

How much an organization needs to be vertically integrated will mostly depend on how interested it is in controlling one part or the whole of the production and commercialization processes. In the print media, this control gives very limited advantages. Companies do not do well in their markets because they own the raw materials, or efficient printing presses, or because they own exclusive news sources or because they have better distribution channels.

In many markets, publishers do not compete for distribution. They share the same outlets, and they purchase the raw material from the same manufacturers. Their competitive edge is sought in the way the products are produced. Despite this, some leading publishing companies maintain structures that have a high level of vertical integration. Bertelsmann owns printing works, publishes books, newspapers, and magazines, and distributes its publications through "readers' clubs" in a number of countries. Hachette is a printer and publisher of newspapers and magazines, but it is also the main shareholder in the "Nouvelles Messaggeries de la Presse Parisienne," which distributes most of the newspapers published in Paris.

It has been observed that in the audiovisual industry integration levels are on the increase contrary to trends in the print media industry. In this sector, a top priority is to secure access to certain key products and to control distribution. Figure 21.2 shows the main stages of distribution and sales of audiovisual products.

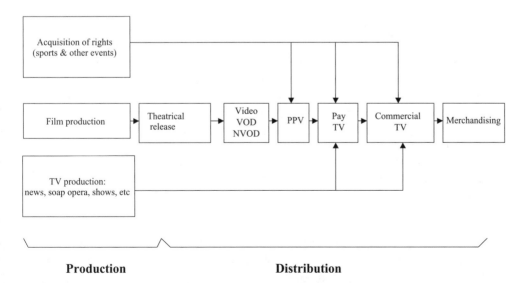

FIG. 21.2.   The audiovisual industry: distribution windows.

Vertical integration can take two forms: (a) upstream, inwhich makers of consumer electronics and distributors acquire television channels, and broadcasting stations enter the production sector, and (b) downstream, where producers acquire or launch television channels and take out shares in cable and satellite television operators.

In Europe, Latin America, and Japan, generalist television channels have dominated the audiovisual industry; therefore, these channels have taken part in processes of downstream vertical integration.

In contrast, in the United States, the leading production companies have held the dominant position. In the late 1990s, Fox and Warner both set up their own networks— Fox Broadcasting Corporation and The WB. Disney acquired the channel ABC, while Viacom, owner of Paramount, bought CBS, and smaller production companies created themed channels such as The National Geographic Channel. These companies were able to dominate the audiovisual sector and undergo the processes of upstream vertical integration because their strength lay in their film and television products, which reach worldwide audiences.

Full vertical integration is achieved when the company is present right along the whole chain, from the production of the instruments—television sets, transmitters, aerials, etc.—down to the sale and rental of films in video shops. Control of some of these phases is not particularly advantageous for companies, for instance, the manufacture of television sets; in contrast, the companies that have access to successful programs and have a dominant position in distribution—terrestrial, cable, or satellite—can raise an almost impenetrable entry barrier for rival companies.

Finally, the degree of integration between production companies and broadcasters depends on legislation: Some governments have stipulated that channels must devote a certain percentage of broadcasting time to independent production companies and have set up mechanisms to promote the vertical disintegration of public and private corporations.

## Horizontal Integration

In one sense, the advantages and disadvantages of horizontal integration are exactly the opposite of vertical integration. It encourages specialization and permits the generation of synergies and scale economies, but it does not give simultaneous control of supply and distribution (Very, 1993).

Horizontally integrated media companies own the same type of media in one or several markets: radio stations, television channels, free publications, etc. These growth strategies enable corporations to introduce a product or service that has already been efficiently managed in its home base into new markets.

Some factors favor horizontal integration processes:

1. Experienced management; additional specific training is not required for their new functions and this means that interruptions to work routines are kept to a minimum.
2. Problems involved in getting to know and penetrating a new market can be solved by linking with local partners.

3. If the new media incorporated into the group are not located in distant markets, they can benefit from the commercial relations the corporation has established with suppliers and advertisers.
4. Bigger size and specialization generate savings in the acquisition of raw material (newsprint) and elaborated products (programs, news services, etc.).
5. With the introduction of a new media product, organizational and accounting systems can be set up that contribute to developing the product. For example, they facilitate access to the general services of the company—databases, reporting services, study reports, specialist advice on design, programming or marketing, etc.—at reduced prices.

But companies that base their growth only on processes of horizontal integration can face certain problems. There is no diversification of risk, because all their activity is concentrated in one type of business; there is no overall control of the different phases in the commercial process, and thus they are dependent on their suppliers or distributors; and their ability to grow is restricted to grouping more media of the same characteristics in a greater number of markets.

Horizontal integration strategies are to be found more in the print media sector, the music industry, and cable television (Parsons, 2003). As mentioned previously, generalist television companies have preferred to have simultaneous control over production and the broadcasting of audiovisual contents.

From the mid-20th century onward, there has been constant debate on the possible dominant position of newspaper groups that followed a model of horizontal integration. Occasionally, these controversies have given rise to anticoncentration laws, forcing newspaper owners to abandon their wish of grouping together different titles of newspapers and magazines.

In most cases, horizontal integration has been accompanied by other growth models. Companies buy up media of a similar nature and penetrate other countries while diversifying into new businesses and buying up shares in companies that supply or distribute their products. This gives rise to groups that are integrated vertically and horizontally and have also achieved a high degree of multimedia diversification.

These multidirectional investment policies give rise to media groups with highly complex structures that seek to integrate the advantages of each growth model. The strategies followed by large companies have at least two points in common. After having reached a sufficient size, they embark on their multimedia diversification, and sooner or later decide on international expansion.

## OWNERSHIP OF MEDIA COMPANIES

One last aspect that has had an important role to play in the globalization of the media market is how company ownership has evolved. Until the end of the 20th century, local proprietors ran businesses on a local scale that targeted the public more or less close to home. As we have already seen, a large number of media companies have now gone global, and media groups' capital is also becoming more and more internationalized.

## From Family-Owned Companies to Public Corporations

It was from the mid 19th century that the media began to form part of profit-making enterprises. Until then, the journals printed were usually linked to the political and literary world. Around 1850, the conjunction of a number of inventions and innovations would permit the development of the popular press: the appearance of the first news agencies, the laying down of the railway lines, improvement in printing systems, and the wider use of the telegraph.

At the start and until the late 20th century, the media were run by families who sought to serve the public, influence their communities; and make a certain amount of profit on their investments. Initially, they launched and bought up daily newspapers and magazines, and in the first 30 years of the 1900s radio stations were launched and the first films were made. Family ownership brought a number of advantages: continuity of the project, long-term direction, a high level of managerial commitment, a strong corporate culture, and frequently a strong desire to serve employees and the community.

These qualities helped many companies survive and prosper, within and outside the media environment. For example, in the early years of this century, 20% of Fortune 500 companies were family run; more than half of the employees in the private sector of the world economy work for family-run businesses; and some of the most well-known brand names in a wide range of commercial sectors—such as Ford, BMW, Mars, Henkel, Wal-Mart, Benetton, Estée Lauder, or Chanel—are still family run.

The great strength of these companies is their owners' determination to protect the future of their businesses. At the other extreme are those companies—an ever-increasing number—whose senior executives management are lacking in long-term commitment.

From the early 1990s certain business management experts began to speak about the risk of placing too much emphasis on immediate results. Reichheld (1996) pointed out that in the United States half of a company's clients change every 5 years, half of the employees change every 4 years, and half of the owners changes every year. With such low levels of staying power—especially of owners—it is hard to establish a corporate culture, to have shared values and working methods, or to set down long-term goals.

In media groups, families have continued to hold a greater share of capital than in many other sectors of the economy. This fact is explained by the particular nature of the products and services that these companies produce and commercialize. They are based on the narration of real events and stories and hence have an influence on society, on the mental outlook of peoples, and on citizens' day-to-day decisions.

Families who have set up or inherited newspapers, radio stations, or television channels are reluctant to sell their media to companies or investors that give priority to corporate profits over public service. The owners' emotional ties with the media mean that certain media firms are managed by the fifth or sixth generation of owners from the same family.

In some countries, most of the media are family-owned. This is the case, for example, in Latin America, where some names have dominated the media sector for over a century: Azcárraga (Mexico), Mariño or Mesquita (Brazil), Cisneros (Venezuela), Miró Quesada (Peru), and Edwards (Chile). The chief reasons why these families still retain their positions of privilege are the legal barriers that hinder the entry of foreign capital and the social, political, and economic structure of these countries.

To a lesser extent in Europe and Asia, there are also some media firms that are still family run. Indeed, some of the biggest media companies in the world are family owned or, at least, the founders' heirs still retain a certain influence; such is the case for Disney, News Corporation (Murdoch), Bertelsmann (Mohn), and Mediaset (Berlusconi).

However, there are circumstances when capital passes from family ownership and is diversified in the hands of many private investors:

1. A customary procedure for raising more capital for debt repayments or to fund expansion plans is to float the company on the stock exchange or to sell off part of the capital to other shareholders.
2. Capital becomes diluted with the progressive handing down of the company from parents to offspring and successive generations. This can be the trigger for internal disputes over the right strategy or who is in control of the company. One way of solving these conflicts is to bring in new owners with the founding family taking a back seat in the running of the business.
3. When family-owned companies grow and begin to turn in high profits, owners see the chance to sell at a highly advantageous price: hence, huge economic success often spells the end of the family's ownership of the company.
4. The fact that media companies come under new ownership may also be the result of seeking greater professionalism in management, more transparency and credibility, and shareholders with new ideas.

## Internationalization of Ownership

With many media companies going public and the dispersion of their capital among many small shareholders, the legal framework drawn up for the sector has become, to some degree, obsolete. Measures referring to "companies with national capital" or the broadcasting of radio and television programs of "national" origin no longer make much sense (Inkeles, 1998; La Porte & Sádaba, 2002).

It is also becoming increasingly difficult to identify a company's nationality. One of the most significant cases illustrative of this problem involved the French company Vivendi, which at the close of 2000 bought up Universal, one of the main Hollywood film production companies in the world and world leader in the music industry. At the time, Vivendi was the leading pay television operator in Europe and still in a phase of rapid growth. For some analysts, this takeover, which ended up 3 years later with Universal being sold again to relieve Vivendi of some of its debts, appeared to represent the first great victory of Europe over North America in the entertainment industry. Other authors, in contrast, argued that the opposite was true (Musso, 2000): 54% of Vivendi's capital was in foreign hands, especially in North American and British pension funds, meaning that the most probable effect of the operation was that the American production company would find it easier to distribute its products on European pay television channels.

It is impossible to avoid controversy on the interpretation of the effects of the internationalization of ownership. First, it must be clarified whether business control is equivalent to editorial control. In most legal systems, the owner of a company has almost total decisionmaking power over content by naming management, determining the competitive strategy, choosing the business plan, and approving staff recruitment.

Managers' room for maneuver in setting out the editorial line depends on the internal rules of each company, institutional culture, the degree of the owner's involvement in content, newsroom statutes, behavior codes, and management negotiating capacity.

In many countries, legislation is changing to deal with the fragmentation and internationalization of companies' capital. Up to a few years ago, the total or partial control of a company depended on the percentage of shares owned by a physical or legal entity. Today, control is associated with the capacity to exert a "decisive influence" on company management. A person controls a company, even though his/her share of the capital is minimal, if in practice, s/he is responsible for appointing managers, has veto rights, decides on investment plans, or takes part in key decisionmaking for the company.

From an economic point of view, the way the structure of the ownership of media companies has evolved holds many advantages. First, when control passes from the family to the stock market, shareholders have a quicker return on their investments because there is absolute liquidity of capital.

Going public also brings the company into the public gaze, which reinforces the corporate image and confers prestige and credibility. Even though these intangible elements do not appear on the company's balance sheets, they are conditioning factors for the type of trade relations that companies establish with suppliers, financial entities, and the public.

Moreover, to compete on a global stage, it is reasonable that ownership is not just concentrated in a small group of people who share similar experiences and cultural traditions. Opening up capital to other investors paves the way for new ideas and perspectives.

Another advantage to going public is that the market is quick to punish unprofessional management: An investor who considers that a company is not making the most of opportunities or is not making proper use of its assets can make a public offer for shares and take over control. This helps to stop owners from becoming inefficient, which can cause the stagnation or bankruptcy of a media group.

Finally, the need for transparency can also aid in internal management. The need to present economic results on a habitual basis and the fact that companies on the stock exchange are under the permanent scrutiny of analysts and investors means that there is a healthy pressure placed on management; they cannot make arbitrary or hasty decisions or sign agreements that cannot be explained to the public.

The challenge facing media companies with a dispersed and internationalized capital is to capitalize on the advantages referred to—financial strength, credibility, a wide range of approaches, transparency, and professionalism—while at the same time avoiding the main risk: overemphasis on the short term.

All of management's decisions have repercussions for the price of the shares, and some owners invest with the aim of obtaining short-term gains. This fact can mean they bring pressure to bear on companies for immediate benefits rather than seeking prestige and long-term results.

To avoid this problem, media groups, regardless of their nationality and the number of their shareholders, need a core of owners committed to the future of the business, interested in the quality of the products, and willing to make investments which do not give immediate returns. With this approach, a company can operate on a sounder basis—creating and protecting valuable brands and talented and highly motivated teams—while at the same time reaching its economic goals.

## CONCLUSIONS AND FURTHER RESEARCH

Political, economic, and cultural globalization is modifying the way media companies compete: there is more competition than ever before; huge conglomerations have emerged; in some cases, news and entertainment products and services cover the globe; and the major companies' capital is now international.

The first of these effects—more competitors in each market—is the result of a progressively shrinking world. The breaking down of national barriers, the potential of new technologies, and the existence of a collective idiom shared by a great range of countries means that far-off and unfamiliar markets offer the right conditions for launching and acquiring new media.

This fact is also directly linked to the growth of giant media groups; a global market has replaced their home countries as their "natural environment." When companies become successful, their strategic decisions all have one factor in common: expansion into foreign markets to widen their scope for action.

In some sectors, such as the film and music industries and on-line services, television production and certain models of themed magazines have led to an increase in the number of products that cross over the boundaries of their respective countries. In contrast, in other areas, such as the daily press or radio news, the local perspective seems to maintain its leading role.

If companies are to compete on the global stage, they need more capital and a wider range of cultural perspectives. This means selling off company shares to a more widely dispersed and international ownership. When this occurs and the most dynamic companies have reached a certain size, they will almost certainly go public.

These facts are accompanied by certain questions that will only be answered when analytical studies produce empirical evidence. These questions, currently the subject of so much debate, address the issue of what management model should be used for media companies and which policies should be pursued by governments.

With regard to management, two fundamental issues require further research. First, it seems necessary to analyze the circumstances under which the advantages of globalization—scale economies, synergies, and risk diversification—may cancel out the problems caused by gigantism such as the coordination costs between the different business units. Second, it is important to discover mechanisms that can counteract the short-term view typical of companies quoted on the stock market. This problem can affect those values that are often the hallmarks of the most prestigious media, such as the emphasis on quality or commitment to the community.

From the policymakers' perspective, the first area to be analyzed is what risk is there of the weaker countries and regions, with smaller populations or a less developed economy, losing their cultural identity faced with the onslaught of the large corporations; fears of possible cultural colonialism must be measured against data that confirm or contradict this hypothesis. A second aspect worthy of particular attention is the way of measuring who exerts effective control over a company with thousands of small shareholders. If this issue is not properly addressed, anticoncentration laws will prove to be ineffective.

Globalization, then, poses problems and provides opportunities as much for media groups as for citizens; both—the latter, through their political representatives—should meet this new phenomenon in a spirit of innovation and creativity, finding ways for companies to grow and develop in harmony with the public interest.

## REFERENCES

Albarran, A., & Dimmick, J. (1996). Concentration and economies of multiformity in the communication industries. *Journal of Media Economics, 9*(4), 410–450.

Alger, D. (1998). *Megamedia: How giant corporations dominate mass media, distort competition and endanger democracy.* Lanham, MD: Littlefield.

Bagdikian, B. (1990). *The media monopoly* (3rd ed.) Boston: Bacon Press.

Boyd-Barret, O. (1998). Media imperialism reformulated. In D. K. Thussu (Ed.), *Electronic empires: Global media and local resistance* (pp. 157–176). London: Arnold.

Christensen, C. (1997). *The innovator's dilemma. When new technologies cause great firms to fail.* Boston: HBS Press.

Croteau, D., & Hoynes, W. (2001). *The business of media: Corporate media and the public interest.* Thousand Oaks, CA: Pine Forge Press.

De Mooij, M. (2002). Convergencia y divergencia en el comportamiento de los consumidores.*Comunicación y Sociedad, 15*(1), 43–69.

Giddens, A. (1994). *Consecuencias de la modernidad* (p. 117). Madrid: Alianza.

Hammer, M. (1996). *Beyond reengineering.* New York: HarperCollins.

Hofstede, G. (2000). *Culture's consequences* (2nd ed.). Thousand Oaks, CA: Sage.

Hughes, J., & Lang, K. R. (2003). If I had a song: The culture of digital community networks and its impact on the music industry. *International Journal on Media Management, 5*(3), 180–190.

Inkeles, A. (1998). *One world emerging? Convergence and divergence in industrial societies.* Boulder, CO: Westview.

Jefferson, Thomas (1787). The Jefferson discussion group of Orlando Florida. Retrieved September 30, 2004, from http://jdg.thejeffersonproject.org/topics/2001-07.html

La Porte, T., & Sádaba, T. (2002). Globalización y diversidad cultural en la política audiovisual europea. *Comunicación y Sociedad, 15*, 101–127.

Le Champion, R. (1991). Une tipologie des strategies d'enterprise dans le secteur de la communication. *Mediaspouvuoirs, 21*(1), 37–51.

Levitt, T. (May–June 1983). The globalization of markets. *Harvard Business Review*, 92–102.

Markides, C. C., & Williamson, P. J. (1994). Related diversification, core competences and corporate performance. *Strategic Management Journal, 15*, 149–165.

Martín Barbero, J. (2002). Identities: Traditions and new communities. *Media, Culture & Society, 24*, 621–641.

Mattelart, A. (1994). *Mapping world communication: war, progress, culture.* Minneapolis: University of Minnesota Press.

McChesney, R. (1999). *Rich media, poor democracy.* Urbana-Chicago, IL: University of Illinois Press.

McLuhan, M. (1960). *Explorations in communication.* London: Bacon Press.

Medina, M. (2001). Algunas claves de la expansión de los grupos de comunicación españoles en Latinoamérica. *Comunicación y Sociedad, 14*(2), 71–99.

Minc, A. (1994). *La nueva edad media. El gran vacío ideológico* (p. 12). Madrid: Temas de hoy.

Musso, P. (2000, December). Vivendi-Universal: l'Amerique gagnante. *Le Monde*, p. 21.

Orihuela, J. L. (1997). Bajo el síndrome de la McDonalización: las Facultades de Comunicación en la era global. *Reflexiones Académicas, 9*, 153–168.

Parsons, P. R. (2003). Horizontal integration in the cable television industry. *Journal of Media Economics, 16*(1), 23–40.

Picard, R. G. (2002). *The economics and financing of media companies.* New York: Fordham University Press.

Picard, R. G., & Brody, J. (1997). *The newspaper publishing industry.* Boston: Allyn & Bacon.

Porter, M. (1985). *Competitive strategy.* New York: The Free Press.

Reichheld, R. (1996). *The loyalty effect.* Boston: HBS Press.

Ritzer, G. (1996). *The MacDonalization of society. An investigation into the changing character of contemporary social life* (3rd ed., p. 16). Thousand Oaks, CA: Pine Forge Press.

Robertson, R. (1992). *Globalization, social theory and global culture* (p. 8). London: Sage.

Sánchez-Tabernero, A., & Carvajal, M. (2002). *Media concentration in the European market. new trends and challenges.* Pamplona, Spain: Media Market Monographs.

Schiller, H. (1976). *Communication and cultural domination.* White Plains, NY: International Arts & Sciencies Press.

Schiller, H. (1991). Not yet the post-imperialist era. *Critical Studies in Mass Communication, 8,* 13–28.

School of Cooperative Individualism (2004). Retrieved March 12, 2004, from http://www.cooperativeindividualism.org/jefferson_c_02.html

Thompson, L. (1999). *Convergence in television and the Internet* (2nd ed.). London: Informa Media.

Veronis, Suhler & Associates (1999). *Communications industry report,* New York: Author.

Very, P. (1993). Success in diversification: Building on core competence. *Long Range Planning, 26,* 80–92.

# 22

# Issues in Political Economy

Phil Graham

University of Waterloo and University of Queensland

## INTRODUCTION AND OVERVIEW

The broad range of studies that fall under the heading of "political economy of communication" has been growing and diversifying these past 50 years or so in much the same way as political economy did from the mid-19th century onward. Some researchers focus on mass media industry structures, emphasizing the effects of media ownership on political systems. For others, it is a study of various moments in what might be called the "commodity" cycle in mass media: production, distribution, exchange, and consumption. For most, it is only one or two of these moments, with production processes being largely ignored. Some approaches emphasize content, others technology. Some emphasize various aspects of social structure, others individual agency.

Generally speaking, political economy of communication is undertaken within a critical research framework and is therefore overtly value-laden. That is to be expected: Political economy first emerged as a branch of moral philosophy and therefore tends to foreground specific ethical orientations. In particular, most political economic studies of communication are concerned with addressing social imbalances of power that flow from the structure and operation of communication systems. In this chapter, I proceed by first providing key definitions and a review of contemporary literature. I then trace the historical development of political economy of communication as a recognizable field of scholarship, identifying the various areas of research that comprise this relatively young field. Finally, I suggest directions for the future development of the field in a new media environment.

## Key Definitions

I define *political economy* here as the study of how values of all kinds are produced, distributed, exchanged, and consumed (the economic); how power is produced, distributed, and exercised (the political); and how these aspects of the social world are related at any given place and time. Studies in *political economy of communication* are therefore concerned with understanding how communication and communication technologies figure in political economic relations. Although such research necessarily includes research into "the production and dissemination of information and culture" within given social systems (Bettig & Hall, 2003, p. 10), it is essential for any such research to understand how these processes figure in economic and political forms at particular times and places. Research within this field must therefore address the relationships between people, their systems of mediation, and how these figure in the development, maintenance, and change of social and political structures.

Although I understand *communication* as the movement of meanings between people, and *communications* (or media technologies) as the means by which those meanings are moved, for the purposes of this chapter I conflate these two definitions in the term *communication*. I am aware that by collapsing the "content" and "technologies" of communication I risk collapsing two very distinct perspectives on how we make, move, and exchange meanings. But that is not a matter of mere convenience, especially given the thoroughly technologized communication environments in which many of us now live.

The perspective such an approach implies can be understood in terms of Roger Silverstone's (1999) "mediation" perspective. It is an approach that has the virtues of not separating meaning from its means of movement from the contexts in which it is produced and through which it is disseminated. The only terminology I use to separate means of communication from communication technologies is *new media*. The term has a specifically technological sense here and denotes the emergence and diffusion of new communication technologies.

## A REVIEW OF CONTEMPORARY RESEARCH

A review of contemporary literature in political economy of communication reveals five main research themes: *ownership, monopoly, audiences, access,* and *democracy*. Dividing the literature into these five thematic areas is a convenience to some extent, but it also identifies emergent and potential fragmentations in the field along specific lines of inquiry. Issues of *ownership* tend to focus on corporate agendas, both in terms of the economic power corporations wield through media ownership, and in terms of the political power that concentrated media ownership confers on corporations and the people who control them. Issues of *monopoly* tend to focus on the role of media corporations in shaping the general character of societies operating in a "monopoly capitalism" framework (Smythe, 1981). Issues surrounding *audiences* tend to focus on the impact of media practices upon people & perceptions; how audiences shape media practices; how media practices function in the commodification of knowledge, epistemology, and communication more generally; and how the work of audiences is appropriated and sold by media corporations.

Issues around the theme of *democracy* tend to focus on how distorted information undermines basic political freedoms, and how new media provide (or do not provide) potential for a more direct and participative form of democracy. Issues of *access* are most clearly marked in the contemporary context by the term "digital divide," denoting class divisions according to levels of access to communication technologies, and by a comparison of the "information rich" and "information poor," denoting a lack of access to media content and content markets.

Most of the literature has developed in the context of mass media environments, and in political economic contexts that were much more clearly capitalistic than current formations, which might be characterized as being more "corporatist" than capitalist (Saul, 1997; Schiller, 1999). There is much to suggest that new approaches are necessary for understanding current changes in the new media environment. The emergence and proliferation of new digital media has not only blurred the relationship between "audiences," "producers," and "distributors" of media content, it has also changed the economic model upon which the development and influence of mass media corporations was based. A key marker in this respect is the fact that in 2004, for the first time in mass media history, consumers spent more on media than did advertisers (Mandese, 2004). The new media environment, combined with what is arguably a qualitatively new, globalized, political economic environment, has therefore brought quite a deal of pressure to bear upon studies in political economy of communication.

## CONTEMPORARY RESEARCH THEMES

### Ownership

A concern with patterns of ownership is predominant in contemporary literature. This is understandable in a recently globalized mass media environment dominated by seven corporations: Viacom, General Electric, Disney, Time Warner, Vivendi Universal, Bertelsmann, and News Corp (Free Press, 2004). The intense concentrations of ownership in recent years have been associated with the rise of neoliberal globalization, a macropolitical trend since the late 1970s. For McChesney, neoliberalism

> refers to the policies and processes whereby a relative handful of private interests are permitted to control as much as possible of social life in order to maximize their personal profit. Associated initially with Reagan and Thatcher, neoliberalism has for the past two decades been the dominant global political economic trend adopted by political parties of the center, much of the traditional left, and the right. These parties and the policies they enact represent the immediate interests of extremely wealthy investors and less than one thousand large corporations. (McChesney, 1999b, p. 40)

The role of the neoliberal agenda in media ownership, according to Dan Schiller (1999), has been to shift media ownership away from public institutions such as "government agencies and educational institutions" to "an autonomous sphere of corporate network applications that was essentially free of regulatory oversight and was parasitic on the existing telecommunications network" (Schiller, 1996, pp. 3–5). Neoliberalism entails the ostensive erosion of regulatory regimes, leaving the ownership and control of media networks to the corporate (or private) sector. But upon closer scrutiny, this is not actually achieved through less regulation. Rather, says Schiller, "a liberalized networking sector required fiendishly complex operational details and consumed an entire generation's regulatory attention" (1999, p. 6). In other words, what first appeared as a push to deregulate media ownership was in fact a proliferation of new regulations oriented toward transferring ownership of media networks from public to corporate interests.

Neoliberal "deregulation" has allowed corporate ownership of communication networks to extends to every sector of the developed world, including "schools, universities, museums, professional societies, [and] government agencies" (Schiller, 1999, p. 205). At the same time, globalized neoliberalism, facilitated by new digital media, has produced a qualitative change in the character of political economy: there has emerged "a change in the sweep of corporate rule," with the result that digital capitalism is now "free to physically transcend territorial boundaries and, more important, to take economic advantage of the sudden absence of geopolitical constraints on its development" (p. 205). The emergent patterns of ownership are typically seen as a function of "monopoly capitalism" that defined most of the twentieth century (McChesney & Foster, 2003; Smythe, 1981).

## Monopoly Capitalism and Media Ownership

Although it is more technically correct to define global media ownership patterns as an oligopoly (a few sellers) rather than a monopoly (a single seller), the term *media monopoly* is most often used in political economy of communication to describe the role of mass media in supporting the kinds of political economic environments that developed during the 20th century (Bagdikian, 1997; McChesney & Foster, 2003; Smythe, 1981):

> For a long time now it has been widely understood within economics that under the capitalism of giant firms, corporations no longer compete primarily through price competition. They engage instead in what economists call "monopolistic competition." This consists chiefly of attempts to create monopoly positions for a particular brand, making it possible for corporations to charge more for the branded product while also expanding their market share. (McChesney & Foster, 2003)

This particular conception of monopoly capitalism is a communication-oriented derivative of Lenin's theory of imperialism, and that originates with Dallas Smythe (1981, p. 24). Smythe defines monopoly capitalism as the form of global political economy in which a "relatively few giant monopoly corporations" engage in the "deliberate collusive avoidance of price competition" (1981, p. 11). Mass media practices are essential to the development and maintenance of mass societies and monopoly capitalism. The most obvious example in this respect is advertising because it is designed to generate the "necessity for consumers to buy new products" based on stylistic obsolescence through the "calculated manipulation of public tastes" (Smythe, 1981, p. 11).

McChesney (1999a) argues that any inquiry into how media ownership in monopoly capitalism inhibits the capacity of citizens to attain a democratic genuinely egalitarian participatory democracy must include studies of how a system-wide propaganda that favors the system itself is maintained. McChesney argues that Herman and Chomsky's (1988) propaganda model is being essential to understanding how this happens. They provide a framework of five filters for understanding how media systems—especially news systems—operate to produce opinions that favor the political economic status quo. Researchers such as Klaehn (2002), however, challenge any unproblematic reading of the relationship between corporate media ownership and public consciousness. The main criticism Klaehn raises is that the propaganda model presupposes audience effects without offering any way to study them (2002, p. 153). He questions whether the propaganda model can actually help us know whether and how media organizations in monopoly capitalism can exercise a successful hegemony because it "does not theorize audience effects, it presumes that news content is framed so as to (re)produce 'privileged' interpretations of the news which are ideologically serviceable to corporate and state monied interests" (p. 153).

Herman's reply to such criticisms is that:

> The propaganda model describes a decentralized and non-conspiratorial market system of control and processing, although at times the government or one or more private actors may take initiatives and mobilize coordinated elite handling of an issue. Propaganda campaigns can occur only when consistent with the interests of those controlling and managing the filters (Herman, 1996, p. 115).

As Schiller (1999) points out, global concentrations of corporate media ownership are the consequence of frenzied regulatory activities—they rely on legislation for their very existence. By controlling flows of both important and trivial information—for example, news and advertising—monopoly capitalism produces media organizations with a significant amount of centralized power, both in terms of setting agendas (Smythe, 1981; Takeshita, 1997) and exercising mass influence over patterns of taste (Smythe, 1981).

## Audiences

Audience research in political economy of communication tends to fall into two categories: those that focus on the effects that media messages have on audiences and those that focus on the role of audiences as co-producers in media processes (cf. Garnham, 1990; Klaehn, 2002; Silverstone, 1999; Smythe, 1981). The first of these categories is more a branch of audience studies in general than an intrinsic part of political economy. It is a field of research in itself, rife with arguments about the role of media consumption patterns in the determination of consciousness, issues of causality, intentionality, and people's capacity to be cynical or playful in respect of media messages (Curtis, 1988; Höijer, 2004; Mansell, 2004). The extremes of the arguments in this field range from the radical postmodern view that makes strong individualist assumptions about people and therefore sees only indeterminate individual differences, to the strong determinisms of advertisers and marketers who claim that audience effects can be calculated according to quantitative formulae (Curtis, 1988). Although there is much of interest to political economy in this field, I am personally disinclined to include such approaches in political economy of communication, even though they are certainly part of the conversation. My argument in this respect is that political economies of communication cannot be derived from the different effects of messages on individuals any more than the nature of capital can be derived from how people react to eating various forms of mass-produced food.

The view that more properly belongs in studies of political economy is, I think, one that sees audiences as productive, definite, and concrete factors in the constitution of political economic forms. In this view, beginning with Horkheimer and Adorno (1947/1998), audiences have been seen as a *primary object* of corporate mass media production systems. The first task of a commercial media venture is to produce an audience of consumers. That is because audiences are media corporations' commodities and are sold to advertisers. Smythe (1981) extends this perspective to elaborate a theory of audience labor, identifying a key fallacy in most audience-focused media studies, and dismissing them as subjective and idealist:

> It is easy to see why conventional, bourgeois theory about communication is idealist. The entire literature—bourgeois and Marxist alike—about mass communications has defined (the principal) product of the mass media as "messages," "information," "images," "meaning," "entertainment," "education," "orientation," "manipulation," etc. *All* these concepts are subjective mental entities; all deal with superficial appearances, divorced from real life processes. The concepts of entertainment, education, orientation, and manipulation do not even refer to any aspects of mass media content but to its *effects*, or *purpose*. (1981, p. 23)

Smythe argues that no Marxist analysis, including that of Horkheimer and Adorno, has addressed the role of "Consciousness Industry from the standpoint of its historical materialist role in making monopoly capitalism function through demand management," because none "take account of how the mass media under monopoly capitalism produce audiences to market commodities, candidates, and issues to themselves" (p. 25).

Smythe's most significant contribution in respect of audiences is an historical materialist theory of audience labor. Smythe sees that participating in media is work: 'Because audience power is produced, sold, purchased, and consumed, it commands a price and is a commodity. Like other 'labor power' it involves work" (1981, p. 26). The point is that mass media corporations must, if they are to flourish, produce audiences for sale to advertisers. Given that audiences now spend more on media than advertisers (Mandese, 2004), audiences have the potential to exercise their economic purchasing power over media content. Instead of being objects of audience production processes, audiences now have the opportunity to demand a place in the production process and to demand content forms oriented towards the promotion of more satisfactory and equitable power relations. Not to say that this will automatically happen, but a necessary condition is access to cultural production processes (Bourdieu, 1998; Lessig, 2004). Gaining access to content production processes is now certainly within reach of many more people outside the corporate sector because the means of production have dropped from costing hundreds of thousands of dollars to almost nothing, with production tools being offered by open source software portals such as Sourceforge (http://www.sourceforge.org) for little or no cost (Berry, 2004; Mansell, 2004).

To achieve the ends of an actively engaged public, Bourdieu (1998) encourages a reasoned utopianism on the part of audiences to correct what he sees as damaging effects of mass media networks. According to Bourdieu, mass media institutions have deleterious effects on virtually every sphere of society, from journalism, justice, and politics; to art, literature, philosophy, and science (1998). His position is that individuals have the right to harness their inherent creativity, construct their media environments without the pervasive control of monopolistic media production systems and, more particularly, media production systems (Bordieu, 1998, p. 130).

Mosco (1987) also argues that a participatory culture can check the power of corporatist media networks. Using Gaudemar's (1979) concept of *mobilization* to frame an analysis of mass media advertising and the liminal force of cross-promotion in public media spectacles:

> The Super Bowl . . . indirectly advertises ideas that support a particular form of consumption by half-time performance that feature leading performers, patriotic addresses and the display of military weaponry. . . . People are mobilized for the purpose of packaging their attention for sale to advertisers (commodification) and for socializing them into particular sets of acceptable values (social control) (Mosco, 1987, p. 31).

Such spectacles are today replete with promotions, and every public activity space, from the Olympics to the University Campus to the home, is a site for the exercise of such activities (Klein, 2000). The ideal, indeed the necessity, of general participation in the production of culture first emerges with Lewis Mumford (1934/1964):

> The essential task of all sound economic activity is to produce a state in which creation will be a common fact in all experience: in which no group will be denied, by reasons of toil or deficient education, their share in the cultural life of the community, up to the limits of their personal capacity. Unless we socialize creation, unless we make production subservient to education, a mechanized system of production, however efficient, will only harden into a servile Byzantine formality, enriched by bread and circuses. (p. 430)

To many pundits, the new media environment offers hope for a reversal in the effects of 20th-century media trends in respect of culture. Among those who have studied political economy in the context of new media, the most utopian analysts have been called, variously, "postmodern," "postindustrial," and "post-everything" (Baudrillard, 1975; Bell, 1976; Robinson & Richardson, 1999).

Nicholas Garnham (1990) criticizes the textual tendency in such studies of political economy because of their political economic implications. Relativist, idealist, radical "postmodern" audience theories that privilege individual agency over longer and larger social structures play directly into the hands of the status quo, offering no grounds for challenge (Garnham, 1990). Similarly, research based on the assumptions of neoliberal theory—perfect markets, radical individualism, perfect and equal access to information, full and democratic participation—combined with the radical semiotic perspective that assumes the complete arbitrariness of signs, the aleatory aspects of meaning, and the unpredictable and creative of nature of individuals, can only lead to more of the same in respect of theory and practice:

> I am concerned to oppose a pluralism, derived from political science and in particular US political science, which sees the media and other cultural institutions as a given, perhaps technologically determined, field upon which a swirling and varying set of social interest groups compete for power. If the textual tendency evacuates the terrain of explanation by giving up on reference, this tendency has no concept of the structured and differential nature of social power or the sources of that power. It pays for its proper respect for human agency with a weak to non-existent concept of social structure. In doing so it idealizes the institution of both bourgeois democracy and the capitalist mixed economy and has a tendency to fall prey to their associated ideologies of freedom of the press and free flow of communication as the transparent mechanisms through which interests group politics are eternally played out. (Garnham, 1990, p. 2)

The new public spaces of interaction facilitated by new media bring new potentials for communicative interactions and interventions with them. Yet such potentials often go unrealized where new media are concerned (McChesney & Schiller, 2003). Communication is an intrinsic part of new media spaces (Thompson, 2003). Recognizing this, and the effects of new value-creating processes that involve audiences as producers, is essential to understanding how contemporary and emerging markets for creative material might better function to produce a more civically oriented media environment (Lessig, 2004). The concept of *value* and its production in new media environments takes on new meaning when the erosion between audiences and producers of content is considered in its fullest sense. Although the notion of redefining the concept of value for the digital age is explored in research concerned with audiences and new potentials to create new media, it is also bound up with larger political economic trends that are partially expressed in the literature on *access*.

## Access

Issues of access have emerged in political economy as a major focus of studies with the development of the new media environment. There are no examples in the history of political economy that speak of the "TV rich and TV poor" or the "radio rich and radio poor" in any systematic way, even though official social indicators of economic progress have, since the early 1990s, included the number of televisions per household (Organization for Economic Co-operation and Development [OECD], 1993). Schiller (1996) is notable for synthesizing issues of access in new and older media environments. According to Schiller, we can expect more of the same from new media in respect of them maintaining and extending the existing corporate media hegemony throughout the global mediascape:

> Two key sectors received special attention, and unstinting resources from the U.S. Government, in the never-ending pursuit of winning and holding the global market for U.S. products

and services. Satellite communications, which radically improve telecommunications, and removed distance as a factor in global production, and computerization, which has become the basis of the information-using economy, have long been the recipients of heavy subsidies and favored treatment, Washington's enthusiasm for "free markets" notwithstanding. . . . Control of information instrumentation, invariably, goes hand in hand with the control of the message flow, its content, surveillance capability, and all forms of communication intelligence. (1996, p. 93)

In short, Herbert Schiller sees the U.S. media corporation assault on global culture, as it was developed in the age of broadcast mass media, merely being exacerbated in the information age through the control of infrastructure and markets.

This is a common theme that is often juxtaposed to discussions of the information-rich and the information-poor. The primary focus is on access to means of communication:

According to the latest UN Human Development Report, industrialized countries, with only 15% of the world's population, are home to 88% of all Internet users. Less than 1% of people in South Asia are online even though it is home to one-fifth of the world's population.

The situation is even worse in Africa. With 739 million people, there are only 14 million phone lines. That's fewer than in Manhattan or Tokyo. Eighty percent of those lines are in only six countries. There are only 1 million Internet users on the entire continent compared with 10.5 million in the UK. (Black, 1999)

The assumption is that not having a computer is an impoverishing state of affairs, and that beneficial access to valuable information is a corollary of access to new media. Such assumptions are based on a mystical "if they build it, service will come" philosophy for the real technological problem of limited access (Schofield, Demont-Heinrich, & Webber, 2004, p. 535).

In comparison, Herbert Schiller's concept of information inequality is a sophisticated synthesis of perspectives that includes issue of control over technological systems, and incorporates conceptions of power structures and political traditions, rather than mere access to technology:

Corporate speech has become a dominant discourse, nationally and internationally. It has also dramatically changed the context in which the concepts of freedom of speech, a free press, and democratic expression have to be considered. While the corporate voice booms across the land, individual expression, at best, trickles through tiny public circuits. (Schiller, 1996, p. 45)

Schiller's perspective on access, or information control, is a synthesis of content, technologies, institutions, and regulatory structures seen as a combined system that functions to inculcate corporate discourse that maintains and increases information inequality on a global scale. This, Schiller argues, will lead to the depleted form of global governance based on the U.S. model (1996, pp. 94–102).

## Democracy

Political economy of communication is principally concerned with the effects of a dominant, global, corporate-owned media system operating in developed capitalist societies that have ostensively democratic systems of governance (Mosco, 1996). With the emergence of new interactive digital media, "e-democracy" has emerged as a distinct field of research, and of national and international policy-making efforts (Dutton & Lin, 2002; OECD, 2003). The more hopeful view is that new media facilitate "a relation based on partnership with government, in which citizens actively participate in policy-making processes" (OECD, 2003, p. 32), and that an issues-based "cyberadvocacy" is emerging as a force for increased democratic participation (Dutton & Lin, 2002). From the less hopeful view, the prediction is that governments will merely use the Web to extend more and less obvious means of surveillance, influence, and opinion manipulation techniques that emerged as systemic tools for the ideological coordination of mass mediated societies throughout the 20th century (McChesney, 1999b).

Issues surrounding the relationships between communication and democracy, and the relationships between democracy and capitalism, exemplify scholarship within this area. Castells (1996, 1997, 1998) claims that the information age has wrought changes in social stratification and, accordingly, in social and political mobilization, whereby forms of class analysis become outdated to the point at which "new social movements have superseded class politics" (Halcli & Webster, 2000, p. 68). Although class relations and "societal orders of discourse" (Fairclough, 1992) have clearly changed, to say that economic class stratifications and class politics have disappeared is tenuous at best, with the gap between rich and poor continuing to grow yearly (Lederer, 2004).

Castells provides analyses of the emergence and significance of identity-based activisms, using the Zapatista movement as an exemplar (1997). His thesis on value production in the network society is summarized as follows: "I think therefore I produce" (1998, p. 359). Castells suggests, therefore, that an industrial labor theory of value should be replaced with an "informational" labor theory of value for the *networker* (1996, pp. 240–251). Halcli and Webster (2000) hold another view:

> Today's informational capitalism manifests radically altered hierarchical arrangements. With these go changes in power relationships, the allocation of resources and prospects for the future. Above all, the axis between the labor and capital which underpinned former political allegiances has apparently been removed . . . we now have capitalism without a capitalist class. Network oriented and adept informational labor is now responsible for running capitalism nowadays. (2000, p. 68).

Capitalism without a capitalist class is not capitalism. "Capital is not a thing, it is a definite social relation of production pertaining to a particular historical social formation, which simply takes the form of a thing and gives this thing a specific social character" (Marx, 1981, p. 953). In other words, no capitalists, no capitalism.

Dan Schiller (1999) asks if democracy can survive a market system that inflicts data deprivation on the social fabric in the interests of corporations. He is not especially concerned with access as the most fundamental problem in respect of democratic progress because the new social space is emerging from an older one and therefore carries with it the characteristics of the system upon which it is built:

> I argue that we should be skeptics about the potential of cyberspace. Knowledge carried through the internet is no less shaped by social forces than it is elsewhere. Far from delivering us into a high-tech Eden, in fact, cyberspace itself is being rapidly colonized by the familiar workings of the market system. Across the breadth and depth, computer networks link with existing capitalism to massively broaden the effective reach of the marketplace. Indeed the Internet comprises nothing less than the central production and control apparatus of an increasingly supranational market system (Schiller, 1999, p. xiv).

That is true, but only partially. The Internet is more than *just* the central production and control system for high finance and globalize transnational interests; it has provided the means for globalized forms of resistance, as Castells (1997) points out, and is the most likely site for collapsing the very system it supports (Silverstone, 1999). The June 2004 network failure at the Royal Bank of Canada gave just a small taste of how vulnerable the market system's base has become as a result of its reliance on an essentially fragile complex of technologies (Bruce, 2004). To organize knowledge and society in such a fragile, high-speed system practically guarantees massive systemic failures.

What Schiller says, though, is true. But *why* it is true also interesting. New media have changed the form and social character of money (Graham, 2000). In present conditions, money—the expression of officially recognized, fully fungible, universal forms of value— has become entirely detached from any referent: it has come to be seen as entirely symbolic value (Bourdieu, 1991). Technology has helped move *value* from being seen as inhering in precious metals and land to being merely a system of numbers circling in cyberspace at close to light speed (Graham, 2002). This has the potential to create significant political changes as money more and more reveals itself to be a contrivance of human abstraction (Graham, 2000, 2002).

## A BRIEF HISTORY OF THE FIELD

> To develop the concept of capital it is necessary to begin not with labor but with value, and, precisely, with exchange value in an already developed movement of circulation. It is just as impossible to make the transition directly from labor to capital as it is to go from the different human races directly to the banker, or from nature to the steam engine. (Marx, 1973, p. 259)

A theory of value is essential for a comprehensive political economy. If for no other reason, it is important to study the history of political economic studies in communication to see how conceptions of value, and the character of money, have changed in such studies with changes in the character of new media environments throughout the 20th century (Graham, 2002). This is reflected in the history of studies in political economy of communication. Somewhat like mainstream political economy throughout the later 19th century, political economy of communication has begun to narrow the range of values it concerns itself with, eventually presupposing the character of money without questioning its social source.

As Harold Innis shows, each civilization has its own means of suicide (1951b, p. 141) and that, with its increased focus on price at the cost of understanding other aspects of value, "economics risks becoming a higher branch of accounting" (p. 141). Every society has an economic history characterized to some significant degree in terms of its successive knowledge monopolies. As a recognized field of study, political economy of communication has its roots in the concept of Innis's "knowledge monopolies" (1942, 1944, 1950, 1951a, 1951b). Innis coined this term to illustrate the fact that throughout history certain privileged groups (priests, kings, bureaucrats, soldiers, scientists, and so on) have enjoyed a monopoly of access to certain kinds of knowledge. Innis tends to appear as the pioneer of all contemporary political economic studies in the field of communication. But even from the period during which Innis wrote we must also acknowledge Horkheimer and Adorno (1947 / 1998), whose essay on the 'culture industry' continues to have relevance for current circumstances (Jarvis, 1998; Silverstone, 1999).

Political economy of communication becomes incipient as a discipline during the second decade of the twentieth century, when figures such as Harold Lasswell (1927, 1941) and Edward Bernays (1928, 1945) appear as significant scholars of wartime propaganda. Following the effects and strategies of propaganda methods in WWI deployed by the Creel Committee, both clearly understand the political economic implications of new media and their attendant capabilities to change the character and functioning of societies. At this time, we see a concern with propaganda, a term that did not have the automatically negative connotations it carries today.

According to Lasswell:

> Propaganda is the management of collective attitudes by the manipulation of significant symbols. The word attitude is taken to mean a tendency to act according to certain patterns of evaluation. The existence of an attitude is not a direct datum of experience, but an inference from science which have a conventionalized significance. . . . The valuational patterns upon which this inference is founded may be primitive gestures of the face and body, or more sophisticated gestures of the pen and voice. Taken together, these objects which have a standard meaning in a group are called significant symbols. The elevated eyebrow, the clenched fist, the sharp voice, the pungent phrase, have their references established within the web of a particular culture. Such significant symbols are paraphernalia employed in expressing the attitudes, and they are also capable of being employed to reaffirm or redefine attitudes. (Lasswell, 1927, p. 627)

Lasswell's is a political economic understanding of communication grounded in a nonpsychological view of the social. "Patterns of evaluation" and "valuational patterns" are other ways to say "value" and indicate the agentive aspect of value and its source: particular groups of people actively value particular ways of being, seeing, and acting; particular types of food, entertainment, and politics; particular codes of morality and traditions of kinship; and so on—evaluations are action (Bourdieu, 1991). By recognizing that "patterns of evaluation" within "the web of a particular culture" are the primary objects of propaganda, Lasswell does not separate the economic from the political. People evaluate aspects of the world in historically and culturally specific ways, and it is this continual doing of evaluations through which specific cultural values get produced and reproduced, and how the most important mass actions flow from these patterns (Lasswell, 1941). This is a far-reaching conception of value; it is an inherent aspect of any social interaction and does not usually appear as a singular form or object.

For Lasswell, propaganda may be positive *or* negative, but its aim is always cultural values (1927, p. 630). Moreover, all means of propaganda are a "form of words," whether "spoken, written, pictorial, or musical, and the number of stimulus carriers is infinite" (1927, p. 631). Because of "technological changes," especially the new medium of radio, increased literacy, and because most of what could "formerly be done by violence and coercion must now be done by argument and persuasion," Lasswell asserts that propaganda is in fact *necessary* for the operation of democracy (1927, p. 631). Laswell's view is that advances in communication technologies, increased literacy, and the widespread "ventilation of opinions and the taking of votes" has created an environment in which democracy "has proclaimed the dictatorship of palaver, and the technique of dictating to the dictator is named propaganda" (1927, p. 631). There is an inseparable relation between the political and the economic here: The production and manipulation of attitudinal patterns (values) is the means by which political power is exercised in mass democracy.

To Bernays (1928), generally considered by the modern Public Relations industry as its pioneer, propaganda is more an internalist endeavor because it is primarily psychological. But he is still oriented towards the social formation of values: "From the broadest standpoint, [propaganda] is the power of the [ruling] group to sway the larger public in its attitude" (1928, p. 958). Knowledge of "group cleavages of society, the importance of group leaders, and the habits of their followers" are essential knowledge for the successful propagandist (p. 961). Bernays considers that "a circumstance or circumstances of dramatic moment" are events that change and establish the "functioning of given attitudes toward given subjects, such as religion, sex, race, morality, nationalism, internationalism, and so forth" (p. 961). Whether the object is attitudes towards hats, sexuality, or God, Bernays argues that, in the "age of mass production," there must be a corresponding "technique for the mass distribution of ideas" and attitudes, and thus for the mass production of public attitudes (p. 971). Bernays is proclaiming the necessity of what Smythe calls "monopoly capitalism."

Gallup (1938) was not the least bit guilty of historical balance in matters of political judgment, preferring to think of the perfect democracy as an immediate relationship between political action and ongoing measurements of public opinion:

> James Bryce said that the next and final stage in our democracy would be reached if the will of the majority of citizens were to be ascertainable at all times. With the development of the science of measuring public opinion, it can be stated with but few qualifications, that this stage in our democracy is rapidly being reached. It is now possible to ascertain, with a high degree of accuracy, the views of the people on all national issues. (Gallup, 1938, p. 9)

The usefulness of polling is not to be confined to government or politics. It can be "equally useful in the field of social problems" (1938, p. 13). Once sufficient is known about specific attitudes—opinions about welfare, religious prejudice, venereal disease, and any problem of attitude whatsoever—they can be addressed "with equal success" (1938, pp. 13–14). Quantitative methods can be used to measure all aspects of value. Therefore "with many of our leading psychologists and social scientists" interested in the problem of measuring public opinion, "it will not be long before the final stage in the development of our democracy, as described by Bryce, has been reached—that the will of the majority of citizens can be ascertained at all times" (p. 14). Questions about the relationship between the facts of public opinion research, about the implications of centrally controlled mass media, and about the inherent rectitude or otherwise of government and its organs elude Gallup in his enthusiasm for an early end to the history of democracy. Such questions, muted and blurred by Gallup's enthusiasms for direct democracy and a utopian attitude toward new statistical methods, were answered by an ugly response from post-Depression Germany.

## Political Economy of Communication in Nazi Germany

The historical exemplar of classical political economic principles being consciously applied to communication policy is Nazi Germany's propagandists, who produced new values and power structures on a massive scale. For the Nazi propagandists propaganda is, *pace* Lasswell and Gallup, a matter of moral obligation to the public, a value and public good in itself:

> When we talk about the necessity of political propaganda, we seek powerful moral goals. We want to make our people a united nation that confidently and clearly understands National Socialism's policies, quickly and correctly. We cannot change our political principles as we would a consumer good, becoming random, irresponsible and immoral. We do not want to distort, confuse or incite, rather clarify, unify, and tell the truth. Political propaganda is the highest responsibility, it is a moral duty, a national duty. We may never think there is too much of it, or that it is superfluous. (Wells, 1936)

Moral, national, biological, aesthetic, spiritual, and ethnic values all figure in Nazi political economy of communication. The following summarizes the position: "For us, gold is not a measure of the value of money. Our foundation is German labor and confidence in the Führer" (Lange, in NSDAP, 1939).

The paranoid values of eugenics, social Darwinism, and the natural state of an all-pervasive competition for survival were propagated throughout Germany, through film (Hippler, 1937); radio (Goebbels, 1933); printed materials, and by every means and available to the propagandists, including cultural gatherings, mass marches, "stickers," and especially through the spoken and written word (Stark, 1930). Appeals to fear; immutable laws of nature; a traumatized national psychology; doctrines of scarce resources; work as the highest good; the necessity of being the dominant nation; racial hygiene and superiority; the utilitarian view of science, technology, and truth—these formed the basic theses of Nazi propaganda. The comprehensive range of the Nazis' appeals, combined with the centralized control of public communication, had intense, widespread, and vicious effects. The nation's patterns of evaluation were successfully manipulated by the

National Socialist Party through centralized control of media, and the rest, as they say, is history. It may seem reductionist and cold to say that Nazi Germany owed its short-lived "successes" to a sophisticated understanding of political economy of communication, but one cannot deny that the regime successfully set out to achieve the production of an entirely new set of values for German people, that its communication strategies were oriented toward the production of those values, and that in achieving its objectives, the Nazi regime produced a literal explosion of activity that followed entirely new patterns of evaluation.

## FORMALIZING THE FIELD AROUND MEANS OF PRODUCTION

Beginning with Harold Innis (1942, 1944, 1950, 1951a, 1951b), political economy of communication became a recognizable field. While it might be said that Innis is responsible to some significant degree for the artificial separation of communication technologies from communication more generally, by focusing on the relationship between new media and new political forms, Innis provides an historical materialist method for studying political economies of communication, one that has proved invaluable. By emphasizing technological form over content, Innis foregrounds how new media can sustain, erode, or otherwise transform civilizations based on the means of production where "knowledge monopolies" are concerned (1942, 1944, 1950, 1951a, 1951b). Innis also expanded conceptions of media, just as the term "the media" was becoming singular and monolithic in everyday speech. Innis helped show that myth, prayer, alphabet, architecture, libraries, transport systems, weaponry, and technologies more generally are means of communication, and therefore means of producing, sustaining, and destroying knowledge monopolies, civilizations, and their associated cultures (1951b).

Innis's most significant contribution to the development of political economy of communication is his staple theory of communication: "Communication, when considered in terms of the medium that facilitated it, might be seen as the basic staple in the growth of Empire" (Carey, 1989/1992, p. 158). From this view flowed a concern with the most basic perspectives on human experience: time and space (Carey, 1989/1992, p. 158; Innis, 1942, 1944, 1950, 1951). Like Marx, in an effort to comprehend classical political economy at the most basic level, Innis's insights lead him to define the character of political economic systems in terms of time and space, focusing on how new media challenge and change relationships between cultures, places, political formations, and time periods. The author's critique of a completely quantitative rationality where conceptions of value are concerned in economics recognizes that money is more or less epiphenomenal of a wider range of cultural values that do not permit of quantitative analysis (Innis, 1944):

> Innis argued that changes in communication technology affected culture by altering the structure of interests (the things thought about) by changing the character of symbols (the things thought with), and by changing the nature of community (in which thought developed). By a space-binding culture he meant literally that: a culture whose predominant interest was in space—land as real estate, voyage, discovery, movement, expansion, empire, control. In the realm of symbols he meant the growth of symbols and conceptions that

supported these interests: the physics of space, the arts of navigation and civil engineering, the price system, the mathematics of tax collectors and bureaucracies, the entire realm of physical science, and the system of affectless, rational symbols that facilitated those interests. In the realm of community's human communities of space: communities that were not in place but in space, mobile, connected over vast distances by appropriate symbols, forms, and interests. (Carey, 1989/1992, p. 160)

At the core of such a theory is an inherent challenge to the narrow conception of value held by researchers in the field of economics (Innis, 1944). We can see such concerns emerging now in the current proliferation of terms such as "social capital," "cultural capital," "symbolic capital," and "the triple bottom line," to name just a few attempts to define value in a nonquantitative, nonmonetary way (Bourdieu, 1988, 1991; Elkington, 1999; Latham, 1998; Putnam, 2000).

While holding a similarly broad view of value as that of the early propagandists, Innis differs from them in an important way. He refuses "to yield to the modern notion that the level of democratic process correlates with the amount of capital invested in communication, capital that can do our knowing for us, and fervently hoped that his work would break modern monopolies of knowledge in communication and further restore the political power of the foot and the tongue" (Carey, 1989/1992, p. 164). By seeing that culture and political power moves along lines of communication, Innis was also foregrounding those aspects of experience that underpin "official" conceptions of value.

Innis's colleague Marshall McLuhan (1964) pushed the technological perspective to the point at which people felt impelled to deploy "technological determinism" as a negative epithet to describe any work in media studies that emphasizes the transformative aspects of new media. The basis of critiques such as these is that, by foregrounding the techno-logical, human agency gets obscured (Klaehn, 2002). Such criticisms notwithstanding, and despite arguments to the contrary, McLuhan remains a key figure in the development of political economy of communication, emphasizing the human sensory apparatus, its relation to various values that, for example, oral and visually oriented media produce, and to the political and cultural effects that technological transformations entail. McLuhan's chapter on "Money" in *Understanding Media* (1964) is most instructive in this respect:

Like any other medium, [money] is a staple, a natural resource. As an outward and visible form of the urge to change and to exchange, it is a corporate image, depending on society for its institutional status. Apart from communal participation, money is meaningless. . . . (1964, p. 133)

Similarly instructive is McLuhan's assessment of new media in shaping power relations:

Ink and photo are supplanting soldiery and tanks. The pen daily becomes mightier than the sword.

The French phrase "guerres des nerfs" . . . has since become to be referred to as "the cold war." It is really an electric battle of information and of images that goes far deeper and is more obsessional than the hot wars of industrial hardware. (1964, p. 339)

McLuhan is especially prescient in respect of contemporary information warfare. The growing importance of information to global political power is evidenced by the U.S. Department of Defense's (DOD) first *Information Operations Doctrine*, which classified "cyberspace," along with "air, land, and sea," as "battlespace" (Brewin, 1998):

> The Information Operations doctrine "moves information operations from an ad hoc process and institutionalizes it." The individual services already had taken steps to formalize their information operations, Kuehl said, and the new doctrine brings these operations into the joint realm.... The doctrine published by the chiefs takes warfare to a new dimension with the "ultimate target human decision-making." (1998).

Particularly since the terrorist attacks of September 11, 2001, Departments of Defense throughout the developed world have begun to react to the need for information and to prioritize the collection and analysis of information in the conduct of warfare (Bonner, 2004).

In many ways, McLuhan and Innis opened the way for the work of social historians of technology, such as Arnold Pacey (2000), Lynne White Jr (1940, 1965, 1974), Lewis Mumford (1961, 1964), Langdon Winner (1986), and David F. Noble (1997), to be included in the political economy of communication literature. Their inclusion in the field recognizes the fact that technologies have a communicative dimension in and of themselves and play a significant role in political economic formations; as much as means of production for capitalism, or whichever system of political economy, they are also means of producing culturally and historically specific systems of meaning. Although such inclusions sometimes threaten to place too much emphasis on the "purely" technological, the foregrounding of the technological and its social character has been an important development in political economies of communication, one that has yet to be fully incorporated into the field.

## Issues in Contemporary Approaches

The single most pressing issue in contemporary political economy of communication is the tendency to unconsciously separate the "economic" from the political and all other social aspects of human interaction. This leads to an artificial separation of "economic" values—by which is generally meant money—from all others. As noted previously, the bulk of the studies focus on mass media ownership and its broad societal effects (e.g., Garnham, 1990; McChesney, 2000; McChesney & Schiller, 2003, Bagdikian, 1997; Mosco, 1996; Mosco & Foster, 2001; Schiller, 1999;Wasko, 2001).

Although most researchers explicitly reject the idea that capitalism should be presupposed in any analysis of political economy, there is still a strong tendency (a) to presuppose the character of money and (b) to present capitalism as if it were an invariable object of studies in political economy:

> Political economy is always concerned with analyzing a structure of social relations and of social power. But it is particularly concerned to analyze peculiarities of a system of social power called capitalism. (Garnham, 1990, p. 7)

McChesney (2000) defines the field as follows:

> First, it addresses the nature of the relationship between media and communication systems on the one hand and the broader social structure of society. In other words, it examines how media and communication systems and content reinforce, challenge or influence existing class and social relations. It does this with a particular interest in how economic factors influence politics and social relations. Second, the political economy of communication looks specifically at *how ownership, support mechanisms (e.g. advertising) and government policies influence media behavior and content.* This line of inquiry emphasizes structural factors and the labor process in the production, distribution and consumption of communication. (McChesney, 2000, p. 109)

McChesney argues here that political economy of communication is the field in which "media and communication systems and content" are seen to link "economic factors" with "politics and social relations" (p. 109). But by separating the economic from the political, and both of these from the rest of social relations, McChesney presents a somewhat artificial challenge for political economy of communication; joining what only appear to be separate aspects of life. The appearance that economics and politics are somehow separate from social relations is itself an achievement of mediation systems. Classical political economy proceeds upon the assumption that social relations are an unbroken whole (Marcuse & Neumann, 1997). It is only very recent developments that have seen the fragmenting of social science into the many disciplines we know today (Graham, 2003). Prior to the mid-19th century, such an explanation would have been unnecessary because the

> intrinsic connection between philosophy and the theory of society . . . formulates the pattern of all particular theories of social change occurring in the ancient world, in the middle ages, and on the commencement of modern times. One decisive result is the emphasis on the fact that social change cannot be interpreted within a particular social science, but must be understood within the social and natural totality of human life. (Marcuse & Neumann, 1942/1998, p. 95)

Implicit in contemporary approaches is a broken theory of value, one that sees money as a relatively fixed and homogeneous form of expression. Within the field of economics, the tendency has been, at least since the late 19th century, to slowly abolish all values other than money from its field of investigation (Graham, 2002; Perry, 1916).

These are not uncommon moves in defining political economy of communication, especially given dominant understandings of what *economics* means, a point that McChesney notes when he says that *media economics*

> often provides microanalysis of how media firms and markets operate but, like the field of mainstream economics, it assumes the existing social and class relations are a given, and a benevolent one at that. Likewise, communication policy studies examine the influence of government policies on media performance, but the work generally presupposes the necessary existence of the market and the broader social situation as the best of all possible worlds. The dominant form of communication research in the USA is drawn from quantitative

behavioral social science. This work tends to be the polar opposite of the political economy of communication: it presupposes capitalist society as a given and then discounts structural factors in explaining media behavior. (McChesney, 2000)

Much of this can be explained by intellectual and institutional histories. Economics, politics, and sociology, along with the totality of social sciences, have been slowly disciplined—separated from each other, first in theory then in practice (Graham, 2003). As McChesney points out, government policies are shaped by quantitative microeconomic analyses, sociologically informed opinion polls, and often Darwinian understandings of humanity. Political economy of communication differs from media economics' view of the world by emphasizing the structural implications of political economic forms.

However, if the primary goal of studies in political economy of communication is to comprehend social inequalities created by communication practices and change them for the better—as most political economists of communication claim it is—then the field requires a comprehensive theory of value at its foundation. Similarly, sound systemic definitions are also necessary if we are to comprehend the nature of the political economic system in which we live.

While noting the rise of massive concentrations of corporate media ownership, and the general trend throughout the world for corporate entities to exert greater and greater amounts of political power (Schiller, D., 1999; Schiller, H., 1989), political economy of communication tends to regard the system as capitalist (Garnham, 1990; McChesney, 2000; Schiller, D., 1999). As it is defined in the mainstream, political economy of communication

> cannot provide a comprehensive explanation of all communication activity, but it can explain certain issues extremely well and it provides a necessary context for most other research questions in communication. Although the political economy of communication can be applied to the study of precapitalist and postcapitalist societies and communication systems, it is primarily concerned with capitalist societies and commercial media systems, as these models dominate across the world (Mosco, 1996).

Although it is necessary to consider political economy of communication as a context for most questions pertaining to communication, I disagree with Mosco's assertion that the capitalist system continues to dominate the world. It ignores the emergence and triumph of corporatism throughout the course of the twentieth century (Graham & Luke, 2003; Saul, 1997; Schiller, H., 1989).

Most political economic formations of communication have emerged under corporatist principles, from the mass mediations of the Creel Committee in 1916; to Hitlerism, Fascism, Stalinist Sovietism, and the many "new-deal" public radio initiatives in the 1930s; to the massive state-approved monopolies that have emerged in the late 20th to early 21st centuries. In France, for instance, "total of 70% of national newspapers are the property of two armament manufacturers" (*Le Monde*, 2004). Political economies of communication must at least comprehend the organizing principles of their political contexts. Capitalism, which assumes relatively free markets, relatively free trade, relatively diverse ownership, and steadily lower labor costs over time, is not the model that characterizes the development of political economies of communication over the past century. It is a commonplace in political economy of communication that trade follows lines of communication rather than the reverse (Carey, 1989). The East India Company of the mercantilist era was no more able to function without its ships than is the Hughes Electronics media corporation able to function without its satellites. Mercantilism, advances in navigation and shipping, the emergence of a general credit system, and the rise of the merchant class as a political force are mutually defining phenomena in history (Nace, 2003). The elements of any political economic formation cannot be separated and understood at the same time.

By definition, capitalism requires the existence of a capitalist class; a class that owns the means of production (Marx, 1976). The current system is not dominated by such a class, although a dominant class of corporatists has emerged (Saul, 1997). There are significant qualitative differences in how capitalists and corporatists organize their worlds (Saul, 1997). Capitalists form an owning class, and its political power comes from ownership; corporatists are a controlling class, and their political power comes from controlling public discourse (Saul, 1997, chap. 3). For example, Rupert Murdoch can exercise control over a global media empire by owning less than 15% of the company's equity. That is what is meant by the notion of 'a controlling interest' in the language of corporatism. A relatively small share in one corporation can be leveraged into controlling a larger share of another, especially when ownership is dispersed among workers and the rest of the public. Here is how such arrangements are communicated:

> This page provides information on the joint application filed by General Motors Corporation ("GM"), Hughes Electronics Corporation ("Hughes") and The News Corporation Limited ("News Corp." and, collectively with GM and Hughes, the "Applicants") to the Commission seeking consent to transfer control of various Commission licenses and authorizations, including direct broadcast satellite ("DBS") and fixed satellite space station, earth station, and terrestrial wireless authorizations held by Hughes and its wholly- or majority-owned subsidiaries to News Corp. ("Application"). The proposed transaction involves the split-off of Hughes from GM, wherein Hughes will become a separate and independent company, followed by a series of transactions where News Corp., through its majority-held subsidiary, Fox Entertainment Group, will acquire a 34% interest in Hughes. The remaining 66% interest in Hughes will be held by three GM employee benefit trusts (managed by an independent trustee), which combined will hold an approximately 20% interest in Hughes, and by the general public, which will hold an approximately 46% interest in Hughes. (Federal Communications Commission, 2003)

The relationships expressed here accurately reflect how far the current system is from being capitalist. Three corporate persons, News Corporation, General Motors, and Hughes Electronics Corporation, have made an arrangement to give a single person (Murdoch) control over a global, extraterrestrial media system by mobilizing employee benefit trusts and the money of the general public. That is not a description of a capitalist phenomenon because there is no capitalist involved; there are only corporate persons and corporatists: legal fictions and the people who control them. The illusion that a capitalist class still exists is an achievement of mass- and micro-mediated corporatist discourse: the active manipulation of laws; the valuation of stocks, bonds, and futures; the continual creation of new forms of money to which the public does not have access; the global dispersion and diffusion of ownership through institutions such as mutual funds and the associated mobilization of the general public's savings that such institutions facilitate; and the ongoing, mass propaganda that the system somehow resembles capitalism (Graham & Luke, 2003).

## UNDERSTANDING POLITICAL ECONOMIES OF COMMUNICATION IN THE FUTURE

It is my contention that political economies have changed to such an extent that an almost total reassessment is required to comprehend the changes (Graham, 2000). Marx's approach to comprehending political economy, especially in his early work, consisted in large part of an analysis of the language of political economy (Fairclough & Graham, 2002). Because the current system has emerged so rapidly (even if one takes a longer historical view and argues that it has been three or more centuries in developing), there are few conceptual means available to analyze it in any clear way. The underpinning assumptions of political economy of communication are that political power follows lines of communication and requires these lines to act effectively; that social relations of production are a function of mediation systems; and that, from these relations, historically specific political economic formations emerge, are sustained, or, upon the introduction of new media, are transformed in some significant way, in both qualitative and quantitative terms.

Four writers stand out as providing the basic elements from which to synthesize a coherent approach to political economy of communication under current conditions: Dallas Smythe (1981), Karl Marx (1973), Roger Silverstone (1999), and Jay Lemke (1995). This perhaps unlikely combination of authors provides four elements that are of direct relevance to understanding political economy of communication in the current context: Smythe for his theory of *consciousness*; Marx for his theory of *value*; Silverstone for his theory of *mediation*; and Lemke for his theory of *meaning*. I only have space here to point out key elements from each of these.

Smythe defines *consciousness* as

> the total awareness of life which people have. It includes their understanding of themselves as individuals and of their relations with other individuals in a variety of forms of organization, as well as with their natural environment. Consciousness is a dynamic process. It grows and decays with the interaction of doing (or practice) and cognition over the life cycle of the individual in the family and other social formations. It draws on emotions, ideas, instincts, memory and all the other sensory apparatus. (1981, pp. 270–271)

Smythe's is a historically and culturally specific, materialist definition of human experience that explains how we comprehend our world as a totality. Consciousness—*being conscious*—is a definitively human activity. Being conscious starts with the ability to evaluate our world and our place in it. As I have said here, perhaps too many times, the ways in which we evaluate various aspects of our world—what are ordinarily called "values"—is an essential inclusion in any political economy of communication.

As our political economic systems have become technically more sophisticated, more intimate facets of human experience have become subsumed formally as part of what is broadly called "the economy." They have been incorporated as saleable aspects of human activity, or what is called *labor* in studies of political economy. The general systemic tendency to appropriate the more abstract aspects of humanity is exemplified in terms such as *knowledge worker* and *knowledge economy*. The emergent political economic formation is organized primarily around the corporate production of symbolic artifacts—especially new financial instruments—and is facilitated by proliferating new media. With this progression, new and more abstract forms of value have developed that correspond to the newly formalized "labors of abstraction" in the knowledge economy. These forms of value are not merely monetary, although they may be traded for money at some stage. It is uncontentious to say that money values have permeated societies everywhere, and that this has had significant impacts on how they operate. But the enthronement of money as the primary evaluative principle cannot be explained by the character of money itself, or by its movement. Money has been sold as having inherent value rather than being seen as an epiphenomenal expression of people evaluating the world and their place in it. This is achieved by the manipulation of other aspects of value, which in turn necessarily requires the movement of meanings from one set of institutional contexts (the commercial) into all other aspects of human experience (Graham, 2001). Consequently political economy of communication requires a theory of *movement* that incorporates the typically irreconcilable dimensions of space and time:

> Mediation involves the movement of meaning from one text to another, from one discourse to another, from one event to another. It involves the constant transformation of meanings, both large scale and small, significant and insignificant, as media texts and texts about media circulate in writing, in speech and audiovisual forms, and as we, individually and collectively, directly and indirectly, contribute to their production (Silverstone, 1999, p. 13)

Seeing movement reconciles the strong division between our experiences of time and space. Mediation sees meanings move through and across spaces and times, linking and delinking them (1999, p. 14). The process of mediation "involves the work of institutions, groups and technologies" and is "the product of textual unraveling in the words, deeds and experiences of everyday life, as much as by the continuities of broadcasting and narrowcasting" (1999, p. 15).

With these three concepts, framed in these particular ways, we have the basis for theoretically grasping the basic elements of political economies of communication. Analytically, this leaves us to understand the various dimensions of meaning. These can be described within a three-term system as defined by Lemke (1995): the *Presentational*, or the "aboutness" of meaning; the *Attitudinal*, or the evaluative aspects of meaning; and the *Organizational*, or how meanings derive coherence. It is in the *Attitudinal* domain that research into political economy of communication must start if it is to comprehend the degree to which the current system differs from any other in history.

Through the synthesis of these approaches, the ways in which social relations are changing can be understood in broad terms. There are many sites that need to be understood in the current context, violent and chaotic as it is. Politics, finance, and military propaganda; resistance, revolution, and technological change; commercial production, distribution, exchange, and consumption; fundamentalisms of all sorts, peace activism, and environmental struggles throughout the world are conducted to some large extent within the spaces of new media networks. This has become so much the case that it may well be that political economies of communication have become the most important aspect of political economy for understanding global social dynamics.

## CONCLUSION

I have outlined contemporary political economy of communication, shown its development as a field of research throughout the 20th century, and described what I think a political economy of communication means in the current context. Of course, much more could be said on the subject, and I hope this chapter will provide the impetus for such studies. Political economy of communication is about the production of values at the most fundamental level—the level of consciousness—and the exercise of power on the broadest possible scale: the totality of human beings now joined in a globally mediated system of social relations. New media inevitably lead to new political economic formations. New political economic formations are new systems that require new understandings. In respect of management, the new political economies of communication require entirely new understandings that can comprehend the ways in which consciousness is produced; ways in which values are produced; the means by which meanings are moved; and the ways in which these aspects are realized in specific meanings. Through the synthesis of these aspects of political economy, we can begin to chart a course through one of the most complex and gigantic systems of social relations that has developed in the history of humanity.

## ACKNOWLEDGMENTS

I thank and acknowledge the Canada Research Chairs Program (http://www.chairs.gc.ca/), the Social Sciences and Humanities Research Council of Canada, The Australian Research Council, and the University of Queensland Foundation for their support.

## REFERENCES

Adorno, T. (1951). *Minima moralia: Reflections from a damaged life* (E.F.N. Jephcott, Trans.). New York: Verso.
Bagdikian, B. H. (1997). *The media monopoly (5th Ed.)*. Boston: Beacon Press.
Baudrillard, J. (1975). *The mirror of production* (J. B. Thompson, Trans.). St. Louis, MO: Telos.
Bell, D. (1976). *The coming of post-industrial society. A venture in social forecasting*. New York: Basic Books.

Bernays, E. L. (1928). Manipulating public opinion: The why and the how. *American Journal of Sociology, 33*(6), 958–971.

Bernays, E. L. (1945). Attitude polls-servants or masters. *Public Opinion Quarterly, 9*(3), 264–268b.

Berry, D. M. (2004). The contestation of code: A preliminary investigation into the discourse of the free software and open software movement. *Critical Discourse Studies, 1*(1), 65–89.

Bettig, R. V., & Hall, J. L. (2003). *Big Media, big money: Cultural texts and political economics.* Lanham, MD: Rowman & Littlefield.

Black, J. (1999). Losing ground bit by bit. *BBC News Online.* Retrieved July 2004, from http://news.bbc.co.uk/1/hi/special_report/1999/10/99/information_rich_information_poor/472621.stm

Bonner, R. C. (2004, August 10). *The rest of the story, securing U.S. borders post 9/11.* Washington: US Department of State. Retrieved August 14, 2004, from http://www.iwar.org.uk/news-archive/2004/08-10-4.htm

Bordieu, P. (1988/1998). *On television and journalism* (P. Parkhurst Ferguson, Trans.). London: Pluto Press.

Bourdieu, P. (1991). *Language and symbolic power* (G. Raymond & M. Adamson, Trans.). London: Polity.

Bourdieu, P. (1998). A reasoned utopia and economic fatalism. *New Left Review, 227,* 125–130.

Brewin, B. (1998, December 2). DOD recognizes info warfare as key battlefield. *Federal Computer Week.* Retrieved December 11, 1998, from http://www.fcw.com/pubs/fcw/1998/1130/web-infowar-12-2-98.html

Bruce, L. (2004, June 4). "RBC fixes 'processing glitch'". It World Canada. Available online at http://www.itworldcanada.com/Pages/Docbase/ViewArticle.aspx?id=idgml-c48456f0-4ed8-4a96&s=395692.

Carey, J. (1989). *Communication as culture: Essays on media and society.* London: Routledge.

Carey, J. W. (1989/1992). *Communication as Culture: Essays on media and society.* New York: Routledge.

Castells, M. (1996). *The information age: Economy, society & culture, Vol. 1: The rise of the network society.* Oxford: Blackwell.

Castells, M. (1997). *The information age: Economy, society & culture, Vol. 2: The power of identity.* Oxford: Blackwell.

Castells, M. (1998). *The information age: Economy, society and culture, Vol. 3: The end of the millennium.* Oxford: Blackwell.

Curtis, T. (1988). The information society: A computer-generated caste system? In V. Mosco & J. Wasko (Eds). *The political economy of information* (pp. 95–107). Madison: University of Wisconsin Press.

Dietz, A. (1934). The nature of contemporary propaganda. *Unser Wille und Weg, 4,* 299–301 (R. Bytwerk, Trans.). Retrieved March 24, 2000 from http://www.calvin.edu/academic/cas/gpa/dietz1.htm

Dutton, W. H., & Lin, W. (2002). E-democracy: A case study of web-orchestrated cyberadvocacy. In J. Armitage & J. Roberts (Eds.), *Living with cyberspace: Technology and society in the 21st century* (pp. 98–108). London: Continuum.

Duvall, M. (July, 2004). Bad code at Canada's largest bank. *Eweek.* Retrieved October 7, 2004, from http://www.findarticles.com/p/articles/mi_zdewk/is_200407/ai_ziff131007

Elkington, J. (1999). *Cannibals with forks: The triple bottom line of 21st century business.* Oxford: Capstone.

Fairclough, N. (1992). *Discourse and social change.* London: Routledge.

Fairclough, N., & Graham, P. (2002). Marx as a critical discourse analyst: The genesis of a critical method. *Estudios de Sociolingüística, 3*(1), 185–229.

Federal Communications Commission. (2003). *General Motors Corporation, Hughes Electronics Corporation, and The News Corporation Limited.* Retrieved February 25, 2004, from http://www.fcc.gov/transaction/news-directv.html

Free Press. (2004). *Who owns the media?* Retrieved August 2004, from http://www.freepress.net/ownership/

Fuller, L. K. (2004). Big money: Cultural texts and political economics. *Journal of Popular Culture 38*(1), 211–212.

Gallup, G. (1938). Testing public opinion. *Public Opinion Quarterly [Special Supplement: Public opinion in a democracy], 2*(1), 8–14.

Garnham, N. (1990). *Capitalism and communication: Global culture and the economics of information.* London: Sage.

Gaudemar, J. (1979). *La mobilisation générale.* Paris: Maspero.

Goebbels, J. (1933). *The radio as the eight great power* (R. Bytwerk, Trans.). In *Signale der neuen Zeit. 25 ausgewählte Reden von Dr. Joseph Goebbels* (pp. 197–207). Munich: Zentralverlag der NSDAP, 1938. Retrieved September 1998 from http://www.calvin.edu/academic/cas/gpa/goeb56.htm

Graham, P. (2000). Hypercapitalism: A political economy of informational idealism. *New Media & Society, 2*(2), 131–156.

Graham, P. (2001). Space: Irrealis objects in technology policy and their role in the creation of a new political economy. *Discourse & Society, 12*(6), 761–788.

Graham, P. (2002). Predication and propagation: A method for analysing evaluative meanings in technology policy. *TEXT 22*(2), 227–268.

Graham, P. (2003). Critical discourse analysis and evaluative meaning; Interdisciplinarity as a critical turn. In G. Weiss & R. Wodak (Eds.), *Critical discourse analysis: Theory and interdisciplinarity* (pp. 130–159). London: Palgrave MacMillan.

Graham, P., & Luke, A. (2003). Militarizing the body politic. New media as weapons of mass instruction. *Body & Society, 9*(4), 149–168.

Guademar, J. P. (1979). *La mobilisation générale*. Paris: Editions Du Champ Urbain.

Halcli, A., & Webster, F. (2000). Inequality and mobilization in the information age. *European Journal of Social Theory, 3*(1), 67–81.

Herman, E. S. (1996). The propaganda model revisited. *Monthly Review, 48*(3), 115–129.

Herman, E. S., & Chomsky, N. (1988). *Manufacturing consent: The political economy of the mass media*. New York: Pantheon Books.

Hippler, F. (1937). Der Film als Waffe [Film as a Weapon]. *Unser Wille und Weg, 7*, 21–23 (R. Bytwerk, Trans.). Retrieved March 24, 2000, from http://www.calvin.edu/academic/cas/gpa/hippler1.htm

Höijer, B. (2004). The discourse of global compassion: The audience and media reporting of human suffering. *Media Culture & Society, 26*(4), 513–531.

Horkheimer, M., & Adorno, T. W. (1947/1998). *The dialectic of enlightenment* (J. Cumming, Trans.). Continuum: New York.

Huffington, A. (2004). Blog heaven. *The American Prospect, 15*(7), 28–29.

Innis, H. A. (1942). The newspaper in economic development. *Journal of Economic History, 2* [Supplement: The Tasks of Economic History], 1–33.

Innis, H. A. (1944). On the economic significance of culture. *Journal of Economic History, 4* [Supplement: The Tasks of Economic History], 80–97.

Innis, H. A. (1950). *Empire and communications*. Oxford: Clarendon Press.

Innis, H. A. (1951a). *The bias of communication*. Toronto: Toronto University Press.

Innis, H. A. (1951b). Industrialism and cultural values. *The American Economic Review, 41*(2), 201–209.

Jarvis, S. (1998). *Adorno: A critical introduction*. London: Polity.

Klaehn, J. (2002). A critical review and assessment of Herman and Chomsky's 'Propaganda Model. *European Journal of Communication, 17*(2), 147–182.

Klein, N. (2000). *No Logo*. New York, New York: Picador.

Klein, N. (2001). *No logo*. London: Flamingo.

Lasswell, H. D. (1927). The theory of political propaganda. *The American Political Science Review, 21*(3), 627–631.

Lasswell, H. D. (1941). World attention survey. *Public Opinion Quarterly, 5*(3), 456–462.

Latham, M. (1998). *Civilising global capital: New thinking for Australian Labor*. Sydney, Australia: Allen & Unwin.

Lederer, E. M. (2004, October 13). "Eighty-five nations endorse U.N. population agenda—but Bush administration refuses to sign." Associated Press, New York, NY. Available online at http://www.aegis.com/news/ap/2004/AP041027.html

Lemke, J. L. (1995). *Textual politics: Discourse and social dynamics*. London: Taylor & Francis.

Le Monde (2004, March 13). The French Exception [Editorial] *Le Monde* (L. Thatcher, Trans.). Retrieved March 16, 2004, from http://www.truthout.org/docs_04/031604H.shtml

Lessig, L. (2004). *Free culture: How big media uses technology and the law to lock down culture and control creativity*. New York: Penguin Press.

Mandese, J. (2004, August 3). Consumers outspend advertisers on media. *Media Daily News*. New York: MediaPost. Retrieved [DATE] from http://www.mediapost.com/dtls_dsp_news.cfm?newsID=262413

Manovich, L. (2001). *The language of new media*. Cambridge, MA: MIT Press.

Mansell, R. (2004). Political economy, power and new media. *New Media & Society, 6*(1), 96–105.

Marcuse, H., and Neumann, F. (1942/1998). A history of the doctrine of social change. In D. Kellner (Ed.) *Collected papers of Herbert Marcuse, Vol. 1: Technology, war and fascism: Herbert Marcuse*. London: Routledge.

Marx, K., & Engels, F. (1848/1932). *The communist manifesto*. Melbourne, Australia: Proletarian Publishing.

Marx, K. (1973). *Grundrisse: Foundations of the critique of political economy (Rough draft)* (M. Nicolaus, Trans.). London: Penguin.

Marx, K. (1976). *Capital: A critique of political economy* (Vol. 1) (B. Fowkes, Trans.). London: Penguin.

Marx, K. (1981). *Capital: A critique of political economy* (Vol. 3) (D. Fernbach, Trans). London: Penguin.

McChesney, R. W. (1999a). Noam Chomsky and the struggle against neoliberalism. *Monthly Review, 50*(11), 40–48.

McChesney, R. W. (1999b). *Rich media poor democracy: Communication politics in a dubious age.* Chicago: University of Illinois Press.

McChesney, R. W. (2000). The political economy of communication and the future of the field. *Media, Culture & Society, 22*(1), 109–116.

McChesney, R. W., & Foster, J. B. (2003). The commercial tidal wave. *Monthly Review, 54,* 10.

McChesney, R. W., & Schiller, D. (2003). *The political economy of international communications: Foundations for the emerging global debate about media ownership and regulation (Technology, Business and Society Programme Paper No. 11).* Geneva: United Nations Research Institute for Social Development.

McLuhan, M. (1964). *Understanding media: The extensions of man.* London: Routledge.

Mosco, V. (1987), *The pay-per society: Computers and communication in the digital age.* New Jersey:Ablex.

Mosco, V. (1996). *The political economy of communication.* Thousand Oaks, CA: Sage.

Mosco, V., & Foster, D. (2001). Cyberspace and the end of politics. *Journal of Communication Inquiry, 25*(3), 218–236.

Mumford, L. (1961). *The city in history: Its origins, its transformations, and its prospects.* New York: Harcourt, Brace & World.

Mumford, L. (1934/1962). *Technics and civilization.* New York: Harcourt Brace & World.

Mumford, L. (1964). *The pentagon of power.* New York: Harcourt Brace Jovanovich.

Nace, T. (2003). *Gangs of America: The rise of corporate power and the disabling of democracy.* San Francisco: Bert Koehler.

Noble, D. (1997). *The religion of technology: The divinity of man and the spirit of invention.* New York: Alfred A. Knopf.

NSDAP (1939). First course for Gau and county propaganda leaders of the NSDAP. In 1. Lehrgang der Gau- und Kreispropagandaleiter der NSDAP. *Unser Wille und Weg, 9,* 124–139 (R. Bytwerk, 1998, Trans.). Retrieved March 24, 2000, from http://www.calvin.edu/academic/cas/gpa/lehrgang.htm

Organization for Economic Co-operation and Development (OECD). (1993). *OECD meeting of national accounts experts.* Paris: Author. Retrieved August 20, 2004, from http://www.oecd.org/dataoecd/54/21/2682315.pdf

OECD. (2003). *Promise and problems of e-democracy: Challenges of online citizen participation.* Paris: Author. Retrieved August 21, 2004 from http://www1.oecd.org/publications/e-book/4204011E.PDF

Pacey, A. (1999/2000). *Meaning in technology.* Cambridge, MA: MIT Press.

Papacharissi, Z. (2002). The virtual sphere: The Internet as a public Sphere. *New Media & Society, 4*(1), 9–27.

Perry, R. B. (1916). Economic value and moral value. *Quarterly Journal of Economics, 30*(3), 443–485.

Poole, D. C. (1939). Public opinion and value judgements. *Public Opinion Quarterly, 3*(3), 371–375.

Putnam, R. D. (2000). *Bowling alone: The collapse and revival of American community.* New York: Simon & Schuster.

Robinson, B., & Richardson, H. (1999, January). *The historical meaning of the crisis of information systems: A Vygotskian analysis.* Paper presented at the *Critical Management Studies Conference.* Retrieved May 12, 1999 from http://dspace.dial.pipex.com/town/close/hr22/cmsconference/

Saul, J. R. (1997). *The unconscious civilization.* Maryborough, Australia: Penguin.

Schiller, H. (1989). *Culture, Inc.: The corporate takeover of public expression.* New York: Oxford.

Schiller, D. (1996). *Theorizing communication: A history.* New York: Oxford University Press.

Schiller, D. (1999). *Digital capitalism.* Cambridge, MA: MIT Press.

Schiller, H. (1996). *Information inequality. The deepening social crisis in America.* New York: Routledge.

Schofield Clark, L., Demont-Heinrich, C., & Webber, S. (2004). Ethnographic interviews on the digital divide. *New Media and Society, 6*(4), 529–547.

Silverstone, R. (1999). *Why study the media?* London: Sage.

Smythe, D. (1981). *Dependency road: Communications, capitalism, consciousness, and Canada.* NJ: Ablex.

Stark, G. (1930). *Modern political propaganda.* (From *Moderne Politische Propaganda*). Munich: Verlag Frz. Eher Nachf. (R. L. Bytwerk, Trans.). Retrieved March 24, 2000, from http://www.calvin.edu/academic/cas/gpa/stark.htm

Takeshita, T. (1997). Exploring the media's roles in defining reality: From issue-agenda setting to attribute-agenda setting. In M. McCombs, L. Shaw, & D. Weaver (Eds.), *Communication and democracy: Exploring the intellectual frontiers in agenda-setting theory* (pp. 15–27). London: Lawrence Erlbaum Associates.

Taylor, B. C., Demont-Heinrich, C., Broadfoot, K. J., Dodge, J., & Jian, G. (2002). New media and the circuit of cyber-culture: Conceptualizing Napster. *Journal of Broadcasting & Electronic Media, 46*(4), 607–630.

Thompson, P. A. (2003). Making the world go round?: Communication, information and global trajectories of finance capital. In C. Greenfield (Ed.), *Economy, communication and neo-liberal politics. Southern Review, 36*(3), 20–43.

Wasko, J. (2001). Challenging Disney myths. *Journal of Communication Inquiry, 25*(3), 237–257.

Wells, J. (1936). Political propaganda as a moral duty. ("Politische Propaganda als sittliche Pflicht"). *Unser Wille und Weg, 6,* 238–241. (R. Bytwerk, Trans.). Retrieved March 24, 2000, from http://www.calvin.edu/academic /cas/gpa/moralpro.htm

White, L., Jr. (1940). Technology and invention in the middle ages. *Speculum, 15*(2), 141–159.

White, L., Jr. (1965). The legacy of the Middle Ages in the American Wild West. *Speculum, 40*(2), 191–202.

White, L., Jr. (1974). Technology assessment from the stance of a medieval historian. *The American Historical Review, 79*(1), 1–13.

Winner, L. (1986). *The whale and the reactor: A search for limits in an age of high technology.* Chicago : University of Chicago Press.

# ANALYTICAL TOOLS IN MEDIA MANAGEMENT AND ECONOMICS

# 23

# Quantitative Methods in Media Management and Economics

Randal A. Beam

Indiana University

What factors motivate consumers to subscribe to pay-per-view television? What is the relationship between a newspaper's subscription price and its circulation? What are the characteristics of radio stations that rely on satellite-delivered programming? Have horizontal mergers led to concentration in the book-publishing industry? What factors influence the commercial success of films?

During the past 15 years, scholars have used quantitative research methods to answer these and many other research questions about media management and media economics (Borrell, 1997; Greco, 1999; LaRose & Atkin, 1991; Lewis, 1995; Litman & Kohl, 1989). Indeed, quantitative methods appear to be the most common approach used for research in these fields. Almost 60% of the articles published in the *Journal of Media Economics (JME)* and the *International Journal on Media Management (JMM)* have been based in whole or in part on quantitative research.[1] The approaches taken in these articles varied considerably. Some researchers collected the data themselves through experiments, content analyses, or surveys. Others relied on commercial or institutional information, such as Nielsen television ratings or government economic statistics. Still others used both. Research questions focused on television, newspapers, books, movies, radio, telecommunications, the Internet, media concentration, economic theory, advertising, and dozens of other topics. For some studies, results were presented as simple tables of averages or percentages. For others, the findings were the product of sophisticated economic models

---

[1] An analysis conducted for this chapter and the chapter about qualitative methods found that about 46% of the articles used primarily quantitative methods and another 12% used a mixture of quantitative and qualitative methods.

or complicated regression analyses. These differences, although considerable, should not mask important similarities among this research. In turning to quantitative methods, all the authors of these studies were embracing a particular philosophy about how to understand the world. This philosophy assumes that researchers can systematically observe and measure social phenomena, and that what they discover can be replicated by others following similar procedures. In other words, these authors shared a similar philosophy about social science.

This chapter is an introduction to quantitative approaches to research on media management and media economics. It will provide an overview of the quantitative techniques used most widely in these fields, will present the kinds of research questions for which these techniques are appropriate, will define key concepts and principles associated with these techniques, and will offer examples that demonstrate how these techniques have been applied in research. The chapter begins by discussing briefly the basic assumptions that underlie quantitative research methods. It then proceeds to an overview of concepts, principles, and data-collection methods used in quantitative research. It concludes with a report on research trends based on the analysis of more than 300 articles published since 1988 in *JME* and *JMM,* the two leading journals on media management and media economics.[2] The goals of the chapter are to provide a general understanding of quantitative approaches to research and to demonstrate how those approaches have been applied in recent research on media management and media economics.

## EXAMINING ASSUMPTIONS ABOUT QUANTITATIVE RESEARCH

In an introduction to *Sociological Paradigms and Organisational Analysis,* Burrell and Morgan (1979) point out that all social scientists either explicitly or implicitly embrace certain assumptions about the nature of the social world and the means by which it can be investigated. These assumptions, which guide research, are related to the issues of ontology, epistemology, human nature and methodology.

Assumptions about ontology come first. They speak to beliefs about the essence of the phenomena under investigation.[3] At one extreme, ontologically speaking, is the *nominalist.* Nominalists assume that the social world is inherently the creation of individuals' cognitions and envision a social world "made up of nothing more than names, concepts and labels which are used to structure reality" (Burrell & Morgan, 1979, p. 4). Pure nominalists believe that social reality is constructed by individuals and does not exist outside of individual consciousness. Alternately, *realists* subscribe to a belief in a "real" social world that is as concrete as the natural world. For realists, the social world existed long before they were born and will continue to exist long after they are gone.

*Epistemology* is concerned with assumptions about ways in which social scientists acquire knowledge. *Positivist* epistemologies emulate the approaches taken in the natural

---

[2]Although other journals of economics, management and mass communication publish studies on media management and media economics, the *Journal of Media Economics* and the *International Journal on Media Management* are the two oldest journals devoted exclusively to research on these topics.

[3]This discussion is based on Burrell and Morgan (1979, pp. 1–37).

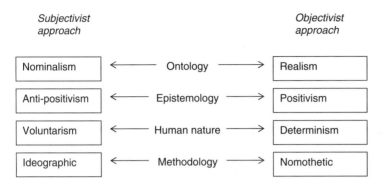

FIG. 23.1. A scheme for analyzing assumptions about social science. Adapted from Burrell and Morgan (1979, p. 3).

sciences. Positivists embrace the belief that knowledge is real and objective; is capable of being acquired and exchanged with others; and is built gradually through a long, cumulative process of inquiry. Positivists subscribe to the role of a neutral observer, and they believe that they create knowledge by offering and testing hypotheses about the social world in a search for underlying regularities or causal relationships. *Antipositivists* think it's foolish to engage in a search for "objective" social knowledge because objective knowledge doesn't exist. To antipositivists, knowledge, by its very nature, is subjective. They dismiss the idea that a social scientist can ever be a neutral observer and assert that the search for knowledge is fundamentally an individualistic pursuit. Antipositivists "understand from the inside rather than outside" (Burrell & Morgan, 1979, p. 5).

Assumptions about human nature speak to the presumed relationship between humans and their environment. At one extreme are those who adopt a *deterministic* perspective. Pure determinism assumes that humans are the products of their environment and that their actions are dictated by the social circumstances in which they find themselves. At the other extreme, a *voluntaristic* view of human nature argues that humans are creatures of free will whose activities are largely unaffected—at least they are not determined—by the social world in which they exist.

In describing key assumptions about ontology, epistemology and human nature, Burrell and Morgan have staked out the ends of three continua that are associated with *subjectivist* and the *objectivist* approaches to social science (see Fig. 23.1). Taken together, these assumptions about ontology, epistemology and human nature influence the choices that scientists make for gathering information about the social world—that is, they influence their *methodology*. Social scientists who embrace a subjectivist approach would be inclined toward *ideographic* methods. Those methods emphasize obtaining firsthand knowledge of a subject through close, detailed, comprehensive investigation. Social scientists who embrace an objectivist approach would be inclined toward *nomothetic* methods, which emulate the research processes followed in the natural sciences. It is the nomothetic method that is associated with quantitative techniques for collecting and analyzing data.

In choosing to use quantitative methods, then, researchers are embracing—either knowingly or naively—a set of fundamental assumptions about the social world and the ways one learns about it. Researchers using quantitative methods are asserting that there's an enduring, tangible social world out there that can be studied effectively by following systematic processes for gathering and analyzing information. Further, the researchers' purpose typically is to look for regularities or causal relationships within that social world, with the ultimate goal being to predict or explain social phenomena.

## Quantitative Versus Qualitative Research: Two Examples

Though quantitative research methods comprise a powerful arsenal of data collection and analysis techniques, they aren't appropriate for every scholar or for every research question. The decision about whether to use quantitative methods begins at a philosophical level with the ontological and epistemological assumptions that researchers are willing to accept. Beyond that, the researchers confront other choices that will help determine which method will be most useful in examining social phenomena.

One important choice relates to whether the researchers want to generalize their findings beyond the entities—the firms, the nations, the people, the articles, the advertisements—that they examine. Typically, researchers are forced to decide whether it's more critical to gain a rich, detailed, textured understanding about a few things or to draw broader, more generalizable conclusions about a relatively large number of things. A comparison of two recent research projects about the television industry illustrates this trade-off between depth and breadth.

Both projects had as a goal trying to better understand strategic competition within the cable television industry. Shrikhande's (2001) study of CNNI and BBC World examined how these two all-news channels sought to establish a presence in Asia. She conducted a qualitative case study in which she collected data by examining news articles and industry studies about those channels. She also interviewed key officials of both organizations, obtaining information that no other researcher had collected before. Ultimately, Shrikhande was able to offer a detailed, textured account of how these channels developed the competitive strategies that they used to start telecasts in Asia. Presumably Shrikhande hoped her study would offer insights into the competitive strategies of TV companies seeking to do business outside their home country. But it's impossible to know how idiosyncratic the experiences of CNNI and BBC World might have been. If Shrikhande could have examined 50 companies using the same method—a daunting task given the amount of detailed information that she collected—it might have enhanced her ability to draw generalizations about strategies that companies follow in situations like this. But the time and cost of such an undertaking would have been prohibitive, and the complexity of the findings would have been almost too overwhelming to present. Shrikhande chose instead to learn a lot about two cable channels. She chose depth over breadth.

Chan-Olmsted and Li (2002) also conducted a study of strategic competition within the cable industry, though they used quantitative techniques. They wanted to know how the different strategies of video programmers related to performance. Their data were obtained primarily from an analyst's report on the cable industry. That report included numerical measurements of a dozen or so characteristics—variables—that Chan-Olmsted and Li believed would be relevant to their research questions. Those quantitative variables included such things as organizational size, product-pricing practices, and operating efficiency. The analyst's report supplied this information for 59 cable channels, though the absence of complete data for 14 of those channels ultimately caused them to be removed from the study. The Chan-Olmsted and Li findings were based on cluster analysis and analysis of variance, two techniques used to analyze quantitative data. Their findings were, in effect, statistics that let them detect patterns within the cable television industry and evaluate relationships among their variables. These statistical findings didn't provide the detail and nuance that Shrikhande offered in her qualitative analysis. But the Chan-Olmsted and Li results were based on information from 45 cable channels, not two. Though they didn't have extensive information about the channels in their study, the size of their data set enhanced their ability to draw generalizations about the relationships among the variables that they studied. They chose breadth over depth.

These examples illustrate appropriate uses of qualitative and quantitative research methods. Qualitative methods were an appropriate choice for Shrikhande because the goal of her research was to see what could be learned from a detailed, comprehensive ex- amination of the strategies of two organizations. Quantitative methods worked well for Chan-Olmsted and Li because their goal was to search for relationships between strategic choices and performance. Their intent was to be able to make statements about relation- ships among key variables related to strategy and performance and to be able to argue that those relationships applied widely to organizations like the ones that they had studied.

## CONCEPTS AND PRINCIPLES IN QUANTITATIVE RESEARCH

In conducting their study on strategic choice and performance, Chan-Olmsted and Li followed a widely accepted process for collecting and analyzing quantitative data. Un- derstanding quantitative research is very much about understanding the concepts and principles that guide that research process. This section gives an overview of those con- cepts and principles and provides examples to illustrate them.

### Concepts and Variables

The building blocks of quantitative research are *concepts* and *variables*. Concepts and variables are the things that researchers study. Though scholars differ on the precise meanings of those terms, they generally concur that concepts are abstract and variables are concrete. Chaffee (1991, p. 1) calls concepts words or labels that represent things that people observe or imagine. They are abstractions formed by generalizing from particulars (Kerlinger, 1986, p. 26). "Job satisfaction" and "personal income" are examples of concepts found in research on media management and economics. One cannot see, feel, or touch "job satisfaction" or, absent a pile of cash in a sack, "personal income." But researchers have found ways to define and measure both of those concepts by creating variables that are concrete *indicators* of them.

The process of moving from a label (i.e., job satisfaction) to a clear definition of a concept and then to a system for measuring that concept is called *explication*.[4] Concept

---

[4]For a discussion of the explication process, see Chaffee (1991).

explication begins with the preliminary identification of or labeling of a state or process that researchers believe might be useful in their work. It then moves toward the statement of a *conceptual definition* that provides a precise and meaningful verbal description of the concept. The process ends with the creation and evaluation of an *empirical definition*, which specifies the way that the concept will be measured in a research study.

"Job satisfaction" is an abstract label that has an intuitive meaning to those who are interested in the management of media organizations. But what exactly is it, and how can it be measured in an employee? Those are questions that concept explication seeks to answer. Those who have done research on job satisfaction have puzzled over exactly how to define the concept, and they haven't always agreed on the best way to do so. But deciding on a useful conceptual definition is essential to conducting quantitative research. One of those who tackled this problem was Kalleberg, who defined job satisfaction conceptually as "an overall affective orientation on the part of individuals toward work roles which they are presently occupying" (1977). Kalleberg's definition is still abstract. It is not yet a system for measuring the level of job satisfaction in a worker, but it is more specific than the broad label that he began with, and it provides the foundation for developing one or more concrete indicators of the concept.

Concepts are not always inherently variable. For example, "capitalism" and "democracy" are concepts but they are not variable. But to be useful in quantitative research, concepts must be transformed into *variables*. Variables are concrete representations of concepts to which numerical values can be attached. Those numerical values vary across the entities being studied, hence the name *variable*. In quantitative research, concepts are measured via one or more variables. For example, to assess an individual's level of job satisfaction, a researcher might ask a question like this: "Overall, how much pleasure do you get from the work that you currently do? Would you say you get a lot of pleasure, some pleasure, a little pleasure, or no pleasure at all?" Numerical values can be attached to each possible response, with a "4" indicating that an individual gets a lot of pleasure from work and a "1" indicating that the individual gets no pleasure at all. Presumably the response to the "how much pleasure" question varies from individual to individual because some get more satisfaction from their work than others. The variable, then, is the set of responses that all individuals have given when asked the question, "Overall, how much pleasure do you get from the work that you currently do?" It is the concrete indicator for the abstract concept of job satisfaction.

The rules of the research game don't require that a single variable be used to measure a single concept. In fact, for a multifaceted concept such as job satisfaction it's better to use a group of related variables that can tap into the different aspects of the concept. Researchers studying job satisfaction might ask a series of questions about attitudes toward pay, fringe benefits, working conditions, feedback from supervisors and so forth. Together, the entire set of responses to those questions—the set of variables—is used to assess the degree of satisfaction that an individual has with a job.

The *operational definition* of job satisfaction will spell out exactly how those individual variables are to be used, collectively, to measure job satisfaction. Two common approaches are to create a composite *scale* or an *index*. A composite scale is a measure composed of several variables that, taken as a group, have a logical structure (Babbie, 1992, p. G7). Those variables produce an ordinal measurement of the concept. A Guttman scale is one type of composite scale (Babbie, 1992, pp. 183–186). A Guttman scale to assess the profit orientation of media companies might include these four true/false statements:

1. At Company X, the management seeks to operate profitably over a period of 3 fiscal years.
2. At Company X, the management seeks to operate profitably over a period of 1 fiscal year.
3. At Company X, the management seeks to operate profitably during every fiscal quarter.
4. At Company X, the management seeks to operate profitably during every monthly accounting period.

In creating a Guttman scale, the assumption would be that if Statement 4 were a truthful description of the profit orientation of Company X, Statements 1 through 3 would be true as well. Further, it would be assumed that Company X would have a stronger profit orientation than Company Y, for which only Statements 1 and 2 were true.

The simple summated index is another kind of composite measure that also combines two or more variables in an effort to provide a better indicator of a concept. In a simple additive index, however, the variables have no logical structure to them and all are of equal importance as indicators of a concept (Babbie, 1992, p. G4). For example, a researcher wanting to measure the profit orientation of daily newspaper firms might ask managers to respond to these four true/false items:

1. Your newspaper firm has been profitable in each of the last four fiscal quarters.
2. For the last fiscal year, the profit margin at your newspaper firm was higher than the average margin for newspapers owned by publicly held corporations.
3. Within the last fiscal year, your newspaper firm has reduced staff size in an effort to meet its profit goals.
4. At your newspaper firm, the profit goal for this fiscal year is higher than the profit goal for last fiscal year.

In creating a simple additive index, the researcher might assign a value of "1" for each "true" answer and a value of "0" for each false answer. The values would be added, and the total for each newspaper firm would become its value on the index—a new composite variable created from the four original variables. The index value would be the indicator of the strength of a newspaper firm's profit orientation. The Guttman scale and a simple summated index are two popular options for creating composite variables, but there are others. For a more complete discussion on scales or indices, consult a text on research methods or on scale and index construction (Babbie, 1992; Wimmer & Dominick, 2003).

In everyday discussion, researchers tend to move back and forth loosely between the terms *concept* and *variable*. Often, they don't bother distinguishing between the terms if the concept is relatively concrete. The concept of personal income, for example, can be defined as "the financial compensation received by persons from participation in production" (U.S. Bureau of Economic Analysis, 2004). In the United States, personal income is almost certainly measured as the number of dollars that someone is paid over a specific period of time for his or her work. Though "personal income" is the concept and the "dollars earned per year for work" is the variable, it's likely that researchers will simply refer to personal income as a variable because it is a relatively concrete concept.

## Unit of Analysis, Level of Measurement

The final stages of explication have as their goal producing an appropriate, reliable, and valid way of measuring a concept for use in quantitative data analysis. The composite measures discussed in the previous section are examples of two approaches to creating variables that become measures or indicators of a concept. On the path toward that goal, researchers must confront other important issues related to measurement. One of the first is to determine the *unit of analysis* for a study. The unit of analysis is the thing—the individual, the collectivity, the object, the event—being studied and about which data are being collected (Babbie, 1992, p. G8). Ultimately, many if not all of the variables in a data set will be characteristics of the unit of analysis. In research on media management and economics, typical units of analysis are the individual, the firm, the market, the industry, the nation, the household, the article, the television program, or the film. Occasionally, an event such as a merger, a transaction, or a complaint is used as a unit of analysis.

Table 23.1 shows how often different units of analysis were used in the primarily quantitative studies in *The Journal of Media Economics* and *The International Journal on*

TABLE 23.1
Percentages of Units of Analysis

| Unit of Analysis | Percent |
| --- | --- |
| Firm | 37 |
| Market | 18 |
| Individual | 12 |
| Industry | 9 |
| TV program | 7 |
| Household | 3 |
| Print article | 2 |
| Print publication | 2 |
| Nation | 1 |
| Organizational collectivity, pair | 1 |
| Year | 1 |
| Movie, film | 1 |
| Other, not categorized | 4 |

*Note:* Figures apply to articles that used primarily quantitative methods. Figures do not add to 100 because of rounding. ($N = 150$.)

*Media Management.* The firm was the most common unit of analysis. Typical variables used to characterize firms include such things as the number of individuals the firm employs, the firm's ownership structure, the number of years it has been in business, the firm's revenues, and the firm's profit margins. A study by Demers (1996) on ownership structure and profit goals is one example of research that used the firm as a unit of analysis. In that study, Demers collected information on the characteristics of 223 daily newspapers. Those characteristics included the degree to which the newspaper firm exhibited traits of a corporate form of organization and the degree to which the newspaper firm emphasized profits as its most important organizational value. Demers found that the more a newspaper firm exhibited traits of corporate organization, the less it emphasized profits as its central goal. His variables tracked the characteristics of firms, and his findings drew generalizations about firms—about his unit of analysis. It's worth noting the unit of analysis is not always the same as the entity from which data are collected. Demers gathered information from people—from 409 employees at the newspapers in his study. At some newspapers, he obtained data from more than one person. But he wanted to generalize about the 223 newspapers in his study, not about the 409 individuals working at those papers. In cases where he obtained information from more than one person at a paper, he combined their responses so that on any given variable (degree of corporate organization, emphasis on profits, organization size and so forth) he had only one value for each unit of analysis—for each newspaper firm.

A second important consideration in measurement is the level at which a variable measured. Four *levels of measurement* exist—the nominal level, ordinal level, interval level, and ratio level. In some cases, the level of measurement is determined by an inherent characteristic of the concept being studied (Wimmer & Dominick, 2003, pp. 50–52). In other cases, the level of measurement is determined by choices that the researcher makes during concept explication.

The lowest level of measurement is the *nominal* level. At the nominal level, the conditions or responses for a variable have no inherent ordinal ranking. Gender is a nominal variable, with the conditions of the variable being "male" and "female." In most quantitative research studies neither gender condition is considered inherently higher than the other. In research on media management and media economics, common nominal variables would be type of media firm (newspaper, television, magazine), type of television program (news, entertainment, sports), or type of ownership structure (public, quasi-public, private).

The other three levels of measurement are associated with an ordinal ranking—with responses or conditions that can be ordered from low to high. The most rudimentary of those levels of measurement is the *ordinal* level. For ordinal-level variables, responses or conditions of a variable can be ranked from low to high, but the differences between those responses or conditions are not uniform. "Job satisfaction" is an example of a variable measured at the ordinal level. To assess job satisfaction among U.S. journalists, Weaver, Beam, Brownlee, Voakes, and Wilhoit (2003) surveyed 1,500 news workers, asking this question: "Overall, how satisfied are you with your current job? Would you say you very satisfied, fairly satisfied, somewhat dissatisfied or very dissatisfied?" Clearly, the journalists who replied "fairly satisfied" rated their job more favorably than the journalists who replied "somewhat dissatisfied," and the journalists who said "somewhat dissatisfied" rated their job more favorably than the journalists who said "very dissatisfied." But nothing can be known about the distance between each of those responses. It's not known whether the individual who was "very satisfied" was three times, five times, or 20 times happier than the individual who was "fairly" satisfied. All that's known is that some responses represented a higher condition of satisfaction than others. Variables measured at the nominal and ordinal levels are examples of *discrete variables*. Discrete variables are those that take on a finite set of values that cannot be meaningfully broken into smaller, equal categories (Wimmer & Dominick, 2003, p. 461).

Variables measured at the *interval* level solve the distance problem that plagues ordinal variables. At the interval level, the distances between response categories are equal. Research methods texts invariably cite temperature as the classic interval-level variable. The distance between 32 degrees Fahrenheit and 33 degrees is the same as between 55 and 56 degrees or between 100 and 101 degrees. In research on media management and media economics, many variables meet the criterion of equidistance between response categories. The Dow Jones Industrial Average for stocks is an interval-level variable. At any given time, any 100-point difference in the Dow average is equivalent to any other 100-point difference.

The highest level of measurement is the *ratio* level. The properties of interval-level and ratio-level measures are the same with this exception: Ratio-level measures have a true zero point. Again, many ratio-level variables are used in research on media management and economics. Revenues, profits, marginal costs, and sales are all examples of variables for which a true zero point could (and sometimes does) exist. Variables measured at the interval and ratio levels are examples of *continuous* variables (Kerlinger, 1986, pp. 35–36). For a continuous variable, response values can be broken into increasingly smaller, equal categories and still have meaning. Time is a continuous variable. Hours can be broken into minutes, minutes into seconds, seconds into fractions of seconds.

The level of measurement of variables has both substantive and practical implications for researchers. Variables must be both reliable and valid indicators of a concept to be useful in quantitative research. Attempting to measure a variable at an inappropriate level threatens both validity and reliability, two terms discussed more fully later. In most instances, for example, it would be inappropriate to try to treat race, gender, or nation as an ordinal-, interval-, or ratio-level variable. That would be inconsistent with the inherent nature of the concept. Similarly, researchers should use caution in imposing interval- or ratio-level measures on concepts that don't naturally lend themselves to that kind of treatment. It might be possible, for example, to ask an individual to rate his level of job satisfaction on a scale of zero to 100, with zero indicating "no satisfaction" and 100 indicating "maximum satisfaction." Though that produces a ratio-like set of responses, the researcher still doesn't know whether the distance between 10 and 20 is truly equivalent to the distance between 70 and 80 on this "yardstick" for assessing job satisfaction. Still, there are practical benefits to using the highest level of measurement possible. Many of the most powerful statistical techniques assume that data have been collected at the interval or ratio levels. Often researchers fudge on these assumptions and treat ordinal-level data as if it were interval-level data. Statisticians disagree about whether this is a serious deviation from rigorous research practice (Wimmer & Dominick, 2003, p. 52).

## Reliability and Validity

Discussions about reliability and validity center around the adequacy of a system used to measure a concept (Babbie, 1992, pp. 127–135; Bryman, 2001; Stamm, 2003, pp. 134–140; Wimmer & Dominick, 2003, pp. 56–60). *Reliability* is perhaps the easier term to understand. It refers to the ability of a system of measurement to consistently produce the same result for the same phenomenon every time the system is used. For example, most households have meters that measure water use. If a meter is reliable, it will register the same usage each time an identical quantity of water passes through it. If the meter said that filling a bathtub took 30 gallons of water this morning, a reliable meter would also say that it took 30 gallons to fill the tub tomorrow morning and 30 gallons the morning after. An unreliable meter would be less consistent. This morning it might report 30 gallons, tomorrow 28 gallons and perhaps 33 gallons the day after.

A reliable water meter is not necessarily an accurate water meter, however. Suppose that by laboriously carting water in a certified 5-gallon can, a homeowner determined that it actually took 35 gallons to fill the bathtub. Though the meter has proved to be a reliable system for measuring water—day in and day out, it registered 30 gallons—it has not provided a valid measure of water use. *Validity* speaks to the "truthfulness" of the measuring system. Is what's being measured actually what the researcher thinks is being measured? Recall one of the systems—one of the questions—used to measure job satisfaction: "Overall, how much pleasure do you get from the work that you currently do? Would you say you get a lot of pleasure, some pleasure, a little pleasure, or no pleasure at all?" When confronting the issue of validity, the researcher must ask himself: Does this question truly measure job satisfaction? Or is it tapping into something else?

Quantitative research provides statistical tools for helping assess the reliability of systems of measurement. Validity is another story. Though research methods books outline several strategies for assessing validity, whether a system of measurement is a valid indicator of a concept is a judgment call. The researcher must be able to make a case for the validity of her approach to measuring a concept.

## Description, Prediction, and Explanation

The fundamental goals of most quantitative research in media management and media economics can be characterized as efforts to describe, to predict, or to explain. Though description is sometimes considered the most rudimentary goal of research, providing data that accurately describe something can be of enormous value.[5] Each day, for example, Nielsen Media Research describes the size and composition of audiences for television programs. Nielsen's descriptions strongly influence advertising rates in the multi-billion-dollar commercial television business.

---

[5]Descriptive research should not be confused with descriptive statistics, though the product of quantitative descriptive research typically is presented using descriptive statistics. *Descriptive statistics* characterize or summarize observations from a sample, either for a single variable or for a relationship involving two or more variables. Descriptive statistics can be contrasted with *inferential statistics*, which are used to draw inferences about a population based on a sample. For a fuller explanation, see Babbie (1992, pp. 432 and G3).

Descriptive studies often provide the foundation for research that seeks to predict or explain. Whereas descriptive research focuses on determining the characteristics of an entity under study, research that has prediction or explanation as its goal examines relationships among concepts or variables. In the early 1990s, the U.S. Federal Communications Commission changed the way that it regulated telecommunication services. Uri (2003) wanted to know whether this change was associated with differences in service quality within the telecommunications industry. A study was conducted to examine the relationship between the two concepts. One of the concepts was the "regulation system" imposed on the telecommunication industry, which as a variable had two conditions—a rate-of-return system and an incentive system. The second concept was "service quality." Four variables were designated as indicators of service quality. Uri proposed that the relationship between the system of regulation and service quality was causal—that is, that a change in the system of regulation from rate-of-return to incentive caused a change in the indicators of service quality. In causal relationships, variables that determine or influence a phenomenon are called *independent variables* or *predictor variables*. Variables that are affected or influenced by an independent or predictor variable are called *dependent variables*. Uri's study demonstrated that there was, indeed, a relationship between the system of regulation and service quality. When the system changed from rate-of-return to incentive, service quality declined. Uri also concluded that this relationship was causal—that the change in the regulatory system was responsible for the decline in service quality, not just associated with it. Uri's research could be considered an attempt to predict or explain in this sense: When the FCC changes its system of regulation from rate-of-return to incentive, it's possible to "predict" what will happen to service quality, other things being equal. Another way to think about that relationship is that under certain conditions, declines in service quality can be "explained" by changes in FCC regulations.

## Univariate, Bivariate, and Multivariate Statistics

In quantitative research, conclusions such as those that Uri reached are dependent on statistical analyses of data. Dozens of statistical techniques are available to help researchers make sense of quantitative data. In choosing from among these techniques, researchers should consider the characteristics of the data collected, the goals of the research, and their understanding of the techniques. The last consideration is sometimes overlooked. If research is done with the goal of improving the understanding of a phenomenon, it's important that researchers work with tools that they understand how to use properly.

The techniques used for analysis of quantitative data can be grouped into three broad categories—univariate analysis, bivariate analysis, and multivariate analysis (Babbie, 1992, pp. 389–408). *Univariate analysis* focuses on the examination of the distribution of answers for a single variable. Descriptive research relies heavily on univariate analysis. Results often are presented in the form of frequencies or percentages. Table 23.1 showed the results of a univarite analysis in which the findings were presented as percentages. In addition to frequencies and percentages, univariate analysis also produces measures of central tendency (mean, median, and mode), measures of dispersion (range and standard deviation)

**TABLE 23.2**
Job Satisfaction by Gender

| Job Satisfaction | Men (N = 768) | Women (N = 379) |
|---|---|---|
| Very satisfied | 34.1% | 31.7% |
| Fairly satisfied | 52.5 | 47.0 |
| Somewhat dissatisfied | 11.8 | 19.5 |
| Very dissatisfied | 1.6 | 1.8 |

Note: From Weaver, Beam, Brownlee, Voakes, and Wilhoit (2003).

and measures of distribution (skewness, kurtosis). For continuous variables such as age or income, measures of central tendency, dispersion and distribution often are the most meaningful *descriptive statistics*. For discrete variables, frequencies and percentages typically are most appropriate.

In *bivariate analyses*, researchers examine the relationship between two variables. *Contingency tables*—sometimes called crosstabs—are a classic example of bivariate analysis. Table 23.2 is a contingency table from Weaver et al.'s (2003) study of U.S. journalists. It expresses the level of job satisfaction by gender, showing the percentages of men and of women for each condition of job satisfaction. The percentages sum down the columns, to 100. Organizing the table this way helps the researcher see the relationship between job satisfaction and gender. Casual inspection of the table suggests that although the majority of both men and women are satisfied with their jobs, satisfaction tends to be somewhat higher among men than women.

Another common bivariate analysis is to compute a *correlation coefficient*, which assesses the strength of the association between two variables. Correlation coefficients can be computed between variables at all levels of measurement, with different coefficients appropriate for variables at different levels of measurement. One of the mostly commonly used correlation coefficients, the Pearson product-moment coefficient, is appropriate for two variables measured at the interval or ratio levels. This coefficient ranges from $-1.0$ to $+1.0$. The sign of the coefficient (plus or minus) describes the nature of the relationship between two variables. A positive value for the coefficient indicates a positive association between the variables—as the value of one variable rises, so does the value of the other variable. A negative value indicates an inverse relationship—as the value of one variable increases, the value of the other variable declines. The magnitude of the coefficient indicates the strength of the relationship between two variables, with values of $+1$ and $-1$ indicating the strongest magnitudes. In their national study of U.S. journalists (Weaver et al., 2003), a Pearson coefficient was computed for the ages of the journalists and the number of years of professional experience that they had. The coefficient was .86, indicating a strong positive association between those variables. As the age of the journalist increased, the number of years of professional experience increased, too, just as one might expect.

As was the case with univariate analyses, the frequencies and percentages in contingency tables and the Pearson correlation coefficient are examples of descriptive statistics. In these examples, however, the statistics are used to describe a relationship between two variables rather than a distribution of cases for a single variable. Under some circumstances, *inferential statistics* also can be used in bivariate analysis. Inferential statistics allow a researcher to draw conclusions about a population of interest based on the characteristics of a sample (Babbie, 1992, pp. 447–456). For example, inferential statistics can help determine how likely it is that the difference found in the sample between men's and women's job satisfaction will also be found in the entire population of U.S. journalists. The contingency-table and correlational analyses are only two of several inferential techniques appropriate for bivariate analysis. Other frequently used techniques include tests of differences between means, one-way analysis of variance, and simple (two-variable) regression analysis.

The most powerful statistical techniques used in quantitative research on media management and economics involve the analysis, simultaneously, of more than two variables. Many of the most popular *multivariate* techniques for data analysis are extensions of those statistical tools used in bivariate analyses. Multivariate analysis is appropriate for the following circumstances:

- Situations in which it's necessary to *control* for one or more variables to get a true sense of the relationship between variables of interest. Controlling for a variable means removing its effect on a relationship of primary interest. For example, researchers studying gender and job satisfaction among U.S. journalists also might believe salary to be associated both with gender and with job satisfaction. To accurately understand the relationship between gender and job satisfaction it would be necessary to remove or to hold constant the influence of salary on this relationship of primary interest. Multivariate techniques allow the influence of a variable such as salary to be controlled.
- Situations in which the researcher wants to look at the impact of two or more independent variables on a dependent variable. Salary and gender are not the only factors that might influence a journalist's job satisfaction. Other influences might include age, the type of assignments the journalist is given, the degree of autonomy the journalist has in her work, and so forth. *Multiple-regression analysis, analysis of variance,* and *analysis of covariance* are multivariate techniques that allow a researcher to better understand how a group of independent variables affect a dependent variable.
- Situations in which the researcher wants to look at changes across time. A cousin of multiple regression, *time-series analysis* is appropriate for analyzing data collected at multiple time periods for the same variable. A study involving changes in advertising expenditures over many years would be a candidate for time-series analysis.
- Situations in which a researcher would like to use a set of variables to predict membership in a group. Employee turnover is a concern of media managers. *Discriminant analysis, logistic regression,* and *cluster analysis* are techniques that could be used to understand the most important factors associated with an employee's membership in one of two groups, those who stay in a job and those who leave a job.
- Situations in which a large group of variables believed to be indicators of a concept or concepts need to be reduced to a more manageable number. *Factor analysis* and

*multidimensional scaling* are multivariate techniques used for data reduction—for creating a relatively small number of composite variables from a relatively large number of individual measures. Those techniques look for statistical associations among individual indicators. Perhaps a researcher interested in job satisfaction has developed 50 measures to tap into different aspects of that concept. Factor analysis could be used to group those indicators into a smaller number of composite items reflecting different *dimensions* of job satisfaction.

• Situations in which the researcher wants to examine systems or models in which variables may act simultaneously both as independent and dependent variables. *LISREL*, an acronym for linear structural relations, and *path analysis* can be used to test such models. A researcher testing a complicated model of consumer behavior might turn to LISREL or techniques like it.

Other statistical techniques are available for the multivariate analysis of quantitative data. Most research methods and statistics texts describe the statistical techniques for analysis of quantitative data in more detail than is possible here (Babbie, 1992; Cohen & Cohen, 1983; Jaeger, 1990; Marascuilo & Serlin, 1988; McClendon, 1994; Wonnacott & Wonnacott, 1969). Other useful sources of information about quantitative data analysis are manuals, guidebooks, and online support for the computer software used in data analysis. SAS/STAT and SPSS are two comprehensive statistical-analysis software packages used widely in the social sciences. The basic SAS/STAT and SPSS programs can compute descriptive and inferential statistics for data sets of the size typically used in academic research. In addition, the companies sell data-analysis software for specialized purposes. Versions of SPSS and SAS/STAT are available for personal computers. The companies sell manuals that describe how to use their programs. Commercial publishers also offer guides to the software that often are cheaper than the manuals. The Web sites for SAS/STAT (www.sas.com) and SPSS (www.spss.com) provide information about buying and using their statistical software packages.

## OBTAINING QUANTITATIVE DATA

Those who use quantitative research methods to study media management and media economics most often rely on one or more of five approaches to obtain their data— they conduct a survey, they do a lab experiment, they execute a content analysis, they undertake a case study, or they use data obtained from institutional sources or other research studies. This section provides brief discussions about the value of each approach to data collection.

### Institutional and Secondary Sources

Almost 60% of the primarily quantitative articles in *JME* and *JMM* were based on analyses of data not collected specifically for the research project for which they were being used (Table 23.3). Occasionally those data came from other scholars who provided access to data that they had collected for previous studies. More often, those analyses were of

**TABLE 23.3**
Frequencies of Data-Collection Methods

| Data-Collection Method | Percent |
| --- | --- |
| Secondary data | 57 |
| Survey | 24 |
| Content analysis | 13 |
| Model specification, simulation | 3 |
| Experiment | 2 |
| Not categorized | 2 |

*Note:* Figures add to more than 100 percent because some studies use multiple methods.

data collected by commercial organizations, trade organizations, and governmental or quasi-governmental agencies. In those instances, the data for these *secondary analyses*[6] were made available free or for a fee. In either situation, researchers have not collected or directed the collection of the data that they are using in their study. That is what distinguishes secondary analysis from *primary analysis*, which is analysis of original data collected by researchers for a specific research purpose.

Secondary analyses are popular because the data are comparatively inexpensive, they can be obtained quickly, and they frequently are of high quality. The expense of collecting the data either has been borne by someone other than the researcher or is shared among a large number of individuals and organizations, lowering the cost to any single user. Economic data from the U.S. decennial census or from Eurostat are examples of information from government or quasi-governmental organizations that are made available for free or for a nominal fee. Ratings for television programs or circulation figures for newspapers are examples of data that have been collected by commercial organizations and sold to users. The appendix to this chapter lists some sources for secondary data used in research on media management and media economics. Although cost, ease of access, and quality are important benefits of conducting secondary analyses of data, this approach also has drawbacks. Perhaps the most important is the inability of researchers to control precisely what information is collected and from whom. For example, researchers who want to use data from the U.S. Bureau of Labor Statistics to study the income of reporters and editors are "stuck with" the bureau's definition of that occupation group. The researchers must make do with what's available, even if it's not ideally suited for the research questions they are trying to answer.

---

[6]Definitions of secondary analysis vary. Heaton (2004) defines secondary analysis as research that uses existing data collected for a prior study. Becker (2003) defines it as the reuse of social data after they have been put aside by the original researcher. The definition used in this chapter is broader. It encompasses not only data collected by researchers for previous studies, but also data collected by governmental, quasi-governmental, and commercial organizations that are made available for general use in research, free or for a fee.

Typical examples of secondary analysis are Borrell's (1997) research on satellite-delivered programs at U.S. radio stations and Jayakar and Waterman's (2000) study of the film industry, both of which were published in *JME*. Borrell's interest was in determining what kinds of U.S. radio stations used satellite-delivered programming. Information about satellite-delivered programming was originally collected by a commercial organization and published in the *M Street Radio Directory*. Borrell sampled the directory's list of 12,600 stations and harvested data for about 500 stations. Those data became the basis for his study, which identified station characteristics associated with use of satellite-delivered programming. Though Borrell used a single source of secondary data in his study, it's common to draw information from several sources. That was the case with the Jayakar and Waterman research on international trade in theatrical films. Their study married national-level economic data with information on box-office receipts collected by a private publication. Their analyses tested economic models that helped explain why U.S.-produced films were popular in foreign markets. In that study, the secondary analyses were done to assist with theory development. That is often a hallmark of research involving secondary analysis. Generally, the interest is less in the data as a way to describe a population than in their value in developing and testing a theory.

## Experiments

Experiments are a relatively uncommon way of collecting data for research on media management and media economics. Of the roughly 150 studies in *JME* and *JMM* that used primarily quantitative methods, only about 2% relied on data from experiments. One reason that experiments are rare is that the unit of analysis is often the individual (or some other animate object). Research questions about media management and media economics tend to require units of analysis above the individual level, such as work groups, organizations, markets, or industries. Indeed, individuals were the unit of analysis in only about 12% of the *JME* and *JMM* quantitative studies.

Experiments are usually conducted in a controlled setting—a laboratory—rather than in the natural environment.[7] The researcher is typically interested in the impact of one or more manipulated *factors* on participants in the experiment, who are called *subjects*. The designs of experiments can be quite complicated, so a reader interested in experimental research should consult the classic treatment of that subject by Campbell and Stanley (1963) or a text on experimental design. The simplest true experiment consists of two groups of subjects, preferably with identical numbers of subjects assigned randomly to each group. Random assignment of subjects renders each group equal, for the purpose of the research, as the experiment begins. A *pretest* is conducted of the two groups, and then a *stimulus*—a manipulated factor—is applied to one group while the other group is left alone.[8] Those receiving the stimulus constitute the *experimental group* or *treatment*

---

[7] Field experiments seek to combine the strength of experimental design with a naturalistic setting. For a description of field experiments, see Hair, Babin, Money & Samouel (2003, pp. 65–67).

[8] Under this design, the pretest also allows the researcher to check the assumption of equality made as a result of random assignment of subjects. If the groups are equal (within reasonable limits) in terms of the variables of interest for the experiment, that can be confirmed by comparing pretest results for the experimental and control groups.

*group* and those left alone constitute the *control group*. A posttest is administered to both groups, and the results of the posttests are analyzed to determine if the stimulus appeared to have any effect. If it did, that effect should be evident in the experimental group but not the control group.

Though rarely used in the study of media management or economics, experiments have an important advantage over other quantitative methods when it comes to establishing causal relationships. Because researchers administer the stimulus themselves, they are able to establish that, without question, a potential cause of a phenomenon occurred prior to the presumed effect of that phenomenon. That is critical in distinguishing between a causal relationship and a simple association between two variables. Though researchers can take advantage of many different kinds of experimental and quasi-experimental designs, all have in common an attempt to assess the effect of one or more manipulated variables on groups of subjects. That was the case in a study in which Maxwell (2003) used a quasi-experimental design to determine how price differences affected the likelihood that students would buy textbooks from an online vendor versus a traditional campus bookstore. Her experimental subjects were 72 undergraduate students to whom she presented different purchase scenarios. In those purchase scenarios, both pricing levels and the kind of bookseller (online vs. traditional bookstore) were manipulated. Those constituted the key independent variables in her experiment. The dependent variables were likelihood that the students would buy books from a particular bookseller and attitudes that the students had toward those booksellers. From the experiment, she concluded that price differences influenced purchase intent but not necessarily other attitudes toward the booksellers.

## Survey Research

Surveys are the most common way that researchers obtain data for quantitative studies on media management and media economics. About a quarter of the primarily quantitative *JME* and *JMM* studies used primary or original survey data—data collected by the author with a specific research purpose in mind. In addition, many other quantitative studies relied on secondary analysis of survey data from governmental, quasi-governmental, or commercial organizations.

Surveys seek to obtain information from relatively large numbers of individuals or collectivities through interviews, written questionnaires, or direct monitoring of behavior. Interviews of *respondents*—individuals or collectivities that complete survey questionnaires—can be conducted by telephone or in person. Respondents also can be asked to complete written questionnaires by themselves. These *self-administered questionnaires* are handed out, mailed, or distributed via the Internet. Sometimes they are published in a newspaper or magazine with a request that readers fill out the questionnaire and send it back to the sponsor. Direct monitoring of respondents is relatively rare in survey research and usually is done as part of a broader data-collection process that also includes an interview or self-administered questionnaire. For example, some Nielsen television ratings are based on a system that electronically monitors the programs that individuals in Nielsen households watch. Those viewing data are then matched to information collected previously about the individuals living in those households. That permits Nielsen to provide clients with age, gender, income, and other information about viewers of particular TV programs.

Surveys are useful ways to obtain both qualitative and quantitative data. However, the analysis of qualitative survey data can be cumbersome if the number of respondents is large. Weaver et al.'s (2003) survey of 1,500 U.S. journalists produced more than 1,200 pages of responses to just 10 *open-ended questions*—questions for which there were no predetermined response options. Open-ended questions provide more flexibility to the respondent, of course, but typically lengthen the data-analysis portion of a research project. Open-ended answers usually must go through an intermediate step of being read and categorized so that they can be converted into numeric form and analyzed using statistical software. Or, only a small sample of the responses is analyzed, which means that a substantial amount of the information collected is discarded.

On the other hand, if the researcher chooses to use *fixed-response questions* that produce quantitative data, information from thousands of survey respondents can be easily and quickly analyzed using statistical software such as Excel, SPSS, or SAS/STAT. Fixed-response questions can seek specific quantitative information, such as the respondent's age at her last birthday, or they can ask the respondent to choose from a relatively small number of potential answers that the researcher has chosen in advance. Those answers can be assigned numeric values. For example, the response options to a question about job satisfaction might be coded "4" for "very satisfied," "3" for "fairly satisfied," "2" for "somewhat dissatisfied," and "1" for "very dissatisfied." Many survey research centers enter information directly into computers as respondents are being interviewed or they scan responses to self-administered questionnaires directly into a computer data file. This allows almost instantaneous data analysis, assuming that the responses have been rendered in quantitative form. That is a powerful incentive to ask fixed-response questions if the researcher is looking for quick results.[9]

Rigorous, standardized procedures are critical in survey research, particularly when it comes to creating and administering items in questionnaires. (Questionnaires are used in other forms of data collection, too, but are the primary tool for collecting information in surveys of individuals and collectivities.) The most successful researchers work hard on concept explication so that the variables that they create measure their key concepts as precisely and usefully as possible. If the tool for data collection is a questionnaire for individuals, every effort is made to make sure that respondents can easily understand the items in it. If an item is ambiguous, there's no certainty that Respondent A and Respondent B will agree on the information that the item is seeking. Survey interviewers are trained to present the items precisely as written so that all respondents are being told or asked exactly the same thing. Items are worded carefully so that they do not predispose respondents to choose a particular answer or leave respondents unable to find appropriate answers from among those that are offered. All this care is taken so that answers from different respondents to the same item can be compared. Careless wording or inconsistency across interviewers or inappropriate response options can undermine

---

[9]These are sometimes called closed-ended questions.

that goal, creating problems with both the validity and reliability of information obtained through the survey.

Using survey research to search for evidence of causal relationships can be more challenging than in a tightly controlled laboratory setting. Whereas it is relatively easy to use survey data to determine if two variables are correlated, it is often more difficult to meet other conditions for establishing that a relationship between those variables is causal—that Variable X caused Variable Y. That is particularly true if the survey data are *cross-sectional*—that is, collected at a single point in time. If the survey data are *longitudinal*—collected at two or more points in time—it's sometimes possible to mimic the administration of a manipulated variable, as in an experiment. That can help establish evidence of a causal relationship.

A key consideration in survey research is how to select the respondents to be surveyed. One approach is to conduct a *census*, which is an attempt to gather information about everyone or everything in a population of interest. An example is the decennial U.S. census in which the government tries to survey every household in the country. Conducting a census would be unusual in fields such as political science, public opinion, or sociology, where the populations being studied are typically large, and fluid, and therefore costly to contact. But a census often is not as daunting in research on media management and media economics.[10] A researcher undertaking a study of a nation's daily newspapers or commercial broadcast stations could readily obtain list of all those firms and, with relatively little money, collect data about each one of them. Van Kranenburg (2002) did just that in his study of market structure in the Dutch daily newspaper market. He used annual circulation data that had been collected from all editorially independent newspapers in The Netherlands after 1950.

Most researchers, however, are satisfied with a *sample* from a population, rather than a census. Sampling is usually cheaper and easier than conducting a census. Samples fall into two broad categories—probability and nonprobability samples. *Nonprobability samples* are also called *informal samples, convenience samples,* or *model samples,* which Kish defines as "a sampling based on broad assumptions about the distribution of survey variables in a population" (Kish, 1995, p. 18). Less technically, nonprobability samples rely on something other than probability theory to determine which potential respondents—called *sample elements*[11]—to include. Sometimes it's serendipity, as in the case of the TV call-in poll that asks who should be the next coach of the local football team. Other times it might be the researcher's hunch that the women in the church auxiliary would be good people to survey about the effectiveness of a new laundry soap or floor cleaner. One common nonprobability sample is the *quota sample*. In a quota sample, the researcher decides in advance what percentage of respondents should have particular characteristics—men and women; professionals and nonprofessionals; Republicans, Democrats, and independents. Respondents are recruited or chosen until those quotas a filled. The quota sample is but one type of nonprobability sample. Readers who want to learn about other kinds should consult a basic social-science research methods text such as Bryman (2001, pp. 83–104).

---

[10]Kish argues that a census can be considered one kind of sample. See Kish (1995, pp. 17–18).

[11]Sample elements are the entities from which information is obtained. See Babbie (1992, p. 232).

A drawback of a nonprobability sample is that it's not possible to estimate how representative the sample is of a population of interest. That's a significant limitation if the goal of research is to draw generalizations about social phenomena in a population. Still, management research often lends itself to nonprobability sampling because it can be impractical to use more complicated—and often more expensive—probability sampling techniques. In his book *When MBAs Rule the Newsroom*, Underwood (1993) used a nonprobability sample of 12 West Coast newspapers to assess whether market-oriented journalism was changing traditional values within the newspaper industry. Underwood and a colleague had managed to elicit the cooperation of those 12 dailies, which were relatively close to their homes in Seattle, so they conducted their research using surveys of more than 400 journalists at those newspapers. Were the journalists at those 12 organizations representative of all U.S. daily newspaper journalists? It's impossible to say. With nonprobability sampling, the degree to which the sample is representative of the population of interest can't be estimated. But a probability sample of either journalists or newspapers would likely have included respondents scattered across the country or would have involved newspapers reluctant to cooperate with this research. The 400-plus journalists in Underwood's study probably gave a reasonable sense of journalists' attitudes toward market-driven journalism. Even so, it was technically not possible to estimate how representative that sample might have been of the population of all U.S. journalists.

Though more difficult to execute, *probability samples* often are worth the extra effort because they allow researchers to make stronger claims about the representativeness of the sample. A probability sample is one where any single element of a population potentially has a known, nonzero probability of being included (Kish, 1995, p. 20). A *simple random sample*, for example, is one well-known type of probability sample. In a simple random sample, each element in a population has an equal chance of being included in the sample. If the population of interest is 10,000 television programs, a simple random sample of 500 shows means that any single show, chosen at random, has a 1-in-20 chance of being included. With that information in hand, researchers would be able to estimate how likely it is that the findings based on the sample of 500 reflect the real values that exist in the population of 10,000. The estimates are based on probability theory, which can be employed as a tool in data analysis if the researcher has used a probability sample. If the probability sample is drawn properly, it's highly likely to produce extremely accurate estimates of the characteristics that the researcher wants to measure in the population of interest.[12] In other words, the sample is likely to be "representative" of that population.

Probability samples are excellent ways to gather accurate information about large populations—firms, programs, advertisements, individuals—without having to talk to or examine every element in the population. Chyi and Lasorsa (2002) used a probability sample of Austin, Texas, residents to estimate how much overlap existed between readership of online and print editions of newspapers and to determine which of those two formats was preferred. Because the 818 participants in their telephone survey were selected using probability sampling, they also were able to use inferential statistics to analyze the data that they collected from the survey.

---

[12]More precisely, the researcher can estimate how often a sample such as the one that was drawn is likely to produce estimates of the population that are accurate within specified limits.

## Content Analysis

More so than experimental research, survey research and secondary analyses of existing data, content analysis is a technique used widely in both qualitative and quantitative research. *Content analysis* is a formal, systematic effort to discern patterns or relationships within a set of symbols—within oral, written or visual content (Riffe, Lacy, & Fico, 1998, pp. 18–32). Qualitative content analyses emphasize a search for underlying meanings within the content, and they pay particular attention to the context in which the content is produced (Altheide, 1996). Quantitative analyses focus more on manifest content and devote substantial effort to the reliable measurement of the symbols. Many definitions of quantitative content analysis describe it as an "objective" process, by which it's meant that the researcher can directly observe the symbols and that the symbols' meanings are shared widely by those within particular community or culture. The presence of these symbols is recorded in numeric form and then subjected to statistical analysis to detect patterns or relationships among the content variables that have been measured.

As with survey research, sampling is an issue in content analysis. Here again, researchers have three broad choices for selecting the symbols to be analyzed. They can conduct a census or draw a probability or nonprobability sample. As with sampling in survey research, a probability sample brings with it greater assurance that the content is representative of the population from which it came and the opportunity to use inferential statistics to test hypotheses about relationships among variables.

In quantitative content analysis, perhaps the key methodological challenge is achieving consistency in the coding of the content. *Coding* is the process of assigning numerical values to the content variables that the researcher considers relevant, such as the topic of a newspaper article or the length of a television story. Achieving consistency across several coders is an issue of reliability in measurement. High reliability implies that identical content is coded in identical ways, regardless of who or what is doing the coding. Sometimes coding of symbols is straightforward, which makes high reliability easy to achieve. If the research calls for coding the number of words in an article or number of references to a specific company, there's little chance for disagreement among coders. Indeed, if the content is in digital form, computer programs can accurately produce estimates for variables such as those, so achieving consistency is seldom a problem. On the other hand, if the goal is to code the number of unfavorable representations of a firm on television news shows, it's easier to imagine how disagreements among coders might arise. If a report characterizes a company's marketing practices as "aggressive," is that a compliment or a criticism?

Researchers conducting content analyses follow procedures to minimize differences among coders. But generally speaking, the more complex the coding scheme, the lower the reliability across coders. Because intercoder agreement is a challenge for those working with quantitative content data, special statistics have been developed to assess reliability. Riffe, Lacy, and Fico (1998, pp. 104–134) provide a comprehensive discussion of reliability in content analysis as well as a summary of common statistical techniques used to estimate reliability. When it comes to other analyses of quantitative content data, most of the techniques used in survey and experimental research are appropriate for content analysis, too. Contingency-table analysis appears to be the most popular technique. Even so, it's not unusual to use bivariate correlational analysis, multiple regression, and analysis of variance, among other techniques.

Content analyses accounted for roughly 15% of the primarily quantitative studies in *JME* and *JMM*. In some cases, the goal of the research was to describe characteristics of the content—television shows, magazine articles, advertisements. In other cases, content was examined to provide insight about the organizations, the market conditions, or the policy decisions that shaped it. A typical example of the latter is the longitudinal study by Li and Chiang (2001) in which they found that as the Taiwan TV market became more competitive, programming diversity declined. Media content was the dependent variable in that study, and that is often the case for content analyses in media management or media economics research.

## Case Studies

*Case studies* are research projects that examine a single case or, perhaps, make a comparison of a handful of cases. The latter are called *comparative case studies*. A *case* might be a group, an organization, a nation, a publication, a situation, an event, or even an individual. Most quantitative research studies include many cases, none of which draw particular attention from the researcher. Rather, the researcher is focused more on understanding the concepts and variables that characterize each of the cases. In case studies, the reverse is true. The case itself becomes the center of attention.

Case studies tend to be associated with qualitative research because qualitative data-collection methods are common in case studies. It wouldn't be unusual to find an organizational case study in which data collection included unstructured interviews with managers, focus groups with employees or customers, historical analyses of the firm's successes and failures, and a qualitative content analysis of articles in trade publications about the organization or its products. But case studies can also make use of quantitative data, either as part of a multimethod research project that that combines both qualitative and quantitative data collection or as a single-method project that relies solely on quantitative data.

What distinguishes a quantitative case study from other kinds of quantitative research is its limited potential for producing generalizations. Indeed, a study—quantitative or qualitative – that confines itself to characteristics of a single case shouldn't be used to draw generalizations about other similar cases. There's no way to know how representative the case under examination is of the other cases—the other firms, the other nations, the other individuals—in the population. Despite their limited capacity to produce generalizations about a population, quantitative case studies have made invaluable contributions to the fields of media management and media economics. One of the best-known management research projects was a case study done at the Western Electric Co. Hawthorne Works plan in Chicago in the 1920s and 1930s. Researchers conducted a *field experiment*—an experiment conducted in a natural setting—in which they varied the level of light in the manufacturing plant (Roethlisberger & Dickson, 1939). They discovered, through the collection of quantitative data, that an increase in lighting was associated with greater productivity at the plant. But so was a decrease in lighting! This finding became known as the "Hawthorne effect," which suggests that behavior can be influenced by individuals' awareness that they are being studied (Frey, Botan & Kreps, 2000, p. 121).

## CHARACTERISTICS OF QUANTITATIVE RESEARCH

The previous sections have provided overviews of the key assumptions that underlie quantitative research and of the ways data are typically obtained and analyzed in quantitative studies. This final section summarizes some characteristics of quantitative research published in *JME* and *JMM* during the past 15 years.

Quantitative research was the dominant form of inquiry during that period, but that is increasingly less the case today. The examination of 309 articles in *JME* and *JMM* found that about 46% were quantitative studies, about 24% were qualitative studies, about 12% used mixed methods, and the remaining 18% were essays, bibliographies, or conceptual discussions in which few or no data were collected. The distribution of quantitative and qualitative studies has changed substantially since 1999 with the launch of *JMM*, a journal edited and published in Europe. *JME*, which was founded in 1988 and is edited in the United States, has tended to publish quantitative research, whereas *JMM* has been more inclined toward qualitative studies. Over the years, about 60% of *JME* articles have relied primarily on quantitative techniques and 24% primarily on qualitative techniques, with another 16% being conceptual articles or essays. That distribution has varied widely year to year (Fig. 23.2). In *JMM*, about 48% of the articles have been based primarily on qualitative research and about 25% primarily on quantitative research. The remaining 27% were conceptual articles or essays. Only in its first year of publication, when just five articles were printed, was quantitative research predominant in *JMM* (Fig. 23.3).

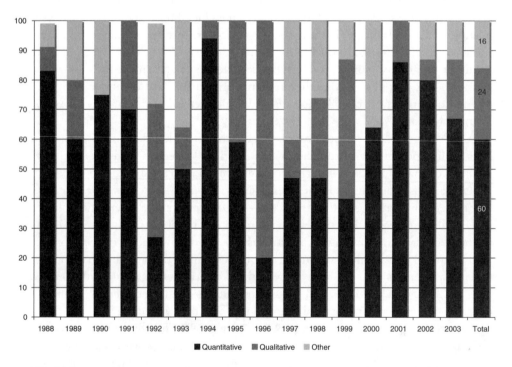

FIG. 23.2.    Articles using primarily quantitative, primarily qualitative, and other methods in *Journal of Media Economics*, 1988–2003 (*N* = 216). Figures are percentages.

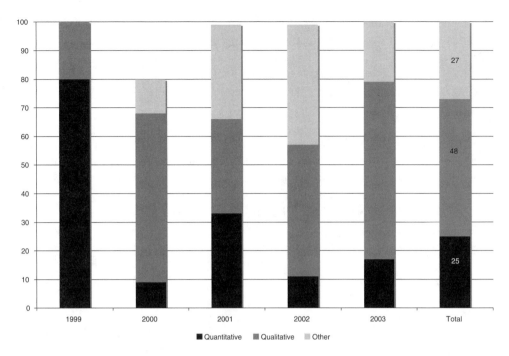

FIG. 23.3. Articles using primarily quantitative, primarily qualitative, and other methods in *International Journal on Media Management*, 1999–2003 (N = 93). Figures are percentages.

Scholars publishing quantitative research in *JME* and *JMM* have been more inclined toward economic research than management research. This finding reflects, in part, that *JME* has been publishing about a decade longer than *JMM* and is focused more directly on economics. But even in *JMM*, there's slightly more quantitative research on economics than on management. Over all, about 60% of the studies in these two journals have focused on economics. Of those, about half have dealt with market issues, primarily the structure-conduct-performance model or industrial-organization economics. Studies relying on management theory, communication theory, or no theory at all represent much smaller percentages of the body of quantitative research. Because economics research often looks at change across time and because many institutional sources collect data about the same way year in and year out, a substantial percentage of this quantitative research—close to 46%—is longitudinal. As might be expected given the subject matter, virtually all of this research was conducted above the individual level of analysis. In terms of industry focus, two segments—the television and newspaper industries—received the lion's share of attention. About 37% of the primarily quantitative research has been on television and about 21% on newspapers. Cross-industry or multiple-industry studies constituted the next-highest category, at only 7%, followed by the film and the new media categories, each at 6%. A smattering of studies on other industries—advertising, books, magazines, radio, telecommunications, broadband—made up the rest. None of those categories accounted for more than 5% of the total.

As mentioned previously, for quantitative research in media management and media economics, the most common practice has been for researchers to analyze data collected by someone else, with about 60% of the quantitative studies making use of data from secondary sources. About half of the studies rely on secondary data exclusively, and another 10% use both primary data and secondary data.

That is a broad description of the quantitative research that has been published in *JME* and *JMM* during the past 15 years. The description suggests several fruitful directions for future research:

• *The management of media organizations needs more attention.* Management research comprised only 15% of the quantitative studies in these fields. The decline of traditional mass media such as daily newspapers and broadcast television; the growth of niche and ethnic media; the convergence of staffs for print, video, and Web platforms under one organizational roof; and the growing commercial pressures facing organizations offer ample challenges to those who manage media companies. Those trends similarly offer ample opportunity for scholarship that seeks to understand how they may affect the ways that media organizations are managed and what that may imply for the news, entertainment, and services that they deliver to the communities they serve.

• *Content deserves more attention, particularly in studies about management.* Within *JME* and *JMM*, only one content analysis examined a question about the impact of management on media content. It's the case, of course, that studies examining the link between management and content have been published in other venues. Still, understanding more about how organizational change, organizational culture, or different management styles may influence content seems to be a fertile area for further research.

• *It is time to broaden the scholarly focus beyond the newspaper and television industries.* Almost 60% of the quantitative studies in *JME* and *JMM* examined those industries, with the majority of the studies about newspapers concentrating on the daily sector. Although these remain large, crucial segments of the media industry, other important vehicles for delivering news and information to society—radio, magazines, and the Internet—have been neglected.

• *More comparative research is needed.* A book such as this, focused as it is on media management and media economics, frames the media as "special businesses" worthy of study in their own right. Certainly that is true, but it is difficult to adequately understand the ways in which media organizations differ from other kinds of commercial enterprises without comparing them to other kinds of organizations.

## APPENDIX

Secondary data sources used in recent research on media management and media economics:

*Bacon's Information:* Bacon's (http://www.bacons.com) publishes directories of newspapers, magazines, and newsletters for North American and some Central American markets. Commercial source.

*BIA Financial Network:* BIAfn (http://www.bia.com) supplies a wide range of information about the newspaper, radio, and television industries to investors and others interested in the media, communications and related industries. Commercial source.

*Editor & Publisher:* E&P (http://www.editorandpublisher.com), a division of the VNU Media Group, publishes an annual directory of North American daily and weekly newspapers, as well as a guide to city, county, MSA, and non-MSA markets. The directory includes partial staff listings, advertising rates, circulation data and production requirements. Commercial source.

*Eurostat:* Eurostat (http://europa.eu.int/comm/eurostat/) collects economic data about countries in the European Union. Quasi-governmental source.

*Federal Communications Commission:* The FCC maintains databases on broadcast licensees available through commission's Media Bureau section on its Web site (http://www.fcc.gov/mb). Government source.

*International Telecommunication Union:* The World Telecommunications Indicators database contains information about telecommunications systems from about 200 countries (http://www.itu.int/home). Quasi-governmental source.

*Moody's Investors Service:* Moody's (http://www.moodys.com) rates bonds and provides current and historical data on yields from bonds. Commercial source.

*National Center for Education Statistics:* The NCES (http://nces.ed.gov), a federal agency, gathers information related to education, including data on telecommunications and Internet access in schools. Government source.

*Newspaper Association of America:* A trade organization for the U.S. newspaper industry, the NAA (http://www.naa.org) collects circulation and other information about weekly and daily newspapers. Trade association.

*Securities and Exchange Commission:* The SEC's Edgar database (http://www.sec.gov) has information about publicly held U.S. companies. SEC filings contain financial and managerial data, including owners, directors, and executive compensation.

*SRDS Media Solutions:* SRDS (http://www.srds.com) databases or publications have information about advertising rates, circulation, share, and lifestyle information for print and broadcast media outlets. Commercial source.

*State newspaper directories:* Many state press associations publish directors of newspapers. Trade association.

*Thomson Corp.:* Thomson (http://www.thomson.com), an international information services company, maintains databases about business activity worldwide, including mergers and acquisitions and joint ventures. Thomson also publishes the Dealmaker's Journal, which covers mergers and acquisitions. Commercial source.

*Tribune Media Services:* TMS (http://tms.tribune.com) produces English and Spanish data related to television schedules and movie schedules for North America. It also provides channel lineups for U.S., Canadian and UK markets. Commercial source.

*U.S. Bureau of Labor Statistics:* The BLS has information on inflation, consumer spending, wages, earnings, benefits, and other data related to employment, including some international data. Much of the information is available at the BLS Web site (http://www.bls.gov). Government source.

*U.S. Census Bureau:* The Census Bureau collects information about individuals, house-holds, and businesses in the United States. Much of the information is available at the bureau's Web site (http://www.census.gov). Government source.

*Value Line:* Value Line is an information service that produces print and electronic products about publicly held corporations, including commentaries from analysts and data about corporate ownership. Commercial source.

## Other Places to Find Information

Many research libraries subscribe to a wide variety of print and electronic products on business and economics. Library home pages often contain special lists of such sources. Often access to these databases is restricted to individuals affiliated with the university. The Media Management and Economics Division of the Association for Education in Journalism and Mass Communication maintains a list of resources for research on media management and media economics at its Web site (http://www.miami.edu/mme/resources.htm).

## ACKNOWLEDGMENTS

The author would like to acknowledge the contributions of his collaborators on the content analyses of the *Journal of Media Economics* and the *International Journal on Media Management:* Dr. C. Ann Hollifield and Amy Jo Coffee of the University of Georgia, and Bozena Izabella Mierzejewska of the University of St. Gallen.

## REFERENCES

Altheide, D. L. (1996). *Qualitative media analysis.* Newbury Park, CA: Sage.

Babbie, E. (1992). *The practice of social research* (6th ed.). Belmont, CA: Wadsworth.

Becker, L. B. (2003). Secondary analysis. In G. H. Stempel III, D. H. Weaver, & G. C. Wilhoit (Eds.), *Mass communication research and theory* (pp. 252–266). Boston: Allyn & Bacon.

Borrell, A. J. (1997). Radio station characteristics and the adoption of satellite-delivered radio programming. *Journal of Media Economics, 10*(1), 17–28.

Bryman, A. (2001). *Social research methods.* Oxford: Oxford University Press.

Burrell, G., & Morgan, G. (1979). Part I: In search of a framework. In *Sociological paradigms and organisational analysis* (pp. 1–37). London: Heinemann.

Campbell, D. T., & Stanley, J. C. (1963). *Experimental and quasi-experimental designs for research.* Boston: Houghton-Mifflin.

Chaffee, S. H. (1991). *Explication.* Newbury Park, CA: Sage.

Chan-Olmsted, S. M., & Li, J. C. C. (2002). Strategic competition in the multi-channel video programming market: An intraindustry strategic group study of cable programming networks. *Journal of Media Economics, 15*(3), 153–174.

Chyi, H. I., & and Lasorsa, D. L. (2002). An explorative study on the market relation between online and print newspapers. *Journal of Media Economics, 15*(2), 91–106.

Cohen, J., & Cohen, P. (1983). *Applied multiple regression/correlation analysis for the behavioral sciences* (2nd ed.). Hillsdale, NJ: Lawrence Erlbaum Associates.

Demers, D. P. (1996). Corporate newspaper structure, profits and organizational goals. *Journal of Media Economics, 9*(2), 1–23.

Frey, L. R, Botan, C. H., & Kreps, G. L. (2000). *Investigating communication: An introduction to research methods* (2nd ed.). Boston: Allyn and Bacon.

Greco, A. N. (1999). The impact of horizontal mergers and acquisitions on corporate concentration in the U.S. book publishing industry, 1989–1994. *Journal of Media Economics, 12*(3), 165–180.

Hair, J. F. Jr., Babin, B., Money, A. H. & Samouel, P. (2003). *Essentials of business research methods*. Indianapolis, IN: Wiley.

Heaton, J. (1998). *Secondary analysis of qualitative data* (Social Research Update, 22). Retrieved August 29, 2004, from the University of Surrey Web site, http:// www.soc.surrey.ac.uk/ sru/ SRU22.html

Jaeger, R. M. (1990). *Statistics: A spectator sport* (2nd ed.). Newbury Park, CA: Sage.

Jayakar, K. P., & Waterman, D. (2000). The economics of American theatrical movie exports: An empirical analysis. *Journal of Media Economics, 13*(3), 153–169.

Kalleberg, A. (1977). Work values and job rewards: A theory of job satisfaction. *American Sociological Review, 42*(1), 124–143.

Kerlinger, F. N. (1986). *Foundations of behavioral research* (3rd ed.). Fort Worth: Holt, Rinehart and Winston.

Kish, L. (1995). *Survey sampling*. New York: Wiley.

LaRose, R., & Atkin, D. (1991). Attributes of movie distribution channels and consumer choice. *Journal of Media Economics, 4*(1), 3–17.

Lewis, R. (1995). Relation between newspaper subscription price and circulation, 1971–1992. *Journal of Media Economics, 8*(1), 25–41.

Li, S. S., & Chiang, C. C. (2001). Market competition and programming diversity: A study on the TV market in Taiwan. *Journal of Media Economics, 14*(2), 105–119.

Litman, B., & Kohl, L. S. (1989). Predicting financial success of motion pictures: The '80s experience. *Journal of Media Economics, 2*(2), 35–50.

Marascuilo, L. A., & Serlin, R. C. (1988). *Statistical methods for the social and behavioral sciences*. New York: W. H. Freeman.

Maxwell, S. (2003). The effects of differential textbook pricing: Online versus in store. *Journal of Media Economics, 16*(2), 87–95.

McClendon, M. J. (1994). *Multiple regression and causal analysis*. Itasca, IL: F. E. Peacock.

Riffe, D., Lacy, S., & Fico, F. G. (1998). Defining content analysis as a social science tool. In *Analyzing media messages: Using quantitative content analysis in research* (pp. 18–32). Mahwah, NJ: Lawrence Erlbaum Associates.

Roethlisberger, F. J., & Dickson, W. J. (1939). *Management and The Worker: An Account of a Research Program Conducted by Western Electric Company, Hawthorne Works, Illinois*. Cambridge, MA: Harvard University Press.

Shrikhande, S. (2001). Competitive strategies in the internationalization of television: CNNI and BBC World in Asia. *Journal of Media Economics, 14*(3), 147–168.

Stamm, K. R. (2003). Measurement decisions. In G. H. Stempel III, D. H. Weaver, & G. C. Wilhoit (Eds.), *Mass communication research and theory* (pp. 129–146) Boston: Allyn & Bacon.

Underwood, D. (1993). *When MBAs Rule the Newsroom*. New York: Columbia University Press.

Uri, N. D. (2003). The impact of incentive regulation on service quality in telecommunications in the United States. *Journal of Media Economics, 16*(4), 265–280.

U.S. Bureau of Economic Analysis (2004). Personal income and per capita personal income. Retrieved August 11, 2004, on the World Wide Web from the Fedstats database.

Van Kranenburg, H. (2002). Mobility and market structure in the Dutch daily newspaper market segments. *Journal of Media Economics, 15*(2), 107–123.

Weaver, D. H., Beam, R., Brownlee, B., Voakes, P., & Wilhoit, G. C. (2003, August). *The American journalist in the 21st century*. Mini-plenary for the Association for Education in Journalism and Mass Communication annual convention, Kansas City, MO.

Wimmer, R. D., & Dominick, J. R. (2003). *Mass media research: An introduction* (7th ed.). Belmont, CA: Thomson Wadsworth.

Wonnacott, T. H., & Wonnacott, R. J. (1969). *Introductory statistics*. New York: Wiley.

# 24

# Methodological Approaches in Media Management and Media Economics Research

Gillian Doyle and Simon Frith
University of Stirling

## INTRODUCTION

Over the past two decades, the number of scholars working on (and students following courses in) media management and media economics has expanded dramatically. There are a number of reasons for this. The digital revolution has transformed both the shape and the scope of media businesses, accelerating the related processes of convergence and globalization. The simultaneous deregulation of national media industries has meant that the attention of both policymakers and media academics has shifted from political to economic issues. At the same time the media have become increasingly important as businesses and as potential employers of ambitious MBAs. Put these changes together and there are a number of new demands for teaching and research focused on the specific economic and management problems raised by media business practice. For media and communications studies departments, economics and management can no longer be treated as irrelevant. For economics departments and business schools, the media can no longer be regarded as marginal. For policymakers, the impacts of media companies on the national economy (on employment, on the balance of payments, on competitiveness and growth) are of increasing importance for economic management. For media entrepreneurs and executives, the problems of managing talent and intellectual property, of retaining and building markets, of operating in a global economy, of responding or not to new technological temptations are ever more complex. Even consumers now face increasingly complicated decisions as to what resources to invest in what media product or experience, as choices of what to buy and how to pay for it proliferate. Media management and media economics may be relatively new subject areas and may have an uneasy relationship with their parent disciplines—economics and management science, on the one hand, media sociology, on the other—but their importance is undeniable, and there is certainly abundant opportunity now for researchers to develop knowledge and shape the analytic concepts of these emerging fields of inquiry.

This chapter sets out to outline the research methods that may be used in addressing issues in media management and economics. It also describes the particular intellectual and practical issues that researchers in this field regularly face. It draws on the experience of several years of working with students preparing postgraduate dissertations in the field of media management as well as on the authors' own research experiences. The range of methods and problems described here is by no means exhaustive, but it is meant to provide a realistic picture of both the most common research strategies and the most likely research pitfalls.

Most (but not all) research carried out in media management and economics is premised on the assumption that the media industry is different from others. The business of communicating with mass audiences—supplying ideas, information, and entertainment to segments of the public—is different from supplying motorcars or pizzas because media output has the potential for serious impact, whether for better or worse, on public welfare. One of the major intellectual challenges that researchers in our field often find themselves grappling with is diversity or even conflict in the expectations that surround the function of media resource management.

Conventional economic theories do not necessarily provide an adequate framework when it comes to the analysis of media companies' market strategies (or even, indeed, the nature of their "failure" or "success"). If they did, the rationale for distinguishing media management and media economics as special fields of inquiry would be considerably diminished! At the same time, and to a different degree than in other industries, media management involves coping with "irrationalities." The economic importance of personal resources such as talent and "star quality," on the one hand, and the way in which personal tastes and collective market choices feed off each other, on the other, problematize conventional assumptions about economic value and rational market behavior.

If one set of problems facing researchers stems from the limitations of generic economic and managerial theories, another challenge is that, by and large, media management and media economics are at an early stage of developing alternative analytical frameworks. Some useful work has been carried out by economists in developing heuristic models that take account of the special contingencies of media provision, but much of the research work conducted in media management is about creating valuable knowledge for and about industry. It does not necessarily help to develop the subject's overall intellectual or theoretical coherence. A tendency toward applied and practical work inevitably means that when compared with more developed and longer-established fields of inquiry, relatively little exists in the way of a prevailing paradigm in either media management or media economics. And, at the same time, there remain significant gaps in empirical knowledge (about media labor markets, for example) that have made it difficult to develop overall unifying theories of media structures.

The challenges faced by researchers in media management and economics, which are discussed in more detail later, can also be viewed as opportunities. One of the obvious characteristics of media management is its interdisciplinarity. It provides a meeting point for a range of disciplines (economics, management studies, political science, and sociology) that each have their own research questions, theoretical concerns, and methodological traditions. Media management has grown in recent years from a subject area comprising a small number of scholars working on topics deriving from their own particular disciplinary backgrounds to a substantive interdisciplinary field in its own right with its own journals (e.g., *The Journal of Media Economics* and *The International Journal on Media Management*) and subject associations (e.g., European Media Management Education Association or EMMA[1]). And the management of media resources remains a compelling focus for research whose potential to contribute to public understanding of sociopolitical, cultural, and economic systems is increasingly recognized.

## THE NATURE OF RESEARCH IN MEDIA MANAGEMENT AND ECONOMICS

Do media firms produce the sorts of goods and services that consumers want and need? Are they supplied in the right quantities and under conditions of optimal efficiency? What is the association between the markets in which media firms operate and how they perform? How can managers of media firms ensure that the resources available for provision of media goods are used as effectively as possible? What special challenges are thrown up by the management of creative processes? Which strategies will ensure that new media technologies are used to best competitive effect? What role should the state play in ensuring that the organization and supply of media output matches societal needs? These are a few examples of questions that researchers interested in media management and economics might reasonably want to ask. How can they be answered?

The typical starting point for research is identifying a question. Good research, irrespective of its discipline, depends on the quality of the question posed as much as getting an answer to it. Questions that are too vague or too muddled, too general or too obscure, too ambitious or too narrow will lead to all kinds of problems. Each of the questions just asked is very broad—too broad put into operation as a specific research question—and each has been investigated many times over in the past. In arriving at a question that is researchable, it is essential to distinguish between the wider issues or concerns related to media management that may provide the overarching context for a study, and the specific topic, investigation of which offers a real chance to add to what is known already.

Arriving at a question is, of course, easy if the topic is chosen for you. Much research related to the management and economics of media can be found not in the academic literature but in management reports and surveys carried out by and within media businesses and public policy offices. Research matters a great deal to the media industry; it is an essential tool of media policymakers. Audience, box office, and sales figures, for example, are central to the production decisions of the music, film, radio, television, publishing, and advertising industries. They determine what programs are made, which records are released, what films are funded; they shape promotional strategies and inform

---

[1] EMMA's Web site can be found at www.the-emma.org/

decisions as to how much money should be invested in each new work. Specialist re-searchers are employed by media firms and media sectors of industry precisely to bring a scientific approach to the analysis of the uncertainties (or irrationality) of taste and talent. Research data is equally important in debates about media policy and regulation, for example, concerning the social effects of particular forms of output or the market consequences of cross-media ownership.

In practice, then, the choice of a research question depends on whom the research is for. When research is carried out directly on behalf of a client (a media organization, for example, or a policymaking body), the agenda is usually clear. Client research can provide relatively generous budgets and may give the researcher access to sensitive management data that would otherwise not be available. However, it is worth remembering that a client's question is itself often ideologically formed and may well involve assumptions about what counts as evidence and how it should be interpreted. In addition, some would argue that client research tends to produce the answers that clients want to hear, that con-firms the wisdom of existing policies or plays well in terms of preferred strategies or office politics. Findings that don't fit with corporate or government policy may well be ignored; neither considered internally nor ever made public. From an academic perspective, what-ever advantages clients bring in terms of resources and access may well be outweighed by the disadvantages of an unsatisfactory brief or possible risk of suppressed findings.

Other research questions in the media field are driven by the curiosity or interest of the researcher rather than by client needs or policy relevance. Curiosity can simply reflect personal interests and experiences, or it may stem from dissatisfaction with existing disciplinary theories of how the media should be assessed economically or managed effectively. It can derive from an urge to test or challenge an assertion, to fill a gap in knowledge, or to apply an existing argument to new data. In all such cases, if to differing degrees, "curiosity" describes a response to a perceived problem in the relationship of a theory (of a given business practice in the media sector, say) to reality. This concern with how theory relates to practice is one of the main factors distinguishing academic from client-based research.

In research that is driven by academic curiosity, the researcher has the freedom (de-pending on available resources) to determine what methods will be used to collect and analyze data. The choice of method adopted has a crucial influence on how research is judged, whether by examiners, academic peers, or media practitioners themselves. A convincing case must be made for the research design chosen, bearing in mind that each method involves opportunity costs and alternative methods will produce different kinds of evidence. Before deciding how a research project will be designed, then, it is essential to have a clear understanding of what particular methods can and cannot do. Some of the main sources of data and tools for investigating media management questions are considered next.

## Documents and Texts as Data Sources

Official data that is available in the public domain is an extremely valuable resource for researchers interested in media management or economics. Indispensable economic media data is usually available, for example, from industry regulators. In the United States the reports of the Federal Communications Commission (FCC) are an important research resource. In the UK, the Independent Television Commission (ITC), the Radio Authority, Oftel (the regulator for telecommunications), and the Copyright Tribunal all publish annual reports, industry surveys, and other working documents that contain useful statistical and financial media industry data.[2] Licence applications to the Radio Authority are publicly available and a useful source of information about radio economics. Likewise, reports produced by government departments, such as the Department of Trade and Industry (DTI) or the Department of Culture, Media and Sport (DCMS) in the UK or the Department of Commerce in the United States, can be excellent sources of survey data about media industries.

Legal rulings and documentation related to, for example, official inquiries by competition authorities are another potential source of relevant economic data. The evidence provided (by command) to such investigations by managers of media firms offers considerable insight into the workings of the broader industry, and as such commercial information is being produced for a public body or inquiry it is, unusually, likely to be publicly accessible. In the UK, for example, the competition authorities—the Competition Commission (previously the Monopolies and Mergers Commission) and the Office of Fair Trading (OFT)—have over the past 20 years conducted public inquiries into the radio, television (terrestrial and satellite), film, newspaper, telecommunications, and music sectors. Such inquiries generate a variety of hearings, reports, and investigations, providing not only statistical information but also insights into working and managerial practices within and across all sectors of the media. For instance, the Competition Commission's report (2000) concerning proposed mergers between Carlton Communications, Granada Group, and/or United News & Media contained much useful information about relevant advertising markets and program supply arrangements in the UK terrestrial television sector.

In addition to the local economic data that may be gleaned from official bodies at the national level, much relevant economic data is also gathered by international policymaking or trade bodies such as the OECD and the World Trade Organization. At the regional level, the Directorate of the European Commission concerned with audiovisual policy, DG15, has published numerous surveys, reports, policy communications, and other documents containing up-to-date statistics and a range of other valuable information about the television and film industries both in Europe and globally.[3] Anyone starting a research project in media management or media economics needs to begin by becoming familiar with what information is already available from such official sources.

Much of this official data is nowadays made available on the various bodies' Web sites, and the Internet has become a very valuable research tool for media management researchers. Indeed, most of the originators of official media industry data, whether public or trade bodies, whether national or international, have Web sites on which information about reports and publications (and, often, full documents in a downloadable form)

---

[2] The Communications Act 2003 provided for a major reorganization of regulation in the UK. The responsibilities of ITC, the Radio Authority, and Oftel have been passed to a new converged broadcasting and telecommunications regulator, OFCOM, which will now be the most important official source of media data.

[3] These reports are available through the Commission's audiovisual Web site.

are readily available. Each sector of the media has its own national and international professional associations and trade organizations (such as the Motion Picture Exporters Association of America, the European Publishers Union, the Radio Advertising Bureau, or the International Federation of Phonograph Industries), and many of these bodies have researchers and research departments that publish reports, newsletters, and surveys on the Web. For the starting researcher, a good way to identify what sources are available for such information about a specific media sector is to examine the bibliographies and sources listed in existing academic literature.

Professional research companies that are specifically hired or created by media industries to research their markets and audiences are another potentially good source of secondary data. The headline sales and audience figures produced by such companies as Nielsen Media Research or Broadcasters' Audience Research Board (for broadcasters and advertisers) or Audit Bureau of Circulations (for newspaper and magazine publishers and advertisers) are usually placed in the public domain, and more data may be available at Web sites or reproduced in industry journals. Detailed figures are typically reserved for paying clients, who may be willing, nonetheless, to share them with academic researchers.

The central focus for a good deal of media management research is the firm. Documentary information about media firms is available from a variety of sources including, most obviously (but not always most easily), the firms themselves. In most countries, companies are required by law to produce annual reports that convey basic financial information about recent trading, assets, directors, etc., and these financial reports and accounts are accessible to the public. Most media companies of any size or stature—and especially those that are publicly listed on stock exchanges—publish documents (trading statements, annual reports and accounts, press releases, etc.) that convey fairly abundant information about their activities and plans and about trading conditions in their sectors, as well as about their finances. Much of this documentation is freely available on company Web sites. A number of databases also exist (FT Index, for example) through which such company information can readily be accessed.

Whatever the value of all this documentation, however, it remains evident that much of the detailed financial and management data that is of particular interest to scholars of media management and economics does not exist. Or, when it does, it is contained in documents that are not in the public domain. Monthly performance reviews, dissections of operating costs, and the sort of management data that would allow a media company's operations to be analyzed in close detail are generally not open to the gaze of outsiders (nor, understandably, to rivals). Such "privileged" commercial information may also be kept from public view even when it has been supplied to regulators. The determined researcher can only get access to this sort of data by negotiating with or talking to its gatekeepers.

## People as a Source of Information

One of the most important sources of information about management practices in the media industry is, of course, people. In order to gather information from media managers or other industry practitioners, the two most commonly used research methods are interviews and questionnaires. Other potentially useful methods include observation and focus groups.

**The Interview Versus the Questionnaire.**    Both these methods are a way of getting information directly from people, whether media producers or consumers, media executives, or regulators. The advantage of a questionnaire survey is that it is a relatively economical way of gathering information from a large number of people in a form that is comparable (in the way that the information is recorded) and that can be aggregated. The disadvantage of the questionnaire is that it produces standardized data that is constructed by the questionnaire itself.

An interview, on the other hand, has the advantage of capturing deeper and more open-ended information. The interviewee determines the narrative and findings can be unexpected. But carrying out interviews is a very time-consuming way of gathering data. The other major disadvantage is that information is gathered in a way that can make comparison difficult; by its nature, interview material tends to stress the uniqueness of an individual's experience.

The choice between carrying out interviews or conducting a questionnaire survey depends on what the researcher hopes to do with the information. If a very clear statement of the research problem can be established from the outset, then it makes sense to adopt a technique that essentially limits the information you gather, especially if the aim is to make generalizations (about managerial behavior or attitudes). If, on the other hand, research is exploratory, or aimed at clarifying a question, then interviews might be a more appropriate technique. The ideal research design probably involves a combination of both techniques, and indeed, many research studies in media management have done exactly that. This allows questionnaires to be designed on the basis of information gathered from interviews or, alternatively, interviews can be used to test conclusions drawn from questionnaires. For example, in Loomis and Albarran's (2004) study of how clusters of radio stations in the United States are managed, responses gathered from an initial set of in-depth interviews with eight radio managers were then used to inform the design of a much wider questionnaire survey covering all the largest radio groups in the country. Limitations on time and other resources, however, do often mean that a researcher has to choose one method or another.

### Interviews

Interviews are very commonly used by both academic researchers and business journalists as a technique for uncovering the workings of the media industry and media firms. An example would be Preston's study (2003) of the culture and practices of program commissioning across UK broadcasters, which was based on more than 70 in-depth interviews with relevant programers and broadcasting personnel carried out over a year-long period. Interviewing describes a variety of approaches ranging from the *structured*, in which a focused series of questions on a specific topic is strictly followed, to the *unstructured*, in which the conversation is guided by a looser set of questions and follows a less predictable line of inquiry (and may, indeed, take place in a less formal setting). Whichever approach is adopted, thorough preparation is essential. Typically, gaining access to busy managers, producers, journalists, and program-makers is not easy. Proper thought must be given to what information is needed and why, before potential subjects are approached.

Even setting aside the time it can take to arrange an interview, the meeting itself is likely to be the shortest part of the research process. Information must be collected in advance about the interviewee, about his or her company and the relevant media sector. The more details relevant to the subject of the investigation that can be gathered in advance, the less time has to be wasted on them during the interview and the clearer the researcher's focus on what information is needed from (can only be obtained from) this specific interviewee. Such advance information gathering is crucial for question framing and equips the researcher to challenge answers and sharpen up responses in follow-up discussion. Practicalities such as pretiming the interview, arranging cue sheets, and checking recording equipment are an equally essential aspect of interview preparation. The more knowledgeable, professional, and prepared the researcher is and appears to be, the better the chance of gaining the respect and co-operation of the person being questioned.

### Questionnaire Surveys

A questionnaire is a highly structured means of collecting information from respondents and, unlike structured interviews, questionnaires are usually self-administered. A questionnaire survey is therefore a more convenient way of gathering data from large numbers of people. Questionnaire surveys have been frequently used in media management research. For example, Mai's (2002) work on the development of the television industry in Taiwan involved the use of a questionnaire survey: Information about their business strategies was collected from senior managers in 29 satellite television companies. Many surveys, of course, are on a larger scale than this.

The extensive literature on questionnaire design provides much instruction on how to ask questions. The most important point is that questions must be clear and unambiguous. The use of internal checks (the same question being asked in different ways, for example, using different words, to see if you get the same answer) helps to ensure the validity of information gathered. Testing for internal validity—the concern here—is a way of checking whether the design of the research is appropriate for its subjects. Do the people answering the questions understand them in the way the researchers intended? Do the researchers understand the answers in the way the respondents intended? This is a necessary stage before one can determine external validity: whether the results uncovered can be generalized beyond the confines of the study in question.

Good questionnaire design dictates that knowledge claimed by respondents in answer to one question should be tested through follow-up questions, and that general claims should be related to specific answers. This is to ensure that data is *reliable*. For example, instead of asking, "How many tracks do you download per week?" or "How many hours of television do you watch per day?" it is better to ask, "How many tracks did you download last week?" or "How many hours of television did you watch yesterday?" And then: "Is this the number you usually download/watch in a week/a day?" "What is the average number of tracks you download a week or hours of television you watch in a day?"

Questionnaire surveys are the usual way of gathering data that is going to be used in *quantitative* and *comparative* research. The design of the questionnaire—the way in which information is recorded—needs to facilitate the sort of analysis that will follow. Whereas factual answers (e.g., responses to "how many hours of television did you watch yesterday?") can easily be quantified and compared, the same is not necessarily true for responses involving subjective opinions or tastes ("What did you think of the BBC's coverage of the Iraq War?"). If comparative analysis is the aim, the range of available responses must be restricted and organized into a limited number of categories.

### Observation

Another valuable research tool available to the media management researcher is observation. Whereas interviews and questionnaires are necessarily obtrusive methods of getting information from people, observation may be unobtrusive and allow information to be gathered from people in the course of their normal working lives.

In research related to media economics and media management, observation can be a better research method than interviews or questionnaires for two kinds of reasons. First, it can get directly at information (about work practices, for example) that individuals don't provide in interviews or surveys because they don't know it, or because they can't articulate it, or because they regard it as commercially sensitive and not to be divulged to strangers. Second, there is a category of institutional knowledge, a knowledge of norms of behavior and networks, that is so taken for granted that individuals don't know they know it! Observational methods are particularly useful in workplace settings because it is here that formal organizations are most obviously underpinned by informal arrangements that are not usually revealed by explicit questioning. Observation also has the advantage that, unlike in more structured forms of investigation, the researcher is able to capitalize on chance remarks or events that open up new or unexpected lines of inquiry.

Processes of production and distribution in the media industry are well suited to investigation by means of observation. Prolonged immersion in the settings where such activities take place allow the researcher to gain firsthand knowledge of how individuals go about their normal work activities and how those activities are managed. For example, to sit in a newsroom or on a newsdesk over a long enough period of time is to get firsthand knowledge of the processes of news creation and delivery. Schlesinger's work on the creation of broadcast news within the BBC relied on an extensive period of participant observation in the 1970s (Schlesinger, 1978).[4] Schlesinger's later analysis of this experience highlights one of the potential drawbacks of participant observation: "The process whereby I got under the BBC's skin was also one whereby it got under mine" (Schlesinger, 1980, p. 353). If the researcher becomes too immersed in or captivated by the view of the world held by the subject of research, by the corporate ideology of the media firm being investigated, then the analytical detachment essential to good research may be compromised or lost.

---

[4]For a recent example of a similar ethnographic study of the BBC (including its News and Current Affairs production) see Born (2004).

The main problem with observation as a research tool, however, is its cost. Extended observation over a long period of time is both time consuming and time intensive, and it is likely to be difficult (and also time consuming) to gain such access to media organizations, especially in the case of commercial media. Understandably objections arise when observation is aimed at activities deemed to be commercially sensitive, such as strategic management decisionmaking. Researchers can find that access agreements are changed or broken as the research proceeds (following personnel changes, for example, when the original facilitator moves on), and the price of access can be restrictions on the publication of findings.

In practice, observation is almost always used with other methods (usually interviews) either in advance (as a way of determining who to talk to about what), afterwards (as a means of checking the meaning of interview data) or in parallel (as in the use of "key informants" in ethnography).

### Focus Groups

The focus group—getting a small sample of people together to discuss a topic or product under the moderation of a researcher—has become the most fashionable of market research methods in the past couple of decades, but it has a long academic history and can usefully be drawn upon by media researchers, particularly those concerned with media effects and media consumers. Focus groups are thus commonly used in studies of the ways in which people with particular social or cultural characteristics respond to certain forms of media experience. For research relying extensively on focus group findings, see, for example, the work carried out at the Stirling Media Research Institute on women and men viewing violences (Schlesinger, 1992; Schlesinger et al., 1998).

## Quantitative and Qualitative Analysis

Existing research studies in media management and economics exemplify a range of analytical approaches, quantitative and qualitative (and often both). Quantitative research is centrally concerned with measurement. Results of questionnaire surveys or of highly structured interviews or numerical and statistical data gathered from primary or secondary sources are equally open to quantitative analysis. At the same time, the systems through which media output is created, supplied, and consumed cannot always be reduced satisfactorily to an inert set of measurable regularities. There will always be an important role for qualitative research techniques in media management research, for data produced by the methods discussed in the last section (semistructured and unstructured interviews; participant observation; the examination of documents).

In qualitative research, the emphasis tends to be on individuals' interpretations of their environments or events taking place within their environments of their own behavior or that of others. Qualitative research is well suited to investigating work practices and managerial styles and carrying out organizational research. The analysis and presentation of qualitative findings allow nuances and contexts to be taken into account. Qualitative methods give the researcher a way of understanding what is going on within media organizations from the perspective of participants (rather than simply according to the researcher's academic assumptions) (Bryman, 1995, pp. 29–30).

Some qualitative techniques used in management research have, by now, been effectively systematized. For example, so-called strategic management studies have developed a variety of tools for analyzing the business environment. Here we find the familiar application of SWOT (strengths, weaknesses, opportunities, and threats) and PEST or PESTEL (political, economic, social, technical, environmental, legal) analyses, which can be as readily applied to media as to any other firms. Conducting a SWOT analysis involves identifying key strengths and weaknesses within a firm and the main opportunities and strengths that are present within its sphere of operations. See, for example, Helgesen's work on internationalization of Norwegian newspaper firms, which uses both a SWOT analysis of the Norwegian newspaper industry as a whole as well as individual case studies of three of its largest players (Helgesen, 2002, pp. 123–138). At their most basic level, such strategic management models mean listing under prescribed headings all the issues that may affect a particular organization. Implementation of these models requires, as a first step, the use of qualitative research methods to gather as much data as possible about that organization and its business environment.

On the other hand, the quantitative techniques predominant in many branches of economics are equally essential in addressing research questions related to the management of the media. Raw data obtained and analyzed in the correct way can provide vital information about audiences or advertising patterns, about productivity and profitability, and about many of the processes involved in the production and supply of media content. Quantitative data gathered by questionnaire surveys or from published sources can be analyzed using a variety of techniques. For single variables much can be revealed by basic calculations of averages or measures of spread such as standard deviation or, where two or more variables are involved, through the use of correlation coefficients. Correlation and regression techniques are the basis of a range of tools used in management and economics for estimating and forecasting. Comparative evaluations of the business performance of media companies also typically rely on quantitative techniques, for example on comparisons of profitability or return on capital employed (ROCE). Quantitative approaches such as the calculation of net present value or the internal rate of return are as widely used to evaluate and compare investment choices in the media business as in any other industry.

Many of the quantitative tools available to media management researchers, in other words, are the same as in any other branch of economics, even if the subject of analysis (audience and advertising data, for example) is different. Straightforward correlation analysis, for instance, is frequently used in research on the relationship between the variables that interest media managers and media economists (such as audience satisfaction levels and particular product attributes, or organizational structure and output). Bakker's work mapping changes in readership and shifts in the newspaper market caused by the arrival of free titles provides another example of a familiar quantitative approach—a substitution/cumulation model—being applied to a media topic. In this model, circulation data (primarily gathered from secondary sources) is used to calculate the extent to which a new market entrant causes consumers to change their purchasing behavior (Bakker, 2002, p. 80). The questions here—Do new products substitute for old ones? To what extent are both are used at the same time? Does the whole market expand?—are obviously of general importance in such a technologically sensitive sector as the media.

Some quantitative approaches are unique to the study of media (Deacon, Pickering, Golding, & Murdock, 1999). For example, a study carried out by Golding and colleagues at Loughborough University monitored the content of all national press and broadcasting news bulletins in the UK for the 2-year period from 1997 to 1999. "In that period, 86,987 news items were coded, from 3,550 separate media" (Golding, 2000, p. 10). The categorization and coding of these items according to a range of key characteristics enabled researchers to carry out quantitative analysis from which significant conclusions could be drawn about patterns and trends within the British news agenda.

Another research issue from which analytic models particular to media economics have emerged concerns media concentration and diversity. Starting from traditional techniques for categorizing and quantifying media content (i.e., content analysis), it is possible to develop measures of content diversity and then to correlate these with patterns of media ownership, on the one hand, and with profiles of consumer taste and preference on the other (Van Cuilenburg, 2000). Such quantitative analysis is a way of uncovering the relationship between media diversity and competitive market structures. Hence studies of the link between diversity in program scheduling strategies and the number and ownership of competing broadcasters (Owen & Wildman, 1992) or between "market concentration and homogeneity of the cultural product" in the music industry (Peterson & Berger, 1975).

Indeed, how media firms behave under different market structures has been a concern for many media economists (Albarran, 1996; Alexander, Owers, & Carveth, 1998; Picard, 1989, 2002; Wirth & Bloch, 1995). But defining media markets and measuring the degree of concentrated ownership within them is no easy task. Traditional concentration indices and ratios can be used. Amongst the most popular of these are the concentration ratio (CR) and the Herfindahl–Hirschman index (HHI). The CR involves summing up the market shares of the biggest firms in a given market sector—for example, $CR_4$ measures the market share of the four largest players ($CR_4 = .85$, denoting a collective market share of 85% for the four biggest firms); $CR_8$ measures the market share of the eight largest firms, etc. HHI involves summing the squared market shares of all firms operating in a given sector of industry (with the index varying between zero and one, the latter denoting monopoly). HHI therefore has the advantage of taking into account the relative size distribution as well as the number of firms in a sector. Conventional indices tend to focus on a single variable (e.g., revenue share or capital employed) as the yardstick for market share. But some interesting developmental approaches taken by media researchers go beyond this to try to capture a closer understanding of where and how control over media provision is located—e.g., by measuring not only concentration of ownership but also, simultaneously, editorial concentration and audience concentration (Van Cuilenburg, 2000).

## Case Studies

Case studies are commonly used in research as well as a teaching tool in management and business studies. To understand in depth how an industry works does not necessarily mean researching a large number of cases. The case study approach involves illuminating a given issue or phenomenon through the detailed examination of one instance of it. This approach is common in media management research because the unit of analysis is often the organization or firm. The complexity of organizational phenomena can be such that a case study provides by far the best sort of data.

The case study should probably be viewed as a research strategy rather than as a research method. If the strategy is to focus on one case and examine this in some depth (rather than carrying out a wider but less penetrating survey), the researcher still has to choose between a variety of methods to carry out the investigation (interviews, questionnaires, observation, etc.). A combination of quantitative and qualitative techniques is usually the preferred option: a questionnaire survey of employees, for example, is combined with interviews with key personnel within the case study organization.

One of the great strengths of case study research is that it allows for thorough and in-depth investigation over a prolonged period, taking account of the complexities of context. Case study research is therefore the best option when the research question concerns a series of events or operational links that need to be traced over time. It is also useful in conducting exploratory research, when the aim is to gain insights about, say, areas of organizational activity that are not yet well documented or understood and that can only be teased out through prolonged, detailed, and multilayered scrutiny.

The problem with case studies, however, is that they don't provide a sufficient basis for scientific generalization. Examining procedures and practices in one particular context or within one particular firm (with all its innate idiosyncrasies) may well produce data that has no wider truth or significance. The problem, to put this another way, is that the researcher has no way of knowing whether or not a case is "typical": whether this particular media firm's management of its resources tells us anything about media management in general. It has been argued in their defense that case studies, like scientific experiments, "are generalizable to theoretical propositions and not to populations or universes" (Yin, 1994, p. 10). In other words, with case studies "the aim is not to infer the findings from a sample to a population, but to engender patterns and linkages of theoretical importance" (Bryman, 1995, p. 173). What's at stake is not a generalization but, as in experimental science, a hypothesis. A case study is not intended to work as a sample of one. Instead, it is about facilitating a more thorough and multifaceted analysis of a particular process or a series of events than would be possible through any alternative research strategy.

Case studies are not always confined to one subject of analysis. For example, the comparative approach taken by Albarran and Moellinger (2002, pp. 103–122) in their analysis of the structure and performance of the top six communication industry firms in the United States might arguably be described as case study rather than survey research—it combines elements of both. The evidence from multiple cases might be considered more compelling or robust than that from a single case projects but it has drawbacks. Multiple-case research study is far more time consuming and may well work against achieving the very depth and detail for which the case-study approach was developed in the first place.

## PROBLEMS AND PITFALLS

Researchers in the fields of media management and media economics are likely to encounter not only the usual practical and theoretical challenges associated with all research, but also particular problems that derive from the distinctive nature of their area of inquiry.

As Alan Peacock observed some years ago, studies of the broadcasting industry that involve "the intrusion of economic analysis" may be confronted by both practical problems (such as the shortage of relevant econometric data) and conceptual pitfalls (how does one measure program quality or viewer welfare?) (Peacock, 1989, pp. 3–4). Cave summarized the problems associated with conducting normative economic analysis of the television as follows:

> Firstly, the public good property of programs and transmissions means that once we move away from the world of the omniscient planner capable of providing an efficient bundle of outputs into the world of private provision, we are at once in "second best" country, where results are both hard to come by and special. Secondly, television is an industry which many people feel should be governed by something other than current household preferences. (Cave, 1989, p. 35)

Problems of this sort can crop up in research related to any sector of the media. As has been discussed elsewhere (Doyle, 2002), the fact that media and other "cultural" output has qualities not shared by other products and services means that the application of economic theory to the media faces a number of unique challenges. Indeed, media output seems to defy the very premise on which the laws of economics are based—scarcity. However much a film, a song, or a television program is consumed, it doesn't ever get used up. Also, its market value as a fashion item isn't predictable—a song or film or program can be more valuable as a "classic" than it was as a new release.

Economics is about promoting efficiency in the allocation of resources. The notion of economic efficiency is inextricably tied up with objectives. But the objectives of media organizations tend to vary widely. Many media organizations do indeed comply with the classical theory of the firm and, like commercial entities in any other industry, are primarily geared toward maximizing profits and satisfying shareholders. A good number of other media organizations, however, even in the commercial sector, appear to be driven by alternative motives (hence the terms *alternative* or *independent* applied to record, film, magazine, or television production companies that are not simply concerned with maximizing financial returns). For companies operating in the public service sector, quality of output and other public service objectives (such as diversity of output or meeting minority audience needs) are an end in themselves. And some broadcasting firms find themselves operating in between the market and the nonmarket sectors, having to fulfill one set of objectives for an industry regulator, and another set for shareholders. Because objectives are both hazy and varied, the application of any all-embracing model based in conventional economic theory to the media business is very difficult.

The central unit of analysis for much research in media economics and media management is the firm. Researchers in our field want to know whether media organizations and the resources they are utilizing are being managed efficiently. We want to compare the performance of media organizations in different circumstances. The task of establishing an appropriate performance measure for firms is, though, bedeviled by what Wirth and Bloch (1995, p. 18) describe as the "multidimensional" nature of performance, and this is particularly a problem in media analysis. In any organization, different constituencies—shareholders, senior management, employees, customers, "the public"—are likely to have different ideas about what the organization's goals are, or ought to be. As already noted, this is especially true in the media sector where, as in other industries involved in cultural provision, some (though by no means all) constituencies may regard social and cultural rather than economic criteria as of uppermost importance in judgments of performance and output. Despite some attempts to develop all-embracing models specifically for the media industry (see, for example, Hendriks, 1995), the problem remains that there is no easy way of conceiving or operationalizing research aimed at quantifying the overall economic performance or effectiveness of media firms.

Other challenges to economic research on the media industry stem from 'distorted' mechanisms and the nature of market failure. In free-market economies, most decisions concerning resource allocation are made through the price system. But the relationship between price and resource allocation in the media is somewhat unusual, most obviously in broadcasting where (notwithstanding the growth of subscription-based channels) many of the services consumers receive still do not involve a direct payment from the viewer. Without price as a direct link between consumers and producers, there is a fundamental failure in the usual means of registering consumer preferences with suppliers. And even where money does change hands, the pricing mechanism may be peculiar: The price of media goods such as CDs or cinema admissions is rarely related to the cost of producing this particular record or film; most magazines' profit figures are determined by advertising rather than consumer sales—the cost of the magazine in the store does not necessarily tell us anything about its consumer value.

In terms of economics, production methods are said to be inefficient if it would be possible to produce more of at least one commodity—without simultaneously producing less of another—by merely reallocating resources. However, when it comes to the production of media output, this approach begins to look inadequate. For example, it might well be possible for a television company to redistribute its resources so as to produce more hours of programming output or bigger audiences for the same cost as before. But if, at the same time, this were to reduce the diversity or quality of media output (or the aggregate utility or welfare generated by this output), could it be said to be a more efficient use of resources? Media output can be classified and quantified in numerous ways, but translating this data into welfare impacts or utility is extremely problematic.

And, again, even without considering welfare issues, the irrationality of the media market makes it difficult to measure the efficiency of production in conventional ways. All media industries operate on the basis of cross subsidy. It has long been calculated, for example, that only about 1 out of 11 albums released covers its costs (and a similar ratio seems to be applicable to books). Much investment in the film and television industries is in the development of scripts and programs that are not made, or if made not released, or if released not promoted, or if promoted not viewed! All such films and programs are "failures," but they don't therefore necessarily indicate the "inefficient" use of resources, given the profit ratio on the output that is successful and the difficulty in predicting how markets will respond. A company that produces one global best-seller or box office smash and ten loss-making records or films is likely to have far higher returns than a company that produces records or films that all just cover their costs. Analyzing "rational" economic production policy in the media market is thus a research ambition fraught with difficulty.

As we've already discussed, one problem that stems from the focus on the firm is getting access to the relevant data. This, of course, is not confined to media research but applies to organizational studies more generally. "Many organizations are resistant to being studied, possibly because they are suspicious about the aims of the researcher. Further, those persons that act as 'gatekeepers' between the researcher and the organization (usually fairly senior managers) are likely to be concerned about the amount of their own and others' time that is likely to be consumed by the investigation" (Bryman, 1995, p. 2). The point to add here is that because some media firms are relatively willing to open their doors to scholarly research whereas other steadfastly refuse, media management or economic theory is in danger of being developed on the basis of systematically unrepresentative findings. There is no doubt in Britain, for example, that the BBC has been much more open to researchers than any other broadcasting company. How has this affected our understanding of television firms?

The problem here is not just which firms are more or less research accessible, but which individuals in these firms. For example, only a limited number of people within an organization are in a position to explain how its strategy is devised, how systems for implementing change work, and so forth. These individuals may or may not be willing to share their knowledge. In other sorts of research into organizational structures and practice, the problem may not be to identify and access the right informants but to decide at what level to carry out the study. If, for example, we want to study journalistic working practices, then do we need to approach editors and more senior managers as well as the journalists themselves? When data is collected at more than one level, new problems arise. How to aggregate it? How to deal with conflicting accounts?

Cost issues—constraints on time and money—are another important consideration. The focus on relatively small samples of media companies and their managers (particularly in, say, master's-level research projects for which time and other resources are limited) raises questions about validity and reliability. One difficulty here is that people and indeed documents sometimes lie! Misleading information may not be given deliberately—firms and individuals may lie unconsciously or omit information perceived as damaging to a company's reputation because they want to represent themselves in the best possible light. Sometimes, interviewees can't remember or don't know the answer to a question but feel obliged to give an answer anyway, and do so based on guesswork. Where the research question is concerned with impressions and opinions rather than hard facts, then ensuring the truth or authenticity of information gathered is very difficult. And a smaller sample size makes it difficult to cross-check findings. These sorts of problem are more likely to emerge if only one or two people within a firm are interviewed (even if they are senior managers); they are not an inevitable drawback to case studies as such.

The other problem with a small sample discussed earlier is determining whether the findings gathered are typical or unique. In the media industry there is a tendency for a small handful of companies to dominate in almost every subsector and territory. This can mean that access to just two or three leading companies provides a data sample that collectively accounts for a highly significant market share. Limited time and money may thus tempt the researcher into focusing on just a small sample of leading companies. But the behaviors and management practices of large media companies are unlikely to be representative of the industry as a whole. Reliance on too narrow a sample can leave doubts about the general significance of research findings even when they are based on the study of major corporations.

In practice (again thinking of problems noticed in master's theses), this is often a particular problem with research using a firm's own corporate and promotional literature (of which financial statements may be seen as a subset). The Web sites of media companies tend to be of high quality, well organized, and informative, and they are therefore particularly valuable to researchers using the Internet as a key information source. Herein lies another pitfall. Analysis of company documentation and data set out on company Web sites must bring to bear a critical understanding that the primary purpose of this information is to present the company, its activities, and its progress as favorably as possible to customers, shareholders, and the wider public.

There is no doubt that unlike media research in some other disciplines (sociology, for example), research in media management and media economics can involve a heavy reliance on secondary sources. Studies may be centered around analysis of the financial or trading statements published by media companies on the Web and elsewhere. Studies may involve analysis of secondary audience data or information about circulation figures, advertising revenues, or sales. Research may be focused on information compiled by relevant trade associations or bodies representing a sector or on industry studies and reports compiled by management or business consultants, by investment analysts or lobby groups. All such data must be treated warily, with proper critical judgment.

Some secondary source data is reliable and some is not. A good starting point in evaluating such material is to examine how—through precisely what methods of research—the information in question has been compiled. This applies especially to data from semiofficial or nonofficial sources. Unless underlying research methods are demonstrably sound, then results cannot be accepted at face value. It is also worth considering why and on whose behalf research has been compiled. Information accepted for everyday trading purposes (for example, the size of television audiences) is not necessarily accurate.[5] Statistical data (for example, annual numbers of pirated recordings or illegal downloads) that are compiled for political lobbying purposes may be selective, unreliable, or incomplete (the problem from the academic researchers' point of view is that although such data is widely disseminated, little information is provided about its source). Similarly, the main purpose of an investment report is not broadly to inform but, rather, to encourage specific investment transactions. Inevitably, information gathered for commercial reasons is weighted toward telling clients what they want to hear. In order to use secondary source data successfully and effectively, all factors liable to distort or undermine its reliability must be fully and carefully assessed.

The final problem with which researchers in media management may have to be concerned is temporal validity (Bryman, 1995). The subject of an investigation will, on occasion, change in such a way as to reduce the validity and relevance of findings that

---

[5] The problems here become evident when such information is not accepted by everyone in an industry. As we write there is a major dispute due to reach the British courts following the refusal of the Wireless Group to accept the validity of the radio listening figures provided the trade's audience research body JICRAR.

have emerged from it.[6] Media organizations evolve constantly. A case study analysis of an organization carried out in one particular time frame may subsequently be discovered to capture events in an uncharacteristic or incomplete state. Temporal validity is a special concern for media researchers because of the industry's reliance on technology. Research focused on 'new' production and distribution devices inevitably bears the risk of being overtaken by events. It is a fact of life in media management research that findings valid at one moment may no longer pertain at the next.

## CONCLUSIONS

Research in media management and media economics covers a wide diversity of themes. Studies in these fields have concerned themselves with all aspects of media organizations and their management, with the use of resources in media production and distribution, with the markets in which media firms operate, and with their wider economic environment. There is certainly research concerned with theoretical and philosophical questions and the general advance of a new academic discipline, but most research studies in the field are probably still "applied," looking at specific problems in specific companies or industry sectors. The diversity of the resulting work reflects the use of a wide range of methodologies and intellectual approaches, drawing on sociology and political science as well as management studies and economics. We hope to have made clear in the preceding discussion that no single methodological approach can be regarded as standard. In the end, carrying out good research depends most importantly on the ability to recognize the strengths and weaknesses of alternative methods in the specific context of a chosen question.

Conducting research in these areas of inquiry is not without its problems. In this chapter we have touched on some of these, such as the absence of unifying theories, the difficulty of accessing relevant data, the limitations associated with the measurement of organizational and managerial effectiveness, the obstacles to data aggregation, and the drawbacks of taking snapshots of an industry that is almost always, for technological reasons, in a state of flux. There is another kind of problem that we would like to mention finally, and that is the odd status of research in the industry itself.

As we noted at the beginning of the chapter, research data (market research data, in particular) is an extremely valuable resource in the media industry, both in determining production policies and in setting terms of trade. One consequence is that media practitioners tend to be suspicious of research that is not market focused—academic work is welcomed when it adds to information about media markets, and often otherwise ignored. There's a strong belief in the media as in other industries that to know about a business one must work in it; academic research is, by definition, "only theoretical," describes only "what is in books." But media executives can often also seem suspicious

---

[6]One of us (Simon Frith) has experienced this somewhat embarrassing problem directly. Between researching and publishing my study of the British rock music industry (Frith, 1978), EMI changed from being an exemplification of the success of a managerial strategy of vertical integration to being a company in crisis (following the 1970s oil crisis and the beginning of the shift from vinyl to CD production).

of *all* systematic thinking about their industry. And this comes back to the experienced irrationality involved in uncovering and nurturing talent and depending on "fickle" public tastes. On the one hand, this means that for all the industry's dependence on market research, success stories are often trumpeted in terms of executives having had the boldness or vision to *ignore* research. A recent *Guardian* story on the remarkable success of the EMAP magazine *Heat* is typical in this respect. *Heat* was launched in 1999 as a UK version of *Entertainment Weekly* and relaunched a year later: "Two years exhaustive research by EMAP had fed into a magazine selling just 65,000 copies a week. In an act of desperation, all the expensive research was binned and it [*Heat*] was relaunched 'on a hunch' as a women's gossip magazine, with the tagline, 'This week's hottest celebrity news.' It now sells 600,000 copies a week."[7]

On the other hand, successful media executives are less likely than their equivalents in other industries to have had a business school education (a significant number have started out in some aspect of the creative process itself; lawyers are more likely than accountants to run media companies). This again means that whatever the corporate reality, irrational qualities (instinct, gut feeling) are more likely to be cited in explaining decisions than the application of management science models (see, for example, Wolff, 2004). Either way, academics may have a difficult job explaining why their kind of media research might matter to media practitioners.

The intellectual and practical challenges confronting those interested in media management and economics should not be regarded, however, as a deterrent to scholarly research. On the contrary, such challenges have inspired and continue to inspire the development of innovative research that explores the economic, financial, managerial, and social aspects of the media industry. Existing research is both a valuable resource for future researchers and an example of the rich opportunities to contribute to existing knowledge and to shape the evolution of the fields of media management and media economics.

## REFERENCES

Albarran, A. (1996). *Media economics: Understanding markets, industries and concepts*. Ames: Iowa State University Press.

Albarran, A., & Moellinger, T. (2002). The top six communications industry firms: Structure, performance and strategy. In Picard, R. (Ed.), *Media firms: Structures, operations and performance* (pp. 103–122). Mahwah, NJ: Lawrence Erlbaum Associates.

Alexander, A., Owers, J., & Carveth, R. (Eds.). (1998). *Media economics: Theory and practice* (2nd ed.). Mahwah, NJ: Lawrence Erlbaum Associates.

Bakker, P. (2002). Reinventing newspapers: Readers and markets of free dailies. In Picard, R. (Ed.). *Media firms: Structures, operations and performance* (pp. 77–86). Mahwah, NJ: Lawrence Erlbaum Associates.

Born, G. (2004). *Uncertain vision. Birt, Dyke and the reinvention of the BBC*. London: Secker and Warburg.

Bryman, A. (1995). *Research methods and organization studies*. London: Routledge.

Cave, M. (1989). An introduction to television economics. In G. Hughes and D. Vines (Eds.), *Deregulation and the future of commercial television* (David Hume Institute Paper No. 12) (pp. 9–37). Aberdeen, UK: Aberdeen University Press.

---

[7] Plunkett (2004).

Competition Commission (2000). *Carlton Communications plc, Granada Group plc and United News & Media plc: A report on the three proposed mergers* (Cm 4781). Norwich, UK: The Stationery Office.

Deacon, D., Pickering, M., Golding, P., & Murdock, G. (1999). *Researching communications*. London: Arnold.

Doyle, G. (2002). *Understanding media economics*. London: Sage.

Frith, S. (1978). *The sociology of rock*. London: Constable.

Golding, P. (2000). Assessing media content: Why, how and what we learnt in a British media content study. In Picard, R. (Ed.), *Measuring media content, quality and diversity: Approaches and issues in content research* (pp. 9–24). Turku; Finland: Turku School of Economics and Business Administration.

Helgesen, J. (2002). The internationalization of Norwegian newspaper companies. In Picard, R. (Ed.), *Media firms: Structures, operations and performance* (pp. 123–38). Mahwah, NJ: Lawrence Erlbaum Associates.

Hendriks, P. (1995). Communication policy and industrial dynamics in media markets: Towards a theoretical framework for analyzing media industry organization. *Journal of Media Economics, 8*(2), 61–76.

Loomis, K., & Albarran, A. (2004). Managing radio market clusters: Orientations of general managers. *Journal of Media Economics, 17*(1), 51–69.

Mai, L. (2002). Company size, operational type, ownership structure and business strategy: An analysis of taiwanese satellite channel companies. In Picard, R. (Ed.), *Media firms: Structures, operations and performance* (pp. 139–168). Mahwah, NJ: Lawrence Erlbaum Associates.

Owen, B., & Wildman, S. (1992). *Video economics*. Cambridge, MA: Harvard University Press.

Peacock, A. (1989). Introduction. In G. Hughes and D. Vines (Eds.), *Deregulation and the future of commercial television* (David Hume Institute paper No. 12) (pp. 1–8). Aberdeen, UK: Aberdeen University Press.

Peterson, R. A., & Berger, D. G. (1975). Cycles in symbol production: The case of popular music. *American Sociological Review, 40*, 158–173.

Picard, R. (1989). *Media economics: Concepts and issues*. London: Sage.

Picard, R. (Ed.). (2002). *Media firms: Structures, operations and performance*. Mahwah, NJ: Lawrence Erlbaum Associates.

Plunkett, J. (2004, February 16). Stirring up the froth. *Media Guardian*, p. 5.

Preston, A. (2003). *Inside the commissioners: The culture and practice of commissioning at UK broadcasters*. Glasgow, UK: The Research Centre for Television and Interactivity.

Schlesinger, P. (1978). *Putting "reality" together: BBC news*. London: Constable.

Schlesinger, P. (1980). Between sociology and journalism. In H. Christian (Ed.), *The sociology of journalism and the press* (Sociological Review Monograph 29) (pp. 341–369). Keele, UK: University of Keele.

Schlesinger, P. (1992). *Women viewing violence*. London: BFI.

Schlesinger, P., Boyle, R., Haynes, R., McNair, B., Dobash, R., and Dobash, R. (1998). *Men viewing violence* (Report for the Broadcasting Standards Commission). Stirling, UK: SMRI.

Van Cuilenburg, J. (2000). On measuring media competition and diversity: Concepts, theories and methods. In Picard, R. (Ed.), *Measuring media content, quality and diversity: Approaches and issues in content research* (pp. 51–84). Turku, Finland: Turku School of Economics and Business Administration.

Wirth, M., & Bloch, H. (1995). Industrial organization theory and media industry analysis. *Journal of Media Economics, 8*(2), 15–26.

Wolff, M. (2004). *Autumn of the moguls. My misadventures with the titans, poseurs and money guys who mastered and messed up big media*. London: Flamingo.

Yin, R. (1994). *Case study research: Design and methods* (2nd ed.). London: Sage.

# Qualitative Research in Media Management and Economics

C. Ann Hollifield and Amy Jo Coffey
University of Georgia

*Qualitative research* refers to methods of inquiry that generate and interpret non-numerical data, with the goal of developing detailed, in-depth understanding of the subject of study. The distinction between qualitative and quantitative methods is, on the surface at least, one of measurement. Qualitative methods generate nominal or categorical data or, in other words, data that describe the subject of study without any type of numerical valuation. The use of qualitative methods in research has a long, rich history (Denzin & Lincoln, 2000; Vidich & Lyman, 2000), and today qualitative methods are widely employed in many academic disciplines including mass communication, business, and management.

This definition of qualitative methods is, however, deceptively simple. Behind it is a topic of immense complexity that encompasses conflicting research paradigms and diverse approaches to research design, measurement, interpretation, and evaluation. So varied and contradictory are the ways of conducting qualitative research that scholars often mean very different things when they use the term, and discussions of the subject frequently are emotionally fraught.

Within media management and economics research, research based in qualitative methods is well established. Although the field has been dominated by quantitative methods, the number of published studies using qualitative methods has steadily increased in recent years. Qualitative methods also are commonly employed by media consultants or by others engaged in action or applied research in media organizations, and the approach is central to the work done by scholars and activists working at the crossroads of media economics and media policy.

It is a fundamental principle, of course, that the research method should be driven by the research question. Although qualitative methods have many applications, they are particularly appropriate to the study of organizational-level phenomena or a small number of cases. In other words, they are especially effective for research in which the goal is to generate detailed or specific findings, rather than generalizable findings. They also are valuable for exploratory research where the researcher is seeking to identify variables and issues. Because qualitative methods provide a more flexible framework for data collection than do most quantitative methods, they are more likely to provide opportunities for research subjects to offer their own explanations and interpretations of events, as opposed to having responses categorized into an analytical framework preset by the researcher. Finally, qualitative methods, like quantitative methods, can be used to test theories and hypotheses.

In media management and economics, much of the qualitative research involving primary data collection is grounded in social science methods, which reflects the field's roots in organizational studies and economics. Interviews and field and participant observation methods are some of the more common primary data collection methods used in published qualitative studies on media industries and organizations. This contrasts with the qualitative work done in the broader field of mass communication, where it is more common for scholars to apply qualitative approaches such as critical or postmodern analysis, which are more closely aligned with the humanities than the social sciences.

Although many people view social science and interpretive research methods as incompatible, in fact both provide valuable contributions to the development of knowledge and understanding of media organizations and industries. That there is controversy regarding the validity of the respective approaches is, however, undeniable. The roots of this tension lie in fundamental epistemological differences between social science and interpretive approaches. These differences influence how scholars approach qualitative research and how they judge the quality of the resulting work, despite what appear to be surface similarities in methodology. Any discussion of qualitative research methods must necessarily address these key epistemological issues.

## THE EPISTEMOLOGICAL FOUNDATIONS OF QUALITATIVE INQUIRY

Social science approaches to research are based in positivist or postpositivist epistemologies. Both positions emerge from the Enlightenment traditions of rationalism and empiricism, which argued that knowledge could be gained from thinking and observation, as contrasted with the religious or metaphysical revelations that had been given primacy prior to that time (Johnson & Duberley, 2000).

There are always differing views and assumptions underlying the work of scholars within even a single tradition, so a brief explanation of any specific epistemology must be, by definition, overly simplistic. However, in general terms, both positivism and postpositivism argue that knowledge is based on observation and evidence.[1] Assertions of

---

[1]For detailed discussions of the epistemological arguments and critiques underlying social science and management research, see Johnson and Duberley (2000); Lincoln and Guba (2000); Schwandt (2000).

truth that cannot be empirically tested are suspect and classified as speculation. The standard for inquiry is the ability to verify claims, and the primary purposes of research are to identify underlying causal processes and to produce useful knowledge that can be applied to solving problems.

As a result of this focus on observation and verification, positivism and postpositivism share an emphasis on methodological transparency and systemization, with the goal of establishing the reliability of the measurement and interpretation and the validity of the findings. Establishing reliability—and therefore, replicability—is a crucial element in social-science-based measurement because measurements that are not reliable cannot be valid. Therefore, the quality of research is judged in large part by the methods and processes that the researcher used, which should be explicitly spelled out so that others may critique the work, replicate it, and confirm it. The scholar must also specifically identify the evidence by which a theory or hypothesis will be deemed incorrect.

The primary difference between the positivist and postpositivist epistemologies lies in their assumptions about the ability of research to create knowledge. The positivist position holds that repeated replication can establish a theory or hypothesis as truth. The postpositivist position is that research can only falsify theories and hypotheses because even after replication, it's always possible that future research will challenge the theory.

Among the underlying assumptions of the positivist and postpositivist epistemologies is that the researcher can be a neutral or objective observer, detached from feelings and motivations that might influence interpretation (Johnson & Duberley, 2000; Wood, 1997). The assumption of neutral observation includes the idea that there also is an external reality that is the same for all people and can be observed with reliability. Johnson and Duberley (2000) note that this assumption of objectivity represents an insurmountable internal contradiction for positivists/postpositivists. Because there can be no empirical verification of the existence of such a neutral observational space, the assumption is metaphysical, although positivism wholly rejects metaphysical revelation as knowledge.

At the other end of the epistemological spectrum are those who consider themselves to be "interpretivists" or "subjectivists." *Interpretivist* epistemologies reject the notion of a single reality that is the same for all people. They argue that human beings are active interpreters and creators of meaning and so, consequently, no single interpretation of an event or phenomenon can be accurate. Events can be and will be interpreted very differently by individuals, shaped by their personal frames of reference and by what they believe they already "know" to be true. For example, what one person sees as a terrorist act, another will interpret as a heroic act of liberation. A person of strong religious belief might credit a friend's unexpected recovery from a life-threatening illness to divine intervention, whereas an atheist looking at the same case might attribute it to medical science. Interpretivists argue that even scientific "knowledge" is really just interpretation because what researchers see as they look at scientific data is influenced by what they believe already is "known" and by political and individual agendas. Additionally, theories are always changing, indicating that the current state of scientific "knowledge" is really just the latest interpretation.

This variability in interpretation inevitably creates multiple versions of reality that interpretivists argue are all equally valid. In the absence of an objective, observable reality, there is no basis for privileging one person's construction of reality over another's. Therefore, knowledge is acquired through personal revelation (Lincoln & Guba, 2000).

As with positivism, the interpretivist approach contains internal contradictions. Among them is that the position renders knowledge relativistic. If all knowledge claims are equally valid, then why should any knowledge claim—including that of interpretivism itself—be valued over any other? Rejection of relativism—the position that one knowledge claim can, in fact, be stronger than another—necessarily assumes the postivist/postpostivist position that there is some form of observable external reality that is not wholly subject to individual interpretation and against which knowledge claims can be judged. Similarly, the idea that it is possible to incorporate the research subject's own interpretations of reality into an analysis assumes the researcher can perfectly reflect the subject's reality without contamination by the researcher's own frames of reference. Interpretivists reject that possibility.

Researchers working from the interpretivist frame employ a variety of research methods, all of which are necessarily qualitative because the use of quantitative methods assumes the existence of an objective, measurable reality. Ethnographic interviews, textual analysis, and historical methods are among the data collection methods commonly used by interpretivist scholars. The standards by which the methodological quality of interpretivist research is judged differ from those used in social science. In general, interpretivist research is viewed as inseparable from the researcher and, because all knowledge claims are the result of individual interpretation, social science standards of reliability and replicability are irrelevant.[2] Transparency is defined not as the careful explanation of the methods and procedures used by the scholar but, rather, as the careful explanation of the scholar's personal interpretive frame and experience. The quality or validity of research is established either through consensus among scholars over time or, in critical research, which focuses on power relationships, by the project's success in stimulating some emancipating action among the subjects of study.

These paradigmatic differences have crucial implications for the credibility of research that uses qualitative methods. Because research based on interpretative paradigms relies exclusively on qualitative methods, many qualitative texts treat qualitative research as if it were synonymous with interpretivist research (Fortner & Christians, 1981; Pauly, 1991). Within that framework, issues of sampling, operational definitions, reliability, and validity are irrelevant in judging the quality of research. From the social science perspective, however, qualitative research is simply research that generates non-numerical or nominal-level data. The use of qualitative methods does not relieve the researcher of the need to meet normal standards of methodological transparency, reliability, replicability, and validity.

Although the mass communication discipline has embraced many interpretivist paradigms, organizational studies and economics remain dominated by positivist and postpositivist research (Clegg & Hardy, 1996; Johnson & Duberley, 2000; Reed, 1996), perhaps at least in part because those epistemologies focus on prediction, control, and problem solving. However, paradigmatic diversity is emerging in management studies, and because of the continual exchange of ideas between management and media

---

[2]Not all scholars agree that reliability and validity issues are irrelevant to research done through interpretive paradigms (Silverman, 2001). However, generally the notion of reliability is considered to be logically inconsistent with the assumption of an interpreted reality.

management scholars, it is likely that interpretivist research approaches will become more central in the media management field in the future. In the meantime, however, the majority of studies published in media management and economics journals continue to use social science methods, including those using qualitative research methods. Consequently, this chapter focuses primarily on the use of qualitative methods as they are applied and evaluated in social science-based media management and economics research.

## THE METHODOLOGICAL PROFILE OF MEDIA MANAGEMENT AND ECONOMICS RESEARCH

In order to understand how qualitative methods have been used by scholars in the field of media management and economics, a meta-analysis of the literature was undertaken using Rogers' propositional inventory method (Rogers, 1981). Only articles that had appeared in *Journal of Media Economics* (*JME*) and *The International Journal on Media Management* (*JMM*) were analyzed because those journals were the leading specialized journals in the field at the time of the analysis. All articles from all issues of both journals were analyzed, including one issue of *JMM* that was still in press. Thus, the meta-analysis covered the period 1988–2003.

The articles were divided among four coders. Categories for coding the theoretical and methodological components of the literature were developed. Although no intercoder reliability tests were conducted, coders were in constant communication and, where differences in coding were found, consensus was reached and the coders recoded material as necessary. Coding focused on the theory, data collection, data analysis, and units of analysis used in each study. The most difficult coding issues occurred in qualitative studies, where the use of multiple methods and a tendency toward lack of methodological transparency often made it difficult to clearly identify the specific methods used.

### Methodological Trends in Media Management and Economics Research

It is clear from the analysis that interest in the field of media management and economics research grew over the 15 years between 1988 and 2003 (Table 25.1). During that time, the number of peer-reviewed articles published each year in specialized media management and economics journals climbed steadily. Additionally, the number of journals devoted exclusively to research on media management and economics grew from one—*Journal of Media Economics*, which began publishing in 1988—to four by early 2004.[3] Research on media management and economics also continued to regularly appear in other leading journals in mass communication, business, and economics.

An examination of the research published in the two most established journals in the field, *JME* and *JMM*, found that 42.5% of the 309 articles analyzed used qualitative

---

[3] *The International Journal on Media Management*, which was started in Switzerland in 1999, *The Journal of Media Economics & Culture*, which began publishing in 2003 in South Korea, and *The Journal of Media Business Studies*, which was launched in Sweden in 2004.

**TABLE 25.1**
Growth in Published Media Management and Economic
Research (MME) and Use of Qualitative Methods Across Time

| Year | Percent of Total MME Studies Published Since 1988 | Percent Qualitative Studies out of Total MME Studies During Period[a] |
|---|---|---|
| 1988–1989 | 7.1 | 18.8 |
| 1990–1995 | 24.7 | 30.7 |
| 1996–2000 | 31.2 | 52.4 |
| 2001–2003 | 37 | 48.1 |
| $N$[b] | 309 | 247 |

[a]Includes studies that used both qualitative and quantitative methods. [b]The difference in the $N$ values of the two columns reflects the fact that 61 articles were coded as not having involved data collection. Typically, these were articles about theoretical issues. Of the 247 articles that involved the use of specific methods, 142 were quantitative, 59 were qualitative, and 46 used both quantitative and qualitative methods.

methods, and that the use of qualitative methods in media management and economics research increased sharply from the mid-1990s onward (Table 25.1). Case studies and comparative case studies were the research designs used most consistently among those employing qualitative methods to study media organizations (Table 25.2). More than half of all the qualitative projects examined used some form of case study. To the degree that it was possible to tell from reading the methodology and findings sections of the published studies, interviews appeared to be the most consistently used method of generating primary data among qualitative researchers, with almost 23% of the qualitative studies using interviews for at least some data collection. Historical methods also were widely employed for primary data collection, with nearly 22% of the studies using some form of historical research. Less common (7.5%) were studies that used field or participant observation as a method for generating primary data.

Because one of the primary objectives of qualitative research is to develop a rich and detailed picture of the issue being studied, many of the studies used multiple methods of data collection. This was particularly common in those studies that used a case-study or comparative case-study design. Also common in qualitative media management research was the use of secondary data—that is, data that originally were collected for some other purpose. In fact, only 34.3% of the studies examined made it clear in their methods sections that the author or authors had engaged in gathering primary data. Among the other methodological trends identified during the meta-analysis was that the majority of studies, nearly 60%, did not gather data over time, providing only a single temporal snapshot of their subject. Additionally, fewer than 5% of the qualitative research projects examined tested hypotheses.

**TABLE 25.2**
Research Design and Data Collection Methods Used in
Published Qualitative Media Management and Economics
Research, 1988–2003

| *Design/Data Collection Method* | *Percent of Qualitative Studies*[a] |
|---|---|
| Case study | 28 |
| Comparative case study | 24.7 |
| Interviews | 22.6 |
| Historical methods | 21.5 |
| Essay | 19.4 |
| Legal/regulatory/policy analysis | 11.8 |
| Literature review/meta-analysis | 8.6 |
| Field observation | 4.3 |
| Participant observation/action research | 3.2 |
| Other methods | 4.3 |
| N of studies | 93[b] |
| N of responses | 141 |

[a] Percentages do not add up to 100% because they include multiple responses where researchers used more than one method in a study.  [b] N does not include 12 studies that coders did not code because it was not possible to clearly identify the methods of data collection.

## Methodological Transparency Issues in Qualitative Research

Perhaps the most striking finding of the analysis was that in the qualitative articles examined, there was a tendency toward methodological fogginess rather than transparency. It was rare to find a qualitative study in which the research design and the methods used to select cases, interview subjects, or sources of information were clearly spelled out so as to invite understanding, critique, or replication. Similarly, in only a handful of studies were the methods used for data analysis and interpretation specified. The lack of methodological transparency was found both in studies grounded in social science approaches, where standards for transparency of method and analysis would be expected to be the same as for quantitative work, and for those based in interpretivist epistemologies, where a discussion of the author's own interpretive frame and limitations would be expected. Finally, it was equally unusual to find a systematic presentation of the data on which the study's conclusions were based.

This lack of transparency about research design and methods of data collection, analysis, and interpretation is problematic. In social-science-based research, methodological transparency is a central requirement because social science assumes that there can be both valid and nonvalid findings. Establishing the validity of findings requires methodological rigor, including the use of a comparative design, an acceptable sampling strategy, clear operational definitions, systematic data collection, and reliable and valid measures.

Consequently, research should contain explicit statements about the design used, the variables studied and how they were defined, the researcher's expectations about the likely findings of the study, how and why cases, documents, studies, or other data sources were selected or rejected, the data collection methods employed, the methods used to increase the reliability of data collection and analysis, details about data analysis techniques, and any limitations or problems the research team encountered.

When qualitative research is based on interpretive paradigms, the standards used to judge the quality of the research include "historical situatedness, erosion of ignorance and misapprehension, action stimulus, trustworthiness and authenticity" (Lincoln & Guba, 2000, p. 170). Arguments about research quality focus less on whether the findings reflect "reality," "than about whose reality their narrative captures" (Pauly, 1991, p. 23). Thus, the need for methodological transparency moves to a focus on the organizational or historical context in which the arguments are situated, the researcher's own personal frames, and the ways in which those frames may have influenced interpretation. For the researcher to ignore the need for transparent self-examination is to assume a position of privilege in which the scholar removes from scrutiny his or her own role in the social construction of knowledge.

The fact that analysis of qualitative research in media management and economics journals shows a consistent lack of the methodological transparency required by either major epistemology is troubling. It suggests that scholars in both paradigmatic traditions are, as Jensen (1991) suggested, assuming that the use of qualitative methods is a license to make research an "easy . . . carefree romp" (p. 1).

## QUALITATIVE RESEARCH DESIGNS

Research design refers to how a research project is planned and structured, including the exemplar to be studied, the variables to be compared and examined, and the data collection methods to be used. The design of a research project is paramount because, if a project's design is flawed by the standards of the paradigm in which the scholar is operating, then the value of the findings will be questionable.

The term "methods" refers to the techniques used for data collection or measurement.

The ideal research design in social science would accomplish three things: simplicity, specificity, and generalizability. In practice, it is virtually impossible to achieve more than two of these three goals in any given study because a design that would produce both specificity and generalizability would have to be complex.

Qualitative data collection methods are often used in projects designed to focus on specificity and simplicity. Generalizability is difficult, although not impossible, to achieve using qualitative methods because in order to generalize research findings to a broad population, it usually is necessary to have a large, randomly selected sample. Because qualitative data collection and analysis tend to be time consuming, qualitative methods are rarely used with large samples. Thus, social-science-based qualitative research usually is not generalizable beyond the dataset.

Generalizability also is not possible for qualitative research based on interpretative paradigms because, in the absence of an objective, observable reality, all knowledge claims are specific to the case and to the individual researcher. It becomes logically inconsistent with the underlying paradigm to argue that any individual scholar's findings can be generalized to other cases or other scholars' work.

What qualitative methods provide to researchers instead of generalizability is the opportunity to develop extremely detailed, context-rich data or interpretations that offer insights into subtle underlying relationships. Because generalizability usually is not a goal, projects using qualitative methods often employ purposive selection of the sample or cases.

Another important element of research design in social science research is the idea of comparison. Without building an element of comparison or control into a research design, it is impossible to determine whether two factors are related. For example, if a researcher were studying the effects of leadership style on employee motivation, it would be impossible to know whether there was a relationship between the two variables if the study observed only one media executive.

For research conducted from an interpretive basis, comparison is less important than triangulation as a design element. Ensuring that the research accurately reflects the context of the research—that is, the conditions and values of the subjects—is of paramount importance in interpretive research. One approach to achieving that is to design the study so that data are gathered from multiple sources. A second approach is theoretical triangulation, that is, studying the problem or condition from multiple theoretical viewpoints and combining the results into a richer, more multifaceted understanding of the issue (Fortner & Christians, 1981).

## QUALITATIVE METHODS

### Case-Study Designs

Although case studies and comparative case studies are often described as qualitative research "methods," a case study is, in fact, not a method but a research design. But because it is such a widely used research design in the field of media management and economics, the case study deserves special discussion.

A *case study* is the focused exploration of a single case of a particular phenomenon (Denzin & Lincoln, 2000). Case studies are frequently used either to conduct a preliminary exploration of a topic so as to identify potential issues and variables for later research, or as a method for showcasing an example of some particular aspect of management or organizational behavior (Bryman, 1989; Williams, Rice, & Rogers, 1988). The goal of the research might be to learn what management strategies are being employed, what current "best practices" are, how organizational processes have changed over time, or to validate previous research, or confirm or disconfirm theory (Bryman, 1989; Gravetter & Forzano, 2003). Although case studies cannot be generalized beyond the particular case, they can set limits for generalizing by identifying cases in which a theory doesn't hold.

In all instances, a case study is a concentrated focus on the particular and the particular alone. Specifically, "the case is expected to be something that functions, that operates; the study is the observation of operations" (Denzin & Lincoln, 2000, p. 444).

Case studies can be methodologically complex. In some instances, both quantitative and qualitative methods may be combined, providing a multifaceted view of the phenomenon under study. For example, in a case study of the Southam newspaper chain in Canada, Edge (2003) used corporate documents and financial reports, secondary sources in the form of news stories about events in the company, and direct knowledge and observation from an earlier period when he had been employed by Southam. Similarly, Gershon and Kanayama (2002) used primary and secondary sources and personal and written interviews in their case study of the Sony Corp.'s development and evolution into a leading transnational media corporation.

The greatest strength of the case study as a design is the richness of detail it provides. Because the project focuses on only one case, the variety and thoroughness of the data developed can be much deeper and more nuanced, providing insights into complex relationships that might be overlooked in other designs (Gravetter & Forzano, 2003; Williams et al., 1988). Finally, the narrative detail in case studies can make them compelling and powerful, potentially increasing their impact on the reader. Consider, for instance, the impact of a case study in which a media executive's leadership style is directly observed, versus a survey of employees' assessment of the executive's style based on preestablished Likert Scale measures.

The primary weakness of the case study design is that it is not grounded in comparison. Therefore, it is difficult to know whether the observed phenomenon is unique to that case and condition or whether it commonly occurs in other circumstances. Consequently, case studies lack internal and external validity. Results are indicative only of that singular entity or event at one point in time, making "alternative explanations . . . always possible" (Gravetter & Forzano, 2003, p. 178). Validity concerns can be remedied somewhat through replication of case studies; however, scholars do not all agree on this, as the circumstances are almost never identical to those of the original case study.

Other criticisms leveled against the case study design include issues of researcher bias and subjectivity. Case studies generate large volumes of data from multiple sources, and few case studies have employed multiple coders and intercoder reliability tests to establish the reliability of observation and interpretation. The gatekeeping process involved in choosing from the available data those events to be highlighted in the findings makes selective bias more likely (Denzin & Lincoln, 2000; Gravetter & Forzano, 2003; Silverman, 2001). Finally, case studies tend not to be accepted when other methods that use large samples or comparisons could have been used (Williams et al., 1988).

The actual process of case study research involves identifying a research question, case selection, data collection, arrangements, analysis, and write-up (Denzin & Lincoln, 2000). Probably the most difficult task is selecting an appropriate case. Considerations include which cases are most typical or representative, which contain elements that address the dominant theme of the project and include variables central to the research question, and which will provide the best access to information.[4] In practice, the different stages of case study research often blend together, and many researchers recommend writing the report as the study progresses (Williams et al., 1988).

---

[4] For a more complete discussion of case study research designs, see Yin (2003) and Williams et al. (1988).

## Comparative Case-Study Designs

Comparative case studies address the central weakness of the single case study method by incorporating comparisons into the research design. As a result, comparative case studies are more revealing and can be highly valuable. Comparing multiple cases provides a reference or control and can reveal patterns that would not be evident in a single case study (Denzin & Lincoln, 2000). Moreover, case patterns and features can be more easily identified and, because the internal validity of the research design is improved by adding the comparisons, it is more likely that an argument can be made for extrapolating findings to other cases with similar conditions (Bryman, 1989).

The research process for the comparative case study is the same as for the single case study, varying only in regard to case selection. In the comparative approach, the researcher must decide whether to select cases based on similarity on the dependent variable, which is called a within-group design, or on difference on the independent variable, known as an across-group design, or both. The trade-off is that the more cases that are added to the study, the more complex the research design grows and the fewer details the researcher will be able to gather about each case. Some of the data richness that the case study method offers starts to be lost.

In media management and economics research, studies using a within-group design (Collette & Litman, 1997; Fedler & Pennington, 2003; Küng, 2003; Shrikhande, 2001) have been more common than those based on an across-group design (Brown, 2002; Pathania-Jain, 2001).

Because multiple cases are involved, comparative case study research tends to be more focused on specific variables than is single case study research. Consequently, it is less effective in incorporating a wide range of potentially relevant data. If the researcher looks only at specific variables or the linkages between cases, otherwise valuable insights into the specific intricacies of the cases involved can be lost and the focus shifts away from the cases themselves (Denzin & Lincoln, 2000).

## Field Observation Methods

*Field observation* is the process of gathering data through direct observation of the phenomenon of interest. Field observation generally involves minimal interaction with the subjects being observed, although it is not necessarily unobtrusive observation. The minimization of interaction makes field observation distinct from participant observation methods, in which the researcher is actively involved in a process even while observing it.

As a data collection method, field observation is appropriate for the study of organizations, cultures, processes and practices, groups, relationships, roles, and the social construction of meaning (Babbie, 1989; Lofland & Lofland, 1984, Schwartzman, 1993). For example, in media management and economics research, field observation has been used to study personnel issues (Becker, Fruit, & Caudill, 1987), the impact of digital media devices on the media industry (Rawolle & Hess, 2000), and news construction and gatekeeping (Abbott & Brassfield, 1989; Heider, 2000).

The strength of observational methods is that they provide direct information about processes. Surveys and interviews can generate expected-response bias, that is, respondents may tell a researcher what they think the researcher wants to hear or what they think they should say in response to a question. Field observation allows the researcher to personally observe what people do, as opposed to relying on what they say they do.

One of the weaknesses of field observation is that the researcher's presence can increase organizational members' self-consciousness and thereby change their behavior. This is known as the *Hawthorne effect*, after the series of studies on the effects of working conditions on employee productivity where it was first observed (Roethlisberger & Dickson, 1939). Unless the observer also has a control group built into the research design, it will be difficult to know whether the behavior is the result of the researcher's presence or whether it is an actual effect of whatever the researcher has identified as the independent variable in the study.

Distortions in behavior caused by the researcher's presence can be somewhat countered by spending an extended period of time in the group or organization until the study subjects begin to ignore the researcher. This, however, makes field observation a very time-intensive method. Unobtrusive observation or deception are other ways researchers avoid distorting the behaviors they are observing. *Unobtrusive observation* occurs when the subjects are unaware they are being watched. *Deception* usually means the researcher pretends to become a member of the group without informing the group that he or she also is conducting research. But deception raises questions about research ethics.

Another issue that arises with field observation is the question of reliability and validity. Because usually only one observer is present, it is difficult to establish reliability for the observations and interpretation. Additionally, a single researcher cannot be in all places at all times and observe all things, so key information may be lost. However, if more than one observer is used in order to address these problems, the costs involved in the research rapidly rise, and the likelihood of causing behavioral changes in the research subjects increases.

The research process for field observations is, in some ways, similar to those for case studies. Once a research question has been developed, the challenge becomes to identify a representative situation where one can observe the phenomenon of interest. If the study involves the effects of leadership style on creativity, for example, it is necessary to ask how representative this organization, its leader, and its creative processes are within the industry as a whole. These issues are, of course, similar to the problems faced when trying to identify an appropriate case for a case study.

Where field observation provides a unique challenge is in gaining access to the organization or setting that is to be observed (Lindlof, 1995). In the media industry, organizations may be hesitant about allowing a researcher to come in out of concern that the research will disrupt work processes, portray the organization in an unflattering light, or reveal trade secrets. Gaining access sometimes requires that the researcher enter into a "bargain" with the organization. These bargains can involve different things, but the researcher has to evaluate whether the requirements of the bargain will affect the scope of observation, the integrity of the research findings, or the security or privacy of the individuals observed to an unacceptable degree.

Data collection in observational research involves watching, listening, and asking questions. One model for organizational field research suggests that researchers should gather data on participants, the space and time of events and interactions, the goals and outcomes of events, power and influence interactions, event cycles, and the channels, codes, norms, and symbols used in interpersonal or intraorganizational communication as they relate to the research topic (Schwartzman, 1993). Recording observations is a major challenge in observational research because, if the researcher visibly takes notes or makes recordings, the observed will be made more conscious of the fact that they are being watched. For the sake of accuracy, it is important that observational researchers record their field notes as soon as possible after a period of observation, but often notes are not taken in the research setting itself.

Although research should be grounded in theory, one of the risks of observational research is that researchers may focus too much on observing the processes they expect to find and thereby miss important factors or misinterpret events in ways that conform to their preexisting expectations. In other words, people tend to see what they expect to see. Because of this, efforts to interpret observational data generally should wait until data collection has been finished.

## Participant Observation Methods

*Participant observation* is a variation on field observation research wherein the researcher becomes an active participant in the events or processes that he or she is observing. This can take place in one of several ways. A researcher may use deception to pose as a participant so that his or her role as an observer remains undetected. It also is possible to identify oneself as a researcher but then to join in the activities being observed so as to become an actual participant. Participation, then, becomes a strategy for making the researcher "invisible," so that the people being observed stop feeling self-conscious (Berg, 1995; Lindlof, 1995).

*Action research* is a distinctive form of participant observation research. Although action research is a comparatively new approach to academic research, it is, in fact, a long-established tradition in organizational studies, where it is known as "management consulting." In action research, the researcher not only participates but acts as a change agent in the process being observed. The researcher is actively observing and interpreting a particular organizational process and making suggestions for changes that may improve outcomes. The quality of action research is judged by whether or not the organization's leadership accepts the suggestions and, if so, whether positive outcomes result.[5]

Among the strengths of participant observation as a research method is its ability to provide a researcher with access to information that otherwise might not be available. For example, it can make it easier to learn about a group's internal cultural and symbolic norms because the researcher will be socialized into group membership. Even when the group is aware that the researcher has the dual roles of group member and observer, the act of participating in the group's activities eventually will reduce most members' self-consciousness and wariness.

---

[5]For more information on action research, see Greenwood and Levin (1998, 2000), Gummesson (2000), and Kemmis and McTaggart (2000).

Conversely, researchers need to be aware that being a participant observer also may reduce access to information, particularly information from elites. If, for example, a senior reporter at a newspaper were fired, the editor might be willing to explain that decision to a researcher who had been given access to the newsroom, with the understanding that the fired employee's privacy would be preserved. However, it is highly unlikely that a coworker would be made privy to the details of such a decision, even if it were known that the coworker also was conducting research.

A key weakness of participant observation research is that it makes the researcher a stakeholder in the organizational game, suffering the small wins and losses that make up the average workday. Such personal involvement can color the researcher's observations, increasing the likelihood that valuable data will be overlooked or misinterpreted. In some cases, the researcher's personal interests may become so aligned with those of the people being observed that he or she begins to "protect" them from potential negative effects of the research.

In media management and economics research, participant observation has not been used as widely as might be expected given the close connections between the media profession and the scholarly community in mass communication. Nevertheless, it has been used effectively on a number of occasions. Examples of the method include Soloski's (1979) use of participation observation to study the organizational effects of an ownership change on a newspaper for which he was working and Edge's (2003) inclusion of his knowledge as a former employee in his study of the effects of public ownership on the Southam newspaper group in Canada. Similarly, Argyris (1974) and Johansson (2002) both used action research models to study internal operations at a U.S. newspaper and a Swedish magazine, respectively.

## Ethnographic Methods

Although defined differently by different scholars, ethnography uses field observation methods but includes a concern with allowing the subjects of study to offer their own explanations and accounts of the events that are observed and the motivations behind them (Berg, 1995). Ethnography is grounded in interpretive paradigms, which has implications for both the methodological practice and interpretation of field observation work.[6]

Ethnographic research, which has its roots in anthropology, focuses on describing the complexities of life and the social relationships that shape human behavior (Wolcott, 1973). Ethnography assumes that the researcher will become immersed in the observed community and serve as the channel through which the group's internal narrative is communicated to the world (Schwartzman, 1993). The basis of ethnography is "thick description" (Geertz, 1973, p. 9), which includes relating rich details of cultural and communication behaviors and events. Generally, ethnography is presented as a narrative account of what was observed. Among ethnographers, controversy swirls over the proper balance between the "natives'" voices and the researcher's voice, and whether it is even

---

[6]For a more thorough discussion of ethnography, see Altheide (1996), Geertz (1973), Lindlof (1995), and Schwartzman (1993).

possible for researchers to accurately mirror the voices of others without coloring them through the researcher's own frames.

## Interview Methods

Interviews are a crucial data collection method in media management and economics research, primarily because very few corporate "elites" will consent to respond to telephone or mail surveys. Consequently, almost any research project that requires data from senior media executives will have to employ interviews (Breed, 1955; Chyi & Sylvie, 2000; Geissler & Einwiller, 2001; Gerpott & Niegel, 2002; Turow, 1982).

Interviews can take three forms: structured, semistructured, and unstructured. A *structured interview* includes a predetermined list of questions from which the interviewer does not vary. *Semistructured interviews* contain preset questions, but the interviewer will add or drop questions as seems appropriate or follow up on new topics or lines of inquiry that may be introduced by the respondent. Consequently, the interview frequently digresses. An *unstructured interview* is free-flowing, with no predetermined topics or questions, and is most commonly used in ethnographic research.

Semistructured interviews are a widely used format with elite respondents and are particularly appropriate to organizational research. Corporate and political leaders tend to respond more positively to a conversational style that allows them some control of the direction of the interview. Additionally, by using a completely predetermined set of questions, a researcher will lose a valuable opportunity to gain rich data and new insights from elite sources, who may never again be accessible. In contrast, executives are less likely to commit the time and patience required for unstructured interviews.

Semistructured or structured interviews are particularly important in comparative research because the structure is necessary to ensure that the researcher has gained comparable data from multiple sources. Structured interviews provide each respondent with the same questions and in the same order, which minimizes the likelihood that respondents' answers will be influenced by information, digressions, or interactions outside of the questions themselves. Semistructured interviews generate comparable data in that respondents answer most of the same questions. However, it is more likely that the answers to some questions will have been influenced by digressions that may have occurred because the question order is not strictly controlled.

The interviewing process involves developing an interview instrument and pretesting the questions to ensure that they will generate the desired data. The interview is a performance on the part of the researcher, and rehearsal is key to success (Berg, 1995; Lindlof, 1995). Practice allows the interviewer to become familiar with the questions and role-play the planned interaction with respondents. During the interview, the researcher must be highly self-aware, adjusting his or her actions as necessary to keep the respondent engaged and the interview on topic.

One of the key challenges of interviews is gaining access to respondents. Gaining access usually requires the researcher to reveal the nature of the research project. But it is important that the researcher's hypotheses or expectations not be revealed, as this may introduce expected response bias or cause the respondent to refuse to participate.

Establishing rapport between the interviewer and interviewee is critical to the success of the interview (Berg, 1995). With in-person interviews, nonverbal communication plays a central role in establishing rapport. Nonverbal communication includes such things as the interviewer's dress, posture, physical proximity to the respondent, and acceptance of amenities the respondent may offer, such as food or drink. The effective interviewer monitors all of these elements and tries to continually match the respondent's nonverbal behavior as closely as possible. Other factors in establishing rapport include nodding, smiling, or giving short verbal encouragements such as "yes," or "uh-huh" during the interview, which helps encourage the speaker to continue. However, such cues can be interpreted by the respondent as approval or disapproval and may generate expected response bias. On the other hand, silence and lack of response also will affect the respondent because a complete lack of communicative cues is unnatural in human interaction. Consequently, the interviewer must constantly monitor his or her own communications during the interview, considering how they may be influencing the respondent.

Although rapport is necessary to the successful interview, it also carries risks. If rapport levels are high, the interview subject may come to believe that the researcher is an ally and will interpret the data the way the respondent wishes. In studies that involve longer interactions such as ethnographic research, high levels of rapport can make it difficult for the researcher to avoid "going native," that is, becoming aligned with the individuals, group, or organization under study (Fontana & Frey, 2000).

For those working from interpretive paradigms, the interview process varies somewhat because of the concern that the interviewer's voice may overpower that of the subject. Postmodern, gender, and critical research tend to rely on unstructured interviews. Interview data often are reported with minimal interpretation and may even be reported only as excerpts from the interviews (Fontana & Frey, 2000). The focus essentially is on collecting oral records from people and sharing them.

Although often viewed as a comparatively easy research method to use because of its similarity to normal conversation, interviewing is actually very difficult and many researchers never master the skill. Additionally, the proper relationship between interviewer and interviewee is increasingly a subject of debate among scholars, as are issues of how interview data should be interpreted and used. These discussions should be thoroughly reviewed before embarking on research in which interviews are the primary method.[7]

## Historical Methods

Historical methods are frequently used in media management and economics research (Buzzard, 2002; Fedler & Pennington, 2003; Picard, 1996; Wolfe & Kapoor, 1996). An obvious use is the development of management or organizational related histories, but a far larger number of scholars use some elements of the historical method in their development of case studies, essays, policy studies, or other projects, even if they don't view themselves as writing histories.

---

[7]Berg (1995), Fontana & Frey (2000), Lindlof (1995), and Silverman (2001) are excellent resources for more information on interviewing.

Within the qualitative methodological framework, historians argue over whether their methods are properly located in the humanities or the social sciences (Howell & Prevenier, 2001; Marwick, 1974; Nord & Nelson, 1981). Although historical research traditionally has been grounded in narrative, interpretive approaches, over the past few decades it has become more common for historians to draw upon social science methods, including quantitative analysis. This reflects both the potential of historical research to identify patterns of human interaction and the hope that understanding history can contribute to understanding current events and issues.

On the other hand, history cannot be separated from the individual actors and their points in time. Additionally, the historical record is rarely complete. Indeed, it has been said that "History is the *memory* of things said and done" (Becker, 1931, p. 22, emphasis added), rather than a record of the actual events themselves. Consequently, historical methods vary widely among historians, but it is not uncommon for historians to use a combination of interpretive and social science methods.

Among historians, epistemological debates focus on what questions to ask, how theory is to be used in the historical research process, how documents, materials, and other data are to be interpreted, and how history is to be read—that is, what it means in the context of the human enterprise. In contrast, there is far more consensus about methodological standards for data collection and measurement (Shafer, 1974; Smith, 1981; Startt & Sloan, 2003).[8]

Among historians, emphasis is placed on gathering primary documentation from original sources that address the research question. Primary sources refer to information about the topic that was produced at the time and by people directly involved in the issue. This may include official records and documents, letters, diaries, or eyewitness accounts. Where the research question directly involves the nature of media content, newspapers, broadcasts, or stories may be considered primary data. The historical method requires more than simply gathering such evidence, however. It also must be authenticated and its credibility established (Bennett, Brown, & Halsey, 1970; Shafer, 1974; Smith, 1981; Startt & Sloan, 2003).

Secondary sources, such as news accounts and books, also are important, although they are viewed with some skepticism as evidence since they represent secondhand knowledge that already has been filtered and interpreted by at least one reporter. Thus, the probability of distortion is high.

A crucial challenge in historical research arises during analysis. It is difficult to analyze previous events in the context of their own time. Language, worldviews, and values change, and one of the problems the historian must address is how to understand and interpret the standards and values of the past. Historical events interpreted through current values will be understood differently than if interpreted through the values of their own times. However, the degree to which it is possible for a historian to accurately mirror the standards and understandings of a time, culture, or event he or she did not personally experience is open to debate. Consequently, historical research is not merely

---

[8]Detailed discussions about the historical method can be found in Barzun and Graff (1992), Brundage (1997), Shafer (1974), Schudson (1997), and Startt and Sloan (2003).

a reflection of the memory of things said and done. At some level, it also is the *creation* of the memory of things said and done.

The quality of historical research is evaluated on the basis of the comprehensiveness and credibility of the evidence gathered, the cohesiveness of the interpretation and its correspondence to the evidence and to the historical context in which the events took place, and its contribution to the solution of historical problems (Shafer, 1974). Scholars who tend toward more of a social science approach to history expect research to be theoretically grounded and findings to contribute to understanding problems or events.

Based on these standards, the quality of mass communication histories has been critiqued as being too often based on one or more unexamined assumptions (Schudson, 1997). Among those assumptions are that commercial forces automatically have negative effects on journalism and its service of the public interest, that media and journalism are in a state of decline as compared to the past, and that economics and technology are deterministic in media industries and practices so that many of the complex events and phenomena observed in media can be explained by these two forces. Although Schudson identifies other unexamined assumptions that he argues underlie much historical research in mass communications, clearly these three assumptions are particularly relevant to historians of media management and economics.

## Focus Group Methods

*Focus groups* are a qualitative data collection method little used by scholarly researchers in media management and economics. Not a single one of the 309 articles published in *The Journal of Media Economics* or *The International Journal on Media Management* between 1988 and 2003 used focus groups as either a primary or secondary method of data collection.

The explanation for this is simple: Data from focus groups are highly suspect from both the social science and interpretive viewpoints. Although some experts disagree (Morgan, 1998), most social scientists are skeptical of the method on grounds that participants in focus groups are not randomly selected—a critique that would apply to much of the data gathered through qualitative methods. However, in the case of focus groups, industry researchers often generalize the data to the population from which participants were drawn despite the sampling method. Scholars also charge that the artificial settings in which focus groups are held and the presence of recording equipment can inhibit participants. Additionally, the focus-group process subjects participants to social forces that make them vulnerable either to being silenced or swayed by other members in the group (Wimmer & Dominick, 1997).

Despite these criticisms, focus groups still are widely used as a research technique by media managers and management consultants (Morgan, 1998). They frequently are used by the media industry to identify emerging trends in popular culture and to gather general responses to media content and format. The television industry, in particular, makes frequent use of focus groups to gather audience feedback on program concepts, episodes, scripts, or storylines, and on individual actors and news anchors.

Within the media industry, sophisticated variations on the focus group have been developed that address at least some of the weaknesses of the method. While watching a television program, for example, focus group participants use individual handheld devices to record their moment-by-moment reactions to the program. The mean of the group's individual responses is tabulated and appears as a rising and falling graph across the face of the program viewed. This visual record of the group's reactions helps provide some protection against pressures to conform during subsequent discussions.[9]

## Literature Reviews and Meta-analysis Methods

It is useful for the media management and economics community to "take stock" of its acquired body of knowledge periodically by evaluating the existing research on specific topics. The value of meta-analyses of literature is evident by their relatively frequent appearance in media management and economics journals (Fu, 2003; Hollifield, 2001; Lacy & Niebauer, 1995; Wirth & Bloch, 1995) Such reviews are even more common in books and other publications.

The primary difference between a formal meta-analysis of literature and a standard literature review for a research project is that, in a meta-analysis, the literature itself is the dataset, with each study providing an individual case. A meta-analysis examines the entire available population of literature in an area and uses a systematic method for breaking down the studies and comparing their internal characteristics, findings, and implications. Thus, the subject of study in a meta-analysis is the state of knowledge on a specific topic.

One of the leading methods for systematizing the analysis of different pieces of research is the *Rogers propositional inventory* (Rogers, 1981). The propositional inventory provides a breakdown of research methods, a comparison of findings, and a synthesis of general conclusions.

There are a couple of ways to conduct a propositional inventory, including the voting method and the word table data-display. The former tabulates the statistical significance of primary research results and then offers a "meta-conclusion" based upon the relationship between variables. The latter is based on a word table where rows represent each study as a "case" and columns represent the aspects of the research that the scholar is studying, such as the theory, sampling methods and operational definitions used, findings, and conclusions.

Once the propositional inventory is concluded, it becomes possible to see whether researchers who appear to be studying the same topics are, in fact, doing so, or whether they are using such different theoretical frameworks, variables, operational definitions, and methods that there is less cohesiveness across the body of research than it first appears. The researcher will be able to use the inventory to synthesize findings, recognize inconclusive data and gaps in the literature, and have an overall picture of the field's—or a topic's—evolution and status.[10]

---

[9] There are many resources available that discuss the focus group methodology. Among them are Morgan and Krueger (1998) and Wimmer and Dominick (1997).

[10] For specifics on how to conduct a propositional inventory, see Rogers' *Methodology for Meta-Research* (1981).

## QUALITATIVE DATA ANALYSIS

### Analyzing Qualitative Data in Social Science Research

The analysis of qualitative data is difficult and time-consuming. By some estimates, data analysis in qualitative projects can take two to three times longer than data collection (Miles & Huberman, 1994). Within the social science framework, there are numerous approaches to systematizing qualitative data analysis so that transparency and reliability can be achieved.

A first step in the process is to transform data into a format that can be used for analysis. This may mean transcribing notes, summarizing documents, entering files into a computer database, etc. Critical to the process is to ensure that the data are reformatted accurately so that error is not introduced into the texts during the transcription process. Given the volumes of data that qualitative research designs usually produce, it is important to develop a data management system that will ensure that key pieces of information can be retrieved and linked to related information across sources.[11] With large qualitative projects, the danger always exists that critical data will be lost.

Once the data have been prepared, a system for coding the data according to the variables in the study must be developed. There are different ways to do this. The *constant comparative approach* (Lincoln & Guba, 1985) requires that all incidents coded into a particular category be compared back to all other incidents coded into the same category and also against incidents coded into similar categories. The coding process then consists of constant coding and recoding until categorical exclusivity is achieved. Another method, *pattern coding*, consists of identifying emergent patterns of events or themes that serve as a type of metacoding (Miles & Huberman, 1994). The pattern coding process is a method of grouping the codes of smaller units of analysis so that larger and perhaps more obscure patterns can emerge. A third approach, *concordances*, focuses on identifying key words in text so that the patterns and context in which certain words or phrases emerge are identified (Ryan & Bernard, 2000). These represent only a few ways in which qualitative data may be coded.

Coding is not simply the act of identifying topics, however. Codes must have some conceptual purpose that is related to the primary research question guiding the study, and they should be carefully operationally defined. The reliability of the methods used to label or code the data also must be established to ensure that the research would be replicable. Reliability is measured by having more than one person code the same material according to the definitions and codes established for the project. There are a number of ways of measuring intercoder reliability, each of which has its strengths and weaknesses (Holsti, 1969; Krippendorff, 1980; Miles & Huberman, 1994). Qualitative data analysis software also can be used to establish reliability for some types of coding.

Once material has been coded, analysis can be approached in several ways. Data can be laid out visually in word tables, flow charts, conceptual maps, or models that create physical representations of the patterns identified through the coding process. Such visual

---

[11] Additional sources on techniques for qualitative data management and analysis include: Altheide (1996), Miles and Huberman (1994), and Silverman (2001).

displays help clarify conceptual links and patterns between variables, across cases, and in the time order of events. The goal of data analysis is to identify patterns, similarities, and differences within and across cases, and to seek theoretically relevant explanations for what is found.

Increasingly, researchers using qualitative methods are employing sophisticated data analysis software that assists with the coding and analysis processes. A number of such programs are on the market. The programs and the tasks for which they are designed vary. Also, of course, the attributes of the specific programs change over time as they are redesigned and updated. Consequently, researchers working with qualitative data should carefully review the current versions of available data-analysis programs according to the specific needs of the project for which it will be used.

## Textual Analysis for Interpretive Research

Textual analysis is a method of analyzing qualitative data frequently used by those working in interpretive paradigms. It is grounded in the assumption that the meaning of texts is found in the ways they were written and the ways they are read, not in the texts themselves (Hodder, 2000). Consequently, there is no single "true" meaning of any text, but only an interpretation of it. The quality of the interpretation depends on whether the researcher has properly situated his or her interpretation in the historical context in which the text was produced.

As a data analysis method, textual analysis is applied to more than written texts. All kinds of physical and visual artifacts are included in the concept of "texts," as are written and spoken narratives. Architecture, landscapes, streetscapes, décor, waste products, art, fashion, advertisements, and symbols of all kinds are considered texts no less than news-paper content or television program episodes. Indeed, culture and all of its products fall within the definition. Ethnographers analyzing the data gathered through organizational observation, critical theorists analyzing organizational power structures, and symbolo-gists studying organizational symbols or symbolic behavior all are likely to employ some form of textual analysis as they seek to understand the data they have collected.

As a method of data analysis, textual analysis is like other techniques in that it seeks to locate and interpret patterns in the artifacts being analyzed. Hodder (2000) defines the method of textual analysis as identifying patterns and evaluating them in three ways: their context; their similarities and differences; and their relevance in terms of the general theories from which the scholar is working. In this, textual analysis does not differ from other qualitative methods of data analysis. Where it does differ is in the acceptance of the scholar's individual interpretation of the text without the need to establish reliability of interpretation. The quality of the interpretations developed through textual analysis are evaluated on the basis of the integrity, persuasiveness, believability, and connections between theory, data, arguments, and conclusions (Hodder, 2000; Jones, 1996).

Textual analysis has not been widely used in media management and economics research to date, although it has been applied in the broader field of organizational studies. Scholars using postmodern feminist theory to study organizations, for example, might use textual analysis to examine internal organizational discourses and how they differentially affect men and women in the organization. Critical theorists might use textual analysis to interpret the power relationships they observe, and symbologists might use the method to interpret organizational symbols and symbolic behaviors (Jones, 1996).

# RESEARCH ETHICS

Although qualitative methods deliver rich detail and incomparable depth, they also present unique risks for ethical breaches. Interviews, case studies, and action research usually require significant human interaction, one-on-one conversation and observation, and a high degree of trust between researcher and subject. Meticulous observation of ethical practices is very important in media management and economics research because a breach of trust can threaten the economic survival of companies or the careers and livelihoods of individuals.

Most social scientists agree upon four basic guidelines for ethical practice: informed consent, criteria for deception, privacy and confidentiality, and accuracy. Institutional Review Boards, or IRBs, are required to review all research designs and instruments used in research at most universities in the United States, providing both guidance and enforcement of ethical standards. However, in qualitative research, issues sometimes arise that are not explicitly covered under IRB guidelines. It is also the case that although many nations have similar systems to ensure ethical research practices, not all do. Consequently, a brief discussion of these fundamental principles is worthwhile.

## Informed Consent and Deception

Participants cannot consent to what they do not know. Informed consent means that participants are fully informed about the processes and risks involved in the research so that their participation is truly voluntary (Stake, 2000). No coercion can be used. Anyone may refuse to answer a question or refuse to participate entirely.

In some cases, full disclosure may distort the study's results and produce an invalid outcome. In such instances, a minimal amount of deception might be acceptable. Deception is the omission of selected information, or "partial truths" told to research subjects. Some researchers believe this is never acceptable, whereas others point to its necessity under certain conditions, for instance to prevent respondent bias or, in the case of management consulting research, to protect the client or sponsor's identity (Cooper & Schindler, 2001).

Participant observation research in which the researcher does not reveal his/her research role would be an example of the first case. In most circumstances, unobtrusive observation in public settings is not considered an ethical problem. However, unobtrusive observation in private settings such as a workplace, where some expectation of privacy exists, falls into the gray area of ethical behavior. In other instances, if stating the identity of the research sponsor or the nature of the study could affect participant responses, cause respondents to question the study's motives, or give a competitor clues as to possible new products or services to be offered, then deception in the form of sponsor or research-question nondisclosure may be considered. Deception should never be used for ill-conceived purposes, such as to increase response rates or where the deception might put the subject at substantial risk (Cooper & Schindler, 2001).

In cases where the researcher deems it necessary to deceive, debriefing is recommended. Debriefing occurs after data collection or at the study's conclusion. It involves the researcher providing the participants with the information previously withheld from them and sharing the results of the research in summary form. The debriefing process may serve an instrumental purpose in that it may leave subjects with a more positive sense of the research. It also allows the researcher to learn the subjects' impressions of the study, which can help improve future research designs.

## Privacy and Confidentiality

Privacy and confidentiality can be challenging in qualitative research because of the nature of the collected data itself. Proprietary company data and interviews pose some of the greatest risks. Despite confidentiality or anonymity guarantees by researchers, quotations excerpted from interviews often contain stylistic expressions, syntax, or content that will make the source of the quote readily identifiable to those who know the respondent. In such cases, paraphrasing is advisable. However, for those working in interpretive paradigms or using ethnographic methods, paraphrasing violates one of the fundamental tenets—and purposes—of the research. Nevertheless, using direct quotations or including detailed behavioral or personality observations in the descriptions indisputably puts the subject at risk of being identified, which, within workplace settings, can put the person at substantial economic risk. The likelihood of this occurrence is greater in small companies or in cases in which a small number of subjects were interviewed.

When working with proprietary company or individual information, an entire research team must have a full understanding of confidentiality, including students or other research assistants who may be helping with the project. Proprietary company data are valuable, as is consumer information. Additionally, once sensitive data are collected, the researcher must protect them by keeping them in a secure location to prevent accidental discovery.

## Accuracy

Credible research demands accuracy. Researcher fraud, concocted datasets, or methodological procedures that never took place are unethical and never permissible. More common than fraud, however, are measurement errors and errors of interpretation. Both are unavoidable in research. The use of precise operational definitions, careful and systematic data collection methods, and reliability tests during both instrument development and data analysis are important elements in reducing measurement error. Errors of interpretation are more difficult to gauge. Indeed, from the perspective of interpretive paradigms, errors of interpretation are impossible to avoid because each individual has a unique interpretation so that no single interpretation is correct. However, both interpretive and social science paradigms share a concern with contextually accurate interpretation. Consequently, in neither paradigm does it meet the standards of quality research to set out to "prove" or "demonstrate" the accuracy of a hypothesis or a preconceived belief where that proof or demonstration involves ignoring or discounting evidence to the contrary.

## Transnational Ethics

As interest in the globalization of media increases, more scholars will find themselves dealing with the ethical issues specific to transnational media management and economics research. Whereas in the developed world the primary concern in management research is protecting research participants from economic risk, there are many nations in which respondents may also be exposed to physical danger, particularly if there is a possibility that the researcher's field notes will be examined by officials. Where government permission is required before conducting the research, participants may be under pressure to participate so that consent is not genuine. In some nations, participants will expect payment or favors in return for participation.

In dealing with such issues, it often helps to team up with a local scholar in the host country (Punnett & Shenkar, 1996). Conducting transnational qualitative research requires a delicate balance between satisfying research goals and doing so in a way that will not offend study participants, produce erroneous results, put subjects at risk, or violate the ethical standards that the researcher is expected to adhere to in his or her own culture. Working with a local partner who is knowledgeable about regional conditions can help avoid such problems.

The welfare of the research subject is paramount, no matter the situation, culture, or nation. This principle should guide all others when making ethical decisions involving transnational research.

## CONCLUSION

Qualitative methods are a crucial tool for media management and economics research. They generate rich, detailed data that can provide nuanced insights into the inner workings of organizations and individuals within organizations. Equally important, qualitative methods bridge the different epistemological paradigms in which mass communication scholars work—being synonymous with neither the positivist/postpositivist nor the interpretivist approaches. They serve as an equally valuable research method to scholars working from all perspectives.

Within social science research, qualitative methods are distinguished from quantitative methods primarily on the basis of the type of data they generate: nominal as opposed to the largely ordinal, interval, and ratio-level data that quantitative methods generate. Consequently, qualitative methods can be used to achieve many of the same research goals as quantitative methods, including hypothesis testing.

Within the interpretive paradigms, qualitative methods are the primary—if not the only—method used in research because the assumptions underlying quantitative methods are logically inconsistent with the assumptions underlying interpretive paradigms. In the interpretive context, qualitative methods are used to raise questions and provide insight, rather than provide concrete data and findings. Although the volume of media management and economics research based in interpretive paradigms has been rather limited in the past, it is likely to increase in the future as more scholars are attracted to the study of media from an organizational perspective.

The paradigmatic flexibility of qualitative methods is, however, also a source of weakness in terms of their application. Examination of media management and economics research that applied qualitative methods indicates that too often researchers try to occupy the middle ground between the paradigms: Some studies clearly based in social science approaches abandon the methodological rigor and transparency required of that paradigm, whereas studies that authors have explicitly defined as grounded in interpretive approaches lack scholarly self-examination and occasionally even incorporate quantitative analysis and make claims of generalizability. Research requires methodological rigor and conceptual consistency regardless of the type of measurement one uses.

Qualitative methods also create key challenges for researchers. Both data collection and analysis can be more time-intensive than is common in quantitative research. Some qualitative approaches also have the potential to create types of ethical problems that would be less likely to occur with other methods. Both issues need to be considered and addressed by the researcher.

Finally, central to any discussion of research is the concept that choice of methodology should be driven by a project's research question, design, and epistemological assumptions. The choice of methodology is simply the choice of the tool to be used to complete the project.

In media management and economics research, qualitative methods have been, and will continue to be, central to understanding the behavior and operations of media organizations and the individuals within them. The rich data generated by observation, interviews, ethnographies, and other qualitative methods provide a strong foundation of specific insights upon which the field can build.

## REFERENCES

Abbott, E. A., & Brassfield, L. T. (1989). Comparing decisions on releases by TV and newspaper gatekeepers. *Journalism Quarterly, 66*, 853–856.

Altheide, D. L. (1996). *Qualitative Research Methods Series: Vol. 38. Qualitative media analysis.* Thousand Oaks, CA: Sage.

Argyris, C. (1974). *Behind the front page: Organizational self-renewal in a metropolitan newspaper.* San Francisco: Jossey-Bass.

Babbie, E. (1989). *The practice of social research* (5th ed.), Belmont, CA: Wadsworth.

Barzun, J., & Graff, H. F. (1992). *The modern researcher* (5th ed.). Fort Worth, TX: Harcourt Brace Jovanovich.

Becker, C. (1931, Dec. 29). *Everyman his own historian.* Annual address of the President of the American Historical Association. Minneapolis, MN. Retrieved June 5, 2004, from http://www.theaha.org/info/AHA_History/clbecker.htm

Becker, L. B., Fruit, J. W., & Caudill, S. L. (1987). *The training and hiring of journalists.* Norwood, NJ: Ablex.

Bennett, P. S., Brown, R. H., & Halsey, V. R. (Eds.). (1970). *What happened on Lexington Green? An inquiry into the nature and method of history.* Parsippany, NJ: Dale Seymour.

Berg, B. L. (1995). *Qualitative research methods for the social sciences* (2nd ed.), Boston: Allyn & Bacon.

Breed, W. (1955). Social control in the newsroom: A functional analysis. *Social Forces, 33*(4), 326–335.

Brown, A. (2002). Different paths: A comparison of the introduction of digital terrestrial television in Australia and Finland. *International Journal on Media Management, 4*(4), 277–286.

Brundage, A. (1997). *Going to the sources: A guide to historical research and writing* (2nd ed.). Wheeling, IL: Harlan Davidson.

Bryman, A. (1989). *Research methods and organization studies*. London: Unwin Hyman.

Buzzard, S. F. K. (2002). The People Meter wars: A case study of technological innovation and diffusion in the ratings industry. *Journal of Media Economics, 15*(4), 273–291.

Chyi, H. I., & Sylvie, G. (2000). Online newspapers in the U.S.: Perceptions of markets, products, revenue, and competition. *International Journal on Media Management, 2*(2), 69–77.

Clegg, S. R., & Hardy, C. (1996). Introduction: Organizations, organization and organizing. In S. R. Clegg, C. Hardy, & W. R. Nord (Eds.)., *Handbook of organization studies* (pp. 1–28). London: Sage.

Collette, L., & Litman, B. R. (1997). The peculiar economics of new broadcast network entry: The case of United Paramount and Warner Bros. *Journal of Media Economics, 10*(4), 3–22.

Cooper, D. R., & Schindler, P. S. (2001). *Business research methods* (7th ed). Boston: McGraw-Hill/Irwin.

Denzin, N. K., & Lincoln, Y. S. (2000). Introduction: The discipline and practice of qualitative research. In N. K. Denzin and Y. S. Lincoln (Eds.), *Handbook of qualitative research* (2nd ed., pp. 1–28). Thousand Oaks, CA: Sage.

Edge, M. (2003). The good, the bad, and the ugly: Financial markets and the demise of Canada's Southam newspapers. *International Journal on Media Management 5*(4), 227–236.

Fedler, F., & Pennington, R. (2003). Employee-owned dailies: The triumph of economic self-interest over journalistic ideals. *International Journal on Media Management, 5*(4), 262–274.

Fontana, A., & Frey, J. H. (2000). The interview: From structured questions to negotiated text. In N. K. Denzin and Y. S. Lincoln (Eds.), *Handbook of qualitative research* (2nd ed., pp. 645–672). Thousand Oaks, CA: Sage.

Fortner, R. S., & Christians, C. G. (1981). Separating wheat from chaff in qualitative studies. In G. H. Stempel & B. H. Westley (Eds.), *Research methods in mass communication* (pp. 363–374). Englewood Cliffs, NJ: Prentice-Hall.

Fu, W. (2003). Applying the structure-conduct-performance framework in the media industry analysis. *International Journal on Media Management, 5*(4), 275–284.

Geertz, C. (1973). *The interpretation of cultures*. New York: Basic Books.

Geissler, U., & Einwiller, S. (2001). A typology of enterpreneurial communicators: Findings from empirical study in E-Business, *International Journal on Media Management, 3*(3), 154–160.

Gerpott, T. J., & Niegel, C. (2002). Mobile business start-ups in Germany: An exploration of the start-up scene and of corporate venture capital firms' views on business success drivers and inhibitors. *International Journal on Media Management, 4*(4), 235–247.

Gershon, R. A., & Kanayama, T. (2002). The Sony Corporation: A case study in transnational media management. *International Journal on Media Management, 4*(2), 105–117.

Gravetter, F. J., & Forzano, L. B. (2003). *Research methods for the behavioral sciences*. Australia: Thomson/Wadsworth.

Greenwood, D. J., & Levin, M. (1998). *Introduction to action research: Social research for social change*. Thousand Oaks, CA: Sage.

Greenwood, D. J., & Levin, M. (2000). Reconstructing the relationships between universities and society through action research. In N. K. Denzin and Y. S. Lincoln (Eds.), *Handbook of qualitative research* (2nd ed., pp. 85–106). Thousand Oaks, CA: Sage.

Gummesson, E. (2000). *Qualitative methods in management research* (2nd ed.). Thousand Oaks, CA: Sage.

Heider, D. (2000). *White news: Why local news programs don't cover people of color*. Mahwah, NJ: Lawrence Erlbaum Associates.

Hodder, I. (2000). The interpretation of documents and material culture. In N. K. Denzin and Y. S. Lincoln (Eds.), *Handbook of qualitative research* (2nd ed., pp. 703–715). Thousand Oaks, CA: Sage.

Hollifield, C. A. (2001). Crossing borders: Media management research in a transnational environment. *Journal of Media Economics, 14*(3), 133–146.

Holsti, O. R. (1969). *Content analysis for the social sciences and humanities*. Reading, MA: Addison-Wesley.

Howell, M. C., & Prevenier, W. (2001). *From reliable sources: An introduction to historical methods*. Ithaca, NY: Cornell University Press.

Jensen, J. (1991). Foreword. *Journalism Monographs, 125*.

Johansson, T. (2002). Lighting the campfire: The creation of a community of interest around a media company. *International Journal on Media Management, 4*(1), 4–12.

Johnson, P., & Duberley, J. (2000). *Understanding management research: An introduction to epistemology.* London: Sage.

Jones, M. O. (1996). *Qualitative Research Methods Series: Vol. 39. Studying organizational symbolism: What, how, why?* Thousand Oaks, CA: Sage.

Kemmis, S., & McTaggart, R. (2000). Participatory action research. In N. K. Denzin and Y. S. Lincoln (Eds.), *Handbook of qualitative research* (2nd ed., pp. 567–605). Thousand Oaks, CA: Sage.

Krippendorff, K. (1980). *Content analysis: An introduction to its methodology.* Newbury Park, CA: Sage.

Küng, L. (2003, October). *What makes media firms tick? Exploring the hidden drivers of firm performance.* In R. G. Picard (ed.), Strategic Responses to Media Market Changes (pp. 65–82), Media Management and Transformation Centre, Jönköping International Business School, Jönköping University, Sweden.

Lacy, S., & Niebauer, W. E. (1995). Developing and using theory for media economics. *Journal of Media Economics, 8*(2), 3–13.

Lincoln, Y. S., & Guba, E. G. (1985). *Naturalistic inquiry.* Beverly Hills, CA: Sage.

Lincoln, Y. S., & Guba, E. G. (2000). Paradigmatic controversies, contradictions, and emerging confluences. In N. K. Denzin and Y. S. Lincoln (Eds.), *Handbook of qualitative research* (2nd ed., pp. 163–188). Thousand Oaks, CA: Sage.

Lindlof, T. R. (1995). *Qualitative communication research methods.* Thousand Oaks, CA: Sage.

Lofland, J., & Lofland, L. H. (1984). *Analyzing social settings: A guide to qualitative observation and analysis* (2nd ed.). Belmont, CA: Wadsworth.

Marwick, A. (1974). *The nature of history* (3rd ed.). Chicago: Lyceum Books.

Miles, M. B., & Huberman, A. M. (1994). *Qualitative data analysis: An expanded sourcebook* (2nd ed.). Thousand Oaks, CA: Sage.

Morgan, D. L. (1998). The Focus Group Guidebook, Vol. 1 in D. L. Morgan & R. A. Krueger (Series Eds.), *The focus group kit, volumes 1–6.* Thousand Oaks, CA: Sage.

Morgan, D. L., & Krueger, R. A. (1998). *The focus group kit, volumes 1–6.* Thousand Oaks, CA: Sage.

Nord, D. P., & Nelson, H. L. (1981). The logic of historical research. In G. H. Stempel & B. H. Westley (Eds.), *Research methods in mass communication* (pp. 278–304). Englewood Cliffs, NJ: Prentice-Hall.

Pathania-Jain, G. (2001). Global parents, local partners: A value-chain analysis of collaborative strategies of media firms in India. *Journal of Media Economics, 14*(3), 169–187.

Pauly, J. J. (1991). A beginner's guide to doing qualitative research in mass communication. *Journalism Monographs, 125,* 1–29.

Picard, R. G. (1996). The rise and fall of communication empires. *Journal of Media Economics, 9*(4), 23–40.

Punnett, B. J., & Shenkar, O. (Eds.). (1996). *Handbook for international management research.* Cambridge, MA: Blackwell Business.

Rawolle, J., & Hess, T., (2000). New digital media and devices—An analysis for the media industry. *International Journal on Media Management, 2*(2), 89–99.

Reed, M. (1996). Organizational theorizing: A historically contested terrain. In S. R. Clegg, C. Hardy, & W. R. Nord (Eds.), *Handbook of organization studies* (pp. 31–56). London: Sage.

Roethlisberger, F. J., & Dickson, W. J. (1939). *Management and the worker: An account of a research program conducted by the Western Electric Company, Hawthorne Works, Chicago.* Cambridge, MA: Harvard University Press.

Rogers, E. H. (1981, May 21–25). *Methodology for meta-research.* Presidential address at the conference of the International Communication Association.

Ryan, G. W., & Bernard, H. R. (2000). Data management and analysis methods. In N. K. Denzin and Y. S. Lincoln (Eds.), *Handbook of qualitative research* (2nd ed., pp. 769–802). Thousand Oaks, CA: Sage.

Schudson, M. (1997). Toward a troubleshooting manual for journalism history. *Journalism & Mass Communication Quarterly, 74,* 463–476.

Schwandt, T. A. (2000). Three epistemological stances for qualitative inquiry: Interpretivism, hermeneutics, and social constructivism. In N. K. Denzin and Y. S. Lincoln (Eds.), *Handbook of qualitative research* (2nd ed., pp. 189–213). Thousand Oaks, CA: Sage.

Schwartzman, H. B. (1993). *Qualitative research methods series: Vol. 27. Ethnography in organizations.* Newbury Park, CA: Sage.

Shafer, R. J. (1974). The nature of history. In R. J. Shafer (Ed.), *A guide to historical method* (rev. ed.). Homewood, IL: Dorsey.

Shrikhande, S. (2001). Competitive strategies in the internationalization of television: CNNI and BBC World in Asia. *Journal of Media Economics, 14*(3), 147–168.

Silverman, D. (2001). *Interpreting qualitative data: Methods for analysing talk, text, and interaction* (2nd ed.). London: Sage.

Smith, M. Y. (1981). The method of history. In G. H. Stempel & B. H. Westley (Eds.), *Research methods in mass communication* (pp. 305–319). Englewood Cliffs, NJ: Prentice-Hall.

Soloski, J. (1979). Economics and management: The real influence of newspaper groups. *Newspaper Research Journal, 1*(1), 19–28.

Stake, R. E. (2000). Case studies. In N. K. Denzin & Y. S. Lincoln (Eds.), *Handbook of qualitative research* (2nd ed., pp. 435–454). Thousand Oaks, CA: Sage.

Startt, J. D., & Sloan, W. D. (2003). *Historical methods in mass communication (rev. ed.).* Northport, AL: Vision Press.

Turow, J. (1982). Unconventional programs on commercial television: An organizational perspective. In J. S. Ettema & D. C. Whitney (Eds.), *Individuals in mass media organizations: Creativity and constraint* (pp. 107–129). Beverly Hills, CA: Sage.

Vidich, A. J., & Lyman, S. M. (2000). Qualitative methods: Their history in sociology and anthropology. In N. K. Denzin and Y. S. Lincoln (Eds.), *Handbook of qualitative research* (2nd ed., pp. 37–84). Thousand Oaks, CA: Sage.

Williams, F., Rice, R. E., & Rogers, E. M. (1988). *Research methods and the new media.* New York: Free Press.

Wimmer, R. D., & Dominick, J. R. (1997). *Mass media research: An introduction* (5th ed.), Belmont, CA: Wadsworth.

Wirth, M. O., & Bloch, H. (1995). Industrial organization theory and media industry analysis. *Journal of Media Economics, 8*(2), 15–26.

Wolcott, H. F. (1973). *The man in the principal's office: An ethnography.* New York: Holt, Rinehart and Winston.

Wolfe, A. S., & Kapoor, S. (1996). The Matsushita takeover of MCA: A critical, materialist, historical and First Amendment view. *Journal of Media Economics, 9*(4), 1–21.

Wood, J. T. (1997). *Communication theories in action: An introduction.* Belmont, CA: Wadsworth.

Yin, R. K. (2003). *Case study research: Design and methods* (3rd ed). Thousand Oaks, CA: Sage.

# Media Finance and Valuation

Gary W. Ozanich
The Kelsey Group

Beginning in the mid-1980s financial management of the enterprise became a principal focus of media companies. Prior to that time, corporate strategy for media companies was primarily concerned with operational issues such as broadcast programming or newspaper circulation. This changed with the advent of leveraged buy-outs, hostile takeovers, and the development of large, vertically integrated media conglomerates. This resulted in a focus on maximizing common stock values. The key to maximizing common stock value is focusing on the performance of assets as measured by financial metrics.

Prior to this emphasis on financial performance measures, publicly traded equities of media companies typically traded below their breakup or "sum of the parts" value. The companies were not fully valued on the operating cash that they generated (Baker & Smith, 1998). These companies became prime targets of leveraged buy-outs, often by investors hostile to existing management. The successful leveraged buy-outs of companies such as Viacom International, Multimedia Inc., and Storer Communications and the acquisition of ABC Corporation by The Walt Disney Company brought an increased focus on financial management and shareholder value maximization. The subsequent consolidation of media industries through mergers and acquisitions throughout the 1990s also reinforced the importance of financial management (Ozanich & Wirth, 2004).

This chapter provides an overview of key financial tools used in media finance and research, many of which have been developed during the past two decades. These tools are based on long-standing finance theory. However, they began to be used in creative and somewhat nontraditional ways by those engaged in media finance. This overview focuses on three primary areas, the use of cash-flow-based measures as the primary determinant of financial performance, methods of valuation, and the issue of accrual versus cash accounting in media industries.

## LITERATURE REVIEW

A literature review is relevant to this analysis in three areas. The first is a review of studies specific to the media industries that use financial measures or tools. The second concerns the more general literature that examines the cash flow measures used in media finance. The third is the literature focused on the theory and methodology of firm valuation.

Relative to finance studies specific to the media industries, there is a very limited amount of literature. Historically, scholarly studies that examine the media tend to rely upon data based at the industry level (e.g., Alexander, Owers, Carveth, Hollifield, & Greco, 2004). An exception to this is studies undertaken by the Federal Communications Commission (FCC). In recent years, FCC researchers have included financial data and analysis at the corporate level in their annual industry reports (FCC, 2002, 2004). Also, from a financial perspective, Vogel (2001) provides a discussion of several key issues in accounting and finance for the media industries at the firm level. However, there is no body of literature or comprehensive review that specifically examines media finance issues.

It is worth noting that with convergence and the broadening of the definition of media companies, telecommunications companies are increasingly being included under the media company umbrella. There is a long history of financial research in the telecommunications industry based upon rate of return regulation. Although largely irrelevant to today's telecommunication's industry, a detailed historical analysis is available in Cave, Majumdar, & Vogelsang (2002).

In terms of the second area, measures used in media finance, the literature is more robust. As described, in some cases, media finance uses nontraditional metrics. These metrics have come under scrutiny by academic studies as their use expanded, particularly during the Internet stock "bubble" from 1998 to 2000. The topic of greatest debate is the use of cash flow measures. They are also a major focus of this chapter.

In practice, cash flow measures came into widespread use during the 1980s, and academic studies began to note these measures as their use became apparent (Foss, 1995). There has been a great debate about the appropriateness and inconsistencies in how these cash flow metrics are calculated (Whitfield, 2004). Some researchers, argue that modern finance strategy should focus on cash flow in lieu of other measures (Barlas, Randall, & Verschoor, 2002; Bhalla, 2004), whereas a more traditional perspective argues that the "use of EBITDA may be dangerous to your career" (King, 2001).

The issues center on two factors: the use of cash flow measures of firm performance such as EBITDA and EBIT instead of profitability measures such as net income, and how these cash flow measures are derived (Bahnson, Paul, & Budge, 1996). Statements of cash flow are themselves governed by the Financial Accounting Standards Board Statement Number 95 (Financial Accounting Standards Board [FASB], 1987). Critics have argued that these FASB standards provide too much discretion in allocating cash flows among operating, financing, and investing activities (Broome, 2004). This issue has been cited as one of the causes of financial scandals such as Enron, Tyco, and Adelphia Communications (Sender, 2002).

The nuance and validity of these arguments are beyond the scope of this chapter. The reality is that, in many industries and particularly in the media sectors, cash flow is used as the key metric of operations. Lin, Fowler, and Hankers (2004) undertook a survey of financial managers in an attempt to "strike a balance between the views of education and practitioners." In attempting to compare traditional versus contemporary techniques, the researchers found the topic of cash flow management to be the single most important issue identified by financial managers.

Thus, as occurs in practice, the analysis provided in this chapter presents cash-flow-based metrics as the most critical tools in the financial analysis of media companies. This includes an appreciation that there is controversy about the use of these measures. However, the fact is that in reality they are standard tools in the world of media businesses and finance.

The third area, that of the theory and methods of firm valuation, is well documented. The basic concepts and methods are included in most graduate-level finance texts. In recent years, and particularly in the media industries, the emphasis has been on the use of discounted cash flow (DCF) models. Rutterford (2004) provides an historical perspective on the evolution toward DCF models in firm valuation.

## THE GOALS OF THE FIRM

The economic literature has substantial research examining the traditional view of profit maximization as the objective of the firm (Scherer & Ross, 1990, pp. 38–55). Arguably, takeovers, mergers and acquisitions, executive stock options, and the general focus on the stock market have shifted management goals toward share price maximization. For media companies, this goal may involve measures other than profits.

The profit of a firm is generally defined as net income after taxes. Media industries tend to focus on operating cash flow, defined as earnings before interest, taxes, depreciation, and amortization (EBITDA), rather than on profitability. Table 26.1 depicts the Operating Statement from Cablevision Systems' Annual Report 10-K (2002). Note that the company's earnings are negative, but if interest, depreciation, and amortization are added back to operating income, the operating cash flow or EBITDA reflects substantial positive cash income.

The reason for using EBITDA is that the net income or profit of the firm is not indicative of the actual cash generated by operations. This is partially due to the large noncash (i.e., paper expenses) associated with the firm's depreciation and amortization expense. EBITDA is an appropriate "profitability" measure for a company whose capital intensive assets are going to last a significant period of time. However, it is a poor measure of "profitability" for a company operating in a rapidly changing industry.

Media companies such as newspapers, broadcasting, and cable TV are in mature industries with stable and predictable revenues and expenses and that enjoy substantial barriers to entry. This is why adding back the interest on the capital used by media companies to build their required technological infrastructure and the substantial noncash expenses of

**TABLE 26.1**
Cablevision System Operating Statement
(Year Ending 12/31/02, in Thousands of Dollars)

| | |
|---|---:|
| Revenues, net | $ 4,003,407 |
| Operating expenses | 3,024,373 |
| Depreciation and amortization | 911,042 |
| Operating income (EBIT) | 67,992 |
| EBITDA | 979,034 |
| Interest expense | 487,113 |
| Other expenses | 36,870 |
| Net investment/affiliate and contract gains (losses) | (242,672) |
| Income (loss) before taxes | (698,663) |
| EBITDA/interest expense | 2.01Xs |
| EBIT/interest expense | 0.14Xs |

*Note:*   From *Cablevision Systems Corporation 10-K Report* (2002).

depreciation and amortization on long-term assets (such as cable networks or broadcast licenses) to operating income better reflects the earning capability of the asset. Thus, most media companies focus on maximizing EBITDA rather than net income, thereby maximizing the performance of the assets as measured by the generation of operating cash flow.

Asset value maximization is a second measure on which management may focus rather than profits. The concept here is that some assets (such as film libraries, various types of intellectual properties, or licenses to use the electromagnetic spectrum) represent long-term assets that will generate future cash flows. Thus, in lieu of earnings or cash flow in the current year, the focus is on building assets that will generate cash flow over a longer period of time. Firms focused on asset value maximization are typically valued on the basis of their *breakup value*, sometimes called their private market value. Value here is based on what other companies would pay for a firm's assets. So called strategic buyers might find such assets a particularly good fit with their existing businesses and be willing to pay a premium for the assets.

In sum, for both EBITDA maximization and asset value maximization, managerial focus is still on maximization of the value of the share price. However, the means to achieve share price maximization has shifted to a focus on other metrics in these two examples and away from net income maximization.

## SHORT- AND LONG-TERM FINANCIAL MANAGEMENT CONSIDERATIONS

Financial management can be considered within the context of the day-to-day or short-term operations of the firm and within a larger context of capital budget decisionmaking for the long-term growth of the firm. Day-to-day financial management is typically categorized as working capital management. If long-term capital budgeting decisionmaking

TABLE 26.2
Key Ratios in Media Finance

| Ratio | Definition |
|---|---|
| **Liquidity ratios** | |
| Operating cash flow coverage | EBITDA/Interest expense |
| Cash flow coverage | EBIT/Interest expense |
| O.C.F. coverage of interest + Maturities | EBITDA/Int. exp.+Short-term debt mat. |
| C.F. coverage of interest + Maturities | EBIT/Int. Exp.+Short-term debt mat. |
| Free cash flow coverage | EBITDA-Cap. ex./Interest expense |
| **Leverage ratios** | |
| Debt to equity | Long-term debt/Common equity |
| Debt to market capitalization | Long-term debt/(Common Share Price × Shares outstanding + Par value preferred shares + Long-term debt − Cash and equivalents) |
| **Profitability ratios** | |
| Operating cash flow per share | EBITDA/Common shares outstanding |
| Cash flow per share | EBIT/Common shares outstanding |
| Earnings per share | Income after taxes/C.S. outstanding |
| Operating cash flow margin | EBITDA/revenues |

is effective and investment and industry strategies are correct, working capital management should be seamless.

Financial management for the long-term growth of the firm should provide flexibility, stability, and security while allowing for share price maximization. Brearley, Myers, and Marcus (2004, p. 482) have identified four elements associated with achieving long-term growth: analyzing investment and financing choices, projecting future consequences, deciding what alternatives to undertake, and measuring performance. There are a number of analytical tools that are commonly used to facilitate the process of media financial management.

## Tools in Media Financial Statement Analysis

The tools used in the financial management of media companies are a subset of standard metrics detailed in most finance textbooks with a primary focus on financial ratios and net present value analysis. Key ratios are provided in Table 26.2 and include ratios focused on liquidity, leverage, and profitability. These measures are primarily derived from balance sheets, operating statements, and statement of changes in cash flows.[1]

In practice liquidity ratios for media companies focus on interest rate coverage and free cash flow. Given the high leverage of media companies and the thin interest expense coverage, this is usually the measure that can best predict a liquidity crisis. As described

---

[1] Although the body of 10-Ks and 10-Qs contain the bulk of financial information, it is imperative to read them in conjunction with the footnotes in the report.

in Table 26.2, EBITDA (i.e., operating cash flow) and EBIT (i.e., cash flow) coverage of interest expense and of interest expense plus short-term debt maturities are standard measures. As detailed earlier, under the assumption that depreciation and amortization expense penalize a company by expensing a long-term stable cash flow generating asset too quickly, EBITDA is usually the preferred coverage measure for media companies. In some cases, however, EBIT may be used instead of EBITDA in calculating coverage. This occurs when the depreciation and amortization schedule is considered appropriate for an asset, such as for telecommunications companies using a network that will be replaced. An alternative measure is to use EBITDA minus capital expenditures (i.e., "free cash flow") in calculating coverage ratios. Free cash flow should be used in the numerator of coverage ratios when companies need to upgrade networks with some frequency (e.g., the cable telecommunications industry) and/or when companies have significant ongoing expenditures that must go into the long-term development of their assets.

Leverage ratios depict the relative balance between debt and equity. Media companies tend to be highly leveraged. Classic finance theory suggests that a firm is indifferent to its capital structure in a perfect world where there are no taxes and financial markets are efficient (Ross, Westerfield, & Jordan, 2003, p. 575). These assumptions are not present in the real world. Likewise, media companies have used debt financing (i.e., leverage) far more than typical industrial companies because of their predictable cash flows and growth rates.

In general, media companies employ above-average levels of debt because they believe that they can generate substantial cash flow or net income that will accrue to shareholders as interest and debt maturity expenses are paid. Thus, companies seek to lever their balance sheets to fund internal operations or pay for mergers and acquisitions under the assumption that growth rates of these assets will outstrip the cost of the debt capital, thereby avoiding any common stock dilution compared to the equity that would be issued to cover these expenses. For management, leveraging a balance sheet also has the advantage of making the firm less susceptible (i.e., attractive) to a takeover through a leveraged buyout.

Measures of the degree of leverage are relatively straightforward. The debt to equity ratio is the most often used by the financial markets. Another popular ratio is long-term debt to market capitalization. *Market capitalization* is defined as the number of common stock shares multiplied by their price plus the par value of outstanding preferred stock plus long-term debt minus cash and equivalents. This has the advantage of putting the amount of debt within the context of the market value of the firm, as opposed to using an accounting measure of the firm's equity value as carried on the balance sheet.

The final category of ratio analysis is profitability ratios. Similar to other industries, in media finance, earnings per share is usually a key benchmark. However, since net income is negative for some media companies, which generate substantial positive cash flow, alternative measures such as EBITDA per share, EBIT per share, and/or free cash flow per share are often used in place of earnings per share.

Another type of useful profitability ratio is an operating ratio. Operating ratios measure the percentage of revenues that is left after meeting operating expenses. The most often used operating ratio for the media industry is operating cash flow margin (EBITDA/revenues). A second ratio that is useful is the operating margin

(EBIT / revenues). Media companies, such as large market TV broadcasters, metropolitan newspapers, and The Yellow Pages, often have operating cash flow margins exceeding 40%. The existence of such high operating cash flow margins shows how hugely valuable these assets are. It is also an indication that the barriers to competitive entry are very high because operating margins, which are well above average, would attract market entry in the absence of significant barriers to entry.

### The Importance of Valuation Analysis

As indicated by the nature of the metrics discussed thus far, the focus of media companies is almost exclusively on their operations or operating statement rather than on balance sheet measures. This is because balance sheet measures such as retained earning or shareholder's equity are often negatively affected by accounting conventions that focus on net earnings, income, and tangible assets. They do not reflect sustainable and predictable operating cash flow, nor are they typically a good proxy for the value of the underlying core company assets. Media assets are dominated by intellectual property, licenses, trademarks, and other intangible assets. As described by Smith and Parr (2000, p. 1), "No longer does the term 'capital resource' bring to mind balance sheets of cash or pictures of sprawling manufacturing plants."

This means that alternative methods must be established in order to determine valuations for media companies. Valuation methods are particularly important in determining the "sum of the parts" of a media company. Deriving a basis for equity valuation for the stock market is critical in order to allow media firms to establish credit facilities and borrow capital as well as to measure the overall performance of media companies.

### FINANCIAL MANAGEMENT AND MEDIA VALUATION

Financial management and asset valuation for media companies is a complex task. Some of this complexity is due to the unique nature of the media industry, whereas other issues are faced by virtually all large companies. There are three primary valuation issues faced by media companies:

1. Because of consolidation and concentration of ownership, media assets are increasingly owned by large complex organizations, some of which are conglomerates with disparate assets.
2. Volatility in the financial markets has created a moving target for equity valuation. The fact that media companies have regularly fallen in and out of favor with institutional and retail investors has had a major impact on the volatility of media company valuations.
3. Technological innovation and convergence are resulting in a new era for both the creation and distribution of media content.

The media industry has undergone unprecedented consolidation during the past two decades (Compaine & Gomery, 2000). Major factors behind increased media consolidation and concentration include the relaxation of ownership restrictions, vertical integration, a general pursuit of "synergy," and the availability of capital (Ozanich & Wirth, 2004). Table 26.3 provides a list of the 10 largest media companies in the United States and a description of their assets.

The size of these companies, coupled with the fact that they have so many lines of business, presents difficult financial management issues. In terms of finance and valuation tools, the wide range of businesses and their geographical dispersion require careful analysis. Today's largest media companies are so huge and their operations so complex that precision is difficult to achieve. This presents a challenge to both management and analysts. As a result, valuation methodologies and forecasts must be developed from the bottom up. Simple approaches such as cash flow multiples at the aggregate level are inadequate and cannot be justified.

An interesting challenge faced by management is sustaining growth and, by implication, firm value in such large conglomerates. It is problematic to significantly increase valuation from internal cash flow growth because it would have to occur simultaneously across all divisions. Thus, many companies turn to acquisitions for growth as opposed to depending only on growth from existing assets. For example, General Electric used an acquisition strategy to provide double-digit earnings and cash flow growth throughout the 1990s. Likewise, recent transactions such as News Corporation's acquisition of DirecTV can be seen as asset growth through acquisition.

A related issue for large media conglomerates is that it is a difficult task to find acquisition targets or new lines of business capable of having a visible effect on revenues, cash flow, or earnings. For huge media companies this requires the identification of very large acquisition targets.

An additional issue in valuation is that of financial market volatility. Media companies were an integral part of the stock market "bubble" of the late 1990s. As depicted in Fig. 26.1, the value of an index of the common equity prices for media companies peaked in 2000 and dramatically declined for $2^{1}/_{2}$ years before subsequently rising through 2004 (but not back to earlier levels). Given that other macroeconomic indicators such as long-term interest rates were relatively stable to declining, it is apparent that media firm valuation has been a moving target. Justifications for such volatility in valuation must rest at least partially with irrational exuberance by investors.

Media firm valuation volatility represents an issue for valuation analysis. However, if the equity market is placing a premium or a discount on the securities of media companies, an arbitrage opportunity exists. That is, if security prices seem either too rich or cheap compared to the underlying "true" value of the assets of the company, then investment or trading opportunities exist. In essence this should be the basis of "buy" or "sell" recommendations by analysts.

A third issue facing the valuation of media companies is that of new and converging technologies. Newer distribution technologies such as the Internet and direct-to-home satellite services are providing new ways to distribute content and are competing with traditional media. For example, more people read *The New York Times* on-line than read the print edition of the newspaper (Steinberg, 2003). Also, the migration to digital technologies has resulted in increased network capacity. For example, migration to digital

## TABLE 26.3
### Ten Largest Media Companies Corporate Holdings (Dollars in Millions)

| 2002 | 2001 | Media Company | Media Revenues 2002 | Total Corp. Revenue | Newspaper | Magazine | Television | Radio | Cable | Other Media |
|---|---|---|---|---|---|---|---|---|---|---|
| 1 | 1 | AOL Time Warner | $28,629 | $40,961 | $0 | $4,850 | $494 | $0 | $14,192 | $9,094 |
| 2 | 3 | Viacom | 16,326 | 24,606 | 0 | 29 | 7,490 | 1,859 | 5,052 | 1,896 |
| 3 | 2 | Comcast Corp. | 16,043 | 21,112 | 0 | 0 | 0 | 0 | 16,043 | 0 |
| 4 | 4 | Walt Disney Co. | 9,763 | 25,329 | 0 | 271 | 4,485 | 579 | 4,428 | 0 |
| 5 | 5 | NBC-TV (General Electric Co.) | 7,390 | 131,698 | 0 | 0 | 6,763 | 0 | 627 | 0 |
| 6 | 6 | Cox Enterprises | 7,349 | 9,900 | 1,350 | 0 | 538 | 421 | 5,040 | 0 |
| 7 | 7 | News Corp. | 6,645 | 17,474 | 140 | 4 | 4,301 | 0 | 1,660 | 540 |
| 8 | 8 | DirecTV (General Motors Corp.) | 6,445 | 186,763 | 0 | 0 | 0 | 0 | 0 | 6,445 |
| 9 | 10 | Clear Channel Communications | 5,851 | 8,421 | 0 | 0 | 274 | 3,717 | 0 | 1,860 |
| 10 | 9 | Gannett Co. | 5,617 | 6,422 | 4,760 | 0 | 771 | 0 | 0 | 86 |

Note: From "Ten largest U.S. media companies." (2004). www.adage.com

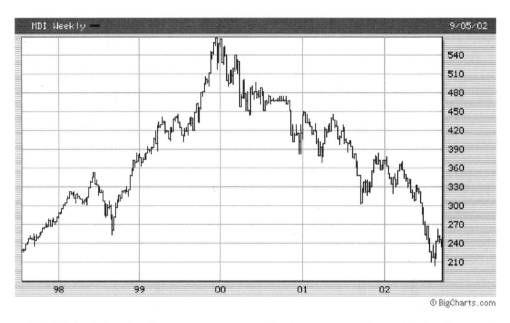

FIG. 26.1.    Index of media company common stock values 1990–2003. Source: Prophet Finance. Available at www.prophet.net

networks has dramatically increased the number of cellular phone subscribers and lowered the cost of cellular telephony (FCC, 2003). For media companies the combination of technological innovation and convergence has resulted in narrowcasting, content personalization, and audience fragmentation. Questions remain as to the degree to which new and converging technologies will create new markets or increased demand as opposed to serving as substitutes for existing media.

The debacle of the AOL acquisition of Time Warner Communications demonstrates the difficulty in forecasting technological evolution, demand, and the ever-allusive synergy that would create greater financial value through the combination of assets (Munk, 2004). To a large extent the Internet stock "bubble," which occurred from 1998 to 2000, resulted from discarding traditional accounting and finance based valuation methods and relying solely on a market comparable approach for valuation. Internet companies were valued based on the equity market valuation of comparable public companies.

Some analysts and investors were believers in a "new economy" where traditional valuation approaches were no longer relevant. New and creative metrics were developed in an attempt to rationalize security values, but ultimately market comparables or the equity values of "peer" companies were primarily used to rationalize security prices (Smith, Craig, & Solomon, 2003).

Stock market volatility aside, new technologies and convergence represent a serious problem when undertaking the financial valuation of media companies. There is no easy solution to this problem. Analyses must take into account competing and complimentary delivery channels as well as shifting cost structures that may result in lowered barriers to entry and increased competition. This must be done on a line-of-business basis within the analysis of a firm, and it is perhaps possible to make generalizations on an industry-wide basis. However, this is a difficult task that should not be underestimated.

## VALUATION METHODS

Similar to all businesses, media companies have both tangible and intangible assets. For example, a cable TV company owns a network, a tangible asset. This company also is dependent on its customer list, an intangible asset. In another media industry, a newspaper has tangible assets in its property, plant, and equipment (PPE). However, intangible assets include the "goodwill" associated with its name and reputation as well as its subscriber list. Other examples of intangible assets include the intellectual property of film and software companies, licenses of broadcasters, and trademarks owned by companies such as Disney. Generally speaking, most of the value of media companies is derived from intangible assets.

As previously described, firm valuation is of particular importance to media companies because traditional earnings per share and accounting values such as balance sheet measures underestimate the cash flow potential of the assets as well as the "true" value of intangible assets of the enterprise. Thus, in practice, valuation analyses of media companies focus on market approaches and operating asset analysis instead of accounting approaches in determining common stock price value, creditworthiness, and firm performance. There are three methodologies available for use: an income/cash flow approach, a cost approach, and a market or "breakup value" approach. Of these three, the first and third are most relevant.

### Income/Cash Flow Analysis

The most common metric in media finance is *discounted cash flow* (DCF) analysis. This allows for the calculation of the net present value (NPV) of an asset. Simply put, a DCF is used to calculate the current value of future cash flows that an asset is expected to generate. Typically the company's (or an acquiring company's) cost of capital is used as the basis for this discounting (i.e., for setting the discount rate). This method provides a value for today based on future cash inflows and outflows (Ross et al., p. 157). This approach has an intuitive appeal in determining the value of a company. In the simplest case a DCF can be done for the operating assets of a company, usually at the line-of-business level. The discounted expected future cash flows are then summed to provide a value for the operating assets of the company at a given discount rate.

There are a number of issues involved with this approach. The first concerns what "cash flow" should be used as the basis for the discounting. As mentioned earlier, EBITDA, or earnings before interest, taxes, depreciation, and amortization, is the most popular measure of cash flow used in media financial analysis. As stated earlier, this is because most media financial analysts believe that the inclusion of depreciation and amortization expenses in "cash flow" would result in an understatement of the true cash being generated by the typical media firm. Thus, EBITDA has been a standard measure in media finance since the mid-1980s, particularly for companies with networks, electromagnetic spectrum licenses, film libraries, and valuable trademarks.

An alternative and more conservative metric is *free cash flow*, or EBITDA net of so-called maintenance capital expenditures. Financial analysts who use free cash flow argue that a portion of depreciation and amortization expense is a legitimate deduction because a certain amount of continuing or capitalized maintenance expense is necessary to keep an asset viable. Utilization of a free cash flow approach is particularly appropriate for network-based assets such as cable TV or cellular telephony. The problem is determining the value for maintenance capital expenditures. Generally, this figure will be generated based on conversations with the company or through the use of outside technical consultants who can provide the financial analyst with an estimate. Another approach is to use the statement of cash flows to determine the additions to property, plant, and equipment and estimate the percentage to allocate to an existing plant.

In practice, EBITDA is typically used as the cash flow measure (rather than free cash flow), and maintenance capital expenditures are assumed to be encompassed in noncapitalized operating expenses. An exception is in the case of distressed companies, where liquidity is so thin that there is a concern that assets will deteriorate because there is a lack of capital to maintain them.

The next issue in a DCF analysis is how to forecast performance. Each individual asset or each line of business must have a forecast for revenues and costs. This is often more art than science. However, there are a number of tools that may be used. The first tool here is the historical performance of the line of business. Historical growth rates and performance are the best yardsticks for forecasting future performance. The second tool is an analysis of future competitive and macroeconomic factors that will affect an industry. This is a complicated task and requires assumptions about interest rates, economic growth, new technologies, and consumer behavior.

A third tool is the use of peer-group analysis. Metrics such as operating cash flow margin can be compared across an industry. This provides a benchmark for the performance of an existing firm and the possibility of improving or deteriorating margins as part of the valuation analysis. Understanding the performance of a line of business relative to its peers provides insight into its operations and can provide some guidelines in the forecasting process. A major forecasting mistake to avoid is assuming a linear growth rate without having a basis on which to do so. The obvious uncertainty in utilizing a future cash flow approach to media firm valuation is the fallibility in the forecasts and the tendency for rosy or best-case scenarios to dominate. Ultimately, a forecast or range of forecasts (e.g., worst case, likely case, and best case) must be assigned to a line of business or operating asset in a DCF analysis.

The economic life of an asset, particularly intangible assets, is also difficult to forecast. This is important to the forecasting process and can determine how many years out the DCF model goes. For example, a successful feature film can generate significant revenues for years in after-market release. Likewise, hit TV series, such as *Seinfeld* or *ER*, can be expected to generate revenues from syndication for decades. Generally a company will do internal forecasts on a 5-year basis. Sometimes a 10-year forecast will be attempted. Another factor is that accounting guidelines require that broadcasting and film production companies define the effective life of their products as less than 10 years (FASB, 2004).

Thus, DCF models and projections for economic life will typically go out 5 to 7 years in most analytical models. This does not mean that the assets won't have an effective life beyond this time frame. However, the discounting mechanism utilized in net present value analysis makes the out years of diminishing value. When this fact is combined with the uncertainty of forecasting so far in advance, it is clear why a 5- to 7-year DCF model is standard practice among media financial analysts.

Media valuation has often been expressed in terms of industry "multiples of operating cash flow" (Vogel, 2001, p. 124). There may be a tendency to use these multiples as shorthand and oversimplify the valuation process being utilized. In fact, valuation multiples are based on two alternative approaches. The first is based upon a DCF model:

$$\text{Multiple model}_1 = \text{DCF of EBITDA} \div \text{Running rate EBITDA}$$

This is a straightforward analysis where the EBITDA is the operating cash flow for a "pure" line of business such as cable TV or radio broadcasting. Running rate EBITDA is defined as the operating cash flow for the latest 12-month period. This is the most direct and the most theoretically defensible approach.

The second multiple model approach is typically used when doing peer-group or industry analyses. This approach is based on market capitalization:

$$\text{Multiple model}_2 = \text{Public market value} \div \text{Running rate EBITDA}$$

This approach is based on the public market value of its issued and outstanding common stock times share price plus par value of the preferred shares plus long-term debt minus cash and cash equivalents. The public market value represents the valuation that investors are placing on a company. This can be a complicated metric. As discussed, few media companies are pure plays in one industry. Thus, the value of a company is better conceptualized as a blended valuation of a number of different businesses. It is possible to attempt to break down this market capitalization measure to different lines of business if the company reports a cash flow measure such as EBITDA on a line-of-business basis in the footnotes of its annual 10-K report.

In doing these analyses, if an aggregation is undertaken for companies or assets within the industry, a range of values will result. For example, television stations typically have an EBITDA multiple of 8 to 12 and cable TV assets typically have an EBITDA multiple of 12 to 15 times.

To the extent that there is a difference between the two multiple models in terms of firm valuation, an arbitrage opportunity exists. If a media company's value using a market capitalization multiple (i.e., multiple model$_2$) is lower than its value as suggested by the DCF approach (i.e., multiple model$_1$), the firm would be an appropriate target for investment or take-over. In the second case, where the market capitalization model values a firm at a level greater than does the DFC model, this would suggest an overvalued stock, which would be a candidate for a short sale.

In summary, while the income/cash flow method approach is subject to the uncertainties of forecasting and the complications of breaking out and recombining lines of business in a "sum of the parts" exercise, it provides an intuitive and rigorous method of valuation. It is perhaps most useful in mergers and acquisitions where a company is purchasing assets and is typically uninterested in the legacy accounting of the selling or target firm.

## Cost Approaches to Valuation

Cost approaches to valuation are based on accountancy measures or actual estimates of replacement costs. A cost approach is not very useful in media finance. Smith and Parr (2000) provide a definition of the cost approach. "The cost approach seeks to measure the future benefits of ownership by quantifying the amount of money that would be required to replace the future service capability of the subject value" (p. 164).

This can be considered the replacement cost of the asset. This is a complicated question, involving issues of depreciation and goodwill or estimates of the cost of actually manufacturing or building a replacement for the asset. Balance sheets include accounting measures for PPE, but, as previously discussed, this measure understates the value of assets such as a cable TV network that has a life that exceeds depreciation and amortization schedules. Balance sheet measures for intangible assets such as broadcast licenses, trademarks, and film libraries reflect costs and not their actual earning capacity. Goodwill is another intangible balance sheet measure that is more reflective of merger and acquisition accounting than actual value (Fraser, 1995, p. 55).

Theoretically it is possible to use expert technicians and consultants to determine the actual replacement cost of media PPE, but it would not be very useful. The true value of media properties is associated with long-term earnings resulting from barriers to entry for new competition. Whether through economies of scale, exclusive licenses, or vertical integration, media companies face limited competition. Thus, they can be expected to generate substantial cash flow. Thus, an estimate of the cost of PPE to manufacture the products is not an accurate valuation of the assets or enterprise.

A final area where cost valuation approaches fall short concerns the nature of intellectual property and intangible assets that are at the core of most media companies. According to Smith and Parr (2000, p. 213) cost valuation approaches do not include the amount of economic benefits associated with the asset, the trend of economic benefits, the duration of economic benefits, the risk associated with economic benefits, or adjustments for any effect of obsolescence. In sum, cost approaches to valuation for media assets are seldom used in practice.

## Market Approaches

Market valuation approaches are based on the concept of *comparables*. This is the assumption that the value of an asset or line of business can be established by comparing it to similar assets or enterprises where a value has been established. There are two sources for comparables: the public market, and public data from transactions such as mergers, acquisitions, and asset sales.

The assumptions in both of these approaches are based on the appropriateness of peer analyses and the efficiency of pricing in the securities markets or asset transactions. The first of these assumptions (i.e., the appropriateness of peer analyses) is the basis for industry and sector studies. It is based on comparing companies within the same industry. As discussed in the previous sections, a range of valuations, such as EBITDA multiples, may exist within an industry. However, the financial tools already described, such as operating margins, liquidity ratios, leverage ratios, and profitability ratios, can be used to understand the differences between the company being valued and the comparables being used. This can result in fine tuning of the peer analysis.

The primary problem with peer analysis is finding appropriate peers or comparables. Because of conglomeration and vertical integration in the media industry, there are few "pure plays" and appropriate comparables are difficult to identify. The only solution is deconstruction of the parts of companies with some comparable assets in an attempt to assign values to the relevant assets.

The second assumption (i.e., the relative efficiency of pricing in the public security markets and asset transactions) is less problematic. The goal of valuation is to determine what a company is worth at a particular point in time. By undertaking a valuation based on the current public market value of comparables, a current valuation is achieved. In terms of comparables based on mergers and acquisitions or asset transactions, a key issue is the recency of the comparable transaction. Given the number of media mergers and acquisitions that have occurred in recent years, this is often not a problem. However, when no recent comparable transactions have occurred, various approaches (i.e., through deflation or inflation) can be used to account for market differentials between the current transaction and older "comparable" transactions.

Public market comparables are based on the current value that the security market places on the company's equity plus long-term debt minus current assets including cash and cash equivalents. If this is a "pure play" comparable, then the company's public market value is typically divided by its running rate EBITDA (see the earlier discussion of multiple models) to establish an appropriate multiple. This value is then used to multiply the EBITDA of the company that is the object of the valuation, and a comparable "market value" is established.

Pure plays are the exception and most public market valuations must be accomplished through a sum-of-the-parts approach. Public companies with similar assets are "deconstructed" in order to provide an EBITDA multiple for these assets. This may involve the examination of several companies, and there is the risk of loss of precision. Once comparable multiples are established, they are applied to the relevant lines of business for the company that is the object of the valuation. By using these comparable multiples against the EBITDA of each line of business, a sum-of-the-parts valuation can be accomplished.

This approach has the advantage of providing a current market value and can be fine tuned by comparing the operating and liquidity ratios of the two companies. This method also has many of the advantages of the income/cash flow valuation approach and is one of the valuation approaches used in mergers and acquisitions or in fairness opinions.

Comparables from mergers and acquisitions or asset sales are referred to as private market transactions. They are not based on the value that security markets place on securities, but rather on prices agreed to by willing buyers and sellers. Between 2000 and 2002, there were more than $300 billion in media mergers and acquisitions in 692 reported transactions (Ozanich & Wirth, 2004). These transactions and other publicly reported asset sales can be used as the basis for deriving comparables. The methodology is similar to that described earlier. "Pure play" transactions can be directly analyzed and conglomerate comparables can be deconstructed to provide estimates on a line-of-business basis.

Market valuations are undertaken whenever practical in financial analysis and are typically used in conjunction with income/cash flow analyses with the two methods used as verification or to provide a range of values.

## ALTERNATIVE MEASURES TO CASH FLOW: ACCOUNTING ISSUES

As discussed above, the use of cash flow, usually defined as EBITDA, has become a standard in media valuation. For some media, this does not represent actual net cash inflows minus outflows. This has to do with the method of revenue and expense recognition in some businesses. Some media businesses such as newspapers, motion pictures, and television production are subject to first copy costs (Picard, 1989). This means that almost all costs occur up front in the production of the first copy of the intellectual property and that most marketing expenses occur during the initial period of distribution.

This is not an issue for newspapers, where costs are recouped on the day of publication. However, consider the film industry. In 2002, there were 467 MPAA-released films. The average negative cost per film was $58.8 million, and the average marketing cost was $30.6 million (Motion Picture Association of America, 2004). Revenues generated from a feature film may be realized over dozens of years as the film reaches theatrical aftermarkets. Besides the film itself, the benefits of the marketing and promotion expenses accrue over the life of the product. Arguably the initial "buzz" of a feature film affects the product's value for many years. These same issues occur for the television production industry, as successful series move into syndication. Likewise, film libraries are purchased with an expectation that the payback will occur over many years.

The issue of accrual accounting versus cash accounting is acute for the film and television production industries. If revenues and costs are recorded as they occur, then significant losses would occur in the first year and significant profits in the later years. This is not a unique problem. To deal with the issue of capital investments, accounting theory has developed the concept of cost capitalization through the use of depreciation and amortization so that investments can be expensed over the life of an asset. This is adequate for most businesses.

However, because of the unique nature of the film and television production industries, special accounting practices have been established for the intellectual property created by firms in these industries. A detailed analysis of the financial accounting policies of these unique industries is beyond the scope this chapter. However, these policies are presented in the context of their relationship to financial tools used in valuation.[2]

Standardized accounting practices in the film and television production industries are relevant not only to the analysis of such firms, but also to the participants in the industry who receive deferred compensation based on future performance of the film or TV show (Blumenthal & Goodenough, 1998). The Financial Accounting Standards

---

[2]Vogel (2001, pp. 104–147) provides a comprehensive analysis of accounting issues in the film industry.

Board first addressed this issue in FASB Statement 53 in 1980. This was superseded by FASB Statement 139 in 2000 (FASB, 2004). Also in 2000, the American Institutes of Certified Public Accountants (AICPA) issued Statement of Position 00-02 (SOP-00-02) (AICPA, 2004). These policies are designed to standardize the accounting practices of these industries and allow for accurate financial statements and comparisons across the industries.

The key points of these standards are as follows:

1. Film revenue estimates, against which negative costs are to be amortized, are to be over no more than 10 years.
2. Marketing costs, for the most part, should be amortized as they occur.
3. TV series are to be recognized over the life of the contract and are subject to criteria designed to ensure that license fees are reasonably likely to be collected.
4. Abandoned projects must be written off directly on the income statement.
5. Films are to be defined as long-term assets, not inventories, and "their worth is to be based upon future cash flow estimates discounted back to the present" (Vogel, 2001, pp. 112–113).

In practice what this means to the tools used in the financial analysis of media companies is that a combination of balance sheets, operating statements, and the statement of changes in cash flow must be very carefully scrutinized. Table 26.4 is based on data filed in a Sony Corporation 10-K (2003) concerning Columbia Tri-Star Film Distribution.

The accounting used by the company is undoubtedly conservative and certainly adheres to all good accounting principles. However, note the contradictory information communicated by the different elements of the financial statement. Columbia Tri-Star reports a 2003 profit of $491 million relative to its income statement. Yet, when the

**TABLE 26.4**

Select Financial Data Columbia Tri-Star Film Distributors International Inc. (in Thousands of Dollars)

|  | 2001 | 2002 | 2003 |
| --- | --- | --- | --- |
| Operating statement |  |  |  |
| Revenues | 4,627,891 | 5,298,675 | 6,689,750 |
| Profit | 36 | 260 | 491 |
| Change in cash flow Statement |  |  |  |
| Amortization of film costs | 2,039 | 2,021 | 2,600 |
| Increase in film costs | (2,242) | (1,967) | (2,645) |
| Balance sheet |  |  |  |
| Motion picture assets | 7,398 | 7,669 | 7,237 |

Note: From Sony Corporation. (2003). 10-K based on 120¥ = $1.

statement of changes in cash flow is examined, Columbia Tri-Star reported a negative cash flow of $2.6 million. This is due to the differences in revenue and cost recognition resulting from the accrual versus cash accounting.

In terms of liquidity in the film and television production industries, the income statement will often look better or worse than the statement of changes in cash flow. For the short term, particularly for companies facing liquidity problems, the statement of changes in cash flow is the more important of the statements. It has not been unusual for film companies to enter bankruptcy protection while showing EBITDA coverage of interest expense on the operating statement in excess of 3 times. However, these companies show a negative flow of funds in the statement of changes in cash flow.

A proper approach to the financial analysis of these industries relative to operations is to ensure that the statements are analyzed in sequence for several years and that the statements are placed within the context of the life of released products. Movie blockbusters can particularly complicate financial analyses since there is risk in assuming that they will occur on a regular basis.

In terms of valuation approaches, as indicated by FASB and AICPA, the worth of films and television shows should be based upon the DCF of their estimated future life, not to exceed 10 years. Theoretically, one approach would be to determine the title and characteristics of the films or shows held as long-term assets and attempt to estimate their licensing value. In practice this would be very difficult for analysts to undertake. The alternative is to use the balance sheet value of the long-term assets that are associated with the films or TV shows held by a firm. This is almost always reported in a firm's annual 10-K Report and represents the single best valuation available for the film and television industry. In Table 26.4, the 2003 film assets of Columbia Tri-Star are reported by its parent company, Sony Corp., to total $7.2 million.

## SUGGESTIONS FOR FUTURE RESEARCH

The area of media finance, and the specific topic of tools used in media finance, has not been subject to systematic research. Arguably, financial decisionmaking is the driving force in determining the industry structure, conduct, and performance. There are two major areas in need of future research in this area: the reliability and validity of financial measures, and the utilization of financial measure tools in public policy and economic research.

Lack of research into the reliability and validity of financial measures for media companies is an acute problem. Cash flow measures are the industry standard, yet they are subject to a great deal of controversy in academic research. Future studies are needed to reconcile these differences and confirm or reject the validity of methodologies based on cash flow measures.

The second area, using financial measures in public policy and economic research, is an overlooked area. The FCC has begun to include such financial data in its annual industry reviews. However, media economic and policy researchers have not used financial measures to any significant extent. Given that they could provide operational measurement of such concepts as competition and supranormal profits, they should be in general use.

Specific research questions that should be addressed going forward include the following:

1. What definitions and accounting provisions can be developed to provide validity and reliability in media cash flow measurement?
2. Are cash flow based valuation methods in reality the best way to ascertain the true long-term value of media assets, or are more traditional methods better suited?
3. Through retrospective analyses, how accurate has accrual accounting been in measuring financial performance for intellectual property assets, such as motion pictures?
4. Have regulations standardizing accounting rules for media companies met their objectives?
5. How can financial measures be used to determine the performance of media companies in terms of the public interest and public good? Specifically, how can conduct and performance concepts for media companies be explicated through the use of financial metrics and measures?

## SOURCES OF DATA

The primary sources of data for conducting media finance research are publicly available. The principal source of data is company filings with the Securities and Exchange Commission. Every company with public ownership is required to file quarterly reports, 10-Q's, within 4 weeks of the end of every quarter of operation. Annual reports, 10-K's, are required to be filed within 6 weeks of the end of the company's fiscal year. The 10-K is comprehensive and is subject to third-party auditing. Of particular use to researchers are the footnotes and line-of-business discussion in the 10-K. Other primary sources of data are the Annual Report to Shareholders and company press releases. All of these reports are typically available on the company's Web site. They are also available through the SEC's Edgar system and through www.lexis-nexis.

## CONCLUSION

This chapter has provided an applied perspective on the tools used in media finance and valuation. The methods and tools described all have a foundation in traditional finance and accountancy theory. Media assets have many unique financial characteristics that result in the most appropriate measures of media firm performance being based on cash flow measures. EBITDA or operating cash flow is the single most important metric in media financial analysis. Likewise, cash accounting measures are often preferred to accrual measures. Finally, valuation measures based on public market comparables, discounted cash flow analysis, and a "sum of the parts" approach are more appropriate than balance sheet measures. It is unlikely that these approaches will change. The long-lived nature of media assets and the substantial barriers to entry in most media businesses should continue to support these very applied approaches.

# REFERENCES

Alexander, A., Owers, J., Carveth, R., Hollifield, A., & Greco, A. (Eds.). (2004). *Media economics: Theory and practice* (3rd ed.). Mahwah, NJ: Lawrence Erlbaum Associates.

American Institutes of Certified Public Accountants. (2004). *Statement of position 00-02*. Retrieved January 31, 2004, from www.aicpa.org/members/div/accstd/general/jpa1.htm

Baker, G., & Smith, G. D. (1998). *The new financial capitalists: Kohlberg, Kravis, Roberts and the creation of corporate value*. New York: Cambridge University Press.

Bahnson, P., Paul, B., & Budge, B. (1996). Nonarticulation in cash flow statements and implications for education, research and practice. *Accounting Horizons, 10*(4), 1–15.

Barlas, S., Randall, R., & Verschoor, C. (2002). EBITDA. *Strategic Finance, 83*(2), 4–12.

Bhalla, V. (2004). Creating wealth: Corporate financial strategy and decision making. *Journal of Management Research, 4*(1), 13–28.

Blumenthal, H., & Goodenough, O. (1998). *This business of television* (2nd ed.). New York: Billboard Press.

Brearley, R., Myers, S., & Marcus, A. (2004). *Fundamentals of corporate finance* (3rd ed.). New York: McGraw-Hill Irwin.

Broome, O. (2004). Statement of cash flows: Time for change. *Financial Analysts Journal, 60*(2), 16–22.

Cablevision Systems Corporation. (2002). *10-K Annual Report*. Retrieved on August 18, 2004, from http://www.cablevision.com/index.jhtml?pageType=investor

Cave, M., Majumdar, S., & Vogelsang, I. (Eds.). (2002). *Handbook of telecommunications economics*: Vol. 1. *Structure, regulation and competition*. Boston: North Holland.

Compaine, B., & Gomery, D. (2000). *Who owns the media? Competition and concentration in the mass media industry* (3rd ed.). Mahwah, NJ: Lawrence Erlbaum Associates.

Federal Communications Commission. (2002). *Radio industry review: Trends in ownership, format and finance*. Retrieved August 18, 2004, from www.fcc.gov/mb/policy/radio.html

Federal Communications Commission. (2003). *In the matter of implementation of section 6002(b) of the omnibus budget reconciliation act of 1993. Annual analysis of competitive market conditions with respect to commercial mobile services, Eighth Report* (WT Docket No. 02-379, adopted June 26, 2003).

Federal Communications Commission. (2004). *Ninth annual report on competition in video markets*. Retrieved August 18, 2004, from http://www.fcc.gov/competition/proceedings.html

Financial Accounting Standard Board. (1987). *Financial statement 95*. Retrieved August 18, 2004, from www.fasb.org/st/#fas95

Financial Accounting Standard Board. (2004). *Financial statement 139*. Retrieved August 18, 2004, from www.fasb.org/st/#fas150

Foss, G. (1995). Quantifying risk in corporate bond markets. *Financial Analysts Journal, 51*(2), 29–43.

Fraser, L. (1995). *Understanding financial statements* (4th ed.). Englewood Cliffs, NJ: Prentice-Hall.

King, A. (2001). Warning: Use of EBITDA may be dangerous to your career. *Strategic Finance, 83*(3), 35–49.

Lin, M., Fowler, M., & Hankers, L. (2004). Management accounting: Striking a balance between the views of education and practitioners. *Accounting Education, 10*, 51–68.

Motion Picture Association of America. (2004). *2002 Economic review*. Retrieved September 28, 2004, from www.mpaa.org/useconomicreview

Munk, N. (2004). *Fools rush in: Steve Case, Jerry Levin, and the unmaking of AOL Time Warner*. New York: Cambridge University Press.

Ozanich, G., & Wirth, M. (2004). Structure and change: An industry overview. In A. Alexander, J. Owers, R. Carveth, A. Hollifield, & A. Greco (Eds.), *Media economics: Theory and practice* (3rd ed., pp. 69–84). Mahwah, NJ: Lawrence Erlbaum Associates.

Picard, R. (1989). *Media economics: Concepts and issues*. Newbury Park, CA: Sage.

Ross, S., Westerfield, R., & Jordan, B. (2003). *Fundamentals of corporate finance* (6th ed.). New York: McGraw-Hill Irwin.

Rutterford, J. (2004). From dividend yield to discounted cash flow: A history of UK and U.S. equity valuation techniques. *Accounting, Business & Financial History, 14*, 115–132.

Scherer, F., & Ross, D. (1990). *Industrial market structure and economic performance* (3rd ed.). Boston: Houghton Mifflin.

Sender, H. (2002, May 8). Cash flow? Is it always as it seems? *The Wall Street Journal*, p. C-1.

Smith, G., & Parr, R. (2000). *Valuation of intellectual property and intangible assets* (3rd ed.). New York: Wiley.

Smith, R., Craig, C., & Solomon, D. (2003, April 29). Wall Street firms settle charges over research in $1.4 billion pact. *The Wall Street Journal*, p. A-1.

Sony Corporation. (2003). *10-K Annual Report*. Retrieved August 18, 2004, from http://www.sony.net/SonyInfo/IR/

Steinberg, J. (2003, December 1). Technology & media: To grab young readers, newspapers print free jazzy editions. *The New York Times*, p. C-1.

Ten largest U.S. media companies. (2004). *Advertising Age*. Retrieved August 18, 2004, from www.adage.com

Vogel, H. (2001). *Entertainment industry economics: A guide for financial analysis* (5th ed.). New York: Cambridge University Press.

Whitfield, B. (2004). Statement of cash flow: Time for change! *Financial Analysts Journal, 60*(2), 16–22.

# Audience Research and Analysis

Patricia F. Phalen

The George Washington University

## INTRODUCTION

Commercial audience research in the United States has changed substantially since its introduction in the 1930s. Throughout the 20th century, the research industry grew to include everything from small, boutique firms to large research corporations. New technologies developed for the distribution of news and entertainment; new methods of estimating media audiences advanced with them. These methods relied on advances in data collection and processing technology as well as modern statistical techniques to improve the collection and analysis of audience information. Advertisers and media organizations accepted the underlying assumptions of commercial research, but they remained vigilant to ensure improvements that would yield more consistent and reliable data.

In the 21st century, the audience research industry faces challenges that will undoubtedly test its resilience. New forms of media require new forms of measurement, and, for traditional electronic media, "good enough" may no longer be acceptable in the increasingly competitive market for audiences. Historically, the research information system that drives media markets evolved through incremental modifications to the existing methods of measurement. Over the next few decades, major transformations in technology and media usage patterns are likely to require major adjustments in the ways audience data are collected and interpreted.

This chapter examines the challenges faced by audience research firms in a rapidly changing media environment. The first section reviews the scholarly literature on media audience research; the second offers a brief historical account of this industry in the United States. The third section analyzes factors that will shape audience measurement over the next few decades, and the final section suggests topics for further academic study of the market for audience research. Although it is impossible to predict the exact ways in which the American research industry will develop, it is certain that the information system that supports media markets will change significantly in the new millennium of the 21st century.

## LITERATURE REVIEW

Scholarly studies of commercial audience research fall into two general, and often contentious, categories. The first includes the work of social scientists who study information system characteristics (the "quality" of information) and the relationships between audience data and media markets. The second deals with the theoretical analyses of commercial audience measurement, usually from a cultural or critical studies perspective.

### Social Science

Academic researchers in this group take as their starting point the recognition that research firms sell audience information to both advertisers and media organizations as a commodity to be used in economic exchange (Beville, 1988; Ettema & Whitney, 1994; Webster & Phalen, 1997; Webster, Phalen, & Lichty, 2005). Although flaws in the system are widely recognized by scholars and media professionals alike, quantitative audience research is accepted as the standard for economic transactions (Phalen, 1998; Webster et al., 2005). As long as buyers and sellers in a market for advertising time accept audience ratings as "good enough," the market can sustain its trade in audiences.[1] The economic viability of new media options depends in large part on the availability of audience data (Banks, 1981).

Several authors provide comprehensive descriptions and analyses of commercial audience research (Beville, 1988; Buzzard, 1992; Webster et al., 2005; Wimmer & Dominick, 2000). They discuss the history and methods of ratings research, and the strengths and weaknesses of the information system. Others consider models of audience behavior in economic theories of program choice (Owen & Wildman, 1992), and the role of audience as product in media markets (Napoli, 2003; Phalen, 1996). This line of inquiry includes research on the ways market participants use audience data to reduce risk in economic transactions, and the strategies they employ to compensate for information deficiencies (Phalen, 1998, 2003b).

A number of academic studies use commercial research to identify listening or viewing patterns (e.g., Napoli, 2003; Webster & Newton, 1988; Webster & Phalen, 1997). These studies, while acknowledging the imperfections of ratings data, accept the underlying assumptions of commercial audience measurement. Specifically, they rely on the

---

[1]*Audience ratings* are the estimates of media audience size and demographics that are provided by third-party research firms. They are not to be confused with content ratings for television and film.

measurability of audiences and the legitimacy of using probability theory to estimate actual audiences from samples of the population.

## Cultural and Critical Studies

Researchers from this perspective are generally less concerned with improving the quality of quantitative audience information or understanding its economic function. They are likely to question the assumptions behind audience measurement, and focus on its place in a larger system of economic power. For the most part, these scholars reject the assumptions of quantitative research and use qualitative methods for understanding media audiences (Hagen & Wasko, 2000; Hay, Grossberg, & Wartella, 1996).

Scholars writing from this perspective criticize the information system as politically suspect and exclusionary, challenging industry claims of objective audience measurement (Ang, 1991; Meehan, 1990). They focus on issues such as the way audiences understand messages (Wicks, 2001), the development and implications of the audience construct (Alasuutari, 1999; Seiter, 1999), and the evolution of qualitative research methods in audience studies (Abercrombie & Longhurst, 1998). Although this body of research enhances our theoretical understanding of audiences, findings are seldom incorporated into the market information system in the same way as the results of quantitative research.

## A BRIEF HISTORY OF AUDIENCE MEASUREMENT

This summary, necessarily selective because of space constraints, highlights the major developments in commercial audience research technology since the 1930s. More detailed historical accounts can be found elsewhere (Banks, 1981; Beville, 1988; Webster et al., 2005). These sources follow closely the evolution of measurement technologies from the use of telephones and hand calculations in the 1930s to the use of computer software and digital data processing.

When mass media consisted of print communication, audience measurement was relatively straightforward. Subscription rates provided a base from which to build readership profiles for newspapers and magazines, and as long as the data supplied by publishers could be verified by an external audit, advertisers could rely on its credibility. Subscriber information could then be combined with marketing research to predict consumer behavior.

The introduction of radio as an advertiser-supported medium made audience research more complicated. The one-time purchase of radio sets indicated potential audience size, but provided no information about program choices. Advertisers would purchase airtime only if they could predict, with a reasonable degree of confidence, that the characteristics of the radio audience matched the characteristics of people who were likely to buy their products. Estimating actual audiences for a program, station, or network, however, required new measurement methods.

In the 1930s, theories of sampling and statistical analysis were developing alongside marketing research and political polling techniques. These methods would prove useful for estimating media audiences as well. From the start, the audience information system for broadcasting was based on the same assumptions that market researchers employed, including the usefulness of probability theory to predict consumer behavior, and the need to capture similarities among people rather than individual differences.

In effect, the system that came to be known as audience ratings served the needs of advertisers rather than programmers. Ratings defined success in terms of audience size rather than the quality of television content. They were a proxy for consumer buying behavior, and the relevant audience characteristics were those that could be measured, such as age, gender, and income. Furthermore, without a full census of the audience similar to that provided by subscription data, the system relied on the assumption that one person with particular characteristics could represent many others with the same traits. In other words, people of the same age, gender, income, etc., would be likely to choose the same programs.

Although this logic might seem faulty to those unfamiliar with quantitative research, the fact was that advertisers saw increases in sales when they placed advertising in this way. They needed an information system that would reduce risks: the risk of spending money to reach people who were not interested in their product and, conversely, the risk of failing to reach people who might buy it. The new system of audience ratings carried out this economic function in the marketplace. Although all parties to a transaction recognized weaknesses in the data, they also realized that ratings could provide a reasonable degree of predictability without being 100% accurate on every measure. The commercial system of audience estimation soon became institutionalized.

To ensure the credibility, comparability, and overall economic efficiency of audience ratings, trading partners relied on third-party research firms to collect and analyze audience data (Phalen, 2003b). Archibald Crossley's research led to the formation of the Cooperative Analysis of Broadcasting (CAB), the first successful research concern linked to the commercial trade in radio audiences. Crossley used the method of telephone recall to survey listeners and, although the system yielded biased information due in large part to unrepresentative samples and response error, these ratings became the generally accepted estimates of radio audiences.

Claude Hooper and Montgomery Clark soon launched a rival service that effectively competed with Crossley's rating system. They used phone coincidentals, which shared the same sampling limitations of the recall design, but offered the advantage of decreasing response error. Whereas Crossley's method required people to remember what they had heard during the previous hours, Clark-Hooper asked them what they were listening to at the time of the phone call. Although both measurement systems were limited, many of the terms and concepts introduced by Crossley and Clark-Hooper are still in common usage today (Webster et al., 2005).

In subsequent years, data collection methods became less dependent on phone technology. These methods included Sydney Roslow's interview technique, A. C. Nielsen's audimeter, and James Seiler's radio listening diary (Webster et al., 2005). Each had, and still has, its own strengths and weaknesses for audience measurement. In-person interviewing yields detailed information about respondents, but its costs are prohibitive as an ongoing data collection technique. The audimeter, or passive meter, provides detailed information about household media usage, but it lacks information about individuals and their program preferences. And diaries yield rich information about individuals, but the data are only reliable to the extent that respondents fill them out accurately.[2]

When radio listening was still a family event, Nielsen used passive meters to collect audience information. The meter was attached to the radio set in each sample home, and it reported when the radio was on and the frequency, or channel, to which it was tuned. But radio became a personal medium during the transition to a television-centered home media environment (Barnes & Thompson, 1988), and meters couldn't work with portable or in-car sets. The listener diary, however, could easily accommodate individual listening outside of the home. Eventually, the diary replaced the passive meter as the standard for radio measurement in local markets.

Passive meters could, however, collect set usage data for the new medium of television. Because the technology offered no insight into specific viewer characteristics, Nielsen and Arbitron used viewer diaries to collect demographic information.[3] Nielsen projected ratings from its national audience sample by combining data from metered sets with demographic information from diary homes. In the largest television markets, both research companies used this dual-methodology system to generate local ratings. In the medium-sized and smaller markets, they collected viewing data with diaries alone.

As noted earlier, the passive meter recorded only the basics: when sets were in use and which channels were tuned. To generate program ratings, research firms had to match this data with program names. This system was relatively straightforward in a three-channel marketplace where stations carried network schedules as they were fed. But as media options expanded, it became more difficult for researchers to know which programs were scheduled at which times. The manual process of compiling station schedules was both cumbersome and highly subject to human error.

To overcome this problem, Nielsen implemented an electronic tracking system called Automated Measurement of Line-ups (AMOL), which reads identification codes on programs and uses them to aggregate viewer statistics (Webster et al., 2005). This became particularly important for syndicators, who sold programs to individual stations across the country. Tracking the audience was complicated because local programmers scheduled syndicated shows in different time periods. Nevertheless, sellers needed credible estimates of program viewing patterns in order to attract national advertisers. AMOL was one solution. The cost of the system, however, was prohibitive for many program providers, who continued to use ratings generated through the manual process of matching schedules to audiences in each market.

The growth of cable television forced audience research firms to adapt their research designs. The increasing number of viewing options continued to fragment audiences at the national and local levels, but samples were generally unreliable for such small segments of the population. Improvements were slow to develop, however, because broadcast media had no economic incentive to help their competition by investing more heavily in sample design. Besides, cable systems and networks operated under a different business model than broadcasters, relying on subscription revenue to generate profits.

---

[2] See Webster et al. (2005) for a detailed summary of the strengths and weaknesses of data collection methods.
[3] Arbitron exited the local television measurement business in 1994.

Cable had no infrastructure to handle the development of ad sales and, consequently, little advertising revenue to justify a major investment in the ratings system.

This situation was short-lived. As soon as cable penetration reached a critical mass of television households, cable networks began to develop their sales capability (Phalen, 1996), and advertisers became interested in placing their messages on targeted cable nets such as ESPN and Lifetime. At first, cable commissioned proprietary studies from audience research firms to support the sale of time to national advertisers. But as their marketing infrastructure expanded, cable networks needed audience data comparable to those of their broadcast counterparts. Otherwise, they could not sell their audiences to buyers at advertising agencies who were used to negotiating based on the ratings.

Once cable networks became part of Nielsen's syndicated ratings service they could compete with broadcasters for advertising revenue. Local cable opportunities also expanded, due in large part to the installation of digital technologies that gave systems more flexibility to insert commercials into the programming lineup. The technology alone, however, did not address all the obstacles to local cable advertising. Buyers and sellers also needed a mechanism to reduce transaction costs so that advertisers could buy time in the cable market as easily as they could in the broadcast national spot market. This problem was solved by the development of cable rep firms, which needed local cable ratings for the systems they represented. Nielsen began providing not only national ratings for cable networks, but also local ratings for some cable companies. As new media enter the television market, and as advertisers are forced to pursue new venues for their messages, Nielsen is likely to serve many more cable clients at the local market level.

To support the market for national ad time, the audience research industry made do with meter/diary methodology until the mid-1980s when they faced competition from a potential market entrant with a better mousetrap—AGB. The British firm offered a peoplemeter that could electronically record not just on/off/channel information, but demographics as well. The new technology could give advertisers more information about their audiences, and data would be available much faster, without the tedious process of manual entry of diary information. AGB looked like a threat to Nielsen.

But Nielsen hadn't been idle. Researchers had already developed similar technology; they just hadn't implemented it yet. Client complaints about the old data collection methods had been largely ineffective because Nielsen faced no real economic threat. AGB's competitive move, however, forced Nielsen to roll out its own all-electronic People Meter. In 1987 the company switched from diary/passive meter data collection to People Meter methodology in the national sample. As with any research technology, the People Meter has its flaws, but the ratings it generates have become the currency with which national audiences are bought and sold. Diaries and passive meters are still used for audience research in local television markets, although, as discussed later, that situation is changing.

Nielsen's introduction of the People Meter forced AGB out of the American audience research market. Neither advertisers nor media organizations would provide the monetary support for two separate ratings systems, although they had welcomed AGB's competitive threat as a way to force improvements in data collection methodologies. This reflects conflicting economic motives in the marketplace. On the one hand clients want competition to ensure quality of information; on the other, they don't want to pay for two separate ratings systems. The industry chose to reject another potential competitor in 1999 when Statistical Research, Inc., tried to introduce SMART, its new metering system. When Nielsen promised to upgrade its own data collection technology, the media industry gave financial backing to the incumbent, and SMART was forced to fold.

Media organizations and advertisers often pressure audience research firms to improve sample designs and data collection methodologies. However, it can't be assumed that those who purchase and use audience data have doggedly pursued every opportunity for innovation. Each improvement has an economic cost, which may or may not outweigh its economic benefits. Market participants want to see smaller error estimates, because this means the ratings are more likely to reflect actual audience size and demographics. But to bring the error estimates down (i.e., to make the data more accurate), they have to increase their monetary investment in the audience ratings system. If the marginal improvements in error estimates aren't likely to yield comparable improvements in profits, then "good enough" becomes the status quo. Trading partners find other ways to lessen the risk of buying and selling time. For example, they develop business practices, such as audience guarantees, that compensate for statistical inaccuracies, and they rely on repeat business to balance out the errors over time (Phalen, 1996, 1998).

The media industry is also affected by economic costs that are not measured by monetary investment in the ratings service. Changes in audience research methods might require the development of new skill sets by the professionals who analyze the data. The new system might also yield vastly different numbers for programs and/or channels, which would make historical trend data obsolete. These costs and others like them may not be immediately apparent to the market observer, but they affect the degree to which market participants actively seek improvements in the ratings system (Phalen, 1996).

Viewers and media critics alike often lament the effects of ratings on production and scheduling decisions. They see the speed of information delivery as a potential drawback because faster data delivery means faster programming decisions. And this means that errors in the data may not balance out over time. Media executives can acquire detailed ratings information within hours of a broadcast, and pressures for profit can drive immediate decisions about a program's fate. One ironic result of this process is that it takes away one of the most valuable advantages that television series have over theatrical films. In television, writers can take time to develop complex stories and characters. But if renewal/cancellation decisions are made based on one or two episodes, the storytelling advantages are lost (D. Batali, personal communication, August 2003). This represents an opportunity cost in the market for television programming.

When the World Wide Web emerged as an advertising opportunity in the 1990s, advertisers needed a system for estimating user characteristics in order to make ad placement decisions. However, Internet technology differed from television and radio in significant ways; established audience research firms did not yet have the capabilities to monitor Web pages.[4] Nor did they have the incentive. Nielsen and Arbitron provided information to broadcast and cable clients, who were unlikely to support a new measurement system to help potential competitors in the ad market. As a consequence, the

---

[4]In this context, *capabilities* does not mean potential—it refers to having the skills and technology within the firm (see Penrose, 1966).

mechanism for tracking Internet user data developed outside traditional audience research organizations.

Two third-party research firms, Media Metrix and NetRatings, were the first to provide advertisers and Web publishers with Internet user data comparable to audience ratings. They developed software that monitored the on-line choices made by respondents, a method of data collection that has been compared to passive metering because it collects data without requiring action on the part of the user (Webster et al., 2005). Internet research didn't remain outside the established audience research industry for long. Nielsen acquired the capabilities it needed for Internet measurement by purchasing NetRatings. The service competes with comScore Networks, which acquired Media Metrix.

Once Internet research firms recruited their samples and began collecting data, they faced the problem of information overload. How could they aggregate user information in ways that would help buyers and sellers in the market for advertising? Not surprisingly, market participants wanted information similar to what they were used to with older forms of electronic media. Categories such as "cumulative audience," "average audience," "reach" and "frequency" would allow them to make inter- and intramedium comparisons (Phalen, 1999). Internet measurement firms provided them with reports containing the same concepts and terminology they used in the broadcast and cable advertising markets. In fact, Nielsen has introduced an "Internet Pocketpiece" modeled after the television Network Pocketpiece that sales representatives and buyers have used for years (Elkin, 2003b).

There are very few companies that provide audience measurement in the radio, television, and Internet markets. Arbitron is the sole provider of local and network radio ratings. Nielsen Media Research, which is now part of the worldwide research company VNU, generates audience ratings for the national, regional, and local television advertising markets in the United States and many European countries. And Nielsen/Netratings shares the Internet usage information market with comScore Media Metrix. This reflects the continuing consolidation of the information industry, and the growing internationalization of marketing research—especially research on media audiences. From the point of view of advertisers, this change has many benefits. They include the potential for standardization of audience measurement across different countries and the lower transaction costs of dealing with few rather than many different ratings providers. But many see the same characteristics as drawbacks. There are sociocultural as well as economic consequences to standardization in research. Uniformity of audience measurement could, for example, limit the ways in which media systems can develop. If profit is the main goal, and packaging audiences for advertisers is the means to that end, then content might follow the same course in other countries as it has in the United States. This development would threaten indigenous programming.

## INTO THE FUTURE: NOT YOUR PARENTS' RATING SYSTEM

In 2005, audience research firms face market changes that test the limitations of existing research methodologies. Electronic media audiences are more fragmented than ever with the average U.S. home receiving 90–100 channels of television content (Bianco, 2004; *TV*

*Dimensions 2004*, 2004). The Internet and consumer technologies, such as the personal video recorder (PVR), continue to gain popularity with television audiences. And, as in most aspects of economic life, advertising continues its trend toward globalization. Market participants recognize that in the face of these changes some metrics used in the marketplace will be inadequate for the future (Johnson, Fine, Linnett, & Teinowitz, 2003). However, because of the economic costs of rendering the accepted system obsolete, buyers and sellers want to address these challenges by enhancing rather than replacing the status quo.

PVRs entered the consumer market in 1999 with the introduction of TiVo (Allan, 2003). Although market penetration of TiVo and other forms of PVR is estimated at only 2% (Posnock, 2004), the Yankee Group predicts that by 2008, more than 20% of U.S. homes will have some type of digital video recorder (Posnock, 2004). This could potentially alter the television advertising market in significant ways. DVR functionality goes well beyond what viewers were used to with videotape recorders: Users can store vast amounts of programming, time-shift in ways that were impossible with older technology, and avoid advertising messages altogether. In fact, one study showed that TiVo customers are four times as likely to timeshift popular programs as to watch them live (Allan, 2003).

In this new home media environment, the traditional gatekeeping role of programmers will become obsolete, and familiar research methodologies will prove inadequate to measure audience behavior. Although Nielsen, under pressure from clients, is including PVR households in the television sample (Johnson et al., 2003), they still cannot collect data on all viewing choices in those homes. To address this problem, the company has developed an active/passive meter, which uses codes embedded in signals to identify individual programs, regardless of when they are viewed. This technology will also facilitate audience measurement for video on demand (VOD), and the availability of ratings for nonlinear programming will allow media organizations to sell commercial time to advertisers. When this happens, consumers are likely to see popular programming migrate to the VOD platform.

Although PVRs and other advanced technologies pose challenges to the current media research system, they also present an opportunity for innovation in audience measurement. Services such as TiVo can compile aggregate data on media use that is unavailable with diaries and meters, including information about time shifting, replay, and program preferences. DBS providers and cable companies that install digital set-top boxes in the home can also collect log file information and make it available to researchers. To take advantage of the possibilities, Nielsen has been forging partnerships with these services to develop a joint measurement system that would combine established Nielsen methods and the data available from the set-top boxes.

One of the most controversial changes in audience measurement technology has been the introduction of People Meters in local markets. As noted earlier, People Meters are the standard data collection method for the national Nielsen sample, while passive meters and diaries are used for local market measurement. In 2004 Nielsen installed People Meters in Boston to test the technology in the local market context. Although clients were not unanimous in their support of this change, Nielsen gained monetary commitments from enough group station owners to start installing the new technology in other local markets, including New York, Chicago and Los Angeles. The company plans to install People Meters in the top 10 television markets first (Tiegel, 2003) and to continue rolling out the technology in less populated markets until the point where the potential advertising income is too small to support the cost of the meters. If stations are able to get continuous data like the data the networks have been using for years, the practice of putting their best programs in sweeps months may, arguably, no longer be necessary. Many see this as a very good development, because the quality of programming would be more consistent throughout the year (Mermigas, 2003).

Although People Meters could soon be the standard for both national and local television measurement, they have several drawbacks as a method of data collection. The major problem is that they require action on the part of respondents, who quickly become tired of pressing buttons when they enter or leave a room. Researchers are trying to develop a solution to this problem—a passive meter that records viewing or listening behavior without any effort on the part of respondents.

Research on a new passive meter has been ongoing. One of the most promising technologies is Arbitron's Personal People Meter (PPM), which was tested first in Britain and then in Philadelphia. It is a small, pager-like device that respondents carry with them throughout the day. By reading inaudible codes on radio and television programming, the PPM records all signals that the respondent is likely to have heard or seen. At the end of the day, the device is placed in a docking station, which sends the data to Arbitron. Not only does this technology have the benefit of requiring minimal effort, it can also provide estimates of cross-media exposure (Chunovic, 2003), which would allow intermedium comparisons that are otherwise unavailable.

The passive meter has other benefits as well. It can measure demographic groups, such as younger males, who traditionally do not fill out diaries. The PPM could also provide information about individual television viewing, unlike the older ratings system that was designed to measure household media usage. Out-of-home viewing, a problem that has plagued Nielsen, could be incorporated into audience measurement through the use of this new technology. Additionally, the PPM could record viewing from any source, whether broadcast, cable, DVR, or Internet.

The technology does, however, have limitations. Critics maintain that the device could easily pick up signals that respondents never even noticed, thereby inflating estimates of media exposure. There is also a likelihood that respondents would forget to carry the meter with them. Nevertheless, the advertising and media industries show enough interest that Arbitron is continuing to test the technology. In fact, the company has extended its testing to Latin America and Canada. Some predict that Nielsen will contract with Arbitron to use the new device for their own ratings estimates.

Changes in broadcast technologies represent just one set of challenges for audience measurement. As the Internet continues to gain popularity as an advertiser-supported medium, researchers face a number of difficulties in providing accurate user estimates. One of the most immediate is ensuring the quality and size of samples (Elkin, 2003a). Advertisers, for example, want research firms to collect user statistics from work computers as well as from home computers. However, employers are concerned with surveillance, so they do not allow workers to participate in the studies. Thus, Internet usage at work is underrepresented in the samples. Recruitment methods can be another source of bias. Nielsen uses random-digit dialing (RDD), and comScore uses RDD plus pop-ups that solicit co-operation by offering virus protection and faster broadband connections ("comScore Inks," 2003). The first method is inefficient, but the second method could bias the sample toward the most technologically literate group of computer users.

Internet content providers are searching for a standard of user measurement that will serve the needs of potential advertisers. This will require not only the use of similar modes of data collection, but also general agreement on the part of audience research firms to define concepts such as "audience" in the same way. If one service defines audience as those users who are exposed to an item of content for 1 minute, and others require a 5-minute exposure, the data will be impossible to compare. Similarly, the definitions of concepts such as *reach* have to be the same, or at least very similar. Without standardization, the numbers generated by research companies have far less value to the buyers and sellers of advertising space/time.

In the Internet measurement system, research firms report numbers according to idiosyncratic criteria. This affects, for example, the designation of Web content as any specific type. If the same item of content is categorized differently in each system, then comparisons are meaningless. For this reason, many in the industry are calling for a third party to review content categories and set transparent criteria (Moore, 2003). Market participants also have to address the problem of disparity between log file data and audience research information. In fact, log files for measured Web pages show different numbers than the two major research firms (Elkin, 2003a).

The measurement of theatrical film audiences is often overlooked in the discussion of commercial audience research, largely because studios have traditionally studied moviegoers for very different reasons than broadcasters study audiences. As early as the 1940s, Hollywood studios commissioned marketing studies from George Gallup, but the data were used to inform production decisions and to develop promotion strategies (Ohmer, 1999). Because feature films did not participate in the advertising market in the same way as their electronic media counterparts, movie audiences were not measured and packaged for advertisers. After a film's release, success could be measured in ticket sales; there was no need for extensive ratings-type demographic data.

Changes in the advertising market will require more ratings-type information for feature films: Television programs have lost audiences, and advertisers are seeking new venues to reach potential customers. An expanded audience information system for feature films will develop if advertisers begin using product placement as a substitute for electronic media ad placement, or if they continue to develop ways to advertise in theatrical films that resemble methods of television advertising. In fact, Nielsen is offering research services that measure cinema and video-on-demand audiences. Advertisers have begun to realize that viewers reached through theatrical exhibition as well as feature film windowing opportunities such as VHS, DVD, video-on-demand, and even commercial airline exhibition have an economic value that can be quantified through systematic research (Phalen, 2003a).

## SUGGESTIONS FOR FURTHER RESEARCH

The challenges and opportunities for audience research that have been reviewed in this chapter raise many questions for academic research. Following are three that the author considers central to understanding the economic functions and effects of audience research.

*How will changes in measurement technology affect business practices in the market for advertising time?* Changes in audience measurement can affect the ways in which market participants conduct business. A specific example will serve to illustrate the point. Media organizations have pressured Nielsen to explain the disappearance of young male viewers in various markets. Viewers in this demographic aren't diligent in filling out diaries, but clients expect better sampling to compensate for the problem. Nielsen, on the other hand, claims that the lower viewing levels reflect what is actually happening in the market—younger viewers are turning to other options for entertainment. Market participants have developed two ways of redistributing the risk of underdelivering this audience. Sellers began offering guarantees in the scatter market (Linnett, 2003), to ensure that the target ratings bought by the advertiser will yield the promised number of viewers. The media are also requiring Nielsen to make a formal agreement to pay a financial penalty if certain sample characteristics fail (McClellan, 2003).

This is just one example of ways in which business practices change with the reliability of ratings. As new research technologies gain acceptance into American homes, advertisers and media organizations will make adjustments to guard against the unbalanced distribution of risk.

*What are the likely effects of new technologies on program decisionmaking?* New electronic media technologies offer programmers a source of feedback that goes beyond ratings information. Viewers can respond directly to programs through chatrooms or program Web sites, and decisionmakers can use these sites to monitor opinions, tastes, and trends. Because the samples are neither random nor representative, the information does not have the same reliability as quantitative research. However, the range of opinions expressed and the ease of discovery could affect decisionmaking processes in production and programming.

*How will the globalization of commercial audience research affect programming in the United States and other countries?* Nielsen is already competing for audience measurement contracts in non-U.S. markets (Wimmer & Dominick, 2000). However, the financial resources and capabilities of its new parent company are likely to extend its reach significantly. The extent to which Nielsen's methods and research designs are standardized across countries will affect international markets for advertising time. To date, no comprehensive studies of the effects of such standardization have been conducted. Of particular interest are the possible effects on local cultures and economies.

## ACKNOWLEDGMENT

The author thanks Todd Schumacher for his research assistance with this project.

# REFERENCES

Abercrombie, N., & Longhurst, B. (1998). *Audiences: A sociological theory of performance and imagination.* Thousand Oaks, CA: Sage.

Alasuutari, P. (1999). *Rethinking the media audience.* Thousand Oaks, CA: Sage.

Allan, R. (February 3, 2003). TiVo box redefines television viewing. *Electronic Design,* 41–46.

Ang, I. (1991). *Desperately seeking the audience.* London: Routledge.

Banks, M. J. (1981). *History of broadcast audience research in the United States, 1920–1980 with an emphasis on the rating services.* Unpublished doctoral dissertation, University of Tennessee, Knoxville, TN.

Barnes, B., & Thompson, L. (1988). The impact of audience information sources on media evolution. *Journal of Advertising Research, 28,* RC9–RC14.

Beville, M. H. (1988). *Audience ratings: Radio, television, cable* (Revised Student Edition). Hillsdale, NJ: Lawrence Erlbaum Associates.

Bianco, A. (2004, July 12). Special report: The vanishing mass market. *Business Week,* 60.

Buzzard, K. (1992). *Electronic media ratings: Turning audiences into dollars and sense.* Boston: Focal Press.

Chunovic, L. (June 2, 2003). When audiences intersect; Philly portable People Meter test helps advertisers make cross-media buys. *Television Week,* 18.

comScore inks largest net audience measurement contract. (2003, August 11). *Electronic Information Report.*

Elkin, T. (2003a). Better at-work data demanded. *Advertising Age, 74*(47), 20.

Elkin, T. (2003b). Nielsen rolls net-traffic gauge. *Advertising Age, 74*(10), 2.

Ettema, J. S., & Whitney, D. C. (1994). *Audiencemaking: How the media create the audience.* Thousand Oaks, CA: Sage.

Hagen, I., & Wasko, J. (2000). *Consuming audiences? Production and reception in media research.* Cresskill, NJ: Hampton Press.

Hay, J., Grossberg, L., & Wartella, E. (1996). *Audience and its landscape.* Boulder, CO: Westview Press.

Johnson, B., Fine, J., Linnett, R., & Teinowitz, I. (2003). Cracks in the foundation. *Advertising Age, 74* (49), 1.

Linnett, R. (2003). Scatter market implodes. *Advertising Age, 74*(42), 1.

McClellan, S. (August 4, 2003). Viacom signs $400M pact with Nielsen; series of contracts supports local people meters in top 10 markets. *Broadcasting & Cable,* 2.

Media Dynamics (2004). *TV Dimensions 2004.* New York: Media Dynamics.

Meehan, E. R. (1990). Why we don't count. The commodity audience. In P. Mellencamp (Ed.), *Logics of television: Cultural criticism* (pp. 117–137). Bloomington, IN: Indiana University Press.

Mermigas, D. (October 1, 2003). Ratings sweeps demise: A tech change overdue. *Mermigas on Media,* 1.

Moore, S. (2003). Let's fix Internet rating flaws. *Advertising Age, 74*(37), 20.

Napoli, P. (2003). *Audience economics: Media institutions and the audience marketplace.* New York: Columbia University Press.

Ohmer, S. (1999). The science of pleasure: George Gallup and audience research in Hollywood. In M. Stokes, & R. Maltby (Eds.), *Identifying Hollywood's audiences: Cultural identity and the movies* (pp. 61–80). London: British Film Institute.

Owen, B., & Wildman, S. (1992). *Video economics.* Cambridge, MA: Harvard University Press.

Penrose, E. (1966). *Theory of the growth of the firm.* Oxford: Basil Blackwell.

Phalen, P. F. (1996). *Information and markets and the market for information: An analysis of the market for television audiences.* Unpublished doctoral dissertation, Northwestern University, Evanston, IL.

Phalen, P. F. (1998). Market information system and personalized exchange: Business practices in the market for television audiences. *Journal of Media Economics, 11*(4), 17–34.

Phalen, P. F. (1999, April). Buying internet audiences: The more things change. Paper presented at the Broadcast Education Association annual conference, Las Vegas, NV.

Phalen, P. F. (2003a, April). Entertainment at 33,000 feet: The history of inflight entertainment. Broadcast Education Association annual conference, Las Vegas, NV.

Phalen, P. F. (2003b). Trading time and money for information in the television advertising market: Strategies and consequences. In A. Albarran & A. Arese (Eds.), *Time and media markets* (pp. 145–159). Mahwah, NJ: Lawrence Erlbaum Associates.

Posnock, S. T. (2004). It can control Madison Avenue. *American Demographics, 26*(1), 28–33.

Seiter, E. (1999). *Television and new media audiences*. New York: Oxford University Press.

Tiegel, E. (2003, September 8). Nielsen delays Hispanic intro; Local people meter overnight to expand to top 10 markets over three years; Spanish language measurements to come in 2006. *Television Week*, 24.

Webster, J. G., & Newton, G. (1988). Structural determinants of the television news audience. *Journal of Broadcasting & Electronic Media, 32*, 381–389.

Webster, J. G., & Phalen, P. F. (1997). *Mass audience: Rediscovering the dominant model*. Mahwah, NJ: Lawrence Erlbaum Associates.

Webster, J. G., Phalen, P. F., & Lichty, L. W. (2005 in press). *Ratings analysis: The theory and practice of audience research* (3rd ed.). Mahwah, NJ: Lawrence Erlbaum Associates.

Wicks, R. H. (2001). *Understanding audiences: Learning to use the media constructively*. Mahwah, NJ: Lawrence Erlbaum Associates.

Wimmer, R. D., & Dominick, J. R. (2000). *Mass media research: An introduction*. Belmont, CA: Wadsworth.

# FUTURE DIRECTIONS
# IN MEDIA MANAGEMENT
# AND ECONOMICS

# 28

# Directions for Media Management Research in the 21st Century

Dan Shaver and Mary Alice Shaver

The University of Central Florida

The research opportunities and challenges in the field of media management are multiplying with incredible speed, reflecting the changing face of media industries chronicled in the preceding chapters. In looking ahead, three factors appear likely to dominate the evolution of media industries and define the challenges facing media managers—digital technologies, consumer adoption patterns, and the global regulatory environment.

Figure 28.1 shows a conceptual schematic of the engines driving the evolution of media industries at the beginning of the 21st century, reflecting some of the issues demanding the attention of media management scholars.

If change is the keyword to describe the direction of media industries, managers must understand media consumers to understand that change. Advances in media technology have occurred—and will continue to occur—with extraordinary speed and, sometimes, in unexpected directions. In less than a decade, the World Wide Web has gone from a curiosity to a major distribution channel for news and information, entertainment, interpersonal communication, and sales of products and services. The on-line developments since the introduction of the protocols underlying the World Wide Web are not, however, primarily a story of technological advancement. They are, more importantly, a reflection of the convergence of a constellation of economic, technological, and social developments that sparked adoption of the new media options at an exponential rate.

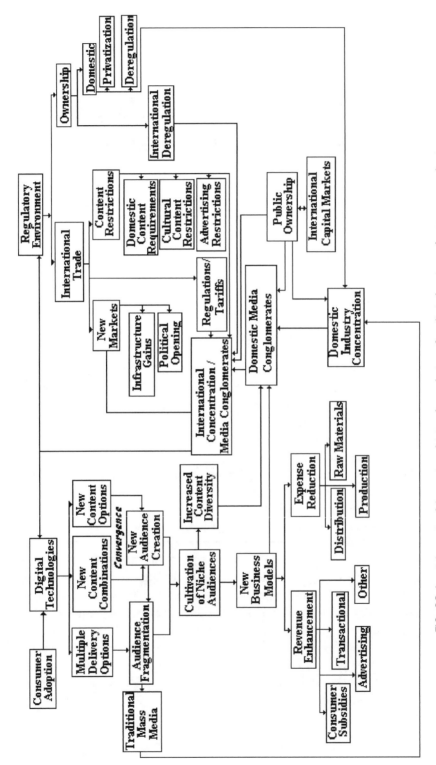

FIG. 28.1.  Schematic of the engines driving the evolution of media industries as the 21st century begins.

## ADOPTION ISSUES

Before one can explore the managerial challenges and opportunities of new technologies, there is a need to understand the dynamics of the market for these technologies. What factors drive, and what barriers prevent, consumer acceptance/adoption of one media product and not another? At what point will technological developments or social currents break through the barriers to adoption? What are the potential market(s) for specific media products? What are the competitive and strategic issues of these markets? What levels of substitutability exist between new and old, current and potential products? What impact will the growth/development of one media product have on other, existing products? In the enthusiastic preview of a new media capability, it is easy to forget that the markets required to introduce and profitably sustain a product or service are affected by considerable social and psychological inertia. To the degree that media scholars can accurately assess these issues, their findings will be of value to both scholars and managers of media industries.

Although markets determine the success and impact of technology, the pace of development of technological capabilities often continues independently of market factors. Technological innovation potentially affects media markets in three ways: multiplication of delivery channel options for content; introduction of new content combinations; and introduction of new content options. Events involving the second and third alternatives may loosely be defined as *convergence effects*.

The issue of multiple delivery options means there is a steady increase in the number of channels through which consumers can obtain media content. This proliferation of channels has a significant potential impact on how the enterprise must be managed, whatever the medium. Consumers of television content have gone from two or three network broadcast channels to hundreds of cable options to hundreds of satellite options. Now, content is even available on-line as producers of afternoon dramas allow—for a fee—the downloading of digital files of each day's installment for viewing on the consumer's computer. The inevitable result of channel proliferation is audience fragmentation. The impact of this fragmentation is felt most heavily by traditional mass media. This, in turn, provides an impetus for industry consolidation, as corporate owners seek larger aggregate audiences by increasing the number of individual outlets under their control, and individual owners are encouraged to sell because of dwindling audience share.

## CONVERGENCE AND NICHE AUDIENCES

Convergence effects result from the ability to deliver either new content combinations or new kinds of content to audiences. On-line news sites, with the ability to offer both print and streaming video to news consumers, are one example. Because of their timeliness, ability to provide greater background material due to lack of space limitations, and high degree of user/consumer control, these sites represent a potential challenge to both traditional print and broadcast/cable news outlets.

New content options offer media consumers technology-driven content that is simply not available through traditional media. On-line gaming, for example, offers entertainment values that challenge traditional entertainment media such as broadcast/ cable and film for audience attention. Similarly, advertising sites with games and other interactive features provide attractive alternatives to existing advertising functions in traditional media. Both of these convergence effects result in the creation of niche audiences, multiply the forces leading to audience fragmentation, and create an imperative for media content providers to develop strategies for cultivation of specialized audiences.

Two effects of the need to cultivate niche audiences are immediately apparent. The first is the need to increase content diversity. As audience segments become more specialized, managers must provide more focused content to appeal to and hold audience attention. Nowhere is this more apparent than in the proliferation of specialized cable/satellite channels. The same effects, of course, can also be seen in print and Internet products. This drive for more varied content generation provides an incentive for media managers to seek opportunities for vertical integration and drives the development of media conglomerates capable of repurposing content from one medium to another.

A second effect of niche audience cultivation is the need for media managers to seek new business models that enhance revenues or reduce costs. As markets shift in scope and competition, a rethinking of existing revenue models is required for traditional media, and new models are necessary for new content and service providers. New or modified forms of consumer subsidies and advertising pricing structures will be necessary. The development of transaction-based and other new revenue streams appears inevitable.

Expense reduction strategies are the complementary strategy to revenue enhancement for media managers seeking to maintain economic growth in the face of fragmenting audiences and increased competition. These strategies are also likely to have significant impact on existing industry practices. The development of new distribution channels, such as those opened to the film industry by the proliferation of videotape and DVDs, has a direct impact on traditional exhibitors. Digital delivery of music files has the potential for a similar impact on music wholesalers and retailers, and the competition between cable and satellite providers for delivery of traditional broadcast content affects all three subindustries.

Initiatives designed to reduce production costs have similar implications, particularly as audience-acceptable digital alternatives to traditional print vehicles evolve. Electronic delivery and print-on-demand technologies offer significant reductions in materials, inventory, returns, labor, and distribution expense for publishers of all kinds, as well as an effective tool for cost-effective creation of materials for specialized audiences.

Strategies for reduction of raw materials content costs often involve acquisition of content that can be repurposed for other media or segmented for specialized audiences. Alternatively, acquisition or partnerships with firms possessing advanced content-creation technologies, such as digital animation, offer opportunities to reduce acquisition costs for basic media content. All of these strategies offer media owners an incentive to diversify their media holdings and become conglomerates. This relatively recent practice of bringing together traditionally separate media industries under a single corporate umbrella—and expectations of closer coordination between traditionally separate enterprises—creates new challenges in terms of managing corporate culture and the debt load generated by merger and acquisition activity.

## REGULATORY ISSUES

The third major factor affecting the evolution of media industries is the regulatory environment. Ownership restrictions, particularly in the telecommunications and broadcast industries, have historically tended to maintain industry integrity, restrain the formation of media conglomerates and industry concentration, and create artificial competitive structures. As accelerating trends toward privatization and deregulation develop around the world, increasing concentration and new competitive forces are emerging. As national governments relax restraints on nondomestic media ownership or partnerships with international firms, the opportunities for increased international ownership concentration and the proliferation of transnational media conglomerates will increase.

Regulations affecting international trade will also play an important role in shaping market opportunities for media managers. Government-imposed content restrictions come in several forms. Requirements for minimum amounts of domestically produced content in broadcast and film—intended to protect domestic industries and native cultures—tend to reduce programming flexibility and increase content costs for transnational media companies. Culturally based restrictions, common in the Middle East and parts of Asia, have similar effects. Restrictions on advertising content and approaches may inhibit revenue flows. Regulations and tariffs on the importation of printed or recorded materials restrict competitiveness and reduce market opportunities. To the degree these barriers are reduced, economic opportunities for managers in transnational media companies are increased.

A final factor affecting the development of transnational media companies lies in the opening of new markets for their content and services. Evolving political contexts favorable to transnational corporations mean that extraordinarily lucrative markets such as China may become increasingly open to both investment and product importation by transnational media companies. This process is aided by advances in wireless digital technologies that bypass the need for a sophisticated wired infrastructure for delivery. The potential for development of new, relatively untapped markets in Africa and South America as a result of these advances is significant.

The combination of these trends supports an evolutionary model for media industry structures. Domestic industry concentration creates an opportunity—and appetite—for domestic media conglomerates, trends that have been observable for many decades. Relaxation of barriers to international expansion and the development of new markets create opportunities for transnational media firms to evolve and expand. The growth of these firms, in turn, affects the key technology and regulatory drivers. Research and development by firms with increasing resources affects the development and application of digital technologies. At the same time, the economic clout provided by increasing size and concentration gives media conglomerates more influence in lobbying for change in domestic and international regulation.

The strategies and resources of these firms are, in turn, affected by the dynamics of public ownership and international capital markets. Public ownership—and the imperatives of meeting the expectations of capital markets—imposes operating constraints that affect resource allocations and marketing strategies in ways that may differ significantly from the decision models used by private owners—or even industry-specific corporations.

Given the interplay of these factors, the impact on industry operations, media content, and audiences represents the major research challenge in media management in the years ahead. This does not imply that today's industry-specific questions will become unimportant; it means that they will become more complex. In the following pages, we examine how this interplay applies to traditional media vehicles.

## BOOK PUBLISHING

The book publishing industry faces a host of potential changes, providing significant research issues. As technological effects proliferate, a looming issue lies in audience adoption of new delivery systems. What barriers exist? What innovations and adaptations will be required by the industry to facilitate consumer acceptance of digital products? What business segments will emerge as early adopters, and what are the implications for other segments?

The e-book technologies, in particular, were widely touted in the mid-1990s but have failed to realize their potential because of consumer resistance. Advances in technology and evolving consumer markets, however, will undoubtedly change the picture at some point. Understanding how and when, and the likely effects on the existing book publishing industry structure, will be important if the transition is to be managed in ways that minimize the negative effects on publishers and other industry players.

The publishing industry distribution chain is already experiencing significant change. The proliferation of chain superstores, with superior purchasing and economic clout, has resulted in a steady decline in privately owned outlets. The chains, in turn, are facing increasing competitive and pricing pressure from on-line vendors such as Amazon.com. In part, they have responded by developing their own on-line ordering services, but as consumer purchasing patterns shift from retail to on-line shopping, even the success of proprietary sites will place economic pressures on their own traditional brick-and-mortar outlets. This competitive dance is further complicated by the uncertain impact of digital content delivery for e-books and the impact of print-on-demand technologies. Although publishing on demand is still too unsophisticated for the consumer mass market, it is unlikely to remain so.

Digital technologies also have the potential to undermine or alter the traditional relationships between authors, content providers, and publishers, content packagers, and distributors. Established authors, with little need for the promotional resources offered by publishers, may find it desirable to distribute directly to their public, creating a content shortage for publishers. Unknown authors may be able to sidestep publisher gatekeepers and market their work directly to the public, building audiences slowly but inexpensively. With the significant reduction in production and distribution costs associated with digital products, even relatively small audiences can offer significant profit. Publishers will need to identify new value-added strategies to address these issues if they are to succeed in a digital environment.

The expansion of technology-driven production, distribution, and consumption options will also complicate the legal and regulatory environment. Publishers will face the same copyright and reproduction issues currently rampant in the music industry and rapidly emerging in the film industry. These forces will require the exploration of new business models, just as the music industry is experimenting with alternative, legal download options for music files and some performers are using free on-line distribution of their music to drive concert revenues.

New models will inevitably affect management's pricing strategies, as is already occurring in the recorded music industry. Cost reductions will permit pricing reductions without sacrificing profitability, adding to the complexity of competition within the industry. The flexibility of digital technologies and the introduction of new business models will also permit the exploration of new revenue strategies. The ability to gather demographic information online and seamlessly and automatically insert content in digital files creates the potential for new advertising revenue streams. Downloading a home improvement book? Why not include institutional ads for suppliers with stores in your area that specialize in tools and supplies relevant to specific chapters in the book? Any consumer resistance to inclusion of nontraditional content is likely to be mitigated by the convenience of knowing exactly where to go to find what is needed to complete that project. Buying a legal text? What about paying a small additional fee that allows you to update the text once a month with the latest rulings and case law?

The implications of these opportunities for industry ownership and management structures are unclear. There has been a trend toward ownership concentration in publishing, reflecting the desire of owners to gain economies of scope and scale and to acquire content suitable for repurposing or merchandising extensions. The economic leverage and resources available to major media conglomerates gives management an advantage in erecting competitive barriers and exploiting new technologies. Alternately, the significant reductions in production and distribution barriers associated with digital technologies increases the ease of entry and exit for start-ups, potentially increasing the complexity of the competitive environment. The likelihood of this occurring is enhanced by the institutional inertia characteristic of bureaucratic organizations.

The book industry is poised for significant turmoil; understanding these events, studying strategic responses, and identifying potential alternatives offers a rich research agenda for media management scholars.

## NEWSPAPERS

The newspaper industry is a particularly rich field for inquiry. After decades of lumbering along like *Tyrannosaurus rex*—the biggest and meanest thing in the jungle—and able to ignore everyone else, the industry saw things begin to change in the 1970s. Although circulation continued to grow, penetration began to decline and competition for advertising revenues intensified. Still, newspapers maintained dominance of price/item advertising, the core of the retail/display advertising revenue stream, and of classified lineage. National revenues were shifting to other media, but the growth of retail and classified revenues made the change relatively painless. And, newspapers were still the dominant provider of news because of the time constraints imposed on television programming.

Then, the creation of all-news cable channels challenged the franchise for national and international news. By the 1990s, the rise of the Internet offered vehicles with which other local media, such as television stations, could challenge the local news franchise. It also allowed traditional nonprint media—and even nonmedia businesses—to compete for price/item and classified advertising revenues. Publishers responded to these new competitive threats by creating their own on-line products. Generally, these launches sought to replicate the print product online and lacked adequate vision, resources, or planning for profitability. The results were generally disappointing and, as the economic environment declined in the late 1990s, publishers began to rethink their strategies.

Today, the newspaper industry is in search of a new identity. Dependent on mass audiences to maintain its advertising revenue streams, it needs new delivery and revenue models that will allow it to leverage its content generation capabilities in the face of an increasingly competitive marketplace and changing media consumption habits. The crux of the dilemma is that to maintain a sufficiently large aggregate audience, newspaper companies must maintain print products suitable to the consumption preferences of their established audiences while developing new digital products to capture that portion of the audience adopting new consumption patterns. A shift to all-digital production and distribution would offer publishers sufficient cost savings to offset any potential reduction in circulation revenues, but neither technology nor consumer adoption patterns will permit that shift for decades. Meanwhile, publishers must maintain two technologies, seeking ways to develop new revenue streams for their electronic products while preparing an ultimate exit strategy from print decades down the road. This dichotomy creates three potential research streams—issues related to managing the print product, issues related to developing and implementing electronic products, and issues related to the development of exit strategies from print over the long term.

Traditional issues related to readership, the development of new products or content targeting increasingly desirable niche audiences, and media competition will continue to be of interest to scholars and of value to the industry for the foreseeable future. Understanding changes in media preferences and consumption, and their impact on newspaper readership and advertising effectiveness, remains a key goal of the industry. Identifying strategies for increasing readership among young and ethnic audiences is critical to maintaining the viability of the print product. The increasing complexity of competition for advertising revenues offers yet another challenge. Direct mail continues to grow, and the proliferation of advertising opportunities on niche-oriented cable channels offers more choice to advertisers with narrowly focused markets. The consolidation of radio ownership that followed the Telecommunications Act of 1996 has enabled owners in key markets to reconfigure formats in ways that provide a more effective vehicle for reaching tailored audiences. The development of the Internet permits advertisers to reach target audiences directly and cost-effectively through email and proprietary Web sites.

The cultivation of digital products—both in building audiences and in developing revenue streams—presents a new set of challenges to newspaper publishers. Most publishers now recognize that simply replicating the print product on-line is an unsatisfactory strategy. The Internet offers a variety of opportunities related to timeliness, content capacity, multimedia presentation, and interactivity that are not possible with a print product. Identifying ways to leverage these potentials in ways that will maximize audience utility and supplement, rather than detract from, the print product is a top priority for the industry. Fundamental to addressing this issue is a clearer understanding of audience perceptions of the relationship between the two content vehicles. Financing the on-line product also requires the development of new pricing, advertising, and business models, as well as a need to ascertain the relative potency of advertising messages delivered in various formats. The rise of on-line products will also create new demands on resources and training. Multimedia content delivery capabilities will require newspapers to develop skills in content areas previously associated with broadcast and will affect training and staffing requirements. There will be incentives to develop partnerships with other media to meet content creation requirements that have unknown implications for media management structures and will inevitably present issues and conflicts of organizational culture.

The effects of media consolidation and public ownership will continue to be of keen interest to scholars, regulators, and the public. The field will become even more complex as regulators open the possibility of cross-ownership of newspapers and television stations in the same market. Even absent cross-ownership of broadcast outlets, news organizations forced to develop multimedia capabilities for on-line products may be tempted to repurpose that content for cable delivery. As the industry moves toward migration to a digital format, an exploration of delivery alternatives and business models becomes essential. Do on-line models offer maximum benefits, or do content downloads to computers or electronic paper? How can newspaper organizations reshape their services to advertisers in order to maintain advertiser loyalty? What strategies are needed to migrate existing print revenue streams to an electronic environment? How can publishers leverage the branding power of their print products to strengthen the competitive advantage of their electronic products? And, finally, at what point does the vision of a digital migration begin to affect resource allocation and investment decisions? What decisions are likely to be affected, and what will be the impact on content and quality?

## RADIO

The Telecommunications Act of 1996 opened the door for a revolution in the radio industry, and it happened. Top markets quickly developed a high level of ownership concentration that enabled broadcasters to rationalize formats in ways that enhanced the demographics of the audiences they could offer advertisers and strengthened their pricing power. Some in the industry boasted that the new ability to aggregate distinct niche audiences presented a unique opportunity to develop strategies for taking market share from newspapers. To offset the debt created by acquisitions and enhance profitability, owners began to consolidate station management structures and increase the use of syndicated and repurposed internally generated content. Resources devoted to news were frequently reduced or outsourced.

The ultimate impact of these developments on the industry and the public is not yet clear, but understanding these issues has important managerial and public policy implications. Indeed, the speed and uncertainty of developments in the radio industry has spawned concern on the part of legislators and regulators with regard to further ownership deregulation in the broadcast television industry.

These developments offer several research streams for scholars. The first is simply to document and understand current trends and events. What are the competitive effects on independent owners when high levels of ownership concentration develop in their markets? What are the effects on advertisers? What are the implications of consolidation on pricing? Has the effectiveness of radio advertising as a tool to reach target audiences increased? What are the effects on programming diversity? There are some indications that the rationalizing of formats under common ownership may have increased the total number of formats available in many markets. But have these increases in apparent diversity actually come at the expense of less commercially desirable formats that appeal to economic or social minorities? To what degree does radio news affect the public debate, and has this role been compromised as a result of deregulation?

As consolidation has occurred in traditional broadcast markets, new competitive factors are entering the mix. The FCC has increased its commitment to licensing new low-power stations, which are presumed to be highly responsive to community needs and tastes. If there is significant growth in this segment, how will broadcast managers compete for audiences and advertisers? Internet radio is gaining increasing audience acceptance and offers the opportunity to aggregate audiences based on common interests rather than geography, yet its future is murky. Compared to traditional broadcast, barriers to entry and exit for Internet radio are virtually nonexistent. No licenses or capital-intensive broadcast facilities are required. Satellite delivery could even make programming accessible in automobiles, the stronghold of broadcast radio. But many questions remain unanswered. Can sufficient advertising revenues be developed to support such an industry? What kinds of advertisers would benefit from a geographically unbounded audience? Would this competition draw revenues from broadcast radio or from another medium, since broadcast radio relies heavily on local advertisers? Although capital investment requirements are low, the music royalty structures for broadcast and Internet radio differ markedly. What implications does this have for broadcast managers considering investment in Internet radio? Is ownership likely to become concentrated in the hands of the recorded music industry, which would not have to pay royalties on its own titles? Will existing broadcast outlets find that simulcasting existing broadcasts leverages their audiences? Will the potential for interactivity on such sites create new advertising and content delivery opportunities that managers can leverage into new revenue streams?

Finally, there is the issue of public ownership. Although publicly traded companies have always owned some radio stations, ownership restrictions meant that the majority of stations were privately owned. Deregulation and the resulting concentration have changed that. The resources required for station acquisition provide an incentive for owner groups to go public. As an increasing proportion of broadcast ownership rests in the hands of publicly held corporations, questions regarding the impact on management's content and operational decisions become increasingly important.

## BROADCAST AND NETWORK TELEVISION

The hallmark of the broadcast television industry for the past quarter-century has been continued erosion of audience share due to fragmentation as a result of the growth of cable penetration and the proliferation of cable channels. With increasing levels of broadband penetration, the Internet is emerging as an additional competitor for audience attention and an alternative delivery vehicle for news and entertainment. Still, network programming offers the broadest mass audiences for entertainment and commercial advertising content. Technologically, the industry is also poised for dramatic change with the conversion to mandated HDTV broadcast standards that affect operational decisions, require significant capital investment, and may affect audiences because of the requirement for additional equipment or new television sets for those relying on a broadcast signal.

By definition a mass medium, broadcast television content is more constrained than cable content, which builds audiences by a sharp niche focus. Broad demographics, particularly related to age and income, define broadcast audiences while cable channels are able to build audiences based on narrow interest/psychographic profiles. The "public" nature of the broadcast signal further limits programming options, whereas cable content producers have more flexibility. Better understanding the nature and impact of these factors would yield insights into strategies for enhancing competitive performance. Another strategic issue is the effect of all-cable networks on traditional broadcasters. Because the number of stations available for affiliate status was limited, the growth of broadcast networks had natural constraints. The growth of cable penetration, however, has made possible the emergence of cable-only networks (and mixed networks, such as FOX) by eliminating a significant barrier to entry. Understanding the current and future implications of this fundamental change on the strategic issues facing the industry provides opportunity for significant research.

Ownership issues are also an important issue. Until the late 20th century, networks were stand-alone entities. Now, all are part of publicly held corporate conglomerates. Identifying the implications and effects of this fundamental change in ownership structure on content and management decisions—including the effects on the way in which programming and resource allocations are made—is important. The potential deregulation of broadcast outlet ownership, and the possible elimination of the ban on cross-ownership, also raises a host of important questions. What is the likely impact on acquisition strategies? What is the impact on advertisers in markets where newspapers and television stations have a common ownership? What are the implications for organizational and management structure of changes designed to reduce costs by repurposing broadcast and print content or resources? How are these changes likely to affect quality and the flow of information necessary for public discourse? Will they affect the quality of local news and entertainment content?

Changing media options and use habits also offer competitive challenges to the broadcast television industry. Entertainment content, the core of television programming, is available through an increasing variety of channels. DVDs and other recording technologies compete for audience attention. Time spent on-line detracts from the time available for consuming other media, and diminished audiences ultimately mean reduced advertising revenues. Identifying strategies and new business models to address these issues is critical for industry management. Some steps, such as offering downloads of daytime television serials for travelers or others who can't watch the original programming, offer promise, but identifying the market potential for such strategies and spotting new opportunities is essential.

Another aspect of the influence of the Internet is the potential for broadcast outlets to expand into new business lines. Broadband offers the opportunity to make content available to audiences without the constraints time imposes on broadcast programming. Repurposing of content through streaming creates the opportunity to develop new audiences with minimum additional costs. To what degree are audiences willing to view the local news broadcast at 8:30 on-line instead of 6:30 live because they were late arriving home? Of what value would these additional viewers be to advertisers? These are all issues of potentially significant importance to broadcasters.

## ACCESS PROVIDERS

This category includes cable, satellite, and wireless service providers. Content is relevant only as a competitive tool; the primary issue is developing technological capabilities to provide content access to media consumers. The cable industry began developing shortly after World War II, but technological advances in the last decades of the 20th century expanded content options and fueled growth in household penetration. Satellite delivery growth, initially hampered by the need for large receiver dishes and high costs, has increased significantly in the past decade with the development of small dishes and the expansion of available channel capacity, significantly increasing competition between the two industries. Technological advances and deregulation now allow access providers to compete with traditional telephone service providers in nontraditional fields such as voice communication, delivery of entertainment content, and interactive services as well as data transmission. New Internet-based "telephone" services represent a sharp challenge to the traditional structure of telephone service, particularly in the United States, and raise a host of structural and competitive issues for the industries affected.

Satellite delivery also offers opportunities for providers to open and develop new markets in areas of the world that lack the wired infrastructure required by traditional delivery systems, whereas greater bandwidth offers the capability to cultivate increased numbers of niche content markets, strengthening the forces driving audience fragmentation.

Managers in these industries—cable, satellite, and traditional telephone companies—face a critical dilemma. Can they compete effectively or will evolving technological and adoption patterns result in their converging into a single industry? If they are to remain separate and competitive, what markets and strategies will provide sources of competitive advantage for each? If they are to converge, what are the implications for management and ownership structures at both the national and international levels? In what ways can access providers leverage their capabilities—particularly in interactivity—to create new revenue streams? What are the implications for traditional broadcast industries? What are the implications for traditional entertainment content providers such as theater chains and recorded music retailers? What are the implications for the advertising industry when technology allows access subscribers to zip past commercials?

## WIRELESS TECHNOLOGIES

The growth of wireless technology is already beginning to have significant impact on both services and traditional industry structures. Traditional telephone service companies, for example, are withdrawing from the pay telephone market as a result of increased cellular service penetration, and there are indications that increasing numbers of consumers are eliminating traditional residential phone service and relying on cell phones for all their voice communication needs.

These trends raise both strategic and public policy issues. Traditional providers of voice services have historically been required to subsidize service in economically nonviable areas in the name of universal access. How does this principle apply when revenues are shifting to other service providers? What is the impact on economically or geographically disadvantaged populations? How can/should government and society address the issue? How will media managers address these issues?

The growth of wireless Internet services in public areas has the potential to affect the economic balance of content access industries. Organizations ranging from coffee houses to universities to cities are installing wireless Internet access systems, and technology is increasing the reliability of such networks. Will these ultimately threaten the key revenue streams of access providers heavily dependent on residential markets?

Wireless telephone service providers are rapidly adding new capabilities and services—at enhanced fees—for their subscribers. Cameras built into cell phones and online transmission of these photos to other users or to Web sites are one example. The ability to access World Wide Web content—albeit somewhat limited for now—is another example. E-mail access via cell phones or personal digital assistants is another. How far can these service extensions develop? What impact will they have on traditional providers of access services in other industry groups? What factors will drive or retard consumer adoptions?

## STREAMING TECHNOLOGIES

Although not a communications industry per se, streaming technology has the potential for significant impact on traditional media industries, particularly when combined with advanced delivery systems.

A simple example of this can be found in the development and evolution of Internet radio. Broadcast radio is a geographically bounded industry dependent primarily on local advertising revenues. Content tends to be determined by the need to attract a sufficiently large audience to appeal to advertisers within a definable demographic. In a sense, it might be termed a "mass niche" audience. Content formats for which there is insufficient demand in the geographic reach of the broadcast signal are, therefore, not economically viable. Additionally, regulatory and capital barriers to entry are relatively high.

Streaming audio, on the other hand, is not geographically bounded. The opportunity to amass a large audience on a national—or global—basis for even relatively obscure formats is very real. Additionally, regulatory and capital barriers to entry and exit are relatively nonexistent. Differentials in music royalties do impose limitations regarding some content, however.

What are the factors likely to stimulate or retard consumer adoption of streaming audio? What competitive advantages does the ability to deliver more than just audio content offer Internet radio managers? What business strategies are likely to make on-line audio services profitable? What sort of audiences might be created, and to what kinds of advertisers might they be of interest? To what degree are streaming audio services likely to be competitive with—or complementary to—traditional broadcast radio? If they are more complementary than competitive, what other advertising media are likely to lose revenue share to streaming audio? What is the likely impact of differentials in music royalty rates on ownership patterns—are recording companies that don't have to pay royalties to themselves at an advantage?

With increases in bandwidth availability and technology, broadcast television and the film exhibition industry are likely to face similar issues, raising complementary research questions.

## RECORDED MUSIC AND MOTION PICTURE INDUSTRIES

Traditional issues will continue to pose research opportunities in these industries, but new questions deriving from digital technologies will also require scholarly attention.

Digital delivery options—downloads, streaming media, movies on demand—are likely to have a significant impact on the film exhibition and distribution industries and to affect content and consumer decisions. Will these technologies increase the variety of content available by creating new niche markets that may not be commercially viable in the traditional exhibition or distribution systems? Will the ability of consumers to interact with digital movie content—choosing alternative camera perspectives or endings—create competitive advantages that disadvantage traditional exhibition venues? Consumer preference for digitally produced special effects and animation is already affecting production decisions. What will the long-term effects be in terms of costs and revenues? Digital delivery of music—whether legally or illegally—appears to be here to stay. Determining the long-term strategic impact on the industry will not be a simple matter. What results will spring from on-line sites allowing legal downloads for a fee? Are there strategies that might allow music content providers to leverage lower-cost or free music content to generate other revenues? What impact might new promotion and delivery options have on traditional relationships between performers and music companies? What impact will there be on traditional music packaging if consumers are allowed to assemble their own CDs from selections of songs from multiple groups? What new opportunities or business models might be created by industry-wide adoption of new delivery technologies?

Firms in the film production/exhibition industry have been aggressively cultivating nontraditional revenue streams for more than two decades. What are the economic trends resulting from increasingly sophisticated windowing, product placement, promotional and merchandising tie-ins, and cross-media packaging? What are the implications of including commercial advertising in trailers? What are likely impacts on the advertising industry?

With the growth of digital content formats, both the film and music industries are facing issues of copyright protection. The recorded music industry claims a significant revenue impact from illegal file sharing. The film industry's future contains similar clouds. What strategies might be developed to minimize these risks or maximize new opportunities?

## THE WORLD WIDE WEB

Despite lingering debate about whether the World Wide Web is truly a mass medium, there is no question that it is a medium offering content access to a mass audience. As the primary vehicle for delivery of converged content—and as the most quickly adopted medium in history—its potential to affect the management environment of traditional media industries is enormous.

In less than one and a half decades, the Web has gone from a simple set of protocols to a pervasive social factor in developed countries and an increasing influence in developing nations. Its evolution has been largely unguided by regulation or social policy; technology, human interests, and economic issues—real or imagined—have determined its direction.

Strategic issues lead the research questions demanding answers about the management of the capabilities of the World Wide Web. The development of business models and new services that ensure profitability for content providers of various kinds—whether information, entertainment, service, or on-line commerce—is a critical issue. The impact of on-line capabilities, ranging from denial of service attacks and theft of economic information by hackers to cash flow issues for pornography, gambling, and uncollected taxes, have both managerial and social implications.

Another important issue involves rates of broadband adoption. What factors—social or technological—account for significantly different rates of broadband growth in different societies?

The development of Web functionality has significant implications for the advertising industry as well. What approaches are effective? How should effectiveness be measured? How should advertising rates be established? How will reallocation of advertising investments affect revenue streams for traditional mass media companies? Who will gain and who will lose? How can managers in traditional industries respond?

Finally, issues of control and concentration are inevitably. Control of browser development and ownership and management of portals and search engines pose both managerial and public policy questions.

## THE ADVERTISING INDUSTRY

The advertising industry, though not a mass medium itself, is integrally linked to the viability of both traditional and new media. It represents the largest or only source of revenues for broadcast and most print media and is at the center of the business strategies being pursued by most on-line and new media companies. Either through revenue subsidies to content producers or through direct creation of commercial messages, the industry contributes more than any other factor to the development of mass media content.

Two challenges appear likely to dominate the advertising industry in the decades ahead: transnational markets and the proliferation of potential channels for delivery of messages. In the last decades of the 20th century, major advertising organizations developed broad international networks based on consolidated ownership or on affiliations to better address the needs of clients with multinational operations. Understanding the implications of managing service operations across a broad variety of political and cultural geographic units—and whether this structure affects overall client results and agency operating structures positively or negatively, and why—will remain a significant challenge for 21st-century researchers. What business models and management structures offer the most effective results? What degrees of autonomy or control result in highest profitability? To what degree can commercial messages be standardized globally? Can managers achieve true economics of scale and scope in advertising services, or is the potential for achieving such economies an illusion? What factors affect home country advantage, and to what degree do they work to assist or impede the workings of transnational advertising companies?

The second theme goes to the heart of the allocation of advertising resources and the assessment of their effectiveness. Potential strategies by existing media channels to develop new revenue streams will provide advertising decisionmakers increased alternatives. New channels—ranging from the development of Internet ads and Web sites to email advertising to on-line streaming audio—will create an array of nontraditional delivery channels that must be assessed. Determining the actual reach and effectiveness of these new approaches, identifying the best way to create messages for new delivery channels, and agreeing on appropriate measurement and rate-setting procedures for new media are all issues that must be examined.

## CONCLUSION

In the history of scholarship, media management is a relatively young field. Through the last decades of the 20th century, research tended—quite successfully—to focus on individual media industries. Researchers would investigate broadcast or newspaper strategies, for example. This approach was successful because media industries tended to be fairly distinct and ownership patterns tended to be industry specific.

Although industry-specific research will continue to have an important role in the 21st century, technology and consumption patterns are blurring industry lines, and ownership patterns are becoming increasingly complex as multinational conglomerates seek opportunities to realize economies and develop synergies by cross-medium packaging and repurposing of content. In the decades ahead, understanding the new management challenges presented by the evolving nature of media will require considering the interrelated developments—technological, economic, and audience—in competing, related media and close attention to the organizational issues generated by new business strategies.

# 29

# Future Directions for Media Economics Research

Stephen Lacy and Johannes M. Bauer
Michigan State University

Research flourishes in a pluralistic environment, and offering directions for the future risks being presumptuous. As this book demonstrates, media economics is indeed a wide-ranging area of research, and scholars pursue their interests as they see fit. Rather than proposing a next grand research design for media economics, this chapter will offer suggestions for incremental next steps that we think will advance the collective body of knowledge about how media firms and consumers behave and the design and effects of policy toward media. These suggestions aim to develop a better understanding of media economics and government regulation of media by adapting existing economic theories to media firms and by developing theories specifically for examining media firms and consumers.

Research contributes to an understanding of media at different levels of abstraction, and knowledge exists at basic and applied levels (Mokyr, 2002). One challenge of media economics is to advance pure theory while not neglecting practical applicability. Even though the two are related and complementary, they are not identical. Each employs different methods and has unique strengths and weaknesses. For example, pure theory necessarily rests on simplifying assumptions and generally cannot be applied directly to specific cases and management practices. To this end, practical knowledge needs to be derived from theory as well as experience. This chapter will address two central issues facing media economic scholars: approaches toward media economic theories and models, and important issues in policy toward media firms and industries.

# APPROACHES TOWARD MEDIA ECONOMIC
# THEORIES AND MODELS

Almost 45 years ago, *Journalism Quarterly* hosted a debate about the relationship between mass media and economic theory. Landau and Davenport (1959) and Davenport and Landau (1960) argued that traditional economic theory could not adequately explain behavior in media industries and that new theories should be developed. Currier (1960a, 1960b) countered that traditional economic theory could explain the behaviors and activities of mass media firms. The disagreement rests more on the various uses of theory rather than on one approach being better. Standard neoclassical economic theory explains and predicts a broad range of, but not all, media economic phenomena. The standard model often does not translate into accurate prescriptions for specific management decisions. This chapter is based on the assumption that understanding economic behavior can be enhanced by applying economic theory to media behavior and by developing theory from other scholarly approaches that address people's allocation of scarce resources under conditions of uncertainty.

## Economic Approaches to Demand Theory

Perfect competition theory states that demand is determined by the price of products, price of substitutes and complements, income, and taste (Stigler, 1952, p. 43). Taste encompasses a wide range of variables, but traditional microeconomic indifference analysis abstracts from this diversity by assuming that taste is constant and that consumers care only about a product's utility relative to its price. The indifference approach further assumes perfect knowledge and homogeneous products. However, taste plays an important role in determining demand for many products, especially media products where monetary price often plays a slight role or none at all (Lacy & Simon, 1993).

In reaction to the limits of perfect competition theory, Chamberlin (1962) developed the theory of monopolistic competition, which includes product differentiation and selling costs as variables that affect demand. However, Chamberlin did not reconsider the theory of demand that underlies perfect competition. Rather, he incorporated taste by proposing that product differentiation and selling costs make demand curves more inelastic. Although Chamberlin advanced understanding of economics, the theory of monopolistic competition fails to specify a process by which product differentiation and advertising altered demand elasticity for individual consumers.

More recently, Becker (1971, 1996) handled the issue of taste by arguing that many goods such as clothes, food, theater tickets, and medical care do not directly provide utility but are used in processes that create commodities and services that in turn give utility. For example, accessing advertising about cars is part of the process of purchasing an automobile that yields utility. Becker and Murphy (2000) followed Becker's early work with a theory of "social economics," which includes social capital as a variable influencing individual utility functions. The theory explains how habit and social capital can be incorporated in an economic model of behavior that allows for a better understanding of the role of taste in demand.

The concept of social capital allows economists to incorporate the impact of social influences in rational consumer theories, which assume that consumers have ordered sets of preferences and that they maximize utility (Becker & Murphy, 2000, p. 23). The ability to develop ordered preferences and maximize utility requires either perfect knowledge on the part of the consumer or repeated identical decisions that facilitate convergence to an optimal choice through trial and error. Simon (1957) studied situations in which this was not the case and individuals were making decisions under conditions of "bounded rationality." He replaced the assumption of utility maximization with the concept of "satisficing," which posits that people determine acceptable levels of utility from their decisions and accept those as goals, rather than unobtainable maximization. Economists respond to criticism of maximization by saying economic models need not reflect reality perfectly to be useful. This response is true for a description of economic behavior in the aggregate, but traditional economic analysis is limited in its ability to predict individual or group behavior well enough for managers to make specific business decisions. This is particularly true for media products because consumers often have strong preferences, have imperfect knowledge of content before use, and contribute meaning to the content. This is not to say that rational theories of demand are not useful. Indeed, as will be demonstrated later, some hold great promise for use with media. However, it would be useful for scholars to expand the narrow scope of the existing models and to develop additional theories of demand that do not depend on assumptions of simple rationality (in the sense of consistency). Such models might concentrate more on the process of preference formation, which allows for better understanding of how to affect variations through policy.

Already, some economists have applied economic theory to media firms and developed models dealing with product quality and utility. Waterman (1989/1990) modeled the impact of diversity and quality in a monopolistically competitive market for information. Litman (1991) stated that television viewers receive utility from three product dimensions—breadth of diversity, depth of diversity, and quality of product—and that demand for hours of television viewing is a function of diversity and quality. One of the difficulties with testing such theories is the limitations of current measures. Just what constitutes quality in any particular medium or type of message remains debatable. The measures of diversity that have been used are fairly simplistic and often deal with a limited number of content dimensions. For example, Litman (1979) advanced diversity measurement by suggesting that diversity includes horizontal and vertical diversity. Other researchers have added additional dimensions, such as programming scenarios (Li & Chiang, 2001). However, these measures only tap the surface of a concept as complex as programming diversity, and many programming categories used in measuring diversity are arbitrary and often overlapping. Additional theoretical and empirical investigation of the concept of diversity would better inform economic theory, media policy, and empirical measurement.

### Communication Scholarship and Demand Theory

Marshall (1930) explained that utility occurs when goods and services satisfy people's desires and wants. However, he said the inability to measure these desires and wants forces economists to concentrate on purchase behaviors in their analysis of utility (1930, p. 92). Since the *Principles of Economics* was first published in 1890, social science has progressed considerably in its understanding of people's behavior (Simon, 1997). Scholars have begun to investigate why people attend to media output. One such area of investigation has been called "uses and gratification" research (McQuail, 1994, pp. 318–321; Severin & Tankard, 2001, pp. 293–303), and a second area is "dependency theory" (DeFluer & Ball-Rokeach, 1989). Both approaches assume the consumer is an active participant in selecting media messages and that stable categories of media uses can be developed. However, existing uses and gratifications research has been criticized as being atheoretical, for having inconsistencies in defining categories of gratifications, and for failing to account for the fact that media consumers vary in how active they are in using media content (Severin & Tankard, 2001). Dependency theory has received little attention in empirical research. Despite criticisms, this research has potential as a starting point for integrated theories that combine economics with communication studies to provide better prediction and explanation of the media economic behavior of consumers.

Dimmick (2003) incorporated the idea of gratifications in his theory of the niche, which concerns media competition and is based on ecological studies about competition among animal species for resources. In a concept he calls "the gratification utility niche," he sees media industries competing for consumers by allowing them to gain gratifications (utility) from content. Dimmick used cognitive and affective gratifications to measure overlap among types of media. Although Dimmick acknowledges the potential for combining gratifications with utility theory, he uses the concept of gratifications as a way to measure degree of competition across media industries rather than a way to evaluate demand.

Adapting concepts from uses and gratifications research, dependency theory, and decisionmaking theory, Lacy (2000) suggested five categories of media use by consumers—surveillance, diversion, social–cultural interaction, decisionmaking, and self-understanding. He stated that consumers' use of media for these reasons provides utility, and that each consumer has a mix of media for producing utility in these five categories. He also presented a series of propositions about the media mix and how it responds to variations across time and across consumers. However, Lacy did not present a method for measuring the mix.

In a different approach, Lacy (2004) proposed that different types of utility exist for different consumers and products, and he suggested three layers of utility that, in turn, yield four types of utility. The first layer includes physiological utility (consumption of goods and services to benefit the body without requiring cognitive processing) and psychological utility (utility from cognitive reaction to the consumption of goods and services). Psychological utility is divided into experiential psychological utility (utility that comes from perceptions derived from experience with goods or services) and symbolic psychological utility (utility that comes from cognitive reaction to goods or services that involves symbols). Finally, symbolic psychological utility is divided into denotative utility (utility that comes from symbols that have a shared meaning with the majority of people) and connotative utility (utility that comes from more personalized meaning of symbols that are shared by smaller social groups).[1] Underlying this approach is the assumption that utility is a function of both the nature of goods and services and of the consumer's perception of those goods and services. Lacy argues that distinguishing among types of

---

[1]The terms *connotative* and *denotative* are commonly used in the study of general semantics. The exact origins of the terms are unclear, but Hayakawa (1941, p. 61) said the terms were borrowed from literary criticism.

utility allows scholars to better understand demand for symbolic products and the impact of advertising on consumer demand. However, he neglects measurement methods for these types of utilities.

Just as the concept of diversity needs to be dealt with in a more sophisticated manner, so does the relationship between content attributes and consumer utility. This could be accomplished using rational consumer models or models with other assumptions about consumers. Of particular use would be theories and models with taxonomies that would explicate the process of preference formation and work with both rational and nonrational assumptions of behavior.

All of these models address demand in the consumer market. Napoli (2003a) pointed out that little systematic study exists about the nature of audiences in the advertising market and the interaction between the consumer and advertising markets. His analysis describes the factors that affect the quality of audiences from an advertiser's perspective, and the current decline in audience quality that stems from the development of new technology that is fragmenting audiences and allowing audience members more autonomy. This analysis suggests a need to develop better theory for both the consumers and advertising markets as a step toward understanding the relationship between the two markets.

Future theories also should deal with this joint product nature of many media goods. Joint products, which involve two markets being served through one production process, were mentioned by Marshall (1930). Picard (1989) called this relationship dual products. Demand in one of these markets influences demand in the other. However, Marshall's discussion of joint products deals with joint products as a zero-sum game. This is inconsistent with media, where an increase in the number of consumers who read a magazine makes the magazine more valuable in the advertising market. Scholars have conducted empirical studies of media as joint products (Kalita & Ducoffe, 1995; Koschat & Putsis, 2000; Ludwig, 2000; Napoli, 2003b; Sonnac, 2000). With few exceptions (Wildman, 2003), however, theories of demand—either for the consumer or the advertising market incorporating the influence of the other dual market—remain underdeveloped. How does preference for media products affect the ability to concentrate consumers for advertising? Does media product differentiation result in more effective and efficient advertising?

## Economic Approaches to Supply Theory

The digitization of media and the globalization of media companies have created new challenges for managers and economists alike. The ability to digitize all forms of media allows for new configurations of existing media and the easy and cheap distribution of those forms. As a result, scholars have examined the impact of digitization on existing media industries. Van der Wurff (2002) found that digitization lowered barriers in professional information markets in The Netherlands. These lower barriers lead to more options for consumers, who redistribute their time to the new media outlets. Nieto (2003) studied audiences in Spain and found that new technology did not increase significantly the time spent with media, but it did redistribute it. Albarran and Dimmick (1996) found that cross-media economies of scope were declining as a result media concentration.

Newspapers took the initiative in repurposing content on-line, not only because they had a great deal of content that could be moved easily across dial-up service, but because they wanted to protect their classified advertising business. However, research indicates that the movement on-line has been haphazard (Saksena & Hollifield, 2002), that on-line newspapers have yet to draw large numbers of unique readers (Chyi & Lasorsa, 2002), and that the market structure of online versions of the newspapers differs from that of the print version (Chyi & Sylvie, 1998, 2001). Although newspapers were on-line early, increasing digitization is drawing cross-platform use of content in all media industries (Chan-Olmsted, 1998; Shaver & Shaver, 2003; Waterman, 2000).

Digitization effects production and distribution costs in a variety of ways. It can lower the costs, as occurs with placing newspaper and magazine content on the Internet, or it can increase costs to enhance quality, as happens with the vastly improved special effects found in popular films. However, the impact of digitization on media goes beyond simply changing cost structures. Digitized information flow, the diffusion of broadband networks, and significant advances in computing power have undermined traditional industry structures, as epitomized by the Internet. This has blurred the boundaries of the classic media industries. It has become fashionable to refer to the convergence of computing, telecommunications, and media as if a new mega-industry were about to emerge. Convergence is often misunderstood, and the diffusion of a general-purpose technology (convergence at the technical level) is confused with convergence at the level of business organizations and markets (Bauer, Weijnen, Turk, & Herder, 2003). Nevertheless, the transformation raises important economic, management, and policy questions. Among these issues are the reshaping of the vertical and horizontal boundaries of the firm, the need to define new business strategies to coordinate the different components of the changing value nets, and the delineation of markets (see Wirth, 2003).

As a result of increased competition from digitization, corporations find themselves moving toward acquisitions and strategic alliances that increase concentration within and across industries. One particular element of this concentration that often falls under the term "globalization" is the creation of transnational corporations. Globalization allows corporations to take advantage of economies of scope and scale by selling media products in multiple countries. Globalization existed before the digital revolution (Bates, 1998), but digitization enhances the advantages of transnational corporations. As a result, globalization has become part of media corporations' strategies (Gershon, 1997). For example, Holtz-Bacha (1997) examined the investment by U.S. companies in the growing German private television market. Andrews (2003) concentrated on content by analyzing transnational sports programming. Chan-Olmsted and Chang (2003) developed an analytical framework for examining variables that affect diversification strategies of global media conglomerates.

Globalization as a market strategy introduces variables related to affiliations and cultural connections, as well as issues of language and cultural differences. All content does not transfer equally well across cultures. Chan-Olmsted and Chang (2003) include these content variables under the heading of knowledge-based resources and argue that they are critical to the success of a transnational transfer of content. Of course, much work remains in developing measures that allow for understanding how content variables affect strategy. This issue is directly tied to the need for better models of consumer demand for media products.

### Industrial Organization Model

So far, the dominant framework in the exploration of media economics has been the industrial organization (IO) model. The original IO model was developed as a way to apply the various elements of microeconomic price theory to practical industrial problems (Caves, 1987, pp. 1–16). It organizes the analysis around the structure, conduct, and performance of firms in an industry and has been the basis of many studies and models examining media (Busterna, 1988; Chan-Olmsted, 1997; Lacy, 1992; Ramstad, 1997; van der Wurff, 2003). Wirth and Bloch criticized the use of the IO model, saying, "Furthermore, there has been a tendency to apply general relations drawn from the industrial organization model without adequate allowance for the specific circumstances of the problem" (1995, p. 23). Picard (2002) said the usual IO approaches to studying media are limited because they do not explain the behavior of individual firms in reaction to the environment. Young (2000) researched the criticisms of the IO model but found, in an empirical investigation of the television systems in Germany and the United Kingdom that market structure continues to play an important role in firm performance.

During the past three decades, the simple structure-conduct-performance model of traditional IO has gradually been augmented and superseded by the new industrial organization model (Tirole, 1988). Whereas the traditional model is built around the assumption of a relatively stable relation between market structure and performance, the new industrial organization model pays more detailed attention to firm decisions, conduct, and strategic interaction in markets. Utilizing game theoretic models, the approach has yielded, and promises further, new insights (see Owen & Wildman, 1992, for a review of the early emerging literature, and Laffont & Tirole, 2000, for its application to telecommunications). On the other hand, the new IO illustrates the sensitivity of market outcomes to the many interacting variables and the difficulty of establishing simple but general models. In this sense, it does not overcome some of the criticisms launched against the old IO model.

The discussion about the limits of the IO model in media economics reflects a larger debate about the role of management in economic theory. The reaction has been to develop a subfield called "managerial economics," which has taken elements of traditional economic theories and combined them with game theory to emphasize strategy selection by managers of firms (Fisher & Waschik, 2002; Png, 2001). Such approaches have the advantage of incorporating product differentiation and advertising into models of competition. For example, Doyle (1998) examined how regulation resulted in certain program types in a competitive broadcast industry. Gal-Or and Dukes (2003) used two-stage game theory to model product differentiation in commercial television, and differentiation's impact on dual markets. Other examples of such models based on rational economic approaches or game theory include a portfolio theory approach (Litman, Shrikhande, & Ahn, 2000) and the linkage between network programming and off-network syndication (Wildman & Robinson, 1995).

### Economics of Network Industries

Digitization and the diffusion of broadband network platforms enable new interactive services. As a result, many media segments will assume features that have recently been studied in the emerging literature on "network industries" (Gottinger, 2003; Shapiro & Varian, 1999; Shy, 2001). This class of models within the new IO seems, therefore, particularly promising for the future study of media industries, offering another conceptual lens with the potential to unify the field. As this perspective has not yet been widely adopted within media economics, it is useful to review some of its key components.

Several features are typical for network industries. First, production is typically characterized by economies of scale and scope. Economies of scale can have three related sources: fixed costs, learning effects, and technological change. Media economics has emphasized the first aspect by recognizing that many media products and services are produced with high fixed and zero (or very low) incremental cost.[2] Learning effects also can lead to a subadditive cost structure. Probably most important for economies of scale is technological change. An important unresolved issue is how improvements in the quality of services can be captured in measurements of technological change.

Network industries also exhibit strong complementarities among their different components. This is apparent in multimedia applications and services, which require the simultaneous interaction of content, software, and hardware, often configured using specific network platforms. For example, the streaming of news via mobile devices (phones, personal digital assistants [PDAs]) requires compatibility along a complex value net including content providers, network platform providers, application providers, and equipment manufacturers. The existence of such complementarities requires coordination among players at different stages of the value net. It has important consequences for the emerging industry structures and also raises complicated competition policy issues as it may increase the incentive for tacit collusion among the stakeholders. Moreover, as components work in a system, consumers typically face costs when switching to another vendor or service provider. Suppliers can take advantage of this fact and artificially increase switching costs. Shapiro and Varian (1999) distinguish among five forms of switching costs: contractual agreements, training and learning costs, search costs, consumer loyalty, and the cost of data conversion. Switching costs enhance the ability of suppliers to manipulate prices and competition, although it is difficult to determine when government intervention may be justified.

Network effects, a third feature, exist if the utility of consuming a media service is dependent on the overall number of users. Not all media industries exhibit network effects. Over-the-air broadcasting and one-way cable television service show weak network effects. Many new media services exhibit stronger positive (and sometimes negative) network effects. The utility of features of interactive television or cable television, such as audience games, or services such as e-mail, mobile messaging, or the World Wide Web is, at least in part, dependent on the number of users. If such effects cannot be internalized, network externalities—and hence a form of market failure—prevail (Liebowitz & Margolis, 2003). The repercussions of network effects on market structure and competition depend on the specific form of the relation between network size and total benefits. In principle, these benefits can grow linearly, slower, or faster than the number of

---

[2]Given nonrivalry in consumption, many authors classify media and information products as public goods. This is at least partially misleading, as pure public goods also require the presence of nonexcludability, which is not the case for most media products.

participants. There is evidence that in many networks the overall benefits to participants follow an S-shaped curve (Gottinger, 2003). Initially, the incremental benefit of a new user increases whereas it starts to decrease in more mature networks. Unless a network reaches the "critical mass" of participants, it will not be able to grow successfully and may eventually disappear. First movers may enjoy critical advantages and, in cases of competing technologies and heterogeneous user preferences, the inferior technology may get locked in. If gateway or converter technologies exist, network effects are mitigated (Gottinger, 2003). Network effects work both ways, and it may be that they aggravate an industry downturn, as seems to have happened during the dot-com crash in 2000.

Media economics could gain tremendously from the adoption of network and game theory as well as other approaches associated with managerial economics. The role of managerial strategy remains central to competition in imperfect markets. At the same time, strategies have beginning points and ending points, and market structures at these points play a role in strategy. The field needs more dynamic, recursive theories that take advantage of the wealth of recent theoretical work as well as the unique position of media as goods that affect the political and cultural nature of societies. Producing media products remains very different from producing shoes. If media firms ignore this simple fact, how does it affect their performance and a country's policy? Such dynamic and cross-disciplinary theories need to be extensive enough to identify with some precision the processes by which relationships among variables develop and change.

## POLICY TOWARD MEDIA FIRMS AND INDUSTRIES

Media have unique features raising special policy issues. The dual nature of media markets, linking the production of content to draw audiences and the selling of the audiences in the advertising markets, have been widely recognized (Owen & Wildman, 1992; Picard, 1989; Wildman, 1998). Most importantly, however, media are self-reflexive: More than other industries, they simultaneously produce economic goods and cultural goods, such as meaning and shared perceptions. Given this important role for society at large, it is not surprising that they are entrenched in intense policy debates and subject to various forms of oversight and control (Napoli, 2001; Owen, 1975). The specific institutional framework of media is contingent upon the broader political and cultural traditions and arrangements of nations and cannot be discussed in detail in this chapter. In the United States, for example, the First Amendment creates particular protections from government oversight of content. Similar provisions, although often not as stringent, can be found in the constitutions of other democratic nations. However, on a global scale, other media models exist that envision and define the role of media differently (see Siebert, Peterson, & Schramm, 1963, for an early study), creating different economic conditions for media.

Just and Latzer (2003) point out that early predecessors of contemporary media economics, such as Karl Marx and Max Weber, understood the twin roles of media and thus developed comprehensive political–economic theories (see also Hardt, 1988). Political economists who study communication continue to pursue such a broader research agenda (Calabrese & Sparks, 2004; Garnham, 1990; Mosco, 1996; Sussman, 1997). With the expansion of interest in media economics, the discipline shifted toward the neoclassical paradigm. A quick glance at introductory texts (Albarran, 1996; Alexander, Owers, & Carveth, 1998; Low, 2000; Picard, 1989) and the journal literature confirms this development. The growing body of media economic research recognizes the role of public policy for media industries and the need to address public policy issues. However, the multiple transformations of media industries (digitization, convergence, and globalization) challenge present policies, and renewed attention to public policy issues within the discipline would be desirable. Media economics could contribute to the resolution of these issues at a conceptual and empirical level. The following sections review the past and potential future role of media economics for selected public policy issues.

## Conceptualizing Government and Governance

During the 20th century, notions of the role of government in the economy underwent several major transitions, and policy research within media economics could benefit from some of the recent insights. Most media economic research models government as an exogenous agent aiming at increasing welfare in situations of market failure (see, for example, Picard, 1989, pp. 94–102). The existence of market power, the prevalence of externalities, or the public and merit good aspects of media are seen as typical reasons for government intervention into media markets. Government action may also be justified in cases where unfettered market outcomes conflict with widely shared views of fairness and equity. This view of government was challenged beginning in the 1960s. Most importantly, it was recognized that government is an endogenous actor within the institutional framework of a society.

The first wave of criticism emanated from research on the informational structure of policymaking and the actual working of policy, which emphasized potential flaws in the functioning of government. Early work emphasized that asymmetric information would render government susceptible to capture by special interests (Becker, 1983; Peltzman, 1976; Stigler, 1971) or that rent-seeking behavior would jeopardize any potential efficiency gains (Buchanan, Tollison & Tullock, 1980). The renewed interest in institutions has demonstrated the flaws in these claims but nevertheless solidified the view of government as endogenous to the overall social system (Denzau & North, 1994; Eggertsson, 1998). Most recently, scholars have begun to rethink the prospects and limits of public policy toward information industries through the lens of complexity theory (Bauer, 2004; Longstaff, 2003).

These conceptual frameworks sharpened the view of government as a self-interested actor, constrained by multiple factors, including legal, economic, and political conditions. As a result, the power of government to effectively regulate and control is seen as significantly reduced. This does not imply, however, that government policy does not matter. It does shape and govern private-sector and individual decisions; institutional arrangements and policy matter, but they do so in complex ways. Such a view of government as an endogenous actor is particularly valuable in modeling its interaction with the media industries, and should help to develop more powerful and comprehensive theories. This conceptual lens could be further expanded to encompass other forms of governance, such as co-regulation and self-regulation (Campbell, 1999; Latzer, Just, Saurwein, & Slominski, 2003).

It would also allow a more systematic study of the unintended consequences of technology and regulation. The proliferation of technology platforms and media have increased the complexity of the sector and greatly complicated the design of effective policy. Incomplete information, institutional constraints, and systemic constraints, because of the need to reconcile many stakeholder interests, are omnipresent. Moreover, the relation between policy instruments and goals may not be stable because of pervasive feedbacks. As a result, technological change and policy actions may result in unintended and unanticipated consequences. Among the few studies of this phenomenon are Einstein (2004), who examined the effects of the Fin/Syn rules, and the work by Walker and Bellamy (1993) on the impact of the remote control. Similar innovative approaches to other media questions, such as the effects of the Internet seem to offer a promising avenue for further research.

## Public Interest Mandate

Over-the-air broadcast media in the United States are granted free spectrum usage rights and, as a quid pro quo, are treated as trustees of the public interest. This setup contributes to an uneasy tension between commercial considerations and public interest demands. The meaning of "public interest" is notoriously difficult to determine (Napoli, 2001). As close substitutes to over-the-air broadcasting can be offered using other platforms, such as cable systems, satellite television, or the Internet, the policy compact upon which this model is based is increasingly fragile. Media economists have contributed extensively to this discussion. Among the conceptual issues that deserve further attention is the question of whether an explicit public interest mandate is desirable or whether the growing diversity of supply options has rendered it obsolete. If a public interest charge is considered necessary, a corollary question is how it should best be implemented.

Attempting to answer the first question, media economists typically look for evidence of market failure. Several authors have emphasized the merit good character of certain types of programming, such as news, documentaries, or educational programming. The merit good argument is predicated on the assumption that an individual's preferences are somewhat distorted. Such deformed preferences can be the result of imperfect information, or they can emanate from the difficulties of evaluating the effects of exposure to media content. In any case, the government is considered a superior judge and a "paternalistic intervention" is thus seen as justified. Certain types of programming, such as violent content, could be modeled as afflicted with externalities, providing a possible rationale for government policy. Building on earlier contributions, Owen and Wildman (1992) showed that in dual markets increased competition does not necessarily enhance the diversity and quality of the program offering. Somewhat along the same line, Berry and Waldfogel (2001) found that mergers actually increase program diversity in radio markets. Although this research has contributed interesting findings, it does not yield unambiguous recommendations as to whether a public interest mandate is desirable.

One interesting problem, related to the public interest remit, is the formation of preferences for content as well as the formation of beliefs as to what content can satisfy certain needs. As discussed earlier, media economics has contributed significantly to an understanding of program choices. Yet it might be promising to enrich the present modeling efforts with insights from behavioral economics and behavioral game theory

(Camerer, 2003; Camerer, Loewenstein, & Rabin, 2004). This research paradigm finds utilitarian theory and revealed preference theory, with its emphasis on consistency, as wanting because they do not address questions of motivation and preference evolution (Bowles, 2004). At least in principle, behavioral and experimental economics could enhance theories of the formation of media preferences and media choices under time constraints. Such a perspective could contribute to a better understanding of the notion of a "marketplace of ideas," in which unrestricted competition among many media outlets is seen as contributing to the emergence of "truth." The limited capacity of individuals for information processing, as well as habit formation with regard to media sources and consumption, may lend credence to interpretations of the First Amendment, expressed most clearly in *Red Lion v. FCC* (1969), that emphasize the right of the audience to receive balanced information. They may also shed new light on the debate on the effects of violent or pornographic content on minors and the related constitutional issues (Saunders, 1996, 2003). From this perspective, and against prevailing wisdom, a public interest mandate may become more important as media proliferate. The media economic research program could also help design the most effective means to realize such objectives, ranging from market-based solutions and self-regulation, to government-adopted standards, cooperative production, or even government supply (Campbell, 1999; Hamilton, 2004).

## Convergence and Internet Policy

Digitization of information flow, significant advances in computing power and the diffusion of broadband networks undermine traditional industry structures. New digital communication platforms allow the configuration of innovative synchronous and asynchronous services such as on-line newspapers, interactive television, virtual worlds, online gaming, and blogs. They easily transcend national boundaries, thus raising new and complicated international policy issues. Media economics has contributed to the convergence discussion (see the special issue of *The International Journal of Media Management* edited by Wirth, 2003), but more work at the conceptual and empirical level seems warranted. Early research on convergence was influenced by the widely shared vision that computing, telecommunications, and content would amalgamate and eventually fuse into a mega–media industry. Recent developments, including the spectacular failures of merger and acquisition strategies premised on this viewpoint, such as the AOL–Time Warner combination or the Vivendi Universal expansion, have challenged this model. Convergence is clearly happening, but it is often misunderstood. It is most visible at the technological level, where it has led to the wide diffusion of general-purpose technologies such as the Internet or other broadband networks. Convergence is also a reality at the level of advanced terminal equipment and selected multimedia services.

Technical convergence must not be confused with a convergence at the level of business organizations and markets. Indeed, the opposite should be expected. If competitive advantage cannot be secured at the level of communication platforms, firms with different resource endowments will make strong efforts to differentiate themselves at the level of business models, applications, and services. Neither does convergence necessitate integrated legal and regulatory frameworks and institutions as is often implied (Garcia-Murillo & MacInnes, 2003; Latzer, 1998).

Convergence raises several important policy issues. One important question is how markets can be delineated to determine their competitive structure and possible regulatory or antitrust action (Just & Latzer, 2000). Convergence may also create new access barriers, as is pinpointed in the debate on the digital divide. Although the digital divide discussion touches an important issue, it is in need of theoretical and conceptual clarification. Convergence also raises the question of what legal and regulatory model should govern the Internet. Until recently, cyberlibertarians and policymakers alike have demanded that the Internet remain free from regulation. As the Internet matures, it is evident that the bottom-up self-regulatory model envisioned by these stakeholders may not be the most effective approach and that other forms of governance may be needed. Melody (2003) distinguishes four areas (infrastructure, technical parameters, security, and applications) that potentially need oversight. Many of these issues will need to be addressed at the international level, and the current second phase of the World Summit on the Information Society (WSIS) is attempting to develop a blueprint for action.

## Media Ownership, Consolidation, and Globalization

Media ownership turned out to be the most contested issue of American communication policy in 2003. This issue is closely related to the public interest mandate of media but deserves treatment in a separate section. In the United States, the First Amendment places stringent constraints on the ability of the government to regulate content directly. Structural rules were historically used as proxy instruments to overcome this constraint and pursue widely accepted policy goals such as localism and diversity (Napoli, 2001). Together with licensing policies, media ownership rules had a major impact on the structure of the media industries. For example, they contributed to the fact that until the 1980s only three commercial networks existed. As the number of licensees expanded, ownership limits were repeatedly relaxed. The Telecommunications Act of 1996, while retaining a relaxed set of local rules, eliminated national radio ownership limits, thus unleashing a major consolidation in this industry.

In the wake of deregulation, industry went to court to challenge the remaining rules, such as national limits on the number of television households reached by stations belonging to one firm. Several court decisions, such as *Sinclair Broadcast Group v. FCC* (2002), challenged the existing ownership rules for lack of empirical evidence that these regulations contributed to the government's stated goals.[3] Media economic research has contributed to addressing open issues both theoretically and empirically (Compaine & Gomery, 2000; see also Noam, 2003). The FCC commissioned 12 background studies to inform its 2003 review of the existing ownership rules.[4] In an attempt to provide empirical support for its decisions, the FCC adopted a "diversity index" modeled after

---

[3]See Federal Communications Commission, Report and Order and Notice of Proposed Rulemaking, *In the Matter of 2002 Biennial Regulatory Review—Review of the Commission's Broadcast Ownership Rules and Other Rules Adopted Pursuant to Section 202 of the Telecommunications Act of 1996* (MB Docket 02-277), *Cross-Ownership of Broadcast Stations and Newspapers* (MM Docket 01-235), *Rules and Policies Concerning Multiple Ownership of Radio Broadcast Stations in Local Markets* (MM Docket 01-317), *Definition of Radio Markets* (MM Docket 00-244), and *Definition of Radio Markets for Areas Not Located in an Arbitron Survey Area* (MB Docket 03-130), 3 July 2003.

[4]The studies are available at http://www.fcc.gov/ownership/studies.html

the Herfindahl–Hirschman index (HHI) to assess diversity in media markets. Although perhaps a step forward, this index does not address the question of diversity of content per se and many of the conceptual issues remain unresolved. There is a danger that the debate over media ownership remains mired in emotional arguments. It would be desirable to ground decisions in solid empirical evidence; further exploration in this area should therefore be pursued. Research along these lines could also improve knowledge of how the organization of media production (public, private, or cooperative) affects innovation and the quality of output.

## Intellectual Property

Media economics is concerned with the production and distribution of content. One of the most significant global public policy issues is the specification of intellectual property rights. Although the traditional rationale for the establishment of intellectual property rights is economic, with very few exceptions (Landes & Posner, 2003), the discipline has relegated this important discussion to the legal profession, and, more recently, to technologists working on methods of digital rights management (DRM). A critical look reveals that many issues of copyright protection, in which media economists should be most interested, are not settled in a theoretically or empirically satisfactory way. It is striking, for example, how little work has been dedicated to exploring the exact relation between copyright protection and creative activity. Likewise, the optimal duration of copyright and the optimal degree of differentiation of rights have not been investigated thoroughly. Information technology allows greater differentiation of copyright, and some experimentation that would allow for empirical work is already going on. One example of this is in the open source movement and the innovative licenses developed by the Creative Commons project. A further, relatively open question is the enforcement of copyright. Gilbert and Katz (2001) have addressed this issue and clarified some of the open research questions. Overall, intellectual property issues promise some low-hanging fruit for media economists.

## FUTURE RESEARCH

The debate Landau and Davenport (1959) had with Currier (1960a) 45 years ago continues to frame the discussion of media economics, but less as a debate and more as a way of suggesting approaches to research. Existing economic models should be used to analyze media industries and firms, but scholars should not be timid in trying theoretical approaches that incorporate variables exogenous to traditional economic analysis.

Media economics is a relatively young field. As it matures, we expect that it will employ a broader range of methods. One particular direction here is the wider application of mathematical models using calculus. Recent research shows that maximization models are relatively good approximations of relatively stable, repeated decisionmaking situations. Even under conditions of incomplete knowledge, an individual's decisions converge toward an optimal choice after several iterations. Calculus is less suited to analysis of decisionmaking under continuously changing conditions, as are typical for many media industries. In these situations, other tools, such as evolutionary models (e.g., urn processes, Markov chain models) could be utilized to expand the present toolkit of media economics. Although formalization forces the researcher to think through the logical structure and consequence of a problem, it is a method a priori. Thus historical, empirical, and applied research will continue to play an important role in media economics in addition to more formal methods.

On the supply side of microeconomics, mainstream economics offers powerful tools to analyze the behavior of media firms. Developments related to managerial economics, such as game theory and network theory, hold great promise. These approaches fit well with the recent emphasis in media economics on market strategy. However, the adoption of the new does not necessitate that all elements of the older approaches be abandoned. The IO model continues to be a framework that can be useful when modified and incorporated with new approaches. Market structure continues to define the environment in which media firms operate. For example, Fisher and Waschik (2002) point out that the application of game theory starts with assumptions about the number of players, which is, in effect, market structure. However, any integration of theoretical approaches must be dynamic and recognize the recursive nature of economic factors.

Market structure also continues to play an important role in media economics because it is the starting point for the interaction between supply and demand. Structure depends on the number of firms and the nature of the product. Both of these elements define competition, but they also reflect consumer demand. One of the problems facing scholars who study media economics, as well as managers of media firms, is the need for demand theory that allows better prediction. For example, the cross-elasticity of demand determines the level of competition for products. However, price cross-elasticity of demand is of limited importance in measuring media competition, and no adequate measure exists for quality cross-elasticity of demand for differentiated products. Efforts to expand the number of endogenous demand variables have made progress (Becker & Murphy, 2000; Camerer, Loewenstein, & Rabin, 2004). Given the unique features of media industries, transdisciplinary collaboration could yield valuable insights as well. Among the disciplines with great promise for media economics are cognitive science, psychology, sociology, and anthropology, all of which could enhance the study of media demand and supply issues. The former two disciplines could strengthen research on the formation of tastes and media preferences as well as the effects of media. The latter two could improve insights as to the use of media (such as mobile devices) at the individual and organizational level.

This integrated approach would involve models that retain assumptions of rational decisionmaking and models that drop assumptions of utility maximization and equilibrium analysis. Nonmaximization models and theory should, however, deal in more detail with the processes underlying economic behavior. Conceptual models that simply identify relationships can be useful, but theories that explain and describe behavioral processes are essential for effective policy and for the evolutionary development of human behavior. Predictive models are not enough if we hope to understand and influence our own behavior.

The call for scholarship that aims to integrate the paradigm of neoclassical economics with other fields is far from new. This cross-disciplinary approach to demand is even hinted at by Marshall. He believed economics should extend beyond the formal analysis because economics is a study of humans as biological entities (1930, p. xv). He wrote about demand theory:

> From this it follows that such a discussion of demand as is possible at this stage of our work, must be confined to an elementary analysis of an almost purely formal kind. The higher study of consumption must come after, and not before, the main body of economic analysis; and, though it may have a beginning within the proper domain of economics, it cannot find its conclusion there, but must extend far beyond. (1930, pp. 90–91)

The digital transformation of mediated content is affecting the supply and demand conditions of media and challenges the established legal and policy framework. These fundamental changes raise many interesting research questions and should serve as catalysts for a continued vigorous research program. Like other disciplines, media economics has spawned research results at different, related levels and will continue to do so. Theoretical work should broaden and deepen the epistemic knowledge base of the field. At the same time, theories have to abstract from the detailed features of specific cases and are thus no direct guide for management decisions. Applied work can complement theoretical work with the creation of practical knowledge, which is rooted in the epistemic base but augmented with insights from experience (Mokyr, 2002). Particularly interesting research areas include but are not limited to:

- Determinants of demand for media and the allocation of time and attention to the proliferating options
- The formation of preferences and tastes for media and content
- Further exploration of the dual nature of media markets
- Application of the new industrial economics and game theory to the study of individual firm behavior and sector performance
- Attempts to reconcile the economic and cultural dimensions of media
- Clarification of the meaning and implications of "convergence" and its repercussions for media policy
- A critical analysis of the relation between intellectual property rights and creative activity
- Media governance and the effects of different governance regimes (private ownership, collective control, commons) and forms of regulation (government regulation, coregulation, self-regulation) and media performance
- Prospects and limits of governance, including unintended consequences, of firm strategies on media policy

New insights are most likely if a methodologically and theoretically pluralistic approach is pursued. At present, a gap seems to exist between media economists working within traditional economics departments and those affiliated with other programs in media management, journalism, information studies, and communications. Bridging this interior gap as well as a willingness to cross-fertilize with other disciplines should maintain and enhance the vitality of the field.

# REFERENCES

Albarran, A. B. (1996). *Media economics: Understanding markets, industries, and concepts*. Ames: Iowa State University Press.

Albarran, A. B., & Dimmick, J. (1996). Concentration and economics of multiformity in the communications industries. *Journal of Media Economics, 9,* 41–50.

Alexander, A., Owers, J., & Carveth, R. (Eds.). (1998). *Media economics: Theory and practice* (2nd ed.). Mahwah, NJ: Lawrence Erlbaum Associates.

Andrews, D. L. (2003). Sport and the trans-nationalizing media corporation. *Journal of Media Economics, 16,* 235–251.

Bates, B. J. (1998). Going global: The economics of transborder video. In R. G. Picard (Ed.), *Evolving media markets: Effects of economic and policy changes* (pp. 82–119). Turku, Finland: Turku School of Economics and Business Administration.

Bauer, J. M. (2004). Harnessing the swarm: Communications policy in an era of ubiquitous networks and disruptive technologies. *Communications & Strategies, 54,* 19–43.

Bauer, J. M., Weijnen, M. P. C., Turk, A. L., & Herder, P. M. (2003). Delineating the scope of convergence in infrastructures: New frontiers for competition. In W. A. H. Thissen & P. M. Herder (Eds.), *Critical infrastructures—State of the art in research and application* (pp. 209–231). Boston: Kluwer.

Becker, G. S. (1971). *Economic theory*. New York: Alfred A. Knopf.

Becker, G. S. (1983). A theory of competition among pressure groups for political influence. *Quarterly Journal of Economics, 98,* 371–400.

Becker, G. S. (1996). *Accounting for tastes*. Cambridge, MA: Harvard University Press.

Becker, G. S., & Murphy, K. M. (2000). *Social economics: Market behavior in a social environment*. Cambridge, MA: The Belknap Press of Harvard University Press.

Berry, S. T., & Waldfogel, J. (2001). Do mergers increase product variety? Evidence from radio broadcasting. *Quarterly Journal of Economics, 116,* 1009–1025.

Bowles, S. (2004). *Microeconomics: Behavior, institutions, and evolution*. New York: Russell Sage Foundation; Princeton, NJ: Princeton University Press.

Buchanan, J. M., Tollison, R. D., & Tullock, G. (Eds.) (1980). *Toward a theory of the rent-seeking society*. College Station: Texas A&M University.

Busterna, J. C. (1988). Concentration and the industrial organization model. In R. G. Picard, J. P. Winter, M. E. McCombs, & S. Lacy (Eds.), *Press concentration and monopoly* (pp. 35–53). Norwood, NJ: Ablex.

Calabrese, A., & Sparks, C. (2004). *Toward a political economy of culture: Capitalism and communication in the twenty-first century*. Lanham, MD: Rowman & Littlefield.

Camerer, C. F. (2003). *Behavioral game theory: Experiments in strategic interaction*. New York: Russell Sage Foundation; Princeton, NJ: Princeton University Press.

Camerer, C. F., Loewenstein, G., & Rabin, M. (2004). *Advances in behavioral economics*. New York: Russell Sage Foundation; Princeton, NJ: Princeton University Press.

Campbell, A. J. (1999). Self-regulation and the media. *Federal Communications Law Journal, 51,* 711–772.

Caves, R. (1987). *American industry: Structure, conduct, performance* (6th ed.). Englewoods Cliffs, NJ: Prentice-Hall.

Chamberlin, E. H. (1962). *The theory of monopolistic competition* (8th ed.). Cambridge, MA: Harvard University Press.

Chan-Olmsted, S. M. (1997). Theorizing multichannel media economics: An exploration of a group-industry strategic competition model. *Journal of Media Economics, 10*(1), 39–49.

Chan-Olmsted, S. M. (1998). Mergers, acquisitions, and convergence: The strategic alliance of broadcasting, cable television, and telephone services. *Journal of Media Economics, 11*(3), 33–46.

Chan-Olmsted, S. M., & Chang, B. H. (2003). Diversification strategy of global media conglomerates: Examining its patterns and determinants. *Journal of Media Economics, 16,* 213–233.

Chyi, H. I., & Lasorsa, D. L. (2002). An explorative study on the market relation between online and print newspapers. *Journal of Media Economics, 15,* 91–106.

Chyi, H. I., & Sylvie, G. (1998). Competing with whom? Where? An how? A structural analysis of the electronic newspaper market. *Journal of Media Economics, 11*(2), 1–18.

Chyi, H. I., & Sylvie, G. (2001). The medium is global, the content is not: The role of geography in online newspaper markets. *Journal of Media Economics, 14*, 231–248.

Compaine, B. M., & Gomery, D. (2000). *Who owns the media? Competition and concentration in the mass media industry.* Mahwah, NJ: Lawrence Erlbaum Associates.

Currier, F. (1960a). Economic theory and its application to newspapers. *Journalism Quarterly, 37*, 255–258.

Currier, F. (1960b). A further comment from Currier. *Journalism Quarterly, 37*, 260.

Davenport, J. S., & Landau, E. (1960). Replies from Davenport and Landau. *Journalism Quarterly, 37*, 258–260.

DeFluer, M. L., & Ball-Rokeach, S. (1989). *Theories of mass communication* (5th ed.). White Plains, NY: Longman.

Denzau, A. T., & North, D. C. (1994). Shared mental models: Ideologies and institutions. *Kyklos, 47*, 3–31.

Dimmick, J. W. (2003). *Media competition and coexistence: The theory of the niche.* Mahwah, NJ: Lawrence Erlbaum Associates.

Doyle, C. (1998). Programming in a competitive broadcasting market: Entry, welfare, and regulation. *Information Economics and Policy, 10*, 23–39.

Eggertsson, T. (1998). Limits to institutional reform. *Scandinavian Journal of Economics, 100*, 335–357.

Einstein, M. (2004). The financial interest and syndication rules and changes in program diversity. *Journal of Media Economics, 17*, 1–18.

Fisher, C. G., & Waschik, R. G. (2002). *Managerial economics: A game theoretical approach.* London: Routledge.

Gal-Or, E., & Dukes, A. (2003). Minimum differentiation in commercial media markets. *Journal of Economics & Management Strategy, 12*, 291–325.

Garcia-Murillo, M., & MacInnes, I. (2003). The impact of technological convergence on the regulation of ICT industries. *International Journal on Media Management, 5*, 57–67.

Garnham, N. (1990). In F. Inglis (Ed.), *Capitalism and communication: Global culture and the economics of information.* Newbury Park, CA: Sage.

Gershon, R. (1997). *The transnational media corporation: Global messages and free market competition.* Mahwah, NJ: Lawrence Erlbaum Associates.

Gilbert, R. J., & Katz, M. E. (2001). When good value chains go bad: The economics of indirect liability for copyright infringement. *The Hastings Law Journal, 52*, 961–990.

Gottinger, H. W. (2003). *Economies of networks.* London: Routledge.

Hamilton, J. T. (2004). *All the news that's fit to sell: How the market transforms information into news.* Princeton, NJ: Princeton University Press.

Hardt, H. (1988). Communication and economic thought: Cultural imagination in German and American scholarship. *Communication, 10*, 141–163.

Hayakawa, S. I. (1941). *Language in action.* New York: Harcourt, Brace, and Company.

Holtz-Bacha, C. (1997). Development of the German media market: Opportunities and challenges for U.S. media firms. *Journal of Media Economics, 10*(4), 39–58.

Just, N., & Latzer, M. (2000). EU competition policy and market power control in the mediamatics era. *Telecommunications Policy, 24*, 395–411.

Just, N., & Latzer, M. (2003). Ökonomische Theorien der Medien. In S. Weber (Ed.), *Theorien der Medien* (pp. 81–107). Konstanz, Germany: UTB.

Kalita, J. K., & Ducoffe, R. H. (1995). A simultaneous-equation analysis of pricing, circulation, and advertising revenue for leading consumer magazines. *Journal of Media Economics, 8*(4), 1–16.

Koschat, M. A., & Putsis, W. P., Jr. (2000). Who wants you when you're old and poor? Exploring the economics of media pricing. *Journal of Media Economics, 13*, 215–232.

Lacy, S. (1992). The financial commitment model of news media competition. *Journal of Media Economics, 5*(2), 5–21.

Lacy, S. (2000). Commitment of resources as a measure of quality. In R. G. Picard (Ed.), *Measuring media content, quality, and diversity: Approaches and issues in content research* (pp. 25–50). Turku, Finland: Turku School of Economics and Business Administration.

Lacy, S. (2004). Fuzzy markets structure and differentiation: One size does not fit all. In R. G. Picard (Ed.), *Strategic responses to media market changes* (pp. 83–95). Jönköping, Sweden: Jönköping International Business School.

Lacy, S., & Simon, T. F. (1993). *The economics and regulation of United States newspapers.* Norwood, NJ: Ablex.

Laffont, J. J., & Tirole, J. (2000). *Competition in telecommunications.* Cambridge, MA: MIT Press.

Landau, E., & Davenport, J. S. (1959). Price anomalies in the mass media. *Journalism Quarterly, 36,* 291–294.

Landes, W. M., & Posner, R. A. (2003). *The economic structure of intellectual property law.* Cambridge, MA: Belknap Press of Harvard University Press.

Latzer, M. (1998). European mediamatics policies: Coping with convergence and globalization. *Telecommunications Policy, 22,* 457–466.

Latzer, M., Just, N., Saurwein, F., & Slominski, P. (2003). Regulation remixed: Institutional change through self and co-regulation in the mediamatics sector. *Communications and Strategies, 50,* 127–157.

Li, S. S., & Chiang, C. (2001). Market competition and programming diversity: A study of the TV market in Taiwan. *Journal of Media Economics, 14,* 105–199.

Liebowitz, S. J., & Margolis, S. E. (2003). Network effects. In M. E. Cave, S. K. Majumdar, & I. Vogelsang (Eds.), *Handbook of telecommunications economics* (Vol. 1, pp. 75–96). Amsterdam: North Holland/Elsevier.

Litman, B. (1979). The television networks, competition and program diversity. *Journal of Broadcasting, 23,* 393–409.

Litman, B. R. (1991). *Economic aspects of program quality.* Unpublished report, East Lansing: Michigan State University.

Litman, B. R., Shrikhande, S., & Ahn, H. (2000). A portfolio theory approach to network program selection. *Journal of Media Economics, 13,* 57–79.

Longstaff, P. (2003, July). *The puzzle of competition in the communications sector: Can complex systems be regulated or managed?* Program on Information Resources Policy Working Paper, Harvard University.

Low, L. (2000). *Economics of information technology and the media.* Singapore: Singapore University Press.

Ludwig, J. (2000). The essential economic problem of the media: Working between market failure and cross-financing. *Journal of Media Economics, 13,* 187–200.

Marshall, A. (1930). *Principles of economics* (8th ed.). London: Macmillan.

McQuail, D. (1994). *Mass communication theory: An introduction* (3rd ed.). London: Sage.

Melody, W. H. (2003, May 1). *Can the Internet economy be governed and if so, how?* Lecture given at the London School of Economics. Retrieved March 2, 2005 from http://www.lse.ac.uk/objects/2003/08/15/20030815t1601z001.pdf

Mokyr, J. (2002). *The gifts of Athena: Historical origins of the knowledge economy.* Princeton, NJ: Princeton University Press.

Mosco, V. (1996). *The political economy of communication: Rethinking and renewal.* London: Sage.

Napoli, P. M. (2001). *Foundations of communications policy: Principles and process in the regulation of electronic media.* Creskill, NJ: Hampton Press.

Napoli, P. M. (2003a). *Audience economics: Media institutions and the audience marketplace.* New York: Columbia University Press.

Napoli, P. M. (2003b). Environmental conditions in a dual-product marketplace: A participant-observation perspective on the U.S. broadcast television industry. *International Journal on Media Management, 5,* 100–108.

Nieto, A. (2003). Media markets as time markets: The case of Spain. In A. B. Albarran & A. Arrese (Eds.), *Time and media markets* (pp. 127–144). Mahwah, NJ: Lawrence Erlbaum Associates.

Noam, E. M. (2003, October 2). *Testimony on media ownership before the U.S. Senate Committee on Commerce, Science, and Transportation.* Retrieved March 2, 2005 from http://commerce.senate.gov/hearings/testimony.cfm?id=950&wit_id=2681

Owen, B. M. (1975). *Economics and freedom of expression: Media structure and the First Amendment.* Cambridge, MA: Ballinger.

Owen, B. M., & Wildman, S. S. (1992). *Video economics.* Cambridge, MA: Harvard University Press.

Peltzman, S. (1976). Toward a more general Theory of regulation. *Journal of Law and Economics, 19,* 211–240.

Picard, R. G. (1989). *Media economics: Concepts and issues.* Newbury Park, CA: Sage.

Picard, R. G. (2002). The centrality of media firms. In R. G. Picard (Ed.), *Media firms: Structures, operations and performance* (pp. 1–7). Mahwah, NJ: Lawrence Erlbaum Associates.

Png, I. (2001). *Managerial economics* (2nd ed.). Oxford: Blackwell.

Ramstad, G. O. (1997). A model for structural analysis of the media market. *Journal of Media Economics, 10*(3), 45–50.

Red Lion Broadcasting Co. v. FCC, 395 U.S 367 (1969).

Saksena, S., & Hollifield, C. A. (2002). U.S. newspapers and the development of online editions. *International Journal on Media Management, 4,* 75–84.

Saunders, K. (1996). *Violence as obscenity: Limiting the media's First Amendment protection.* Durham, NC: Duke University Press.

Saunders, K. (2003). *Saving our children from the First Amendment.* New York: New York University Press.

Severin, W. J., & Tankard, J. W., Jr. (2001). *Communication theories: Origins, methods, and uses in the mass media* (5th ed.). New York: Longman.

Shapiro, C., & Varian, H. (1999). *Information rules.* Boston: Harvard University Press.

Shaver, D., & Shaver, M. A. (2003). Books and digital technology: A new industry model. *Journal of Media Economics, 16,* 71–86.

Shy, O. (2001). *The economics of network industries.* Cambridge, MA: Cambridge University Press.

Siebert, F. S., Peterson, T., & Schramm, W. (1963). *Four theories of the press: The authoritarian, libertarian, social responsibility, and Soviet communist concepts of what the press should be and do.* Urbana: University of Illinois Press.

Simon, H. A. (1957). *Models of man.* New York: Wiley.

Simon, H. A. (1997). *An empirically based microeconomic.* Cambridge: Cambridge University Press.

Sinclair Broadcast Group v. FCC, 284 F.3d 148 (D.C. Cir. 2002).

Sonnac, N. (2000). Readers' attitudes toward press advertising: Are they ad-lovers or ad-averse? *Journal of Media Economics, 13,* 249–259.

Stigler, G. J. (1952). *The theory of price* (Rev. ed.). New York: The Macmillan Co.

Stigler, G. J. (1971). The economic theory of regulation, *Bell Journal of Economics and Management Science, 2,* 3–21.

Sussman, G. (1997). *Communication, technology, and politics in the information age.* Thousand Oaks, CA: Sage.

Tirole, J. (1988). *The theory of industrial organization.* Cambridge, MA: MIT Press.

van der Wurff, R. (2002). Competition, innovation and performance of professional information providers. In R. G. Picard (Ed.), *Media firms: Structures, operations, and performance* (pp. 41–58). Mahwah, NJ: Lawrence Erlbaum Associates.

van der Wurff, R. (2003). Structure, conduct, and performance of the agricultural trade journal market in the Netherlands. *Journal of Media Economics, 16,* 121–138.

Walker, J. R., & Bellamy, V. R., Jr. (Eds.). (1993). *The remote control in the new age of television.* Westport, CT: Praeger.

Waterman, D. (1989/1990). Diversity and quality of information products in a monopolistically competitive industry. *Information Economics and Policy, 4,* 291–303.

Waterman, D. (2000). CBS–Viacom and the effects of media mergers: An economic perspective. *Federal Communication Law Journal, 52,* 531–550.

Wildman, S. S. (1998). Toward a better integration of media economics and media competition policy. In R. G. Noll & M. E. Price (Eds.), *A communications cornucopia: Markle Foundation essays on information policy* (pp. 573–593). Washington, DC: The Brookings Institution.

Wildman, S. S. (2003). Modeling the ad revenue potential of media audiences: An underdeveloped side of media economics, *Journal of Media Economics & Culture, 1,* 7–37.

Wildman, S. S., & Robinson, K. S. (1995). Network programming and off-network syndication profits: Strategic links and implication for television policy. *Journal of Media Economics, 8*(2), 27–48.

Wirth, M. O. (Ed.). (2003). The future of convergence [Special issue]. *International Journal on Media Management, 5*(1).

Wirth, M. O., & Bloch, H. (1995). Industrial organization theory and media industry analysis. *Journal of Media Economics, 8*(2), 15–26.

Young, D. P. T. (2000). Modeling media markets: How important is market structure? *Journal of Media Economics, 13,* 27–44.

# Global Media Management and Economics

David H. Goff
University of West Georgia

Scholarly works addressing media management and economics (including many of the preceding chapters of this volume) acknowledge the profound trends that have affected the media (or more broadly, "communications") over the past two decades. Technological, political, and economic forces have reshaped the media and communications industries of the world with significant consequences including the emergence of distinctly global communication enterprises. The desire to claim a share of the post–Cold War global economy led to significant policy shifts geared toward encouraging massive private sector investment in new communications infrastructure. National policies have typically shifted from tight government control toward the privatization and deregulation of the telecommunications and electronic media industries in order to foster competition, innovation, and investment in advanced digital technologies and to wring opportunity out of the apparent convergence of the formerly distinct and separate communications technologies.

Just a few years ago Albarran and Chan-Olmsted (1998) examined media and telecommunications in the world's major national and regional markets. The work provided valuable insights into ongoing policy and economic changes within these markets and the movement toward transnational or global operations of media firms. The editors concluded the volume with a chapter devoted to a discussion of five emerging patterns shaping the global media marketplace. They are worth restating here because to a large extent these same five patterns continue to affect global media and the study of media management and economics:

1. Many countries are experiencing rapid change and transformation.
2. The emergence of aggressive media conglomerates and expanded concentration.
3. Liberalization of media industries.
4. Increasing strategic alliances between local media conglomerates and foreign multinational media conglomerates.
5. Digitalization (Albarran & Chan-Olmsted, 1998, pp. 331–335).

Although the same five factors are still important, the economic and policy developments of the past few years have made us more aware of the interaction and interrelationships among them. Media management and economics scholarship, still a relatively young field, has expanded and matured as a growing international community of scholars has continued to explore the influence of these factors and to build a coherent literature of theory and practice. The preceding chapters provide a comprehensive look at the evolution of the field. The purpose of this chapter is to suggest future directions for global media management and economics research. A number of the preceding chapters offer their own suggestions for future inquiry, and the reader is advised that this chapter does not attempt to summarize the advice of the other contributors in this volume. Rather, this chapter frames three broad interrelated areas that pose new or continuing challenges for media management and economics scholarship.

1. The continuing impact of digital media technologies.
2. The continuing and evolving impact of policy and regulation.
3. The need to develop an improved understanding of global dynamics to better understand global media.

## THE CONTINUING IMPACT OF DIGITAL MEDIA TECHNOLOGIES

Digital technology remains the key enabling technology of the current era of globalization. The post–World War II era development of computer technology powered a gradual but accelerating diffusion of digital technologies that encompassed data storage, data networks, telephony, and finally the electronic media. From its 1968 origins, the Internet pioneered the revolutionary packet-switched network technology that has become the basis for virtually all fixed and wireless digital communications. Through what Goff (2000) calls a "remarkable accident of timing," technological, political, and economic forces combined during the decade of the 1990s to speed the deployment of high-speed and high-capacity digital networks (p. 240). The digital network infrastructure built by communications firms near the end of the 20th century provides "the necessary coordination ability" for international investment and trade (Picard, 2004, p. 5). However, technology is a double-edged sword for media managers.

The evolution of digital communication systems continues to afford new means of delivering media content, expanding audience reach and frequency. These systems allow larger established media firms to use and repurpose content within a variety of commonly owned distribution channels. For example, GE's NBC Universal media holdings routinely share news and feature content, presenting it at different times to the audiences of the NBC broadcast network and the CNBC cable network, whereas MSNBC delivers content via both cable and the Internet. NBC entertainment programs are often replayed on the Bravo cable channel. The same technologies can foster competition by enabling newer innovative firms, small and large, to offer new services, often for underserved niche audiences. U.S.-based Bloomberg Media distributes business news in real time via both a proprietary subscription network and the Internet as well as through print, radio, and television. Three important areas of technology development pose issues for management and economic decisions that merit further examination: digital television, broadband delivery, and wireless personal communications devices and systems.

Digital television services are increasingly available in national and transnational markets via satellite, cable, terrestrial broadcast, and online broadband delivery. Picard (2002a) has noted that digital television will not offer any new products or services, but will make available more content from the same amount of spectrum and will extend to viewers new options of control and choice, including the ability to interact with the medium. The transition to digital television will occupy the attention of practitioners and media management and economics scholars for much of the next decade as media firms continue to adopt to the opportunities and challenges posed by digital technology.

Different technical standards and regulatory philosophies affect the diffusion of DTV worldwide and within the U.S. market. For the most part these approaches all offer improved picture quality and a 16:9 aspect ratio (the screen dimensions of feature films). In addition, digital television enables more efficient use of electromagnetic spectrum and the ability to simultaneously multicast (or multiplex) four to six different signals from the same channel assignment. The initial U.S. plan envisioned replacing analog television with digital high definition television (HDTV), a standard that would deliver an electronic image that rivals the quality of feature film. However, the demanding technical standards of HDTV transmission currently use so much spectrum that an HDTV signal basically eliminates the prospect of multicasting several channels from the same source.

Congress mandated the change from analog to digital broadcasting and broadcasters were given both new frequencies for digital broadcasting and a timetable for utilizing them beginning in late 1998 with an initial 2006 goal of abandoning the analog spectrum. However, both broadcasters and consumers have been slow to respond, and the target for the changeover is now expressed in terms of an 85% household penetration level. In January 2004 the FCC reported that nearly 80% of all digital commercial television stations were transmitting content. However, viewing these signals is not easy, and the research firm IDC noted in June 2004 that fewer than 20% of the U.S. households that had purchased the expensive digital receivers were actually accessing HDTV content (IDC, 2004). According to Adams Media Research, the other 80% of digital set owners are still watching standard definition broadcasts and only experience their digital receiver's advanced capabilities when watching DVDs (Taub, 2004). For the most part digital transmissions are only accessible via rooftop or indoor antennas, whereas 86.9% of U.S. television households receive television signals via cable, satellite, or another type of multichannel delivery system, and these services carry few HDTV signals (Television Bureau of Advertising, 2004).

The United Kingdom took another approach and has achieved more success. As of January 2004 almost 50% of households had acquired digital television service and the market was expanding at a rate of 30,000 households per week (Office of Communications, 2004, p. 8). UK digital television offers improved picture and sound qualities with the 16:9 screen dimensions, but not the spectrum-intensive HDTV standard. Instead of HDTV, UK policymakers opted for achieving a wider array of channels through multiplex broadcasts of several channels from each digital transmitter ("HDTV," 2004). Subscriber-funded satellite services BSkyB and the UK's small cable sector led the transition to digital. However, the recent driving force behind digital growth is a free multichannel terrestrial broadcast service called Freeview, a model that has attracted attention in the United States, where broadcasters are searching for a viable digital television business model.

As of July 1, 2004, a total of 1,216 television stations in 207 U.S. markets had begun digital broadcasting ("DTV Stations," 2004). Each of these stations has incurred conversion costs averaging from $1 to $3 million. Because broadcasters are operating both analog and digital transmitters, their electricity costs (for transmission) have increased dramatically. All of these costs are balanced by minimal advertising revenue due to small audiences. What advertising revenue has been generated largely comes at the expense of advertising revenue for the same broadcaster's analog service. Digital technologies allow signals to be compressed, enabling multiple channels to be carried in the same bandwidth. Although government policy still prods the industry toward HDTV, broadcasters are most interested in pursuing the multicasting opportunities to offer more content choices and to extend the repurposing of content.

Increasing the number of channels obviously adds to the fragmentation of audiences, but at the same time it affords opportunities to develop niche content and to generate subscription revenue by offering packages of channels accessed by set-top boxes or plug-and-play devices. A number of ideas exist for what manner of content might prove viable for additional signals including localized weather, traffic, and travel-related information, 24-hour news, sports, and feature films. Managers recognize that local content has special value for audiences and local advertisers, but the cost and logistics of producing such content pose formidable problems. Subscription revenues typically elude terrestrial broadcasters, but the UK service Freeview has demonstrated a successful scheme for combining the spectrum of several terrestrial broadcasters in order to offer 30 channels that provide television content, text, and interactive features along with 20 radio signals. As the name implies, Freeview is actually free to viewers after a one-time set-top box purchase costing less than $100. However, set-top box technology can just as easily enable delivery of a subscription service. Developing a similar multiplex-based subscription service in the United States would require payment for spectrum or modification of current regulation. Nonetheless, the National Association of Broadcasters began to examine Freeview as a prospective business model in early 2004 (Eggerton, 2004). Whether delivered free or by subscription, the prospect of transmitting multiple signals is dampened by the stance of the U.S. cable television industry. Currently analog broadcasters achieve cable carriage of their solitary signal through a "must carry" provision of law. However, the cable industry is generally resistant to carrying more than the one broadcast signal from a station that splits its bandwidth into several. The issue is expected to require intervention of the Federal Communications Commission for resolution.

Digital television technology also affords interactivity, enabling firms to offer games and other new multimedia experiences to consumers, to become more engaged in e-commerce, and even to offer Internet access. Picard (2002b) notes that media firms have been slow to pursue content distribution via e-commerce. Interactivity affords media and advertisers opportunities for direct selling of goods and content.

According to e-Marketer, broadband moved past the early-adopter stage of diffusion by passing the 100 million subscriber mark just 6 years after passing the 1 million mark. By 2007 broadband penetration will reach 250 million worldwide with the Asia-Pacific region dominant, followed by North America and Europe ("Broadband Worldwide," 2004). Broadband is often regarded as high-speed Internet access. However, as the speed and bandwidth of broadband continues to improve (along with digital compression algorithms and other network technologies), broadband is expected to stream high-quality full-motion digital video to digital television receivers, to digital recording devices, and to fixed and mobile computers. This scenario makes broadband a competing delivery platform for digital television and the key to any true convergence between television and computers. Broadband is typically delivered via telephone lines or cable connections, but the next major advances are expected in wireless broadband delivery. Both telephone companies and cable firms have invested heavily in broadband infrastructure in order to capture the Internet access market. In the United States the top 20 cable and DSL (telephone) broadband providers command 98% of the market according to Leichtman Research Group (2004). At the end of the first quarter of 2004 cable broadband in the United States held a 62% market share to 38% for DSL, but the gap is narrowing. In this same quarter the nine largest DSL providers gained more new subscribers than did the top 11 cable companies (Leichtman Research Group, 2004).

Broadband networks also enable firms to engage in telephony and video content delivery. Local phone service revenue has declined in recent years and the cable industry is growing at a glacial 1% per year. On the other hand, revenue from providing high-speed Internet access is increasing 25% per year, and firms from both telephony and cable are envisioning capturing market share from the opposing sector by offering bundled services (Internet access, telephony, and video) as well as mobile phone services (Kharif, 2004). In this environment mergers and acquisitions make sense as firms seek to garner market share and build scale and scope sufficient to discourage new market entrants. Fixed-line telephone firms will continue to expand into the expanding wireless market, and further consolidation in mobile telephony (like the acquisition of AT&T Wireless by Cingular) is likely. Speculation has increased regarding the prospect of mergers between telephone companies and media content providers (Kharif, 2004). SBC Yahoo!, a DSL-delivered broadband content venture, has formed a video-on-demand service by partnering with CinemaNow, an online platform that currently delivers feature films and other content to both computer and TV platforms (Whitney, 2004). Microsoft, Lions Gate Entertainment and Blockbuster own part of CinemaNow (CinemaNow, 2004). At the same time, Movielink has partnered with Intel to stream films from the libraries of the universal, MGM, Sony, Paramount, Universal, and Warner Brothers studios to the television receivers of subscribers (Whitney, 2004).

Some of the most exciting technological developments exist in the area of wireless mobile personal communications devices and systems. These technologies were trapped in a nascent stage by an economic downturn at the turn of the century and are expanding rapidly in 2004. After a slow economy-delayed start, third-generation (3G) mobile phone systems are growing in Europe, the United States, and Asia. Originally intended to enable mobile phone users to access content that was not limited to simple text and graphics, 3G technologies also connect laptop computers, personal data assistants, and other devices. However, some recent technologies such as Wi-Fi and others in the testing stage (WiMax, and Mobile-Fi) will enable mobile broadband access comparable to fixed access as well as ubiquitous remote sensing (through a technology called ZigBee). Wi-Fi is based on the Intel Centrino chip and "hotspots," numerous wireless access areas limited to several hundred feet from a central antenna. WiMax, a technology in the trial stage, operates with a stronger signal that extends outward 25 to 30 miles from the antenna. Mobile-Fi, also in the developmental stages, offers the potential of online broadband access from moving vehicles, and a mobile version of WiMax is planned. Finally, another wireless technology, Ultrawideband, will enable the rapid transfer of large files over short distances (Green, 2004).

Some of these systems may not make it into the mainstream, but the trend they represent is clear. Broadband communications systems will become increasingly wireless and reach almost everywhere, and mobile and fixed devices will interact. Chip makers, computer hardware and software firms, the converged communications systems industry, and the media all have a stake in a wireless broadband future. More spectrum will be needed, increasing on the one hand the potential for new licensing requirements and on the other hand, incentives for governments to speed the turnover of the analog broadcast television frequencies. Either way, governments stand to generate more revenue from auctioning spectrum access. Broadband access is currently dominated by telephone and cable companies. Wi-Fi is largely a complementary technology, extending the reach of fixed line broadband. However, technologies such as WiMax and Mobile-Fi threaten the established order. The leading firms in broadband delivery and mobile telephony will seek to control these technologies. The first signs of the impact of broadband on content markets have appeared. In the United States, Major League Baseball is offering free online archived Webcasts of games. Deals have been struck with AOL, MSN, and several cable systems that provide broadband to provide large packages of live Webcast games each month for the whole baseball season (Lowry, 2004). The prospect of deals like this has been at the center of European Union media competition concerns.

The EU views broadband as an important new communication technology that is poised for explosive growth rivaling that of mobile telephony in its economic impact. Ideally, broadband growth will bring new competitors to media markets. The EU is concerned that large communications firms will use their market power to negotiate exclusive deals for rights to premium content such as sports and recent motion pictures, creating a bottleneck that disadvantages small, newer players (Lowe, 2004; Ungerer, 2003)

## THE CONTINUING AND EVOLVING IMPACT OF POLICY AND REGULATION

The most significant changes affecting regulation and policy over the past 20 years have emerged from the liberalization of media policy in the United States and the European Union. In terms of the world's established media markets, these two entities are home to most of the largest global media firms and provide the locations of the vast majority of the subsidiary operations of the dominant global firms (Kratke, 2003, discussed in the following section). The policy issues that arose with the deregulation and privatization of national media markets (first in Europe and later in other nations) and the effects of the convergence of media, telecom, and information technology are still in play around the world. Very specific trends have been observed. These include the paradoxical emergence of both competition and consolidation in deregulated markets and the status of both media pluralism and public service broadcasting.

Competition in media markets continues to increase as new technologies emerge and the phenomenon of convergence enables communications industries and firms to cross former legal and technical boundaries to compete in several areas of communications (e.g., newspapers, broadcasting, cable). Firms meet present-day challenges with strategies aimed at growth and critical mass (usually in terms of market share) achieved through strategies of vertical and horizontal integration and diversification resulting in increased economic efficiency through economies of scale and scope. Firms such as News Corporation, Viacom, Disney, and NBC Universal are well-known examples. Growth strategies typically lead to mergers and acquisitions with the result that media and communications industries become more consolidated.

The ITV (Channel 3) commercial television service in the United Kingdom provides an excellent example. Following relaxation of ownership rules in 1996, the national broadcast service once operated by 16 licensees was consolidated in the hands of two, Carlton and Grenada (Doyle, 2002a, pp. 124–128), and new policy (the Communications Act 2003) has enabled these two to merge, forming an entity called ITV plc. Regulators asserted that this consolidation would be good for the country because the size and scope of ITV plc would balance that of News Corporation's Sky TV satellite service and the BBC (Tryhorn, 2003).

Herein lies the central paradox of modern media policy. Policies intended to foster competition and encourage new market entrants create competitive economic conditions that are best met by firms that grow, causing consolidation that protects large, dominant, indigenous firms from encroachment by new market entrants. Further, despite their interest in competition, policymakers have an incentive to protect the interests of indigenous firms, as they are often essential to national interests and function as major players in regional or global markets. The same type of paradox affects the historic view that media play important social and political as well as economic roles.

U.S. broadcast media have been privately owned and operated commercially, but required to meet general and specific obligations to serve the public interest. In much of the rest of the world broadcast facilities were initially financed and operated by the government as noncommercial enterprises intended to provide universal service and benefits to society (Picard, 2002b). Both approaches reflect the unique economics of media. By operating apart from the interaction of supply and demand, an economic condition called market failure results. Market failure often implies the inability of a market to provide more intrinsic benefits to society, for example, the information needed for the public to participate in a democratic system. However, in an economic context, market failure results when the free market forces of supply and demand do not yield the optimal provision of products and utilization of resources. Content deemed valuable from a social standpoint often stimulates weak consumer response. Economic theory would dictate that broadcasters would seek to maximize profits and supply less of this type of content and more programming that the audience will consume, with the result that societal interests are underserved (Doyle, 2002b; Murschetz, 2002). Consequently, electronic media typically have operated either with public service requirements or as public service (government controlled) media.

In markets where broadcasting was once government controlled and noncommercial, additional commercial licensees were typically authorized after World War II. In most cases, though, these commercial broadcasters had public service obligations. Policy controlled carefully the ownership of media in the interest of sustaining pluralism (access to diverse media, information, and opinion necessary for an informed citizenry).

In the view of van Cuilenburg and McQuail (2003) policymaking has become a "schizoid" task (p. 195). Governments seek to maintain vestiges of a public interest policy that supports media pluralism as well as the general welfare of society (in all areas of communications) and national culture. At the same time governments support policy that is increasingly driven by economic considerations including reduction of ownership limitations that historically ensured the presence of a number of media voices. Doyle (2002a) reviewed efforts to promote media diversity and pluralism within the UK and the other European Union nations. The study found general agreement among political groups on the value of pan-European policy on media ownership that would limit concentration, but noted that policy had become skewed toward the view of industry groups that regulation should favor the economic fortunes of media firms.

In most nations where publicly funded national public service broadcast media exist a fierce debate is ongoing about the continuing need for such media. Public service broadcasters and the governments that sustain them are being asked "to define their mission and to clarify their financial relationship with their national government" (Meier, 2003, p. 337). Many countries support public service broadcasters either with direct government subsidy or with revenue from a license fee paid by viewers and listeners. Across Europe, where public service broadcasters are common, the audience shares of public service stations are down significantly in the face of increasing competition for audiences. The loss of audience share factors into the argument against sustaining current funding levels and the methods of funding employed. In the United Kingdom the venerable BBC, a public corporation supported by licensee fee revenue, is viewed as something of an anachronism. As part of its mammoth set of first-year tasks, the new UK communications regulatory agency, OFCOM (the Office of Communications) is undertaking a comprehensive review of public service broadcasting. In the UK, the commercial services Channel 3, Channel 4, and Channel 5 all bear public service responsibilities. The review will be completed during 2004.

In other European countries similar concerns exist. Recent research in Germany (Meier, 2003) found that public service broadcasters had adapted to commercial competition by developing a franchise in informational and cultural programming that attracted an audience sufficient to justify the medium's legitimacy. Picard (2002c) examined public service broadcaster shares across Europe and noted their decline from almost universal viewing to shares in the 20–40% range. However, Picard points out that these may be respectable shares in the more crowded and competitive markets of today. The analysis found that the majority of public service broadcasters were reaching audiences larger than a proportionate share based on number of competitors would entail.

Public service broadcasters are sharing in the transition to digital broadcasting, and the provision of even more channels of content, combined with other multichannel services such as satellite broadcasting, cable, and the emerging broadband sector all factor into the debate about public service broadcasting. Increasing numbers of channels provide greater consumer choice and continue to undercut old rationales about the need for public service broadcasters based on limited numbers of outlets.

## DEVELOP AN IMPROVED UNDERSTANDING OF GLOBAL DYNAMICS TO BETTER UNDERSTAND GLOBAL MEDIA

Friedman (2000) characterizes the current era of globalization as an international economic system, one that replaced "the Cold War system" (p. 7) after the fall of the Berlin Wall. International competition increased, the economies of individual nations became increasingly interconnected, and as a result, markets came to be defined globally rather than nationally. As part of this trend, communications policy and regulation were liberalized in many countries in order to encourage competition and the investment in new technologies needed to support overall economic growth, as well as to enable indigenous firms to develop as major players on the global stage. As media firms shifted their orientation from national markets they responded to market liberalization by pursuing logical strategies of vertical and horizontal growth at home and abroad. This era gave rise to the global media conglomerate, a type of firm that typically operates in a number of national media markets and in several media simultaneously (Chan-Olmsted, 2004; Doyle, 2002b; Picard, 1996, 2002a). Examples include Sony, News Corporation, Bertelsmann AG, and Disney.

The evolution of both national and global media firms in this era of significant political and economic change has dominated the agenda of media management and economics scholarship over the past decade. Globalization is typically viewed as a framework that favors the pursuit of competitive advantage by media firms through strategies that favor international expansion. A study by Yang and Shanahan (2003) suggests the value of treating globalization as an operationally defined variable in future research.

Yang and Shanahan (2003) examined the influence of globalization on the consumption and penetration of domestic media and communications technologies (measured by UNESCO in terms of newspaper circulation, numbers of televisions and radios owned, and numbers of Internet hosts and telephone lines for each country). Globalization was defined and measured in terms of "economic openness," a variable derived from country-level GDP and trade data. Data analysis controlled per capita GDP, literacy rates, degree of urbanization, population, and country democracy ratings. Results showed that countries with higher levels of economic openness showed higher penetration rates on all media and communications technologies included in the analysis except ownership of televisions and radios. While expressing the need for additional analyses over time, the authors believe that their findings "demonstrate the potential link between increasing globalization and the importance of information industries and the telecommunications sector" (p. 570).

Many authors have noted the very uneven distribution of communication assets around the world (Albarran & Chan-Olmsted, 1998; Mowlani, 1996). Global and transnational firms pursue competitive advantage and firm sustainability by expanding into carefully selected world markets. There is a need for greater attention to the size, location, and geographic distribution of these markets as well as a deeper analysis of the ways in which geographically dispersed media firm assets relate to each other and to the economic functioning of the firms that own them.

Kratke (2003) offers an example of the value of such an approach with a study oriented toward expanding the understanding the relationship between globalization and urban development. Noting the trend toward transnational operations of media firms, Kratke examined the pattern that has emerged of the location in "globally linked media cities" of the dispersed business units of the global conglomerates (p. 613). Kratke analyzed the locations of 2,766 business units of 33 large and small global media firms. A firm was considered global if it operated in at least three different countries and two continents or world regions. The analysis ranked the cities based on the number of media firm business units present in each. Kratke classified three groups of cities. Cities with more than 60 business units and more than 50% of the global firms represented were classified as alpha cities. Beta cities required more than 30 business units and more than a third of the firms to be represented. Finally, a city needed more than 20 business units and more than 25% of the global firms present to be counted as a gamma-level media city.

Kratke was struck by the uneven distribution of media firm operations among a small number (39) of global media cities. "The organizational units of the globalized cultural economy and media industry reveal a highly selective locational concentration on a global scale" (p. 618). The alpha group (New York, London, Paris, Los Angeles, Munich, Berlin, and Amsterdam) provided the locations of 835 business units. All of the beta group cities except Sydney and Toronto are in Europe. Only three Asian cities (Singapore, Tokyo, and Hong Kong) emerge from the analysis, and they are gamma-level cities. Similarly, only three Latin American cities made the gamma list, and no African or Middle Eastern cities were noted (p. 619). Kratke treats the structure of globally distributed media conglomerate subsidiaries as a network of business units, between which "there are many and varied information and communication flows that enable special regional or local impulses to be picked up and processed . . . world-wide" (p. 624). This process enables global media firms to adapt to trends in consumer behavior and preferences in a rapidly changing and competitive cultural economy.

In an effort to explain the "phenomenon of global communication" (p. 245), McPhail (2002) has suggested using a blend of world system theory and electronic colonialism theory. World system theory describes the economic significance of nations as "core, semiperipheral, and peripheral" (p. 244), with power and influence concentrated in the core sector (e.g., United States, European Union, and Japan). The peripheral nations are developing countries, and the semiperipheral occupy the middle ground, trading with the core but lacking the economic wherewithal to be a part of it. Because the largest global media institutions are found in the core nations, they enjoy dominant positions as purveyors of media content. Electronic colonialism theory is concerned with the ability of media products from core nations to dominate the markets of the other sectors, displacing the culturally specific media products of these countries. Although the globalization of communication enhances the position of core nation firms, "at the same time, many of the same firms and phenomena, such as the Internet, are fueling a resurgence of nationalism and localism, and are a means of protecting and reinforcing indigenous cultures, groups, and languages" (p. 247). Nonetheless, McPhail warns that the global spread of the policies of globalization, deregulation, and privatization are challenging the role of the nation-state just as digital technologies (including the Internet) challenge national borders, citing the increasing importance of pan-national trade / communication agreements and bodies such as the European Union, International Telecommunications Union, and OECD.

The major share of media management and economics scholarship has been naturally devoted to studying the operations of the world's major media firms as they have responded to their changing environments. In recent years the field has become more international as increasing numbers of scholars from outside the United States have made significant contributions to the literature. The majority come from the United States and Europe, but an increasing number of academics from the Asia-Pacific region are active. Still, the amount of research focused on Latin America, Africa, and the Middle East remains small. Scholarship examining firms, policy issues, and developments in the semiperipheral and peripheral nations should be encouraged.

## DISCUSSION

This chapter has examined three areas that pose challenges for media management and economics practice and scholarship: the continuing impact of digital media technologies, the evolving impact of policy and regulation, and the need to develop an improved understanding of global dynamics to better understand global media.

The significance of the continuing diffusion of digital broadcasting (terrestrial and satellite) and fixed broadband networks, combined with the rapid advance toward wireless broadband, will provide ubiquitous access to communication, information, and media networks. Content will, as observers have noted for years, be king and will be available anywhere at any time to everyone equipped with any of a wide array of fixed and mobile network devices: television, computer, mobile phone, PDA, or a hybrid device that combines these capabilities. In this environment the digital television will become another networked device, and computer-related firms such as Microsoft and Intel will see their roles in media competition increase. Digital video recorders, following the lead of most of the devices that preceded them, will become increasingly sophisticated and less expensive. The diffusion of these devices will largely end discussions of time shifting begun with the emergence of the VCR in the 1980s. Consumers will control both the time and place of increasingly personalized media consumption. The key to this scenario of ubiquitous content and connectivity is to make the technology as transparent and as simple to use as possible.

For management at the corporate level the new digital technology of greatest interest will be wireless broadband. The long-debated marriage of television and computer technology is at hand as new digital television receivers have become digital monitors with multiple-function signal input / tuning capabilities. Wireless broadband is a logical extension of fixed broadband, and key players such as cable giant Comcast and the major telephone companies are likely to acquire wireless assets to protect and extend their franchises. Such a move will also support plans of cable firms to offer telephony and telephone companies to provide video services. Larger media conglomerates with significant content assets, such as Disney and Viacom, will need to consider merger or acquisition activity directed toward the emerging content delivery segment represented by CinemaNow and Movielink. Should these changes come about, scholars of media management and economics will have a new wave of merger and acquisition activity to investigate.

At all levels media managers already face significant challenges posed by the increasing number and variety of consumer (media/entertainment/recreation) choices. Obviously, these challenges will continue as more content/delivery options appear in the market-place. For broadcasters still seeking a viable business model for digital television, the challenges of ubiquitous content and connectivity will compound their problems. Audience shares will likely decline further as fragmentation of audiences increases. However, most of the emerging forms of content delivery will operate as subscription or on-demand pay-per-view services. Advertisers, national and especially local, will continue to need locally delivered media forms to reach consumers, and policymakers will need to remain aware of this fact if the viability of local media is increasingly threatened. Both the industry and media scholarship can profit from more research into media consumer behavior in media-rich markets.

Many local television station managers in the United States fear the eventual abandonment of the analog system because nearly 90% of viewers receive their signals via cable or satellite, and carriage of local broadcast signals by these methods remains an issue of contention. Now broadband appears ready to emerge as yet another viable signal delivery platform. In this environment it appears that local broadcasters could indeed benefit from forming market or cluster networks of their own by applying the concepts pioneered by Freeview in the United Kingdom. Local broadcasters and content distributors including syndication companies and small (start-up or regional) networks will be able to use the ubiquitous network connectivity to their mutual advantage. Although there remain technological issues to surmount, local digital television networking could eventually provide the full range of communications services used by consumers, generating subscription revenue and pay-per-view/use revenue. Any movement toward a functional business model for digital television broadcasting in the United States will demand the attention of media management and economics scholars.

Faced with increasing competition and audience fragmentation it is likely that media at the local level will have further incentives to consolidate. Policymakers and regulators in the United States and Europe have acknowledged the economic logic of such consolidation by relaxing ownership restrictions. However, each time ownership limits are increased, fears concerning the public service responsibilities of local media increase as well. Almost all democratic nations value a wide array of media voices as possible, so the ownership of both print (particularly outside the United States) and electronic media is regulated. Broadcast media have historically operated with the most restrictive regulation because of the concept of scarcity of the electromagnetic spectrum.

Print media face significant economic challenges related to competition, readership levels, and the cost of operation. Although the collective audience for electronic media is large and growing with the population, competition for the public's attention is at an all-time high and increasing. With the proliferation of the Internet and the transition to broadband network technologies, an increasing array of diverse electronic media sources continues to emerge online. The electromagnetic spectrum is used more efficiently than ever and policymakers are working to reallocate portions of the spectrum to increase this efficiency so that the burgeoning demand for wireless applications can be met. The eventual switchover from analog to digital broadcasting will free a great deal of spectrum for other uses. More research is needed on the economic and management issues of spectrum utilization. Recent work by Cave (2002) in the UK is an excellent example.

If the matters of the number and diversity of media voices and spectrum are being resolved by new media forms and technological advances, then consolidation of media ownership, especially at the local level, can continue. To the extent that policymakers continue to value local media sources, the practical reality of their economic survival will increasingly drive ownership/control policy in the near term. Especially in small markets it may, in the end, be better to have one local entity operate both the newspaper and television station than to lose one (or both). Scholars need to examine more directly the media behavior of consumers and the economic implications of audience media consumption patterns in a changing media environment.

Public service broadcasting and especially the matter of government subsidies will continue to be debated in many countries. Given the expanding number of digital broadcast sources in the UK, it is likely that the role of the BBC will change. Limited commercial support (perhaps similar to corporate underwriter's announcements that support U.S. public broadcasting) is an option. All UK terrestrial broadcasters have public service responsibilities, and this is unlikely to change. If the BBC becomes partly commercial, the license fee paid by media users could be reduced and/or shared by all broadcasters to support public service programming. The prospects of changing the public service role of broadcasters in Britain or elsewhere have implications for management in both the noncommercial and commercial segments of the industry. The noncommercial side will have the task of developing new revenue sources to support ongoing operations. These managers have hardly been immune to the issues of financing the shift to digital operation and competition from a growing array of other electronic media. Commercial managers may face the prospect of competing for advertising dollars as well as for viewers with former noncommercial broadcasters in addition to the growing list of present competitors. The impact of changes in the public service responsibilities of broadcasters on management and the economic operation of media will provide opportunity for expanded scholarship in this area.

Scholars studying international and transnational media should explore these firms in more depth. A great deal of literature addresses the strategic operation of these media, but we know relatively little about how the component parts of these firms operate in relationship to the local environments in which they are located. How do transnational firms adapt managerially to the political, economic, and social culture of different countries? How do purely economic issues determine the geographic location of a firm's global distribution of assets? More research is needed that examines media management and economics in China and in the nations McPhail places outside the core.

Finally, in order to better understand the global forces affecting media, it may be beneficial for those studying media management and economics media to partner with scholars interested in the linkage between history and economic forces. This type of collaboration may be able to help management understand and prepare for the challenges to global media posed by market changes and by social and political movements.

## REFERENCES

Albarran, A. B., & Chan-Olmsted, S. M. (1998). Global patterns and issues. In A. B. Albarran & S.M. Chan-Olmsted (Eds.), *Global media economics: Commercialization, concentration and integration of world media markets* (pp. 99–118). Ames: Iowa State University Press.

*Broadband worldwide 2004: Subscriber update* (2004). (Report overview). New York: eMarketer, Inc. Retrieved April 24, 2004, from http://www.emarketer.com/products/report.php?bband_apr04

Cave, M. (2002, March). *Review of radio spectrum management.* London: Department of Trade and Industry and HM Treasury.

Chan-Olmsted, S. M. (2004). In search of partnerships in a changing global media market: Trends and drivers of international strategic alliances. In R. G. Picard (Ed.), *Strategic responses to media market changes* (JIBS Research Report Series No. 2004-2) (pp. 47–64). Jönköping, Sweden: Jönköping International Business School.

CinemaNow (2004). *About CinemaNow—Company Background.* Retrieved June 30, 2004, from http://www.cinemanow.com/abt_back.aspx

Doyle, G. (2002a). *Media ownership: The economics and politics of convergence and concentration in the UK and European media.* London: Sage.

Doyle, G. (2002b). *Understanding media economics.* London: Sage.

"DTV stations: 2004. (2004, July 1). National Association of Broadcasters Newsroom. Retrieved July 1, 2004, from http://www.nab.org/Newsroom/Issues/digitaltv/DTVStations.asp

Eggerton, J. (2004, January 5). NAB explores UK's Freeview DTV success. *Broadcasting and Cable, 134*(1), 14.

Friedman, T. (2000). *The Lexus and the olive tree.* New York: Anchor Books.

Goff, D. H. (2000). Issues of Internet infrastructure. In A. B. Albarran & D. H. Goff (Eds.), *Understanding the web: Social, political, and economic dimensions of the Internet* (pp. 239–265). Ames: Iowa State University Press.

Green, H. (2004, April 26). No wires, no rules. *Business Week Online.* Retrieved April 24, 2004, from http://www.businessweek.com/print/magazine/content/04_17/b3880601.htm?mz

*HDTV—High definition television* (2004). Department for Culture, Media and Sport Digital Television Project. Retrieved April 27, 2004, from http://www.digitaltelevision.gov.uk/switchover/hdtv.html

IDC (2004, June 29). I want my DTV: Global digital television market to reach sales of $70 billion in 2008, IDC says. Retrieved June 30, 2004, from http://www.idc.com/getdoc.jsp?containerId=pr2004_06_17_113757

Kharif, O. (2004, March 2). Tearing down the walls in telecom. *Business Week Online.* Retrieved April 24, 2004, from http://www.businessweek.com/print/technology/content/mar2004/tc2004032_4116_tc076.htm?tc

Kratke, S. (2003, September). Global media cities in a world-wide urban network. *European Planning Studies, 11*(6), 605–628.

Leichtman Research Group, Inc. (2004, May 11). *A record 2.3 million add broadband in first quarter of 2004* [Press release]. Retrieved June 30, 2004, from http://www.leichtmanresearch.com/press/051104release.html

Lowe, P. (2004, January 13). *Media concentration & convergence: Competition in communications.* Speech before the Oxford Media Convention 2004. Retrieved April 4, 2004, from http://www.ippr.org.uk/events/files/Philip%20Lowe%20speech.doc

Lowry, T. (2004, April 12). Take me out to the webcast? *Business Week Online*. Retrieved April 24, 2004, from http://www.businessweek.com/print/magazine/content/04_15/b3878055.htm?tc

McPhail, T. L. 2002. *Global communication: Theories, stakeholders, and trends*. Boston: Allyn & Bacon.

Meier, H. K. (2003, September) Beyond convergence. *European Journal of Communication, 18*(3), 337–365.

Mowlani, H. (1996). *Global communication in transition: The end of diversity?* Thousand Oaks, CA: Sage.

Murschetz, P. (2002). Public service television at the digital crossroads—The case of Austria. *JMM—The International Journal on Media and Markets, 4*(2), 85–94.

Office of Communications (2004, 22 January). Ofcom's annual plan: April 2004–March 2005. London: OFCOM. Retrieved April 14 2004, from http://www.ofcom.org.uk/consultations/past/plan/annual_plan/annual_plan.pdf?a=87101

Picard, R. G. (1996). The rise and fall of communication empires. *Journal of Media Economics, 9*(4), 23–40.

Picard, R. G. (2002a). *The economics and financing of media companies*. New York: Fordham University Press.

Picard, R. G. (2002b). Preface: Electronic commerce in entertainment and media. *Electronic Markets, 12*(4), 217.

Picard, R. G. (2002c). Research Note: Assessing audience performance of public service broadcasters. *European Journal of Communication, 17*(2), 227–235.

Picard, R. G. (2004). Environmental and market changes driving strategic planning in media firms. In R. G. Picard (Ed.), *Strategic responses to media market changes* (JIBS Research Report Series No. 2004-2) (pp. 1–17). Jönköping, Sweden: Jönköping International Business School.

Taub, E. A. (2004, June 29). Finding digital signal a blast from past. HoustonChronicle.com. Retrieved June 30, 2004, from http://www.chron.com/cs/CDA/ssistory.mpl/tech/news/2651982

Television Bureau of Advertising (2004). TV basics. Retrieved June 30, 2004, from http://www.tvb.org/rcentral/mediatrendstrack/tvbasics/index.asp

Tryhorn, C. (2003, October 7). ITV merger gets go-ahead. *Guardian Limited*. Retrieved April 17, 2004, from http://media.guardian.co.uk/itvunderpressure/story/0,1430,1057655,00.html

Ungerer, H. (2003, December 10). *Impact of competition law on media—Some comments on current developments*. Speech before the 4th ECTA Regulatory Conference. Brussels: European Commission.

van Cuilenburg, J., & McQuail, D. (2003). Media policy paradigm shifts: Towards a new communications policy paradigm. *European Journal of Communication, 18*(2), 181–207.

Whitney, D. (2004, April 19). Serving it from the web. *Television Week 23*(16), 20.

Yang, F., & Shanahan, J. (2003, October). Economic openness and media penetration. *Communication Research, 30*(5), 557–573.

# Author Index

Butcher, S., 118, 134, *140*
Buzzard, K., 622, *635*
Buzzard, S. F. K., 586, *598*
Byrne, J. C., 121, *139*


**C**


Calabrese, A., 661, *671*
Callingham, M., 240, 241, *248*
Camerer, C., 84, *88*
Camerer, C. F., 664, 667, *671*
Cameron, K., 121, 135, *144*
Camp, S. M., 253, *272*
Campbell, A. J., 278, *291*, 662, 664, *671*
Campbell, D. T., 71, *88*, 539, *550*
Carey, J., 507, 508, 512, *516*
Carlton, D., 356, *360*
Carroll, B., 449, 456, *460*
Carroll, G. R., 329, 330, 331, 332, 337, *342, 343*
Carter, B., 306, *321*
Carvajal, M., 467, 478, *491*
Carveth, R., 26, 29, *33*, 348, *361*, 562, 571, 600, 620, 662, *671*
Castells, M., 502, 503, *516*
Cate, F., 206, *226*
Caudill, S. L., 56, *60*, 581, *597*
Cavazos, R. J., 409, *414*
Cave, D., 316, *321*
Cave, M., 27, *34*, 564, 571, 600, 620, 685, *688*
Caves, R. E., 3, *18*, 186, 187, *198*, 337, 339, *343*, 659, *671*
Chae, S., 395, 398, *414*
Chaffee, E., 163, *178*
Chaffee, S. H., 527, *550*
Chakravarthy, B., 166, 168, *179*
Chamberlin, E. H., 74, *88*, 654, *671*
Chambers, L. T., 14, *18*, 26, *34*, 44, *60*, 236, *248*, 374, *381*, 408, *414*, 428, *443*
Chandler, A., 163, *178*
Chang, B. H., 45, *60*, 145, 155, *158*, 170, *178*, 213, *226*, 658, *699*
Chan-Olmsted, S. M., 13, 14, 15, *18, 20*, 26, 27, *33, 34*, 42, 43, 45, *50, 60*, 62, 63, 116, 126, *139*, 145, 155, *158*, 162, 166, 167, 168, 170, 172, *178, 179*, 194, *198*, 203, 212, 213, 225, *226*, 236, 239, 243, 247, *248, 249, 250*, 256, 266, 267, *272, 273*, 302, 307, *321*, 347, 356, *360*, 373, 374, 378, 380, *381*, 410, *414*, 448, 449, 450, 452, 453, 454, 455, *460, 461*, 526, *550*, 658, 659, *671, 673, 674*, 681, 682, *688*

Charran, R., 221, *226*
Chatterjee, S., 173, 174, *178*, 257, *272*
Chen, M. J., 262, 267, *273*, 330, *344*
Chen, Y., 351, *361*
Cheng, J. L. C., 50, *60*
Chernin, P., 211, 224, *226*
Cherry, B., 92, 93, 94, 95, 97, 101, 102, 103, 105, 106, 107, 108, *109, 110*
Chestnut, B., 47, *64*
Chiang, C. C., 406, *415*, 545, *551*, 655, *673*
Chmielewski, D. C., 301, *321*
Cho, H., 311, *322*
Choi, C., 190, *199*
Choi, J. H., 49, *60*, 348, *361*, 448, 449, 452, 453, *460*
Chomsky, N., 497, *517*
Chon, B. S., 49, *60*, 348, *361*, 448, 449, 452, 453, *460*
Christensen, C. M., 37, *60*, 263, *272*, 474, *490*
Christians, C. G., 574, 579, *598*
Christie, E., 310, *321*
Chua Han Ming, M., 241, *250*
Chuanzhi, L., 118, 134, *140*
Chunovic, L., 630, *635*
Chyi, H. I., 12, 13, *18*, 50, *60*, 310, *321*, 449, 457, *460*, 543, *550*, 585, *598*, 658, *671, 672*
Clark, J. M., 118, *140*
Clark, K. B., 50, *66*
Clark, R. K., 13, *17*
Claybaugh, J., 303, *321*
Clegg, S. R., 574, *598*
Coase, R. H., 25, *34*, 82, *88*
Coate, S., 183, *198*
Cockburn, I., 172, *179*
Coffman, C., 11, *17*
Cohan, J., 221, *226*
Cohen, J., 537, *550*
Cohen, P., 537, *550*
Cohen, W. M., 336, *343*
Cohen-Avigdor, N., 195, *198*
Coit, P., 346, *361*
Colledge, J. A., 447, 450, *461*
Collette, L., 581, *598*
Collins, J., 223, *226*
Collins, R., 26, *34*
Collis, D. J., 163, *179*, 447, 448, 451, 458, *460*
Compaine, B. M., 25, 29, *34*, 42, *60*, 155, *158*, 213, *226*, 256, *272*, 286, 287, *291*, 364, 371, 373, *381*, 605, *620*, 665, *672*
Conneely, C., 237, *248*
Cook, T., 275, *291*
Cooper, A. C., 162, *179*, 266, *272*
Cooper, D. R., 592, *598*
Copeland, T., 151, *158*

# Subject Index

3G mobile phones, 679–680
10-K's, 618, 619
10-Q's, 619
24-hour news channels, localization of, 477

## A

ABC, 123, 252, 406, 484
  acquisition of, 601
  Cap Cities merger, 131
  merger with Disney, 155
Academic jargon, branding, 232–233
*Academy of Management Journal,* 177
*Academy of Management Review,* 177
Access
  for field observation, 584
  to interview respondents, 587–588
  as political economy theme, 494, 495,
    500–501
Access-based pricing, 438–439,
  440
Access providers, 650
Accounting issues, 616–618
Accrual accounting, 616
Accuracy, research and, 595

Acquisitions, 481
  cost reduction and, 642
  growth through, 608
  *See also* Mergers and acquisitions
Across-group design, 583
Action research, 585
Activism, Internet and, 502–503
Adaptive strategy, 163
Adelphia Communications, 603
Administrative management, 4–5
Adoption economies, 420
Adoption externalities, 418–419
Adoption of new technologies, 50, 641
Ad Tag/Ad Copy, 307
Advanced Intelligent Network, 430
Advertiser-supported television, 391–399, 402
Advertising
  classified, 309, 310
Advertising/advertisers
  audience information for, 624, 629
  cable television and, 309, 429
  classified, 309, 310
  as engine of mass media, 122
  ethnic/racial programming and, 409
  expenditures, 351
  financing by, 193